FEMINIST FRONTIERS 5

LAUREL RICHARDSON
VERTA TAYLOR
NANCY WHITTIER

McGraw Hill

Boston   Burr Ridge, IL   Dubuque, IA   Madison, WI   New York   San Francisco   St. Louis
Bangkok   Bogotá   Caracas   Lisbon   London   Madrid
Mexico City   Milan   New Delhi   Seoul   Singapore   Sydney   Taipei   Toronto

McGraw-Hill Higher Education

A Division of The McGraw-Hill Companies

FEMINIST FRONTIERS

Published by McGraw-Hill, an imprint of The McGraw-Hill Companies, Inc., 1221 Avenue of the Americas, New York, NY, 10020. Copyright © 2001, 1997, 1993, 1989, 1983, by The McGraw-Hill Companies, Inc. All Rights reserved. No part of this publication may be reproduced or distributed in any form or by any means, or stored in a database or retrieval system, without the prior written consent of The McGraw-Hill Companies, Inc., including, but not limited to, in any network or other electronic storage or transmission, or broadcast for distance learning. Some ancillaries, including electronic and print components, may not be available to customers outside the United States.

This book is printed on acid-free paper.

1 2 3 4 5 6 7 8 9 0 FGR/FGR 0 9 8 7 6 5 4 3 2 1 0

ISBN 0072321369

Editorial director: *Phillip A. Butcher*
Senior sponsoring editor: *Sally Constable*
Development editor: *Katherine Blake*
Marketing manager: *Leslie Kraham*
Senior project manager: *Mary Conzachi*
Senior production supervisor: *Lori Koetters*
Coordinator freelance design: *Laurie Entringer*
Supplement coordinator: *Susan Lombardi*
New Media: *Kimberly Stark*
Compositor: *Shepherd Incorporated*
Typeface: *9/11 Times Roman*
Printer: *Quebecor Printing Book Group/Fairfield*

Library of Congress Cataloging-in-Publication Data

Feminist frontiers 5 / [edited by] Laurel Richardson, Verta Taylor, Nancy Whittier.
        p. cm.
    Includes bibliographical references.
    ISBN 0-07-232136-9 (softcover : alk. paper)
    1. Feminism—United States. 2. Women—United States. 3. Sex role—United States. 4. Women—Cross-cultural studies. I. Title: Feminist frontiers five. II. Richardson, Laurel, III. Taylor, Verta A. IV. Whittier, Nancy, 1966-

HQ1426 .F472 2001
305.42'0973—dc21   00-031892

www.mhhe.com

A B O U T   T H E   A U T H O R S

LAUREL RICHARDSON has multiple attachments to The Ohio State University. She is Professor Emerita of Sociology, Adjunct Professor of Women's Studies, and Visiting Distinguished Professor of Cultural Studies. She has published seven books and over 100 articles. Her most recent book, *Fields of Play: Constructing an Academic Life* (Rutgers University Press, 1997), tells the story of her strategies to create a university that is more inviting to women and minorities. The book has been multiply honored, including being the recipient of the prestigious C. H. Cooley award.

VERTA TAYLOR is Professor of Sociology and a member of the Graduate Faculty of the Center for Women's Studies at The Ohio State University, where she teaches courses on gender, women's studies, and social movements. She has won numerous teaching awards at Ohio State, including a University Distinguished Teaching Award, and a multicultural teaching award. She also received the Sociologists for Women in Society's Mentoring Award and served as Feminist Lecturer for Sociologists for Women in Society. In addition, she has served as chair of the Section on Sex and Gender, the Section on Collective Behavior and Social Movements, and the Committee on the Status of Gay, Lesbian, Bisexual, and Transgendered Sociologists of the American Sociological Association. She has written and co-authored many books, and her writings have appeared in numerous scholarly collections and in journals such as *Signs, Gender & Society, The American Sociological Review, Social Problems,* and the *Journal of Marriage and Family.*

NANCY WHITTIER is Associate Professor of Sociology and a member of the Women's Studies Program Committee at Smith College. She teaches courses on gender, social movements, queer politics, and research methods. She is the author of *Feminist Generations: The Persistence of the Radical Women's Movement,* which traces the evolution of radical feminism over the past 25 years and examines intergenerational differences within the women's movement. Her work on the women's movement, social movement culture and collective identity, and activist generations has appeared in numerous scholarly collections and journals. She is currently working on a book about the gender politics of the movement against child sexual abuse and its opponents, co-editing a volume on new directions in social movement theory, and co-editing (with Verta Taylor) a book on gender and social movements.

P R E F A C E

The first edition of *Feminist Frontiers* was conceived in the late 1970s, at a time when many women inside and outside academia were beginning to recognize and challenge male domination. At the time of its publication, only a handful of books and anthologies written for classroom use presented a feminist perspective on women's status. The evolution of this book through five editions reflects both the successes of the women's movement and the development of feminist scholarship over the past three decades. Women's studies courses have blossomed and spread to campuses in even the most conservative regions of the country. Feminist scholars in the meantime have refined and enlarged our understanding of how gender inequality operates and how it intersects with other systems of domination based on race, ethnicity, nationality, class, and sexuality. There is no doubt that the situation of women has changed since the publication of the first edition of *Feminist Frontiers*. Gender inequality has not, however, disappeared.

With pride and excitement we write this preface to *Feminist Frontiers 5*. We are proud to be part of the continuing women's movement; we are excited by the burgeoning of knowledge about how gender is connected to race, class, sexuality, nationality, and other differences. We feel fortunate to be writing, teaching, and learning at a time when feminist thought and research are flourishing and deepening. It is simultaneously a time to enjoy the bounty of feminist scholarship and to sow new feminist seeds. We are proud as well that this book is the collective effort of scholars from two different feminist generations. We have enjoyed our collaboration across intellectual and generational perspectives, and we think that it has enriched the book.

We developed this book for use as the major or supplementary text in courses on the sociology of women, women's studies, gender studies, or sex roles. In addition, because the book offers a general framework for analyzing women's status, it can be used as a supplementary text in introductory sociology courses and in courses on social problems, foundations of society, comparative studies, and American studies. Although we have retained some of the articles from previous editions of *Feminist Frontiers*, particularly writings that have become feminist classics, the book has been comprehensively updated to include the most recent scholarship on gender; approximately half of the readings are new to this edition. We have selected readings that continue to emphasize the diversity of women's experiences and multicultural perspectives, while strengthening several sections and bringing in the most current issues in feminist scholarship, including more thorough coverage of men and masculinity.

Feminist Frontiers 5 is organized into four parts, each introduced by a sociological–feminist analysis. Part One, "Introduction," begins with a section representing the diversity of women's experiences and gender systems. Its section on "Theoretical Perspectives" presents engaging and accessible feminist theoretical approaches. Part Two, "Gender, Culture, and Representation," has two sections, "Representation, Language, and Culture," and "Socialization." The five sections of Part Three, "Social Organization of Gender," provide readings on work, families, sexuality, bodies and medicine, and violence against women. Part Four, "Social Change," includes articles on politics and the state and on social protest and the feminist movement.

The new edition has considerably strengthened coverage of culture and representation. The expanded section on "Representation, Language, and Culture" contains many new selections that improve our coverage of television, mass media, intersections of race and gender in representation, and beauty standards. We have also added a selection by Judith Butler in Section Two ("Theoretical Perspectives") that covers performative theories of gender, which will be useful to instructors who want to cover representation at a more theoretically sophisticated level. This selection is easily omitted for lower-level courses.

Throughout the book, we have added new selections that reflect the most current research on such topics as racialized masculinity, cosmetic surgery, talk shows, media images of Asian Americans, child-raising in egalitarian families, affirmative action, women in the trades, peer marriage, men and sexuality, medical treatment of intersexual children, rape prevention, boys and violence, electoral politics, sweatshop labor, queer politics, men's movements, and third-wave feminism. We have added many new boxed inserts that keep the text lively and raise important issues not dealt with in the regular selections. Although the book's core focus remains on women and gender, we have added articles in every section dealing with men and masculinity and/or both men and women.

In addition, we have updated the book to reflect the activism and perspectives of third-wave feminism. We have added coverage of third-wave organizing in the last section ("Social Protest and the Feminist Movement") and have added throughout the volume pieces by third-wave authors and pieces dealing with the experiences of recent generations.

As we set about selecting articles for this edition, we found an abundance of excellent pieces. We used the following criteria for choosing what to include: First, we wanted each selection to be engagingly written and accessible in style and language to readers from different disciplinary backgrounds. Second, as a testament to the tremendous growth in depth and understanding of feminist scholarship, we sought selections exploring a wide range of theoretical and substantive issues. Third, we wanted the anthology to reflect a diversity of racial, ethnic, generational, sexual, and cultural experiences. Fourth, we sought to capture the cross-disciplinary nature of gender research. The result is a collection that links well-written and significant articles within a general feminist sociological perspective.

We gratefully acknowledge the support, skill, and help of many people. We extend thanks to contribution authors, not only for writing the selected pieces but also for allowing us to reprint them here. At McGraw-Hill, we especially thank our editorial director, Phil Butcher, for believing in and supporting this project; Sally Constable, our sponsoring editor, for her encouragement and help in shaping the book; and Kathy Blake, developmental editor, for shepherding the book through its development. We also thank Mary Conzachi for overseeing the final manuscript through editing and production, and Fred Courtright, permissions editor. Amber Ault was instrumental in shaping some section introductions for the third edition of the book; we appreciate her contributions. Nicole Raeburn provided invaluable research assistance on earlier editions of the book, and we continue to be grateful for her work on revising the Instructor's Manual. Rose Foster, Betsy Kaminski, Meg Chilton, and Morgan Lynn provided clerical support and feedback from students' perspectives. In addition, Mary Margaret Fonow and Claire Robertson have given us valuable feedback on their teaching experiences with earlier editions of *Feminist Frontiers*. Finally, we express our appreciation to students in our classes on the sociology of women, sex and gender, and women's studies at Smith College and Ohio State University. They have contributed to the development of this anthology by their thoughtful responses to proposed articles.

The following scholars served as reviewers for *Feminist Frontiers 4* or *5,* and we thank them for their expert and generous comments: Kal Alston, University of Illinois; Lisa Brush, University of Pittsburgh; Mary Ann Clawson, Wesleyan University; Naomi Gerstel, University of Massachusetts; Tace Hedrick, University of Florida; Elizabeth Higginbotham, University of Memphis; Valerie Jenness,

University of California, Irvine; Michael Kimmel, State University of New York—Stony Brook; Donna Langston, Minnesota State University—Mankato; Amy Lind, Arizona State University; Jackie Litt, Iowa State University; Judith Lorber, City University of New York Graduate Center; Debra Minkoff, Yale University; Kim Nielsen, University of Wisconsin—Green Bay; Robbie Pfeufer Kahn, University of Vermont; Sarah Projansky, University of California—Davis; Brenda Phillips, Texas Woman's University; Jennifer Reed, California State University—San Bernadino; and Shirley Yee, University of Washington.

Special thanks go to those close to us who inspired both the work and the authors. Ernest Lockridge has been steadfast in his belief in and support for the project. Leila Rupp critically reviewed the entire collection at every stage of the revision and offered the friendship and support needed to carry out the project. Kate Weigand provided feedback and insight into the collection's organization and offered consistent encouragement and companionship. Jonah Weigand-Whittier is a constant source of inspiration as we seek to reconstruct gender. To them and to the many others who have touched our lives positively, we express our gratitude.

Laurel Richardson
Verta Taylor
Nancy Whittier

CONTENTS

P A R T   O N E

Introduction

What is gender? Consider your answers to that question now, and again at the end of this course. To answer the question requires thinking about what it means to individuals to be men or women and how these meanings affect the ways we interact with each other, the kinds of relationships we form, our positions in our communities. It also entails thinking about the institutions that distribute power, resources, and status among various groups of women and men.

What does it mean to be a woman? Thinking about women's experiences is a complicated task because women have as many differences from each other as commonalities. On the one hand, women everywhere suffer restrictions, oppression, and discrimination because they are living in patriarchal societies. Yet gender is not the sole influence on any woman's life. Differences of race, ethnicity, class, sexuality, age, nation, region, and religion shape women's experiences. Moreover, these differences intersect with each other. For example, Asian-American women of various ages, sexual orientations, classes, and ethnic and national origins, have different experiences.

The experience of being a woman may be quite different for distinct groups of women. For a white, upper-class, heterosexual American woman, for example, femininity might entail being economically dependent on her husband, perfecting a delicate and refined physical appearance, and achieving social influence through child-raising and volunteer work. Womanhood for a middle-class African-American woman might mean providing financial support for her children, holding influential and respected positions within her church and community, yet being stereotyped by the dominant white culture as sexually promiscuous or unintelligent. For a Mexican immigrant to the United States, femininity might mean being a good mother—which, as Denise Segura suggests in Reading 29, may mean working long hours in order to support her children.

The experiences of men are similarly varied. Although men benefit from power and privilege over women, some groups of men also exercise power over other men, while other men are excluded from economic or political influence. To understand the position of a particular man, we must consider his gender, race, class, sexuality, age, and so forth, in order to understand the particular advantages and disadvantages he faces.

In short, gender is defined in various ways for different groups. Gender definitions bring with them a distinct set of restrictions and disadvantages for members in each group, as well as privileges and sources of power or resistance. The task for you, as students, as for scholars of gender, is to recognize the patterns and persistence of male dominance while simultaneously recognizing these variations.

As if matters were not complex enough, feminist scholars also recognize that individuals have unique constellations of experiences. Each of us has our own story to tell. Each of us has multiple alliances and identifications with groups that shift through time and social context. The religious identity of childhood may be shunted aside during young adulthood, for example, only to be reclaimed in

1

later years. Self-definitions as heterosexual may give way later in life to new identities as lesbian or bisexual. As biracial or bicultural or mixed-religion daughters, we might identify with the heritage of either parent or both. Social forces such as sexism, racism, heterosexism, and class inequality shape our biographies, but it is as individuals that we experience and make sense of our lives. Individuals do not easily attribute our experiences to class, race, or gender as *separate* or *separable* entities. We rarely see our own biographies as sociohistorically situated.

The task of feminist scholarship, and of this volume, is to illuminate the social and structural roots of our gendered experiences while simultaneously recognizing the complicated and unique factors that shape our lives. Feminist research builds upon and links two levels of analysis: structure and biography. The *structural* level looks at social institutions and cultural practices that create and sustain gender inequalities and links those inequalities to other systems of oppression, such as racism, ageism, and homophobia. The *biographical* level honors each individual's expression of her own experience. It pays attention to how individuals represent themselves and recognizes personal voice. As a result, we can learn how difference and commonality are structurally rooted and personally experienced. We can see how larger social forces affect our own and others' lives.

Feminist research is not just about analyzing the ways that social structures shape and restrict the lives of women. Of course, it is important to document the inequalities faced by various groups of women and to examine the ways that women have been oppressed and victimized based on gender. Experiences such as discrimination in hiring and pay, sexual violence, and legal subordination, for example, are undeniably central to gender. Yet feminist scholarship also emphasizes the sources of power that women find: how they define themselves, influence their social contexts, and resist the restrictions that they face. The articles in this volume view women not as passive victims of patriarchal social structures but as actors who exercise control over their own lives, find pleasure and fulfillment, and resist social constraints.

Further, feminist research is not just about documenting women's experiences. It is about recognizing the ways that gender shapes the lives of both women and men and analyzing a broad system of gender. By documenting the influence of social structures and highlighting individuals' complex mixture of domination, resistance, and complicity, feminist scholarship leads us to rethink the structural changes needed to meet the needs of actual women and men.

Feminist theory and scholarship on gender, then, face a broad set of questions. The approaches to answering these questions vary enormously; we hope that you will recognize disagreement and debate, as well as cooperation, in the readings that follow. There are, however, some shared assumptions that run through the chapters in this book.

First, feminist scholars view gender as *pervasive,* as part of every feature of social life and individual identity. It is impossible, therefore, to analyze any part of social life as if it were gender neutral. As a result, feminist scholars challenge the male bias hidden under claims of scientific objectivity in academic research. As you read these articles and those in other classes, ask yourself how the social conditions and practices of doing research reinforce or challenge gender inequities.

Second, feminist researchers understand systems of oppression as *interlocking.* Race, class, ethnicity, sexuality, and other systems of domination affect how one experiences gender. Therefore, although gender is a basic fact of social life, women and men in different positions in society experience their gender and the power or oppression that results from it differently. Just as feminist researchers challenge knowledge claims about "people" based on research on men, they question knowledge about "women" based on research on white, middle-class women.

Third, feminist scholars experiment with new ways of doing research, rethinking the relationship between the researcher and the researched. Scientific research assumes that there is a separation between the scholar and the subjects of research and that this separation is necessary to produce "objective" and "valid" research. Feminist researchers challenge this tenet. Treating women as "objects" of research contravenes feminist goals of equality by elevating the researcher's agenda and perspective above those of the researched. One of the major questions of feminist thought is how to do research that empowers both the researcher and the researched. How do we create social research practices in which researcher and researched collaborate in the process of interpreting the world? For some, the solution has been to write about their own lives; some acknowledge directly how their own biases affect their work; some study groups of which they are a part; others do "participatory" or "action" research in which the researcher and the researched determine together the topics, methods, goals, and political action to follow from the project, so that the scholar is a participant in the project, but not its leader.

These are not only theoretical concerns; they are important *ethical* questions. What right does a scholar have to write about another woman's life? How should scholars write about the lives of those women and men who are different from themselves? How can feminist scholars use the skills and privileges of academic practice to diminish social inequality?

We invite you to engage in reading, thinking about, and doing feminist research. We hope that you will consider some of the central questions that run through this book. What are the commonalities and differences among women (or among men)? What, if anything, do women of different classes, races, or sexualities share in common? We hope you will reflect on the complicated balance between oppression and resistance, between the pervasive influence of the society and the ways that individuals and groups find to define themselves and carve out meaningful lives. We encourage you to discuss your ideas, to debate the issues this volume raises with your friends and classmates, to agree or disagree with the authors here, and to come to your own conclusions. We hope that through this engagement, you will consider how gender has shaped your life and how gender intersects with the other systems of inequality that affect you. We hope that you will share your understandings with others, becoming a researcher yourself and a theorist of your own and others' lives so that you might help empower us all and transform society.

Diversity and Difference

Conducting research about women has been the focus of feminist scholars from the 1960s to the present. In recent years, researchers have looked especially closely at the differences and commonalities among women and have also begun to examine how men's lives are shaped by cultural expectations of masculinity. Scholars are interested in learning about the rich complexities of how gender shapes women's and men's lives and in discovering ways of knowing that stand true to these experiences and also offer the prospect of effecting positive change. Women everywhere live with a ubiquitous "monotone" of male advantage, in all its manifestations. Yet differences among women arise from factors like race, ethnicity, class, sexual orientation, age, geographic region, and religion. Further, not all men possess the same advantages or social power. Men of subordinate racial or ethnic groups, classes, or sexual orientations may have power relative to women in their own group but are subordinate in some ways to other men and to women in more powerful groups.

Recognizing that women are not a homogeneous group raises questions about the basis of comparison and the grounds for affiliation among women. Can we even speak of "women" as a meaningful category, or is the diversity among women too great for any generalization? The readings in this section discuss points of similarity and difference among women and among men. They illustrate the vast range of meanings that gender has for women and men in different groups.

One source of commonality that has attracted and shaped feminist understanding is the idea of *oppression*. As a concept, oppression has a long history in contemporary feminist scholarship. What does it mean? Why is it important to think about? The first selection, "Oppression," addresses these questions and raises some others. In that article, Marilyn Frye defines oppression as "living one's life confined and shaped by forces and barriers which are not accidental or occasional and hence avoidable, but are systematically related to each other in such a way as to catch one between and among them and restrict or penalize motion in any direction."

The multiple sources of interrelated oppressions make it difficult for people to recognize how the systems of oppression impinge on their lives or the lives of others. Knowing about the larger social forces helps one to understand the shape of one's life and the difference between "suffering" and "suffering from oppression." As you read the other articles in this section, can you use Frye's concept of oppression to think about the experiences they describe?

Whereas Frye emphasizes how structures of oppression constrict all women, the remaining readings in this section examine the distinctions among women's experiences. Rosalinda Méndez González discusses the history of the western United States from the point of view of women of various classes and ethnicities in "Distinctions in Western Women's Experience: Ethnicity, Class, and Social Change." She suggests that the traditional history of westward expansion across the frontier is the story of only one group of women, the "pioneer" settlers of European descent. Considering the lives of Indian, Mexican, and Chinese women means reconstructing our understanding of the development of the West. This article illustrates the task of contemporary feminist researchers: to examine the experiences of diverse groups of women, consider the impact of class and race inequalities, and rethink the biased assumptions and histories that scholars have long taken for granted.

Paula Gunn Allen, similarly, suggests that assumptions about what it means to be a woman in Anglo-European culture do not hold in American Indian cultures. In "Where I Come From Is Like This," she draws on her bicultural experiences to explore the incongruity of the images of women embedded in Anglo and American Indian cultures. The images of American Indian women she grew up with are images of "practicality, strength, reasonableness, intelligence, wit, and competence," in contrast to non-Indian ideas about women as "passive and weak." Again, we see the difficulty of generalizing about women's experiences. What are the assumptions about women embedded in your own culture?

The next selection emphasizes the difficulties of accurately analyzing how systems of oppression affect peoples' lives. In "The Master's Tools Will Never Dismantle the Master's House," Audre Lorde argues that feminists must critically examine their own use of dominant concepts in their analyses of women's lives. She suggests that academic knowledge is based in an institution that historically has excluded women and people of color, and asks whether academic knowledge can undermine the inequalities on which it is based. Do you think that the "regular" methods of scholarship and science are adequate to the task of understanding the diversity among women? Will new tools be necessary? Lorde argues that encouraging women to relate to each other at the points of their differences promotes growth, creativity, and social change. Do these conversations across differences happen on your campus?

In "Confessions of a Nice Negro" Robin D. G. Kelley shows that just as gender varies for different groups of women, men also are not an undifferentiated group. He examines the complex constructions of African-American masculinity, describing how the myth of Black men as hypermasculine justifies Whites' fear and repression of them. Kelley's mild-mannered intellectual persona means that he is perceived as a "nice Negro," accessible and safe to Whites, but is simultaneously defined as less than fully masculine. Despite his commitment to a gentle, nonsexist masculinity, Kelley describes his pleasure when others perceive him as dangerous after he shaves his head. Although the power to make Whites afraid is a false power, Kelley suggests that its appeal stems from the larger overlaps between masculinity and race. What are the varieties of African-American masculinity? What are some of the varieties of masculinity for White Americans, and how are these different? Can you think of examples of other racialized masculinities?

Peggy McIntosh describes "White Privilege and Male Privilege" as part of invisible systems of domination that not only penalize women and people of color but privilege men and whites. Documenting her own largely unrecognized white privilege helps her understand how she benefits from this system. She argues that members of dominant groups are taught to see themselves as individuals and to attribute their successes to merit. In fact, McIntosh argues that she benefits in her job and daily life from advantages due to race, not merit. How does her list of benefits from white privilege change your understanding of racism? What might a similar list for male privilege look like? If you are a member of a dominant group, can you construct a list of the benefits you receive by virtue of your race, gender, sexual orientation, or class? If you are a member of a subordinated group, can you list some of the ways you are disadvantaged?

Oppression

MARILYN FRYE

It is a fundamental claim of feminism that women are oppressed. The word "oppression" is a strong word. It repels and attracts. It is dangerous and dangerously fashionable and endangered. It is much misused, and sometimes not innocently.

The statement that women are oppressed is frequently met with the claim that men are oppressed too. We hear that oppressing is oppressive to those who oppress as well as to those they oppress. Some men cite as evidence of their oppression their much-advertised inability to cry. It is tough, we are told, to be masculine. When the stresses and frustrations of being a man are cited as evidence that oppressors are oppressed by their oppressing, the word "oppression" is being stretched to meaninglessness; it is treated as though its scope includes any and all human experience of limitation or suffering, no matter the cause, degree, or consequence. Once such usage has been put over on us, then if ever we deny that any person or group is oppressed, we seem to imply that we think they never suffer and have no feelings. We are accused of insensitivity; even of bigotry. For women, such accusation is particularly intimidating, since sensitivity is one of the few virtues that have been assigned to us. If we are found insensitive, we may fear we have no redeeming traits at all and perhaps are not real women. Thus are we silenced before we begin: the name of our situation drained of meaning and our guilt mechanisms tripped.

But this is nonsense. Human beings can be miserable without being oppressed, and it is perfectly consistent to deny that a person or group is oppressed without denying that they have feelings or that they suffer. . . .

The root of the word "oppression" is the element "press." *The press of the crowd; pressed into military service; to press a pair of pants; printing press; press the button.* Presses are used to mold things or flatten them or reduce them in bulk, sometimes to reduce them by squeezing out the gases or liquids in them. Something pressed is something caught between or among forces and barriers which are so related to each other that jointly they restrain, restrict, or prevent the thing's motion or mobility. Mold. Immobilize. Reduce.

The mundane experience of the oppressed provides another clue. One of the most characteristic and ubiquitous features of the world as experienced by oppressed people is the double bind—situations in which options are reduced to a very few and all of them expose one to penalty, censure or deprivation. For example, it is often a requirement upon oppressed people that we smile and be cheerful. If we comply, we signal our docility and our acquiescence in our situation. We need not, then, be taken note of. We acquiesce in being made invisible, in our occupying no space. We participate in our own erasure. On the other hand, anything but the sunniest countenance exposes us to being perceived as mean, bitter, angry, or dangerous. This means, at the least, that we may be found "difficult" or unpleasant to work with, which is enough to cost one one's livelihood; at worst, being seen as mean, bitter, angry, or dangerous has been known to result in rape, arrest, beating, and murder. One can only choose to risk one's preferred form and rate of annihilation.

Another example: It is common in the United States that women, especially younger women, are in a bind where neither sexual activity nor sexual inactivity is all right. If she is heterosexually active, a woman is open to censure and punishment for being loose, unprincipled, or a whore. The "punishment" comes in the form of criticism, snide and embarrassing remarks, being treated as an easy lay by men, scorn from her more restrained female friends. She may have to lie and hide her behavior from her parents. She must juggle the risks of unwanted pregnancy and dangerous contraceptives. On the other hand, if she refrains from heterosexual activity, she is fairly constantly harassed by men who try to persuade her into it and pressure her to "relax" and "let her hair down"; she is threatened with labels like "frigid," "uptight," "man-hater," "bitch" and "cocktease." The same parents who would be disapproving of her sexual activity may be worried by her inactivity because it suggests she is not or will not be popular, or is not sexually normal. She may be charged with lesbianism. If a woman is raped, then if she has been heterosexually active she is subject to the presumption that she liked it (since her activity is presumed to show that she likes sex), and if she has not been heterosexually active, she is subject to the presumption that she liked it (since she is supposedly "repressed and frustrated"). Both heterosexual activity and heterosexual nonactivity are likely to be taken as proof that you wanted to be raped, and hence, of course, weren't *really* raped at all. You can't win. You are caught in a bind, caught between systematically related pressures.

Women are caught like this, too, by networks of forces and barriers that expose one to penalty, loss, or contempt whether one works outside the home or not, is on welfare or not, bears children or not, raises children or not, marries or not, stays married or not, is heterosexual, lesbian, both, or neither. Economic necessity; confinement to racial and/or sexual job ghettos; sexual harassment; sex discrimination; pressures of competing expectations and judgments about *women, wives,* and *mothers* (in the society at large, in racial and ethnic subcultures, and in one's own mind); dependence (full or partial) on husbands, parents, or the state; commitment to political ideas; loyalties to racial or ethnic or other "minority" groups; the demands of self-respect and responsibilities to others. Each of these factors exists in complex tension with every other, penalizing or prohibiting all of the apparently available options. And nipping at one's heels, always, is the endless pack of little things. If one dresses one way, one is subject to the assumption that one is advertising one's sexual availability; if one dresses another way, one appears to "not care about oneself" or to be "unfeminine." If one uses "strong language," one invites categorization as a whore or slut; if one does not, one invites categorization as a "lady"—one too delicately constituted to cope with robust speech or the realities to which it presumably refers.

The experience of oppressed people is that the living of one's life is confined and shaped by forces and barriers which are not accidental or occasional and hence avoidable, but are systematically related to each other in such a way as to catch one between and among them and restrict or penalize motion in any direction. It is the experience of being caged in: all avenues, in every direction, are blocked or booby trapped.

Cages. Consider a birdcage. If you look very closely at just one wire in the cage, you cannot see the other wires. If your conception of what is before you is determined by this myopic focus, you could look at that one wire, up and down the length of it, and be unable to see why a bird would not just fly around the wire any time it wanted to go somewhere. Furthermore, even if, one day at a time, you myopically inspected each wire, you still could not see why a bird would have trouble going past the wires to get anywhere. There is no physical property of any one wire, *nothing* that the closest scrutiny could discover, that will reveal how a bird could be inhibited or harmed by it except in the most accidental way. It is only when you step back, stop looking at the wires one by one, microscopically, and take a macroscopic view of the whole cage, that you can see why the bird does not go anywhere; and then you will see it in a moment. It will require no great subtlety of mental powers. It is perfectly *obvious* that the bird is surrounded by a network of systematically related barriers, no one of which would be the least hindrance to its flight, but which, by their relations to each other, are as confining as the solid walls of a dungeon.

It is now possible to grasp one of the reasons why oppression can be hard to see and recognize: one can study the elements of an oppressive structure with great care and some good will without seeing the structure as a whole, and hence without seeing or being able to understand that one is looking at a cage and that there are people there who are caged, whose motion and mobility are restricted, whose lives are shaped and reduced.

The arresting of vision at a microscopic level yields such common confusion as that about the male door-opening ritual. This ritual, which is remarkably widespread across classes and races, puzzles many people, some of whom do and some of whom do not find it offensive. Look at the scene of the two people approaching a door. The male steps slightly ahead and opens the door. The male holds the door open while the female glides through. Then the male goes through. The door closes after them. "Now how," one innocently asks, "can those crazy women's libbers say that is oppressive? The guy *removed* a barrier to the lady's smooth and unruffled progress." But each repetition of this ritual has a place in a pattern, in fact in several patterns. One has to shift the level of one's perception in order to see the whole picture.

The door-opening pretends to be a helpful service, but the helpfulness is false. This can be seen by noting that it will be done whether or not it makes any practical sense. Infirm men and men burdened with packages will open doors for able-bodied women who are free of physical burdens. Men will impose themselves awkwardly and jostle everyone in order to get to the door first. The act is not determined by convenience or grace. Furthermore, these very numerous acts of unneeded or even noisome "help" occur in counterpoint to a pattern of men not being helpful in many practical ways in which women might welcome help. What *women* experience is a world in which gallant princes charming commonly make a fuss about being helpful and providing small services when help and services are of little or no use, but in which there are rarely ingenious and adroit princes at hand when substantial assistance is really wanted either in mundane affairs or in situations of threat, assault, or terror. There is no help with the (his) laundry; no help typing a report at 4:00 AM; no help in mediating disputes among relatives or children. There is nothing but advice that women should stay indoors after dark, be chaperoned by a man, or when it comes down to it, "lie back and enjoy it."

The gallant gestures have no practical meaning. Their meaning is symbolic. The door-opening and similar services provided are services which really are needed by people who are for one reason or another incapacitated—unwell, burdened with parcels, etc. So the message is that women are incapable. The detachment of the acts from the concrete realities of what women need and do not need is a vehicle for the message that women's actual needs and interests are unimportant or irrelevant. Finally, these gestures imitate the behavior of servants toward masters and thus mock women, who are in most respects the servants and caretakers of men. The message of the false helpfulness of male gallantry is female dependence, the invisibility or insignificance of women, and contempt for women.

One cannot see the meanings of these rituals if one's focus is riveted upon the individual event in all its particularity, including the particularity of the individual man's present conscious intentions and motives and the individual woman's conscious perception of the event in the moment. It seems sometimes that people take a deliberately myopic view and fill their eyes with things seen microscopically in order not to see macroscopically. At any rate, whether it is deliberate or not, people can and do fail to see the oppression of women because they fail to see macroscopically and hence fail to see the various elements of the situation as systematically related in larger schemes.

As the cageness of the birdcage is a macroscopic phenomenon, the oppressiveness of the situations in which women live our various and different lives is a macroscopic phenomenon. Neither can be *seen* from a microscopic perspective. But when you look macroscopically you can see it—a network of forces and barriers which are systematically related and which conspire to the immobilization, reduction, and molding of women and the lives we live.

Distinctions in Western Women's Experience: Ethnicity, Class, and Social Change

ROSALINDA MÉNDEZ GONZÁLEZ

The issues of ethnicity, class, and social change as they relate to women in western history and to historical reevaluation derive in part from the social-change movements of the 1950s and 1960s. Until then academic research had tended to neglect the experiences of minorities, women, and the laboring classes or to justify their subordinate social condition. Then the civil rights, feminist, and nationalist movements raised challenges to these approaches.

The new research born of the rebellions of those exciting years sought to uncover and document the historical facts of the neglected groups; to critique the existing myths, stereotypes, and paradigms that veiled or rationalized the inequalities and the historical contributions of the affected social groups; and to examine and expose the structures of domination and subordination in our society.

At first, these investigations took a rigidly protective stance toward their subjects. Black or Chicano nationalist analyses tended to question all traditional assumptions and to defend all that was black or brown; women's analyses attacked institutions and ideologies as patriarchal without distinction as to class or ethnic inequalities; radicals imbued with class analysis criticized imperialism abroad and class structures at home without considering the ramifications of sex or ethnic discrimination. Those who sought to integrate the analyses of the various forms of social inequality were at first in the minority.

By the 1970s the diverse groups had successfully documented the importance of their subjects' contributions to historical development and demonstrated the existence of

social structures of domination over each group. An effort began then to integrate this analysis and to arrive at a more complex, fundamental explanation of the interconnections among these distinct social-historical experiences.

The process of including women's history, black history, Indian, Chicano, Asian, immigrant, and labor histories in the chronicles of United States history has been a first step toward an integrated history. Now we are confronted with the next step of jointly interpreting our interrelated histories. This requires going beyond the empirical combination of facts, names, and dates to the conceptual problem of seeking an explanation of how the diverse experiences were daily woven by individual human beings into a single and common historical reality.

In outlining the factors involved in these interconnected experiences, we must be careful to search for both the subjective, cultural conditions that motivated the individual woman's experiences and perceptions, and the objective, political-economic conditions that shaped the experiences of each social group.

The use of diaries, personal testimonies, oral histories, and literature has proved to be effective for uncovering the first set of conditions: women's personal or subjective experiences. But there are shortcomings to this approach. Women of the poor, slave, or laboring classes do not tend to leave diaries. Different methods and different questions have to be posed if one is to recapture the personal experiences of Indian, Hispanic, black, Asian, and poor white women of the laboring classes.

To find a conceptual interpretation of these diverse personal experiences, we must address the objective conditions of western life. This involves first challenging the traditional Turnerian interpretation of western history as the "frontier" period. The evolution of the West spans hundreds of years of Indian society before the American frontier. It is important to understand Indian social relations and the role of women before the Europeans imposed a class society.

Four centuries of Spanish conquest and settlement left a legacy of cultural development and social relations which is still in force today as, for example, in the legislation of western states.[1] Then, overlapping the three decades of Mexican rule over large parts of the West, comes the relatively brief period of United States conquest, the "frontier" period which has so absorbed myopic western historians. Finally, it is important to keep in mind that western history also comprises the twentieth-century development of women in the West.[2]

THE QUESTION OF CLASS

In studying western history since European penetration, one of the most obvious but often ignored conditions is the existence of social classes.[3] A class system was first introduced in the sixteenth century by the conquering Spaniards into the area that is now the southwestern United States.

Acknowledging the class character of Spanish and Mexican society in the Southwest penetrates the mist of generalizations which inaccurately assume classless homogeneity. Albert Camarillo's study of the Chicano communities in Santa Barbara and Los Angeles, California, delineates the four classes that comprised Mexican society: the elite rich "Californios," wealthy land-owning ranchers whose holdings averaged 25,000 acres; the middle class of small property owners and ranchers; the majority class of artisans and laborers living in humble dwellings; and the Indian population which was converted into laborers for the missions and menial servants for the wealthy Californios.[4]

In this society, what would it mean to talk about the life cycles of women? Certainly women's lives would appear different within the same household, where the wealthy Californios lived with their slavelike Indian female servants. Historian Elinor Burkett encountered this problem when she set out to study the relations of class, race, and sex in Spanish colonial South America. In feminist studies, Burkett notes, we often assume that:

> sex is as important a force in the historical process as class. Thus, we deal with the domestic squabbles of the aristocracy and the survival trials of the black female in the same conference without feeling uncomfortable; frequently forget that the position of the one is maintained only through the exploitation of the other and that such a relationship leaves little concrete room for sisterhood.[5]

If western historians raised these questions they might uncover in verbal records the gulf between the experiences of women of different classes. For example, the following black lullaby from the southern United States laments a black mother's inability to be with her newborn child through early motherhood and nursing because she had to tend to the baby of her mistress.[6]

All the Pretty Little Horses
Hushaby, don't you cry.
Go to sleepy, little baby.
When you wake, you shall have cake,
And all the pretty little horses.
Blacks and bays, dapples and grays,
Coach and six-a little horses.
Way down yonder in the meadow,
There's a poor little lambie;
The bees and the butterflies pickin' out his eyes,
The poor little thing cries, "Mammy."
Hushaby, don't you cry,
Go to sleepy, little baby.

The evidence of working-class women's experience is there, but the prevailing orientations of studying history, even women's history, steer us toward elite or educated women and their written records; then from this limited and class-biased evidence generalizations are drawn and applied to all women.[7]

In fact, if one looks at history through the eyes of the majority of women, the poor and the laboring classes, a very different picture of society emerges; the picture is far more complete, for elite eyes take *their* world as the standard and assume that all society exists, or should exist, in their image.

But to see through the eyes of the women on the bottom is to see not only the lives of the vast majority, but also to look upward through all levels of society; the flaws and contradictions of the upper classes and of the social structure they maintain become exposed from this perspective. The elite class perspective tends to be biased, myopic, and class-centered; the majority laboring class perspective tends to be more critical and encompassing.

WESTWARD EXPANSION

A second major historical consideration in studying the objective conditions that shaped women's experiences is the process of United States "westward expansion," which ultimately resulted in the appropriation of Indian, French, Spanish, and Mexican territories by the United States and the subordination of local ethnic groups as dispossessed cultural or national "minorities."

The process of westward expansion brings into play a host of major economic, political, and social developments. In a historical and economic sense the conquest of the West can be interpreted as corresponding to the similar process undergone by the western European countries in the sixteenth, seventeenth, and eighteenth centuries; known as the original or "primitive" accumulation of land and resources, this process constituted the preliminary stage for the development of industrial capitalist society.[8] In what sense is the conquest of the West a primitive accumulation?[9] And what is the significance of this process for women's experiences in the West?

Frederick Jackson Turner wrote that "the existence of an area of free land, its continuous recession, and the advance of American settlement westward, explain American development." Yet in the process of westward expansion the leading political actors clearly recognized the true character of that expansion: not an acquisition of an unclaimed territory free for the taking, not the expansion of "free land," but a military and political conquest of an already inhabited territory.[10]

Without the United States Army, in fact, the West could never have been "taken" by the settlers and pioneers. What effect did the army, both in the conquest and in its subsequent preservation, have on women in the West? What effect did it have on creating, altering, or maintaining class, ethnic, or racial divisions? Indian reservations in California were inevitably placed next to army posts and outposts.[11] What impact did the army have on Indian women who survived the devastating wars of extermination against their people?

The railroads were also instrumental in the penetration of the West. The building of the railroads was a key to expansion, not just as a means of military transportation but more fundamentally because of what lay behind the conquest: the penetration of the West by eastern capital. Linking the West Coast to the East Coast not only opened up the ports and raw materials of the West for exploitation by eastern bankers, industrialists, and land speculators but, far beyond that, opened up the Asian subcontinent for exploitation in such a way that it placed the United States at the crossroads of international commerce between the Far East and western Europe. Thus, the military conquest of the Indian and Mexican West and the construction of the transcontinental railroads opened up both a national market and an international empire for giant eastern capitalists.[12]

The building of the transcontinental railroads affected women of diverse ethnic and class backgrounds in a variety of ways; the full effects remain to be studied. We know, for example, that the railroads, after the military, provided one of the most effective ways of destroying American Indian people's subsistence on the Plains, by establishing the policy of paying sharpshooters to kill the buffalo.

The railroads stimulated mass immigration from Europe into the United States and mass migration into the West and Southwest. The construction of the railroads was accomplished by exploiting immigrant laborers: the Chinese, Japanese, and Mexicans on the West Coast, the Irish and European immigrants on the East Coast.[13]

Yet the treatment of European immigrant laborers was qualitatively different, in a political sense, from that of the Asian and Mexican immigrants.[14] Chinese laborers, for example, were brought in as bound labor, as "coolies," a politically unfree form of contract labor. They were forbidden to bring their wives or families. This restriction had a negative and long-lasting impact on the development of Chinese communities in the West, and it led to the importation of Chinese women in the most brutal form of "white slave traffic," an experience quite distinct from that of European immigrant women in the East.[15]

The importation of Mexican labor by the railroads has also left a deep legacy. As with the placement of Indian reservations next to army forts, maps show that the *colonias* or Mexican settlements in the first half of the twentieth century were invariably located along the railroad routes, since whole Mexican families were imported by the companies to clear, lay, and maintain the tracks. The railroad companies would segregate their work force along ethnic lines and establish Mexican colonies of boxcar residences in certain places along the track; thus, the phrase "the wrong side of the tracks" came to be applied to Mexican barrios.[16] In the growing search for roots among Chicanas and Chicanos, the oral histories and family records that are surfacing reveal, in instance after instance, the ties to the railroads among our parents, grandparents, and great-grandparents.[17]

Today many Chicano barrios are still alongside the "wrong side of the tracks." They developed on the original sites of the old railroad-track Mexican colonies; in cities throughout the Southwest from California to Texas, these barrios are still distinguished by adobe houses, unpaved dirt streets, lack of sidewalks, often in direct proximity to walled, modern, Anglo middle-class housing tracts with multitiered, air-conditioned, carpeted homes.

PROPERTY, PATRIARCHY, AND THE NUCLEAR FAMILY

What did the settlement of the land itself mean for women of different classes and ethnicity? Much of the preliminary analysis on women in the West focuses on pioneer women, and their lives are studied through the diaries or literature they left behind. But the majority of women in the nineteenth-century West neither read nor wrote English. Barbara Mayer Wertheimer points out that the ordinary American could not pack up and head West. "It took capital, about $1,500, to outfit a wagon, buy supplies, and tide the family over until the land began to produce. This was an impossible sum for most working-class families to come by."[18]

Without detracting from the courage and endurance of these pioneer women, we have to ask what the takeover and settlement of western lands really represent for the majority of Indian, Mexican, and immigrant women in the West. A more comprehensive answer has to be found by studying first what western conquest and settlement represented in American economic and historical development. The West was not really developed by individual pioneering men and women seeking land. Rather, the West was made economically exploitable by federal intervention in the form of massive land grants to railroads, mining companies, timber companies, and land speculators, and by virtue of federal legislation and funding that subsidized these private profit-making ventures and speculators at public expense.[19]

Industrial and financial magnates did not operate simply out of greed for lucrative profits; they were driven by the economic necessity for expansion, which is at the heart of this system of competition and property. When the United States broke away from England in 1783, capitalist expansion was faced with three obstacles: the plantation slave economy of the South, which held onto a bound labor force, raw materials, and productive lands; the Indian tribes and nations, which had been pushed together into the West; and the Mexican Northwest.

These barriers could be overcome only by the usurpation and appropriation that have characterized the birth of capitalism wherever it has appeared. This process essentially involves breaking up the existing economic system (e.g., feudalism, tribal societies, peasant communities), concentrating land and wealth in the hands of a few entrepreneurs, and uprooting the native peoples from their land and mode of living to provide a source of wage labor.

A bloody Civil War was launched to remove the first obstacle. Wars against the Indians removed the second, and an unprovoked war against Mexico eliminated the third obstacle. After the defeat of the slave plantation economy, Indian tribal societies, and Mexican feudalism in the Southwest, the United States engaged in accelerated expansion and conquest of western territories. This process involved plunder, massacres, swindling, and bribery. It succeeded in imposing capitalist private property and, equally important, individualism and the patriarchal nuclear family, which is so necessary to sustain this form of property.

Various methods were used to impose this system of property and family in the West. In the accumulation of Indian lands, force was not the only technique applied. Andrew Jackson and subsequent presidents attempted to deprive the Indians of their lands by refusing to deal with them as tribes or to negotiate treaties with them as nations. Instead the government forced the Indians, through bribery, treachery, and legislation, to deal with the government as individuals; this policy set them up against each other with the incentive of immediate cash payment to individuals selling plots of land. By forcing the foreign system of private property onto them, the government was attempting to destroy the fundamental communal basis of Indian tribes.

The General Allotment Act, or Dawes Act, of 1883 sought to push the Indians out of the way of western penetration and open up their lands to exploitation, by alloting parcels of tribal land to individuals. The bill was condemned by Senator Henry Teller of Colorado as "a bill to despoil the Indians of their lands and to make them vagabonds on the face of the earth," yet Congress passed it with the justification that "Indians needed to become competitive." Senator Henry Dawes, principal proponent of the measure, argued that Indians "needed to become selfish."[20]

Two centuries earlier the French colonizers in Canada had been amazed at the egalitarianism and freedom among the women and men of the Montagnais tribe, at their disdain for formal authority and domination, and at the respect and independence between husbands and wives. Yet the Jesuit policy of colonization sought to "give authority to one of them to rule the others," and to teach them "to elect and obey 'Captains,' inducing them to give up their children for schooling, and above all, attempting to introduce the principle of binding monogamy and wifely fidelity and obedience to male authority."[21]

In a similar manner the United States recognized that to break down Indian resistance it was necessary to undermine the tribal and clan social organization of the Indians and to enforce upon them the individual nuclear family, with the husband the authority figure over the women and children. This attempt had the multiple purposes of forcing the

Indians to alienate their communal tribal lands, breaking their economic and social clan organization, transforming them into individualist and competitive capitalist farmers, and providing the nuclear family institution through which the ideology of private property, individualism, and dominant–subordinate relations could be passed on.

Other American people—the small farmers, European immigrants, and settlers—also were subject to official policies promoting individualism in the process of westward expansion. The Homestead Act of 1862, which preceded the Dawes Act by almost three decades, forced individuals and individual families to settle independently; no land was made available for whole communities. On the other hand, huge tracts of land were made available only to the big companies penetrating the West: the railroads, banks, land speculators, and mining companies. While the individual homesteaders were told, "The government bets 160 acres against the entry fee of $14 that the settler can't live on the land for five years without starving to death,"[22] the financial and industrial giants were granted all the land they wanted; the government even provided capital for the infrastructural construction they needed to operate and extract their private profits.

The fostering of private property, individualism, and the nuclear family in the West thus resulted on the one hand in the breakup of the population into individual, isolated, competitive minuscule units: nuclear families; and the concentration of wealth and power in the hands of an increasingly smaller elite on the other—monopolies. For monopolization to take place, it was necessary to fragment the population through the imposition of private property.

The United States government promoted this process in the West. Neither the government's nor the monopolies' intention, however, was to perpetuate small-scale production and independence. Rather, they brought people in to clear the land, develop the resources, and make the area productive and, when this was done, usurped this settled population from their small plots and transformed them into the wage-labor force needed in the West. Both stages were accomplished by fostering private property, individual ownership of land, and the privatization of the nuclear family.

EXPLOITATION OF WOMEN'S DOMESTIC LABOR

The patriarchal nuclear family was important, not just as a means of preserving and transferring private property and the values associated with it, but also, for the families of the laboring classes, as a means of privately producing through the domestic labor of women the goods and services necessary to sustain the agricultural or industrial labor force needed by capitalist enterprises.[23]

Among Mexican immigrant families in the early twentieth-century Southwest, women's domestic labor was exploited indirectly by large employers as a means of subsidizing the payment of discriminatory and substandard wages to their Mexican workers.[24] This policy was refined by the monopolies engaged in developing the Southwest; these companies in the extractive, infrastructural, and agricultural industries first imported Mexican immigrants in large numbers at the turn of the century.[25]

The monopolistic pattern of southwestern land ownership and industry in many places retained vestiges of the feudal system, such as tenant or sharecropping systems in agriculture or debt peonage in company mining towns. These practices retarded the assimilation of Mexican immigrants into the working class, and had the effect of perpetuating the bondage of the wife and children under the patriarchal family. Patriarchal family relations were particularly strong in rural areas. Women who were hired as agricultural laborers to pick cotton were never paid their own wages; rather, these were paid to the father, husband, or brother. Because of this system of "family wages," feudal relations in the countryside were not easily broken down, and wage labor did not offer women the economic independence that weakened patriarchal relations as did urban or industrial employment.[26]

Even in urban areas, Mexican families found themselves segregated and living in boxcars or makeshift housing. Mario Garcia, in a study of Mexican families in El Paso, Texas, at the turn of the century, documented how their reduced standard of living provided a justification for the payment of wages far below the "American standard." Mexican families were forced to live "75 percent cheaper than Americans" by a series of economic and political mechanisms. Racial discrimination and starvation wages confined Mexicans to the worst slums, with overcrowded, inferior housing in adobes or shacks. These settlements were denied public services (water, paved streets, electricity, sewers) because the Anglo property owners refused to pay taxes to provide them and because the city, in turn, argued that Mexican residents were not property owners and taxpayers, and therefore not entitled to services.[27]

Given this living situation, the domestic labor of women and children was particularly arduous. They hauled water long distances from the river in buckets, hand-ground corn for hours, gathered and chopped wood for fuel, to make up for the lack of adequate wages and public services.

This extreme exploitation of family labor and the intense immiseration of the laboring communities caused high infant mortality rates, infectious diseases, and malnourishment, while providing the justification for lower wages. It also provided a pool of severely underpaid Mexican female servants whose dusk-to-dawn exploitation in the homes of Anglo-American families freed the women of these families to seek outside employment and enter the industrial world. The economic advancement of many Anglo-American women in the Southwest was carried out on the backs of Mexican-American women, as it was in the South on the backs of black women, and the immediate beneficiaries were the banks and monopolies dominating the South and West.

THE QUESTION OF RESEARCH AND SOCIAL CHANGE

My discussion has not centered on individual heroines of different ethnic or class backgrounds nor on the important subject of women's struggles to change the conditions of ethnic, class, racial, or sex discrimination. I have sought to demonstrate the necessity of taking into consideration the larger, more fundamental political-economic forces in the development of the West, which must be studied if one is to understand the experiences of *all* women.

The forces that had come to dominate the West at the end of the nineteenth century have continued to shape the experiences of women in the twentieth century, the more so as economic concentration and its influence through the growth of government power have expanded. In 1962, the wealthiest 10 percent of the United States population controlled close to 70 percent of all personal wealth, while the other 90 percent of the population shared a little over 30 percent.[28] Even this small share of the pie was unevenly divided. Poverty in the United States was concentrated in the South and West, and among blacks and Mexican-Americans. In 1960, for example, official figures showed that in the Southwest 35 percent of the Spanish-surnamed families and 42 percent of non-white families were living in poverty. Among Anglo families, only 16 percent were listed in poverty, and yet this represented a very large number, since Anglos comprised 66 percent of all poor in the Southwest.[29]

Today we know that poverty and unemployment have worsened, that two out of every three persons in poverty are women, and that black women and Chicanas are among those most affected. This situation continues as the "minority" peoples of the Southwest are rapidly becoming the majority.

The trend toward greater inequality is growing. Richard M. Cyert, president of Pittsburgh's Carnegie-Mellon University, which houses the most advanced research and experimentation center in the robotics fields, recently stated. "I don't think there's any question that we're moving toward a society where income distribution will be even more unequal than it is at present and where unemployment is going to be even greater than it is now."[30]

The issue of inequality confronts anyone seeking to develop a historically accurate, comprehensive analysis that integrates the experiences of the majority of poor and working-class women, the experiences of black, Chicana, Indian, Asian, and immigrant women. We have been dealing with the divisions among us: while these divisions of race and class have existed, we also have to deal with the fundamental unity among us.

Our task is to discover both the causes of the artificial, socially created divisions that have kept us apart and ways to make our fundamental unity a reality. If we are concerned with social change, if our research is to involve a commitment to shedding light on the historical roots of contemporary problems and inequalities so that these inequalities can be abolished, then our research will have to address the issues of inequality, exploitation, and the related political question of democracy. For the history of the West, as the history of the United States, is a history of exploitation of the labor, land, and resources of diverse groups of peoples: Indians, indentured servants, black slaves, farmers, the working class, immigrants, and, not least, the exploitation of women in the home.

For this reason it is also a history of the unfolding struggle over democratic rights and against the powerful minority of antidemocratic forces who have sought to monopolize political power to ensure their economic concentration. This struggle for democracy has involved the Indians' struggle for their land and sovereignty; the struggle of immigrants, of blacks, of Chicanos; working-class and socialist struggles; and, integral to all of these, women's struggle for equality and political emancipation.

ACKNOWLEDGMENTS

Special thanks to Nancy Paige Fernandez, of the Program in Comparative Culture at the University of California at Irvine, for her thoughtful critique of my first draft, and to Lisa Rubens, Lyn Reese, Deanne Thompson, and all the other women at the Women's West Conference whose warm encouragement and extensive discussions and comments enlightened my analysis and understanding.

NOTES

1. E.g., community-property laws for married couples in many southern and western states (especially in former Spanish and French territories); and the Texas "cuckoo law," which allowed a husband to kill his wife's lover if he caught them "in the act." On community property consult Barbara Allen Babcock et al., *Sex Discrimination and the Law* (Boston: Little, Brown, 1975), pp. 604–13. On the Texas "cuckoo law" see "The 'Equal Shooting Rights,'" *Texas Observer,* Mar. 16, 1965; and "Origins of the Cuckoo Law," Apr. 2, 1965. The latter article observes, "Like so many of our especially Texan legal institutions (our homestead law, our venue statute, the independent executor, our adoption law, and our community property system), our legal attitude toward the cuckold's right to take vengeance for an affront to his conjugal honor is Spanish in origin." More accurately, they are feudal in origin.

2. If we include the twentieth century, certain "academic" problems are resolved, such as that there were few black women in "the West" narrowly defined as the frontier period. If we define the West more fully, the presence of black women emerges as a real issue. How, for example, did the development of Jim Crow in the South in the early twentieth century under the sponsorship of the large propertied and monied interests affect women when Jim Crow was imposed on black, Mexican, and Asian communities in the West?

3. Louis M. Hacker, in "Sections—or Classes?" *The Nation* 137, no. 355 (26 July 1933): 108–10 leveled a sharp critique at the Turnerian thesis of a unique and democratic frontier environment in the West. See also Barry D. Karl, "Frederick Jackson Turner: The Moral Dilemma of Professionalization," *Reviews in American History* 3 (March 1975): 1–7.

4. Albert Camarillo, *Chicanos in a Changing Society: From Mexican Pueblos to American Barrios in Santa Barbara and Southern California, 1848–1930* (Cambridge, Mass.: Harvard University Press, 1979). Other studies of sixteenth- to nineteenth-century Mexican families or women include Leonard Pitt, *The Decline of the Californios: A Social History of the Spanish-Speaking Californians, 1846–1890* (Berkeley: University of California Press, 1971); Richard Griswold del Castillo, *The Los Angeles Barrio, 1850–1890: A Social History* (Berkeley: University of California Press, 1979); Richard Griswold del Castillo, *La Familia: Chicano Families in the Urban Southwest, 1848 to the Present* (Notre Dame, Ind.: University of Notre Dame Press, 1984); Frances Leon Swadesh, *Los Primeros Pobladores, Hispanic Americans of the Ute Frontier* (Notre Dame, Ind.: University of Notre Dame Press, 1974); Ramon A. Gutierrez, *Marriage, Sex, and the Family: Social Change in Colonial New Mexico, 1690–1846* (Ph.D. diss., University of Wisconsin, Madison, 1980); Ramon A. Gutierrez, "From Honor to Love: Transformation of the Meaning of Sexuality in Colonial New Mexico," in Raymond T. Smith, ed., *Love, Honor, and Economic Fate: Interpreting Kinship Ideology and Practice in Latin America* (Chapel Hill: University of North Carolina Press, 1983); Ramon A. Gutierrez, "Marriage and Seduction in Colonial New Mexico," in Adelaida del Castillo, ed., *Between Borders: Essays on Mexicana/Chicana Women's History,* Chicana Studies Research Center (Encino, CA: Floricanto Press, 1990); Gloria E. Miranda, *"Gente De Razon* Marriage Patterns in Spanish and Mexican California: A Case Study of Santa Barbara and Los Angeles," *Southern California Quarterly* 39 no. 1 (March 1957): 149–66; Jane Dysart, "Mexican Women in San Antonio, 1830–1860: The Assimilation Process," *Western Historical Quarterly* 7 no. 4 (October 1976): 365–75; Fray Angelico Chavez, "Dona Tules, Her Fame and Her Funeral," *Palacio* 57 (August 1950): 227–34; Marcela Lucero Trujillo, "The Spanish Surnamed Woman of Yester Year," in José Otero and Evelio Echevarria, eds., *Hispanic Colorado* (Fort Collins, Colo.: Centennial Publications, 1977); Daniel J. Garr, "A Rare and Desolate Lane: Population and Race in Hispanic California," *Western Historical Quarterly* 6, no. 2 (April 1975): 133–48. A masterful bibliography on the "Borderlands," containing hundreds of references for further research, is Charles C. Cumberland, *The United States–Mexican Border: A Selective Guide to the Literature of the Region,* published by *Rural Sociology* as vol. 25, no. 2 (June 1970): 230 pp. The work includes references to Spanish–Indian relations in the region.

5. Elinor C. Burkett, "In Dubious Sisterhood: Race and Class in Spanish Colonial South America," *Latin American Perspectives* 4 nos. 1–2 (Winter–Spring, 1977): 18–26.

6. "All the Pretty Little Horses," in Middleton Harris et al., *The Black Book* (New York: Random House, 1974), p. 65. The book is a photographic documentary history of the Black experience in the United States, including documents and graphics of blacks in the West.

7. For example, Barbara Welter's "The Cult of True Womanhood: 1820–1860," *American Quarterly* 18, no. 2 (1966): 151–74, reprinted in Michael Gordon, ed., *The American Family in Socio-Historical Perspective* (New York: St. Martin's Press, 1973). Welter assumes an upper-class, native WASP homogeneity of all women in America: "It was a fearful obligation, a solemn responsibility, which the nineteenth century *American woman* had—to uphold the pillars of the temple with her frail *white hand*" (p. 225, emphasis added). Her article provides no discussion of property or of women and the family's relation to property. In her only (indirect) reference to the economic character of American society and its class divisions, she blithely passes by without acknowledging these contradictions: "America was a land of precarious fortunes. . . . the woman who had servants today, might tomorrow, because of a depression or panic, be forced to do her own work. . . . she was to be the same cheerful consoler of her husband in their cottage as in their mansion" (p. 238).

In fact, this section contains the only references to the existence of other classes of women: ". . . the value of a wife in case of business reverses . . . of course she had a little help from 'faithful Dinah' who absolutely refused to leave her beloved mistress" (pp. 238–239). Welter cites quotations linking the Cult of True Womanhood to a certain order of society ("that a stable order of society depended upon her maintaining her traditional place in it" [p. 242]), yet she never questions that order, never examines that society and why its maintenance depended on women's domestic subordination.

8. Cf. Leo Huberman, *Man's Worldly Goods: The Story of the Wealth of Nations* (New York: Monthly Review Press, 1936); Maurice Dobb, *Studies in the Development of Capitalism* (New York: International Publishers, 1947). An incisive presentation of primitive accumulation and its devastating impact on peasant families in Europe is found in Karl Marx, *Capital,* vol. 1, part 8, "The So-Called Primitive Accumulation."

9. Raul A. Fernandez, in *The United States–New Mexico Border: A Politico-Economic Profile* (Notre Dame, Ind.: University of Notre Dame Press, 1977), presents an analysis of the complex character of this process in the Southwest. Ray Allen Billington's classic *Westward Expansion* traces the historical facts of the process of westward expansion, though from the perspective of Frederick Jackson Turner's "frontier thesis."

10. Both Jefferson Davis and Captain Randolph B. Marcy compared the conquest of the West with the French imperialist conquest of Algeria, and both argued that the United States Army should apply the French tactics in that conquest to the conquest of the Indians in the West. Walter Prescott Webb, *The Great Plains* (Lincoln: University of Nebraska Press, ca. 1931), pp. 194, 195, 196.

11. Lynwood Carranco, *Genocide and Vendetta: The Round Valley Wars in Northern California* (Norman: University of Oklahoma Press, 1981). An excellent survey of government–Indian relations is found in D'Arcy McNichols, *Native American Tribalism: Indian Survivals and Renewals* (published for the Institute of Race Relations, London, by Oxford University Press, 1973). Indian women's resistance in the face of both the Spanish and United States conquests is presented in Victoria Brady, Sarah Crome, and Lyn Reese's "Resist and Survive, Aspects of Native Women of California," (MS Sarah Crome, Institute for the Study of Social Change, University of California, Berkeley, Calif.)

12. For a very explicit account of the connections between this internal conquest and the creation of a foreign empire by the United States, see Scott Nearing, *The American Empire* (New York: Rand School of Social Science, 1921). See also Leo Huberman, *We, the People* (New York, London: Harper Brothers, 1947).

13. A good overview of immigration in the United States is found in Barbara Kaye Greenleaf, *America Fever: The Story of American Immigration* (New York: New American Library, 1974).

14. Rosalinda M. González, "Capital Accumulation and Mexican Immigration to the United States" (Ph.D. diss., University of California at Irvine, 1981) offers a political-economic analysis of the discriminatory treatment of Asian and Mexican immigrants that differs from the traditional explanations in terms of racism.

15. Dorothy Gray, "Minority Women in the West, Juanita, Biddy Mason, Donaldina Cameron," in *Women of the West* (Millbrae, Calif.: Les Femmes Publishing, 1976), pp. 62–75; *Asian Women* (Berkeley: University of California, Dwinelle Hall, 1971); Ruthanne Lum McCunn, *An Illustrated History of the Chinese in America* (San Francisco: Design Enterprises, 1979).

16. Case studies of these barrios and their twentieth-century development appear in Arthur J. Rubel, *Across the Tracks: Mexican-Americans in a Texas City* (Austin: University of Texas Press, 1966); and Ricardo Romo, *East Los Angeles, History of a Barrio* (Austin: University of Texas Press, 1983). The historical development of the Chicano people is examined in Carey McWilliams's classic *North from Mexico: The Spanish Speaking People of the United States* (New York: Greenwood Press, 1968); Rodolfo Acuna, *Occupied America: A History of Chicanos* (New York: Harper & Row, 1981); and the excellent bilingual pictorial history by Chicano Communications Center, *450 Years of Chicano History in Pictures* (South Pasadena, Calif.: Bilingual Educations Services, n.d.). A case study of how monopoly-motivated reforms of the Progressive Era were applied to Mexican immigrant communities at the turn of the century is found in Gilbert G. Gonzalez, *Progressive Education: A Marxist Interpretation* (Minneapolis: Marxist Educational Press, 1982). A historical analysis of Chicanas is presented in Martha P. Cotera, *Diosa y Hembra: The History and Heritage of Chicanas in the U.S.* (Austin, Tex.: Information Systems Development, 1976).

17. See, e.g., the beautiful and poignant description in Jose Lona's "Biographical Sketch of the Life of an Immigrant Woman," in Maria Linda Apodaca, "The Chicana Woman: An Historical Materialist Analysis," *Latin American Perspectives* 4, nos. 1–2:

pp. 70–89. The Institute of Oral History at the University of Texas at El Paso has a growing collection of over 500 taped interviews, many of which relate to the railroads.

18. Barbara Mayer Wertheimer, *We Were There: The Story of Working Women in America* (New York: Pantheon Books, 1977), p. 249. Lillian Schlissel, in *Women's Diaries of the Westward Journey* (New York: Schocken Books, 1982), pointed out that most of the western pioneers were landowners and that their parents had also been landowners, "a class of 'peasant proprietors'" (pp. 10–11).

19. See, e.g., Gabriel Kolko, *Railroads and Regulation* (Westport, Conn.: Greenwood Press, 1976); Robert Wiebe, *The Search for Order, 1877–1920* (New York: Hill and Wang, 1968); James Weinstein, *The Corporate Idea in the Liberal State, 1900–1918* (Boston: Beacon Press, 1968); Matthew Josephson, *The Robber Barons* (New York: Harcourt Brace, 1934); and Matthew Josephson, *The Money Lords* (New York: Weybright and Talley, 1972).

20. McNichols, *Native American Tribalism.* For a brief description of the negative effects on tribal solidarity from the imposition of individualism and the nuclear family on Indian society, see the first two chapters of Keith Basso's *The Cibecue Apache* (New York: Holt, Rinehart and Winston, 1970).

21. Eleanor Leacock, "Women in Development: Anthropological Facts and Fictions, " *Latin American Perspectives* 4, nos. 1–2.

22. Sheryll and Gene Pattersen-Black, *Western Women in History and Literature* (Crawford, Neb.: Cottonwood Press, 1978), p. 5.

23. An important article by Joan Jensen, "Cloth, Bread, and Boarders: Women's Household Production for the Market," *The Review of Radical Political Economics* 12, no. 2 (Summer 1980): 14–24, examines women's household production from the late-eighteenth to early-twentieth centuries. Jensen concludes that it increased the economic productivity of the family through women's provision of services and the home production of produce for domestic consumption and for local and regional markets. In rural areas the domestic labor of women allowed men to increase production of cash crops for urban markets without increasing food costs. "Low food costs combined with taking in boarders allowed the males of American urban families to work for lower wages than they might have required had women not contributed to the family income."

24. Rosalinda M. González, "Mexican Immigrants in the United States: Cultural Conflict and Class Transformation," *Labor History,* forthcoming; and Rosalinda M. González, "Chicanas and Mexican Immigrant Families, 1920–1940" in Joan Jensen and Lois Scharf, eds., *Decades of Discontent: The Women's Movement, 1920–1940* (Westport, Conn.: Greenwood Press, 1983).

25. Many of the leading entrepreneurs in western expansion also had their stakes in foreign conquest. In the Southwest, for example, Adolph Spreckles, who built his fortune in California and Hawaii sugar plantations, merged with Henry C. Havemeyer, the eastern sugar king, to form the sugar trust, which was obtaining concessions in Mexico to grant it complete monopolization. Spreckles was a close friend of the Southern Pacific Railroad, which under the leadership of Henry Huntington and subsequently under William Harriman was gobbling up railroads in the United States and Mexico and absorbing steamship lines and ports. John Kenneth Turner, *Barbarous Mexico* (Austin: University of Texas Press, 1969); Carey McWilliams, *Factories in the Field* (Santa Barbara, Calif.: Peregrine Publishers, 1971).

26. Ruth Allen, *The Labor of Women in the Production of Cotton* (Austin, Tex.: University of Texas Press, 1931).

27. Mario T. Garcia, *Desert Immigrants: The Mexicans of El Paso, 1880–1920* (New Haven, Conn.: Yale University Press, 1981).

28. Institute for Labor Education and Research, *What's Wrong with the U.S. Economy?* (Boston: South End Press, 1982), pp. xi, 32.

29. Leo Grebler et al., in "A Preview of Socioeconomic Conditions," *The Mexican American People* (New York: The Free Press, 1970), pp. 13–34.

30. Donald Dewey, "Robots Reach Out," *United* (August 1983): 92–99.

Where I Come From Is Like This

PAULA GUNN ALLEN

I

Modern American Indian women, like their non-Indian sisters, are deeply engaged in the struggle to redefine themselves. In their struggle they must reconcile traditional tribal definitions of women with industrial and postindustrial non-Indian definitions. Yet while these definitions seem to be more or less mutually exclusive, Indian women must somehow harmonize and integrate both in their own lives.

An American Indian woman is primarily defined by her tribal identity. In her eyes, her destiny is necessarily that of her people, and her sense of herself as a woman is first and foremost prescribed by her tribe. The definitions of woman's roles are as diverse as tribal cultures in the Americas. In some she is devalued, in others she wields considerable power. In some she is a familial/clan adjunct, in some she is as close to autonomous as her economic circumstances and psychological traits permit. But in no tribal definitions is she perceived in the same way as are women in western industrial and postindustrial cultures.

In the West, few images of women form part of the cultural mythos, and these are largely sexually charged. Among Christians, the madonna is the female prototype, and she is portrayed as essentially passive: her contribution is simply that of birthing. Little else is attributed to her and she certainly possesses few of the characteristics that are attributed to mythic figures among Indian tribes. This image is countered (rather than balanced) by the witch/goddess/whore characteristics designed to reinforce cultural beliefs about women, as well as western adversarial and dualistic perceptions of reality.

The tribes see women variously, but they do not question the power of femininity. Sometimes they see women as fearful, sometimes peaceful, sometimes omnipotent and omniscient, but they never portray women as mindless, helpless, simple, or oppressed. And while the women in a given tribe, clan, or band may be all these things, the individual woman is provided with a variety of images of women from the interconnected supernatural, natural, and social worlds she lives in.

As a half-breed American Indian woman, I cast about in my mind for negative images of Indian women, and I find none that are directed to Indian women alone. The negative images I do have are of Indians in general and in fact are more often of males than of females. All these images come to me from non-Indian sources, and they are always balanced by a positive image. My ideas of womanhood, passed on largely by my mother and grandmothers, Laguna Pueblo women, are about practicality, strength, reasonableness, intelligence, wit, and competence. I also remember vividly the women who came to my father's store, the women who held me and sang to me, the women at Feast Day, at Grab Days, the women in the kitchen of my Cubero home, the women I grew up with; none of them appeared weak or helpless, none of them presented herself tentatively. I remember a certain reserve on those lovely brown faces; I remember the direct gaze of eyes framed by bright-colored shawls draped over their heads and cascading down their backs. I remember the clean cotton dresses and carefully pressed hand-embroidered aprons they always wore; I remember laughter and good food, especially the sweet bread and the oven bread they gave us. Nowhere in my mind is there a foolish woman, a dumb woman, a vain woman, or a plastic woman, though the Indian women I have known have shown a wide range of personal style and demeanor.

My memory includes the Navajo woman who was badly beaten by her Sioux husband; but I also remember that my grandmother abandoned her Sioux husband long ago. I recall the stories about the Laguna woman beaten regularly by her husband in the presence of her children so that the children would not believe in the strength and power of femininity. And I remember the women who drank, who got into fights with other women and with the men, and who often won those battles. I have memories of tired women, partying women, stubborn women, sullen women, amicable women, selfish women, shy women, and aggressive women. Most of all I remember the women who laugh and scold and sit uncomplaining in the long sun on feast days and who cook wonderful food on wood stoves, in beehive mud ovens, and over open fires outdoors.

Among the images of women that come to me from various tribes as well as my own are White Buffalo Woman, who came to the Lakota long ago and brought them the religion of the Sacred Pipe, which they still practice; Tinotzin the goddess, who came to Juan Diego to remind him that she still walked the hills of her people and sent him with her message, her demand, and her proof to the Catholic bishop in the city nearby. And from Laguna I take the images of Yellow Woman, Coyote Woman, Grandmother Spider (Spider Old Woman), who brought the light, who gave us weaving and medicine, who gave us life. Among the Keres she is known as Thought Woman, who created us all and who keeps us in creation even now. I remember Iyatiku, Earth Woman, Corn Woman, who guides and counsels the people to peace and who welcomes us home when we cast off this coil of flesh as huskers cast off the leaves that wrap the corn. I remember Iyatiku's sister, Sun Woman, who held metals and cattle, pigs and sheep, highways and engines and so many things in her bundle, who went away to the east saying that one day she would return.

II

Since the coming of the Anglo-Europeans beginning in the fifteenth century, the fragile web of identity that long held tribal people secure has gradually been weakened and torn. But the oral tradition has prevented the complete destruction of the web, the ultimate disruption of tribal ways. The oral tradition is vital; it heals itself and the tribal web by adapting to the flow of the present while never relinquishing its connection to the past. Its adaptability has always been required, as many generations have experienced. Certainly the modern American Indian woman bears slight resemblance to her forebears—at least on superficial examination—but she is still a tribal woman in her deepest

being. Her tribal sense of relationship to all that is continues to flourish. And though she is at times beset by her knowledge of the enormous gap between the life she lives and the life she was raised to live, and while she adapts her mind and being to the circumstances of her present life, she does so in tribal ways, mending the tears in the web of being from which she takes her existence as she goes.

My mother told me stories all the time, though I often did not recognize them as that. My mother told me stories about cooking and childbearing; she told me stories about menstruation and pregnancy; she told me stories about gods and heroes, about fairies and elves, about goddesses and spirits; she told me stories about the land and the sky, about cats and dogs, about snakes and spiders; she told me stories about climbing trees and exploring the mesas; she told me stories about going to dances and getting married; she told me stories about dressing and undressing, about sleeping and waking; she told me stories about herself, about her mother, about her grandmother. She told me stories about grieving and laughing, about thinking and doing; she told me stories about school and about people; about darning and mending; she told me stories about turquoise and about gold; she told me European stories and Laguna stories; she told me Catholic stories and Presbyterian stories; she told me city stories and country stories; she told me political stories and religious stories. She told me stories about living and stories about dying. And in all of those stories she told me who I was, who I was supposed to be, whom I came from, and who would follow me. In this way she taught me the meaning of the words she said, that all life is a circle and everything has a place within it. That's what she said and what she showed me in the things she did and the way she lives.

Of course, through my formal, white, Christian education, I discovered that other people had stories of their own—about women, about Indians, about fact, about reality—and I was amazed by a number of startling suppositions that others made about tribal customs and beliefs. According to the un-Indian, non-Indian view, for instance, Indians barred menstruating women from ceremonies and indeed segregated them from the rest of the people, consigning them to some space specially designed for them. This showed that Indians considered menstruating women unclean and not fit to enjoy the company of decent (nonmenstruating) people, that is, men. I was surprised and confused to hear this because my mother had taught me that white people had strange attitudes toward menstruation: they thought something was bad about it, that it meant you were sick, cursed, sinful, and weak and that you had to be very careful during that time. She taught me that menstruation was a normal occurrence, that I could

AIN'T I A WOMAN?

SOJOURNER TRUTH

Well, children, where there is so much racket there must be something out of kilter. I think that 'twixt the negroes of the South and the women of the North, all talking about rights, the white men will be in a fix pretty soon. But what's all this here talking about?

That man over there says that women need to be helped into carriages, and lifted over ditches, and to have the best place everywhere. Nobody ever helps me into carriages, or over mud-puddles, or gives me any best place! An ain't I a woman? Look at me! Look at my arm! I have ploughed and planted, and gathered into barns, and no man could head me! And ain't I a woman? I could work as much and eat as much as a man—when I could get it—and bear the lash as well! And ain't I a woman? I have borne thirteen children, and seen them most all sold off to slavery, and when I cried out with my mother's grief, none but Jesus heard me! and ain't I a woman?

Then they talk about this thing in the head; what's this they call it? [Intellect, someone whispers.] That's it, honey. What's that got to do with women's rights or negro's rights? If my cup won't hold but a pint, and yours holds a quart, wouldn't you be mean not to let me have my little half-measure full?

Then that little man in black there, he says women can't have as much rights as men, 'cause Christ wasn't a woman! Where did your Christ come from? Where did your Christ come from? From God and a woman! Man had nothing to do with Him.

If the first woman God ever made was strong enough to turn the world upside down all alone, these women together ought to be able to turn it back, and get it right side up again! And now they is asking to do it, the men better let them.

Obliged to you for hearing me, and now old Sojourner ain't got nothing more to say.

Sojourner Truth, excerpt from "Ain't I a Woman?" as found in *Women, Children, and Society: Popular Readings in Women's Studies,* edited by Mary Margaret Fonow and Cathy Rakowski (New York: Simon & Schuster Custom Publishing, 1994).

go swimming or hiking or whatever else I wanted to do during my period. She actively scorned women who took to their beds, who were incapacitated by cramps, who "got the blues."

As I struggled to reconcile these very contradictory interpretations of American Indians' traditional beliefs concerning menstruation, I realized that the menstrual taboos were about power, not about sin or filth. My conclusion was later borne out by some tribes' own explanations, which, as you may well imagine, came as quite a relief to me.

The truth of the matter as many Indians see it is that women who are at the peak of their fecundity are believed to possess power that throws male power totally out of kilter. They emit such force that, in their presence, any male-owned or -dominated ritual or sacred object cannot do its usual task. For instance, the Lakota say that a menstruating woman anywhere near a yuwipi man, who is a special sort of psychic, spirit-empowered healer, for a day or so before he is to do his ceremony will effectively disempower him. Conversely, among many if not most tribes, important cere-

monies cannot be held without the presence of women. Sometimes the ritual woman who empowers the ceremony must be unmarried and virginal so that the power she channels is unalloyed, unweakened by sexual arousal and penetration by a male. Other ceremonies require tumescent women, others the presence of mature women who have borne children, and still others depend for empowerment on postmenopausal women. Women may be segregated from the company of the whole band or village on certain occasions, but on certain occasions men are also segregated. In short, each ritual depends on a certain balance of power, and the positions of women within the phases of womanhood are used by tribal people to empower certain rites. This does not derive from a male-dominant view; it is not a ritual observance imposed on women by men. It derives from a tribal view of reality that distinguishes tribal people from feudal and industrial people.

Among the tribes, the occult power of women, inextricably bound to our hormonal life, is thought to be very great; many hold that we possess innately the blood-given power to kill—with a glance, with a step, or with a judicious mixing of menstrual blood into somebody's soup. Medicine women among the Pomo of California cannot practice until they are sufficiently mature; when they are immature, their power is diffuse and is likely to interfere with their practice until time and experience have it under control. So women of the tribes are not especially inclined to see themselves as poor helpless victims of male domination. Even in those tribes where something akin to male domination was present, women are perceived as powerful, socially, physically, and metaphysically. In times past, as in times present, women carried enormous burdens with aplomb. We were far indeed from the "weaker sex," the designation that white aristocratic sisters unhappily earned for us all.

I remember my mother moving furniture all over the house when she wanted it changed. She didn't wait for my father to come home and help—she just went ahead and moved the piano, a huge upright from the old days, the couch, the refrigerator. Nobody had told her she was too weak to do such things. In imitation of her, I would delight in loading trucks at my father's store with cases of pop or fifty-pound sacks of flour. Even when I was quite small I could do it, and it gave me a belief in my own physical strength that advancing middle age can't quite erase. My mother used to tell me about the Acoma Pueblo women she had seen as a child carrying huge ollas (water pots) on their heads as they wound their way up the tortuous stairwell carved into the face of the "Sky City" mesa, a feat I tried to imitate with books and tin buckets. ("Sky City" is the term used by the Chamber of Commerce for the mother village of Acoma, which is situated atop a high sandstone table mountain.) I was never very successful, but even the attempt reminded me that I was supposed to be strong and balanced to be a proper girl.

Of course, my mother's Laguna people are Keres Indian, reputed to be the last extreme mother-right people on earth. So it is no wonder that I got notably nonwhite notions about the natural strength and prowess of women. Indeed, it is only when I am trying to get non-Indian approval, recognition, or acknowledgment that my "weak sister" emotional and intellectual ploys get the better of my tribal woman's good sense. At such times I forget that I just moved the piano or just wrote a competent paper or just completed a financial transaction satisfactorily or have supported myself and my children for most of my adult life.

Nor is my contradictory behavior atypical. Most Indian women I know are in the same bicultural bind: we vacillate between being dependent and strong, self-reliant and powerless, strongly motivated and hopelessly insecure. We resolve the dilemma in various ways: some of us party all the time; some of us drink to excess; some of us travel and move around a lot; some of us land good jobs and then quit them; some of us engage in violent exchanges; some of us blow our brains out. We act in these destructive ways because we suffer from the societal conflicts caused by having to identify with two hopelessly opposed cultural definitions of women. Through this destructive dissonance we are unhappy prey to the self-disparagement common to, indeed demanded of, Indians living in the United States today. Our situation is caused by the exigencies of a history of invasion, conquest, and colonization whose searing marks are probably ineradicable. A popular bumper sticker on many Indian cars proclaims: "If You're Indian You're In," to which I always find myself adding under my breath, "Trouble."

III

No Indian can grow to any age without being informed that her people were "savages" who interfered with the march of progress pursued by respectable, loving, civilized white people. We are the villains of the scenario when we are mentioned at all. We are absent from much of white history except when we are calmly, rationally, succinctly, and systematically dehumanized. On the few occasions we are noticed in any way other than as howling, bloodthirsty beings, we are acclaimed for our noble quaintness. In this definition, we are exotic curios. Our ancient arts and customs are used to draw tourist money to state coffers, into the pocketbooks and bank accounts of scholars, and into support of the American-in-Disneyland promoters' dream.

As a Roman Catholic child I was treated to bloody tales of how the savage Indians martyred the hapless priests and missionaries who went among them in an attempt to lead them to the one true path. By the time I was through high school I had the idea that Indians were people who had benefited mightily from the advanced knowledge and superior morality of the Anglo-Europeans. At least I had, perforce, that idea to lay beside the other one that derived from my daily experience of Indian life, an idea less dehumanizing and more accurate because it came from my mother and the other Indian people who raised me. That idea was that Indians are a people who don't tell lies, who care for their children and their old people. You never see an Indian orphan, they said. You always know when you're old that someone will take care of you—one of your children will. Then they'd list the old folks who were being taken care of by this child or that. No child is ever considered illegitimate among the Indians, they said. If a girl gets pregnant, the baby is still part of the family, and the mother is too. That's what they said, and they showed me real people who lived according to those principles.

Of course the ravages of colonization have taken their toll; there are orphans in Indian country now, and abandoned, brutalized old folks; there are even illegitimate children, though the very concept still strikes me as absurd. There are battered children and neglected children, and there are battered wives and women who have been raped by Indian men. Proximity to the "civilizing" effects of white Christians has not improved the moral quality of life in Indian country, though each group, Indian and white, explains the situation differently. Nor is there much yet in the oral tradition that can enable us to adapt to these inhuman changes. But a force is growing in that direction, and it is helping Indian women reclaim their lives. Their power, their sense of direction and of self will soon be visible. It is the force of the women who speak and work and write, and it is formidable.

Through all the centuries of war and death and cultural and psychic destruction have endured the women who raise the children and tend the fires, who pass along the tales and the traditions, who weep and bury the dead, who are the dead, and who never forget. There are always the women, who make pots and weave baskets, who fashion clothes and cheer their children on at powwow, who make fry bread and piki bread, and corn soup and chili stew, who dance and sing and remember and hold within their hearts the dream of their ancient peoples—that one day the woman who thinks will speak to us again, and everywhere there will be peace. Meanwhile we tell the stories and write the books and trade tales of anger and woe and stories of fun and scandal and laugh over all manner of things that happen every day. We watch and we wait.

My great-grandmother told my mother: Never forget you are Indian. And my mother told me the same thing. This, then, is how I have gone about remembering, so that my children will remember too.

R E A D I N G 4

The Master's Tools Will Never Dismantle the Master's House

AUDRE LORDE

I agreed to take part in a New York University Institute for the Humanities conference a year ago, with the understanding that I would be commenting upon papers dealing with the role of difference within the lives of american [sic] women: difference of race, sexuality, class, and age. The absence of these considerations weakens any feminist discussion of the personal and the political.

It is a particular academic arrogance to assume any discussion of feminist theory without examining our many dif-

Audre Lorde, "The Master's Tools Will Never Dismantle the Master's House" from *Sister Outsider: Essays and Speeches.* Copyright © 1984 by Audre Lorde. Reprinted with the permission of The Crossing Press, Freedom, California.

ferences, and without a significant input from poor women, Black and Third World women, and lesbians. And yet, I stand here as a Black lesbian feminist, having been invited to comment within the only panel at this conference where the input of Black feminists and lesbians is represented. What this says about the vision of this conference is sad, in a country where racism, sexism, and homophobia are inseparable. To read this program is to assume that lesbian and Black women have nothing to say about existentialism, the erotic, women's culture and silence, developing feminist theory, or heterosexuality and power. And what does it mean in personal and political terms when even the two Black women who did present here were literally found at the last hour? What does it mean when the tools of a racist patriarchy are used to examine the fruits of that same patriarchy? It means that only the most narrow perimeters of change are possible and allowable.

The absence of any consideration of lesbian consciousness or the consciousness of Third World women leaves a serious gap within this conference and within the papers presented here. For example, in a paper on material relationships between women, I was conscious of an either/or model of nurturing which totally dismissed my knowledge as a Black lesbian. In this paper there was no examination of mutuality between women, no systems of shared support, no interdependence as exists between lesbians and women-identified women. Yet it is only in the patriarchal model of nurturance that women "who attempt to emancipate themselves pay perhaps too high a price for the results," as this paper states.

For women, the need and desire to nurture each other is not pathological but redemptive, and it is within that knowledge that our real power is rediscovered. It is this real connection which is so feared by a patriarchal world. Only within a patriarchal structure is maternity the only social power open to women.

Interdependency between women is the way to a freedom which allows the *I* to *be,* not in order to be used, but in order to be creative. This is a difference between the passive *be* and the active *being*.

Advocating the mere tolerance of difference between women is the grossest reformism. It is a total denial of the creative function of difference in our lives. Difference must be not merely tolerated, but seen as a fund of necessary polarities between which our creativity can spark like a dialectic. Only then does the necessity for interdependency become unthreatening. Only within that interdependency of different strengths, acknowledged and equal, can the power to seek new ways of being in the world generate, as well as the courage and sustenance to act where there are no charters.

Within the interdependence of mutual (nondominant) differences lies that security which enables us to descend into the chaos of knowledge and return with true visions of our future, along with the concomitant power to effect those changes which can bring that future into being. Difference is that raw and powerful connection from which our personal power is forged.

As women, we have been taught either to ignore our differences or to view them as causes for separation and suspicion rather than as forces for change. Without community there is no liberation, only the most vulnerable and temporary armistice between an individual and her oppression.

But community must not mean a shedding of our differences, nor the pathetic pretense that these differences do not exist.

Those of us who stand outside the circle of this society's definition of acceptable women; those of us who have been forged in the crucibles of difference—those of us who are poor, who are lesbians, who are Black, who are older—know that *survival is not an academic skill.* It is learning how to stand alone, unpopular and sometimes reviled, and how to make common cause with those others identified as outside the structures in order to define and seek a world in which we can all flourish. It is learning how to take our differences and make them strengths. *For the master's tools will never dismantle the master's house.* They may allow us temporarily to beat him at his own game, but they will never enable us to bring about genuine change. And this fact is threatening only to those women who still define the master's house as their only source of support.

Poor women and women of Color know there is a difference between the daily manifestations of marital slavery and prostitution because it is our daughters who line 42nd Street. If white american [*sic*] feminist theory need not deal with the differences between us, and the resulting difference in our oppressions, then how do you deal with the fact that the women who clean your houses and tend your children while you attend conferences on feminist theory are, for the most part, poor women and women of Color? What is the theory behind racist feminism?

In a world of possibility for us all, our personal visions help lay the groundwork for political action. The failure of academic feminists to recognize difference as a crucial strength is a failure to reach beyond the first patriarchal lesson. In our world, divide and conquer must become define and empower.

Why weren't other women of Color found to participate in this conference? Why were two phone calls to me considered a consultation? Am I the only possible source of names of Black feminists? And although the Black panelist's paper ends on an important and powerful connection of love between women, what about interracial cooperation between feminists who don't love each other?

In academic feminist circles, the answer to these questions is often, "We did not know who to ask." But that is the same evasion of responsibility, the same copout, that keeps Black women's art out of women's exhibitions, Black women's work out of most feminist publications except for the occasional "Special Third World Women's Issue," and Black women's texts off your reading lists. But as Adrienne Rich pointed out in a recent talk, white feminists have educated themselves about such an enormous amount over the past ten years, how come you haven't also educated yourselves about Black women and the differences between us—white and Black—when it is key to our survival as a movement?

Women of today are still being called upon to stretch across the gap of male ignorance and to educate men as to our existence and our needs. This is an old and primary tool of all oppressors to keep the oppressed occupied with the master's concerns. Now we hear that it is the task of women of Color to educate white women—in the face of tremendous resistance—as to our existence, our differ-

ences, our relative roles in our joint survival. This is a diversion of energies and a tragic repetition of racist patriarchal thought.

Simone de Beauvoir once said: "It is in the knowledge of the genuine conditions of our lives that we must draw our strength to live and our reasons for acting."

Racism and homophobia are real conditions of all our lives in this place and time. *I urge each one of us here to reach down into that deep place of knowledge inside herself and touch that terror and loathing of any difference that lives there. See whose face it wears.* Then the personal as the political can begin to illuminate all our choices.

R E A D I N G   5

Confessions of a Nice Negro,
or Why I Shaved My Head

ROBIN D. G. KELLEY

It happened just the other day—two days into the new year, to be exact. I had dashed into the deserted lobby of an Ann Arbor movie theater, pulling the door behind me to escape the freezing winds Michigan residents have come to know so well. Behind the counter knelt a young white teenager filling the popcorn bin with bags of that awful pre-popped stuff. Hardly the enthusiastic employee; from a distance it looked like she was lost in deep thought. The generous display of body piercing suggested an X-generation flower child—perhaps an anthropology major into acid jazz and environmentalism, I thought. Sporting a black New York Yankees baseball cap and a black-and-beige scarf over my nose and mouth, I must have looked like I had stepped out of a John Singleton film. And because I was already late, I rushed madly toward the ticket counter.

Robin D. G. Kelley, "Confessions of a Nice Negro, or Why I Shaved My Head" from *Speak My Name: Black Men on Masculinity and the American Dream,* edited by Don Belton (Boston: Beacon Press, 1995). Reprinted with the permission of the author.

The flower child was startled: "I don't have anything in the cash register," she blurted as she pulled the bag of popcorn in front of her for protection.

"Huh? I just want one ticket for *Little Women,* please— the two-fifteen show. My wife and daughter should already be in there." I slowly gestured to the theater door and gave her one of those innocent childlike glances I used to give my mom when I wanted to sit on her lap.

"Oh god . . . I'm so sorry. A reflex. Just one ticket? You only missed the first twenty minutes. Enjoy the show."

Enjoy the show? Barely 1995 and here we go again. Another bout with racism in a so-called liberal college town; another racial drama in which I play the prime suspect. And yet I have to confess the situation was pretty funny. Just two hours earlier I couldn't persuade Elleza, my four-year-old daughter, to put her toys away; time-out did nothing, yelling had no effect, and the evil stare made no impact whatsoever. Thoroughly frustrated, I had only one option left: "Okay, I'm gonna tell Mommy!" Of course it worked.

So those five seconds as a media-made black man felt kind of good. I know it's a product of racism. I know that the myth of black male violence has resulted in the deaths of many innocent boys and men of darker hue. I know that the power to scare is not real power. I know all that—after all, I study this stuff for a living! For the moment, though, it felt good. (Besides, the ability to scare with your body can come in handy, especially when you're trying to get a good seat in a theater or avoid long lines.)

I shouldn't admit this, but I take particular pleasure in putting fear into people on the lookout for black male criminality mainly because those moments are so rare for me. Indeed, my *inability* to employ black-maleness as a weapon is the story of my life. Why I don't possess it, or rather possess so little of it, escapes me. I grew up poor in Harlem and Afrodena (the Negro West Side of Pasadena/Altadena, California). My mom was single during my formative preadolescent years, and for a brief moment she even received a welfare check. A hard life makes a hard nigga, so I've been told.

Never an egghead or a dork, as a teenager I was pretty cool. I did the house-party circuit on Friday and Saturday nights and used to stroll down the block toting the serious Radio Raheem boombox. Why, I even invaded movie theaters in the company of ten or fifteen hooded and high-topped black bodies, colonizing the balconies and occupying two seats per person. Armed with popcorn and Raisinets as our missiles of choice, we dared any usher to ask us to leave. Those of us who had cars (we called them hoopties or rides back in the day) spent our lunch hours and precious class time hanging out in the school parking lot, running down our Die Hards to pump up Cameo, Funkadelic, Grandmaster Flash from our car stereos. I sported dickies and Levis, picked up that gangsta stroll, and when the shag came in style I was with it—always armed with a silk scarf to ensure that my hair was laid. Granted, I vomited after drinking malt liquor for the first time and my only hit of a joint ended abruptly in an asthma attack. But I was cool.

Sure, I was cool, but nobody feared me. That I'm relatively short with dimples and curly hair, speak softly in a rather medium to high-pitched voice, and have a "girl's name" doesn't help matters. And everyone knows that light skin is less threatening to white people than blue-black or midnight brown. Besides, growing up with a soft-spoken, uncharacteristically passive West Indian mother deep into East Indian religions, a mother who sometimes walked barefoot in the streets of Harlem, a mother who insisted on proper diction and never, ever, ever used a swear word,

screwed me up royally. I could never curse right. My mouth had trouble forming the words—"fuck" always came out as "fock" and "goddamn" always sounded like it's spelled, not "gotdayum," the way my Pasadena homies pronounced it in their Calabama twang. I don't even recall saying the word "bitch" unless I was quoting somebody or some authorless vernacular rhyme. For some unknown reason, that word scared me.

Moms dressed me up in the coolest mod outfits—short-pants suits with matching hats, Nehru jackets, those sixties British-looking turtlenecks. Sure, she got some of that stuff from John's Bargain Store or Goodwill, but I always looked "cute." More stylish than roguish. Kinda like W. E. B. Du Bois as a toddler, or those turn-of-the-century photos of middle-class West Indian boys who grow up to become prime ministers or poets. Ghetto ethnographers back in the late sixties and early seventies would not have found me or my family very "authentic," especially if they had discovered that one of my middle names is Gibran, after the Lebanese poet Kahlil Gibran.

Everybody seemed to like me. Teachers liked me, kids liked me; I even fell in with some notorious teenage criminals at Pasadena High School because *they* liked me. I remember one memorable night in the ninth grade when I went down to the Pasadena Boys' Club to take photos of some of my partners on the basketball team. On my way home some big kids, eleventh-graders to be exact, tried to take my camera. The ringleader pulled out a knife and gently poked it against my chest. I told them it was my stepfather's camera and if I came home without it he'd kick my ass for a week. Miraculously, this launched a whole conversation about stepfathers and how messed up they are, which must have made them feel sorry for me. Within minutes we were cool; they let me go unmolested and I had made another friend.

In affairs of the heart, however, "being liked" had the opposite effect. I can only recall having had four fights in my entire life, all of which were with girls who supposedly liked me but thoroughly beat my behind. Sadly, my record in the boxing ring of puppy love is still 0–4. By the time I graduated to serious dating, being a nice guy seemed like the root of all my romantic problems. I resisted jealousy, tried to be understanding, brought flowers and balloons, opened doors, wrote poems and songs, and seemed to always be on my knees for one reason or another. If you've ever watched "Love Connection" or read *Cosmopolitan,* you know the rest of the story: I practically never had sex and most of the women I dated left me in the cold for roughnecks. My last girlfriend in high school, the woman I took to my prom, the woman I once thought I'd die for, tried to show me the light: "Why do you always ask me what I want? Why don't you just *tell* me what you want me to do? Why don't you take charge and *be a man?* If you want to be a real man you can't be nice all the time!"

I always thought she was wrong; being nice has nothing to do with being a man. While I still think she's wrong, it's an established fact that our culture links manhood to terror and power, and that black men are frequently imaged as the ultimate in hypermasculinity. But the black man as the prototype of violent hypermasculinity is as much a fiction as the happy Sambo. No matter what critics and stand-up comics might say, I know from experience that not all black men—and here I'm only speaking of well-lighted or daytime situations—generate fear. Who scares and who doesn't has a lot to do with the body in question; it is dependent on factors such as age, skin color, size, clothes, hairstyle, and even the sound of one's voice. The cops who beat Rodney King and the jury who acquitted King's assailants openly admitted that the size, shape, and color of his body automatically made him a threat to the officers' safety.

On the other hand, the threatening black male body can take the most incongruous forms. Some of the hardest brothas on my block in West Pasadena kept their perms in pink rollers and hairnets. It was not unusual to see young black men in public with curlers, tank-top undershirts, sweatpants, black mid-calf dress socks, and Stacey Adams shoes, hanging out on the corner or on the basketball court. And we all knew that these brothas were not to be messed with. (The rest of the world probably knows it by now, too, since black males in curlers are occasionally featured on "Cops" and "America's Most Wanted" as notorious drug dealers or heartless pimps.)

Whatever the source of this ineffable terror, my body simply lacked it. Indeed, the older I got and the more ensconced I became in the world of academia, the less threatening I seemed. Marrying and having a child also reduced the threat factor. By the time I hit my late twenties, my wife, Diedra, and I found ourselves in the awkward position of being everyone's favorite Negroes. I don't know how many times we've attended dinner parties where we were the only African Americans in the room. Occasionally there were others, but we seemed to have a monopoly on the dinner party invitations. This not only happened in Ann Arbor, where there is a small but substantial black population to choose from, but in the Negro mecca of Atlanta, Georgia. Our hosts always felt comfortable asking us "sensitive" questions about race that they would not dare ask other black colleagues and friends: What do African Americans think about Farrakahn? Ben

Chavis? Nelson Mandela? Most of my black students are very conservative and career-oriented—why is that? How can we mend the relations between blacks and Jews? Do you celebrate Kwanzaa? Do you put anything in your hair to make it that way? What are the starting salaries for young black faculty nowadays?

Of course, these sorts of exchanges appear regularly in most black autobiographies. As soon as they're comfortable, it is not uncommon for white people to take the opportunity to find out everything they've always wanted to know about "us" (which also applies to other people of color, I'm sure) but were afraid to ask. That they feel perfectly at ease asking dumb or unanswerable questions is not simply a case of (mis)perceived racelessness. Being a "nice Negro" has a lot to do with gender, and my peculiar form of "left-feminist-funny-guy" masculinity—a little Kevin Hooks, some Bobby McFerrin, a dash of Woody Allen—is regarded as less threatening than that of most other black men.

Not that I mind the soft-sensitive masculine persona—after all, it is the genuine me, a product of my mother's heroic and revolutionary child-rearing style. But there are moments when I wish I could invoke the intimidation factor of blackmaleness on demand. If I only had that look—that Malcolm X/Mike Tyson/Ice Cube/Larry Fishburne/Bigger Thomas/Fruit of Islam look—I could keep the stupid questions at bay, make college administrators tremble, and scare editors into submission. Subconsciously, I decided that I had to do something about my image. Then, as if by magic, my wish was fulfilled.

Actually, it began as an accident involving a pair of electric clippers and sleep deprivation—a bad auto-cut gone awry. With my lowtop fade on the verge of a Sly Stone Afro, I was in desperate need of a trim. Diedra didn't have the time to do it, and as it was February (Black History Month), I was on the chitlin' lecture circuit and couldn't spare forty-five minutes at a barbershop, so I elected to do it myself. Standing in a well-lighted bathroom, armed with two mirrors, I started trimming. Despite a steady hand and what I've always believed was a good eye, my hair turned out lopsided. I kept trimming and trimming to correct my error, but as my flattop sank lower, a yellow patch of scalp began to rise above the surrounding hair, like one of those big granite mounds dotting the grassy knolls of Central Park. A nice yarmulke could have covered it, but that would have been more difficult to explain than a bald spot. So, bearing in mind role models like Michael Jordan, Charles Barkley, Stanley Crouch, and Onyx (then the hip-hop group of the hour), I decided to take it all off.

I didn't think much of it at first, but the new style accomplished what years of evil stares and carefully crafted sartorial statements could not: I began to scare people. The effect was immediate and dramatic. Passing strangers avoided me and smiled less frequently. Those who did smile or make eye contact seemed to be deliberately trying to disarm me—a common strategy taught in campus rape-prevention centers. Scaring people was fun for a while, but I especially enjoyed standing in line at the supermarket with my bald head, baggy pants, high-top Reeboks, and long black hooded down coat, humming old standards like "Darn That Dream," "A Foggy Day," and "I Could Write a Book." Now *that* brought some stares. I must have been convincing, since I adore those songs and have been humming them ever since I can remember. No simple case of cultural hybridity here, just your average menace to society with a deep appreciation for Gershwin, Rodgers and Hart, Van Heusen, Cole Porter, and Jerome Kern.

Among my colleagues, my bald head became the lead subject of every conversation. "You look older, more mature." "With that new cut you come across as much more serious than usual." "You really look quite rugged and masculine with a bald head." My close friends dispensed with the euphemisms and went straight to the point: "Damn. You look scary!" The most painful comment was that I looked like a "B-Boy wannabe" and was "too old for that shit." I had to remind my friend that I'm an OBB (Original B-Boy), that I was in the eleventh grade in 1979 when the Sugar Hill Gang dropped "Rapper's Delight," and that *his* tired behind was in graduate school at the time. Besides, B-Boy was not the intent.

In the end, however, I got more questions than comments. Was I in crisis? Did I want to talk? What was I trying to say by shaving my head? What was the political point of my actions? Once the novelty passed, I began getting those "speak for the race" questions that irritated the hell out of me when I had hair. Why have *black men* begun to shave their heads in greater numbers? Why have so many black athletes decided to shave their heads. Does this new trend have some kind of phallic meaning? Against my better judgment, I found myself coming up with answers to these questions—call it an academician's reflex. I don't remember exactly what I said, but it usually began with black prizefighter Jack Johnson, America's real-life "baaad nigger" of the early twentieth century, whose head was always shaved and greased, and ended with the hip-hop community's embrace of an outlaw status. Whatever it was, it made sense at the time.

The publicity photo for my recent book, *Race Rebels,* clearly generated the most controversy among my colleagues. It diverged dramatically from the photo on my first book, where I look particularly innocent, almost angelic. In that first photo I smiled just enough to make my dimples visible; my eyes gazed away from the camera in sort of a dreamy, contemplative pose; my haircut was nondescript and the natural sunlight had a kind of halo effect. The Izod shirt was the icing on the cake. By contrast, the photograph for *Race Rebels* (which Diedra set up and shot, by the way) has me looking directly into the camera, arms folded, bald head glistening from baby oil and rear window light, with a grimace that could give Snoop Doggy Dogg a run for his money. The lens made my arms appear much larger than they really are, creating a kind of Popeye effect. Soon after the book came out, I received several email messages about the photo. A particularly memorable one came from a friend and follow historian in Australia. In the course of explaining to me how he had corrected one of his students who had read an essay of mine and presumed I was a woman, he wrote: "Mind you, the photo in your book should make things clear—the angle and foreshortening of the arms, and the hairstyle make it one of the more masculine author photos I've seen recently????!!!!!"

My publisher really milked this photo, which actually fit well with the book's title. For the American Studies Association meeting in Nashville, Tennessee, which took place the week the book came out, my publisher bought a full-page ad on the back cover of an ASA handout, with my mug staring dead at you. Everywhere I turned—in hotel elevators, hallways, lobbies, meeting rooms—I saw myself, and it was not exactly a pretty sight. The quality of the reproduction (essentially a high-contrast Xerox) made me appear harder, meaner, and crazier than the original photograph.

The situation became even stranger since I had decided to abandon the skinhead look and grow my hair back. In fact, by the time of the ASA meeting I was on the road (since abandoned) toward a big Black Power Afro—a retro style that at the time seemed to be making a comeback. Worse still, I had come to participate in a roundtable discussion on black hair! My paper, titled "Nap Time: Historicizing the Afro," explored the political implications of competing narratives of the Afro's origins and meaning. Overall, it was a terrific session; the room was packed and the discussion was stimulating. But inevitably the question came up: "Although this isn't directly related to his paper, I'd like to find out from Professor Kelley why he shaved his head. Professor Kelley, given the panel's topic and in light of the current ads floating about with your picture on them, can you shed some light on what is attractive to black men about baldness?" The question was posed by a very distinguished and widely read African-American literary scholar. Hardly the naif, he knew the answers as well as I did, but wanted to generate a public discussion. And he succeeded. For ten minutes the audience ran the gamut of issues revolving around race, gender, sexuality, and the politics of style. Even the issue of bald heads as phallic symbols came up. "It's probably true," I said, "but when I was cutting my hair at three o'clock in the morning I wasn't thinking 'penis.' "   Eventually the discussion drifted from black masculinity to the tremendous workloads of minority scholars, which, in all honesty, was the source of my baldness in the first place. Unlike the golden old days, when doing hair was highly ritualized and completely integrated into daily life, we're so busy mentoring and publishing and speaking and fighting that we have very little time to attend to our heads.

Beyond the session itself, that ad continued to haunt me during the entire conference. Every ten minutes, or so it seemed, someone came up to me and offered unsolicited commentary on the photo. One person slyly suggested that in order to make the picture complete I should have posed with an Uzi. When I approached a very good friend of mine, a historian who is partly my Jewish mother and partly my confidante and *always* looking out for my best interests, the first words out of her mouth were, "Robin, I hate that picture! It's the worst picture of you I've ever seen. It doesn't do you justice. Why did you let them use it?"

"It's not that bad," I replied. "Diedra likes it—she took the picture. You just don't like my bald head."

"No, that's not it. I like the bald look on some men, and you have a very nice head. The problem is the photo and the fact that I know what kind of person you are. None of your gentleness and lovability comes out in that picture. Now, don't get a swelled head when I say this, but you have a delightful face and expression that makes people feel good, even when you're talking about serious stuff. The way you smile, there's something unbelievably safe about you."

It was a painful compliment. And yet I knew deep down that she was telling the truth. I've always been unbelievably safe, not just because of my look but because of my actions. Not that I consciously try to put people at ease, to erase conflict and difference, to remain silent on sensitive issues. I can't quite put my finger on it. Perhaps it's my mother's politeness drills? Perhaps it's a manifestation of my continuing bout with shyness? Maybe it has something to do with the sense of joy I get from stimulating conversations? Or maybe it's linked to the fact that my mom refused to raise me in a manner boys are accustomed to? Most likely it is a product of cultural capital—the fact that I *can* speak the language, (re)cite the texts, exhibit the manners and mannerisms that are inherent to bourgeois academic culture. My colleagues identify with me because I can talk intelligently about their scholarship on their terms, which invariably has

the effect of creating an illusion of brilliance. As Frantz Fanon said in *Black Skin, White Masks,* the mere fact that he was an articulate *black* man who read a lot rendered him a stunning specimen of erudition in the eyes of his fellow intellectuals in Paris.

Whatever the source of my ineffable lovability, I've learned that it's not entirely a bad thing. In fact, if the rest of the world could look a little deeper, beyond the hardcore exterior—the wide bodies, the carefully constructed grimaces, the performance of terror—they would find many, many brothas much nicer and smarter than myself. The problem lies in a racist culture, a highly gendered racist culture, that is so deeply enmeshed in the fabric of daily life that it's practically invisible. The very existence of the "nice Negro," like the model-minority myth pinned on Asian Americans, renders the war on those "other," hard-core niggas justifiable and even palatable. In a little-known essay on the public image of world champion boxer Joe Louis, the radical Trinidadian writer C. L. R. James put it best: "This attempt to hold up Louis as a model Negro has strong overtones of condescension and race prejudice. It implies: 'See! When a Negro knows how to conduct himself, he gets on very well and we all love him.' From there the next step is: 'If only all Negroes behaved like Joe, the race problem would be solved.' "[1]

Of course we all know this is a bunch of fiction. Behaving "like Joe" was merely a code for deference and patience, which is all the more remarkable given his vocation. Unlike his predecessor Jack Johnson—the baldheaded prize fighter who transgressed racial boundaries by sleeping with and even marrying white women, who refused to apologize for his "outrageous" behavior, who boasted of his prowess in every facet of life (he even wrapped gauze around his penis to make it appear bigger under his boxing shorts)—Joe Louis was America's hero. As James put it, he was a credit to his race, "I mean the human race."[2] (Re)presented as a humble Alabama boy, God-fearing and devoid of hatred, Louis was constructed in the press as a raceless man whose masculinity was put to good, patriotic use. To many of his white fans, he was a man in the ring and a boy—a good boy—outside of it. To many black folks, he was a hero because he had the license to kick white men's butts and yet maintain the admiration and respect of a nation. Thus, despite similarities in race, class, and vocation, and their common iconization, Louis and Johnson exhibited public behavior that reflected radically different masculinities.

Here, then, is a lesson we cannot ignore. There is some truth in the implication that race (or gender) conflict is partly linked to behavior and how certain behavior is perceived. If our society, for example, could dispense with rigid, archaic notions of appropriate masculine and feminine behavior, perhaps we might create a world that nurtures, encourages, and even rewards nice guys. If violence were not so central to American culture—to the way manhood is defined, to the way in which the state keeps African-American men in check, to the way men interact with women, to the way oppressed peoples interact with one another—perhaps we might see the withering away of white fears of black men. Perhaps young black men wouldn't feel the need to adopt hardened, threatening postures merely to survive in a Doggy-Dogg world. Not that black men ought to become colored equivalents of Alan Alda. Rather, black men ought to be whomever or whatever they want to be, without unwarranted criticism or societal pressures to conform to a particular definition of manhood. They could finally dress down without suspicion, talk loudly without surveillance, and love each other without sanction. Fortunately, such a transformation would also mean the long-awaited death of the "nice Negro."

Not in my lifetime. Any fool can look around and see that the situation for race and gender relations in general, and for black males in particular, has taken a turn for the worse—and relief is nowhere in sight. In the meantime, I will make the most of my "nice Negro" status. When it's all said and done, there is nothing romantic or interesting about playing Bigger Thomas. Maybe I can't persuade a well-dressed white couple to give up their box seats, but at least they'll listen to me. For now . . . .

NOTES

1. C. L. R. James, "Joe Louis and Jack Johnson," *Labor Action,* July 1, 1946.
2. Ibid.

R E A D I N G   6

White Privilege and Male Privilege: A Personal Account of Coming to See Correspondences through Work in Women's Studies

PEGGY MCINTOSH

Through work to bring materials and perspectives from Women's Studies into the rest of the curriculum, I have often noticed men's unwillingness to grant that they are overprivileged in the curriculum, even though they may grant that women are disadvantaged. Denials that amount to taboos surround the subject of advantages that men gain

from women's disadvantages. These denials protect male privilege from being fully recognized, acknowledged, lessened, or ended.

Thinking through unacknowledged male privilege as a phenomenon with a life of its own, I realized that since hierarchies in our society are interlocking, there was most likely a phenomenon of white privilege that was similarly denied and protected, but alive and real in its effects. As a white person, I realized I had been taught about racism as something that puts others at a disadvantage, but had been taught not to see one of its corollary aspects, White privilege, which puts me at an advantage.

I think whites are carefully taught not to recognize white privilege, as males are taught not to recognize male privilege. So I have begun in an untutored way to ask what it is like to have white privilege. This paper is a partial record of my personal observations and not a scholarly analysis. It is based on my daily experiences within my particular circumstances.

I have come to see white privilege as an invisible package of unearned assets that I can count on cashing in each day, but about which I was "meant" to remain oblivious. White privilege is like an invisible weightless knapsack of special provisions, assurances, tools, maps, guides, codebooks, passports, visas, clothes, compass, emergency gear, and blank checks.

Since I have had trouble facing white privilege, and describing its results in my life, I saw parallels here with men's reluctance to acknowledge male privilege. Only rarely will a man go beyond acknowledging that women are disadvantaged to acknowledging that men have unearned advantage, or that unearned privilege has not been good for men's development as human beings, or for society's development, or that privilege systems might ever be challenged and *changed.*

I will review here several types or layers of denial that I see at work protecting, and preventing awareness about, entrenched male privilege. Then I will draw parallels, from my own experience, with the denials that veil the facts of white privilege. Finally, I will list forty-six ordinary and daily ways in which I experience having white privilege, by contrast with my African-American colleagues in the same building. This list is not intended to be generalizable. Others can make their own lists from within their own life circumstances.

Writing this paper has been difficult, despite warm receptions for the talks on which it is based.[1] For describing white privilege makes one newly accountable. As we in Women's Studies work to reveal male privilege and ask men to give up some of their power so one who writes about having white privilege must ask, "Having described it, what will I do to lessen or end it."

The denial of men's overprivileged state takes many forms in discussions of curriculum change work. Some claim that men must be central in the curriculum because they have done most of what is important or distinctive in life or in civilization. Some recognize sexism in the curriculum but deny that it makes male students seem unduly important in life. Others agree that certain *individual*

thinkers are male-oriented but deny that there is any *systemic* tendency in disciplinary frameworks or epistemology to overempower men as a group. Those men who do grant that male privilege takes institutionalized and embedded forms are still likely to deny that male hegemony has opened doors for them personally. Virtually all men deny that male overreward alone can explain men's centrality in all the inner sanctums of our most powerful institutions. Moreover, those few who will acknowledge that male privilege systems have overempowered them usually end up doubting that we could dismantle these privilege systems. They may say they will work to improve women's status, in the society or in the university, but they can't or won't support the idea of lessening men's. In curricular terms, this is the point at which they say that they regret they cannot use any of the interesting new scholarship on women because the syllabus is full. When the talk turns to giving men less cultural room, even the most thoughtful and fair-minded of the men I know will tend to reflect, or fall back on, conservative assumptions about the inevitability of present gender relations and distributions of power, calling on precedent or sociobiology and psychobiology to demonstrate that male domination is natural and follows inevitably from evolutionary pressures. Others resort to arguments from "experience" or religion or social responsibility or wishing and dreaming.

After I realized, through faculty development work in Women's Studies, the extent to which men work from a base of unacknowledged privilege, I understood that much of their oppressiveness was unconscious. Then I remembered the frequent charges from women of color that white women whom they encounter are oppressive. I began to understand why we are justly seen as oppressive, even when we don't see ourselves that way. At the very least, obliviousness of one's privileged state can make a person or group irritating to be with. I began to count the ways in which I enjoy unearned skin privilege and have been conditioned into oblivion about its existence, unable to see that it put me "ahead" in any way, or put my people ahead, over-rewarding us and yet also paradoxically damaging us, or that it could or should be changed.

My schooling gave me no training in seeing myself as an oppressor, as an unfairly advantaged person, or as a participant in a damaged culture. I was taught to see myself as an individual whose moral state depended on her individual moral will. At school, we were not taught about slavery in any depth; we were not taught to see slaveholders as damaged people. Slaves were seen as the only group at risk of being dehumanized. My schooling followed the pattern which Elizabeth Minnich has pointed out: whites are taught to think of their lives as morally neutral, normative, and average, and also ideal, so that when we work to benefit others, this is seen as work that will allow "them" to be more like "us." I think many of us know how obnoxious this attitude can be in men.

After frustration with men who would not recognize male privilege, I decided to try to work on myself at least by identifying some of the daily effects of white privilege in my life. It is crude work, at this stage, but I will give here a list of special circumstances and conditions I experience that I did not earn but that I have been made to feel are mine by birth, by citizenship, and by virtue of being a conscientious law-abiding "normal" person of goodwill. I have chosen those conditions that I think in my case *attach somewhat more to skin-color privilege* than to class, religion, ethnic status, or geographical location, though these other privileging factors are intricately intertwined. As far as I can see, my Afro-American co-workers, friends, and acquaintances with whom I come into daily or frequent contact in this particular time, place, and line of work cannot count on most of these conditions.

1. I can, if I wish, arrange to be in the company of people of my race most of the time.
2. I can avoid spending time with people whom I was trained to mistrust and who have learned to mistrust my kind or me.
3. If I should need to move, I can be pretty sure of renting or purchasing housing in an area which I can afford and in which I would want to live.
4. I can be reasonably sure that my neighbors in such a location will be neutral or pleasant to me.
5. I can go shopping alone most of the time, fairly well assured that I will not be followed or harassed by store detectives.
6. I can turn on the television or open to the front page of the paper and see people of my race widely and positively represented.
7. When I am told about our national heritage or about "civilization," I am shown that people of my color made it what it is.
8. I can be sure that my children will be given curricular materials that testify to the existence of their race.
9. If I want to, I can be pretty sure of finding a publisher for this piece on white privilege.
10. I can be fairly sure of having my voice heard in a group in which I am the only member of my race.

11. I can be casual about whether or not to listen to another woman's voice in a group in which she is the only member of her race.
12. I can go into a bookshop and count on finding the writing of my race represented, into a supermarket and find the staple foods that fit with my cultural traditions, into a hairdresser's shop and find someone who can deal with my hair.
13. Whether I use checks, credit cards, or cash, I can count on my skin color not to work against the appearance that I am financially reliable.
14. I could arrange to protect our young children most of the time from people who might not like them.
15. I did not have to educate our children to be aware of systemic racism for their own daily physical protection.
16. I can be pretty sure that my children's teachers and employers will tolerate them if they fit school and workplace norms; my chief worries about them do not concern others' attitudes toward their race.
17. I can talk with my mouth full and not have people put this down to my color.
18. I can swear, or dress in secondhand clothes, or not answer letters, without having people attribute these choices to the bad morals, the poverty, or the illiteracy of my race.
19. I can speak in public to a powerful male group without putting my race on trial.
20. I can do well in a challenging situation without being called a credit to my race.
21. I am never asked to speak for all the people of my racial group.
22. I can remain oblivious to the language and customs of persons of color who constitute the world's majority without feeling in my culture any penalty for such oblivion.
23. I can criticize our government and talk about how much I fear its policies and behavior without being seen as a cultural outsider.
24. I can be reasonably sure that if I ask to talk to "the person in charge," I will be facing a person of my race.
25. If a traffic cop pulls me over or if the IRS audits my tax return, I can be sure I haven't been singled out because of my race.
26. I can easily buy posters, postcards, picture books, greeting cards, dolls, toys, and children's magazines featuring people of my race.
27. I can go home from most meetings of organizations I belong to feeling somewhat tied in, rather than

isolated, out of place, outnumbered, unheard, held at a distance, or feared.

28. I can be pretty sure that an argument with a colleague of another race is more likely to jeopardize her chances for advancement than to jeopardize mine.

29. I can be fairly sure that if I argue for the promotion of a person of another race, or a program centering on race, this is not likely to cost me heavily within my present setting, even if my colleagues disagree with me.

30. If I declare there is a racial issue at hand, or there isn't a racial issue at hand, my race will lend me more credibility for either position than a person of color will have.

31. I can choose to ignore developments in minority writing and minority activist programs, or disparage them, or learn from them, but in any case, I can find ways to be more or less protected from negative consequences of any of these choices.

32. My culture gives me little fear about ignoring the perspectives and powers of people of other races.

33. I am not made acutely aware that my shape, bearing, or body odor will be taken as a reflection on my race.

34. I can worry about racism without being seen as self-interested or self-seeking.

35. I can take a job with an affirmative action employer without having my co-workers on the job suspect that I got it because of my race.

36. If my day, week, or year is going badly, I need not ask of each negative episode or situation whether it has racial overtones.

37. I can be pretty sure of finding people who would be willing to talk with me and advise me about my next steps, professionally.

38. I can think over many options, social, political, imaginative, or professional, without asking whether a person of my race would be accepted or allowed to do what I want to do.

39. I can be late to a meeting without having the lateness reflect on my race.

40. I can choose public accommodation without fearing that people of my race cannot get in or will be mistreated in the places I have chosen.

41. I can be sure that if I need legal or medical help, my race will not work against me.

42. I can arrange my activities so that I will never have to experience feelings of rejection owing to my race.

43. If I have low credibility as a leader, I can be sure that my race is not the problem.

44. I can easily find academic courses and institutions that give attention only to people of my race.

45. I can expect figurative language and imagery in all of the arts to testify to experiences of my race.

46. I can choose blemish cover or bandages in "flesh" color and have them more or less match my skin.

I repeatedly forgot each of the realizations on this list until I wrote it down. For me, white privilege has turned out to be an elusive and fugitive subject. The pressure to avoid it is great, for in facing it I must give up the myth of meritocracy. If these things are true, this is not such a free country; one's life is not what one makes it; many doors open for certain people through no virtues of their own. These perceptions mean also that my moral condition is not what I had been led to believe. The appearance of being a good citizen rather than a troublemaker comes in large part from having all sorts of doors open automatically because of my color.

A further paralysis of nerve comes from literary silence protecting privilege. My clearest memories of finding such analysis are in Lillian Smith's unparalleled *Killers of the Dream* and Margaret Andersen's review of Karen and Mamie Fields' *Lemon Swamp*. Smith, for example, wrote about walking toward black children on the street and knowing they would step into the gutter; Andersen contrasted the pleasure that she, as a white child, took on summer driving trips to the south with Karen Fields' memories of driving in a closed car stocked with all necessities lest, in stopping, her black family should suffer "insult, or worse." Adrienne Rich also recognizes and writes about daily experiences of privilege, but in my observation, white women's writing in this area is far more often on systemic racism than on our daily lives as light-skinned women.[2]

In unpacking this invisible knapsack of white privilege, I have listed conditions of daily experience that I once took for granted, as neutral, normal, and universally available to everybody, just as I once thought of a male-focused curriculum as the neutral or accurate account that can speak for all. Nor did I think of any of these perquisites as bad for the holder. I now think that we need a more finely differentiated taxonomy of privilege, for some of these varieties are only what one would want for everyone in a just society, and others give license to be ignorant, oblivious, arrogant, and destructive. Before proposing some more finely tuned categorization, I will make some observations about the general effects of these conditions on my life and expectations.

In this potpourri of examples, some privileges make me feel at home in the world. Others allow me to escape penalties or dangers that others suffer. Through some, I escape fear, anxiety, insult, injury, or a sense of not being welcome, not being real. Some keep me from having to hide, to be in disguise, to feel sick or crazy, to negotiate each transaction from the position of being an outsider or, within my group, a person who is suspected of having too close links with a dominant culture. Most keep me from having to be angry.

I see a pattern running through the matrix of white privilege, a pattern of assumptions that were passed on to me as a white person. There was one main piece of cultural turf; it was my own turf, and I was among those who could control the turf. I could measure up to the cultural standards and take advantage of the many options I saw around me to make what the culture would call a success of my life. *My skin color was an asset for any move I was educated to want to make.* I could think of myself as "belonging" in major ways and of making social systems work for me. I could freely disparage, fear, neglect, or be oblivious to anything outside of the dominant cultural forms. Being of the main culture, I could also criticize it fairly freely. My life was reflected back to me frequently enough so that I felt, with regard to my race, if not to my sex, like one of the real people.

Whether through the curriculum or in the newspaper, the television, the economic system, or the general look of people in the streets, I received daily signals and indications that my people counted and that others *either didn't exist or must be trying, not very successfully, to be like people of my race.* I was given cultural permission not to hear voices of people of other races or a tepid cultural tolerance for hearing or acting on such voices. I was also raised not to suffer seriously from anything that darker-skinned people might say about my group, "protected," though perhaps I should more accurately say *prohibited,* through the habits of my economic class and social group, from living in racially mixed groups or being reflective about interactions between people of differing races.

In proportion as my racial group was being made confident, comfortable, and oblivious, other groups were likely being made unconfident, uncomfortable, and alienated. Whiteness protected me from many kinds of hostility, distress, and violence, which I was being subtly trained to visit in turn upon people of color.

For this reason, the word "privilege" now seems to me misleading. Its connotations are too positive to fit the conditions and behaviors which "privilege systems" produce. We usually think of privilege as being a favored state, whether earned or conferred by birth or luck. School graduates are reminded they are privileged and urged to use their (enviable) assets well. The word "privilege" carries the connotation of being something everyone must want. Yet some of the conditions I have described here work to systemically overempower certain groups. Such privilege simply *confers dominance,* gives permission to control, because of one's race or sex. The kind of privilege that gives license to some people to be, at best, thoughtless and, at worst, murderous should not continue to be referred to as a desirable attribute. Such "privilege" may be widely desired without being in any way beneficial to the whole society.

Moreover, though "privilege" may confer power, it does not confer moral strength. Those who do not depend on conferred dominance have traits and qualities that may never develop in those who do. Just as Women's Studies courses indicate that women survive their political circumstances to lead lives that hold the human race together, so "underprivileged" people of color who are the world's majority have survived their oppression and lived survivors' lives from which the white global minority can and must learn. In some groups, those dominated have actually become strong through *not* having all of these unearned advantages, and this gives them a great deal to teach the others. Members of so-called privileged groups can seem foolish, ridiculous, infantile, or dangerous by contrast.

I want, then, to distinguish between earned strength and unearned power conferred systemically. Power from unearned privilege can look like strength when it is, in fact, permission to escape or to dominate. But not all of the privileges on my list are inevitably damaging. Some, like the expectation that neighbors will be decent to you, or that your race will not count against you in court, should be the norm in a just society and should be considered as the entitlement of everyone. Others, like the privilege not to listen to less powerful people, distort the humanity of the holders as well as the ignored groups. Still others, like finding one's staple foods everywhere, may be a function of being a member of a numerical majority in the population. Others have to do with not having to labor under pervasive negative stereotyping and mythology.

We might at least start by distinguishing between positive advantages that we can work to spread, to the point where they are not advantages at all but simply part of the normal civic and social fabric, and negative types of advantage that unless rejected will always reinforce our present hierarchies. For example, the positive "privilege" of belonging, the feeling that one belongs within the human circle, as Native Americans say, fosters development and should not be seen as privilege for a few. It is, let us say, an entitlement that none of us should have to earn; ideally it is an *unearned entitlement*. At present, since only a few have it, it is an *unearned advantage* for them. The negative "privilege" that gave me cultural permission not to take darker-skinned Others seriously can be seen as arbitrarily conferred dominance and should not be desirable for anyone. This paper results from a process of coming to see that some of the power that I originally saw as attendant on being a human being in the United States consisted in *unearned advantage* and *conferred dominance,* as well as other kinds of special circumstance not universally taken for granted.

In writing this paper I have also realized that white identity and status (as well as class identity and status) give me considerable power to choose whether to broach this subject and its trouble. I can pretty well decide whether to disappear and avoid and not listen and escape the dislike I may engender in other people through this essay, or interrupt, answer, interpret, preach, correct, criticize, and control to some extent what goes on in reaction to it. Being white, I am given considerable power to escape many kinds of danger or penalty as well as to choose which risks I want to take.

There is an analogy here, once again, with Women's Studies. Our male colleagues do not have a great deal to lose in supporting Women's Studies, but they do not have a great deal to lose if they oppose it either. They simply have the power to decide whether to commit themselves to more equitable distributions of power. They will probably feel few penalties whatever choice they make; they do not seem, in any obvious short-term sense, the ones at risk, though they and we are all at risk because of the behaviors that have been rewarded in them.

Through Women's Studies work I have met very few men who are truly distressed about systemic, unearned male advantage and conferred dominance. And so one question for me and others like me is whether we will be like them, or whether we will get truly distressed, even outraged, about unearned race advantage and conferred dominance and if so, what we will do to lessen them. In any case, we need to do more work in identifying how they actually affect our daily lives. We need more down-to-earth writing by people about these taboo subjects. We need more understanding of the ways in which white "privilege" damages white people, for these are not the same ways in which it damages the victimized. Skewed white psyches are an inseparable part of the picture, though I do not want to confuse the kinds of damage done to the holders of special assets and to those who suffer the deficits. Many, perhaps most, of our white students in the United States think that

racism doesn't affect them because they are not people of color; they do not see "whiteness" as a racial identity. Many men likewise think that Women's Studies does not bear on their own existences because they are not female; they do not see themselves as having gendered identities. Insisting on the universal "effects" of "privilege" systems, then, becomes one of our chief tasks, and being more explicit about the *particular* effects in particular contexts is another. Men need to join us in this work.

In addition, since race and sex are not the only advantaging systems at work, we need to similarly examine the daily experience of having age advantage, or ethnic advantage, or physical ability, or advantage related to nationality, religion, or sexual orientation. Professor Marnie Evans suggested to me that in many ways the list I made also applies directly to heterosexual privilege. This is a still more taboo subject than race privilege: the daily ways in which heterosexual privilege makes some persons comfortable or powerful, providing supports, assets, approvals, and rewards to those who live or expect to live in heterosexual pairs. Unpacking that content is still more difficult, owing to the deeper embeddedness of heterosexual advantage and dominance and stricter taboos surrounding these.

But to start such an analysis I would put this observation from my own experience: The fact that I live under the same roof with a man triggers all kinds of societal assumptions about my worth, politics, life, and values and triggers a host of unearned advantages and powers. After recasting many elements from the original list I would add further observations like these:

1. My children do not have to answer questions about why I live with my partner (my husband).
2. I have no difficulty finding neighborhoods where people approve of our household.
3. Our children are given texts and classes that implicitly support our kind of family unit and do not turn them against my choice of domestic partnership.
4. I can travel alone or with my husband without expecting embarrassment or hostility in those who deal with us.
5. Most people I meet will see my marital arrangements as an asset to my life or as a favorable comment on my likability, my competence, or my mental health.
6. I can talk about the social events of a weekend without fearing most listeners' reactions.
7. I will feel welcomed and "normal" in the usual walks of public life, institutional and social.
8. In many contexts, I am seen as "all right" in daily work on women because I do not live chiefly with women.

Difficulties and dangers surrounding the task of finding parallels are many. Since racism, sexism, and heterosexism are not the same, the advantages associated with them should not be seen as the same. In addition, it is hard to isolate aspects of unearned advantage that derive chiefly from social class, economic class, race, religion, region, sex, or ethnic identity. The oppressions are both distinct and interlocking, as the Combahee River Collective statement of 1977 continues to remind us eloquently.[3]

One factor seems clear about all of the interlocking oppressions. They take both active forms that we can see and embedded forms that members of the dominant group are taught not to see. In my class and place, I did not see myself as racist because I was taught to recognize racism only in individual acts of meanness by members of my group, never in invisible systems conferring racial dominance on my group from birth. Likewise, we are taught to think that sexism or heterosexism is carried on only through intentional, individual acts of discrimination, meanness, or cruelty, rather than in invisible systems conferring unsought dominance on certain groups. Disapproving of the systems won't be enough to change them. I was taught to think that racism could end if white individuals changed their attitudes; many men think sexism can be ended by individual changes in daily behavior toward women. But a man's sex provides advantage for him whether or not he approves of the way in which dominance has been conferred on his group. A "white" skin in the United States opens many doors for whites whether or not we approve of the way

dominance has been conferred on us. Individual acts can palliate, but cannot end, these problems. To redesign social systems, we need first to acknowledge their colossal unseen dimensions. The silences and denials surrounding privilege are the key political tool here. They keep the thinking about equality or equity incomplete, protecting unearned advantage and conferred dominance by making these taboo subjects. Most talk by whites about equal opportunity seems to me now to be about equal opportunity to try to get into a position of dominance while denying that *systems* of dominance exist.

Obliviousness about white advantage, like obliviousness about male advantage, is kept strongly inculturated in the United States so as to maintain the myth of meritocracy, the myth that democratic choice is equally available to all. Keeping most people unaware that freedom of confident action is there for just a small number of people props up those in power and serves to keep power in the hands of the same groups that have most of it already. Though systemic change takes many decades, there are pressing questions for me and I imagine for some others like me if we raise our daily consciousness on the perquisites of being light-skinned. What will we do with such knowledge? As we know from watching men, it is an open question whether we will choose to use unearned advantage to weaken invisible privilege systems and whether we will use any of our arbitrarily awarded power to try to reconstruct power systems on a broader base.

ACKNOWLEDGMENTS

I have appreciated commentary on this paper from the Working Papers Committee of the Wellesley College Center for Research on Women, from members of the Dodge seminar, and from many individuals, including Margaret Andersen, Sorel Berman, Joanne Braxton, Johnnella Butler, Sandra Dickerson, Marnie Evans, Beverly Guy-Sheftall, Sandra Harding, Eleanor Hinton Hoytt, Pauline Houston, Paul Lauter, Joyce Miller, Mary Norris, Gloria Oden, Beverly Smith, and John Walter.

NOTES

1. This paper was presented at the Virginia Women's Studies Association conference in Richmond in April 1986, and the American Educational Research Association conference in Boston in October 1986, and discussed with two groups of participants in the Dodge seminars for Secondary School Teachers in New York and Boston in the spring of 1987.

2. Andersen, Margaret, "Race and the Social Science Curriculum: A Teaching and Learning Discussion," *Radical Teacher,* November 1984, pp. 17–20. Smith, Lillian, *Killers of the Dream,* New York: W. W. Norton, 1949.

3. "A Black Feminist Statement," The Combahee River Collective, pp. 13–22 in G. Hull, P. Scott, B. Smith, Eds., *All the Women Are White, All the Blacks Are Men, But Some of Us Are Brave: Black Women's Studies,* Old Westbury, NY: The Feminist Press, 1982.

Theoretical Perspectives

Feminist scholars generally distinguish between *sex,* or the biological or innate characteristics of males and females, and *gender,* or the social statuses and meanings assigned to women and men. Gender is one of the most important social distinctions. Societies define men and women as separate and distinct categories, and gender or sex-based stratification is ubiquitous. An individual's gender is one of the first things we notice about her or him, and our own gender is central to our sense of who we are. Not only individuals but also behaviors (aggression, nurturing), traits (strong, delicate), and even objects (pink or blue clothes) are viewed in gendered terms. As we saw in the previous section, gender distinctions overlap with race, class, sexuality, nationality, and other inequalities. Feminist scholars seek to understand how societies construct the meaning of being a woman or a man and how gender affects individual identities, the ways people interact with each other, and inequality.

Explanations of gender inequality fall into two basic schools of thought: the essentialist and the social constructionist. The essentialist position holds that the behaviors of men and women are rooted in biological and genetic factors, including differences in hormonal patterns, physical size, aggressiveness, the propensity to "bond" with members of the same sex, and the capacity to bear children. For the essentialist, the sexual division of labor in human societies is rooted in the sexual determination to be found in all species, from ants to deer to felines to primates. Viewing such differences as a natural outgrowth of human evolution, essentialists contend that sex-based inequality and the natural superiority of the male are inevitable, functional, and necessary for the survival of the species.

The second school of thought, the social constructionist approach, bases its position on a growing body of historical and anthropological research that points to wide variations in gender behavior and in the sexual division of labor among human societies throughout time. Social constructionists contend that the diversity of cultural understandings of gender is too great to be explained by biological factors. Instead, they argue, male dominance appears to be inevitable because cultural ideas and beliefs have arisen to justify and perpetuate sex-based stratification systems that entitle men to greater power, prestige, and wealth than women. While such ideologies do not cause gender inequality, they certainly justify it as natural.

The readings in this section present various approaches to understanding gender. In " 'Night to His Day': The Social Construction of Gender," Judith Lorber outlines a social constructionist approach. She defines gender as a social institution that rests on the "socially constructed statuses" of "man" and "woman." Even the apparently dimorphic physical characteristics of the two sexes, Lorber argues, are socially interpreted and emphasized. How does the social institution of gender create *sameness* among members of each gender and *difference* between women and men? How are the genders ranked in a hierarchy that privileges men over women?

37

The next article builds on Marxist feminist analyses to construct a *structural* explanation of gender inequality. Evelyn Nakano Glenn emphasizes the structural roots of gender and racial stratification in her analysis of paid reproductive work, "From Servitude to Service Work: Historical Continuities in the Racial Division of Paid Reproductive Labor." Reproductive labor, which is the paid or unpaid work necessary to sustain and reproduce the population, includes child-raising, food preparation, housecleaning, and the like, and historically has been assigned to women. Glenn argues that reproductive labor has also been stratified by race, with women of color assigned to perform domestic work for white women and given the dirtiest and most demeaning tasks. Categories of race and gender, Glenn argues, are thus overlapping, and are constructed in part by women's different positions in the labor force. The article illustrates a structuralist theory of the intersections of gender and race in its examination of the connections between the labor women perform and women's positions in the social hierarchy. Who performs the reproductive labor—cooking, cleaning—at your college or university?

In "The Medical Construction of Gender," Suzanne Kessler illustrates the powerful role medicine plays in the social construction of the categories of male and female. Kessler challenges the notion that the biological distinctions between women and men are natural rather than subject to social construction. Drawing from interviews with medical experts who have had extensive clinical experience managing babies born with genitals that are neither clearly male nor clearly female, Kessler discusses the standard practices used by the medical establishment to define the gender of intersexed infants. The primary consideration in physicians' gender assignments and corrective surgery is the ability to construct correctly formed genitals, not the other potential gender markers such as chromosomes, hormones, or psychological factors. Kessler argues that the equation of gender with a two-genital culture helps create and maintain the view that gender consists of two mutually exclusive types—female and male—despite biological evidence of greater natural variation in actual gender markers. Do you agree with the medical view that gender must be assigned immediately, decisively, and irreversibly when an intersexed child is born? What role, if any, do you think social factors should play in making decisions about gender identity? What does Kessler's article suggest about the relationship (if any) between biological differences and societal gender systems?

In addition to the labor market, other social institutions are central to the construction of gender. Central among these is what Adrienne Rich, in a classic article, called "compulsory heterosexuality."[1] Rich argued that heterosexuality is enforced through the organization of marriage, threats of violence against women who are unprotected by men, the legal system, and cultural norms. Under this system, women's romantic relationships with other women pose a threat to male dominance. Other close emotional connections between women—friendships, family relationships—also are a form of resistance to the societal demand that women cast their lot emotionally with men. Adrienne Rich and others encourage us to consider heterosexuality as a cultural ideology and social institution that proscribes and devalues all forms of female friendship and community as it perpetuates women's subordination to men. The concept of compulsory heterosexuality reminds us to consider the role of sexuality in systems of gender inequality. As you read the other selections in this section, can you find examples of how sexuality is connected to the patterns of gender inequality they describe?

Making a black woman's standpoint visible is the goal of Patricia Hill Collins's article, "The Social Construction of Black Feminist Thought." Hill Collins draws on the structural approaches emphasized by Glenn as well as an analysis of cultural beliefs about gender and race. She posits that African-American women's political and economic experiences have allowed them to develop a particular analysis of racism and sexism in the United States, as well as specific strategies of resistance. Her analysis challenges the notions that oppressed groups are not conscious of their oppression or are less capable than their oppressors of understanding the relations of ruling. It also challenges the idea that there can be one "feminist theory" or "feminist perspective" because different positions in the social structure give rise to distinct standpoints on knowledge and social relations. Hill Collins suggests that an inclusive feminist vision will arise only from the patchwork of many distinct standpoints; it will rest on diversity among women, rather than seek to transcend or cover up such variations. What are the elements of a black feminist theory, according to Hill Collins? How is this approach similar to and different from the approaches used in the other articles in this section?

In the final selection, "Subjects of Sex/Gender/ Desire," Judith Butler further examines the construction of the categories of sex and gender. According to Butler, the category "woman" exists only because it is produced through legal and political power structures. She argues that feminist theory has wrongly sought to establish the existence of a universal patriarchy and to construct the category "woman" as if all women shared experiences in common. In contrast, Butler suggests that gender is constructed in various ways in various locations and times, and intersects with race, class, ethnicity, sexuality, and region. Further, Butler argues that even the notion of "sex," as the innate biological differences between women and men that exist before and separate from "gender," is socially constructed. Gender, then, is not just the social manifestations of biological sex; it is also the construction of the apparently "natural" or inevitable sex categories themselves. A feminist politics, Butler proposes, must take the shape not of an assertion of commonality that inevitably excludes many women, but of a coalition among those with different identities. She emphasizes that such efforts must not presuppose the form that those coalitions will take, or insist on unity as a goal. Instead, she suggests; we need a politics that acknowledges fragmentation and difference and proceeds nevertheless. How does Butler's approach challenge the other theorists in this section?

As you consider the various ways of thinking about gender presented in these articles, with which do you agree? As you read the selections in the rest of the book, consider the questions raised here about what gender is, the extent to which women share commonalities of oppression or experience, how gender intersects with other forms of inequality such as race, class, or nationality, and how gender is part of our cultural systems of meaning and our institutions and social structures.

NOTE

1. Rich, Adrienne. "Compulsory Heterosexuality and Lesbian Experience," *Blood, Bread, and Poetry: Selected Prose 1979–1985* (New York: Norton, 1986).

"Night to His Day": The Social Construction of Gender

JUDITH LORBER

Talking about gender for most people is the equivalent of fish talking about water. Gender is so much the routine ground of everyday activities that questioning its taken-for-granted assumptions and presuppositions is like thinking about whether the sun will come up.[1] Gender is so pervasive that in our society we assume it is bred into our genes. Most people find it hard to believe that gender is constantly created and recreated out of human interaction, out of social life, and is the texture and order of that social life. Yet gender, like culture, is a human production that depends on everyone constantly "doing gender" (West and Zimmerman 1987).

And everyone "does gender" without thinking about it. Today, on the subway, I saw a well-dressed man with a year-old child in a stroller. Yesterday, on a bus, I saw a man with a tiny baby in a carrier on his chest. Seeing men taking care of small children in public is increasingly common—at least in New York City. But both men were quite obviously stared at—and smiled at, approvingly. Everyone was doing gender—the men who were changing the role of fathers and the other passengers, who were applauding them silently. But there was more gendering going on that probably fewer people noticed. The baby was wearing a white crocheted cap and white clothes. You couldn't tell if it was a boy or a girl. The child in the stroller was wearing a dark blue T-shirt and dark print pants. As they started to leave the train, the father put a Yankee baseball cap on the child's head. Ah, a boy, I thought. Then I noticed the gleam of tiny earrings in the child's ears, and as they got off, I saw the lit-

tle flowered sneakers and lace-trimmed socks. Not a boy after all. Gender done.

Gender is such a familiar part of daily life that it usually takes a deliberate disruption of our expectations of how women and men are supposed to act to pay attention to how it is produced. Gender signs and signals are so ubiquitous that we usually fail to note them—unless they are missing or ambiguous. Then we are uncomfortable until we have successfully placed the other person in a gender status; otherwise, we feel socially dislocated. In our society, in addition to man and woman, the status can be *transvestite* (a person who dresses in opposite-gender clothes) and *transsexual* (a person who has had sex-change surgery). Transvestites and transsexuals carefully construct their gender status by dressing, speaking, walking, gesturing in the ways prescribed for women or men—whichever they want to be taken for—and so does any "normal" person.

For the individual, gender construction starts with assignment to a sex category on the basis of what the genitalia look like at birth.[2] Then babies are dressed or adorned in a way that displays the category because parents don't want to be constantly asked whether their baby is a girl or a boy. A sex category becomes a gender status through naming, dress, and the use of other gender markers. Once a child's gender is evident, others treat those in one gender differently from those in the other, and the children respond to the different treatment by feeling different and behaving differently. As soon as they can talk, they start to refer to themselves as members of their gender. Sex doesn't come into play again until puberty, but by that time, sexual feelings and desires and practices have been shaped by gendered norms and expectations. Adolescent boys and girls approach and avoid each other in an elaborately scripted and gendered mating dance. Parenting is gendered, with different expectations for mothers and for fathers, and people of different genders work at different kinds of jobs. The work adults do, as mothers and fathers and as low-level workers and high-level bosses, shapes women's and men's life experiences, and these experiences produce different feelings, consciousness, relationships, skills—ways of being that we call feminine or masculine.[3] All of these processes constitute the social construction of gender.

Gendered roles change—today fathers are taking care of little children, girls and boys are wearing unisex clothing and getting the same education, women and men are working at the same jobs. Although many traditional social groups are quite strict about maintaining gender differences, in other social groups they seem to be blurring. Then why the one-year-old's earrings? Why is it still so important to mark a child as a girl or a boy, to make sure she is not taken for a boy or he for a girl? What would happen if they were? They would, quite literally, have changed places in their social world.

To explain why gendering is done from birth, constantly and by everyone, we have to look not only at the way individuals experience gender but at gender as a social institution. As a social institution, gender is one of the major ways that human beings organize their lives. Human society depends on a predictable division of labor, a designated allocation of scarce goods, assigned responsibility for children and others who cannot care for themselves, common values and their systematic transmission to new members, legitimate leadership, music, art, stories, games, and other symbolic productions. One way of choosing people for the different tasks of society is on the basis of their talents, motivations, and competence—their demonstrated achievements. The other way is on the basis of gender, race, ethnicity—ascribed membership in a category of people. Although societies vary in the extent to which they use one or the other of these ways of allocating people to work and to carry out other responsibilities, every society uses gender and age grades. Every society classifies people as "girl and boy children," "girls and boys ready to be married," and "fully adult women and men," constructs similarities among them and differences between them, and assigns them to different roles and responsibilities. Personality characteristics, feelings, motivations, and ambitions flow from these different life experiences so that the members of these different groups become different kinds of people. The process of gendering and its outcome are legitimated by religion, law, science, and the society's entire set of values.

In order to understand gender as a social institution, it is important to distinguish human action from animal behavior. Animals feed themselves and their young until their young can feed themselves. Humans have to produce not only food but shelter and clothing. They also, if the group is going to continue as a social group, have to teach the children how their particular group does these tasks. In the process, humans reproduce gender, family, kinship, and a division of labor—social institutions that do not exist among animals. Primate social groups have been referred to as families, and their mating patterns as monogamy, adultery, and harems. Primate behavior has been used to prove the universality of sex differences—as built into our evolutionary inheritance (Haraway 1978). But animals' sex differences are not at all the same as humans' gender differences; animals' bonding is not kinship; animals' mating is not ordered by marriage; and animals' dominance hierarchies are not the equivalent of human stratification systems. Animals group on sex and age, relational categories that are physiologically, not socially, different. Humans create gender and age-group categories that are socially, and not necessarily physiologically, different.[4]

For animals, physiological maturity means being able to impregnate or conceive; its markers are coming into heat (estrus) and sexual attraction. For humans, puberty means being available for marriage; it is marked by rites that demonstrate this marital eligibility. Although the onset of physiological puberty is signaled by secondary sex characteristics (menstruation, breast development, sperm ejaculation, pubic and underarm hair), the onset of social adulthood is ritualized by the coming-out party or desert walkabout or bar mitzvah or graduation from college or first successful hunt or dreaming or inheritance of property. Humans have rituals that mark the passage from childhood into puberty and puberty into full adult status, as well as for marriage, childbirth, and death; animals do not (van Gennep 1960). To the extent that infants and the dead are differentiated by whether they are male or female, there are different birth rituals for girls and boys and different funeral rituals for men and women (Biersack 1984, 132–33). Rituals of puberty, marriage, and becoming a parent are gendered, creating a "woman," a "man," a "bride," a "groom," a "mother," a "father." Animals have no equivalents for these statuses.

Among animals, siblings mate and so do parents and children; humans have incest taboos and rules that encourage or forbid mating between members of different kin groups (Lévi-Strauss 1956, [1949] 1969). Any animal of the same species may feed another's young (or may not, depending on the species). Humans designate responsibility for particular children by kinship; humans frequently limit responsibility for children to the members of their kinship group or make them into members of their kinship group with adoption rituals.

Animals have dominance hierarchies based on size or on successful threat gestures and signals. These hierarchies are usually sexed, and in some species, moving to the top of the hierarchy physically changes the sex (Austad 1986). Humans have stratification patterns based on control of surplus food, ownership of property, legitimate demands on others' work and sexual services, enforced determinations of who marries whom, and approved use of violence. If a woman replaces a man at the top of a stratification hierarchy, her social status may be that of a man, but her sex does not change.

Mating, feeding, and nurturant behavior in animals is determined by instinct and imitative learning and ordered by physiological sex and age (Lancaster 1974). In humans, these behaviors are taught and symbolically reinforced and ordered by socially constructed gender and age grades. Social gender and age statuses sometimes ignore or override physiological sex and age completely. Male and female animals (unless they physiologically change) are not interchangeable; infant animals cannot take the place of adult animals. Human females can become husbands and fathers, and human males can become wives and mothers, without sex-change surgery (Blackwood 1984). Human infants can reign as kings or queens.

Western society's values legitimate gendering by claiming that it all comes from physiology—female and male procreative differences. But gender and sex are not equivalent, and gender as a social construction does not flow automatically from genitalia and reproductive organs, the main physiological differences of females and males. In the construction of ascribed social statuses, physiological differences such as sex, stage of development, color of skin, and size are crude markers. They are not the source of the social statuses of gender, age grade, and race. *Social statuses* are carefully constructed through prescribed processes of teaching, learning, emulation, and enforcement. Whatever genes, hormones, and biological evolution contribute to human social institutions is materially as well as qualitatively transformed by social practices. Every social institution has a material base, but culture and social practices transform that base into something with qualitatively different patterns and constraints. The economy is much more than producing food and goods and distributing them to eaters and users; family and kinship are not the equivalent of having sex and procreating; morals and religions cannot be equated with the fears and ecstasies of the brain; language goes far beyond the sounds produced by tongue and larynx. No one eats "money" or "credit"; the concepts of "god" and "angels" are the subjects of theological disquisitions; not only words but objects, such as their flag, "speak" to the citizens of a country.

Similarly, gender cannot be equated with biological and physiological differences between human females and males. The building blocks of gender are *socially constructed statuses*. Western societies have only two genders, "man" and "woman." Some societies have three genders—men, women, and *berdaches* or *hijras* or *xaniths*. Berdaches, hijras, and xaniths are biological males who behave, dress, work, and are treated in most respects as social women; they are therefore not men, nor are they female women; they are, in our language, "male women."[5] There are African and American Indian societies that have a gender status called *manly hearted women*—biological females who work, marry, and parent as men; their social status is "female men" (Amadiume 1987; Blackwood 1984). They do not have to behave or dress as men to have the social responsibilities and prerogatives of husbands and fathers; what makes them men is enough wealth to buy a wife.

Modern Western societies' *transsexuals* and *transvestites* are the nearest equivalent of these crossover genders, but they are not institutionalized as third genders (Bolin 1987). Transsexuals are biological males and females who have sex-change operations to alter their genitalia. They do so in order to bring their physical anatomy into congruence with the way they want to live and with their own sense of gender identity. They do not become a third gender; they change genders. Transvestites are males who live as women and females who live as men but do not intend to have sex-change surgery. Their dress, appearance, and mannerisms fall within the range of what is expected from members of the opposite gender, so that they "pass." They also change genders, sometimes temporarily, some for most of their lives. Transvestite women have fought in wars as men soldiers as recently as the nineteenth century; some married women, and others went back to being women and married men once the war was over.[6] Some were discovered when their wounds were treated; others not until they died. In order to work as a jazz musician, a man's occupation, Billy Tipton, a woman, lived most of her life as a man. She died recently at seventy-four, leaving a wife and three adopted sons for whom she was husband and father, and musicians with whom she had played and traveled, for whom she was "one of the boys" (*New York Times* 1989).[7] There have been many other such occurrences of women passing as men to do more prestigious or lucrative men's work (Matthaci 1982, 192–93).[8]

Genders, therefore, are not attached to a biological substratum. Gender boundaries are breachable, and individual and socially organized shifts from one gender to another call attention to "cultural, social, or aesthetic dissonances" (Garber 1992, 16). These odd or deviant or third genders show us what we ordinarily take for granted—that people have to learn to be women and men. Men who cross-dress for performances or for pleasure often learn from women's magazines how to "do femininity" convincingly (Garber 1992, 41–51). Because transvestism is direct evidence of how gender is constructed, Marjorie Garber claims it has "extraordinary power . . . to disrupt, expose, and challenge, putting in question the very notion of the 'original' and of stable identity" (1992, 16).

GENDER BENDING

It is difficult to see how gender is constructed because we take it for granted that it's all biology, or hormones, or human nature. The differences between women and men seem to be self-evident, and we think they would occur no matter what society did. But in actuality, human females and males are physiologically more similar in appearance than are the two sexes of many species of animals and are more alike than different in traits and behavior (C. F. Epstein 1988). Without the deliberate use of gendered clothing, hairstyles, jewelry, and cosmetics, women and men would look far more alike.[9] Even societies that do not cover women's breasts have gender-identifying clothing, scarification, jewelry, and hairstyles.

The ease with which many transvestite women pass as men and transvestite men as women is corroborated by the common gender misidentification in Westernized societies of people in jeans, T-shirts, and sneakers. Men with long hair may be addressed as "miss," and women with short hair are often taken for men unless they offset the potential ambiguity with deliberate gender markers (Devor 1987, 1989). Jan Morris, in *Conundrum,* an autobiographical account of events just before and just after a sex-change operation, described how easy it was to shift back and forth from being a man to being a woman when testing how it would feel to change gender status. During this time, Morris still had a penis and wore more or less unisex clothing; the context alone made the man and the woman:

Sometimes the arena of my ambivalence was uncomfortably small. At the Travellers' Club, for example, I was obviously known as a man of sorts—women were only allowed on the premises at all during a few hours of the day, and even then were hidden away as far as possible in lesser rooms or alcoves. But I had another club, only a few hundred yards away, where I was known only as a woman, and often I went directly from one to the other, imperceptibly changing roles on the way—"Cheerio, sir," the porter would say at one club, and "Hello, madam," the porter would greet me at the other. (1975, 132)

Gender shifts are actually a common phenomenon in public roles as well. Queen Elizabeth II of England bore children, but when she went to Saudi Arabia on a state visit, she was considered an honorary man so that she could confer and dine with the men who were heads of a state that forbids unrelated men and women to have face-to-unveiled-face contact. In contemporary Egypt, lower-class women who run restaurants or shops dress in men's clothing and engage in unfeminine aggressive behavior, and middle-class educated women of professional or managerial status can take positions of authority (Rugh 1986, 131). In these situations, there is an important status change: These women are treated by the others in the situation as if they are men. From their own point of view, they are still women. From the social perspective, however, they are men.[10]

In many cultures, gender bending is prevalent in theater or dance—the Japanese kabuki are men actors who play both women and men; in Shakespeare's theater company, there were no actresses—Juliet and Lady Macbeth were played by boys. Shakespeare's comedies are full of witty comments on gender shifts. Women characters frequently masquerade as young men, and other women characters fall in love with them; the boys playing these masquerading women, meanwhile, are acting out pining for the love of men characters.[11] In *As You Like It,* when Rosalind justifies her protective cross-dressing, Shakespeare also comments on manliness:

Were it not better,
Because that I am more than common tall,
That I did suit me all points like a man:
A gallant curtle-axe upon my thigh,
A boar-spear in my hand, and in my heart
Lie there what hidden women's fear there will,
We'll have a swashing and martial outside,
As many other mannish cowards have
That do outface it with their semblances.   *(I, i, 115–22)*

Shakespeare's audience could appreciate the double subtext: Rosalind, a woman character, was a boy dressed in

PORTRAIT OF A MAN

LOREN CAMERON

I suppose I have told the same old story countless times now. I mean, every transsexual man I've ever met tells the same story: "I never felt like a girl; I played with boys' toys and liked boys' games, etc." Then a rehash about pubescent anxiety, how your body betrays you and you begin to develop very clever coping mechanisms to manage the stress. Like bad posture to hide your budding breasts and big boots and baggy shirts—and lesbianism, if you're lucky.

That was my story, anyway. I figured out early on that I had somehow gotten a square peg, and I wasn't too happy about it. Right from the start this skin of mine just didn't fit. Maybe it was because Mom was going through a divorce when she carried me in her womb. Maybe she was having some survival issues, causing her to put me awash in testosterone.

Or maybe it was those G.I. Joes I played with. Did you ever have one? They had the best uniforms. Lots of outfits to choose from—and boots, don't forget the boots. Big guns and grenades and cool scars. (Scars. I see a real early influence here.) Or it could be that I noticed I always got KP duty and was never promoted above the rank of private when I played Army with the

boys on my block. Girls were never allowed to go into combat.

I don't really know what felt so out of whack, and I don't think I really care. I guess there are as many reasons why a transsexual is transsexual as there are people in the world. All that matters is that it's my body and I can do what I want with it.

It's too bad that my days in Lesbiana had to come to an end. After about ten years of Butch Camp, I graduated to Boy World, big time. All of a sudden, one year I woke up and realized that the boobs had to go. What's more, I wanted a beard too. And a nice, hard, lean body to go with it. A penis? I would settle for an oversize clitoris; it was cheaper, and it works better.

I guess that mean I wanted to be a man. But that felt so alien in the beginning of my change. I was still very socialized as Butch Lesbian. (That isn't the same as Female. Do ya get it?) I felt like a boy in the first few years, and I looked like one too: lots of pimples and a breaking voice, a bad temper and a randy disposition. I remember one occasion when I was shopping for clothes with my girlfriend Isabella. She was High Femme (I was still into femmes in those days), a few inches taller, and a little older than I was. We were in the boys' clothing department at Macy's, which was the only place I could find shirts to fit me. (Besides, I was in my second adolescence.) The salesperson looked at

girl's clothing who then dressed as a boy; like bravery, masculinity and femininity can be put on and taken off with changes of costume and role (Howard 1988, 435).[12]

M Butterfly is a modern play of gender ambiguities, which David Hwang (1989) based on a real person. Shi Peipu, a male Chinese opera singer who sang women's roles, was a spy as a man and the lover as a woman of a Frenchman, Gallimard, a diplomat (Bernstein 1986). The relationship lasted twenty years, and Shi Peipu even pretended to be the mother of a child by Gallimard. "She" also pretended to be too shy to undress completely. As "Butterfly," Shi Peipu portrayed a fantasy Oriental woman who made the lover a "real man" (Kondo 1990b). In Gallimard's words, the fantasy was "of slender women in chong sams and kimonos who die for the love of unworthy

foreign devils. Who are born and raised to be perfect women. Who take whatever punishment we give them, and bounce back, strengthened by love, unconditionally" (D. H. Hwang 1989, 91). When the fantasy woman betrayed him by turning out to be the more powerful "real man," Gallimard assumed the role of Butterfly and, dressed in a geisha's robes, killed himself: "because 'man' and 'woman' are oppositionally defined terms, reversals . . . are possible" (Kondo 1990b, 18).[13]

But despite the ease with which gender boundaries can be traversed in work, in social relationships, and in cultural productions, gender statuses remain. Transvestites and transsexuals do not challenge the social construction of gender. Their goal is to be feminine women and masculine men (Kando 1973). Those who do not want to change their

Isabella and then at me and said, "Oh, is that your son?" I was mortified. I was twenty-nine years old; Isabella was thirty-six. People used to think she was some kind of pervert or something. She was a real trouper, stayed with me through teenage zits, disapproving lesbians, and hetero assumptions. Life was pretty weird in those first years of transition, but it was exciting as well.

It was then that I picked up a camera for the first time. Around '93, I guess. I was taking really bad snapshots of myself to send to friends and family. You know, the kind that are sort of out of focus and lop off the top of your head because you're holding the camera at arm's length. I really got it that visuals were essential to help the folks back home keep up with me as I went through this strange body transformation, this chemical and surgical reinvention of self. That's when I realized that visuals were useful in helping everybody else understand it too.

I knew I had to photograph us. Transsexuals, I mean. Us—that's what was new and different about the idea. I was going to be a photographer who was like them. I believed that we needed that, to see images of ourselves by one of us whose eye through the lens looked for a reflection. Self-portraiture. An eye that didn't see anything odd or freakish. An eye that looked for beauty.

I began meeting more transsexual people, listening to their stories of change, and I started taking their pictures. I took more photos of myself and watched eagerly as the hormones, body building, and chest surgery sculpted my female form more and more into a male one. I was proud of what I saw, in me and in them. We all had one thing in common, if nothing else: We were hell-bent on becoming the people we believed ourselves to be. We had to; we didn't feel it was a matter of choice.

By 1996 my book *Body Alchemy* was published. It's a collection of photographs that will show you just about everything you ever wanted to know about female-to-male bodies and is chock-full of proud, handsome trans men. I have tried to represent some measure of my community in an effort to provide bolstering and informative images with text for both trans and nontrans readers. I feel it has been a needed contribution in a new wave of transsexual activism, very much a part of a burgeoning movement that began about the time I was figuring out what an f-stop was.

Finally, nearly twelve years later, I am feeling just fine. I look in the mirror, and I see the man I've worked so hard to grow up to be. My body has that muscular and hard build like those comic-book heroes that I always wanted to look like. (Well, maybe not quite as big, especially in the crotch. Did you ever notice how big they look in those tights?) My beard, at long last, has filled in, while my head begins to bald, and my photography career goes skipping down its path. I've got a delicious pup of a girlfriend (partner) who, ironically (or maybe not so ironically), is a very handsome butch, indeed. Everybody thinks that Stephanie is my son—or my boy—and that I am some kind of old pervert queer. I tell you, being a man can be a very confusing thing sometimes.

anatomy but do want to change their gender behavior fare less well in establishing their social identity. The women Holly Devor called "gender blenders" wore their hair short, dressed in unisex pants, shirts, and comfortable shoes, and did not wear jewelry or makeup. They described their everyday dress as women's clothing: One said, "I wore jeans all the time, but I didn't wear men's clothes" (Devor 1989, 100). Their gender identity was women, but because they refused to "do femininity," they were constantly taken for men (1987, 1989, 107–42). Devor said of them: "The most common area of complaint was with public washrooms. They repeatedly spoke of the humiliation of being challenged or ejected from women's washrooms. Similarly, they found public change rooms to be dangerous territory and the buying of undergarments to be a difficult feat to accomplish" (1987, 29). In an ultimate ironic twist, some of these women said "they would feel like transvestites if they were to wear dresses, and two women said that they had been called transvestites when they had done so" (1987, 31). They resolved the ambiguity of their gender status by identifying as women in private and passing as men in public to avoid harassment on the street, to get men's jobs, and, if they were lesbians, to make it easier to display affection publicly with their lovers (Devor 1989, 107–42). Sometimes they even used men's bathrooms. When they had gender-neutral names, like Leslie, they could avoid the bureaucratic hassles that arose when they had to present their passports or other proof of identity, but because most had names associated with women, their appearance and their cards of identity were not conventionally congruent, and their gender status was in constant jeopardy.[14] When they could, they found it easier to pass as men than to try to change the stereotyped notions of what women should look like.

Paradoxically, then, bending gender rules and passing between genders does not erode but rather preserves gender boundaries. In societies with only two genders, the gender dichotomy is not disturbed by transvestites, because others feel that a transvestite is only transitorily ambiguous—is "really a man or woman underneath." After sex-change surgery, transsexuals end up in a conventional gender status—a "man" or a "woman" with the appropriate genitals (Eichler 1989). When women dress as men for business reasons, they are indicating that in that situation, they want to be treated the way men are treated; when they dress as women, they want to be treated as women:

> By their male dress, female entrepreneurs signal their desire to suspend the expectations of accepted feminine conduct without losing respect and reputation. By wearing what is "unattractive" they signify that they are not intending to display their physical charms while engaging in public activity. Their loud, aggressive banter contrasts with the modest demeanor that attracts men. . . . Overt signalling of a suspension of the rules preserves normal conduct from eroding expectations. (Rugh 1986, 131)

FOR INDIVIDUALS, GENDER MEANS SAMENESS

Although the possible combinations of genitalia, body shapes, clothing, mannerisms, sexuality, and roles could produce infinite varieties in human beings, the social institution of gender depends on the production and maintenance of a limited number of gender statuses and of making the members of these statuses similar to each other. Individuals are born sexed but not gendered, and they have to be taught to be masculine or feminine.[15] As Simone de Beauvoir said: "One is not born, but rather becomes, a woman . . .; it is civilization as a whole that produces this creature . . . which is described as feminine." (1952, 267).

Children learn to walk, talk, and gesture the way their social group says girls and boys should. Ray Birdwhistell, in his analysis of body motion as human communication, calls these learned gender displays *tertiary sex characteristics* and argues that they are needed to distinguish genders because humans are a weakly dimorphic species—their only sex markers are genitalia (1970, 39–46). Clothing, paradoxically, often hides the sex but displays the gender.

In early childhood, humans develop gendered personality structures and sexual orientations through their interactions with parents of the same and opposite gender. As adolescents, they conduct their sexual behavior according to gendered scripts. Schools, parents, peers, and the mass media guide young people into gendered work and family roles. As adults, they take on a gendered social status in their society's stratification system. Gender is thus both ascribed and achieved (West and Zimmerman 1987).

The achievement of gender was most dramatically revealed in a case of an accidental transsexual—a baby boy whose penis was destroyed in the course of a botched circumcision when he was seven months old (Money and Ehrhardt 1972, 118–23). The child's sex category was changed to "female," and a vagina was surgically constructed when the child was seventeen months old. The parents were advised that they could successfully raise the child, one of identical twins, as a girl. Physicians assured them that the child was too young to have formed a gender identity. Children's sense of which gender they belong to usually develops around the age of three, at the time that they start to group objects and recognize that the people around them also fit into categories—big, little; pink-skinned, brown-skinned; boys, girls. Three has also been the age when children's appearance is ritually gendered, usually by cutting a boy's hair or dressing him in distinctively masculine clothing. In Victorian times, English boys wore dresses up to the age of three, when they were put into short pants (Garber 1992, 1–2).

The parents of the accidental transsexual bent over backward to feminize the child—and succeeded. Frilly dresses, hair ribbons, and jewelry created a pride in looks, neatness, and "daintiness." More significant, the child's dominance was also feminized:

> The girl had many tomboyish traits, such as abundant physical energy, a high level of activity, stubbornness, and being often the dominant one in a girls' group. Her mother tried to modify her tomboyishness: ". . . I teach her to be more polite and quiet. I always wanted those virtues. I never did manage, but I'm going to try to manage them to—my daughter—to be more quiet and lady-like." From the beginning the girl had been the dominant twin. By the age of three, her dominance over her brother was, as her mother described it, that of a mother hen. The boy in turn took up for his sister, if anyone threatened her. (Money and Ehrhardt 1972, 122)

This child was not a tomboy because of male genes or hormones; according to her mother, she herself had also been a tomboy. What the mother had learned poorly while growing up as a "natural" female she insisted that her physically reconstructed son–daughter learn well. For both mother and child, the social construction of gender overrode any possibly inborn traits.

[Editors' note: For a variety of social, psychological, and medical reasons, this often-cited case of gender reassignment was not, in fact, a success. As a teenager, the child discovered that he had been born male and chose to return to living in the male sex category. Studies of other cases of gender reassignment show that as adults some individuals remain in their assigned gender, while others return to their original sex category. See John Colapinto, As Nature Made Him: The Boy Who Was Made a Girl (New York: Harper Collins, 2000) for a discussion of the twins case. Suzanne Kessler (Reading 9) discusses the complex factors that influence the gender reassignment of infants.]

People go along with the imposition of gender norms because the weight of morality as well as immediate social pressure enforces them. Consider how many instructions for properly gendered behavior are packed into this mother's admonition to her daughter: "This is how to hem a dress when you see the hem coming down and so to prevent yourself from looking like the slut I know you are so bent on becoming" (Kincaid 1978).

Gender norms are inscribed in the way people move, gesture, and even eat. In one African society, men were supposed to eat with their "whole mouth, wholeheartedly, and not, like women, just with the lips, that is halfheartedly, with reservation and restraint" (Bourdieu [1980] 1990, 70). Men and women in this society learned to walk in ways that proclaimed their different positions in the society:

> The manly man . . . stands up straight into the face of the person he approaches, or wishes to welcome. Ever on the alert, because ever threatened, he misses nothing of what happens around him. . . . Conversely, a well brought-up woman . . . is expected to walk with a slight stoop, avoiding every misplaced movement of her body, her head or her arms, looking down, keeping her eyes on the spot where she will next put her foot, especially if she happens to have to walk past the men's assembly. (70)

Many cultures go beyond clothing, gestures, and demeanor in gendering children. They inscribe gender directly into bodies. In traditional Chinese society, mothers bound their daughters' feet into three-inch stumps to enhance their sexual attractiveness. Jewish fathers circumcise their infant sons to show their covenant with God. Women in African societies remove the clitoris of prepubescent girls, scrape their labia, and make the lips grow together to preserve their chastity and ensure their mar-

riageability. In Western societies, women augment their breast size with silicone and reconstruct their faces with cosmetic surgery to conform to cultural ideals of feminine beauty. Hanna Papanek (1990) notes that these practices reinforce the sense of superiority or inferiority in the adults who carry them out as well as in the children on whom they are done: The genitals of Jewish fathers and sons are physical and psychological evidence of their common dominant religious and familial status; the genitals of African mothers and daughters are physical and psychological evidence of their joint subordination.[16]

Sandra Bem (1981, 1983) argues that because gender is a powerful "schema" that orders the cognitive world, one must wage a constant, active battle for a child not to fall into typical gendered attitudes and behavior. In 1972, *Ms.* magazine published Lois Gould's fantasy of how to raise a child free of gender-typing. The experiment calls for hiding the child's anatomy from all eyes except the parents' and treating the child as neither a girl nor a boy. The child, called X, gets to do all the things boys *and* girls do. The experiment is so successful that all the children in X's class at school want to look and behave like X. At the end of the story, the creators of the experiment are asked what will happen when X grows up. The scientists' answer is that by then it will be quite clear what X is, implying that its hormones will kick in and it will be revealed as a female or male. That ambiguous, and somewhat contradictory, ending lets Gould off the hook; neither she nor we have any idea what someone brought up totally androgynously would be like sexually or socially as an adult. The hormonal input will not create gender or sexuality but will only establish secondary sex characteristics; breasts, beards, and menstruation alone do not produce social manhood or womanhood. Indeed, it is at puberty, when sex characteristics become evident, that most societies put pubescent children through their most important rites of passage, the rituals that officially mark them as fully gendered—that is, ready to marry and become adults.

Most parents create a gendered world for their newborn by naming, birth announcements, and dress. Children's relationships with same-gendered and different-gendered caretakers structure their self-identifications and personalities. Through cognitive development, children extract and apply to their own actions the appropriate behavior for those who belong in their own gender, as well as race, religion, ethnic group, and social class, rejecting what is not appropriate. If their social categories are highly valued, they value themselves highly; if their social categories are low status, they lose self-esteem (Chodorow 1974). Many feminist parents who want to raise androgynous children soon lose their children to the pull of gendered norms (T. Gordon 1990, 87–90). My son attended a carefully nonsexist elementary school, which didn't even have girls' and boys' bathrooms. When he was seven or eight years old, I attended a class play about "squares" and "circles" and their need for each other and noticed that all the girl squares and circles wore makeup, but none of the boy squares and circles did. I asked the teacher about it after the play, and she said, "Bobby said he was not going to wear makeup, and he is a powerful child, so none of the boys would either." In a long discussion about conformity, my son confronted me with the question of who the conformists were, the boys who followed their leader or the girls who listened to the woman teacher. In actuality, they both were, because they both followed same-gender leaders and acted in gender-appropriate ways. (Actors may wear makeup, but real boys don't.)

For human beings there is no essential femaleness or maleness, femininity or masculinity, womanhood or manhood, but once gender is ascribed, the social order constructs and holds individuals to strongly gendered norms and expectations. Individuals may vary on many of the components of gender and may shift genders temporarily or permanently, but they must fit into the limited number of gender statuses their society recognizes. In the process, they recreate their society's version of women and men: "If we do gender appropriately, we simultaneously sustain, reproduce, and render legitimate the institutional arrangements. . . . If we fail to do gender appropriately, we as individuals—not the institutional arrangements—may be called to account (for our character, motives, and predispositions)" (West and Zimmerman 1987, 146).

The gendered practices of everyday life reproduce a society's view of how women and men should act (Bourdieu [1980] 1990). Gendered social arrangements are justified by religion and cultural productions and backed by law, but the most powerful means of sustaining the moral hegemony of the dominant gender ideology is that the process is made invisible; any possible alternatives are virtually unthinkable (Foucault 1972; Gramsci 1971).[17]

FOR SOCIETY, GENDER MEANS DIFFERENCE

The pervasiveness of gender as a way of structuring social life demands that gender statuses be clearly differentiated. Varied talents, sexual preferences, identities, personalities, interests, and ways of interacting fragment the individ-

ual's bodily and social experiences. Nonetheless, these are organized in Western cultures into two and only two socially and legally recognized gender statuses, "man" and "woman."[18] In the social construction of gender, it does not matter what men and women actually do; it does not even matter if they do exactly the same thing. The social institution of gender insists only that what they do is *perceived* as different.

If men and women are doing the same tasks, they are usually spatially segregated to maintain gender separation, and often the tasks are given different job titles as well, such as executive secretary and administrative assistant (Reskin 1988). If the differences between women and men begin to blur, society's "sameness taboo" goes into action (G. Rubin 1975, 178). At a rock-and-roll dance at West Point in 1976, the year women were admitted to the prestigious military academy for the first time, the school's administrators "were reportedly perturbed by the sight of mirror-image couples dancing in short hair and dress gray trousers," and a rule was established that women cadets could dance at these events only if they wore skirts (Barkalow and Raab 1990, 53).[19] Women recruits in the U.S. Marine Corps are required to wear makeup—at a minimum, lipstick and eye shadow—and they have to take classes in makeup, hair care, poise, and etiquette. This feminization is part of a deliberate policy of making them clearly distinguishable from men Marines. Christine Williams quotes a twenty-five-year-old woman drill instructor as saying: "A lot of the recruits who come here don't wear makeup; they're tomboyish or athletic. A lot of them have the preconceived idea that going into the military means they can still be a tomboy. They don't realize that you are a *Woman* Marine" (1989, 76–77).[20]

If gender differences were genetic, physiological, or hormonal, gender bending and gender ambiguity would occur only in hermaphrodites, who are born with chromosomes and genitalia that are not clearly female or male. Since gender differences are socially constructed, all men and all women can enact the behavior of the other, because they know the other's social script: " 'Man' and 'woman' are at once empty and overflowing categories. Empty because they have no ultimate, transcendental meaning. Overflowing because even when they appear to be fixed, they still contain within them alternative, denied, or suppressed definitions." (J. W. Scott 1988, 49). Nonetheless, though individuals may be able to shift gender statuses, the gender boundaries have to hold, or the whole gendered social order will come crashing down.

Paradoxically, it is the social importance of gender statuses and their external markers—clothing, mannerisms, and spatial segregation—that makes gender bending or gender crossing possible—or even necessary. The social viability of differentiated gender statuses produces the need or desire to shift statuses. Without gender differentiation, transvestism and transsexuality would be meaningless. You couldn't dress in the opposite gender's clothing if all clothing were unisex. There would be no need to reconstruct genitalia to match identity if interests and lifestyles were not gendered. There would be no need for women to pass as men to do certain kinds of work if jobs were not typed as "women's work" and "men's work." Women would not have to dress as men in public life in order to give orders or aggressively bargain with customers.

Gender boundaries are preserved when transsexuals create congruous autobiographies of always having felt like what they are now. The transvestite's story also "recuperates social and sexual norms" (Garber 1992, 69). In the transvestite's normalized narrative, he or she "is 'compelled' by social and economic forces to disguise himself or herself in order to get a job, escape repression, or gain artistic or political 'freedom' " (Garber 1992, 70). The "true identity," when revealed, causes amazement over how easily and successfully the person passed as a member of the opposite gender, not a suspicion that gender itself is something of a put-on.

GENDER RANKING

Most societies rank genders according to prestige and power and construct them to be unequal, so that moving from one to another also means moving up or down the social scale. Among some North American Indian cultures, the hierarchy was male men, male women, female men, female women. Women produced significant durable goods (basketry, textiles, pottery, decorated leather goods), which could be traded. Women also controlled what they produced and any profit or wealth they earned. Since women's occupational realm could lead to prosperity and prestige, it was fair game for young men—but only if they became women in gender status. Similarly, women in other societies who amassed a great deal of wealth were allowed to become men—"manly hearts." According to Harriet Whitehead (1981):

> Both reactions reveal an unwillingness or inability to distinguish the sources of prestige—wealth, skill, personal efficacy (among other things)—from masculinity. Rather there is the innuendo that if a person performing female tasks can attain excellence, prosperity, or social power, it must be because that person is, at some level, a

man. . . . A woman who could succeed at doing the things men did was honored as a man would be. . . . What seems to have been more disturbing to the culture—which means, for all intents and purposes, to the men—was the possibility that women, within their own department, might be onto a good thing. It was into this unsettling breach that the berdache institution was hurled. In their social aspect, women were complimented by the berdache's imitation. In their anatomic aspect, they were subtly insulted by his vaunted superiority. (108)

In American society, men-to-women transsexuals tend to earn less after surgery if they change occupations; women-to-men transsexuals tend to increase their income (Bolin 1988, 153–60; Brody 1979). Men who go into women's fields, like nursing, have less prestige than women who go into men's fields, like physics. Janice Raymond, a radical feminist, feels that transsexual men-to-women have advantages over female women because they were not socialized to be subordinate or oppressed throughout life. She says:

> We know that we are women who are born with female chromosomes and anatomy, and that whether or not we were socialized to be so-called normal women, patriarchy has treated and will treat us like women. Transsexuals have not had this same history. No man can have the history of being born and located in this culture as a woman. He can have the history of *wishing* to be a woman and of *acting* like a woman, but this gender experience is that of a transsexual, not of a woman. Surgery may confer the artifacts of outward and inward female organs but it cannot confer the history of being born a woman in this society. (1979, 114)

Because women who become men rise in the world and men who become women fall, Elaine Showalter (1987) was very critical of the movie *Tootsie,* in which Dustin Hoffman plays an actor who passes as a woman in order to be able to get work. "Dorothy" becomes a feminist "woman of the year" for standing up for women's rights not to be demeaned or sexually harassed. Showalter feels that the message of the movie is double-edged: "Dorothy's 'feminist' speeches . . . are less a response to the oppression of women than an instinctive situational male reaction to being treated like a woman. The implication is that women must be taught by men how to win their rights. . . . It says that feminist ideas are much less threatening when they come from a man" (123). Like Raymond, Showalter feels that being or having been a man gives a transsexual man-to-woman or a man cross-dressed as a woman a social advantage over those whose gender status was always "woman."[21] The implication here is that there is an experiential superiority that doesn't disappear with the gender shift.

For one transsexual man-to-woman, however, the experience of living as a woman changed his/her whole personality. As James, Morris had been a soldier, foreign correspondent, and mountain climber; as Jan, Morris is a successful travel writer. But socially, James was far superior to Jan, and so Jan developed the "learned helplessness" that is supposed to characterize women in Western society:

> We are told that the social gap between the sexes is narrowing, but I can only report that having, in the second half of the twentieth century, experienced life in both roles, there seems to me no aspect of existence, no moment of the day, no contact, no arrangement, no response, which is not different for men and for women. The very tone of voice in which I was now addressed, the very posture of the person next in the queue, the very feel in the air when I entered a room or sat at a restaurant table, constantly emphasized my change of status.
>
> And if other's responses shifted, so did my own. The more I was treated as woman, the more woman I became. I adapted willy-nilly. If I was assumed to be incompetent at reversing cars, or opening bottles, oddly incompetent I found myself becoming. If a case was thought too heavy for me, inexplicably I found it so myself. . . . Women treated me with a frankness which, while it was one of the happiest discoveries of my metamorphosis, did imply membership of a camp, a faction, or at least a school of thought; so I found myself gravitating always towards the female, whether in sharing a railway compartment or supporting a political cause. Men treated me more and more as junior, . . . and so, addressed every day of my life as an inferior, involuntarily, month by month I accepted the condition. I discovered that even now men prefer women to be less informed, less able, less talkative, and certainly less self-centered than they are themselves; so I generally obliged them. (1975, 165–66) [22]

COMPONENTS OF GENDER

By now, it should be clear that gender is not a unitary essence but has many components as a social institution and as an individual status.[23]

As a social institution, gender is composed of:

Gender statuses, the socially recognized genders in a society and the norms and expectations for their enactment behaviorally, gesturally, linguistically, emotionally, and physically. How gender statuses are evaluated depends on historical development in any particular society.

Gendered division of labor, the assignment of productive and domestic work to members of different gender statuses. The work assigned to those of different gender statuses strengthens the society's evaluation of those statuses—the higher the status, the more prestigious and valued the work and the greater its rewards.

Gendered kinship, the family rights and responsibilities for each gender status. Kinship statuses reflect and reinforce the prestige and power differences of the different genders.

Gendered sexual scripts, the normative patterns of sexual desire and sexual behavior, as prescribed for the different gender statuses. Members of the dominant gender have more sexual prerogatives; members of a subordinate gender may be sexually exploited.

Gendered personalities, the combinations of traits patterned by gender norms of how members of different gender statuses are supposed to feel and behave. Social expectations of others in face-to-face interaction constantly bolster these norms.

Gendered social control, the formal and informal approval and reward of conforming behavior and the stigmatization, social isolation, punishment, and medical treatment of nonconforming behavior.

Gender ideology, the justification of gender statuses, particularly, their differential evaluation. The dominant ideology tends to suppress criticism by making these evaluations seem natural.

Gender imagery, the cultural representations of gender and embodiment of gender in symbolic language and artistic productions that reproduce and legitimate gender statuses. Culture is one of the main supports of the dominant gender ideology.

For an individual, gender is composed of:

Sex category, to which the infant is assigned at birth based on appearance of genitalia. With prenatal testing and sex-typing, categorization is prenatal. Sex category may be changed later through surgery or reinspection of ambiguous genitalia.

Gender identity, the individual's sense of gendered self as a worker and family member.

Gendered marital and procreative status, fulfillment or nonfulfillment of allowed or disallowed mating, impregnation, childbearing, kinship roles.

Gendered sexual orientation, socially and individually patterned sexual desires, feelings, practices, and identification.

Gendered personality, internalized patterns of socially normative emotions as organized by family structure and parenting.

Gendered processes, the social practices of learning, being taught, picking up cues, enacting behavior already learned to be gender appropriate (or inappropriate, if rebelling, testing), developing a gender identity, "doing gender" as a member of a gender status in relationships with gendered others, acting deferent or dominant.

Gender beliefs, incorporation of or resistance to gender ideology.

Gender display, presentation of self as a certain kind of gendered person through dress, cosmetics, adornments, and permanent and reversible body markers.

For an individual, all the social components are supposed to be consistent and congruent with perceived physiology. The actual combination of genes and genitalia, prenatal, adolescent, and adult hormonal input, and procreative capacity may or may not be congruous with each other and with sex-category assignment, gender identity, gendered sexual orientation and procreative status, gender display, personality, and work and family roles. At any one time, an individual's identity is a combination of the major ascribed statuses of gender, race, ethnicity, religion, and social class, and the individual's achieved statuses, such as education level, occupation or profession, marital status, parenthood, prestige, authority, and wealth. The ascribed statuses substantially limit or create opportunities for individual achievements and also diminish or enhance the luster of those achievements.

GENDER AS PROCESS, STRATIFICATION, AND STRUCTURE

As a social institution, gender is a process of creating distinguishable social statuses for the assignment of rights and responsibilities. As part of a stratification system that ranks these statuses unequally, gender is a major building block in the social structures built on these unequal statuses.

As a *process,* gender creates the social differences that define "woman" and "man." In social interaction throughout their lives, individuals learn what is expected, see what is expected, act and react in expected ways, and thus simultaneously construct and maintain the gender order: "The very injunction to be a given gender takes place through discursive routes: to be a good mother, to be a heterosexually desirable object, to be a fit worker, in sum, to signify a multiplicity of guarantees in response to a variety of different demands all at once" (J. Butler 1990, 145). Members of a social group neither make up gender as they go along nor exactly replicate in rote fashion what was done before. In almost every encounter, human beings produce gender, behaving in the ways they learned were appropriate for their gender status, or resisting or rebelling against these norms. Resistance and rebellion have altered gender norms, but so far they have rarely eroded the statuses.

Gendered patterns of interaction acquire additional layers of gendered sexuality, parenting, and work behaviors in childhood, adolescence, and adulthood. Gendered norms and expectations are enforced through informal sanctions of gender-inappropriate behavior by peers and by formal punishment or threat of punishment by those in authority should behavior deviate too far from socially imposed standards for women and men.

Everyday gendered interactions build gender into the family, the work process, and other organizations and institutions, which in turn reinforce gender expectations for individuals.[24] Because gender is a process, there is room not only for modification and variation by individuals and small groups but also for institutionalized change (J. W. Scott 1988, 7).

As part of a *stratification* system, gender ranks men above women of the same race and class. Women and men could be different but equal. In practice, the process of creating difference depends to a great extent on differential evaluation. As Nancy Jay (1981) says: "That which is defined, separated out, isolated from all else is A and pure. Not-A is necessarily impure, a random catchall, to which nothing is external except A and the principle of order that separates it from Not-A" (45). From the individual's point of view, whichever gender is A, the other is Not-A; gender boundaries tell the individual who is like him or her, and all the rest are unlike. From society's point of view, however, one gender is usually the touchstone, the normal, the dominant, and the other is different, deviant, and subordinate. In Western society, "man" is A, "wo-man" is Not-A. (Consider what a society would be like where woman was A and man Not-A.)

The further dichotomization by race and class constructs the gradations of a heterogeneous society's stratification scheme. Thus, in the United States, white is A, African American is Not-A; middle class is A, working class is Not-A, and "African-American women occupy a position whereby the inferior half of a series of these dichotomies converge" (P. H. Collins 1990, 70). The dominant categories are the hegemonic ideals, taken so for granted as the way things should be that white is not ordinarily thought of as a race, middle class as a class, or men as a gender. The characteristics of these categories define the Other as that which lacks the valuable qualities the dominants exhibit.

In a gender-stratified society, what men do is usually valued more highly than what women do because men do it, even when their activities are very similar or the same. In different regions of southern India, for example, harvesting rice is men's work, shared work, or women's work: "Wherever a task is done by women it is considered easy, and where it is done by [men] it is considered difficult" (Mencher 1988, 104). A gathering and hunting society's survival usually depends on the nuts, grubs, and small animals brought in by the women's foraging trips, but when the men's hunt is successful, it is the occasion for a celebration. Conversely, because they are the superior group, white men do not have to do the "dirty work," such as housework; the most inferior group does it, usually poor women of color (Palmer 1989).

Freudian psychoanalytic theory claims that boys must reject their mothers and deny the feminine in themselves in order to become men: "For boys the major goal is the achievement of personal masculine identification with their father and sense of secure masculine self, achieved through superego formation and disparagement of women" (Chodorow 1978, 165). Masculinity may be the outcome of boys' intrapsychic struggles to separate their identity from that of their mothers, but the proofs of masculinity are culturally shaped and usually ritualistic and symbolic (Gilmore 1990).

The Marxist feminist explanation for gender inequality is that by demeaning women's abilities and keeping them from learning valuable technological skills, bosses preserve them as a cheap and exploitable reserve army of labor. Unionized men who could be easily replaced by women collude in this process because it allows them to monopolize the better paid, more interesting, and more autonomous jobs: "Two factors emerge as helping men maintain their separation from women and their control of technological occupations. One is the active gendering of jobs and people. The second is the continual creation of sub-divisions in the work processes, and levels in work hierarchies, into

which men can move in order to keep their distance from women" (Cockburn 1985, 13).

Societies vary in the extent of the inequality in social status of their women and men members, but where there is inequality, the status "woman" (and its attendant behavior and role allocations) is usually held in lesser esteem than the status "man." Since gender is also intertwined with a society's other constructed statuses of differential evaluation—race, religion, occupation, class, country of origin, and so on—men and women members of the favored groups command more power, more prestige, and more property than the members of the disfavored groups. Within many social groups, however, men are advantaged over women. The more economic resources, such as education and job opportunities, are available to a group, the more they tend to be monopolized by men. In poorer groups that have few resources (such as working-class African Americans in the United States), women and men are more nearly equal, and the women may even outstrip the men in education and occupational status (Almquist 1987).

As a *structure,* gender divides work in the home and in economic production, legitimates those in authority, and organizes sexuality and emotional life (Connell 1987, 91–142). As primary parents, women significantly influence children's psychological development and emotional attachments, in the process reproducing gender. Emergent sexuality is shaped by heterosexual, homosexual, bisexual, and sadomasochistic patterns that are gendered—different for girls and boys, and for women and men—so that sexual statuses reflect gender statuses.

When gender is a major component of structured inequality, the devalued genders have less power, prestige, and economic rewards than the valued genders. In countries that discourage gender discrimination, many major roles are still gendered; women still do most of the domestic labor and child-rearing, even while doing full-time paid work; women and men are segregated on the job and each does work considered "appropriate"; women's work is usually paid less than men's work. Men dominate the positions of authority and leadership in government, the military, and the law; cultural productions, religions, and sports reflect men's interests.

In societies that create the greatest gender difference, such as Saudi Arabia, women are kept out of sight behind walls or veils, have no civil rights, and often create a cultural and emotional world of their own (Bernard 1981). But even in societies with less rigid gender boundaries, women and men spend much of their time with people of their own gender because of the way work and family are organized.

This spatial separation of women and men reinforces gendered differentness, identity, and ways of thinking and behaving (Coser 1986).

Gender inequality—the devaluation of "women" and the social domination of "men"—has social functions and a social history. It is not the result of sex, procreation, physiology, anatomy, hormones, or genetic predispositions. It is produced and maintained by identifiable social processes and built into the general social structure and individual identities deliberately and purposefully. The social order as we know it in Western societies is organized around racial, ethnic, class, and gender inequality. I contend, therefore, that the continuing purpose of gender as a modern social institution is to construct women as a group to be the subordinates of men as a group. The life of everyone placed in the status "woman" is "night to his day—that has forever been the fantasy. Black to his white. Shut out of his system's space, she is the repressed that ensures the system's functioning" (Cixous and Clément [1975] 1986, 67).

THE PARADOX OF HUMAN NATURE

To say that sex, sexuality, and gender are all socially constructed is not to minimize their social power. These categorical imperatives govern our lives in the most profound and pervasive ways, through the social experiences and social practices of what Dorothy Smith calls the "everyday/everynight world" (1990, 31–57). The paradox of human nature is that it is *always* a manifestation of cultural meanings, social relationships, and power politics; "not biology, but culture, becomes destiny" (J. Butler 1990, 8).

Gendered people emerge not from physiology or sexual orientation but from the exigencies of the social order, mostly from the need for a reliable division of the work of food production and the social (not physical) reproduction of new members. The moral imperatives of religion and cultural representations guard the boundary lines among genders and ensure that what is demanded, what is permitted, and what is tabooed for the people in each gender are well known and followed by most (C. Davies 1982). Political power, control of scarce resources, and, if necessary, violence uphold the gendered social order in the face of resistance and rebellion. Most people, however, voluntarily go along with their society's prescriptions for those of their gender status, because the norms and expectations get built into their sense of worth and identity as a certain kind of human being, and because they believe their society's way is the natural way. These beliefs emerge from the imagery that pervades the way we think, the way we see and hear and speak, the way we fantasize, and the way we feel.

There is no core or bedrock human nature below these endlessly looping processes of the social production of sex and gender, self and other, identity and psyche, each of which is a "complex cultural construction" (J. Butler 1990, 36). *For humans, the social is the natural.* Therefore, "in its feminist senses, gender cannot mean simply the cultural appropriation of biological sexual difference. Sexual difference is itself a fundamental—and scientifically contested—construction. Both 'sex' and 'gender' are woven of multiple, asymmetrical strands of difference, charged with multifaceted dramatic narratives of domination and struggle" (Haraway 1990, 140).

NOTES

1. Gender is, in Erving Goffman's words, an aspect of *Felicity's Condition*: "any arrangement which leads us to judge an individual's . . . acts not to be a manifestation of strangeness. Behind Felicity's Condition is our sense of what it is to be sane" (1983, 27). Also see Bem 1993; Frye 1983, 17–40; Goffman 1977.

2. In cases of ambiguity in countries with modern medicine, surgery is usually performed to make the genitalia more clearly male or female.

3. See J. Butler 1990 for an analysis of how doing gender *is* gender identity.

4. Douglas 1973; MacCormack 1980; Ortner 1974; Ortner and Whitehead 1981; Yanagisako and Collier 1987. On the social construction of childhood, see Ariès 1962; Zelizer 1985.

5. On the hijras of India, see Nanda 1990; on the xaniths of Oman, Wikan 1982, 168–86; on the American Indian berdaches, W. L. Williams 1986. Other societies that have similar institutionalized third-gender men are the Koniag of Alaska, the Tanala of Madagascar, the Mesakin of Nuba, and the Chukchee of Siberia (Wikan 1982, 170).

6. Durova 1989; Freeman and Bond 1992; Wheelwright 1989.

7. Gender segregation of work in popular music still has not changed very much, according to Groce and Cooper 1989, despite considerable androgyny in some very popular figures. See Garber 1992 on the androgyny. She discusses Tipton on pp. 67–70.

8. In the nineteenth century, not only did these women get men's wages, but they also "had male privileges and could do all manner of things other women could not: open a bank account,

write checks, own property, go anywhere unaccompanied, vote in elections" (Faderman 1991, 44).

9. When unisex clothing and men wearing long hair came into vogue in the United States in the mid-1960s, beards and mustaches for men also came into style again as gender identifications.

10. For other accounts of women being treated as men in Islamic countries, as well as accounts of women and men cross-dressing in these countries, see Garber 1992, 304–52.

11. Dollimore 1986; Garber 1992, 32–40; Greenblatt 1987, 66–93; Howard 1988. For Renaissance accounts of sexual relations with women and men of ambiguous sex, see Laqueur 1990a, 134–39. For modern accounts of women passing as men that other women find sexually attractive, see Devor 1989, 136–37; Wheelwright 1989, 53–59.

12. Females who passed as men soldiers had to "do masculinity," not just dress in a uniform (Wheelwright, 1989, 50–78). On the triple entendres and gender resonances of Rosalind-type characters, see Garber 1992, 71–77.

13. Also see Garber 1992, 234–66.

14. Bolin describes how many documents have to be changed by transsexuals to provide a legitimizing "paper trail" (1988, 145–47). Note that only members of the same social group know which names are women's and which men's in their culture, but many documents list "sex."

15. For an account of how a potential man-to-woman transsexual learned to be feminine, see Garfinkel 1967, 116–85, 285–88. For a gloss on this account that points out how, throughout his encounters with Agnes, Garfinkel failed to see how he himself was constructing his own masculinity, see Rogers 1992.

16. Paige and Paige (1981, 147–49) argue that circumcision ceremonies indicate a father's loyalty to his lineage elders— "visible public evidence that the head of a family unit of their lineage is willing to trust others with his and his family's most valuable political asset, his son's penis" (147). On female circumcision, see El Dareer 1982; Lightfoot-Klein 1987; van der Kwaak 1992; Walker 1992. There is a form of female circumcision that removes only the prepuce of the clitoris and is similar to male circumcision, but most forms of female circumcision are far more extensive, mutilating, and spiritually and psychologically shocking than the usual form of male circumcision. However, among the Australian aborigines, boys' penises are slit and kept open, so that they urinate and bleed the way women do (Bettelheim 1962, 165–206).

17. The concepts of moral hegemony, the effects of everyday activities (praxis) on thought and personality, and the necessity of consciousness of these processes before political change can occur are all based on Marx's analysis of class relations.

18. Other societies recognize more than two categories, but usually no more than three or four (Jacobs and Roberts 1989).

19. Carol Barkalow's book has a photograph of eleven first-year West Pointers in a math class, who are dressed in regulation pants, shirts, and sweaters, with short haircuts. The caption challenges the reader to locate the only woman in the room.

20. The taboo on males and females looking alike reflects the U.S. military's homophobia (Bérubé 1989). If you can't tell those with a penis from those with a vagina, how are you going to determine whether their sexual interest is heterosexual or homosexual unless you watch them having sexual relations?

21. Garber feels that *Tootsie* is not about feminism but about transvestism and its possibilities for disturbing the gender order (1992, 5 –9).

22. See Bolin 1988, 149–50, for transsexual men-to-women's discovery of the dangers of rape and sexual harassment. Devor's "gender blenders" went in the opposite direction. Because they found that it was an advantage to be taken for men, they did not deliberately cross-dress, but they did not feminize themselves either (1989, 126–40).

23. See West and Zimmerman 1987 for a similar set of gender components.

24. On the "logic of practice," or how the experience of gender is embedded in the norms of everyday interaction and the structure of formal organizations, see Acker 1990; Bourdieu [1980] 1990; Connell 1987; Smith 1987a.

REFERENCES

Acker, Joan. 1990. Hierarchies, jobs, and bodies: A theory of gendered organizations. *Gender & Society* 4: 139–58.

Almquist, Elizabeth M. 1987. Labor market gendered inequality in minority groups. *Gender & Society* 1:400–14.

Amadiume, Ifi. 1987. *Male Daughters, Female Husbands: Gender and Sex in an African Society.* London: Zed Books.

Ariès, Philippe. 1962. *Centuries of childhood: A social history of family life,* translated by Robert Baldick. New York: Vintage.

Austad, Steven N. 1986. Changing sex nature's way. *International Wildlife,* May–June, 29.

Barkalow, Carol, with Andrea Raab. 1990. *In the Men's House.* New York: Poseidon Press.

Bem, Sandra Lipsitz. 1981. Gender schema theory: A cognitive account of sex typing. *Psychological Review* 88:354–64.

———. 1983. Gender schema theory and its implications for child development: Raising gender-aschematic children in a gender-schematic society. *Signs* 8: 598–616.

———. 1993. *The lense of gender: Transforming the debate on sexual inequality.* New Have: Yale University Press.

Bernard, Jessie. 1981. *The Female World.* New York: Free Press.

Bernstein, Richard. 1986. France jails 2 in odd case of espionage. *New York Times,* 11 May.

Berube, Allan, and John D'Emilio. 1984. The military and lesbians during the McCarthy years. *Signs* 9 759–75.

Bettelheim, Bruno. 1962. *Symbolic wounds: Puberty rites and the envious male.* London: Thames and Hudson.

Biersack, Aletta. 1984. Paiela "women-men": The reflexive foundations of gender ideology. *American Ethnologist* 11:118–38.

Birdwhistell, Ray L. 1970. *Kinesics and context: Essays on body motion communications.* Philadelphia: University of Pennsylvania Press.

Blackwood, Evelyn. 1984. Sexuality and gender in certain Native American tribes: The case of cross-gender females. *Signs* 10:27–42.

Bolin, Anne. 1987. Transsexualism and the limits of traditional analysis. *American Behavioral Scientist* 31:41–65.

———. 1988. *In Search of Eve: Transsexual Rites of Passage.* South Hadley, Mass.: Bergin & Garvey.

Bourdieu, Pierre. [1980] 1990. *The Logic of Practice.* Stanford, Calif.: Stanford University Press.

Brody, Jane E. 1979. Benefits of transsexual surgery disputed as leading hospital halts the procedure. *New York Times,* 2 October.

Butler, Judith. 1990. *Gender trouble: Feminism and the Subversion of Identity.* New York and London: Routledge.

Chodorow, Nancy. 1974. Family structure and feminine personality. In Rosaldo and Lamphere.

———. 1978. *The Reproduction of Mothering.* Berkeley: University of California Press.

Cixous, Hélène, and Catherine Clément. [1975] 1986. *The Newly Born Woman,* translated by Betsy Wing. Minneapolis: University of Minnesota Press.

Cockburn, Cynthia. 1985. *Machinery of Dominance: Women, Men and Technical Know-how.* London: Pluto Press.

Collins, Patricia Hill. 1990. *Black Feminist Thought: Knowledge, Consciousness, and the Politics of Empowerment.* Boston: Unwin Hyman.

Connell, R. [Robert] W. 1987. *Gender and Power: Society, the Person, and Sexual Politics.* Stanford, Calif.: Stanford University Press.

Coser, Rose Laub. 1986. Cognitive structure and the use of social space. *Sociological Forum* 1:1–26.

Davies, Christie. 1982. Sexual taboos and social boundaries. *American Journal of Sociology* 87:1032–63.

de Beauvoir, Simone. 1953. *The Second Sex,* translated by H. M. Parshley. New York: Knopf.

Devor, Holly. 1987. Gender blending females: Women and sometimes men. *American Behavioral Scientist* 31:12–40.

———. 1989. *Gender Blending: Confronting the Limits of Duality.* Bloomington: Indiana University Press.

Dollimore, Jonathan. 1986. Subjectivity, sexuality, and transgression: The Jacobean connection. *Renaissance Drama,* n.s. 17:53–81.

Douglas, Mary. 1973. *Natural Symbols.* New York: Vintage.

Durova, Nadezhda. 1989. *The calvary maiden: Journals of a Russian officer in the Nepoleonic Wars,* translated by Mary Fleming Zirin. Bloomington: Indiana University Press.

Eichler, Margrit. 1989. Sex change operations: The last bulwark of the double standard. In Richardson and Taylor.

El Dareer, Asma. 1982. *Woman, why do you weep? Circumcision and its consequences.* London: Zed Books.

Epstein, Cynthia Fuchs, 1988. *Deceptive Distinctions: Sex, Gender and the Social Order.* New Haven: Yale University Press.

Faderman, Lillian. 1981. *Surpassing the love of men: Romantic friendship and love between women from the Renaissance to the present.* New York: William Morrow.

Foucault, Michel. 1972. *The Archeology of Knowledge and the Discourse on Language,* translated by A. M. Sheridan Smith. New York: Pantheon.

Freeman, Lucy, and Alma Halbert Bond. 1992. *America's first woman warrior: The courage of Deborah Sampson.* New York: Paragon.

Frye, Marilyn. 1983. *The politics of reality: Essays in feminist theory.* Trumansburg, N.Y.: Crossing Press.

Garber, Marjorie. 1992. *Vested Interests: Cross-dressing and Cultural Anxiety.* New York and London: Routledge.

Garfinkel, Harold. 1967. *Studies in ethnomethodology.* Endgelwood Cliffs, N.J.: Prentice-Hall.

Gilmore, David D. 1977. *The arrangement between the sexes.* Theory and Society 4: 301–33.

Gilmore, David D. 1990. *Manhood in the Making: Cultural concepts of Masculinity.* New Haven: Yale University Press.

Gordon, Tuula. 1990. *Feminist Mothers.* New York: New York University Press.

Gramsci, Antonio. 1971. *Selections from the Prison Notebooks,* translated and edited by Quintin Hoare and Geoffrey Nowell Smith. New York: International Publishers.

Greenblatt, Stephen. 1987. *Shakespearean negotiations: The circulation of social energy in Renaissance England.* Berkeley: University of California Press.

Groce, Stephen B., and Margaret Cooper. 1990. Just me and the boys? Women in local-level rock and roll. *Gender & Society* 4:220–29.

Haraway, Donna. 1978. Animal sociology and a natural economy of the body politic. Part I: A political physiology of dominance. *Signs* 4:21–36.

———. 1990. Investment strategies for the evolving portfolio of primate females. In Jacobus, Keller, and Shuttleworth.

Howard, Jean E. 1988. Crossdressing, the theater, and gender struggle in early modern England. *Shakespeare Quarterly* 39:418–41.

Hwang, David Henry. 1989. *M Butterfly.* New York: New American Library.

Jacobs, Sue-Ellen, and Christine Roberts. 1989. Sex, sexuality, gender, and gender variance. In *Gender and anthropology,* edited by Sandra Morgen. Washington, D.C.: American Anthropological Association.

Jay, Nancy. 1981. Gender and dichotomy. *Feminist Studies* 7:38–56.

Kando, Thomas. 1973. *Sex Change: The Achievement of Gender Identity among Feminized Transsexuals.* Springfield, Ill.: Charles C. Thomas.

Kincaid, Jamaica. 1978. Girl. *The New Yorker,* 26 June.

Kondo, Dorinne K. 1990a. *Crafting Selves: Power, Gender, and Discourses of Identity in a Japanese Workplace.* Chicago: University of Chicago Press.

———. 1990b. *M. Butterfly:* Orientalism, gender, and a critique of essentialist identity. *Cultural Critique,* no. 16 (Fall):5–29.

Lancaster, Jane Beckman. 1974. *Primate Behavior and the Emergence of Human Culture.* New York: Holt, Rinehart and Winston.

Laqueur, Thomas. 1990a. *Making sex: Body and gender from the Greeks to Freud.* Cambridge, Mass.: Harvard University Press.

Lévi-Strauss, Claude. 1956. The family. In *Man, Culture, and Society,* edited by Harry L. Shapiro, New York: Oxford.

———. [1949] 1969. *The Elementary Structures of Kinship,* translated by J. H. Bell and J. R. von Sturmer. Boston: Beacon Press.

Lightfoot-Klein, Hanny. 1989. *Prisoners of ritual: An odyssey into female circumcision in Africa.* New York: Harrington Park Press.

MacCormack, Carol P. 1980. Nature, culture and gender: A critique. In *Nature, culture and gender,* edited by Carol P. MacCormack and Marilyn Strathern. Cambridge, England: Cambridge University Press.

Matthaei, Julie A. 1982. *An Economic History of Women's Work in America.* New York: Schocken.

Mencher, Joan. 1988. Women's work and poverty: Women's contribution to household maintenance in South India. In Dwyer and Bruce.

Money, John, and Anke A. Ehrhardt. 1972. *Man & Woman, Boy & Girl.* Baltimore, Md.: Johns Hopkins University Press.

Morris, Jan. 1975. *Conundrum.* New York: Signet.

Nanda, Serena. 1990. *Neither man nor woman: The hijiras of India.* Belmont, Calif.: Wadsworth.

New York Times. 1989. Musician's death at 74 reveals he was a woman. 2 February.

Ortner, Sherry B. 1974. Is female to male as nature is to culture? In Rosaldo and Lamphere.

Ortner, Sherry B., and Harriet Whitehead. 1981a. Introduction: Accounting for sexual meanings. In Ortner and Whitehead (eds.).

Paige, Karen Ericksen, and Jeffrey M. Paige 1981. *The politics of reproductive ritual.* Berkeley: University of California Press.

Palmer, Phyllis. 1989. *Domesticity and Dirt: Housewives and Domestic Servants in the United States, 1920–1945.* Philadelphia: Temple University Press.

Papanek, Hanna. 1979. Family status production: The "work" and "non-work" of women. *Signs* 4:775–81.

Raymond, Janice G. 1979. *The Transsexual Empire: The Making of the She-male.* Boston: Beacon Press.

Reskin, Barbara F. 1988. Bringing the men back in: Sex differentiation and the devaluation of women's work. *Gender & Society* 2:58–81.

Rogers, Mary F. 1992. They were all passing: Agnes, Garfinkel, and company. *Gender & Society* 6:169–91.

Rubin, Gayle. 1975. The traffic in women: Notes on the political economy of sex. In *Toward an Anthropology of Women,* ed. Rayna R[app] Reiter. New York: Monthly Review Press.

Rugh, Andrea B. 1986. *Reveal and Conceal: Dress in Contemporary Egypt.* Syracuse, N.Y.: Syracuse University Press.

Scott, Joan Wallach. 1988. *Gender and the Politics of History.* New York: Columbia University Press.

Showalter, Elaine. 1987. Critical cross-dressing: Male feminists and the woman of the year. In *Men in Feminism,* edited by Alice Jardine and Paul Smith. New York: Methuen.

Smith, Dorothy E. 1987. *The everyday world as problematic: A feminist sociology.* Toronto: University of Toronto Press.

Smith, Dorothy E. 1990. *The Conceptual Practices of Power: A Feminist Sociology of Knowledge.* Toronto: University of Toronto Press.

van der Kwaak, Anke. 1992. Female circumcision and gender identity: A questionable alliance? *Social Science and Medicine* 35:777–87.

van Gennep, Arnold. 1960. *The Rites of Passage,* trans. Monika B. Vizedom and Gabrielle L. Caffee. Chicago: University of Chicago Press.

Walker, Molly K. 1992. Maternal reactions to fetal sex. *Health Care for Women International* 13:293–302.

West, Candace, and Don Zimmerman. 1987. Doing gender. *Gender & Society* 1: 125–51.

Wheelright, Julie. 1989. *Amazons and Military Maids: Women Who Cross-dressed in Pursuit of Life, Liberty and Happiness.* London: Pandora Press.

Whitehead, Ann. 1981. "I'm hungry, Mum": The politics of domestic budgeting. In Young, Wolkowitz, and McCullagh.

Wikan, Unni. 1982. *Behind the veil in Arabia: Women in Oman.* Baltimore, Md.: Johns Hopkins University Press.

Williams, Christine L. 1989. *Gender Differences at Work: Women and Men in Nontraditional Occupations.* Berkeley: University of California Press.

Williams, Walter L. 1986. *The spirit and the flesh: Sexual diversity in American Indian culture.* Boston: Beacon Press.

Yanagisako, Sylvia Junko, and Jane Fishburne Collier. 1987. Toward a unified analysis of gender and kinship. In *Gender and kinship: Essays toward a unified analysis,* edited by Jane Fishburne Collier and Sylvia Junko Yanagisako. Berkeley: University of California Press.

Zelizer, Viviana A. 1985. *Pricing the priceless child: The changing social value of children.* New York: Basic Books.

From Servitude to Service Work: Historical Continuities in the Racial Division of Paid Reproductive Labor

EVELYN NAKANO GLENN

Recent scholarship on African-American, Latina, Asian-American, and Native American women reveals the complex interaction of race and gender oppression in their lives. These studies expose the inadequacy of additive models that treat gender and race as separate and discrete systems of hierarchy (Collins 1986; King 1988; Brown 1989). In an additive model, white women are viewed solely in terms of gender, while women of color are thought to be "doubly" subordinated by the cumulative effects of gender plus race. Yet achieving a more adequate framework, one that captures the interlocking, interactive nature of these systems, has been extraordinarily difficult. Historically, race and gender have developed as separate topics of inquiry, each with its own literature and concepts. Thus features of social life considered central in understanding one system have been overlooked in analyses of the other.

One domain that has been explored extensively in analyses of gender but ignored in studies of race is social reproduction. The term *social reproduction* is used by feminist scholars to refer to the array of activities and relationships involved in maintaining people both on a daily basis and intergenerationally. Reproductive labor includes activities such as purchasing household goods, preparing and serving food, laundering and repairing clothing, maintaining furnishings and appliances, socializing children, providing

care and emotional support for adults, and maintaining kin and community ties.

Marxist feminists place the gendered construction of reproductive labor at the center of women's oppression. They point out that this labor is performed disproportionately by women and is essential to the industrial economy. Yet because it takes place mostly outside the market, it is invisible, not recognized as real work. Men benefit directly and indirectly from this arrangement—directly in that they contribute less labor in the home while enjoying the services women provide as wives and mothers and indirectly in that, freed of domestic labor, they can concentrate their efforts in paid employment and attain primacy in that area. Thus the sexual division of reproductive labor in the home interacts with and reinforces sexual division in the labor market.[1] These analyses draw attention to the dialectics of production and reproduction and male privilege in both realms. When they represent gender as the sole basis for assigning reproductive labor, however, they imply that all women have the same relationship to it and that it is therefore a universal female experience.[2]

In the meantime, theories of racial hierarchy do not include any analysis of reproductive labor. Perhaps because, consciously or unconsciously, they are male centered, they focus exclusively on the paid labor market and especially on male-dominated areas of production.[3] In the 1970s several writers seeking to explain the historic subordination of peoples of color pointed to dualism in the labor market—its division into distinct markets for white workers and for racial-ethnic workers—as a major vehicle for maintaining white domination (Blauner 1972; Barrera 1979).[4] According to these formulations, the labor system has been organized to ensure that racial-ethnic workers are relegated to a lower tier of low-wage, dead-end, marginal jobs; institutional barriers, including restrictions on legal and political rights, prevent their moving out of that tier and competing with Euro-American workers for better jobs. These theories draw attention to the material advantages whites gain from the racial division of labor. However, they either take for granted or ignore women's unpaid household labor and fail to consider whether this work might also be "racially divided."

In short, the racial division of reproductive labor has been a missing piece of the picture in both literatures. This piece, I would contend, is key to the distinct exploitation of women of color and is a source of both hierarchy and interdependence among white women and women of color. It is thus essential to the development of an integrated model of race and gender, one that treats them as interlocking, rather than additive, systems.

In this article I present a historical analysis of the simultaneous race and gender construction of reproductive labor in the United States, based on comparative study of women's work in the South, the Southwest, and the Far West. I argue that reproductive labor has divided along racial as well as gender lines and that the specific characteristics of the division have varied regionally and changed over time as capitalism has reorganized reproductive labor, shifting parts of it from the household to the market. In the first half of the century racial-ethnic women were employed as servants to perform reproductive labor in white households, relieving white middle-class women of onerous aspects of that work; in the second half of the century, with the expansion of commodified services (services turned into commercial products or activities), racial-ethnic women are disproportionately employed as service workers in institutional settings to carry out lower-level "public" reproductive labor, while cleaner white-collar supervisory and lower professional positions are filled by white women.

I will examine the ways race and gender were constructed around the division of labor by sketching changes in the organization of reproductive labor since the early nineteenth century, presenting a case study of domestic service among African-American women in the South, Mexican-American women in the Southwest, and Japanese-American women in California and Hawaii . . . . Race and gender emerge as socially constructed, interlocking systems that shape the material conditions, identities, and consciousnesses of all women.

HISTORICAL CHANGES IN THE ORGANIZATION OF REPRODUCTION

The concept of reproductive labor originated in Karl Marx's remark that every system of production involves both the production of the necessities of life and the reproduction of the tools and labor power necessary for production (Marx and Engels 1969, 31). Recent elaborations of the concept grow out of Engels's dictum that the "determining force in history is, in the last resort, the production and reproduction of immediate life." This has, he noted, "a two-fold character, on the one hand the production of subsistence and on the other the production of human beings themselves" (Engels 1972, 71). Although often equated with domestic labor or defined narrowly as referring to the renewal of labor power, the term *social reproduction* has come to be more broadly conceived, particularly by social historians, to refer to the creation and recreation of people as cultural and social, as well as physical, beings (Ryan 1981, 15). Thus, it involves mental, emotional, and manual labor (Brenner and Laslett 1986, 117). This labor can be organized in myriad ways—in and out of the household, as paid or unpaid work, creating exchange value or only use value—and these ways are not mutually exclusive. An example is the preparation of food, which can be done by a family member as unwaged work in the household, by a servant as waged work in the household, or by a short-order cook in a fast-food restaurant as waged work that generates profit for the employer. These forms exist contemporaneously.

Prior to industrialization, however, both production and reproduction were organized almost exclusively at the household level. Women were responsible for most of what might be designated as reproduction, but they were simultaneously engaged in the production of foodstuffs, clothing, shoes, candles, soap, and other goods consumed by the household. With industrialization, production of these basic goods gradually was taken over by capitalist industry. Reproduction, however, remained largely the responsibility of individual households. The ideological separation between men's "productive" labor and women's nonmarket-based activity that had evolved at the end of the eighteenth century was elaborated in the early decades of the nineteenth. An idealized division of labor arose in which men's work was to follow production outside the home, while women's work was to remain centered in the household (Boydston 1990, esp. 46–48). Household work continued to include the production of many goods consumed by members (Smuts 1959, 11–13; Kessler-Harris 1981), but as an expanding range of outside-manufactured goods became available, household work became increasingly focused on reproduction.[5] This idealized division of labor was largely illusory for working-class households, including immigrant and racial-ethnic families, in which men seldom earned a family wage; in these households women and children were forced into income-earning activities in and out of the home (Kessler-Harris, 1982).

In the second half of the twentieth century, with goods production almost completely incorporated into the market, reproduction has become the next major target for commodification. Aside from the tendency of capital to expand into new areas for profit making, the very conditions of life brought about by large-scale commodity production have increased the need for commercial services. As household members spend more of their waking hours employed outside the home, they have less time and inclination to provide for one another's social and emotional needs. With the growth of a more geographically mobile and urbanized society, individuals and households have become increasingly cut off from larger kinship circles, neighbors, and traditional communities. Thus, as Harry Braverman notes, "The population no longer relies upon social organization in the form of family, friends, neighbors, community, elders, children, but with few exceptions must go to the market and only to the market, not only for food, clothing, and shelter, but also for recreation, amusement, security, for the care of the young, the old, the sick, the handicapped. In time not only the material and service needs but even the emotional patterns of life are channeled through the market" (Braverman 1974, 276). Conditions of capitalist urbanism also have enlarged the population of those requiring daily care and support: elderly and very young people, mentally and physically disabled people, criminals, and other people incapable of fending for themselves. Because the care of such dependents becomes difficult for the "stripped-down" nuclear family or the atomized community to bear, more of it becomes relegated to institutions outside the family.[6]

The final phase in this process is what Braverman calls the "product cycle," which "invents new products and services, some of which become indispensable as the conditions of modern life change and destroy alternatives" (Braverman 1974, 281). In many areas (e.g., health care), we no longer have choices outside the market. New services and products also alter the definition of an acceptable standard of living. Dependence on the market is further

reinforced by what happened earlier with goods production, namely, an "atrophy of competence," so that individuals no longer know how to do what they formerly did for themselves.

As a result of these tendencies, an increasing range of services has been removed wholly or partially from the household and converted into paid services yielding profits. Today, activities such as preparing and serving food (in restaurants and fast-food establishments), caring for handicapped and elderly people (in nursing homes), caring for children (in child care centers), and providing emotional support, amusement, and companionship (in counseling offices, recreation centers, and health clubs) have become part of the cash nexus. In addition, whether impelled by a need to maintain social control or in response to pressure exerted by worker and community organizations, the state has stepped in to assume minimal responsibility for some reproductive tasks, such as child protection and welfare programs.[7] Whether supplied by corporations or the state, these services are labor-intensive. Thus, a large army of low-wage workers, mostly women and disproportionately women of color, must be recruited to supply the labor.

Still, despite vastly expanded commodification and institutionalization, much reproduction remains organized at the household level. Sometimes an activity is too labor-intensive to be very profitable. Sometimes households or individuals in them have resisted commodification. The limited commodification of child care, for example, involves both elements. The extent of commercialization in different areas of life is uneven, and the variation in its extent is the outcome of political and economic struggles (Brenner and Laslett 1986, 121; Laslett and Brenner 1989, 384). What is consistent across forms, whether commodified or not, is that reproductive labor is constructed as "female." The gendered organization of reproduction is widely recognized. Less obvious, but equally characteristic, is its racial construction: historically, racial-ethnic women have been assigned a distinct place in the organization of reproductive labor.

Elsewhere I have talked about the reproductive labor racial-ethnic women have carried out for their own families; this labor was intensified as the women struggled to maintain family life and indigenous cultures in the face of cultural assaults, ghettoization, and a labor system that relegated men and women to low-wage, seasonal, and hazardous employment (Glenn 1985; 1986, 86–108; Dill 1988). . . .

DOMESTIC SERVICE AS THE RACIAL DIVISION OF REPRODUCTIVE LABOR

Both the demand for household help and the number of women employed as servants expanded rapidly in the latter half of the nineteenth century (Chaplin 1978). This expansion paralleled the rise of industrial capital and the elaboration of middle-class women's reproductive responsibilities. Rising standards of cleanliness, larger and more ornately furnished homes, the sentimentalization of the home as a "haven in a heartless world" (Lasch 1977), and the new emphasis on childhood and the mother's role in nurturing children all served to enlarge middle-class women's responsibilities for reproduction at a time when technology had done little to reduce the sheer physical drudgery of housework.[8]

By all accounts middle-class women did not challenge the gender-based division of labor or the enlargement of their reproductive responsibilities. Indeed, middle-class women—as readers and writers of literature; as members and leaders of clubs, charitable organizations, associations, reform movements, and religious revivals; and as supporters of the cause of abolition—helped to elaborate the domestic code (Brenner and Laslett 1986).[9] Feminists seeking an expanded public role for women argued that the same nurturant and moral qualities that made women centers of the home should be brought to bear in public service. In the domestic sphere, instead of questioning the inequitable gender division of labor, they sought to slough off the more burdensome tasks onto more oppressed groups of women.[10]

Phyllis Palmer observes that at least through the first half of the twentieth century, "most white middle class women could hire another woman—a recent immigrant, a working-class woman, a woman of color, or all three—to perform much of the hard labor of household tasks" (Palmer 1987, 182–83). Domestics were employed to clean house, launder and iron clothes, scrub floors, and care for infants and children. They relieved their mistresses of the heavier and dirtier domestic chores.[11] White middle-class women were thereby freed for supervisory tasks and for cultural, leisure, and volunteer activity or, more rarely during this period, for a career.[12]

Palmer suggests that the use of domestic servants also helped resolve certain contradictions created by the domestic code. She notes that the early twentieth-century housewife confronted inconsistent expectations of middle-class womanhood: domesticity and "feminine virtue." Domesticity—defined as creating a warm, clean, and attractive home for husband and children—required hard physical labor and meant contending with dirt. The virtuous woman, however, was defined in terms of spirituality, refinement, and the denial of the physical body. Additionally, in the 1920s and 1930s there emerged a new ideal of the modern wife as an intelligent and attractive companion. If the heavy parts of household work could be transferred to paid help, the middle-class housewife could fulfill her domestic duties, yet distance herself from the physical labor and dirt and also have time for personal development (Palmer 1990, 127–51).

Who was to perform the "dirty work" varied by region. In the Northeast, European immigrant women, particularly those who were Irish and German, constituted the majority of domestic servants from the mid-nineteenth century to World War I (Katzman 1978, 65–70). In regions where there was a large concentration of people of color, subordinate-race women formed a more or less permanent servant stratum. Despite differences in the composition of the populations and the mix of industries in the regions, there were important similarities in the situation of Mexicans in the Southwest, African Americans in the South, and Japanese people in northern California and Hawaii. Each of these groups was placed in a separate legal category from whites, excluded from rights and protections accorded full citizens. This severely limited their ability to organize, compete for jobs, and acquire capital (Glenn 1985). The racial division of private reproductive work mirrored this racial dualism in the legal, political, and economic systems.

In the South, African-American women constituted the main and almost exclusive servant caste. Except in times of extreme economic crisis, whites and Blacks did not compete for domestic jobs. Until the First World War 90 percent of all nonagriculturally employed Black women in the South were employed as domestics. Even at the national level, servants and laundresses accounted for close to half (48.4 percent) of nonagriculturally employed Black women in 1930.[13]

In the Southwest, especially in the states with the highest proportions of Mexicans in the population—Texas, Colorado, and New Mexico—Chicanas were disproportionately concentrated in domestic service.[14] In El Paso nearly half of all Chicanas in the labor market were employed as servants or laundresses in the early decades of the century (Garcia 1981, 76). In Denver, according to Sarah Deutsch, perhaps half of all households had at least one female member employed as a domestic at some time, and if a woman became a widow, she was almost certain to take in laundry (Deutsch 1987a, 147). Nationally, 39.1 percent of nonagriculturally employed Chicanas were servants or laundresses in 1930.[15]

In the Far West—especially in California and Hawaii, with their large populations of Asian immigrants—an unfavorable sex ratio made female labor scarce in the late nineteenth and early twentieth centuries. In contrast to the rest of the nation, the majority of domestic servants in California and Hawaii were men: in California until 1880 (Katzman 1978, 55) and in Hawaii as late as 1920 (Lind 1951, table 1). The men were Asian—Chinese and later Japanese. Chinese houseboys and cooks were familiar figures in late nineteenth-century San Francisco; so too were Japanese male retainers in early twentieth-century Honolulu. After 1907 Japanese women began to immigrate in substantial numbers, and they inherited the mantle of service in both California and Hawaii. In the pre-World War II years, close to half of all immigrant and native-born Japanese American women in the San Francisco Bay area and in Honolulu were employed as servants or laundresses (U.S. Bureau of the Census 1932, table 8; Glenn 1986, 76–79). Nationally, excluding Hawaii, 25.4 percent of nonagricultural Japanese American women workers were listed as servants in 1930.[16]

In areas where racial dualism prevailed, being served by members of the subordinate group was a prerequisite of membership in the dominant group. According to Elizabeth Rae Tyson, an Anglo woman who grew up in El Paso in the early years of the century, "almost every Anglo-American family had at least one, sometimes two or three servants: a maid and laundress, and perhaps a nursemaid or yardman. The maid came in after breakfast and cleaned up the breakfast dishes, and very likely last night's supper dishes as well; did the routine cleaning, washing and ironing, and after the family dinner in the middle of the day, washed dishes again, and then went home to perform similar services in her own home" (Garcia 1980, 327). In southwest cities, Mexican-American girls were trained at an early age to do domestic work and girls as young as nine or ten were hired to clean house.[17]

In Hawaii, where the major social division was between the haole (Caucasian) planter class and the largely Asian plantation worker class, haole residents were required to employ one or more Chinese or Japanese servants to demonstrate their status and their social distance from those less privileged. Andrew Lind notes that "the literature on Hawaii, especially during the second half of the nineteenth century, is full of references to the open-handed hospitality of Island residents, dispensed by the ever-present maids and houseboys" (Lind 1951, 73). A public school teacher who arrived in Honolulu in 1925 was placed in a teacher's cottage with four other mainland teachers. She discovered a maid had already been hired by the principal: "A maid! None of us had ever had a maid. We were all used to doing our own work. Furthermore, we were all in debt and did not feel that we wanted to spend even four dollars a month on a maid. Our principal was quite insistent. Everyone on the plantation had a maid. It was, therefore, the thing to do" (Lind 1951, 76).

In the South, virtually every middle-class housewife employed at least one African-American woman to do cleaning and child care in her home. Southern household workers told one writer that in the old days, "if you worked for a family, your daughter was expected to, too" (Tucker 1988, 98). Daughters of Black domestics were sometimes inducted as children into service to baby-sit, wash diapers, and help clean (Clark-Lewis 1987, 200–201).[18] White-skin privilege transcended class lines, and it was not uncommon for working-class whites to hire Black women for housework (Anderson and Bowman 1953). In the 1930s white women tobacco workers in Durham, North Carolina, could mitigate the effects of the "double day"—household labor on top of paid labor—by employing Black women to work in their homes for about one-third of their own wages (Janiewski 1983, 93). Black women tobacco workers were too poorly paid to have this option and had to rely on the help of overworked husbands, older children, Black women too old to be employed, neighbors, or kin.

Where more than one group was available for service, a differentiated hierarchy of race, color, and culture emerged. White and racial-ethnic domestics were hired for different tasks. In her study of women workers in Atlanta, New Orleans, and San Antonio during the 1920s and 1930s, Julia Kirk Blackwelder reported that "anglo women in the employ of private households were nearly always reported as housekeepers, while Blacks and Chicanas were reported as laundresses, cooks, or servants" (Blackwelder 1978, 349).[19]

In the Southwest, where Anglos considered Mexican or "Spanish" culture inferior, Anglos displayed considerable ambivalence about employing Mexicans for child care. Although a modern-day example, this statement by an El Paso businessman illustrates the contradictions in Anglo attitudes. The man told an interviewer that he and his wife were putting off parenthood because "the major dilemma would be what to do with the child. We don't really like the idea of leaving the baby at home with a maid . . . for the simple reason if the maid is Mexican, the child may assume that the other person is its mother. Nothing wrong with

Mexicans, they'd just assume that this other person is its mother. There have been all sorts of cases where the infants learned Spanish before they learned English. There've been incidents of the Mexican maid stealing the child and taking it over to Mexico and selling it" (Ruíz 1987b, 71).

In border towns, the Mexican group was further stratified by English-speaking ability, place of nativity, and immigrant status, with non-English-speaking women residing south of the border occupying the lowest rung. In Laredo and El Paso, Mexican-American factory operatives often employed Mexican women who crossed the border daily or weekly to do domestic work for a fraction of a U.S. operative's wages (Hield 1984, 95; Ruíz 1987a, 64).

THE RACE AND GENDER CONSTRUCTION OF DOMESTIC SERVICE

Despite their preference for European immigrant domestics, employers could not easily retain their services. Most European immigrant women left service upon marriage, and their daughters moved into the expanding manufacturing, clerical, and sales occupations during the 1910s and twenties.[20] With the flow of immigration slowed to a trickle during World War I, there were few new recruits from Europe. In the 1920s, domestic service became increasingly the specialty of minority-race women (Palmer 1990, 12). Women of color were advantageous employees in one respect: they could be compelled more easily to remain in service. There is considerable evidence that middle-class whites acted to ensure the domestic labor supply by tracking racial-ethnic women into domestic service and blocking their entry into other fields. Urban school systems in the Southwest tracked Chicana students into homemaking courses designed to prepare them for domestic service. The El Paso school board established a segregated school system in the 1880s that remained in place for the next thirty years; education for Mexican children emphasized manual and domestic skills that would prepare them to work at an early age. In 1909 the Women's Civic Improvement League, an Anglo organization, advocated domestic training for older Mexican girls. Their rationale is explained by Mario Garcia: "According to the league the housegirls for the entire city came from the Mexican settlement and if they could be taught housekeeping, cooking, and sewing, every American family would benefit. The Mexican girls would likewise profit since their services would improve and hence be in greater demand" (Garcia 1981, 113).

The education of Chicanas in the Denver school system was similarly directed toward preparing students for domestic service and handicrafts. Sarah Deutsch found that Anglo women there persisted in viewing Chicanas and other "inferior-race" women as dependent, slovenly, and ignorant. Thus, they argued, training Mexican girls for domestic service not only would solve "one phase of women's work we seem to be incapable of handling" but it would simultaneously help raise the (Mexican) community by improving women's standard of living, elevating their morals, and facilitating Americanization (Deutsch 1987b, 736). One Anglo writer, in an article published in 1917 titled "Problems and Progress among Mexicans in Our Own Southwest," claimed, "When trained there is no better servant than the gentle, quiet Mexicana girl" (Romero 1988a, 16).

In Hawaii, with its plantation economy, Japanese and Chinese women were coerced into service for their husbands' or fathers' employers. According to Lind, prior to World War II:

> It has been a usual practice for a department head or a member of the managerial staff of the plantation to indicate to members of his work group that his household is in need of domestic help and to expect them to provide a wife or daughter to fill the need. Under the conditions which have prevailed in the past, the worker has felt obligated to make a member of his own family available for such service, if required, since his own position and advancement depend upon keeping the goodwill of his boss. Not infrequently, girls have been prevented from pursuing a high school or college education because someone on the supervisory staff has needed a servant and it has seemed inadvisable for the family to disregard the claim. [Lind 1951, 77]

Economic coercion also could take bureaucratic forms, especially for women in desperate straits. During the Depression, local officials of the federal Works Progress Administration (WPA) and the National Youth Administration (NYA), programs set up by the Roosevelt administration to help the unemployed find work, tried to direct Chicanas and Blacks to domestic service jobs exclusively (Blackwelder 1984, 120–22; Deutsch 1987a, 182–83). In Colorado, local officials of the WPA and NYA advocated household training projects for Chicanas. George Bickel, assistant state director of the WPA for Colorado, wrote: "The average Spanish-American girl on the NYA program looks forward to little save a life devoted to motherhood often under the most miserable circumstances" (Deutsch 1987a, 183). Given such an outlook, it made sense to provide training in domestic skills.

Young Chicanas disliked domestic service so much that slots in the programs went begging. Older women, especially single mothers struggling to support their families, could not afford to refuse what was offered. The cruel dilemma that such women faced was poignantly expressed in one woman's letter to President Roosevelt:

My name is Lula Gordon. I am a Negro woman. I am on the relief. I have three children. I have no husband and no job. I have worked hard ever since I was old enough. I am willing to do any kind of work because I have to support myself and my children. I was under the impression that the government or the W.P.A. would give the Physical [sic] fit relief clients work. I have been praying for that time to come. A lady, Elizabeth Ramsie, almost in my condition, told me she was going to try to get some work. I went with her. We went to the Court House here in San Antonio, we talked to a Mrs. Beckmon. Mrs. Beckmon told me to phone a Mrs. Coyle because she wanted some one to clean house and cook for ($5) five dollars a week. Mrs. Beckmon said if I did not take the job in the Private home I would be cut off from everything all together. I told her I was afraid to accept the job in the private home because I have registered for a government job and when it opens up I want to take it. She said that she was taking people off of the relief and I have to take the job in the private home or none. . . . I need work and I will do anything the government gives me to do. . . . Will you please give me some work. [Blackwelder 1984, 68–69]

Japanese-American women were similarly compelled to accept domestic service jobs when they left the internment camps in which they were imprisoned during World War II. To leave the camps they had to have a job and a residence, and many women were forced to take positions as live-in servants in various parts of the country. When women from the San Francisco Bay area returned there after the camps were closed, agencies set up to assist the returnees directed them to domestic service jobs. Because they had lost their homes and possessions and had no savings, returnees had to take whatever jobs were offered them. Some became live-in servants to secure housing, which was in short supply after the war. In many cases domestic employment became a lifelong career (Glenn 1986).

In Hawaii the Japanese were not interned, but there nonetheless developed a "maid shortage" as war-related employment expanded. Accustomed to cheap and abundant household help, haole employers became increasingly agitated about being deprived of the services of their "mamasans." The suspicion that many able-bodied former maids were staying at home idle because their husbands or fathers had lucrative defense jobs was taken seriously enough to prompt an investigation by a university researcher.[21]

Housewives told their nisei maids it was the maids' patriotic duty to remain on the job. A student working as a live-in domestic during the war was dumbfounded by her mistress's response when she notified her she was leaving to take a room in the dormitory at the university. Her cultured and educated mistress, whom the student had heretofore admired, exclaimed with annoyance: " 'I think especially in war time, the University should close down the dormitory.' Although she didn't say it in words, I sensed the implication that she believed all the (Japanese) girls should be placed in different homes, making it easier for the haole woman."[22] The student noted with some bitterness that although her employer told her that working as a maid was the way for her to do "your bit for the war effort," she and other haole women did not, in turn, consider giving up the "conveniences and luxuries of pre-war Hawaii" as their bit for the war.[23]

The dominant group ideology in all these cases was that women of color—African-American women, Chicanas, and Japanese-American women—were particularly suited for service. These racial justifications ranged from the argument that Black and Mexican women were incapable of governing their own lives and thus were dependent on whites—making white employment of them an act of benevolence—to the argument that Asian servants were naturally quiet, subordinate, and accustomed to a lower standard of living. Whatever the specific content of the racial characterizations, it defined the proper place of these groups as in service: they belonged there, just as it was the dominant group's place to be served.

David Katzman notes that "ethnic stereotyping was the stock in trade of all employers of servants, and it is difficult at times to figure out whether blacks and immigrants were held in contempt because they were servants or whether urban servants were denigrated because most of the servants were blacks and immigrants" (Katzman 1978, 221). Even though racial stereotypes undoubtedly preceded their entry into domestic work, it is also the case that domestics were forced to enact the role of the inferior. Judith Rollins and Mary Romero describe a variety of rituals that affirmed the subordination and dependence of the domestic; for example, employers addressed household workers by their first names and required them to enter by the back door, eat in the kitchen, and wear uniforms. Domestics understood they were not to initiate conversation but were to remain standing or visibly engaged in work whenever the employer was in the room. They also had to accept with gratitude "gifts" of discarded clothing and leftover food (Rollins 1985, chap. 5; Romero 1987).

For their part, racial-ethnic women were acutely aware that they were trapped in domestic service by racism and not by lack of skills or intelligence. In their study of Black life in prewar Chicago, St. Clair Drake and Horace Cayton found that education did not provide African-Americans with an entree into white-collar work. They noted, "Colored girls are often bitter in their comments about a society which condemns them to the 'white folks' kitchen' " (Drake and Cayton [1945] 1962, 246). Thirty-five years later, Anna May Madison minced no words when she declared to anthropologist John Gwaltney: "Now, I don't do nothing for white women or men that they couldn't do for themselves. They don't do anything I couldn't learn to do every bit as well as they do it. But, you see, that goes right back to the life that you have to live. If that was the life I had been raised up in, I could be President or any other thing I got a chance to be" (Gwaltney 1980, 173).

Chicana domestics interviewed by Mary Romero in Colorado seemed at one level to accept the dominant culture's evaluation of their capabilities. Several said their options were limited by lack of education and training. However, they also realized they were restricted just because they were Mexican. Sixty-eight-year-old Mrs. Portillo told Romero: "There was a lot of discrimination, and Spanish people got just regular housework or laundry work. There was so much discrimination that Spanish people couldn't get jobs outside of washing dishes—things like that" (Romero 1988b, 86).

Similarly, many Japanese domestics reported that their choices were constrained because of language difficulties and lack of education, but they, too, recognized that color was decisive. Some nisei domestics had taken typing and business courses and some had college degrees, yet they had to settle for "schoolgirl" jobs after completing their schooling. Mrs. Morita, who grew up in San Francisco and was graduated from high school in the 1930s, bluntly summarized her options: "In those days there was no two ways about it. If you were Japanese, you either worked in an art store ('oriental curios' shop) where they sell those little junks, or you worked

as a domestic. . . . There was no Japanese girl working in an American firm" (Glenn 1986, 122).

Hanna Nelson, another of Gwaltney's informants, took the analysis one step further; she recognized the coercion that kept African-American women in domestic service. She saw this arrangement as one that allowed white women to exploit Black women economically and emotionally and exposed Black women to sexual assaults by white men, often with white women's complicity. She says, "I am a woman sixty-one years old and I was born into this world with some talent. But I have done the work that my grandmother's mother did. It is not through any failing of mine that this is so. The whites took my mother's milk by force, and I have lived to hear a human creature of my sex try to force me by threat of hunger to give my milk to an able man. I have grown to womanhood in a world where the saner you are, the madder you are made to appear" (Gwaltney 1980, 7).

RACE AND GENDER CONSCIOUSNESS

Hanna Nelson displays a consciousness of the politics of race and gender not found among white employers. Employers' and employees' fundamentally different positions within the division of reproductive labor gave them different interests and perspectives. Phyllis Palmer describes the problems the YWCA and other reform groups encountered when they attempted to establish voluntary standards and working hours for live-in domestics in the 1930s. White housewives invariably argued against any "rigid" limitation of hours; they insisted on provisions for emergencies that would override any hour limits. Housewives saw their own responsibilities as limitless, and apparently felt there was no justification for boundaries on domestics' responsibilities. They did not acknowledge the fundamental difference in their positions: they themselves gained status and privileges from their relationships with their husbands—relationships that depended on the performance of wifely duties. They expected domestics to devote long hours and hard work to help them succeed as wives, without, however, commensurate privileges and status. To challenge the inequitable gender division of labor was too difficult and threatening, so white housewives pushed the dilemma onto other women, holding them to the same high standards by which they themselves were imprisoned (Kaplan 1987; Palmer 1990).

Some domestic workers were highly conscious of their mistresses' subordination to their husbands and condemned their unwillingness to challenge their husbands' authority. Mabel Johns, a sixty-four-year-old widow, told Gwaltney:

> I work for a woman who has a good husband; the devil is good to her, anyway. Now that woman could be a good person if she didn't think she could just do everything and have everything. In this world whatsoever you get you will pay for. Now she is a grown woman, but she won't know that simple thing. I don't think there's anything wrong with her mind, but she is greedy and she don't believe in admitting that she is greedy. Now you may say what you willormay [*sic*] about people being good to you, but there just ain' a living soul in this world that thinks more of you than you do of yourself. . . . She's a grown woman, but she have to keep accounts and her husband tells her whether or not he will let her do thus-and-so or buy this or that. [Gwaltney 1980, 167]

Black domestics are also conscious that a white woman's status comes from her relationship to a white man, that she gains privileges from the relationship that blinds her to her own oppression, and that she therefore willingly participates in and gains advantages from the oppression of racial-ethnic women. Nancy White puts the matter powerfully when she says,

> My mother used to say that the black woman is the white man's mule and the white woman is his dog. Now, she said that to say this: we do the heavy work and get beat whether we do it well or not. But the white woman is closer to the master and he pats them on the head and lets them sleep in the house, but he ain' gon' treat neither one like he was dealing with a person. Now, if I was to tell a white woman that, the first thing she would do is to call you a nigger and then she'd be real nice to her husband so he would come out here and beat you for telling his wife the truth. [Gwaltney 1980, 148]

Rather than challenge the inequity in the relationship with their husbands, white women pushed the burden onto women with even less power. They could justify this only by denying the domestic worker's womanhood, by ignoring the employee's family ties and responsibilities. Susan Tucker found that southern white women talked about their servants with affection and expressed gratitude that they shared work with the servant that they would otherwise have to do alone. Yet the sense of commonality based on gender that the women expressed turned out to be one-way.

Domestic workers knew that employers did not want to know much about their home situations (Kaplan 1987, 96; Tucker 1988). Mostly, the employers did not want domestics' personal needs to interfere with serving them. One domestic wrote that her employer berated her when she asked for a few hours off to pay her bills and take care of pressing business (Palmer 1990, 74). Of relations between white mistresses and Black domestics in the period from 1870 to 1920, Katzman says that in extreme cases "even the shared roles of motherhood could be denied." A Black child nurse reported in 1912 that she worked fourteen to sixteen hours a day caring for her mistress's four children. Describing her existence as a "treadmill life," she reported that she was allowed to go home "only once in every two weeks, every other Sunday afternoon—even then I'm not permitted to stay all night. I see my own children only when they happen to see me on the streets when I am out with the children [of her mistress], or when my children come to the yard to see me, which isn't often, because my white folks don't like to see their servants' children hanging around their premises."[24]

While this case may be extreme, Tucker reports, on the basis of extensive interviews with southern African-American domestics, that even among live-out workers in the 1960s,

> White women were also not noted for asking about child care arrangements. All whites, said one black woman, "assume you have a mother, or an older daughter to keep your child, so it's all right to leave your kids." Stories of white employers not believing the children of domestics were sick, but hearing this as an excuse not to work, were also common. Stories, too, of white women who did not inquire of a domestic's family— even when that domestic went on extended trips with the family—were not uncommon. And work on Christmas morning and other holidays for black mothers was not considered by white employers as unfair. Indeed, work on these days was seen as particularly important to the job. [Tucker 1988, 99]

The irony is, of course, that domestics saw their responsibilities as mothers as the central core of their identity. The Japanese-American women I interviewed, the Chicana day workers Romero interviewed, and the African-American domestics Bonnie Thornton Dill interviewed all emphasized the primacy of their role as mothers (Dill 1980; Glenn 1986; Romero 1988b). As a Japanese immigrant single parent expressed it, "My children come first. I'm working to upgrade my children." Another domestic, Mrs. Hiraoka, confided she hated household work but would keep working until her daughter graduated from optometry school.[25] Romero's day workers arranged their work hours to fit around their children's school hours so that they could be there when needed. For domestics, then, working had meaning precisely because it enabled them to provide for their children.

Perhaps the most universal theme in domestic workers' statements is that they are working so their own daughters will not have to go into domestic service and confront the same dilemmas of leaving their babies to work. A Japanese-American domestic noted, "I tell my daughters all the time, 'As long as you get a steady job, stay in school. I want you to get a good job, not like me.' That's what I always tell my daughters: make sure you're not stuck."[26]

In a similar vein, Pearl Runner told Dill, "My main goal was I didn't want them to follow in my footsteps as far as working" (Dill 1980, 109). Domestic workers wanted to protect their daughters from both the hardships and the dangers that working in white homes posed. A Black domestic told Drake and Cayton of her hopes for her daughters: "I hope they may be able to escape a life as a domestic worker, for I know too well the things that make a girl desperate on these jobs" (Drake and Cayton 1962, 246).

When they succeed in helping their children do better than they themselves did, domestics may consider that the hardships were worthwhile. Looking back, Mrs. Runner is able to say, "I really feel that with all the struggling that I went through, I feel happy and proud that I was able to keep helping my children, that they listened and that they all went to high school. So when I look back, I really feel proud, even though at times the work was very hard and I came home very tired. But now, I feel proud about it. They all got their education" (Dill 1980, 113). Domestics thus have to grapple with yet another contradiction. They must confront, acknowledge, and convey the undesirable nature of the work they do to their children, as an object lesson and an admonition, and at the same time maintain their children's respect and their own sense of personal worth and dignity (Dill 1980, 110). When they successfully manage that contradiction, they refute their white employers' belief that "you are your work" (Gwaltney 1980, 174). . . .

CONCLUSIONS AND IMPLICATIONS

This article began with the observation that the racial division of reproductive labor has been overlooked in the sepa-

rate literatures on race and gender. The distinct exploitation of women of color and an important source of difference among women have thereby been ignored. How, though, does a historical analysis of the racial division of reproductive labor illuminate the lives of women of color and white women? What are its implications for concerted political action? In order to tackle these questions, we need to address a broader question, namely, how does the analysis advance our understanding of race and gender? Does it take us beyond the additive models I have criticized?

The Social Construction of Race and Gender

Tracing how race and gender have been fashioned in one area of women's work helps us understand them as socially constructed systems of relationships—including symbols, normative beliefs, and practices—organized around perceived differences. This understanding is an important counter to the universalizing tendencies in feminist thought. When feminists perceive reproductive labor only as gendered, they imply that domestic labor is identical for all women and that it therefore can be the basis of a common identity of womanhood. By not recognizing the different relationships women have had to such supposedly universal female experiences as motherhood and domesticity, they risk essentializing gender—treating it as static, fixed, eternal, and natural. They fail to take seriously a basic premise of feminist thought, that gender is a social construct.

If race and gender are socially constructed systems, then they must arise at specific moments in particular circumstances and change as these circumstances change. We can study their appearance, variation, and modification over time. I have suggested that one vantage point for looking at their development in the United States is in the changing division of labor in local economies. A key site for the emergence of concepts of gendered and racialized labor has been in regions characterized by dual labor systems.

As subordinate-race women within dual labor systems, African-American, Mexican-American, and Japanese-American women were drawn into domestic service by a combination of economic need, restricted opportunities, and educational and employment tracking mechanisms. Once they were in service, their association with "degraded" labor affirmed their supposed natural inferiority. Although ideologies of "race" and "racial difference" justifying the dual labor system already were in place, specific ideas about racial-ethnic womanhood were invented and enacted in everyday interactions between mistresses and workers. Thus ideologies of race and gender were created and verified in daily life (Fields 1982).

Two fundamental elements in the construction of racial-ethnic womanhood were the notion of inherent traits that suited the women for service and the denial of the women's identities as wives and mothers in their own right. Employers accepted a cult of domesticity that purported to elevate the status of women as mothers and homemakers, yet they made demands on domestics that hampered them from carrying out these responsibilities in their own households. How could employers maintain such seemingly inconsistent orientations? Racial ideology was critical in resolving the contradiction: it explained why women of color were suited for degrading work. Racial characterizations effectively neutralized the racial-ethnic woman's womanhood, allowing the mistress to be "unaware" of the domestic's relationship to her own children and household. The exploitation of racial-ethnic women's physical, emotional, and mental work for the benefit of white households thus could be rendered invisible in consciousness if not in reality.

With the shift of reproductive labor from household to market, face-to-face hierarchy has been replaced by structural hierarchy. In institutional settings, stratification is built into organizational structures, including lines of authority, job descriptions, rules, and spatial and temporal segregation. Distance between higher and lower orders is ensured by structural segregation. Indeed, much routine service work is organized to be out of sight: it takes place behind institutional walls where outsiders rarely penetrate (e.g., nursing homes, chronic care facilities), in back rooms (e.g., restaurant kitchens), or at night or other times when occupants are gone (e.g., in office buildings and hotels). Workers may appreciate this time and space segregation because it allows them some autonomy and freedom from demeaning interactions. It also makes them and their work invisible, however. In this situation, more privileged women do not have to acknowledge the workers or to confront the contradiction between shared womanhood and inequality by race and class. Racial ideology is not necessary to explain or justify exploitation, not for lack of racism, but because the justification for inequality does not have to be elaborated in specifically racial terms: instead it can be cast in terms of differences in training, skill, or education.[27]

Because they are socially constructed, race and gender systems are subject to contestation and struggle. Racial-ethnic women continually have challenged the devaluation of their womanhood. Domestics often did so covertly. They learned to dissemble, consciously "putting on an act" while inwardly rejecting their employers' premises and maintaining a separate identity rooted in their families and communities. . . . In domestic service, women have transcended the limitations of their work by focusing on longer-term goals, such as their children's future.

Beyond Additive Models: Race and Gender as Interlocking Systems

As the foregoing examples show, race and gender constructs are inextricably intertwined. Each develops in the context of the other; they cannot be separated. This is important because when we see reproductive labor only as gendered, we extract gender from its context, which includes other interacting systems of power. If we begin with gender separated out, then we have to put race and class back in when we consider women of color and working-class women. We thus end up with an additive model in which white women have only gender and women of color have gender plus race.

The interlock is evident in the case study of domestic workers. In the traditional middle-class household, the availability of cheap female domestic labor buttressed white male privilege by perpetuating the concept of reproductive labor as women's work, sustaining the illusion of a protected private sphere for women and displacing conflict away from husband and wife to struggles between housewife and domestic.

The racial division of labor also bolstered the gender division of labor indirectly by offering white women a slightly more privileged position in exchange for accepting domesticity. Expanding on Judith Rollins's notion that white housewives gained an elevated self-identity by casting Black domestics as inferior contrast figures, Phyllis Palmer suggests the dependent position of the middle-class housewife made a contrasting figure necessary. A dualistic conception of women as "good" and "bad," long a part of western cultural tradition, provided ready-made categories for casting white and racial-ethnic women as oppositional figures (Davidoff 1979; Palmer 1990, 11, 137–39). The racial division of reproductive labor served to channel and recast these dualistic conceptions into racialized gender constructs. By providing them an acceptable self-image, racial constructs gave white housewives a stake in a system that ultimately oppressed them.

The racial division of labor similarly protects white male privilege in institutional settings. White men, after all, still dominate in professional and higher management positions, where they benefit from the paid and unpaid services of women. And as in domestic service, conflict between men and women is redirected into clashes among women. . . . In both household and institutional settings, white professional and managerial men are the group most insulated from dirty work and contact with those who do it. White women are frequently the mediators who have to negotiate between white male superiors and racial-ethnic subordinates. Thus race and gender dynamics are played out in a three-way relationship involving white men, white women, and women of color.

Beyond Difference: Race and Gender as Relational Constructs

Focusing on the racial division of reproductive labor also uncovers the relational nature of race and gender. By "relational" I mean that each is made up of categories (e.g., male/female, Anglo/Latino) that are positioned, and therefore gain meaning, in relation to each other (Barrett 1987). Power, status, and privilege are axes along which categories are positioned. Thus, to represent race and gender as relationally constructed is to assert that the experiences of white women and women of color are not just different but connected in systematic ways.

The interdependence is easier to see in the domestic work setting because the two groups of women confront one another face to face. That the higher standard of living of one woman is made possible by, and also helps to perpetuate, the other's lower standard of living is clearly evident. In institutional service work the relationship between those who do the dirty work and those who benefit from it is mediated and buffered by institutional structures, so the dependence of one group on the other for its standard of living is not apparent. Nonetheless, interdependence exists, even if white women do not come into actual contact with women of color.[28]

The notion of relationality also recognizes that white and racial-ethnic women have different standpoints by virtue of their divergent positions. This is an important corrective to feminist theories of gendered thought that posit universal female modes of thinking growing out of common experiences such as domesticity and motherhood. When they portray reproductive labor only as gendered, they assume there is only one standpoint—that of white women. Hence, the activities and experiences of middle-class women become generic "female" experiences and activities, and those of other groups become variant, deviant, or specialized.

In line with recent works on African-American, Asian-American, and Latina feminist thought, we see that taking the standpoint of women of color gives us a different and more critical perspective on race and gender systems (Garcia 1989; Anzaldúa 1990; Collins 1990.) Domestic workers in particular—because they directly confront the contradictions in their lives and those of their mistresses—develop an acute consciousness of the interlocking nature of race and gender oppression.

Perhaps a less obvious point is that understanding race and gender as relational systems also illuminates the lives of white American women. White womanhood has been constructed not in isolation but in relation to that of women of color. Therefore, race is integral to white women's gender identities. In addition, seeing variation in racial division of labor across time in different regions gives us a more variegated picture of white middle-class womanhood. White women's lives have been lived in many circumstances; their "gender" has been constructed in relation to varying others, not just to Black women. Conceptualizing white womanhood as monolithically defined in opposition to men or to Black women ignores complexity and variation in the experiences of white women.

Implications for Feminist Politics

Understanding race and gender as relational, interlocking, socially constructed systems affects how we strategize for change. If race and gender are socially constructed rather than being "real" referents in the material world, then they can be deconstructed and challenged. Feminists have made considerable strides in deconstructing gender; we now need to focus on deconstructing gender and race simultaneously. An initial step in this process is to expose the structures that support the present division of labor and the constructions of race and gender around it.

Seeing race and gender as interlocking systems, however, alerts us to sources of inertia and resistance to change. The discussion of how the racial division of labor reinforced the gender division of labor makes clear that tackling gender hierarchy requires simultaneously addressing race hierarchy. As long as the gender division of labor remains intact, it will be in the short-term interest of white women to support or at least overlook the racial division of labor because it ensures that the very worst labor is performed by someone else. Yet, as long as white women support the racial division of labor, they will have less impetus to struggle to change the gender division of labor. This quandary is apparent in cities such as Los Angeles, which have witnessed a large influx of immigrant women fleeing violence and poverty in Latin America, Southeast Asia, and the Caribbean. These women form a large reserve army of low-wage labor for both domestic service and institutional service work. Anglo women who ordinarily would not be able to afford servants are employing illegal immigrants as maids at below-minimum wages (McConoway 1987). Not only does this practice diffuse pressure for a more equitable sharing of household work but it also recreates race and gender ideologies that justify the subordination of women of color. Having a Latino or Black maid picking up and cleaning after them teaches Anglo children that some people exist primarily to do work that Anglos do not want to do for themselves.

Acknowledging the relational nature of race and gender and therefore the interdependence between groups means that we recognize conflicting interests among women. Two examples illustrate the divergence. With the move into the labor force of all races and classes of women, it is tempting to think that we can find unity around the common problems of "working women." With that in mind, feminist policymakers have called for expanding services to assist employed mothers in such areas as child care and elderly care. We need to ask, Who is going to do the work? Who will benefit from increased services? The historical record suggests that it will be women of color, many of them new immigrants, who will do the work and that it will be middle-class women who will receive the services. Not so coincidentally, public officials seeking to reduce welfare costs are promulgating regulations requiring women on public assistance to work. The needs of employed middle-class women and women on welfare might thus be thought to coincide: the needs of the former for services might be met by employing the latter to provide the services. The divergence in interest becomes apparent, however, when we consider that employment in service jobs at current wage levels guarantees that their occupants will remain poor. However, raising their wages so that they can actually support themselves and their children at a decent level would mean many middle-class women could not afford these services.

A second example of an issue that at first blush appears to bridge race and ethnic lines is the continuing earnings disparity between men and women. Because occupational segregation, the concentration of women in low-paying, female-dominated occupations, stands as the major obstacle to wage equity, some feminist policymakers have embraced the concept of comparable worth (Hartmann 1985; Acker 1989). This strategy calls for equalizing pay for "male" and "female" jobs requiring similar levels of skill and responsibility, even if differing in content. Comparable worth accepts the validity of a job hierarchy and differential pay based on "real" differences in skills and responsibility. Thus, for example, it attacks the differential between nurses and pharmacists but leaves intact the differential between nurses and nurse's aides. Yet the division between "skilled" and "unskilled" jobs is exactly where the racial division typically falls. To address the problems of women of color service workers would require a fundamental attack on the concept of a hierarchy of worth; it would call for flattening the wage differentials between highest- and lowest-paid ranks. A claim would have to be made for the right of all workers to a living wage, regardless of skill or responsibility.

These examples suggest that forging a political agenda that addresses the universal needs of women is highly problematic not just because women's priorities differ but because gains for some groups may require a corresponding loss of advantage and privilege for others. As the history of the racial division of reproductive labor reveals, conflict and contestation among women over definitions of womanhood, over work, and over the conditions of family life are part of our legacy as well as the current reality. This does not mean we give up the goal of concerted struggle. It means we give up trying falsely to harmonize women's interests. Appreciating the ways race and gender division of labor creates both hierarchy and interdependence may be a better way to reach an understanding of the interconnectedness of women's lives.

ACKNOWLEDGMENTS

Work on this project was made possible by a Title F leave from the State University of New York at Binghamton and a visiting scholar appointment at the Murray Research Center at Radcliffe College. Discussions with Elsa Barkley Brown, Gary Glenn, Carole Turbin, and Barrie Thorne contributed immeasurably to the ideas developed here. My thanks to Joyce Chinen for directing me to archival materials in Hawaii. I am also grateful to members of the Women and Work Group and to Norma Alarcon, Gary Dymski, Antonia Glenn, Margaret Guilette, Terence Hopkins, Eileen McDonagh, JoAnne Preston, Mary Ryan, and four anonymous *Signs* reviewers for their suggestions.

NOTES

1. For various formulations, see Benston (1969), Secombe (1974), Barrett (1980), Fox (1980), and Sokoloff (1980).

2. Recently, white feminists have begun to pay attention to scholarship by and about racial-ethnic women and to recognize racial stratification in the labor market and other public arenas. My point here is that they still assume that women's relationship to domestic labor is universal; thus they have not been concerned with explicating differences across race, ethnic, and class groups in women's relationship to that labor.

3. See, e.g., Reisler (1976), which, despite its title, is exclusively about male Mexican labor.

4. I use the term *racial-ethnic* to refer collectively to groups that have been socially constructed and constituted as racially as well as culturally distinct from European Americans and placed in separate legal statuses from "free whites" (c.f. Omi and Winant 1986). Historically, African Americans, Latinos, Asian Americans, and Native Americans were so constructed. Similarly, I have capitalized the word *Black* throughout this article to signify the racial-ethnic construction of that category.

5. Capitalism, however, changed the nature of reproductive labor, which became more and more devoted to consumption activities, i.e., using wages to acquire necessities in the market and then processing these commodities to make them usable (see Weinbaum and Bridges 1976; and Luxton 1980).

6. This is not to deny that family members, especially women, still provide the bulk of care of dependents, but to point out that there has been a marked increase in institutionalized care in the second half of the twentieth century.

7. For a discussion of varying views on the relative importance of control versus agency in shaping state welfare policy, see Gordon (1990). Piven and Cloward note that programs have been created only when poor people have mobilized and are intended to defuse pressure for more radical change (1971, 66). In their *Poor People's Movements* (Piven and Cloward 1979), they document the role of working-class struggles to win concessions from the state. For a feminist social control perspective, see Abramovitz (1988).

8. These developments are discussed in Degler (1980), Strasser (1982), Cowan (1983), and Dudden (1983, esp. 240–42).

9. See also Blair (1980); Epstein (1981); Ryan (1981); Dudden (1983); and Brenner and Laslett (1986).

10. See, e.g., Kaplan (1987).

11. Phyllis Palmer, in her *Domesticity and Dirt,* found evidence that mistresses and servants agreed on what were the least desirable tasks—washing clothes, washing dishes, and taking care of children on evenings and weekends—and that domestics were more likely to perform the least desirable tasks (1990, 70).

12. It may be worth mentioning the importance of unpaid cultural and charitable activities in perpetuating middle-class privilege and power. Middle-class reformers often aimed to mold the poor in ways that mirrored middle-class values but without actually altering their subordinate position. See, e.g., Sanchez (1990) for discussion of efforts of Anglo reformers to train Chicanas in domestic skills.

13. U.S. Bureau of the Census 1933, chap. 3, "Color and Nativity of Gainful Workers," tables 2, 4, 6. For discussion of the concentration of African-American women in domestic service, see Glenn (1985).

14. I use the terms *Chicano, Chicana,* and *Mexican American* to refer to both native-born and immigrant Mexican people/women in the United States.

15. U.S. Bureau of the Census 1933.

16. Ibid.

17. For personal accounts of Chicano children being inducted into domestic service, see Ruíz (1987a) and interview of Josephine Turietta in Elsasser, MacKenzie, and Tixier y Vigil (1980, 28–35).

18. See also life history accounts of Black domestics, such as that of Bolden (1976) and of Anna Mae Dickson by Wendy Watriss (Watriss 1984).

19. Blackwelder also found that domestics themselves were attuned to the racial-ethnic hierarchy among them. When advertising for jobs, women who did not identify themselves as Black overwhelmingly requested "housekeeping" or "governess" positions, whereas Blacks advertised for "cooking," "laundering," or just plain "domestic work."

20. This is not to say that daughters of European immigrants experienced great social mobility and soon attained affluence. The nondomestic jobs they took were usually low paying and the conditions of work often deplorable. Nonetheless, white native-born and immigrant women clearly preferred the relative freedom of industrial, office, or shop employment to the constraints of domestic service (see Katzman 1978, 71–72).

21. Document Ma 24, Romanzo Adams Social Research Laboratory papers. I used these records when they were lodged in the sociology department; they are currently being cataloged by the university archives and a finding aid is in process.

22. Ibid., document Ma 15, 5.

23. Ibid.

24. "More Slavery at the South: A Negro Nurse," from the *Independent* (1912), in Katzman and Tuttle (1982, 176–85, 179).

25. From an interview conducted by the author in the San Francisco Bay area in 1977.

26. Ibid.

27. That is, the concentration of minority workers in lower-level jobs can be attributed to their lack of "human capital"—qualifications—needed for certain jobs.

28. Elsa Barkley Brown pointed this out to me in a personal communication.

REFERENCES

Abramovitz, Mimi. 1988. *Regulating the Lives of Women: Social Welfare Policy from Colonial Times to the Present.* Boston: South End Press.

Acker, Joan. 1989. *Doing Comparable Worth: Gender, Class, and Pay Equity.* Philadelphia: Temple University Press.

Adams, Romanzo. Social Research Laboratory papers. University of Hawaii Archives, Manoa.

American Nurses' Association. 1965. *Health Occupations Supportive to Nursing.* New York: American Nurses' Association.

Anderson, C. Arnold, and Mary Jean Bowman. 1953. "The Vanishing Servant and the Contemporary Status System of the American South." *American Journal of Sociology* 59:215–30.

Anzaldúa, Gloria. 1990. *Making Face, Making Soul—Haciendo Caras: Creative Critical Perspectives by Women of Color.* San Francisco: Aunt Lute Foundation.

Barrera, Mario. 1979. *Race and Class in the Southwest: A Theory of Racial Inequality.* Notre Dame, Ind., and London: University of Notre Dame Press.

Barrett, Michèle. 1980. *Women's Oppression Today: Problems in Marxist Feminist Analysis.* London: Verso.

———. 1987. "The Concept of 'Difference.' " *Feminist Review* 26(July):29–41.

Benson, Susan Porter. 1986. *Counter Cultures: Saleswomen, Customers, and Managers in American Department Stores, 1890–1940.* Urbana and Chicago: University of Illinois Press.

Benston, Margaret. 1969. "The Political Economy of Women's Liberation." *Monthly Review* 21(September):13–27.

Blackwelder, Julia Kirk. 1978. "Women in the Work Force: Atlanta, New Orleans, and San Antonio, 1930 to 1940." *Journal of Urban History* 4(3):331– 58, 349.

———. 1984. *Women of the Depression: Caste and Culture in San Antonio, 1929–1939.* College Station: Texas A&M University Press.

Blair, Karen. 1980. *The Clubwoman as Feminist: True Womanhood Redefined, 1868–1914.* New York: Holmes & Meier.

Blauner, Robert. 1972. *Racial Oppression in America.* Berkeley: University of California Press.

Bolden, Dorothy. 1976. "Forty-two Years a Maid: Starting at Nine in Atlanta." In *Nobody Speaks for Me! Self-Portraits of American Working Class Women,* ed. Nancy Seifer. New York: Simon & Schuster.

Boydston, Jeanne. 1990. *Home and Work: Housework, Wages, and the Ideology of Labor in the Early Republic.* New York: Oxford University Press.

Braverman, Harry. 1974. *Labor and Monopoly Capital: The Degradation of Labor in the Twentieth Century.* New York and London: Monthly Review Press.

Brenner, Johanna, and Barbara Laslett. 1986. "Social Reproduction and the Family." In *Sociology, from Crisis to Science?* vol. 2, *The Social Reproduction of Organization and Culture,* ed. Ulf Himmelstrand, 116–31. London: Sage.

Brown, Elsa Barkley. 1989. "Womanist Consciousness: Maggie Lena Walker and the Independent Order of Saint Luke." *Signs: Journal of Women in Culture and Society* 14(3):610–33.

Cannings, Kathleen, and William Lazonik. 1975. "The Development of the Nursing Labor Force in the United States: A Basic Analysis." *International Journal of Health Sciences* 5(2): 185–216.

Carnegie, Mary Elizabeth. 1986. *The Path We Tread: Blacks in Nursing, 1854 –1954.* Philadelphia: Lippincott.

Chaplin, David. 1978. "Domestic Service and Industrialization." *Comparative Studies in Sociology* 1:97–127.

Clark-Lewis, Elizabeth. 1987. "This Work Had an End: African American Domestic Workers in Washington, D.C., 1910–1940." In *"To Toil the Livelong Day": America's Women at Work, 1780–1980,* ed. Carole Groneman and Mary Beth Norton. Ithaca, N.Y.: Cornell University Press.

Coleman, Barbara. 1989. "States Grapple with New Law." *AARP News Bulletin,* 30(2):4–5.

Collins, Patricia Hill. 1986. "Learning from the Outsider Within: The Sociological Significance of Black Feminist Thought." *Social Problems* 33 (6):14–32.

———. 1990. *Black Feminist Thought: Knowledge, Consciousness, and the Politics of Empowerment.* New York: Allen & Unwin.

Cowan, Ruth Schwartz. 1983. *More Work for Mother: The Ironies of Household Technology from the Open Hearth to the Microwave.* New York: Basic.

Davidoff, Lenore. 1979. "Class and Gender in Victorian England: The Diaries of Arthur J. Munby and Hannah Cullwick." *Feminist Studies* 5(Spring):86–114.

Degler, Carl N. 1980. *At Odds: Women and the Family in America from the Revolution to the Present.* New York: Oxford University Press.

Deming, Dorothy. 1947. *The Practical Nurse.* New York: Commonwealth Fund.

Deutsch, Sarah. 1987a. *No Separate Refuge: Culture, Class, and Gender on an Anglo-Hispanic Frontier in the American Southwest, 1880–1940.* New York: Oxford University Press.

———. 1987b. "Women and Intercultural Relations: The Case of Hispanic New Mexico and Colorado." *Signs* 12(4):719–39.

Diamond, Timothy. 1988. "Social Policy and Everyday Life in Nursing Homes: A Critical Ethnography." In *The Worth of Women's Work: A Qualitative Synthesis,* ed. Anne Statham, Eleanor M. Miller, and Hans O. Mauksch. Albany, N.Y.: SUNY Press.

Dill, Bonnie Thornton. 1980. "The Means to Put My Children Through: Childrearing Goals and Strategies among Black Female Domestic Servants." In *The Black Woman,* ed. La Frances Rodgers-Rose. Beverly Hills and London: Sage.

———. 1988. "Our Mothers' Grief: Racial Ethnic Women and the Maintenance of Families." *Journal of Family History* 12(4):415–31.

Drake, St. Clair, and Horace Cayton. (1945) 1962. *Black Metropolis: A Study of Negro Life in a Northern City,* vol. 1. New York: Harper Torchbook.

Dudden, Faye E. 1983. *Serving Women: Household Service in Nineteenth Century America.* Middletown, Conn.: Wesleyan University Press.

Elsasser, Nan, Kyle MacKenzie, and Yvonne Tixier y Vigil. 1980. *Las Mujeres: Conversations from a Hispanic Community.* Old Westbury, N.Y.: Feminist Press.

Engels, Friedrich. 1972. *The Origins of the Family, Private Property and the State.* New York: International Publishers.

Epstein, Barbara. 1981. *The Politics of Domesticity: Women, Evangelism, and Temperance in Nineteenth Century America.* Middletown, Conn.: Wesleyan University Press.

Fields, Barbara. 1982. "Ideology and Race in American History." In *Region, Race, and Reconstruction: Essays in Honor of C. Vann Woodward,* ed. J. Morgan Kousser and James M. McPherson. New York: Oxford University Press.

Fink, Leon, and Brian Greenberg. 1979. "Organizing Montefiore: Labor Militancy Meets a Progressive Health Care Empire." In *Health Care in America: Essays in Social History,* ed. Susan Reverby and David Rosner. Philadelphia: Temple University Press.

Fox, Bonnie, ed. 1980. *Hidden in the Household: Women's Domestic Labour under Capitalism.* Toronto: Women's Press.

Gamarinikow, Eva. 1978. "Sexual Division of Labour: The Case of Nursing." In *Feminism and Materialism: Women and Modes of Production,* ed. Annette Kuhn and Ann-Marie Wolpe, 96–123. London: Routledge & Kegan Paul.

Game, Ann, and Rosemary Pringle. 1983. *Gender at Work.* Sydney: Allen & Unwin.

Garcia, Alma. 1989. "The Development of Chicana Feminist Discourse, 1970– 1980." *Gender and Society* 3(2):217–38.

Garcia, Mario T. 1980. "The Chicana in American History: The Mexican Women of El Paso, 1880–1920: A Case Study." *Pacific Historical Review* 49(2): 315–39.

———. 1981. *Desert Immigrants: The Mexicans of El Paso, 1880–1920.* New Haven, Conn.: Yale University Press.

Glazer, Nona. 1988. "Overlooked, Overworked: Women's Unpaid and Paid Work in the Health Services' 'Cost Crisis,'" *International Journal of Health Services* 18(2):119–37.

Glenn, Evelyn Nakano. 1985. "Racial Ethnic Women's Labor: The Intersection of Race, Gender and Class Oppression." *Review of Radical Political Economy* 17(3):86–108.

———. 1986. *Issei, Nisei, Warbride: Three Generations of Japanese American Women in Domestic Service.* Philadelphia: Temple University Press.

Gordon, Linda. 1990. "The New Feminist Scholarship on the Welfare State." In *Women, the State, and Welfare,* ed. Linda Gordon, 9–35. Madison: University of Wisconsin Press.

Gwaltney, John, ed. 1980. *Drylongso: A Self-Portrait of Black America.* New York: Random House.

Hartmann, Heidi I., ed. 1985. *Comparable Worth: New Directions for Research.* Washington, D.C.: National Academy Press.

Hield, Melissa. 1984. "Women in the Texas ILGWU, 1933–50." In *Speaking for Ourselves: Women of the South,* ed. Maxine Alexander, 87–97. New York, Pantheon.

Hine, Darlene Clark, ed. 1985. *Black Women in the Nursing Profession: A Documentary History.* New York: Pathfinder.

———. 1989. *Black Women in White: Racial Conflict and Cooperation in the Nursing Profession, 1890–1950.* Bloomington: Indiana University Press.

Janiewski, Delores. 1983. "Flawed Victories: The Experiences of Black and White Women Workers in Durham during the 1930s." In *Decades of Discontent: The Women's Movement, 1920–1940,* ed. Lois Scharf and Joan M. Jensen, 85–112. Westport, Conn., and London: Greenwood.

Kaplan, Elaine Bell. 1987. "'I Don't Do No Windows': Competition between the Domestic Worker and the Housewife." In *Competition: A Feminist Taboo?* ed. Valerie Miner and Helen E. Longino. New York: Feminist Press at CUNY.

Katzman, David M. 1978. *Seven Days a Week: Women and Domestic Service in Industrializing America.* New York: Oxford University Press.

Katzman, David M., and William M. Tuttle, Jr., eds. 1982. *Plain Folk: The Life Stories of Undistinguished Americans.* Urbana and Chicago: University of Illinois Press.

Kessler-Harris, Alice. 1981. *Women Have Always Worked: A Historical Overview.* Old Westbury, N.Y.: Feminist Press.

———. 1982. *Out to Work: A History of Wage-earning Women in the United States.* New York: Oxford University Press.

King, Deborah K. 1988. "Multiple Jeopardy, Multiple Consciousness: The Context of a Black Feminist Ideology." *Signs* 14(1):42–72.

Lamphere, Louise. 1987. *From Working Daughters to Working Mothers: Immigrant Women in a New England Industrial Community.* Ithaca, N.Y.: Cornell University Press.

Lasch, Christopher. 1977. *Haven in a Heartless World: The Family Besieged.* New York: Basic.

Laslett, Barbara, and Johanna Brenner. 1989. "Gender and Social Reproduction: Historical Perspectives." *Annual Review of Sociology* 15:381–404.

Lind, Andrew. 1951. "The Changing Position of Domestic Service in Hawaii." *Social Process in Hawaii* 15:71–87.

Luxton, Meg. 1980. *More than a Labour of Love: Three Generations of Women's Work in the Home.* Toronto: Women's Press.

McConoway, Mary Jo. 1987. "The Intimate Experiment." *Los Angeles Times Magazine,* February 19, 18–23, 37–38.

Marx, Karl, and Friedrich Engels. 1969. *Selected Works,* vol. 1. Moscow: Progress.

Mellor, Earl F. 1987. "Workers at the Minimum Wage or Less: Who They Are and the Jobs They Hold." *Monthly Labor Review,* July, 34–38.

Omi, Michael, and Howard Winant. 1986. *Racial Formation in the United States.* New York: Routledge.

Palmer, Phyllis. 1987. "Housewife and Household Worker: Employer-Employee Relations in the Home, 1928–1941." In

"To Toil the Livelong Day": America's Women at Work, 1780–1980, ed. Carole Groneman and Mary Beth Norton, 179–95. Ithaca, N.Y.: Cornell University Press.

———. 1990. *Domesticity and Dirt: Housewives and Domestic Servants in the United States, 1920–1945.* Philadelphia: Temple University Press.

Piven, Frances Fox, and Richard A. Cloward. 1971. *Regulating the Poor: The Functions of Public Welfare.* New York: Pantheon.

———. 1979. *Poor People's Movements: Why They Succeed, How They Fail.* New York: Pantheon.

Reisler, Mark. 1976. *By the Sweat of Their Brow: Mexican Immigrant Labor in the United States, 1900–1940.* Westport, Conn.: Greenwood.

Reverby, Susan M. 1979. "From Aide to Organizer: The Oral History of Lillian Roberts." In *Women of America: A History,* ed. Carol Ruth Berkin and Mary Beth Norton. Boston: Houghton Mifflin.

———. 1987. *Ordered to Care: The Dilemma of American Nursing, 1850–1945.* Cambridge: Cambridge University Press.

Rollins, Judith. 1985. *Between Women: Domestics and Their Employers.* Philadelphia: Temple University Press.

Romero, Mary. 1987. "Chicanas Modernize Domestic Service." Unpublished manuscript.

———. 1988a. "Day Work in the Suburbs: The Work Experience of Chicana Private Housekeepers." In *The Worth of Women's Work: A Qualitative Synthesis,* ed. Anne Statham, Eleanor M. Miller, and Hans O. Mauksch, 77–92. Albany: SUNY Press.

———. 1988b. "Renegotiating Race, Class, and Gender Hierarchies in the Everyday Interactions between Chicana Private Household Workers and Employers." Paper presented at the 1988 meetings of the Society for the Study of Social Problems, Atlanta.

Rose, Hilary. 1986. "Women's Work: Women's Knowledge." In *What Is Feminism?* ed. Juliet Mitchell and Ann Oakley, 161–83. Oxford: Basil Blackwell.

Ruíz, Vicki L. 1987a. "By the Day or the Week: Mexicana Domestic Workers in El Paso." In *Women on the U.S.-Mexico Border: Responses to Change,* ed. Vicki L. Ruíz and Susan Tiano, 61–76. Boston: Allen & Unwin.

———. 1987b. "Oral History and La Mujer: The Rosa Guerrero Story." In *Women on the U.S.-Mexico Border: Responses to Change,* ed. Vicki L. Ruíz and Susan Tiano, 219–32. Boston: Allen & Unwin.

Ryan, Mary P. 1981. *Cradle of the Middle Class: The Family in Oneida County, New York, 1790–1865.* Cambridge: Cambridge University Press.

Sacks, Karen Brodkin. 1988. *Caring by the Hour: Women, Work, and Organizing at Duke Medical Center.* Urbana and Chicago: University of Illinois Press.

Sacks, Karen Brodkin, and Dorothy Remy, eds. 1984. *My Troubles Are Going to Have Trouble with Me: Everyday Trials and Triumphs of Women Workers.* New Brunswick, N.J.: Rutgers University Press.

Sanchez, George J. 1990. " 'Go after the Women': Americanization and the Mexican Immigrant Woman, 1915–1929." In *Unequal Sisters: A Multicultural Reader in Women's History,* ed. Ellen Carol DuBois and Vicki L. Ruíz, 250–63. New York: Routledge.

Secombe, Wally. 1974. "The Housewife and Her Labour under Capitalism." *New Left Review* 83(January–February):3–24.

Sekcenski, Edward S. 1981. "The Health Services Industry: A Decade of Expansion. " *Monthly Labor Review* (May):10–16.

Silvestri, George T., and John M. Lukasiewicz. 1987. "A Look at Occupational Employment Trends to the Year 2000." *Monthly Labor Review* (September): 46–63.

Smuts, Robert W. 1959. *Women and Work in America.* New York: Schocken.

Sokoloff, Natalie J. 1980. *Between Money and Love: The Dialectics of Women's Home and Market Work.* New York: Praeger.

Starr, Paul. 1982. *The Social Transformation of American Medicine.* New York: Basic.

Strasser, Susan. 1982. *Never Done: A History of American Housework.* New York: Pantheon.

Tucker, Susan. 1988. "The Black Domestic in the South: Her Legacy as Mother and Mother Surrogate." In *Southern Women,* ed. Carolyn Matheny Dillman, 93–102. New York: Hemisphere.

U.S. Bureau of the Census. 1932. *Fifteenth Census of the United States: 1930, Outlying Territories and Possessions.* Washington, D.C.: Government Printing Office.

———. 1933. *Fifteenth Census of the United States: 1930, Population,* vol. 5, *General Report on Occupations.* Washington, D.C.: Government Printing Office.

———. 1984. *Census of the Population, 1980,* vol. 1, *Characteristics of the Population.* Washington, D.C.: Government Printing Office.

U.S. Department of Labor. 1987a. *Industry Wage Survey: Hospitals, August 1985.* Bureau of Labor Statistics Bulletin 2273. Washington, D.C.: Government Printing Office.

———. 1987b. *Industry Wage Survey: Nursing and Personal Care Facilities, September 1985.* Bureau of Labor Statistics Bulletin 2275. Washington, D.C.: Government Printing Office.

———. 1989. *Employment and Earnings, January 1989.* Bureau of Labor Statistics Bulletin. Washington, D.C.: Government Printing Office.

Wagner, David. 1980. "The Proletarianization of Nursing in the United States, 1932–1945." *International Journal of Health Services* 10(2):271–89.

Watriss, Wendy. 1984. "It's Something Inside You." In *Speaking for Ourselves: Women of the South,* ed. Maxine Alexander. New York: Pantheon.

Weinbaum, Batya, and Amy Bridges. 1976. "The Other Side of the Paycheck." *Monthly Review* 28:88–103.

The Medical Construction of Gender

SUZANNE KESSLER

The birth of intersexed infants, babies born with genitals that are neither clearly male nor clearly female, has been documented throughout recorded time.[1] In the late twentieth century, medical technology has become sufficiently advanced to allow scientists to determine chromosomal and hormonal gender, which is typically taken to be the real, natural, biological gender, usually referred to as "sex."[2] Nevertheless, physicians who handle cases of intersexed infants consider several factors beside biological ones in determining, assigning, and announcing the gender of a particular infant. Indeed, biological factors are often preempted in physicians' deliberations by such cultural factors as the "correct" length of the penis and capacity of the vagina.

In the literature on intersexuality, issues such as announcing a baby's gender at the time of delivery, post-delivery discussions with the parents, and consultations with patients in adolescence are considered only peripherally to the central medical issues—etiology, diagnosis, and surgical procedures.[3] Yet members of medical teams have standard practices for managing intersexuality, which rely ultimately on cultural understandings of gender. The process and guidelines by which decisions about gender (re)construction are made reveal the model for the social construction of gender generally. Moreover, in the face of apparently incontrovertible evidence—infants born with some combination of "female" and "male" reproductive and sexual features—physicians hold an incorrigible belief that female and male are the only "natural" options. This paradox highlights and calls into question the idea that female and male are biological givens compelling a culture of two genders.

Ideally, to undertake an extensive study of intersexed infant case management, I would like to have had direct access to particular events, for example the deliveries of intersexed infants and the initial discussions among physicians, between physicians and parents, between parents, and among parents and family and friends of intersexed infants. The rarity with which intersexuality occurs, however, made this unfeasible.[4] Alternatively, physicians who have had considerable experience dealing with this condition were interviewed. I do not assume that their "talk" about how they manage such cases mirrors their "talk" in the situation, but their words do reveal that they have certain assumptions about gender and that they impose those assumptions via their medical decisions on the patients they treat.

Interviews were conducted with six medical experts (three women and three men) in the field of pediatric intersexuality: one clinical geneticist, three endocrinologists (two of them pediatric specialists), one psychoendocrinologist, and one urologist. All of them have had extensive clinical experience with various intersexed syndromes, and some are internationally known researchers in the field of intersexuality. They were selected on the basis of their prominence in the field and their representing four different medical centers in New York City. Although they know one another, they do not collaborate on research and are not part of the same management team. All were interviewed in the spring of 1985 in their offices. The interviews lasted between forty-five minutes and one hour. Unless further referenced, all quotations in this chapter are from these interviews.[5]

THE THEORY OF INTERSEXUALITY MANAGEMENT

The sophistication of today's medical technology has led to an extensive compilation of various intersex categories based on the various causes of malformed genitals. The "true hermaphrodite" condition, where both ovarian and testicular tissue are present either in the same gonad or in opposite gonads, accounts for fewer than 5 percent of all cases of ambiguous genitals:[6] More commonly, the infant has either ovaries or testes, but the genitals are ambiguous. If the infant has two ovaries, the condition is referred to as female pseudohermaphroditism. If the infant has two testes, the condition is referred to as male pseudohermaphroditism. There are numerous causes of both forms of pseudohermaphroditism, and although there are life-threatening aspects to some of these conditions, having ambiguous genitals per se is not harmful to the infant's health.[7] Although most cases of ambiguous genitals do not represent true hermaphroditism, in keeping with the contemporary literature I will refer to all such cases as intersexed.

Current attitudes toward the intersex condition have been primarily influenced by thee factors. First are the developments in surgery and endocrinology. Diagnoses of specific intersex conditions can be made with greater precision. Female genitals can be constructed that look much like "natural" ones, and some small penises can be enlarged with the exogenous application of hormones, although surgical skills are not sufficiently advanced to construct a "normal"-looking and -functioning penis out of other tissue.[8] Second, in the contemporary United States, the influence of the feminist movement has called into question the valuation of women according to strictly reproductive functions, and the presence or absence of functional gonads is no longer the only or the definitive criterion for gender assignment. Third, psychological theorists focus on "gender identity" (one's sense of oneself as belonging to the female or male category) as distinct from "gender role" (cultural expectations of one's behavior as "appropriate" for a female or male).[9] The relevance of this new gender identity theory for rethinking cases of ambiguous genitals is that gender must be assigned as early as possible if gender identity is to develop successfully. As a result of these three factors, intersexuality is considered a treatable condition of the genitals, one that needs to be resolved expeditiously.

According to all of the specialists interviewed, management of intersexed cases is based upon the theory of gender proposed first by John Money, J. G. Hampson, and J. L. Hempson in 1955 and developed in 1972 by Money and Anke A. Ehrhardt. The theory argues that gender identity is changeable until approximately eighteen months of age.[10] "To use the Pygmalion allegory, one may begin with the same clay and fashion a god or a goddess."[11] The theory rests on satisfying several conditions: The experts must

ensure that the parents have no doubt about whether their child is male or female; the genitals must be made to match the assigned gender as soon as possible; gender-appropriate hormones must be administered at puberty; and intersexed children must be kept informed about their situation with age-appropriate explanations. If these conditions are met, the theory proposes, the intersexed child will develop a gender identity in accordance with the gender assignment (regardless of the chromosomal gender) and will not question her or his assignment and request reassignment at a later age.

Supportive evidence for Money and Ehrhardt's theory is based on only a handful of repeatedly cited cases, but it has been accepted because of the prestige of the theoreticians and its resonance with contemporary ideas about gender, children, psychology, and medicine. Gender and children are malleable; psychology and medicine are the tools used to transform them. This theory is so strongly endorsed that it has taken on the character of gospel. "I think we [physicians] have been raised in the Money theory," one endocrinologist said. Another claimed, "We always approach the problem in a similar way and it's been dictated, to a large extent, by the work of John Money and Anke Ehrhardt because they are the only people who have published, at least in medical literature, any data, any guidelines." It is provocative that this physician immediately followed this assertion with: "And I don't know how effective it really is." Contradictory data are rarely cited in reviews of the literature, were not mentioned by any of the physicians interviewed, and have not reduced these physicians' belief in the theory's validity.[12]

The doctors interviewed concur with the argument that gender must be assigned immediately, decisively, and irreversibly, and that professional opinions be presented in a clear and unambiguous way. The psychoendocrinologist said that when doctors make a statement about the infant, they should "stick to it." The urologist said, "If you make a statement that later has to be disclaimed or discredited, you've weakened your credibility." A gender assignment made decisively, unambiguously, and irrevocably contributes, I believe, to the general impression that the infant's true, natural "sex" has been discovered, and that something that was there all along has been found. It also serves to maintain the credibility of the medical profession, reassure the parents, and reflexively substantiate Money and Ehrhardt's theory.

Also according to this theory, if corrective surgery is necessary, it should take place as soon as possible. If the infant is assigned the male gender, the initial stage of penis repair is usually undertaken in the first year, and further surgery is completed before the child enters school. If the infant is assigned the female gender, vulva repair (including clitoral reduction) is usually begun by three months of age. Money suggests that if reduction of phallic tissue were delayed beyond the neonatal period, the infant would have traumatic memories of having been castrated.[13] Vaginoplasty, in those females having an adequate internal structure (e.g., the vaginal canal is near its expected location), is done between the ages of one and four years. Girls who require more complicated surgical procedures might not be surgically corrected until preadolescence.[14] The complete vaginal canal is typically constructed only when the body is fully grown, following pubertal feminization with estrogen, although some specialists have claimed surgical success with vaginal construction in the early childhood years.[15] Although physicians speculate about the possible trauma of an early-childhood "castration" memory, there is no corresponding concern that vaginal reconstructive surgery delayed beyond the neonatal period is traumatic.

Even though gender identity theory places the critical age limit for gender reassignment between eighteen months and two years, the physicians acknowledge that diagnosis, gender assignment, and genital reconstruction cannot be delayed for as long as two years, since a clear gender assignment and correctly formed genitals will determine the kind of interactions parents will have with their child.[16] The geneticist argued that when parents "change a diaper and see genitalia that don't mean much in terms of gender assignment, I think it prolongs the negative response to the baby. . . . If you have clitoral enlargement that is so extraordinary that the parents can't distinguish between male and female, it is sometimes helpful to reduce that somewhat so that the parent views the child as female." Another physician concurred: Parents "need to go home and do their job as child rearers with it very clear whether it's a boy or a girl."

DIAGNOSIS

A premature gender announcement by an obstetrician, prior to a close examination of an infant's genitals, can be problematic. Money and his colleagues claim that the primary complications in case management of intersexed infants can be traced to mishandling by medical personnel untrained in sexology.[17] According to one of the pediatric endocrinologists interviewed, obstetricians improperly educated about intersexed conditions "don't examine the babies closely

enough at birth and say things just by looking, before separating legs and looking at everything, and jump to conclusions, because 99 percent of the time it's correct. . . . People get upset, physicians I mean. And they say things that are inappropriate." For example, he said that an inexperienced obstetrician might blurt out, "I think you have a boy, or no, maybe you have a girl." Other inappropriate remarks a doctor might make in postdelivery consultation with the parents include, "You have a little boy, but he'll never function as a little boy, so you better raise him as a little girl." As a result, said the pediatric endocrinologist, "the family comes away with the idea that they have a little boy, and that's what they wanted, and that's what they're going to get." In such cases, parents sometimes insist that the child be raised male despite the physicians' instructions to the contrary. "People have in mind certain things they've heard, that this is a boy, and they're not likely to forget that, or they're not likely to let it go easily." The urologist agreed that the first gender attribution is critical: "Once it's been announced, you've got a big problem on your hands." "One of the worst things is to allow them [the parents] to go ahead and give a name and tell everyone, and it turns out the child has to be raised in the opposite sex."[18]

Physicians feel that the mismanagement of such cases requires careful remedying. The psychoendocrinologist asserted, "When I'm involved, I spend hours with the parents to explain to them what has happened and how a mistake like that could be made, *or not really a mistake but a different decision*" [my emphasis]. One pediatric endocrinologist said, "I try to dissuade them from previous misconceptions and say, 'Well, I know what they meant, but the way they said it confused you. This is, I think, a better way to think about it.' " These statements reveal physicians' efforts not only to protect parents from concluding that their child is neither male nor female or both, but also to protect other physicians' decision-making processes. Case management involves perpetuating the notion that good medical decisions are based on interpretations of the infant's real "sex" rather than on cultural understandings of gender.

"Mismanagements" are less likely to occur in communities with major medical centers where specialists are prepared to deal with intersexuality and a medical team (perhaps drawing physicians from more than one teaching hospital) can be quickly assembled. The team typically consists of the original referring doctor (obstetrician or pediatrician), a pediatric endocrinologist, a pediatric surgeon (urologist or gynecologist), and a geneticist. In addition, a psychologist, psychiatrist, or psychoendocrinologist might play a role. If an infant is born with ambiguous genitals in a small community hospital without the relevant specialists on staff, the baby is likely to be transferred to a hospital where diagnosis and treatment is available. Intersexed infants born in poor rural areas where there is less medical intervention might never be referred for genital reconstruction. Many of these children, like those born in earlier historical periods, will grow up and live through adulthood with the genital ambiguity—somehow managing.

The diagnosis of intersexed conditions includes assessing the chromosomal sex and the syndrome that produced the genital ambiguity and may include medical procedures such as cytologic screening, chromosomal analysis; assessing serum electrolytes; hormone, gonadotropin, and steroids evaluation; digital examination; and radiographic genitography.[19] In any intersexed condition, if the infant is determined to be a genetic female (having an XX chromosome makeup), then the treatment—genital surgery to reduce the phallus size—can proceed relatively quickly, satisfying what the doctors believe are psychological and cultural demands. For example, 21-hydroxylase deficiency, a form of female pseudohermaphroditism and one of the most common conditions, can be determined by a blood test within the first few days.

If, on the other hand, the infant is determined to have at least one Y chromosome, then surgery may be considerably delayed. A decision must be made whether to test the ability of the phallic tissue to respond to human chorionic gonadotropin (HCG), a treatment intended to enlarge the microphallus enough to be a penis. The endocrinologist explained, "You do HCG testing and you find out if the male can make testosterone. . . . You can get those results back probably within three weeks. . . . You're sure the male is making testosterone—but can he respond to it? It can take three months of waiting to see whether the phallus responds."

If the Y-chromosome infant cannot make testosterone or cannot respond to the testosterone it makes, the phallus will not develop, and the Y-chromosome infant will not be considered to be a male after all. Should the infant's phallus respond to the local application of testosterone or a brief course of intramuscular injections of low-potency androgen, the gender assignment problem is resolved, but possibly at some later cost, since the penis will not grow again at puberty when the rest of the body develops.[20] Money's case-management philosophy assumes that while it may be difficult for an adult male to have a much smaller than average penis, it is very detrimental to the morale of the young boy to have a micropenis.[21] In the former case, the male's manliness might be at stake, but in the latter case, his essential maleness might be. Although the psychological consequences of these experiences have not been empirically documented, Money and his colleagues suggest that it is wise to avoid the problems of both the micropenis in childhood and the still-undersized penis postpuberty by reassigning many of these infants to the female gender.[22] This approach suggests that for Money and his colleagues, chromosomes are less relevant in determining gender than penis size, and, by implication, that "male" is defined not by the genetic condition of having one Y and one X chromosome or by the production of sperm but by the aesthetic condition of having an "appropriately" sized penis.

The tests and procedures required for diagnosis (and consequently for gender assignment) can take several months.[23] Although physicians are anxious not to make premature gender assignments, their language suggests that it is difficult for them to take a completely neutral position and to think and speak only of *phallic tissue* that belongs to an infant whose gender has not yet been determined or decided. Comments such as "seeing whether the male can respond to testosterone" imply at least a tentative male gender assignment of an XY infant. The psychoendocrinologist's explanations to parents of their infant's treatment program also illustrate this implicit male gender assignment. "Clearly this baby has an underdeveloped phallus. But if the phallus responds to this treatment, we are fairly confident that surgical techniques and hormonal techniques will help this child to look like a boy. But we want to make absolutely sure and use some hormone treatments and see whether the tissue reacts." The mere fact that this doctor refers to the genitals as an "underdeveloped" phallus rather than an overdeveloped clitoris suggests that the infant has been judged to be, at least provisionally, a male. In the case of the undersized phallus, what is ambiguous is not whether this is a penis but whether it is "good enough" to remain one. If, at the end of the treatment period, the phallic tissue has not responded, what had been a potential penis (referred to in the medical literature as a "clitoropenis") is now considered an enlarged clitoris (or "penoclitoris"), and reconstructive surgery is planned as for the genetic female.

The time-consuming nature of intersex diagnosis and the assumption, based on the gender identity theory, that gender be assigned as soon as possible thus present physicians with difficult dilemmas. Medical personnel are committed to discovering the etiology of the condition in order to determine the best course of treatment, which takes time. Yet they feel an urgent need to provide an immediate assignment and genitals that look and function appropriately. An immediate assignment that will need to be retracted is more problematic than a delayed assignment, since reassignment carries with it an additional set of social complications. The endocrinologist interviewed commented: "We've come very far in that we can diagnose, eventually, many of the conditions. But we haven't come far enough. . . . We can't do it early enough. . . . Very frequently a decision is made before all this information is available, simply because it takes so long to make the correct diagnosis. And you cannot let a child go indefinitely, not in this society you can't. . . . There's pressure on parents [for a decision], and the parents transmit that pressure onto physicians."

A pediatric endocrinologist agreed: "At times you may need to operate before a diagnosis can be made. . . . In one case parents were told to wait on the announcement while the infant was treated to see if the phallus would grow when treated with androgens. After the first month passed and there was some growth, the parents said they had given the child a boy's name. They could only wait a month."

Deliberating out loud on the judiciousness of making parents wait for assignment decisions, the endocrinologist asked rhetorically, "Why do we do all these tests if in the end we're going to make the decision simply on the basis of the appearance of the genitalia?" This question suggests that the principles underlying physicians' decisions are cultural rather than biological, based on parental reaction and the medical team's perception of the infant's societal adjustment prospects given the way the child's genitals look or could be made to look. Moreover, as long as the decision rests largely on the criterion of genital appearance, and male is defined as having a "good-sized" penis, more infants will be assigned to the female gender than the male.

THE WAITING PERIOD: DEALING WITH AMBIGUITY

During the period of ambiguity between birth and assignment, physicians not only must evaluate the infant's prospects of becoming a good male but also must manage the parents' uncertainty about a genderless child. Physicians advise that parents postpone announcing the gender of the infant until a gender has been explicitly assigned. They believe that parents should not feel compelled to disclose the baby's "sex" to other people. The clinical geneticist interviewed said that physicians "basically encourage them [parents] to treat it [the infant] as neuter." One of the pediatric endocrinologists reported that

in France parents confronted with this dilemma sometimes give the infant a neuter name such as Claude. The psychoendocrinologist concurred: "If you have a truly borderline situation, and you want to make it dependent on the hormone treatment. . . . then the parents are . . . told, 'Try not to make a decision. Refer to the baby as "baby." Don't think in terms of boy or girl.' " Yet, when asked whether this is a reasonable request to make of parents in our society, the physician answered: "I don't think so. I think parents can't do it."[24]

New York State requires that a birth certificate be filled out within forty-eight hours of delivery, but the certificate need not be filed with the state for thirty days. The geneticist tells parents to insert "child of" instead of a name. In one case, parents filled out two birth registration forms, one for each gender, and they refused to sign either until a final gender assignment had been made.[25] One of the pediatric endocrinologists claimed, "I heard a story, I don't know if it's true or not. There were parents of a hermaphroditic infant who told everyone they had twins, one of each gender. When the gender was determined, they said the other had died."

The geneticist explained that when directly asked by parents what to tell others about the gender of the infant, she says, "Why don't you just tell them that the baby is having problems and as soon as the problems are resolved we'll get back to you." A pediatric endocrinologist echoes this suggestion in advising parents to say, "Until the problem is solved, [we] would really prefer not to discuss any of the details." According to the urologist, "If [the gender] isn't announced, people may mutter about it and may grumble about it, but they haven't got anything to get their teeth into and make trouble over for the child, or the parents, or whatever." In short, parents are asked to sidestep the infant's gender rather than admit that the gender is unknown, thereby collaborating in a web of white lies, ellipses, and mystifications.[26]

Even as physicians teach parents how to deal with those who may not find the infant's condition comprehensible or acceptable, they also must make the condition comprehensible and acceptable to the parents, normalizing the intersexed condition for them. In doing so, they help the parents consider the infant's condition in the most positive way. There are four key aspects to this "normalizing" process.

First, physicians teach parents usual fetal development and explain that all fetuses have the potential to be male or female. One of the endocrinologists explains, "In the absence of maleness, you have femaleness. . . . It's really the basic design. The other [intersex] is really a variation on a theme." This explanation presents the intersex condition as a natural phase of fetal development. Another endocrinologists "like[s] to show picture[s] to them and explain that at a certain point in development males and females look alike and then diverge for such and such reason." The professional literature suggests that doctors use diagrams that illustrate "nature's principle of using the same anlagen to produce the external genital parts of the male and female."[27]

Second, physicians stress the normalcy of other aspects of the infant. For example, the geneticist tells parents, "The baby is healthy, but there was a problem in the way the baby was developing." The endocrinologists says the infant has "a mild defect, [which] just like anything could be considered a birth defect, a mole, or a hemangioma." This language not only eases the blow to the parents but also redirects their attention. Terms like "hermaphrodite" or "abnormal" are not used. The urologist said that he advised parents "about the generalization of sticking to the good things and not confusing people with something that is unnecessary."

Third, physicians (at least initially) imply that it is not the gender of the child that is ambiguous but the genitals. They talk about "undeveloped," "maldeveloped," or "unfinished" organs. From a number of the physicians interviewed came the following explanations:

At a point in time the development proceeded in a different way, and sometimes the development isn't complete and we may have some trouble . . . in determining what the *actual* sex is. And so we have to do a blood test to help us. [my emphasis]

The baby may be a female, which you would know after the buccal smear, but you can't prove it yet. If so, then it's a normal female with a different appearance. This can be surgically corrected.

The gender of your child isn't apparent to us at the moment.

While this looks like a small penis, it's actually a large clitoris. And what we're going to do is put it back in its proper position and reduce the size of the tip of it enough so it doesn't look funny, so it looks right.

Money and his colleagues report a case in which parents were advised to tell their friends that the reason their infant's gender was reannounced from male to female is that "the baby was . . . 'closed up down there.' [. . .] When the closed skin was divided, the female organs were revealed, and the baby discovered to be, *in fact,* a girl." [my emphasis] It was mistakenly assumed to be a male at first because "there was an excess of skin on the clitoris."[28]

The message in these examples is that the trouble lies in the doctor's ability to determine the gender, not in the baby's gender per se. The real gender will presumably be determined/proven by testing, and the "bad" genitals (which are confusing the situation for everyone) will be "repaired." The emphasis is not on the doctors' creating gender but in their completing the genitals. Physicians say that they "reconstruct" the genitals rather than "construct" them. The surgeons reconstitute from remaining parts what should have been there all along. The fact that gender in an infant is "reannounced" rather than "reassigned" suggests that the first announcement was a mistake because the announcer was confused by the genitals. The gender always was what it is now seen to be.[29]

Finally, physicians tell parents that social factors are more important in gender development than biological ones, even though they are searching for biological causes. In essence, the physicians teach the parents Money and Ehrhardt's theory of gender development.[30] In doing so, they shift the emphasis from the discovery of biological factors that are a sign of the "real" gender to providing the appropriate social conditions to produce the "real" gender. What remains unsaid is the apparent contradiction in the assumption that a "real" or "natural" gender can be or needs to be produced artificially. The physician/parent discussions make it clear to family members that gender is not a biological given [even though, of course, the physicians' own procedures for diagnosis assume that it is] and that gender is fluid: The psychoendocrinologist paraphrased an explanation to parents thus: "It will depend, ultimately, on how everybody treats your child and how your child is looking as a person. . . . I can with confidence tell them that generally gender [identity] clearly agrees with the assignment." A pediatric endocrinologist explained: "I try to impress upon them that there's an enormous amount of clinical data to support the fact that if you sex-reverse an infant . . . the majority of the time the alternative gender identity is commensurate with the socialization, the way that they're raised, and how people view them, and that seems to be the most critical."

The implication of these comments is that gender identity (of all children, not just those born with ambiguous genitals) is determined primarily by social factors, that the parents and community always construct the child's gender. In the case of intersexed infants, the physicians merely provide the right genitals to go along with the socialization. Of course at so-called normal births, when the infant's genitals are unambiguous, the parents are not told that the child's gender is ultimately up to socialization. In those cases, doctors do treat gender as a biological given.

SOCIAL FACTORS IN DECISION MAKING

Most of the physicians interviewed claimed that personal convictions of doctors ought to play no role in the decision-making process. The psychoendocrinologist explained:

> I think the most critical factors [are] what is the possibility that this child will grow up with genitals which look like that of the assigned gender and which will ultimately function according to gender. . . . That's why it's so important that it's a well-established team, because [personal convictions] can't really enter into it. It has to be what is surgically and endocrinologically possible for that baby to be able to make it. . . . It's really much more within medical criteria. I don't think many social factors enter into it.

While this doctor eschews the importance of social factors in gender assignment, she argues forcefully that social factors are extremely important in the development of gender identity. Indeed, she implies that social factors primarily enter the picture once the infant leaves the hospital.

In fact, doctors make decisions about gender on the basis of shared cultural values that are unstated, perhaps even unconscious, and therefore considered objective rather than subjective. Money states the fundamental rule for gender assignment: "Never assign a baby to be reared, and to surgical and hormonal therapy, as a boy, unless the phallic structure, hypospadiac or otherwise, is neonatally of at least the same caliber as that of same-aged males with small–average penises."[31] Elsewhere, he and his colleagues provide specific measurements for what qualities as a micropenis: "A penis is, by convention, designated as a micropenis when at birth its dimensions are three or more standard deviations below the mean. . . . When it is correspondingly reduced in diameter with corpora that are vestigial, . . . it unquestionably qualifies as a micropenis."[32] A pediatric endocrinologist claimed that although "the [size of the] phallus is not the deciding factor, . . . if the phallus is less than two centimeters long at birth and won't respond to androgen treatments, then it's made into a female." There is no clearer statement of the formula for gender assignment than the one given by one well-published pediatric surgeon: "The decision to raise the

child with male pseudohermaphroditism as a male or female is dictated entirely by the size of the phallus."[33]

These guidelines are clear, but they focus on only one physical feature, one that is distinctly imbued with cultural meaning. This becomes especially apparent in the case of an XX infant with normal female reproductive gonads and a "perfect" penis. Would the size and shape of the penis, in this case, be the deciding factor in assigning the infant as a "male," or would the "perfect" penis be surgically destroyed and female genitals created? Money notes that this dilemma would be complicated by the anticipated reaction of the parents to seeing "their apparent son lose his penis."[34] Other researchers concur that parents are likely to want to raise a child with a normal-shaped penis (regardless of size) as "male," particularly if the scrotal area looks normal and if the parents have had no experience with intersexuality.[35] Elsewhere, Money argues in favor of not neonatally amputating the penis of XX infants since fetal masculinization of brain structures would predispose them "almost invariably [to] develop behaviorally as tomboys, even when reared as girls."[36] This reasoning implies first that tomboyish behavior in girls is bad and should be avoided and second that it is preferable to remove the internal female organs, implant prosthetic testes, and regulate the "boy's hormones for his entire life than to overlook or disregard the perfection of the penis."[37]

The ultimate proof to the physicians that they intervened appropriately and gave the intersexed infant the correct gender assignment is that the reconstructed genitals look normal and function normally in adulthood. The vulva, labia, and clitoris should appear ordinary to the woman and her partner(s), and the vagina should be able to receive a normal-sized penis. Similarly, the man and his partner(s) should feel that his penis (even if somewhat smaller than the norm) looks and functions in an unremarkable way. Although there are no published data on how much emphasis the intersexed person, him- or herself, places upon genital appearance and functioning, physicians are absolutely clear about what they believe is important. The clinical geneticist said, "If you have . . . a seventeen-year-old young lady who has gotten hormone therapy and has breast development and pubic hair and no vaginal opening, I can't even entertain the notion that this young lady wouldn't want to have corrective surgery." The urologist summarized his criteria: "Happiness is the biggest factor. Anatomy is part of happiness." Money states, "The primary deficit [of not having sufficient penis]—and destroyer of morale—lies in being unable to satisfy the partner."[38] Another team of clinicians reveals its phallocentrism and argues that the most serious mistake in gender assignment is to create "an individual unable to engage in genital [heterosexual] sex."[39]

The equation of gender with genitals could have emerged only in an age when medical science can create genitals that appear to be normal and to function adequately, and an emphasis on the good phallus above all else could have emerged only in a culture that has rigid aesthetic and performance criteria for what constitutes maleness. The formulation "Good penis equals male; absence of good penis equals female" is treated in the literature and by the physicians interviewed as an objective criterion, operative in all cases. There is a striking lack of attention to the size and shape requirements of the female genitals, other than that the clitoris not be too big and that the vagina be able to receive a penis.[40]

In the late nineteenth century, when women's reproductive function was culturally designated as their essential characteristic, the presence or absence of ovaries (whether or not they were fertile) was held to be the ultimate criterion of gender assignment for hermaphrodites. As recently as 1955, there was some concern that if people with the same chromosomes or gonads paired off, even if they had different genitals, that "might bring the physician in conflict with the law for abetting the pursuit of (technically) illegal sex practices."[41] The urologist interviewed recalled a case from that period of a male child reassigned to "female" at the age of four or five because ovaries had been discovered. Nevertheless, doctors today, schooled in the etiology and treatment of the various intersex syndromes, view decisions based primarily on chromosomes or gonads as wrong, although, they complain, the conviction that the presence of chromosomes or gonads is the ultimate criterion "still dictates the decisions of the uneducated and uninformed."[42] Presumably the educated and informed now know that decisions based primarily on phallic size, shape, and sexual capacity are right.

While the prospect of constructing good genitals is the primary consideration in physicians' gender assignments, another extramedical factor was repeatedly cited by the six physicians interviewed—the specialty of the attending physician. Although intersexed infants are generally treated by teams of specialists, only the person who coordinates the team is actually responsible for the case. This person, acknowledged by the other physicians as having chief responsibility, acts as spokesperson to the parents. Although all of the physicians claimed that these medical teams work smoothly, with few differences of opinion, several of them mentioned decision-making orientations that are grounded in particular medical specializations. One

endocrinologist stated, "The easiest route to take, where there is ever any question, . . . is to raise the child as female. . . . In this country, that is usual if the infant falls into the hands of a pediatric endocrinologist. . . . If the decision is made by the urologists, who are mostly males, . . . they're always opting, because they do the surgery, they're always feeling they can correct anything." Another endocrinologist concurred: "[Most urologists] don't think in terms of dynamic processes. They're interested in fixing pipes and lengthening pipes, and not dealing with hormonal, and certainly not psychological issues. . . . 'What can I do with what I've got?' " Urologists were defended by the clinical geneticist: "Surgeons here, now I can't speak for elsewhere, they don't get into a situation where the child is a year old and they can't make anything."

Whether or not urologists "like to make boys," as one endocrinologist claimed, the following example from a urologist who was interviewed explicitly links a cultural interpretation of masculinity to the medical treatment plan. The case involved an adolescent who had been assigned the female gender at birth but was developing some male pubertal signs and wanted to be a boy. "He was ill-equipped," said the urologist, "yet we made a very respectable male out of him. He now owns a huge construction business—those big cranes that put stuff up on the building."

POSTINFANCY CASE MANAGEMENT

After the infant's gender has been assigned, parents generally latch onto the assignment as the solution to the problem—and it is. The physician as detective has collected the evidence, as lawyer has presented the case, and as judge has rendered a verdict. Although most of the interviewees claimed that parents are equal participants in the whole process, they gave no instances of parental participation prior to the gender assignment.[43] After the physicians assign the infant's gender, the parents are encouraged to establish the credibility of that gender publicly by, for example, giving a detailed medical explanation to a leader in their community, such as a physician or pastor, who will explain the situation to curious casual acquaintances. Money argues that "medical terminology has a special layman's magic in such a context, it is final and authoritative and closes the issue."[44] He also recommends that eventually the mother "settle [the] argument once and for all among her women friends by allowing some of them to see the baby's reconstructed genitalia." Apparently, the powerful influence of normal-looking genitals helps overcome a history of ambiguous gender.

Some of the same issues that arise in assigning gender recur some years later when, at adolescence, the child may be referred to a physician for counseling.[45] The physician then tells the adolescent many of the same things his or her parents had been told years before, with the same language. Terms like "abnormal," "disorder," "disease," and "hermaphroditism" are avoided; the condition is normalized and the child's gender is treated as unproblematic. One clinician explains to his patients that sex organs are different in appearance for each person, not just those who are intersexed. Furthermore, he tells the girls "that while most women menstruate, not all do . . . that conception is only one of a number of ways to become a parent; [and] that today some individuals are choosing not to become parents."[46] The clinical geneticist tells a typical female patient: "You are female. Female is not determined by your genes. Lots of other things determine being a woman. And you are a woman but you won't be able to have babies."

A case reported by one of the pediatric endocrinologists involving an adolescent female with androgen insensitivity provides an intriguing insight into the postinfancy gender-management process. She was told at the age of fourteen "that her ovaries weren't normal and had been removed. That's why she needed pills to look normal. . . . I wanted to convince her of her femininity. Then I told her she could marry and have normal sexual relations. . . . [Her] uterus won't develop but [she] could adopt children." The urologist interviewed was asked to comment on this handling of the counseling. "It sounds like a very good solution to it. He's stating the truth, and if you don't state the truth . . . then you're in trouble later." This is a strange version of "the truth," however, since the adolescent was chromosomally XY and was born with normal testes that produced normal quantities of androgen. There *were* no ovaries or uterus. Another pediatric endocrinologist, in commenting on the management of this case, hedged the issue by saying that he would have used a generic term like "the gonads." A third endocrinologist said she would say that the uterus had never formed.

Technically, these physicians are lying when, for example, they explain to an adolescent XY female with an intersexed history that her "ovaries . . . had to be removed because they were unhealthy or were producing 'the wrong balance of hormones.' "[47] We can presume that these lies are told in the service of what physicians consider a greater good—keeping individual/concrete genders as clear and uncontaminated as the notions of female and male are in the abstract. One clinician suggests that with some female patients it eventually may be possible to talk to them "about their gonads having some structures and features that are testicular-like."[48] This call for honesty may be based, at least partly, on the possibility of the child's discovering his or her chromosomal sex inadvertently from a buccal smear taken in a high school biology class. Today's litigious climate may be another encouragement.

In sum, the adolescent is typically told that certain internal organs did not form because of an endocrinological defect, not because those organs could never have developed in someone with her or his sex chromosomes. The topic of chromosomes is skirted.

There are no published studies on how these adolescents experience their condition and their treatment by doctors. An endocrinologist interviewed mentioned that her adolescent patients rarely ask specifically what is wrong with them, suggesting that they are accomplices in this evasion. In spite of the "truth" having been evaded, the clinician's impression is that "their gender identities and general senses of well-being and self-esteem appear not to have suffered."[49]

LESSONS FROM INTERSEX MANAGEMENT

Physicians conduct careful examinations of the intersexed infant's genitals and perform intricate laboratory procedures. They are interpreters of the body, trained and committed to uncovering the "actual" gender obscured by ambiguous genitals. Yet they also have considerable leeway in assigning gender, and their decisions are influenced by cultural as well as medical factors. What is the relationship between the physician as discoverer and the physician as determiner of gender? Where is the relative emphasis placed in discussions with parents and adolescents and in the consciousness of the physicians? It is misleading to characterize the doctors whose words are provided here as presenting themselves publicly to the parents as discoverers of the infant's real gender but privately acknowledging that the infant has no real gender other than the one being determined or constructed by the medical professionals. They are not hypocritical. It is also misleading to claim that the physicians' focus shifts from discovery to determination over the course of treatment: first the doctors regard the infant's gender as an unknown but discoverable reality; then the doctors relinquish their attempts to find the real gender and treat the infant's gender as something they must construct. They are not medically incompetent or deficient. Instead, I am arguing that the peculiar balance of discovery and determination throughout treatment permits physicians to handle very problematic cases of gender in the most unproblematic of ways.

This balance relies fundamentally on a particular conception of "natural."[50] Although the "deformity" of intersexed genitals would be immutable were it not for medical interference, physicians do not consider it natural. Instead, they think of, and speak of, the surgical/hormonal alteration of such "deformities" as natural because such intervention returns the body to what it ought to have been if events had taken their typical course. The nonnormative is converted into the normative, and the normative state is considered natural.[51] The genital ambiguity is remedied to conform to a "natural," that is, culturally indisputable gender dichotomy. Sherry Ortner's claim that the culture/nature distinction is itself a construction—a product of culture—is relevant here. Language and imagery help create and maintain a specific view of what is natural about the two genders, and I would argue, about the very idea of gender—that it consists of two exclusive types: female and male.[52] The belief that gender consists of two exclusive types is maintained and perpetuated by the medical community in the face of incontrovertible physical evidence that this is not mandated by biology.

The lay conception of human anatomy and physiology assumes a concordance among clearly dimorphic gender markers—chromosomes, genitals, gonads, hormones—but physicians understand that concordance and dimorphism do not always exist. Their understanding of biology's complexity, however, does not inform their understanding of gender's complexity. In order for intersexuality to be managed differently than it currently is, physicians would have to take seriously Money's assertion that it is a misrepresentation of epistemology to consider any cell in the body authentically male or female.[53] If authenticity for gender resides not in a discoverable nature but in someone's

proclamation, then the power to proclaim something else is available. If physicians recognized that implicit in their management of gender is the notion that finally, and always, people construct gender, as well as the social systems that are grounded in gender-based concepts, the possibilities for real societal transformations would be unlimited. Unfortunately, neither in their representations to the families of the intersexed nor among themselves do the physicians interviewed for this study draw such far-reaching implications from their work. Their "understanding" that particular genders are medically (re)constructed in these cases does not lead them to see that gender is *always* constructed. Accepting genital ambiguity as a natural option would require that physicians also acknowledge that genital ambiguity is "corrected" not because it is threatening to the infant's life but because it is threatening to the infant's culture.

Rather than admit to their role in perpetuating gender, physicians "psychologize" the issue by talking about the parents' anxiety and humiliation in being confronted with an anomalous infant. They talk as though they have no choice but to respond to the parents' pressure for a resolution of psychological discomfort and as though they have no choice but to use medical technology in the service of a two-gender culture. Neither the psychology nor the technology is doubted, since both shield physicians from responsibility. Indeed, for the most part, neither physicians nor parents emerge from the experience of intersex case management with a greater understanding of the social construction of gender. Society's accountability, like their own, is masked by the assumption that gender is a given. Thus, the medical management of intersexuality, instead of illustrating nature's failure to ordain gender in these isolated, "unfortunate" instances, illustrates physicians' and western society's failure of imagination—the failure to imagine that each of their management decisions is a moment when a specific instance of biological "sex" is transformed into a culturally constructed gender.

NOTES

1. For historical reviews of the intersexed person in ancient Greece and Rome, see Leslie Fiedler, *Freaks: Myths and Images of the Second Self* and Vern Bullough, *Sexual Variance in Society and History.* For the Middle Ages and Renaissance, see Michel Foucault, *History of Sexuality.* For the eighteenth and nineteenth centuries, see Michel Foucault, *Herculine Barbin* and Alice

Domurat Dreger, *Hermaphrodites and the Medical Invention of Sex* (Cambridge: Harvard University Press, 1998). For the early twentieth century, see Havelock Ellis, *Studies in the Psychology of Sex.*

2. Traditionally, the term "gender" has designated psychological, social, and cultural aspects of maleness and femaleness, and the term "sex" has specified the biological and presumably more

objective components. Twenty years ago, Wendy McKenna and I introduced the argument that "gender" should be used exclusively to refer to anything related to the categories "female" and "male," replacing the term "sex," which would be restricted to reproductive and "lovemaking" activities (Kessler and McKenna). Our reasoning was (and still is) that this would emphasize the socially constructed, overlapping nature of all category distinctions, even the biological ones. We wrote about gender chromosomes and gender hormones even though, at the time, doing so seemed awkward. I continue this practice here, but I follow the convention of referring to people with mixed biological gender cues as "intersexed" or "intersexuals" rather than as "intergendered" or "intergenderals." The latter is more consistent with my position, but I want to reflect both medical and vernacular usage without using quotation marks each time.

3. See, for example: M. Bolkenius, R. Daum, and E. Heinrich, "Paediatric Surgical Principles in the Management of Children with Intersex"; Kenneth I. Glassberg, "Gender Assignment in Newborn Male Pseudohermaphrodites"; and Peter A. Lee et al., "Micropenis. I. Criteria, Etiologies and Classification."

4. It is difficult to get accurate statistics on the frequency of intersexuality. Chromosomal abnormalities (like XOXX or XXXY) are registered, but those conditions do not always imply ambiguous genitals, and most cases of ambiguous genitals do not involve chromosomal abnormalities. None of the physicians interviewed would venture a guess on frequency rates, but all claimed that intersexuality is rare. One physician suggested that the average obstetrician may see only two cases in twenty years. Another estimated that a specialist may see only one a year or possibly as many as five a year. A reporter who interviewed physicians at Johns Hopkins Medical Center wrote that they treat, at most, ten new patients a year (Melissa Hendricks, "Is It a Boy or a Girl?"). The numbers are considerably greater if one adopts a broader definition of intersexuality to include all "sex chromosome" deviations and any genitals that do not look, according to the culturally informed view of the moment, "normal" enough. A urologist at a Mr. Sinai School of Medicine symposium on Pediatric Plastic and Reconstructive Surgery (New York City, 16 May 1996) claimed that one of every three hundred male births involves some kind of genital abnormality. A meticulous analysis of the medical literature from 1955 to 1997 led Anne Fausto-Sterling and her students to conclude that the frequency of intersexuality may be as high as 2 percent of live births, and that between 0.1 and 0.2 percent of newborns undergo some sort of genital surgery (Melanie Blackless et al., "How Sexually Dimorphic Are We?"). The Intersex Society of North America (ISNA) estimates that about five intersex surgeries are performed in the United States each day.

5. Although the interviews in this chapter were conducted more than ten years ago, interviews with physicians conducted in the mid- to late 1990s and interviews conducted with parents of intersexed children during that same time period (both reported on in later chapters) indicate that little has changed in the medical management of intersexuality. This lack of change is also evident in current medical management literature. See, for example, F. M. E. Slijper et al.,

"Neonates with Abnormal Genital Development Assigned the Female Sex: Parent Counseling" and M. Rohatgi, "Intersex Disorders: An Approach to Surgical Management."

6. Mariano Castro-Magana, Moris Angulo, and Platon J. Collipp, "Management of the Child with Ambiguous Genitalia."

7. For example, infants whose intersexuality is caused by congenital adrenal hyperplasia can develop severe electrolyte disturbances unless the condition is controlled by cortisone treatments. Intersexed infants whose condition is caused by androgen insensitivity are in danger of eventual malignant degeneration of the testes unless these are removed. For a complete catalog of clinical syndromes related to the intersexed condition, see Arye Lev-Ran, "Sex Reversal as Related to Clinical Syndromes in Human Beings."

8. Much of the surgical experimentation in this area has been accomplished by urologists who are trying to create penises for female-to-male transsexuals. Although there have been some advancements in recent years in the ability to create a "reasonable-looking" penis from tissue taken elsewhere on the body, the complicated requirements of the organ (requiring both urinary and sexual functioning) have posed surgical problems. It may be, however, that the concerns of the urologists are not identical to the concerns of the patients. While data are not yet available from the intersexed, we know that female-to-male transsexuals place greater emphasis on the "public" requirements of the penis (for example, being able to look normal while standing at the urinal or wearing a bathing suit) than on its functional requirements (for example, being able to achieve an erection) (Kessler and McKenna, 128–132). As surgical techniques improve, female-to-male transsexuals (and intersexed males) might increase their demands for organs that look and function better.

9. Historically, psychology has tended to blur the distinction between the two by equating a person's acceptance of her or his genitals with gender role and ignoring gender identity. For example, Freudian theory posited that if one had a penis and accepted its reality, then masculine gender role behavior would naturally follow (Sigmund Freud, "Some Psychical Consequences of the Anatomical Distinctions between the Sexes").

10. Almost all of the published literature on intersexed infant case management has been written or co-written by one researcher, John Money, professor of medical psychology and professor of pediatrics, emeritus, at Johns Hopkins University and Hospital, where he is director of the Psychohormonal Research Unit. Even the publications that are produced independently of Money reference him and reiterate his management philosophy. Although only one of the physicians interviewed has published with Money, they all essentially concur with his views and give the impression of a consensus that is rarely encountered in science. The one physician who raised some questions about Money's philosophy and the gender theory on which it is based has extensive experience with intersexuality in a nonindustrialized culture where the infant is matured differently with no apparent harm to gender development. Even though psychologists fiercely argue issues of gender identity and gender role development, doctors who treat intersexed infants seem untouched by these debates. There are still, in the late 1990s, few

renegade voices from within the medical establishment. Why Money has been so single-handedly influential in promoting his ideas about gender is a question worthy of a separate substantial analysis. His management philosophy is conveyed in the following sources: John Money, J. G. Hampson, and J. L. Hampson, "Hermaphroditism: Recommendations Concerning Assignment of Sex, Change of Sex, and Psychologic Management"; John Money, *Sex Errors of the Body: Dilemmas, Education, Counseling;* John Money, Reynolds Potter, and Clarice S. Stoll, "Sex Reannouncement in Hereditary Sex Deformity: Psychology and Sociology of Habilitation"; Money and Ehrhardt; John Money, "Psychologic Consideration of Sex Assignment in Intersexuality"; John Money, "Psychological Counseling: Hermaphroditism"; John Money, Tom Mazur, Charles Abrams, and Bernard F. Norman, "Micropenis, Family Mental Health, and Neonatal Management: A Report on Fourteen Patients Reared as Girls"; and John Money, "Birth Defect of the Sex Organs: Telling the Parents and the Patient."

11. Money and Ehrhardt, 152.

12. One exception is the case followed by Milton Diamond in "Sexual Identity, Monozygotic Twins Reared in Discordant Sex Roles and a BBC Follow-up" and, with Keith Sigmundson, in "Sex Reassignment at Birth: Long-term Review and Clinical Applications."

13. Money, "Psychologic Consideration of Sex Assignment in Intersexuality."

14. Castro-Magana, Angulo, and Collipp.

15. Victor Braren et al., "True Hermaphroditism: A Rational Approach to Diagnosis and Treatment."

16. Studies of nonintersexed newborns have shown that, from the moment of birth, parents respond to their infant based on her or his gender. Jeffrey Rubin, F. J. Provenzano, and Z. Luria, "The Eye of the Beholder: Parents' Views on Sex of Newborns."

17. Money, Mazur, Abrams, and Norman.

18. There is evidence from other kinds of sources that once a gender attribution is made, all further information buttresses that attribution, and only the most contradictory new information will cause the original gender attribution to be questioned. Kessler and McKenna.

19. Castro-Magana, Angulo, and Collipp.

20. Money, "Psychologic Consideration of Sex Assignment in Intersexuality."

21. Technically, the term "micropenis" should be reserved for an exceptionally small but well-formed structure, a small, malformed "penis" should be referred to as a "microphallus" (Peter A. Lee et al.).

22. Money, Mazur, Abrams, and Norman, 26. A different view is argued by another leading gender-identity theorist: "When a little boy (with an imperfect penis) knows he is a male, he creates a penis that functions symbolically the same as those of boys with normal penises" (Robert J. Stoller, *Sex and Gender*).

23. W. Ch. Hecker, "Operative Correction of Intersexual Genitals in Children."

24. This way of presenting advice fails to understand that parents are part of a larger system. A pediatric endocrinologist told

biologist Anne Fausto-Sterling that parents, especially young ones, are not independent actors. They rely on the advice of grandparents and older siblings, who, according to the physician, are more hysterical and push for an early gender assignment before all the medical data are analyzed (private communication, summer 1996).

25. Elizabeth Bing and Esselyn Rudikoff, "Divergent Ways of Parental Coping with Hermaphrodite Children."

26. These evasions must have many ramifications in everyday social interactions between parents, family, and friends. How people "fill in" the uncertainty such that interactions remain relatively normal is an interesting question that warrants further study. One of the pediatric endocrinologists interviewed acknowledged that the published literature discusses intersex management only from the physicians' point of view. He asks, "How [do parents] experience what they're told, and what [do] they remember . . . and carry with them?" One published exception to this neglect of the parents' perspective is a case study comparing two different coping strategies. The first couple, although initially distressed, handled the traumatic event by regarding the abnormality as an act of God. The second couple, more educated and less religious, put their faith in medical science and expressed a need to fully understand the biochemistry of the defect. Bing and Rudikoff.

27. Tom Mazur, "Ambiguous Genitalia: Detection and Counseling" and Money "Psychologic Consideration of Sex Assignment in Intersexuality," 218.

28. Money, Potter, and Stoll, 211.

29. The term "reassignment" is more commonly used to describe the gender changes of those who are cognizant of their earlier gender, e.g., transsexuals—people whose gender itself was a mistake.

30. Although Money and Ehrhardt's socialization theory is uncontested by the physicians who treat intersexuality and is presented to parents as a matter of fact, there is actually much debate among psychologists about the effect of prenatal hormones on brain structure and ultimately on gender-role behavior and even on gender identity. The physicians interviewed agreed that the animal evidence for prenatal brain organization is compelling but that there is no evidence in humans that prenatal hormones have an inviolate or unilateral effect. If there is any effect of prenatal exposure to androgen, they believe it can easily be overcome and modified by psychosocial factors. It is this latter position, not the controversy in the field, that is communicated to the parents. For an argument favoring prenatally organized gender differences in the brain, see Milton Diamond, "Human Sexual Development: Biological Foundations for Social Development"; for a critique of that position, see Ruth Bleier, *Science and Gender. A Critique of Biology and Its Theories on Women.*

31. Money, "Psychological Counseling: Hermaphroditism," 610.

32. Money, Mazur, Abrams, and Norman, 18.

33. P. Donahoe, "Clinical Management of Intersex Abnormalities."

34. John Money, "Hermaphroditism and Pseudohermaphroditism."

35. Mojtaba Beheshti, Brian E. Hardy, Bernard M. Churchill, and Denis Daneman, "Gender Assignment in Male

Pseudohermaphrodite Children" Of course, if the penis looked normal and the empty scrotum was overlooked, it might not be discovered until puberty that the male child was XX with a female internal structure.

36. Money, "Psychologic Consideration of Sex Assignment in Intersexuality," 216.

37. Weighing the probability of achieving a "perfect" penis against the probable trauma such procedures may entail is another social factor in decision making. According to an endocrinologist interviewed, if it seems that an XY infant with an inadequate penis would require as many as ten genital operations over a six-year period in order to have an adequate penis, the infant would be assigned the female gender. In this case, the endocrinologist's practical and compassionate concerns would override purely genital criteria.

38. Money, "Psychologic Consideration of Sex Assignment in Intersexuality," 217.

39. Castro-Magana, Angulo, and Collipp, 180.

40. It is unclear how much of this bias is the result of a general cultural devaluation of the female and how much is the result of physicians' belief in their ability to construct anatomically correct and functional female genitals.

41. John F. Oliven, *Sexual Hygiene and Pathology: A Manual for the Physician.*

42. Money, "Psychologic Consideration of Sex Assignment in Intersexuality," 215. Remnants of this anachronistic view can still be found, however, when doctors justify the removal of contradictory gonads on the grounds that they are typically sterile or at risk for malignancy (J. Dewhurst and D. B. Grant, "Intersex Problems.") Presumably, if the gonads were functional and healthy, their removal would provide an ethical dilemma for at least some medical professionals.

43. Although one set of authors argued that the views of the parents on the most appropriate gender for their child must be taken into account (Dewhurst and Grant, 1192), the physicians interviewed here denied direct knowledge of this kind of participation. They claimed that they personally had encountered few, if any, cases of parents who insisted on their child being assigned a particular gender. Yet each had heard about cases where a family's ethnicity or religious background biased them toward males. None of the physicians recalled whether this preference for male offspring meant the parents wanted a male regardless of the "inadequacy" of the penis, or whether it meant that the parents would have greater difficulty with a less-than-perfect-male than with a "normal" female.

44. Money, "Psychological Counseling: Hermaphroditism," 613.

45. As with the literature on infancy, most of the published material on adolescents is on surgical and hormonal management rather than on social management. See, for example, Joel J. Roslyn, Eric W. Fonkalsrud, and Barbara Lippe, "Intersex Disorders in Adolescents and Adults."

46. Mazur, 421.

47. Dewhurst and Grant, 1193.

48. Mazur, 422.

49. Ibid.

50. For an extended discussion of different ways of conceptualizing what is natural, see Richard W. Smith, "What Kind of Sex Is Natural?"

51. This supports sociologist Harold Garfinkel's argument that we treat routine events as our *due* as social members and that we treat gender, like all normal forms, as a moral imperative. It is no wonder, then, that physicians conceptualize what they are doing as natural and unquestionably "right." Harold Garfinkel, *Studies in Ethnomethodology.*

52. Sherry B. Ortner, "Is Female to Male as Nature Is to Culture?"

53. Money, "Psychological Counseling: Hermaphroditism," 618.

REFERENCES

Beheshti, Mojtaba, Brian E. Hardy, Bernard M. Churchill, and Denis Daneman. "Gender Assignment in Male Pseudohermaphrodite Children." *Urology* 22, no. 6 (December 1983):604–607.

Bing, Elizabeth and Esselyn Rudikoff. "Divergent Ways of Parental Coping with Hermaphrodite Children." *Medical Aspects of Human Sexuality* (December 1970):73–88.

Blackless, Melanie, Anthony Charuvastra, Amanda Derryck, Anne Fausto-Sterling, Karl Lauzanne, and Ellen Lee. "How Sexually Dimorphic Are We?" Unpublished manuscript, 1997.

Bleier, Ruth. *Science and Gender: A Critique of Biology and Its Theories on Women.* New York: Pergamon Press, 1984.

Bolkenius, M., R. Daum, and E. Heinrich. "Paediatric Surgical Principles in the Management of Children with Intersex." *Progress in Pediatric Surgery* 17 (1984):33–38.

Braren, Victor, John J. Warner, Ian M. Burr, Alfred Slonim, James A. O'Neill Jr., and Robert K. Rhamy. "True Hermaphroditism: A Rational Approach to Diagnosis and Treatment." *Urology* 15 (June 1980):569–574.

Bullough, Vern. *Sexual Variance in Society and History.* New York: John Wiley and Sons, 1976.

Castro-Magana, Mariano, Moris Angulo, and Platon J. Collipp. "Management of the Child with Ambiguous Genitalia." *Medical Aspects of Human Sexuality* 18, no. 4 (April 1984):172–188.

Dewhurst, J., and D. B. Grant. "Intersex Problems." *Archives of Disease in Childhood* 59 (July–December 1984):1191–1194.

Diamond, Milton. "Human Sexual Development: Biological Foundations for Social Development." In *Human Sexuality in*

Four Perspectives, ed. Frank A. Beach, 22–61. Baltimore: The Johns Hopkins University Press, 1976.

———. "Sexual Identity, Monozygotic Twins Reared in Discordant Sex Roles and a BBC Follow-Up." *Archives of Sexual Behavior* 11, no. 2 (1982):181–186.

———, and Keith Sigmundson. "Sex Reassignment of Birth: Long-term Review and Clinical Applications." *Archives of Pediatric and Adolescent Medicine* 151 (May 1997):298–304.

Donahoe, P. "Clinical Management of Intersex Abnormalities." *Current Problems in Surgery* 28 (1991):519–579.

Dreger, Alice Domurat. *Hermaphrodites and the Medical Invention of Sex.* Cambridge: Harvard University Press, 1998.

Ellis, Havelock. *Studies in the Psychology of Sex.* New York: Random House, 1942.

Fiedler, Leslie. *Freaks: Myths and Images of the Second Self.* New York: Simon and Schuster, 1978.

Foucault, Michael. *Herculine Barbin.* New York: Pantheon Books, 1978.

———. *History of Sexuality.* New York: Pantheon Books, 1980.

Freud, Sigmund. "Some Psychical Consequences of the Anatomical Distinctions between the Sexes" (1925). In *The Complete Psychological Works,* trans. and ed. J. Strachy, vol. 18. New York: Norton, 1976.

Garfinkel, Harold. *Studies in Ethnomethodology.* Englewood Cliffs, N.J.: Prentice Hall, 1967.

Glassberg, Kenneth I. "Gender Assignment in Newborn Male Pseudohermaphodites." *Urologic Clinics of North America* 7 (June 1980):409–421.

Hecker, W. Ch. "Operative Correction of Intersexual Genitals in Children." *Progress in Pediatric Surgery* 17 (1984):21–31.

Hendricks, Melissa. "Is It a Boy or a Girl?" *Johns Hopkins Magazine* 45, no. 5 (November 1993):10–16.

Kessler, Suzanne J., and Wendy McKenna. *Gender: An Ethnomethodological Approach.* New York: Wiley-Interscience, 1978; Chicago: University of Chicago Press, 1985.

Lee, Peter A., Thomas Mazur, Robert Danish, James Amrhein, Robert M. Blizzard, John Money, and claude J. Migeon. "Micropenis: I. Criteria, Etiologies and Classification." *The Johns Hopkins Medical Journal* 146 (1980):156–163.

Lev-Ran, Arye. "Sex Reversal as Related to Clinical Syndromes in Human Beings." In *Handbook of Sexology II: Genetics, Hormones and Behavior,* ed. John Money and H. Musaph, 157–173. New York: Elsevier, 1978.

Mazur, Tom. "Ambiguous Genitalia: Detection and Counseling." *Pediatric Nursing* 9 (November/December 1983):417–431.

Money, John. "Birth Defect of the Sex Organs: Telling the Parents and the Patient." *British Journal of Sexual Medicine* 10 (March 1983):14.

———. "Hermaphroditism and Pseudohermaphroditism." In *Gynecologic Endocrinology,* ed. Jay J. Gold, 449–464. New York: Hoeber, 1968.

———. "Psychologic Consideration of Sex Assignment in Intersexuality." *Clinics in Plastic Surgery* 1 (April 1974):215–222.

———. "Psychological Counseling: Hermaphroditism." In *Endocrine and Genetic Diseases of Childhood and Adolescence,* ed. L. I. Gardner, 609–618. Philadelphia: W. B. Saunders, 1975.

———. *Sex Errors of the Body: Dilemmas, Education, Counseling.* Baltimore: The Johns Hopkins University Press, 1968. Reprint, 1994.

———, and Anke A. Ehrhardt. *Man & Woman, Boy & Girl.* Baltimore: The Johns Hopkins University Press, 1972.

———, J. G. Hampson, and J. L. Hampson. "Hermaphroditism: Recommendations Concerning Assignment of Sex, Change of Sex, and Psychologic Management." *Bulletin of The Johns Hopkins Hospital* 97 (1955):284–300.

———, Tom Mazur, Charles Abrams, and Bernard F. Norman. "Micropenis, Family Mental Health, and Neonatal Management: A Report on Fourteen Patients Reared as Girls." *Journal of Preventive Psychiatry* 1, no. 1 (1981):17–27.

———, Reynolds Potter, and Clarice S. Stoll. "Sex Reannouncement in Hereditary Sex Deformity: Psychology and Sociology of Habilitation." *Social Science and Medicine* 3 (1969):207–216.

Oliven, John F. *Sexual Hygiene and Pathology: A Manual for the Physician.* Philadelphia: J. B. Lippincott Co., 1955.

Ortner, Sherry B. "Is Female to Male as Nature Is to Culture?" In *Woman, Culture, and Society,* ed. Michelle Zimbalist Rosaldo and Louise Lamphere, 67–87. Stanford, Calif.: Stanford University Press, 1974.

Rohatgi, M. "Intersex Disorders: An Approach to Surgical Management." *Indian Journal of Pediatrics* 59 (1992):523–530.

Roslyn, Joel J., Eric W. Fonkalsrud, and Barbara Lippe. "Intersex Disorders in Adolescents and Adults." *The American Journal of Surgery* 146 (July 1983):138–144.

Rubin, Jeffrey, F. J. Provenzano, and Z. Luria. "The Eye of the Beholder: Parents' Views on Sex of Newborns." *American Journal of Orthopsychiatry* 44, no. 4 (1974):512–519.

Slijper, F. M. E., S. L. S. Drop, J. C. Molenaar, and R. J. Scholtmeijer. "Neonates with Abnormal Genital Development Assigned the Female Sex: Parent Counseling." *Journal of Sex Education and Therapy* 20, no. 1 (1994):9–17.

Smith, Richard W. "What Kind of Sex is Natural?" In *The Frontiers of Sex Research,* ed. Vern Bullough, 103–111. Buffalo: Prometheus, 1979.

Stoller, Robert J. *Sex and Gender,* vol. 1. New York: J. Aronson, 1968.

The Social Construction of Black Feminist Thought

PATRICIA HILL COLLINS

Sojourner Truth, Anna Julia Cooper, Ida Wells Barnett, and Fannie Lou Hamer are but a few names from a growing list of distinguished African-American women activists. Although their sustained resistance to Black women's victimization within interlocking systems of race, gender, and class oppression is well known, these women did not act alone.[1] Their actions were nurtured by the support of countless ordinary African-American women who, through strategies of everyday resistance, created a powerful foundation for this more visible Black feminist activist tradition.[2] Such support has been essential to the shape and goals of Black feminist thought.

The long-term and widely shared resistance among African-American women can only have been sustained by an enduring and shared standpoint among Black women about the meaning of oppression and the actions that Black women can and should take to resist it. Efforts to identify the central concepts of this Black women's standpoint figure prominently in the works of contemporary Black feminist intellectuals.[3] Moreover, political and epistemological issues influence the social construction of Black feminist thought. Like other subordinate groups, African-American women not only have developed distinctive interpretations of Black women's oppression but have done so by using alternative ways of producing and validating knowledge itself. . . .

THE CONTOURS OF AN AFROCENTRIC FEMINIST EPISTEMOLOGY

Africanist analyses of the Black experience generally agree on the fundamental elements of an Afrocentric standpoint.

Patricia Hill Collins, "The Social Construction of Black Feminist Thought," from *Signs: Journal of Women in Culture and Society* 14, no.4 (1989): 745–773 (excerpted). Copyright © 1989 by The University of Chicago. Reprinted with the permission of the author and The University of Chicago Press.

In spite of varying histories, Black societies reflect elements of a core African value system that existed prior to and independently of racial oppression.[4] Moreover, as a result of colonialism, imperialism, slavery, apartheid, and other systems of racial domination, Blacks share a common experience of oppression. These similarities in material conditions have fostered shared Afrocentric values that permeate the family structure, religious institutions, culture, and community life of Blacks in varying parts of Africa, the Caribbean, South America, and North America.[5] This Afrocentric consciousness permeates the shared history of people of African descent through the framework of a distinctive Afrocentric epistemology.[6]

Feminist scholars advance a similar argument. They assert that women share a history of patriarchal oppression through the political economy of the material conditions of sexuality and reproduction.[7] These shared material conditions are thought to transcend divisions among women created by race, social class, religion, sexual orientation, and ethnicity and to form the basis of a women's standpoint with its corresponding feminist consciousness and epistemology.[8]

Since Black women have access to both the Afrocentric and the feminist standpoints, an alternative epistemology used to rearticulate a Black women's standpoint reflects elements of both traditions.[9] The search for the distinguishing features of an alternative epistemology used by African-American women reveals that values and ideas that Africanist scholars identify as being characteristically "Black" often bear remarkable resemblance to similar ideas claimed by feminist scholars as being characteristically "female."[10] This similarity suggests that the material conditions of oppression can vary dramatically and yet generate some uniformity in the epistemologies of subordinate groups. Thus, the significance of an Afrocentric feminist epistemology may lie in its enrichment of our understanding of how subordinate groups create knowledge that enables them to resist oppression.

The parallels between the two conceptual schemes raise a question: Is the worldview of women of African descent more intensely infused with the overlapping feminine/Afrocentric standpoints than is the case for either African-American men or white women?[11] While an Afrocentric feminist epistemology reflects elements of epistemologies used by Blacks as a group and women as a group, it also paradoxically demonstrates features that may be unique to Black women. On certain dimensions, Black women may more closely resemble Black men, on others, white women, and on still others, Black women may stand apart from both groups. Black feminist sociologist Deborah K. King describes this phenomenon as a "both/or" orientation, the act of being simultaneously a member of a group and yet standing apart from it. She suggests that multiple realities among Black women yield a "multiple consciousness in Black women's politics" and that this state of belonging yet not belonging forms an integral part of Black women's oppositional consciousness.[12] Bonnie Thornton Dill's analysis of how Black women live with contradictions, a situation she labels the "dialectics of Black womanhood," parallels King's assertions that this "both/or" orientation is central to an Afrocentric feminist consciousness.[13] Rather than emphasizing how a Black women's standpoint and its accompanying epistemology are different than those in Afrocentric and feminist analyses, I use Black women's experiences as a point of contact between the two.

Viewing an Afrocentric feminist epistemology in this way challenges analyses claiming that Black women have a more accurate view of oppression than do other groups. Such approaches suggest that oppression can be quantified and compared and that adding layers of oppression produces a potentially clearer standpoint. While it is tempting to claim that Black women are more oppressed than everyone else and therefore have the best standpoint from which to understand the mechanisms, processes, and effects of oppression, this simply may not be the case.[14]

African-American women do not uniformly share an Afrocentric feminist epistemology since social class introduces variations among Black women in seeing, valuing, and using Afrocentric feminist perspectives. While a Black women's standpoint and its accompanying epistemology stem from Black women's consciousness of race and gender oppression, they are not simply the result of combining Afrocentric and female values—standpoints are rooted in real material conditions structured by social class.[15]

Concrete Experience as a Criterion of Meaning

Carolyn Chase, a thirty-one-year-old inner-city Black woman, notes, "My aunt used to say, 'A heap see, but a few know.' "[16] This saying depicts two types of knowing, knowledge and wisdom, and taps the first dimension of an Afrocentric feminist epistemology. Living life as Black women requires wisdom since knowledge about the dynamics of race, gender, and class subordination has been essential to Black women's survival. African-American women give such wisdom high credence in assessing knowledge.

Allusions to these two types of knowing pervade the words of a range of African-American women. In explaining the tenacity of racism, Zilpha Elaw, a preacher of the mid-1800s, noted: "The pride of a white skin is a bauble of great value with many in some parts of the United States, who readily sacrifice their intelligence to their prejudices, and possess more knowledge than wisdom."[17] In describing differences separating African-American and white women, Nancy White invokes a similar rule: "When you come right down to it, white women just *think* they are free. Black women *know* they ain't free."[18] Geneva Smitherman, a college professor specializing in African-American linguistics, suggests that "from a black perspective, written documents are limited in what they can teach about life and survival in the world. Blacks are quick to ridicule 'educated fools,' . . . they have 'book learning' but no 'mother wit,' knowledge but not wisdom."[19] Mabel Lincoln eloquently summarizes the distinction between knowledge and wisdom: "To black people like me, a fool is funny—you know, people who love to break bad, people you can't tell anything to, folks that would take a shotgun to a roach."[20]

Black women need wisdom to know how to deal with the "educated fools" who would "take a shotgun to a roach." As members of a subordinate group, Black women cannot afford to be fools of any type, for their devalued status denies them the protections that white skin, maleness, and wealth confer. This distinction between knowledge and wisdom, and the use of experience as the cutting edge dividing them, have been key to Black women's survival. In the context of race, gender, and class oppression, the distinction is essential since knowledge without wisdom is adequate for the powerful, but wisdom is essential to the survival of the subordinate.

For ordinary African-American women, those individuals who have lived through the experiences about which they claim to be experts are more believable and credible than those who have merely read or thought about such experiences. Thus, concrete experience as a criterion for credibility frequently is invoked by Black women when making knowledge claims. For instance, Hannah Nelson describes the importance that personal experience has for her: "Our speech is most directly personal, and every black person assumes that every other black person has a right to a personal opinion. In speaking of grave matters, your personal experience is considered very good evidence. With us, distant statistics are certainly not as important as the actual experience of a sober person."[21] Similarly, Ruth Shays uses her concrete experiences to challenge the idea that formal education is the only route to knowledge: "I am the kind of person who doesn't have a lot of education, but both my mother and my father had good common sense. Now, I think that's all you need. I might not know how to use thirty-four words where three would do, but that does not mean that I don't know what I'm talking about . . . I know what I'm talking about because I'm talking about myself. I'm talking about what I have lived."[22] Implicit in Shays's self-assessment is a critique of the type of knowledge that obscures the truth, the "thirty-four words" that cover up a truth that can be expressed in three.

Even after substantial mastery of white masculinist epistemologies, many Black women scholars invoke their own concrete experiences and those of other Black women in selecting topics for investigation and methodologies used. For example, Elsa Barkley Brown subtitles her essay on Black women's history "how my mother taught me to be an historian in spite of my academic training."[23] Similarly, Joyce Ladner maintains that growing up as a Black woman in the South gave her special insights in conducting her study of Black adolescent women.[24]

Henry Mitchell and Nicholas Lewter claim that experience as a criterion of meaning with practical images as its symbolic vehicles is a fundamental epistemological tenet in African-American thought-systems.[25] Stories, narratives, and Bible principles are selected for their applicability to the lived experiences of African-Americans and become symbolic representations of a whole wealth of experience. For example, Bible tales are told for their value to common life, so their interpretation involves no need for scientific historical verification. The narrative method requires that the story be "told, not torn apart in analysis, and trusted as core belief, not admired as science."[26] Any biblical story contains more than characters and a plot—it presents key ethical issues salient in African-American life.

June Jordan's essay about her mother's suicide exemplifies the multiple levels of meaning that can occur when concrete experiences are used as a criterion of meaning.

Jordan describes her mother, a woman who literally died trying to stand up, and the effect that her mother's death had on her own work:

> I think all of this is really about women and work. Certainly this is all about me as a woman and my life work. I mean I am not sure my mother's suicide was something extraordinary. Perhaps most women must deal with a similar inheritance, the legacy of a woman whose death you cannot possibly pinpoint because she died so many, many times and because, even before she became your mother, the life of that woman was taken. . . . I came too late to help my mother to her feet. By way of everlasting thanks to all of the women who have helped me to stay alive I am working never to be late again.[27]

While Jordan has knowledge about the concrete act of her mother's death, she also strives for wisdom concerning the meaning of that death.

Some feminist scholars offer a similar claim that women, as a group, are more likely than men to use concrete knowledge in assessing knowledge claims. For example, a substantial number of the 135 women in a study of women's cognitive development were "connected knowers" and were drawn to the sort of knowledge that emerges from firsthand observation. Such women felt that since knowledge comes from experience, the best way of understanding another person's ideas was to try to share the experiences that led the person to form those ideas. At the heart of the procedures used by connected knowers is the capacity for empathy.[28]

In valuing the concrete, African-American women may be invoking not only an Afrocentric tradition, but a women's tradition as well. Some feminist theorists suggest that women are socialized in complex relational nexuses where contextual rules take priority over abstract principles in governing behavior. This socialization process is thought to stimulate characteristic ways of knowing.[29] For example, Canadian sociologist Dorothy Smith maintains that two modes of knowing exist, one located in the body and the space it occupies and the other passing beyond it. She asserts that women, through their child-rearing and nurturing activities, mediate these two modes and use the concrete experiences of their daily lives to assess more abstract knowledge claims.[30]

Amanda King, a young Black mother, describes how she used the concrete to assess the abstract and points out how difficult mediating these two modes of knowing can be:

WOMANIST

ALICE WALKER

Womanist 1. From *womanish*. (Opp. of "girlish," i.e., frivolous, irresponsible, not serious.) A black feminist or feminist of color. From the black folk expression of mothers to female children, "You acting womanish," i.e., like a woman. Usually referring to outrageous, audacious, courageous or *willful* behavior. Wanting to know more and in greater depth than is considered "good" for one. Interested in grown-up doings. Acting grown up. Being grown up. Interchangeable with another black folk expression: "You trying to be grown." Responsible. In charge. *Serious.*

. . .

2. *Also:* A woman who loves other women, sexually and/or nonsexually. Appreciates and prefers women's

culture, women's emotional flexibility (values tears as natural counterbalance of laughter), and women's strength. Sometimes loves individual men, sexually and/or nonsexually. Committed to survival and wholeness of entire people, male *and* female. Not a separatist, except periodically, for health. Traditionally universalist, as in: "Mama, why are we brown, pink, and yellow, and our cousins are white, beige, and black?" Ans.: "Well, you know the colored race is just like a flower garden, with every color flower represented." Traditionally capable, as in: "Mama, I'm walking to Canada and I'm taking you and a bunch of other slaves with me." Reply: "It wouldn't be the first time."

. . .

3. Loves music. Loves dance. Loves the moon. *Loves* the Spirit. Loves love and food and roundness. Loves struggle. *Loves* the Folk. Loves herself. *Regardless.*

. . .

4. Womanist is to feminist as purple to lavender.

Alice Walker, "Womanist" from *In Search of Our Mothers' Gardens: Womanist Prose*. Copyright © 1983 by Alice Walker. Reprinted with the permission of Harcourt, Inc.

The leaders of the ROC [a labor union] lost their jobs too, but it just seemed like they were used to losing their jobs. . . . This was like a lifelong thing for them, to get out there and protest. They were like, what do you call them—intellectuals. . . . You got the ones that go to the university that are supposed to make all the speeches, they're the ones that are supposed to lead, you know, put this little revolution together, and then you got the little ones . . . that go to the factory every day, they be the ones that have to fight. I had a child and I thought I don't have the time to be running around with these people. . . . I mean I understand some of that stuff they were talking about, like the bourgeoisie, the rich and the poor and all that, but I had surviving on my mind for me and my kid.[31]

For King, abstract ideals of class solidarity were mediated by the concrete experience of motherhood and the connectedness it involved.

In traditional African-American communities, Black women find considerable institutional support for valuing concrete experience. Black extended families and Black churches are two key institutions where Black women experts with concrete knowledge of what it takes to be self-defined Black women share their knowledge with their younger, less experienced sisters. This relationship of sisterhood among Black women can be seen as a model for a whole series of relationships that African-American women have with each other, whether it is networks among women in extended families, among women in the Black church, or among women in the African-American community at large.[32]

Since the Black church and the Black family are both woman-centered and Afrocentric institutions, African-American women traditionally have found considerable institutional support for this dimension of an Afrocentric feminist epistemology in ways that are unique to them. While white women may value the concrete, it is questionable whether white families, particularly middle-class nuclear ones, and white community institutions provide comparable types of support. Similarly, while Black men are supported by Afrocentric institutions, they cannot participate in Black women's sisterhood. In terms of Black women's relationships with one another, then, African-American women may indeed find it easier than others to recognize connectedness as a primary way of knowing, simply because they are encouraged to do so by Black women's tradition of sisterhood.

The Use of Dialogue in Assessing Knowledge Claims

For Black women, new knowledge claims are rarely worked out in isolation from other individuals and are usually developed through dialogues with other members of a community. A primary epistemological assumption underlying the use of dialogue in assessing knowledge claims is that connectedness rather than separation is an essential component of the knowledge-validation process.[33]

The use of dialogue has deep roots in an African-based oral tradition and in African-American culture.[34] Ruth Shays describes the importance of dialogue in the knowledge-validation process of enslaved African-Americans: "They would find a lie if it took them a year . . . the foreparents found the truth because they listened and they made people tell their part many times. Most often you can hear a lie. . . . Those old people was everywhere and knew the truth of many disputes. They believed that a liar should suffer the pain of his lies, and they had all kinds of ways of bringing liars to judgement."[35]

The widespread use of the call and response discourse mode among African-Americans exemplifies the importance placed on dialogue. Composed of spontaneous verbal and nonverbal interaction between speaker and listener in which all of the speaker's statements or "calls" are punctuated by expressions or "responses" from the listener, this Black discourse mode pervades African-American culture. The fundamental requirement of this interactive network is active participation of all individuals.[36] For ideas to be tested and validated, everyone in the group must participate. To refuse to join in, especially if one really disagrees with what has been said, is seen as "cheating."[37]

June Jordan's analysis of Black English points to the significance of this dimension of an alternative epistemology.

Our language is a system constructed by people constantly needing to insist that we exist. . . . Our lan-

guage devolves from a culture that abhors all abstraction, or anything tending to obscure or delete the fact of the human being who is here and now/the truth of the person who is speaking or listening. Consequently, *there is no passive voice construction possible in Black English.* For example, you cannot say, "Black English is being eliminated." You must say, instead, "White people eliminating Black English." The assumption of the presence of life governs all of Black English . . . every sentence assumes the living and active participation of at least two human beings, the speaker and the listener.[38]

Many Black women intellectuals invoke the relationships and connectedness provided by use of dialogue. When asked why she chose the themes she did, novelist Gayle Jones replied: "I was . . . interested . . . in oral traditions of storytelling—Afro-American and others, in which there is always the consciousness and importance of the hearer."[39] In describing the difference in the way male and female writers select significant events and relationships, Jones points out that "with many women writers, relationships within family, community, between men and women, and among women—from slave narratives by black women writers on—are treated as complex and significant relationships, whereas with many men the significant relationships are those that involve confrontations—relationships outside the family and community."[40] Alice Walker's reaction to Zora Neale Hurston's book *Mules and Men* is another example of the use of dialogue in assessing knowledge claims. In *Mules and Men,* Hurston chose not to become a detached observer of the stories and folktales she collected but instead, through extensive dialogues with the people in the communities she studied, placed herself at the center of her analysis. Using a similar process, Walker tests the truth of Hurston's knowledge claims: "When I read *Mules and Men* I was delighted. Here was this perfect book! The 'perfection' of which I immediately tested on my relatives, who are such typical Black Americans they are useful for every sort of political, cultural, or economic survey. Very regular people from the South, rapidly forgetting their Southern cultural inheritance in the suburbs and ghettos of Boston and New York, they sat around reading the book themselves, listening to me read the book, listening to each other read the book, and a kind of paradise was regained."[41]

Their centrality in Black churches and Black extended families provides Black women with a high degree of support from Black institutions for invoking dialogue as a dimension of an Afrocentric feminist epistemology.

However, when African-American women use dialogues in assessing knowledge claims, they might be invoking a particularly female way of knowing as well. Feminist scholars contend that males and females are socialized within their families to seek different types of autonomy, the former based on separation, the latter seeking connectedness, and that this variation in types of autonomy parallels the characteristic differences between male and female ways of knowing.[42] For instance, in contrast to the visual metaphors (such as equating knowledge with illumination, knowing with seeing, and truth with light) that scientists and philosophers typically use, women tend to ground their epistemological premises in metaphors suggesting speaking and listening.[43]

While there are significant differences between the roles Black women play in their families and those played by middle-class white women, Black women clearly are affected by general cultural norms prescribing certain familial roles for women. Thus, in terms of the role of dialogue in an Afrocentric feminist epistemology, Black women may again experience a convergence of the values of the African-American community and woman-centered values.

The Ethic of Caring

"Ole white preachers used to talk wid dey tongues widdout sayin' nothin', but Jesus told us slaves to talk wid our hearts."[44] These words of an ex-slave suggest that ideas cannot be divorced from the individuals who create and share them. This theme of "talking with the heart" taps another dimension of an alternative epistemology used by African-American women, the ethic of caring. Just as the ex-slave used the wisdom in his heart to reject the ideas of the preachers who talked "wid dey tongues widdout sayin' nothin'," the ethic of caring suggests that personal expressiveness, emotions, and empathy are central to the knowledge-validation process.

One of three interrelated components making up the ethic of caring is the emphasis placed on individual uniqueness. Rooted in a tradition of African humanism, each individual is thought to be a unique expression of a common spirit, power, or energy expressed by all life.[45] This belief in individual uniqueness is illustrated by the value placed on personal expressiveness in African-American communities.[46] Johnetta Ray, an inner-city resident, describes this Afrocentric emphasis on individual uniqueness: "No matter how hard we try, I don't think black people will ever develop much of a herd instinct. We are profound individualists with a passion for self-expression."[47]

A second component of the ethic of caring concerns the appropriateness of emotions in dialogues. Emotion indicates that a speaker believes in the validity of an argument.[48] Consider Ntozake Shange's description of one of the goals of her work: "Our [western] society allows people to be absolutely neurotic and totally out of touch with their feelings and everyone else's feelings, and yet be very respectable. This, to me, is a travesty. . . . I'm trying to change the idea of seeing emotions and intellect as distinct faculties."[49] Shange's words echo those of the ex-slave. Both see the denigration of emotion as problematic, and both suggest that expressiveness should be reclaimed and valued.

A third component of the ethic of caring involves developing the capacity for empathy. Harriet Jones, a sixteen-year-old Black woman, explains why she chose to open up to her interviewer: "Some things in my life are so hard for me to bear, and it makes me feel better to know that you feel sorry about those things and would change them if you could."[50]

These three components of the ethic of caring—the value placed on individual expressiveness, the appropriateness of emotions, and the capacity for empathy—pervade African-American culture. One of the best examples of the interactive nature of the importance of dialogue and the ethic of caring in assessing knowledge claims occurs in the use of the call and response discourse mode in traditional Black church services. In such services, both the minister and the congregation routinely use voice rhythm and vocal inflection to convey meaning. The sound of what is being said is just as important as the words themselves in what is, in a sense, a dialogue between reason and emotions. As a result, it is nearly impossible to filter out the strictly linguistic-cognitive abstract meaning from the sociocultural psycho-emotive meaning.[51] While the ideas presented by a speaker must have validity, that is, agree with the general body of knowledge shared by the Black congregation, the group also appraises the way knowledge claims are presented.

There is growing evidence that the ethic of caring may be part of women's experience as well. Certain dimensions of women's ways of knowing bear striking resemblance to Afrocentric expressions of the ethic of caring. Belenky, Clinchy, Goldberger, and Tarule point out that two contrasting epistemological orientations characterize knowing—one, an epistemology of separation based on impersonal procedures for establishing truth, and the other, an epistemology of connection in which truth emerges through care. While these ways of knowing are not gender specific, disproportionate numbers of women rely on connected knowing.[52]

The parallels between Afrocentric expressions of the ethic of caring and those advanced by feminist scholars are noteworthy. The emphasis placed on expressiveness and emotion in African-American communities bears marked resemblance to feminist perspectives on the importance of personality in connected knowing. Separate knowers try to subtract the personality of an individual from his or her ideas because they see personality as biasing those ideas. In contrast, connected knowers see personality as adding to an individual's ideas, and they feel that the personality of each group member enriches a group's understanding.[53] Similarly, the significance of individual uniqueness, personal expressiveness, and empathy in African-American communities resembles the importance that some feminist analyses place on women's "inner voice."[54]

The convergence of Afrocentric and feminist values in the ethic-of-care dimension of an alternative epistemology seems particularly acute. While white women may have access to a women's tradition valuing emotion and expressiveness, few white social institutions except the family validate this way of knowing. In contrast, Black women have long had the support of the Black church, an institution with deep roots in the African past and a philosophy that accepts and encourages expressiveness and an ethic of caring. While Black men share in this Afrocentric tradition, they must resolve the contradictions that distinguish abstract, unemotional Western masculinity from an Afrocentric ethic of caring. The differences among race/gender groups thus hinge on differences in their access to institutional supports valuing one type of knowing over another. Although Black women may be denigrated within white-male-controlled academic institutions, other institutions, such as Black families and churches, which encourage the expression of Black female power, seem to do so by way of their support for an Afrocentric feminist epistemology.

The Ethic of Personal Accountability

An ethic of personal accountability is the final dimension of an alternative epistemology. Not only must individuals develop their knowledge claims through dialogue and present those knowledge claims in a style proving their concern for their ideas, people are expected to be accountable for their knowledge claims. Zilpha Elaw's description of slavery reflects this notion that every idea has an owner and that the owner's identity matters: "Oh, the abominations of slavery! . . . every case of slavery, however lenient its inflictions and mitigated its atrocities, indicates an oppressor, the oppressed, and oppression."[55] For Elaw, abstract

definitions of slavery mesh with the concrete identities of its perpetrators and its victims. Blacks "consider it essential for individuals to have personal positions on issues and assume full responsibility for arguing their validity."[56]

Assessments of an individual's knowledge claims simultaneously evaluate an individual's character, values, and ethics. African-Americans reject Eurocentric masculinist beliefs that probing into an individual's personal viewpoint is outside the boundaries of discussion. Rather, all views expressed and actions taken are thought to derive from a central set of core beliefs that cannot be other than personal.[57] From this perspective, knowledge claims made by individuals respected for their moral and ethical values will carry more weight than those offered by less respected figures.[58]

An example drawn from an undergraduate course composed entirely of Black women, which I taught, might help clarify the uniqueness of this portion of the knowledge-validation process. During one class discussion, I assigned the students the task of critiquing an analysis of Black feminism advanced by a prominent Black male scholar. Instead of dissecting the rationality of the author's thesis, my students demanded facts about the author's personal biography. They were especially interested in concrete details of his life such as his relationships with Black women, his marital status, and his social class background. By requesting data on dimensions of his personal life routinely excluded in positivist approaches to knowledge validation, they were invoking concrete experience as a criterion of meaning. They used this information to assess whether he really cared about his topic and invoked this ethic of caring in advancing their knowledge claims about his work. Furthermore, they refused to evaluate the rationality of his written ideas without some indication of his personal credibility as an ethical human being. The entire exchange could only have occurred as a dialogue among members of a class that had established a solid enough community to invoke an alternative epistemology in assessing knowledge claims.[59]

The ethic of personal accountability is clearly an Afrocentric value, but is it feminist as well? While limited by its attention to middle-class white women, Carol Gilligan's work suggests that there is a female model for moral development where women are more inclined to link morality to responsibility, relationships, and the ability to maintain social ties.[60] If this is the case, then African-American women again experience a convergence of values from Afrocentric and female institutions.

The use of an Afrocentric feminist epistemology in traditional Black church services illustrates the interactive nature of all four dimensions and also serves as a metaphor for the distinguishing features of an Afrocentric feminist way of knowing. The services represent more than dialogues between the rationality used in examining biblical texts/stories and the emotion inherent in the use of reason for this purpose. The rationale for such dialogues addresses the task of examining concrete experiences for the presence of an ethic of caring. Neither emotion nor ethics is subordinated to reason. Instead, emotion, ethics, and reason are used as interconnected, essential components in assessing knowledge claims. In an Afrocentric feminist epistemology, values lie at the heart of the knowledge-validation process such that inquiry always has an ethical aim. . . .

ACKNOWLEDGMENTS

Special thanks go out to the following people for reading various drafts of this manuscript: Evelyn Nakano Glenn, Lynn Weber Cannon, and participants in the 1986 Research Institute, Center for Research on Women, Memphis State University; Elsa Barkley Brown, Deborah K. King, Elizabeth V. Spelman, and Angelene Jamison-Hall; and four anonymous reviewers at *Signs*.

NOTES

1. For analyses of how interlocking systems of oppression affect Black women, see Frances Beale, "Double Jeopardy: To Be Black and Female," in *The Black Woman,* ed. Toni Cade (New York: Signet, 1970); Angela Y. Davis, *Women, Race and Class* (New York: Random House, 1981); Bonnie Thornton Dill, "Race, Class, and Gender: Prospects for an All-Inclusive Sisterhood," *Feminist Studies* 9, no. 1 (1983): 131–50; bell hooks, *Ain't I a Woman? Black Women and Feminism* (Boston: South End Press, 1981); Diane Lewis, "A Response to Inequality: Black Women, Racism, and Sexism," *Signs: Journal of Women in Culture and Society* 3, no. 2 (Winter 1977): 339–61; Pauli Murray, "The Liberation of Black Women," in *Voices of the New Feminism,* ed. Mary Lou Thompson (Boston: Beacon, 1970), 87–102; and the introduction in Filomina Chioma Steady, *The Black Woman Cross-Culturally* (Cambridge, Mass.: Schenkman, 1981), 7–41.

2. See the introduction in Steady (n. 1 above) for an overview of Black women's strengths. This strength-resiliency perspective has greatly influenced empirical work on African-American women. See, e.g., Joyce Ladner's study of low-income Black adolescent girls, *Tomorrow's Tomorrow* (New York: Doubleday, 1971); and Lena Wright Myers's work on Black women's self-concept, *Black Women: Do They Cope Better?* (Englewood Cliffs, N.J.: Prentice-Hall, 1980). For discussions of Black women's resistance, see Elizabeth Fox-Genovese, "Strategies and Forms of Resistance: Focus on Slave Women in the United States," in *In Resistance: Studies in African, Caribbean and Afro-American History,* ed. Gary Y. Okihiro (Amherst, Mass.: University of Massachusetts Press, 1986), 143–65; and Rosalyn Terborg-Penn, "Black Women in Resistance: A Cross-Cultural Perspective," in Okihiro, ed., 188–209. For a comprehensive discussion of everyday resistance, see James C. Scott, *Weapons of the Weak: Everyday Forms of Peasant Resistance* (New Haven, Conn.: Yale University Press, 1985).

3. See Patricia Hill Collins's analysis of the substantive content of Black feminist thought in "Learning from the Outsider Within: The Sociological Significance of Black Feminist Thought," *Social Problems* 33, no. 6 (1986): 14–32.

4. For detailed discussions of the Afrocentric worldview, see John S. Mbiti, *African Religions and Philosophy* (London: Heinemann, 1969); Dominique Zahan, *The Religion, Spirituality, and Thought of Traditional Africa* (Chicago: University of Chicago Press, 1979); and Mechal Sobel, *Trabelin' On: The Slave Journey to an Afro-Baptist Faith* (Westport, Conn.: Greenwood Press, 1979), 1–76.

5. For representative works applying these concepts to African-American culture, see Niara Sudarkasa, "Interpreting the African Heritage in Afro-American Family Organization," in *Black Families,* ed. Harriette Pipes McAdoo (Beverly Hills, Calif.: Sage, 1981); Henry H. Mitchell and Nicholas Cooper Lewter, *Soul Theology: The Heart of American Black Culture* (San Francisco: Harper & Row, 1986); Robert Farris Thompson, *Flash of the Spirit: African and Afro-American Art and Philosophy* (New York: Vintage, 1983); and Ortiz M. Walton, "Comparative Analysis of the African and the Western Aesthetics," in *The Black Aesthetic,* ed. Addison Gayle (Garden City, N.Y.: Doubleday, 1971), 154–64.

6. One of the best discussions of an Afrocentric epistemology is offered by James E. Turner, "Foreword: Africana Studies and Epistemology; a Discourse in the Sociology of Knowledge," in *The*

Next Decade: Theoretical and Research Issues in Africana Studies, ed. James E. Turner (Ithaca, N.Y.: Cornell University Africana Studies and Research Center, 1984), v–xxv. See also Vernon Dixon, "World Views and Research Methodology," summarized in Sandra Harding, *The Science Question in Feminism* (Ithaca, N.Y.: Cornell University Press, 1986), 170.

7. See Hester Eisenstein, *Contemporary Feminist Thought* (Boston: G. K. Hall, 1983). Nancy Hartsock's *Money, Sex, and Power* (Boston: Northeastern University Press, 1983), 145–209, offers a particularly insightful analysis of women's oppression.

8. For discussions of feminist consciousness, see Dorothy Smith, "A Sociology for Women," in *The Prism of Sex: Essays in the Sociology of Knowledge,* ed. Julia A. Sherman and Evelyn T. Beck (Madison: University of Wisconsin Press, 1979); and Michelle Z. Rosaldo, "Women, Culture, and Society: A Theoretical Overview," in *Woman, Culture, and Society,* ed. Michelle Z. Rosaldo and Louise Lamphere (Stanford, Calif.: Stanford University Press, 1974), 17– 42. Feminist epistemologies are surveyed by Alison M. Jaggar, *Feminist Politics and Human Nature* (Totowa, N.J.: Rowan & Allanheld, 1983).

9. One significant difference between Afrocentric and feminist standpoints is that much of what is termed women's culture is, unlike African-American culture, created in the context of and produced by oppression. Those who argue for a women's culture are electing to value, rather than denigrate, those traits associated with females in white patriarchal societies. While this choice is important, it is not the same as identifying an independent, historic culture associated with a society. I am indebted to Deborah K. King for this point.

10. Critiques of the Eurocentric masculinist knowledge-validation process by both Africanist and feminist scholars illustrate this point. What one group labels "white" and "Eurocentric," the other describes as "male-dominated" and "masculinist." Although he does not emphasize its patriarchal and racist features, Morris Berman's *The Reenchantment of the World* (New York: Bantam, 1981) provides a historical discussion of western thought. Afrocentric analyses of this same process can be found in Molefi Kete Asante, "International/Intercultural Relations," in *Contemporary Black Thought,* ed. Molefi Kete Asante and Abdulai S. Vandi (Beverly Hills, Calif.: Sage, 1980), 43–58; and Dona Richards, "European Mythology: The Ideology of 'Progress,' " in Asante and Vandi, eds., 59–79. For feminist analyses, see Hartsock, *Money, Sex, and Power* (n. 7 above). Harding also discusses this similarity (see chap. 7, "Other 'Others' and Fractured Identities: Issues for Epistemologists," 163–96).

11. Harding, 166.

12. Deborah K. King, "Race, Class, and Gender Salience in Black Women's Womanist Consciousness" (Dartmouth College, Department of Sociology, Hanover, N. H., 1987, typescript).

13. Bonnie Thornton Dill, "The Dialectics of Black Womanhood," *Signs* 4, no. 3 (Spring 1979): 543–55.

14. One implication of standpoint approaches is that the more subordinate the group, the purer the vision of the oppressed group. This is an outcome of the origins of standpoint approaches in Marxist social theory, itself a dualistic analysis of social structure. Because such approaches rely on quantifying and ranking human oppressions—familiar tenets of positivist approaches—they are rejected by Blacks and feminists alike. See Harding (n. 6 above) for a discussion of this point. See also Elizabeth V. Spelman's discussion of the fallacy of additive oppression in "Theories of Race and Gender: The Erasure of Black Women," *Quest* 5, no. 4 (1982): 36–62.

15. Class differences among Black women may be marked. For example, see Paula Giddings's analysis in *When and Where I Enter: The Impact of Black Women on Race and Sex in America* (New York: William Morrow, 1984) of the role of social class in shaping Black women's political activism; or Elizabeth Higginbotham's study of the effects of social class in Black women's college attendance in "Race and Class Barriers to Black Women's College Attendance," *Journal of Ethnic Studies* 13, no. 1 (1985): 89–107. Those African-American women who have experienced the greatest degree of convergence of race, class, and gender oppression may be in a better position to recognize and use an alternative epistemology.

16. John Langston Gwaltney, *Drylongso: A Self-Portrait of Black America* (New York: Vintage, 1980), 83.

17. William L. Andrews, *Sisters of the Spirit: Three Black Women's Autobiographies of the Nineteenth Century* (Bloomington: Indiana University Press, 1986), 85.

18. Gwaltney, 147.

19. Geneva Smitherman, *Talkin and Testifyin: The Language of Black America* (Detroit: Wayne State University Press, 1986), 76.

20. Gwaltney, 68.

21. Ibid., 7.

22. Ibid., 27, 33.

23. Elsa Barkley Brown, "Hearing Our Mothers' Lives" (paper presented at the Fifteenth Anniversary Faculty Lecture Series, African-American and African Studies, Emory University, Atlanta, 1986).

24. Ladner (n. 2 above).

25. Mitchell and Lewter (n. 5 above). The use of the narrative approach in African-American theology exemplifies an inductive system of logic alternately called "folk wisdom" or a survival-based, need-oriented method of assessing knowledge claims.

26. Ibid., 8.

27. June Jordan, *On Call: Political Essays* (Boston: South End Press, 1985), 26.

28. Mary Belenky, Blythe Clinchy, Nancy Goldberger, and Jill Tarule, *Women's Ways of Knowing* (New York: Basic, 1986), 113.

29. Hartsock, *Money, Sex and Power* (n. 7 above), 237; and Nancy Chodorow, *The Reproduction of Mothering* (Berkeley and Los Angeles: University of California Press, 1978).

30. Dorothy Smith, *The Everyday World as Problematic* (Boston: Northeastern University Press, 1987).

31. Victoria Byerly, *Hard Times Cotton Mill Girls: Personal Histories of Womanhood and Poverty in the South* (New York: ILR Press, 1986), 198.

32. For Black women's centrality in the family, see Steady (n. 1 above): Ladner (n. 2 above); Brown (n. 23 above); and

McAdoo, ed. (n. 5 above). See Cheryl Townsend Gilkes, " 'Together and in Harness': Women's Traditions in the Sanctified Church," *Signs* 10, no. 4 (Summer 1985): 678–99, for Black women in the church; and chap. 4 of Deborah Gray White, *Ar'n't I a Woman? Female Slaves in the Plantation South* (New York: Norton, 1985). See also Gloria Joseph, "Black Mothers and Daughters: Their Roles and Functions in American Society," in *Common Differences: Conflicts in Black and White Feminist Perspectives,* ed. Gloria Joseph and Jill Lewis (Garden City, N.Y.: Anchor, 1981), 75–126. Even though Black women play essential roles in Black families and Black churches, these institutions are not free from sexism.

33. As Belenky et al. note, "Unlike the eye, the ear requires closeness between subject and object. Unlike seeing, speaking and listening suggest dialogue and interaction" (18).

34. Thomas Kochman, *Black and White: Styles in Conflict* (Chicago: University of Chicago Press, 1981); and Smitherman (n. 19 above).

35. Gwaltney (n. 16 above), 32.

36. Smitherman, 108.

37. Kochman, 28.

38. Jordan (n. 27 above), 129.

39. Claudia Tate, *Black Women Writers at Work* (New York: Continuum, 1983) , 91.

40. Ibid., 92.

41. Alice Walker, *In Search of Our Mothers' Gardens* (New York: Harcourt Brace Jovanovich, 1974), 84.

42. Evelyn Fox Keller, *Reflections on Gender and Science* (New Haven, Conn.: Yale University Press, 1985); Chodorow (n. 29 above).

43. Belenky et al. (n. 28 above), 16.

44. Thomas Webber, *Deep Like the Rivers* (New York: Norton, 1978), 127.

45. In her discussion of the West African Sacred Cosmos, Mechal Sobel (n. 4 above) notes that Nyam, a root word in many West African languages, connotes an enduring spirit, power, or energy possessed by all life. In spite of the pervasiveness of this key concept in African humanism, its definition remains elusive. She points out, "Every individual analyzing the various Sacred Cosmos of West Africa has recognized the reality of this force, but no one has yet adequately translated this concept into Western terms" (13).

46. For discussions of personal expressiveness in African-American culture, see Smitherman (n. 19 above); Kochman (n. 34 above), esp. chap. 9; and Mitchell and Lewter (n. 5 above).

47. Gwaltney (n. 16 above), 228.

48. For feminist analyses of the subordination of emotion in western culture, see Arlie Russell Hochschild, "The Sociology of Feeling and Emotion: Selected Possibilities," in *Another Voice: Feminist Perspectives on Social Life and Social Science,* ed. Marcia Millman and Rosabeth Kanter (Garden City, N.Y.: Anchor, 1975), 280–307; and Chodorow.

49. Tate (n. 39 above), 156.

50. Gwaltney, 11.

51. Smitherman, 135 and 137.

52. Belenky et al. (n. 28 above), 100–130.

53. Ibid., 119.

54. See ibid., 52–75, for a discussion of inner voice and its role in women's cognitive styles. Regarding empathy, Belenky et al. note: "Connected knowers begin with an interest in the facts of other people's lives, but they gradually shift the focus to other people's ways of thinking. . . . It is the form rather than the content of knowing that is central. . . . Connected learners learn through empathy" (115).

55. Andrews (n. 17 above), 98.

56. Kochman (n. 34 above), 20 and 25.

57. Ibid, 23.

58. The sizable proportion of ministers among Black political leaders illustrates the importance of ethics in African-American communities.

59. Belenky et al. discuss a similar situation. They note, "People could critique each other's work in this class and accept each other's criticisms because members of the group shared a similar experience. . . . Authority in connected knowing rests not on power or status or certification but on commonality of experience" (118).

60. Carol Gilligan, *In a Different Voice* (Cambridge, Mass.: Harvard University Press, 1982). Carol Stack critiques Gilligan's model by arguing that African-Americans invoke a model of moral development similar to that used by women (see "The Culture of Gender: Women and Men of Color," *Signs* 11, no. 2 [Winter 1986]: 321–24). Another difficulty with Gilligan's work concerns the homogeneity of the subjects whom she studied.

Subjects of Sex/Gender/Desire

JUDITH BUTLER

One is not born a woman, but rather becomes one.

—Simone de Beauvoir

Strictly speaking, "women" cannot be said to exist.

—Julia Kristeva

Woman does not have a sex.

—Luce Irigaray

The deployment of sexuality . . . established this notion of sex.

—Michel Foucault

The category of sex is the political category that founds society as heterosexual.

—Monique Wittig

"WOMEN" AS THE SUBJECT OF FEMINISM

For the most part, feminist theory has assumed that there is some existing identity, understood through the category of women, who not only initiates feminist interests and goals within discourse, but constitutes the subject for whom political representation is pursued. But *politics* and *representation* are controversial terms. On the one hand, repre-

sentation serves as the operative term within a political process that seeks to extend visibility and legitimacy to women as political subjects; on the other hand, representation is the normative function of a language which is said either to reveal or to distort what is assumed to be true about the category of women. For feminist theory, the development of a language that fully or adequately represents women has seemed necessary to foster the political visibility of women. This has seemed obviously important considering the pervasive cultural condition in which women's lives were either misrepresented or not represented at all.

Recently, this prevailing conception of the relation between feminist theory and politics has come under challenge from within feminist discourse. The very subject of women is no longer understood in stable or abiding terms. There is a great deal of material that not only questions the viability of "the subject" as the ultimate candidate for representation or, indeed, liberation, but there is very little agreement after all on what it is that constitutes, or ought to constitute, the category of women. The domains of political and linguistic "representation" set out in advance the criteria by which subjects themselves are formed, with the result that representation is extended only to what can be acknowledged as a subject. In other words, the qualifications for being a subject must first be met before representation can be extended.

Foucault points out that juridical systems of power *produce* the subjects they subsequently come to represent.[1] Juridical notions of power appear to regulate political life in purely negative terms—that is, through the limitation, prohibition, regulation, control, and even "protection" of individuals related to that political structure through the contingent and retractable operation of choice. But the subjects regulated by such structures are, by virtue of being subjected to them, formed, defined, and reproduced in accordance with the requirements of those structures. If this analysis is right, then the juridical formation of language and politics that represents women as "the subject" of feminism is itself a discursive formation and effect of a given version of representational politics. And the feminist subject turns out to be discursively constituted by the very political system that is supposed to facilitate its emancipation. This becomes politically problematic if that system can be shown to produce gendered subjects along a differential axis of domination or to produce subjects who are presumed to be masculine. In such cases, an uncritical appeal to such a system for the emancipation of "women" will be clearly self-defeating.

The question of "the subject" is crucial for politics, and for feminist politics in particular, because juridical subjects are invariably produced through certain exclusionary practices that do not "show" once the juridical structure of politics has been established. In other words, the political construction of the subject proceeds with certain legitimating and exclusionary aims, and these political operations are effectively concealed and naturalized by a political analysis that takes juridical structures as their foundation. Juridical power inevitably "produces" what it claims merely to represent; hence, politics must be concerned with this dual function of power: the juridical and the productive. In effect, the law produces and then conceals the notion of "a subject before the law"[2] in order to invoke that discursive formation as a naturalized foundational premise that subsequently legitimates that law's own regulatory hegemony. It is not enough to inquire into how women might become more fully represented in language and politics. Feminist critique ought also to understand how the category of "women," the subject of feminism, is produced and restrained by the very structures of power through which emancipation is sought.

Indeed, the question of women as the subject of feminism raises the possibility that there may not be a subject who stands "before" the law, awaiting representation in or by the law. Perhaps the subject, as well as the invocation of a temporal "before," is constituted by the law as the fictive foundation of its own claim to legitimacy. The prevailing assumption of the ontological integrity of the subject before the law might be understood as the contemporary trace of the state of nature hypothesis, that foundationalist fable constitutive of the juridical structures of classical liberalism. The performative invocation of a nonhistorical "before" becomes the foundational premise that guarantees a presocial ontology of persons who freely consent to be governed and, thereby, constitute the legitimacy of the social contract.

Apart from the foundationalist fictions that support the notion of the subject, however, there is the political prob-

lem that feminism encounters in the assumption that the term *women* denotes a common identity. Rather than a stable signifier that commands the assent of those whom it purports to describe and represent, *women,* even in the plural, has become a troublesome term, a site of contest, a cause for anxiety. As Denise Riley's title suggests, *Am I That Name?* is a question produced by the very possibility of the name's multiple significations.[3] If one "is" a woman, that is surely not all one is; the term fails to be exhaustive, not because a pregendered "person" transcends the specific paraphernalia of its gender, but because gender is not always constituted coherently or consistently in different historical contexts, and because gender intersects with racial, class, ethnic, sexual, and regional modalities of discursively constituted identities. As a result, it becomes impossible to separate out "gender" from the political and cultural intersections in which it is invariably produced and maintained.

The political assumption that there must be a universal basis for feminism, one which must be found in an identity assumed to exist cross-culturally, often accompanies the notion that the oppression of women has some singular form discernible in the universal or hegemonic structure of patriarchy or masculine domination. The notion of a universal patriarchy has been widely criticized in recent years for its failure to account for the workings of gender oppression in the concrete cultural contexts in which it exists. Where those various contexts have been consulted within such theories, it has been to find "examples" or "illustrations" of a universal principle that is assumed from the start. That form of feminist theorizing has come under criticism for its efforts to colonize and appropriate nonwestern cultures to support highly western notions of oppression, but because they tend as well to construct a "Third World" or even an "Orient" in which gender oppression is subtly explained as symptomatic of an essential, nonwestern barbarism. The urgency of feminism to establish a universal status for patriarchy in order to strengthen the appearance of feminism's own claims to be representative has occasionally motivated the shortcut to a categorial or fictive universality of the structure of domination, held to produce women's common subjugated experience.

Although the claim of universal patriarchy no longer enjoys the kind of credibility it once did, the notion of a generally shared conception of "women," the corollary to that framework, has been much more difficult to displace. Certainly, there have been plenty of debates: Is there some commonality among "women" that preexists their oppression, or do "women" have a bond by virtue of their oppression alone? Is there a specificity to women's cultures that is independent of their subordination by hegemonic, masculinist cultures? Are the specificity and integrity of women's cultural or linguistic practices always specified against and, hence, within the terms of some more dominant cultural formation? If there is a region of the "specifically feminine," one that is both differentiated from the masculine as such and recognizable in its difference by an unmarked and, hence, presumed universality of "women"? The masculine/feminine binary constitutes not only the exclusive framework in which that specificity can be recognized, but in every other way the "specificity" of the feminine is once again fully decontextualized and separated off analytically and politically from the constitution of class, race, ethnicity, and other axes of power relations that both constitute "identity" and make the singular notion of identity a misnomer.[4]

My suggestion is that the presumed universality and unity of the subject of feminism are effectively undermined by the constraints of the representational discourse in which it functions. Indeed, the premature insistence on a stable subject of feminism, understood as a seamless category of women, inevitably generates multiple refusals to accept the category. These domains of exclusion reveal the coercive and regulatory consequences of that construction, even when the construction has been elaborated for emancipatory purposes. Indeed, the fragmentation within feminism and the paradoxical opposition to feminism from "women" whom feminism claims to represent suggest the necessary limits of identity politics. The suggestion that feminism can seek wider representation for a subject that it itself constructs has the ironic consequence that feminist goals risk failure by refusing to take account of the constitutive powers of their own representational claims. This problem is not ameliorated through an appeal to the category of women for merely "strategic" purposes, for strategies always have meanings that exceed the purposes for which they are intended. In this case, exclusion itself might qualify as such an unintended yet consequential meaning. By conforming to a requirement of representational politics that feminism articulate a stable subject, feminism thus opens itself to charges of gross misrepresentation.

Obviously, the political task is not to refuse representational politics—as if we could. The juridical structures of language and politics constitute the contemporary field of power; hence, there is no position outside this field, but only a critical genealogy of its own legitimating practices. As such, the critical point of departure is *the historical present,* as Marx put it. And the task is to formulate within this constituted frame a critique of the categories of identity that contemporary juridical structures engender, naturalize, and immobilize.

Perhaps there is an opportunity at this juncture of cultural politics, a period that some would call "postfeminist," to reflect from within a feminist perspective on the injunction to construct a subject of feminism. Within feminist political practice, a radical rethinking of the ontological constructions of identity appears to be necessary in order to formulate a representational politics that might revive feminism on other grounds. On the other hand, it may be time to entertain a radical critique that seeks to free feminist theory from the necessity of having to construct a single or abiding ground which is invariably contested by those identity positions or anti-identity positions that it invariably excludes. Do the exclusionary practices that ground feminist theory in a notion of "women" as subject paradoxically undercut feminist goals to extend its claims to "representation."[5]

Perhaps the problem is even more serious. Is the construction of the category of women as a coherent and stable subject an unwitting regulation and reification of gender relations? And is not such a reification precisely contrary to feminist aims?

To what extent does the category of women achieve stability and coherence only in the context of the heterosexual matrix?[6] If a stable notion of gender no longer proves to be the foundational premise of feminist politics, perhaps a new sort of feminist politics is now desirable to contest the very reifications of gender and identity, one that will take the variable construction of identity as both a methodological and normative prerequisite, if not a political goal.

To trace the political operations that produce and conceal what qualifies as the juridical subject of feminism is precisely the task of a *feminist genealogy* of the category of women. In the course of this effort to question "women" as the subject of feminism, the unproblematic invocation of that category may prove to *preclude* the possibility of feminism as a representational politics. What sense does it make to extend representation to subjects who are constructed through the exclusion of those who fail to conform to unspoken normative requirements of the subject? What relations of domination and exclusion are inadvertently sustained when representation becomes the sole focus of politics? The identity of the feminist subject ought not to be the foundation of feminist politics, if the formation of the subject takes place within a field of power regularly buried through the assertion of that foundation. Perhaps, paradoxically, "representation" will be shown to make sense for feminism only when the subject of "women" is nowhere presumed.

THE COMPULSORY ORDER OF SEX/GENDER/DESIRE

Although the unproblematic unity of "women" is often invoked to construct a solidarity of identity, a split is introduced in the feminist subject by the distinction between sex and gender. Originally intended to dispute the biology-is-destiny formulation, the distinction between sex and gender serves the argument that whatever biological intractability sex appears to have, gender is culturally constructed: hence, gender is neither the causal result of sex nor as seemingly fixed as sex. The unity of the subject is thus already potentially contested by the distinction that permits gender as a multiple interpretation of sex.[7]

If gender is the cultural meanings that the sexed body assumes, then a gender cannot be said to follow from a sex in any one way. Taken to its logical limit, the sex/gender distinction suggests a radical discontinuity between sexed bodies and culturally constructed genders. Assuming for the moment the stability of binary sex, it does not follow that the construction of "men" will accrue exclusively to the bodies of males or that "women" will interpret only female bodies. Further, even if the sexes appear to be unproblematically binary in their morphology and constitution (which will become a question), there is no reason to assume that genders ought also to remain as two.[8] The presumption of a binary gender system implicitly retains the belief in a mimetic relation of gender to sex whereby gender mirrors sex or is otherwise restricted by it. When the constructed status of gender is theorized as radically independent of sex, gender itself becomes a free-floating artifice, with the consequence that *man* and *masculine* might just as easily signify a female body as a male one, and *woman* and *feminine* a male body as easily as a female one.

This radical splitting of the gendered subject poses yet another set of problems. Can we refer to a "given" sex or a "given" gender without first inquiring into how sex and/or gender is given, through what means? And what is "sex" anyway? Is it natural, anatomical, chromosomal, or hormonal, and how is a feminist critic to assess the scientific discourses which purport to establish such "facts" for us?[9] Does sex have a history?[10] Does each sex have a different history, or histories? Is there a history of how the duality of sex was established, a genealogy that might expose the binary options as a variable construction? Are the ostensibly natural facts of sex discursively produced by various scientific discourses in the service of other political and social interests? If the immutable character of sex is contested, perhaps this construct called "sex" is as culturally constructed as gender; indeed, perhaps it was always already gender, with the consequence that the distinction between sex and gender turns out to be no distinction at all.[11]

It would make no sense, then, to define gender as the cultural interpretation of sex, if sex itself is a gendered category. Gender ought not to be conceived merely as the cultural inscription of meaning on a pre-given sex (a juridical conception); gender must also designate the very apparatus of production whereby the sexes themselves are established. As a result, gender is not to culture as sex is to nature; gender is also the discursive/cultural means by which "sexed nature" or "a natural sex" is produced and established as "prediscursive," prior to culture, a politically neutral surface *on which* culture acts. It is already clear that one way the internal stability and binary frame for sex are effectively secured is by casting the duality of sex in a prediscursive domain. This production of sex *as* the prediscursive ought to be understood, however, as the effect of the apparatus of cultural construction designed by *gender*. How, then, does gender need to be reformulated to encompass the power relations that produce the effect of a prediscursive sex and so conceal that very operation of discursive production?

GENDER: THE CIRCULAR RUINS OF CONTEMPORARY DEBATE

Is there "a" gender which persons are said *to have,* or is it an essential attribute that a person is said *to be,* as implied in the question 'What gender are you?'? When feminist theorists claim that gender is the cultural interpretation of sex or that gender is culturally constructed, what is the manner or mechanism of this construction? If gender is constructed, could it be constructed differently, or does its constructedness imply some form of social determinism, foreclosing the possibility of agency and transformation? Does 'construction' suggest that certain laws generate gender differences along universal axes of sexual difference? How and where does the construction of gender take place? What sense can we make of a construction that cannot assume a human constructor prior to that construction? On some accounts, the notion that gender is constructed suggests a certain determinism of gender meanings inscribed on anatomically differentiated bodies, where those bodies are understood as passive recipients of an inexorable cultural law. When the relevant "culture" that "constructs" gender is understood in terms of such a law or set of laws, then it seems that gender is as determined and fixed as it was under the biology-is-destiny formulation. In such a case, not biology, but culture, becomes destiny.

On the other hand, Simone de Beauvoir suggests in *The Second Sex* that "one is not born a woman, but rather, becomes one."[12] For de Beauvoir, gender is "constructed," but implied in her formulation is an agent, a *cogito,* who somehow takes on or appropriates that gender and could, in principle, take on some other gender. Is gender as variable and volitional as de Beauvoir's account seems to suggest? Can "construction" in such a case be reduced to a form of choice? De Beauvoir is clear that one "becomes" a woman, but always under a cultural compulsion to become one. And clearly, the compulsion does not come from "sex." There is nothing in her account that guarantees that the "one" who becomes a woman is necessarily female. It "the body is a situation,"[13] as she claims, there is no recourse to a body that has not always already been interpreted by cultural meanings; hence, sex could not qualify as a prediscursive anatomical facticity. Indeed, sex, by definition, will be shown to have been gender all along.[14]

The controversy over the meaning of *construction* appears to founder on the conventional philosophical polarity between free will and determinism. As a consequence, one might reasonably suspect that some common linguistic restriction on thought both forms and limits the terms of the debate. Within those terms, "the body" appears as a passive medium on which cultural meanings are inscribed or as the instrument through which an appropriative and interpretive will determines a cultural meaning for itself. In either case, the body figures as a mere *instrument* or *medium* for which a set of cultural meanings are only externally related. But "the body" is itself a construction, as are the myriad "bodies" that constitute the domain of gendered subjects. Bodies cannot be said to have a signifiable existence prior to the mark of their gender; the question then emerges: To what extent does the body *come into being* in and through the mark(s) of gender? How do we reconceive the body no longer as a passive medium or instrument awaiting the enlivening capacity of a distinctly immaterial will?[15]

Whether gender or sex is fixed or free is a function of a discourse which, it will be suggested, seeks to set certain limits to analysis or to safeguard certain nets of humanism as presuppositional to any analysis of gender. The locus of intractability, whether in "sex" or "gender" or in the very meaning of "construction," provides a clue to what cultural possibilities can and cannot become mobilized through any further analysis. The limits of the discursive analysis of gender presuppose and preempt the possibilities of imaginable and realizable gender configurations within culture.

This is not to say that any and all gendered possibilities are open, but that the boundaries of analysis suggest the limits of a discursively conditioned experience. These limits are always set within the terms of a hegemonic cultural discourse predicated on binary structures that appear as the language of universal rationality. Constraint is thus built into what that language constitutes as the imaginable domain of gender.

Although social scientists refer to gender as a "factor" or a "dimension" of an analysis, it is also applied to embodied persons as "a mark" of biological, linguistic, and/or cultural difference. In these latter cases, gender can be understood as a signification that an (already) sexually differentiated body assumes, but even then that signification exists only *in relation* to another, opposing signification. Some feminist theorists claim that gender is "a relation," indeed, a set of relations, and not an individual attribute. Others, following de Beauvoir, would argue that only the feminine gender is marked, that the universal person and the masculine gender are conflated, thereby defining women in terms of their sex and extolling men as the bearers of a body-transcendent universal personhood. . . .

THEORIZING THE BINARY, THE UNITARY, AND BEYOND

Is it possible to identify a monolithic as well as a monologic masculinist economy that traverses the array of cultural and historical contexts in which sexual difference takes place? Is the failure to acknowledge the specific cultural operations of gender oppression itself a kind of epistemological imperialism, one which is not ameliorated by the simple elaboration of cultural differences as "examples" of the selfsame phallogocentrism? The effort to *include* "Other" cultures as variegated amplifications of a global phallogocentrism constitutes an appropriative act that risks a repetition of the self-aggrandizing gesture of phallogocentrism, colonizing under the sign of the same those differences that might otherwise call that totalizing concept into question.[16]

Feminist critique ought to explore the totalizing claims of a masculinist signifying economy, but also remain self-critical with respect to the totalizing gestures of feminism. The effort to identify the enemy as singular in form is a reverse-discourse that uncritically mimics the strategy of the oppressor instead of offering a different set of terms. That the tactic can operate in feminist and antifeminist contexts alike suggests that the colonizing gesture is not primarily or irreducibly masculinist. It can operate to affect other relations of racial, class, and heterosexist subordination, to name but a few. And clearly, listing the varieties of oppression, as I began to do, assumes their discrete, sequential coexistence along a horizontal axis that does not describe their convergences within the social field. A vertical model is similarly insufficient; oppressions cannot be summarily ranked, causally related, distributed among planes of "originality" and "derivativeness."[17] Indeed, the field of power structured in part by the imperializing gesture of dialectical appropriation exceeds and encompasses the axis of sexual difference, offering a mapping of intersecting differentials which cannot be summarily hierarchized within the terms of either phallogocentrism or any other candidate for the position of "primary condition of oppression." Rather than an exclusive tactic of masculinist signifying economies, dialectical appropriation and suppression of the Other is one tactic among many, deployed centrally but not exclusively in the service of expanding and rationalizing the masculinist domain.

The contemporary feminist debates over essentialism raise the question of the universality of female identity and masculinist oppression in other ways. Universalistic claims are based on a common or shared epistemological standpoint, understood as the articulated consciousness or shared structures of oppression or in the ostensibly transcultural structures of femininity, maternity, sexuality, and/or *écriture feminine*. The opening discussion in this chapter argued that this globalizing gesture has spawned a number of criticisms from women who claim that the category of "women" is normative and exclusionary and is invoked with the unmarked dimensions of class and racial privilege intact. In other words, the insistence upon the coherence and unity of the category of women has effectively refused the multiplicity of cultural, social, and political intersections in which the concrete array of "women" is constructed.

Some efforts have been made to formulate coalitional politics which do not assume in advance what the content of "women" will be. They propose instead a set of dialogic encounters by which variously positioned women articulate separate identities within the framework of an emergent coalition. Clearly, the value of coalitional politics is not to be underestimated, but the very form of coalition of an emerging and unpredictable assemblage of positions, cannot be figured in advance. Despite the clearly democratizing impulse that motivates coalition building, the coalitional theorist can inadvertently reinsert herself as sovereign of the process by trying to assert an ideal form for coalitional structures *in advance*, one that will effectively guarantee unity as the outcome. Related efforts to determine what is and is not the true shape of a dialogue, what constitutes a subject-position, and, most importantly, when "unity" has been reached, can impede the self-shaping and self-limiting dynamics of coalition.

The insistence in advance on coalitional "unity" as a goal assumes that solidarity, whatever its price, is a prerequisite for political action. But what sort of politics demands that kind of advance purchase on unity? Perhaps a coalition needs to acknowledge its contradictions and take action with those contradictions intact. Perhaps also part of what dialogic understanding entails is the acceptance of divergence, breakage, splinter, and fragmentation as part of the often tortuous process of democratization. The very notion of "dialogue" is culturally specific and historically bound, and while one speaker may feel secure that a conversation is happening, another may be sure it is not. The power relations that condition and limit dialogic possibilities need first to be interrogated. Otherwise, the model of dialogue risks relapsing into a liberal model that assumes that speaking agents occupy equal positions of power and speak with the same presuppositions about what constitutes "agreement" and "unity" and, indeed, that those are the goals to be sought. It would be wrong to assume in advance that there is a category of "women" that simply needs to be filled in with various components of race, class, age, ethnicity, and sexuality in order to become complete. The assumption of its essential incompleteness permits that category to serve as a permanently available site of contested meanings. The definitional incompleteness of the category might then serve as a normative ideal relieved of coercive force.

Is "unity" necessary for effective political action? Is the premature insistence on the goal of unity precisely the cause of an ever more bitter fragmentation among the ranks? Certain forms of acknowledged fragmentation might facilitate coalitional action precisely because the "unity" of the category of women is neither presupposed nor desired. Does "unity" set up an exclusionary norm of solidarity at the level of identity that rules out the possibility of a set of actions which disrupt the very borders of identity concepts, or which seek to accomplish precisely that disruption as an explicit political aim? Without the presupposition or goal of "unity," which is, in either case, always instituted at a conceptual level, provisional unities might emerge in the context of concrete actions that have purposes other than the articulation of identity. Without the compulsory expectation that feminist actions must be instituted from some stable, unified, and agreed-upon identity, those actions might well get a quicker start and seem more congenial to a number of "women" for whom the meaning of the category is permanently moot.

This antifoundationalist approach to coalitional politics assumes neither that "identity" is a premise nor that the shape or meaning of a coalitional assemblage can be known prior to its achievement. Because the articulation of an identity within available cultural terms instates a definition that forecloses in advance the emergence of new identity concepts in and through politically engaged actions, the foundationalist tactic cannot take the transformation or expansion of existing identity concepts as a normative goal. Moreover, when agreed-upon identities or agreed-upon dialogic structures, through which already established identities are communicated, no longer constitute the theme or

subject of politics, then identities can come into being and dissolve depending on the concrete practices that constitute them. Certain political practices institute identities on a contingent basis in order to accomplish whatever aims are in view. Coalitional politics requires neither an expanded category of "women" nor an internally multiplicitous self that offers its complexity at once.

Gender is a complexity whose totality is permanently deferred, never fully what it is at any given juncture in time. An open coalition, then, will affirm identities that are alternately instituted and relinquished according to the purposes at hand; it will be an open assemblage that permits multiple convergences and divergences without obedience to a normative telos of definitional closure.

NOTES

1. See Michel Foucault, "Right of Death and Power over Life," in *The History of Sexuality,* vol. I, *An Introduction,* trans. Robert Hurley (New York: Vintage, 1980), originally published as *Histoire de la sexualité I: La volonté de savoir* (Paris: Gallimard, 1978). In that final chapter, Foucault discusses the relation between the juridical and productive law. His notion of the productivity of the law is clearly derived from Nietzsche, although not identical with Nietzsche's will-to-power. The use of Foucault's notion of productive power is not meant as a simple-minded "application" of Foucault to gender issues. The consideration of sexual difference within the terms of Foucault's own work reveals central contradictions in his theory.

2. References throughout this work to a subject before the law are extrapolations of Derrida's reading of Kafka's parable "Before the Law" in *Kafka and the Contemporary Critical Performance: "Centenary Readings,* ed. Alan Udoff (Bloomington: Indiana University Press, 1987).

3. See Denise Riley, *Am I That Name?: Feminism and the Category of "Women" in History* (New York: Macmillan, 1988).

4. See Sandra Harding, "The Instability of the Analytical Categories of Feminist Theory," in *Sex and Scientific Inquiry,* eds. Sandra Harding and Jean F. O'Barr (Chicago: University of Chicago Press, 1987), 283–302.

5. I am reminded of the ambiguity inherent in Nancy Cott's title, *The Grounding of Modern Feminism* (New Haven: Yale University Press, 1987). She argues that the early-twentieth-century US feminist movement sought to "ground" itself in a program that eventually "grounded" that movement. Her historical thesis implicitly raises the question of whether uncritically accepted foundations operate like the "return of the repressed": based on exclusionary practices, the stable political identities that found political movements may invariably become threatened by the very instability that the foundationalist move creates.

6. I use the term *heterosexual matrix* throughout the text to designate that grid of cultural intelligibility through which bodies, genders, and desires are naturalized. I am drawing from Monique Wittig's notion of the "heterosexual contract" and, to a lesser extent, on Adrienne Rich's notion of "compulsory heterosexuality" to characterize a hegemonic discursive/epistemic model of gender intelligibility that assumes that for bodies to cohere and make sense there must be a stable sex expressed through a stable gender (masculine expresses male, feminine expresses female) that is oppositionally and hierarchically defined through the compulsory practice of heterosexuality.

7. For a discussion of the sex/gender distinction in structuralist anthropology and feminist appropriations and criticisms of that formulation, see chapter 2. section i, "Structuralism's Critical Exchange," in my *Gender Trouble: Feminism and the Subversion of Identity* (Routledge, 1990).

8. For an interesting study of the *berdache* and multiple-gender arrangements in Native American cultures, see Walter L. Williams, *The Spirit and the Flesh. Sexual Diversity in American Indian Culture* (Boston: Beacon Press, 1988). See also Sherry B. Ortner and Harriet Whitehead, eds., *Sexual Meanings: The Cultural Construction of Sexuality* (New York: Cambridge University Press, 1981). For a politically sensitive and provocative analysis of the *berdache,* transsexuals, and the contingency of gender dichotomies, see Suzanne J. Kessler and Wendy McKenna, *Gender: An Ethnomethodological Approach* (Chicago: University of Chicago Press, 1978).

9. A great deal of feminist research has been conducted within the fields of biology and the history of science that assesses the political interests inherent in the various discriminatory procedures that establish the scientific basis for sex. See Ruth Hubbard and Marian Lowe, eds., *Genes and Gender,* 1 and 2 (New York: Gordian Press, 1978, 1979); the two issues on feminism and sci-

ence of *Hypatia: A Journal of Feminist Philosophy,* 2/3 (Fall 1987), and 3/1 (Spring 1988), and especially The Biology and Gender Study Group, "The Importance of Feminist Critique for Contemporary Cell Biology," (Spring 1988); Sandra Harding, *The Science Question in Feminism* (Ithaca: Cornell University Press, 1986); Evelyn Fox-Keller, *Reflections on Gender and Science* (New Haven: Yale University Press, 1984); Donna Haraway, "In the Beginning was the Word: The Genesis of Biological Theory," *Signs: Journal of Women in Culture and Society,* 6/3 (1981); Donna Haraway, *Primate Visions* (New York: Routledge, 1989); Sandra Harding and Jean F. O'Barr, *Sex and Scientific Inquiry* (Chicago: University of Chicago Press, 1987); Anne Fausto-Sterling, *Myths of Gender: Biological Theories About Women and Men* (New York: Norton, 1979).

10. Clearly Foucault's *History of Sexuality* offers one way to rethink the history of "sex" within a given modern Eurocentric context. For a more detailed consideration see Thomas Lacquer and Catherine Gallagher, eds., *The Making of the Modern Body: Sexuality and Society in the 19th Century* (Berkeley: University of California Press, 1987), originally published as an issue of *Representations,* 14 (Spring 1986).

11. See my "Variations on Sex and Gender: Beauvoir, Wittig, Foucault," in *Feminism as Critique,* eds. Seyla Benhabib and Drucilla Cornell (Basil Blackwell, dist. by University of Minnesota Press, 1987).

12. Simone de Beauvoir, *The Second Sex,* trans. E. M. Parshley (New York: Vintage, 1973), 301.

13. Ibid. 38.

14. See my "Sex and Gender in de Beauvoir's *Second Sex,*" *Yale French Studies, Simone de Beauvoir: Witness to a Century,* 72 (Winter 1986).

15. Note the extent to which phenomenological theories such as Sartre's, Merleau Ponty's, and de Beauvoir's tend to use the term *embodiment.* Drawn as it is from theological contexts, the term tends to figure "the" body as a mode of incarnation, and hence to preserve the external and dualistic relationship between a signifying immateriality and the materiality of the body itself.

16. Gayatri Spivak most pointedly elaborates this particular kind of binary explanation as a colonizing act of marginalization. In a critique of the "self-presence of the cognizing supra-historical self," which is characteristic of the epistemic imperialism of the philosophical cogito, she locates politics in the production of knowledge that creates and censors the margins that constitute, through exclusion, the contingent intelligibility of that subject's given knowledge-regime: "I call ` politics as such' the prohibition of marginality that is implicit in the production of any explanation. From that point of view, the choice of particular binary oppositions . . . is no mere intellectual strategy. It is, in each case, the condition of the possibility for centralization (with appropriate apologies) and, correspondingly, marginalization." Gayatri Chakravorty Spivak, "Explanation and Culture: Marginalia," in *In Other Worlds: Essays in Cultural Politics* (New York: Routledge, 1987), 113.

17. See the argument against "ranking oppressions" in Cherrie Moraga, "La Güera," in *This Bridge Called My Back: Writings of Radical Women of Color,* eds. Gloria Anzaldua and Cherrie Moraga (New York: Kitchen Table, Women of Color Press, 1982).

PART TWO

Gender, Culture, and Socialization

Everyone is born into a *culture*—a set of shared ideas about the nature of reality, standards of right and wrong, and concepts for making sense of social interactions. These ideas are put into practice in behaviors and material objects. As totally dependent infants we are *socialized*—taught the rules, roles, and relationships of the social world we will inherit. In the process of growing up, we learn to think, act, and feel as we are "supposed to." As adults, we are embedded in our culture's assumptions and images of gender.

One of the earliest and most deeply seated ideas to which we are socialized is that of gender identity: the idea that "I am a boy" or "I am a girl." Because the culture promotes strong ideas about what boys and girls are like, we learn to think of ourselves in terms of our gender identity (our "boyness" or "girlness") and adopt behaviors that are sex-assigned in our culture. Thus, for example, a girl who plays quietly with dolls is viewed as behaving in a feminine or "ladylike" manner and a boy who plays with trucks is seen as appropriately masculine, "all boy." Consciously or unconsciously, adults and peers categorize children as boys or girls, respond to and regard them differently, and encourage them to adopt behaviors and attitudes on the basis of their sex. We raise, in effect, two different kinds of children: girls and boys.

Parents are strong socializing influences, and they provide the first and most deeply experienced socialization. Despite claims to the contrary, American parents treat girls and boys differently. Boys and girls have different toys, names, and room decor and are played with in different ways. Even the stores in which parents shop for children's toys or clothing have separate aisles for boys' and girls' items. Even if parents monitor their actions in the hope of preventing sexism from affecting their child, other socializing influences—peers, schools, mass media— bear down on the child.

One of the primary socializing influences is *language*. When we learn to talk we also learn the thought patterns and communication styles of our culture. Those patterns and styles reinforce differentiation by sex and perpetuate sex stereotyping, although the kind of stereotyping may vary from language to language. All languages teach their cultures' ideas about men and women. They do it "naturally": as one learns a language, one learns the viewpoint of one's culture.

In the English language, for example, the generic *man* is supposed to include males and females, as well as people of all races and ethnicities; but in linguistic practice it does not. People other than white and male are linguistically tagged in writing and in speech. For example, occupational categories are sex- or race-tagged if the person's sex or race does not fit cultural stereotypes about who will be in those occupations. Consider: doctor/woman doctor/ Black woman doctor; nurse/male nurse/ Asian male nurse. Linguistic tags teach normative expectations about who should occupy particular positions in society and about the normalcy or legitimacy of white men's claim to powerful positions.

As societies become more complex, increasingly the mass media have become centralized agents that transmit dominant cultural beliefs. Movements toward cultural heterogeneity are thwarted through the homogenizing effects of television in particular. TV presents sex stereotypes in their purest and simplest forms. Whether the program is about African-American families, lawyers at work, white teenagers, or talking animals, the stereotyping messages about sex and race are endlessly repetitive. Children in the United States spend more time watching television than they spend in school or interacting with parents or peers. Moreover, they believe that what they see on television is an accurate representation of how the world is and should be organized. White middle-class male dominance and sexualized, passive femininity are the repetitive themes.

The socialization effected by the family, language, and the mass media is continued in the educational system. Schools are formally charged with teaching the young. While teaching them reading, writing, and arithmetic, however, the schools also teach the conventional views of gender. They do so through the pattern of staffing (male principals and custodians, female teachers and food servers), curriculum, the sex segregation of sports and activities, and different expectations for boys and girls. Children themselves reinforce these messages through sex-segregated play and teasing of children who do not conform.

Socialization—whether through the home, the school, language, or the mass media—creates and sustains gender differences. Boys are taught that they will inherit the privileges and prestige of manhood, and that they must be tough, aggressive, and interested in trucks, airplanes, and sports. Girls, in contrast, learn that they are less socially valuable than boys and that they should be quiet, pretty, and interested in dolls, fashion, and boys. Subcultures that promote values and beliefs different from the mainstream do exist, and individuals do not necessarily internalize every message from the dominant culture. Nevertheless, traditional cultural views of gender are ubiquitous and powerful.

Through powerful social institutions, then, children and adults learn and consume a culture. Our culture views men and masculinity as superior to women and femininity. It is a system that assigns different behaviors and attitudes to males and females and that further distinguishes between people of different racial and ethnic groups. As adults we continue to be shaped by the books we read, the movies we see, and the people we spend time with. The ways that gender is portrayed or represented in the culture—in mass media, schools, public discussions— provide us with our only conceptual tools for thinking about men and women. It becomes nearly impossible to think about gender without having our thoughts shaped by the images that surround us.

The readings in this part of *Feminist Frontiers V* illustrate and explain different aspects of cultural constructions of gender and the socialization process. These systems of meaning shape how we understand ourselves and the social institutions that form our society. The readings document both the prevalence of conventional understanding in the culture and the presence of alternative messages. As you read, consider what kinds of influences conventional representations of gender have and what sources exist for challenging these images.

Representation, Language, and Culture

Images of gender are pervasive in our lives. In our language, mass media, and daily lives, we encounter particular images of what it means to be a woman or a man. Often we take these images for granted, and the ways that women and men are represented seem natural or inevitable. Language and media representations of gender shape the way we view ourselves and our relationships to each other and to the world around us. This section explores the images of women and men expressed in language and mass media.

Laurel Richardson's "Gender Stereotyping in the English Language" demonstrates the major ways in which sexism pervades the structure and standard usage of modern American English. Her analysis reveals different expectations of women and men embedded in the language and shows how we internalize and reinforce gender differences. as we read, write, and speak English or hear it spoken. The reading raises questions about the relationships between language and social life, including connections between linguistic change and other forms of social change. What are some examples of sexist or non-sexist language? Do you think using nonsexist language affects people's attitudes about women? How?

Language is one among many aspects of cultural conceptions of women. In many societies, standards of beauty and eroticism require women's bodies to conform to unrealistic and distorted ideals. Kathryn Pauly Morgan describes one of the consequences of cultural messages of beauty on women: the high rates of cosmetic surgery. In "Women and the Knife," Morgan discusses the phenomenal rise in the United States of elective cosmetic surgeries, such as liposuction, breast augmentation and reduction, facelifts, nose jobs, and various "nips" and "tucks" performed on the hips, buttocks, thighs, belly, and breasts. She points out that the pressure to take advantage of new medical technologies to achieve male-defined standards of beauty and restore the appearance of youth is becoming so intense that women who fail to take advantage of modern surgical techniques may be stigmatized as not caring about their appearances or as unliberated.

Morgan encourages women not to embrace the procedures and products of the cosmetic industry that reinforce dominant heterosexual norms of femininity. She identifies two strategies feminists might use to resist the surgical objectification and commodification of women's bodies. Do you agree with Morgan that feminists should avoid having elective cosmetic surgeries? How important do you think being stereotypically attractive is for college women? Is beauty a higher priority than academic success? Do you think that as you grow older you might find it difficult to resist the growing pressure to have cosmetic surgery to restore your youthful appearance?

Compulsory heterosexuality promotes the acceptance of male-defined standards and ideals of beauty. However, racial, ethnic, and class inequalities also influence contemporary thinking about female bodies. Bell hooks argues in "Selling Hot Pussy: Representations of Black Female Sexuality in the Cultural Marketplace" that contemporary images of black female bodies perpetuate racist assumptions about black women that can be traced to slavery, when white Europeans developed a fascination with the bodies of black people. When black women are included in films, television, and advertising, they usually play sluts or mammies. Almost always, the black women playing these roles are biracial or light-skinned. Drawing from the songs and performances of entertainers such as Tina Turner, Anita Baker, and Diana Ross, hooks shows that black women are represented in magazines, popular music, and advertising in ways that tend to reinforce prevailing stereotypes of them as highly sexualized. What images of black women are embedded in your favorite movies, TV shows, music videos, and popular songs? Are there any that present new and different representations of the black female body and black female sexuality?

Standards and ideals that uphold gender and racial inequality are indeed pervasive. However, not all popular representations of gender in television, films, popular music, and magazines endorse traditional notions of femaleness. As Corinne Squire suggests in "Empowering Women? The Oprah Winfrey Show," alternate images of women are making inroads into popular culture. The Oprah show, one of the most watched daytime talk programs on American television, seeks to empower women through a *televisual feminism*. Not only the host but many of the guests and the majority of the studio and home audience members are women. Most episodes examine woman-identified topics, such as relationships, communication, and physical appearance, and the show routinely features personal suffering—domestic violence, child abuse, eating disorders, and so on—that brings to light various forms of gender oppression. In addressing women's problems, Oprah translates black feminism to television.

Squire argues that the program owes its success to the use of exaggerated displays of intense emo-

tions that promote the kind of consciousness-raising that feminist writing often cannot accomplish. Do you agree that the Oprah show is feminist and anti-racist in its message? Are there aspects of the show that promote traditional gender relations? What gender images are conveyed in other daytime talk and television shows?

Cultural representations of gender and sexuality are central to racial, patriarchal, and class domination. Focusing on the lives of Asian Americans in the United States, Yen Le Espiritu examines the way cultural symbols pertaining to masculinity and femininity are used to objectify and exploit Asian-American women and men. In "Ideological Racism and Cultural Resistance," Espiritu describes the way both Asian-American women and men have been femininized, contributing to the group's marginalization and role as the compliant "model minority" in contemporary U.S. cultural ideology.

She views the rise of Asian-American nationalist culture, which presents images of Asian-American men as strong, independent, and self-defined, as a form of resistance to the ideological assaults on their gender identities. At the same time, the masculinist underpinnings of Asian nationalist culture and politics marginalize Asian-American women and their needs. Can you think of some examples of movies, TV shows, videos, and popular music that portray Asian-American men and women in feminine terms? Can you think of examples of other social movements that accentuate men's identities and interests and marginalize women and their interests?

In "En Rapport, In Opposition: Cobrando cuentas a las nuestras," Gloria Anzaldúa discusses why it is both important and difficult for women of color to establish self-defined cultures and identities. Anzaldúa argues that infighting in the name of "ethnic correctness"—over who is "really Latina" or "Black enough"—merely recreates the ideologies of racial purity that uphold inequality. Instead, she proposes a politics rooted in the "borderlands" that recognize the intermixing of various ethnic cultures in families and individuals. Such a politics entails abandoning the search for a fixed and consistent cultural identity, but it holds the promise of a new kind of community that is not based on defining some women as fundamentally different—*Other*—and therefore inferior. Have you observed the kind of infighting that Anzaldúa describes? What would the new politics she proposes look like on your campus?

We cannot emphasize too strongly the importance of language and media images in the construction of our understanding of women's and men's positions in society. We are exposed to these images continually. Because the language we have acquired and the images we use are so deeply rooted and inseparable, it is very difficult for us to break free of them, to see and describe the world and our experiences in nonsexist ways. Yet women and other subordinate groups do attempt to construct alternate systems of meaning and draw strength from cultures of resistance. The power to define has a major influence on our conceptions of others and ourselves.

Gender Stereotyping in the English Language

LAUREL RICHARDSON

Everyone in our society, regardless of class, ethnicity, sex, age, or race, is exposed to the same language, the language of the dominant culture. Analysis of verbal language can tell us a great deal about a people's fears, prejudices, anxieties, and interests. A rich vocabulary on a particular subject indicates societal interests or obsessions (e.g., the extensive vocabulary about cars in America). And different words for the same subject (such as *freedom fighter* and *terrorist, passed away* and *croaked, make love* and *ball*) show that there is a range of attitudes and feelings in the society toward that subject.

It should not be surprising, then, to find differential attitudes and feelings about men and women rooted in the English language. Although English has not been completely analyzed, six general propositions concerning these attitudes and feelings about males and females can be made.

First, in terms of grammatical and semantic structure, women do not have a fully autonomous, independent existence; they are part of man. The language is not divided into male and female with distinct conjugations and declensions, as many other languages are. Rather, *women* are included under the generic *man*. Grammar books specify that the pronoun *he* can be used generically to mean *he or she*. Further, *man,* when used as an indefinite pronoun, grammatically refers to both men and women. So, for example, when we read *man* in the following phrases we are to interpret it as applying to both men and women: "man the oars," "one small step for man, one giant step for mankind," "man, that's tough," "man overboard," "man the toolmaker," "alienated man," "garbageman." Our rules of

etiquette complete the grammatical presumption of inclusivity. When two persons are pronounced "man and wife," Miss Susan Jones changes her entire name to Mrs. Robert Gordon (Vanderbilt, 1972). In each of these correct usages, women are a part of man; they do not exist autonomously. The exclusion of women is well expressed in Mary Daly's ear-jarring slogan "the sisterhood of man" (1973:7–21).

However, there is some question as to whether the theory that *man* means everybody is carried out in practice (see Bendix, 1979; Martyna, 1980). For example, an eight-year-old interrupts her reading of "The Story of the Cavemen" to ask how we got here without cavewomen. A ten-year-old thinks it is dumb to have a woman post*man.* A beginning anthropology student believes (incorrectly) that all shamans ("witch doctors") are males because her textbook and professor use the referential pronoun *he.*

But beginning language learners are not the only ones who visualize males when they see the word *man.* Research has consistently demonstrated that when the genetic *man* is used, people visualize men, not women (Schneider & Hacker, 1973; DeStefano, 1976; Martyna, 1978; Hamilton & Henley, 1982). DeStefano, for example, reports that college students choose silhouettes of males for sentences with the word *man* or *men* in them. Similarly, the presumably generic *he* elicits images of men rather than women. The finding is so persistent that linguists doubt whether there actually is a semantic generic in English (MacKay, 1983).

Man, then, suggests not humanity but rather male images. Moreover, over one's lifetime, an educated American will be exposed to the prescriptive *he* more than a million times (MacKay, 1983). One consequence is the exclusion of women in the visualization, imagination, and thought of males and females. Most likely this linguistic practice perpetuates in men their feelings of dominance over and responsibility for women, feelings that interfere with the development of equality in relationships.

Second, in actual practice, our pronoun usage perpetuates different personality attributes and career aspirations for men and women. Nurses, secretaries, and elementary school teachers are almost invariably referred to as *she;* doctors, engineers, electricians, and presidents as *he.* In one classroom, students referred to an unidentified child as *he* but shifted to *she* when discussing the child's parent. In a faculty discussion of the problems of acquiring new staff, all architects, engineers, security officers, faculty, and computer programmers were referred to as *he;* secretaries and file clerks were referred to as *she.* Martyna (1978) has noted that speakers consistently use *he* when the referent has a high-status occupation (e.g., doctor, lawyer, judge) but shift to *she* when the occupations have lower status (e.g., nurse, secretary).

Even our choice of sex ascription to nonhuman objects subtly reinforces different personalities for males and females. It seems as though the small (e.g., kittens), the graceful (e.g., poetry), the unpredictable (e.g., the fates), the nurturant (e.g., the church, the school), and that which is owned and/or controlled by men (e.g., boats, cars, governments, nations) represent the feminine, whereas that which is a controlling forceful power in and of itself (e.g., God, Satan, tiger) primarily represents the masculine. Even athletic teams are not immune. In one college, the men's teams are called the Bearcats and the women's teams the Bearkittens.

Some of you may wonder whether it matters that the female is linguistically included in the male. The inclusion of women under the pseudogeneric *man* and the prescriptive *he,* however, is not a trivial issue. Language has tremendous power to shape attitudes and influence behavior. Indeed, MacKay (1983) argues that the prescriptive *he* "has all the characteristics of a highly effective propaganda technique": frequent repetition, early age of acquisition (before age six), covertness (*he* is not thought of as propaganda), use by high-prestige sources (including university texts and professors), and indirectness (presented as though it were a matter of common knowledge). As a result, the prescriptive affects females' sense of life options and feelings of well-being. For example, Adamsky (1981) found that women's sense of power and importance was enhanced when the prescriptive *he* was replaced by *she.*

Awareness of the impact of the generic *man* and prescriptive *he* has generated considerable activity to change the language. One change, approved by the Modern Language Association, is to replace the prescriptive *he* with the plural *they*—as was accepted practice before the eighteenth century. Another is the use of *he or she.* Although it sounds awkward at first, the *he or she* designation is increasingly being used in the media and among people who have recognized the power of the pronoun to perpetuate sex stereotyping. When a professor, for example, talks about "the lawyer" as "he or she," a speech pattern that counteracts sex stereotyping is modeled. This drive to neutralize the impact of pronouns is evidenced further in the renaming of occupations: a policeman is now a police officer, a postman is a mail carrier, a stewardess is a flight attendant.

Third, linguistic practice defines females as immature, incompetent, and incapable and males as mature, complete, and competent. Because the words *man* and *woman* tend to connote sexual and human maturity, common speech, organizational titles, public addresses, and bathroom doors frequently designate the women in question as *ladies.* Simply contrast the different connotations of *lady* and *woman* in the following common phrases:

> *Luck, be a lady (woman) tonight.*
> *Barbara's a little lady (woman).*
> *Ladies' (Women's) Air Corps.*

In the first two examples, the use of *lady* desexualizes the contextual meaning of *woman.* So trivializing is the use of *lady* in the last phrase that the second is wholly anomalous. The male equivalent, *lord,* is never used, and its synonym, *gentleman,* is used infrequently. When *gentleman* is used, the assumption seems to be that certain culturally condoned aspects of masculinity (e.g., aggressivity, activity, and strength) should be set aside in the interests of maturity and order, as in the following phrases:

> *A gentlemen's (men's) agreement.*
> *A duel between gentlemen (men).*
> *He's a real gentleman (man).*

Rather than feeling constrained to set aside the stereotypes associated with *man,* males frequently find the opposite process occurring. The contextual connotation of *man* places a strain on males to be continuously sexually and socially potent, as the following examples reveal:

> *I was not a man (gentleman) with her tonight.*
> *This is a man's (gentleman's) job.*
> *Be a man (gentleman).*

Whether males, therefore, feel competent or anxious, valuable or worthless in particular contexts is influenced by the demands placed on them by the expectations of the language.

Not only are men infrequently labeled *gentlemen,* but they are infrequently labeled *boys.* The term *boy* is reserved for young males, bellhops, and car attendants, and as a put-down to those males judged inferior. *Boy* connotes immaturity and powerlessness. Only occasionally do males "have a night out with the boys." They do not talk "boy talk" at the office. Rarely does our language legitimize carefreeness in males. Rather, they are expected, linguistically, to adopt the responsibilities of manhood.

On the other hand, women of all ages may be called *girls.* Grown females "play bridge with the girls" and indulge in "girl talk." They are encouraged to remain child-like, and the implication is that they are basically immature and without power. Men can become men, linguistically, putting aside the immaturity of childhood; indeed, for them to retain the openness and playfulness of boyhood is linguistically difficult.

Further, the presumed incompetence and immaturity of women are evidenced by the linguistic company they keep. Women are categorized with children ("women and children first"), the infirm ("the blind, the lame, the women"), and the incompetent ("women, convicts, and idiots"). The use of these categorical designations is not accidental happenstance; "rather these selectional groupings are powerful forces behind the actual expressions of language and are based on distinctions which are not regarded as trivial by the speakers of the language" (Key, 1975:82). A total language analysis of categorical groupings is not available, yet it seems likely that women tend to be included in groupings that designate incompleteness, ineptitude, and immaturity. On the other hand, it is difficult for us to conceive of the word *man* in any categorical grouping other than one that extends beyond humanity, such as "Man, apes, and angels" or "Man and Superman." That is, men do exist as an independent category capable of autonomy; women are grouped with the stigmatized, the immature, and the foolish. Moreover, when men are in human groupings, they are invariably first on the list ("men and women," "he and she," "man and wife"). This order is not accidental but was prescribed in the sixteenth century to honor the worthier party.

Fourth, in practice women are defined in terms of their sexual desirability (to men); men are defined in terms of their sexual prowess (over women). Most slang words in reference to women refer to their sexual desirability to men (e.g., *dog, fox, broad, ass, chick*). Slang about men refers to their sexual prowess over women (e.g., *dude, stud, hunk*). The fewer examples given for men is not an oversight. An analysis of sexual slang, for example, listed more than a thousand words and phrases that derogate women sexually but found "nowhere near this multitude for describing men" (Kramarae, 1975:72). Farmer and Henley (cited in Schulz, 1975) list five hundred synonyms for *prostitute,* for example, and only sixty-five for *whoremonger.* Stanley (1977) reports two hundred twenty terms for a sexually promiscuous woman and only twenty-two for a sexually promiscuous man. Shuster (1973) reports that the passive verb form is used in reference to women's sexual experiences (e.g., *to be laid, to be had, to be taken*), whereas the active tense is used in reference to the male's sexual experience (e.g., *lay, take, have*). Being sexually attractive to males is culturally condoned for women and being sexually powerful is approved for males. In this regard, the slang of the street is certainly not countercultural; rather, it perpetuates and reinforces different expectations in females and males as sexual objects and performers.

Further, we find sexual connotations associated with neutral words applied to women. A few examples should suffice. A male academician questioned the title of a new course, asserting it was "too suggestive." The title? "The Position of Women in the Social Order." A male tramp is simply a hobo, but a female tramp is a slut. And consider the difference in connotation of the following expressions:

> *It's easy.*
> *He's easy.*
> *She's easy.*

In the first, we assume something is "easy to do"; in the second, we might assume a professor is an "easy grader" or a man is "easygoing." But when we read "she's easy," the connotation is "she's an easy lay."

In the world of slang, men are defined by their sexual prowess. In the world of slang and proper speech, women are defined as sexual objects. The rule in practice seems to be: If in doubt, assume that *any* reference to a women has a sexual connotation. For both genders, the constant bombardment of prescribed sexuality is bound to have real consequences.

Fifth, women are defined in terms of their relations to men; men are defined in terms of their relations to the world at large. A good example is seen in the words *master* and *mistress.* Originally these words had the same meaning—"a person who holds power over servants." With the demise of the feudal system, however, these words took on different meanings. The masculine variant metaphorically refers to power over something; as in "He is the master of his trade"; the feminine variant metaphorically (although probably not in actuality) refers to power over a man sexually, as in "She is Tom's mistress." Men are defined in terms of their power in the occupational world, women in terms of their sexual power over men.

The existence of two contractions for Mistress (*Miss* and *Mrs.*) and but one for Mister *(Mr.)* underscores the cultural concern and linguistic practice: women are defined in relation to men. Even a divorced woman is defined in terms of her no-longer-existing relation to a man (she is still *Mrs. Man's Name*). But apparently the divorced state is not relevant enough to the man or to the society to require a label. A divorced woman is a *divorcée,* but what do you call a divorced man? The recent preference of many women to be called *Ms.* is an attempt to provide for women an equivalency title that is not dependent on marital status.

Sixth, a historical pattern can be seen in the meanings that come to be attached to words that originally were neutral: those that apply to women acquire obscene and/or debased connotations, but no such pattern of derogation holds for neutral words referring to men. The processes of *pejoration* (the acquiring of an obscene or debased connotation) and *amelioration* (the reacquiring of a neutral or positive connotation) in the English language in regard to terms for males and females have been studied extensively by Muriel Schulz (1975).

Leveling is the least derogative form of pejoration. Through leveling, titles that originally referred to an elite class of persons come to include a wider class of persons. Such democratic leveling is more common for female designates than for males. For example, contrast the following: *lord—lady; baronet—dame; governor—governess.*

Most frequently what happens to words designating women as they become pejorated, however, is that they come to denote or connote sexual wantonness. *Sir* and *mister,* for example, remain titles of courtesy, but at some time *madam, miss,* and *mistress* have come to designate, respectively, a brothelkeeper, a prostitute, and an unmarried sexual partner of a male (Schulz, 1975:66).

Names for domestic helpers, if they are females, are frequently derogated. *Hussy,* for example, originally meant "housewife." *Laundress, needlewoman, spinster* ("tender of the spinning wheel"), and *nurse* all referred to domestic occupations within the home, and all at some point became slang expressions for prostitute or mistress.

Even kinship terms referring to women become denigrated. During the seventeenth century, *mother* was used to mean "a bawd"; more recently *mother (mothuh f—)* has become a common derogatory epithet (Cameron, 1974). Probably at some point in history every kinship term for females has been derogated (Schulz, 1975:66).

Terms of endearment for women also seem to follow a downward path. Such pet names as Tart, Dolly, Kitty, Polly, Mopsy, Biddy, and Jill all eventually became sexually derogatory (Schulz, 1975:67). *Whore* comes from the same Latin root as *care* and once meant "a lover of either sex."

Indeed, even the most neutral categorical designations—*girl, female, woman, lady*—at some point in their history have been used to connote sexual immorality. *Girl* originally meant "a child of either sex"; through the process of semantic degeneration it eventually meant "a prostitute." Although *girl* has lost this meaning, *girlie* still retains sexual connotations. *Woman* connoted "a mistress" in the early nineteenth century; *female* was a degrading epithet in the latter part of the nineteenth century; and when *lady* was introduced as a euphemism, it too became deprecatory. "Even so neutral a term as *person,* when it was used as substitute for *woman,* suffered [vulgarization]" (Mencken, 1963: 350, quoted in Schulz, 1975:71).

Whether one looks at elite titles, occupational roles, kinship relationships, endearments, or age–sex categorical designations, the pattern is clear. Terms referring to females are pejorated—"become negative in the middle instances and abusive in the extremes" (Schulz, 1975:69). Such semantic derogation, however, is not evidenced for male referents. *Lord, baronet, father, brother, nephew, footman, bowman, boy, lad, fellow, gentleman, man, male,* and so on "have failed to undergo the derogation found in the history of their corresponding feminine designations" (Schulz, 1975:67). Interestingly, the male word, rather than undergoing derogation, frequently is replaced by a female referent when the speaker wants to debase a male. A weak man, for example, is referred to as a *sissy* (diminutive of *sister*), and an army recruit during basic training is called a *pussy.* And when one is swearing at a male, he is referred to as a *bastard* or a *son of a bitch*—both appellations that impugn the dignity of a man's mother.

In summary, these verbal practices are consistent with the gender stereotypes that we encounter in everyday life. Women are thought to be a part of man, nonautonomous, dependent, relegated to roles that require few skills, characteristically incompetent and immature, sexual objects, best defined in terms of their relations to men. Males are visible, autonomous and independent, responsible for the protection and containment of women, expected to occupy positions on the basis of their high achievement or physical power, assumed to be sexually potent, and defined primarily by their relations to the world of work. The use of the language perpetuates the stereotypes for both genders and limits the options available for self-definition.

REFERENCES

Adamsky, C. 1981. "Changes in pronominal usage in a classroom situation." *Psychology of Women Quarterly* 5:773–79.

Bendix, J. 1979. "Linguistic models as political symbols: Gender and the generic 'he' in English." In J. Orasanu, M. Slater, and L. L. Adler, eds., *Language, Sex and Gender: Does la différence Make a Difference?* pp. 23–42. New York: New Academy of Science Annuals.

Cameron, P. 1974. "Frequency and kinds of words in various social settings, or What the hell's going on?" In M. Truzzi, ed., *Sociology for Pleasure,* pp. 31–37. Englewood Cliffs, N.J.: Prentice-Hall.

Daly, M. 1973. *Beyond God the Father.* Boston: Beacon Press.

DeStefano, J. S. 1976. Personal communication. Columbus: Ohio State University.

Hamilton, N., & Henley, N. 1982. "Detrimental consequences of the generic masculine usage." Paper presented to the Western Psychological Association meetings, Sacramento.

Key, M. R. 1975. *Male/Female Language.* Metuchen, N.J.: Scarecrow Press.

Kramarae, Cheris. 1975. "Woman's speech: Separate but unequal?" In Barrie Thorne and Nancy Henley, eds., *Language and Sex: Difference and Dominance,* pp. 43–56. Rowley, Mass.: Newbury House.

MacKay, D. G. 1983. "Prescriptive grammar and the pronoun problem." In B. Thorne, C. Kramarae, and N. Henley, eds., *Language, Gender, and Society,* pp. 38–53. Rowley, Mass.: Newbury House.

Martyna, W. 1978. "What does 'he' mean? Use of the generic masculine." *Journal of Communication* 28:131–38.

Martyna, W. 1980. "Beyond the 'he/man' approach: The case for nonsexist language." *Signs* 5:482–93.

Mencken, H. L. 1963. *The American Language.* 4th ed. with supplements. Abr. and ed. R. I. McDavis. New York: Knopf.

Schneider, J., & Hacker, S. 1973. "Sex role imagery in the use of the generic 'man' in introductory texts: A case in the sociology of sociology." *American Sociologist* 8:12–18.

Schulz, M. R. 1975. "The semantic derogation of women." In B. Thorne and N. Henley, eds., *Language and Sex: Difference and Dominance,* pp. 64–75. Rowley, Mass.: Newbury House.

Shuster, Janet. 1973. "Grammatical forms marked for male and female in English." Unpublished paper. Chicago: University of Chicago.

Stanley, J. P. 1977. "Paradigmatic woman: The prostitute." In D. L. Shores, ed., *Papers in Language Variation.* Birmingham: University of Alabama Press.

Vanderbilt, A. 1972. *Amy Vanderbilt's Etiquette.* Garden City, N.Y.: Doubleday.

R E A D I N G I 3

Women and the Knife: Cosmetic Surgery and the Colonization of Women's Bodies

KATHRYN PAULY MORGAN

INTRODUCTION

Consider the following passages:

If you want to wear a Maidenform Viking Queen bra like Madonna, be warned: A body like this doesn't just

Kathryn Pauly Morgan. "Women and the Knife: Cosmetic Surgery and the Colonization of Women's Bodies." from *Hypatia* 6 no. 3. (1991). Reprinted with the permission of the author.

happen. . . . Madonna's kind of fitness training takes time. The rock star, *whose muscled body was recently on tour,* spends a minimum of three hours a day working out (*Toronto Star* 1990d; emphasis added).

A lot of the contestants [in the Miss America Pageant] do not owe their beauty to their Maker but to their Re-Maker. Miss Florida's nose came courtesy of her surgeon. So did Miss Alaska's. And Miss Oregon's breasts came from the manufacturers of silicone (Goodman 1989).

Jacobs [a plastic surgeon in Manhattan] constantly answers the call for cleavage. "Women need it for their holiday ball gowns" (*Sheboygan Press* 1985).

We hadn't seen or heard from each other for twenty-eight years. . . . Then he suggested it would be nice if we could meet. I was very nervous about it. How much had I changed? I wanted a facelift, tummy tuck and liposuction, all in one week. (A woman, age forty-nine, being interviewed for an article on "older couples" falling in love; *Toronto Star* 1990c).

"It's hard to say why one person will have cosmetic surgery done and another won't consider it, but generally I think people who go for surgery are more aggressive, they are the doers of the world. It's like makeup. You see some women who might be greatly improved by wearing makeup, but they're, I don't know, granola-heads or something, and they just refuse." (Dr. Ronald Levine, director of plastic surgery education at the University of Toronto and vice chairman of the plastic surgery section of the Ontario Medical Association; *Toronto Star* 1990a).

Another comparable limitation [of the women's liberation movement] is a tendency to reject certain good things only in order to punish men. . . . There is no reason why a women's liberation activist should not try to look pretty and attractive (Markovic 1976).

Now [imagine] *needles and knives . . . cutting into your skin.* Imagine that you have been given this surgery as a gift from your loved one, who read a persuasive and engaging press release from Drs. John and Jim Williams that ends by saying "The next morning the limo will chauffeur your loved one back home again, with a gift of beauty that will last a lifetime" (Williams and Williams, 1990). Imagine the beauty that you have been promised. . . .

We need a feminist analysis to understand why actual, live women are reduced and reduce themselves to "potential women" and choose to participate in anatomizing and fetishizing their bodies as they buy "contoured bodies," "restored youth," and "permanent beauty." In the face of a growing market and demand for surgical interventions in women's bodies that can and do result in infection, bleeding, embolisms, pulmonary edema, facial nerve injury, unfavorable scar formation, skin loss, blindness, crippling, and death, our silence becomes a culpable one. . . .

Not only is elective cosmetic surgery moving out of the domain of the sleazy, the suspicious, the secretively deviant, or the pathologically narcissistic, it is *becoming the norm.* This shift is leading to a predictable inversion of the domains of the deviant and the pathological, so that women who contemplate *not using* cosmetic surgery will increasingly be stigmatized and seen as deviant. . . .

Cosmetic surgery entails the ultimate envelopment of the lived temporal *reality* of the human subject by technologically created appearances that are then regarded as "the real." Youthful appearance triumphs over aged reality.

I. "JUST THE FACTS IN AMERICA, MA'AM"

As of 1990, the most frequently performed kind of cosmetic surgery is liposuction, which involves sucking fat cells out from underneath our skin with a vacuum device. This is viewed as the most suitable procedure for removing specific bulges around the hips, thighs, belly, buttocks, or chin. It is most appropriately done on thin people who want to get rid of certain bulges, and surgeons guarantee that even if there is weight gain, the bulges won't reappear since the fat cells have been permanently removed. At least twelve deaths are known to have resulted from complications such as hemorrhages and embolisms. "All we know is there was a complication and that complication was death," said the partner of Toni Sullivan, age forty-three ("hardworking mother of two teenage children" says the press; *Toronto Star* 1989b). Cost: $1,000 to $7,500.

The second most frequently performed kind of cosmetic surgery is breast augmentation, which involves an implant, usually of silicone. Often the silicone implant hardens over time and must be removed surgically. Over one million women in the United States are known to have had breast augmentation surgery. Two recent studies have shown that breast implants block X-rays and cast a shadow on surrounding tissue, making mammograms difficult to interpret, and that there appears to be a much higher incidence of cancerous lumps in "augmented women" (*Toronto Star* 1988). Cost: $1,500 to $3,000.

"Facelift" is a kind of umbrella term that covers several sorts of procedures. In a recent Toronto case, Dale Curtis "decided to get a facelift for her fortieth birthday. . . . Bederman used liposuction on the jowls and neck, removed the skin and fat from her upper and lower lids and tightened up the muscles in the neck and cheeks. . . . 'She was supposed to get a forehead lift but she chickened out,' Bederman says" (*Toronto Star* 1989a). Clients are now being advised to begin their facelifts in their early forties and are also told that they will need subsequent facelifts every five to fifteen years. Cost: $2,500 to $10,500.

"Nips" and "tucks" are cute, camouflaging labels used to refer to surgical reduction performed on any of the following areas of the body: hips, buttocks, thighs, belly, and breasts. They involve cutting out wedges of skin and fat and sewing up the two sides. These are major surgical procedures that cannot be performed in outpatient clinics because of the need for anaesthesia and the severity of possible postoperative complications. Hence, they require access to costly operating rooms and services in hospitals or clinics. Cost: $3,000 to $7,000.

The number of "rhinoplasties," or nose jobs, has risen by 34 percent since 1981. Some clients are coming in for second and third nose jobs. Nose jobs involve either the inserting of a piece of bone taken from elsewhere in the body or the whittling down of the nose. Various styles of noses go in and out of fashion, and various cosmetic surgeons describe the noses they create in terms of their own surnames, such as "the Diamond nose" or "the Goldman nose" (*Sheboygan Press* 1985). Cost: $2,000 to $3,000.

More recent types of cosmetic surgery, such as the use of skin-expanders and suction lipectomy, involve inserting tools, probes, and balloons under the skin either for purposes of expansion or reduction (Hirshson 1987).

Lest one think that women (who represent between 60 and 70 percent of all cosmetic surgery patients) choose only one of these procedures, heed the words of Dr. Michael Jon Bederman of the Center for Cosmetic Surgery in Toronto:

We see working girls, dental technicians, middle-class women who are unhappy with their looks or are aging prematurely. And we see executives—both male and female. . . . Where before someone would have a tummy tuck and not have anything else done for a year, frequently we will do liposuction and tummy tuck and then the next day a facelift, upper and lower lids, rhinoplasty and *other things*. The recovery time is the same whether a person has one procedure or *the works,* generally about two weeks (*Toronto Star* 1989a; emphasis added).

In principle, there is no area of the body that is not accessible to the interventions and metamorphoses performed by cosmetic surgeons intent on creating twentieth-century versions of "femina perfecta."

II. FROM ARTIFICE TO ARTIFACT: THE CREATION OF ROBO WOMAN?

[Today, what] is designated "the natural" functions primarily as a frontier rather than as a barrier. While genetics, human sexuality, reproductive outcome, and death were previously regarded as open to variation primarily in evolutionary terms, they are now seen by biotechnologists as domains of creation and control. Cosmetic surgeons claim a role here too. For them, human bodies are the locus of challenge. As one plastic surgeon remarks:

Patients sometimes misunderstand the nature of cosmetic surgery. It's not a shortcut for diet or exercise. *It's a way to override the genetic code (Toronto Star* 1990b; emphasis added).

. . . Practices of coercion and domination are often camouflaged by practical rhetorical and supporting theories that appear to be benevolent, therapeutic, and voluntaristic. Previously, for example, colonizing was often done in the name of bringing "civilization" through culture and morals to "primitive, barbaric people," but contemporary colonizers mask their exploitation of "raw materials and human labor" in the name of "development."

The beauty culture is coming to be dominated by a variety of experts, and consumers of youth and beauty are likely to find themselves dependent not only on cosmetic surgeons but on anesthetists, nurses, aestheticians, nail technicians, manicurists, dietitians, hairstylists, cosmetologists, masseuses, aromatherapists, trainers, pedicurists, electrolysists, pharmacologists, and dermatologists. All these experts provide services that can be bought; all these experts are perceived as administering and transforming the human body into an increasingly artificial and ever more perfect object. . . .

For virtually all women as women, success is defined in terms of interlocking patterns of compulsion: compulsory attractiveness, compulsory motherhood, and compulsory heterosexuality, patterns that determine the legitimate limits of attraction and motherhood.[1] Rather than aspiring to self-determined and woman-centered ideals of health or integrity, women's attractiveness is defined as attractive-to-men; women's eroticism is defined as either nonexistent, pathological, or peripheral when it is not directed to phallic goals; and motherhood is defined in terms of legally sanctioned and constrained reproductive service to particular men and to institutions such as the nation, the race, the owner, and the class—institutions that are, more often than not, male-dominated. Biotechnology is now making beauty, fertility, the appearance of heterosexuality through surgery, and the appearance of youthfulness accessible to virtually all women who can afford that technology—and growing numbers of women are making other sacrifices in their lives in order to buy access to the technical expertise.

In western industrialized societies, women have also become increasingly socialized into an acceptance of technical knives. We know about knives that can heal: the knife that saves the life of a baby in distress, the knife that cuts out the cancerous growths in our breasts, the knife that straightens our spines, the knife that liberates our arthritic fingers so that we may once again gesture, once again touch, once again hold. But we also know about other knives: the knife that cuts off our toes so that our feet will fit into elegant shoes, the knife that cuts out ribs to fit our bodies into corsets, the knife that slices through our labia in episiotomies and other forms of genital mutilation, the knife that cuts into our abdomens to remove our ovaries to cure our "deviant tendencies" (Barker-Benfield 1976), the knife that removes our breasts in prophylactic or unnecessary radical mastectomies, the knife that cuts out our "useless bag" (the womb) if we're the wrong color and poor or if we've "outlived our fertility," the knife that makes the "bikini cut" across our pregnant bellies to facilitate the cesarean section that will allow the obstetrician to go on holiday. We know these knives well.

And now we are coming to know the knives and needles of the cosmetic surgeons—the knives that promise to sculpt our bodies, to restore our youth, to create beauty out of what was ugly and ordinary. What kind of knives are these? Magic knives. Magic knives in a patriarchal context. Magic knives in a Eurocentric context. Magic knives in a white supremacist context. What do they mean? I am afraid of these knives.

III. LISTENING TO THE WOMEN

In order to give a feminist reading of any ethical situation we must listen to the women's own reasons for their actions (Sherwin 1984–85, 1989). It is only once we have listened to the voices of women who have elected to undergo cosmetic surgery that we can try to assess the extent to which the conditions for genuine choice have been met and look at the consequences of these choices for the position of women. Here are some of those voices:

VOICE 1: (*a woman looking forward to attending a prestigious charity ball*): "There will be a lot of new faces at the Brazilian Ball" (*Toronto Star* 1989a). [Class/status symbol]

VOICE 2: "You can keep yourself trim. . . . But you have no control over the way you wrinkle, or the fat on your hips, or the skin of your lower abdomen. If you are *hereditarily predestined* to stretch out or wrinkle in your face, you will. If your parents had puffy eyelids and saggy jowls, you're going to have puffy eyelids and saggy jowls" (*Toronto Star* 1989a). [Regaining a sense of control; liberation from parents; transcending hereditary predestination]

VOICE 3: "Now we want a nose that makes a statement, with tip definition and a strong bridge line" (*Toronto Star* 1989a). [Domination; strength]

VOICE 4: "I decided to get a facelift for my fortieth birthday after ten years of living and working in the tropics had taken its toll" (*Toronto Star* 1989a). [Gift to the self; erasure of a decade of hard work and exposure]

VOICE 5: "I've gotten my breasts augmented. I can use it as a tax write-off" (*Toronto Star* 1989a). [Professional advancement; economic benefits]

VOICE 6: "I'm a teacher and kids let schoolteachers know how we look and they aren't nice about it. A teacher who looks like an old bat or has a big nose will get a nickname" (*Toronto Star* 1990b). [Avoidance of cruelty; avoidance of ageist bias]

VOICE 7: "I'll admit to a boob job." (Susan Akin, Miss America of 1986, quoted in Goodman 1989). [Prestige; status; competitive accomplishments in beauty contest]

VOICE 8: (*forty-five-year-old grandmother and proprietor of a business*): "In my business, the customers expect you to look as good as they do" (Hirschson 1987). [Business asset; economic gain; possible denial of grandmother status]

VOICE 9: "People in business see something like this as showing an overall aggressiveness and go-forwardness. *The trend is to, you know, be all that you can be*" (*Sheboygan Press* 1985). [Success; personal fulfillment]

VOICE 10: (*paraphrase*): "I do it to fight holiday depression" (*Sheboygan Press* 1985). [Emotional control; happiness]

VOICE 11: "I came to see Dr. X for the holiday season. I have important business parties, and the man I'm trying to get to marry me is coming in from Paris" (*Sheboygan Press* 1985). [Economic gain; heterosexual affiliation]

Women have traditionally regarded (and been taught to regard) their bodies, particularly if they are young, beautiful, and fertile, *as a locus of power* to be enhanced through artifice and, now, through artifact. In 1792, in *A Vindication of the Rights of Woman,* Mary Wollstonecraft remarked: "Taught from infancy that beauty is woman's scepter, the mind shapes itself to the body and roaming round its gilt cage, only seeks to adorn its prison." How ironic that the mother of the creator of *Frankenstein* should be the source of that quote. We need to ask ourselves whether today, involved as we are in the modern inversion of "our bodies shaping themselves to our minds," we are creating a new species of woman-monster with new artifactual bodies that function as prisons or whether cosmetic surgery for women does represent a potentially liberating field of choice.

When Snow White's stepmother asks the mirror, "Who is fairest of all?" she is not asking simply an empirical question. In wanting to continue to be "the fairest of all," she is striving, in a clearly competitive context, for a prize, for a position, for power. The affirmation of her beauty brings with it privileged heterosexual affiliation, privileged access to forms of power unavailable to the plain, the ugly, the aged, and the barren.

The Voices are seductive—they speak the language of gaining access to transcendence, achievement, liberation, and power. And they speak to a kind of reality. First, electing to undergo the surgery necessary to create youth and beauty artificially not only appears to but often actually does give a woman a sense of identity that, to some extent, she has chosen herself. Second, it offers her the potential to raise her status both socially and economically by increasing her opportunities for heterosexual affiliation (especially with white men). Third, by committing herself to the pursuit of beauty, a woman integrates her life with a consistent set of values and choices that bring her widespread approval and a resulting sense of increased self-esteem. Fourth, the pursuit of beauty often gives a woman access to a range of individuals who administer to her body in a caring way, an experience often sadly lacking in the day-to-day lives of many women. As a result, a woman's pursuit of beauty through transformation is often associated with lived experiences of self-creation, self-fulfillment, self-transcendence, and being cared for. The power of these experiences must not be underestimated.

While I acknowledge that these choices can confer a kind of integrity on a woman's life, I also believe that they are likely to embroil her in a set of interrelated contradictions. I refer to these as "Paradoxes of Choice."

IV. THREE PARADOXES OF CHOICE

In exploring these paradoxes, I appropriate Foucault's analysis of the diffusion of power in order to understand forms of power that are potentially more personally invasive than are more obvious, publicly identifiable aspects of power. In the chapter "Docile Bodies" in *Discipline and Punish,* Foucault (1979, 136–37) highlights three features of what he calls disciplinary power:

1. The *scale* of the control. In disciplinary power the body is treated individually and in a coercive way because the body itself is the *active* and hence apparently free body that is being controlled through movements, gestures, attitudes, and degrees of rapidity.
2. The *object* of the control, which involves meticulous control over the efficiency of movements and forces.
3. The *modality* of the control; which involves constant, uninterrupted coercion.

Foucault argues that the outcome of disciplinary power is the docile body, a body "that may be subjected, used, transformed, and improved" (Foucault 1979, 136). Foucault is discussing this model of power in the context of prisons and armies, but we can adapt the central insights of this notion to see how women's bodies are entering "a machinery of power that explores it, breaks it down, and rearranges it" through a recognizably political metamorphosis of embodiment (Foucault 1979, 138).[2] What is important about this notion in relation to cosmetic surgery is the extent to which it makes it possible to speak about the diffusion of power throughout western industrialized cultures that are increasingly committed to a technological beauty imperative. It also makes it possible to refer to a set of experts—cosmetic surgeons—whose explicit power mandate is to explore, break down, and rearrange women's bodies.

Paradox One: The Choice of Conformity—Understanding the Number 10

While the technology of cosmetic surgery could clearly be used to create and celebrate idiosyncrasy, eccentricity, and uniqueness, it is obvious that this is not how it is presently being used. Cosmetic surgeons report that legions of women appear in their offices demanding "Bo Derek" breasts (*Sheboygan Press* 1985). Jewish women demand reductions of their noses so as to be able to "pass" as one of their Aryan sisters who form the dominant ethnic group (Lakoff and Scherr 1984). Adolescent Asian girls who bring in pictures of Elizabeth Taylor and of Japanese movie actresses (whose faces have already been reconstructed) demand the "westernizing" of their own eyes and the creation of higher noses in hopes of better job and marital prospects (*Newsweek* 1985). Black women buy toxic bleaching agents in hopes of attaining lighter skin. What is being created in all of these instances is not simply beautiful bodies and faces but white, western, Anglo-Saxon bodies in a racist, antisemitic context.

More often than not, what appear at first glance to be instances of choice turn out to be instances of conformity. The women who undergo cosmetic surgery in order to compete in various beauty pageants are clearly choosing to conform. So is the woman who wanted to undergo a facelift, tummy tuck, and liposuction all in one week, in order to win heterosexual approval *from a man she had not seen in twenty-eight years* and whose individual preferences she could not possibly know. In some ways, it does not matter who the particular judges are. Actual men—brothers, fathers, male lovers, male beauty "experts"—and hypothetical men live in the aesthetic imaginations of women. Whether they are male employers, prospective male spouses, male judges in the beauty pageants, or male-identified women, these modern day Parises are generic and live sometimes ghostly but powerful lives in the reflective awareness of women (Berger 1972). A woman's makeup, dress, gestures, voice, degree of cleanliness, degree of muscularity, odors, degree of hirsuteness, vocabulary, hands, feet, skin, hair, and vulva can all be evaluated, regulated, and disciplined in the light of the hypothetical often-white male viewer and the male viewer present in the assessing gaze of other women (Haug 1987). Men's appreciation and approval of achieved femininity becomes all the more invasive when it resides in the incisions, stitches, staples, and scar tissue of women's bodies as women choose to conform. And . . . women's public conformity to the norms of beauty often signals a deeper conformity to the norms of compulsory heterosexuality along with an awareness of the violence that can result from violating those norms. Hence the first paradox: that what looks like an optimal situation of reflection, deliberation, and self-creating choice often signals conformity at a deeper level.

Paradox Two: Liberation into Colonization

As argued above, a woman's desire to create a permanently beautiful and youthful appearance that is not vulnerable to the threats of externally applied cosmetic artifice or to the natural aging process of the body must be understood as a deeply significant existential project. It deliberately involves the exploitation and transformation of the most intimately experienced domain of immanence, the body, in the name of transcendence: transcendence of hereditary predestination, of lived time, of one's given "limitations." What I see as particularly alarming in this project is that

what comes to have primary significance is not the real given existing woman but her body viewed as a "primitive entity" that is seen only as potential, as a kind of raw material to be exploited in terms of appearance, eroticism, nurturance, and fertility as defined by the colonizing culture.[3]

But for whom is this exploitation and transformation taking place? Who exercises the power here? Sometimes the power is explicit. It is exercised by brothers, fathers, male lovers, male engineering students who taunt and harass their female counterparts, and male cosmetic surgeons who offer "free advice" in social gatherings to women whose "deformities" and "severe problems" can all be cured through their healing needles and knives. And the colonizing power is transmitted through and by those women whose own bodies and disciplinary practices demonstrate the efficacy of "taking care of herself" in these culturally defined feminine ways. Sometimes, however, the power may be so diffused as to dominate the consciousness of a given woman with no other subject needing to be present. . . .

In electing to undergo cosmetic surgery, women appear to be protesting against the constraints of the "given" in their embodied lives and seeking liberation from those constraints. But I believe they are in danger of retreating and becoming more vulnerable, at that very level of embodiment, to those colonizing forms of power that may have motivated the protest in the first place. Moreover, in seeking independence, they can become even more dependent on male assessment and on the services of all those experts they initially bought to render them independent.

Here we see a second paradox bound up with choice: that the rhetoric is that of liberation and care, of "making the most of yourself," but the reality is often the transformation of oneself as a woman for the eye, the hand, and the approval of the Other—the lover, the taunting students, the customers, the employers, the social peers. And the Other is almost always affected by the dominant culture, which is male supremacist, racist, ageist, heterosexist, antisemitic, ableist and class-biased.[4]

Paradox Three: Coerced Voluntariness and the Technological Imperative

Where is the coercion? At first glance, women who choose to undergo cosmetic surgery often seem to represent a paradigm case of the rational chooser. Drawn increasingly from wider and wider economic groups, these women clearly make a choice, often at significant economic cost to the rest of their life, to pay the large sums of money demanded by cosmetic surgeons (since American health insurance plans do not cover this elective cosmetic surgery).

Furthermore, they are often highly critical consumers of these services, demanding extensive consultation, information regarding the risks and benefits of various surgical procedures, and professional guarantees of expertise. Generally they are relatively young and in good health. Thus, in some important sense, they epitomize relatively invulnerable free agents making a decision under virtually optimal conditions.

Moreover, on the surface, women who undergo cosmetic surgery choose a set of procedures that are, by definition, "elective." This term is used, quite straightforwardly, to distinguish cosmetic surgery, from surgical intervention for reconstructive or health-related reasons (following massive burns, cancer-related forms of mutilation, etc.). The term also appears to distinguish cosmetic surgery from apparently involuntary and more pathologically transforming forms of intervention in the bodies of young girls in the form of, for example, foot-binding or extensive genital mutilation.[5] But I believe that this does not exhaust the meaning of the term "elective" and that the term performs a seductive role in facilitating the ideological camouflage of the *absence of choice.* Similarly, I believe that the word "cosmetic" serves an ideological function in hiding the fact that the changes are *noncosmetic:* they involve lengthy periods of pain, are permanent, and result in irreversibly alienating metamorphoses such as the appearance of youth on an aging body. . . .

There are two important ideological, choice-diminishing dynamics at work that affect women's choices in the area of . . . cosmetic surgery. The first of these is the *pressure to achieve perfection through technology.*

The second . . . is the *double-pathologizing of women's bodies.* The history of western science and western medical practice is not altogether a positive one for women. As voluminous documentation has shown, cell biologists, endocrinologists, anatomists, sociobiologists, gynecologists, obstetricians, psychiatrists, surgeons, and other scientists have assumed, hypothesized, or "demonstrated" that women's bodies are generally inferior, deformed, imperfect, and/or infantile. . . .

[Now, women are being pressured to see plainness or being ugly as a form of pathology. Consequently, there is strong pressure] to be beautiful in relation to the allegedly voluntary nature of "electing" to undergo cosmetic surgery. It is clear that pressure to use this technology is on the increase. Cosmetic surgeons report on the wide range of clients who buy their services, pitch their advertising to a large audience through the use of the media, and encourage women to think, metaphorically, in terms of the seemingly trivial "nips" and "tucks" that will transform their lives. As cosmetic surgery becomes increasingly normalized through the concept of the female "makeover" that is translated into columns and articles in the print media or made into nationwide television shows directed at female viewers, as the "success stories" are invited onto talk shows along with their "makers," and as surgically transformed women win the Miss America pageants, women who refuse to submit to the knives and to the needles, to the anesthetics and the bandages, will come to be seen as deviant in one way or another. Women who refuse to use these technologies are already becoming stigmatized as "unliberated," "not caring about their appearance" (a sign of disturbed gender identity and low self-esteem according to various health care professionals), as "refusing to be all that they could be" or as "granola-heads."

And as more and more success comes to those who do "care about themselves" in this technological fashion, more coercive dimensions enter the scene. In the past, only those women who were perceived to be *naturally* beautiful (or rendered beautiful through relatively conservative superficial artifice) had access to forms of power and economic social mobility closed off to women regarded as plain or ugly or old. But now womanly beauty is becoming technologically achievable, a commodity for which each and every woman can, in principle, sacrifice if she is to survive and succeed in the world, particularly in industrialized western countries. Now technology is making obligatory the appearance of youth and the reality of "beauty" for every woman who can afford it. Natural destiny is being supplanted by technologically grounded coercion, and the coercion is camouflaged by the language of choice, fulfillment, and liberation.

Similarly, we find the dynamic of the double-pathologizing of the normal and of the ordinary at work here. In the technical and popular literature on cosmetic surgery, what have previously been described as normal variations of female bodily shapes or described in the relatively innocuous language of "problem areas," are increasingly being described as "deformities," "ugly protrusions," "inadequate breasts," and "unsightly concentrations of fat cells"—a litany of descriptions designed to intensify feelings of disgust, shame, and relief at the possibility of recourse for these "deformities." Cosmetic surgery promises virtually all women the creation of beautiful, youthful-appearing bodies. As a consequence, more and more women will be labeled "ugly" and "old" in relation to this more select population of surgically created beautiful faces and bodies that have been contoured and augmented, lifted and tucked into a state of achieved feminine excellence. I suspect that the naturally "given," so to speak, will increasingly come to be seen as the technologically "primitive"; the "ordinary" will come to be perceived and evaluated as the "ugly." Here, then, is the *third paradox:* that the technological beauty imperative and the pathological inversion of the normal are coercing more and more women to "choose" cosmetic surgery.

V. ARE THERE ANY POLITICALLY CORRECT FEMINIST RESPONSES TO COSMETIC SURGERY?

Attempting to answer this question is rather like venturing forth into quicksand. Nevertheless, I will discuss two very different sorts of responses that strike me as having certain plausibility: the response of refusal and the response of appropriation.[6] I regard both of these as utopian in nature.

The Response of Refusal

In her witty and subversive parable, *The Life and Loves of a She-Devil,* Fay Weldon puts the following thoughts into the mind of the cosmetic surgeon whose services have been bought by the protagonist, "Miss Hunter," for her own plans for revenge:

> He was her Pygmalion, but she would not depend upon him, or admire him, or be grateful. He was accustomed to being loved by the women of his own construction. A soft sigh of adoration would follow him down the corridors as he paced them, visiting here, blessing there, promising a future, regretting a past: cushioning his footfall, and his image of himself. But no soft breathings came from Miss Hunter. [He adds, ominously,] . . . he would bring her to it (Weldon 1983, 215–16).

But Miss Hunter continues to refuse, and so will many feminist women. The response of refusal can be recognizably feminist at both an individual and a collective level. It results from understanding the nature of the risks involved—those having to do with the surgical procedures and those related to a potential loss of embodied personal integrity in a patriarchal context. And it results from understanding the conceptual shifts involved in the political technologizing of women's bodies and contextualizing them so that their oppressive consequences are evident precisely as

they open up more "choices" to women. "Understanding" and "contextualizing" here mean seeing clearly the ideological biases that frame the material and cultural world in which cosmetics surgeons practice, a world that contains racist, antisemitic, eugenicist, and ageist dimensions of oppression, forms of oppression to which current practices in cosmetic surgery often contribute.

The response of refusal also speaks to the collective power of women as consumers to affect market conditions. If refusal is practiced on a large scale, cosmetic surgeons who are busy producing new faces for the "holiday season" and new bellies for the "winter trips to the Caribbean" will find few buyers of their services. Cosmetic surgeons who consider themselves body designers and regard women's skin as a kind of magical fabric to be draped, cut, layered, and designer-labeled may have to forgo the esthetician's ambitions that occasion the remark that "the sculpting of human flesh can never be an exact art" (Silver 1989). They may, instead, (re)turn their expertise to the victims in the intensive burn unit and to the crippled limbs and joints of arthritic women. This might well have the consequence of (re)converting those surgeons into healers.

Although it may be relatively easy for some individual women to refuse cosmetic surgery even when they have access to the means, one deep, morally significant facet of the response of refusal is to try to understand and to care about individual women who do choose to undergo cosmetic surgery. It may well be that one explanation for why a woman is willing to subject herself to surgical procedures, anaesthetic, postoperative drugs, predicted and lengthy pain, and possible "side effects" that might include her own death is that her access to other forms of power and empowerment or appear to be so limited that cosmetic surgery is the primary domain in which she can experience some semblance of self-determination. . . . Choosing an artificial and technologically designed creation of youthful beauty may not only be necessary to an individual woman's material, economic, and social survival. It may also be the way that she is able to choose, to elect a kind of subjective transcendence against a backdrop of constraint, limitation, and immanence. . . .

As a feminist response, individual and collective refusal may not be easy. As Bartky, I, and others have tried to argue, it is crucial to understand the central role that socially sanctioned and socially constructed femininity plays in a male supremacist, heterosexist society. And it is essential not to underestimate the gender-constituting and identity-confirming role that femininity plays in bringing woman-as-subject into existence while simultaneously creating her as patriarchally defined object (Bartky 1988; Morgan 1986). In these circumstances, refusal may be akin to a kind of death, to a kind of renunciation of the only kind of life-conferring choices and competencies to which a woman may have access. And, under those circumstances, it may not be possible for her to register her resistance in the form of refusal. The best one can hope for is a heightened sense of the nature of the multiple double-binds and compromises that permeate the lives of virtually all women and are accentuated by the cosmetic surgery culture. As a final comment, it is worth remarking that although the response of refusal has a kind of purity to recommend it, it is unlikely to have much impact in the current ideological and cultural climate. . . .

The Response of Appropriation

Rather than viewing the womanly/technologized body as a site of political refusal, the response of appropriation views it as the site for feminist action through transformation, appropriation, parody, and protest. This response grows out of that historical and often radical feminist tradition that regards deliberate mimicry, alternative valorization, hyperbolic appropriation, street theater, counterguerrilla tactics, destabilization, and redeployment as legitimate feminist politics. Here I am proposing a version of what Judith Butler regards as "Femininity Politics" and what she calls "Gender Performatives." . . .

Rather than agreeing that participation in cosmetic surgery and its ruling ideology will necessarily result in further colonization and victimization of women, this feminist strategy advocates appropriating the expertise and technology for feminist ends. One advantage of the response of appropriation is that it does not recommend involvement in forms of technology that clearly have disabling and dire outcomes for the deeper feminist project of engaging "in the historical, political, and theoretical process of constituting ourselves as subjects as well as objects of history" (Hartsock 1990, 170).[7] Women who are increasingly immobilized bodily through physical weakness, passivity, withdrawal, and domestic sequestration in situations of hysteria, agoraphobia, and anorexia cannot possibly engage in radical gender performatives of an active public sort or in other acts by which the feminist subject is robustly constituted. In contrast, healthy women who have a feminist understanding of cosmetic surgery are in a situation to deploy cosmetic surgery in the name of its feminist potential for parody and protest. . . .

As Butler correctly observes, parody "by itself is not subversive" (1990, 139) since it always runs the risk of becoming "domesticated and recirculated as instruments of cultural hegemony." She then goes on to ask, in relation to gender identity and sexuality, what words or performances would

compel a reconsideration of the *place* and stability of the masculine and the feminine? And what kind of gender performance will enact and reveal the performativity of gender itself in a way that destabilizes the naturalized categories of identity and desire? (Butler 1990, 139)

We might, in parallel fashion, ask what sorts of performances would sufficiently destabilize the norms of femininity, what sorts of performances will sufficiently expose the truth of the slogan "Beauty is always made, not born." In response I suggest two performance-oriented forms of revolt.

The first form of revolt involves revalorizing the domain of the "ugly" and all that is associated with it. Although one might argue that the notion of the "ugly" is parasitic on that of "beauty," this is not entirely true since the ugly is also contrasted with the plain and the ordinary, so that we are not even at the outset constrained by binary oppositions. The ugly, even in a beauty-oriented culture, has always held its own fascination, its own particular kind of splendor. Feminists can use that and explore it in ways that might be integrated with a revalorization of being old, thus simultaneously attacking the ageist dimension of the reigning ideology. Rather than being the "culturally enmired subjects" of Butler's analysis, women might constitute themselves as culturally liberated subjects through public participation in Ms. Ugly Canada/America/Universe/Cosmos pageants *and use the technology of cosmetic surgery to do so.*

Contemplating this form of revolt as a kind of imaginary model of political action is one thing; actually altering our bodies is another matter altogether. And the reader may well share the sentiments of one reviewer of this paper who asked: "Having oneself surgically mutilated in order to prove a point? Isn't this going too far?" I don't know the answer to that question. If we cringe from contemplating this alternative, this may, in fact, testify (so to speak) to the hold that the beauty imperative has on our imagination and our bodies. If we recoil from *lived* alteration of the contours of our bodies and regard it as "mutilation," then so, too, ought we to shrink from contemplation of cosmetic surgeons who de-skin and alter the contours of women's bodies so that we become more and more like athletic or emaciated (depending on what's in vogue) mannequins with large breasts in the shop windows of modern patriarchal culture. In what sense are these not equivalent mutilations?

What this feminist performative would require would be not only genuine celebration of but *actual* participation in the fleshly mutations needed to produce what the culture constitutes as "ugly" so as to destabilize the "beautiful" and expose its technologically and culturally constitutive origin and its political consequences. Bleaching one's hair white and applying wrinkle-inducing "wrinkle creams," having one's face and breasts surgically pulled down (rather than lifted), and having wrinkles sewn and carved into one's skin might also be seen as destabilizing actions with respect to aging. And analogous actions might be taken to undermine the "lighter is better" aspect of racist norms of feminine appearance as they affect women of color.

A second performative form of revolt could involve exploring the commodification aspect of cosmetic surgery. One might, for example, envision a set of "Beautiful Body Boutique" franchises, responsive to the particular "needs" of a given community. Here one could advertise and sell a whole range of bodily contours; a variety of metric containers of freeze-dried fat cells for fat implantation and transplant; "body configuration" software for computers; sewing kits of needles, knives, and painkillers; and "skin-Velcro" that could be matched to fit and drape the consumer's body; variously sized sets of magnetically attachable breasts complete with discrete nipple pumps; and other inflation devices carefully modulated according to bodily aroma and state of arousal. Parallel to the current marketing strategies for cosmetic breast surgeries, commercial protest booths, complete with "before and after" surgical makeover displays for penises, entitled "The Penis You Were Always Meant to Have," could be set up at various medical conventions and health fairs; demonstrations could take place outside the clinics, hotels, and spas of particularly eminent cosmetic surgeons—the possibilities here are endless. Again, if this ghoulish array offends, angers, or shocks the reader, this may well be an indication of the extent to which the ideology of compulsory beauty has anesthetized our sensibility in the reverse direction, resulting in the domesticating of the procedures and products of the cosmetic surgery industry.

In appropriating these forms of revolt, women might well accomplish the following: acquire expertise (either in fact or in symbolic form) of cosmetic surgery to challenge the coercive norms of youth and beauty, undermine the power dynamic built into the dependence on surgical experts who define themselves as aestheticians of women's bodies, demonstrate the radical malleability of the cultural commodification of women's bodies, and make publicly explicit the political role that technology can play in the construction of the feminine in women's flesh.

CONCLUSION

I have characterized both these feminist forms of response as utopian in nature. What I mean by "utopian" is that these responses are unlikely to occur on a large scale even though they may have a kind of ideal desirability. In any culture that defines femininity in terms of submission to men, that makes the achievement of femininity (however culturally specific) in appearance, gesture, movement, voice, bodily contours, aspirations, values, and political behavior obligatory for any woman who will be allowed to be loved or hired or promoted or elected or simply allowed to live, and in any culture that increasingly requires women to purchase femininity through submission to cosmetic surgeons and their magic knives, refusal and revolt exact a high price. I live in such a culture.

ACKNOWLEDGMENTS

Many thanks to the members of the Canadian Society for Women in Philosophy for their critical feedback, especially my commentator, Karen Weisbaum, who pointed out how strongly visualist the cosmetic surgery culture is. I am particularly grateful to Sarah Lucia Hoagland, keynote speaker at the 1990 C-SWIP conference, who remarked at my session, "I think this is all wrong." Her comment sent me back to the text to rethink it in a serious way. . . .

NOTES

1. I say "virtually all women" because there is now a nascent literature on the subject of fat oppression and body image as it affects lesbians. For a perceptive article on this subject, see Dworkin (1989). I am, of course, not suggesting that compulsory heterosexuality and obligatory maternity affect all women equally. Clearly women who are regarded as "deviant" in some respect or other—because they are lesbian or women with disabilities or "too old" or poor or of the "wrong race"—are under enormous pressure from the dominant culture *not* to bear children, but this, too, is an aspect of patriarchal pronatalism.

2. I view this as a recognizably *political* metamorphosis because forensic cosmetic surgeons and social archaeologists will be needed to determine the actual age and earlier appearance of women in cases where identification is called for on the basis of existing carnal data. See Griffin's (1978) poignant description in "The Anatomy Lesson" for a reconstruction of the life and circumstances of a dead mother from just such carnal evidence. As we more and more profoundly artifactualize our own bodies, we become more sophisticated archaeological repositories and records that both signify and symbolize our culture.

3. I intend to use "given" here in a relative and political sense. I don't believe that the notion that biology is somehow "given" and culture is just "added" is a tenable one. I believe that we are intimately and inextricably encultured and embodied, so that a reductionist move in either direction is doomed to failure. For a persuasive analysis of this thesis, see Lowe (1982) and Haraway (1978, 1989). For a variety of political analyses of the "given" as primitive, see Marge Piercy's poem "Right to Life" (1980), Morgan (1989), and Murphy (1984).

4. The extent to which ableist bias is at work in this area was brought home to me by two quotations cited by a woman with a disability. She discusses two guests on a television show. One was "a poised, intelligent young woman who'd been rejected as a contestant for the Miss Toronto title. She is a paraplegic. The organizers' excuse for disqualifying her: 'We couldn't fit the choreography around you.' Another guest was a former executive of the Miss Universe contest. He declared, 'Her participation in a beauty contest would be like having a blind man compete in a shooting match' " (Matthews 1985).

5. It is important here to guard against facile and ethnocentric assumptions about beauty rituals and mutilation. See Lakoff and Scherr (1984) for an analysis of the relativity of these labels and for important insights about the fact that use of the term "mutilation" almost always signals a distancing from and reinforcement of a sense of cultural superiority in the speaker who uses it to denounce what other cultures do in contrast to "our culture."

6. One possible feminist response (that, thankfully, appears to go in *and* out of vogue) is that of feminist fascism, which insists on a certain particular and quite narrow range of embodiment and appearance as the only range that is politically correct for a feminist. Often feminist fascism sanctions the use of informal but very powerful feminist "embodiment police," who feel entitled to identify and denounce various deviations from this normative range. I find this feminist political stance incompatible with any movement I would regard as liberatory for women and here I admit that I side with feminist liberals who say that "the presumption must be on the side of freedom" (Warren 1989) and see that as the lesser of the two evils.

7. In recommending various forms of appropriation of the practices and dominant ideology surrounding cosmetic surgery, I think it important to distinguish this set of disciplinary practices from those forms of simultaneous Retreat-and-Protest that Susan Bordo (1989, 20) so insightfully discusses in "The Body and the Reproduction of Femininity": hysteria, agoraphobia, and anorexia. What cosmetic surgery shares with these gestures is what Bordo remarks upon, namely, the fact that they may be "viewed as a surface on which conventional constructions of femininity are exposed starkly to view, through their inscription in extreme or hyperliteral form." What is different, I suggest, is that although submitting to the procedures of cosmetic surgery involves pain, risks, undesirable side effects, and living with a heightened form of patriarchal anxiety, it is also fairly clear that, most of the time, the pain and risks are relatively short term. Furthermore, the outcome often appears to be one that generally enhances women's confidence, confers a sense of well-being, contributes to a greater comfortableness in the public domain, and affirms the individual woman as a self-determining and risk-taking individual. All these outcomes are significantly different from what Bordo describes as the "languages of horrible suffering" (Bordo 1989, 20) expressed by women experiencing hysteria, agoraphobia, and anorexia.

REFERENCES

Barker-Benfield, G. J. 1976. *The Horrors of the Half-Known Life.* New York: Harper and Row.

Bartky, Sandra Lee. 1988. Foucault, feminity, and the modernization of patriarchal power. In *Feminity and Foucault: Reflections on Resistance,* ed. Irene Diamond and Lee Quimby: Boston: Northeastern University Press.

Berger, John. 1972. *Ways of Seeing.* New York: Penguin Books.

Bordo, Susan R. 1989. The body and the reproduction of feminity: A feminist appropriation of Foucault. In *Gender/body/ knowledge: Feminist Reconstructions of Being and Knowing,* ed. Alison Jagger and Susan Bordo. New Brunswick, NJ: Rutgers University Press.

Butler, Judith. 1990. *Gender Trouble: Feminism and the Subversion of Identity.* New York: Routledge.

Dworkin, Sari. 1989. Not in man's image. Lesbians and the cultural oppression of body image. *Women and Therapy* 8:27–39.

Foucault, Michel. 1979. *Discipline and Punish: The Birth of the Prison.* Alan Sheridan, trans. New York: Pantheon.

Goodman, Ellen. 1989. A plastic surgeon. *Boston Globe,* September 19.

Griffin, Susan. 1978. *Woman and Nature: The Roaring Inside Her.* New York: Harper and Row.

Haraway, Donna. 1978. Animal sociology and a natural economy of the body politic, Parts I, II. *Signs: Journal of Women in Culture and Society* 4:21–60.

———. 1989. *Primate Visions.* New York: Routledge.

Hartsock, Nancy. 1990. Foucault on power: A theory for women? In *Feminism/postmodernism,* ed. Linda Nicholson. New York: Routledge.

Haug, Frigga, ed. 1987. *Female Sexualization: A Collective Work of Memory.* Erica Carter, trans. London: Verso.

Hirshson, Paul. 1987. New wrinkles in plastic surgery: An update on the search for perfection. *Boston Globe Sunday Magazine.* May 24.

Lakoff, Robin Tolmach, and Raquel Scherr. 1984. *Face Value: The Politics of Beauty.* Boston: Routledge and Kegan Paul.

Lowe, Marion. 1982. The dialectic of biology and culture. In *Biological Woman: The Convenient Myth,* ed. Ruth Hubbard, Mary Sue Henifin, and Barbara Fried. Cambridge, MA. Schenkman.

Markovic, Mihailo. 1976. Women's liberation and human emancipation. In *Women and Philosophy: Toward a Theory of Liberation,* ed. Carol Gould and Marx Wartofsky. New York: Capricorn Books.

Matthews, Gwyneth Ferguson. 1985. Mirror, mirror: Self-image and disabled women. *Women and Disability: Resources for Feminist Research,* 14:47–50.

Morgan, Kathryn Pauly. 1986. Romantic love, altruism and self-respect: An analysis of Simone De Beauvoir. *Hypatia* 1:117–148.

———. 1989. Of woman born: How old-fashioned! New reproductive technologies and women's oppresion. In *The Future of Human Reproduction,* ed. Christine Overall. Toronto: The Women's Press.

Murphy, Julie [Julien S]. 1984. Egg farming and women's future. In *Test-tube Women: What Future for Motherhood?,* ed. Rita Arditti, Renate Duelli-Klein, and Shelley Minden. Boston: Pandora Press.

Newsweek. 1985. New bodies for sale. May 27.

Piercy, Marge. 1980. *The Moon Is Always Female.* New York: A. Knopf.

Sheboygan Press. 1985. Cosmetic surgery for the holidays. New York Times News Service.

Sherwin, Susan. 1984–85. A feminist approach to ethics. *Dalbousie Review* 64:704–13.

———. 1989. Feminist and medical ethics: Two different approaches to contextual ethics. *Hypatia* 4:57–72.

Silver, Harold. 1989. Liposuction isn't for everyone. *Toronto Star,* October 20.

Toronto Star. 1988. Implants hide tumors in breasts, study says. July 29.

———. 1989a. Changing Faces. May 25.

———. 1989b. Woman, 43, dies after cosmetic surgery. July 7.

———. 1990a. The quest to be a perfect 10. February 1.

———. 1990b. Retouching nature's way: Is cosmetic surgery worth it? February 1.

———. 1990c. Falling in love again. July 23.

———. 1990d. *Madonna passionate about fitness. August 16.*

Warren, Virginia. 1989. Feminist directions in medical ethics. *Hypatia* 4:73–87.

Weldon, Fay. 1983. *The Life and Loves of a She-Devil.* London: Coronet Books; New York: Pantheon Books.

Williams, John, and Jim Williams. 1990. Say it with liposuction. *Harper's.* August.

THE MYTH OF THE PERFECT BODY

ROBERTA GALLER

A woman was experiencing severe abdominal pain. She was rushed to the emergency room and examined, then taken to the operating room, where an appendectomy was performed. After surgery, doctors concluded that her appendix was fine but that she had VD. It never occurred to them that this woman had a sexual life at all, because she was in a wheelchair.

I saw a woman who had cerebral palsy at a neuromuscular clinic. She was covered with bruises. After talking with her, it became clear that she was a battered wife. I brought her case to the attention of the medical director and social worker, both progressive practitioners who are knowledgeable about resources for battered women. They said, "But he supports her. Who else will take care of her? And besides, if she complains, the court might take custody of her children."

As a feminist and psychotherapist I am politically and professionally interested in the impact of body image on a woman's self-esteem and sense of sexuality. However, it is as a woman with a disability that I am personally involved with these issues. I had polio when I was ten years old, and now with arthritis and some new aches and pains I feel in a rather exaggerated fashion other effects of aging, a progressive disability we all share to some degree.

Although I've been disabled since childhood, until the past few years I didn't know anyone else with a disability and in fact *avoided* knowing anyone with a disability. I had many of the same fears and anxieties which many of you who are currently able-bodied might feel about close association with anyone with a disabili-

ty. I had not opted for, but in fact rebelled against, the prescribed role of dependence expected of women growing up when I did and which is still expected of disabled women. I became the "exceptional" woman, the "super-crip," noted for her independence. I refused to let my identity be shaped by my disability. I wanted to be known for *who* I am and not just by what I physically cannot do.

Although I was not particularly conscious of it at the time, I was additionally burdened with extensive conflicts about dependency and feelings of shame over my own imperfections and realistic limitations. So much of my image and definition of myself had been rooted in a denial of the impact of my disability. Unfortunately, my values and emphasis on independence involved an assumption that any form of help implied dependence and was therefore humiliating.

As the aging process accelerated the impact of my disability, it became more difficult to be stoic or heroic or ignore my increased need for help at times. This personal crisis coincided in time with the growing national political organization of disabled persons who were asserting their rights, demanding changes in public consciousness and social policy, and working to remove environmental and attitudinal barriers to the potential viability of their lives.

Disabled women also began a dialogue within the feminist community. On a personal level it has been through a slow process of disability consciousness-raising aided by newly found "sisters in disability," as well as through profoundly moving discussions with close, nondisabled friends that we, through mutual support and self-disclosure, began to explore our feelings and to shed the shame and humiliation associated with needing help. We began to understand that to need help did not imply helplessness nor was it the opposite of independence.

This increased appreciation of mutual interdependence as part of the human condition caused us to reexamine the feminist idea of autonomy versus dependence.

Feminists have long attacked the media image of "the Body Beautiful" as oppressive, exploitative, and objectifying. Even in our attempts to create alternatives. however, we develop standards which oppress some of us. The feminist ideal of autonomy does not take into account the realistic needs for help that disabled, aging—and, in fact, most—women have. The image of the physically strong "superwoman" is also out of reach for most of us.

As we began to develop disability consciousness, we recognized significant parallels to feminist consciousness. For example, it is clear that just as society creates an ideal of beauty which is oppressive for us all, it creates an ideal model of the physically perfect person, who is not beset with weakness, loss, or pain. It is toward these distorted ideals of perfection in form and function that we all strive and with which we identify.

The disabled (and aging) woman poses a symbolic threat by reminding us how tenuous that model, "the myth of the perfect body," really is, and we might want to run from this thought. The disabled woman's body may not meet the standard of "perfection" in either image, form, or function. On the one hand, disabled women share the social stereotype of women in general as being weak and passive, and in fact are depicted as the epitome of the incompetent female. On the other hand, disabled women are not viewed as women at all, but portrayed as helpless, dependent children in need of protection. She is not seen as the sexy, but the sexless object, asexual, neutered, unbeautiful and unable to find a lover. This stigmatized view of the disabled woman reflects a perception of assumed inadequacy on the part of the nondisabled.

For instance, disabled women are often advised by professionals not to bear children, and are (within race and class groupings) more likely to be threatened by or be victims of involuntary sterilization. Concerns for reproductive freedom and child custody, as well as rape and domestic violence, often exclude the disabled woman by assuming her to be an asexual creature. The perception that a disabled woman couldn't possibly get a man to care for or take care of her underlies the instances where professionals have urged disabled women who have been victims of brutal battery to stay with abusive males. Members of the helping professions often assume that no other men would want them.

Disability is often associated with sin, stigma, and a kind of "untouchability." Anxiety, as well as a sense of vulnerability and dread, may cause others to respond to the "imperfections" of a disabled woman's body with terror, avoidance, pity and or guilt. In a special *Off Our Backs* issue on disabled women, Jill Lessing postulated that it is "through fear and denial that attitudes of repulsion and oppression are acted out on disabled people in ways ranging from our solicitous good intentions to total invisibility and isolation."*

Even when the disabled woman is idealized for surmounting all obstacles, she is the recipient of a distancing admiration, which assumes her achievement to be necessary compensation for a lack of sexuality, intimacy, and love. The stereotype of the independent "supercrip," although embodying images of strength and courage, involves avoidance and denial of the realities of disability for both the observer and the disabled woman herself.

These discomforts may evoke a wish that disabled women remain invisible and that their sexuality be a hidden secret. However, disabled (and aging) women are coming out; we are beginning to examine our issues publicly, forcing other women to not only address the issues of disability but reexamine their attitudes toward their own limitations and lack of perfection, toward oppressive myths, standards, and social conditions which affect us all. . . .

*Jill Lessing. "Denial and Disability," *Off Our Backs,* vol. xi, no. 5. May 1981, p. 21.

BULLY IN THE MIRROR

STEPHEN S. HALL

On an insufferably muggy afternoon in July, with the thermometer pushing 90 degrees and ozone alerts filling the airwaves, Alexander Bregstein was in a foul mood . . . Working on just three hours of sleep, and having spent the last eight hours minding a bunch of preschool kids in his summer job as a camp counselor, Alexander was itching to kick back and relax. So there he was, lying on his back in the weight room of his gym, head down on an incline bench, earphones pitching three-figure decibels of the rock band Finger Eleven into his ears as he gripped an 85-pound weight in each hand and then, after a brief pause to gather himself, muscled them into the air with focused bursts of energy. Each life was accompanied by a sharp exhalation, like the quick, short stroke of a piston.

The first thing you need to know about Alexander is that he is sixteen years old, bright, articulate and funny in that self-deprecating and almost wise teenage way. However, about a year ago, Alexander made a conscious decision that those weren't the qualities he wanted people to recognize in him, at least not at first. He wanted people to *see* him first, and what they see these days are thick neck muscles, shoulders so massive that he can't scratch his back, a powerful bulge in his arms and a chest that has been deliberately chiseled for the two-button look—what Alexander now calls "my most endearing feature." He walks with a kind of cocky gravity-testing bounce in his step that derives in part from his muscular build but also from the confidence of knowing he looks good in his tank top and baggy shorts.

As his spotter, Aaron Anavim, looked on, Alexander lifted the 85-pound weights three more times, arms quivering, face reddening with effort. Each dumbbell, I realized as I watched, weighed more than I did when I entered high school. Another half-dozen teenagers milled around the weight room, casting glances at themselves and one another in the mirror. They talked of looking "cut," with sharp definition to their muscles, and of developing "six-packs," crisp divisions of the abdominals, but of all the muscles that get a workout in rooms like these, the most important may be the ones that move the eyes in restless sweeping arcs of comparison and appraisal. . . . Until recently, Alexander carried nearly 210 pounds on a 5-foot-6 frame, and when I asked if he was teased about his weight, he practically dropped a dumbbell on my feet. "Oh! Oh, man, was I *teased?* Are you kidding?" he said in his rapid, agreeable patter. "When I was fat, people must have gone home and thought of nothing else except coming in with new material the next day. They must have had *study groups* just to make fun of people who were overweight." . . .

And so Alexander decided to do something about it, something drastic.

There is a kind of timeless, archetypal trajectory to a teenager's battle with body image, but in most accounts the teenager is female and the issue is anorexia or bulimia. As any psychologist knows, however, and as any sufficiently evolved adult male could tell you, boys have body-image problems, too. Traditionally, they have felt pressure to look not thin, but rather strong and virile, which increasingly seems to mean looking bulked up and muscular, and that is why I was interested in talking to Alexander.

Although more than thirty years in age separates us, hearing him give voice to his insecurities, to imagined physical flaws, reminded me all over again of my own tortured passage through adolescence, my own dissatisfaction with a body that seemed punitively untouched by any growth spurt, and my own reluctant accommodation with certain inalienable facts of nature. Like me, Alexander had been teased and harassed about being short in stature. Like me, he had struggled to overcome his physical shortcomings as a member of the high school wrestling team. Unlike me, he also battled a severe weight problem, but at a similar moment in life, we had both looked in the mirror and hadn't liked what we'd seen.

Still, a lot has changed since I was fifteen. Consider the current batch of cold messages from the culture at large. The new anabolic Tarzan. "Chicks dig the long ball." Littleton. (Buried beneath a ton of prose about gun control was the report that Eric Harris apparently felt dissatisfied with his height, repeatedly complaining that he was smaller than his brother.) Aggressive advertising campaigns showing half-naked men in which the Obsession could just as easily be about your own very toned body as about someone else's. Even a lawsuit at the higher echelons of American business peeled away the pretense of adult civility to show that the classic junior-high body-image put-down—Michael Eisner dissing Jeffrey Karzenberg as a "little midget"—is alive and well in the boardroom, as it has been in the locker room for decades. You would never know that for the past quarter-century, feminist thought and conversation have created room for alternatives to traditional masculinity, in which toughness is equated with self-worth and physical stature is equated with moral stature.

No one can quite cite any data, any scientific studies proving that things are different, but a number of psychologists with whom I spoke returned to the same point again and again: the cultural messages about an ideal male body, if not new, have grown more insistent, more aggressive, more widespread and more explicit in recent years.

Since roughly 90 percent of teenagers who are treated for eating disorders are female, boys still have a way to go. Young girls have suffered greatly from insecurity about appearance and body image, and the scientific literature on anorexia and related body-image disorders depicts a widespread and serious health problem in adolescent females. But to hear some psychologists tell it, boys may be catching up in terms of insecurity and even psychological pathology. . . . A number of studies in the past decade—of men, not boys—have suggested that "body-image disturbances," as researchers sometimes call them, may be more prevalent in men than previously believed and almost always begin in the teen-age years. . . .

Recent figures on cosmetic surgery indirectly confirm the anecdotal sense that men are going to greater extremes to improve their appearances. Women still account for about 90 percent of all procedures, but the number of men undergoing cosmetic surgery rose about 34 percent between 1996 and 1998, with liposuction being the most sought service. "Basically men in general are getting the same medicine that women have had to put up with for years, which was trying to match an unattainable ideal in terms of body image," says Harrison G. Pope, Jr., of Harvard Medical School, who has focused his studies on college-age men just past adolescence. "Boys are much more prone at this point to worry about being beefed up, about having muscles," says Mary Pipher, a psychologist and the author of *Reviving Ophelia,* a book about adolescent girls. "As we've commodified boys' bodies to sell products, with advertisements that show boys as bodies without heads, we've had this whole business about focusing on the body." And, she adds, families move so often that teenagers "don't really know each other very well, so the only piece of information that's really accessible is your appearance."

There is one trenchant piece of research that justifies the sudden new focus on male development. Inspired by the AIDS epidemic, government-sponsored researchers began an enormous survey of sexual attitudes in teenage boys called the 1988 National Survey of Adolescent Males. Joseph H. Pleck, a psychologist at the University of Illinois at Urbana-Champaign and one of the principal investigators of the study, reported in 1993 a factor called "masculinity ideology," which indicates the degree to which boys subscribe to the more traditional standards of male comportment: the need for respect from peers and spouses, a reliance on physical toughness, a reluctance to talk about problems, even a reluctance to do housework. "The more traditional the attitude about masculinity in adolescent males," Pleck found, "the higher their risk for risky sexual behavior, substance use, educational problems and problems with the law."

"This one variable is a really powerful predictor of behavior," says Dan Kindlon, a researcher at the School of Public Health at Harvard and co-author, with Michael Thompson, of *Raising Cain,* "When you look at the kinds of kids who are in trouble in terms of—you name it—drugs and alcohol, suicide, attention-deficit disorder and learning disabilities, the prevalence statistics are so skewed toward boys that it's enough to knock you over. And when they looked at kids over time, the kids who had the highest risk were the highest in terms of this masculinity ideology." Since this ideology is so pervasive in boys, Kindlon says, it creates a kind of social pecking order based on physical size and the *appearance* of toughness.

The confusions that arise in young males as they try to reconcile the traditional masculine values of their fathers, for example, with a post-feminist culture that celebrates sensitivity and openness have created a "national crisis of boyhood," according to some psychologists. . . . Some academics claim to have seen the crisis coming for years. After the recent outbreaks of school violence in Littleton, Jonesboro, and Springfield, Pollack said, "It's boys who are doing this, because of this code about what they can say and can't say, how they feel about their body self, how they feel about their self-image, how they feel about themselves in school." There's "no coincidence," he added, that boys are unleashing this violence in school.

You don't have to buy the alarmism implicit in Pollack's point to appreciate that body-image concerns form part of a larger, more complex and in some ways changeless ethos of male adolescence that would be trite and obvious if it weren't so true: boys, like girls, are keenly aware of, and insecure about, their physical appearance. Boys, unlike some girls, do not talk about it with their parents, with other adults, or even among themselves, at least in part for fear of being perceived as "sensitive," a code word for "weak." Indeed, they tease each other, on a scale from casually nasty to obsessively cruel, about any perceived flaws, many of which involve some physical difference—size, shape, complexion, coordination—and since adolescent teasing begs for an audience, much of this physical ridicule occurs in school. If you don't change the "culture of cruelty," as Kindlon and Thompson put it in their book, you'll never defuse the self-consciousness and concerns about body image in boys. . . .

In 1965, just shy of fourteen, I was not only the shortest kid in my freshman gym class; but also the new kid in school, my family having just moved to a suburb west of Chicago. It had rained heavily the day before,

and there were huge puddles on the fields around which we were ordered to take the obligatory lap at the end of calisthenics. As I was running along, two larger boys— football players, it turned out—came up behind me, knocked me down and then, each taking a leg as if grabbing a wishbone, dragged my 4-foot-9, 82-pound frame along the ground and through several pond-size puddles. It is part of the dynamic of stoic boyhood, of suffering the routine bullying and hazing in resentful silence, that my parents will learn of this incident for the first time when they read this article.

As I spoke with adolescent boys and psychologists, it became clear that of all body-image issues, size is the most important, in part because it leads to a kind of involuntary self-definition. One morning I met with a group of boys attending a summer session at the Chelsea Center of the McBurney Y.M.C.A. in Manhattan. I asked them if they had nicknames, and almost every name referred to a physical quality. Mouse. String Bean. Little J. Leprechaun. Shortie. Half Pint. Spaghetti. . . .

A boy's body image is shaped, if not determined, by the cruelest, most unforgiving and meanest group of judges imaginable: other boys. And even if you outgrow, physically and emotionally, the body image that oppressed you as an adolescent, it stays with you in adult life as a kind of subdermal emotional skin that can never be shed, only incorporated into the larger person you try to become. I think that's what Garry Trudeau, the formerly small cartoonist, had in mind when he described life as a tall adult as that of a "recovering short person."

It was during his sophomore year, getting "the day-lights pounded out of him" in wrestling and gaining even more weight, that Alexander began what he calls, with justification, his "drastic transformation." He started by losing thirty pounds in one month. For a time, he consumed only 900 calories a day, and ultimately got down to 152 pounds. He began to lift weights seriously, every day for three months straight. He started to read magazines like *Flex* and *Men's Fitness*. He briefly dabbled with muscle-building supplements like creatine. He got buff, and then beyond buff.

By the time his sophomore year in high school began, Alexander had packaged his old self in a phenomenally new body, and it has had the desired effect. "My quality of social life changed dramatically when I changed my image," he said. . . . Alexander was especially pleased by the good shape he was in. . . . But fitness was only part of what he was after. As he put it: "No one's looking for a natural look, of being thin and in shape. It's more of looking toward a level beyond that." He added that "guys who work out, especially guys who have six-packs and are really cut up, are the ones girls go after."

To be honest, I was a little dubious about this until I spoke with an admittedly unscientific sampling of teenage girls. It turned out that they not only agreed with the sentiment, but also spoke the same lingo. "If you're going swimming or something like that, girls like the stomach best," said Elizabeth, a fourteen-year old. "Girls like it if they have a six-pack, or if they're really ripped, as they say. That's the most important thing. And arms too."

"But not too much," added her friend Kane, also fourteen. "You don't like it if the muscles are too huge."

"It changes your perspective on them if they have a flabby stomach," Elizabeth continued. "And the chest is important too." . . .

"The feminist complaint all along has been that women get treated as objects, that they internalize this and that it damages their self-esteem," says Kelly D. Brownell, director of the Yale Center for Eating and Weight Disorders. "And more and more, guys are falling into that same thing. They're getting judged not by who they are, but how they look."

There is no way to plug popular culture into an equation and see what effect it has on mass psychology, of course, but there is widespread sentiment that these provocative images of buff males have really upped the ante for boys. . . . Some of the research on body-image disorders in males indirectly makes that connection to cultural images.

[Roberto] Olivardia, who conducted extensive interviews with men suffering from body dysmorphic disorder, says the patients bring up Hollywood movie stars all the time. "Arnold Schwarzenegger, Stallone, Jean-Claude Van Damme. And Calvin Klein—that name has been brought up quite a lot of times." If you pick up an issue of *GQ* or *Men's Health* or *Teen People,* you'll see the trickle-down effect: a boy removes a tank top for Guess jeans. Firemen drop trou for Jockey shorts. Even the recent ads for "Smart Start" cereals by Kellogg's feature a naked torso. Consider: a six-pack in a cereal ad. . . .

This male preoccupation with appearance seems to herald a dubious, regressive form of equality—now boys can become as psychologically and physically debilitated by body-image concerns as girls have been for decades. After all, this vast expenditure of teenage male energy, both psychic and kinetic, is based on the premise that members of the opposite sex are attracted to a retro, rough-hewn, muscular look. . . .

Because he's a perceptive kid, Alexander recognizes how feckless, how disturbing, how *crazy* this all is. "I tell you, it's definitely distressing," he said, "the fact that as much as girls get this anorexic thing and they're going through these image things with dolls and stuff, guys are definitely doing the same." True, he admitted, his social life has never been better. "But in a way it depresses me," he said, before heading off to a party, "that I had to do this for people to get to know me."

Selling Hot Pussy: Representations of Black Female Sexuality in the Cultural Marketplace

BELL HOOKS

Friday night in a small midwestern town—I go with a group of artists and professors to a late-night dessert place. As we walk past a group of white men standing in the entryway to the place, we overhear them talking about us, saying that my companions, who are all white, must be liberals from the college, not regular "townies," to be hanging out with a "nigger." Everyone in my group acts as though they did not hear a word of this conversation. Even when I call attention to the comments, no one responds. It's like I am not only not talking, but suddenly, to them, I am not there. I am invisible. For my colleagues, racism expressed in everyday encounters—this is our second such experience together—is only an unpleasantness to be avoided, not something to be confronted or challenged. It is just something negative disrupting the good time, better to not notice and pretend it's not there.

As we enter the dessert place they all burst into laughter and point to a row of gigantic chocolate breasts complete with nipples—huge edible tits. They think this is a delicious idea—seeing no connection between this racialized image and the racism expressed in the entryway. Living in a world where white folks are no longer nursed and nurtured primarily by black female caretakers, they do not look at these symbolic breasts and consciously think about "mammies." They do not see this representation of chocolate breasts as a sign of displaced longing for a racist past when the bodies of black women were commodity, available to anyone white who could pay the price. I look at these dark breasts and think about the representation of black female bodies in popular culture. Seeing them, I think about the

connection between contemporary representations and the types of images popularized from slavery on. I remember Harriet Jacobs' powerful exposé of the psychosexual dynamics of slavery in *Incidents in the Life of a Slave Girl*. I remember the way she described that "peculiar" institution of domination and the white people who constructed it as "a cage of obscene birds."

Representations of black female bodies in contemporary popular culture rarely subvert or critique images of black female sexuality which were part of the cultural apparatus of nineteenth-century racism and which still shape perceptions today. Sander Gilman's essay, "Black Bodies, White Bodies: Toward an Iconography of Female Sexuality in Late Nineteenth-Century Art, Medicine, and Literature," calls attention to the way black presence in early North American society allowed whites to sexualize their world by projecting onto black bodies a narrative of sexualization disassociated from whiteness. Gilman documents the development of this image, commenting that "by the eighteenth century, the sexuality of the black, male and female, becomes an icon for deviant sexuality." He emphasizes that it is the black female body that is forced to serve as "an icon for black sexuality in general."

Most often attention was not focused on the complete black female on display at a fancy ball in the "civilized" heart of European culture, Paris. She is there to entertain guests with the naked image of Otherness. They are not to look at her as a whole human being. They are to notice only certain parts. Objectified in a manner similar to that of black female slaves who stood on auction blocks while owners and overseers described their important, salable parts, the black women whose naked bodies were displayed for whites at social functions had no presence. They were reduced to mere spectacle. Little is known of their lives, their motivations. Their body parts were offered as evidence to support racist notions that black people were more akin to animals than other humans. When Sarah Bartmann's body was exhibited in 1810, she was ironically and perversely dubbed "the Hottentot Venus." Her naked body was displayed on numerous occasions for five years. When she died, the mutilated parts were still subject to scrutiny. Gilman stressed that: "The audience which had paid to see her buttocks and had fantasized about the uniqueness of her genitalia when she was alive could, after her death and dissection, examine both." Much of the racialized fascination with Bartmann's body concentrated attention on her buttocks.

A similar white European fascination with the bodies of black people, particularly black female bodies, was manifest during the career of Josephine Baker. Content to "exploit" white eroticization of black bodies, Baker called attention to the "butt" in her dance routines. Phyllis Rose, though often condescending in her recent biography, *Jazz Cleopatra: Josephine Baker in Her Time,* perceptively explores Baker's concentration on her ass:

> She handled it as though it were an instrument, a rattle, something apart from herself that she could shake. One can hardly overemphasize the importance of the rear end. Baker herself declared that people had been hiding their asses too long. "The rear end exists. I see no reason to be ashamed of it. It's true there are rear ends so stupid, so pretentious, so insignificant that they're good only for sitting on." With Baker's triumph, the erotic gaze of a nation moved downward: she had uncovered a new region for desire.

Many of Baker's dance moves highlighting the "butt" prefigure movements popular in contemporary black dance.

Although contemporary thinking about black female bodies does not attempt to read the body as a sign of "natural" racial inferiority, the fascination with black "butts" continues. In the sexual iconography of the traditional black pornographic imagination, the protruding butt is seen as an indication of a heightened sexuality. Contemporary popular music is one of the primary cultural locations for discussions of black sexuality. In song lyrics, "the butt" is talked about in ways that attempt to challenge racist assumptions that suggest it is an ugly sign of inferiority, even as it remains a sexualized sign. The popular song, "Doin' the Butt," fostered the promotion of a hot new dance favoring those who could most protrude their buttocks with pride and glee. A scene in Spike Lee's film *School Daze* depicts

an all-black party where everyone is attired in swimsuits dancing—doing the butt. It is one of the most compelling moments in the film. The black "butts" on display are unruly and outrageous. They are not the still bodies of the female slave made to appear as mannequin. They are not a silenced body. Displayed as playful cultural nationalist resistance, they challenge assumptions that the black body, its skin color and shape, is a mark of shame. Undoubtedly the most transgressive and provocative moment in *School Daze,* this celebration of buttocks either initiated or coincided with an emphasis on butts, especially the buttocks of women, in fashion magazines. Its potential to disrupt and challenge notions of black bodies, specifically female bodies, was undercut by the overall sexual humiliation and abuse of black females in the film. Many people did not see the film, so it was really the song "Doin' the Butt" that challenged dominant ways of thinking about the body, which encourage us to ignore asses because they are associated with undesirable and unclean acts. Unmasked, the "butt" could be once again worshiped as an erotic seat of pleasure and excitement.

When calling attention to the body in a manner inviting the gaze to mutilate black female bodies yet again, to focus solely on the "butt," contemporary celebrations of this part of the anatomy do not successfully subvert sexist/racist representations. Just as nineteenth-century representations of black female bodies were constructed to emphasize that these bodies were expendable, contemporary images (even those created in black cultural production) give a similar message. When Richard Wright's protest novel *Native Son* was made into a film in the 1980s, the film did not show the murder of Bigger's black girlfriend Bessie. This was doubly ironic. She is murdered in the novel and then systematically eliminated in the film. Painters exploring race as artistic subject matter in the nineteenth century often created images contrasting white female bodies with black ones in ways that reinforced the greater value of the white female icon. Gilman's essay colludes in this critical project: he is really most concerned with exploring white female sexuality.

A similar strategy is employed in the Wright novel and in the film version. In the novel, Bessie is expendable because Bigger has already committed the more heinous crime of killing a white woman. The first and more important murder subsumes the second. Everyone cares about the fate of Mary Dalton, the ruling-class white female daughter; no one cares about the fate of Bessie. Ironically, just at the moment when Bigger decides that Bessie's body is expendable, that he will kill her, he continues to demand that she help him, that she "do the right thing." Bigger intends to use her, then throw her away, a gesture reinforcing that hers is an expendable body. While he must transgress dangerous boundaries to destroy the body of a white female, he can invade and violate a black female body with no fear of retribution and retaliation.

Black and female, sexual outside the context of marriage, Bessie represents "fallen womanhood." She has no protectors, no legal system will defend her rights. Pleading her cause to Bigger, she asks for recognition and compassion for her specific condition.

> Bigger, please! Don't do this to me! Please! All I do is work, work like a dog! From morning till night. I ain't got no happiness. I ain't never had none. I ain't got nothing and you do this to me. . . .

Poignantly describing the lot of working-class poor black women in the 1940s, her words echo those of poet Nikki Giovanni describing the status of black women in the late 1960s. The opening lines to "Woman Poem" read: "You see my whole life is tied up to unhappiness." There is a radical difference, however. In the 1960s, the black female is naming her unhappiness to demand a hearing, an acknowledgment of her reality, and change her status. This poem speaks to the desire of black women to construct a sexuality apart from that imposed upon us by a racist/sexist culture, calling attention to the ways we are trapped by conventional notions of sexuality and desirability:

> . . . It's a sex object if you're pretty and no love or love and no sex if you're fat get back fat black woman be a mother grandmother strong thing but not woman gameswoman romantic woman love needer man seeker dick eater sweat getter fuck needing love seeking woman

"Woman Poem" is a cry of resistance urging those who exploit and oppress black women, who objectify and dehumanize, to confront the consequences of their actions. Facing herself, the black female realizes all that she must struggle against to achieve self-actualization. She must counter the representation of herself, her body, her being as expendable.

Bombarded with images representing black female bodies as expendable, black women have either passively absorbed this thinking or vehemently resisted it. Popular culture provides countless examples of black female appropriation and exploitation of "negative stereotypes" to either assert control over the representation or at least reap the benefits of it. Since black female sexuality has been represented in racist/sexist iconography as more free and liberated, many black women singers, irrespective of the quality of their voices, have cultivated an image which suggests they are sexually available and licentious. Undesirable in the conventional sense, which defines beauty and sexuality as desirable only to the extent that it is idealized and unattainable, the black female body gains attention only when it is synonymous with accessibility, availability, when it is sexually deviant.

Tina Turner's construction of a public sexual persona most conforms to this idea of black female sexuality. In her recent autobiography *I, Tina* she presents a sexualized portrait of herself—providing a narrative that is centrally "sexual confession." Even though she begins by calling attention to the fact that she was raised with puritanical notions of innocence and virtuous womanhood which made her reticent and fearful of sexual experience, all that follows contradicts this portrait. Since the image that has been cultivated and commodified in popular culture is of her as "hot" and highly sexed—the sexually ready and free black woman—a tension exists in the autobiography between the reality she presents and the image she must uphold. Describing her first sexual experience, Turner recalls:

> Naturally, I lost my virginity in the backseat of a car. This was the fifties, right? I think he had planned it, the little devil—he knew by then that he could get into my pants, because there's already been a lot of kissing and touching inside the blouse, and then under the skirt and so forth. The next step was obvious. And me, as brazen as I was, when it came down to finally doing the real thing, it was like: "Uh-oh, it's time." I mean, I was scared. And then it happened.
>
> Well, it hurt so bad—I think my earlobes were hurting. I was just dying, God. And he wanted to do it two or three times! It was like poking an open wound. I could hardly walk afterwards.
>
> But I did it for love. The pain was excruciating; but I loved him and he loved me, and that made the pain less—Everything was right. So it was beautiful.

Only there is nothing beautiful about the scenario Turner describes. A tension exists between the "cool" way she describes this experience, playing it off to suggest she *was* in control of the situation, and the reality she recounts where she succumbs to male lust and suffers sex. After describing a painful rite of sexual initiation, Turner undermines the confession by telling the reader that she felt good. Through retrospective memory, Turner is able to retell this experience in a manner that suggests she was comfortable with sexual experience at an early age, yet cavalier language does not completely mask the suffering evoked by the details she gives. However, this cavalier attitude accords best with how her fans "see" her. Throughout the biography she will describe situations of extreme sexual victimization and then undermine the impact of her words by evoking the image of herself and other black women as sexually free, suggesting that we assert sexual agency in ways that are never confirmed by the evidence she provides.

Tina Turner's singing career has been based on the construction of an image of black female sexuality that is made synonymous with wild animalistic lust. Raped and exploited by Ike Turner, the man who made this image and imposed it on her, Turner describes the way her public persona as singer was shaped by his pornographic misogynist imagination:

> Ike explained: As a kid back in Clarksdale, he'd become fixated on the white jungle goddess who romped through Saturday matinee movie serials—revealing rag-clad women with long flowing hair and names like Sheena, Queen of the Jungle, and Nyoka—particularly Nyoka. He still remembered *The Perils of Nyoka,* a fifteen-part Republic Picture serial from 1941, starring Kay Alridge in the title role and featuring a villainess named Vultura, an ape named Satan, and Clayton Moore (later to be TV's Lone Ranger) as love interest. Nyoka, Sheena—Tina! Tina Turner—Ike's own personal Wild Woman. He loved it.

Turner makes no comment about her thoughts about this image. How can she? It is part of the representation which makes and maintains her stardom.

Ike's pornographic fantasy of the black female as wild sexual savage emerged from the impact of a white patriarchal controlled media shaping his perceptions of reality. His decision to create the wild black woman was perfectly compatible with prevailing representations of black female sexuality in a white supremacist society. Of course the Tina Turner story reveals that she was anything but a wild woman; she was fearful of sexuality, abused, humiliated, fucked, and fucked over. Turner's friends and colleagues document the myriad ways she suffered about the experience of being brutally physically beaten prior to appearing on stage to perform, yet there is no account of how she coped with the contradiction (this story is told by witnesses in *I, Tina*). She was on one hand in excruciating pain inflicted by a misogynist man who dominated her life and her sexuality, and on the other hand projecting in every performance the image of a wild tough sexuality liberated woman. Not unlike the lead character in the novel *Story of O* by Pauline Reage, Turner must act as though she glories in her submission, that she delights in being a slave of love. Leaving Ike, after many years of forced marital rape and physical abuse, because his violence is utterly uncontrollable, Turner takes with her the "image" he created.

Despite her experience of abuse rooted in sexist and racist objectification, Turner appropriated the "wild woman" image, using it for career advancement. Always fascinated with wigs and long hair, she created the blonde lioness mane to appear all the more savage and animalistic. Blondeness links her to jungle imagery even as it serves as an endorsement of a racist aesthetics which sees blonde hair as the epitome of beauty. Without Ike, Turner's career has soared to new heights, particularly as she works harder to exploit the visual representation of woman (and particularly black woman) as sexual savage. No longer caught in the sadomasochistic sexual iconography of black female in erotic war with her mate that was the subtext of the Ike and Tina Turner show, she is now portrayed as the autonomous black woman whose sexuality is solely a way to exert power. Inverting old imagery, she places herself in the role of dominator.

Playing the role of Aunty Entity in the film *Mad Max: Beyond the Thunderdome,* released in 1985, Turner's character evokes two racist/sexist stereotypes, that of the black "mammy" turned power hungry and the sexual savage who uses her body to seduce and conquer men. Portrayed as lusting after the white male hero who will both conquer and reject her, Aunty Entity is the contemporary reenactment of that mythic black female in slavery who supposedly "vamped" and seduced virtuous white male slave owners. Of course the contemporary white male hero of *Mad Max* is stronger than his colonial forefathers. He does not succumb to the dangerous lure of the deadly black seductress who rules over a mini-nation whose power is based on the use of shit. Turner is the bad black woman in this film, an image she will continue to exploit.

Turner's video "What's Love Got to Do with It" also highlights the convergence of sexuality and power. Here, the black woman's body is represented as potential weapon. In the video, she walks down rough city streets, strutting her stuff, in a way that declares desirability, allure, while denying access. It is not that she is no longer represented as available; she is "open" only to those whom she chooses.

Assuming the role of hunter, she is the sexualized woman who makes men and women her prey (in the alluring gaze of the video, the body moves in the direction of both sexes). This tough black woman has no time for woman bonding, she is out to "catch." Turner's fictive model of black female sexual agency remains rooted in misogynist notions. Rather than being a pleasure-based eroticism, it is ruthless, violent; it is about women using sexual power to do violence to the male Other.

Appropriating the wild woman pornographic myth of black female sexuality created by men in a white supremacist patriarchy, Turner exploits it for her own ends to achieve economic self-sufficiency. When she left Ike, she was broke and in serious debt. The new Turner image conveys the message that happiness and power come to women who learn to beat men at their own game, to throw off any investment in romance and get down to the real dog-eat-dog thing. "What's Love Got to Do with It" sung by Turner evokes images of the strong bitchified black woman who is on the make. Subordinating the idea of romantic love and praising the use of sex for pleasure as commodity to exchange, the song had great appeal for contemporary postmodern culture. It equates pleasure with materiality, making it an object to be sought after, taken, acquired by any means necessary. When sung by black women singers, "What's Love Got to Do with It" called to mind old stereotypes which make the assertion of black female sexuality and prostitution synonymous. Just as black female prostitutes in the 1940s and 1950s actively sought clients in the streets to make money to survive, thereby publicly linking prostitution with black female sexuality, contemporary black female sexuality is fictively constructed in popular rap and R&B songs solely as commodity—sexual service for money and power, pleasure is secondary.

Contrasted with the representation of wild animalistic sexuality, black female singers like Aretha Franklin and younger contemporaries like Anita Baker fundamentally link romance and sexual pleasure. Aretha, though seen as a victim of no-good men, the classic "woman who loves too much" and leaves the lyrics to prove it, also sang songs of resistance. "Respect" was heard by many black folks, especially black women, as a song challenging black male sexism and female victimization while evoking notions of mutual care and support. In a recent PBS special highlighting individual musicians, Aretha Franklin was featured. Much space was given in the documentary to white male producers who shaped her public image. In the documentary, she describes the fun of adding the words "sock it to me" to "Respect" as a powerful refrain. One of the white

male producers, Jerry Wexler, offers his interpretation of its meaning, claiming that it was a call for "sexual attention of the highest order." His sexualized interpretations of the song seemed far removed from the way it was heard and celebrated in black communities. Looking at this documentary, which was supposedly a tribute to Aretha Franklin's power, it was impossible not to have one's attention deflected away from the music by the subtext of the film, which can be seen as a visual narrative documenting her obsessive concern with the body and achieving a look suggesting desirability. To achieve this end, Franklin constantly struggles with her weight, and the images in the film chronicle her various shifts in body size and shape. As though mocking this concern with her body, throughout most of the documentary Aretha appears in what seems to be a household setting, a living room maybe, wearing a strapless evening dress, much too small for her breast size, so her breasts appear like two balloons filled with water about to burst. With no idea who shaped and controlled this image, I can only reiterate that it undermined the insistence in the film that she has overcome sexual victimization and remained a powerful singer; the latter seemed more likely than the former.

Black female singers who project a sexualized persona are as obsessed with hair as they are with body size and body parts. As with nineteenth-century sexual iconography, specific parts of the anatomy are designated more sexual and worthy of attention than others. Today much of the sexualized imagery for black female stars seems to be fixated on hair; it and not buttocks signifies animalistic sexuality. This is quintessentially so for Tina Turner and Diana Ross. It is ironically appropriate that much of this hair is synthetic and man-made, artificially constructed as is the sexualized image it is meant to evoke. Within a patriarchal culture where women over forty are not represented as sexually desirable, it is understandable that singers exploiting sexualized representations who are near the age of fifty place less emphasis on body parts that may reflect aging while focusing on hair.

In a course I teach on "The Politics of Sexuality," where we often examine connections between race and sex, we once critically analyzed a *Vanity Fair* cover depicting Diana Ross. Posed on a white background, apparently naked with the exception of white cloth draped loosely around her body, the most striking element in the portrait was the long mane of jet black hair cascading down. There was so much hair that it seemed to be consuming her body (which looked frail and anorexic), negating the possibility that this naked flesh could represent active female sexual agency. The white diaperlike cloth reinforced the idea that this was a portrait of an adult female who wanted to be seen as child-like and innocent. Symbolically, the hair that is almost a covering hearkens back to early pictorial images of Eve in the garden. It evokes wildness, a sense of the "natural" world, even as it shrouds the body, repressing it, keeping it from the gaze of a culture that does not invite women to be sexual subjects. Concurrently, this cover contrasts white-ness and blackness. Whiteness dominates the page, obscur-ing and erasing the possibility of any assertion of black power. The longing that is most visible in this cover is that of the black woman to embody and be encircled by white-ness, personified by the possession of long straight hair. Since the hair is produced as commodity and purchased, it affirms contemporary notions of female beauty and desir-ability as that which can be acquired.

According to postmodern analyses of fashion, this is a time when commodities produce bodies, as this image of Ross suggests. In her essay "Fashion and the Cultural Logic of Postmodernity," Gail Faurshou explains that beauty is no longer seen as a sustained "category of precapitalist cul-ture." Instead, "the colonization and the appropriation of the body as its own production/consumption machine in late capitalism is a fundamental theme of contemporary socialization." This cultural shift enables the bodies of black women to be represented in certain domains of the "beautiful" where they were once denied entry, i.e., high-fashion magazines. Reinscribed as spectacle, once again on display, the bodies of black women appearing in these mag-azines are not there to document the beauty of black skin, of black bodies, but rather to call attention to other con-cerns. They are represented so readers will notice that the magazine is racially inclusive even though their features are often distorted, their bodies contorted into strange and bizarre postures that make the images appear monstrous or grotesque. They seem to represent an anti-aesthetic, one that mocks the very notion of beauty.

Often black female models appear in portraits that make them look less like humans and more like mannequins or robots. Currently, black models whose hair is not straight-ened are often photographed wearing straight wigs; this seems to be especially the case if the model's features are unconventional, i.e., if she has large lips or particularly dark skin, which is not often featured in the magazine. The October 1989 issue of *Elle* presented a short profile of designer Azzedine Alaia. He stands at a distance from a black female body holding the sleeves of her dress. Wearing a ridiculous straight hairdo, she appears naked, holding the dress in front of her body. The caption reads, "THEY ARE BEAUTIFUL AREN'T THEY!" His critical gaze is on the model and not the dress. As commentary it suggests that even black women can look beautiful in the right outfit. Of course when you read the piece, this state-ment is not referring to the model but is a statement Alaia makes about his clothes. In contemporary postmodern fash-ion sense, the black female is the best medium for the showing of clothes because her image does not detract from the outfit; it is subordinated.

Years ago, when much fuss was made about the reluc-tance of fashion magazines to include images of black women, it was assumed that the presence of such represen-tations would in and of themselves challenge racist stereo-types that imply black women are not beautiful. Nowadays, black women are included in magazines in a manner that tends to reinscribe prevailing stereotypes. Darker-skinned models are most likely to appear in photographs where their features are distorted. Biracial women tend to appear in sexualized images. Trendy catalogues like Tweeds and J. Crew make use of a racialized subtext in their layout and advertisements. Usually they are emphasizing the connec-tion between a white European and American style. When they began to include darker-skinned models, they chose biracial or fair-skinned black women, particularly with blonde or light-brown long hair. The nonwhite models appearing in these catalogues must resemble as closely as possible their white counterparts so as not to detract from the racialized subtext. A recent cover of Tweeds carried this statement:

> Color is, perhaps, one of the most important barometers of character and self-assurance. It is as much a part of the international language of clothes as silhouette. The message colors convey, however, should never over-whelm. They should speak as eloquently and intelligent-ly as the wearer. Whenever colors have that intelligence, subtlety, and nuance we tend to call them European. . . .

Given the racialized terminology evoked in this copy, it follows that when flesh is exposed in attire that is meant to evoke sexual desirability it is worn by a nonwhite model. As sexist/racist sexual mythology would have it, she is the embodiment of the best of the black female savage tem-pered by those elements of whiteness that soften this image, giving it an aura of virtue and innocence. In the racialized pornographic imagination, she is the perfect combination of virgin and whore, the ultimate vamp. The impact of this image is so intense that Iman, a highly paid black fashion model who once received worldwide acclaim because she was the perfect black clone of a white ice-goddess beauty, has had to change. Postmodern notions that black female beauty is constructed, not innate or inherent, are personified by the career of Iman. Noted in the past for features this culture sees as "Caucasian"—thin nose, lips, and limbs— Iman appears in the October 1989 issue of *Vogue* "made over." Her lips and breasts are suddenly full. Having once had her "look" destroyed by a car accident and then remade, Iman now goes a step further. Displayed as the embodiment of a heightened sexuality, she now looks like the racial/sexual stereotype. In one full-page shot, she is naked, wearing only a pair of brocade boots, looking as though she is ready to stand on any street corner and turn a trick, or worse yet, as though she just walked off one of the pages of *Players* (a porn magazine for blacks). Iman's new image appeals to a culture that is eager to reinscribe the image of black woman as sexual primitive. This new representation is a response to contemporary fascination with an ethnic look, with the exotic Other who promises to fulfill racial and sexual stereotypes, to satisfy longings. This image is but an extension of the edible black tit.

Currently, in the fashion world the new black female icon who is also gaining greater notoriety, as she assumes both the persona of sexually hot "savage" and white-identified black girl, is the Caribbean-born model Naomi Campbell. Imported beauty, she, like Iman, is almost constantly visually portrayed nearly nude against a sexualized background. Abandoning her "natural" hair for blonde wigs or ever-lengthening weaves, she has great crossover appeal. Labeled by fashion critics as the black Brigitte Bardot, she embodies an aesthetic that suggests black women, while appealingly "different," must resemble white women to be considered really beautiful.

Within literature and early film, this sanitized ethnic image was defined as that of the "tragic mulatto." Appearing in film, she was the vamp that white men feared. As Julie Burchill puts it outrageously in *Girls on Film:*

> In the mature Forties, Hollywood decided to get to grips with the meaty and messy topic of multiracial romance, but it was a morbid business. Even when the girls were gorgeous white girls—multiracial romance brought tears, traumas, and suicide. The message was clear: you intelligent white men suffer enough guilt because of what your grandaddy did—you want to suffer some more! Keep away from those girls. . . .

Contemporary films portraying biracial stars convey this same message. The warning for women is different from that given men—we are given messages about the danger of asserting sexual desire. Clearly the message from *Imitation of Life* was that attempting to define oneself as sexual subject would lead to rejection and abandonment. In the film *Choose Me,* Rae Dawn Chong plays the role of the highly sexual black woman chasing and seducing the white man who does not desire her (as was first implied in *Imitation of Life*) but instead uses her sexually, beats her, then discards her. The biracial black woman is constantly "gaslighted" in contemporary film. The message her sexualized image conveys does not change even as she continues to chase the white man as if only he had the power to affirm that she is truly desirable.

European films like *Mephisto* and the more recent *Mona Lisa* also portray the almost white, black woman as tragically sexual. The women in the films can only respond to constructions of their reality created by the more powerful. They are trapped. Mona Lisa's struggle to be sexually self-defining leads her to choose lesbianism, even though she is desired by the white male hero. Yet her choice of a female partner does not mean sexual fulfillment, as the object of her lust is a drug-addicted young white woman who is always too messed up to be sexual. Mona Lisa nurses and protects her. Rather than asserting sexual agency, she is once again in the role of mammy.

In a more recent film, *The Virgin Machine,* a white German woman obsessed by the longing to understand desire goes to California where she hopes to find a "paradise of black Amazons." However, when she arrives and checks out the lesbian scene, the black women she encounters are portrayed as mean fat grotesques, lewd and licentious. Contemporary films continue to place black women in two categories, mammy or slut, and occasionally a combination of the two. In *Mona Lisa,* one scene serves as powerful commentary on the way black sexuality is perceived in a racist and imperialist social context. The white male who desires the black prostitute Mona Lisa is depicted as a victim of romantic love who wishes to rescue her from a life of ruin. Yet he is also the conqueror, the colonizer, and this is most evident in the scene where he watches a video wherein she engages in fellatio with the black male pimp who torments her. Both the black man and the black woman are presented as available for the white male's sexual consumption. In the context of postmodern sexual practice, the masturbatoryvoyeuristictechnologically based fulfillment of desire is more exciting than actually possessing any real Other.

There are few films or television shows that attempt to challenge assumptions that sexual relationships between black women and white men are not based solely on power relationships which mirror master/slave paradigms. Years ago, when soap operas first tried to portray romantic/sexual involvement between a black woman and a white man, the station received so many letters to protest from outraged viewers that they dropped this plot. Today many viewers are glued to the television screen watching the soap opera *All My Children* primarily to see if the black woman played by Debbie Morgan will win the white man she so desperately loves. These two lovers are never portrayed in bedroom scenes so common now in daytime soaps. Morgan's character is not just competing with an old white woman flame to get her white man, she is competing with a notion of family. And the story poses the question of whether white male desire for black flesh will prevail over commitments to blood and family loyalty.

Despite this plot of interracial sexual romance on the soaps, there is little public discussion of the connections between race and sexuality. In real life, it was the Miss America pageant where a black woman was chosen to represent beauty and therefore desirability which forced a public discussion of race and sex. When it was revealed that Vanessa Williams, the fair-skinned straightened-hair "beauty," had violated the representation of the Miss America girl as pure and virtuous by having posed nude in a series of photographs showing her engaged in sexual play with a white woman, she lost her crown but gained a different status. After her public "disgrace," she was able to remain in the limelight by appropriating the image of sexualized vamp and playing sexy roles in films. Unmasked by a virtuous white public, she assumed (according to their standards) the rightful erotic place set aside for black women in the popular imagination. The American public that had so brutally critiqued Williams and rejected her had no difficulty accepting and applauding her when she accepted the image of fallen woman. Again, as in the case of Tina Turner, Williams's bid for continued success necessitated her acceptance of conventional racist/sexist representations of black female sexuality.

The contemporary film that has most attempted to address the issue of black female sexual agency is Spike Lee's *She's Gotta Have It.* Sad to say, the black woman does not get "it." By the end of the film, she is still unable to answer the critical question, posed by one of her lovers as he rapes her, "whose pussy is this?" Reworded the question might be: How and when will black females assert sexual agency in ways that liberate us from the confines of colonized desire, of racist/ sexist imagery and practice? Had Nola Darling been able to claim her sexuality and name its power, the film would have had a very different impact.

There are few films that explore issues of black female sexuality in ways that intervene and disrupt conventional representations. The short film *Dreaming Rivers,* by the British black film collective Sankofa, juxtaposes the idealized representation of black woman as mother with that of sexual subject, showing adult children facing their narrow notions of black female identity. The film highlights the autonomous sexual identity of a mature black woman which exists apart from her role as mother and caregiver. *Passion of Remembrance,* another film by Sankofa, offers exciting new representations of the black female body and black female sexuality. In one playfully erotic scene, two young black women, a lesbian couple, get dressed to go out. As part of their celebratory preparations they dance together, painting their lips, looking at their images in the mirror, exulting in their black female bodies. They shake to a song that repeats the refrain "let's get loose" without conjuring images of a rotgut colonized sexuality on display for the racist/sexist imagination. Their pleasure, the film suggests, emerges in a decolonized erotic context rooted in commitments to feminist and antiracist politics. When they look in the mirror and focus on specific body parts (their full thick lips and buttocks), the gaze is one of recognition. We see their pleasure and delight in themselves.

Films by African-American women filmmakers also offer the most oppositional images of black female sexuality. Seeing for a second time Kathleen Collin's film *Losing Ground,* I was impressed by her daring, the way she portrays black female sexuality in a way that is fresh and exciting. Like *Passion of Remembrance* it is in a domestic setting, where black women face one another (in Collin's film—as mother and daughter), that erotic images of black female sexuality surface outside a context of domination and exploitation. When daughter and mother share a meal, the audience watches as a radical sexual aesthetics emerges as the camera moves from woman to woman, focusing on the shades and textures of their skin, the shapes of their bodies, and the way their delight and pleasure in themselves is evident in their environment. Both black women discreetly flaunt a rich sensual erotic energy that is not directed outward, it is not there to allure or entrap; it is a powerful declaration of black female sexual subjectivity.

When black women relate to our bodies, our sexuality, in ways that place erotic recognition, desire, pleasure, and fulfillment at the center of our efforts to create radical black female subjectivity, we can make new and different representations of ourselves as sexual subjects. To do so we must be willing to transgress traditional boundaries. We

THE BEAUTY MYTH

NAOMI WOLF

. . . Beauty pornography looks like this: The perfected woman lies prone, pressing down her pelvis. Her back arches, her mouth is open, her eyes shut, her nipples erect; there is a fine spray of moisture over her golden skin. The position is female superior; the stage of arousal, the plateau phase just preceding orgasm. On the next page, a version of her, mouth open, eyes shut, is about to tongue the pink tip of a lipstick cylinder. On the page after, another version kneels in the sand on all fours, her buttocks in the air, her face pressed into a towel, mouth open, eyes shut. The reader is looking through an ordinary women's magazine. In an ad for Reebok shoes, the woman sees a naked female torso, eyes averted. In an ad for Lily of France lingerie, she sees a naked female torso, eyes shut; for Opium perfume, a naked woman, back and buttocks bare, falls facedown from the edge of a bed; for Triton showers, a naked woman, back arched, flings her arms upward; for Jogbra sports bras, a naked female torso is cut off at the neck. In these images, where the face is visible, it is expressionless in a rictus of ecstasy. The reader understands from them that she will have to look like that if she wants to feel like that.

Beauty sadomasochism is different: In an ad for Obsession perfume, a well-muscled man drapes the naked, lifeless body of a woman over his shoulder. In an ad for Hermès perfume, a blond woman trussed in black leather is hanging upside down, screaming, her wrists looped in chains, mouth bound. In an ad for Fuji cassettes, a female robot with a playmate's body, but made of steel, floats with her genitals exposed, her ankles bolted and her face a steel mask with slits for the eyes and mouth. In an ad for Erno Laszlo skin care products, a woman sits up and begs, her wrists clasped together with a leather leash that is also tied to her dog, who is sitting up in the same posture and begging. In an American ad for Newport cigarettes, two men tackle one woman and pull another by the hair; both women are screaming. In another Newport ad, a man forces a woman's head down to get her distended mouth around a length of spurting hose gripped in his fist; her eyes are terrified. In an ad for Saab automobiles, a shot up a fashion model's thighs is captioned. "Don't worry. It's ugly underneath." In a fashion layout in *The Observer* (London), five men in black menace a model, whose face is in shock, with scissors and hot iron rods. In *Tatler* and *Harper's and Queen,* "designer rape sequences (women beaten, bound, and abducted, but immaculately turned out and artistically photographed)" appear. In Chris von Wangenheim's *Vogue* layout, Doberman pinschers attack a model. Geoffrey Beene's metallic sandals are displayed against a background of S and M accessories. The woman learns from these images that no matter how assertive she may be in the world, her private submission to control is what makes her desirable. . . .

must no longer shy away from the critical project of openly interrogating and exploring representations of black female sexuality as they appear everywhere, especially in popular culture. In *The Power of the Image: Essays on Representation and Sexuality,* Annette Kuhn offers a critical manifesto for feminist thinkers who long to explore gender and representation:

. . . in order to challenge dominant representations, it is necessary first of all to understand how they work, and thus where to seek points of possible productive transformation. From such understanding flow various politics and practices of oppositional cultural production, among which may be counted feminist interventions . . . there is another justification for a feminist analysis of main-

Sexual "explicitness" is not the issue. We could use a lot more of that, if explicit meant honest and revealing; if there were a full spectrum of erotic images of uncoerced real women and real men in contexts of sexual trust, beauty pornography could theoretically hurt no one. Defenders of pornography base their position on the idea of freedom of speech, casting pornographic imagery as language. Using their own argument, something striking emerges about the representation of women's bodies: The representation is heavily censored. Because we see many versions of the naked Iron Maiden, we are asked to believe that our culture promotes the display of female sexuality. It actually shows almost none. It censors representations of women's bodies, so that only the official versions are visible. Rather than seeing images *of* female desire or that cater *to* female desire, we see mock-ups of living mannequins, made to contort a grimace, immobilized and uncomfortable under hot lights, professional set/pieces that reveal little about female sexuality. In the United States and Great Britain, which have no tradition of public nakedness, women rarely—and almost never outside a competitive context—see what other *women* look like naked; we see only identical humanoid products based loosely on women's bodies. . . .

. . . Leaving aside the issue of what violent sexual imagery does, it is still apparent that there is an officially enforced double standard for men's and women's nakedness in mainstream culture that bolsters power inequities.

The practice of displaying breasts, for example, in contexts in which the display of penises would be unthinkable, is portrayed as trivial because breasts are not "as naked" as penises or vaginas; and the idea of half exposing men in a similar way is moot because men don't have body parts comparable to breasts. But if we think about how women's genitals are physically concealed, unlike men's, and how women's breasts are phydically exposed, unlike men's, it can be seen differently: women's breasts, then, correspomd to men's penises as the vulnerable "sexual flower" on the body, so that to display the former and conceal the latter makes women's bodies vulnerable while men's are protected. Cross-culturally, unequal nakedness almost always expresses power relations: In modern jails, male prisoners are stripped in front of clothed prison guards; in the antebellum South, young black male slaves were naked while serving the clothed white masters at table. To live in a culture in which women are routinely naked where men aren't is to learn inequality in little ways all day long. So even if we agree that sexual imagery is in fact a language, it is clearly one that is already heavily edited to protect men's sexual—and hence social—confidence while undermining that of women. . . .

When they discuss [their bodies], women lean forward, their voices lower. They tell their terrible secret. It's my breasts, they say. My hips. It's my thighs. I hate my stomach. This is not aesthetic distaste, but deep sexual shame. The parts of the body vary. But what each woman who describes it shares is the conviction that *that* is what the pornography of beauty most fetishizes. Breasts, thighs, buttocks, bellies: the most sexually central parts of women, whose "ugliness" therefore becomes an obsession. Those are the parts most often battered by abusive men. The parts that sex murderers most often mutilate. The parts most often defiled by violent pornography. The parts that beauty surgeons most often cut open. The parts that bear and nurse children and feel sexual. A misogynist culture has succeeded in making women hate what misogynists hate. . . .

stream images of women: may it not teach us to recognize inconsistencies and contradictions within dominant traditions of representation, to identify points of leverage for our own intervention: cracks and fissures through which may be captured glimpses of what in other circumstance might be possible, visions of "a world outside the order not normally seen or thought about?"

This is certainly the challenge facing black women, who must confront the old painful representations of our sexuality as a burden we must suffer, representations still haunting the present. We must make the oppositional space where our sexuality can be named and represented, where we are sexual subjects—no longer bound and trapped.

Empowering Women? The Oprah Winfrey Show

CORINNE SQUIRE

WINFREY: Listen . . . obviously I come from a very
   biased point of view here.
FEMALE GUEST: Because you're a woman.
WINFREY: Yes. Well, and because I—what we try to do—
   we do program these shows to empower women.

THE OPRAH WINFREY SHOW, 1989B

INTRODUCTION

Every weekday in the USA 20 million people watch *The Oprah Winfrey Show,* making it the most-watched daytime talk program. Snaring an unassailable 35 per cent of the audience, it acts as a lead-in for local stations' lucrative early evening news programmes (McClellan, 1993; Boemer, 1987). The show has become a common source of information and opinions about relationships, psychopathology, and gender. It is a cultural icon, signifying at the same time lurid dilemmas, emotional intensity, fame, and black women's success. It is even a well-known chronological marker, as in "I worked so hard I was done in time for *Oprah,*" or, "I did my shopping so quick I was home by *Oprah.*"

Winfrey, the first African-American woman to host a national talk show[1] is also well known for her television specials on self-esteem and child abuse, for her role as Sophia in the film *The Color Purple,* as an advocate for abused children, and as a philanthropist supporting programs for poor black youth. The tabloids chronicle her fluctuating weight and self-esteem and her long-standing relationship with a businessman, Stedman Graham. She is one of the richest women in the world, with a yearly income of around $40 million, $16 million more than Madonna (Goodman, 1991). In 1989 she was voted the second most admired woman in the USA—after Nancy Reagan. The Oprah phenomenon is interesting in itself but this essay will restrict itself to considering Oprah, "daytime queen" (Guider, 1987), in the context of the show.

In this study I will treat the television program as a polysemous, difficult but readable text; examine its compliance with and departure from television conventions; investigate its framing by broader "texts" of social power and history; and see it as suffused with the intensity and fragmentariness of subjectivity. While psychologists are increasingly taking on such modes of analysis, psychological studies of television generally use more traditional methods, like content analysis or the microanalysis of speech and nonverbal communication. An exception is Valerie Walkerdine's "Video Replay" (1989), which provides an exemplary reading of the criss-crossed narratives of gender and class that inhabit our subjective responses to the small screen.

Like other daytime talk shows, *Oprah* aims to entertain, inform, and encourage communication about difficult issues. It is a kind of popular psychology, lacing advice and catharsis with comedy and melodrama. But the show also tries, Winfrey says, to empower women: to be a televisual feminism. Not only the host but many guests and the majority of the studio and watching audiences are women, and most episodes address female-identified topics: relationships, communication, physical appearance. Host, guests, and the studio audience also spend a lot of time in animated, messy discussions of injustices that are at the center of much contemporary feminist campaigning, like job discrimination, male violence, and sexual abuse.

While Winfrey often says the show transcends "race," it features black guests and issues of concern to black people in the USA more than comparable shows and focuses particularly on black women's perspectives. Since the 1980s such perspectives have had a major impact on U.S. feminism as black women activists and writers make their voices heard within the largely U.S. women's movement (see, for instance, Butler, 1990; de Lauretis, 1986; Hill Collins, 1990; hooks, 1981, 1989; Moraga and Anzaldúa, 1981; Spelman, 1990; Spivak, 1988). Differences in class and sexuality between women, which are also concerns of contemporary feminism (Lorde, 1984; Rich, 1986), have only a small place on the *Oprah* show, however. Edginess characterizes *Oprah*'s occasional mentions of lesbian and gay sexuality, and class is rarely explicitly discussed.

I am going to explore the show's diverse and intricate representations of gender, "race," sexuality, class, and subjectivity, and how the nature of television affects these representations. In the process I aim to develop an account of *Oprah*'s relationship to feminism. I am adopting a very general definition of feminism here, assuming that it is concerned, first, to understand gender relationships as fully as possible, in their interrelationships with other social differences, with history, with subjectivity, and with different representational media like television; and second, that it tries to make gender relations and relationships between women less oppressive (Coward, 1983). Does *Oprah*, much watched by women, and a secular authority on gender issues, speak to these feminist concerns? I shall argue that it does and that its most interesting contributions are first, a feminism generalized from black women's histories and writing, and second, its superrealism—an unsettling combination of emotional and empirical excess that puts common assumptions about gendered subjectivities in doubt.

ANALYZING *OPRAH*

Western feminists were slow to pay attention to television, despite its dominant position in their culture. Television representations of gender seemed dauntingly conventional in the face of feminists' limited power to effect change. Left analyses of the media as ideological control also contributed to feminist dismissals of television as shallow, repetitive, and emotionally manipulative. Since the 1970s, however, a number of feminists have treated the pleasures and powers of television seriously, recognizing that they must pay attention to this engrossing cultural form if they are to address the realities and fantasies of gender with which we all live (Kaplan, 1987). Such analyses have to balance an awareness of feminist elements in television messages and in audience understanding of them with a recognition of television's traditionalism and of the ways in which the television message and the power relations of television consumption constrain viewer interpretations (Brunsdon, 1989; Morris, 1988, Nightingale, 1990). Recent analyses of film and television by black writers and by theorists of queer representations start from this complexity, taking it for granted and then compounding it (Bad Object-Choices, 1991; Dent, 1992; Doty, 1992; Julien and Mercer, 1988).

The study draws on a regular monitoring of *The Oprah Winfrey Show* from late 1988 to mid-1993 but its core is an analysis of episodes shown during two weeks in May 1990. Throughout the study, the contents of the show have been fairly constant. Episodes split evenly between "self-help" topics—obsessions, disobedient children, and destructive relationships—*and an "all others"* category which includes shows on appearance (cosmetic surgery, dieting, people who think they are ugly) and physical, mental, or behavioral abnormality (disabling allergies, multiple personality, women who murder their children) and, more rarely, shows on social issues (buying a house, education, poverty), "cute" shows ("Alaskan men," people who can't throw anything away), and celebrity interviews (Joan Rivers, Barbara Bush). The show's form, too, is consistent. Winfrey introduces each episode by reading an outline of the day's topic to camera, talks to guests, solicits a few questions from the audience, brings in some expert opinions, and then alternates guests', experts', and audience members' comments while she roams around the audience with a mike in the style Phil Donahue brought to talk-show prominence. The representations of gender, "race," sexuality, class, and subjectivity with which I am concerned are also highly consistent across shows. I shall go through each of these as elements in a sequential manner, but the intersections should soon become apparent.

Representations of Gender on *Oprah*

Sometimes the *Oprah* show seems simply to endorse traditional notions of femaleness. In the woman-dominated world of daytime television, it appears, the predominantly female audience watches the mainly female casts of the early afternoon soap operas endlessly play out relationship dilemmas—and then listens to a female talk-show host, her many female guests, and her largely female studio audience discuss how to improve your looks, marriage, and parenting. The advertisements in the breaks, like most advertisements and indeed most programming (Bretl and Cantor, 1988; Davis, 1990), show women in traditional roles, worrying about their weight and their children. While the show encourages women to speak frankly about their lives, including their sexualities, the conventional limits apply. In one episode Winfrey assured a woman who had employed a male surrogate sex therapist to teach her to reach orgasm that she could be "explicit." "Well, he started by using his finger inside me, very gently. I felt a contraction . . ," the woman said, and was abruptly cut off by a commercial. During the break Winfrey said, "I didn't mean *that* explicit" (King, 1987:126). Conventionally, the show uses women to conjure prohibited pleasures; their transgressive, cathartic confessions become the apotheosis of television's voyeurism (Ellis, 1982).

Winfrey touches audience members a lot, cries and laughs, and they touch, laugh, and cry back. These exchanges signify an empathy that is traditionally feminine, but also feminist in its insistence on the "personal," and that is largely free of the inflections of authority and sexuality mixed in with male hosts' touching.

The show also presents feminist arguments about women's lower economic and social status, men's difficulties in close relationships, women's difficulties in combining paid work and parenting, the suppression of women's sexuality, and men's physical and sexual abuse. Moreover, since television representations often have more than one meaning, even the show's apparently conservative representations of gender can support feminist readings. The show's representations of the female body, for instance, are not simply incitements to female self-hatred. In one notorious episode Winfrey hauled on stage sixty-seven pounds of lard—the amount of weight she had lost; since then she has forsworn dieting. Today, the show routinely notes the oppressiveness and irrelevance of dominant images of the female body, explores how preoccupations with food and weight cloak depression and feelings of low self-worth, and acknowledges the comforting, social and sensual nature of eating, and one episode focused exclusively on discrimination against fat people. Winfrey's own size acts as a reminder of how women's bigness can be a form of power, perhaps especially when they are black women in a field dominated by white men. As Gracie Mae Still, the narrator of Alice Walker's "1955," put it, "fat like I is looks distinguished. You see me coming and know somebody's *there!*" (1982: 13).

The show sometimes considers motherhood with conventional reverence, but also treats it as a matter of hard work or discusses it in a more flexible way, as when Maya Angelou calls Winfrey her "daughter-friend" (*Oprah*

Winfrey Show, 1993). It has also problematized motherhood, as in an episode on maternal child abuse.

The show's feminism is most explicit, however, in its often-declared commitment to empowering women. This term has multiple meanings, indicating variously an interest in women's political, economic, and educational advancement; in women getting help for personal and relationship problems; and most generally, in women perceiving a range of individual and social choices as open to them and deciding among them. Each meaning implies a different version of feminism. The first suggests a public, the second a personal, focus for feminism, and the last founds feminist politics in psychological well-being. Nevertheless the show's representations of empowerment all assume a commonality between women that allows the representations to make the category "women" their unproblematic center. Feminism must use this category to ground its analyses and claims, but the category always has a social and historical context that gives it a specific meaning (Riley, 1988; Spelman, 1990). *Oprah,* however, represents women as sharing emotional and social qualities—communication skills, for instance—regardless of the differences between women. The show's aim is to empower this shared womanhood.

The dominant presence of women on the show is underwritten by a complementary male presence. The show continually solicits men's opinions, runs episodes on men as lovers and parents, and raises and counters the suggestion that *Oprah* is "anti-men." The show's "woman-centered" talk is always, silently, about men, for gender is a relationship: one term evokes the other.

The complementariness of *Oprah*'s representations of gender raises an important question about its relationship to feminism. Might women's disempowerment, against which the show defines itself, nevertheless be its most powerful message? A narrative of empowerment structures each episode but the show's repeated accounts of victimization often seem to overwhelm them. After the daily success story of women getting their lives in order, you know that tomorrow you will start off once more with the harrowing experiences of women whose lives have been taken from them by abuse, illness, or poverty. Feminism has to describe structures of male power in order to resist them and to this degree it is complicit with them. But on *The Oprah Winfrey Show,* self-consciously complicit description often seems to collapse into a fruitless reiteration of stories of personal suffering. Domestic violence, child abuse, and eating disorders support regular episodes, each claiming to bring to light a horrible and hitherto secret oppression, each by this claim implicitly reinstating the horror and prohibitions around the topic; for talking about a forbidden subject may maintain as much as disperse a taboo. *Oprah*'s current emphasis on health and exercise at the expense of diets, for example, is undercut by a conventional subtext of the female body as subject to control (Bordo, 1989; Coward, 1989), and by the frequency with which diets are mentioned, only to be dismissed.

The show's complementary meanings have some promising feminist implications as well. The show often presents women as objects of beauty: in makeover episodes, for instance; or on the daily credits, shot when Winfrey was near her thinnest, had a Revlon modeling contract, and could operate as a powerful screen player in the cultural and psychic masquerade of femininity (Heath, 1985). The credits show Winfrey in a series of slowed, staggered close-ups and medium close-ups, listening sympathetically to guests, laughing, swinging her hair, bouncing across the screen. Beginning with Laura Mulvey, feminist film theorists have argued that such representations of femininity put the spectator in a complementarily masculine position of pleasure and desire (Mulvey, 1975, 1981). *Oprah*'s predominantly female studio and viewing audience is thus set up to look at the feminine object, Winfrey, from a patriarchal position: as men. The audience may either adopt this masculine spectatorship or abdicate spectatorship for an identification with the femininity on screen (see also de Lauretis, 1991; Doane, 1987). Such work suggests that *Oprah* offers women a variety of psychic investments, so its feminism will not be a simple matter of women watching women but will filter through the multiple subjectivities of spectatorship.

If we view *Oprah*'s multiple representations of gender in a context wider than the show, their relationship to feminism often starts to seem closer. Despite the limits the show sets on what can be said, for instance, and its tendency to present talk as a cure-all, its stress on "explicit" speech seems oppositional in the broader context of U.S. procensorship campaigns, especially since explicit talk on *Oprah* is often talk about a common censorship target, female sexuality. The show's representations of men also appear more resistant if they are read against the power relationships generally obtaining between women and men. Episodes shift from description to prescription, from problems with men or men's problems to women's solutions. Even if a similar move will be made all over again in the very next episode, the move cuts against the cultural grain. Viewed historically, too, *Oprah*'s repeated and apparently unchang-

ing considerations of some sensational topics may indicate not just unsated voyeurism or stalled feminism but a series of historically distinct concerns. A show about rape survivors, for example, means something different after the Palm Beach case, in which William Smith, a nephew of Edward Kennedy, was acquitted of raping a lower-middle-class white woman, than it does after the Central Park case, in which black youths were convicted of beating and raping a white woman stockbroker who was running in the park.

"Race" and Racism

Henry Louis Gates (1989) describes how, in the 1950s, his family would rush to see African Americans on television, and how concerned they were that the performers be good. More African Americans are on television now but blacks are still underrepresented and appear mainly as a set of sitcom and drama clichés or as news anchors. The concern of people of color about their television representation remains strong (Fife, 1987; Grey, 1989; Ziegler and White, 1990). Shows like *Oprah* generate big expectations and concomitant criticism. *Oprah* has been said to absolve white guilt by presenting a rags-to-riches black, unthreatening female, who hugs whites in the audience more than people of color. The show has also been accused of being negative about African-American men, having few minorities on the production team, and giving racist white organizations airtime rather than confronting more subtle and pervasive racisms. Winfrey ridicules calls for her to be more black, asking, "How black do you have to be?" (King, 1987: 187). The demand that she "represent" African Americans is indeed a sign of her token status on television. As Isaac Julien and Kobena Mercer have written of film, the notion that one instance "could 'speak for' an entire community of interests reinforces the perceived secondariness of that community" (1988:4).

The *Oprah* show is, in any case, permeated with "race" as much as it is with gender. Winfrey's own Chicago-based production company, the first owned by an African American, makes it. This, together with her ratings, gives her Cosby-like powers—to determine topics and how to treat them, for instance—that black people rarely have in television. The show itself consistently addresses racism, explicitly, by calling for equal opportunities and recruiting people of color for the production team and, implicitly, by challenging casual instances of racism. In an episode on interracial relationships, Winfrey ironizes a white male guest's history of dating only black women, saying. "It's that melanin that got you . . . that melanin count just overwhelmed him." *Oprah* avoids overt racial politics but toward the end this episode featured audience members' political analyses of interracial relationships:

FEMALE AUDIENCE MEMBER: . . . the reason people are taking it so terribly is that we are part of a racist society, period, and that has to change for anything to change.

FEMALE GUEST: That's right. (*Oprah Winfrey Show,* 1989a)

Less overtly, the show often features visual representations of racial difference without verbal comment, a silence that may be the result of television's caution about "race" but that may work, as Kum-Kum Bhavnani (1990) has described, as antiracist empowerment. In one segment of the "1991 Follow-up Show" (*Oprah Winfrey Show,* 1992), for instance, an African-American family, identified simply as a "family" living in a project, got a "dream house." Two other segments showed dramatic reunions between adopted children and birth parents. In both cases children of mixed parentage met previously unknown white or black parents, while "race" went unmentioned. These silences allowed racial differences to appear but refused them legitimacy in the narratives. In the silences, the cultural mythology of de-raced all-American "family" achieved a tactical defeat of other more clearly racist mythologies of black welfare mothers and tragic mulatto children.

The show's representations of black America are also telling. It regularly features successful African-American businesspeople, professionals, and entertainers, generating a picture of black culture and achievement rare in mainstream media. After a long absence, rappers now appear on the show occasionally; there are indeed parallels between *Oprah*'s woman-empowering aims and those some women rappers express (Rose, 1990). The show regularly considers issues that are important and controversial among blacks: education, self-esteem, class tensions, conflicts between black women and men over black women's alleged disrespectful and money-grabbing, "ain't nothing going on but the rent" approach to black men and black men's claimed irresponsibility, black discrimination against dark-skinned black people, interracial adoption and relationships, and black hair and skin care. Black-oriented advertisements and public service announcements are more frequent than on most other network shows. More generally, Winfrey's and her black guests' stories of their lives combine with the show's references to black struggles, especially those of strong black women, to provide a perpetually renewed and

reformulated television history of African America, not as comprehensive as those produced during Black History Month, but there all year round.

Winfrey sometimes talks black American, usually to make a joke. Television conventionally allows such language for comedic purposes but it remains language infrequently heard outside sitcoms, dramas, and documentary representations of inner cities. Winfrey even induces similar speech in others. Once, trailing one of her specials on the early evening news after her show, she talked with the black newsreader Roz Abrams, and the somewhat formal Abrams called her "girlfriend." For a hallucinatorily brief moment black women's acquaintanceship and talk displaced the bland chumminess and linguistics common in such exchanges.

Occasionally Winfrey addresses whites in the studio audience to explain some aspect of black life. This move homogenizes both the life and the audience, and can seem to offer a quasi-anthropological supplement to talk shows' usual peeping-tom pleasures. But it gives a public voice to marginalized phenomena and acknowledges an ignorance and distance that usually go unspoken, while Winfrey's blunt pedagogy circumvents voyeurism.

Finally, black feminism seems, as much as woman-centered feminism, to define the show. This black feminism recognizes the different history of patriarchy among African Americans (Gaines, 1988), writes the history of black women's resistance in the antislavery and civil rights movements and in every family, and celebrates the strength and creativity of black women (Walker, 1983). Winfrey often invokes the film *The Color Purple,* the writing of Gloria Naylor (1982), and the work of Maya Angelou (1970), whose account of growing up in the black South she says describes her own life and whom she calls her mentor (*Oprah Winfrey Show,* 1993). Men's abuse, which Patricia Hill Collins (1990: 185) says needs to be the object of black feminist analysis, implicitly receives this attention through the host's and black audience members' repeated engagement with it. Angelou and Walker are often said to ignore the history and problematic of black masculinity and in the process collude with white racism. *Oprah* is subject to similar criticisms but tackles the issues by presenting positive images of African-American fatherhood and male mentoring. Winfrey still Signifies on black men though, as Gloria-Jean Masciorotte (1991), citing Gates (1988) citing Hurston, says; and other African-American women on the show do the same. This Signifyin(g) is, as Gates says, both a verbal game and a serious cultural engagement. A black woman in the audience raised a laugh when she admonished a black male guest, a lothario vacillating between two white women, one with dark, one with light hair, "She over there on the light side, she over there on the dark side, you in the middle on the *gray* side" (*Oprah Winfrey Show,* 1992). The show itself also Signifies, in Gates's broad sense of textual revision, on the texts of African-American women writers, rewriting them in a different medium and for a larger, racially diverse audience. For many of the white and black viewers of *Oprah,* the show's enduring canon of these writers—along with the more variable set of female self-help gurus and high-achieving women who guest—must constitute the dominant cultural representation of feminism.

Sexualities

In common with the rest of television, *The Oprah Winfrey Show* is heterosexist. Openly lesbian or gay guests appear rarely, the show carefully establishes the heterosexuality of well-known guests, and when it addresses homosexuality directly it tends either to problematize it or to mainstream it as a human issue, distanced from sex and politics (Gross, 1989). Bisexuality is a special problem. In an episode presented jointly with the hunt-the-criminal program *America's Most Wanted,* a man's bisexuality became the emblem of his ability to elude the criminal justice system: "The problem with John Hawkins is he's a very good-looking guy, he's a very good con, and he's bisexual, so he has the ability to basically adapt into any community or any type of social structure," said a police officer (reshown on *Oprah Winfrey Show,* 1992).

Sometimes *Oprah* gives screen time to camp men who function briefly and conventionally as jesters. More of a challenge to dominant assumptions about sexuality is the show's marking of differences within heterosexuality, for instance the line it draws between abusive and nonabusive heterosexual relationships. This acknowledgment of plural heterosexualities coexists with the show's more traditional representations of sexual relationships between women and men either as always involving the same desires and social patterns, as in episodes along the lines of "Save Your Marriage" and "Best Husband Contest" or as infinitely various, as in "Men Who Married Their Divorced Wives" and "Women Who Married Their Stepsons." Finally, the show's overwhelmingly female spectacle and spectatorship might conceivably be read as a kind of televisual lesbianism but the link between female spectatorship, sexuality, and sexual politics is very unclear (de Lauretis, 1991; Stacey, 1988).

Class

Despite a late-1980s burst of class-conscious sitcoms, television is not very interested in class relationships. On *Oprah,* though, the all-American narrative of Winfrey's progress from poverty to wealth is often invoked, and her riches legitimized as the rightful reward of her struggle for a piece of the pie. The wealth is frequently represented as exuberant consumption by references to Winfrey's restaurant, her condo, her farm, and her furs. In a study of women's reactions to *Dynasty,* Andrea Press (1990) writes that working-class women have a particular affinity with such representations; the *Oprah* show's periodic ditchings of gritty emotion in favour of glitz may then be part of its success. But the show represents Winfrey's good works and her dispensations of wealth to the poor too. Taken together, these representations turn wealth into something new, strange, and full of responsibilities. The show also refers often and unromantically to poverty, in episodes on project life for instance, and points up class differences in values and lifestyles. At the start of a show on "Stressed-out Dads," Winfrey showed two clips from *thirtysomething* of yuppie fathers caring for their children and then said, laughing and sarcastic, "I know that happens in y'alls' house every night" (*Oprah Winfrey Show,* 1990b).

The show may present Winfrey as a de-raced all-American success story but it gives a strong presence to middle-class African Americans and pays attention to the responsibilities and close historical relationships middle-class blacks have with and for poorer blacks, especially young people. Many issues debated between black women and men on the show involve class: the averred paucity of suitable black men available to educated black women; these women's alleged prejudices about ordinary working black men, and whether black women or men, especially those in the middle class, should have interracial relationships. No other networked shows give these topics the acrimonious airings they get on *Oprah;* the other daytime talk shows seem unable to see their contentiousness. *Oprah* is indeed at times better able to recognize the shifting and intersecting agendas of class, gender, and "race" than is much feminist theory.

Oprah as Psychology

Alongside the show's investment in social relationships runs a much more explicit preoccupation with psychological issues and explanations. The daytime talk show is a psychological genre (Carbaugh, 1988). Most *Oprah* episodes focus on overtly psychological phenomena like "obses-sions" and "negotiation skills," psychologists are the show's commonest "expert" guests, Winfrey's interventions and those of audience members are mostly directed at clarifying experiences and emotions, and interpersonal communica-tion is presented as a cathartic and enabling solution to social as well as personal problems. The show gives almost all the problems it addresses, even those like unemploy-ment, some psychological content, usually in terms of "feelings." Each episode's narrative moves toward psycho-logical closure: people end up "feeling" better because they have "expressed themselves" or "started to think about what they really want." Winfrey's psychological democra-cy, her representation as a person just like the audience members, is also very powerful. Showing an extreme ver-sion of the usual perception of television as the mass medi-um closest to interpersonal communication (Ellis, 1982; Pfau, 1990), women in *Oprah*'s audience frequently preface their contributions by telling Winfrey how much they like her and the show, and how they feel they know her almost as a friend (Waldron, 1987: 182).

The ubiquity of psychological discourse on *Oprah* is important to recognize at a time psychology has wide-ranging social power in the overdeveloped world, and in view of the female-identified and often feminist-approved status of explanations in "personal" terms. Psychologism has been indicted as the filling of talk shows generally. Aaron Fogel (1986) describes the genre as a collective psy-chological reaction to puritanism, and Giuseppe Minnini (1989) characterizes it as pure ego, a "talk-showman"[*sic*] holding forth in a way that does not allow dialogue, let alone productive engagement with issues. Less moralisti-cally, it could be argued that *Oprah*'s psychologism some-times drowns out its, at times, more complicated represen-tations of power relationships. In an episode on obsessional jealousy, one woman's account of how her youth had facili-tated her husband's manipulation of her was invalidated and replaced by Winfrey's, a psychologist's, and audience members' declarations that people can only do things to you if you let them.

The show mirrors psychologists' professional confi-dence in their ability to improve things with a relentless optimism that leaves little room for persistent problems or imperfect solutions. Psychologists do not, however, have an easy ride on the show. They are often drowned out by audi-ence members' and Winfrey's own floods of psychological pronouncements and Winfrey jokes about these appropria-tions of expertise. The show steers its audience toward self-help groups or books written by its guest rather than toward

professional help. In an episode that featured women living with men who would not marry them, first the audience and then Winfrey made restrained fun of the guest psycholo-gists' zeal:

PSYCHOLOGIST 1:   . . . counseling would really be appro-priate (audience laughter starts) for a couple who seems to be, stuck, no, I'm talking about together, and together with a counselor establishing an agenda for themselves as a couple . . .

WINFREY: All therapists want everybody to go to counsel-ing, yeah (laughs).

PSYCHOLOGIST 2:   Orpah, it helps . . . it helps a lot.

WINFREY: Oh I know it does, I know it helps a lot. (*Oprah Winfrey Show,* 1990a)

Antiprofessionalism is a common stance in the USA but *Oprah*'s lay psychology has other connotations too. Its emphasis on getting people to communicate is part of a utopian picture of a viewing community and a world in which everyone knows they are not alone. Often the stress on communication recalls a religious commitment to testi-fying (see also Masciarotte, 1991), and this convergence of talk show with worship (Fogel, 1986) takes on a specific resonance in *Oprah* from the history of black churches as places where African-American women's voices could be raised and heard. The show's persistent focus on self-esteem ties into an implicit liberal democratic politics of rights, responsibilities, and choice, and, through the non-specific spirituality the show attaches to self-worth, to New Ageism. *Oprah*'s optimism about psychological improve-ment is associated with beliefs in religious redemption and in social progress, for which redemption is itself a metaphor. Andrea Stuart (1988; see also Bobo, 1988) has suggested that black women watching *The Color Purple* read its happy ending not within the film narrative, where it seems inconsistent and sentimental, but within broader reli-gious, social and historical narratives, where it offers an important antidote to hopelessness. Perhaps *Oprah*'s daily psychological resolutions of dramatic suffering support a similar reading.

An individual woman may be represented on *Oprah* as shaped by social forces like racism and male violence but also as fully and only responsible for her own actions. An odd mélange can result, of growth psychology, religious devotion, political analysis, and personal hubris. An emble-matic example on *Oprah* itself was Angelou's presentation of herself and her work. Describing her composition of a poem for Clinton's inauguration, she said she was not nervous: all she had to do was "get centered" and write. No false humility was required: after all, "I come from the Creator trailing wisps of glory." And telling of her own overcoming of abuse, poverty, and racism, she recalled the key realization: "God loves *me,* Oprah, Oprah, the skies opened up. I can do *anything*" (*Oprah Winfrey Show,* 1993). Winfrey looked deeply touched, they clasped hands, and the show broke for commercials. The show's loose concatenations of ideas are easy to deride but they build up a complicated picture of psychological as well as social and historical relationships, relationships which the show does not try to resolve. Some might see the ambiguities as disabling and claim television audiences cannot cope with them. But I think it is productive for a talk show to display, as *Oprah* does, the contradictions that traverse our subjectivities, rather than to opt for social determinist explanations of problems, victimologies that allow subjectivity no clear place, or to invoke an unproblematic human agency as the general solution, as talk shows usually do. *Oprah's* infusion by black feminism seems to be what generates this complexity.

Oprah, Television, and Superrealism

Oprah's reflexivity about being television calls attention to how the characteristics of television, and of the daytime talk show in particular, shape it. More than most television (see Ellis, 1982), the daytime talk show is a casual form, not watched continuously. To compensate, it is made eyecatching, with clear, immediate images and plenty of camera movement and cutting to offset the slowness of talk. Daytime viewers may be attending to things other than television or just passing through a room where the television is on, so the shows favor sound bites: punchy questions; short, clear encapsulations of arguments and feelings; brief passages of incoherent speech, tears, or silence to signal deep emotion; bursts of laughter and applause, snatches of theme music bracketing breaks and the program itself, and enticing cliffhanger trails before each break: "When we get back, are strong-thinking, decisive women a threat to you men?" (*Oprah Winfrey Show,* 1989b). These characteristics produce a currency of rapid, intense, simple, and repetitive aural and visual representations, from the sixnote sequence that means *Oprah* to the screwed-up, crying faces of incest survivors asked "How did it feel?" These fragmented representations are always breaking up the coherence and continuity of the talk show's narrative of psychological improvement.

It might be said of *Oprah,* as is often argued of talk shows and television in general, that its dispersed, atomistic

representations do not disturb but only support the cultural consensus (Ellis, 1982; Fogel, 1986; Miller, 1990; Minnini, 1989). From this perspective, *Oprah* is too frivolous to be feminist. Some feminists have, however, interpreted television representations that reach *Oprah's* level of disruption as carnivalesque or melodramatic challenges to television's conventional representations of gender (Ang, 1985; Brown, 1990; Deming, 1990). I am going to argue that *Oprah's* televisual characteristics produce rather a *superrealism* that has some modest feminist value.

Daytime talk shows like *Oprah* try to reach a realist truth by interleaving information and entertainment and deploying narratives of psychological growth to pull this "infotainment" together. Sometimes they do not manage the integration, and superrealism, a realism torn out of shape by excesses of emotion or empiricism, disrupts the explanatory framework. On *Oprah,* this disruption happens in one of two ways. First, superrealism may take over when a "psychological" truth recurs so often on the show that it begins to shed its individual psychological character and starts to look more like a social, political, or religious fact. The narratives of sexual abuse on *Oprah,* for example, very similar and endlessly repeated, seem to go beyond psychological understanding to become facts about gender relationships that demand explanation in other, social terms. It is the televisual superficiality and facility of the show that allows this superreal excess to register.

Oprah's second type of superrealism appears when the emotions in the show get so intense that the show forgoes any claim to provide information and simply displays an extreme effect—accessible to psychoanalytic interpretation, perhaps, but not to the kinds of psychological explanations most of us are familiar with and use. For instance, when the show featured an abused woman with ninety-two personalities, it could not provide a coherent account of her subjectivity. Abuse started to seem utterly idiosyncratic and affectively overwhelming. Again, this registering of excess relied on the show's superreal televisual character: on snappy formulations of monstrous feelings and quick moves to commercial breaks ("back in a moment") that left the unspeakable and the unimaginable resounding around American living rooms.

I would argue that *Oprah* owes its cultural effects largely to its superrealist emotional and empirical excesses, which rework or Signify on television and culture, something talk shows' more conventional psychological explanations are unlikely to do. Its contribution to U.S. debates about the education of black children or the relationships between black women and black men comes not so much from its explicit consideration of these debates as from their unannounced, unasked for, and unmarked recurrence within the show, so frequently and pervasively that they become superreal facts, uncontainable within the show's psychological narratives.

Henry Louis Gates (1989) wrote that he hopes "blacks will stop looking to TV for (their) social liberation." Feminists of color and white feminists rarely look to television for social liberation. But television can achieve what feminist writing finds difficult: *Oprah*'s interwoven explorations of "race," class, and gender and its popularization of aspects of black feminist thought are examples. And feminists may discover something about how to deal with the complex connections between subjectivity, gender, and other social relationships from the suspension of *The Oprah Winfrey Show* between fluff and gravity; psychology, social analysis, and emotions; realism and superrealism; and from their own difficulties in addressing this mixture.

ACKNOWLEDGMENTS

I would like to thank Ann Phoenix, Kum-Kum Bhavnani, Chris Griffin, and an unnamed reviewer for their helpful comments and encouragement.

NOTE

1. Another African-American woman, the comedian Marsha Warfield, has had a half-hour networked morning show, and Montel Williams, the "male Oprah," has an hour-long morning show on CBS. A new crop of *Oprah* challengers, several with African-American hosts, appeared in 1993 (Freeman, 1992). The earliest African-American talk-show host was Ellis Haizlip, who, in the late 1960s and early 1970s, fronted *Soul,* "a live performance/talk show inspired by the burgeoning cultural nationalist movement" (Jones, 1991).

REFERENCES

Ang, I. (1985), *Watching Dallas: Soap Opera and the Melodramatic Imagination* (London: Methuen).

Angelou, M. (1970), *I Know Why the Caged Bird Sings* (New York: Random House).

Bad Object-Choices (1991) (ed.), *How Do I Look? Queer Film and Video* (Seattle: Bay Press).

Bhavnani, K.-K. (1990). "What's Power Got To Do It?" In I. Parker and J. Shotter (eds.), *Deconstructing Social Psychology* (London: Routledge).

Bobo, J. (1988), "*The Color Purple:* Black Women as Cultural Readers," in D. Pribram (ed.), *Female Spectators Looking at Film and Television* (London: Verso).

Boemer, M. (1987), "Correlating Lead-in Show Ratings with Local Television News Rating," *Journal of Broadcasting and Electronic Media* 31:89–94.

Bordo, S. (1989), "Reading the Slender Body," in M. Jacobus, E. Foxkeller, and S. Shuttleworth (eds.), *Body/Politics* (New York: Routledge).

Bretl, D., and Cantor, J. (1988), "The Portrayal of Men and Women in U.S. Television Commercials: A Recent Content Analysis and Trends over 15 Years," *Sex Roles,* 18:595–609.

Brown, M. E. (1990), "Motley Moments: Soap Operas, Carnival, Gossip and the Power of the Utterance," in M. E. Brown (ed,), *Television and Women's Culture: The Politics of the Popular* (London: Sage).

Brunsdon, C. (1989), "Text and Audience," in E. Sieter, H. Borchers, G. Kreutzner, and E. Warth (eds.), *Remote Control* (New York: Routledge).

Butler, J. (1990), *Gender Trouble* (New York: Routledge).

Carbaugh, D. (1988), *Talking American: Cultural Discourses on Donahue* (Norwood, NJ: Ablex).

Coward, R. (1983), *Patriarchal Precedents* (London: Routledge & Kegan Paul).

——— (1989), *The Whole Truth* (London: Faber & Faber).

Davis, D. (1990), "Portrayals of Women in Prime-time Network Television: Some Demographic Characteristics," *Sex Roles,* 23:325–32.

de Lauretis, T. (1986) (ed.), *Feminist Studies/Critical Studies* (Bloomington: Indiana Univ. Press).

—— (1991), "Film and the Visible," in Bad Object-Choices (1991).

Deming, C. (1990), "For Television-Centered Television Criticism: Lessons from Feminism," in M. E. Brown (ed.), *Television and Women's Culture: The Politics of the Popular* (London: Sage).

Dent, G. (1992) (ed.), *Black Popular Culture* (Seattle: Bay Press).

Doane, M. A. (1987), *The Desire to Desire* (Bloomington: Indiana Univ. Press).

Doty, A. (1992), *Making Things Perfectly Queer* (Minneapolis: Univ. of Minnesota Press).

Ellis, J. (1982), *Visible Fictions* (London: Routledge & Kegan Paul).

Fife, M. (1987), "Promoting Racial Diversity in U.S. Broadcasting: Federal Policies Versus Social Realities," *Media, Culture and Society,* 9:431–505.

Fogel, A. (1986), "Talk Shows: On Reading Television," in S. Donadio, S. Railton, and S. Ormond (eds.), *Emerson and His Legacy* (Carbondale: Southern Illinois Univ. Press).

Freeman, M. (1992), "Can We Talk? New for 1993," *Broadcasting and Cable* (Dec.), 14.

Gaines, J. (1988), "White Privilege and Looking Relations: Race and Gender in Feminist Film Theory," Last Special Issue on "Race," *Screen,* 29:12–27.

Gates, H. L. (1988), *The Signifying Monkey* (New York: Oxford Univ. Press).

—— (1989), "TV's Black World Turns—But Stays Unreal," *New York Times* (Nov.), 12.

Goodman, F. (1991), "Madonna and Oprah: The Companies They Keep," *Working Women,* 16:52–5.

Grey, H. (1989), "Television, Black Americans, and the American Dream," *Critical Studies in Mass Communication,* 6:376–86.

Gross, L. (1989), "Out of the Mainstream: Sexual Minorities and the Mass Media," in E. Seiter, H. Borchers, G. Kreutzner, and E. Warth (eds.), *Remote Control* (New York: Routledge).

Guider, E. (1987), "Katz Advises How to Handle Daytime Queen," *Variety* (July), 8.

Harrison, B. (1989), "The Importance of Being Oprah," *New York Times Magazine* (June), 11.

Heath, S. (1985), "Joan Riviere and the Masquerade," in V. Burgin, J. Donald, and C. Kaplan (eds.), *Formations of Fantasy* (London: Methuen).

Hill Collins, P. (1990), *Black Feminist Thought* (Cambridge, Mass: Unwin Hyman).

hooks, b. (1981), *Ain't I A Woman? Black Women and Feminism* (Boston: South End Press).

—— (1989), *Talking Back: Thinking Feminist, Thinking Black* (Boston: South End Press).

Jones, L. (1991), "Hot Buttered 'Soul,' " *Village Voice* (Mar.), 12.

Julien, I., and Mercer, K. (1988), "Introduction: De Margin and De Center," Last special Issue on "Race," *Screen,* 29:2–10.

Kaplan, E. A. (1987), "Feminism Criticism and Television," in R. Allen (ed.), *Channels of Discourse* (Chapel Hill: Univ. of North Carolina Press).

King, N. (1987), *Everybody Loves Oprah* (New York: Morrow).

Lorde, A. (1984), *Sister Outsider: Essays and Speeches* (Trumansburg, NY: Crossing Press).

Masciarotte, G. -J. (1991), "C'mon Girl: Oprah Winfrey and the Discourse of Feminine Talk," *Genders,* 11:81–110.

McClellan, S. (1993), "Freshman 'Deep Space Nine' Records Stellar Sweep Debut," *Broadcasting and Cable* (Apr.), 24–6.

Miller, M. C. (1990), *Boxed In: The Culture of Television* (Evanston, Ill.: Northwestern Univ. Press).

Minnini, G. (1989), "Genres de discours et types de dialogue: Le 'Talk-show,' " in E. Weigand and F. Hundnurscher (eds.), *Dialoganalyze,* ii (Tübingen: Niemeyer).

Moraga, C., and Anzaldúa, G. (1981), *This Bridge Called My Back* (Watertown, Mass.: Persephone Press).

Morris, M. (1988), "Banality in Cultural Studies," *Block,* 14:15–26.

Mulvey, L. (1975), "Visual Pleasure and Narrative Cinema," *Screen,* 16:6–18.

—— (1981), "Afterthoughts on 'Visual Pleasure and Narrative Cinema' Inspired by 'Duel in the Sun,' " *Framework,* 15/16/17:12–15.

Naylor, G. (1982), *The Women of Brewster Place* (New York: Viking).

Nightingale, V. (1990), "Women as Audiences," in M. E. Brown (ed.), *Television and Women's Culture: The Politics of the Popular* (London: Sage).

Oprah Winfrey Show (1989a) "Blacks and Whites Dating" (New York: Journal Graphics, 1 Mar.).

—— (1989b), "Home Fights" (New York: Journal Graphics, 25 Apr.).

—— (1990a), "A Mother's Plea: Marry My Daughter" (23 May, author's transcript).

—— (1990b), "Stressed-Out Dads" (30 May, author's transcript).

—— (1992), "1991 Follow-up Show" (8 Jan., Channel 4, Britain, author's transcript).

—— (1993), "Maya Angelou Interview" (13 July, author's transcript).

Pfau, M. (1990), "A Channel Approach to Television Influence," *Journal of Broadcasting and Electronic Media,* 34:195–214.

Press, A. (1990), "Class, Gender and the Female Viewer: Women's Responses to 'Dynasty,' " in M. E. Brown (ed.), *Television and Women's Culture: The Politics of the Popular* (London: Sage).

Rich, A. (1986), "Compulsory Heterosexuality and Lesbian Existence," *Blood, Bread and Poetry* (New York: Norton).

Riley, D. (1988), *Am I That Name? Feminism and the Category of "Women" in History* (Minneapolis: Univ. of Minnesota Press).

Rose, T. (1990), "Never Trust a Big Butt and a Smile," *Camera Obscura,* 23:109–32 (in this volume).

Spelman, E. (1990), *Inessential Women* (London: Women's Press).

Spivak, G. (1988), *In Other Worlds* (New York: Routledge, Chapman and Hall).

Stacey, J. (1988), "Desperately Seeking Difference," in L. Gamman and M. Marshment (eds.), *The Female Gaze* (London: Women's Press).

Stuart, A. (1988), "*The Color Purple:* In Defence of Happy Endings," in L. Gamman and M. Marshment (eds.), *The Female Gaze* (London: Women's Press).

Waldron, R. (1987), *Oprah!* (New York: St Martin's Press).

Walker, A. (1982), *You Can't Keep A Good Woman Down* (London: Women's Press).

———— (1983), *In Search of Our Mothers' Gardens* (New York: Harcourt Brace Jovanovich).

Walkerdine, V. (1989), "Video Replay," in V. Burgin (ed.), *Formations of Pleasure* (London: Methuen).

Ziegler, D., and White, A. (1990), "Women and Minorities on Network Television News: An Examination of Correspondents and Newsmakers." *Journal of Broadcasting and Electronic Media*, 34:2 215–23.

WOMEN RAP BACK

MICHELE WALLACE

Like many black feminists, I look on sexism in rap as a necessary evil. In a society plagued by poverty and illiteracy, where young black men are as likely to be in prison as in college, rap is a welcome articulation of the economic and social frustrations of black youth.

It offers the release of creative expression and historical continuity; it draws on precedents as diverse as jazz, reggae, calypso, Afro-Cuban, African and heavy metal, and its lyrics include rudimentary forms of political, economic, and social analysis.

But though there are exceptions, like raps advocating world peace, (The W.I.S.E. Guyz's "Time for Peace") and opposing drug use (Ice T's "I'm Your Pusher"), rap lyrics can be brutal, raw, and, where women are the subject, glaringly sexist.

Though styles vary—from that of the X-rated Ice T to the sybaritic Kwamé to the hyperpolitics of Public Enemy—what seems universal is how little male rappers respect sexual intimacy and how little regard they have for the humanity of the black woman.

At present there is only a small platform for black women to address the problems of sexism in rap and in their community. For a black feminist to chastise misogyny in rap publicly would be viewed as divisive and counterproductive. The charge is hardly new. Such a reaction greeted Ntozake Shange's play, *For Colored Girls Who Have Considered Suicide When the Rainbow Is Enuf,* my own essays, *Black Macho and the Myth of the Superwoman,* and Alice Walker's novel *The Color*

Purple, all of which were perceived as being critical of black men.

Rap is rooted not only in the blaxploitation films of the 1960s but also in an equally sexist tradition of black comedy. In the use of four-letter words and explicit sexual references, both Richard Pryor and Eddie Murphy, who themselves drew upon the earlier examples of Redd Foxx, Pigment Markham, and Moms Mabley, are conscious reference points for the 2 Live Crew. Black comedy, in turn, draws on an oral tradition in which black men trade "toasts," stories in which dangerous badmen and trickster figures like Stackolee and Dolomite sexually exploit women and promote violence among men.

Rap remains almost completely dominated by black males and this mindset. Although women have been involved in rap since at least the mid-1980s, record companies have only recently begun to promote them. And as women rappers like Salt-N-Pepa, Monie Love, M.C. Lyte, L.A. Star, and Queen Latifah slowly gain more visibility, rap's sexism may emerge as a subject for scrutiny. Indeed, the answer may lie with women, expressing in lyrics and videos the tensions between the sexes in the black community.

Today's women rappers range from a high ground that refuses to challenge male rap on its own level (Queen Latifah) to those who subscribe to the same sexual high jinks as male rappers (Oaktown 3.5.7.). M.C. Hammer launched Oaktown 3.5.7., made up of his former backup dancers. These female rappers manifest the worst-case scenario: their skimpy, skintight leopard costumes in the video of "Wild and Loose (We Like It)" suggest an exotic animalistic sexuality. Clearly, their bodies are more important than rapping. And in a field in which writing one's own rap is crucial, their lyrics are written by their former boss, M.C. Hammer.

Most women rappers constitute the middle ground: they talk of romance, narcissism, and parties. On the other hand, Salt-N-Pepa on "Shake Your Thang" uses the structure of the 1969 Isley Brothers song "It's Your Thing" to insert a protofeminist rap response: "Don't try to tell me how to party. It's my dance and it's my body." M.C. Lyte, in a dialogue with Positive K on "I'm Not Havin' It," comes down hard on the notion that women can't say no and criticizes the shallowness of the male rap.

Queen Latifah introduces her video "Ladies First," performed with the English rapper Monie Love, with photographs of black political heroines like Winnie Mandela, Sojourner Truth, Harriet Tubman, and Angela Davis. With a sound that resembles scat as much as rap, Queen Latifah chants "Stereotypes they got to go" against a backdrop of newsreel footage of the apartheid struggle in South Africa. The politically sophisticated Queen Latifah seems worlds apart from the adolescent, buffoonish sex orientation of most rap. In general, women rappers seem so much more grown up.

Can they inspire a more beneficent attitude toward sex in rap?

What won't subvert rap's sexism is the actions of men; what will is women speaking in their own voice.

R E A D I N G   1 6

Ideological Racism and Cultural Resistance: Constructing Our Own Images

YEN LE ESPIRITU

The slit-eyed, bucktooth Jap thrusting his bayonet, thirsty for blood. The inscrutable, wily Chinese detective with his taped eyelids and wispy moustache. The childlike, indolent Filipino houseboy. Always giggling. Bowing and scraping. Eager to please, but untrustworthy. The sexless, hairless Asian male. The servile, oversexed Asian female. The Geisha. The sultry, sarong-clad, South Seas maiden. The serpentine, cunning Dragon Lady. Mysterious and evil, eager to

please. Effeminate. Untrustworthy. Yellow Peril. Fortune Cookie Psychic. Savage. Dogeater. Invisible. Mute. Faceless peasants breeding too many children. Gooks. Passive Japanese Americans obediently marching off to "relocation camps" during the Second World War.

Jessica Hagedorn (1993, p. xxii)

Focusing on the material lives of Asian Americans, racist and gendered immigration policies and labor conditions have worked in tandem to keep Asian Americans in an assigned, subordinate place. But as is evident from the stereotypes listed above, besides structural discrimination, Asian American men and women have been subject to ideological assaults. Focusing on the ideological dimension of Asian American oppression, this chapter examines the cultural symbols—or what Patricia Hill Collins (1991) called "controlling images" (pp. 67–68)—generated by the dominant group to help justify the economic exploitation and social oppression of Asian-American men and women over time. Writing on the objectification of black women, Collins (1991) observed that the exercise of political-economic domination by racial elites "always involves attempts to objectify the subordinate group" (p. 69). Transmitted through cultural institutions owned, controlled, or supported by various elites, these "controlling images" naturalize racism, sexism, and poverty by branding subordinate groups as alternatively inferior, threatening, or praiseworthy. These controlling images form part of a larger system of what Donald G. Baker (1983) referred to as "psychosocial dominance" (p. 37). Along with the threat and occasional use of violence, the psychosocial form of control conditions the subject minority to become the stereotype, to "live it, talk it, embrace it, measure group and individual worth in its terms, and believe it" (Chin & Chan, 1972, pp. 66–67). In so doing, minority members reject their own individual and group identity and accept in its stead "a white supremacist complex that establishes the primacy of Euro-American cultural practices and social institutions" (Hamamoto, 1994, p. 2). But the objectification of Asian Americans as the exotic and inferior "other" has never been absolute. Asian Americans have always, but particularly since the 1960s, resisted race, class, and gender exploitation not only through political and economic struggles but also through cultural activism. This chapter surveys the range of oppositional projects in which Asian-American cultural workers have engaged to deconstruct the conceptual apparatus of the dominant group and to defend Asian-American manhood and womanhood. My goal is to understand how the internalization and renunciation of these stereotypes have shaped sexual and gender politics within Asian America. In particular, I explore the conflicting politics of gender between Asian-American men and women as they negotiate the difficult terrain of cultural nationalism—the construction of an antiassimilationist, native Asian-American subject—and gender identities.

YELLOW PERIL, CHARLIE CHAN, AND SUZIE WONG

A central aspect of racial exploitation centers on defining people of color as "the other" (Said, 1979). The social construction of Asian American "otherness"—through such controlling images as the Yellow Peril, the model minority,

the Dragon Lady, and the China Doll—is "the precondition for their cultural marginalization, political impotence, and psychic alienation from mainstream American society" (Hamamoto, 1994, p. 5). As indicated by these stereotypes, representations of gender and sexuality figure strongly in the articulation of racism. These racist stereotypes collapse gender and sexuality: Asian men have been constructed as hypermasculine, in the image of the "Yellow Peril," but also as effeminate, in the image of the "model minority," and Asian women have been depicted as superfeminine, in the image of the "China Doll," but also as castrating, in the image of the "Dragon Lady" (Mullings, 1994, pp. 279–280; Okihiro, 1995). As Mary Ann Doane (1991) suggested, sexuality is "indissociable from the effects of polarization and differentiation, often linking them to structures of power and domination" (p. 217). In the Asian-American case, the gendering of ethnicity—the process whereby white ideology assigns selected gender characteristics to various ethnic "others"—cast Asian-American men and women as simultaneously masculine and feminine but also as neither masculine nor feminine. On the one hand, as part of the Yellow Peril, Asian-American men and women have been depicted as a *masculine* threat that needs to be contained. On the other hand, both sexes have been skewed toward the female side: an indication of the group's marginalization in U.S. society and its role as the compliant "model minority" in contemporary U.S. cultural ideology. Although an apparent disjunction, both the feminization and masculinization of Asian men and women exist to define and confirm the white man's superiority (Kim, 1990).

The Yellow Peril

In the United States, Asia and America—East and West—are viewed as mutually exclusive binaries (Kim, 1993, p. viii). Within this exclusive binary system, Asian Americans, even as citizens, are designated Asians, not Americans. Characterizing Asian Americans as "permanent houseguests in the house of America," Sau-Ling Cynthia Wong (1993) stated that "Asian Americans are put in the niche of the 'unassimilable alien': . . . they are alleged to be self-disqualified from full American membership by materialistic motives, questionable political allegiance, and, above all, outlandish, overripe, 'Oriental' cultures" (p. 6). Sonia Shah (1994) defined this form of "cultural discrimination" as a "peculiar blend of cultural and sexist oppression based on our accents, our clothes, our foods, our values, and our commitments" (p. 182). This cultural discrimination brands Asians as perpetual foreigners and thus perpetuates the notion of their alleged racial unassimilability. For example, although Japanese Americans have lived in the United States since the turn of the century, many television programs, such as "Happy Days" (1974–1984) and "Gung Ho" (1986–1987), have continued to portray them as newly arrived foreigners (Hamamoto, 1994, p. 13).

As the unassimilable alien, Asian Americans embody for many other Americans the "Yellow Peril"—the threat that Asians will one day unite and conquer the world. This threat includes military invasion and foreign trade from Asia, competition to white labor from Asian labor, the alleged moral degeneracy of Asian people, and potential miscegenation between whites and Asians (Wu, 1982, p. 1). Between 1850 and 1940, U.S. popular media consistently portrayed Asian men as a military threat to the security and welfare of the United States *and* as a sexual danger to innocent white women (Wu, 1982). In numerous dime novels, movies, and comic strips, Asians appeared as feral, rat-faced men lusting after virginal white women. Arguing for racial purity, these popular media depicted Asian–white sexual union as "at best, a form of beastly sodomy, and, at worst, a Satanic marriage" (Hoppenstand, 1983, p. 174). In these popular depictions, the white man was the desirable sexual partner and the hero who rescued the white woman from "a fate worse than death" (Hoppenstand, 1983, pp. 174–175). By the mid-1880s, hundreds of garishly illustrated and garishly written dime novels were being disseminated among a wide audience, sporting such sensational titles as *The Bradys and the Yellow Crooks, The Chase for the Chinese Diamonds, The Opium Den Detective* and *The Stranglers of New York*. As portrayed in these dime novels, the Yellow Peril was the Chinatown district of a big city "in which decent, honest white folk never ventured" (Hoppenstand, 1983, p. 177).

In twentieth-century U.S. popular media, the Japanese joined the Chinese as a perceived threat to Europe and the United States (Wu, 1982, p. 2). In 1916, William Randolph Hearst produced and distributed *Petria,* a movie about a group of fanatical Japanese who invade the United States and attempt to rape a white woman (Quinsaat, 1976, p. 265). After the Japanese bombing of Pearl Harbor on December 7, 1941, the entire Yellow Peril stereotype became incorporated in the nation's war propaganda, quickly whipping white Americans into a war fever. Along with the print media, Hollywood cranked up its anti-Japanese propaganda and produced dozens of war films that centered on the Japanese menace. The fiction of the Yellow Peril stereotype became intertwined with the fact of the United States' war with Japan and the two became one in the mindset of the American public (Hoppenstand, 1983, pp. 182–183). It was fear of the Yellow Peril—fear of the rise of nonwhite people and their contestation of white supremacy—that led to the declaration of martial law in Hawaii on December 7, 1941, and to the internment of over 110,000 Japanese on the mainland in concentration camps (Okihiro, 1994, p. 137). In subsequent decades, reflecting changing geopolitical concerns, U.S. popular media featured a host of new Yellow Peril stereotypes. During the 1950s Cold War years, in television programs as well as in movies, the Communist Chinese evil-doers replaced the Japanese monster; during the Vietnam war of the 1970s, the Vietnamese Communists emerged as the new Oriental villains.

Today, Yellow Perilism takes the forms of the greedy, calculating, and clever Japanese businessman aggressively buying up U.S. real estate and cultural institutions *and* the superachieving but nonassimilating Asian Americans (Hagedorn, 1993, p. xxii). In a time of rising economic powers in Asia, declining economic opportunities in the United States, and growing diversity among America's people, this new Yellow Perilism—the depiction of Asia and Asian Americans as economic and cultural threats to mainstream United States—supplies white Americans with a united identity and provides ideological justification for U.S. isolationist policy toward Asia, increasing restrictions against Asian (and Latino) immigration,[1] and the invisible institutional racism and visible violence against Asians in the United States (Okihiro, 1994, pp. 138–139).

The Racial Construction of Asian-American Manhood

Like other men of color, Asian-American men have been excluded from white-based cultural notions of the masculine. Whereas white men are depicted both as virile and as protectors of women, Asian men have been characterized both as asexual *and* as threats to white women. It is important to note the historical contexts of these seemingly divergent representations of Asian-American manhood. The racist depictions of Asian men as "lascivious and predatory" were especially pronounced during the nativist movement against Asians at the turn of the century (Frankenberg, 1993, pp. 75–76). The exclusion of Asian women from the United States and the subsequent establishment of bachelor societies eventually reversed the construction of Asian masculinity from "hypersexual" to "asexual" and even "homosexual." The contemporary model-minority stereotype further emasculates Asian-American men as passive and malleable. Disseminated and perpetuated through the popular media, these stereotypes of the emasculated Asian male construct a reality in which social and economic discrimination against these men appears defensible. As an example, the desexualization of Asian men naturalized their inability to establish conjugal families in pre-World War II United States. Gliding over race-based exclusion laws that banned the immigration of most Asian women and antimiscegenation laws that prohibited men of color from marrying white women, these dual images of the eunuch and the rapist attributed the "womanless households" characteristic of prewar Asian America to Asian men's lack of sexual prowess and desirability.

A popular controlling image applied to Asian-American men is that of the sinister Oriental—a brilliant, powerful villain who plots the destruction of western civilization. Personified by the movie character of Dr. Fu Manchu, this Oriental mastermind combines western science with eastern magic and commands an army of devoted assassins (Hoppenstand, 1983, p. 178). Though ruthless, Fu Manchu lacks masculine heterosexual prowess (Wang, 1988, p. 19), thus privileging heterosexuality. Frank Chin and Jeffrey Chan (1972), in a critique of the desexualization of Asian men in western culture, described how the Fu Manchu character undermines Chinese-American virility:

> Dr. Fu, a man wearing a long dress, batting his eyelashes, surrounded by muscular black servants in loin cloths, and with his habit of caressingly touching white men on the leg, wrist, and face with his long fingernails, is not so much a threat as he is a frivolous offense to white manhood. (p. 60)

In another critique that glorifies male aggression, Frank Chin (1972) contrasted the neuterlike characteristics assigned to Asian men to the sexually aggressive images associated with other men of color. "Unlike the white stereotype of the evil black stud, Indian rapist, Mexican macho, the evil of the evil Dr. Fu Manchu was not sexual, but homosexual" (p. 66). However, Chin failed to note that as a homosexual, Dr. Fu (and by extension, Asian men) threatens and offends white masculinity—and therefore needs to be contained ideologically and destroyed physically.[2]

Whereas the evil Oriental stereotype marks Asian-American men as the white man's enemy, the stereotype of the sexless Asian sidekick—Charlie Chan, the Chinese laundryman, the Filipino houseboy—depicts Asian men as devoted and impotent, eager to please. William Wu (1982) reported that the Chinese servant "is the most important single image of the Chinese immigrants" in American fiction about Chinese Americans between 1850 and 1940 (p. 60). More recently, such diverse television programs as "Bachelor Father" (1957–1962), "Bonanza" (1959–1973), "Star Trek" (1966–1969), and "Falcon Crest" (1981–1990) all featured the stock Chinese bachelor domestic who dispenses sage advice to his superiors in addition to performing traditional female functions within the household (Hamamoto, 1994, p. 7). By trapping Chinese men (and by extension, Asian men) in the stereotypical "feminine" tasks of serving white men, American society erases the figure of the Asian "masculine" plantation worker in Hawaii or railroad construction worker in the western United States, thus perpetuating the myth of the androgynous and effeminate Asian man (Goellnicht, 1992, p. 198). This feminization, in turn, confines Asian immigrant men to the segment of the labor force that performs women's work.

The motion-picture industry has been key in the construction of Asian men as sexual deviants. In a study of Asians in the U.S. motion pictures, Eugene Franklin Wong (1978) maintained that the movie industry filmically castrates Asian males to magnify the superior sexual status of white males (p. 27). As on-screen sexual rivals of whites, Asian males are neutralized, unable to sexually engage Asian women and prohibited from sexually engaging white women. By saving the white woman from sexual contact with the racial "other," the motion-picture industry protects the Anglo-American, bourgeois male establishment from any challenges to its hegemony (Marchetti, 1993, p. 218). At the other extreme, the industry has exploited one of the most potent aspects of the Yellow Peril discourses—the sexual danger of contact between the races—by concocting a sexually threatening portrayal of the licentious and aggressive Yellow Man lusting after the White Woman (Marchetti, 1993, p. 3). Heedful of the larger society's taboos against Asian male–white female sexual union, white male actors donning "yellowface"—instead of Asian male actors—are used in these "love scenes." Nevertheless, the message of the perverse and animalistic Asian male attacking helpless white women is clear (Wong, 1978). Though depicting sexual aggression, this image of the rapist, like that of the eunuch, casts Asian men as sexually undesirable. As Wong (1978) succinctly stated, in Asian male–white female relations, "There can be rape, but there cannot be romance" (p. 25). Thus, Asian males yield to the sexual superiority of the white males who are permitted filmically to maintain their sexual dominance over both white women and women of color. A young Vietnamese-American man describes the damaging effect of these stereotypes on his self-image:

Every day I was forced to look into a mirror created by white society and its media. As a young Asian man, I shrank before white eyes. I wasn't tall, I wasn't fair, I wasn't muscular, and so on. Combine that with the enormous insecurities any pubescent teenager feels, and I have no difficulty in knowing now why I felt naked before a mass of white people. (Nguyen, 1990, p. 23)

White cultural and institutional racism against Asian males is also reflected in the motion-picture industry's preoccupation with the death of Asians—a filmic solution to the threats of the Yellow Peril. In a perceptive analysis of Hollywood's view of Asians in films made from the 1930s to the 1960s, Tom Engelhardt (1976) described how Asians, like Native Americans, are seen by the movie industry as inhuman invaders, ripe for extermination. He argued that the theme of the nonhumanness of Asians prepares the audience to accept, without flinching, "the leveling and near-obliteration of three Asian areas in the course of three decades" (Engelhardt, 1976, p. 273). The industry's death theme, though applying to all Asians, is mainly focused on Asian males, with Asian females reserved for sexual purposes (Wong, 1978, p. 35). Especially in war films, Asian males, however advantageous, their initial position, inevitably perish at the hands of the superior white males (Wong, 1978, p. 34).

The Racial Construction of Asian-American Womanhood

Like Asian men, Asian women have been reduced to one-dimensional caricatures in western presentation. The condensation of Asian women's multiple differences into gross character types—mysterious, feminine, and nonwhite—obscures the social injustice of racial, class, and gender oppression (Marchetti, 1993, p. 71). Both western film and literature promote dichotomous stereotypes of the Asian woman: Either she is the cunning Dragon Lady or the servile Lotus Blossom Baby (Tong, 1994, p. 197). Though connoting two extremes, these stereotypes are interrelated: Both eroticize Asian women as exotic "others"—sensuous, promiscuous, but untrustworthy. Whereas American popular culture denies "manhood" to Asian men, it endows Asian women with an excess of "womanhood," sexualizing them but also impugning their sexuality. In this process, sexism and racism have been blended together to produce the sexualization of white racism (Wong, 1978, p. 260). Linking the controlling images of Asian men and women, Elaine Kim (1990) suggested that Asian women are portrayed as sexual for the same reason that men are asexual: "Both exist to define the white man's virility and the white man's superiority" (p. 70).

As the racialized exotic "others," Asian-American women do not fit the white-constructed notions of the feminine. Whereas white women have been depicted as chaste and dependable, Asian women have been represented as promiscuous and untrustworthy. In a mirror image of the evil Fu Manchu, the Asian woman was portrayed as the castrating Dragon Lady who, while puffing on her foot-long cigarette holder, could poison a man as easily as she could seduce him. "With her talonlike six-inch fingernails, her skintight satin dress slit to the thigh," the Dragon Lady is desirable, deceitful, and dangerous (Ling, 1990, p. 11). In the 1924 film *The Thief of Baghdad,* Anna May Wong, a pioneer Chinese-American actress, played a handmaid who employed treachery to help an evil Mongol prince attempt to win the hand of the Princess of Baghdad (Tajima, 1989, p. 309). In so doing, Wong unwittingly popularized a common Dragon Lady social type: treacherous women who are partners in crime with men of their own kind. The publication of *Daughter of Fu Manchu* (1931) firmly entrenched the Dragon Lady image in white consciousness. Carrying on her father's work as the champion of Asian hegemony over the white race, Fah Lo Sue exhibited, in the words of American studies scholar William F. Wu, "exotic sensuality, sexual availability to a white man, and a treacherous nature" (cited in Tong, 1994, p. 197). A few years later, in 1934, Milton Caniff inserted into his adventure comic strip "Terry and the Pirates" another version of the Dragon Lady who "combines all the best features of past moustache twirlers with the lure of the handsome wench" (Hoppenstand, 1983, p. 178). As such, Caniff's Dragon Lady fuses the image of the evil male Oriental mastermind with that of the Oriental prostitute first introduced some fifty years earlier in the dime novels.

At the opposite end of the spectrum is the Lotus Blossom stereotype, reincarnated throughout the years as the China Doll, the Geisha Girl, the War Bride, or the Vietnamese prostitute—many of whom are the spoils of the last three wars fought in Asia (Tajima, 1989, p. 309). Demure, diminutive, and deferential, the Lotus Blossom Baby is "modest, tittering behind her delicate ivory hand, eyes downcast, always walking ten steps behind her man, and, best of all, devot[ing] body and soul to serving him" (Ling, 1990, p. 11). Interchangeable in appearance and name, these women have no voice; their "nonlanguage" includes uninterpretable chattering, pidgin English, giggling, and silence (Tajima, 1989). These stereotypes of

Asian women as submissive and dainty sex objects not only have impeded women's economic mobility but also have fostered an enormous demand for X-rated films and pornographic materials featuring Asian women in bondage, for "Oriental" bathhouse workers in U.S. cities, and for Asian mail-order brides (Kim, 1984, p. 64)

Sexism, Racism, and Love

The racialization of Asian manhood and womanhood upholds white masculine hegemony. Cast as sexually available, Asian women become yet another possession of the white man. In motion pictures and network television programs, interracial sexuality, though rare, occurs principally between a white male and an Asian female. A combination of sexism and racism makes this form of miscegenation more acceptable: Race mixing between an Asian male and a white female would upset not only racial taboos but those that attend patriarchal authority as well (Hamamoto, 1994, p. 39). Whereas Asian men are depicted as either the threatening rapist or the impotent eunuch, white men are endowed with the masculine attributes with which to sexually attract the Asian woman. Such popular television shows as "Gunsmoke" (1955–1975) and "How the West Was Won" (1978–1979) clearly articulate the theme of Asian female sexual possession by the white male. In these shows, only white males have the prerogative to cross racial boundaries and to choose freely from among women of color as sex partners. Within a system of racial and gender oppression, the sexual possession of women and men of color by white men becomes yet another means of enforcing unequal power relations (Hamamoto, 1994, p. 46).

The preference for white male–Asian female is also prevalent in contemporary television news broadcasting, most recently in the 1993– 1995 pairing of Dan Rather and Connie Chung as coanchors of the "CBS Evening News." Today, virtually every major metropolitan market across the United States has at least one Asian-American female newscaster (Hamamoto, 1994, p. 245). While female Asian-American anchorpersons—Connie Chung, Tritia Toyota, Wendy Tokuda, and Emerald Yeh—are popular television news figures, there is a nearly total absence of Asian-American men. Critics argue that this is so because the white male hiring establishment, and presumably the larger American public, feels more comfortable (i.e., less threatened) seeing a white male sitting next to a minority female at the anchor desk than the reverse. Stephen Tschida of WDBJ-TV (Roanoke, Virginia), one of only a handful of male Asian-American television news anchors, was informed early in his career that he did not have the proper "look" to qualify for the anchorperson position. Other male broadcast news veterans have reported being passed over for younger, more beauteous, female Asian Americans (Hamamoto, 1994, p. 245). This gender imbalance sustains the construction of Asian-American women as more successful, assimilated, attractive, and desirable than their male counterparts.

To win the love of white men, Asian women must reject not only Asian men but their entire culture. Many Hollywood narratives featuring romances between Anglo-American men and Asian women follow the popular Pocahontas mythos: The Asian woman, out of devotion for her white American lover, betrays her own people and commits herself to the dominant white culture by dying, longing for, or going to live with her white husband in his country. For example, in the various versions of *Miss Saigon,* the contemporary version of *Madame Butterfly,* the tragic Vietnamese prostitute eternally longs for the white boy soldier who has long abandoned her and their son (Hagedorn, 1993, p. xxii). These tales of interracial romance inevitably have a tragic ending. The Asian partner usually dies, thus providing a cinematic resolution to the moral lapse of the Westerner. The Pocahontas paradigm can be read as a narrative of salvation; the Asian woman is saved either spiritually or morally from the excesses of her own culture, just as she physically saves her western lover from the moral degeneracy of her own people (Marchetti, 1993, p. 218). For Asian women, who are marginalized not only by gender but also by class, race, or ethnicity, the interracial romance narratives promise "the American Dream of abundance, protection, individual choice, and freedom from the strictures of a traditional society in the paternalistic name of heterosexual romance" (Marchetti, 1993, p. 91). These narratives also carry a covert political message, legitimizing a masculinized Anglo-American rule over a submissive, feminized Asia. The motion picture *China Gate* (1957) by Samuel Fuller and the network television program "The Lady from Yesterday" (1985), for example, promote an image of Vietnam that legitimizes American rule. Seduced by images of U.S. abundance, a feminized Vietnam sacrifices herself for the possibility of future incorporation into America, the land of individual freedom and economic opportunities. Thus, the interracial tales function not only as a romantic defense of traditional female roles within the patriarchy but also as a political justification of American hegemony in Asia (Marchetti, 1993, p. 108).

Fetishized as the embodiment of perfect womanhood and genuine exotic femininity, Asian women are pitted against their more modern, emancipated western sisters (Tajima, 1989). In two popular motion pictures, *Love Is a Many-Splendored Thing* (1955) and *The World of Suzie Wong* (1960), the white women remain independent and potentially threatening, whereas both Suyin and Suzie give up their independence in the name of love. Thus, the white female characters are cast as calculating, suffocating, and thoroughly undesirable, whereas the Asian female characters are depicted as truly "feminine"—passive, subservient, dependent, and domestic. Implicitly, these films warn white women to embrace the socially constructed passive Asian beauty as the feminine ideal if they want to attract and keep a man. In pitting white women against Asian women, Hollywood affirms white male identity against the threat of emerging feminism and the concomitant changes in gender relations (Marchetti, 1993, pp. 115–116). As Robyn Wiegman (1991) observed, the absorption of women of color into gender categories traditionally reserved for white women is "part of a broader program of hegemonic recuperation, a program that has at its main focus the reconstruction of white masculine power" (p. 320). It is also important to note that as the racialized exotic "other," Asian women do not replace but merely substitute for white women, and thus will be readily dismissed once the "real" mistress returns.

The controlling images of Asian men and Asian women, exaggerated out of all proportion in western representation, have created resentment and tension between Asian-American men and women. Given this cultural milieu, many American-born Asians do not think of other Asians in sexual terms (Fung, 1994, p. 163). In particular, due to the persistent desexualization of the Asian male, many Asian females do not perceive their ethnic counterparts as desirable marriage partners (Hamamoto, 1992, p. 42). In so doing, these women unwittingly enforce the Eurocentric gender ideology that objectifies both sexes and racializes all Asians (see Collins, 1990, pp. 185–186). In a column to *Asian Week,* a weekly Asian-American newspaper, Daniel Yoon (1993) reported that at a recent dinner discussion hosted by the Asian-American Students Association at his college, the Asian-American women in the room proceeded, one after another, to describe how "Asian-American men were too passive, too weak, too boring, too traditional, too abusive, too domineering, too ugly, too greasy, too short, too . . . Asian. Several described how they preferred white men, and how they never had and never would date an Asian man" (p. 16). Partly as a result of the racist constructions of Asian-American womanhood and manhood and their acceptance by Asian Americans, intermar-

riage patterns are high, with Asian-American women intermarrying at a much higher rate than Asian-American men.[3] Moreover, Asian women involved in intermarriage have usually married white partners (Agbayani-Siewert & Revilla, 1995, p. 156; Min, 1995, p. 22; Nishi, 1995, p. 128). In part, these intermarriage patterns reflect the sexualization of white racism that constructs white men as the most desirable sexual partners, frowns on Asian male–white women relations, and fetishizes Asian women as the embodiment of perfect womanhood. Viewed in this light, the high rate of outmarriage for Asian-American women is the "material outcome of an interlocking system of sexism and racism" (Hamamoto, 1992, p. 42).[4]

CULTURAL RESISTANCE: RECONSTRUCTING OUR OWN IMAGES

"One day/I going to write/about you," wrote Lois-Ann Yamanaka (1993) in "Empty Heart" (p. 548). And Asian Americans did write—"to inscribe our faces on the blank pages and screens of America's hegemonic culture" (Kim,1993, p. xii). As a result, Asian Americans' objectification as the exotic aliens who are different from, and other than, Euro-Americans has never been absolute. Within the confines of race, class, and gender oppression, Asian Americans have maintained independent self-definitions, challenging controlling images and replacing them with Asian-American standpoints. The civil rights and ethnic studies movements of the late 1960s were training grounds for Asian-American cultural workers and the development of oppositional projects. Grounded in the U.S. black power movement and in anticolonial struggles of Third World countries, Asian-American antihegemonic projects have been unified by a common goal of articulating cultural resistance. Given the historical distortions and misrepresentations of Asian Americans in mainstream media, most cultural projects produced by Asian-American men and women perform the important tasks of correcting histories, shaping legacies, creating new cultures, constructing a politics of resistance, and opening spaces for the forcibly excluded (Kim, 1993, p. xiii; Fung, 1994, p. 165).

Fighting the exoticization of Asian Americans has been central in the ongoing work of cultural resistance. As discussed above, Asian Americans, however rooted in this country, are represented as recent transplants from Asia or as bearers of an exotic culture. The Chinese American playwright Frank Chin noted that New York critics of his play *Chickencoop Chinaman* complained in the early 1970s that his characters did not speak, dress, or act "like Orientals" (Kim, 1982, p. xv). Similarly, a reviewer described Maxine Hong Kingston's *The Woman Warrior* as a tale of "East meets West" and praised the book for its "myths rich and varied as Chinese brocade"—even though *The Woman Warrior* is deliberately antiexotic and antinostalgic (quoted in Kim, 1982, p. xv). In both of these examples, the qualifier *American* has been blithely excised from the term *Asian American*.

Asian-American cultural workers simply do not accept the exotic, one-dimensional caricatures of themselves in U.S. mass media. In the preface of *Aiiieeeee!*, a landmark collection of Asian-American writers (in this case, Chinese, Japanese, and Filipinos), published in the mid-1970s, the editors announced that the anthology, and the title *Aiiieeeee!* itself, challenged the exoticization of Asian Americans:

> The pushers of white American culture . . . pictured the yellow man as something that when wounded, sad, angry, or swearing, or wondering whined, shouted, or screamed "aiiieeeee!" Asian America, so long ignored and forcibly excluded from creative participation in American culture, is wounded, sad, angry, swearing, and wondering, and this is his AIIIEEEEE!!! It is more than a whine, shout, or scream. It is fifty years of our whole voice. (Chan et al., 1974, p. xii)

The publication of *Aiiieeeee!* gave Asian-American writers visibility and credibility and sparked other oppositional projects. Jessica Hagedorn, a Filipina-American writer, described the legacy of *Aiiieeeee!:* "We could not be ignored; suddenly, we were no longer silent. Like other writers of color in America, we were beginning to challenge the long-cherished concepts of a xenophobic literary canon dominated by white heterosexual males" (Hagedorn, 1993, p. xviii). Inspired by *Aiiieeeee!* and by other "irreverent and blasphemous" American writers, Hagedorn created an anthology of contemporary Asian-American fiction in 1993—"a book I wanted to read but had never been available to me" (Hagedorn, 1993, p. xxx). In the tradition of *Aiiieeeee!,* the title of Hagedorn's anthology, *Charlie Chan Is Dead,* is vigorously political, defying and stamping out the vestiges of a "fake 'Asian' pop icon" (Hagedorn, 1993, p. xxi). In the anthology's preface, Elaine Kim (1993) contested the homogenization of Asian American by juxtaposing the one-dimensional Charlie Chan to the many ways of being Asian American in the contemporary United States:

> Charlie Chan is dead, never to be revived. Gone for good his yellowface asexual bulk, his fortune-cookie English, his stereotypical Orientalist version of "the [Confucian] Chinese family," challenged by an array of characters, some hip and articulate, some brooding and sexy, some insolent and others innocent, but all as unexpected as a Korean American who writes in French, a Chinese-Panamanian-German who longs too late to know her father, a mean Japanese-American grandmother, a Chinese-American flam-dive, or a teenage Filipino-American male prostitute. Instead of "model minorities," we find human beings with rich and complex pasts and brave, often flamboyant dreams of the future. (p. xiii)

Taking up this theme, Wayne Chang's commercial film *Chan Is Missing* (1981) offers a range of Chinatown characters who indirectly convey the message that Chinese Americans, like other Americans, are heterogeneous (Chan, 1994, p. 530). Portraying Asian Americans in all our contradictions and complexities—as exiled, assimilated, rebellious, noble—Asian-American cultural projects reveal heterogeneity rather than "producing regulating ideas of cultural unity or integration" (Lowe, 1994, p. 53). In so doing, these projects destabilize the dominant racist discourse that constructs Asians as a homogeneous group who are "all alike" and readily conform to "types" such as the Yellow Peril, the Oriental mastermind, and the sexy Suzie Wong (Lowe, 1991).

Asian-American cultural projects also deconstruct the myth of the benevolent United States promised to women and men from Asia. Carlos Bulosan's *America Is in the Heart* (1943/1973), one of the core works of Asian-American literature, challenges the narrative of the United States as the land of opportunity. Seduced by the promise of individual freedom through education, the protagonist Carlos discovers that as a Filipino immigrant in the United States, he is denied access to formal schooling. This disjunction between the promise of education and the unequal access of different racial and economic groups to that education—reinforced by Carlos's observations of the exploitation, marginality, and violence suffered by his compatriots in the United States—challenges his faith in the promise of US democracy and abundance (Lowe, 1994, p. 56). John Okada's *No-No Boy* (1957) is another searing indictment of U.S. racist hysteria. In this portrayal of the aftermath of the internment of Japanese Americans during World War II, the protagonist, Ichiro, angrily refuses to adjust to his postinternment and postimprisonment circumstances, thus dramatizing the Asian-American subject's refusal to accept the subordinating terms of assimilation (Lowe, 1994, p. 59). In the following excerpt from the poem by Cao Tan, "Tomorrow I Will Be Home," a Vietnamese refugee describes the emasculating effect of U.S. society:

Tomorrow I will be home and someone will ask
What have you learned in the States?
If you want to give me a broom
I'll tell you, I am a first class janitor.
I wash dishes much faster than the best housewife
And do a vacuum job better than any child
Every day I run like a madman in my brand new car
Every night I bury my head in my pillow and cry . . . .

Bich (1989)

To reject the myth of a benevolent United States is also to refute ideological racism: the justification of inequalities through a set of controlling images that attribute physical and intellectual traits to racially defined groups (Hamamoto, 1994, p. 3). In the 1980 autobiographical fiction *China Men*, Maxine Hong Kingston smashed the controlling image of the emasculated Asian man by foregrounding the legalized racism that turned immigrant Chinese "men" into "women" at the turn of the century. In his search for the Gold Mountain, the novel's male protagonist Tang Ao finds instead the Land of Women, where he is caught and transformed into an Oriental courtesan. Because Kingston reveals at the end of the legend that the Land of Women was in North America, readers familiar with Chinese-American history will readily see that "the ignominy suffered by Tang Ao in a foreign land symbolizes the emasculation of Chinamen by the dominant culture" (Cheung, 1990, p. 240). Later in the novel, the father's failure as a provider—his emasculation—inverts the sexual roles in the family. His silence and impotent rage deepen as his wife takes on active power in the family and assumes the "masculine" traits of aggressiveness and authority. As a means of releasing his sense of frustration and powerlessness in racist America, the father lapses into silence, screams "wordless male screams in his sleep," and spouts furious misogynistic curses that frighten his daughter (Sledge, 1980, p. 10). The author/narrator Maxine traces her father's abusive behavior back to his feeling of emasculation in America: "We knew that it was to feed us you had to endure demons and physical labor" (cited in Goellnicht, 1992, p. 201). Similarly, in Louis Chu's 1961 novel *Eat a*

Bowl of Tea, the protagonist's sexual impotence represents the social powerlessness of generations of Chinatown bachelors prevented by discriminatory laws and policies from establishing a traditional family life (Kim, 1982, p. xviii).

More recently, Steven Okazaki's film *American Sons* (1995)[5] tells the stories of four Asian-American men who reveal how incidents of prejudice and bigotry shaped their identity and affected the way they perceived themselves and society. About his film, Okazaki (1995) explained, "Prejudice, bigotry, and violence twist and demean individual lives. *American Sons* looks at difficult issues, such as hate violence, in order to show this intimate and disturbing examination of the deep psychological damage that racism causes over generations." Asian-American men's increasing involvement in hip-hop—a highly masculinized cultural form and a distinctly American phenomenon—is yet another contemporary denouncement of the stereotype of themselves as "effeminate, nerdy, asocial foreigners" (Choe, 1996). By exposing the role of the larger society in the emasculation and oppression of Asian men, Kingston, Chu, and Okazaki invalidated the naturalization and normalization of Asian men's asexuality in U.S. popular culture.

Finally, Asian-American cultural workers reject the narrative of salvation: the myth that Asian women (and a feminized Asia) are saved, through sexual relations with white men (and a masculinized United States), from the excesses of their own culture. Instead, they underscore the considerable potential for abuse in these inherently unequal relationships. Writing in Vietnamese, transplanted Vietnamese writer Tran Dieu Hang described the gloomy existence of Vietnamese women in sexist and racist U.S. society—an accursed land that singles out women, especially immigrant women, for oppression and violence. Her short story "Roi Ngay Van Moi" ("There Will Come New Days," 1986) depicts the brutal rape of a young refugee woman by her American sponsor despite her tearful pleas in limited English (Tran, 1993, pp. 72–73). Marianne Villanueva's short story "Opportunity" (1991) also calls attention to the sexualization and racialization of Asian women. As the protagonist Nina, a "mail-order bride" from the Philippines, enters the hotel lobby to meet her American fiance, the bellboys snicker and whisper *puta,* whore: a reminder that U.S. economic and cultural colonization of the Philippines always forms the backdrop to any relations between Filipinos and Americans (Wong, 1993, p. 53). Characterizing Filipino-American literature as a "literature of exile," Oscar Campomanes (1992) underscored the legacy of U.S. colonization of the Philippines: "The signifiers 'Filipinos' and 'Philippines' evoke colonialist meanings and cultural redactions which possess inordinate power to shape the fates of the writers and of Filipino peoples everywhere" (p. 52). Theresa Hak Kyung Cha's *Dictee* (1982), a Korean-American text, likewise challenges the myth of U.S. benevolence in Asia by tracing the impact of colonial and imperial damage and dislocation on the Korean subject (Lowe, 1994, p. 61). As Sau-Ling Cynthia Wong (1993) suggested, "To the extent that most typical cases of Asian immigration to the United States stem from an imbalance of resources writ large in the world economy, it holds in itself the seed of exploitation" (p. 53).

CONTROLLING IMAGES, GENDER, AND CULTURAL NATIONALISM

Cultural nationalism has been crucial in Asian Americans' struggles for self-determination. Emerging in the early 1970s, this unitary Asian-American identity was primarily racial, male, and heterosexual. Asian-American literature produced in those years highlighted Chinese- and Japanese-American male perspectives, obscuring gender and other intercommunity differences (Kim, 1993). Asian-American male writers, concerned with recuperating their identities as men and as Americans, objectified both white and Asian women in their writings (Kim, 1990, p. 70). In a controversial essay entitled "Racist Love," Frank Chin and Jeffrey Paul Chan (1972) pointed to the stereotype of the emasculated Asian-American man:

> The white stereotype of Asian is unique in that it is the only racial stereotype completely devoid of manhood. Our nobility is that of an efficient housewife. At our worst we are contemptible because we are womanly, effeminate, devoid of all the traditionally masculine qualities of originality, daring, physical courage, creativity. (p. 68)

In taking whites to task for their racist debasement of Asian-American men, however, Chin and Chan succumbed to the influence of Eurocentric gender ideology, particularly its emphasis on oppositional dichotomous sex roles (Collins, 1991, p. 184). In a critique of "Racist Love," King-Kok Cheung (1990) contended that Chin and Chan buttressed patriarchy "by invoking gender stereotypes, by disparaging domestic efficiency as 'feminine,' and by slotting desirable traits such as originality, daring, physical courage, and creativity under the rubric of masculinity" (p. 237). Similarly, Wong (1993) argued that in their influ-

ential "Introduction" to *Aiiieeeee! An Anthology of Asian American Writers* (1974), Chan, Chin, Inada, and Wong operated on the premise that a true Asian-American sensibility is "non-Christian, nonfeminine, and nonimmigrant" (p. 8).

Though limited and limiting, a masculinist cultural nationalist agenda appealed to Asian-American activists because of its potential to oppose and disrupt the logic of racial domination. In the following excerpt, Elaine Kim (1993), a pioneer in the field of Asian-American literature, explained the appeal of cultural nationalism:

> Certainly it was possible for me as a Korean-American female to accept the fixed masculinist Asian-American identity posited in Asian-American cultural nationalism, even when it rendered invisible or at least muted women's oppression, anger, and ways of loving and interpreted Korean Americans as imperfect imitations of Chinese Americans; because I could see in everyday life that not all material and psychic violence to women of color comes from men, and because, as my friends used to say, "No Chinese [American] ever called me a 'Gook.'" (p. x)

Kim's statement suggests that for Asian-American women, and for other women of color, gender is only a part of a larger pattern of unequal social relations. Despite the constraints of patriarchy, racism inscribes these women's lives and binds them to Asian-American men in what Collins (1991) called a "love and trouble" tradition (p. 184).

Because the racial oppression of Asian Americans involves the "feminization" of Asian men (Said, 1979), Asian-American women are caught between the need to expose the problems of male privilege and the desire to unite with men to contest the overarching racial ideology that confines them both. As Cheung (1990) suggested, Asian-American women may be simultaneously sympathetic and angry toward the men in their ethnic community: sensitive to the men's marginality but resentful of their sexism (p. 239). Maxine Hong Kingston's writings seem to reflect these conflicting emotions. As discussed above, in the opening legend of *China Men*, the male protagonist Tang Ao is captured in the Land of Women (North America), where he is forced to become a woman—to have his feet bound, his ears pierced, his eyebrows plucked, his cheeks and lips painted. Cheung (1990) argued that this legend is double-edged, pointing not only to the racist debasement of Chinese Americans in their adopted country but also to the subjugation of Chinese women both in China and in the United States (p. 240). Although the effeminization suffered by Tang Ao is brutal, it is the same mutilation that many Chinese women were for centuries forced to bear. According to Goellnicht's (1992) reading of Kingston's work, this opening myth suggests that the author both deplores the emasculation of her forefathers by mainstream America and critiques the Confucian patriarchal practices of her ancestral homeland (p. 194). In *China Men,* Kingston also showed no acceptance of sexist practices by immigrant men. The father in this novel/autobiography is depicted as a broken man who attempts to reassert male authority by denigrating those who are even more powerless—the women and children in his family (Cheung, 1990, p. 241; Goellnicht, 1992, p. 200).

Along the same lines, Maxine Hong Kingston's *The Woman Warrior* (1977) reveals the narrator's contradictory attitudes toward her childhood "home," which is simultaneously a site of "woman hatred" and an area of resistance against the racism of the dominant culture. The community that nourishes her imagination and suffuses her with warmth is the same community that relegates women to an inferior position, limiting them to the role of serving men (Rabine, 1987, pp. 477–478). In the following passage, the narrator voices her mixed feelings toward the Chinese-American community:

> I looked at their ink drawings of poor people snagging their neighbors' flotage with long flood hooks and pushing the girl babies on down the river. And I had to get out of hating range. . . . I refuse to shy my way anymore through our Chinatown, which tasks me with the old sayings and the stories. The swordswoman and I are not so dissimilar. May my people understand the resemblance so that I can return to them. (Kingston, 1977, p. 62)

Similarly, in a critique of Asian-American sexual politics, Kayo Hatta's short video *Otemba* (1988) depicts a girl's-eye view of the final days of her mother's pregnancy as her father hopes and prays for the birth of a boy (see Tajima, 1991, p. 26).

Stripped of the privileges of masculinity, some Asian-American men have attempted to reassert male authority by subordinating feminism to nationalist concerns. Lisa Lowe (1991) argued that this identity politics displaces gender differences into a false opposition of "nationalism" and "assimilation." From this limited perspective, Asian-American feminists who expose Asian-American sexism are cast as "assimilationist," as betraying Asian-American "nationalism." Maxine Hong Kingston's *The Woman Warrior* (1977) and Amy Tan's *The Joy Luck Club* (1989) are the targets of such nationalist criticisms. Frank Chin, Ben Tong, and others have accused these and other women novelists of feminizing Asian-American literature by exaggerating the community's patriarchal structure, thus undermining the power of Asian-American men to combat the racist stereotypes of the dominant white culture. For example, when Kingston's *The Woman Warrior* received favorable reviews, Chin accused her of attempting to "cash in on the feminist fad" (Chan, 1994, p. 528). Another Asian-American male had this to say about the movie *The Joy Luck Club:*

> The movie was powerful. But it could have been powerful *and inclusive,* if at least one of the Asian male characters was portrayed as something other than monstrously evil or simply wimpy. We are used to this message coming out of Hollywood, but it disturbed me deeply to hear the same message coming from Amy Tan and Wayne Wang—people of my own color. (Yoon, 1993)

Whereas Chin and others cast this tension in terms of nationalism and assimilationism, Lisa Lowe (1991) argued that it is more a debate between nationalist and feminist concerns in Asian-American discourse. This insistence on a fixed masculinist identity, according to Lowe (1991), "can be itself a colonial figure used to displace the challenges of heterogeneity, or subalternity, by casting them as assimilationist or anti-ethnic" (pp. 33–34).

But cultural nationalism need not be patriarchial. Rejecting the ideology of oppositional dichotomous sex roles, Asian-American cultural workers have also engaged in cross-gender projects. In a recent review of Asian-American independent filmmaking, Renee Tajima (1991) reported that some of the best feminist films have been made by Asian-American men. For example, Arthur Dong's *Lotus* (1987) exposes women's exploitation through the practice of footbinding (Tajima, 1991, p. 24). Asian-American men have also made use of personal documentary, in both diary and autobiographical form—an approach known to be the realm of women filmmakers. Finally, there is no particular gender affiliation in subject matters: Just as Arthur Dong profiles his mother in *Sewing Woman;* Lori Tsang portrays her father's life in *Chinaman's Choice* (Tajima, 1991, p. 24).

CONCLUSION

Ideological representations of gender and sexuality are central in the exercise and maintenance of racial, patriarchal, and class domination. In the Asian-American case, this ideological racism has taken seemingly contrasting forms: Asian men have been cast as both hypersexual and asexual, and Asian women have been rendered both superfeminine and masculine. Although in apparent disjunction, both forms exist to define, maintain, and justify white male supremacy. The racialization of Asian-American manhood and womanhood underscores the interconnections of race, gender, and class. As categories of difference, race and gender relations do not parallel but intersect and confirm each other, and it is the complicity among these categories of difference that enables U.S. elites to justify and maintain their cultural, social, and economic power. Responding to the ideological assaults on their gender identities, Asian-American cultural workers have engaged in a wide range of oppositional projects to defend Asian-American manhood and womanhood. In the process, some have embraced a masculinist cultural nationalism, a stance that marginalizes Asian-American women and their needs. Though sensitive to the emasculation of Asian-American men, Asian-American feminists have pointed out that Asian-American nationalism insists on a fixed masculinist identity, thus obscuring gender differences. Though divergent, both the nationalist and feminist positions advance the dichotomous stance of man or woman, gender or race or class, without recognizing the complex relationality of these categories of oppression. It is only when Asian Americans recognize the intersections of race, gender, and class that we can transform the existing hierarchical structure.

ACKNOWLEDGMENT

The excerpt from Cao Tan's poem "Tomorrow I Will Be Home" appeared in *War and Exile: A Vietnamese Anthology,* edited by N. N. Bich, 1989, Springfield, VA: Vietnam PEN Abroad.

NOTES

1. In 1996, the U.S. Congress deliberated on but did not pass two bills (S. 1394/269 and H.R. 2202) that would have sharply cut legal immigration by removing the family preferences from the existing immigration laws.

2. I thank Mary Romero for pointing this out to me.

3. Filipino Americans provide an exception in that Filipino-American men tend to intermarry as frequently as Filipina-American women. This is so partly because they are more Americanized and have a relatively more egalitarian gender-role orientation than other Asian-American men (Agbayani-Siewert & Revilla, 1995, p. 156).

4. In recent years, Asian Americans' rising consciousness, coupled with their phenomenal growth in certain regions of the United States, has led to a significant increase in inter-Asian marriages (e.g., Chinese Americans to Korean Americans). In a comparative analysis of the 1980 and 1990 Decennial Census, Larry Hajimi Shinigawa and Gin Young Pang (forthcoming) found a dramatic decrease of interracial marriages and a significant rise of inter-Asian marriages. In California (where 39% of all Asian Pacific Americans reside), inter-Asian marriages increased from 21.1% in 1980 to 64% in 1990 of all intermarriages for Asian-American husbands and from 10.8% to 45.% for Asian-American wives during the same time period.

5. I thank Takeo Wong for calling my attention to this film.

REFERENCES

Agbayani-Siewert, P., & Revilla, L. (1995). Filipino Americans. In P. G. Min (Ed.), *Asian Americans: Contemporary Trends and Issues* (pp. 134–168). Thousand Oaks, CA: Sage.

Baker, D. G. (1983). *Race, Ethnicity, and Power: A Comparative Study.* New York: Routledge.

Bich, N. N. (Ed.). (1989). *War and Exile: A Vietnamese Anthology.* Springfield, VA: Vietnam PEN Abroad.

Chan, J. P., Chin, F., Inada, L. F., & Wong, S. (1974). *Aiiieeeee! An Anthology of Asian American Writers.* Washington, DC: Howard University Press.

Chan, S. (1994). The Asian-American Movement, 1960s–1980s. In A. S. Chan, D. H. Daniels, M.T. Garcia, and T.P. Wilson (Eds.), *Peoples of Color in the American West* (pp. 525–533). Lexington, MA: D. C. Heath.

Cheung, K.-K. (1990). The woman warrior versus the Chinaman pacific: Must a Chinese American critic choose between feminism and heroism? In M. Hirsch & E. F. Keller (Eds.), *Conflicts in Feminism* (pp. 234–251). New York: Routledge.

Chin, F. (1972). Confessions of the Chinatown cowboy. *Bulletin of Concerned Asian Scholars,* 4(3), 66.

Chin, F., & Chan, J. P. (1972). Racist love. In R. Kostelanetz (Ed.), *Seeing through Shuck* (pp. 65–79). New York: Ballantine.

Choe, Laura. 1996, February 10. "Versions": Asian Americans in Hip Hop. Paper presented at the California Studies Conference, Long Beach, CA.

Collins, P. H. (1991). *Black Feminist Thought: Knowledge, Consciousness, and the Politics of Empowerment.* New York: Routledge.

Doane, M. A. (1991). *Femme Fatales: Feminism, Film Theory, Psychoanalysis.* New York: Routledge.

Engelhardt, T. (1976). Ambush at Kamikaze Pass. In E. Gee (Ed.), *Counterpoint: Perspectives on Asian America* (pp. 270–279). Los Angeles: University of California at Los Angeles, Asian American Studies Center.

Frankenberg, R. (1993). *White Women, Race Matters: The Social Construction of Whiteness.* Minneapolis: University of Minnesota Press.

Fung, R. (1994). Seeing yellow: Asian identities in film and video. In K. Aguilar-San Juan (Ed.), *The State of Asian America* (pp. 161–171). Boston: South End.

Goellnicht, D. C. (1992). Tang Ao in America: Male subject positions in *China Men.* In S. G. Lim & A. Ling (Eds.), *Reading the Literatures of Asian America* (pp. 191–212). Philadelphia: Temple University Press.

Hagedorn, J. (1993). Introduction: "Role of dead man require very little acting." In J. Hagedorn (Ed.), *Charlie Chan Is Dead: An Anthology of Contemporary Asian American Fiction* (pp. xxi–xxx). New York: Penguin.

Hamamoto, D. Y. (1994). *Monitored Peril: Asian Americans and the Politics of Representation.* Minneapolis: University of Minnesota Press.

Hoppenstand, G. (1983). Yellow devil doctors and opium dens: A survey of the yellow peril stereotypes in mass media entertainment. In C. D. Geist & J Nachbar (Eds.), *The Popular Culture Reader* (3rd ed., pp. 171–185). Bowling Green, OH: Bowling Green University Press.

Kim, E. (1982). *Asian American Literature: An Introduction to the Writings and Their Social Context.* Philadelphia: Temple University Press.

Kim, E. (1984). Asian American writers: A bibliographical review. *American Studies International,* 22, 2.

Kim, E. (1990). "Such opposite creatures": Men and women in Asian American literature. *Michigan Quarterly Review,* 29, 68–93.

Kim, E. (1993). Preface. In J. Hagedorn (Ed.), *Charlie Chan Is Dead: An Anthology of Contemporary Asian American Fiction* (pp. vii–xiv). New York: Penguin.

Kingston, M.H. (1977). *The Woman Warrior.* New York: Vintage.

Ling, A. (1990). *Between Worlds: Women Writers of Chinese Ancestry.* New York: Pergamon.

Lowe, L. (1991). Heterogeneity, hybridity, multiplicity: Marking Asian American difference. *Diaspora, 1,* 24–44.

Lowe, L. (1994). Canon, institutionalization, identity: Contradictions for Asian American studies. In D. Palumbo-Liu (Ed.), *The Ethnic Canon: Histories, Institutions, and Interventions* (pp. 48–68). Minneapolis: University of Minnesota Press.

Lowe, L. (1996). *Immigrant Acts: On Asian American Cultural Politics.* Durham, NC: Duke University Press.

Marchetti, G. (1993). *Romance and the "Yellow Peril": Race, Sex, and Discursive Strategies in Hollywood Fiction.* Berkeley: University of California Press.

Min, P. G. (1995). Korean Americans. In P. G. Min (Ed.), *Asian Americans: Contemporary Trends and Issues* (pp. 199–231). Thousand Oaks, CA: Sage.

Mullings, L. (1994). Images, ideology, and women of color. In M. Baca Zinn & B. T. Dill (Eds.), *Women of Color in U.S. Society* (pp. 265–289). Philadelphia: Temple University Press.

Nguyen, V. (1990, December 7). Growing up in white America. *Asian Week,* p. 23.

Nishi, S. M. (1995). Japanese Americans. In P. G. Min (Ed.), *Asian Americans: Contemporary Trends and Issues* (pp. 95–133). Thousand Oaks, CA: Sage.

Okazaki, S. (1995). *American Sons.* Promotional brochure for the film of that name.

Okihiro, G. Y. (1994). *Margins and Mainstreams: Asians in American History and Culture.* Seattle: University of Washington Press.

Okihiro, G. Y. (1995, November). *Reading Asian Bodies, Reading Anxieties.* Paper presented at the University of California, San Diego Ethnic Studies Colloquium, La Jolla.

Quinsaat, J. (1976). Asians in the media: The shadows in the spotlight. In E. Gee (Ed.), *Counterpoint: Perspectives on Asian America* (pp. 264–269). Los Angeles: University of California at Los Angeles, Asian American Studies Center.

Rabine, L. W. (1987). No lost paradise: Social gender and symbolic gender in the writings of Maxine Hong Kingston. *Signs: Journal of Women in Culture and Society,* 12, 471–511.

Said, E. (1979). *Orientalism.* New York: Random House.

Shah, S. (1994). Presenting the Blue Goddess: Toward a national, Pan-Asian feminist agenda. In K. Aguilar-San Juan (Ed.), *The State of Asian America: Activism and Resistance in the 1990s* (pp. 147–158). Boston: South End.

Sledge, L. C. (1980). Maxine Kingston's *China Men:* The family historian as epic poet. *MELUS, 7,* 3–22.

Tajima, R. (1989). Lotus blossoms don't bleed: Images of Asian Women. In Asian Women United of California (Ed.), *Making Waves: An Anthology of Writings by and about Asian American Women* (pp. 308–317). Boston: Beacon.

Tajima, R. (1991). Moving the image: Asian American independent filmmaking 1970–1990. In R. Leong (Ed.), *Moving the Image: Independent Asian Pacific American Media Arts* (pp. 10–33). Los Angeles: University of California at Los Angeles, Asian American Studies Center, and Visual Communications, Southern California Asian American Studies Central.

Tong, B. (1994). *Unsubmissive Women: Chinese Prostitutes in Nineteenth-Century San Francisco*. Norman: University of Oklahoma Press.

Tran, Q. P. (1993). Exile and home in contemporary Vietnamese American feminine writing. *Amerasia Journal, 19,* 71–83.

Wang, A. (1988). Maxine Hong Kingston's reclaiming of America: The birthright of the Chinese American male. *South Dakota Review, 26,* 18–29.

Wiegman, R. (1991). Black bodies/American commodities: Gender, race, and the bourgeois ideal in contemporary film. In L. D. Friedman (Ed.), *Unspeakable Images: Ethnicity and the American Cinema* (pp. 308–328). Urbana: University of Illinois Press.

Wong. E. F. (1978). *On Visual Media Racism: Asians in the American Motion Pictures*. New York: Arno.

Wong, S.-L. C. (1993). *Reading Asian American Literature: From Necessity to Extravagance*. Princeton, NJ: Princeton University Press.

Wu, W. F. (1982). *The Yellow Peril: Chinese Americans in American Fiction 1850–1940*. Hamden, CT: Archon.

Yamanaka, L.A. (1993). Empty heart. In J. Hagedorn (Ed.), *Charlie Chan is dead: An anthology of contemporary Asian American Fiction* (pp. 544–550). New York: Penguin.

Yoon, D. D. (1993, November 26). Asian American male: Wimp or what? *Asian Week*, p. 16.

R E A D I N G   1 7

En Rapport, In Opposition: Cobrando cuentas a las nuestras

GLORIA ANZALDÚA

WATCH FOR FALLING ROCKS

The first time I drove from El Paso to San Diego, I saw a sign that read *Watch for Falling Rocks*. And though I watched and waited for rocks to roll down the steep cliff walls and attack my car and me, I never saw any falling rocks. Today, one of the things I'm most afraid of are the rocks we throw at each other. And the resultant guilt we carry like a corpse strapped to our backs for having thrown rocks. We colored women have memories like elephants. The slightest hurt is recorded deep within. We do not forget the injury done to us and we do not forget the injury we have done another. For unfortunately we do not have hides like elephants. Our vulnerability is measured by our capacity for openness, intimacy. And we all know that our own kind is driven through shame or self-hatred to poke at all our open wounds. And we know they know exactly where the hidden wounds are.

> I keep track of all distinctions. Between past and present. Pain and pleasure. Living and surviving. Resistance and capitulation. Will and circumstances. Between life and death. Yes. I am scrupulously accurate. I have become a keeper of accounts.
>
> *Irena Klepfisz*[1]

One of the changes that I've seen since *This Bridge Called My Back* was published[2] is that we no longer allow white women to efface us or suppress us. Now we do it to each other. We have taken over the missionary's "let's civilize the savage role," fixating on the "wrongness" and moral or political inferiority of some of our sisters, insisting on a profound difference between oneself and the *Other*. We have been indoctrinated into adopting the old imperialist ways of conquering and dominating, adopting a way of confrontation based on differences while standing on the ground of ethnic superiority.

In the "dominant" phase of colonialism, European colonizers exercise direct control of the colonized, destroy the native legal and cultural systems, and negate non-European civilizations in order to ruthlessly exploit the resources of the subjugated with the excuse of attempting to "civilize" them. Before the end of this phase, the natives internalize western culture. By the time we reach the "neocolonialist" phase, we've accepted the white colonizers' system of values, attitudes, morality, and modes of production.[3] It is not by chance that in the more rural towns of Texas, Chicano neighborhoods are called *colonias* rather than *barrios*.

There have always been those of us who have "cooperated" with the colonizers. It's not that we have been "won" over by the dominant culture, but that it has exploited preexisting power relations of subordination and subjugation within our native societies.[4] The great White ripoff and they are still cashing in. Like our exploiters who fixate on the inferiority of the natives, we fixate on the fucked-upness of our sisters. Like them we try to impose our version of "the ways things should be"; we try to impose one's self on the *Other* by making her the recipient of one's negative elements, usually the same elements that the Anglo projected on us. Like them, we project our self-hatred on her; we stereotype her; we make her generic.

JUST HOW ETHNIC ARE YOU?

One of the reasons for this hostility among us is the forced cultural penetration, the rape of the colored by the white, with the colonizers depositing their perspective, their language, their values in our bodies. External oppression is paralleled with our internalization of that oppression. And our acting out from that oppression. They have us doing to those within our own ranks what they have done and continue to do to us—*Othering* people. That is, isolating them, pushing them out of the herd, ostracizing them. The internalization of negative images of ourselves, our self-hatred, poor self-esteem, makes our own people the *Other*. We shun the white-looking Indian, the "high yellow" Black woman, the Asian with the white lover, the Native woman who brings her white girlfriend to the Pow Wow, the

Chicana who doesn't speak Spanish, the academic, the uneducated. Her difference makes her a person we can't trust. *Para que sea "legal,"* she must pass the ethnic legitimacy test we have devised. And it is exactly our internalized whiteness that desperately wants boundary lines (this part of me is Mexican, this Indian) marked out and woe to any sister or any part of us that steps out of our assigned places, woe to anyone who doesn't measure up to our standards of ethnicity. *Si no cualifica,* if she fails to pass the test, *le aventamos mierda en la cara, le aventamos piedras, la aventamos*. We throw shit in her face, we throw rocks, we kick her out. *Como gallos de pelea nos atacamos unas a las otras—mexicanas de nacimiento contra* the born-again *mexicanas*. Like fighting cocks, razor blades strapped to our fingers, we slash out at each other. We have turned our anger against ourselves. And our anger is immense. *Es un acido que corroe.*

INTERNAL AFFAIRS

o las que niegan a su gente

> *Tu traición yo la llevo aquá muy dentro,*
> *la llevo dentro de mi alma*
> *dentro de mi corazón.*
> *Tu traicón.*
>
> *Cornelio Reyna*[5]

I get so tired of constantly struggling with my sisters. The more we have in common, including love, the greater the heartache between us, the more we hurt each other. It's excruciatingly painful, this constant snarling at our own shadows. Anything can set the conflict in motion: the lover getting more recognition by the community, the friend getting a job with higher status, a breakup. As one of my friends said, "We can't fucking get along."

So we find ourselves *entreguerras*,[6] a kind of civil war among intimates, an in-class, in-race, in-house fighting, a war with strategies, tactics that are our coping mechanisms, that once were our survival skills and which we now use upon one another,[7] producing intimate terrorism—a modern form of *las guerras floridas,* the war of flowers that the Aztecs practiced in order to gain captives for the sacrifices. Only now we are each other's victims, we offer the *Other* to our politically correct altar.

El deniego   The hate we once cast at our oppressors we now fling at women of our own race. Reactionary—we have gone to the other extreme—denial of our own. We struggle for power, compete, vie for control. Like kin, we are there for each other, but like kin we come to blows. And the differences between us and this new *Other* are not racial but ideological, not metaphysical but psychological. *Nos negamos a si mismas y el deniego nos causa daño.*

BREAKING OUT OF THE FRAME

I'm standing at the sea end of the truncated Berkeley pier. A boat had plowed into the black posts, gouging out a few hundred feet of structure, cutting the pier in two. I stare at the sea, surging silver-plated, between me and the lopped-off corrugated arm, the wind whipping my hair. I look down, my head and shoulders a shadow on the sea. Yemaya pours strings of light over my dull jade, flickering body, bubbles pop out of my ears. I feel the tension easing and, for the first time in months, the litany of work yet to do, of deadlines, that sings incessantly in my head, blows away with the wind.

    Oh, Yemaya, I shall speak the words
      you lap against the pier.

But as I turn away I see in the distance a ship's fin fast approaching. I see fish heads lying listless in the sun, smell the stench of pollution in the waters.

From where I stand, *queridas carnalas*—in a feminist position—I see, through a critical lens with variable focus, that we must not drain our energy breaking down the male/white frame (the whole of western culture) but turn to our own kind and change our terms of reference. As long as we see the world and our experiences through white eyes—in a dominant/subordinate way—we're trapped in the tar and pitch of the old manipulative and strive-for-power ways.

Even those of us who don't want to buy in get sucked into the vortex of the dominant culture's fixed oppositions, the duality of superiority and inferiority, of subject and object. Some of us, to get out of the internalized neocolonial phase, make for the fringes, the Borderlands. And though we have not broken out of the white frame, we at least see it for what it is. Questioning the values of the dominant culture, which imposes fundamental difference on those of the "wrong" side of the good/bad dichotomy, is the first step. Responding to the *Other* not as irrevocably different is the second step. By highlighting similarities, downplaying divergences, that is, by *rapprochement* between self and *Other,* it is possible to build a syncretic relationship. At the

basis of such a relationship lies an understanding of the effects of colonization and its resultant pathologies.

We have our work cut out for us. Nothing is more difficult than identifying emotionally with a cultural alterity, with the *Other. Alter:* to make different; to castrate. *Altercate:* to dispute angrily. *Alter ego:* another self or another aspect of oneself. *Alter idem:* another of the same kind. Nothing is harder than identifying with an interracial identity, with a mestizo identity. One has to leave the permanent boundaries of a fixed self, literally "leave" oneself and see oneself through the eyes of the *Other.* Cultural identity is "nothing more nor less than the mean between selfhood and otherness. . . ."[8] Nothing scares the Chicana more than a quasi Chicana; nothing disturbs a Mexican more than an acculturated Chicana; nothing agitates a Chicana more than a Latina who lumps her with the *norteamericanas.* It is easier to retreat to the safety of difference behind racial, cultural, and class borders. Because our awareness of the *Other* as object often swamps our awareness of ourselves as subject, it is hard to maintain a fine balance between cultural ethnicity and the continuing survival of that culture, between traditional culture and an evolving hybrid culture. How much must remain the same, how much must change.

For most of us our ethnicity is still the issue. Ours continues to be a struggle of identity—not against a white background so much as against a colored background. *Ya no estamos afuera o atras del marco de la pintura*—we no longer stand outside nor behind the frame of the painting. We are both the foreground, the background, and the figures predominating. Whites are not the central figure, they are not even in the frame, though the frame of reference is still white, male, and heterosexual. But the white is still there, invisible, under our skin—we have subsumed the white.

EL DESENGAÑO/DISILLUSIONMENT

And yes I have some criticism, some self-criticism. And no I will not make everything nice. There is shit among us we need to sift through. Who knows, there may be some fertilizer in it. I've seen collaborative efforts between us end in verbal abuse, cruelty, and trauma. I've seen collectives fall apart, dumping their ideals by the wayside and treating each other worse than they'd treat a rabid dog. My momma said, "Never tell other people our business, never divulge family secrets." Chicano dirt you do not air out in front of white folks, nor lesbian dirty laundry in front of heterosexuals. The cultural things stay with la Raza. Colored feminists must present a united front in front of white and other groups. But the fact is we are not united. (I've come to suspect that unity is another Anglo invention like their one sole god and the myth of the monopole.[9]) We are not going to cut through la mierda by sweeping the dirt under the rug.

We have a responsibility to each other, certain commitments. The leap into self-affirmation goes hand in hand with being critical of self. Many of us walk around with reactionary, self-righteous attitudes. We preach certain political behaviors and theories and we do fine with writing about them. Though we want others to live their lives by them, we do not live them. When we are called on it, we go into a self-defensive mode and denial just like whites did when we started asking them to be accountable for their race and class biases.

LAS OPUESTAS/THOSE IN OPPOSITION

In us, intra- and cross-cultural hostilities surface in not so subtle put-downs. *Las no comprometidas, las que negan a sus gente. Fruncemos las caras y negamos toda responsabilidad.* Where some of us racially mixed people are stuck in now is denial and its damaging effects. Denial of the white aspects that we've been forced to acquire, denial of our sisters who for one reason or another cannot "pass" as 100 percent ethnic—as if such a thing exists. Racial purity, like language purity, is a fallacy. Denying the reality of who we are destroys the basis needed from which to talk honestly and deeply about the issues between us. We cannot make any real connections because we are not touching each other. So we sit facing each other and before the words escape our mouths the real issues are blanked in our consciousness, erased before they register because it hurts too much to talk about them, because it makes us vulnerable to the hurt the *carnala* may dish out, because we've been wounded too deeply and too often in the past. So we sit, a paper face before another paper face—two people who suddenly cease to be real. *La no compasiva con la complaciente, lo incomunicado atorado en sus gargantas.*

We, the new Inquisitors, swept along with the "swing to the right" of the growing religious and political intolerance, crusade against racial heretics, mow down with the sickle of righteous anger our dissenting sisters. The issue (in all aspects of life) has always been when to resist changes and when to be open to them. Right now, this rigidity will break us.

RECOBRANDO/RECOVERING

Una luz fria y cenicienta bañada en la plata palida del amanecer entra a mi escritorio and I think about the critical stages we feminists of color are going through, chiefly that of learning to live with each other as *carnalas, parientes, amantes,* as kin, as friends, as lovers. Looking back on the road that we've walked on during the last decade, I see many emotional, psychological, spiritual, political gains—primarily developing an understanding and acceptance of the spirituality of our root ethnic cultures. This has given us the ground from which to see that our spiritual lives are not split from our daily acts. *En recobrando* our affinity with nature and her forces (deities), we have "recovered" our ancient identity, digging it out like dark clay, pressing it to our current identity, molding past and present, inner and outer. Our clay-streaked faces acquiring again images of our ethnic self and self-respect taken from us by the colonizadores. And if we've suffered losses, if often in the process we have momentarily "misplaced" our *carnala-* hood, our sisterhood, there beside us always are the women, *las mujeres.* And that is enough to keep us going.

By grounding in the earth of our native spiritual identity, we can build up our personal and tribal identity. We can reach out for the clarity we need. Burning sage and sweetgrass by itself won't cut it, but it can be a basis from which we act.

And yes, we are elephants with long memories, but scrutinizing the past with binocular vision and training it on the juncture of past with present, and identifying the options on hand and mapping out future roads, will ensure us survival.

So if we won't forget past grievances, let us forgive. Carrying the ghosts of past grievances *no vale la pena.* It is not worth the grief. It keeps us from ourselves and each other; it keeps us from new relationships. We need to cultivate other ways of coping. I'd like to think that the infighting that we presently find ourselves doing is only a stage in the continuum of our growth, an offshoot of the conflict that the process of biculturation spawns, a phase of the internal colonization process, one that will soon cease to hold sway over our lives. I'd like to see it as a skin we will shed as we are born into the twenty-first century.

And now in these times of the turning of the century, of harmonic *conversion,* of the end of *El Quinto Sol* (as the ancient Aztecs named our present age), it is time we began to get out of the state of opposition and into *rapprochment,* time to get our heads, words, ways out of white territory. It is time that we broke out of the invisible white frame and stood on the ground of our own ethnic being.

NOTES

1. Irena Klepfisz, *Keeper of Accounts* (Montpelier, VT: Sinister Wisdom, 1982), 85.

2. According to Chela Sandoval, the publication of *Bridge* marked the end of the second wave of the women's movement in its previous form. *U.S. Third World Feminist Criticism: The Theory and Method of Oppositional Consciousness,* a dissertation in process.

3. Abdul R. JanMohamed, "The Economy of Manichean Allegory: The Function of Racial Difference in Colonialist Literature," *"Race," Writing, and Difference,* ed. Henry Louis Gates, Jr. (Chicago: University of Chicago Press, 1985), 80–81.

4. JanMohamed, 81.

5. Cornelio Reyna is a Chicano from Texas who sings and plays *bajo-sexto* in his *música norteña/conjunto. "Tu Traición"* is from the album *15 Exitasos,* Reyna Records, 1981.

6. *Entreguerras, entremundos/Inner Wars among the Worlds* is the title of a forthcoming book of narratives/novel.

7. Sarah Hoagland, "Lesbian Ethics: Intimacy & Self-Understanding," *Bay Area Women's News,* May/June 1987, vol. 1, no. 2, 7.

8. Nadine Gordimer is quoted in JanMohamed's essay, 88.

9. Physicists are searching for a single law of physics under which all other laws will fall.

Socialization

We are born into cultures that have definite ideas about men and women and their appropriate attitudes, values, and behaviors. Dominant American culture defines certain traits as masculine or feminine and values behaviors, occupations, and attitudes deemed masculine more highly than those associated with women. It assumes that what men do is right and normal. Women are judged in accordance with how well they conform to the male standard. This way of thinking is known as *androcentrism*. As children, we learn to see ourselves and others as girls or boys and to judge our own and others behaviors according to standards of gender-appropriate behavior. The articles in this section analyze the complex process of gender socialization from various perspectives.

Learning about our culture begins in the family. We learn about gender not only from what our parents say but also from what they do. Some theorists argue that women's mothering role has consequences for both the development of gender-related personality differences and the unequal social status of women and men. Nancy Chodorow, in "Family Structure and Feminine Personality," proposes that because women do the mothering, men are more powerful socially but feel an enduring need to distance themselves from women and feminine traits, a need that leaves them insecure and isolated. Women occupy a secondary social position, in her view, but retain stronger connections to others and a greater capacity for intimacy.

Elizabeth Spelman, however, takes issue with Chodorow's basic assumptions, pointing out that a theoretical explanation of how individuals acquire gender cannot be detached from a discussion of how individuals of different races and classes acquire different definitions of gender. In short, Spelman contends that there can be no universal theory of gender identity. Do you think Chodorow's theory is useful despite its lack of attention to differences of race and class?

Because the culture differentiates not only along gender lines but according to race, ethnicity, and class as well, our socialization experiences also differ along these lines. What an African-American mother, for example, needs to teach her sons and daughters to enable them to survive in a white-male-dominated society is different from what a white mother needs to teach her children. These kinds of racial differences, in turn, are compounded by differences in class status. In " 'The Means to Put My Children Through': Child-Rearing Goals and Strategies among Black Female Domestic Servants," Bonnie Thornton Dill writes about the complexity of race and gender issues. Contrasting the race and class advantages available to white employers' children with the goals domestic workers held for their own children, Dill outlines the reactions and responses of black female domestic workers who cared for white children to provide income but who reared their own children to enter the middle class. What differences are apparent between the child-raising patterns that Dill describes and the model that Chodorow proposes?

Gender socialization is carried out in schools as well as in homes. By the time children are in school, they not only have been socialized into their gender but also are able to negotiate how and in which situations gender will be socially salient. Barrie Thorne, in "Girls and Boys Together . . . But Mostly Apart: Gender Arrangements in Elementary Schools," argues for a more complex idea of gender as socially constructed and context specific. In her observations of social relations among children in elementary school, she finds that boys and girls are segregated and seen as different in the classroom and on the playground both because of teachers' actions and because children socialize each other. Did your own experiences in elementary school conform to the patterns Thorne describes?

As a result of gender socialization, by adolescence many girls experience a loss of self-confidence and self-definition, as Carol Gilligan describes in "Women's Psychological Development: Implications for Psychotherapy." The adolescent girls Gilligan interviewed feel a daunting social pressure to deny their own perceptions as they struggle between asserting their own identities and conforming to societal definitions of womanhood. They are caught between their desire to forge genuine relationships in which they can be themselves and the growing disconnection between what they know to be true and how they are expected to behave. Each finds her own path through the obstacles of gender socialization, resisting some prescriptions for femininity, accepting others, and seeking to make sense of her experiences through her relationships with family and friends. How is Gilligan's article influenced by the model of psychological development that Nancy Chodorow proposes in this section?

Some parents try to raise children without these gender stereotypes. In "Ideology, Experience, Identity: The Complex Worlds of Children in Fair Families," Barbara Risman describes how children with egalitarian parents understand gender. She suggests that children acquire gender identities and ideologies from both their parents and their peers. When mothers and fathers both work outside the home, share child-raising, and are committed to gender equality, their children also believe that men and women should be equal. Yet, Risman finds, these same children believe that girls and boys are very different from each other, and their own identities are at least partially gender-traditional. What do the children she interviews think boys and girls are like? How do they view their own nonconformity with gender roles? In your observation, are traditional views of what girls and boys are like still prevalent?

Family Structure and Feminine Personality

NANCY CHODOROW

I propose here[1] a model to account for the reproduction within each generation of certain general and nearly universal differences that characterize masculine and feminine personality and roles. My perspective is largely psychoanalytic. Cross-cultural and social-psychological evidence suggests that an argument drawn solely from the universality of biological sex differences is unconvincing.[2] At the same time, explanations based on patterns of deliberate socialization (the most prevalent kind of anthropological, sociological, and social-psychological explanation) are in themselves insufficient to account for the extent to which psychological and value commitments to sex differences are so emotionally laden and tenaciously maintained, for the way gender identity and expectations about sex roles and gender consistency are so deeply central to a person's consistent sense of self.

This paper suggests that a crucial differentiating experience in male and female development arises out of the fact that women, universally, are largely responsible for early child care and for (at least) later female socialization. This points to the central importance of the mother–daughter relationship for women, and to a focus on the conscious and unconscious effects of early involvement with a female for children of both sexes. The fact that males and females experience this social environment differently as they grow up accounts for the development of basic sex differences in personality. In particular, certain features of the mother–daughter relationship are internalized universally as basic elements of feminine ego structure (although not necessarily what we normally mean by "femininity").

Specifically, I shall propose that, in any given society, feminine personality comes to define itself in relation and connection to other people more than masculine personality does. (In psychoanalytic terms, women are less individuated than men; they have more flexible ego boundaries.)[3] Moreover, issues of dependency are handled and experienced differently by men and women. For boys and men, both individuation and dependency issues become tied up with the sense of masculinity, or masculine identity. For girls and women, by contrast, issues of femininity, or feminine identity, are not problematic in the same way. The structural situation of child rearing, reinforced by female and male role training, produces these differences, which are replicated and reproduced in the sexual sociology of adult life.

The paper is also a beginning attempt to rectify certain gaps in the social-scientific literature, and a contribution to the reformulation of psychological anthropology. Most traditional accounts of family and socialization tend to emphasize only role training, and not unconscious features of personality. Those few that rely on Freudian theory have abstracted a behaviorist methodology from this theory, concentrating on isolated "significant" behaviors like weaning and toilet training. The paper advocates instead a focus on the ongoing interpersonal relationships in which these various behaviors are given meaning.[4]

More empirically, most social-scientific accounts of socialization, child development, and the mother–child relationship refer implicitly or explicitly only to the development and socialization of boys and to the mother–son relationship. There is a striking lack of systematic description about the mother–daughter relationship, and a basic theoretical discontinuity between, on the one hand, theories about female development, which tend to stress the development of "feminine" qualities in relation to and comparison with men, and on the other hand, theories about women's ultimate mothering role. This final lack is particularly crucial, because women's motherhood and mothering role seem to be the most important features in accounting for the universal secondary status of women (Chodorow, 1971; Ortner, Rosaldo, this volume). The present paper describes the development of psychological qualities in women that are central to the perpetuation of this role.

In a formulation of this preliminary nature, there is not a great body of consistent evidence to draw upon. Available evidence is presented that illuminates aspects of the theory—for the most part psychoanalytic and social-psychological accounts based almost entirely on highly industrialized western society. Because aspects of family structure are discussed that are universal, however, I think it is worth considering the theory as a general model. In any case, this is in some sense a programmatic appeal to people doing research. It points to certain issues that might be especially important in investigations of child development and family relationships, and suggests that researchers look explicitly at female versus male development and that they consider seriously mother–daughter relationships even if these are not of obvious "structural importance" in a traditional anthropological view of that society.

THE DEVELOPMENT OF GENDER PERSONALITY

According to psychoanalytic theory,[5] personality is a result of a boy's or girl's social-relational experiences from earliest infancy. Personality development is not the result of conscious parental intention. The nature and quality of the social relationships that the child experiences are appropriated, internalized, and organized by her or him and come to constitute her or his personality. What is internalized from an ongoing relationship continues independent of that original relationship and is generalized and set up as a permanent feature of the personality. The conscious self is usually not aware of many of the features of personality, or of its total structural organization. At the same time, these are important determinants of any person's behavior, both that which is culturally expected and that which is idiosyncratic or unique to the individual. The conscious aspects of personality, like a person's general self-concept and, importantly, her or his gender identity, require and depend upon the consistency and stability of its unconscious organization. In what follows I shall describe how contrasting male and female experiences lead to differences in the way the developing masculine or feminine psyche resolves certain relational issues.

Separation and Individuation (Preoedipal Development)

All children begin life in a state of "infantile dependence" (Fairbairn, 1952) upon an adult or adults, in most cases their mother. This state consists first in the persistence of primary identification with the mother: the child does not differentiate herself or himself from her or his mother but experiences a sense of oneness with her. (It is important to distinguish this from later forms of identification, from "secondary identification," which presuppose at least some degree of experienced separateness by the person who identifies.) Second, it includes an oral-incorporative mode of relationship to the world, leading, because of the infant's total helplessness, to a strong attachment to and dependence upon whoever nurses and carries her or him.

Both aspects of this state are continuous with the child's prenatal experience of being emotionally and physically part of the mother's body and of the exchange of body material through the placenta. That this relationship continues with the natural mother in most societies stems from the fact that women lactate. For convenience, and not because of biological necessity, this has usually meant that mothers, and females in general, tend to take all care of babies. It is probable that the mother's continuing to have major responsibility for the feeding and care of the child (so that the child interacts almost entirely with her) extends and intensifies her or his period of primary identification with her more than if, for instance, someone else were to take major or total care of the child. A child's earliest experience, then, is usually of identity with and attachment to a single mother, and always with women.

For both boys and girls, the first few years are preoccupied with issues of separation and individuation. This includes breaking or attenuating the primary identification with the mother and beginning to develop an individuated sense of self, and mitigating the totally dependent oral attitude and attachment to the mother. I would suggest that, contrary to the traditional psychoanalytic model, the preoedipal experience is likely to differ for boys and girls. Specifically, the experience of mothering for a woman involves a double identification (Klein & Rivière, 1937). A woman identifies with her own mother and, through identification with her child, she (re)experiences herself as a cared-for child. The particular nature of this double identification for the individual mother is closely bound up with her relationship to her own mother. As Deutsch expresses it, "In relation to her own child, woman repeats her own mother–child history" (1944:205). Given that she was a female child, and that identification with her mother and mothering are so bound up with her being a woman, we might expect that a woman's identification with a girl child might be stronger; that a mother, who is, after all, a person who is a woman and not simply the performer of a formally defined role, would tend to treat infants of different sexes in different ways.

There is some suggestive sociological evidence that this is the case. Mothers in a women's group in Cambridge, Massachusetts (see note 1), say that they identified more with their girl children than with boy children. The perception and treatment of girl versus boy children in high-caste, extremely patriarchal, patrilocal communities in India are in the same vein. Families express preference for boy children and celebrate when sons are born. At the same time, Rajput mothers in North India are "as likely as not" (Minturn & Hitchcock, 1963) to like girl babies better than boy babies once they are born, and they and Havik Brahmins in South India (Harper, 1969) treat their daughters with greater affection and leniency than their sons. People in both groups say that this is out of sympathy for the future plight of their daughters, who will have to leave their natal family for a strange and usually oppressive postmarital household. From the time of their daughters' birth, then, mothers in these communities identify anticipatorily, by reexperiencing their own past, with the experiences of separation that their daughters will go through. They develop a particular attachment to their daughters because of this and by imposing their own reaction to the issue of separation on this new external situation.

It seems, then, that a mother is more likely to identify with a daughter than with a son, to experience her daughter (or parts of her daughter's life) as herself. Fliess's description (1961) of his neurotic patients who were the children of ambulatory psychotic mothers presents the problem in its psychopathological extreme. The example is interesting, because, although Fliess claims to be writing about people defined only by the fact that their problems were tied to a particular kind of relationship to their mothers, an overwhelmingly large proportion of the cases he presents are women. It seems, then, that this sort of disturbed mother inflicts her pathology predominantly on daughters. The mothers Fliess describes did not allow their daughters to perceive themselves as separate people, but simply acted as if their daughters were narcissistic extensions or doubles of themselves, extensions to whom were attributed the mothers' bodily feelings and who became physical vehicles for their mothers' achievement of autoerotic gratification. The daughters were bound into a mutually dependent "hyper-symbiotic" relationship. These mothers, then, perpetuate a mutual relationship with their daughters of both primary identification and infantile dependence.

A son's case is different. Cultural evidence suggests that insofar as a mother treats her son differently, it is usually by emphasizing his masculinity in opposition to herself and by pushing him to assume, or acquiescing in his assumption of, a sexually toned male-role relation to her. Whiting (1959) and Whiting et al. (1958) suggest that mothers in societies with mother–child sleeping arrangements and postpartum sex taboos may be seductive toward infant sons. Slater (1968) describes the socialization of precarious masculinity in Greek males of the classical period through their mothers' alternation of sexual praise and seductive behavior with hostile deflation and ridicule. This kind of behavior contributes to the son's differentiation from his mother and to the formation of ego boundaries (I will later discuss certain problems that result from this).

Neither form of attitude or treatment is what we would call "good mothering." However, evidence of differentiation of a pathological nature in the mother's behavior toward girls and boys does highlight tendencies in "normal" behavior. It seems likely that from their children's earliest childhood, mothers and women tend to identify more with daughters and to help them to differentiate less, and that processes of separation and individuation are made more difficult for girls. On the other hand, a mother tends to identify less with her son, and to push him toward differentiation and the taking on of a male role unsuitable to his age, and undesirable at any age in his relationship to her.

For boys and girls, the quality of the preoedipal relationship to the mother differs. This, as well as differences in development during the oedipal period, accounts for the persisting importance of preoedipal issues in female development and personality that many psychoanalytic writers describe.[6] Even before the establishment of gender identity, gender personality differentiation begins.

Gender Identity (Oedipal Crisis and Resolution)

There is only a slight suggestion in the psychological and sociological literature that preoedipal development differs for boys and girls. The pattern becomes explicit at the next developmental level. All theoretical and empirical accounts agree that after about age three (the beginning of the "oedipal" period, which focuses on the attainment of a stable gender identity) male and female development becomes radically different. It is at this stage that the father, and men in general, begin to become important in the child's primary object world. It is, of course, particularly difficult to generalize about the attainment of gender identity and sex-role assumption, since there is such wide variety in the sexual sociology of different societies. However, to the extent that in all societies women's life tends to be more private and domestic, and men's more public and social, . . . we can make general statements about this kind of development.

In what follows, I shall be talking about the development of gender personality and gender identity in the tradition of psychoanalytic theory. Cognitive psychologists have established that by the age of three, boys and girls have an irreversible conception of what their gender is (see Kohlberg, 1966). I do not dispute these findings. It remains true that children (and adults) may know definitely that they are boys (men) or girls (women), and at the same time experience conflicts or uncertainty about "masculinity" or "femininity," about what these identities require in behavioral or emotional terms, etc. I am discussing the development of "gender identity" in this latter sense.

A boy's masculine gender identification must come to replace his early primary identification with his mother. This masculine identification is usually based on identification with a boy's father or other salient adult males. However, a boy's father is relatively more remote than his mother. He rarely plays a major care-taking role even at this period in his son's life. In most societies, his work and social life take place farther from the home than do those of his wife. He is, then, often relatively inaccessible to his son, and performs his male role activities away from where the son spends most of his life. As a result, a boy's male gender identification often becomes a "positional" identification, with aspects of his father's clearly or not-so-clearly defined male role, rather than a more generalized "personal" identification—a diffuse identification with his father's personality, values, and behavioral traits—that could grow out of a real relationship to his father.[7]

Mitscherlich (1963), in his discussion of western advanced capitalist society, provides a useful insight into the problem of male development. The father, because his work takes him outside of the home most of the time, and because his active presence in the family has progressively decreased, has become an "invisible father." For the boy, the tie between affective relations and masculine gender identification and role learning (between libidinal and ego development) is relatively attenuated. He identifies with a fantasied masculine role, because the reality constraint that contact with his father would provide is missing. In all societies characterized by some sex segregation (even those in which a son will eventually lead the same sort of life as his father), much of a boy's masculine identification must be of this sort, that is, with aspects of his father's role, or what he fantasies to be a male role, rather than with his father as a person involved in a relationship to him.

There is another important aspect to this situation, which explains the psychological dynamics of the universal social and cultural devaluation and subordination of women.[8] A boy, in his attempt to gain an elusive masculine identification, often comes to define this masculinity largely in negative terms, as that which is not feminine or involved with women. There is an internal and external aspect to this. Internally, the boy tries to reject his mother and deny his attachment to her and the strong dependence upon her that he still feels. He also tries to deny the deep personal identification with her that has developed during his early years. He does this by repressing whatever he takes to be feminine inside himself, and, importantly, by denigrating and devaluing whatever he considers to be feminine in the outside world. As a societal member, he also appropriates to himself and defines as superior particular social activities and cultural (moral, religious, and creative) spheres—possibly, in fact, "society" and "culture" themselves.[9]

Freud's description of the boy's oedipal crisis speaks to the issues of rejection of the feminine and identification with the father. As his early attachment to his mother takes on phallic-sexual overtones, and his father enters the picture as an obvious rival (who, in the son's fantasy, has apparent power to kill or castrate his son), the boy must radically deny and repress his attachment to his mother and replace it with an identification with his loved and admired, but also potentially punitive, therefore feared, father. He internalizes a superego.[10]

To summarize, four components of the attainment of masculine gender identity are important. First, masculinity becomes and remains a problematic issue for a boy. Second, it involves denial of attachment or relationship, particularly of what the boy takes to be dependence or need for another, and differentiation of himself from another. Third, it involves the repression and devaluation of femininity on both psychological and cultural levels. Finally, identification with his father does not usually develop in the context of a satisfactory affective relationship, but consists in the attempt to internalize and learn components of a not immediately apprehensible role.

The development of a girl's gender identity contrasts with that of a boy. Most important, femininity and female-role activities are immediately apprehensible in the world of her daily life. Her final role identification is with her mother and women, that is, with the person or people with whom she also has her earliest relationship of infantile dependence. The development of her gender identity does not involve a rejection of this early identification, however. Rather, her later identification with her mother is embedded in and influenced by their ongoing relationship of both primary identification and preoedipal attachment. Because her mother is around, and she has had a genuine relationship to her as a person, a girl's gender and gender-role identification are mediated by and depend upon real affective relations. Identification with her mother is not positional—the narrow learning of particular role behaviors—but rather a personal identification with her mother's general traits of character and values. Feminine identification is based not on fantasied or externally defined characteristics and negative identification, but on the gradual learning of a way of being familiar in everyday life, and exemplified by the person (or kind of people—women) with whom she has been most involved. It is continuous with her early childhood identifications and attachments.

The major discontinuity in the development of a girl's sense of gender identity, and one that has led Freud and other early psychoanalysts to see female development as exceedingly difficult and tortuous, is that at some point she must transfer her primary sexual object choice from her mother and females to her father and males, if she is to attain her expected heterosexual adulthood. Briefly, Freud considers that all children feel that mothers give some cause for complaint and unhappiness: they give too little milk; they have a second child; they arouse and then forbid their child's sexual gratification in the process of caring for her or him. A girl receives a final blow, however: her discovery that she lacks a penis. She blames this lack on her mother, rejects her mother, and turns to her father in reaction.

Problems in this account have been discussed extensively in the general literature that has grown out of the women's movement, and within the psychoanalytic tradition itself. These concern Freud's misogyny and his obvious assumption that males possess physiological superiority, and that a woman's personality is inevitably determined by her lack of a penis.[11] The psychoanalytic account is not completely unsatisfactory, however. A more detailed consideration of several theorists[12] reveals important features of female development, especially about the mother–daughter relationship, and at the same time contradicts or mitigates the absoluteness of the more general Freudian outline.

These psychoanalysts emphasize how, in contrast to males, the female oedipal crisis is not resolved in the same absolute way. A girl cannot and does not completely reject her mother in favor of men, but continues her relationship of dependence upon and attachment to her. In addition, the strength and quality of her relationship to her father is completely dependent upon the strength and quality of her relationship to her mother. Deutsch suggests that a girl wavers in a "bisexual triangle" throughout her childhood and into puberty, normally making a very tentative resolution in favor of her father, but in such a way that issues of separation from and attachment to her mother remain important throughout a woman's life (1944:205):

> It is erroneous to say that the little girl gives up her first mother relation in favor of the father. She only gradually draws him into the alliance, develops from the mother–child exclusiveness toward the triangular parent–child relationship and continues the latter, just as she does the former, although in a weaker and less elemental form, all her life. Only the principal part changes: now the mother, now the father plays it. The ineradicability of affective constellations manifests itself in later repetitions.

We might suggest from this that a girl's internalized and external object-relations become and remain more complex, and at the same time more defining of her, than those of a boy. Psychoanalytic preoccupation with constitutionally based libidinal development, and with a normative male model of development, has obscured this fact. Most women are genitally heterosexual. At the same time, their lives always involve other sorts of equally deep and primary relationships, especially with their children, and, importantly, with other women. In these spheres also, even more than in the area of heterosexual relations, a girl imposes the sort of object-relations she has internalized in her preoedipal and later relationship to her mother.

Men are also for the most part genitally heterosexual. This grows directly out of their early primary attachment to their mother. We know, however, that in many societies their heterosexual relationships are not embedded in close personal relationship but simply in relations of dominance and power. Furthermore, they do not have the extended personal relations women have. They are not so connected to children, and their relationships with other men tend to be based not on particularistic connection or affective ties, but rather on abstract, universalistic role expectations.

Building on the psychoanalytic assumption that unique individual experiences contribute to the formation of individual personality, culture and personality theory has held that early experiences common to members of a particular society contribute to the formation of "typical" personalities organized around and preoccupied with certain issues: "Prevailing patterns of child-rearing must result in similar internalized situations in the unconscious of the majority of individuals in a culture, and these will be externalized back into the culture again to perpetuate it from generation to generation" (Guntrip, 1961:378). In a similar vein, I have tried to show that to the extent males and females, respectively, experience similar interpersonal environments as they grow up, masculine and feminine personality will develop differently.

I have relied on a theory which suggests that features of adult personality and behavior are determined, but which is not biologically determinist. Culturally expected personality and behavior are not simply "taught," however. Rather, certain features of social structure, supported by cultural beliefs, values, and perceptions, are internalized through the family and the child's early social object-relationships. This largely unconscious organization is the context in which role training and purposive socialization take place.

SEX-ROLE LEARNING AND ITS SOCIAL CONTEXT

Sex-role training and social interaction in childhood build upon and reinforce the largely unconscious development I have described. In most societies (ours is a complicated exception) a girl is usually with her mother and other female relatives in an interpersonal situation that facilitates continuous and early role learning and emphasizes the mother–daughter identification and particularistic, diffuse, affective relationships between women. A boy, to a greater or lesser extent, is also with women for a large part of his childhood, which prevents continuous or easy masculine role identification. His development is characterized by discontinuity.

Ariès (1962:61), in his discussion of the changing concept of childhood in modern capitalist society, makes a distinction that seems to have more general applicability. Boys, he suggests, became "children" while girls remained "little women." "The idea of childhood profited the boys first of all, while the girls persisted much longer in the traditional way of life which confused them with the adults: we shall have cause to notice more than once this delay on the part of the women in adopting the visible forms of the essentially masculine civilization of modern times." This took place first in the middle classes, as a situation developed in which boys needed special schooling in order to prepare for their future work and could not begin to do this kind of work in childhood. Girls (and working-class boys) could still learn work more directly from their parents, and could begin to participate in the adult economy at an earlier age. Rapid economic change and development have exacerbated the lack of male generational role continuity. Few fathers now have either the opportunity or the ability to pass on a profession or skill to their sons.

Sex-role development of girls in modern society is more complex. On the one hand, they go to school to prepare for life in a technologically and socially complex society. On the other, there is a sense in which this schooling is a pseudotraining. It is not meant to interfere with the much more important training to be "feminine" and a wife and mother, which is embedded in the girl's unconscious development and which her mother teaches her in a family context, where she is clearly the salient parent.

This dichotomy is not unique to modern industrial society. Even if special, segregated schooling is not necessary for adult male work (and many male initiation rites remain a form of segregated role training), boys still participate in more activities that characterize them as a category apart from adult life. Their activities grow out of the boy's need to fill time until he can begin to take on an adult male role. Boys may withdraw into isolation and self-involved play or join together in a group that remains more or less unconnected with either the adult world of work and activity or the familial world.

Jay (1969) describes this sort of situation in rural Modjokuto, Java. Girls, after the age of five or so, begin gradually to help their mothers in their work and spend time with their mothers. Boys at this early age begin to form bands of age mates who roam and play about the city, relating neither to adult men nor to their mothers and sisters. Boys, then, enter a temporary group based on universalistic membership criteria, while girls continue to participate in particularistic role relations in a group characterized by continuity and relative permanence.

The content of boys' and girls' role training tends in the same direction as the context of this training and its results. Barry, Bacon, and Child, in their well-known study (1957), demonstrate that the socialization of boys tends to be oriented toward achievement and self-reliance and that of girls toward nurturance and responsibility. Girls are thus pressured to be involved with and connected to others, boys to deny this involvement and connection.

ADULT GENDER PERSONALITY AND SEX ROLE

A variety of conceptualizations of female and male personality all focus on distinctions around the same issue and provide alternative confirmation of the developmental model I have proposed. Bakan (1966: 15) claims that male personality is preoccupied with the "agentic," and female personality with the "communal." His expanded definition of the two concepts is illuminating:

I have adopted the terms "agency" and "communion" to characterize two fundamental modalities in the existence of living forms, agency for the existence of an organism as an individual and communion for the participation of the individual in some larger organism of which the individual is a part. Agency manifests itself in self-protection, self-assertion, and self-expansion; communion manifests itself in the sense of being at one with other organisms. Agency manifests itself in the formation of separations; communion in the lack of separations. Agency manifests itself in isolation, alienation, and aloneness; communion in contact, openness, and union. Agency manifests itself in the urge to master; communion in noncontractual cooperation. Agency manifests itself in the repression of thought, feeling, and impulse; communion in the lack and removal of repression.

Gutmann (1965) contrasts the socialization of male personalities in "allocentric" milieux (milieux in which the individual is part of a larger social organization and system of social bonds) with that of female personalities in "autocentric" milieux (in which the individual herself or himself is a focus of events and ties).[13] Gutmann suggests that this leads to a number of systematic differences in ego functioning. Female ego qualities, growing out of participation in autocentric milieux, include more flexible ego boundaries (i.e., less insistent self–other distinctions), present orientation rather than future orientation, and relatively greater subjectivity and less detached objectivity.[14]

Carlson (1971) confirms both characterizations. Her tests of Gutmann's claims lead her to conclude that "males represent experiences of self, others, space, and time in individualistic, objective, and distant ways, while females represent experiences in relatively interpersonal, subjective, immediate ways" (p. 270). With reference to Bakan, she claims that men's descriptions of affective experience tend to be in agentic terms and women's in terms of communion, and that an examination of abstracts of a large number of social-psychological articles on sex differences yields an overwhelming confirmation of the agency/communion hypothesis.

Cohen (1969) contrasts the development of "analytic" and "relational" cognitive style, the former characterized by a stimulus-centered, parts-specific orientation to reality, the latter centered on the self and responding to the global characteristics of a stimulus in reference to its total context. Although focusing primarily on class differences in cognitive style, she also points out that girls are more likely to mix the two types of functioning (and also to exhibit inter-

nal conflict about this). Especially, they are likely to exhibit at the same time both high field dependence and highly developed analytic skills in other areas. She suggests that boys and girls participate in different sorts of interactional subgroups in their families: boys experience their family more as a formally organized primary group; girls experience theirs as a group characterized by shared and less clearly delineated functions. She concludes (p. 836): "Since embedded responses covered the gamut from abstract categories, through language behaviors, to expressions of embeddedness in their social environments, it is possible that embeddedness may be a distinctive characteristic of female sex-role learning in this society regardless of social class, native ability, ethnic differences, and the cognitive impact of the school."

Preliminary consideration suggests a correspondence between the production of feminine personalities organized around "communal" and "autocentric" issues and characterized by flexible ego boundaries, less detached objectivity, and relational cognitive style, on the one hand, and important aspects of feminine as opposed to masculine social roles, on the other.

Most generally, I would suggest that a quality of embeddedness in social interaction and personal relationships characterizes women's life relative to men's. From childhood, daughters are likely to participate in an intergenerational world with their mother, and often with their aunts and grandmothers, whereas boys are on their own or participate in a single-generation world of age mates. In adult life, women's interaction with other women in most societies is kin-based and cuts across generational lines. Their roles tend to be particularistic and to involve diffuse relationships and responsibilities rather than specific ones. Women in most societies are *defined* relationally (as someone's wife, mother, daughter, daughter-in-law; even a nun becomes the bride of Christ). Men's association (although it too may be kin-based and intergenerational) is much more likely than women's to cut across kinship units, to be restricted to a single generation, and to be recruited according to universalistic criteria and involve relationships and responsibilities defined by their specificity.

EGO BOUNDARIES AND THE MOTHER–DAUGHTER RELATIONSHIP

The care and socialization of girls by women ensures the production of feminine personalities founded on relation and connection, with flexible rather than rigid ego boundaries, and with a comparatively secure sense of gender identity. This is one explanation for how women's relative embeddedness is reproduced from generation to generation, and why it exists within almost every society. More specific investigation of different social contexts suggests, however, that there are variations in the kind of relationship that can exist between women's role performance and feminine personality.

Various kinds of evidence suggest that separation from the mother, the breaking of dependence, and the establishment and maintenance of a consistently individuated sense of self remain difficult psychological issues for western middle-class women (i.e., the women who become subjects of psychoanalytic and clinical reports and social–psychological studies). Deutsch (1944, 1945) in particular provides extensive clinical documentation of these difficulties and of the way they affect women's relationships to men and children and, because of their nature, are reproduced in the next generation of women. Mothers and daughters in the women's group mentioned in note 1 describe their experiences of boundary confusion or equation of self and other, for example, guilt and self-blame for the other's unhappiness; shame and embarrassment at the other's actions; daughters' "discovery" that they are "really" living out their mothers' lives in their choice of career; mothers' not completely conscious reactions to their daughters' bodies as their own (overidentification and therefore often unnecessary concern with supposed weight or skin problems, which the mother is really worried about in herself); etc.

A kind of guilt that western women express seems to grow out of and to reflect lack of adequate self–other distinctions and a sense of inescapable embeddedness in relationships to others. Tax describes this well (1970:2; italics mine):

> Since our awareness of others is considered our duty, the price we pay when things go wrong is guilt and self-hatred. And things always go wrong. We respond with apologies; we continue to apologize long after the event is forgotten—and *even if it had no causal relation to anything we did to begin with.* If the rain spoils someone's picnic, we apologize. We apologize for taking up space in a room, for living.

As if the woman does not differentiate herself clearly from the rest of the world, she feels a sense of guilt and responsibility for situations that did not come about through her actions and without relation to her actual ability to determine the course of events. This happens, in the most famil-iar instance, in a sense of diffuse responsibility for everything connected to the welfare of her family and the happiness and success of her children. This loss of self in overwhelming responsibility for and connection to others is described particularly acutely by women writers (in the work, for instance, of Simone de Beauvoir, Kate Chopin, Doris Lessing, Tillie Olsen, Christina Stead, Virginia Woolf).

Slater (1961) points to several studies supporting the contention that western daughters have particular problems about differentiation from their mother. These studies show that though most forms of personal parental identification correlate with psychological adjustment (i.e., freedom from neurosis or psychosis, *not* social acceptability), personal identification of a daughter with her mother does not. The reason is that the mother–daughter relation is the one form of personal identification that, because it results so easily from the normal situation of child development, is liable to be excessive in the direction of allowing no room for separation or difference between mother and daughter.

The situation reinforces itself in circular fashion. A mother, on the one hand, grows up without establishing adequate ego boundaries or a firm sense of self. She tends to experience boundary confusion with her daughter and does not provide experiences of differentiating ego development for her daughter or encourage the breaking of her daughter's dependence. The daughter, for her part, makes a rather unsatisfactory and artificial attempt to establish boundaries: she projects what she defines as bad within her onto her mother and tries to take what is good into herself. (This, I think, is the best way to understand the girl's oedipal "rejection" of her mother.) Such an arbitrary mechanism cannot break the underlying psychological unity, however. Projection is never more than a temporary solution to ambivalence or boundary confusion.

The implication is that, contrary to Gutmann's suggestion (see note 3), "so-called ego pathology" may not be "adaptive" for women. A woman's biosexual experiences (menstruation, coitus, pregnancy, childbirth, lactation) all involve some challenge to the boundaries of her body ego ("me"/"not-me" in relation to her blood or milk, to a man who penetrates her, to a child once part of her body). These are important and fundamental human experiences that are probably intrinsically meaningful and at the same time complicated for women everywhere. However, a western woman's tenuous sense of individuation and of the firmness of her ego boundaries increases the likelihood that experiences challenging these boundaries will be difficult for her and conflictive.

Nor is it clear that this personality structure is "functional" for society as a whole. The evidence presented in this paper suggests that satisfactory mothering, which does not reproduce particular psychological problems in boys and girls, comes from a person with a firm sense of self and of her own value, whose care is a freely chosen activity rather than a reflection of a conscious and unconscious sense of inescapable connection to and responsibility for her children.

SOCIAL STRUCTURE AND THE MOTHER–DAUGHTER RELATIONSHIP

Clinical and self-analytic descriptions of women and of the psychological component of mother–daughter relationships are not available from societies and subcultures outside of the western middle class. However, accounts that are primarily sociological about women in other societies enable us to infer certain aspects of their psychological situation. In what follows, I am not claiming to make any kind of general statement about what constitutes a "healthy society," but only to examine and isolate specific features of social life that seem to contribute to the psychological strength of some members of a society. Consideration of three groups with matrifocal tendencies in their family structure (Tanner, 1971) highlights several dimensions of importance in the developmental situation of the girl.

Young and Willmott (1957) describe the daily visiting and mutual aid of working-class mothers and daughters in East London. In a situation where household structure is usually nuclear, like the western middle class, grown daughters look to their mothers for advice, for aid in childbirth and child care, for friendship and companionship, and for financial help. Their mother's house is the ultimate center of the family world. Husbands are in many ways peripheral to family relationships, possibly because of their failure to provide sufficiently for their families as men are expected to do. This becomes apparent if they demand their wife's disloyalty toward or separation from her mother: "The great triangle of childhood is mother–father–child; in Bethnal Green the great triangle of adult life is Mum–wife–husband" (p. 64).

Geertz (1961)[15] and Jay (1969) describe Javanese nuclear families in which women are often the more powerful spouse and have primary influence upon how kin relations are expressed and to whom (although these families are formally centered upon a highly valued conjugal relationship based on equality of spouses). Financial and decision-making control in the family often rests largely in the hands of its women. Women are potentially independent of men in a way that men are not independent of women. Geertz points to a woman's ability to participate in most occupations, and to own farmland and supervise its cultivation, which contrasts with a man's inability, even if he is financially independent, to do his own household work and cooking.

Women's kin role in Java is important. Their parental role and rights are greater than those of men; children always belong to the woman in case of divorce. When extra members join a nuclear family to constitute an extended family household, they are much more likely to be the wife's relatives than those of the husband. Formal and distant relations between men in a family, and between a man and his children (especially his son), contrast with the informal and close relations between women, and between a woman and her children. Jay and Geertz both emphasize the continuing closeness of the mother–daughter relationship as a daughter is growing up and throughout her married life. Jay suggests that there is a certain amount of ambivalence in the mother–daughter relationship, particularly as a girl grows toward adulthood and before she is married, but points out that at the same time the mother remains a girl's "primary figure of confidence and support" (1969:103).

Siegel (1969) describes Atjehnese families in Indonesia in which women stay on the homestead of their parents after marriage and are in total control of the household. Women tolerate men in the household only as long as they provide money, and even then treat them as someone between a child and a guest. Women's stated preference would be to eliminate even this necessary dependence on men: "Women, for instance, envision paradise as the place where they are reunited with their children and their mothers; husbands and fathers are absent, and yet there is an abundance all the same. Quarrels over money reflect the women's idea that men are basically adjuncts who exist only to give their families whatever they can earn" (p. 177). A woman in this society does not get into conflicts in which she has to choose between her mother and her husband, as happens in the western working class (see above; also Komarovsky, 1962), where the reigning ideology supports the nuclear family.

In these three settings, the mother–daughter tie and other female kin relations remain important from a woman's childhood through her old age. Daughters stay closer to home in both childhood and adulthood and remain involved in particularistic role relations. Sons and men are more likely to feel uncomfortable at home and to spend work and play time away from the house. Male activities and spheres emphasize universalistic, distancing qualities: men in Java are the bearers and transmitters of high culture and formal relationships; men in East London spend much of their time in alienated work settings; Atjehnese boys spend their time in school, and their fathers trade in distant places.

Mother–daughter ties in these three societies, described as extremely close, seem to be composed of companionship and mutual cooperation and to be positively valued by both mother and daughter. The ethnographies do not imply that women are weighed down by the burden of their relationships or by overwhelming guilt and responsibility. On the contrary, they seem to have developed a strong sense of self and self-worth, which continues to grow as they get older and take on their maternal role. The implication is that "ego strength" is not completely dependent on the firmness of the ego's boundaries.

Guntrip's distinction between "immature" and "mature" dependence clarifies the difference between mother–daughter relationships and women's psyche in the western middle class and in the matrifocal societies described. Women in the western middle class are caught up to some extent in issues of infantile dependence, while the women in matrifocal societies remain in definite connection with others, but in relationships characterized by mature dependence. As Guntrip describes it (1961:291): "*Mature dependence* is characterized by full differentiation of ego and object (emergence from primary identification) and therewith a capacity for valuing the object for its own sake and for giving as well as receiving; a condition which should be described not as independence but as mature dependence." This kind of mature dependence is also to be distinguished from the kind of forced independence and denial of need for relationship that I have suggested characterizes masculine personality and that reflects continuing conflict about infantile dependence (Guntrip, 1961:293; my italics): "Maturity is not equated with independence though it includes a certain capacity for independence. . . . The independence of the mature person is simply that he does not collapse when he has to stand alone. It is not an independence of needs for other persons with whom to have relationship: *that would not be desired by the mature.*"

Depending on its social setting, women's sense of relation and connection and their embeddedness in social life provide them with a kind of security that men lack. The quality of a mother's relationship to her children and maternal self-esteem, on the one hand, and the nature of a daughter's developing identification with her mother, on the other, make crucial differences in female development.

Women's kin role, and in particular the mother role, is central and positively valued in Atjeh, Java, and East London. Women gain status and prestige as they get older; their major role is not fulfilled in early motherhood. At the same time, women may be important contributors to the family's economic support, as in Java and East London, and in all three societies they have control over real economic resources. All these factors give women a sense of self-esteem independent of their relationship to their children. Finally, strong relationships exist between women in these societies, expressed in mutual cooperation and frequent contact. A mother, then, when her children are young, is likely to spend much of her time in the company of other women, not simply isolated with her children.

These social facts have important positive effects on female psychological development. (It must be emphasized that all the ethnographies indicate that these same social facts make male development difficult and contribute to psychological insecurity and lack of ease in interpersonal relationships in men.) A mother is not invested in keeping her daughter from individuating and becoming less dependent. She has other ongoing contacts and relationships that help fulfill her psychological and social needs. In addition, the people surrounding a mother while a child is growing up become mediators between mother and daughter, by providing a daughter with alternative models for personal identification and objects of attachment, which contribute to her differentiation from her mother. Finally, a daughter's identification with her mother in this kind of setting is with a strong woman with clear control over important spheres of life, whose sense of self-esteem can reflect this. Acceptance of her gender identity involves positive valuation of herself, and not an admission of inferiority. In psychoanalytic terms, we might say it involves identification with a preoedipal, active, caring mother. Bibring points to clinical findings supporting this interpretation: "We find in the analysis of the women who grew up in this 'matriarchal' setting the rejection of the feminine role less frequently than among female patients coming from the patriarchal family culture" (1953:281).

There is another important aspect of the situation in these societies. The continuing structural and practical importance of the mother–daughter tie not only ensures that a daughter develops a positive personal and role identification with her mother, but also requires that the close psychological tie between mother and daughter become firmly grounded in real role expectations. These provide a certain constraint and limitation upon the relationship, as well as an avenue for its expression through common spheres of interest based in the external social world.

All these societal features contrast with the situation of the western middle-class woman. Kinship relations in the middle class are less important. Kin are not likely to live near each other, and, insofar as husbands are able to provide adequate financial support for their families, there is no need for a network of mutual aid among related wives. As the middle-class woman gets older and becomes a grandmother, she cannot look forward to increased status and prestige in her new role.

The western middle-class housewife does not have an important economic role in her family. The work she does and the responsibilities that go with it (household management, cooking, entertaining, etc.) do not seem to be really necessary to the economic support of her family (they are crucial contributions to the maintenance and reproduction of her family's class position, but this is not generally recognized as important either by the woman herself or by the society's ideology). If she works outside the home, neither she nor the rest of society is apt to consider this work to be important to her self-definition in the way that her housewife role is.

Child care, on the other hand, is considered to be her crucially important responsibility. Our post-Freudian society in fact assigns to parents (and especially to the mother)[16] nearly total responsibility for how children turn out. A middle-class mother's daily life is not centrally involved in relations with other women. She is isolated with her children for most of her workday. It is not surprising, then, that she is likely to invest a lot of anxious energy and guilt in her concern for her children and to look to them for her own self-affirmation, or that her self-esteem, dependent on the lives of others than herself, is shaky. Her life situation leads her to an overinvolvement in her children's lives.

A mother in this situation keeps her daughter from differentiation and from lessening her infantile dependence. (She also perpetuates her son's dependence, but in this case society and his father are more likely to interfere in order to assure that, behaviorally, at least, he doesn't *act* dependent.) And there are no other people around to mediate in the mother–daughter relationship. Insofar as the father is actively involved in a relationship with his daughter and his daughter develops some identification with him, this helps her individuation, but the formation of ego autonomy through identification with and idealization of her father may be at the expense of her positive sense of feminine self. Unlike the situation in matrifocal families, the continu-

ing closeness of the mother–daughter relationship is expressed only on a psychological, interpersonal level. External role expectations do not ground or limit it.

It is difficult, then, for daughters in a western middle-class family to develop self-esteem. Most psychoanalytic and social theorists[17] claim that the mother inevitably represents to her daughter (and son) regression, passivity, dependence, and lack of orientation to reality, whereas the father represents progression, activity, independence, and reality orientation.[18] Given the value implications of this dichotomy, there are advantages for the son in giving up his mother and identifying with his father. For the daughter, feminine gender identification means identification with a devalued, passive mother, and personal maternal identification is with a mother whose own self-esteem is low. Conscious rejection of her oedipal maternal identification, however, remains an unconscious rejection and devaluation of herself, because of her continuing preoedipal identification and boundary confusion with her mother.

Cultural devaluation is not the central issue, however. Even in patrilineal, patrilocal societies in which women's status is very low, women do not necessarily translate this cultural devaluation into low self-esteem, nor do girls have to develop difficult boundary problems with their mother. In the Moslem Moroccan family, for example, a large amount of sex segregation and sex antagonism gives women a separate (domestic) sphere in which they have a real productive role and control, and also a life situation in which any young mother is in the company of other women.[19] Women do not need to invest all their psychic energy in their children, and their self-esteem is not dependent on their relationship to their children. In this and other patrilineal, patrilocal societies, what resentment women do have at their oppressive situation is more often expressed toward their sons, whereas daughters are seen as allies against oppression. Conversely, a daughter develops relationships of attachment to and identification with other adult women. Loosening her tie to her mother therefore does not entail the rejection of all women. The close tie that remains between mother and daughter is based not simply on mutual overinvolvement but often on mutual understanding of their oppression.

CONCLUSION

Women's universal mothering role has effects both on the development of masculine and feminine personality and on the relative status of the sexes. This paper has described the development of relational personality in women and of personalities preoccupied with the denial of relation in men. In its comparison of different societies it has suggested that men, while guaranteeing to themselves sociocultural superiority over women, always remain psychologically defensive and insecure. Women, by contrast, although always of secondary social and cultural status, may in favorable circumstances gain psychological security and a firm sense of worth and importance in spite of this.

Social and psychological oppression, then, is perpetuated in the structure of personality. The paper enables us to suggest what social arrangements contribute (and could contribute) to social equality between men and women and their relative freedom from certain sorts of psychological conflict. Daughters and sons must be able to develop a personal identification with more than one adult, and preferably one embedded in a role relationship that gives it a social context of expression and provides some limitation upon it. Most important, boys need to grow up around men who take a major role in child care, and girls around women who, in addition to their child care responsibilities, have a valued role and recognized spheres of legitimate control. These arrangements could help to ensure that children of both sexes develop a sufficiently individuated and strong sense of self, as well as a positively valued and secure gender identity that does not bog down either in ego-boundary confusion, low self-esteem, and overwhelming relatedness to others or in compulsive denial of any connection to others or dependence upon them.

NOTES

1. My understanding of mother–daughter relationships and their effect on feminine psychology grows out of my participation beginning in 1971 in a women's group that discusses mother–daughter relationships in particular and family relationships in general. All the women in this group have contributed to this understanding. An excellent dissertation by Marcia Millman (1972) first suggested to me the importance of boundary issues for women and became a major organizational focus for my subsequent work. Discussions with Nancy Jay, Michelle Rosaldo, Philip Slater, Barrie Thorne, Susan Weisskopf, and Beatrice Whiting have been central to the development of the ideas presented here. I am grateful to George Goethals, Edward Payne, and Mal Slavin for their comments and suggestions about earlier versions of this paper.

2. Margaret Mead provides the most widely read and earliest argument for this viewpoint (cf., e.g., 1935 and 1949); see also Chodorow (1971) for another discussion of the same issue.

3. Unfortunately, the language that describes personality structure is itself embedded with value judgment. The implication in most studies is that it is always better to have firmer ego boundaries, that "ego strength" depends on the degree of individuation. Gutmann, who recognizes the linguistic problem, even suggests that "so-called ego pathology may have adaptive implications for women" (1965:231). The argument can be made that extremes in either direction are harmful. Complete lack of ego boundaries is clearly pathological, but so also, as critics of contemporary western men point out (cf., e.g., Bakan, 1966, and Slater, 1970), is individuation gone wild, what Bakan calls "agency unmitigated by communion," which he takes to characterize, among other things, both capitalism based on the Protestant ethic and aggressive masculinity. With some explicit exceptions that I will specify in context, I am using the concepts solely in the descriptive sense.

4. Slater (1968) provides one example of such an investigation. LeVine's recent work on psychoanalytic anthropology (1971a, b) proposes a methodology that will enable social scientists to study personality development in this way.

5. Particularly as interpreted by object-relations theorists (e.g., Fairbairn, 1952, and Guntrip, 1961) and, with some similarity, by Parsons (1964) and Parsons and Bales (1955).

6. See, e.g., Brunswick, 1940; Deutsch, 1932, 1944; Fliess, 1948; Freud, 1931; Jones, 1927; and Lampl-de Groot, 1927.

7. The important distinction between "positional" and "personal" identification comes from Slater, 1961, and Winch, 1962.

8. For more extensive arguments concerning this, see, e.g., Burton & Whiting (1961), Chodorow (1971), and Slater (1968).

9. The processes by which individual personal experiences and psychological factors contribute to or are translated into social and cultural facts, and, more generally, the circularity of explanations in terms of socialization, are clearly very complicated. A discussion of these issues, however, is not within the scope of this paper.

10. The question of the universality of the oedipus complex as Freud describes it is beyond the scope of this paper. Bakan (1966, 1968) points out that in the original Oedipus myth, it was the father who first tried to kill his son, and that the theme of paternal infanticide is central to the entire Old Testament. He suggests that for a variety of reasons, fathers probably have hostile and aggressive fantasies and feelings about their children (sons). This more general account, along with a variety of psychological and anthropological data, convinces me that we must take seriously the notion that members of both generations may have conflicts over the inevitable replacement of the elder generation by the younger, and that children probably feel both guilt and (rightly) some helplessness in this situation.

11. These views are most extreme and explicit in two papers (Freud, 1925, 1933) and warrant the criticism that has been directed at them. Although the issue of penis envy in women is not central to this paper, it is central to Freud's theory of female development. Therefore I think it worthwhile to mention three accounts that avoid Freud's ideological mistakes while allowing that his clinical observations of penis envy might be correct.

Thompson (1943) suggests that penis envy is a symbolic expression of women's culturally devalued and underprivileged position in our patriarchal society; that possession of a penis symbolizes the possession of power and privilege. Bettelheim (1954) suggests that members of either sex envy the sexual functions of the other, and that women are more likely to express this envy overtly, because, since men are culturally superior, such envy is considered "natural." Balint (1954) does not rely on the fact of men's cultural superiority, but suggests that a little girl develops penis envy when she realizes that her mother loves people with penises, i.e., her father, and thinks that possession of a penis will help her in her rivalry for her mother's attentions.

12. See, e.g., Brunswick, 1940; Deutsch, 1925, 1930, 1932, 1944; Freedman, 1961; Freud, 1931; Jones, 1927.

13. Following Cohen (1969), I would suggest that the external structural features of these settings (in the family or in school, for instance) are often similar or the same for boys and girls. The different kind and amount of adult male and female participation in these settings account for their being experienced by children of different sexes as different sorts of milieux.

14. Gutmann points out that all these qualities are supposed to indicate lack of adequate ego strength and suggests that we ought to evaluate ego strength in terms of the specific demands of different people's (e.g., women's as opposed to men's) daily lives. Bakan goes even further and suggests that modern male ego qualities are a pathological extreme. Neither account is completely adequate. Gutmann does not consider the possibility (for which we have good evidence) that the everyday demands of an autocentric milieu

are unreasonable: although women's ego qualities may be "functional" for their participation in these milieux, they do not necessarily contribute to the psychological strength of the women themselves. Bakan, in his (legitimate) preoccupation with the lack of connection and compulsive independence that characterize western masculine success, fails to recognize the equally clear danger (which, I will suggest, is more likely to affect women) of communion unmitigated by agency—of personality and behavior with no sense of autonomous control or independence at all.

I think this is part of a more general social-scientific mistake, growing out of the tendency to equate social structure and society with male social organization and activities within a society. This is exemplified, for instance, in Erikson's idealistic conception of maternal qualities in women (1965) and, less obviously, in the contrast between Durkheim's extensive treatment of "anomic" suicide (1897) and his relegation of "fatalistic" suicide to a single footnote (p. 276).

15. This ethnography and a reading of it that focuses on strong female kin relations (Siegel, 1969) were brought to my attention by Tanner (1971).

16. See Slater (1970) for an extended discussion of the implications of this.

17. See, e.g., Deutsch, 1944, passim; Erikson, 1964:162; Klein & Rivière, 1937:18; Parsons, 1964, passim; Parsons & Bales, 1955, passim.

18. Their argument derives from the universal fact that a child must outgrow her or his primary identification with and total dependence upon the mother. The present paper argues that the value implications of this dichotomy grow out of the particular circumstances of our society and its devaluation of relational qualities. Allied to this is the suggestion that it does not need to be, and often is not, relationship to the father that breaks the early maternal relationship.

19. Personal communication from Fatima Mernissi, based on her experience growing up in Morocco and her sociological fieldwork there.

REFERENCES

Ariès, P. 1962. *Centuries of Childhood: A Social History of Family Life.* New York.

Bakan, D. 1966. *The Duality of Human Existence: Isolation and Communion in Western Man.* Boston.

———. 1968. *Disease, Pain, and Sacrifice: Toward a Psychology of Suffering.* Boston.

Balint, A. 1954. *The Early Years of Life: A Psychoanalytic Study.* New York.

Barry, H., Bacon, M., & Child, I. 1957. "A cross-cultural survey of some sex differences in socialization." *Journal of Abnormal and Social Psychology* 55:327–32.

Bettelheim, B. 1954. *Symbolic Wounds: Puberty Rites and the Envious Male.* New York.

Bibring, G. 1953. "On the 'passing of the Oedipus complex' in a matriarchal family setting." In R. Lowenstein, ed., *Drives, Affects and Behavior: Essays in Honor of Marie Bonaparte,* pp. 278–84. New York.

Brunswick, R. 1940. "The preoedipal phase of the libido development." In R. Fliess, ed., pp. 231–53.

Burton, R., & Whiting, J. 1961. "The absent father and cross-sex identity." *Merrill-Palmer Quarterly of Behavior and Development* 7 (2):85–95.

Carlson, R. 1971. "Sex differences in ego functioning: Exploratory studies of agency and communion." *Journal of Consulting and Clinical Psychology* 37:267–77.

Chodorow, N. 1971. "Being and doing. A cross-cultural examination of the socialization of males and females." In V. Gornick & B. Moran, eds., *Woman in Sexist Society: Studies in Power and Powerlessness.* New York.

Cohen, R. 1969. "Conceptual styles, culture conflict, and nonverbal tests of intelligence." *American Anthropologist* 71:828–56.

Deutsch, H. 1925. "The psychology of woman in relation to the functions of reproduction." In R. Fliess, ed., pp. 165–79.

———. 1930. "The significance of masochism in the mental life of women." In R. Fliess, ed., pp. 195–207.

———. 1932. "On female homosexuality." In R. Fliess, ed., pp. 208–30.

———. 1944, 1945. *Psychology of Women.* Vols. I & II. New York.

Durkheim, E. 1897. *Suicide.* New York, 1968.

Erikson, E. 1964. *Insight and Responsibility.* New York.

———. 1965. "Womanhood and the inner space." In R. Lifton, ed., *The Woman in America.* Cambridge, Mass.

Fairbairn, W. 1952. *An Object-Relations Theory of the Personality.* New York.

Fliess, R. 1948. "Female and preoedipal sexuality: A historical survey." In R. Fliess, ed., pp. 159–64.

———. 1961. *Ego and Body Ego: Contributions to Their Psychoanalytic Psychology.* New York, 1970.

Fliess, R., ed. 1969. *The Psychoanalytic Reader: An Anthology of Essential Papers with Critical Introductions.* New York. Originally published in 1948.

Freedman, D. 1961. "On women who hate their husbands." In H. Ruitenbeek, ed., pp. 221–37.

Freud, S. 1925. "Some psychological consequences of the anatomical distinction between the sexes." In J. Strachey, ed., *The Standard Edition of the Complete Psychological Works of Sigmund Freud,* Vol. XIX, pp. 248–58. London.

———. 1931. "Female sexuality." In H. Ruitenbeek, ed., pp. 88–105.

———. 1933. "Femininity." In *New Introductory Lectures in Psychoanalysis,* pp. 112–35. New York, 1961.

Geertz, H. 1961. *The Javanese Family: A Study of Kinship and Socialization.* New York.

Guntrip, H. 1961. *Personality Structure and Human Interaction: The Developing Synthesis of Psycho-dynamic Theory.* New York.

Gutmann, D. 1965. "Women and the conception of ego strength." *Merrill-Palmer Quarterly of Behavior and Development* 2:229–40.

Harper, E. 1969. "Fear and the status of women." *Southwestern Journal of Anthropology* 25:81–95.

Jay, R. 1969. *Javanese Villagers: Social Relations in Rural Modjokuto.* Cambridge, Mass.

Jones, E. 1927. "The early development of female sexuality." In H. Ruitenbeek, ed., pp. 21–35.

Klein, M., & Rivière, J. 1937. *Love, Hate and Reparation.* New York, 1964.

Kohlberg, L. 1966. "A cognitive-developmental analysis of children's sex-role concepts and attitudes." In E. Maccoby, ed., *The Development of Sex Differences,* pp. 82–173. Stanford, Calif.

Komarovsky, M. 1962. *Blue-collar Marriage,* New York, 1967.

Lampl-de Groot, J. 1927. "The evolution of the Oedipus complex in women." In R. Fliess, ed., pp. 180–94.

LeVine, R. 1971a. "The psychoanalytic study of lives in natural social settings." *Human Development* 14:100–109.

———. 1971b. "Re-thinking psychoanalytic anthropology." Paper presented at the Institute on Psychoanalytic Anthropology, 70th Annual Meeting of the American Anthropological Association, New York.

Mead, M. 1935. *Sex and Temperament in Three Primitive Societies.* New York, 1963.

———. 1949. *Male and Female: A Study of Sexes in a Changing World.* New York, 1968.

Millman, M. 1972. "Tragedy and exchange: Metaphoric understandings of interpersonal relationships." Ph.D. dissertation, Department of Sociology, Brandeis University.

Minturn, L., & Hitchcock, J. 1963. "The Rajputs of Khalapur, India." In B. Whiting, ed., *Six Cultures: Studies in Child Rearing.* New York.

Mitscherlich, A. 1963. *Society without the Father.* New York, 1970.

Ortner, S. 1974. "Is Female to Male as Nature is to Culture?" In Michelle Zembalist Rosaldo and Louise Lamphere, ed., *Women, Culture, and Society,* pp. 67–88. Stanford University Press.

Parsons, T., 1964. *Social Structure and Personality.* New York.

Parsons, T., & Bales, R. 1955. *Family, Socialization and Interaction Process.* New York.

Rosaldo, M. 1974. "Women, Culture, and Society: A Theoretical Overview." In Michelle Zimbalist Rosaldo and Louise Lamphere, ed., *Women, Culture, and Society,* pp. 17–42. Stanford University Press.

Ruitenbeek, H., ed. 1966. *Psychoanalysis and Female Sexuality.* New Haven.

Siegel, J. 1969. *The Rope of God.* Berkeley, Calif.

Slater, P. 1961. "Toward a dualistic theory of identification." *Merrill-Palmer Quarterly of Behavior and Development* 7:113–26.

———. 1968. *The Glory of Hera: Greek Mythology and the Greek Family.* Boston.

———. 1970. *The Pursuit of Loneliness: American Culture at the Breaking Point.* Boston.

Tanner, N. 1971. "Matrifocality in Indonesia and among Black Americans." Paper presented at the 70th Annual Meeting of the American Anthropological Association, New York.

Tax, M. 1970. *Woman and Her Mind: The Story of Daily Life.* Boston.

Thompson, C. 1943. " 'Penis envy' in women." In H. Ruitenbeek, ed., pp. 246–51.

Whiting, J. 1959. "Sorcery, sin and the superego: A cross-cultural study of some mechanisms of social control." In C. Ford, ed., *Cross-Cultural Approaches: Readings in Comparative Research,* pp. 147–68. New Haven, 1967.

Whiting, J., Kluckhohn, R., & Anthony, A. 1958. "The function of male initiation rites at puberty." In E. Maccoby, T. Newcomb, & E. Hartley, eds., *Readings in Social Psychology,* pp. 359–70. New York.

Winch, R. 1962. *Identification and Its Familial Determinants.* New York.

Young, M., & Willmott, P. 1957. *Family and Kinship in East London.* London, 1966.

GENDER IN THE CONTEXT OF RACE AND CLASS: NOTES ON CHODOROW'S "REPRODUCTION OF MOTHERING"

ELIZABETH V. SPELMAN

. . . Much of feminist theory has proceeded on the assumption that gender is indeed a variable of human identity independent of other variables such as race and class, that whether one is a woman is unaffected by what class or race one is.[1] Feminists have also assumed that sexism is distinctly different from racism and classism, that whether and how one is subject to sexism is unaffected by whether and how one is subject to racism or classism.

The work of Nancy Chodorow has seemed to provide feminist theory with a strong foundation for these arguments. It has explicitly and implicitly been used to justify the assumption that there is nothing problematic about trying to examine gender independently of other variables such as race, class, and ethnicity. Though Chodorow's writings have received sometimes scathing criticism from feminists, more often they have been seen by feminist scholars in many different disciplines as providing a particularly rich understanding of gender.[2] Indeed, Chodorow offers what appears to be a very promising account of the relations between gender identity and other important aspects of identity such as race and class. For while she treats gender as separable from race and class, she goes on to suggest ways in which the sexist oppression intimately connected to gender differences is related to racism and classism.

. . . While Chodorow's work is very compelling, it ought to be highly problematic for any version of feminism that demands more than lip service to the significance of race and class, racism and classism, in the lives of the women on whom Chodorow focuses. The problem, as I see it, is not that feminists have taken Chodorow seriously, but that we have not taken her seriously enough. Her account points to a more complicated understanding of gender and the process of becoming gendered than she herself develops. She tells us to look at the social context of mothering in order to understand the effect of mothering on the acquisition of gender identity in children; but if we follow her advice, rather than her own practice, we are led to see that gender identity is not neatly separable from other aspects of identity such as race and class. They couldn't be if, as Chodorow insists, the acquisition of gender occurs in and helps perpetuate the "hierarchical and differentiated social worlds" we inhabit. . . . It is a general principle of feminist inquiry to be skeptical about any account of human relations that fails to mention gender or consider the possible effects of gender differences: for in a world in which there is sexism, obscuring the workings of gender is likely to involve—whether intentionally or not—obscuring the workings of sexism. We thus ought to be skeptical about any account of gender relations that fails to mention race and class or to consider the possible effects of race and class differences on gender: for in a world in which there is racism and classism, obscuring the workings of race and class is likely to involve—whether intentionally or not—obscuring the workings of racism and classism.

For this reason alone we may have a lot to learn from the following questions about any account of gender relations that presupposes or otherwise insists on the separability of gender, race, and class: Why does it seem possible or necessary to separate them? Whatever the motivations for doing so, does it serve the interests of some people and not others? Does methodology ever express race or class privilege—for example, do any of the methodological reasons that might be given for trying to investigate gender in isolation from race and class in fact serve certain race or class interests?

These questions are not rhetorical. For very good and very important reasons, feminists have insisted on asking how gender affects or is affected by every branch of human inquiry (even those such as the physical sciences, which seem to have no openings for such questions). And with very good reason we have been annoyed by the absence of reference to gender in inquiries about race or class, racism and classism. Perhaps it seems the best response to such a state of affairs, first to focus on gender and sexism and then to go on to think about how gender and sexism are related to race and racism, class and classism. Hence the appeal of the work of Nancy Chodorow and the variations on it by others. But however logically, methodologically, and politically sound such inquiry seems, it obscures the ways in which race and class identity may be intertwined with gender identity. Moreover, since in a racist and classist society the racial and class identity of those who are subject to racism and classism are not obscured, all it can really mask is the racial and class identity of white middle-class women. It is because white middle-class women have something at stake in not having their racial and class identity made and kept visible that we must question accepted feminist positions on gender identity.

If feminism is essentially about gender, and gender is taken to be neatly separable from race and class, then race and class don't need to be talked about except in some peripheral way. And if race and class are peripheral to women's identities as women, then racism and classism can't be of central concern to feminism. Hence the racism and classism some women face and other women help perpetuate can't find a place in feminist theory unless we keep in mind the race and class of all women (not just the race and class of those who are the victims of racism and classism). I have suggested here that one way to keep them in mind is to ask about the extent to which gender identity exists in concert with these other aspects of identity. This is quite different from saying either (1) we need to talk about race and class instead of gender or (2) we need to talk about race and class in addition to gender. Some feminists may be concerned that focus on race and class will deflect attention away from gender and from what women have in common and thus from what gives feminist inquiry its distinctive cast. This presupposes not only that we ought not spend too much time on what we don't have in common but that we have gender in common. But do we have gender identity in common? In one sense, of course, yes: all women are women. But in another sense, no: not if gender is a social construction and females become not simply women but particular kinds of women. If I am justified in thinking that what it means for me to be a woman must be exactly the same as what it means for you to be a woman (since we both are women), I needn't bother to find out anything from you or about you in order to find out what it means for you to be a woman: I can simply deduce what it means from my own case. On the other hand, if the meaning of what we apparently have in common (being women) depends in some ways on the meaning of what we don't have in common (for example, our different racial or class identities), then far from distracting us from issues of gender, attention to race and class in fact helps us to understand gender. In this sense it is only if we pay attention to how we differ that we come to an understanding of what we have in common.[3]

NOTES

1. Notice how different this is from saying that whether one is *female* is unaffected by what race or class one is.

2. Among the philosophers and political theorists who have incorporated Chodorow's work into their own analyses are Jane Flax, "Political Philosophy and the Patriarchal Unconscious: A Psychoanalysis Perspective on Epistemology and Metaphysics," Nancy C. M. Hartsock, "The Feminist Standpoint: Developing the Ground for a Specifically Feminist Historical Materialism," Naomi Scheman, "Individualism and the Objects of Psychology," and Sandra Harding, "Why Has the Sex/Gender System Become Visible Only Now?"—all in *Discovering Reality,* ed. Harding and Hintikka. See also Isaac D. Balbus, *Marxism and Domination* (Princeton: Princeton University Press, 1982). Chodorow's work also has been incorporated into the literary criticism of Judith Kegan Gardiner, "On Female Identity and Writing by Women," *Critical Inquiry* 8, no. 2 (1981): 347–61, and of Elizabeth Abel,

"(E)Merging Identities: The Dynamics of Female Friendship in Contemporary Fiction by Women," *Signs* 6, no. 3 (1981): 413–35. Students of psychoanalysis such as Jessica Benjamin and Evelyn Fox Keller have found Chodorow's work helpful in explaining their own positions, Benjamin in "Master and Slave: The Fantasy of Erotic Domination," in *Powers of Desire: The Politics of Sexuality,* ed. Ann Snitow, Christine Stansell, and Sharon Thompson (New York: Monthly Review Press, 1983), 280–99; Keller in "Gender and Science," *Psychoanalysis and Contemporary Thought* 2, no. 3 (1978): 409–33. Chodorow's work has also influenced the far-reaching work of Carol Gilligan. *In a Different Voice* (Cambridge: Harvard University Press, 1982). Chodorow's book and earlier articles were the subject of a critical symposium in *Signs* 6, no. 3 (1981), with comments from Judith Lorber, Rose Laub Coser, and Alice S. Rossi and a response from Chodorow. Iris Young recently has expressed doubts about the wisdom of Flax's,

Hartsock's, and Harding's use of Chodorow, in "Is Male Gender Identity the Cause of Male Domination?" in *Mothering: Essays in Feminist Theory,* ed. Joyce Trebilcot (Totowa, N.J.: Rowman and Allanheld, 1983). In the *Mothering* volume also appears Pauline Bart's highly critical review of Chodorow's book, a review first found in *off our backs* 11, no. 1 (1981). Adrienne Rich has pointed out the heterosexist bias in *The Reproduction of Mothering* in "Compulsory Heterosexuality and Lesbian Existence," *Signs* 5, no. 4 (1980): 631–60. Gloria Joseph has addressed the fact of the absence of a discussion of race and racism in accounts like Chodorow's.

3. Thanks to Helen Longino, Monica Jakuc, and Marilyn Schuster for helpful comments on a very early draft of this chapter.

R E A D I N G 1 9

"The Means to Put My Children Through": Child-Rearing Goals and Strategies among Black Female Domestic Servants

BONNIE THORNTON DILL

This essay explores the family and child-rearing strategies presented by a small group of Afro-American women who held jobs as household workers while raising their children. The data are drawn from a study of the relationship of work and family among American-born women of African descent who were private household workers (domestic servants) for most of their working lives.

The primary method of data collection was life histories, collected through open-ended, in-depth interviews with twenty-six women living in the northeastern United States. All participants were between sixty and eighty years old. A word of caution in reading this essay: The conclusions are not meant to apply to all Black female domestic servants, but represent only my interpretation of the experiences of these twenty-six women.

The life history method is particularly useful in studying Black female domestic workers whose stories and experiences have largely been distorted or ignored in the social science literature.[1] According to Denzin (1970:220), the

Bonnie Thornton Dill. " 'The Means to Put My Children Through': Child-Rearing Goals and Strategies among Black Female Domestic Servants" from *The Black Woman,* edited by La Frances Rodgers-Rose. (Newbury Park, Calif.: Sage Publications, 1980). Reprinted with the permission of the author.

method "presents the experiences and definitions held by one person, group, or organization as that person, group, or organization interprets those experiences." As such, it provides a means of exploring the processes whereby people construct, endure, and create meaning in both the interactional and structural aspects of their lives. It aids in the identification and definition of concepts appropriate to a sociological understanding of the subject's experience, and moves toward building theory that is grounded in imagery and meanings relevant to the subject. Collected through in-depth interviews, life histories are active processes of rendering meaning to one's life—its conflicts, ambiguities, crises, successes, and significant interpersonal relationships. Subjects are not merely asked to "report" but rather to reconstruct and interpret their choices, situations, and experiences.[2] The study of Black Americans cries out for such a sensitized approach to their lives.

The child-rearing goals and strategies adopted by the women who participated in this study are particularly revealing of the relationship of work and family. As working mothers, they were concerned with providing safe and secure care for their children while they were away from home. As working-class people, seeking to advance their children beyond their own occupational achievements, they confronted the problem of guiding them toward goals that were outside of their own personal experience. These issues, as well as others, take on a particular form for women who were household workers primarily because of the nature of their work.

Unlike many other occupations, domestic work brings together, in a closed and intimate sphere of human interaction, people whose paths would never cross were they to conduct their lives within the socioeconomic boundaries to which they were ascribed. These intimate interactions across the barriers of income, ethnicity, religion, and race occur within a sphere of life that is private and has little public exposure—the family.

As household workers, these women often become vital participants in the daily lives of two separate families: their employer's and their own. In fact, they have often been described as being "like one of the family" (Childress, 1956), and yet the barriers between them and their employers are real and immutable ones. In addition, working-class Black women employed by middle- and upper-class white families observe and experience vast differences in the material quality of life in the two homes. With regard to child-rearing, employers could provide luxuries and experiences for their children that were well beyond the financial means of the employee.

This essay, therefore, presents some of the ways in which the women talked about their reactions and responses to the discrepancies in life chances between those of their children and those of their employers. To some extent, these discrepancies became the lens through which we viewed their goals for their children and their child-rearing practices. At the same time, the contrast in objective conditions provides a background against which the women's perceptions of similarities between themselves and their employers are made more interesting.

The data from this study indicate that the relationship between the employee's family life and her work was shaped by four basic factors. First, there was the structure of the work. Whether she worked full-time or part-time and lived in, lived out, or did day work determined the extent to which she became involved in the employer's day-to-day life. It also determined the amount of time she had to share with her own family. Second were the tasks and duties she was assigned. With regard to her own child-rearing goals and strategies, the intermingling of employer and employee lifestyles occurred most frequently among those women who took care of the employer's children. It is through their discussion of these activities that the similarities and differences between the two families are most sharply revealed. A third factor is the degree of employer–employee intima-

cy. An employee who cared for the employer's children was more likely to have an intimate relationship with her employing family, but not always. Though the employer–employee relationship in domestic service is characterized as a personalized one when compared with other work relationships, this does not presume intimacy between the two parties, that is, a reciprocal exchange of interests and concerns. Among the women who participated in this study, those who did not share much of their own life with their employers appeared to minimize the interaction of work and family. Finally were the employee's goals for her children. Those women who felt that their employers could aid them in achieving the educational or other goals they had set for their children were more likely to encourage an intermingling of these two parts of their lives.

On domestic work and upward mobility:

> Strangely enough, I never intended for my children to have to work for anybody in the capacity that I worked. Never. And I never allowed my children to do any baby-sitting or anything of the sort. I figured it's enough for the mother to do it and in this day and time you don't have to do that. . . . So they never knew anything about going out to work or anything. They went to school.

Given the low social status of the occupation, the ambivalent and defensive feelings many of the women expressed about their work and the eagerness with which women left the occupation when other opportunities were opened to them, it is not at all surprising that most of the women in this study said they did not want their children to work in domestic service. Their hopes were centered upon "better" jobs for their children: jobs with more status, income, security, and comfort. Pearl Runner[3] recalled her goals for her children:

> My main goal was I didn't want them to follow in my footsteps as far as working. I always wanted them to please go to school and get a good job because it's important. That was really my main object.

Lena Hudson explained her own similar feelings this way:

> They had a better chance than I had, and they shouldn't look back at what I was doing. They had a better chance and a better education than I had, so look out for something better than I was doing. And they did. I haven't had a one that had to do any housework or anything like that. So I think that's good.

The notion of a better chance is a dominant one in the women's discussions of their goals for their children. They portray themselves as struggling to give their children the skills and training they did not have; and as praying that opportunities which had not been open to them would be open to their children. In their life histories, the women describe many of the obstacles they encountered in this quest. Nevertheless, there are dilemmas which, though not discussed explicitly, are implicit in their narratives and a natural outgrowth of their aspirations.

First of these is the task of guiding children toward a future over which they had little control and toward occupational objectives with which they had no direct experience. Closely tied to this problem was their need to communicate the undesirability of household work and at the same time maintain their personal dignity despite the occupation. While these two problems are not exceptional for working-class parents in an upwardly mobile society, they were mediated for Black domestic workers through the attitudes toward household work held by members of the Black communities in which the women lived and raised their children.

Had domestic work not been the primary occupation of Black women and had racial and sexual barriers not been so clearly identifiable as the reason for their concentration in this field of employment, these problems might have been viewed more personally and the women's histories might have been more self-deprecating than in fact they were. This particular set of circumstances would suggest that the women at least had the option of directing their anger and frustration about their situation outward upon the society rather than turning it inward upon themselves. Drake and Cayton (1945) confirm this argument in their analysis of domestic work, saying that "colored girls are often bitter in their comments about a society which condemns them to the *white folks'* kitchen" (p. 246). In addition, attitudes in the Black community toward domestic service work mediated some of the more negative attitudes which were prevalent in the wider society. Thus, the community could potentially become an important support in the child-rearing process, reinforcing the idea that while domestic service was low-status work, the people who did it were not necessarily low-status people.

The data in this study do not include the attitudes of the children of domestic servants toward their mothers' occupation. To my knowledge, there has been no systematic study of this issue. However, some biographies and community studies have provided insight into the range of feelings children express. Drake and Cayton (1945), for example, cite one woman who described her daughter as being "bitter against what she calls the American social system." DuBois talks about feeling an instinctive hatred toward the occupation (1920:110). I have had employers tell me that their domestics' children hated their children because the employer's kids got the best of their mother's time. I have also heard Black professionals speak with a mixture of pride, anger, and embarrassment about the fact that their mother worked "in the *white folks'* kitchen" so that they could get an education. Clearly, these issues deserve further study.

Throughout these histories, the women identified education as the primary means through which mobility could be achieved. As with many working-class people, education was seen as a primary strategy for upward mobility, a means to a better-paying and more prestigious job. Most of the women who participated in this study had not completed high school (the mean years of schooling completed for the group were 9.2 years). They reasoned that their limited education in combination with racial discrimination had hindered their own chances for upward mobility. Zenobia King explained her attitudes toward education in this way:

In my home in Virginia, education, I don't think, was stressed. The best you could do was be a schoolteacher. It wasn't something people impressed upon you you could get. I had an aunt and cousin who were trained nurses and the best they could do was nursing somebody at home or something. They couldn't get a job in a hospital. . . . I didn't pay education any mind really until I came to New York. I'd gotten to a certain stage in domestic work in the country and I didn't see the need for it. When I came, I could see opportunities that I could have had if I had a degree. People said it's too bad I didn't have a diploma.

From Mrs. King's perspective and from those of some of the other women, education for a Black woman in the South before World War II did not seem to offer any tangible rewards. She communicates the idea that an education was not only unnecessary but could perhaps have been a source of even greater frustration and dissatisfaction. This idea was reemphasized by other women who talked about college-educated women they knew who could find no work other than domestic work. In fact, both Queenie Watkins and Corrinne Raines discussed their experiences as trained teachers who could not find suitable jobs and thus took work in domestic service. Nevertheless, Corrinne Raines maintained her belief in education as a means of upward mobility, a belief that was rooted in her family of orientation. She said:

> I am the twelfth child [and was] born on a farm. My father was—at that day, you would call him a successful farmer. He was a man who was eager for his children to get an education. Some of the older ones had gotten out of school and were working and they were able to help the younger ones. That's how he was able to give his children as much education as he gave them, because the older ones helped him out.

Given this mixed experience with education and social mobility, it might be expected that many of the women would have expressed reservations about the value of an education for their children's mobility. However, this was not the case. Most of them, reflecting on their goals for their children, expressed sentiments similar to Pearl Runner's:

> This is the reason why I told them to get an education. . . . If they want to go to college it was fine because the higher you go the better jobs you get. They understood that because I always taught that into them. Please try to get an education so you can get a good job 'cause it was hard for colored girls to get jobs, period. They had to have an education.

Mrs. Runner's statement is important because it contains the rudiments of an explanation for why she and other women stressed education in the face of discriminatory practices that frequently discounted even their best efforts. Opallou Tucker elaborates on this theme and provides a somewhat more detailed explanation:

> It's [domestic work] all right if you want to do it and if you can't do anything else, but it's not necessary now. If you prepare yourself for something that's better, the doors are open now. I know years ago there was no such thing as a Black typist. I remember girls who were taking typing when I was going to school. They were never able to get a job at it. So it really [was] for their own personal use. My third child, and a niece, after they got up some size, started taking typing. And things began to open up after she got grown up. But in my day and time you could have been the greatest typist in the world, but you would never have gotten a job. It's fine to prepare yourself so that when opportunity knocks, you'll be able to catch up.

In these statements, Mrs. Runner and Mrs. Tucker convey a complex and subtle understanding of the interaction of racism and opportunity. They recognize the former as a real and tangible barrier, but they do not give in to it. They describe themselves as having taught their children to be prepared. Education was seen as a means of equipping oneself for whatever breaks might occur in the nation's patterns of racial exclusion. Thus, key to their aspirations for their children was the hope and belief that opportunities would eventually open and permit their children to make full use of the skills and knowledge they encouraged them to attain.

Nevertheless, maintaining these hopes could not have been as easy and unproblematic as hindsight makes it seem. The fact that many of the women who expressed this strong commitment to education at the time of the interview had seen their children complete a number of years of schooling and enter jobs which would never have been open to them when they were young was clearly a source of pride and satisfaction which could only have strengthened their beliefs. Thus, as they recalled their goals and aspirations for their children, they tended to speak with a sense of self-affirmation about their choices, confidence that may not have been present years earlier. As Mrs. Runner expressed,

> I tell you I feel really proud and I really feel that with all the struggling that I went through, I feel happy and proud that I was able to keep helping my children, that they listened and that they all went to high school. So when I look back, I really feel proud, even though at times the work was very hard and I came home very tired. But now, I feel proud about it. They all got their education.

Perhaps reflective of their understanding of the complex interaction of racism and opportunity, most of the women described limited and general educational objectives for their children. Although a few women said they had wanted their children to go to college and one sent her son to a private high school with the help of scholarships, most women saw high school graduation as the concrete, realizable objective which they could help their children attain. Willie Lee Murray's story brings out a theme that was recurrent in several other histories:

> My children did not go to college. I could not afford to send them to college. And they told me, my younger one especially, he said: Mommy, I don't want to go to college at your expense. When I go to college, I'll go on my own. I would not think of you workin' all your

days—sometimes you go sick and I don't know how you gonna get back. You put us through school and you gave us a beautiful life. We'll get to college on our own.

Mrs. Murray seems to indicate that while she would have liked her children to go to college, she limited her goals and concentrated her energies upon their completing high school.

In addition to limited educational objectives, most of the women did not describe themselves as having had a specific career objective in mind for their children. They encouraged the children to get an education in order to get a better job. Precisely what those jobs would be was left open, to be resolved through the interaction of their son or daughter's own luck, skill, perseverance, and the overall position of the job market vis-à-vis Black entrants.

Closely related to the goals the women expressed about their children's future position in society were their goals relative to their child's development as a person. Concern that their children grow up to be good, decent, law-abiding citizens was a dominant theme in these discussions. Most of the women in the study described their employers as having very specific career goals for their children, usually goals that would have the children following their parents' professional footsteps. In characterizing the differences between their goals and those of their employers, the women stressed the differences in economic resources. Johnnie Boatwright was quite explicit on this point:

There was a lot of things they [employers] did that I wanted to do for mine, but I just couldn't afford it. . . . Like sending them to school. Then they could hire somebody; child slow, they could hire a tutor for the child. I wish I could have been able to do what they done. And then too, they sent them to camps, nice camps, not any camp but one they'd pick out. . . . So that's what I wished I could had did for him [her son]. . . . See, whether it was right or wrong, mines I couldn't do it because I didn't have the money to do it. I wasn't able to do it. So that's the way it was. I did what I could and that was better than nothing.

In light of these discrepancies in resources, personal development was an important and realizable goal which may have been an adaptive response to the barriers which constricted the women's range of choices. This was an area over which the women had greater influence and potential control. It was also an area in which they probably received considerable community support, since values in the Black community, as pointed out above, attribute status to success along personal and family dimensions in addition to the basic ones of occupation, education, and income.

While Mrs. Boatwright conveys a sense of resignation and defeat in discussing her inability to do for her son what the employers did for theirs, Pearl Runner is more optimistic and positive about what she was able to do for her children.

Their money may be a little more, but I felt my goal was just as important as long as they [the children] got their education. They [employers] had the money to do lots more than I did, but I felt that if I kept working, my goals was just as important. I felt my children were just as important.

Feelings like those expressed by both Mrs. Runner and Mrs. Boatwright are reflected throughout the data in the women's comparisons of their aspirations and expectations for their children's future with those of their employers. However, it also seems apparent that their intimate participation in families in which the husbands were doctors, lawyers, stockbrokers, college professors, writers, and housewives provided considerable support for their more limited educational objectives. While not everyone had the specific experience of Lena Hudson, whose employer provided an allowance for her daughter which permitted the girl to stay in high school, the model of the employer's life with regard to the kinds of things they were able to give their children was a forceful one and is repeatedly reflected in the women's discussions of their child-rearing goals.

When asked: "What do you think were the goals that the Wallises [her employers] had for their children? What did they want for their children? What did they want them to become in life?" Lena Hudson replied:

Well, for *their* children, I imagine they wanted them to become like they were, educators or something that like. What they had in mind for *my* children, they saw in me that I wasn't able to make all of that mark. But raised my children in the best method I could. Because I wouldn't have the means to put *my* children through like they could for *their* children. And they see I wasn't the worst person in the world, and they saw I meant *some* good to my family, you see, so I think that was the standard with them and my family.

Her answers provide insight into the personal and social relationship between the two families and into her recognition of the points of connectedness and distance between them. The way in which she chose to answer the question reflects her feelings about working for the Wallis family and how that helped her accomplish the goals she had set for her own family.

MRS. HUDSON: And in the meantime, they owned a big place up in Connecticut. And they would take my children, and she, the madam, would do for my children just what she did for theirs.

INTERVIEWER: What kinds of things do you think your children learned from that, from the time that they spent with them?

MRS. HUDSON: Well, I think what they learnt from them, to try to live a decent life themselves, and try to make the best out of their life and the best out of the education they had. So I think that's what they got from them.

INTERVIEWER: What would you say you liked most about the work that you did?

MRS. HUDSON: Well, what I liked most about it, the things that I weren't able to go to school to do for my children. I could kinda pattern from the families that I worked for, that I could give my children the best of my abilities. And I think that's the thing I got from them, though they [her children] couldn't become professors, but they could be good in whatever they did.

The warm personal relationship between the two families was based not only on the direct assistance which the Wallises gave Mrs. Hudson, but also on the ways in which she was able to utilize her position in their family to support and sustain her personal goals. Thus, we can understand why she saw work as an ability rather than a burden. Work was a means for attaining her goals; it provided her with the money she needed to be an independent person, and it exposed her and her children to "good" things—values and a style of life which she considered important. To some extent, Lena Hudson found the same things in her work that she found in her church; reinforcement for the standards which she held for her children and for herself.

The women who stressed education for their children and saw their children attain it were most frequently women like Mrs. Hudson who were closely tied to one or two employing families for a long period of time. For the most part, they were the women who had careers in domestic service. However, ties with employers were not crucial even within this small group, because some women said they had received very little support from their employers along these lines. Several women, as indicated above, pointed to a strong emphasis upon education in their families of orientation. Additionally, education as a means of upward mobility is a fundamental element in American social ideology. It appears, therefore, that the importance of the employer–employee relationship was in the support and reinforcement these middle-class families' goals, aspirations, and style of life provided the women. The amount of support varied, of course, with the particular relationship the employee had with her employer's family and the degree of the employer's interest in and commitment to the employee's personal life. On the spectrum presented by the women in this study, Mrs. Hudson's relationship with the Wallis family would be at one end; the relationship between Georgia Sims and the family for whom she worked longest at the other. The following segment of the interview with Mrs. Sims is a good example of a minimally interactive employer–employee relationship:

INTERVIEWER: What were your goals for your children?

MRS. SIMS: Well, to be decent, law-abiding men. That's all.

INTERVIEWER: Do you think there were any similarities between your goals for your children and the goals your employers, the Peterses, had for their children?

MRS. SIMS: Oh, sure! Oh, yes, because I mean you must remember, they had the money; now I didn't have it. Oh, definitely there was different goals between us. [*Note:* Mrs. Sims obviously understood the question to be about *differences* rather than similarities, so the question was asked again.]

INTERVIEWER: Do you think there were any things that were alike in terms of your goals for your children and their goals for their children?

MRS. SIMS: No. Nothing.

INTERVIEWER: Nothing at all?

MRS. SIMS: No.

INTERVIEWER: What kinds of goals did they have for their children?

MRS. SIMS: Oh, I mean education, going on to be, you know, upstanding citizens, and they had the jobs— My children couldn't get up, I mean when they become twenty, twenty one, they couldn't get up and go out and say, well, I'm gonna get an office job, I'm gonna get this kind of job. No. The best thing they could do is go and be a porter in the subway.

Mrs. Sims was very detached from her occupation. She was not a career household worker. In fact, she described herself as having had very limited contact with her employers, arriving when they were all on their way to work and school and often departing before they returned home. She said that she had no specific child care duties. Thus, her description of the employers' goals for their children is probably more of a projection on her part than it is based on discussion or direct participation in the employers' life.

Two types of child-rearing goals have been identified thus far: goals regarding the child's future position in the society and goals regarding his or her personal development. In addition to these two types of goals, the women aspired to provide their children with some accoutrements of a middle-class lifestyle. Their discussion of these desires often reflects the discrepancies between their lives and those of their employers. Jewell Prieleau describes her employer's children as follows:

> Her children always dress nice. Whenever her daughter was going to music school or anyplace, I had to take her in a taxi. Whenever she finish, she had to be picked up. I had to go get her.

In describing her own grandchildren, she said:

> I went to three nice department stores and I opened up credit for them so I could send them to school looking nice. I got up early in the morning and sent them off to school. After school I would pick them up in a taxi and bring them here [the job].

Mrs. Prieleau is not the only woman in this study who talked about going into debt to give her children some of the material things that she never had and that were part of her image of a "better life" for her children. Willa Murray told the following story:

> I remember when my sons wanted that record player. I said I'm gonna get a record player; I'm gonna do days work. But I had to get AC current for this record player. I called up this lady [her employer] and I said, I'm goin' to Household Finance this morning. If they call you for a reference would you give me some reference. She said, sure. I sat down and the man said come in. He said, Miz Murray, do you have a co-signer. I said, no. He said, well what's your collateral? I said something about the furniture. He said, do you work? I said, yeah, I do days work. He said, days work? You don't have a steady job? I said yes sir, days work. He said, who do you work for? I told him. He said, we'll see what we can do. He

gave the hundred and fifty dollars. I came home, phone the electric company, told them they could send the man to put the current in.

In these statements and some of the ones quoted earlier, we begin to see how the employer's style of life influenced these women. However, it cannot be assumed that the women's desires were merely an outgrowth of the employer–employee relationship. The material products which they sought are so widely available in the culture that they are considered general symbols of upward mobility. Upward mobility for their children was the basic goal of most of the women who participated in this study. It was a goal which seems to have existed prior to and apart from their work situation and the values of their employers. Nevertheless, in some cases the women found reinforcement for and regeneration of these goals within the work situation, just as they found supports within their community and family lives.

RAISING THE "WHITE FOLKS'" CHILDREN

The women's discussion of child-rearing strategies, particularly such issues as discipline, exemplify both the class and cultural differences between employer and employee. For private household workers, these differences are expressed within a relationship of inequality. The data collected in this study permitted an examination of employer parent–child interactions as it was perceived and constructed by the household workers. This has benefits as well as liabilities. As outsiders whose child-rearing practices and lifestyle differed from those of the employers, the women in this study provide a particularly revealing picture of parent–child relationships in the employing family. However, they were not mere observers of the process; they participated in it and thereby restructured it. The women's insights, therefore, offer a unique critical perspective that is found only in subordinates' characterizations of their superiors. However, as participants in the process, their observations are limited to the time frame in which they were present and make it virtually impossible to assess the women's impact on the process. Nevertheless, their stories about their own role in rearing the employer's children provide considerable understanding of how they saw their work and, more importantly, how their work affected their own style of parenting. Willa Murray's comments illuminate this:

> Throughout, the people that I worked for taught their children that they can talk back. They would let them

[the children] say anything they wanted to say to them. I noticed a lot of times they [the children] would talk back or something and they [the parents] would be hurt. They would say to me, I wish they [the children] wouldn't. I wish they were more like your children. They allowed them to do so much. But they taught them a lot of things. I know one thing, I think I got a lot of things from them. . . . I think I've learnt a lot about [how to do] with my children by letting them do and telling them—like the whites would tell them—that I trust you. I think a lot of Black mothers when we come along, they didn't trust us. They were telling us what we were gonna do. . . . But I think they [whites] talk to their children about what's in life, what's for them, what not to do. And they let them talk, they tell them all the things that we didn't tell our children. We're beginning to tell our children. . . . The alternative is that I told my children straight, that if a boy and a girl have sexual intercourse—I learned that from the white people—and you don't have anything to protect it, that girl will get a baby. So my children were looking out for that. I learned that from my people. I listened to what they tell [their children].

Talk between parents and children is a dominant theme of Mrs. Murray's comments. She is critical of her employers for permitting their children to "talk back" to them; to question their instructions, to respond impertinently or otherwise mock or demean the parents' authority. Yet, talking *with* the children, reasoning with them, explaining things and hearing their thoughts and opinions on various matters, is behavior which she admired enough to try to emulate. Telling the children that you "trust them" places greater emphasis upon self-direction than upon following orders. Clearly, the line between letting the children talk and permitting them to "talk back" is a difficult one to draw, yet Mrs. Murray draws it in transferring her work-learned behavior to her own child-rearing circumstances.

It should not be surprising that there would be behavioral characteristics which employers would admire in employee children, just as there were traits which Mrs. Murray and others admired in their employers' interactions with their children. In fact, it is striking that each would admire aspects of the other and seek to incorporate them within their own lives while the circumstances that generated those particular patterns were quite different. Nevertheless, reorienting the parent–child relationship in the employer's family was frequently described as a regular part of the worker's child care activity. In fact, the women's

discussions of their experiences in caring for their employers' children are variations upon the stories of resistance which characterized their establishing themselves in the employer–employee relationship. Queenie Watkins's description of the following child care incident provides a good example:

> One morning I was feeding Stevie oatmeal and I was eating oatmeal. His uncle, the little girl and I were all sitting at the table together eating. He said, I don't want this and I'm gonna spit it out. I said, you better not, Stevie. With that he just let it all come into my face. I took myself a big mouthful and let it go right back in his face. He screamed, and his uncle said, what did you do that for? I said, you fight fire with fire. My psychology is to let a child know he can't do to you what you can't do to him. The mother came running. I said, this ends my work here, but she said, just wash Stevie's face. I said, I'm not gonna wash it; let him wash it himself—he wasn't two years old. Finally, I said, I'll take him and wash his face but who's gonna wash my face? His mother started to laugh and said, you're some character. And you know what, he never did that again. He ate his food and I never had to chastise Stevie about anything after that.

Zenobia King told a slightly different story about the way in which she inserted her values into the parent–child relationship of an employing family:

> One time the daughter went out and she stayed all day. She didn't tell her mother where she was. And when she came back, her mother jumped on her in a really bad way. She told her she wished she had died out there, etc., etc., and her daughter said if her mother had loved her she would have asked where she was going. So, I separated them. I sent the daughter to one room and the mother to the other and talked to both of them and I brought them back together.

In both of these stories, as in others in this genre, the women see themselves as the instructor of both the children and the parents. They characterize themselves as helping the parent learn how to parent while simultaneously setting rules and regulations as to the kind of treatment they should expect from the children. Queenie Watkins's philosophy of fighting fire with fire was reiterated by Oneida Harris in describing her relations with one of the children whom she cared for:

He was nine years old and he rate me the worst maid they'd ever had because I wouldn't take any of his foolishness. If he kicked me in the shins, I'd kick him back. . . . I said he hasn't any bringing up, and if I stay here he's gonna listen. I said to his mother, if you don't want me, tell me tomorrow and I'll go. So anyway, the next day he would bring me up a little bit; she's the next-to-the-worst maid we ever had. Each week I came up till I was the best one.

As in the stories of resistance, both Queenie Watkins and Oneida Harris depict themselves as setting guidelines for respect from the children in the same way respect was established in the employer–employee relationship. The additional dimension of instructing parents in the ways of handling their children was another recurrent theme in the life histories.

Through these and other similar anecdotes which the women used to describe their participation in caring for their employers' children, they communicate a perception of their employers as uncomfortable in exercising the power associated with the parenting role. To a large degree, they depict their employers as either inconsistent and afraid of their children or ignorant of child-rearing strategies that would develop obedience and respect. The women see this as their forte; in many instances they describe themselves as exercising power on behalf of the parents and teaching the children to obey them and respect their parents. In so doing, they also present themselves as teaching the parents. Willa Murray is keenly aware of the paradoxical nature of this situation when she says: "Now I'm the maid, not the mistress." In the maid–mistress relationship, the latter gives instructions, which the former carries out. In a sense, Willa Murray's story presents a role reversal, one which she finds both surprising and amusing but also appropriate. It is akin to the anecdote in which she described herself telling her employers that they had more education than she did but their behavior was not intelligent. These presentations suggest that despite stereotypic conceptions of the maid–mistress relationship, women in these roles could gain considerable power and influence within a family, particularly where they had worked for a number of years and had considerable responsibility.

The household workers' impact on the parent–child relationship is only one aspect of their child care role. The other, equally important, aspect of this role is their relationship with the children they cared for and the fact, implicit in our earlier discussion, that they describe themselves as surrogate mothers for these children:

There's a long time she [the child] use to thought I was her mamma. She would ask me why is my skin white and yours brown, you my mamma? I tell her I'm not your mamma and I see the hurt coming in her eye. You know, like, she didn't want me to say that. I said there's your mamma in there, I'm just your nurse. She said no, you my mamma. [Mattie Washington]

I took care of the children. In fact, the children would call me when they had a problem or something, before they would call her [their mother]. [Zenobia King]

He [the boy] looked at me as a mother. When he went away to school he just would not come home if I wasn't there. And even when he was at home, if he was out playing with the boys he'd come in, his mother, grandmother and father would be sitting around, he'd say, where is everybody? His mother would look around and say well if you mean Oneida, I think she's upstairs. Upstairs he'd come. And they couldn't get that. It was sad, you see. They give him everything in the world but love. [Oneida Harris]

I was more like a mother to them, and you see she didn't have to take too much time as a mother should to know her children. They were more used to me because I put them to bed. The only time she would actually be with them was like when I'm off Thursday and on Sundays. They would go out sometimes, but actually I was really the mother because I raised them from little. [Pearl Runner]

Without exception, the women in this study who had child-care responsibilities talked about themselves as being "like a mother" to the employers' children. Their explanations of the development of this kind of relationship tended to follow those of Oneida Harris and Pearl Runner: their employers were frequently unavailable and spent less time with the children than they did. Because they interacted with the children on a daily basis and often had responsibility for their care, discipline, play, and meals, their role was a vital and important one in the eyes of both child and parent. This explains, in part, some of their power in affecting the parent–child relationship, as discussed above. The fact that the women had such an important and pivotal role in the development of the employer's children and at the same time held a job in which they could be replaced gave the entire relationship of parent, child, and housekeeper a particularly intense quality. For the most part, workers developed their strongest emotional ties to the children in the employing family.

Because the women saw themselves as surrogate mothers, the children whom they cared for could easily become their surrogate children. This is particularly apparent when we compare their comments and discussions about their own and their employers' children. One of the most prevalent patterns was to talk with pride and satisfaction about the accomplishments of their surrogate children. In general, the women would talk about how frequently they heard from these children and whether they got cards, letters, or money at Mother's Day or Christmas. In addition, they would describe the (now grown) children's occupations and family and, if they had pictures available, they would show them to me. This type of commentary provided an interesting parallel to their discussions of their own children. But even more important, it was designed to communicate the closeness that they felt existed between them and the children they had raised; closeness which was maintained over a number of years even after the children were grown.

Surrogate mothering, as pointed out in Opallou Tucker's case study, had the prospect of tying the worker into the emotional life of the employing family. For the women who lived outside the employer's household and were actively engaged in rearing their own children and caring for their own families, as were most of the women in this study, the prospect was minimized. However, for a woman like Mattie Washington, who lived in for most of the thirty years that she worked for one family, the potential for becoming enveloped in their life, at the expense of her own, was much greater.

In most instances, the women described themselves as caretakers, playmates, disciplinarians, confidantes, and friends of the employer's children. Nevertheless, it is clear from their discussions that in most cases the real ties of affection between themselves and their employer came through the children.

The children, therefore, provided the ties that bound the women to their employers as well as the mark of their difference. The role of surrogate mother allowed the women to cross these barriers and, for a fleeting moment, express their love and concern for a child without regard to the obstacles that lay ahead. Also, because most young children readily return love that is freely given and are open and accepting of people without regard to status factors that have meaning for their parents, the workers probably felt that they were treated with greater equality and more genuine acceptance by the children of the household.

NOTES

1. There is a very limited body of literature directly focused upon Black women in domestic service in the United States. Many of these studies are confined to the southern experience. Among the most important containing data on Black women in northern cities are Haynes (1923). Eaton (1967), and Chaplin (1964). Some discussion of the subject was also found in community studies, particularly those conducted before World War II (Drake & Cayton, 1945; Ovington, 1969). Labor studies provided a third source of data (among these were Greene & Woodson, 1930, and Haynes, 1912).

2. This discussion is largely drawn from a paper by Dill and Joselin (1977).

3. The names used for the participants in the study are fictitious.

REFERENCES

Chaplin, D. 1964. "Domestic service and the Negro." In A. Shostak and W. Gamberg, eds., *Blue Collar World*. Englewood Cliffs, N.J.: Prentice-Hall.

Childress, A. 1956. *Like One of the Family*. Brooklyn: Independence Publishers.

Denzin, N. K. 1970. *The Research Act*. Chicago: AVC.

Dill, B. T., & Joselin, D. 1977. "The limit of quantitative methods: The need of life histories." Paper presented at the Society for the Study of Social Problems Annual Meetings, Chicago.

Drake, S. C., & Cayton, H. 1945. *Black Metropolis*. New York: Harper & Row.

DuBois, W. E. B. 1920. *Darkwater*. New York: Harcourt Brace.

Eaton, I. 1967. "Negro domestic service in Seventh Ward Philadelphia." In W. E. B. DuBois, *The Philadelphia Negro*. New York: Schocken.

Greene, L. J., & Woodson, C. G. 1930. *The Negro Wage Earner*. Washington, D.C.: Association for the Study of Negro Life and History.

Haynes, G. 1912. *The Negro at Work in New York City: A Study in Economic Progress*. New York: Longmans.

Haynes, G. 1923. "Negroes in domestic service in the United States." *Journal of Negro History* 8:384–442.

Ovington, M. W. 1969. *Half a Man*. New York: Schocken.

Girls and Boys Together . . . But Mostly Apart: Gender Arrangements in Elementary Schools

BARRIE THORNE

Throughout the years of elementary school, children's friendships and casual encounters are strongly separated by sex. Sex segregation among children, which starts in preschool and is well established by middle childhood, has been amply documented in studies of children's groups and friendships (e.g., Eder & Hallinan, 1978; Schofield, 1981) and is immediately visible in elementary school settings. When children choose seats in classrooms or the cafeteria, or get into line, they frequently arrange themselves in same-sex clusters. At lunchtime, they talk matter-of-factly about "girls' tables" and "boys' tables." Playgrounds have gendered turfs, with some areas and activities, such as large playing fields and basketball courts, controlled mainly by boys, and others—smaller enclaves like jungle-gym areas and concrete spaces for hopscotch or jump rope—more often controlled by girls. Sex segregation is so common in elementary schools that it is meaningful to speak of separate girls' and boys' worlds.

Studies of gender and children's social relations have mostly followed this "two worlds" model, separately describing and comparing the subcultures of girls and boys (e.g., Lever, 1976; Maltz & Borker, 1983). In brief summary: Boys tend to interact in larger, more age-heterogeneous groups (Lever, 1976; Waldrop & Halverson, 1975; Eder & Hallinan, 1978). They engage in more rough and tumble play and physical fighting (Maccoby & Jacklin, 1974). Organized sports are both a central activity and a major

metaphor in boys' subcultures; they use the language of "teams" even when not engaged in sports, and they often construct interaction in the form of contests. The shifting hierarchies of boys' groups (Savin-Williams, 1976) are evident in their more frequent use of direct commands, insults, and challenges (Goodwin, 1980).

Fewer studies have been done of girls' groups (Foot, Chapman, & Smith, 1980; McRobbie & Garber, 1975), and—perhaps because categories for description and analysis have come more from male than female experience—researchers have had difficulty seeing and analyzing girls' social relations. Recent work has begun to correct this skew. In middle childhood, girls' worlds are less public than those of boys; girls more often interact in private places and in smaller groups or friendship pairs (Eder & Hallinan, 1978; Waldrop & Halverson, 1975). Their play is more cooperative and turn-taking (Lever, 1976). Girls have more intense and exclusive friendships, which take shape around keeping and telling secrets, shifting alliances, and indirect ways of expressing disagreement (Goodwin, 1980; Lever, 1976; Maltz & Borker, 1983). Instead of direct commands, girls more often use directives which merge speaker and hearer, e.g., "let's" or "we gotta" (Goodwin, 1980).

Although much can be learned by comparing the social organization and subcultures of boys' and of girls' groups, the separate-worlds approach has eclipsed full, contextual understanding of gender and social relations among children. The separate-worlds model essentially involves a search for group sex differences and shares the limitations of individual sex difference research. Differences tend to be exaggerated and similarities ignored, with little theoretical attention to the integration of similarity and difference (Unger, 1979). Statistical findings of difference are often portrayed as dichotomous, neglecting the considerable individual variation that exists; for example, not all boys fight, and some have intense and exclusive friendships. The sex difference approach tends to abstract gender from its social context, to assume that males and females are qualitatively and permanently different (with differences perhaps unfolding through separate developmental lines). These assumptions mask the possibility that gender arrangements and patterns of similarity and difference may vary by situation, race, social class, region, or subculture.

Sex segregation is far from total, and is a more complex and dynamic process than the portrayal of separate worlds reveals. Erving Goffman (1977) has observed that sex segregation has a "with–then apart" structure; the sexes segregate periodically, with separate spaces, rituals, groups, but they also come together and are, in crucial ways, part of the same world. This is certainly true in the social environment of elementary schools. Although girls and boys do interact as boundaried collectivities—an image suggested by the separate-worlds approach—there are other occasions when they work or play in relaxed and integrated ways. Gender is less central to the organization and meaning of some situations than others. In short, sex segregation is not static, but is a variable and complicated process.

To gain an understanding of gender which can encompass both the "with" and the "apart" of sex segregation, analysis should start not with the individual, nor with a search for sex differences, but with social relationships. Gender should be conceptualized as a system of relationships rather than as an immutable and dichotomous given. Taking this approach, I have organized my research on gender and children's social relations around questions like the following: How and when does gender enter into group formation? In a given situation, how is gender made more or less salient or infused with particular meanings? By what rituals, processes, and forms of social organization and conflict do "with–then apart" rhythms get enacted? How are these processes affected by the organization of institutions (e.g., different types of schools, neighborhoods, or summer camps), varied settings (e.g., the constraints and possibilities governing interaction on playgrounds vs. classrooms), and particular encounters?

METHODS AND SOURCES OF DATA

This study is based on two periods of participant observation. In 1976–1977 I observed for eight months in a largely working-class elementary school in California, a school with 8 percent Black and 12 percent Chicana/o students. In 1980 I did fieldwork for three months in a Michigan ele-

mentary school of similar size (around 400 students), social class, and racial composition. I observed in several classrooms—a kindergarten, a second grade, and a combined fourth–fifth grade—and in school hallways, cafeterias, and playgrounds. I set out to follow the round of the school day as children experience it, recording their interactions with one another, and with adults, in varied settings.

Participant observation involves gaining access to everyday, "naturalistic" settings and taking systematic notes over an extended period of time. Rather than starting with preset categories for recording, or with fixed hypotheses for testing, participant observers record detail in ways which maximize opportunities for discovery. Through continuous interaction between observation and analysis, "grounded theory" is developed (Glaser & Strauss, 1967).

The distinctive logic and discipline of this mode of inquiry emerges from: (1) theoretical sampling—being relatively systematic in the choice of where and whom to observe in order to maximize knowledge relevant to categories and analysis which are being developed; and (2) comparing all relevant data on a given point in order to modify emerging propositions to take account of discrepant cases (Katz, 1983). Participant observation is a flexible, open-ended and inductive method, designed to understand behavior within, rather than stripped from, social context. It provides richly detailed information anchored in everyday meanings and experience.

DAILY PROCESSES OF SEX SEGREGATION

Sex segregation should be understood not as a given, but as the result of deliberate activity. The outcome is dramatically visible when there are separate girls' and boys' tables in school lunchrooms or sex-separated groups on playgrounds. But in the same lunchroom one can also find tables where girls and boys eat and talk together, and in some playground activities the sexes mix. By what processes do girls and boys separate into gender-defined and relatively boundaried collectivities? And in what contexts, and through what processes, do boys and girls interact in less gender-divided ways?

In the school settings I observed, much segregation happened with no mention of gender. Gender was implicit in the contours of friendship, shared interest, and perceived risk which came into play when children chose companions—in their prior planning, invitations, seeking of access, saving of places, denials of entry, and allowing or protesting of "cuts" by those who violated the rules for lining up.

Sometimes children formed mixed-sex groups for play, eating, talking, working on a classroom project, or moving through space. When adults or children explicitly invoked gender—and this was nearly always in ways which separated girls and boys—boundaries were heightened and mixed-sex interaction became an explicit arena of risk.

In the schools I studied, the physical space and curricula were not formally divided by sex, as they have been in the history of elementary schooling (a history evident in separate entrances to old school buildings, where the words "Boys" and "Girls" are permanently etched in concrete). Nevertheless, gender was a visible marker in the adult-organized school day. In both schools, when the public address system sounded, the principal inevitably opened with: "Boys and girls . . . ," and in addressing clusters of children, teachers and aides regularly used gender terms ("Heads down, girls"; "The girls are ready and the boys aren't"). These forms of address made gender visible and salient, conveying an assumption that the sexes are separate social groups.

Teachers and aides sometimes drew upon gender as a basis for sorting children and organizing activities. Gender is an embodied and visual social category which roughly divides the population in half, and the separation of girls and boys permeates the history and lore of schools and playgrounds. In both schools—although through awareness of Title IX, many teachers had changed this practice—one could see separate girls' and boys' lines moving, like caterpillars, through the school halls. In the fourth–fifth-grade classroom the teacher frequently pitted girls against boys for spelling and math contests. On the playground in the Michigan school, aides regarded the space close to the building as girls' territory, and the playing fields "out there" as boys' territory. They sometimes shooed children of the other sex away from those spaces, especially boys who ventured near the girls' area and seemed to have teasing in mind.

In organizing their activities, both within and apart from the surveillance of adults, children also explicitly invoked gender. During my fieldwork in the Michigan school, I kept daily records of who sat where in the lunchroom. The amount of sex segregation varied: it was least at the first-grade tables and almost total among sixth-graders. There was also variation from classroom to classroom within a given age and from day to day. Actions like the following heightened the gender divide: In the lunchroom, when the two second-grade tables were filling, a high-status boy walked by the inside table, which had a scattering of both boys and girls, and said loudly, "Oooo, too many girls," as he headed for a seat at the far table. The boys at the inside table picked up their trays and moved, and no other boys sat at the inside table, which the pronouncement had effectively made taboo. In the end, that day (which was not the case every day), girls and boys ate at separate tables.

Eating and walking are not sex-typed activities, yet in forming groups in lunchrooms and hallways children often separated by sex. Sex segregation assumed added dimensions on the playground, where spaces, equipment, and activities were infused with gender meanings. My inventories of activities and groupings on the playground showed similar patterns in both schools: boys controlled the large fixed spaces designated for team sports (baseball diamonds, grassy fields used for football or soccer); girls more often played closer to the building, doing tricks on the monkey bars (which, for sixth-graders, became an area for sitting and talking) and using cement areas for jump rope, hopscotch, and group games like four-square. (Lever, 1976, provides a good analysis of sex-divided play.) Girls and boys most often played together in kickball, and in group (rather than team) games like four-square, dodgeball, and handball. When children used gender to exclude others from play, they often drew upon beliefs connecting boys to some activities and girls to others: A first-grade boy avidly watched an all-female game of jump rope. When the girls began to shift positions, he recognized a means of access to the play and he offered, "I'll swing it." A girl responded, "No way, you don't know how to do it, to swing it. You gotta be a girl." He left without protest. Although children sometimes ignored pronouncements about what each sex could or could not do, I never heard them directly challenge such claims.

When children had explicitly defined an activity or a group as gendered, those who crossed the boundary—especially boys who moved into female-marked space—risked being teased. ("Look! Mike's in the girls' line!"; "That's a girl over there," a girl said loudly, pointing to a boy sitting at an otherwise all-female table in the lunchroom.) Children, and occasionally adults, used teasing—especially the tease of "liking" someone of the other sex, or of "being" that sex by virtue of being in their midst—to police gender boundaries. Much of the teasing drew upon heterosexual romantic definitions, making cross-sex interaction risky and increasing social distance between boys and girls.

RELATIONSHIPS BETWEEN THE SEXES

Because I have emphasized the "apart" and ignored the occasions of "with," this analysis of sex segregation falsely implies that there is little contact between girls and boys in daily school life. In fact, relationships between girls and boys—which should be studied as fully as, and in connection with, same-sex relationships—are of several kinds:

1. "Borderwork," or forms of cross-sex interaction which are based upon and reaffirm boundaries and asymmetries between girls' and boys' groups.
2. Interactions which are infused with heterosexual meanings.
3. Occasions where individuals cross gender boundaries to participate in the world of the other sex.
4. Situations where gender is muted in salience, with girls and boys interacting in more relaxed ways.

Borderwork

In elementary school settings, boys' and girls' groups are sometimes spatially set apart. Same-sex groups sometimes claim fixed territories such as the basketball court, the bars, or specific lunchroom tables. However, in the crowded, multifocused, and adult-controlled environment of the school, groups form and disperse at a rapid rate and can never stay totally apart. Contact between girls and boys sometimes lessens sex segregation, but gender-defined groups also come together in ways which emphasize their boundaries.

"Borderwork" refers to interaction across, yet based upon and even strengthening, gender boundaries. I have drawn this notion from Fredrik Barth's (1969) analysis of social relations which are maintained across ethnic boundaries without diminishing dichotomized ethnic status.[1] His focus is on more macro, ecological arrangements; mine is on face-to-face behavior. But the insight is similar: groups may interact in ways which strengthen their borders, and the maintenance of ethnic (or gender) groups can best be understood by examining the boundary that defines the groups, "not the cultural stuff that it encloses" (Barth, 1969:15). In elementary schools there are several types of borderwork: contests or games where gender-defined teams compete; cross-sex rituals of chasing and pollution; and group invasions. These interactions are asymmetrical, challenging the separate-but-parallel model of "two worlds."

Contests   Boys and girls are sometimes pitted against each other in classroom competitions and playground games. The fourth–fifth-grade classroom had a boys' side and a girls' side, an arrangement that reemerged each time the teacher asked children to choose their own desks.

Although there was some within-sex shuffling, the result was always a spatial moiety system—boys on the left, girls on the right—with the exception of one girl (the "tomboy" whom I'll describe later), who twice chose a desk with the boys and once with the girls. Drawing upon and reinforcing the children's self-segregation, the teacher often pitted the boys against the girls in spelling and math competitions, events marked by cross-sex antagonism and within-sex solidarity. The teacher introduced a math game; she would write addition and subtraction problems on the board, and a member of each team would race to be the first to write the correct answer. She wrote two scorekeeping columns on the board: "Beastly Boys" . . . "Gossipy Girls." The boys yelled out, as several girls laughed, "Noisy girls! Gruesome girls!" The girls sat in a row on top of their desks; sometimes they moved collectively, pushing their hips or whispering "Pass it on." The boys stood along the wall, some reclining against desks. When members of either group came back victorious from the front of the room, they would do the "giving five" hand-slapping ritual with their team members.

On the playground a team of girls occasionally played a team of boys, usually in kickball or team two-square. Sometimes these games proceeded matter-of-factly, but if gender became the explicit basis of team solidarity, the interaction changed, becoming more antagonistic and unstable. Two fifth-grade girls played against two fifth-grade boys in a team game of two-square. The game proceeded at an even pace until an argument ensued about whether the ball was out or on the line. Karen, who had hit the ball, became annoyed, flashed her middle finger at the other team, and called to a passing girl to join their side. The boys then called out to other boys, and cheered as several arrived to play. "We got five and you got three!" Jack yelled. The game continued, with the girls yelling, "Bratty boys! Sissy boys!" and the boys making noises—"Weee haw," "Ha-ha-ha"—as they played.

Chasing   Cross-sex chasing dramatically affirms boundaries between girls and boys. The basic elements of chase and elude, capture and rescue (Sutton-Smith, 1971) are found in various kinds of tag with formal rules and in informal episodes of chasing which punctuate life on playgrounds. These episodes begin with a provocation (taunts like "You can't get me!" or "Slobber monster!"; bodily pokes or the grabbing of possessions). A provocation may be ignored or responded to by chasing. Chaser and chased may then alternate roles. In an ethnographic study of chase sequences on a school playground, Christine Finnan (1982) observes that chases vary in number of chasers to chased (e.g., one chasing one or five chasing two); form of provocation (a taunt or a poke); outcome (an episode may end when the chased outdistances the chaser, or with a brief touch, being wrestled to the ground, or the recapturing of a hat or a ball); and use of space (there may or may not be safety zones).

Like Finnan (1982) and Sluckin (1981), who studied a playground in England, I found that chasing has a gendered structure. Boys frequently chase one another, an activity which often ends in wrestling and mock fights. When girls chase girls, they are usually less physically aggressive; they less often, for example, wrestle one another to the ground.

Cross-sex chasing is set apart by special names—"girls chase the boys"; "boys chase the girls"; "the chase"; "chasers"; "chase and kiss"; "kiss chase"; "kissers and chasers"; "kiss or kill"—and by children's animated talk about the activity. The names vary by region and school, but contain both gender and sexual meanings (this form of play is mentioned, but only briefly analyzed, in Finnan, 1982; Sluckin, 1981; Parrott, 1972; and Borman, 1979).

In "boys chase the girls" and "girls chase the boys" (the names most frequently used in both the California and Michigan schools) boys and girls become, by definition, separate teams. Gender terms override individual identities, especially for the other team ("Help, a girl's chasin' me!"; "C'mon, Sarah, let's get that boy"; "Tony, help save me from the girls"). Individuals may also grab someone of their sex and turn them over to the opposing team: Ryan grabbed Billy from behind, wrestling him to the ground. "Hey, girls, get 'im," Ryan called.

Boys more often mix episodes of cross-sex with same-sex chasing. Girls more often have safety zones, places like the girls' restroom or an area by the school wall, where they retreat to rest and talk (sometimes in animated postmortems) before new episodes of cross-sex chasing begin.

Early in the fall in the Michigan school, where chasing was especially prevalent, I watched a second-grade boy teach a kindergarten girl how to chase. He slowly ran backwards, beckoning her to pursue him, as he called, "Help, a girl's after me." In the early grades chasing mixes with fantasy play, e.g., a first-grade boy who played "sea monster," his arms outflung and his voice growling, as he chased a group of girls. By third grade, stylized gestures—exaggerated stalking motions, screams (which only girls do), and karate kicks—accompany scenes of chasing.

Names like "chase and kiss" mark the sexual meanings of cross-sex chasing, a theme I return to later. The threat of kissing—most often girls threatening to kiss boys—is a rit-ualized form of provocation. Cross-sex chasing among sixth-graders involves elaborate patterns of touch and touch avoidance, which adults see as sexual. The principal told the sixth-graders in the Michigan school that they were not to play "pom-pom," a complicated chasing game, because it entailed "inappropriate touch."

Rituals of Pollution   Cross-sex chasing is sometimes entwined with rituals of pollution, as in "cooties," where specific individuals or groups are treated as contaminating or carrying "germs." Children have rituals for transfering cooties (usually touching someone else and shouting, "You've got cooties!"), for immunization (e.g., writing "CV" for "cootie vaccination" on their arms), and for eliminating cooties (e.g., saying "no gives" or using "cootie catchers" made of folded paper) (described in Knapp & Knapp, 1976). While girls may give cooties to girls, boys do not generally give cooties to one another (Samuelson, 1980).

In cross-sex play, either girls or boys may be defined as having cooties, which they transfer through chasing and touching. Girls give cooties to boys more often than vice versa. In Michigan, one version of cooties is called "girl stain"; the fourth-graders whom Karkau (1973) describes used the phrase "girl touch." "Cootie queens" or "cootie girls" (there are no "kings" or "boys") are female pariahs, the ultimate school untouchables, seen as contaminating not only by virtue of gender, but also through some added stigma such as being overweight or poor.[2] That girls are seen as more polluting than boys is a significant asymmetry, which echoes cross-cultural patterns, although in other cultures female pollution is generally connected to menstruation and not applied to prepubertal girls.

Invasions   Playground invasions are another asymmetric form of borderwork. On a few occasions I saw girls invade and disrupt an all-male game, most memorably a group of tall sixth-grade girls who ran onto the playing field and grabbed a football which was in play. The boys were surprised and frustrated, and, unusual for boys this old, finally tattled to the aide. But in the majority of cases, boys disrupt girls' activities rather than vice versa. Boys grab the ball from girls playing four-square, stick feet into a jumprope and stop an ongoing game, and dash through the area of the bars where girls are taking turns performing, sending the rings flying. Sometimes boys ask to join a girls' game and then, after a short period of seemingly earnest play, disrupt the game. Two second-grade boys begged to "twirl" the jump rope for a group of second-grade girls who had been jumping for some time. The girls agreed, and the boys began to twirl. Soon, without announcement, the boys changed from "seashells, cockle bells" to "hot peppers" (spinning the rope very fast), and tangled the jumper in the rope. The boys ran away laughing.

Boys disrupt girls' play so often that girls have developed almost ritualized responses: they guard their ongoing play, chase boys away, and tattle to the aides. In a playground cycle which enhances sex segregation, aides who try to spot potential trouble before it occurs sometimes shoo boys away from areas where girls are playing. Aides do not anticipate trouble from girls who seek to join groups of boys, with the exception of girls intent on provoking a chase sequence. And indeed, if they seek access to a boys' game, girls usually play with boys in earnest rather than breaking up the game.

A close look at the organization of borderwork—or boundaried interactions between the sexes—shows that the worlds of boys and girls may be separate, but they are not parallel, nor are they equal. The worlds of girls and boys articulate in several asymmetric ways:

1. On the playground, boys control as much as ten times more space than girls, when one adds up the area of large playing fields and compares it with the much smaller areas where girls predominate. Girls, who play closer to the building, are more often watched over and protected by the adult aides.
2. Boys invade all-female games and scenes of play much more than girls invade boys'. This, and boys' greater control of space, correspond with other findings about the organization of gender, and inequality, in our society: compared with men and boys, women and girls take up less space, and their space and talk are more often violated and interrupted (Greif, 1982; Henley, 1977; West & Zimmerman, 1983).
3. Although individual boys are occasionally treated as contaminating (e.g., a third-grade boy who both boys and girls said was "stinky" and "smelled like pee"), girls are more often defined as polluting. This pattern ties to themes that I discuss later: it is more taboo for a boy to play with (as opposed to invade) girls, and girls are more sexually defined than boys.

A look at the boundaries between the separated worlds of girls and boys illuminates within-sex hierarchies of status and control. For example, in the sex-divided seating in the fourth–fifth-grade classroom, several boys recurringly sat near "female space": their desks were at the gender divide in the classroom, and they were more likely than other boys to sit at a predominantly female table in the lunchroom. These boys—two nonbilingual Chicanos and an overweight "loner" boy who was afraid of sports—were at the bottom of the male hierarchy. Gender is sometimes used as a metaphor for male hierarchies; the inferior status of boys at the bottom is conveyed by calling them "girls." Seven boys and one girl were playing basketball. Two younger boys came over and asked to play. While the girl silently stood, fully accepted in the company of players, one of the older boys disparagingly said to the younger boys, "You girls can't play."[3]

In contrast, the girls who more often travel in the boys' world, sitting with groups of boys in the lunchroom or playing basketball, soccer, and baseball with them, are not stigmatized. Some have fairly high status with other girls. The worlds of girls and boys are asymmetrically arranged, and spatial patterns map out interacting forms of inequality.

Heterosexual Meanings

The organization and meanings of gender (the social categories "woman/man," "girl/boy") and of sexuality vary cross-culturally (Ortner & Whitehead, 1981)—and, in our society, across the life course. Harriet Whitehead (1981) observed that in our (western) gender system, and that of many traditional North American Indian cultures, one's choice of a sexual object, occupation, and dress and demeanor are closely associated with gender. However, the "center of gravity" differs in the two gender systems. For Indians, occupational pursuits provide the primary imagery of gender; dress and demeanor are secondary, and sexuality is least important. In our system, at least for adults, the order is reversed: heterosexuality is central to our definitions of "man" and "woman" ("masculinity/femininity") and the relationships that obtain between them, whereas occupation and dress/demeanor are secondary.

Whereas erotic orientation and gender are closely linked in our definitions of adults, we define children as relatively asexual. Activities and dress/demeanor are more important than sexuality in the cultural meanings of "girl" and "boy." Children are less heterosexually defined than adults, and we have nonsexual imagery for relations between girls and boys. However, both children and adults sometimes use heterosexual language—"crushes," "like," "goin' with," "girlfriends," and "boyfriends"—to define cross-sex relationships. This language increases through the years of elementary school; the shift to adolescence consolidates a gender system organized around the institution of heterosexuality.

In everyday life in the schools, heterosexual and romantic meanings infuse some ritualized forms of interaction between groups of boys and girls (e.g., "chase and kiss") and help maintain sex segregation. "Jimmy likes Beth" or "Beth likes Jimmy" is a major form of teasing, which a child risks in choosing to sit by or walk with someone of the other sex. The structure of teasing and children's sparse vocabulary for relationships between girls and boys are evident in the following conversation, which I had with a group of third-grade girls in the lunchroom. Susan asked me what I was doing, and I said I was observing the things children do and play. Nicole volunteered, "I like running, boys chase all the girls. See Tim over there? Judy chases him all around the school. She likes him." Judy, sitting across the table, quickly responded, "I hate him. I like him for a friend." "Tim loves Judy," Nicole said in a loud, singsong voice.

In the younger grades, the culture and lore of girls contain more heterosexual romantic themes than those of boys. In Michigan, the first-grade girls often jumped rope to a rhyme which began: "Down in the valley where the green grass grows, there sat Cindy [name of jumper], as sweet as a rose. She sat, she sat, she sat so sweet. Along came Jason and kissed her on the cheek. First comes love, then comes marriage, then along comes Cindy with a baby carriage." Before a girl took her turn at jumping, the chanters asked her, "Who do you want to be your boyfriend?" The jumper always proffered a name, which was accepted matter-of-factly. In chasing, a girl's kiss carried greater threat than a boy's kiss; "girl touch," when defined as contaminating, had sexual connotations. In short, starting at an early age, girls are more sexually defined than boys.

Through the years of elementary school, and increasing with age, the idiom of heterosexuality helps maintain the gender divide. Cross-sex interactions, especially when children initiate them, are fraught with the risk of being teased about "liking" someone of the other sex. I learned of several close cross-sex friendships, formed and maintained in neighborhoods and church, which went underground during the school day.

By the fifth grade a few children began to affirm, rather than avoid, the charge of having a girlfriend or a boyfriend; they introduced the heterosexual courtship rituals of adolescence. In the lunchroom in the Michigan school, as the tables were forming, a high-status fifth-grade boy called out from his seat at the table: "I want Trish to sit by me." Trish came over, and almost like a king and queen, they sat at the gender divide—a row of girls down the table on her side, a row of boys on his. In this situation, which inverted earlier forms, it was not a loss but a gain in status to publicly choose a companion of the other sex. By affirming his choice, the boy became unteasable (note the familiar asymmetry of heterosexual courtship rituals: the male initiates). This incident signals a temporal shift in arrangements of sex and gender.

Traveling in the World of the Other Sex

Contests, invasions, chasing, and heterosexually defined encounters are based upon and reaffirm boundaries between girls and boys. In another type of cross-sex interaction, individuals (or sometimes pairs) cross gender boundaries, seeking acceptance in a group of the other sex. Nearly all the cases I saw of this were tomboys—girls who played organized sports and frequently sat with boys in the cafeteria or classroom. If these girls were skilled at activities central in the boys' world, especially games like soccer, baseball, and basketball, they were pretty much accepted as participants.

Being a tomboy is a matter of degree. Some girls seek access to boys' groups but are excluded; other girls limit their "crossing" to specific sports. Only a few—such as the tomboy I mentioned earlier, who chose a seat with the boys in the sex-divided fourth–fifth grade—participate fully in the boys' world. That particular girl was skilled at the various organized sports which boys played in different seasons of the year. She was also adept at physical fighting and at using the forms of arguing, insult, teasing, naming, and sports-talk of the boys' subculture. She was the only Black child in her classroom, in a school with only 8 percent Black students; overall that token status, along with unusual athletic and verbal skills, may have contributed to her ability to move back and forth across the gender divide. Her unique position in the children's world was widely recognized in the school. Several times, the teacher said to me, "She thinks she's a boy."

I observed only one boy in the upper grades (a fourth-grader) who regularly played with all-female groups, as opposed to "playing at" girls' games and seeking to disrupt them. He frequently played jump rope and took turns with girls doing tricks on the bars, using the small gestures—for example, a helpful push on the heel of a girl who needed momentum to turn her body around the bar—which mark skillful and earnest participation. Although I never saw him play in other than an earnest spirit, the girls often chased him away from their games, and both girls and boys teased him. The fact that girls seek and have more access to boys'

LEARNING TO FIGHT

GEOFFREY CANADA

On Union Avenue, failure to fight would mean that you would be set upon over and over again. Sometimes for years. Later I would see what the older boys did to Butchie.

Butchie was a "manchild," very big for his age. At thirteen he was the size of a fully grown man. Butchie was a gentle giant. He loved to play with the younger boys and was not particularly athletic. Butchie had one flaw: he would not fight. Everyone picked on him. The older teenagers (fifteen and sixteen) were really hard on him. He was forever being punched in the midsection and chest by the older boys for no reason. (It was against the rules to punch in the face unless it was a "fair fight.")

I don't know what set the older boys off, or why they picked that Saturday morning, but it was decided that Butchie had to be taught a lesson. The older boys felt that Butchie was giving the block a bad reputation. Everyone had to be taught that we didn't tolerate cowards. Suddenly two of them grabbed Butchie. Knowing that something was wrong, that this was not the rough and tumble play we sometimes engaged in, Butchie broke away. Six of the older boys took off after him. Butchie zigzagged between the parked cars, trying desperately to make it to his building and the safety of his apartment. One of the boys cut him off and, kicking and yelling, Butchie was snagged.

By the time the other five boys caught up, Butchie was screaming for his mother. We knew that his mother often drank heavily on the weekends and were not surprised when her window did not open and no one came to his aid. One of the rules of the block was that you were not allowed to cry for your mother. Whatever happened you had to "take it like man." A vicious punch to the stomach and a snarled command, "Shut the fuck up," and Butchie became quiet and stopped struggling. The boys marched him up the block, away from his

apartment. Butchie, head bowed, hands held behind his back, looked like a captured prisoner.

There are about twelve of us younger boys out that morning playing football in the street. When the action started we stopped playing and prepared to escape to our individual apartment buildings. We didn't know if the older boys were after us, too—they were sometimes unpredictable—and we nervously kept one eye on them and one on a clear avenue of escape. As they marched Butchie down the block it became apparent that we were meant to learn from what was going to [happen] to Butchie, that they were really doing this for us.

The older boys took Butchie and "stretched" him. This was accomplished by four boys grabbing Butchie, one on each arm, one on each leg. Then they placed him on the trunk of a car (in the early 1960s the cars were all large) and pulled with all their might until Butchie was stretched out over the back of the car. When Butchie was completely, helplessly exposed, two of the boys began to punch him in his stomach and chest. The beating was savage. Butchie's cries for help seemed only to infuriate them more. I couldn't believe that a human body could take that amount of punishment. When they finished with him, Butchie just collapsed in the fetal position and cried. The older boys walked away talking, as if nothing had happened.

To those of us who watched, the lesson was brutal and unmistakable. No matter who you fought, he could never beat you *that* bad. So it was better to fight even if you couldn't win than to end up being "stretched" for being a coward. We all fought, some with more skill and determination than others, but we all fought. The day my brother John went out to play on the block and had to fight Paul Henry, there was plenty of wild swinging and a couple of blows landed, but they did no real damage. When no one got the better of the other after six or seven minutes, the fight was broken up. John and Paul Henry were made to shake hands and became best of friends in no time.

John was free. He could go outside without fear. I was still trapped. I needed help figuring out what would happen when I went outside. John was not much help to me about how the block worked. He was proud that he could go out and play while we were still stuck in the house. I mentioned something about going downstairs and having Ma come down to watch over me and John laughed at me, called me a baby. He had changed, he had accepted the rules—no getting mothers to fight your battles. His only instructions to me were to fight back, don't let the boys your age hit you without hitting back. Within a week I decided I just couldn't take it, and I went downstairs.

The moment I went outside I began to learn about the structure of the block and its codes of conduct. Each excursion taught me more. The first thing I learned was that John, even though he was just a year older than me, was in a different category than I was. John's peers had some status on the block; my peers were considered too young to have any.

At the top of the pecking order were the young adults in their late teens (seventeen, eighteen, and nineteen). They owned the block; they were the strongest and the toughest. Many of them belonged to a gang called the Disciples. Quite a few had been arrested as part of a police crackdown on gangs in the late fifties and early sixties. Several came out of jail during my first few years on Union Avenue. They often spent large amounts of time in other areas of the Bronx, so they were really absentee rulers.

At this time there were some girls involved in gang activities as well; many of the larger male gangs had female counterparts whose members fought and intimidated other girls. On Union Avenue there was a group of older girls who demanded respect, and received it, from even the toughest boys on the block. Some of these girls were skilled fighters, and boys would say "she can fight like a boy" to indicate that a girl had mastered the more sophisticated techniques of fistfighting. Girls on Union Avenue sometimes found themselves facing the same kind of violence as did boys, but this happened less often. All in all there was less pressure on girls to fight for status, although some did; for girls to fight there usually had to be a major triggering incident.

But status was a major issue for boys on the block. The next category in the pecking order was the one we all referred to as the "older boys," fifteen and sixteen years old. They belonged to a group we sometimes called the Young Disciples, and they were the real rulers of Union Avenue. This was the group that set the rules

of conduct on the block and enforced law and order. They were the ones who had stretched Butchie.

Next were boys nine, ten, and eleven, just learning the rules. While they were allowed to go into the street and play, most of them were not allowed off the block without their mother's permission. My brother John belonged to this group.

The lowest group was those children who could not leave the sidewalk, children too young to have any status at all. I belonged to this group and I hated it. The sidewalk, while it provided plenty of opportunity to play with other children, seemed to me to be the sidelines. The real action happened in the street.

There were few expectations placed on us in terms of fighting, but we were not exempt. There was very little natural animosity among us. We played punchball, tag, and "red light, green light, one-two-three." It was the older boys who caused the problems. Invariably, when the older boys were sitting on the stoop and one of them had a brother or cousin amongst us, it would be he who began the prelude to violence.

I'd been outside for more than a week and thought that I had escaped having to fight anyone because all the boys were my friends. But sure enough, Billy started in on me.

"David, can you beat Geoff?"

David looked at me, then back at Billy. "I don't know."

"What! You can't beat Geoff? I thought you was tough. You scared? I know you ain't scared. You betta not be scared."

I didn't like where this conversation was heading. David was my friend and I didn't know Billy, he was just an older boy who lived in my building. David looked at me again and this time his face changed, he looked threatening, he seemed angry.

"I ain't scared of him."

I was lost. Just ten minutes before, David and I were playing, having a good time. Now he looked like I was his worst enemy. I became scared, scared of David, scared of Billy, scared of Union Avenue. I looked for help to the other boys sitting casually on the stoop. Their faces scared me more. Most of them barely noticed what was going on, the rest were looking half interested. I was most disheartened by the reaction of my brother John. Almost in a state of panic, I looked to him for help. He looked me directly in the eye, shook his head no, then barely perceptibly pointed his chin toward David as if to say, Quit stalling, you know what you have to do. Then he looked away as if this didn't concern him at all.

The other sidewalk boys were the only ones totally caught up in the drama. They knew that their day would also come, and they were trying to learn what they could about me in case they had to fight me tomorrow, or next week, or whenever.

During the time I was sizing up my situation I made a serious error. I showed on my face what was going on in my head. My fear and my confusion were obvious to anyone paying attention. This, I would later learn, was a rookie mistake and could have deadly consequences on the streets.

Billy saw my panic and called to alert the others. "Look at Geoff, he's scared. He's scared of you, David. Go kick his ass."

It was not lost on me that the questioning part of this drama was over. Billy had given David a direct command. I thought I was saved, however, because Billy had cursed. My rationale was that no big boy could use curses at a little boy. My brother would surely step in now and say, "C'mon, Billy, you can't curse at my little brother. After all, he's only seven." Then he would take me upstairs and tell Ma.

When I looked at John again I saw only that his eyes urged me to act, implored me to act. There would be no rescue coming from him. What was worse, the other older boys had become interested when Billy yelled, "Kick his ass," and were now looking toward David and me. In their eyes this was just a little sport, not a real fight, but a momentary distraction that could prove to be slightly more interesting than talking about the Yankees, or the Giants, or their girlfriends. They smiled at my terror. Their smiles seemed to say, "I remember when I was like that. You'll see, it's not so bad."

Thinking on your feet is critical in the ghetto. There was so much to learn and so much of it was so important. It was my brother's reaction that clued me in. I knew John. He was a vicious tease at times, but he loved me. He would never allow me to be harmed and not help or at least go for help. He was telling me I had to go through this alone. I knew I could run upstairs, but what about tomorrow? Was I willing to become a prisoner in my apartment again? And what about how everyone was smiling at me? How was I ever going to play in the street with them if they thought I was such a baby? So I made the decision not to run but to fight.

I decided to maximize the benefits the situation afforded. I said, not quite with the conviction that I'd hoped for, "I'm not afraid of David. He can't beat me. C'mon, David, you wanna fight?"

There was only one problem—I didn't know how to fight. I hadn't seen Dan taking back John's coat, or John's fight with Paul Henry. But a funny thing happened after I challenged David. When I looked back at him, he didn't look quite so confident. He didn't look like he wanted to fight anymore. This gave me courage.

Billy taunted David, "You gonna let him talk to you like that? Go on, kick his ass."

Then Paul Henry chimed in, "Don't be scared, little Geoff. Go git him."

I was surprised. I didn't expect anyone to support me, especially not Paul Henry. But as I would learn

---

worlds than vice versa, and the fact that girls who travel with the other sex are less stigmatized for it, are obvious asymmetries, tied to the asymmetries previously discussed.

Relaxed Cross-Sex Interactions

Relationships between boys and girls are not always marked by strong boundaries, heterosexual definitions, or interacting on the terms and turfs of the other sex. On some occasions girls and boys interact in relatively comfortable ways. Gender is not strongly salient nor explicitly invoked, and girls and boys are not organized into boundaried collectivities. These "with" occasions have been neglected by those studying gender and children's relationships, who have emphasized either the model of separate worlds (with little attention to their articulation) or heterosexual forms of contact.

Occasions when boys and girls interact without strain, when gender wanes rather than waxes in importance, frequently have one or more of the following characteristics:

1. The situations are organized around an absorbing task, such as a group art project or creating a radio show, which encourages cooperation and lessens attention to gender. This pattern accords with other studies finding that cooperative activities reduce group antagonism

later, most of these fights were viewed as sport by the bystanders. You rooted for the favorite or the underdog. Almost everyone had someone to root for them when they fought.

David put up his balled-up fists and said, "Come on." I didn't know how to fight, but I knew how to pretend fight. So I "put up my dukes" and stood like a boxer. We circled one another.

"Come on."

"No, *you* come on."

Luckily for me, David didn't know how to fight either. The older boys called out encouragement to us, but we didn't really know how to throw a punch. At one point we came close enough to one another for me to grab David, and we began to wrestle. I was good at this, having spent many an hour wrestling with my three brothers.

Wrestling wasn't allowed in a "real" fight, but they let us go at it a few moments before they broke us up. The older boys pronounced the fight a tie and made us shake hands and "be friends." They rubbed our heads and said, "You're all right," and then gave us some pointers on how to really fight. We both basked in the glory of their attention. The other sidewalk boys looked at us with envy. We had passed the first test. We were on our way to becoming respected members of Union Avenue.

David and I became good friends. Since we'd had a tie we didn't have to worry about any other older boys making us fight again. The rule was that if you fought an opponent, and could prove it by having witnesses, you didn't have to fight that person again at the command of the older boys. This was important, because everyone, and I mean everyone, had to prove he could beat other boys his age. Union Avenue, like most other inner-city neighborhoods, had a clear pecking order within the groups as well as between them when it came to violence. The order changed some as boys won or lost fights, but by and large the same boys remained at the top. New boys who came on the block had to be placed in the pecking order. If they had no credentials, no one to vouch for their ability, they had to fight different people on the block until it could be ascertained exactly where they fit in. If you refused to fight, you moved to the bottom of the order. If you fought and lost, your status still remained unclear until you'd won a fight. Then you'd be placed somewhere between the person you lost to and the person you beat.

The pecking order was important because it was used to resolve disputes that arose over games, or girls, or money, and also to maintain order and discipline on the block. Although we were not a gang, there were clear rules of conduct, and if you broke those rules there were clear consequences. The ranking system also prevented violence because it gave a way for boys to back down; if everybody knew you couldn't beat someone and you backed down, it was no big deal most of the time.

My "fight" with David placed me on top of the pecking order for boys on the sidewalk. I managed to get through the rest of the summer without having to fight anyone else. I had learned so much about how Union Avenue functioned that I figured I would soon know all I needed about how to survive on the block.

(e.g., Sherif & Sherif, 1953, who studied divisions between boys in a summer camp; and Aronson et al., 1978, who used cooperative activities to lessen racial divisions in a classroom).

2. Gender is less prominent when children are not responsible for the formation of the group. Mixed-sex play is less frequent in games like football, which require the choosing of teams, and more frequent in games like handball or dodgeball, which individuals can join simply by getting into a line or a circle. When adults organize mixed-sex encounters—which they frequently do in the classroom and in physical education periods on the playground—they legitimize cross-sex contact. This removes the risk of being teased for choosing to be with the other sex.

3. There is more extensive and relaxed cross-sex interaction when principles of grouping other than gender are explicitly invoked—for example, counting off to form teams for spelling or kickball, dividing lines by hot lunch or cold lunch, or organizing a work group on the basis of interests or reading ability.

4. Girls and boys may interact more readily in less public and crowded settings. Neighborhood play, depending on demography, is more often sex- and age-integrated than play at school, partly because with fewer numbers, one may have to resort to an array of social categories to

find play partners or to constitute a game. And in less crowded environments there are fewer potential witnesses to "make something of it" if girls and boys play together.

Relaxed interactions between girls and boys often depend on adults to set up and legitimize the contact.[4] Perhaps because of this contingency—and the other, distancing patterns which permeate relations between girls and boys—the easeful moments of interaction rarely build to close friendship. Schofield (1981) makes a similar observation about gender and racial barriers to friendship in a junior high school.

IMPLICATIONS FOR DEVELOPMENT

I have located social relations within an essentially spatial framework, emphasizing the organization of children's play, work, and other activities within specific settings and in one type of institution, the school. In contrast, frameworks of child development rely upon temporal metaphors, using images of growth and transformation over time. Taken alone, both spatial and temporal frameworks have shortcomings; fitted together, they may be mutually correcting.

Those interested in gender and development have relied upon conceptualizations of "sex-role socialization" and "sex differences." Sexuality and gender, I have argued, are more situated and fluid than these individualist and intrinsic models imply. Sex and gender are differently organized and defined across situations, even within the same institution. This situational variation (e.g., in the extent to which an encounter heightens or lessens gender boundaries, or is infused with sexual meanings) shapes and constrains individual behavior. Features which a developmental perspective might attribute to individuals and understand as relatively internal attributes unfolding over time may, in fact, be highly dependent on context. For example, children's avoidance of cross-sex friendship may be attributed to individual gender development in middle childhood. But attention to varied situations may show that this avoidance is contingent on group size, activity, adult behavior, collective meanings, and the risk of being teased.

A focus on social organization and situation draws attention to children's experiences in the present. This helps correct a model like "sex-role socialization," which casts the present under the shadow of the future, or presumed "endpoints" (Speier, 1976). A situated analysis of arrangements of sex and gender among those of different ages may

point to crucial disjunctions in the life course. In the fourth and fifth grades, culturally defined heterosexual rituals ("goin' with") begin to suppress the presence and visibility of other types of interaction between girls and boys, such as nonsexualized and comfortable interaction and traveling in the world of the other sex. As "boyfriend/girlfriend" definitions spread, the fifth-grade tomboy I described had to work to sustain "buddy" relationships with boys. Adult women who were tomboys often speak of early adolescence as a painful time when they were pushed away from participation in boys' activities. Other adult women speak of the loss of intense, even erotic ties with other girls when they entered puberty and the rituals of dating, that is, when they became absorbed into the situation of heterosexuality (Rich, 1980). When Lever (1976) describes best-friend relationships among fifth-grade girls as preparation for dating, she imposes heterosexual ideologies onto a present which should be understood on its own terms.

As heterosexual encounters assume more importance, they may alter relations in same-sex groups. For example, Schofield (1981) reports that for sixth- and seventh-grade children in a middle school, the popularity of girls with other girls was affected by their popularity with boys, while boys' status with other boys did not depend on their relations with girls. This is an asymmetry familiar from the adult world; men's relationships with one another are defined through varied activities (occupations, sports), while relationships among women—and their public status—are more influenced by their connections to individual men.

A full understanding of gender and social relations should encompass cross-sex as well as within-sex interactions. "Borderwork" helps maintain separate, gender-linked subcultures, which, as those interested in development have begun to suggest, may result in different milieux for learning. Daniel Maltz and Ruth Borker (1983), for example, argue that because of different interactions within girls' and boys' groups, the sexes learn different rules for creating and interpreting friendly conversation, rules which carry into adulthood and help account for miscommunication between men and women. Carol Gilligan (1982) fits research on the different worlds of girls and boys into a theory of sex differences in moral development. Girls develop a style of reasoning, she argues, which is more personal and relational; boys develop a style which is more positional, based on separateness. Eleanor Maccoby (1982), also following the insight that because of sex segregation, girls and boys grow up in different environments, suggests implications for gender-differentiated prosocial and antisocial behavior.

This separate-worlds approach, as I have illustrated, also has limitations. The occasions when the sexes are together should also be studied, and understood as contexts for experience and learning. For example, asymmetries in cross-sex relationships convey a series of messages: that boys are more entitled to space and to the nonreciprocal right of interrupting or invading the activities of the other sex; that girls are more in need of adult protection, lower in status, more defined by sexuality, and may even be polluting. Different types of cross-sex interaction—relaxed, boundaried, sexualized, or taking place on the terms of the other sex—provide different contexts for development.

By mapping the array of relationships between and within the sexes, one adds complexity to the overly static and dichotomous imagery of separate worlds. Individual experiences vary, with implications for development. Some children prefer same-sex groupings; some are more likely to cross the gender boundary and participate in the world of the other sex; some children (e.g., girls and boys who frequently play "chase and kiss") invoke heterosexual meanings, while others avoid them.

Finally, after charting the terrain of relationships, one can trace their development over time. For example, age variation in the content and form of borderwork, or of cross- and same-sex touch, may be related to differing cog-nitive, social, emotional, or physical capacities, as well as to age-associated cultural forms. I earlier mentioned temporal shifts in the organization of cross-sex chasing, from mixing with fantasy play in the early grades to more elaborately ritualized and sexualized forms by the sixth grade. There also appear to be temporal changes in same- and cross-sex touch. In kindergarten, girls and boys touch one another more freely than in fourth grade, when children avoid relaxed cross-sex touch and instead use pokes, pushes, and other forms of mock violence, even when the touch clearly expresses affection. This touch taboo is obviously related to the risk of seeming to *like* someone of the other sex. In fourth grade, same-sex touch begins to signal sexual meanings among boys as well as between boys and girls. Younger boys touch one another freely in cuddling (arm around shoulder) as well as mock-violence ways. By fourth grade, when homophobic taunts like "fag" become more common among boys, cuddling touch begins to disappear for boys, but less for girls.

Overall, I am calling for more complexity in our conceptualizations of gender and of children's social relationships. Our challenge is to retain the temporal sweep, looking at individual and group lives as they unfold over time, while also attending to social structure and context and to the full variety of experiences in the present.

ACKNOWLEDGMENTS

I would like to thank Jane Atkinson, Nancy Chodorow, Arlene Daniels, Peter Lyman, Zick Rubin, Malcolm Spector, Avril Thorne, and Margery Wolf for comments on an earlier version of this paper. Conversations with Zella Luria enriched this work.

NOTES

1. I am grateful to Frederick Erickson for suggesting the relevance of Barth's analysis.

2. Sue Samuelson (1980) reports that in a racially mixed playground in Fresno, California, Mexican-American but not Anglo children gave cooties. Racial as well as sexual inequality may be expressed through these forms.

3. This incident was recorded by Margaret Blume, who, for an undergraduate research project in 1982, observed in the California school where I earlier did fieldwork. Her observations and insights enhanced my own, and I would like to thank her for letting me cite this excerpt.

4. Note that in daily school life., depending on the individual and the situation, teachers and aides sometimes lessened and at other times heightened sex segregation.

REFERENCES

Aronson, E., et al. 1978. *The Jigsaw Classroom.* Beverly Hills, Calif.: Sage.

Barth, F., ed. 1969. *Ethnic Groups and Boundaries.* Boston: Little, Brown.

Borman, K. M. 1979. "Children's interactions in playgrounds," *Theory into Practice* 18:251–57.

Eder, D., & Hallinan, M. T. 1978. "Sex differences in children's friendships." *American Sociological Review* 43:237–50.

Finnan, C. R. 1982. "The ethnography of children's spontaneous play." In G. Spindler, ed., *Doing the Ethnography of Schooling,* pp. 358–80. New York: Holt, Rinehart & Winston.

Foot, H. C.; Chapman, A. J.; & Smith, J. R. 1980. "Introduction." *Friendship and Social Relations in Children,* pp. 1–14. New York: Wiley.

Gilligan, C. 1982. *In a Different Voice: Psychological Theory and Women's Development.* Cambridge: Harvard University Press.

Glaser, B. G., & Strauss, A. L. 1967. *The Discovery of Grounded Theory.* Chicago: Aldine.

Goffman, E. 1977. "The arrangement between the sexes." *Theory and Society* 4:301–36.

Goodwin, M. H. 1980. "Directive-response speech sequences in girls' and boys' task activities." In S. McConnell-Ginet, R. Borker, & N. Furman, eds., *Women and Language in Literature and Society,* pp. 157–73. New York: Praeger.

Greif, E. B. 1982. "Sex differences in parent–child conversations." *Women's Studies International Quarterly* 3:253–58.

Henley, N. 1977. *Body Politics: Power, Sex, and Nonverbal Communication.* Englewood Cliffs, N.J.: Prentice-Hall.

Karkau, K. 1973. *Sexism in the Fourth Grade.* Pittsburgh: KNOW, Inc. (pamphlet).

Katz, J. 1983. "A theory of qualitative methodology: The social system of analytic fieldwork." In R. M. Emerson, ed., *Contemporary Field Research,* pp. 127–48. Boston: Little, Brown.

Knapp, M., & Knapp, H. 1976. *One Potato, Two Potato: The Secret Education of American Children.* New York: W. W. Norton.

Lever, J. 1976. "Sex differences in the games children play." *Social Problems* 23:478–87.

Maccoby, E. 1982. "Social groupings in childhood: Their relationship to prosocial and antisocial behavior in boys and girls." Paper presented at conference on The Development of Prosocial and Antisocial Behavior, Voss, Norway.

Maccoby, E., & Jacklin, C. 1974. *The Psychology of Sex Differences.* Stanford, Calif.: Stanford University Press.

Maltz, D. N., & Borker, R. A. 1983. "A cultural approach to male–female miscommunication." In J. J. Gumperz, ed., *Language and Social Identity,* pp. 195–216. New York: Cambridge University Press.

McRobbie, A., & Garber, J. 1975. "Girls and subcultures." In S. Hall & T. Jefferson, eds., *Resistance through Rituals,* pp. 209–23. London: Hutchinson.

Ortner, S. B., & Whitehead, H. 1981. *Sexual Meanings.* New York: Cambridge University Press.

Parrott, S. 1972. "Games children play: Ethnography of a second-grade recess." In J. P. Spradley & D. W. McCurdy, eds., *The Cultural Experience,* pp. 206–19. Chicago: Science Research Associates.

Rich, A. 1980. "Compulsory heterosexuality and lesbian existence." *Signs,* 5:631–60.

Samuelson, S. 1980. "The cooties complex." *Western Folklore* 39:198–210.

Savin-Williams, R. C. 1976. "An ethological study of dominance formation and maintenance in a group of human adolescents." *Child Development* 47:972–79.

Schofield, J. W. 1981. "Complementary and conflicting identities: Images and interaction in an interracial school." In S. R. Asher & J. M. Gottman, eds., *The Development of Children's Friendships,* pp. 53–90. New York: Cambridge University Press.

Sherif, M., & Sherif, C. 1953. *Groups in Harmony and Tension.* New York: Harper.

Sluckin, A. 1981. *Growing Up in the Playground.* London: Routledge & Kegan Paul.

Speier, M. 1976. "The adult ideological viewpoint in studies of childhood." In A. Skolnick, ed., *Rethinking Childhood,* pp. 168–86. Boston: Little, Brown.

Sutton-Smith, B. 1971. "A syntax for play and games." In R. E. Herron and B. Sutton-Smith, eds., *Child's Play,* pp. 298–307. New York: Wiley.

Unger, R. K. 1979. "Toward a redefinition of sex and gender." *American Psychologist* 34:1085–94.

Waldrop, M. F., & Halverson, C. F. 1975. "Intensive and extensive peer behavior: Longitudinal and cross-sectional analysis." *Child Development* 46:19–26.

West, C., & Zimmerman, D. H. 1983. "Small insults: A study of interruptions in cross-sex conversations between unacquainted persons." In B. Thorne, C. Kramarae, & N. Henley, eds., *Language, gender, and society.* Rowley, Mass.: Newbury House.

Whitehead, H. 1981. "The bow and the burden strap: A new look at institutionalized homosexuality in Native America." In S. B. Ortner & H. Whitehead, eds., *Sexual Meanings,* pp. 80–115. New York: Cambridge University Press.

Women's Psychological Development:
Implications for Psychotherapy*

CAROL GILLIGAN

REVISION

. . . I am in a room filled with thirteen-year-old girls—the eighth grade of the Laurel School in Cleveland. Portraits of women hang on the walls, looking down decorously at the sprawl of girls, backpacks, sweaters. The five-year study of girls' development which these girls have been part of has ended, and I want to know how they want to be involved, now that we are writing about this work and presenting it in public.[1] A consensus silently forms and Zoe speaks: "We want you to tell them everything we said, and we want our names in the book." We begin to talk about the details, and Paula raises her hand. "When we were in fourth grade, we were stupid," she says. I say it would never have occurred to me to use the word "stupid" to describe them as fourth graders, since what impressed me most when they were nine was how much they knew. "I mean," Paula corrects herself, "when we were in fourth grade, we were honest."

Adrienne Rich (1979) writes about re-vision as an act of survival for women:

> Until we can understand the assumptions in which we are drenched we cannot know ourselves. And this drive to self-knowledge, for women, is more than a search for identity: it is part of our refusal of the self-destructiveness of male-dominated society. (p. 35)

Writing as revision—the subject of Rich's essay—becomes an act of political resistance, offering writers in particular "the challenge and promise of a whole new psychic geography to be explored."

But an exploration of the landscape of women's psychology reveals a resistance of a different sort: a revision which covers over the world of girls' childhood, as girls, coming of age, name the relational life they have lived, often most intensely with their mothers, as "false," or "illogical," or "stupid." This act of revision washes away the grounds of girls' feelings and thoughts and undermines the transformatory potential which lies in women's development by leaving girls-turning-into-women with the sense that their feelings are groundless, their thoughts are about nothing real, what they experienced never happened, or at the time they could not understand it.

As girls at adolescence revise the story of their childhood, however, they draw attention to a relational crisis which is at the center of women's development—a crisis which has generally been seen retrospectively.[2] In conversations between girls and women, this relational struggle tends to stir when the subject turns to knowing and not knowing. I begin with examples taken from different school settings. . . .

* * *

It is early in the morning in the middle of winter, and I am sitting with Sheila in a quiet room in the coeducational school she is attending. Outside the window, light spreads across fields of snow. Inside it is dim; we have lit a lamp and I begin with my first question. "Looking back over the past year, what stands out for you?" It is the third year of the study, and Sheila, now sixteen, says that all her relationships

Carol Gilligan. "Women's Psychological Development: Implications for Psychotherapy" from *Women, Girls, & Psychotherapy: Reframing Resistance,* edited by Carol Gilligan, Annie G. Rogers, and Deborah L. Tolman. Copyright © 1991 by The Haworth Press, Inc. Reprinted with the permission of the publishers.

*See acknowledgments at end of reading.

have changed. They "used to be stable and long-lasting, and they are very unstable now." She dates this upheaval to the betrayal of a confidence by a girl she had thought her best friend. Since then, she has "gotten very close and in insane arguments with people, and so relationships go to more extremes: hot and extremely cold. . . . I have come together and grown apart with a lot of people."

Reflecting on these changes, Sheila says that she does not "really like myself enough to look out for myself." Stirred by the sadness of this statement, I ask, "Do you really feel that way?" She says, "Yeah. I mean I do look out for myself, but I care about other people, I think, more than I care about myself. I don't know." And with this string of self-portraying statements—"I mean I do . . . but I care . . . I think . . . I care . . . I don't know"— Sheila unravels a relational crisis which leaves her feeling disconnected from others, out of touch with the world, and essentially all alone.

Asked about a time when she felt down on herself, Sheila says, "the last five years"—since she was eleven. And she has developed an intricate strategy for protection, taking herself out of relationship for the sake of "relationships" with people whom she feels do not know or value her. Lori Stern writes about Sheila as exemplifying girls' puzzling tendency to disavow themselves (see Gilligan, Rogers, & Tolman, 1991). Extending Stern's analysis, I wish to focus on Sheila's experience of relational impasse—the logic of which Sheila lays out clearly in the course of the following dialogue between us. Sheila describes an internal conversation between a voice which asks her, "What do you want in relationships?" and another voice which essentially cuts off the question and functions as a kind of internalized backseat driver. I begin with this voice:

SHEILA: There is always that little part jumping up in the back saying, "Hey me, hey me, you are not worth-while."

CAROL: And why not?

SHEILA: Because people have shown it. Because my relationships have proven that.

CAROL: How can they show that? How can other people know?

SHEILA: Other people say, "It has to be true because you are stupid. You don't know it yourself, you are not even worthwhile to know the truth." Other people must know it.

CAROL: Do you believe that?

SHEILA: In a way.

CAROL: And in another way?

SHEILA: In another way, I think I must be smarter because I haven't let them in.

CAROL: Ah, so if you haven't let them in, then they can't know.

SHEILA: I am safe, right?

CAROL: But if you let them in all the way?

SHEILA: Then it's not safe. Then if I do something, then I know it's me.

CAROL: I see. This way you could always say they don't know the real you.

SHEILA: Uh-huh. Sane, isn't it?

CAROL: It's a very good hedge. But at the cost [of what you have said you want]. It precludes . . . what you have called "honesty in relationships."

As I question the seemingly unquestionable voice which Sheila heeds but does not believe or agree with, Sheila describes her feelings of helplessness in the face of others whom she has in fact outsmarted, keeping herself safe but at the cost of sacrificing the relationships she wanted.

The previous year, Sheila had created a powerful image of relational crisis in describing her relationship with her boyfriend. Her striking and witty description of standing helplessly in a relationship which is sinking captures her own situation and also the feelings of other girls and women who, like Sheila, are reluctant to say what they clearly know is happening:

> It is like two people standing in a boat that they both know is sinking. I don't want to say anything to you because it will upset you, and you don't want to say anything to me because it will upset you. And we are both standing here in water up to about our ankles, watching it rise, and I don't want to say anything to you, you know.

Girls often use the phrase "I don't know" to cover knowledge which they believe may be dangerous, and the phrase "you know," correspondingly to discover what it is possible for them to know and still be connected with other people.

* * *

I am sitting with Rosie in the teachers' lounge—a small room on the second floor of her school.[3] A coffee pot, unplugged, sits on the wooden desk, and wooden crosspanes mark off the daylight into even squares. Rosie is fifteen, and she says, "I am confused." She knows the disparities between the way she is and the way her mother wants to see her ("as close to the perfect child") and she also knows the differences between the way she sees her mother and the way her mother wants to be seen by Rosie. Caught between viewpoints, she becomes confused in describing herself:

> When I am describing myself, I am confused. Just really trying to sort everything out and figure out what exactly my viewpoints are. Putting things in order and deciding how to think about things.

Rosie knows she is not the perfect girl whom her ambitious and successful Latina mother imagines—the girl who "gets straight A's and has a social life but still gets home exactly on the dot, on time, and does everything her parents say, and keeps her room neat." I ask, "Are there girls like that?" Rosie says, "Perhaps, saints." "Do saints have sex," I wonder aloud, thinking of Rosie, whose mother has just discovered that she is having sex with her boyfriend. And Rosie begins, "I don't know," but then fills in what has been her solution: "If they want, as long as they don't get caught, as long as nobody knows."

Yet Rosie intensely wants to be known by her mother. Once her mother knows about her sexuality, Rosie says, "I hunted her down and made her talk to me, and it wasn't like a battle or anything. I just wanted to see what she had to say." But Rosie's viewpoints are so radically disruptive of the order of her mother's household that Rosie may wonder whether, by changing her own viewpoint or perhaps arranging things differently, she might be able to repair what otherwise seems an irreparable division: between staying in touch with herself, thereby knowing what she is seeing and feeling ("I looked at her little study and bedroom, and they are a mess too") and staying in connection with her mother's way of seeing herself and Rosie. "So," Rosie concludes, "I don't know."

A PERSISTENT OBSERVATION

Beginning in the nineteenth century, psychiatrists and psychologists have consistently marked adolescence as a particularly difficult time in women's development—a time when girls "are more liable to suffer" (Henry Maudsley, 1879, cited in Showalter, 1985, p. 130). And among the girls who suffer in adolescence are those who seem most psychologically vital. Elaine Showalter quotes the following passage from Josef Breuer as illustrative:

Adolescents who are later to become hysterical are for the most part lively, gifted, and full of intellectual interests before they fall ill. Their energy of will is often remarkable. They include girls who get out of bed at night so as secretly to carry out some study that their parents have forbidden for fear of their overworking. The capacity for forming sound judgments is certainly not more abundant in them than in other people; but it is rare to find in them simple, dull intellectual inertia or stupidity. (p. 158)

Michelle Fine (1986), studying high school dropouts at the end of the twentieth century, notes that the girls who drop out of inner-city schools—at the time they drop out—are among the least depressed and the brightest. Lively, intelligent, and willful girls at both ends of the century and the social class spectrum thus find themselves in trouble at adolescence.

Anne Petersen (1988), reviewing the literature on adolescence, pulls together a series of findings which provide further evidence that girls are likely to experience psychological problems at this time. Adolescence witnesses a marked increase in episodes of depression, eating disorders, poor body image, suicidal thoughts and gestures, and a fall in girls' sense of self-worth. Petersen's review extends the impressions of clinicians across the century that girls at adolescence experience a kind of psychic constraint or narrowing (Freud, 1905, 1933; Horney, 1926; Miller, 1984; Thompson, 1964) and suffer from a range of depressive symptoms, dissociative processes, and "as if" phenomena (Demitrack et al., 1990; Deutsch, 1944; Rutter, 1986).

Epidemiological studies offer further evidence. Elder and Caspi (1990) report that when families are under stress—whether from marital conflict, economic hardship, or fathers going off to war—the children who are most psychologically at risk are boys in childhood and girls at adolescence. Block (1990) reports a sudden drop in girls' resiliency around the age of eleven, with no corresponding finding for boys. Seligman (1991) finds that "girls, at least up to puberty, are more noticeably optimistic than boys," (p. 125) and concludes that "whatever causes the huge difference in depression in adulthood, with women twice as vulnerable as men, it does not have its roots in childhood. Something must happen at or shortly after puberty that causes a flip-flop—and hits girls very hard indeed" (pp. 149–150). And a recent national survey (Greenberg-Lake Analysis Group, 1991) finds that white girls tend to experience a drop in feelings of self-worth around the age of eleven, Latinas experience a more precipitous drop a few years later—around the beginning of high school—and black girls tend to sustain their feelings of self-worth but at the expense, perhaps, of dissociating themselves from school and disagreeing publicly with their teachers.

Taken together, this evidence suggests that girls face a psychological crisis at the time of adolescence—a crisis to which some girls respond by devaluing themselves and feeling themselves to be worthless, while others disagree publicly and dissociate themselves from institutions which devalue them—in this case, the schools. Both solutions, however, are costly for girls. Yet despite this remarkable convergence of clinical observation, developmental findings, and epidemiological data, pointing repeatedly to a striking asymmetry between girls' and boys' development—and one which has clear implications for preventing suffering and fostering development—this persistent observation of difference has, until recently, remained unexplored and unexplained theoretically (see Brown & Gilligan, 1990b; Gilligan, 1990a; Gilligan, Brown, & Rogers, 1990; Rogers, 1990).

GIRLS

Sounds, touching memory, filtering through theory, collecting, like water slowly filling a basin and then suddenly overflowing or rain falling steadily onto the afternoon streets of childhood—girls' voices, shouting, screaming, whispering, speaking, singing, running up and down the octaves of feelings. And the silence. Faces calm, eyes steady, ears open, girls sitting in a circle and then suddenly rising—like a flock of birds. Taking off and then settling, as if by prearrangement. And yet, nothing has been said, nothing is spoken. Only girls' faces and bodies taking in, registering the tides of daily living, following the drifts of thoughts and feelings, picking up the currents of relationship. I wade in.

It is Tuesday afternoon in the beginning of November—just after Halloween. The Theater, Writing, and Outing Club is meeting for the second year—part of a project designed by three women to learn from girls about girls' experience in the time when childhood turns into adolescence and to offer girls in return our help in sustaining and strengthening their voices, their resistance, their courage and their relationships.[4] Ten girls, ages ten and eleven—three African-American, five European-American, one Asian-American, one with a parent from India—and three women (Annie Rogers and me—European-American psychologists—and Normi Noel, a Canadian-born actor,

theater director, and voice teacher) stream into the science room of the public school which the girls are attending. The girls have decided this year to teach us what they know.

Two girls stand side by side in the center of the clearing we have created. Two other girls—"their thoughts"—stand behind them. The drama begins. One girl says that she wants to play with the other; the other clearly does not want to. As the two girls face into this relational impasse, their "thoughts" articulate the stream of their consciousness—a brilliant rendering of each girl's thoughts and feelings in response to what is happening between them. Finally, the thoughts take over, and speaking now directly to one another, set into motion feelings and thoughts which initially seemed fixed, unchangeable and settled, and in doing so begin to work out the relational problem.

What girls know about relationships and feelings unfolded steadily through our weekly meetings in the second year of the group. The immediate grasp of psychological processes, the keeping of a watchful eye and open ear constantly tuned to the relational surround which we had observed in girls and heard in interview settings (Brown & Gilligan, 1990b; Gilligan, Brown, & Rogers, 1990), now was dramatized directly for us by girls who seemed to want to leave no question in our minds about the strength of their voices and the depths of their knowing and the intensity of their desire for honest relationships between us. The week Normi introduced neutral masks from Greek theater by demonstrating how a face can mask feelings, each girl, going around one by one in a circle, turned her face into a mask and then named the feelings in the mask and the feelings which the mask was hiding. The feelings masked were feeling "ordinary, nothing special" (covered over by a mask that was "snooty") and feeling angry, not wanting to be with someone, hating someone, being bored (covered over by masks that were "nice," "smiling" and "interested"). "But Normi," eleven-year-old Joan says at the end of the exercise, "people always mask their feelings."

Girls' facility in turning their faces into the faces of nice, smiling, and interested girls was coupled by their ear for false voices—especially the false voices of women in false relationships. On Halloween, when Annie and I brought pieces of costumes, including angel wings for "someone too good to be true," the girls, putting on the wings, instantly raised their voices to the high-pitched breathiness of good-woman conversation, dramatizing both the persona of the too-good-to-be-true woman and the mechanism of disconnection—the use of voice to cover rather than to convey thoughts and feelings and thus to close rather than to open a channel of connection between people. Separating their voices from the well of feelings and thoughts which lies deep in the body, girls did precise imitations of women's greeting rituals and social gestures and in doing so revealed how well they know the timbre and pitch of false female friendships.

Daily, girls take in evidence from the human world around them—the world which is open for psychological observation all day long, every day, "for free." And in this way, girls often see what is not supposed to be seen and hear what supposedly was unspoken. Like anthropologists, they pick up the culture; like sociologists, they observe race, class and sex differences; like psychologists, they come to know what is happening beneath the surface; like naturalists, they collect their observations, laying them out, sorting them out, discussing them between themselves in an ongoing conversation about relationships and people which goes on, on and off, for much of the day, every day. . . . This relational capacity may well underlie the psychological resiliency which girls show throughout childhood—an ability to tune themselves into the relational world, to connect with different people. . . .

It was surprising to discover the readiness with which younger girls—seven- and eight-year-olds—tell people how they feel, mark relational violations, and openly respond to what is happening in relationships, even when their response leads them to experience painful feelings or cause others to be upset.[5] This relational honesty is vividly caught in Lyn Mikel Brown's (1989) example of Diane, an eight-year-old whistle-blower in the relational world. When Diane is asked about a time when someone was not being listened to, she speaks of her experience at dinner when her brother and sister interrupt her and "steal [her] mother's attention." Diane's solution is to bring a whistle to dinner and to blow the whistle when she is interrupted. Mother, brother, and sister, she reports, suddenly stopped talking and turned to her, at which point she said, "in a normal voice, 'that's much nicer.' " Karin, her classmate, walks out of the room on the second day when the teacher ignores her hand and calls on others "to do all the hard problems." Karin (see Brown, 1989; Brown & Gilligan, 1990b) knows that people seeing her in the hall will think that she is in trouble, but she also knows "I wasn't in trouble. I just couldn't take it. So I guess I just left." Asked if her teacher knows why she left, Karin makes a fine distinction between knowing and listening, saying "She wouldn't listen to me, but I told her, so I guess she knows."

Girls' willingness to voice painful relational realities is rawly evident as eight-year-old Jesse, in Brown's description (see Gilligan, Rogers, & Tolman, 1991) tells of the time when she went to play with a friend and the friend had another friend over and they would not play with Jesse. Jesse told her friend that she wasn't having any fun "just sitting there" and that she would go home if they did not play with her, at which point her friend, she reports, said "Just go home." In contrast, Tanya, at thirteen, reveals the treachery which flows from not speaking about painful relational realities. She and another friend backed out of a plan to go to camp with a third girl who was, Tanya says, "supposedly my best friend." When the girl discovers what has happened and asks if she can go to the other camp with them, Tanya says to her, "If you want to; it's up to you," while being perfectly clear that "I didn't want her to come." Tanya feels trapped because "I can't say so. . . . I can't say anything to her. Because she'll be hurt, so I have no idea what to do."

Victoria, at eleven, in the face of such relational treachery, opts for radical isolation—"independence from everyone." Describing her withdrawal from relationships in an effort to stay with her own experience, she is unequivocal in her judgment that what she is doing is harmful: "I try to build, it's kind of bad really to do it, but I try to build a little shield."

* * *

Learning from girls what girls are doing at the time they reach adolescence, I mark the places that are both familiar to me and surprising. And notice the sensations which bring back memories, like the feeling of moving without hesitation and the sound of a voice speaking directly without qualification—the open sounds of voices coming directly from the center of girls' bodies. Picking up from girls the feeling of moving freely in a girl's body, I find myself running with girls as I remember running in childhood.

And listening to girls' voices, I also begin to listen with girls to the voices which they are taking in. Opening their ears to the world, listening in, eavesdropping on the daily conversations, girls take in voices which silence their relational knowledge. And as their experience and their bodies change with adolescence, girls are more apt to discount the experiences of their childhood or to place a cover over their childhood world so that it remains intact. Yet, closing the door on their childhood, girls are in danger of knocking out what are in effect the T-cells of their psychological immune system—their seemingly effortless ability to tune into the relational world. Voices which intentionally or unintentionally interfere with girls' knowing, or encourage girls to silence themselves, keep girls from picking up or bringing out into the open a series of relational violations which they are acutely keyed into, such as not being listened to, being ignored, being left out, being insulted, being criticized, being spoken about meanly, being humiliated or made fun of, being whispered about, being talked about behind one's back, being betrayed by a friend, or being physically overpowered or hurt.

Tanya, at sixteen, writes a letter to Lyn Mikel Brown—the director of the Harvard-Laurel Project—about her feelings in response to a paper which Lyn and I had written (a paper which she and Lyn had discussed together at some length) (see Brown & Gilligan, 1990a, 1990b). She speaks of "a voice inside" her which "has been muffled." She explains, "The voice that stands up for what I believe in has been buried deep inside of me." Tanya wants to be in honest relationship with people. And yet, taking in what she is hearing about perfect girls whom people seem to love and admire, Tanya finds herself paying attention to voices which impede her relational desires. "I do not want the image of a 'perfect girl' to hinder myself from being a truly effective human being," she writes. "Yet, I still want to be nice, and I never want to cause any problem." . . .

"Cover up," girls are told as they reach adolescence, daily, in innumerable ways. Cover your body, cover your feelings, cover your relationships, cover your knowing, cover your voice, and perhaps above all, cover desire (see also Debold & Tolman, 1991; Gilligan, Rogers, & Tolman, 1991). And the wall that keeps memory from seeping through these covers may be the wall with the sign which labels body, feelings, relationships, knowing, voice, and desire as bad.

A THEORY OF DEVELOPMENT

If psychological health consists, most simply, of staying in relationship with oneself, with others, and with the world, then psychological problems signify relational crises: losing touch with one's thoughts and feelings, being isolated from others, cut off from reality. The zen of development which makes human growth such a fascinating journey is that relationships, which are the channels of growth, are also the avenues through which people are psychically wounded. Vulnerability—the opening to experience which is at the heart of development—thus always carries with it the risk of being seriously hurt or diminished, and this play of opening and closing, embodiment and disembodiment, is reflected in the two meanings of the word "courage" (see Rogers, 1990).

The evidence that boys are more likely than girls to suffer psychologically in early childhood whereas girls are more at risk for developing psychological difficulties in adolescence calls for explanation and implies a revision—a new way of speaking about psychological development. This difference, I will suggest, also contains a hope for transformation.

Learning from girls about the relational crisis which girls experience as they approach adolescence—a place where development seems impassable—I offer as a working thesis that adolescence is a comparable time in women's psychological development to early childhood for men. It precipitates a relational crisis which poses an impasse in psychological development, a place where for the sake of relationship (with other people and with the world), one must take oneself out of relationship. Because this separation of self from relationship is psychologically untenable and also essentially confusing (if one is not in one's relationships, then the word "relationships" loses meaning), this division must be resisted and some compromise arrived at.

Freud (1899/1900) suggested as much for boys when he spoke about the "oedipus complex" as a turning point in boys' early childhood and also as the foundation for neurotic suffering and for civilization. The pressure girls are under as they reach adolescence and girls' experience of severe relational crisis similarly marks a turning point or watershed in girls' development. But girls' relationship to the culture is different, and also girls at adolescence are at a very different point in their own development than boys in early childhood—with far more experience of relationships and also perhaps with less incentive to give up relationship as the cost, ironically, of entering society. Consequently, women's psychological development—as others have observed (see Miller, 1986)—is profoundly transformational.

The relational crisis of boys' early childhood and of girls' adolescence is marked by a struggle to stay in relationship—a healthy resistance to disconnections which are psychologically wounding (from the body, from feelings, from relationships, from reality). This struggle takes a variety of forms, but at its center is a resistance to loss—to giving up the reality of relationships for idealizations or, as it is sometimes called, identifications. As young boys are pressured to take on images of heroes, or superheroes, as the grail which informs their quest to inherit their birthright or their manhood, so girls are pressed at adolescence to take on images of perfection as the model of the pure or perfectly good woman: the woman whom everyone will promote and value and want to be with (see Gilligan, 1990a; Brown & Gilligan, 1990b; Jack, 1991).

Children's healthy resistance to disconnection—the intense human desire for relationship which now is generally taken as foundational of psychic life—thus tends to lead children into a political struggle. Boys in early childhood resist leaving the comforts and pleasures, as well as the discomforts and pains, of their relational life: They want to stay with the people who have been with them. And girls at adolescence resist leaving the rich relational tapestry of their childhood. This resistance calls into question the prevailing order of social relationships and calls forth counter-pressures to enforce that order in the name, currently, of psychological health, as well as for the sake of civilization.

Thus at the time of early childhood for boys, when masculinity seems in question, and in early adolescence for girls, when femininity seems on the line, a healthy resistance to disconnections which turns into a political struggle comes under pressure to turn into a psychological resistance—that is, a resistance to knowing what is happening and an impulse to cover the struggle.

Here, the differences observed over the century between the times of seemingly heightened vulnerability or openness to growth and wounding in boys' and girls' lives contain a promise of transformation. If girls can sustain in adolescence a resistance which is more easily overwhelmed in boys' childhood, then women's psychological development will change the prevailing order of relationships. Compared with boys, whose desires for relationship, although strongly felt, tend to be less articulate, more inchoate, more laced with early loss and terror, girls' desires for relationship, leavened through years of childhood experience, tend to be hardier, more easily spoken, better known, more finely textured or differentiated, and consequently less frightening, although no less painful. Girls' healthy resistance to disconnection, which springs up at the edge of adolescence as girls approach a culture of relationships which has been built largely by men, thus calls into question what has been accepted as the canonical story of human development: the story which takes separation for granted, the story which seems logical, the story which rejects the possibility of honest or genuine relationship. . . .

IMPLICATIONS FOR PSYCHOTHERAPY

In my dream, I am wearing my glasses over my contact lenses. I am literally seeing double, although I do not realize this in the dream. I sit with a woman and remorsefully realize that I have wanted too much in the relationship—that I cannot possibly have what I want. She says, "I cannot offer you myself," and the logic of her statement feels overwhelming. And then—still in the dream—I take off my glasses and suddenly say, "No," because I suddenly know that this is not it—this remorseful wanting of what cannot be given. "No," I say, and then go on to speak the truth of my experience in the relationship. With this, my head suddenly swivels, like an owl's head turning 180 degrees around, and I feel—in the dream—a strong jolt, like a shock, and overwhelmingly dizzy, as if I am seeing double. Only after I wake up do I realize that when I felt dizzy was when I was seeing straight, and that in the dream when I felt I was seeing clearly, I was literally seeing double—wearing two sets of lenses, which made it impossible to see straight.

I dream this dream on the first night of the second year of the Theater, Writing, and Outing Club, which Annie Rogers, Normi Noel and I have formed with eight girls from the Atrium School. We are in New Hampshire, near Mount Sunapee, for the weekend. And I realize the next morning that this work with girls is seeping deeply into my dream life, leading me to re-vision—to a new seeing and naming of my experience; taking me back to the time of adolescence, the time, I realize, when straight-seeing became shocking, surprising really in the manner Nina describes in speaking about the girl in her story; angering and yet, at bottom, somehow more sorrowful. The time when relationships flowed—albeit through some rocky places; the time before voice and vision doubled.

Adolescent girls offer a key to understanding women's psychological development. And they offer some suggestions for preventing and treating psychological suffering. To catch girls in the moment of their revision—at the time just before or around adolescence—is to see a world disappearing: a rich world of relationships which seems so powerful in part because it feels so ordinary. To see this world disappearing while girls are saying that nothing is being lost, or at least nothing of value, and to hear one story of love begin to cover and eclipse another until, like the moon in the sun's shadow, the under story glows faintly red, is to ask the question which is at the heart of therapy and prevention: is this loss necessary, is this suffering and psychic diminution inevitable—a question which ties in with girls' healthy resistance and girls' courage (also see Rogers, 1990).

Then the central paradox of women's—and men's—psychological development becomes opened for re-examination: the taking of oneself out of relationship for the sake of relationships. And the incoherence at the center of this sentence—the dizzying black spot where the word "relationship" loses or changes meaning—then becomes the focus of a new question: what would it mean not to give up relationship?

Heads swirl, dizziness descends, threatening blackness, a voice whispers "take cover." As in speaking with Gail or Sheila or Rosie, I am asking myself the question which leads into the underground: the healthy resistance to disconnection which becomes a political resistance or struggle, which then is under pressure to turn into a psychological resistance: a seeing double, a not knowing.

Because women and girls who resist disconnections are likely to find themselves in therapy—for having gotten themselves into some combination of political and psychological trouble—therapists are in a key position to strength-

en healthy resistance and courage, to help women recover lost voices and tell lost stories, and to provide safe houses for the underground. Tuning themselves into the voices of girls in the time before the re-vision, therapists can be good company for women as they return through the passages—going backward now—from a psychological resistance which takes the form of not knowing and covers a series of disconnections, to a political resistance which exposes false relationships and brings relational violations out into the open, to a healthy resistance to disconnection which grants immunity to psychological illness—the resistance which is rooted in wanting and having honest relationships.

ACKNOWLEDGMENTS

I am most grateful for the support and encouragement of Joan Lipsitz and the Lilly Endowment, the late Lawrence Cremin and the Spencer Foundation, and Wendy Puriefoy and the Boston Foundation. The work described in this paper would not have been possible without grants from the Geraldine Rockefeller Dodge Foundation, the Joseph S. Klingenstein Foundation, the Cleveland Foundation, the Gund Foundation, and Mrs. Marilyn Brachman Hoffman. Lyn Mikel Brown, the director of the Harvard-Laurel Project, and Annie Rogers, the director of the "Strengthening Healthy Resistance and Courage in Girls" project, have contributed centrally to my understanding of girls' voices and my thinking about women's psychological development. I wish to thank Lyn and Annie, the other members of the Harvard Project on the Psychology of Women and the Development of Girls—Elizabeth Debold, Judy Dorney, Barbara Miller, Mark Tappan, Jill Taylor, Deborah Tolman, and Janie Ward, Sarah Hanson (the project assistant), and all of the girls who have joined with us in this work and taught us about girls' experience.

NOTES

1. The Harvard Project on the Psychology of Women and the Development of Girls began in the early 1980s to explore a series of questions about women's psychological development by joining women and girls, research and clinical practices, psychology and politics. Over the course of the decade, the Project has conducted a variety of studies, retreats, and prevention projects at a range of locations designed to ensure the inclusion of different voices—from girls at Emma Willard School for girls (1981–84); to girls and boys in Boys' and Girls' Clubs in three ethnically different Boston neighborhoods and coeducational public and private schools in and around the city (1984–90); to girls ages six to seventeen at the Laurel School in Cleveland—a project that expanded to include women who as teachers, psychologists, and mothers were involved in teaching girls (1985–90); and beginning in 1989, to more intensive work involving women from the Harvard Project and girls

from the Atrium School in Watertown, Massachusetts, and from a public school in the vicinity of Boston, as well as other women who as mothers, teachers, psychotherapists, ministers, and policy makers have become involved with us in this project.

2. For the relational crisis in women's psychological development, see Gilligan, 1982, and Miller, 1986, 1988. See also Belenky et al. (1986), Gilligan, Lyons, & Hanmer (1990), and the Stone Center Working Papers Series. For a retrospective view of the crisis in girls' lives at adolescence, see Hancock (1990).

3. For a fuller discussion of Rosie, see Gilligan, 1990a.

4. The Theater, Writing, and Outing Club is a central part of the project "Strengthening Healthy Resistance and Courage in Girls." This prevention project is designed to help girls sustain their knowledge of relationships and the clarity of their voices into adolescence through theater and writing exercises created to strength-

en and expand the range of girls' voices and girls' relationships and outings designed to encourage girls' active responses to the natural and cultural worlds. The project works centrally through developing healthy relationships between girls and women.

5. My analysis of Diane, Karin, Jesse and Victoria draws heavily on Lyn Mikel Brown's work on girls' narratives of relationships (Brown, 1989, in press, see also Brown & Gilligan, 1990b).

REFERENCES

Belenky, M., Clinchy, B., Goldberger, N., & Tarule, J. (1986). *Women's Ways of Knowing: The Development of Self, Voice, and Mind.* New York: Basic Books.

Block, J. (1990, October). Ego resilience through time: Antecedents and ramifications. In *Resilience and Psychological Health.* Symposium of the Boston Psychoanalytic Society, Boston, MA.

Brown, L. M. (1989). *Narratives of Relationship: The Development of a Care Voice in Girls Ages 7 to 16.* Unpublished doctoral dissertation, Harvard University Graduate School of Education, Cambridge, MA.

Brown, L. M. (in press). A problem of vision: The development of voice and relational knowledge in girls ages 7 to 16. *Women's Studies Quarterly.*

Brown, L. M. (1991). Telling a girl's life. *Women & Therapy.*

Brown, L. M., & Gilligan, C. (1990a, August). Listening for self and relational voices: A responsive/resisting reader's guide. In M. Franklin (Chair), *Literary Theory as a Guide to Psychological Analysis.* Symposium conducted at the annual meeting of the American Psychological Association, Boston, MA.

Brown, L. M., & Gilligan, C. (1990b). Meeting at the crossroads: The psychology of women and the development of girls. Manuscript submitted for publication.

Debold, E. (1991). The body at play. *Women & Therapy.*

Debold, E., & Tolman, D. (1991, January). Made in whose image? Paper presented at the Ms. Foundation's Fourth Annual Women Managing Wealth Conference, New York.

Demitrack, M., Putnam, F., Brewerton, T., Brandt, H., & Gold, P. (1990). Relation of clinical variables to dissociative phenomena in eating disorders. *The American Journal of Psychiatry,* 147(9), 1184–1188.

Deutsch, H. (1944). *Psychology of Women,* Vol. I. New York: Grune & Stratton.

Elder, G., & Caspi, A. (1990). Studying lives in a changing society: Sociological and personological explorations. In A. Rabin, R. Zucker, R. Emmons, & S. Frank (Eds.), *Studying Persons and Lives* (pp. 226–228). New York: Springer.

Fine, M. (1986). Why urban adolescents drop into and out of public high school. *Teachers College Record,* 87(3), 393–409.

Freud, S. (1899/1900). The interpretation of dreams. In J. Strachey (Ed. and Trans.), *The Standard Edition of the Complete Psychological Works of Sigmund Freud* (Vols. IV & V). London: Hogarth Press.

Freud, S. (1905). Three essays on the theory of sexuality. In J. Strachey (Ed. and Trans.), *The Standard Edition of the Complete Psychological Works of Sigmund Freud* (Vol. VII). London: The Hogarth Press.

Freud, S. (1933). New introductory lectures on psychoanalysis (Lecture XXXIII: Femininity). In J. Strachey (Ed. and Trans.), *The Standard Edition of the Complete Psychological Works of Sigmund Freud* (Vol. XXII). London: The Hogarth Press.

Gilligan, C. (1982). *In a Different Voice: Psychological Theory and Women's Development.* Cambridge, MA: Harvard University Press.

Gilligan, C. (1990a). Joining the resistance: Psychology, politics, girls and women. *Michigan Quarterly Review,* 29(4), 501–536.

Gilligan, C. (1990b). Teaching Shakespeare's sister: Notes from the underground of female adolescence. In C. Gilligan, N. Lyons, & T. Hanmer (Eds.), *Making Connections: The Relational Worlds of Adolescent Girls at Emma Willard School* (pp. 6–29). Cambridge, MA: Harvard University Press.

Gilligan, C., Brown, L. M., & Rogers, A. (1990). Psyche embedded: A place for body, relationships, and culture in personality theory. In A. Rabin, R. Zucker, R. Emmons, & S. Frank (Eds.), *Studying Persons and Lives* (pp. 86–147). New York: Springer.

Gilligan, C., Lyons, N., & Hanmer, T. (Eds.). (1990). *Making Connections: The Relational Worlds of Adolescent Girls at Emma Willard School.* Cambridge, MA: Harvard University Press.

Gilligan, C., Rogers, A. G., and Tolman, D. L. (Eds.) (1991). *Women, Girls, and Psychotherapy.* New York: Haworth Press.

Greenberg-Lake Analysis Group Inc. (1991, January). Shortchanging girls, shortchanging America: A nationwide poll to assess self esteem, educational experiences, interest in math and science, and career aspirations of girls and boys ages 9–15. (Available from The American Association of University Women, 515 Second Street NE, Washington, DC 20002).

Hancock, E. (1989). *The Girl Within: A Groundbreaking New Approach to Female Identity.* New York: Fawcett Columbia.

Horney, K. (1926). The flight from womanhood. *International Journal of Psychoanalysis,* 7, 324–339.

Jack, D. (1991). *Silencing the Self: Depression and Women.* Cambridge, MA: Harvard University Press.

Kincaid, J. (1985). *Annie John.* New York: Farrar Straus Giroux.

Kingston, M. H. (1977). *The Woman Warrior.* New York: Alfred A. Knopf.

Miller, J. B. (1984). The development of women's sense of self. Work in Progress, No. 12. Wellesley, MA: Stone Center Working Papers Series.

Miller, J. B. (1986). *Toward a New Psychology of Women* (2nd edition). Boston: Beacon.

Miller, J. B. (1988). Connections, disconnections and violations. Work in Progress, No. 33. Wellesley, MA: Stone Center Working Papers Series.

Petersen, A. (1988). Adolescent development. *Annual Review of Psychology, 39*, 583–607.

Rich, A. (1979). *On Lies, Secrets, and Silence: Selected Prose, 1966–1978.* New York: Norton.

Rogers, A. (1990). The development of courage in girls and women. Unpublished manuscript, Harvard University, Project on the Psychology of Women and the Development of Girls, Cambridge, MA.

Rogers, A. (1991). A feminist poetics of psychotherapy. *Women & Therapy.*

Rutter, M. (1986). The developmental psychopathology of depression: Issues and perspectives. In M. Rutter, C. Izzard, & P. Read (Eds.), *Depression in Young People: Developmental and Clinical Perspectives.* New York: Guilford Press.

Seligman, M. E. P. (1991). *Learned Optimism.* New York: Random House.

Showalter, E. (1985). *The Female Malady.* New York: Penguin.

Stern, Lori. (1991). Disavowing the self in female adolescence. *Women & Therapy.*

Stone Center Working Papers Series. Work in Progress. Wellesley, MA: Wellesley College.

Thompson, C. (1964). *Interpersonal Psychoanalysis.* New York: Basic.

Tolman, D. (1991). Adolescent girls, women and sexuality: Discerning dilemmas of desire. *Women & Therapy.*

R E A D I N G   2 2

Ideology, Experience, Identity
The Complex Worlds of Children in Fair Families

BARBARA RISMAN

In this chapter I follow what happens when marital partners committed to fairness become parents. In these households there are few interactional expectations attached to gender. But children grow up not only in their families but also in their schools and with their friends. In this chapter I explore what happens when gendered expectations are changed within the family but not outside of it. What are the consequences for the children's gendered identities, and for their social lives?[1]

There has been no previous research, to my knowledge, on how and whether children raised in egalitarian house-

holds differ from those in more traditional families. We found two patterns: the children faced serious inconsistencies between their egalitarian beliefs and their experiences with peers, and their identities seem to be forged more from lived experiences than from ideology (see Risman and Myers 1997 for an earlier discussion of these findings). The disjunction between ideology, experience, and identity seems to be common to all these children's stories. I cannot conclusively show that the patterns identified here are not true for all upper-middle-class white children in contemporary America, but I do not believe that they are. First, as a parent, I have direct access to my daughter's friends and to their families, and I rarely see any evidence that most of those children deal with the same issues as those salient to children in these fair families. Second, I can compare these children's experiences to some new gender research on children and make some educated guesses about what makes these children different.

PREVIOUS LITERATURE: DEVELOPING GENDERED IDENTITIES

Sociologists have only rarely—and quite recently—studied children's gender. Most of the literature that needs to be reviewed originates in other disciplines. When children are studied in both sociology and psychology, the predominant questions center on how children learn to be boys or girls. That is, most of the past literature falls squarely into the individualist level of analysis—seeking to explain how male and female babies develop into gendered boys and girls. This individualist literature on children can be organized analytically by presumptions about children's role in their own socialization. I divide this scholarship into three categories: that which sees children as the primary *actors* in the gendering process; that which sees children's gender as something *imposed* by the larger culture and reinforced by rewards and punishments; and that which argues that children are constrained by longstanding gender norms but which sees children as *participating in and negotiating* the enactment of gender.

Self-Gendering

Theories of cognitive development have addressed children's role in learning gendered expectations. Piaget (1932) and Kohlberg (1966) argued that children play an active role in gender acquisition. Children do not passively absorb information from their parents and peers but seek relevant information, and they organize it into predictable patterns. They begin to do this at a young age in order to make sense of their worlds. According to Kohlberg, children choose gender as a major organizing principle because it jibes with their desire for order. Children come to view gender as "natural" differences between males and females. Piaget and other cognitive development theorists argue that children see same-sex modeling as morally necessary and invariant (Kohlberg 1966; Maccoby 1992; Martin 1993). This perspective puts undue emphasis on the child as a rational actor who freely selects gender from the available options. There is a chicken-and-egg conundrum here. Children are born into the existing social structure and are affected accordingly; they do not randomly reproduce gender. Writers in this perspective have tended to presume that gender dichotomies are not only salient but necessary for the psychological development of children. Thus, while children are seen as actors, this perspective ignores the power of gender stratification on children's cognitive processes. Still, one could imagine that children raised in a family without gender dichotomies might self-gender less systematically.

Socialization Imposed on Passive Recipients

Scholars at the other end of the spectrum have often focused on how the existing gender order constrains the socialization of children. Beginning with Parsons and Bales (1955) and Inkeles (1968), scholars in this tradition see socialization as a one-way conduit of information from adult to child. In particular, parents and other adults apply to children stereotypes of behavior based on the child's sex. This typing begins at birth (Deaux 1984; Fagot, Leinbach, and C. O'Boyle 1992; Hutson 1983; Stern and Karraker 1989). Bandura (1962, 1971) argues that parents, teachers, and peers all reward children for learning the behavior of the same sex. Because they receive positive feedback for "correct" behavior, children imitate same-sex behavior and "encode" it into their behavioral repertoires. Once encoded, the child's gender is set.

Scholars of sex roles assert that the gendering of children is complete at an early age. The acquisition of appropriate gender characteristics and expectations is not optional for the child. The important impact of scholarship on gender socialization is the realization that, because we treat boys and girls differently, they develop different skills and desires (Renzetti and Curan 1992; Richardson 1981). In this view, different treatment helps to create people who *are* socially different. By imposing different constraints and expectations society helps to create a self-fulfilling prophecy that perpetuates gender inequality. However, the socialization perspective of gender learning offers a static picture of gender, with the child as a relatively acquiescent recipient of appropriate models of behavior that in turn offer little room for improvisation and change (Kreps et al. 1994). Within this perspective one would logically argue that children rewarded for gender-atypical behavior would develop less gender-typed personalities and identities.

Acting, Not Just Reacting

Sociologists have begun to argue that gender socialization of children is more than just adults providing role models and sanctions, with children hitting, missing, and eventually getting it "right" (Corsaro 1985; Alanen 1988). Instead, they are finding that children actually participate in the process. This emerging tradition integrates a concern with the development of gendered selves via cognitive schemas with attention to the power of interactional expectations. Children are influenced not only by the adult world (self-gendering and socialization) but also by each other. For example, Borman and O'Reilly (1987) find that kindergarteners in same-sex play groups initiate play in similar ways but that the topics for play vary by gender. That is, boys and girls play different types of games, creating different conversational and negotiation demands. Thorne (1993) observed groups of children in classrooms and school yards, noting how they create and police gender boundaries and form various strata among themselves. She asserts that gender relations are not invariant but can change according to the context and the actors involved. Thorne has criticized most socialization and development frameworks because they presuppose a certain outcome: that boys will learn appropriate masculinities, girls will learn appropriate femininities, and if they fail to do so they will either be punished or relegated to the ranks of deviants. She argues that such a future-oriented perspective distorts children's everyday realities, which are crucial to their ongoing gendered negotiations. "Children's interactions are not preparation for life," she writes. "They are life itself" (3).

Bem (1993) similarly improves on both cognitive and socialization theories by linking them. She argues that children try to make sense of the world by forming categories, or schemas, but says that these categories are shaped by existing gender categories in society. Gender is subtly transmitted to children by adults both consciously and unconsciously, so that the dominant way of understanding the social world is usually seen as the best way to understand it. Existing gender divisions are nearly hegemonic and often unquestioned by both children and adults. Therefore, questioning the taken-for-granted gendered organization of society is difficult and unlikely.

It seems reasonable that all three processes occur. Children who live in gendered societies no doubt develop gender schemas and will code themselves, as well as the world around them, in gendered terms. But this seems much more likely to be the result of their lived experiences in patriarchal societies than the consequence of an innate drive for cognitive development. While children are developing cognitive gender schemas, adults and older children are treating boys and girls quite differently. Gender socialization is apparent in any observation of children's lives. And while children are being socialized they react to, negotiate, and even reject some societal pressures. Although

children are actors in the gendering process, we must not ignore the impact of differential reinforcement of gender-appropriate behavior. The cognitive effects of living in a gendered (and sexist) society, the reality of gender socialization, and the active efforts of boys and girls to negotiate their own worlds interact to shape their daily lives, and perhaps to affect their future options.

Unequal Outcomes: Reproducing Gender Difference and Inequality

Even when we recognize that children are both actors and reactors in the gendering process, we cannot overlook the strong empirical data which suggest that most boys and girls are differentially prepared for adulthood. Boys are still routinely socialized to learn to work in teams and to compete, and girls are still routinely socialized to value nurturing (note the relative numbers of boys and girls in team sports versus those dedicated to the popular Babysitters Club book series). Thorne (1993) has shown convincingly that there is much more crossover gender play than dichotomous thinking presumes, yet other research continues to indicate the consequences of gender socialization on children (Lever 1978; Luttrell 1993; Hawkins 1985; Wilder, Mackie, and Cooper 1985; Signorelli 1990; Maccoby 1992; Hutson 1983). There is also much evidence that gender socialization differs by social class, ethnicity, and religion (Peterson and Rollins 1987; Collins 1990).

Socialization clearly happens both in children's play and in their families. Lever's (1978) classic study of boys' and girls' play offers insight into how boys and girls are prepared for a future in which men are presumed to belong in the public, competitive sphere and women to the private, nurturing sphere. Boys' games were more likely to be outside, involve teams, and be age-integrated. Girls were more likely to play make-believe games with one or two others and to break up a game rather than work through conflict. These differences are well developed by the middle of elementary school. Parents and immediate family are also obviously an important source of transmission for gendered expectations (Maccoby 1992). Research indicates that parents participate in gender-typing by often rewarding gender-typical play and punishing gender-atypical play (Bem 1993; Hutson 1983).

While several scholars have documented that some families are moving toward shared parenting and more liberal gender socialization for children, we have little information about how effective such changes in parenting style might be in a society in which gendering processes continue to occur (Coltrane 1996; Schwartz 1994; Segal 1990). It is to this question of how children in egalitarian families fare that I now turn our attention.

CHILDREN IN FAIR FAMILIES

The parents of the children discussed here have attempted to break the chain of gender inequality that typically begins at birth. These children are living in a context different from that in more mainstream families: most of these parents make a conscious effort *not* to replicate what Connell (1987) calls hegemonic masculinities and emphasized femininities. They have an ideological and practical commitment to organizing their homes and families in an egalitarian manner. Whereas mainstream parents may react with delight when their daughter wants to be Barbie for Halloween and their son wants toy guns for his birthday, these parents are likely to be dismayed. Their children are growing up in a world where gender does not dictate who does what or who has more power, at least not in the family. Rather than receiving reinforcement from their parents when they enact hegemonic behavior, these children are likely to encounter disappointment or concern. So how do these children negotiate gender, given their atypical parents?

To understand these children's perspectives on their own lives we had to create cognitively appropriate research instruments. After six months of planning we decided on three separate formats for the children: an interview schedule with questions resembling stories for the four- through six-year-olds; an interview format that included some questions, some writing of poems, and some free play for seven- through ten-year-olds; and interviews that included open-ended questions and some paper-and-pencil items for the older children. There were twenty-six children in these fifteen families, but five were under four years of age, too young to interview. We interviewed twelve boys and nine girls. Ten of the children were between four and six, seven children were between seven and ten, and four children were at least eleven. Three of the four older children were from the same family, so I refrain from making any generalizations about that group.

These children live in complex worlds. They must navigate complicated social and cognitive landscapes. Three themes emerged from our conversations and observations. First, the parents seem to be very successful at transferring their ideological values to their children. The youngsters believe that men and women are equal, or ought to be.

Second, these children's experiences at school and with their peers have taught them unequivocally that boys and girls are not similar, nor do they think they should be. Boys and girls are—in these children's minds—totally different kinds of people. Third, identities seem more forged from experiences with peers than from ideology. The boys in particular seem to struggle to reconcile their identities and their beliefs.

Ideology

Sixteen of the twenty-one children we interviewed had entirely adopted their parents' egalitarian or feminist views on gender, and two of the children without such views were four-year-olds whose answers were better described as inconsistent than traditional. The children know that occupations are currently sex-segregated but believe they should not be. They do not see any tasks in families that ought to be exclusively for either men or women. One nine-year-old boy actually became annoyed at the line of questioning about what men and women should do. He rolled his eyes and retorted, "I told you I think anybody can do these jobs. . . . I think that saying just men or just women could do these jobs isn't being equal." In contrast, most four-year-olds assign sex-stereotypic labels to activities, occupations, and playthings (Bornstein and Lamb 1988).

Most of the children, both boys and girls, not only believe that men and women should be free to work in any occupation and should share the family labor, but also understand that male privilege exists in contemporary society. A nine-year-old girl told us that she believes very much in feminism because "I don't think that it is the least bit fair that in most places males have the main power. I think that women play an important part and should be free to do what they want to do." Similarly, a fifteen-year-old told us, in response to a question about what he likes about being a boy, "It's probably easier being a guy. At least it is now because of stereotypes and prejudices and everything." Overall, most of these children were sophisticated true believers in the capabilities of men and women to perform the same jobs and family roles. The influence of their parents as ideological conduits and role models is evident in their attitudes.

Experiences

These children may have liberal attitudes about gender equality for men and women, but when that ideology contradicts their experiences as boys and girls, life wins hands down. Despite their post-gender answers to what is appropriate for adults, these children give stereotypical answers about the differences between boys and girls. In order to find out their gut beliefs about boys and girls we probed their experiences with a variety of techniques. We asked how their lives would be different if a magician turned them into the opposite sex. We provided short scenarios using stereotypically male and female adjectives (e.g., weak, strong, fearful, adventure-some) and asked them to tell us which adjectives described girls and which described boys and why. We asked what they liked and disliked about being a girl or boy. We asked them to write poems beginning with the line "If I were a boy/girl" using the opposite sex category. We showed them pictures of a boy and a girl, sitting side by side on a sofa, and asked them to tell us a story about each child. We followed up every comment that would help us assess their attitudes.

Although none of the four- to six-year-olds have begun to believe that boys and girls are different, most children from mainstream families clearly have strong gender schemas by this age (Bem 1993). Their egalitarian parents have managed to insulate the preschoolers from typical American norms, perhaps by their choice of paid care-giving arrangements and friends. Once the children reached seven years of age, however, their nonfamilial experiences broadened considerably, as did their ideas about differences between the sexes. We find the descriptions of school-age children remarkably consistent and stereotypical across sex and age categories. Girls are sweet and neat; boys are athletic and disruptive. And these descriptions are consistent with those given by children, presumably from more mainstream families, in other research (Bornstein and Lamb 1988). Table 1 contains adjectives used in direct quotes about boys. The age and sex of the speakers who use each adjective at least once are indicated. Of the sixteen adjectives used, half describe socially disruptive personality traits, often considered aspects of masculinity. The rest are more neutral descriptors but are still stereotypically male. The world that these school-age children know is one in which boys as a group are athletic and mean.

We elicited more comments about boys than about girls— girls are described almost as a second species. But again the comments were remarkably consistent. All of the adjectives describe traditional feminine stereotypes (Table 2). Six of the

TABLE 1   ADJECTIVES USED TO DESCRIBE BOYS

Adjective	Speakers by Gender and Age				
Active	7-year-old girl				
Into sports	7-year-old girl	12-year-old boy	10-year-old boy	10-year-old boy	9-year-old girl
Mean	7-year-old girl	15-year-old boy	4-year-old girl		
Bad	7-year-old girl	9-year-old girl			
More free	11-year-old girl				
Sarcastic	15-year-old boy				
Cool	4-year-old girl				
Aggressive	12-year-old boy	10-year-old boy	9-year-old girl		
Athletic	12-year-old boy	10-year-old boy			
Tough	12-year-old boy				
Stronger	6-year-old boy	10-year-old boy			
Into fighting	10-year-old boy	9-year-old girl			
Troublemaking	10-year-old boy	9-year-old girl			
Competitive	9-year-old girl				
Bully	10-year-old boy				
Into computers	4-year-old boy				

adjectives are socially valued personality traits, the others more neutral. The children voiced unequivocal belief in major sex differences between boys and girls just minutes after parroting their parents' feminist views about the equality and similarity of men and women.

Three of these children did qualify their stereotypical answers. One eight-year-old boy made a point of telling us that he knew that girls could be into sports or computers, he just did not know any who were. A seven-year-old girl was sure that girls were better behaved and that boys were mean, but she also sometimes wanted to be a boy because they seemed to have more playful and active games. A ten-year-old boy knew that some girls were "like boys," and he was even letting such a girl try out for his spy club. And one five-year-old boy made the acute observation that girls played different games than boys did when at school on the playground, but when in the neighborhood they played the same games together.

When family experiences collided with experiences with peers, the family influences were dwarfed. For example, a six-year-old boy told us that if a magician were to turn him into a girl, he'd be different because he would have long hair. This boy's father had a ponytail that reached the middle of his back, and the mother's hair was hardly below her ears. A four-year-old boy told us that if a magician were to turn him into a girl, he'd have to do housework—this from the son of a father whose flexible work schedule has allowed him to spend more time in domestic pursuits than his wife does.

It almost seems as if these children believe that boys and girls are opposites but that men and women are magically transformed into equal and comparable people. The children know that men and women are equal; it is boys and girls who are totally different.

Seven of these children spoke explicitly about male privilege among peers or at school. An eleven-year-old girl told us that sometimes she wished to be a boy because when

> teachers need help like to carry a box to their classroom, they always come in and say, like, "Can I borrow a couple of your boys," and never say, "Can I borrow a couple of your students?" And so the girls never get to do any of the stuff and leave the classroom. . . . It's always the boys that get to leave. And, like, little trips and stuff, when we used to go on field trips, the boys would always have to carry a basket of lunches and go ahead, and when they had stuff to bring from the car, it'd always be boys that would get to go to the car. . . . The girls, like, had to stay on the bus and just sit there and wait while some boys got to go there and the girls never got to do it, do that stuff . . . You get left out because you're a girl. . . . But I'm not wimpy.

A seven-year-old girl told us that she was "more hyper" than most girls and that many of her friends were boys because they were more active and playful. A ten-year-old boy mentioned "racism against women" in sports. A nine-year-old-girl was an avowed feminist with implicit essentialist notions about girls' innate cooperativeness versus boys' innate combativeness. She thought girls ought to have more power in the world because they were better people.

TABLE 2   ADJECTIVES USED TO DESCRIBE GIRLS

Adjective	Speakers by Gender and Age		
Nice	10-year-old boy	4-year-old girl	12-year-old boy
Well-behaved	10-year-old boy	7-year-old girl	
Quiet	10-year-old boy	10-year-old boy	7-year-old girl
Cooperative	9-year-old girl		
Good	9-year-old girl		
Sweet	7-year-old girl		
Not into sports	10-year-old boy		
Not sneaky	12-year-old boy		
Nicer to friends	12-year-old boy		
Less free	11-year-old girl		

This is the response an eight-year-old boy gave to us when he was asked to write a poem about what it would be like to be a girl. His understanding of male privilege was widely shared if not usually so well articulated.

If I were a girl I'd have to attract a guy
wear makeup; sometimes.
Wear the latest style of clothes and try to be likable.
I probably wouldn't play any physical sports like football
or soccer.
I don't think I would enjoy myself around men
in fear of rejection
or under the pressure of attracting them.

While both boys and girls "knew" that boys were trouble-makers, sarcastic, and athletic, this boy also saw clearly that girls had major disadvantages.

Only a few of the boys were aware that they belonged to a group for which they had internalized negative character-istics. One such boy answered our question about how he was different from other guys this way: "I think I'm taller. I don't like bullying people around that much. . . . When one of my friends starts fighting somebody or arguing with somebody I don't join in. I steer clear of them. I try to get in as few fights as possible." This boy built his identity on sports (his room was a baseball shrine, and his activities were sports, sports, and more sports) but tried to distance himself from the violent aspects of peer-group masculinity. Another boy told us that if he were transformed into a girl he would be nicer to his friends. These boys had internal-ized negative attitudes toward their own group and, at some level, themselves. In no case did any girl tell us how bad girls were as a group. When girls talked about how they were similar to and different from other girls, their answers were idiosyncratic (e.g., taller or shorter, longer hair, better reader). These children "know" that boys and girls are dif-ferent, they "know" that boys have advantages, but they also "know" that girls are nicer people.

Identity

These children are very consistent when they explain how boys and girls are different. The unanimity dissolves when we begin to look at how they are forging their own identi-ties. Only six of the children seem to have fashioned selves that unambiguously fit their own stereotyped notions about childhood gender. The interview and observational data col-lected in these families identify six children who describe themselves in consistently gendered fashion and were so identified in observational data.

The first obvious finding is that these children's attitudes and identities are not necessarily correlated. Of the six chil-dren with stereotypical gendered selves, one boy and three girls are also self-consciously egalitarian, even feminist. The two other children in this category had more traditional beliefs about gender.

As the tables show, the children suggested that boys were active, into sports, mean, bad, freer than girls, sarcas-tic, cool, aggressive, athletic, tough, stronger than girls, into fights, troublemakers, competitive, bullies, and into com-puters. I use the label "all-boy" boys and "all-girl" girls to describe children who portray characteristics exclusively in one of the two tables. No child manifested every character-istic on our list, but the two children in the all-boy category and the four girls in the all-girl group could not be described with any of the adjectives on the opposite-sex list. For example, there was no indication that the Pretzman boy was mean or a troublemaker—just the opposite. He fol-lowed our directions closely and appeared to be very sweet. Yet all his interests were stereotypically masculine—sports, Legos, "Star Trek," computers. He described himself as "strong" and used that criterion to differentiate boys and girls. He didn't play much with girls, and there was no indi-cation of cross-gender behavior or traits either in the inter-view or as we watched him at home. The twelve-year-old Potadman boy was similar. His main interest and identity seemed to be attached to sports. He answered us with short, not-too-reflective comments. In traditionally masculine fashion, he described his friendships almost entirely in terms of sharing activities.

I categorize the four girls as all-girl because they can be described using the characteristics the children provided for us about girls: nice, well-behaved, quiet, cooperative, good, sweet, not into sports, not sneaky, nice to friends. None of these girls embodied every one of these traits, but it is unlikely that they would be described by any of the traits on the other list. One shared characteristic was their distaste for competitive sports. The eleven-year-old Germane girl provides an easy comparison with the twelve-year-old Potadman boy. Her favorite games were fantasies, her favorite activity was dance, her favorite possessions were dolls and stuffed animals. The Stokes ten-year-old was sim-ilarly gendered. Her favorite activities were reading, writing poems, and art. She is adamant about disliking sports, and she knows why: she doesn't like any activity where you have to be pushy or aggressive. The six-year-old Green daughter had three dollhouses, and there was not a "boy" toy in the house. Her parents were very conscious of encouraging her to make her own choices and to develop her own potential; the mother told us she was trying to get her daughter to be willing to play some sports, at least at school during recess.

These six children, raised by egalitarian parents and often holding feminist attitudes themselves, have nevertheless fashioned selves that are unambiguously gendered. The following poem sums up what these children think about even imagining being the opposite sex. The poem was written by the Sykes girl in response to our request to write a verse that begins "If I were a boy": "If I were a boy, I'd know my parents had made a mistake and that I should have been a girl. I'd always feel that I didn't belong because the girls were who I wanted to play with but they wouldn't let me, and I didn't want to be with the boys."

This nine-year-old provides an interesting example of the disjunction between identity and ideology. She lives in one of the most self-consciously feminist and progressive families in our study. They see themselves as outside the mainstream. They have no television set so that their daughter will avoid excess materialism. Both parents and daughter are avowed feminists. The daughter is one of the most feminine in the sample—her long wavy hair flows below her waist. She collects china teacups, hates competitive sports, and loves nature and hiking. She saved a bug from death during my home observation and carried it tenderly outside. In my honor she put on her favorite nightgown, ankle-length and with a pink bow. This child is very smart, and she intends to succeed professionally, maybe in a scientific career. So despite her feminine self-presentation and dislike for most things male, she actually crosses gender boundaries in other ways.

The other fifteen children have also fashioned gendered selves. The boys are much more likely to like sports, the girls to like dance. Despite their parents' role-modeling, despite their own ideology, all these girls are more feminine than masculine and all these boys are more masculine than feminine. But the rest of the children, to varying degrees, cross gender lines in interests and interpersonal style. All but one of the girls is either involved in at least one competitive sport or expects to be when she is a little older. All the boys stand out in some way as exceptions to hegemonic masculinity. An interesting sex difference exists, however. All the girls told us in quite explicit terms just how they were different from other girls, but the boys often denied any differences from other boys—differences that our interview and observational team noted. For example, the Cody daughter knows that she is different from other girls because she loves team sports, and she would like to be a boy except that she knows "they aren't always very nice." A four-year-old girl likes to climb trees as well as play fantasy games about babies. She knows she is "nice, like other girls," but she wants to be "cool," like boys. She told us her future goal was to "be a mommy so I can work hard and like my job." The Cross girl believes that she is more active than other girls, but she is also "real sweet," likes horses, and is nice to her friends (all characteristics that she says make her different from boys). The Relux six-year-old told us that she is "not like other girls particularly." She has friends who are boys, although her best friend is another girl. But she likes being a girl because she can do whatever she wants.

The boys coded as portraying some crossover behaviors and interpersonal style were much less likely than the girls to notice it themselves. Although some of the data reported here come directly from the interviews, this analysis also relies on subtle inconsistencies in their own words, body language, and to some extent intuition of the part of the interview and observational team, as recorded in field notes. The older Potadman boys (fifteen and seventeen years of age) told us of some hopes and dreams that seemed to cross gender stereotypes. The fifteen-year-old baby-sits and loves to vacuum and cook. He would like to stay home with his children if his wife could earn a high enough income. His very tall older brother, whose ponytail reaches below his waist, hates to work out and finds it unfair that women can be considered sexy without being muscular but that men cannot. He writes poetry and never had been much into sports, though he does like volleyball. He describes himself as an intellectual outsider and seems comfortable—if somewhat vulnerable—with the status.

Four little boys also reported androgynous preferences. The four-year-old Cody boy likes many boys' games, particularly baseball. But he also wants to be like his sister, plays housekeeping at day care, and enjoys playing dress-up in his sister's clothes. The four-year-old Trexler son has favorite movie characters: Aladdin and the Little Mermaid. The four-year-old Relux boy thinks that being "silly" is the best part of being a boy. While he likes guns and has mostly boys as friends, his answers to most questions seem gender-neutral. Similarly, the five-year-old Cary boy likes boys' toys and baseball, but many of his favorite activities seem to be gender-neutral, such as board games and playing outside with both boys and girls. His body language and self-presentation led to the description of him as "gentle" in the field notes. The six-year-old Staton son prefers stereotypically boys' toys, and he takes tai kwon do lessons, but, like the fifteen-year-old Potadman boy, he would like to not work at all so that he could "spend more time with his kids." These boys never seemed rough or tough; even when talking about their stereotypical behaviors they seemed warm and caring.

There were two boys whose words contradicted their behavior (as reported by their parents) and our observations. The ten-year-old Oakley boy seemed to try too hard at his self-presentation. He wanted us to think he was tough, mean, and sneaky, a "real" boy. But the boy we met was warm, kind, and soft-spoken, even as he told us about his war games. This son of two writers wanted a blue-collar job for which he could wear "lots of armor" and be tough. But these words didn't square with what we saw: a ten-year-old who played gently with his four-year-old sister. He interrupted his own and his sister's interview to take her to look out the bathroom window so that she did not miss the full moon. They fought during our home interview, and he hurt her by mistake. He was genuinely sorry, offering his "butt" for her to hit in response. When we noticed some Barbie dolls in his closet and asked what kind of games he played with them, he answered, "Oh, I mostly kill them in war games. They're my sisters." But his mother told us that both children played fantasy games with the dolls. He alluded to this himself later: "I like the Ken doll because he is a basketball star." This boy twitched when he spoke about gender preferences. I found the interview poignant: he knew that boys were supposed to be mean and sneaky, and he wanted very much to fulfill those expectations, or at least to make us believe that he did. But we couldn't believe it. He was too nice a child.

Another interviewer had a similar experience with the ten-year-old Woods boy. His identity was sports based: he was a baseball fanatic, and his room was entirely in Carolina Blue. He talked about liking to compete. And yet he described his baby brother in loving terms, and in three straight losses in a card game he showed no competitive spirit or disappointment. He emanated warmth, as did his father. He also differentiated himself from other boys because he was not a bully and did not like to fight.

CONCLUSION

These data illustrate the usefulness of the theoretical model offered in this book. Although gender structure exists at the institutional, interactional, and individual levels, its consequences are far from predetermined. The children discussed here are being raised in social settings in which gender expectations and interactional demands have been consciously changed to value gender equality. And the children in fair families have adopted their parents' egalitarian views. They say that men and women are equal and that no jobs—inside or outside the family—ought to be sex-typed. But beyond these abstract belief statements these children depend on their own lived experiences for understanding gender. And they "know" that boys and girls are very different.

Boys, as a group, are described—even by boys themselves—as not only athletic but also mean and troublesome. Girls are described as sweet, quiet, and well behaved. And yet it is clear that both boys and girls value, at some level, the masculine over the feminine, or at least the privileges that accompany male status. They notice that boys have more freedom at school and that most boys play harder and with more autonomy. Six of these children met their own criteria for being all boy or all girl; the rest exhibited some cross-gender behavior. The girls knew and reported how they were different from other girls; the boys did not. Gendered selves are changing here, but the change is uneven, with attitudes toward others changing faster than identities. Thorne (1993) shows that children from more mainstream families also cross gender boundaries. Some boys from traditional families also develop soft and gentle selves, and girls from traditional homes can be seen aggressively entering boys' games on the playground. But Thorne gives no indication that children from more traditional families struggle with the inconsistencies among their beliefs, their extrafamilial experiences, and their developing identities.

The parents in fair families are transmitting new cognitive images or gender rules to their children. And though this process is hardly direct or perfectly effective, the children of these families seem to be adopting their parents' gender rules about adult responsibilities. But when it comes to developing their own identities, these children seem to be at least as influenced by the cognitive images and folk knowledge learned from peers as those messages from home. The children struggle with the contradictions between their parentally influenced ideologies and the cognitive images that dominate peer-group culture. In how they fashion their identities, their gendered selves, we can see why social change moves so slowly at the individual level.

Yet the parents in fair families also were raised in peer cultures with traditional cognitive images about gender and somehow have managed to create new ones for themselves. Their children are the product of a gender structure in flux. Most of them, while clearly developing gendered selves, are also crossing gender boundaries even as they subscribe to the ruling cognitive images in their own culture, which still define boys and girls as opposites. Each time a girl admits that she is not like other girls because she likes sports, each time a little boy differentiates himself from boys as a group because he does not like to fight, the cognitive image begins to blur. Eventually, perhaps, with some adult intervention, those childhood cognitive images might crack and dissolve, to be re-created in a post-gendered society. What is even more clear, however, is that as these children grow into adulthood and move into more egalitarian settings, they are well prepared to reconstruct post-gendered identities. There is no reason to believe that the identities and selves they adopt to negotiate their sexist and gendered childhood worlds will determine the selves they adopt later in life, as their social situations and the expectations they face change.

These data are very clear on another important point, too. These children are growing up to be happy, healthy, and well adjusted in egalitarian, gender-atypical families. They are doing well in families in which both parents are committed to labor-force participation and in which fathers are actively nurturing their children. These families dramatically depart from what many fundamentalist Judeo-Christian traditionalists and contemporary political conservatives have argued is the "natural" family—with patriarchal breadwinning fathers and homemaking mothers. Children raised in families with attentive and loving feminist parents do just fine.

But what is also clear is that changing families alone does not allow children to live post-gendered lives. Parents may have the power to change their marriage and their child-rearing techniques, but effective social change requires collective action and coalitions across families, schools, and friendship networks. Social change cannot be effective at the level of identities only; it must occur simultaneously at the level of identities, interactions, and institutions.

NOTE

1. An earlier report of these data about children in fair families is available in Risman and Myers (1997).

REFERENCES

Alanen, L. 1988. "Rethinking Childhood." *Acta Sociologica* 31:53–67.

Bandura, A. 1962. "Social Learning Through Imitation." In *Nebraska Symposium on Motivation,* vol. 10, 211–274, edited by M. Jones. Lincoln: University of Nebraska Press.

———. 1971. *Psychological Modeling: Conflicting Themes.* Chicago: Aldine-Atherton.

Bem, Sandra L. 1993. *The Lenses of Gender: Transforming the Debate on Sexual Inequality.* New Haven: Yale University Press.

Borman, K. M., and P. O'Reilly. 1987. "Learning Gender Roles in Three Urban U.S. Kindergarten Classrooms." *Child and Youth Services* 8:43–66.

Bornstein, Marc H., and Michael E. Lamb. 1988. *Developmental Psychology: An Advanced Textbook.* Hillsdale, N.J.: Erlbaum.

Collins, Patricia Hill. 1990. *Black Feminist Thought: Knowledge, Consciousness, and the Politics of Empowerment.* Boston: Unwin, Hyman.

Coltrane, Scott. 1996. *Family Man: Fatherhood, Housework, and Gender Equity.* Oxford: Oxford University Press.

Connell, Robert W. 1987. *Gender and Power: Society, the Person, and Sexual Politics.* Stanford, Calif: Stanford University Press.

Corsaro, W. A. 1985. *Friendship and Peer Culture in the Early Years.* Norwood, N.J.: Ablex.

Deaux, Kay. 1984. "From Individual Differences to Social Categories: Analysis of a Decade's Research on Gender." *American Psychologist* 39:105–116.

Fagot, B. I., M. D. Leinbach, and C. O'Boyle. 1992. "Gender Labeling, Gender Stereotyping, and Parenting Behaviors." *Development Psychology* 28:225–230.

Hawkins, J. 1985. "Computers and Girls: Rethinking the Issues." *Sex Roles* 13:165–180.

Inkeles, A. 1968. "Society, Social Structure, and Child Socialization." In *Socialization and Society,* ed. J. Clausen. Boston: Little, Brown.

Kohlberg, Lawrence. 1966. "A Cognitive-Developmental Analysis of Children's Sex-Role Concepts and Attitudes." In *The Development of Sex Differences,* 82–172, ed. Eleanor Maccoby. Stanford, Calif.: Stanford University Press.

Kreps, G. A., and S. L. Bosworth with J. A. Mooney, S. T. Russell, and K. A. Myers. 1994. *Organizing, Role Enactment, and Disaster: A Structural Theory.* Newark: University of Delware Press.

Lever, Janet. 1978. "Sex Differences in the Complexity of Children's Play and Games." *American Sociological Review* 43:471–483.

Luttrell, W. 1993. "The Teachers, They All Had Their Pets: Concepts of Gender, Knowledge, and Power." *Signs* 18:505–546.

Maccoby, E. E. 1992. "The Role of Parents in the Socialization of Children: An Historical Overview." *Developmental Psychology* 28:1006–1017.

Martin, C. L. 1993. "New Directions for Investigating Children's Gender Knowledge." *Developmental Review* 13:184–204.

Parsons, T., and R. Bales. 1955. *Family Socialization and Interaction Process.* Glencoe, Ill.: Free Press.

Peterson, G. W., and B. C. Rollins. 1987. "Parent-Child Sociali-zation." In *Handbook of Marriage and the Family,* ed. M. Sussman and S. Steinmetz. New York: Plenum.

Piaget, J. 1932. *The Moral Judgement of the Child.* London: Kegan Paul.

Renzetti, C. M., and D. J. Curran. 1992. *Women and Men in Society.* Boston: Allyn and Bacon.

Richardson, L. W. 1981. *The Dynamics of Sex and Gender.* 2nd ed. Boston: Houghton-Mifflin.

Risman, Barbara, and Kristen Myers. 1997. "As the Twig Is Bent: Children Reared in Feminist Households." *Qualitative Sociology* 20:2.

Schwartz, Pepper. 1994. *Peer Marriage: How Love between Equals Really Works.* New York: Free Press.

Segal, L. 1990. *Slow Motion: Changing Masculinities, Changing Men.* New Brunswick, N.J.: Rutgers University Press.

Signorelli, N. 1990. "Children, Television, and Gender Roles." *Journal of Adolescent Health Care* 11:50–58.

Stern, M., and K. H. Karraker. 1989. "Sex Stereotyping of Infants: A Review of Gender Labeling Studies." *Sex Roles* 20:501–522.

Thorne, Barrie. 1993. *Gender Play.* New Brunswick, N.J.: Rutgers University Press.

Wilder, G., D. Mackie, and J. Cooper. 1985. "Gender and Computers: Two Surveys of Gender-Related Attitudes." *Sex Roles* 13:215–228.

P A R T   T H R E E

Social Organization of Gender

The processes of gender socialization that begin in early childhood prepare us for participation in society as adult women and men. Socialization alone, however, cannot account for the differences in power and prestige between men and women in almost all societies. Gender encompasses more than the socialized differences between individual women and men. As Judith Lorber pointed out in Section Two, gender also affects the way that social institutions—from family to medicine to politics—are structured. Key to feminist analyses is an understanding of the role of a society's *institutions* in perpetuating gender inequality.

Like other forms of social inequality, *gender inequality* includes the unequal distribution of three different kinds of valued commodities. First, inequality entails differential access to power, defined as the ability to carry out one's will despite opposition. Second, inequality includes differential access to the sources of prestige, defined as the ability to command respect, honor, and deference. Third, differential access to wealth, or economic and material resources, is important to inequality. Those who have access to any one of these resources—power, prestige, or wealth—occupy a position from which they are likely to achieve access to the others and thereby reinforce their status over those who have less. In the case of gender-stratified social systems, men's greater access to power, prestige, and wealth enhances their opportunities to exploit women and decreases women's ability to resist.

Of course, not all men have equal access to prestige, power, or wealth. Men of subordinate racial or ethnic groups, working-class and poor men, and many gay or elderly men are also excluded from socially sanctioned sources of power, prestige, and wealth. Women, too, vary in their degree of access to power, prestige, and wealth; white or upper-class women receive benefits from their class and race even while they are penalized for their gender. Patricia Hill Collins suggests that we think of gender as one system of domination, which interacts with other systems of domination such as racism, class inequality, and heterosexism (Collins 1990). The task of feminist scholars is to trace the intersections of gender and other systems of domination, examining the varied ways that gender inequality is expressed and reinforced in social institutions.

Institutions construct systems of inequality in a variety of ways. Economic and legal systems; political, educational, medical, religious, and familial institutions; mass media; and the institutions of science and technology reinforce the ideology of women's inferiority and preserve men's greater access to power, wealth, and prestige. How? The *structures* of institutions are gendered in that they privilege men and those traits labeled masculine and they penalize women and the traits labeled feminine. Such institutions engage in practices that discriminate against women, exclude or devalue women's perspectives, and perpetuate the idea that differences between women and men and the dominance of men are natural. In addition, the control of these institutions usually rests in the hands of men, and social scientists understand that dominant groups tend to behave in ways that enhance their own power.

Institutions establish various kinds of rewards and punishments that encourage women to behave in submissive ways, and such submissive behavior in turn perpetuates the idea that women are naturally submissive. For example, a complex social system in the United States exerts strong pressures on women to marry heterosexually. Families train daughters to be wives and mothers; high school events require opposite-sex dates; college fraternities and sororities promote heterosexual coupling; widespread violence against women encourages them, ironically, to seek male protection; and men's higher incomes mean that heterosexual marriage tends to improve a woman's standard of living.

A woman's failure to marry constitutes a violation of social prescriptions and often leaves her economically disadvantaged and socially suspect. On the other hand, despite women's increasing participation in the paid labor force, in heterosexual marriage the burden of domestic labor still usually falls disproportionately on women, a dynamic that helps maintain the inequality between men and women in the work world.

It is important to reiterate that gender stratification is not the only form of inequality affecting women's and men's lives and the structure of social institutions. Institutions that disadvantage racial or ethnic groups, older people, the disabled, the poor, or particular religious or class-based groups also discriminate against both women and men who belong to those groups. Understanding women's oppression as a function of the social organization of gender necessitates understanding the overlaps between sexism and other forms of subordination.

The following articles examine how particular institutions express, construct, and maintain gender inequality. They analyze the ways that women's subordination is maintained in work, families, sexuality, medical treatment of bodies, and violence against women. The articles do not simply document women's submission, however. They also describe the ways that women and men in various groups resist oppression and attempt to exercise control over their choices and their lives. To what extent are women or men able to resist the structures of gender, and to what extent are they controlled by gendered institutions?

REFERENCE

Collins, Patricia Hill. 1990. *Black Feminist Thought.* New York: Routledge.

SECTION FIVE

Work

Work for pay influences many aspects of our lives: our economic prosperity, our social status, where we live, our relationships with family members and friends, our health, and our access to health care. Our work experiences influence how we come to view others, ourselves, and the social world around us. Reciprocally, how we are situated in society often influences the kind of work we do and our compensation for that work.

In traditional societies, division of labor based on sex and age did not necessarily correspond to differences in the importance assigned to different tasks: "women's work" might be considered just as socially valuable as "men's work." In societies like the United States, however, social divisions of labor based on gender, race, and age reflect and perpetuate power differences among groups.

This section begins with Alice Kessler-Harris's examination of the historical justifications of pay inequities between women and men. "The Wage Conceived: Value and Need as Measures of a Woman's Worth" explores the ideological bases of the differential economic rewards available to women and men and the implications of both gender ideologies and the economic practices for women's participation in the workforce. Can you think of ways in which these historical justifications for paying women less than men are still influential today?

Inequities between women and men in earnings often exist because the sexes are concentrated in different occupations. In "Sex Differences in Moving Up and Taking Charge," Barbara Reskin and Irene Padavic examine the continuing existence of a promotion gap between men and women and between whites and minorities of both sexes. Even if women have made some strides in recent decades, in all countries for which data are available women are still vastly underrepresented in top-level jobs. Reskin and Padavic assess the evidence for the three most common explanations for the promotion gap: human capital inequalities, concentrations in sex-segregated occupations with different job ladders, and discrimination. They conclude by outlining legal and organizational remedies for the problem. In thinking about the promotion gap discussed by Reskin and Padavic, ask how many women department chairs, deans, and vice presidents there are at your college or university. If there is a discrepancy between the numbers of men and of women who have reached these high-level positions, which explanation do you think is the most plausible?

The remaining articles in this section offer focused examinations of the work experiences of particular groups. Beverly W. Jones traces the interplay of race, class, and gender in "Race, Sex, and Class: Female Tobacco Workers in Durham, North Carolina, 1920–1940, and the Development of Female Consciousness." Jones describes a tobacco company's relegation of black women to unhealthy working conditions because of race, and to the lowest-paying jobs because of sex. In response to their oppression, black women tobacco workers developed a class identity, and from it emerged a sisterhood of struggle, support, dignity, and resistance. What enabled them to maintain a sense of self-worth despite their working conditions?

Robin Leidner examines the construction of gender identity in two common contemporary occupations: fast-food service, a job performed primarily by women, and insurance sales, a job performed primarily by men. Leidner shows how workers and managers in both jobs interpreted the skills and tasks required as best suited for either women (in the case of fast food) or men (in insurance sales). Workers, Leidner suggests, are not just doing their jobs. They are also constructing and reaffirming cultural definitions of gender and their own gender identities. In jobs that you have held, how did gender affect the ways that you and others thought about your work?

Stereotyped assumptions about the types of jobs that should be assigned to women (jobs that accommodate women's involvement in home life) and the types that should be assigned to men (jobs that are consistent with men's noninvolvement in home life) help to produce a gendered work environment. Employers' and workers' assumptions about gender and jobs can create an environment that fosters harassment when women enter predominantly male

occupations. In "Marking Gender Boundaries: Porn, Piss, Power Tools," Susan Eisenberg describes various forms of harassment and hostility encountered by women working construction. On job sites, male co-workers use strategies such as failing to train women in the operation of dangerous tools, displaying pornography, and setting up injuries and accidents for women or people of color to exercise male domination. So powerful are the pressures to create an all-male work environment that co-workers and foremen in positions of authority, when given the choice between male bonding and loyalty to their particular trade or union, are likely to allow the harassment of women workers to continue. Have you ever experienced sexual harassment on the job? How was it manifested? What effect did it have on your ability to do your work? What strategies can counter sexual harassment on the job and facilitate women's entry into male-dominated jobs?

As these articles demonstrate, women's ethnicities, ages, and class backgrounds affect both the structural opportunities available to them in the labor force and their interpretations of these experiences. What experiences, if any, do women in the labor force *share* by virtue of their gender?

The Wage Conceived:
Value and Need as Measures of a Woman's Worth

ALICE KESSLER-HARRIS

When a person complains that a certain wage rate is unduly low, he may be making that judgment in the light of what he thinks is due the kind of person *performing that work, e.g. a married man. Others may regard the same rate as not unreasonable in view of the kind of* work *it is.*

—*Henry A. Landsberger*[1]

In 1915 New York State's Factory Investigating Commission asked some seventy-five prominent individuals—economists, social reformers, businessmen, and publicists among them—what factors determined the rate of wages. The answers varied. Some suggested that workers' organizations were most important; others believed the size of a business's profits could enhance or restrain the wages of employees. Another key factor was the standard of living anticipated by workers. But the majority of those interviewed believed the efficiency of the worker and the supply of labor constituted by far the two most powerful determinants of wages.[2] These traditional explanations for wage rates would have found favor with the proponents of the economic theory then popular.

Widely accepted wage theory at the turn of the century was rooted in, though not limited to, the law of supply and demand. If that phrase, as economic historian Arnold Tolles implies, does not do economists justice, it does, at least, convey the economists' belief "that the reward for every

kind of human effort is controlled by some kind of impersonal and irresistible force, similar to the force of gravity."[3] Theory held that wages would rise or fall in response to employers' fluctuating willingness to pay. That willingness in turn was predicated on what employers thought they could earn from labor as well as on how much labor was available at different wage rates. Thus, in theory, the demand for labor (measured by the additional revenue labor could produce) and the supply (which took into account the differences in education and training of the worker) together determined the wage.[4]

Despite the apparent certainty of economists such as Professor Roy Blakely of Cornell, who testified before the commission that "wages tend to approximate the value of what they produce,"[5] the theory left room for a substantial degree of subjective judgment on the part of employers as to the value of particular workers. A critical part of the chemical mix that determined the wages of workers in general involved something intangible called "custom." If a male worker was paid according to some formula that reflected the value of what he produced and the difficulty of replacing him, he was also paid according to what he and other workers thought he was worth. Custom, or tradition, played an acknowledged but uncalculated role in regulating the wage. But custom and tradition were gendered. They influenced male and female wages in different ways. And especially in the female wage, they played a far larger role than we have earlier been willing to concede. The women's wage, at least for the early twentieth century, rested in large measure on conceptions of what women needed.

The distinction alerts us to the rich possibilities contained in the wage conceived as a social rather than as a theoretical construct. If the wage is, as most economists readily acknowledge, simultaneously a set of ideas about how people can and should live and a marker of social status, then it contains within it a set of social messages and a system of meanings that influence the way women and men behave. We are all familiar with the capacity of these social meanings to reduce the wages of recent immigrants, of African-Americans, and of other groups. But, partly because it is so apparently natural, the capacity of the wage to speak to issues of gender is less clear. Yet the language with which the women's wage is conceived throws into relief the same process that exists for men. The wage frames gendered messages; it encourages or inhibits certain forms of behavior; it can reveal a system of meaning that shapes the expectations of men and women and anticipates their struggles over power; it participates in the negotiations that influence the relationships of the sexes inside and outside the family. In all these capacities, the wage functions as a terrain of contest over visions of fairness and justice. This essay will attempt to illustrate some of these processes in the early twentieth century.

The structure of wages that emerged in the course of industrialization in the late nineteenth century reflected a long tradition that revolved around what has become known as the family wage—the sum necessary to sustain family members. That sum had been earned by several family members for most of the history of capitalism. Family income was typically pooled and then redistributed by one family member. But the dream of a family wage that could be earned by a male breadwinner alone had long been an object of struggle among organized working people who thought of it as a mechanism for regulating family life and allowing women to work in their own homes.[6] Ideally, and sometimes in practice, the family wage was a male wage, a wage that went to a male breadwinner.[7]

What then of a woman's wage? It reflected not what was but what ought to be. That men ought to be able to support wives and daughters implied that women need not engage in such support. They ought to be performing home duties. Thus, if a woman earned wages, the normal expectation was that she did so to supplement those of other family wage earners. Theoretically, at least, the decision as to who would and would not earn was regulated by the family unit. The wage belonged to her family. Until the third quarter of the nineteenth century, U.S. law and practice reflected these assumptions. Typically, a woman's wage was legally the property of her husband or father. The average wage of women workers was little more than half of the male wage. And even the most skilled women rarely earned as much as two-thirds of the average paid to unskilled men. If a woman

lived independently, her wage was normally not sufficient to support her. Nor was it intended to do so.

The nineteenth century fight for a family wage was thus simultaneously a fight for a social order in which men could support their families and receive the services of women; and women, dependent on men, could stay out of the labor force. Historians have debated the advantages and disadvantages of this mode of thinking, but for our purposes it is important to note only that the family wage reflected popular thinking—a sense of what was right and just.[8] Widely supported by working-class men and women at the end of the nineteenth century, it rested on what seemed to many to be a desirable view of social order.

Its incarnation in the form of the living wage more clearly isolated the female role. Though the content of a living wage varied, like the family wage, it was imbued with gendered expectations. John Ryan, the Catholic priest who was the United States' most prolific exponent of the living wage, for example, asserted the laborer's right to a "decent and reasonable" life that meant to him "the right to exercise one's primary faculties, supply one's essential needs, and develop one's personality."[9] Others were somewhat more specific. British economist William Smart thought the living wage ought to pay for "a well-drained dwelling, with several rooms, warm clothing with some changes of underclothing, pure water, a plentiful supply of cereal food with a moderate allowance of meat and milk and a little tea, etc., some education, and some recreation, and lastly sufficient freedom for his wife from other work to enable her to perform properly her maternal and her household duties."[10] John Mitchell, head of the United Mine Workers union, was somewhat more ambitious. The wage, he thought, ought to be enough to purchase "the American standard of living." This included, but was not limited to, "a comfortable house of at least six rooms," which contained a bathroom, good sanitary plumbing, parlor, dining room, kitchen, sleeping rooms, carpets, pictures, books, and furniture.[11]

For Ryan, as for other proponents of the living wage, the "love and companionship of a person of the opposite sex"[12] was an essential element of what a living wage should purchase. The bottom line, according to Ryan, was the laborer's capacity "to live in a manner consistent with the dignity of a human being."[13] The *Shoe Workers' Journal* proposed that "everything necessary to the life of *a normal man* be included in the living wage: the right to marriage, the right to have children and to educate them."[14]

As the family wage held the promise of female homemaking, the living wage, which explicitly incorporated wife and children, excluded the possibility that female dignity

the prevailing at
all working wom
provided them wi
use this idealized
mine women's wa

For all the elab
tom line turned
sense of what w
noted, came into
Women came into
female workers—
level of the occupa
women generally
social worker M
Investigating Com
one of the most im
laundry work, fact
and home work, ef
wages," she decla
judgment, was the
productivity and er
workers than to di
those who could be
marized the proces
there is a definite
the worker and t
Gompers would ha
little connection be
paid; the employer

While from the
gross oversimplific
all accepted the cri
structure. A vice pr
ing before the comi
of 1894, acknowled
based on the comp
for ten hours . . .
pany discovered "t
less competent and
making an unreaso
that the piece price
was what was "rea
productivity or effic
part of the content
worker appears to
International Harves
gating commission
efforts to set a mini
company's desire, he

could inhere either in a woman's ability to earn wages or in her capacity to support a family. Because the living wage idealized a world in which men had the privilege of caring for women and children, it implicitly refused women that privilege. And, because it assumed female dependency, to imagine female independence impugned male roles and male egos. Ground rules for female wage earners required only self-support, and even that was estimated at the most minimal level. Champions of the living wage for women counted among her necessities food, clothing, rent, health, savings, and a small miscellaneous fund.[15] Nothing in the arguments for a female living wage vitiates the harsh dictum of John Stuart Mill. The wages of single women, asserted that famous economist, "must be equal to their support, but need not be more than equal to it; the minimum in their case is the pittance absolutely required for the sustenance of one human being."[16] "Women who are forced to provide their own sustenance have a right," echoed Ryan, "to what is a living wage *for them*." Their compensation, he argued, with apparent generosity, "should be sufficient to enable them to live decently."[17]

At the time Ryan wrote, women constituted close to 25 percent of the industrial work force. More than one-third of wage-earning women in urban areas lived independently of their families, and three-quarters of those living at home helped to support other family members. False conceptions of women who needed only to support themselves did a particular disservice to Black women, who were eight times as likely to earn wages as white women. For Black women racial discrimination and its attendant poverty meant that more that one-third of those who were married would continue to earn wages, and virtually all of those who earned wages participated in family support.[18] Yet the real needs of these women were rarely acknowledged. Nor did the brief, dismissive commentary on "a woman's living wage" mention recreation or comfort or human dignity or the capacity to care for others.

Ryan readily conceded that men without families to support and/or with other means of support were entitled to draw a living wage because "they perform as much labor as their less fortunate fellows."[19] His proposals generously allocated a living wage to men who never intended to marry because "rights are to be interpreted according to the average conditions of human life."[20] But the same generosity was not evident in notions of the living wage for women workers. Rather, it seemed fair to reduce women to the lowest levels of bestiality. Advocates of the living wage confidently explained that women's "standard of physical comfort, in other words, their standard of life" was lower than

that of men." While her ideals were "naturally higher than those of men, her physical wants are simpler. The living wage for a woman is lower than the living wage for a man because it is possible for her as a result of her traditional drudgery and forced tolerance of pain and suffering to keep alive upon less."[21] Women, with a single set of exceptions, were to be paid only according to their most minimal needs. Only to women who were employed in the same jobs as men did Ryan concede the need for equal pay because, he argued, "when women receive less pay than men, the latter are gradually driven out of the occupation."[22]

Ryan failed to acknowledge that in attributing to women "average conditions" that reflected social myth rather than reality he undermined his own cause. While his vision and that of most living wage advocates came from a desire to protect the home, not from antagonism to the pitiable condition of those women who worked for wages, his proposals left the home vulnerable. "The welfare of the whole family," he noted, "and that of society likewise, renders it imperative that the wife and mother should not engage in any labor except that of the household. When she works for hire, she can neither care properly for her own health, rear her children aright, nor make her home what it should be for her husband, her children, herself."[23] Theoretically, that might have been true; but in practice, by reducing women's potential capacity to earn adequate incomes, he diminished their ability to support themselves and their homes.

Without negating the good intentions of Ryan and others on behalf of the family and without imposing anachronistic judgments about their desire to protect the family and to place family needs ahead of women's individual rights, one can still see that the consequences of their rhetoric for women who earned wages were no mere abstractions. They assumed a hard and concrete reality, for example, in discussions of the minimum wage for women that took place between about 1911 and 1913. To alleviate the plight of women workers, social reformers attempted to pass legislation that would force employers to pay a wage sufficient to meet a woman's minimal needs. Between 1912 and 1923, thirteen states and the District of Columbia passed such legislation in one form or another. Each statute was preceded by a preamble that declared the legislators' intentions to offer protection that ranged from providing a sum "adequate for maintenance" to ensuring enough to "maintain the worker in health" and guaranteeing her "moral well-being." Whatever the language of the preamble, and whatever the mechanism by which the wage was ultimately to be decided, the minimum was invariably rooted in what was determined to be a "living" wage for women workers.[24] But the

discussion require
might be. Elizabet
ing women in Pitts
could "not live dec
of less than $7 a v
estimated the livin
$9 to $11 a week-
from dying of cold
sibility of efficien
ation.[25] The questi
was whether "it is
the bare necessarie
sion for comforts, r

The budgets dr;
for the necessities
uncover the actual
heavily reliant on
women to perpetua
beyond the barest s
taken by Sue Ainsle
and Edith Wyatt ir
1910.[28] The author
make ends meet, tu
feat. They exuded s
fast," whose "lunch
cents," and who, as
her own laundry, .
done. Her regular w
ing, 42 cents; board
all other expenses
encouraged social
much a female wa
from undergarments

The debate over
outward order dicta
exercise of thrift, se
warned fiercely ag;
pleasure, or recreati
access to a walk in
wage prescribed a s[
to preserve moralit)
generous as to temp
It limited fantasy to
door of ambition onl
are grimly reflected
published in *Harpe*
Girl Who Comes to t

Offering to pay
solicited brief essay

rather than to either the value of the product or the level of the worker's productivity. For if custom was inscribed into the wage and the wage was conceived male, what *women* earned was not in the same sense as *males* a "wage." In the minds of employers and of male workers, the wage was to be paid to those who supported families.[48] If part of its function was to reflect the value of the product made, another and equally important part was to make a statement about the value of the worker who made the product. As long as female workers were not—could not be—male workers, their wages could not hope to touch those of their male peers.

We can guess that employers thought of it that way by their responses to questions about how much they paid women. Louise Bosworth cited the case of a woman who told her employer, "We cannot live on what we earn," and was asked in response, "Then what wages can you live on?"[49] The same paternalistic assumptions appear among employers who testified before the commission that investigated Illinois's *white slave* traffic in 1912. *[Editors' note: "White slavery" was the phrase used in the early 1900s to refer to forced prostitution.]* The employers interviewed reported unhesitatingly that they paid their male and female workers on the basis of what they estimated each needed. Julius Rosenwald, head of Sears, Roebuck and Company, then a mail-order house, told an investigative commission that "the concern made it a point not to hire girls not living at home at less than $8 a week."[50] A Montgomery Ward vice president echoed the sentiment: "We claim that all our employees without homes are on a self-supporting basis, and if we discover they are not we will put them there in an hour."[51] One department store executive described how his store asked all job applicants to sign a form "giving their estimate of necessary expenses in addition to family particulars. The girls who are not receiving sufficient to live on come to us. There are many instances of such receiving an increase." No one ever investigated the accuracy of the application forms, and even the commission chair was dubious as to who the procedure protected. A girl might readily lie about home support, he noted, "to assure herself of a job."[52] But at bottom, this was less the issue than the prevailing assumption that "girls" could and should be paid at a minimum that relied on family subsidy rather than on what their labor was worth.

If employers and popular opinion are any guide, and the question of what appeared to be reasonable lay at the heart of the wage structure, then all wages—not only those of women—contained a greater proportion of wants than most

of us have recognized. Women's wages, then, are only uniquely vulnerable in the sense that they participate in popular definitions of gender that denigrate the needs of one sex. The wage simultaneously framed job-related expectation in the light of existing gender roles and shaped gender experiences to avoid disappointment in view of the prevailing wage structure. More than exploitation of women, or paternalism toward them, the wage reflected a rather severe set of injunctions about how men and women were to live. These injunctions could be widely negated only at the peril of social order. Thus, part of the function of the female wage was to ensure attachment to family. The male wage, in contrast, provided incentives to individual achievement. It promoted geographical mobility and sometimes hinted at the possibility of social mobility as well. The female wage allowed women to survive; the male wage suggested a contribution to national economic well-being. These messages affirmed existing values and integrated all the parties into a set of understandings that located the relationships of working men and women to each other.

Some of these messages are powerful. Existing wage fund theory posited a limited sum available for all wages. It reduced the incentive to provide a higher wage for women by suggesting that their gain would come at the cost of male raises and therefore threaten the family's well-being. Smart put it this way: "Women's wages are, after all, part and parcel of the one share in the distribution of income which falls to labor."[53] What followed from that, of course, was that raising women's wages would merely reduce those of the men in their class by a similar proportion, leaving families in the same place economically and depriving them of maternal care to boot. Samuel Gompers translated this into a warning to members of the American Federation of Labor: "In industries where the wives and children toil, the man is often idle because he has been supplanted, or because the aggregate wages of the family are no higher than the wages of the adult man—the husband and father of the family."[54]

If women's wage gains could come only at the cost of the family, then their low wages affirmed and supported existing family life. As the renowned economist Alfred Marshall put it, a higher wage for women might be "a great gain in so far as it tends to develop their faculties, but an injury in so far as it tempts them to neglect their duty of building up a true home, and of investing their efforts in the personal capital of their children's character and abilities."[55] To Marshall the clear social choice implicit in the wage payment was between individual achievement and family well-being. His statement affirms the use of wages to preserve what is desirable to him: that all women are or will be married, that marriage is a normal state, that women will be continuously supported by men with sufficient wages, and that under these circumstances a wage that might be translated into an incentive not to marry or remain within families poses a challenge. Moreover, Marshall's view reflected the prevailing belief that a man was entitled to a wife to serve him and their home. It contained the assumption that a female who did not have a husband had erred. The differential female wage thus carried a moral injunction, a warning to women to follow the natural order.

The absence, by choice or necessity, of a family of her own did not excuse a woman from adherence to familial duties or morals, nor did it impel a more generous attitude toward wages. In fact, the level of the wage, which signaled an affirmation of family life, simultaneously threw out a challenge to preserve morality. In a March 1913 letter to the *New York Herald,* the head of Illinois's vice commission commented that "our investigations . . . show conclusively that thousands of good girls are going wrong every year merely because they can not live upon the wages paid them by employers."[56] But this was not necessarily an invitation to raise wages. Since not to live within a family was itself immoral, and the wage was seen as primarily a contribution to family life, a higher wage would only contribute to immorality. An ongoing debate over the fine line between a wage high enough to tempt women into supporting themselves and one so low that it could push the unwary into prostitution placed the wage in thrall to morality. Social worker Jeannette Gilder found herself in the awkward position of testifying against a pay raise for working women because "it seems to me to be paying a pretty poor compliment to the young women of this country to suggest that their virtue hangs upon such a slender thread that its price can be fixed somewhere between $6 and $8 a week."[57] And yet those who insisted that a low wage was an invitation to prostitution dominated the debate.

The wage also transmitted messages about the workforce. Employers feared that a rise in women's wages would trigger a demand for higher wages for men. As the wage captured social restrictions on female aspirations at work, so it conveyed the male potential for advancement, promotion, loyalty, and persistence. Contemporaries understood this well. When Elizabeth Butler remarked that "boys are often preferred to girls . . . because they can be relied on to learn the trade and women cannot,"[58] she captured the notion that implicit in the wage is the assumption that a man's wage is an investment in the future, while a woman's wage assumes only that the work at hand will be done.

Economist Francis Walker said this in a different way. If a man marries, he "becomes a better and more notable workman on that account." In contrast, if a woman marries, "it is most probable that she will . . . be a less desirable laborer than she was before."[59] Yet these statements promote the self-fulfilling function they simultaneously reflect. Lacking a man's wage, women were not normally given the opportunity to demonstrate that they too could be an investment in the future. Such experiments would be dangerous. Not only would a higher wage for women convey an inaccurate estimate of the potential occupational mobility of females, but it might inhibit the employer's capacity to use wages to construct the work force to his liking.

Finally, the wage made a familiar statement about female personality. Holding the stereotypical male as the norm, it claimed recompense for the costs of translating female qualities into the marketplace. Francis Walker exaggerated but caught the point when *he* insisted that the wage reflected women's character traits as well as their domestic orientation. It took account, *he* noted, of personalities that were "intensely sensitive to opinion, [and] shrink from the familiar utterances of blame." Coldness and indifference alone, he thought, were often sufficient to repress women's "impulses to activity."[60] These qualities of character exacted supervisory costs of the employer that were recaptured in the lower pay of women. As Charles Cheney, a South Manchester, Connecticut, manufacturer, put it, part of the reason women were paid less than men was because "they are sensitive and require extraordinarily tactful and kindly treatment and much personal consideration."[61]

Restrictive as the messages thrown out by a woman's wage were clearly intended to be, they were by no means the only messages that reached women. The very existence of a wage, the possibility of earning income evoked a contrary set of images: images that derived some support from the promise of American success. The same wage that evoked a struggle to survive and placed a lid on social mobility, the same wage that obscured women's visions of independence and citizenship had the capacity to conjure contrary images as well. It could even point the way to potential equality for women. These tensions are visible in the huge strikes that wracked the garment industry beginning in 1909–10, in the energy of young female labor leaders, and in the quest of more affluent women for lives that combined career and motherhood. Such events indicate that the notion of wages rooted in wants existed in a contested sphere—tempered by a broader ideology of individualism. They lead us to wonder about the role played by a woman's wage in a period of changing wants and rising levels of personal ambition.

The wage that in some measure helped to affirm and construct gendered expectations in the period before World War I continued to play that role afterward. But the dramatic social changes that came during and after the war, particularly the rise of a consumer culture, created their own pressures on the structure of gender. Because for most people the wage offered access to consumption, it mediated some of the tensions in gender roles that emerged in the 1920s. While public perception of a woman's wage remained conceptually "needs-based," continuing to limit female expectations, it quickly became clear that changing needs demanded some concessions to women's individual aspirations. These mixed messages contributed to arguments among women about who deserved a wage.[62]

In the statistical tables, the war appears as a small blip in the history of working women. New entrants into the labor force were relatively few, and the teens ended with little apparent increase in the numbers of women who earned wages. But the big surprise lay in the numbers of women who switched jobs. About half a million women, it seemed, chose to move into men's jobs. The *New York Times* commented on these figures with surprise: "The world of men woke up and took a second look at the world of women during the World War. It is still looking." And, it continued, "the Great War has in many cases been responsible for a change of premise as well as job."[63]

The primary explanation for these job shifts seems to have been the attraction of the male wage. Historian Maurine Greenwald estimates, for example, that women who became streetcar conductors immediately increased their wages by about *one-third* over those they had earned in traditional female jobs.[64] Daniel Nelson, who has explored the transformation of the factory, notes that after 1915 "the wages offered by machinery and munitions makers" drew an increasing number of women who had worked in traditional women's fields.[65] Though women's productivity was frequently acknowledged to be as high as that of the men they replaced, women were not, on principle, offered the same wage. A twenty-six-city survey by the New York State Industrial Commission at the end of the war revealed that *less* than 10 percent of the women who replaced men received pay equal to that of the men who had preceded them. The commission reported that "in many cases the production of women was equal to that of men, in others it was greater, and in still others, less. The wages paid had little, if anything, to do with productive efficiency."[66] Since women who were paid less than men still earned far more than they could have at women's jobs, few of those who benefited from wartime opportunities complained. But the

pressure of a dual wage structure on male wages posed a problem. Fearing a breakdown of social order, men and women began to call for a wage paid for the job—or equal pay. This slogan, as we will see later, was designed primarily to reduce pressure on men's wages.

Though most of the wartime job shifts proved to be temporary, they signaled an incipient dissatisfaction among some wage-earning women over the issue of wages—a dissatisfaction that could no longer be contained by rationalizations over social role. These struggles frequently pitted women who earned wages against those who did not, revealing something about contested definitions of womanhood among white women. For example, when female streetcar conductors in several large cities waged largely futile battles to hang on to their high-paying jobs, they were fighting not only the men who wanted their jobs back but a conception of womanliness that restricted access to outdoor work. And the female printers in New York State who successfully struggled to exempt themselves from legislation that precluded their working during the lucrative night hours simultaneously attacked rigid conceptions of family life.

Such campaigns were opposed by clear signals from government and corporations to women not to expect too much. The Women's Bureau of the Department of Labor offers a case in point. In 1920, when the bureau was created, it received a meagre $75,000 lump-sum appropriation and distributed it as effectively as it could. In 1922 a House proviso "stipulated that no salary in the Women's Bureau should be more than $1800, except three at $2000, and the director's and assistant director's salaries which have been fixed by statute." If effected, the proviso, as the Women's Bureau pointed out, would have left it with "no staff of technically trained, experienced people to direct and supervise its work." But more important, the bureau noted that other agencies of the government paid their male employees with the same qualifications "very much higher salaries than any that have even been suggested by the Women's Bureau—twice as much in many instances."[67]

Such policies were routine in industry. In the electrical industry of the 1920s, Ronald Schatz reports that "corporations maintained separate pay scales for men and women. Male wage keysheets began where female keysheets left off; the least skilled male workers earned more than the most capable female employee."[68] Still, the point for women was that even this low pay exceeded that of such traditionally female jobs as laundry work and waiting on tables. "For this reason, many young women preferred jobs in electrical factories." When the Ford Motor Company instituted a five-dollar day for its male employees after the war, it deliberately omitted women workers. According to Vice President James Couzens, women "are not considered such economic factors as men."[69]

Corporations carefully distinguished between the kinds of social welfare programs offered as extensions of cash wages to women and men. General Electric and Westinghouse offered men programs that stressed financial and job security, such as a 5 percent bonus every six months after five years of service, a pension after twenty years, and group life insurance and paid vacations after ten years of service. Women, for whom longevity was not encouraged and for whom it was thought not to matter, got programs that emphasized sociability, such as "dances, cooking classes, secretarial instruction, picnics, clubs, and summer camps."[70]

The not-so-subtle relationship between policy and practice is beautifully illustrated in the self-confirming apparatus in effect at the General Electric Company, where President Gerard Swope defended his policies on the grounds that "our theory was that women did not recognize the responsibilities of life and were hoping to get married soon and would leave us, and therefore, this insurance premium deduction from the pay would not appeal to them."[71] As historian Ronald Schatz notes, because GE compelled women to quit if they married, women rarely acquired enough seniority to obtain pensions or vacations with pay. Women's aspirations could not be entirely stilled by these measures. The Ford Motor Company, according to historian Stephen Meyer III, "considered all women, regardless of their family stakes, as youths: that is as single men under twenty-two without dependents, and therefore ineligible for Ford profits." Yet "as the result of criticism from women's rights advocates, the company eventually allowed some women, who were the heads of households, to participate in its welfare plan."[72]

One result of such policies and an instrument in their perpetuation as well was that women carefully rationalized their increasing workforce participation and defended themselves by comparing their wages only to those of other women. The model was familiar. The numerous investigating commissions of the prewar period had already asserted the injustice of paying women as much as men. Thus, investigators exploring the feasibility of a higher wage for women raised such issues as what, for instance, a firm would "have to pay a man with a family if it paid $2 a day to girls with no one but themselves to support?"[73] This does not seem to have inhibited women's desire for higher incomes. But it seems to have channeled their grievances away from men who earned far more than they and toward women instead. Among Western Electric workers interviewed in the late 1920s, a typical female who complained about wages tended to be distressed not at her absolute wage but at how it compared with those of other women. As one female employee complained, "the girl next to me, her job pays $39.80 per hundred, and mine pays $28.80 and I work just as hard as she does. I don't see how they figure that out. She makes ten cents more on every one she makes."[74]

These powerful and sometimes explicit barriers extended across race lines and to the social wages offered by modern corporations. In their presence Black women were paid less than white women for the same or similar jobs. Employers utilized them to sanction distinctions in the amenities they offered to Black and white women. An early survey of the tobacco industry in Virginia reflects the value of such circumscribed comparisons. "Tuesday and Friday," the report noted matter of factly, "the white girls have 15 minutes extra in order to dance, but the 15 minutes is paid for by the firm."[75]

What kept the "wage" pot bubbling, then, was not women's desire to achieve male pay but their urge to satisfy more concrete wants. As mass production jobs and clerical work opened up to white women, some factory jobs became available to Black women. New, relatively well-paying jobs and rising real wages for both men and women contributed to the advent of the consumer society and helped to create a new definition of wants that drew on a prevailing individualism from which women could hardly be excluded. Marketing techniques, installment buying, and the increasing value placed on consumption replaced thrift and postponed gratification as appropriate spirits of the time. New definitions of wants attracted new groups of women to the workforce and suggested new rationales for staying there.

The changing population of female workers challenged perceptions of a wage that spoke to simpler needs. To women for whom the prewar women's wage had offered little apart from the despair of poverty, the wage now stretched to encompass the hope of individual achievement measured by material goals. Defined in prewar practice as the minimum required to sustain a single woman partially supported by her family, the postwar wage at least suggested the capacity to earn a living.[76] Ronald Edsforth, who studied auto workers in the 1920s, notes that government investigators discovered among the women working in auto factories in the 1920s a "genuinely modern level of individual materialism . . . guiding . . . life-shaping decisions."

They concluded that "jobs in the auto factories were most desired simply because auto workers' earnings were high."[77] But even the rising wage was clearly inadequate to reconcile the competing needs of an increasingly heterogeneous group of female wage earners. Less immigrant than native born, containing a small but steadily growing proportion of married women, and with a still tiny but slowly growing representation of Black women in mainstream jobs that had long been closed to them, women with competing views of the wage attempted to participate in what some called the "American standard of living." In the process they helped to establish a new set of gendered definitions about self and others.

For middle-class, single, adventurous women, work and a wage meant escape from boredom, a bit of rebellion, a purpose in life—the means to a relatively autonomous existence. Fueled by the rhetoric of the women's movement and energized by a successful campaign for the vote, single women, no longer subsidized by families and increasingly eager to live outside them, craved the independence that wages potentially offered. To some, participation in wage work offered to contribute economic equality to the political citizenship they had won with suffrage.[78] To others, as economist Theresa Wolfson suggested, the wage bought the liberty to live "comparatively free lives outside of their working hours."[79]

For poorer women, including immigrants and women of color, and for most of the married women who earned, the wage became a measure of the capacity to participate in an increasingly pervasive consumer society. "I would like to work," commented one young assembly line worker, "until I get my furniture paid for. My husband is young and hasn't got much of a start yet and I want to help him."[80] A woman's wage represented, still, a supplement to male earnings—an extension of family life. Less a vehicle to sheer survival in the 1920s, it promised access to the new wants generated by an ethic of consumption. If it still continued to preclude freedom for most women, it offered a way to sustain and even enhance family life and exacted, in return, the price of women's continuing commitment to the workforce.[81] It should not surprise us then that the changing material content of the wage did not diminish either the effort to earn it or its importance in women's lives. And it dramatically expanded the numbers of women willing and able to earn wages. A young woman who had worked at the Western Electric company for a year complained that her feet swelled on the job. She didn't want to sit down, however, because "I can't turn out the rates when I sit down." She had, she said, returned to Western Electric after a year

at another job because "I couldn't earn near as much money, and I couldn't save any."[82]

Because a woman's wage had to serve the increasingly fragmented needs of a diverse array of women, the rhetoric surrounding it became more complex. It is best uncovered in the efforts of the newly created Women's Bureau of the Department of Labor to represent women workers of all kinds. The bureau's official position consistently upheld wages for women based on the value of the job. Yet its public posture simultaneously affirmed the need for a minimum wage based on the needs of the worker. Wages, wrote Mary Anderson, head of the bureau, "should be established on the basis of occupation and not on the basis of sex or race." At the same time, she added, the minimum wage rate that was available to women only, if at all, "should cover the cost of living in health and decency, instead of a bare existence, and should allow for dependents and not merely for the individual."[83]

The compromise, then, appeared to lie not in abandoning a needs-based assessment of women's wages so much as in an effort to understand that any definition of "wants" encompassed a broad range of human needs. While fewer than 15 percent of all married women, and about 30 percent of Black married women, with wage-earning husbands were regularly employed before the 1930s, those who earned wages had a complicated series of wants. For example, well-paid male and female hosiery workers in the Piedmont Valley of North Carolina and Tennessee flaunted their capacity to buy consumer goods.[84] In the same region, the poorly paid white textile workers could and frequently did hire Black women to take care of their children while white husbands and wives worked in the mills.[85] Black women used their tiny pay to feed and clothe their children and to support those who cared for them in their absence. Such enormous differences in the uses of wages notwithstanding, the image of women paid at a rate regulated by public perceptions of abstract needs helped to perpetuate the sense that, in the competition for jobs among women, what was at stake was not skill or the nature of work but the capacity to contribute to family support. This image perpetuated a low wage for all women. In exactly the way that employers had earlier chosen to believe that young, single women were supported by their parents, so, in the period after World War I, an idealized image of marriage with its attendant financial subsidy served to define a woman's role and threatened to regulate the level of wages for all women.

Partly in consequence, single women, inside and outside the Women's Bureau, were haunted by visions of married women subsidized by their husbands and therefore able to accept lower wages. Public debate over the wage question in the 1920s turned on the issue of whose needs the wage was intended to meet—the married woman working for "pin money" or the independent self-supporting woman of all classes. Neither category encompassed the reality of women workers, more than three-quarters of whom, according to contemporary studies, supported themselves and their families. While in the prewar period, questions about "workers who are in part supported by parents or other members of the family"[86] had captured a certain unease about independent women who transcended traditional roles, the 1920s attack on pin-money workers focused on the distress of single working women who feared competition from women whose families partially supported them. The competition, muted by the prosperity of the 1920s, did not explode until the 1930s. In the meantime, the question of married women in industry was argued pro and con, with such stalwart champions of working women as Mary Gilson, Melinda Scott, and Sophonisba Breckinridge protesting that married women ought not to be in the labor force. Breckinridge proposed instead "a living wage for men based on their own needs and those of their wives and a standard family of three children; disciplinary measures for husbands who are unwilling to work, and state aid for wives of those who cannot work."[87]

In the face of the commitment to a needs-based wage, proponents of individualism and some champions of the Women's Bureau fought a losing battle for "a rate for the job." The new consumerism required a more complex set of messages than simple individualism. While it offered support for raising the wage enough to accommodate both new social relations and new needs, it would not, and did not, challenge conceptions of the wage that sustained family life. Thus, one group of women struggled to elevate a woman's wage by asking that all workers receive value for the job, while a second declared itself in need of protective legislation and advocated a minimum wage to legitimate women's capacity to work at all. A woman's wage still refused to incorporate the capacity to earn a living. At most, it offered a fling at independence to those who did not need to contribute to family support. For the poor it could enhance a family's standard of living. But in no sense was a woman's wage intended to promote the desire for a self-sufficient existence.

Yet to women who worked, the capacity to improve the standard of living was not mere ideology. The reification of an "American" standard of living offered a rationale for continuing wage work among married women. As consumer expectations rose, the purchase of what some might have called pin-money goods became not a luxury but part of the quality of life. Because a woman's wage appeared as largely contributory, it neither undermined male egos nor fomented female independence. Men understood the wage as an indication of whether they were "getting ahead." Women understood it as an indication of whether they could keep up with their work, their status among their peers, and their position in the eyes of the boss. And yet women's capacity to enhance the family standard contributed to denuding the notion that the family wage either could or should be earned by men alone. At the same time, women established new sources of comparisons that enabled them to maintain status and self-esteem even as they continued to earn less than two-thirds of the wage of the average male worker.

But women's wages, restricted by an ethos of need and locked into comparisons with other women, still could not rise high enough to compete with the wages of men. If the message of the wage differed for men and women, it failed to prevent women from seeking the same kinds of material gains acquired by men. At some level the "woman's wage" decisively relegated females to a plateau of citizenship that could not be equated with that of men. As much as suffrage had seemed to extend citizenship to women, a women's wage suggested the limits of their aspirations and assigned them to sometimes objectionable social roles. A "rate for the job"—a wage equivalent to that of similarly situated men working in the same firm—would have trumpeted a message of aspiration and ambition that few in the 1920s were ready to hear. But the value that a woman worker created was never the central issue of women's wage work. Rather, the wage sought to identify the boundaries within which economic inequality could be used to constrain the prerogatives of citizenship. The sex of a worker remained safely more important than what that worker did. With some few exceptions, equality was not at issue; the wage did not contest male prerogatives in the workplace. Rather, it symbolized the limits of political citizenship.

NOTES

1. Henry A. Landsberger, *Hawthorne Revisited: Management and the Worker, Its Critics, and the Developments in Human Relations in Industry* (Ithaca, N.Y.: Cornell University, 1958), 19.

2. New York State, *Factory Investigating Commission,* Fourth Report (Albany: S.B. Lyon Co., 1915), vol. 1, app. 3, passim. (Hereinafter referred to as FIC.)

3. N. Arnold Tolles, *Origins of Modern Wage Theories* (Englewood Cliffs, N.J.: Prentice-Hall, 1964), 8.

4. This theory, known as marginal productivity theory, was predicated on the assumption of perfect competition and emphasized the demands of employers in calculating the wage. Its classic exposition is John Bates Clark, *The Distribution of Wealth* (New York: Macmillan, 1899).

5. FIC, Fourth Report, vol. 4, 435.

6. In the United States, organized workers agitated for the idea beginning in the 1830s.

7. Melton McLaurin, *Paternalism and Protest: Southern Cotton Mill Workers and Organized Labor, 1875–1905* (Westport, Conn.: Greenwood Press, 1971), 23, describes how the notion of a family wage that rested on the labor of all family members could contribute to expectations of female and child labor. In southern textile mills, "mill management argued that the total annual income of a mill family was far greater than that of a farm family. Thus the 'family wage' was used as a cover for the low wages paid individuals" (23). But this is not the usual understanding. See Martha May, "The Historical Problem of the Family Wage: The Ford Motor Company and the Five Dollar Day," *Feminist Studies,* 8 (Summer 1982), 394–424.

8. For access to the opposing positions, see Jane Humphries, "The Working Class Family, Women's Liberation, and Class Struggle: The Case of Nineteenth Century British History," *Review of Radical Political Economics,* 9 (Fall 1977), 25–41; Michelle Barrett and Mary McIntosh, "The Family Wage: Some Problems for Socialists and Feminists," *Capital and Class,* 11 (1980), 51–72; and Hilary Land, "The Family Wage," *Feminist Review,* 6 (1980), 55–78.

9. John A. Ryan, *A Living Wage: Its Ethical and Economic Aspects* (New York: Macmillan, 1906), 117.

10. William Smart, *Studies in Economics* (London: Macmillan, 1985), 34. Smart added that "in addition perhaps some consumption of alcohol and tobacco, and some indulgence in fashionable dress are, in many places, so habitual that they may be said to be 'conventionally necessary' " (34).

11. Cited by Ryan, *Living Wage,* 130, from the *American Federationist,* 1898.

12. Ryan, *Living Wage,* 117.

13. Ibid., vii.

14. Italics mine. Quoted in May, "Historical Problem of the Family Wage," 402. Samuel Gompers believed the worker's living wage should "be sufficient to sustain himself and those dependent upon him in a manner to maintain his self-respect, to educate his children, supply his household with literature, with opportunities to spend a portion of his life with his family." In Samuel Gompers, "A Minimum Living Wage," *American Federationist,* 5 (April 1898), 26.

15. See, for example, the list compiled by F. Spencer Baldwin in Louise Bosworth, *The Living Wage of Women Workers* (New York: Longmans Green and Co., 1911), 7; see also Elizabeth Beardsley Butler, *Women and the Trades: Pittsburgh, 1907–1908* (Pittsburgh: University of Pittsburgh Press, 1984 [1909]), 346–47.

16. J. Laurence Laughlin, ed., *Principles of Political Economy by John Stuart Mill* (New York: D. Appleton and Company, 1885), 214.

17. Italics mine. Ryan, *Living Wage,* 107.

18. Lynn Y. Wiener, *From Working Girl to Working Mother: The Female Labor Force in the United States, 1820–1980* (Chapel Hill: University of North Carolina, 1985), 19, 26, 84.

19. Ryan, *Living Wage,* 107.

20. Ibid., 120.

21. Kellogg Durland, "Labor Day Symposium," *American Federationist* 12 (September 1905), 619.

22. Ryan, *Living Wage,* 107.

23. Ibid., 133.

24. Dorothy W. Douglas, *American Minimum Wage Laws at Work* (New York: National Consumers' League, 1920), 14.

25. Butler, *Women and the Trades,* 346; Bosworth, *Living Wage of Women Workers,* 9. The Women's Bureau estimated that the minimums in effect from 1913 to 1915 ranged from $8.50 to $10.74. See Bulletin no. 61, *The Development of Minimum Wage Laws in the United States: 1912–1927* (Washington, D.C.: Government Printing Office, 1928).

26. Thomas Herbert Russell, *The Girl's Fight for a Living: How to Protect Working Women from Dangers Due to Low Wages* (Chicago: M.A. Donahue, 1913), 108.

27. Elizabeth Brandeis, "Labor Legislation," vol. 3 of John Commons, *History of Labor in the United States* (New York: Macmillan, 1935), 524–25, makes the point that these budgets were calculated in one of two ways: on the basis of actual expenditures (a problem because women had to live on what they earned, however small) or on the basis of theoretical budgets (a problem because employer-members of boards resisted the inclusion of such items as recreation, "party dress," etc.). They were then "modified" by estimates of prevailing wages, consideration of the amounts of the proposed increases, and possible consequences for business conditions.

28. Sue Ainslee Clark and Edith Wyatt, "Working-Girls' Budgets: A Series of Articles Based upon Individual Stories of Self-Supporting Girls," *McClure's,* 35 (October 1910). Additional articles appeared in *McClure's* in vol. 36 in November and December 1910 and February 1911. They were published in book form under the title *Making Both Ends Meet: The Income and Outlay of New York Working-Girls* (New York: Macmillan, 1911). The classic study is that of Louise Bosworth, cited in note 25.

29. Clark and Wyatt, "Working-Girls' Budgets," *McClure's,* 35 (October 1910), 604. See the discussion of these budgets in

Wiener, *From Working Girl to Working Mother*, 75–77; and Joanne Meyerowitz, *Women Adrift: Independent Wage Earners in Chicago, 1880–1930* (Chicago: University of Chicago Press, 1988), 33–35.

30. The magazine advertised for contributions in January 1908 and published from four to six contributions from February 1908 to January 1909. In September 1908 it announced that it was flooded with contributions and would no longer accept any more. There is no way of knowing how heavily these were edited, so they have been used here only to extract a broad gauge of opinion.

31. "The Girl Who Comes to the City," *Harper's Bazaar,* 42 (January 1908), 54.

32. "The Girl Who Comes to the City," 42 (October 1908), 1005; 42 (July 1908), 694.

33. "The Girl Who Comes to the City," 42 (August 1908), 776. The maximum achieved by any of these women was the $100 a month earned by a Washington D.C., civil servant (42 [November 1908], 1141). That sum was sufficient for a single woman not only to live reasonably well but to save and invest some of her income. It was rarely achieved by women.

34. "The Girl Who Comes to the City," 42 (November 1908), 1141; see also October 1908, 1007.

35. See, for example, Alice Kessler-Harris, *Out to Work: A History of Wage Earning Women in the United States* (New York: Oxford, 1982), 99–101; Meyerowitz, *Women Adrift,* 34–36.

36. "The Girl Who Comes to the City," 42 (March 1908), 277; 42 (May 1908), 500. The widespread nature of this assumption is apparent in "Women's Wages," *Nation,* 108 (February 22, 1919), 270–71: "The employer of women today is in a large proportion of cases heavily subsidized; for there is a considerable gap between the $9 a week that is paid to a girl and her actual cost of maintenance. Who makes up the difference? In the employer's mind it is usually the girl's family—which is often mythical."

37. Smart, *Studies in Economics,* 115.

38. Butler, *Women and the Trades,* 346.

39. Meyerowitz, *Women Adrift,* 33.

40. Butler, *Women and the Trades,* 344.

41. FIC, Fourth Report, vol. 4, app. 3, 450.

42. Scott Nearing, "The Adequacy of American Wages," *Annals of the American Academy of Political and Social Sciences,* 59 (May 1915), 2.

43. "Women's Wages and Morality," *American Federationist,* 20 (June 1913), 467.

44. Smart, *Studies in Economics,* 125.

45. Russell, *Girl's Fight for a Living,* 21. On pay differences by race, see Meyerowitz, *Women Adrift,* 36; and Dolores Janiewski, *Sisterhood Denied: Race, Gender and Class in a New South Community* (Philadelphia: Temple University Press, 1985), 110–13.

46. FIC, Fourth Report, vol. 2, app. 3, 468; Don D. Lescohier, then a Minnesota statistician and later to become an eminent gatherer of labor statistics, commented at the same hearings that "custom . . . plays a far larger part in holding wages stationary than we have been accustomed to think" (ibid., 459).

47. Smart, *Studies in Economics,* 116. The radical Scott Nearing, in a minority opinion, held that the male wage was not determined by another principle at all. He protested industry's lack of attention to social relations: "The man with a family is brought into active competition with the man who has no family obligations. The native-born head of a household must accept labor terms which are satisfactory to the foreign-born single man. Industry does not inquire into a worker's social obligations" (Nearing, "Adequacy of American Wages," 123).

48. Which is not, of course, to imply that all males who earned wages were paid enough to support families. See Janiewski, *Sisterhood Denied,* for illustrations of wages in the southern tobacco and textile industries that required the labor of three or more people to sustain a family.

49. Bosworth, *Living Wage,* 4.

50. Russell, *Girl's Fight for a Living,* 73.

51. Ibid., 108.

52. Ibid., 83.

53. Smart, *Studies in Economics,* 107.

54. Samuel Gompers, "Woman's Work, Rights and Progress," *American Federationist,* 20 (August 1913), 625.

55. Alfred Marshall, *Principles of Economics,* 8th ed. (New York: Macmillan, 1953), 685.

56. Quoted in Russell, *Girl's Fight for a Living,* 16; and see "Women's Wages and Morality," 465.

57. Russell, *Girl's Fight for a Living,* 38; cf. also the testimony of Ida Tarbell in ibid., 39.

58. Butler, *Women and the Trades,* 342–43.

59. Francis Amasa Walker, *The Wages Question: A Treatise on Wages and the Wages Class* (New York: Henry Holt and Company, 1876), 374.

60. Ibid., 378.

61. Quoted in Marjorie Shuler, "Industrial Women Confer," *Woman Citizen,* 8 (January 27, 1923), 25.

62. Such arguments were prefigured in the late nineteenth century by assertions that the greedy were taking jobs from the needy. See Kessler-Harris, *Out to Work,* 99ff.

63. "Women as Wage Earners," *New York Times,* January 28, 1923, 26.

64. Maurine Greenwald, *Women, War, and Work: The Impact of World War One on Women in the United States* (Westport, Conn.: Greenwood Press, 1980), 155. Greenwald notes that a female janitor who might have made $35 a month earned $75–80 a month as a conductor.

65. Daniel Nelson, *Managers and Workers: Origins of the New Factory System in the United States* (Madison: University of Wisconsin Press, 1975), 145.

66. Quoted in "Women and Wages," *The Woman Citizen,* 4 (June 7, 1919), 8. The article went on to report that one plant had "reckoned women's production as 20 per cent greater than that of the men preceding them. But this did not prevent the same plant from cutting down the women's pay one-third."

67. Typescript, "Memoranda Regarding Women's Bureau," in National Archives, Record Group 86, Box 4, File: WTUL Action

on Policies. The bureau lost this battle. As a result, its professional staff tended to work more out of loyalty and commitment than for monetary gain. See Judith Sealander, *As Minority Becomes Majority: Federal Reaction to the Phenomenon of Women in the Work Force, 1920–1963* (Westport, Conn.: Greenwood Press, 1983), chap. 3, for the early days of the Women's Bureau.

68. Ronald W. Schatz, *The Electrical Workers: A History of Labor at General Electric and Westinghouse, 1923–60* (Urbana: University of Illinois Press, 1983), 32.

69. Quoted in Stephen Meyer III, *The Five Dollar Day: Labor Management and Social Control in the Ford Motor Company, 1908–1921* (Albany: State University of New York Press, 1981), 140.

70. Schatz, *Electrical Workers,* 20–21.

71. Quoted in Schatz, *Electrical Workers,* 21; Nelson, *Managers and Workers,* 118, confirms that the wage as welfare differed for men and women: "Manufacturers who employed large numbers of women usually emphasized measures to make the factory more habitable. Lunchrooms, restrooms, landscaping and other decorative features conveyed the idea of a home away from home. At the same time, the classes in domestic economy and child rearing, social clubs, outings and dances (women only) assured the worker that she need not sacrifice her femininity when she entered the male world of the factory. But, because the female operative was (or was thought to be) a secondary wage earner and probably a transient, she was not offered pensions, savings programs and insurance plans."

72. Meyer, *Five Dollar Day,* 140; implicit in the Ford policy was a quite conscious attempt to circumscribe the roles and self-perceptions of men as well as of women. Meyer quotes a Ford policy manual from the 1920s to the effect that "if a man wants to remain a profit sharer, his wife should stay at home and assume the obligations she undertook when married" (141). See the commentary on this issue in "Housework Wages," *The Woman Citizen,* 4 (October 4, 1919), 449.

73. Russell, *Girl's Fight for a Living,* 101; the same investigator asked an employer, "If you raised a little girl from $3 to $8 would a man getting $15 feel aggrieved?" (112)—a question that loads the dice by imagining women as no more than children.

74. Microfilm records, Western Electric Plant, Hawthorne Works, Operating Branch M., interviews, Reel 6, July 8, 1929. Records of individuals are not identified or tagged beyond the branch where the interviews were taken. The growing sense of entitlement to comparable wages was captured by an experienced female worker who declared herself satisfied with her work "because it was more interesting and I could make my rate" but nevertheless complained that "I don't see why they didn't raise me anyway like they did the other girls, every half year or every year."

In ibid., July 9, 1929. This phenomenon was not specific to women alone. F. J. Roethlisberger and William Dickson, analyzing the Western Electric research, commented, "The results of the inter- viewing program show very clearly that the worker was quite as much concerned with these differentials, that is the relation of his wages to that of other workmen as with the absolute amount of his wages." See *Management and the Worker: An Account of a Research Program Conducted by the Western Electric Company, Hawthorne Works, Chicago* (Cambridge, Mass.: Harvard University Press, 1946), 543. But nothing in the interviews indi- cates that women compared their wages with those of men, nor did men with those of women.

75. Mary Schaill and Ethel Best to Mary Anderson, Novem- ber 5, 1919, Virginia Survey, Bulletin no. 10, National Archives, Record Group 86: Records of the Women's Bureau, Box 2.

76. Pauline Newman, veteran trade unionist, challenged old notions of a living wage in "The 'Equal Rights' Amendment," *American Federationist,* 45 (August 1938), 815. She wrote, "It is not a wage which affords an opportunity for intellectual develop- ment; it is not a wage which allows for spiritual growth; it is not a wage on which wage-earning women can enjoy the finer things of life."

77. Ronald Edsforth, *Class Conflict and Cultural Consensus: The Making of a Mass Consumer Society in Flint, Michigan* (New Brunswick, N.J.: Rutgers University Press, 1987), 95.

78. Daniel T. Rodgers, *The Work Ethic in Industrial America: 1850–1920* (Chicago: University of Chicago Press, 1974), 196.

79. Theresa Wolfson, *The Woman Worker and the Trade Unions* (New York: International Publishers, 1926), 42.

80. Microfilm records, Western Electric Plant, Hawthorne Works, Operating Branch M., interviews, Reel 6, July 8, 1929.

81. Wolfson, *Woman Worker,* 42–43.

82. Microfilm records, Western Electric Plant, Hawthorne Works, Operating Branch M., interviews, Reel 6, Folder 1, Box 14, July 1, 1929.

83. Mary Anderson, "Industrial Standards for Women," *American Federationist,* 32 (July 1925), 565.

84. Jacquelyn Dowd Hall et al., *Like a Family: The Making of a Southern Cotton Mill World* (Chapel Hill: University of North Carolina Press, 1987), 255–56.

85. See interviews with Ada Mae Wilson, Mary Ethel Shockley, Ina Wrenn, and Gertrude Shuping in Southern Oral History Project Collection, Martin Wilson Library, University of North Carolina, Chapel Hill. Used with the kind help of Jacquelyn Dowd Hall.

86. The quotation is from FIC, Fourth Report, vol. 4, 440. The percentage of married black women working and supporting fami- lies was far higher than that for white women.

87. Shuler, "Industrial Women Confer," 12.

Sex Differences in Moving up and Taking Charge

BARBARA RESKIN and IRENE PADAVIC

Until twenty years ago, few employers even considered women for promotions that would take them outside the female clerical or assembly-line ghetto. Although more women have been promoted in recent years, women still have a long way to go. Now they may get some help from the legal system, however. For instance, the Supreme Court ruled in 1990 that Ann Hopkins should be promoted to partner status at the Big Six accounting firm of Price Waterhouse. The decision put other companies on notice that discriminating in promotions could be costly. Then in 1991 a jury awarded $6.3 million to a woman whom Texaco had twice passed over for promotion. On the legislative front, the Civil Rights Act of 1991 now allows employees to sue not merely for lost wages and litigation expenses but also for punitive damages. Similarly, the Glass Ceiling Act of 1991—designed to encourage employers to remove barriers to the progress of women and minorities—reflects increasing public concern with barriers to job mobility. But how effective this legislation will be remains to be seen.

As for access to authority, women have also made some strides. In 1940 many firms explicitly prohibited women from occupying managerial positions (Goldin 1990). By the 1970s, with women flooding the labor market and the number of managerial jobs expanding dramatically, unprecedented numbers of women were entering the ranks of management. Since then, American women have increased their representation in management ranks from 18 percent of all managers in 1970 to 30 percent in 1980 and 40 percent in 1990. These figures indisputably show that thousands of

women are gaining access to jobs that usually confer organizational power. Whether women in these positions actually are able to act on the authority typical of managerial positions is a question we address in this chapter.

WOMEN, MEN, AND PROMOTIONS

Television shows and movies offer a distorted image of women who have done well in the business and professional world. The successful woman is depicted as beautiful, white, and heterosexual. She has a spectacular wardrobe and plenty of money, and the people she works with take her seriously. She is sometimes ruthless in exerting her power. Few real women match this glamorous image.

The Promotion Gap

In the real world of work, just a handful of women reach the top of the corporate hierarchy. In 1990, only nineteen—or fewer than 0.5 percent—of the 4,012 highest-paid officers and directors in top companies were women (Fierman 1990). Within Fortune 500 companies, women and minorities held fewer than 5 percent of senior management posts (Fierman 1990), indicating snail-like progress from the early 1970s, when 1 to 3 percent of senior managers were women (Segal 1992).

A glass ceiling blocks the on-the-job mobility of women of all classes, as well as minorities of both sexes. Indeed, in some organizations the glass ceiling may be quite low; for many women of all traces, the problem is the sticky floor, which keeps them trapped in low-wage, low-mobility jobs (Berheide 1992). Data from a study conducted in the early 1980s in Illinois found that the average man had 0.83 promotion and the average woman 0.47 promotion (Spaeth 1989). National data for 1991 show a smaller but still significant promotion gap: 48 percent of men had been promoted by their current employer but only 34 percent of women (Reskin and Kalleberg 1993). Both these studies underestimate the promotion gap by failing to distinguish between small-step promotions (for example, clerk-typist 1 to clerk-typist 2) and larger ones (for example, sales representative to sales manager).

Historically, African-American women and men have fared worse in promotions than other groups have (Jones 1985).[1] In 1988, 72 percent of managers in companies employing more than 100 people were white men, 23 percent were white women, 3 percent were African-American men, and 2 percent were African-American women (Alexander 1990). Although some people believe that affirmative action programs give women of color an undue advantage over other groups, this is not the case (McGuire and Reskin 1993; Sokoloff 1992). Being a "twofer" (a term that personnel directors sometimes use for people who fill two Equal Employment Opportunity categories) may help some minority women get jobs, but it hurts them in promotions because it undermines their credibility. Many people assume that minorities—and especially minority women—are hired or promoted only to fill quotas. According to Ella Bell, an organizational behavior professor and consultant. "Being a twofer doesn't give you legitimization, doesn't give you a voice or power, and doesn't move you up" (Alexander 1990).

Several studies have indicated that men do not confront blocked opportunities because of their sex; in fact, as one sociologist noted, men tend to "rise to the top like bubbles in wine bottles" (Grimm 1978). Christine Williams (1992) found that employers singled out male workers in traditionally female jobs—nurse, librarian, elementary school teacher, social worker, and the like—for an express ride to the top on a "glass escalator." Some of the men in William's study faced pressure to accept promotions, like the male children's librarian who received negative evaluations for not "shooting high enough."

The country's largest employer, the U.S. government, has a better record in promoting women and African Americans than private industry does. Historically, the government has been the only place outside the black community where African-American female managers, administrators, and professionals could find jobs in their fields (Higginbotham 1987). Even now, African-American women do better in government jobs than in private industry. In 1992 both black and white women were better represented in governor-appointed cabinet-level positions than in top jobs in private industry (Harlan 1992). In other nations as well, women tend to do better in the public sector than in the private sector (Antal and Izraeli 1993).

Even inside government, however, men have a substantial edge in access to top jobs. In this country, women accounted for 43.5 percent of the workforce in state and local governments but only 31.3 percent of high-level state and local government jobs (Harlan 1991). Minority women were 9.8 percent of jobholders but only 5.1 percent of top-level jobholders. Although women held half of all federal government jobs in 1992 and made up 86 percent of the government's clerical workers, they were only a quarter of supervisors and only a tenth of senior executives (U.S. Merit Systems Protection Board 1992). Minority women were fewer than 2 percent of senior executives and were promoted less often than white women with equivalent experience (U.S. Merit Systems Protection Board 1992).

What is striking about these disparities among government workers is that they exist fifteen years after the 1978 Civil Service Reform Act. In fact, a government report declared that the 1980s had brought "a resurgence of discrimination" (U.S. Merit Systems Protection Board 1992). Ironically, senior-level women and minorities employed in the Department of Labor division that is charged with enforcing discrimination regulations recently filed a grievance, claiming that sex discrimination has prevented their advancement. Alluding to the glass ceiling, one worker told the *Wall Street Journal* (1992), "We need Windex and paper towels because we can't even see [it]!"

Although American women lag behind men in promotions, compared to women in most other countries American women are doing relatively well. American women were four times more likely than French women to hold administrative and managerial jobs and six and a half times more likely to do so than British women (Crompton and Sanderson 1990:176). In no country, however, were women represented in top-level jobs on a par with their numbers in administrative and managerial positions (Farley 1993). In Denmark, women were 14.5 percent of administrators and managers in 1987 but only between 1 and 5 percent of top management; in Japan, women were 7.5 percent of administrators and managers but only 0.3 percent of top management in the private sector (Antal and Izraeli 1993:58; Steinhoff and Kazuko 1988). In all the countries for which information was available, women were vastly underrepresented in top-level jobs (Antal and Izraeli 1993).

Consequences of the Promotion Gap

Does it matter that women are locked out of the higher-level jobs? Yes. First of all, the practice is unfair. Americans of both sexes value promotions as a path to greater pay, authority, autonomy, and job satisfaction (Markham et al. 1987:227). And both sexes are ready to work hard for a promotion. In a recent survey of federal employees, 78 percent of the women and 74 percent of the men agreed that they were willing to devote whatever time was necessary in order to advance in their career (U.S. Merit Systems Protection Board 1992). Among minority women, 86 percent were willing to devote as much time as it takes (minority men's responses were not reported separately). Upward mobility is the heart of the American dream, and its denial to women reflects poorly on our society. A second reason to be concerned about the promotion gap is that it depresses women's wages. At a time when women's wages average only 70 percent of men's this is a serious consideration. Third, promotion barriers reduce women's opportunities to exercise authority on the job (as we discuss later) and to have autonomy from close supervision. Autonomy—the freedom to design aspects of one's work, to decide the pace and hours of work, and to not have others exercising authority over oneself (M. Adler 1993)—enhances job satisfaction. A fourth consequence of women's blocked mobility is that it often leads women to quit in frustration.

Some women try to get around blocked mobility by starting their own business. In 1990 women owned 30 percent of all businesses, and the Small Business Administration expects the number to rise to 40 percent by the year 2000 (Shellenbarger 1993). Yet women are less successful than men in these ventures; in 1982 the average business run by a woman grossed only 35 percent of what the average man-run business grossed (U.S. Small Business Administration 1988). A partial explanation is that women-run businesses are usually economically marginal. Many women business owners have the legal status of entrepreneur but are independent contractors: workers hired on a freelance basis to do work that regular employees otherwise would do in-house (Christensen 1989). Far fewer women own a business that employs others. The median hourly wage for a full-time, self-employed woman was $3.75 in 1987, compared to $8.08 for a full-time female employee (Collins 1993). Often self-employed women provide services that help other employed women cope with domestic work, such as catering, housecleaning, caring for children, and being a "mother's helper."

Explanations for the Promotion Gap

Many factors impede women's mobility. Although women are as committed to their careers as men are, women have less of the education, experience, and training that employers desire. Women also tend to be located in jobs that do not offer the same diversity of experience or the same opportunities for upward mobility as men's jobs. Finally, in making promotion decisions, employers discriminate against women. These are the three basic explanations of why companies still promote more white men than women and minorities.

Human-Capital Inequities and Promotion Human-capital theorists claim that sex differences in promotion rates are due to sex differences in commitment, education, and experience. These differences are presumed to make women less productive than men.

The claim that men are more committed than women to their jobs is based on the idea that women place family responsibilities ahead of career commitment. According to this reasoning, family demands do not allow women to devote as much time to their careers as men, and therefore women are unable to do all the things necessary to get promoted rapidly. Although employers act on this stereotype of women's lesser commitment, it is not founded in reality. . . . Women's career commitment does not differ from men's.

The second human-capital claim is that educational differences account for the promotion gap. Indeed, in 1992, women earned 47 percent of the bachelor's degrees in business administration but only 34 percent of the master's degrees. Thus educational differences do contribute to the sex disparity in promotion rates. However, they do not account for all of the disparity. Women with the same educational credentials as men are not attaining top-management jobs at the same rate. When told that women will slowly make their way to the top as more get advanced degrees, one woman manager countered, "My generation came out of graduate school fifteen or twenty years ago. The men are now in line to run major corporations. The women are not. Period" (Fierman 1990).

As for the third human-capital claim, women do receive less training and have less experience both within a firm and within the labor force. It is implausible, however, that women voluntarily acquire less experience. In many settings, employers prevent women from acquiring the essential experiences needed for advancement. For example, military promotion to the rank of commissioned officer is usually reserved for people with combat experience, but Congress and the military have banned women from combat positions. In banking, managers who hope for a top spot need extensive experience in commercial lending. But until recently, most women bank managers were not given the chance to work in commercial lending, so few women could acquire the expertise needed to rise beyond middle management. In the same way, the sex segregation of blue-collar production jobs denies women the experience they need to rise to management positions in manufacturing firms.

Similarly, in an increasingly global economy, some corporations are requiring international experience for future executives. However, women are far less likely than men to receive international assignments. According to the *Wall Street Journal,* international experience is increasingly crucial for advancement, and researchers agree (N. Adler 1984; Antal and Izraeli 1993). A human-resources vice president admitted, "No one will be in general management [in this company] by the end of the decade who didn't have international exposure and experience" (Bennett 1993). This trend will benefit white men more than women and minorities (Antal and Izraeli 1993). Many companies think twice before posting a woman or an African American to a foreign assignment, partly because they fear that sexist or racist attitudes will hinder their employee's ability to get the job done. Among industrial and service companies that regularly post employees to international assignments, 36 percent post men exclusively (Moran, Stahl & Boyer, Inc. 1988). Employers' fears are often unfounded, however: Most women posted to foreign assignments have succeeded in them, and their employers subsequently have made women a large proportion of the employees sent on international missions (N. Adler 1988). Those women will be in a better position than many others to advance in their careers.

Segregation and Promotion   The segregation explanation of the promotion gap focuses on differences between men and women's organizational locations. A key concept in this explanation is the internal labor market, or a firm's system for filling jobs by promoting experienced employees. Internal labor markets are composed of related jobs (or job families) connected by job ladders, which are promotion or transfer paths that connect lower- and higher-level jobs. These ladders may have only two rungs (as in a take-out restaurant that promotes counter workers to delivery persons), or they may span an entire organization. Job ladders also differ in shape. Some are shaped like a ladder—for example, a company's sales division whose job ladder

includes one stock clerk, one sales trainee, one sales representative, one assistant sales manager, and one sales manager. When the vice president in this division retires, everyone moves up one step. In contrast, other job ladders are shaped like a pyramid, with many entry-level jobs feeding into smaller and smaller numbers of jobs at progressively higher levels of the organization, so many workers compete for relatively few jobs. The broader the base of the pyramid, the smaller a worker's odds of being promoted.

The basic idea behind the segregation explanation is that women are promoted less often than men partly because access to internal labor markets is gendered. Women workers are more likely than men to be in jobs with short job ladders or to be in dead-end jobs. This sort of sex segregation begins with entry-level jobs. Men are more often placed in jobs with long job ladders and chances at top jobs.

Many traditionally female jobs, such as switchboard operator or teacher, do not have job ladders (Tomaskovic-Devey 1993). Employers have often designed these sorts of jobs without job ladders because they were not interested in reducing turnover and in fact wanted to encourage turnover in order to keep wages low. (Job ladders discourage turnover by giving workers an incentive to stay.) Women in traditionally male occupations are also more likely than men to have dead-end jobs. Women faculty in law schools, for example, disproportionately work as clinical instructors or instructors of research and writing, where they teach professional skills; these jobs usually are not on the tenure ladder (Reskin and Merritt 1993).

For workers who are on job ladders, men tend to be found on longer ladders that reach higher in the organization. In contrast, women and minorities are concentrated on short ladders, with just one or two rungs above the entry level. Clerical work, for example, is usually part of a two-rung system. A typical word-processing office, for instance, consists of many word-processing workers and one supervisor; a travel agency employs many reservation agents and one supervisor (Gutek 1988:231).

An illustration of how internal labor markets can affect promotion comes from a grocery chain whose female employees sued for discrimination because it had promoted almost no women or minorities to store manager. A diagram of this chain's internal labor market (Figure 1) shows that women's underrepresentation in the top jobs stemmed largely from sex segregation of lower-level jobs. Job ladders in the predominantly male produce departments led to top management. In contrast, the most heavily female departments—bakery/deli and general merchandise—were

FIGURE 1   INTERNAL LABOR MARKET FOR GROCERY STORE CHAIN, 1981 TO 1984
Source: Unpublished data from *Marshall et al. v. Alpha Beta.*

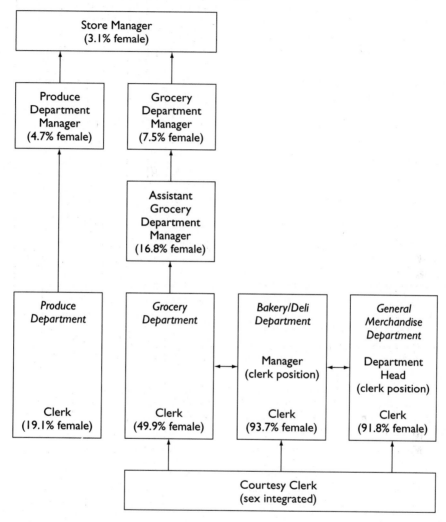

on short job ladders not directly connected to the ladder to top management.

The different kinds of establishments that employ women and men explain much of the promotion gap. Large organizations are more likely to have the resources that allow them to create promotion ladders. Moreover, their sheer size lets them create more opportunities to promote deserving workers (Spaeth 1989). Therefore, women's greater concentration in small, entrepreneurial firms and nonprofit organizations and men's concentration in large

corporations and for-profit companies also reduce women's odds of promotion relative to men. In one survey, corporations employed 47 percent of a random sample of men, compared to 34 percent of women (Reskin and Kalleberg 1993).

Segregation also contributes to the promotion gap by making women's accomplishments invisible. In prestigious Wall Street law firms, for example, senior partners have tended to assign women lawyers to research rather than litigation. Appearing in the courtroom less often than their male peers made women less visible, thus hampering their promotion to partner (Epstein 1993). In corporations, women managers are concentrated in staff positions, such as personnel or public relations, and men are concentrated in the more visible and important line positions, such as sales or production. Staff positions involve little risk and therefore provide few opportunities for workers to show senior management their full capabilities. When top executives are looking for people to promote to senior management, they seldom pick vice presidents of personnel management or public relations. They usually pick vice presidents in product management or sales, who more often than not are male.

Discrimination and Promotion　Sex discrimination by employers is a third explanation for the promotion gap. In brief, it recognizes that employers reward men's qualifications more than women's. The case of Ann Hopkins illustrates blatant discrimination. Despite having brought more money into Price Waterhouse than any other contender for promotion had done, Hopkins was denied promotion to partner. According to the court that ruled in her favor, the senior partners based their evaluation on her personality and appearance and ignored her accomplishments. Her male mentor had advised Hopkins that her chances of promotion would improve if she would "walk more femininely, talk more femininely, wear makeup, have [her] hair styled, and wear jewelry" (White 1992:192).

Actually, appearing feminine does not help a woman get a promotion. In fact, the mere fact of being a woman may be an insurmountable barrier. A male personnel officer told a female bank manager that her career had stalled because

> what the chairman and presidents want are people that they are comfortable with, and they are not . . . comfortable with women. It doesn't even get to the . . . level of you as an individual and [your] personality; *it is the skirt that's the problem.* (Reskin and Roos 1990:156).

Top-level management is a male environment, and some men feel uncomfortable with women. The result is discrimination. The Federal Bureau of Investigation (FBI), for example, refused to even hire women as agents until the death of Director J. Edgar Hoover in 1972 (Johnson 1993). The lingering effect of this discrimination is that the highest-ranking woman is the agent in charge of the FBI's smallest field office, in Anchorage, Alaska.

Statistical discrimination comes into play as well. Employers statistically discriminate against women when they stereotype them as uninterested in advancement or as lacking the attributes needed in higher-level jobs. According to Rosabeth Moss Kanter (1977), when managers are uncertain about the qualifications necessary to do a job, they prefer to promote people who have social characteristics like their own. Kanter called this practice homosocial reproduction. Presumably managers believe that similar people are likely to make the same decisions they would. Thus they seek to advance others who are the same sex, race, social class, and religion; who belong to the same clubs; who attended the same colleges; and who enjoy the same leisure activities. Homosocial reproduction is especially likely in risky ventures, like launching a new TV series. Denise Bielby and William Bielby (1992) argued that, because most studio and network executives are male, they view male writers and producers as "safer" than women with equally strong qualifications and are more likely to give men rather than women long-term deals and commitments for multiple series. The fear that someone who seems different—a woman, perhaps, or a Hispanic—will conform to executives' negative stereotypes results in a cadre of top managers who look alike and think alike.

WOMEN, MEN, AND AUTHORITY

In addition to getting promoted less often than men, women are allowed to exercise less authority. Exercising authority means, broadly, having power: the capacity to mobilize people, to get their cooperation, to secure the resources to do the job (Kanter 1983). A person with job authority is someone who sets policy or makes decisions about organizational goals, budgets, production, and subordinates (for example, about hiring, firing, and pay).

Women's lack of authority in the workplace appears in two guises. First, women usually do not occupy the kinds of positions that offer opportunities to exert power. Second, when they are in such positions, they are not usually given as much power as men are. These barriers affect women at all levels, including managers, professionals, and blue-collar workers.

The belief that women should not have authority over men is embedded in employers' personnel practices. According to Barbara Bergmann (1986:114–6), many employers adhere to an informal segregation code that keeps women from supervising men and that reserves the training slots leading to higher-level jobs for men. Men rule over women and junior men, women rule over women, but women rarely if ever rule over men. This code applied to minorities as well: Minorities may give orders to one another but not to members of the dominant group.

Bergmann (1986:114–6) dubbed this set of principles the segregation code. In many lines of work, co-workers often help enforce the code. Many men resent women who are promoted above them, and they often make their resentment known. According to one male corporate manager, "It's okay for women to have these jobs, as long as they don't go zooming by *me*" (Kanter 1977:218). A woman pipe fitter recalled how,

> when I first made [pipe] fitter, the helpers were really pissed and angry that they were going to have to work with me. There was a lot of talk about having to work for a woman, take orders from a woman. Some of them came right out in saying I didn't know what I was doing. . . . One man [was] marching around telling everybody that he was . . . too important to have to work for a woman. (Schroedel 1985:23)

Similarly, male bus drivers found it difficult to take a female supervisor seriously. According to the female supervisor,

> It was a blow to their ego to have a woman tell them what to do. . . . Some would not respond at all, and there was no way you could make them do it. . . . A lot of the drivers tell me now that they're glad I'm not in [supervision] any more. They couldn't handle a woman telling 'em what to do on the road. (Schroedel 1985:209–211)

As one woman said, "Let's face it, how is an employer going to think a woman is manager material if he thinks her maternal instincts have primacy over business priorities?" (Kleiman 1993). Such deep-seated cultural stereotypes allow the segregation code to remain.

REMEDIES FOR THE PROMOTION AND AUTHORITY GAPS

The social forces that maintain sex differences in opportunities to move up and take charge are resistant to change. Yet employers can help increase women's access to promotion and authority in many ways. To improve advancement opportunities for clerical and service workers, for example, companies could create "bridge" positions that help workers to switch job ladders—for example, move from a clerical ladder to an administrative one—without penalty (Kanter 1976). Some large companies have already made such changes, usually in response to court decrees that they promote more women. USX (formerly U.S. Steel) changed its rules so that women in traditionally female jobs could transfer to more promising steelworker jobs without losing their seniority (Ullman and Deaux 1981). The plan was highly successful: In just four years, the number of women in production and maintenance jobs in two steel mills increased threefold (Reskin and Hartmann 1986:93). AT&T's modifications of its promotion and training policies brought similar results. In the early 1970s, the Equal Employment Opportunity Commission required the company to improve its record of promotions for minorities and women. The nondiscriminatory promotion policies that the company instituted yielded a 300 percent increase in the number of women in middle- and upper-management positions (Northrup and Larson 1979).

Another way that organizations can shrink the promotion and authority gaps is by replacing informal promotion practices with formal ones. In the absence of formal criteria for personnel decisions, managers' biases are more likely to come into play (Roos and Reskin 1984). Lucky Grocery Stores, for example, did not formally post announcements of promotion opportunities because male store managers thought they knew which employees were interested in promotion. The result was that few women were promoted, prompting a successful lawsuit by women who had been passed up (*Stender et al. v. Lucky* 1992). In general, formal recruitment methods and promotion procedures—such as job advertisements, objective hiring criteria, and open transfer policies—help ensure women's access to jobs that bring authority (Szafran 1982; Roos and Reskin 1984).

Raising the price that employers pay to discriminate would help eliminate several of the obstacles described in this chapter. Despite the wastefulness of excluding potentially productive people from top jobs on the basis of their sex and color, employers have done just that. Organizations have multiple goals, and they act on the ones that have the highest priority. Making a profit is usually the highest goal, so higher fines and other financial sanctions could raise equal opportunity on the agenda of priorities.

Another avenue that women and minorities can follow to increase their promotion opportunities is to pursue additional litigation and legislation. However, powerful remedies are necessary in the wake of the Reagan and Bush administrations, which severely undermined laws intended to protect women and minorities from discriminatory practices in the workplace. In addition, anti-affirmative action decisions of the Supreme Court have now trickled down into lower courts, slowing the pace of change (White 1992:201). Still, the courts and the legislature have provided some help in recent years. For example, a 1991 court case led Marriott Corporation to pay $3 million to women managers who had been denied promotions. At fault were the company's informal promotion policy and a work culture that "froze women out" (Goozner 1991). A legislative example is the Glass Ceiling Division within the U.S. Department of Labor, established by Congress in 1991, which is supposed to eliminate the barriers to women's and minorities' promotion to top posts. Although the division has little enforcement power, it works with the Office of Federal Contract Compliance, which has the rarely used power to debar discriminating companies from receiving government contracts. It is too soon to tell if enforcement agencies will actively enforce the Glass Ceiling Act. Much depends on the political process that allocates budget resources and penalties. In addition, the 1992 Civil Rights Act, which allows for punitive damages, may help increase promotion opportunities for excluded groups.

These are potentially powerful weapons because they impose a cost on employers. However, their ability to close the promotion and authority gaps still depends on two things: the willingness of aggrieved parties to press for change and the willingness of enforcement agencies to enforce.

SUMMARY

In the past twenty years, women have made progress in closing the promotion and authority gaps, but they still have a long way to go. Will the outlook be better for the college students of today? We don't know. History shows that women's job options do not improve automatically. They improved during the 1970s through the efforts of federal agencies enforcing new laws, advocacy groups, and companies voluntarily establishing Equal Employment Opportunity programs (Reskin and Hartmann 1986:97). Further progress depends on similar efforts in the 1990s and beyond.

NOTE

1. A study in the late 1920s of a northern meat-packing plant found that African-American women were assigned to the worst departments—hog killing and beef casing—and had no access to the better jobs. They were denied promotion to jobs in the bacon room, supposedly because the public did not want black hands to touch meat in the last stages of processing (Jones 1985:177).

REFERENCES

Adler, Marina A. 1993. "Gender Differences in Job Autonomy: The Consequences of Occupational Segregation and Authority Position." *Sociological Quarterly* 34:449–66.

Adler, Nancy J. 1984. "Women Do Not Want International Careers: And Other Myths About International Management." *Organizational Dynamics* 13:66–79.

———. 1988. "Pacific Basin Managers: A Gaijin, Not a Woman." Pp. 226–49 in Nancy J. Adler and Dafna N. Izraeli (eds.), *Women in Management Worldwide.* New York: M. E. Sharpe.

Alexander, Keith L. 1990. "Minority Women Feel Racism, Sexism Are Blocking Path to Management." *Wall Street Journal.* (July 25):B1.

Antal, Ariane B., and Dafna N. Izraeli. 1993. "A Global Comparison of Women in Management: Women Managers in Their Homelands and as Expatriates." 52–96 in Ellen A. Fagenson (ed.), *Women in Management: Trends, Issues and Challenges in Managerial Diversity.* Newbury Park, CA: Sage.

Bennett, Amanda. 1993. "Path to Top Jobs Now Twists and Turns." *Wall Street Journal* (March 15):D1, D6.

Bergmann, Barbara R. 1986. *The Economic Emergence of Women.* New York: Basic Books.

Berheide, Catherine W. 1992. "Women Still 'Stuck' in Low-Level Jobs." *Women in Public Services: A Bulletin for the Center for Women in Government* 3 (Fall).

Bielby, Denise D., and William T. Bielby. 1992. "Cumulative Versus Continuous Disadvantage in an Unstructured Labor Market." *Work and Occupations* 19:366–87.

Christensen, Kathleen. 1989. "Flexible Staffing and Scheduling in U.S. Corporations." *Research Bulletin No. 240.* New York: The Conference Board.

Collins, Nancy. 1993. "Self-Employment Versus Wage and Salary Jobs: How Do Women Fare?" *Research-in-Brief.* Washington, DC: Institute for Women's Policy Research.

Crompton, Rosemary, and Kay Sanderson. 1990. *Gendered Jobs and Social Change.* Boston: Unwyn Hyman.

Epstein, Cynthia F. 1993. *Women in Law.* Urbana: University of Illinois Press.

Farley, Jennie. 1993. "Commentary." 97–102 in Ellen A. Fagenson (ed.), *Women in Management: Trends, Issues and Challenges in Managerial Diversity.* Newbury Park, CA: Sage.

Fierman, Jaclyn. 1990. "Why Women Still Don't Hit the Top." *Fortune* (July 30):40, 42, 46, 50, 54, 58, 62.

Goldin, Claudia. 1990. *Understanding the Gender Gap.* New York: Oxford University Press.

Goozner, Merrill. 1991. "$3 Million Sex-Bias Accord at Marriott." *Chicago Tribune* (March 6):sec. 3, p. 3.

Grimm, James W. 1978. "Women in Female-Dominated Professions." 293–315 in Ann Stromberg and Shirley Harkess (eds.), *Women Working: Theories and Facts in Perspective.* Palo Alto, CA: Mayfield.

Gutek, Barbara. 1988. "Women in Clerical Work." 225–40 in Ann H. Stromberg and Shirley Harkess (ed.), *Women Working: Theories and Facts in Perspective.* Mountain View, CA: Mayfield.

Harlan, Sharon. 1991. "Number of Women in Government Increasing." *Women in Public Services: A Bulletin for the Center for Women in Government* 1 (Summer).

———. 1992. "Women Face Barriers in Top Management." *Women in Public Services: A Bulletin for the Center for Women in Government* 2 (Winter 1991/92).

Higginbotham, Elizabeth. 1987. "Employment for Professional Black Women in the Twentieth Century." 73–99 in Christine Bose and Glenna Spitze (eds.), *Ingredients for Women's Employment Policy.* Albany, NY: SUNY Press.

Johnston, David. 1993. "FBI Agent to Quit Over Her Treatment in Sexual Harassment Case." *New York Times* (October 11):A7.

Jones, Jacquelyn. 1985. *Labor of Love, Labor of Sorrow.* New York: Vintage.

Kanter, Rosabeth Moss. 1976. "The Policy Issues: Presentation VI." 282–91 in Martha Blaxall and Barbara Reagan (eds.), *Women and the Workplace.* Chicago: University of Chicago Press.

———. 1977. *Men and Women of the Corporation.* New York: Basic Books.

———. 1983. "Women Managers: Moving Up in a High Tech Society." 21–36 in Jennie Farley (ed.), *The Woman in Management: Career and Family Issues.* Ithaca: New York State School of Industrial and Labor Relations, Cornell University.

Kleiman, Carol. 1993. "Women End Up Sacrificing Salary for Children." *Tallahassee Democrat* (March 3):D8.

Markham, William T., Sharon Harlan, and Edward J. Hackett. 1987. "Promotion Opportunity in Organizations." *Research in Personnel and Human Resource Management* 5:223–87.

McGuire, Gail M., and Barbara F. Reskin. 1993. "Authority Hierarchies at Work: The Impacts of Race and Sex." *Gender & Society* 7:487–506.

Moran, Stahl & Boyer, Inc. 1988. *Status of American Female Expatriate Employees: Survey Results.* Boulder, CO: International Division, Moran, Stahl & Boyer, Inc.

Northrup, Herbert R., and John A. Larson. 1979. *The Impact of the AT&T–EEO Consent Decrees.* Labor Relations and Public Policy Series, No. 20. Philadelphia: Industrial Research Unit, University of Pennsylvania.

Reskin, Barbara F., and Heidi Hartmann. 1986. *Women's Work, Men's Work: Sex Segregation on the Job.* Washington, DC: National Academy Press.

Reskin, Barbara F., and Anne L. Kalleberg. 1993. "Sex Differences in Promotion Experiences in the United States and Norway." R.C. No. 28, Presented at the International Sociological Association meeting, Durham, NC.

Reskin, Barbara F., and Deborah J. Merritt. 1993. "Sex Segregation among Law Faculty Members." Unpublished paper.

Reskin, Barbara F., and Patricia A. Roos. 1990. *Job Queues, Gender Queues: Explaining Women's Inroads into Male Occupations.* Philadelphia: Temple University Press.

Roos, Patricia A., and Barbara F. Reskin. 1984. "Institutionalized Barriers to Sex Integration in the Workplace." 235–60 in Barbara F. Reskin (ed.), *Sex Segregation in the Workplace.* Washington, DC: National Academy Press.

Schroedel, Jean Reith. 1985. *Alone in a Crowd: Women in the Trades Tell Their Stories.* Philadelphia: Temple University Press.

Segal, Amanda T., *with Wendy Zellner.* 1992. "Corporate Women." *Business Week* (June 8):74–8.

Shellenbarger, Sue. 1993. "Work and Family: Women Start Younger at Own Businesses." *Wall Street Journal* (March 15):B1.

Sokoloff, Natalie J. 1992. *Black Women and White Women in the Professions.* New York: Routledge.

Spaeth, Joe L. 1989. *Determinants of Promotion in Different Types of Organizations.* Unpublished manuscript. Urbana: University of Illinois.

Steinhoff, P.G., and T. Kazuko. 1988. "Woman Managers in Japan." 103–21 in Nancy J. Adler and Dafna N. Izraeli (eds.), *Women in Management Worldwide.* New York: M. E. Sharpe.

Stender et al. v. Lucky. 1992. "Findings of Fact and Conclusion of Law," *Federal Reporter,* vol. 803, Fed. Supplement, p. 259.

Szafran, Robert F. 1982. "What Kinds of Firms Hire and Promote Women and Blacks? A Review of the Literature." *Sociological Quarterly* 23:171–90.

Tomaskovic-Devey, Donald. 1993. *Gender and Racial Inequality at Work.* Ithaca: New York State School of Industrial and Labor Relations, Cornell University.

Ullman, Joseph P., and Kay Deaux. 1981. "Recent Efforts to Increase Female Participation in Apprenticeship in the Basic

Steel Industry in the Midwest." 133–49 in Vernon M. Briggs, Jr., and Felician Foltman (eds.), *Apprenticeship Research: Emerging Findings and Future Trends.* Ithaca: New York State School of Industrial and Labor Relations, Cornell University.

U.S. Merit Systems Protection Board. 1992. *A Question of Equity: Women and the Glass Ceiling in the Federal Government. A Report to the President and Congress by the U.S. Merit Systems Protection Board.* Washington, DC: U.S. Merit Systems Protection Board.

U.S. Small Business Administration. 1988. *Small Business in the American Economy.* Washington, DC: U.S. Government Printing Office.

White, Jane. 1992. *A Few Good Women: Breaking the Barriers to Top Management.* Englewood Cliffs, NJ: Prentice-Hall.

Williams, Christine L. 1992. "The Glass Escalator: Hidden Advantages for Men in the 'Female' Professions." *Social Problems* 39:253–67.

THE MOMMY TEST

BARBARA EHRENREICH

My, my, girls, what's all the fuss over the new "mommy test"? Hundreds of eager young female job seekers have written to me in the last few weeks alone, confident of being able to pass the drug test, the polygraph test, Exxon's new Breathalyzer test—but panicked over the mommy test. Well, the first thing you have to grasp if you hope to enter the ranks of management is that corporations have a perfect *right* to separate the thieves from the decent folk, the straights from the druggies, and, of course, the women from the mommies.

For starters, you should know that thousands of U.S. women, even those afflicted with regular ovulatory cycles and patent fallopian tubes, have been taking—and *passing*—the mommy test for decades. In fact, it used to be almost the first question (just after "Can you type?") in the standard female job interview: "Are you now, or have you ever, contemplated marriage, motherhood, or the violent overthrow of the U.S. government?"

Today, thanks to women's lib, you won't be out on the street even if you fail. All right, there are disadvantages to the mommy track: mandatory milk and cookies at ten, quiet time at three, and so forth. But many women are happy to get a paycheck of any kind, even if it is a gift certificate to Toys 'R' Us. And if you *still* want to be on the fast track, with the grown-ups and the men, here are a few simple tips for acing the mommy test:

1. Be prepared for tricky psychological questions, such as: Would you rather (a) spend six straight hours in a windowless conference room with a group of arrogant, boorish men fighting over their spreadsheets, or (b) scrape congealed pabulum off a linoleum floor? (The answer, surprisingly is *a.*) Or try this one: Would you rather (a) feed apple juice to a hungry baby, or (b) figure out how to boost profits by diluting the company's baby apple juice product with wastewater from the local nuclear power plant? But you get the idea. . . .
2. Bring proof of infertility: your uterus in a mason jar, for example. Alternatively, tell the interviewer that you already had a child, but—and at this point

you stare pensively into space—it didn't work out. . . .

3. Your interviewer will no doubt have framed photos of his own wife and children displayed prominently on his desk. Do not be misled, this is *part of the test.* Be sure to display appropriate levels of disgust and commiseration. You might ask, in a pitying tone, "Oh, did you marry a *mommy?*"

4. If, you actually are a mommy, and have small children of your own who, for some reason, are still living with you, the case is almost hopeless. Unless you can prove that, as a result of some bioengineering feat or error on their birth certificates, you are actually their daddy and hence have no day-to-day responsibility for their care.

But the key thing is *attitude.* If you go for your job interview in a hostile, self-pitying mood, if you're convinced that the mommy test is an example of discrimination or prejudice, believe me, it will show. And there isn't prejudice against mommies today, not really. They're no longer subject to the extreme residential segregation imposed in the fifties, when mommies were required to live in special suburban compounds, far from the great centers of commerce. Today, you'll find them living just about everywhere, even in jaunty little cardboard structures within walking distance of Wall Street.

Today it is no longer necessary (as it was for poor Nancy Reagan) for a woman who aspires to public recognition to renounce all knowledge of, and contact with, her children. We even have a special day devoted to the distribution of flowers on the graves of dead mothers, as well as to those mothers who, for some reason, still linger on.

However, even if we acknowledge all the tremendous contributions mothers have made—and there were mommies at Plymouth Rock, at Gettysburg, possibly even at the Republican National Convention—we must admit that they have, as a race, shown remarkably little aptitude for the fine points of corporate management. When have you ever seen a get-rich-quick book titled *Leveraged Buyouts: A Mother's Secrets,* or *Swimming with the Sharks: A Mommy's Guide to Eating the Competition (And Finishing Every Last Bite)?*

But the bottom line (not to be confused, gals, with the mark left by overly tight Pampers!) is: Even if you respect mommies, like mommies, and are aware of the enormous diversity among them, would you really want to work with one? This is the question that thousands of top U.S. male managers have had to face: Would you want to be at a $100 power lunch and risk being told to polish your plate? Hence the mommy track. It just makes *sense* to segregate them in special offices equipped with extra umbrellas, sweaters, raincoats, and toothbrushes—for their own sake as much as anything.

Personally, I think the mommy track may be just the first step in a new wave of corporate cost cutting. There's a new approach based on the experience of a brilliant young fast-track executive who got pregnant unbeknownst to herself and handily delivered in the ladies' room during a break in the third-quarter sales conference. The baby was raised on phenobarbital and take-out food until it outgrew the lower right-hand desk drawer, at which point our fast tracker hired a babysitter—to take over her corporate responsibilities!

For the truth is, all you eager young job seekers, that no one knows for sure what the management of top U.S. corporations does all day or well into the night. Sitting at desks has been observed. Sitting at meetings has been observed. Initialing memos has been observed. Could a woman—even a mommy—do all this? Certainly, and with time left over for an actual job of some sort. So the question that our corporate leaders must ultimately face is: What does our vast army of pin-striped managers do anyway, and could it be done by a reliable baby-sitter?

THE REALITIES OF AFFIRMATIVE ACTION IN EMPLOYMENT

BARBARA RESKIN

Affirmative action policies and practices reduce job discrimination against minorities and white women, although their effects have not been large. Some critics charge that affirmative action's positive effects have been offset by its negative effects on white men, on productivity, and on the merit system.

For many people, the most troubling aspect of affirmative action is that it may discriminate against majority-group members (Lynch 1997). According to 1994 surveys, 70 to 80 percent of whites believed that affirmative action sometimes discriminates against whites (Steeh and Krysan 1996, p. 139). Men are more likely to believe that a woman will get a job or promotion over an equally or more qualified man than they are to believe that a man will get a promotion over an equally or more qualified women (Davis and Smith 1996).

Several kinds of evidence indicate that whites' fears of reverse discrimination are exaggerated. Reverse discrimination is rare both in absolute terms and relative to conventional discrimination.[1] On every measured outcome, African-American men were much more likely than white men to experience discrimination, and Latinos were more likely than non-Hispanic men to experience discrimination (Heckman and Siegelman 1993, p. 218). Statistics on the numbers and outcomes of complaints of employment discrimination also suggest that reverse discrimination is rare.

According to national surveys, relatively few whites have experienced reverse discrimination. Only 5 to 12 percent of whites believe that their race has cost them a job or a promotion, compared to 36 percent of African Americans (Steeh and Krysan 1996, pp. 139–40). Of

4,025 Los Angeles workers, 45 percent of African Americans and 16 percent of Latinos said that they had been refused a job because of their race, and 16 percent of African Americans and 8 percent of Latinos reported that they had been discriminated against in terms of pay or a promotion (Bobo and Suh 1996, Table 1). In contrast, of the 863 whites surveyed, less than 3 percent had ever experienced discrimination in pay or promotion, and only one mentioned reverse discrimination. Nonetheless, two-thirds to four-fifths of whites (but just one-quarter of African Americans) surveyed in the 1990s thought it likely that less qualified African Americans won jobs or promotions over more qualified whites (Taylor 1994a; Davis and Smith 1994; Steeh and Krysan 1996, p. 139).[2]

Alfred Blumrosen's (1996, pp. 5–6) exhaustive review of discrimination complaints filed with the Equal Employment Opportunity Commission offers additional evidence that reverse discrimination is rare. Of the 451,442 discrimination complaints filed with the EEOC between 1987 and 1994, only 4 percent charged reverse discrimination (see also Norton 1996, pp. 44–5).[3] Of the 2,189 discrimination cases that federal appellate courts decided between 1965 and 1985, *less* than 5 percent charged employers with reverse discrimination (Burstein 1991, p. 518).

Allegations of reverse discrimination are less likely than conventional discrimination cases to be supported by evidence. Of the approximately 7,000 reverse-discrimination complaints filed with the EEOC in 1994, the EEOC found only 28 credible (Crosby and Herzberger 1996, p. 55). Indeed, U.S. district and appellate courts dismissed almost all the reverse-discrimination cases they heard between 1990 and 1994 as lacking merit.

How can we reconcile the enormous gulf between whites' perceptions that they are likely to lose jobs or promotions because of affirmative action and the small risk of this happening? The white men who brought reverse-discrimination suits presumably concluded that their employers' choices of women or minorities could not have been based on merit, because men are accustomed to being selected for customarily male jobs (*New York Times*, March 31, 1995).[4] Most majority-group members who have not had a firsthand experience of competing unsuccessfully with a minority man or woman or a white woman cite media reports as the source of their impression that affirmative action prompts employers to favor minorities and women (Hochschild 1995, pp. 144, 308).[5] It seems likely that politicians' and the media's emphasis on "quotas" has distorted the public's understanding of what is required and permitted in the name of affirmative action (Entman 1997).

There is no evidence that affirmative action reduces productivity or that workers hired under affirmative action are less qualified than other workers. In the first place, affirmative action plans that compromise valid educational and job requirements are illegal. Hiring unqualified workers or choosing a less qualified person over a more qualified one because of their race or sex is illegal and is not condoned in the name of affirmative action (U.S. Department of Labor, Employment Standards Administration n.d. (b), p. 2). Second, to the extent that affirmative action gives women and minority men access to jobs that more fully exploit their productive capacity, their productivity and that of their employers should increase.

Although many Americans believe that affirmative action means that less qualified persons are hired and promoted (Verhovek 1997, p. 32), the evidence does not bear this out. According to a study of more than 3,000 workers hired in entry-level jobs in a cross-section of firms in Atlanta, Boston, Detroit, and Los Angeles, the performance evaluations of women and minorities hired under affirmative action did not differ from those of white men or female or minority workers for whom affirmative action played no role in hiring (Holzer and Neumark 1998). In addition, Columbus, Ohio, female and minority police officers hired under an affirmative action consent decree performed as well as white men

(Kern 1996). Of nearly 300 corporate executives surveyed in 1979, 72 percent believed that minority hiring did not impair productivity (*Wall Street Journal* 1979); 41 percent of CEOs surveyed in 1995 said affirmative action improved corporate productivity (Crosby and Herzberger 1996, p. 86).[6]

The consequences of affirmative action reach beyond workers and employers by increasing the pools of skilled minority and female workers. When affirmative action prompts employers to hire minorities or women for positions that serve the public, it can bring services to communities that would otherwise be underserved. For example, African-American and Hispanic physicians are more likely than whites and Anglos to practice in minority communities (Komaromy et al. 1996). Graduates of the Medical School at the University of California at San Diego who were admitted under a special admissions program were more likely to serve inner-city and rural communities and saw more poor patients than those admitted under the regular procedures (Penn, Russell, and Simon 1986).

Women's and minorities' employment in nontraditional jobs also raises the aspirations of other members of excluded groups by providing role models and by signaling that jobs are open to them. Some minorities and women do not pursue jobs or promotions because they expect to encounter discrimination (Mayhew 1968, p. 313). By reducing the perception that discriminatory barriers block access to certain lines of work, affirmative action curtails this self-selection (Reskin and Roos 1990, p. 305). In addition, the economic gains provided by better jobs permit beneficiaries to invest in the education of the next generation.

The tension between affirmative action and merit is the inevitable result of the conflict between our national values and what actually occurs in the nation's workplaces. As long as discrimination is more pervasive than affirmative action, it is the real threat to meritocracy. But because no one will join the debate on behalf of discrimination, we end up with the illusion of a struggle between affirmative action and merit.

NOTES

1. Lynch's (1989, p. 53) search for white male Southern Californians who saw themselves as victims of reverse discrimination turned up only 32 men.

2. Younger whites, those from more privileged backgrounds, and those from areas with larger black populations—especially black populations who were relatively well off—were the most likely to believe that blacks benefited from preferential treatment (Taylor 1994b).

3. Two percent were by white men charging sex, race, or national-origin discrimination (three-quarters of these charged sex discrimination), and 1.8 percent were by white women charging race discrimination (Blumrosen 1996, p. 5).

4. Occupational segregation by sex, race, and ethnicity no doubt contribute to this perception by reinforcing the notion that one's sex, color, or ethnicity is naturally related to the ability to perform a particular job.

5. The disproportionate number of court-ordered interventions to curtail race and sex discrimination in cities' police and fire departments (Martin 1991) and the large number of court challenges by white men (Bureau of National Affairs 1995, pp. 5–12) probably contributed to the public's impression that hiring quotas are common.

6. No data were provided on the proportion who believed that affirmative action hampered productivity.

REFERENCES

Blumrosen, Alfred W. 1996. *Declaration.* Statement Submitted to the Supreme Court of California in Response to Proposition 209, September 26.

Bobo, Larry, and Susan A. Suh. 1996. "Surveying Racial Discrimination: Analyses from a Multi-Ethnic Labor Market." Working Paper No. 75, Russell Sage Foundation, New York.

Bureau of National Affairs. 1995. *Affirmative Action after Adarand: A Legal, Regulatory, Legislative Outlook.* Washington, DC: The Bureau of National Affairs.

Burstein, Paul. 1991. " 'Reverse Discrimination' Cases in the Federal Courts: Mobilization by a Countermovement." *Sociological Quarterly* 32:511–28.

Crosby, Faye J., and Sharon D. Herzberger. 1996. "For Affirmative Action." p. 3–109 in *Affirmative Action: Pros and Cons of Policy and Practice,* ed. R. J. Simon. Washington, DC: American University Press.

Davis, James A., and Tom W. Smith. 1994. *General Social Survey* [MRDF]. Chicago, IL: National Opinion Research Center [producer, distributor].

———. 1996. *General Social Survey* [MRDF]. Chicago, IL: National Opinion Research Center [producer, distributor].

Entman, Robert M. 1997. "Manufacturing Discord: Media in the Affirmative Action Debate." *Press/Politics* 2:32–51.

Heckman, James J., and Peter Siegelman. 1993. "The Urban Institute Audit Studies: Their Methods and Findings." 187–229 in *Clear and Convincing Evidence: Measurement of Discrimination in America,* ed. M. Fix and R. J. Struyk. Washington, DC: The Urban Institute.

Hochschild, Jennifer. 1995. *Facing Up to the American Dream.* Princeton, NJ: Princeton University Press.

Holzer, Harry J. and David Neumark. Forthcoming 1998. "Are Affirmative Action Hires Less Qualified? Evidence from Employer–Employee Data on New Hires." *Journal of Labor Economics.*

Kern, Leesa. 1996. "Hiring and Seniority: Issues in Policing in the Post-Judicial Intervention Period." Department of Sociology, Ohio State University, Columbus, OH: Unpublished manuscript.

Komaromy, Miriam, Kevin Grumbach, Michael Drake, Karen Vranizan, Nicole Lurie, Dennis Keane, and Andrew Bindman. 1996. "The Role of Black and Hispanic Physicians in Providing Health Care for Underserved Populations." *New England Journal of Medicine* 334:1305–10.

Lynch, Frederick R. 1989. *Invisible Victims: White Males and the Crisis of Affirmative Action.* New York: Greenwood.

———. 1997. *The Diversity Machine: The Drive to Change the White Male Workplace.* New York: Free Press.

Martin, Susan E. 1991. "The Effectiveness of Affirmative Action: The Case of Women in Policing." *Justice Quarterly* 8:489–504.

Mayhew, Leon. 1968. *Law and Equal Opportunity: A Study of Massachusetts Commission against Discrimination.* Cambridge, MA: Harvard University Press.

New York Times. 1995. "Reverse Discrimination Complaints Rare, Labor Study Reports." *New York Times,* March 31, p. A23.

Norton, Eleanor Holmes. 1996. "Affirmative Action in the Workplace." 39–48 in *The Affirmative Action Debate,* ed. G. Curry. Reading, MA: Addison-Wesley.

Penn, Nolan E., Percy J. Russell, and Harold J. Simon. 1986. "Affirmative Action at Work: A Survey of Graduates of the University of California at San Diego Medical School." *American Journal of Public Health* 76:1144–46.

Reskin, Barbara F., and Patricia Roos. 1990. *Job Queues, Gender Queues.* Philadelphia, PA: Temple University Press.

Steeh, Charlotte, and Maria Krysan. 1996. "The Polls—Trends: Affirmative Action and the Public, 1970–1995." *Public Opinion Quarterly* 60:128–58.

Taylor, Marylee C. 1994a. "Beliefs about the Preferential Hiring of Black Applicants: Sure It Happens, But I've Never Seen It."

Pennsylvania State University, University Park, PA. *Unpublished manuscript.*

———. 1994b. "Impact of Affirmative Action on Beneficiary Groups: Evidence from the 1990 General Social Survey." *Basic and Applied Social Psychology* 15:143–78.

U.S. Department of Labor, Employment Standards Administration, Office of Federal Contract Compliance Programs [cited as OFCCP]. The Rhetoric and the Reality about Federal Affirmative Action at the OFCCP." Washington, DC: U.S. Department of Labor.

Verhovek, Sam Howe. 1997. "In Poll, Americans Reject Means but Not Ends of Racial Diversity." *New York Times,* December 14, 1, 32.

Wall Street Journal. 1979. "Labor Letter: A Special News Report on People and Their Jobs in Offices, Fields and Factories: Affirmative Action Is Accepted by Most Corporate Chiefs." *Wall Street Journal,* April 3, p. 1.

READING 25

Race, Sex, and Class: Black Female Tobacco Workers in Durham, North Carolina, 1920–1940, and the Development of Female Consciousness

BEVERLY W. JONES

This article examines how race, sex, and class affected the lives and consciousness of black female tobacco workers in Durham, North Carolina, and how they conceptualized work and its meaning in their lives. The research was based on fifteen interviews. The interviewees fall into three broad age categories: five were born before 1908, seven between 1908 and 1916, and three between 1916 and 1930. All were born in the rural South. The majority migrated to Durham in the 1920s, subsequently entering the labor force.

Historically, black labor of both females and males has been critical to the tobacco manufacturing industry. As cigarette manufacture became mechanized, blacks were hired as stemmers, sorters, hangers, and pullers. These "dirty" jobs were seen as an extension of field labor and therefore as "Negro work" for which whites would not compete.[1] The rapidly expanding number of tobacco factories employed the thousands of black females and males migrat-

Beverly W. Jones, "Race, Sex, and Class: Black Female Tobacco Workers in Durham, North Carolina, 1920–1940, and the Development of Female Consciousness," from *Feminist Studies* 10, no. 3 (Fall 1984). Copyright © 1984 by Feminist Studies, Inc. Reprinted with the permission of Feminist Studies, Inc.

ing from the rural South. The pull of better-paying jobs and the push of falling farm prices, perennial pests, and hazardous weather induced a substantial number of black sharecroppers, renters, and landowners to seek refuge in Durham.

Charlie Necoda Mack, the father of three female future tobacco workers, remembered the difficulties of making an adequate living out of farming in Manning, South Carolina. "I was a big cotton farmer; I made nine bales of cotton one year. Next year I made, I think, one or two, and the next year I didn't make none. I left in July, I had to leave. I borrowed money to get up here—Durham. I had six children and I know no jobs available. Well, then I came up here in July in 1922 and got a job at the factory. And by Christmas I had all my children with clothes and everything." Unlike the Mack family, who were pushed out of South Carolina, others were pulled into the city. Dora Miller, after marrying in 1925, left Apex, North Carolina, because she heard of the "better-paying jobs in Durham." Mary Dove, at age ten and accompanied by her family, left Roxboro, North Carolina, because a "Duke agent told us that a job in the factory at Liggett Myers was waiting for my daddy." Rosetta Branch, age eighteen and single, left Wilmington,

TABLE I TOBACCO INDUSTRY EMPLOYMENT BY RACE AND GENDER

| DURHAM COUNTY: 1930 | | | |
| White | | Negro | |
Male	Female	Male	Female
2,511	2,932	1,336	1,979
NORTH CAROLINA: 1940			
White		Negro	
Male	Female	Male	Female
6,517	3,175	5,899	5,898

SOURCE: U.S. Bureau of the Census, *Population: 1930* (Washington D.C.: GPO, 1930), vol. 3, pt. 2, pp. 355, 378; *Labor Force: 1940* (Washington, D.C.: GPO, 1940), vol. 3, pt. 4, p. 566.

North Carolina, because her mother had died, and "there were no other kinfolks."[2]

Thus, Durham's gainfully employed black population swelled from 6,869 in 1910 to 12,402 in 1930. (The city's total black population in 1930 was 23,481.) According to the census, the number of black female tobacco workers in 1930 was 1,979 out of a total black female population of 12,388. (See Table 1.) Durham and Winston-Salem tobacco factories employed more black females than other cities: one-half of the number of women employed in tobacco factories in 1930 in these cities were black, compared with the 19.7 [percent], in Petersburg and Richmond in Virginia.[3]

Upon disembarking at the central train station, the newly arrived southern migrants were immediately faced with race restrictions. Rigidly segregated communities were the dominant feature of Durham's black life. Many of the migrants settled in the dilapidated housing in the larger communities of East End and Hayti, a bustling commercial district of black businesses, and in the smaller areas of Buggy Bottom and Hickstown. Almost all black workers rented either from the company and white landlords or from black real estate agents. The comments of Annie Barbee, the daughter of Necoda Mack, reflect her first impressions of Durham.

We were renting in the southern part of Durham—the Negro section—on Popular Street, second house from the corner, across the railroad tracks. The house was small, two rooms, but somehow we managed. The street was not paved and when it rained it got muddy and in the fall, the wind blew all the dust into your eyes and face. There were no private family bathrooms. But it was an exciting life. See, in the country things were so dull—no movie houses. . . . Up here people were always fighting and going on all the time.[4]

Despite the exploitive living conditions described by Barbee, urban employment did have some liberating consequences for rural daughters.

Race restricted the black population to segregated neighborhoods and also determined the kinds of jobs black females could get. Black female tobacco workers also faced discrimination as poor people and as females. Although class and sex restraints punctuated the lives of white female tobacco workers, their impact was reinforced by management policies. Although white females' wages were a fraction of white males' and inadequate to support a family, black females' wages were even lower. According to some black female tobacco workers, the wage inequity led many white women to consider black women inferior. This in turn led to an atmosphere of mistrust between black and white females. Management strengthened racial and class inequities in hiring practices, working conditions, and spatial organization of the factory, and therefore impeded the formation of gender bonds among working-class women.

Black females were usually hired as if they were on an auction block. "Foremen lined us up against the walls," one worker stated, "and chose the sturdy robust ones." Mary Dove recalled that she had "to hold up one leg at a time and then bend each backwards and forwards."[5] Once hired, black and white women were separated on different floors at the American Tobacco Company and in entirely different buildings at the Liggett & Myers Tobacco Company. In the 1920s and 1930s, according to a report by the Women's Bureau (the federal agency created in 1920), and confirmed by my interviews, 98 percent of these black females were confined to the prefabrication department, where they performed the "dirty" jobs—sorting, cleaning, and stemming tobacco.[6] White females had the "cleaner" jobs in the manufacturing and packing department as they caught, inspected, and packed the tobacco. However, both jobs were defined by the sex division of labor—jobs to be performed by women. Black men moved between the areas pushing 500-pound hogsheads of tobacco while white men worked as inspectors, safeguarding the sanctity of class and sex segregation.[7]

Reflecting on these blatant differences in working conditions, some fifty years later many black women expressed anger at the injustice. Annie Barbee recalled: "You're over here doing all the nasty dirty work. And over there on the cigarette side white women over there wore white uniforms. . . . You're over here handling all the old sweaty tobacco. There is a large difference. It ain't right!" Rosetta Branch spoke of her experience with anger. "They did not treat us Black folks right. They worked us like dogs. Put us in separate buildings . . . thinking maybe we were going to hurt those white women. Dirty work, dirty work we had to do. Them white women think they something working doing the lighter jobs."[8] These comments reflect the effectiveness of management policies to aggravate racial and sexual differences in order to preclude any possible bonds of gender and also illustrate the unhealthy working conditions to which black women were exposed.

In fact, the interviews indicate that the health of some black women suffered in the factories. Pansy Cheatham, another daughter of Necoda Mack, maintained that the Georgia leaf tobacco "was so dusty that I had to go to the tub every night after work. There was only one window and it got so hot that some women just fainted. The heat and smell was quite potent." Mary Dove recounted one of her fainting spells. "You know on the floor there was a salt dispenser, because it would get so hot. I did not feel so well when I came to work but I had to work. After about two hours standing on my feet, I got so dizzy—I fell out. My clothes was soaking wet from my head to my feet. When I woke up I was in the dispensary."[9]

Blanche Scott and another worker were forced to quit for health reasons. Scott, who began working for Liggett & Myers in 1919, quit four years later. "When I left the factory, it became difficult for me to breathe. The dust and fumes of the burly tobacco made me cough. The burly tobacco from Georgia had chicken feathers and even manure in it. Sometimes I would put an orange in my mouth to keep from throwing up. I knew some women who died of TB." The other worker had miscarried twice. Pregnant again, she decided not to return to the American Tobacco Company. "I felt that all that standing while I stemmed tobacco," she stated, "was the reason I lost my two children." Some women found momentary relief from the dust by retreating outside the confines of the factory complex to breathe the fresh air while sitting under trees or on the sidewalk during lunch.[10]

These comments on the poor, unhealthy working conditions were verified by research on Durham's death records between 1911 and 1930. In many instances, the records were imprecise and failed to provide information about race and occupation. Of the 105 certificates that identified black women as tobacco workers who died between 1911 and 1920, forty-eight (about 46 percent) died of tuberculosis, sometimes listed as phthisis and consumption. Of the 134 recorded deaths of black female tobacco workers between 1920 and 1930, eighty-six (64.5 percent) died of tuberculosis. Because tuberculosis is caused by a bacillus that can be transmitted by a tubercular person through the cough, it is likely that poorly ventilated rooms and incessant coughing by workers, possibly by a carrier, made some workers susceptible to the disease, although deplorable living conditions for workers cannot be dismissed as a contributing factor.[11]

As studies have found in other cities, black females in Durham were more likely to work than white females.[12] Black females also earned lower wages than white females. In the early 1900s, wages for black tobacco workers, both female and male, ranked the lowest in the nation. In 1930, 45.5 percent of native-born white women in Durham were gainfully employed—27.7 percent in tobacco. While 44 percent of black women were working, 36.2 percent were employed in tobacco. From 1920 to 1930, Durham's white female tobacco workers averaged about 29 cents per hour, while black female hand stemmers earned about 11.9 cents an hour. However, black men, as well as black women who stemmed tobacco by machine, averaged about 27 cents an hour, still less than white women.[13]

Wage differentials continued and worsened throughout the 1930s. By the eve of the New Deal, a Women's Bureau survey reported figures for North Carolina which revealed an even higher wage discrepancy. White women working in the making and packing departments reported a median weekly wage of $15.35. Wages ranged from $14.10 earned as catchers to $20.50 on older packing machines. On the newest packing machines, the median wage was $18.15. Black women, working in the leaf department, reported a median weekly wage of $7.95. Hand stemmers earned a median wage of $6.50.[14]

The low wage was itself demeaning to black female workers. But the inadequate wages also forced many into the labor force at an early age. Black women thus worked for a longer part of their lives, and henceforth were more vulnerable to diseases and other health problems. Blanche Scott, for example, began working at the age of twelve. "Since my mother stayed so sick, I had to go to work. I worked at Liggett Myers after school got out. I attended West End School. I'd normally get out at 1:30 and worked from two o'clock to 6 PM. I was just twelve years old. In the summer, they'd let children come and work all day until four o'clock." Pansy Cheatham began working at age thirteen. "My father talked to the foreman," she stated. "I worked because my sisters Mae and Annie worked; I stemmed tobacco by hand. But Papa did collect the money and use it for food and clothing." Cheatham's statement would indicate that at the top of the gender hierarchy of the black family was the father, who controlled the daughter's wages.[15]

Many women saw their employment as a means of "helping out the family." Better stated in the words of Margaret Turner, "that's what a family is all about, when we—the children—can help out our parents."[16] Out of the fifteen interviewees, the ten women who entered the work force at an early age all conceptualized the central meaning of their work in relation to their families.

By the late 1920s and early 1930s, the enforcement of the Child Labor Law of 1917 arrested the practice of employing children under the age of sixteen. "They began to ask for your birth certificate," one worker stated. A study done by Hugh Penn Brinton substantiated the decrease of child labor employment in Durham's factories. Brinton found that from 1919 to 1930 the percentage of black laboring-class households sending children into the labor force had decreased from 35 to 14 percent.[17]

However, the legislation against child labor did not force the wages up for black tobacco workers, and the constant low earning power of both female and male breadwinners continued to affect the lives of black female workers psychologically. Many women submitted to the demands of the foreman and other company officials. Viewed as short-term cheap labor, some females submitted to physical and verbal harassment, because in many instances defiance would have certainly resulted in the loss of jobs. Dora Miller asserted that "since the foreman knew you needed the job, you obeyed all of his demands without question. He called you dirty names and used foul language but you took it." Mary Dove recalled what it was like to work under one "of the toughest bosses." "Our, foreman was a one-eyed fella named George Hill. He was tight! He was out of South Carolina, and he was tight. I mean tight! He'd get on top of them machines—they had a machine that altered the tobacco—he'd get on top of that machine and watch you, see if you was working all right and holler down and curse. Holler down and say, 'GD . . . get to work! GD . . . go to work there, you ain't doin' nothing.' Janie Mae Lyons remembered one who walked in on her while she "was in the sitting position on the stool" and told her "that if you ain't finished then you can pack up and leave. I was so embarrassed and that's what I did."[18]

Lyons's departure from the factory represented a form of militancy—a definitive stance against further harassment. Other women resisted verbally. Annie Barbee publicly castigated "women who allowed the foreman to fumble their behind" and further stated that if "one did that to me he would be six feet under." She indicated no one ever did. One worker resisted "by playing the fool." "The foreman thought I was crazy and left me alone."[19]

Constantly resisting physical and verbal abuse and trying to maintain their jobs, the workers were further threatened by increased mechanization. "I don't think it is right," one woman stated, "to put them machines to take away from us poor people." "Because of the strain we work under," another maintained, "they don't care nothing for us." One woman recalled crying at the machines because she could not quit in the face of high unemployment. "With them machines you have to thread the tobacco in. Them machines run so fast that after you put in one leaf you got to be ready to thread the other. If you can't keep pace the foreman will fire you right on the spot. Sometimes I get so nervous but I keep on going."[20]

The increased mechanization of the tobacco factories, resulting in physical hardships of female workers, can to some degree be attributed to Franklin D. Roosevelt's National Industrial Recovery Acts of 1933 and 1934. On the one hand, President Roosevelt's New Deal measures fostered economic stability for many black families by establishing standard minimum wages and maximum hours. On the other hand, this standardization exacerbated the job insecurity of black workers by indirectly catalyzing many companies to maximize profits by replacing hand labor with technology. During the latter part of the 1930s, Liggett & Myers closed its green-leaf department, which had employed the majority of black women.[21]

The long-term insecurities of their jobs led black female stemmers to organize Local 194. The limited success of the union was reflected in the decline of its membership of two thousand in January 1935 to less than two hundred by May 1935. Black female union members found little support from either Local 208, black controlled, or Local 176, white controlled. In the eyes of the male unionists, the temporary nature of women's jobs excluded them from any serious consideration by the locals.[22] Conscious of their auxiliary position and the lack of support from male-led unions, black females chose not to support the April 16, 1939, strike at Liggett & Myers. Reporting for work on that day, they were turned away, as management had no other recourse but to close the factory. Dora Miller recalled that the black stemmery workers "were never involved in the strike because demands for wage increases did not include us." [23] On April 26, 1939, the company capitulated. The contract indeed reaffirmed Miller's assessment because the stemmery workers were not mentioned.[24]

The factory policies of hiring, wages, working conditions, and spatial segregation, inherently reinforced by racism, the "cult of true white womanhood," and the inadvertent effect of New Deal governmental measures, all came together to touch the lives of black women tobacco workers with sex, race, and class exploitation. These practices further dissipated any possible gender bonds between black women and white women workers. As a race, black female tobacco workers were confined to unhealthy, segregated areas either in separate buildings or on separate floors. As a working class, they were paid inadequate wages. As a sex, they were relegated to the worst, lowest-paid, black women's jobs.

Black females conceptualized work as a means of "helping out the family." Denied self-respect and dignity in the factory, black female tobacco workers felt a need to validate themselves in other spheres. Victimized by their working conditions, female tobacco workers looked to the home as a preferred if not powerful arena. The home became the inner world that countered the factory control over their physical well-being. The duality of their lives—workers of production and nurturers of the family—could be assessed as a form of double jeopardy. But it was their role as nurturers, despite the hardship of work, that provided them with a sense of purpose and "joy." As Pansy Cheatham described her daily routine, "I get up at 5:30 AM. I feed, clothe, and kiss my children. They stay with my sister while I work. At 7 AM I am on the job. A half-hour for lunch at about 12 noon. At 4 PM I quit work. At home about 4:30, then I cook, sometimes mend and wash clothes before I retire. About 11:30 I go to bed with joy in my heart for my children are safe and I love them so."[25]

Black females who worked together in the tobacco factories also had the positive experience of creating networks of solidarity. Viewing their plight as one, black females referred to one another as "sisters." This sisterhood was displayed in the collection of money during sickness and death and celebration of birthdays. The networks established in the factory overlapped into the community and church. Many of these workers belonged to the same churches—Mount Vernon, Mount Gilead, and White Rock Baptist churches—and functioned as leaders of the usher boards, missionary circles, and Sunday School programs. These bonds were enhanced in the community by the development of clubs. These church groups and females' clubs overlapped the factory support networks and functioned in similar ways.

Finally, the resistance to the physical and verbal abuse that was a constant in the work lives of black women fostered among some a sense of autonomy, strength, and self-respect. Annie Barbee was one of those women. The assertiveness, dignity, and strength she developed through work became an intricate part of her private life. At age forty and pregnant, she decided to obtain private medical assistance despite her husband's resistance. "When you know things ain't right God gave you a head and some sense. That's my body. I knew I wasn't going to Duke Clinic. And I was working and making my own money, I went where I wanted to go. You see, being married don't mean that your husband controls your life. That was my life and I was carrying his child, it's true, but I was going to look after myself."[26]

Although the work experience of black women tobacco workers was one of racial, sex, and class oppression, the early entrance into the labor force, the resistance to exploitation, and the longevity of work created a consciousness that fostered a sense of strength and dignity among some women in this working class. Management tactics of wage inequity, hiring practices, and racial-sexual division of labor pitted black women against white women economically as workers, and made the formation of gender bonds across race lines all but impossible. Yet among black women, the linkages of sisterhood engendered a consciousness of female strength, if not feminism.

ACKNOWLEDGMENTS

I am deeply grateful to North Carolina Central University for a Faculty Research Grant and for the excellent editorial comments of the *Feminist Studies* editors.

NOTES

1. For discussion of the historical involvement of black labor in tobacco manufacturing, see Joseph C. Robert, *The Tobacco Kingdom* (Durham, N.C.: Duke University Press, 1938).

2. Author's interviews with Charlie Necoda Mack, 22 May 1979; Dora Miller, 6 June 1979; Mary Dove, 7 July 1979; Rosetta Branch, 15 August 1981; all on file in the Southern Oral History Program, University of North Carolina, Chapel Hill, hereafter cited as SOHP/UNC.

3. The 1940 labor force figures do not include information for Durham County. U.S. Bureau of the Census, *Population: 1930* (Washington, D.C.: GPO, 1930), 3:341. In 1900, the major tobacco industries in the South were the American Tobacco Company and Liggett & Myers in Durham; R. J. Reynolds in Winston-Salem; and P. Lorillard in Richmond, Virginia.

4. Annie Barbee, interview, 28 May 1979, SOHP/UNC.

5. Mary Dove, interviews, 7 July 1971 and 30 May 1981.

6. Women's Bureau, *The Effects of Changing Conditions in the Cigar and Cigarette Industries,* Bulletin no. 110 (Washington, D.C.: GPO, 1932), 774–75. The Women's Bureau was established by Congress in 1920 under the aegis of the United States Department of Labor. Its purpose was to gather information and to provide advice to working women.

7. Mary Dove, interviews, 7 July 1971, 15 and 28 August 1981.

8. Annie Barbee and Rosetta Branch, interviews.

9. Pansy Cheatham, interview, 9 July 1979, SOHP/UNC; Mary Dove, interview, 7 July 1971.

10. Blanche Scott, interviews, 11 July 1979 (SOHP/UNC), 8 and 15 June, 1981; Mary Dove, Annie Barbee interviews.

11. Death certificates, 1911–1930, Durham County Health Department, Vital Records, Durham, North Carolina. I was also interested in the correlation of working conditions and female-related maladies such as stillbirths, miscarriages, and uterine disorders. Further perusal of death certificates of stillbirths was less valuable, for there were no indications of mothers' occupations. Even hospital statistics lacked occupational data. This area of inquiry as it relates to the health of black female workers and working conditions needs further research. Further questions that will have to be explored include: Was there a higher percentage of female tobacco workers dying of tuberculosis than nonfemale tobacco workers? How long were stricken female workers employed in the factory? How much weight must be given to the working environment over that of home environs? Despite the lack of solid data on these questions, the interviews and death records clearly indicate that racial division of labor negatively impacted upon the health of many black female tobacco workers.

12. Elizabeth H. Pleck, "A Mother's Wage: Income Earning among Married Italian and Black Women, 1896–1911," in *The American Family in Social-Historical Perspective,* 2d ed, ed. Michael Gordon (New York: St. Martin's Press, 1978), 490–510; "Culture, Class, and Family Life among Low-Income Urban Negroes," in *Employment, Race, and Poverty,* ed. Arthur M. Ross and Herbert Hill (New York: Harcourt Brace & World, 1967), 149–72; "The Kindred of Veola Jackson: Residence and Family Organization of an Urban Black American Family," in *Afro-American Anthropology: Contemporary Perspectives,* ed. Norman E. Whitten, Jr., and John F. Szwed (New York: Free Press, 1970), chap. 16.

13. U.S. Bureau of the Census, *Population: 1930,* vols. 3 and 4; U.S. Department of Labor, Women's Bureau, *Hours and Earning in Tobacco Stemmeries,* Bulletin no. 127 (Washington, D.C.: GPO, 1934).

14. Women's Bureau, *Effects of Changing Conditions,* 172–75.

15. Blanche Scott and Pansy Cheatham, interviews.

16. Margaret Turner, interview with author, 25 September 1979, SOHP/UNC.

17. Interview, 8 June 1981; Hugh Penn Brinton, "The Negro in Durham: A Study in Adjustment to Town Life" (Ph.D. diss., University of North Carolina, Chapel Hill, 1930).

18. Dora Miller and Mary Dove, interviews; Janie Mae Lyons, interview with author, 4 August 1981.

19. Annie Barbee, interviews 28 May 1979, 10 July 1981.

20. Interviews, 4 and 15 June 1981.

21. For the best discussions of the National Industrial Recovery Act's impact on blacks, see Raymond Wolters, *Negroes and the Great Depression: The Problem of Economic Recovery,* ed. Stanley E. Kutler (Westport, Conn.: Greenwood, 1970); and Bernard Sternsher, ed., *The Negro in the Depression and War: Prelude to Revolution, 1930–45* (Chicago: Quadrangle, 1969). Also see Dolores Janiewski, "From Field to Factory: Race, Class, and Sex and the Woman Worker in Durham, 1880–1940" (Ph.D. diss., Duke University, 1979).

22. *Durham* (N.C.) *Morning Herald,* 17, 18 April 1939, p. 1; Janiewski.

23. Dora Miller, interview.

24. For terms of contract, see *Durham Morning Herald* and *Durham Sun,* 27 April 1939, pp. 1, 2; Janiewski.

25. Pansy Cheatham, interview.

26. Annie Barbee, interview.

R E A D I N G   2 6

Serving Hamburgers and Selling Insurance: Gender, Work, and Identity in Interactive Service Jobs

ROBIN LEIDNER

All workers look for ways to reconcile the work they do with an identity they can accept, either by interpreting the work positively or by discounting the importance of the work as a basis of identity. Hughes, emphasizing the active process of interpretation, recommended examining the "social and social-psychological arrangements and devices by which men [*sic*] make their work tolerable, or even make it glorious to themselves and others" ([1951] 1984, 342). If the work cannot be construed as glorious, or even honorable, workers will look for ways to distance themselves from their jobs, assuring themselves that the work they are doing does not reflect their true worth. One of the most important determinants of the meaning of a type of work, as well as of how the work is conducted and rewarded, is its association with a particular gender. Acceptance by a worker of the identity implied by a job is therefore determined in part by the degree to which the job can be interpreted as allowing the worker to enact gender in a way that is satisfying.

Much contemporary theory and research on gender shares an emphasis on its active and continual construction through social interaction (Garfinkel 1967; Goffman 1977; Kessler and McKenna 1978; West and Zimmerman 1987). West and Zimmerman argue that "participants in interaction organize their various and manifold activities to reflect or express gender, and they are disposed to perceive the behavior of others in a similar light" (1987, 127). One of the most striking aspects of the social construction of gen-

der is that its successful accomplishment creates the impression that gender differences in personality, interests, character, appearance, manner, and competence are natural—that is, that they are not social constructions at all. Gender segregation of work reinforces this appearance of naturalness. When jobholders are all of one gender, it appears that people of that gender must be especially well suited to the work, even if at other times and places, the other gender does the same work. Thus Milkman's analysis of industrial work during World War II demonstrates "how idioms of sex-typing can be flexibly applied to whatever jobs women and men happen to be doing" (1987, 50).

In this article, I will argue that jobholders and their audiences may make this interpretation even under the most unlikely conditions: when the work might easily be interpreted as more suitable for the other gender, and when many aspects of the workers' presentations of self are closely dictated by superiors and are clearly not spontaneous expressions of the workers' characters, interests, or personalities. My analysis of the flexibility of interpretations of gender-appropriate work draws on research on the routinization of jobs that involve direct interaction with customers or clients—what I call "interactive service work" (see Leidner 1988). These sorts of jobs merit attention, since service work is increasingly central to the U.S. economy: The service sector is expected to continue to provide most new jobs through the year 2000 (Personick 1987; Silvestri and Lukasiewic 1987).

Interactive service jobs have several distinctive features that make them especially revealing for investigation of the interrelation of work, gender, and identity. These jobs differ from other types of work in that the distinctions among product, work process, and worker are blurred or nonexistent, since the quality of the interaction may itself be part of

Robin Leidner, "Serving Hamburgers and Selling Insurance: Gender, Work, and Identity in Interactive Service Jobs," *Gender & Society 5*, no. 2 (June 1991). Copyright © 1991 by Sociologists for Women in Society. Reprinted with the permission of Sage Publications, Inc.

the service offered (Hochschild 1983). In many kinds of interactive service work, workers' identities are therefore not incidental to the work but are an integral part of it. Interactive jobs make use of workers' looks, personalities, and emotions, as well as their physical and intellectual capacities, sometimes forcing them to manipulate their identities more self-consciously than do workers in other kinds of jobs. The types of relations with service recipients structured by the jobs may also force workers to revise taken-for-granted moral precepts about personal interaction. Workers who feel that they owe others sincerity, individual consideration, nonmanipulativeness, or simply full attention may find that they cannot be the sort of people they want to be and still do their jobs adequately (Hochschild 1983). While a variety of distancing strategies and rationalizations are possible (Rollins 1985), it may be difficult for interactive service workers to separate themselves from the identities implied by their jobs (Leidner 1988).

When interactive work is routinized, workers' interactions are directly controlled by employers, who may use scripting, uniforms, rules about proper demeanor and appearance, and even far-reaching attempts at psychological reorientation to standardize service encounters. The interactions are expressly designed to achieve a certain tone (friendliness, urgency) and a certain end (a sale, a favorable impression, a decision). Analysis of how employers try to combine the proper interactive elements to achieve the desired effects can make visible the processes by which meaning, control, and identity are ordinarily created through interaction in all kinds of settings. Workers' and service recipients' acceptance or rejection of the terms of the standardized interactions and their efforts to tailor the prescribed roles and routines to suit their own purposes are similarly revealing about the extent to which people sustain beliefs about who they are through how they treat others and are treated by them.

Gender is necessarily implicated in the design and enactment of service interactions. In order to construct routines for interactions, especially scripts, employers make many assumptions about what customers like, what motivates them, and what they consider normal interactive behavior. Some of the assumptions employers make concern how men and women should behave. Once these assumptions about proper gender behavior are built into workers' routines, service recipients may have to accept them in order to fit smoothly into the service interaction. My research on the routinization of service jobs was inspired in part by my astonishment at one such script: I learned that employees of Gloria Marshall Figure Salons were expected to ask their customers, "Have you and your husband discussed your figure needs?" (Lally-Benedetto 1985). The expectation that workers could toss out the term *figure needs* as if it were everyday speech was startling in itself, but I was especially intrigued by the layers of assumptions the question implied about the natures of women and men and the power relations between them.

As this example illustrates, scripts can embody assumptions about proper gendered behavior in fairly obvious ways. To do such jobs as intended, workers must "do gender" in a particular way (Berk 1985b; West and Zimmerman 1987). Even where the gender component is less obvious, workers in all kinds of jobs need to consider how their work relates to their own identities, including their gender identities. Whether workers take pride in the work itself or see it as stigmatizing, whether they work harder than is required or put in the least effort they can get away with, and whether they identify themselves with the job or seek self-definition elsewhere are related not just to job tasks and working conditions but to the extent that the jobs can be interpreted as honorable, worthwhile, and suitable for persons of their gender (Ouellet 1986).

This process of interpretation may be unusually salient and unusually open to analysis in routinized interactive service work. In such jobs, a convincing performance is important, and so employers are concerned about the degree to which workers enact their roles with conviction. The employers may therefore participate in reconciling workers' selves with the identities demanded by the work by providing positive interpretations of the work role or psychic strategies for dealing with its potentially unpleasant or demeaning aspects. In short, employers of interactive service workers may be unusually open in their attempts to channel workers' attitudes and manipulate workers' identities.

Gender is more salient in some service jobs than others, of course. There are routinized interactive service jobs for which the gender of employees and customers is not particularly relevant to how the jobs were constructed or how the interactions are carried out—telephone interviewing, for example, is apparently gender neutral and is done by men and women. However, the gender of workers is not irrelevant in these jobs, since respondents may react differently to men and women interviewers. Similarly, while airplane flight attendant is a job currently held by men as well as women, Hochschild found that men flight attendants were more likely to have their authority respected and less likely to be subjected to emotional outbursts from passengers than were their women co-workers (Hochschild 1983). At the other extreme are jobs that are gender segregated and that would be virtually incomprehensible without extensive assumptions about how both workers and customers enact gender. The Gloria Marshall salon workers' job assumed that both workers and customers would be women. The script used by Playboy bunnies, who were trained to respond to being molested by saying, "Please, sir, you are not allowed to touch the bunnies" (Steinem 1983, 48), took for granted a male customer (see also Spradley and Mann 1975). Both scripts dictated "common understandings" about what men and women are like and how power is distributed between them.

I studied two jobs that fall between these extremes; they are neither gender neutral nor entirely saturated with assumptions about gender. I conducted fieldwork at McDonald's and at Combined Insurance Company of America. At McDonald's, my research centered on the food servers who dealt directly with the public (*window crew,* in McDonald's parlance), and at Combined Insurance, I studied life insurance agents. These jobs were not strictly gender segregated, but they were held predominantly by either women or men, influencing how workers, employers, and customers thought about the jobs. Most, but not all, of McDonald's window crew were young women, and almost all of Combined Insurance's agents were men. Their gender attributes were not essential to their jobs. In fact, both jobs can be gender typed in the opposite direction—in its early years, McDonald's hired only men (Boas and Chain 1976), and in Japan, door-to-door insurance sales is a woman's job (*Life Insurance Business in Japan, 1987/88*).

Workers in both jobs tried to make sense of de facto job segregation by gender, interpreting their jobs as congruent with proper gender enactment. Examination of these two jobs and of how workers thought about them highlights a central paradox in the construction of gender: The considerable flexibility of notions of proper gender enactment does not undermine the appearance of inevitability and naturalness that continues to support the division of labor by gender. Although the work of the insurance agents required many of the same kinds of interactive behavior as the McDonald's job, including behavior that would ordinarily be considered feminine, the agents were able to interpret the work as suitable only for men. They did so by emphasizing aspects of their job that required "manly" attributes and by thinking about their interactive work in terms of control rather than deference. Their interpretation suggests not only the plasticity of gender idioms but the asymmetry of those idioms: Defining work as masculine has a different

meaning for men workers than defining work as feminine has for women workers.

Because interactive service work by definition involves nonemployees in the work process, the implications of the gender constructions of the routines extend beyond the workers. When service jobs are done predominantly by men or predominantly by women, the gender segregation provides confirming "evidence" to the public that men and women have different natures and capabilities. This appearance is especially ironic when employers, treating their workers' selves as fairly malleable, reshape the self-presentations and interactional styles of the service workers. A brief account of my fieldwork and of the routinization of the two jobs precedes further discussion of how work, gender, and identity are enmeshed in these jobs.

ROUTINIZED INTERACTIONS

My data were gathered from participant observation and interviewing. I attended classes at McDonald's management training center, Hamburger University, in June 1986, and spoke with "professors" and trainees there. I conducted research at a local McDonald's franchise from May through November 1986, going through orientation and window-crew training, working on the window, interviewing window workers and managers, and hanging around the crew room to observe and talk with workers. At Combined Insurance, I went through the two-week training for life insurance agents in January 1987. Between January and March, I interviewed trainees and managers and spent one-and-a-half weeks in the field with a sales team, observing sales calls and talking to agents. Since insurance agents must be licensed and bonded, I did not actually sell insurance myself. I also conducted follow-up interviews with Combined Insurance managers in the summer of 1989. The workers and managers with whom I worked at both companies were aware that I was conducting research.

These two jobs were similar in a number of ways. Both were filled, by and large, with young, inexperienced workers, and both had extremely high rates of employee turnover. Neither job is held in high esteem by the public, which affected both customers' treatment of workers and the workers' willingness to embrace their roles (see Zelizer 1979, on the low prestige of life insurance agents). The companies, however, took training very seriously, and they carried the routinization of service interactions very far indeed. McDonald's and Combined Insurance each tried to exercise extensive control over their workers' presentation of themselves. However, they went about this task different-ly and placed different sorts of demands on their workers' psyches. The differences largely have to do with the kinds of relations that the companies established between workers and customers and are related to the gender typing of the work.

McDonald's

McDonald's has been a model of standardization for many kinds of service businesses, and its success, based upon the replication of standard procedures, has been truly phenom-enal. The goal is to provide the same quality of food and service every day at every McDonald's, and the company tries to leave nothing to chance. Individual franchises have considerable leeway in some matters, including labor prac-tices, but they are held to strict standards when it comes to the McDonald's basics of QSC—quality, service, and cleanliness.

At the McDonald's where I worked, all of the workers were hired at the minimum wage of $3.35. There were no fringe benefits and no guarantee of hours of work. As is typical at McDonald's, most men worked on the grill, and most women worked serving customers—about three-quarters of the window workers were women. About 80 percent of the restaurant's employees were Black, though Blacks were a minority of the city's population. Few of the workers were older than their early twenties, but most were out of high school—65 percent of my sample were eighteen or over. The clientele, in contrast, was quite diverse in class, race, age, and gender.

The window workers were taught their jobs in a few hours and were fully trained in a couple of days. The job involved carrying out the "Six Steps of Window Service," an unvarying routine for taking and delivering orders. The modern cash registers used at this McDonald's made it unnecessary for window workers to remember prices or to know how to calculate change. The machines also remind-ed workers to "suggestive sell": For example, if someone ordered a Big Mac, french fries, and a shake, the cash regis-ter's buttons for apple pies, ice cream, and cookies would light up, to remind the worker to suggest dessert. (Garson [1988] provides a scathing view of McDonald's routiniza-tion and computerization.) These workers were closely supervised, not only by McDonald's managers, but also by customers, whose constant presence exerted pressure to be diligent and speedy.

The workers wore uniforms provided by McDonald's and were supposed to look clean-cut and wholesome—for instance, a young man with a pierced ear had to wear a Band-Aid on his earlobe. The lack of control workers had over their self-presentations was brought home clearly when a special promotion of Shanghai McNuggets began, and window workers were forced to wear big Chinese peas-ant hats made of Styrofoam, which most felt made them look ridiculous.

Workers were told to be themselves on the job, but they were also told to be cheerful and polite at all times. Crew people were often reprimanded for not smiling. Almost all of the workers I interviewed said that most customers were pleasant to deal with, but the minority of rude or unreason-able customers had a disproportionate impact. Enduring customers' behavior, no matter how obnoxious, was a basic part of the job. Unfortunately for the workers, they com-pletely lacked what Hochschild calls a "status shield" (1983, 163). Some customers who might have managed to be polite to higher-status workers seemed to have no com-punction at all about snarling at McDonald's employees. The window crew could not escape from angry customers by leaving, and they were not allowed to argue or make smart-alecky remarks. Their only legitimate responses to rudeness or angry outbursts from customers were to control their anger, apologize, try to correct the problem, and in extreme cases, ask a manager to handle it.

The major task for the workers was to serve, and their major psychic task was to control or suppress the self. Workers were required to be nice to one person after anoth-er in a way that was necessarily unindividualized and to keep their tempers no matter how they were treated. What McDonald's demanded of its workers was a stripped-down interactive style, with some *pseudo-gemeinschaft* thrown in. The workers were supposed to be efficient, courteous, and friendly, but in short bursts and within a very narrow range. While they were told to be themselves, there was obviously not much range for self-expression.

Combined Insurance

Combined Insurance placed very different sorts of demands on its workers. The company's business is based on door-to-door sales in rural areas and small towns, and its profits depend on a high volume of sales of relatively inexpensive policies. Combined Insurance was founded in the 1920s by W. Clement Stone, and its agents still use many of the sales and self-conditioning techniques that he developed when he started out in the business—*The Success System That Never Fails* (Stone 1962). Almost all of the company's life insur-ance agents are men, most are white, and most are young—

all of the members of the sales team I studied were in their early twenties. The prospects I called on with the agents were all white, about equally men and women, and quite varied in age.

The agents' initial training was more extensive than the McDonald's workers', involving two weeks of lectures, script memorization, and role playing. During sales school, trainees were taught what to say and do in almost hilarious detail. They memorized scripts for the basic sales presentations, for Rebuttals 1 through 5, corresponding to Objections 1 through 5, and for Interruption-stoppers. They were taught exactly how to stand while waiting for a door to be opened, how to position themselves and the potential customers (known as "prospects"), when to make and break eye contact, how to deliver the Standard Joke, and so on. A lot of class time was spent chanting the scripts in unison and rehearsing proper body movements, as well as in practicing responses to be used in various sales situations.

The trainer underlined the possibility of success through standardization with stories of foreign-born agents who succeeded even before they could speak English—they allegedly learned their sales presentations phonetically. It might seem that the message of these stories was that a parrot could succeed in this job, but in fact, the trainer argued that personal characteristics were vitally important to success, and the most important of these was a Positive Mental Attitude—what Stone called PMA. While McDonald's merely instructed workers to smile and behave pleasantly to customers, Combined Insurance tried to affect its employees' psyches quite fundamentally—to inculcate optimism, determination, enthusiasm, and confidence and to destroy habits of negative thinking. The trainees were taught that through proper self-conditioning, they could learn to suppress negative thoughts altogether. The message for agents was somewhat paradoxical: You should do everything exactly the way we tell you to, but success depends on your strength of character.[1]

While McDonald's workers' main task was to serve people who had already chosen to do business with McDonald's, Combined Insurance's agents had to sell, to take prospects and turn them into customers. The agents' job was to establish rapport quickly with the people they called on (by "warming up the prospect"), to go through the basic sales presentation, to counter any objections raised by the prospects, and to persuade them to buy as much life insurance as possible. Naturally, most of the people they called on were strongly motivated to prevent them from going through this sequence, so their task was not easy. Since the agents' incomes were entirely based on commis-

sion, and their desire to handle their interactions successfully was of course very great, the detailed instructions for proper behavior provided by the company did not seem to strike them as ludicrous or intrusive.

Because the agents worked on their own, rather than in a central workplace, and because their interactions with customers could be much longer and cover a broader range than those of McDonald's workers, the agents were called on to use much more of their selves than the window workers were. They had to motivate themselves and keep up their enthusiasm, and they had to respond appropriately to a wide variety of situations, adjusting their behavior to suit the problems presented by each prospect. Although their basic routine was unvaried, they needed to be chameleon-like to a certain extent and adapt to circumstances. They were, like the McDonald's workers, required to control themselves, but their focus was always on controlling the prospect and the interaction. Virtually every detail of their routines was designed to help them do just that.

DOING GENDER WHILE DOING THE JOB

Although their jobs were largely segregated by gender, McDonald's and Combined Insurance workers interacted with both men and women as customers or prospects. Neither company suggested significantly different approaches to men and women service recipients; the Combined Insurance trainer recommended slightly varied techniques for persuading men and women to buy policies without first consulting their spouses. While the gender of the service recipient might well have influenced how the workers experienced their interactions, I did not find consistent patterns of variation in workers' behavior along this dimension.

At McDonald's, most of the window crew took the division of labor by gender for granted and did not seem to feel any need to account for it. Since there were no differences in the pay or prestige of window and grill work, and since there were exceptions to the pattern of gender segregation, few workers considered the division of labor by gender unfair.[2] When I asked the workers why they thought that there were more women than men working the window, about two-thirds of the twenty-three respondents said that they did not know, with about half offering a guess based on stereotypes about proper gender roles, whether or not they thought the stereotype was justified. About one-quarter of the sample, however, stated explicitly that they disapproved of the division of labor by gender, and three women said that they had asked a manager about it. The store's manager told me that women were typically assigned to start work on the window because "more females have an aversion to grill." Two of the window workers, however (both Black men), thought that men might have an aversion to window because that job required swallowing one's pride and accepting abuse calmly:

THEO: [More women than men work window] because women are afraid of getting burned [on the grill], and men are afraid of getting aggravated and going over the counter and smacking someone.

ALPHONSE: I found the men who work here on window have a real quick temper. You know, all of them. And women can take a lot more. They deal with a lot of things, you know.

Although I never heard the masculinity of the few male window workers impugned, it was commonly taken for granted that men were naturally more explosive than women and would find it more difficult to accept abuse without answering back. The male window workers were usually able to reconcile themselves to swallowing insults, as the women were, either by dissociating themselves from their role or by telling themselves that by keeping their tempers they were proving themselves superior to the rude customers. Refusing to become riled when provoked is consistent with "the cool pose," which Majors says Black men use to "fight to preserve their dignity, pride, respect and masculinity" by enacting an imperviousness to hurt (1989, 86). Thus, while the job did not allow workers to try to get the better of opponents, its demands were not seen as irreconcilable with enacting masculinity. However, no workers argued that men's capacity to tolerate abuse made them especially well-suited to the job, and the Black men quoted above made the opposite argument. Moreover, the job requirements of smiling and otherwise demonstrating deference are not in keeping with the cool pose. Those committed to that stance might well find such behavior demeaning, especially in interactions with white customers or those of higher status.

Other explanations given by workers of the predominance of women on window crew included assertions that women were more interested in dealing with people, that women "were more presentable" and looked better on window, that their nimble fingers suited them to working the registers, and that customers were more likely to find them trustworthy. Several of the workers who offered such stereotyped responses indicated that they did not believe

that the stereotypes were sufficient justification for the predominance of women on the window crew.

It might easily have been argued that men were unsuited to work on the grill—cooking, after all, is usually considered women's work. As the work was understood at McDonald's, however, cooking presented no challenge to masculinity. Serving customers, which involved adopting an ingratiating manner, taking orders from anyone who chose to give them, and holding one's tongue when insulted, was more difficult to conceive as congruent with the proper enactment of manliness. Thus, while the crew people did not argue that window work was especially expressive of femininity, most found it unremarkable that women predominated in that job.

The work of Combined Insurance's agents, in contrast, was defined as properly manly, even though the job presented interactive imperatives that are generally identified with femininity, along with some stereotypically masculine elements. The life insurance sales force was almost entirely composed of men, and the agents on the sales team I observed felt strongly that women would be unlikely to succeed in the job.[3] Moreover, the twenty-two-year-old manager of this sales team told me bluntly (without my having raised the question) that he "would never hire a woman."[4] Since some aspects of the agents' job required skills that are not generally considered manly, the agents' understanding of the job as demanding masculine attributes meant that these skills had to be reinterpreted or de-emphasized.

Like many other kinds of interactive service jobs, including McDonald's window work, insurance sales requires that workers adopt an attitude of congeniality and eagerness to please. This in itself may strike some men as incompatible with the proper enactment of gender, as suggested by the cool pose, which associates masculinity with toughness and detachment (Majors 1989, 84). In *America's Working Man,* Halle records that a few of the chemical workers he studied did not support Jimmy Carter's presidential candidacy because they "suspected that a man who smiled all the time might be a homosexual" (1984, 246). To them, behavior that is transparently intended to please others, to encourage liking, is not considered masculine. Toughness, gruffness, and pride are taken-for-granted elements of masculinity to many blue-collar men (Gray 1987; Willis 1977), and Combined's agents come largely from blue-collar or agricultural backgrounds. For such men, deferential behavior and forced amiability are often associated with servility, and occasions that call for these attitudes—dealings with superiors, for instance—may feel humiliating. Such behavior is not easy to reconcile with the autonomy and assertiveness that are considered central to "acting like a man." The rebellious working-class "lads" Willis studied were therefore concerned to find jobs with "an essentially masculine ethos," jobs "where you would not be expected to be subservient" (1977, 96). Sennett and Cobb, drawing on their interviews with blue-collar men, interpret the low prestige ratings of many service jobs relative to blue-collar jobs as a response to the perceived dependence of service workers on other people, whose shifting demands they must meet (1972, 236).

Thus the glad-handing insincerity required of many sorts of businessmen may seem effete and demeaning to working-class men. The job of salesman, which is on the lower end of the white-collar hierarchy, would seem especially degrading from this point of view. Since success is largely dependent on ingratiating oneself with customers, playing up to others is an essential part of the agent's job, rather than just a demand of the social milieu. Salesmen must swallow insults, treat even social inferiors with deference, and keep smiling.

These aspects of the sales job were quite pronounced for Combined Insurance's life agents. The warming-up-the-prospect phase of the routine called for agents to figure out what topics might interest the prospects and display a flattering enthusiasm for those topics and for the prospects' accomplishments. Agents had to be willing to disguise their true feelings and to seem to accept the prospect's view of the world in order to ingratiate themselves. It was crucial that they not lose their tempers with prospects but remain polite and respectful at all times. Like most salespeople, they had to try to change prospective customers' minds while never seeming to argue with them and to stay pleasant even when rudely dismissed.

The skills required for establishing and maintaining rapport—drawing people out, bolstering their egos, displaying interest in their interests, and carefully monitoring one's own behavior so as not to offend—are usually considered womanly arts. In analyses of a small sample of conversations, Fishman (1978) found that women had to do much more interactive work than men simply to sustain dialogues; men largely took for granted that their conversational attempts would succeed in engaging their partner's interest. Judging only by these interactive demands of insurance sales work, it would seem that women are especially well suited to be agents. We might even expect that the association of ingratiating conversational tactics with women would lead men to view the extensive interactive work required of salespeople as degrading, since it requires

that they assume the role of the interactive inferior who must constantly negotiate permission to proceed. Given the additional attack on personal autonomy implicit in Combined Insurance's programming of employees to follow scripts, it would seem to be difficult for men to combine successful enactment of the role of Combined Insurance agent with the successful enactment of gender.

On the contrary, Combined Insurance's trainers and agents interpreted the agent's job as demanding manly attributes. They assigned a heroic character to the job, framing interactions with customers as contests of will. To succeed, they emphasized, required determination, aggressiveness, persistence, and stoicism. These claims were accurate, but qualities in which women excel, including sensitivity to nuance and verbal dexterity, were also important for success. While the sales training did include tips on building such skills, determination and aggressiveness were treated as the decisive factors for career success. It was through this need for toughness that the work was constructed as manly.[5]

Of course it was quite true that considerable determination, self-motivation, and persistence were required to do this job. The agents had to make numerous sales calls every day, despite the knowledge that many people would be far from glad to see them. They had to keep making calls, even after meeting with repeated rejection and sometimes hostility. And in sales interactions, they had to stick to their objectives even when prospects displayed reluctance to continue the conversation, as most did. Some agents and managers believed that women were unlikely to meet these job demands because they are too sensitive, too unaggressive, and not able to withstand repeated rejection. Josh, one of the agents, claimed, "Most girls don't have what it takes. They don't have that killer instinct." Josh had, however, recruited a woman he knew to join Combined's sales force. "She does have [the killer instinct], if I can bring it out," he said. Ralph, the sales manager, also acknowledged that there might be some exceptional women who could do the job. He amended his statement that he would never hire a woman by saying, "Only if she had a kind of bitchy attitude." "A biker woman" is the kind he meant, he said, "someone hard-core." Obviously, he did not believe it was possible to combine the traits necessary for success as an agent with femininity.[6]

One manager attributed women's assumed deficiencies not to their nature but to economics, arguing that women whose husbands provided an income were unlikely to have the requisite "burning need" to succeed that financial necessity provides. An obvious factor that would prevent most mothers from taking the job—at least one week a month was spent away from home—was not mentioned by any agents in explaining the dearth of women agents, though two managers did mention it. Two agents told me that they "wouldn't want their wives doing this" because of the unpleasant or potentially dangerous places agents must sometimes visit.

This emphasis on aggression, domination, and danger is only one possible construction of sales work. Biggart (1989) and Connelly and Rhoton (1988) discuss in detail the very different ways that direct sales organizations that rely on a female labor force characterize sales work. These organizations, some of which are hugely successful, emphasize nurturance, helpfulness, and service both in relations with customers and among salespeople. Combined Insurance's training also encouraged agents to think of themselves as providing a service to prospective customers, largely in order to overcome trainees' reluctance to impose on others, and some of the agents I spoke with did use the service ideology to counter demeaning images of insurance sales as high-pressure hucksterism. For the most part, however, the agents emphasized the more "manly" dimensions of the work, though there is ample evidence that women can succeed in life insurance sales. For example, Thomas (1990) notes that after the Equitable Life Assurance Society made a commitment to recruiting and supporting women agents, the company's saleswomen outperformed salesmen in sales and commissions.

While most agents would not feel the need, on a daily basis, to construct an explanation for why there were so few women selling life insurance for their company, they did need to construct an interpretation of their work as honorable and fitting for a man if they were to maintain their positive attitudes and do well at their jobs, which required much more self-motivation than did McDonald's jobs. The element of competition, the battle of wills implicit in their interactions with customers, seemed to be a major factor that allowed the agents to interpret their work as manly. Virtually every step of the interaction was understood as a challenge to be met—getting in the door, making the prospect relax and warm up, being allowed to start the presentation, getting through the presentation despite interruptions, overcoming prospects' objections and actually making the sale, and perhaps even increasing the size of the sale. Since many prospects did their best to prevent the agents from continuing, going through these steps did not simply represent following a prescribed routine; it was experienced by agents as proof of their skill and victories of their wills. Each sales call seemed an uphill battle, as the

interactions took place on the prospects' turf and prospects always had the option of telling the agent to leave.

The spirit of jousting was especially clear in some of the techniques taught for closing sales. As the trainer explained "The Assumptive Close," the agents were supposed to "challenge customers"; it was up to the prospects to object if they did not want to go along with the sales. The routine allowed agents to limit the customers' options without seeming to do so, to let prospects believe that they were making decisions while the agents remained in control of the interaction. The pattern bears some resemblance to the seduction of an initially unwilling partner, and the satisfaction that the agents took in "winning" such encounters is perhaps similar to the satisfaction some men take in thinking of sexual encounters as conquests. The agents seemed to approach sales interactions with men in much the same spirit as those with women, however, though they often adjusted their presentation of self to suit a particular prospect's gender, age, and manner—subtly flirtatious, respectfully deferential, or efficient and businesslike.

This sort of manipulation of interactions required a peculiar combination of sensitivity to other people and callousness. The agent had to figure out which approach would work best at any given moment and avoid seeming cold or aggressive but still disregard the customers' stated wishes. The required mix of deference and ruthlessness was well illustrated in an exchange that took place during a sales-team training session. The agents were discussing how to deal with interruptions during a presentation: One of their superiors had advised ignoring them altogether, but the "training module" stated that it was insulting to fail to acknowledge a prospect's comment. When the sales manager instructed, "You have to let them know that you heard them," one of the agents finished the sentence for him: "and that you don't give a shit."

All kinds of interactive service workers—including McDonald's window crew—try to exercise control over their interactions with customers, though not all of them are given organizational resources to help them do so (see, e.g., Whyte 1962, on waitresses, and Benson 1986, on department store saleswomen). Women who can successfully dominate interactions at work might well take pleasure in doing so, as did Combined's life insurance agents. However, it is unlikely that these women's capacity to control other people would be taken as evidence that the work was womanly, unless it were reinterpreted in less aggressive terms, such as "skill in dealing with people."

If following a script could be given a manly cast when it involved asserting one's will through controlling an interaction, it was more difficult to do so when the interactions did not go the agents' way. Refusals were such a routine part of the job, however, that agents could accept most of them as inevitable, not a result of lack of skill or determination. In sales school, the trainers emphasized that not everyone was going to buy—some people really do not need or cannot afford the product; some are just close-minded and would not listen to any salesperson. A greater challenge to the agent's definition of himself was presented by customers who were actively hostile. Some people were angry at being interrupted; some had a grievance against the company; some became furious if they felt that they were being manipulated. In any case, it was not unusual for agents to meet with loud insults, condescending sneers, and slammed doors. To accept this sort of treatment passively could certainly be seen as unmanly. However, the agents were expected to keep their cool, refrain from rudeness, and leave graciously. Some agents did tell me, with glee, of instances when they shouted obscenities once they got out the door, in response to particularly outrageous treatment from a customer. For the most part, however, passive acceptance of ill-treatment was reconciled with manly honor by defining it as maintaining one's control and one's positive attitude, a strategy similar to that used by male and female McDonald's workers. In this view, screaming back at a customer would not be considered standing up for yourself but letting the customer get the better of you, "letting them blow your attitude." Agents proved themselves to be above combative and insulting customers by maintaining their dignity and holding on to their self-concepts as winners, not by sinking to the customers' level.

Other attributes of the job, not directly connected with job routinization, also contributed to the salesmen's ability to define their jobs as compatible with properly enacting gender. The most important of these were the sense of independence agents felt and their belief that they could earn as much as they were worth. Within the limits of their work assignments, agents could set their own schedules, behave as they chose, and work only as hard as they felt like. Because of the importance of self-motivation to success, those who did well could feel justifiably proud, and those lacking in motivation could appreciate the freedom from pressure. The agents thus felt that their jobs provided some of the benefits of self-employment. They could live with the knowledge that many people looked down on them, put up with insults, endure futile days of failure, and still maintain a sense that their work was compatible with manliness and social honor, as long as there was the possibility of "making it big."

DISCUSSION

Until the 1970s, most sociological work concerning the connection between workers' genders and their jobs mirrored the commonsense view that men and women hold different sorts of jobs because of differing physical capacities, psychological orientations, and family responsibilities. Kanter (1977) reversed the traditional argument that women's traits determine the sorts of jobs they hold, claiming instead that the structural features of most women's jobs determine characteristic attitudinal and behavioral responses, which are then interpreted as reflecting women's natures. She focused on power, opportunity, and numbers of like individuals in the workplace as the factors determining workers' responses to jobs. In her analysis, preexisting gender segregation leads workers, managers, and observers to believe incorrectly that gender explains how workers respond to their jobs. As Berk (1985b) has argued, Kanter understated the distinctive properties of gender and minimized the extent to which gender assumptions are built into jobs by work organizations (see also Acker 1990).

More recently, analysts have called attention to the ways that occupations are gendered—they are designed and evolve in particular ways because of the gender of typical incumbents (Cockburn 1985; Reverby 1987). Moreover, theorists have argued that gender is not simply imported into the workplace: Gender itself is constructed in part through work (Beechey 1988; Berk 1985a, 1985b). This argument applies both to the gender identities of individual workers and to cultural understandings of women's and men's natures and capacities and is supported by the cases of McDonald's and Combined Insurance.

Just how jobs are gendered and how doing these jobs affects workers' gender identities remain to be clarified, however. Cockburn describes the gendering of jobs and people as a two-way process: "People have a gender and their gender rubs off on the jobs they mainly do. The jobs in turn have a gender character which rubs off on the people who do them" (1985, 169). While acknowledging that the gender designation of jobs, tools, fields of knowledge, and activities may shift over time, she treats these designations as cultural givens. For example, Cockburn writes (1985, 70):

An 18th-century man no doubt felt effeminate using a spinning wheel, though he would have felt comfortable enough repairing one. Today it is difficult to get a teenage lad to use a floor mop or a typewriter because they contradict his own gender identity.

Cockburn correctly perceives the relevance of work tasks to the workers' gender identity, but overstates the rigidity of the gender typing of those tasks: At McDonald's, mopping has largely become low-status men's work. I argue that despite the existence of culturally shaped gender designations of work activities, employers and workers retain the flexibility to reinterpret them in ways that support jobholders' gender identities. However, the gender designation of work is likely to have different kinds of significance for women and men.

Workers at both McDonald's and Combined Insurance were expected to adjust their moods and demeanors to the demands of their jobs and to learn to handle customers in ways that might be very different from their ordinary styles of interaction. To some extent, workers in both jobs had to take on the role of interactive inferior, adjusting themselves to the styles and apparent preferences of their customers. They were supposed to paste on smiles when they did not feel like smiling and to behave cheerfully and deferentially to people of every status and with every attitude. The workers were not permitted to respond to rudeness in kind but had to try to remain pleasant even in the face of insult.

This sort of behavior is usually associated with femininity, but in fact the two jobs were interpreted quite differently. At McDonald's, many workers and managers considered it natural, even self-evident, that women were best suited to deal with customers. At Combined Insurance, women were generally seen as ill equipped to handle such work. The insurance agents were able to define their job as masculine by emphasizing those aspects of the work that require "manly" traits (control and self-direction) and by reinterpreting some of the more "feminine" job requirements in ways that were not degrading. McDonald's workers' superiors emphasized that the crew's role was to serve, and attempts by window workers to assert their wills in interactions with customers were strongly discouraged. Combined Insurance's agents, on the other hand, were taught that their job was to establish and maintain control in interactions with prospects. They were told that they control their own destinies and were urged to cultivate the qualities of aggressiveness, persistence, and belief in themselves. While success might require that they take on a deferential manner, it was seen as a matter of skill in manipulating situations, not as servility, and therefore was not taken to be inconsistent with manliness. Similarly, accepting abuse calmly was interpreted as a refusal to let someone else dictate the terms of the interaction, not as a loss of control. This conceptualization of the work as an arena for enacting masculinity allowed the agents to accept working conditions that might otherwise have been seen as unacceptably frustrating and demeaning.

When Hughes called attention to the "social and social–psychological arrangements and devices by which men make their work tolerable, or even make it glorious to themselves and others," he apparently meant "men" to include men and women. In fact, the case of Combined Insurance's agents suggests that defining a job as "men's work" is precisely how some men make their work tolerable or even glorious. Willis (1977) and Ouellet (1986) have shown how ideas about masculinity can transform what otherwise might be considered negative job features—danger, hard physical labor, dirt—into badges of honor. In other circumstances, work that seems "glorious" on its own merits—because it is understood to be important, highly skilled, responsible, powerful—is defined as masculine (see, e.g., Cockburn 1985). Identifying work as manly, then, can compensate male workers for hardships, but it also justifies privilege.

Some working-class boys and men insist that only jobs that are physically demanding, exhausting, or dangerous can be considered manly (cf. Halle 1984; Willis 1977), but in fact, the gender designation of particular job tasks is quite plastic, a matter of interpretation in which jobholders, employers, and customers may participate. The actual features of the work do not rigidly determine its gender designation. Nevertheless, the association of a job with manliness serves to elevate the work itself and allows men to construe success on the job as proof of masculinity. The importance of manly work for constructing and maintaining masculine identity may explain some of the resistance of men working in gender-segregated occupations to women co-workers; they tend to define their work not just as particularly appropriate for men but as work that women would not be able to do (Cockburn 1983, 1985; Halle 1984; Swerdlow 1989; Willis 1977). The experiences of women entering previously male-dominated occupations bear out this interpretation. For example, Schroedel (1985, 20–21) quotes a female pipe fitter:

> You see it is just very hard for them to work with me because they're really into proving their masculinity and being tough. And when a woman comes on a job that can work, get something done as fast and efficiently, as well as they can, it really affects them. Somehow if a woman can do it, it ain't that masculine, not that tough.

The Combined Insurance agents sustained the belief that women could not handle their job, even though the work required some skills and qualities typically associated with women.

Interpreting work as womanly has a different meaning for women than interpreting work as manly has for men.

Certain jobs, including nursing and elementary-school teaching, are understood to require some positively valued "female" traits, such as nurturance or sensitivity, and the identification of the work with femininity significantly determines how the work is organized (Melosh 1982; Reverby 1987). Even when the work is seen as expressive of feminine capacities, however, it is not seen as offering proof of female identity in quite the same way that manly work supports male identity, because adult female identity has not traditionally been regarded as something that is achieved through paid work. In other words, while women in traditionally female-defined jobs might well take pleasure in doing work that supports their self-identification as feminine, they are unlikely to think of such work as a necessary part of their gender identity. Thus men and women respond differently to challenges to gender segregation of work. Williams (1989) found that women nurses did not feel threatened when men joined their ranks, though male marines much preferred to keep women out of the corps. Furthermore, while male nurses were concerned to differentiate their activities from those of their women co-workers, female marines did not feel that doing quintessentially masculine work was a challenge to their femininity.

Williams draws on the work of Chodorow (1978) to provide a psychoanalytic explanation for male workers' concern with defining their work as masculine and with maintaining gender segregation at work. She argues that because men, whose original identification is with a female caretaker, must achieve masculinity by distancing themselves from femininity, they are psychologically threatened when one proof of their masculinity is challenged by evidence that women can do the work they have defined as manly. Women, who need not alter their original identification with a female caretaker, have no corresponding need to prove their femininity: "What one *does* has little bearing on how feminine one is" (Williams 1989, 140; emphasis in original). Whether or not the psychoanalytic explanation is valid, Williams persuasively demonstrates that gendered jobs have different meanings for men and women.

The different cultural valuation of behavior labeled masculine and feminine also contributes to the different meanings that enacting gender at work has for women and men. While the constant "doing" of gender is mandatory for everyone, many theorists have noted that the effects of this demand are asymmetrical, since doing masculinity generally means asserting dominance, while doing femininity often means enacting submission (Acker 1990; Berk 1985a). Frye claims (1983, 33) that the female "cannot move or speak without engaging in self-deprecation. The male cannot move or speak without engaging in self-aggrandizement." Thus

many men value the opportunity to do work that supports cultural understandings of masculinity and their own sense of manliness, but we cannot assume that job features that allow or require gender-appropriate behavior will necessarily be welcomed by women workers in the same way. In some cases, women may appreciate the opportunity to enact such "womanly" attributes as nurturance, helpfulness, or sexiness at work, because that behavior affirms their gender identity. On the other hand, servility may be congruent with femininity, but we would hardly expect female McDonald's workers to take the same pleasures in enacting it at work that Combined's agents take in asserting control.

Job features that allow or require gender-appropriate behaviors are not necessarily welcomed, then, but work routines that prevent workers from enacting gender in ways that they are comfortable with are resented and may contribute to workers' decisions to limit their investments of energy, effort, and self-definition in their jobs. Job features that allow gender enactment in ways workers find gratifying, on the other hand, may make up for deficiencies in more objective job benefits. In any case, the variation in the interpretations of similar job demands at McDonald's and Combined Insurance demonstrates that the actual features of the jobs do not themselves determine whether the work will be defined as most appropriate for men or women. Rather, these job features are resources for interpretation that can be drawn on by workers, their superiors, and other audiences.

Despite this flexibility in the interpretation of gender appropriateness, in these two work settings the association of the work with either women or men was made to seem natural—an expression of the essential natures of women and men. Even though the workers' behavior was largely dictated by routines they had no part in creating, and even where the job drew on traits associated with both femininity and masculinity, job segregation by gender was interpreted largely as an outgrowth of inherent gender differences in attitudes and behavior. In trying to make sense of the fact of gender segregation, many of the workers and managers I spoke with drew on taken-for-granted beliefs about the qualities and preferences of women and men. The prevalence of either men or women in a job became evidence that the job demanded specifically masculine or feminine qualities and that the jobholders must be best suited for the work. For the public, as well as for employers and workers, gender segregation of service jobs contributes to the general perception that differences in men's and women's social positions are straightforward reflections of differences in their natures and capabilities.

ACKNOWLEDGMENTS

This article is the 1989 winner of the American Sociological Association Sex and Gender Section Dissertation Paper Award.

I would like to thank Carol A. Heimer, Arthur L. Stinchcombe, Arlene Kaplan Daniels, Sam Kaplan, Judith Lorber, and the *Gender & Society* reviewers for their help and suggestions.

NOTES

1. Combined Insurance has recently made changes in its life insurance products and sales techniques. Agents are now taught a more interactive sales routine ("needs selling") for a policy that can be tailored to suit customers' circumstances, allowing the agents somewhat greater flexibility. The company's largest division, which sells accident insurance, continues to follow Stone's original techniques closely. Positive Mental Attitude training is still stressed for all agents.

2. The job of "host," however, was viewed as less prestigious by some workers. That polite job title referred to those whose main responsibilities were to empty the trash and keep the lobby, windows, bathrooms, and dining areas clean. When one woman took this job, I heard two women window workers express their disapproval; they felt that "girls" should not have to do the dirty work of handling garbage.

3. I learned, in fact, that the two other women in my training class had lasted, respectively, only one day and three weeks in the field. Managers interviewed in 1989 reported that the number of women agents had increased since the new selling system was introduced, though women were still a small minority of the sales force. Reduced travel demands were one reason given for the job's increasing attractiveness to women. See also note 5.

4. The higher-level managers I interviewed did not endorse these discriminatory views, and some commented on the many successful women in the insurance industry. See Thomas (1990) for a discussion of the growth of women's employment in insurance sales. She shows that by 1980, women were 25 percent of U.S. insurance agents.

5. Some managers believe that the new needs-selling approach is better suited to women agents because it requires a less domineering stance and allows them to draw on their understanding of families' needs.

6. Similarly, Williams (1989, 32) reports a backlash against women in the military among male soldiers during World War II. She argues that military men claimed that women soldiers must be unfeminine because the men did not want to accept the alternative explanation for the women's presence—that military service is not inherently masculine.

REFERENCES

Acker, Joan. 1990. Hierarchies, jobs, bodies: A theory of gendered organizations. *Gender & Society* 4:139–58.

Beechey, Veronica. 1988. Rethinking the definition of work: Gender and work. In *Feminization of the Labor Force: Paradoxes and Promises,* ed. Jane Jenson, Elisabeth Hagen, and Ceallaigh Reddy. New York: Oxford University Press.

Benson, Susan Porter. 1986. *Counter Cultures: Saleswomen, Managers, and Customers in American Department Stores, 1890–1940.* Urbana: University of Illinois Press.

Berk, Sarah Fenstermaker. 1985a. *The Gender Factory: The Apportionment of Work in American Households.* New York: Plenum.

———. 1985b. Women's work and the production of gender. Paper presented at the annual meeting of the American Sociological Association, Washington, DC.

Biggart, Nicole. 1989. *Charismatic Capitalism: Direct Selling Organizations in America.* Chicago: University of Chicago Press.

Boas, Max, and Steve Chain. 1976. *Big Mac: The Unauthorized Story of McDonald's.* New York: Mentor, New American Library.

Chodorow, Nancy. 1978. *The Reproduction of Mothering: Psychoanalysis and the Sociology of Gender.* Berkeley: University of California Press.

Cockburn, Cynthia. 1983. *Brothers: Male Dominance and Technological Change.* London: Pluto.

———. 1985. *Machinery of Dominance: Women, Men and Technical Know-how.* London: Pluto.

Connelly, Maureen, and Patricia Rhoton. 1988. Women in direct sales: A comparison of Mary Kay and Amway sales workers. In *The Worth of Women's Work: A Qualitative Synthesis,* ed. Anne Statham, Eleanor M. Miller, and Hans O. Mauksch. Albany: State University of New York Press.

Fishman, Pamela M. 1978. Interaction: The work women do. *Social Problems* 25:397–406.

Frye, Marilyn. 1983. Sexism. In *The Politics of Reality.* Trumansberg, NY: Crossing Press.

Garfinkel, Harold. 1967. *Studies in Ethnomethodology.* Englewood Cliffs, NJ: Prentice-Hall.

Garson, Barbara. 1988. *The Electronic Sweatshop.* New York: Simon & Schuster.

Goffman, Erving. 1977. The arrangements between the sexes. *Theory and Society* 4:301–31.

Gray, Stan. 1987. Sharing the shop floor. In *Beyond Patriarchy: Essays by Men on Pleasure, Power, and Change,* ed. Michael Kaufman. Toronto: Oxford University Press.

Halle, David. 1984. *America's Working Man.* Chicago: University of Chicago Press.

Hochschild, Arlie Russell. 1983. *The Managed Heart: Commercialization of Human Feeling.* Berkeley: University of California Press.

Hughes, Everett C. [1951] 1984. Work and self. In *The Sociological Eye.* New Brunswick, NJ: Transaction.

Kanter, Rosabeth Moss. 1977. *Men and Women of the Corporation.* New York: Basic Books.

Kessler, Suzanne J., and Wendy McKenna. 1978. *Gender: An Ethnomethodological Approach.* Chicago: University of Chicago Press.

Lally-Benedetto, Corinne. 1985. Women and the tone of the body: An analysis of a figure salon. Paper presented at the annual meeting of the Midwest Sociological Society, St. Louis, MO.

Leidner, Robin. 1988. Working on people: The routinization of interactive service work. Ph.D. diss., Northwestern University, Evanston, IL.

Life Insurance Business in Japan, 1987/88. Tokyo: Life Assurance Association of Japan.

Majors, Richard. 1989. Cool pose: The proud signature of Black survival. In *Men's Lives,* ed. Michael S. Kimmel and Michael A. Messner. New York: Macmillan.

Melosh, Barbara. 1982. *"The Physician's Hand": Work Culture and Conflict in American Nursing.* Philadelphia: Temple University Press.

Milkman, Ruth. 1987. *Gender at Work: The Dynamics of Job Segregation by Sex during World War II.* Urbana: University of Illinois Press.

Ouellet, Lawrence J. 1986. Work, commitment, and effort: Truck drivers and trucking in small, non-union, West Coast trucking companies. Ph.D. diss., Northwestern University, Evanston, IL.

Personick, Valerie A. 1987. Industry output and employment through the end of the century. *Monthly Labor Review* 10 (September): 30–45.

Reverby, Susan M. 1987. *Ordered to Care: The Dilemma of American Nursing, 1850–1945.* Cambridge: Cambridge University Press.

Rollins, Judith. 1985. *Between Women: Domestics and Their Employers.* Philadelphia: Temple University Press.

Schroedel, Jean Reith. 1985. *Alone in a Crowd: Women in the Trades Tell Their Stories.* Philadelphia: Temple University Press.

Sennett, Richard, and Jonathan Cobb. 1972. *The Hidden Injuries of Class.* New York: Knopf.

Silvestri, George T., and John M. Lukasiewic. 1987. A look at occupational employment trends to the year 2000. *Monthly Labor Review* 10 (September): 46–63.

Spradley, James P., and Brenda J. Mann. 1975. *The Cocktail Waitress: Woman's Work in a Man's World.* New York: Wiley.

Steinem, Gloria. 1983. I was a Playboy bunny. In *Outrageous Acts and Everyday Rebellions.* New York: Holt, Rinehart & Winston.

Stone, W. Clement. 1962. *The Success System That Never Fails.* Englewood Cliffs, NJ: Prentice-Hall.

Swerdlow, Marian. 1989. Men's accommodations to women entering a nontraditional occupation: A case of rapid transit operatives. *Gender & Society* 3:373–87.

Thomas, Barbara J. 1990. Women's gains in insurance sales: Increased supply, uncertain demand. In *Job Queues, Gender Queues: Women's Movement into Male Occupations,* ed. Barbara Reskin and Patricia Roos. Philadelphia: Temple University Press.

West, Candace, and Don Zimmerman. 1987. Doing gender. *Gender & Society* 1: 125–51.

Whyte, William F. 1962. When workers and customers meet. In *Man, Work, and Society,* ed. Sigmund Nosow and William H. Form. New York: Basic Books.

Williams, Christine. 1989. *Gender Differences at Work: Women and Men in Nontraditional Occupations.* Berkeley: University of California Press.

Willis, Paul. 1977. *Learning to labor: How Working Class Kids Get Working Class Jobs.* New York: Columbia University Press.

Zelizer, Viviana A. Rotman. 1979. *Morals and Markets: The Development of Life Insurance in the United States.* New York: Columbia University Press.

Marking Gender Boundaries:
Porn, Piss, Power Tools

SUSAN EISENBERG

I don't worry about the ones who say things to me. That quiet person with that very controlled anger is the one I worry about. You can feel the anger, they don't have to voice it, you know it's there.

And those are sometimes the ones who try to be the nicest to you. You have to watch them.

—Gay Wilkinson, Boston

Close to eleven on a Friday morning, the steward was walking around the 44-story job collecting $2 each from the roughly sixty electricians on the site to celebrate the general foreman's fiftieth birthday with a drinking party in the shack. The party would start at lunchtime and extend into the afternoon. A stripper would be performing.

I was, at that point, less than a year out of my time.

Several of the new journeywomen in my local, including myself, and several of our business agents had only recently gone through a training together on sexual harassment. Earlier that week a highly publicized rape in the Boston area—on a poolroom table at Big Dan's Tavern—had called public attention to sexual violence. And it was the same week as International Women's Day. Ignoring the situation didn't feel like an option.

The steward told me that I didn't have to contribute or come to the party. I countered that, if the steward was organizing a celebration of the GF's birthday, it should be done so that everyone could participate. And I explained why I didn't think there should be a drinking party with a stripper on a union job site. "Just because we have to take you in," the steward said, "doesn't mean anything has to change because you're here."

I knew I didn't want to go to the party or be working on the job that afternoon, I told my foreman I was going home. Before leaving, I called the union hall and told my business agent that I was walking off the job and why. He asked what the other two female electricians there thought. I said that since both were apprentices and more vulnerable, I hadn't talked with them. He explained that, given how late it was, there wasn't really anything he could do. I said I understood. And I went home. Expecting the party to go on.

Monday morning on the bus ride to work, I learned from a woman plumber who worked on the site that, after I'd left on Friday, my business agent had asked the steward to cancel the party and return everyone's money. My breath caught. I was surprised and impressed that the hall had acted, but I knew there would be retribution.

—Susan

On job sites the behavior of those in authority—the foreman or general foreman representing the contractor (though they are also union members) and the steward representing the union—set a tone and an example for the crew to follow, and strongly affected a tradeswoman's sense of her welcome and safety. On her first job as an apprentice carpenter Lorraine Bertosa felt protected.

I remember my first foreman literally saying to the guys, "Watch how you talk." He said that in the first week I was on the job site. He was one of these guys that felt confident himself, wasn't out to prove anything. It was fine that women were there. A really unbelievable guy to get as a first foreman. If you were willing, then he was willing to meet you halfway. He would say to the guys, "Don't talk like that. You can't talk like that around here" (cuss words, certain things they were saying). I think that pressure came directly from the office, from the contractor. We want to keep these women.

Where contractors and unions did not make such a clear commitment to "keep these women," new tradeswomen were less fortunate. Co-workers, foremen, or stewards who felt that women did not belong in the industry at times expressed that opinion through words, actions, or silence. Before affirmative action brought government support for a more diverse workforce, harassment, ranging from petty to criminal, had been a standard means to discourage those who strayed across the industry's gender and racial boundaries. It did not end when the government regulations began.

Tradeswomen were sharp observers, and most perceived themselves to be on their own in handling any hostility. They worried that requesting assistance could as likely bring retribution as help. Given the imbalance of power, many women put blinders on, kept their focus on the day's work, and waited for a bad situation to end by itself. Women, especially those unfamiliar with the safety practices of tools and equipment, were particularly vulnerable on their first jobs. Not only were they green, but they were not yet sworn into union membership. Probationary periods could range from a few months to two years, for those entering under special affirmative action guidelines. Kathy Walsh was sent driving on a wild-goose chase looking for the foreman on her first day at work—hazing that might have happened to any new apprentice. But on her second day, when she knew where she was going, the ironworker who'd verbally expressed his resentment about having a woman on the job expressed those feelings again, this time physically.

Everybody parked up on top of this embankment. It was about forty feet down to where we were working, very steep, and it was muddy and slippery. An ironworker pushed me from behind. And I slid most of the way down that embankment face first.

Getting up from there—I can't remember whether I was crying or not, if I wasn't I was almost—and getting the mud off of my face and out of my tool pouch and going to work that day was one of the hardest things I'd ever done at that point. Mark, the guy that was nice to me, was like *so nice* to me that day. He gave the guy shit about it, and he came down as quick as he could and helped me get up. At the end of the day he said, "I don't know anybody that wouldn't have walked away at that point. You just keep it up, and fuck these guys." My first day I slammed my hand in the car door. My second day I went down face first down a muddy forty-foot embankment.

The job lasted for about two weeks. They laid me off and I was like—*uh*. I think I made it back to my car before I started crying.

Loyalty by trade is very strong in construction. Workers generally spend coffee breaks and lunch: carpenters with carpenters, ironworkers with ironworkers, painters with painters. For a journeyman of one trade to push down an apprentice of another trade is highly unusual, because normally the full crew would rally to defend *their* apprentice. Attacks on women put men in the position of choosing between male bonding and union or trade solidarity. Only one of the carpenters came to Kathy's assistance. When she reported back to her apprenticeship coordinator after the layoff, she never mentioned the ironworker's action, or the tacit approval of most of her crew. "I was totally intimidated by the whole process, all of it. We didn't even join the union until we had at least 600 hours in."

The behavior of the union representatives a tradeswoman happened to encounter was critical to shaping her expectations of whether or not the union would assist her in handling harassment or discrimination. Although MaryAnn Cloherty would return to union construction years later and complete her apprenticeship with a different local, she quit the first time around. She was a second-year apprentice on a job where having a steward on the site only added to her problems.

There was a lot of pornography on the job, and when I would complain about it they would take it down and they would put up more. Crotch shots, legs spread, blown up. I mean there was a crotch shot that was blown up that was at least three feet by five feet. I walked by it for three days, I didn't know what it was. I did not know what it was until I was on the other side of the picture and I saw a whole series of porno shots. I realized what the other shot must be. That was when I complained.

The offending stuff came down. And then the next day the whole job site was littered with it.

There was a union steward who was the worst offender. I really felt like there was nowhere to go. My steward when I first arrived on the job said, "Put your tools over here." After I put my tools down he said, "One thing you got to understand is, I used to throw gooks from helicopters in Vietnam." I didn't know what was that supposed to mean to me. I think he was trying to scare me or intimidate me or paint himself as a big ogre. I didn't really think I could relate to this guy.

A skilled construction worker must be able to climb scaffolding, use power tools, lift heavy objects, and perform countless other tasks that are inherently dangerous. But like driving a car on a freeway, they can be accomplished with relative safety given proper training, support, and equipment. Just as a student driver wouldn't feel comfortable in high-speed traffic accompanied by a driving instructor who was threatening, someone learning to splice live wires, walk an I-beam, or maneuver their way through the obstacle course of a construction site needed to trust their supervision in order to focus on the actual task at hand.

As a first-year apprentice plumber in Boston, Maura Russell was sent to a new building under construction, a good opportunity to see a project from the ground up. On the crew, though,

One guy was really a very sick fella. One day we were both carrying a length of 6- or 8-inch cast iron pipe. It was a stage of the underground, and he was on one end and I was on the other. We were carrying it from one place to a trench on another part of the job. We were walking by this one big pit that had all this rebar, re-inforcing bar, sticking up in various patterns because they were going to be pouring a floor and also have some starts for some columns.

He gave me a shove with that pipe so that I went down into that pit with the pipe—which is heavy pipe. And it was really lucky—luck had a lot to do with it—that I landed on my feet, still holding the pipe. That I did not end up in a perforated sandwich, with the pipe on top of me, landing on a lot of that rebar which was vertical. I can still see him standing at the top of that pit

with his little Carhartt jacket and reflector shades and Arctic CAT hat looking down. And with his little psycho voice saying, "Gotta watch out. You could get killed around here."

He was really creepy.

I'd be pouring lead in a pit, in a trench. It's a sunny day. This is totally outside. All of a sudden, cloud. And there'd be this Dick—which was his name, actually—totally bending over me, blocking the sun and whispering in my ear in his little creepy voice, "Watch out that you don't get any water in that lead. It could pop up and you'd get a face full of lead and that wouldn't be too pretty, would it?"

Rather than bring the danger she felt from this journeyman to the attention of any authority, Maura just dodged him as best she could. She recognized the box he had her in—it was her word against his. And what's wrong with his warning her to be careful? And who wouldn't believe that a green girl apprentice simply lost her balance carrying heavy pipe?

Women who had no reason to perceive the union as offering them protection, but were still committed to staying in the trade, often chose not to report even very serious harassment. Karen Pollak had applied to several Kansas City unions over the years before affirmative action regulations created an opening in the Carpenters. Having learned the trade from her grandfather, she passed the journeyman's test. She was allowed to enter as a first-year apprentice. Despite the opportunity to hire a skilled mechanic at apprentice rate, it was a year before a contractor would hire her. On her first day on the job as an apprentice carpenter, she could have reported her treatment to the union. Or to the police. Committed to keeping the job, she chose instead the silence she felt was required.

Since none of the carpenters wanted to work with her, Karen was partnered with a laborer who was "none too happy to be working with me. He was trying to do everything he could to drive me crazy. I lost him for several hours in the afternoon. I couldn't find him." Assigned to put in insulation at the edge of the building, Karen was given a safety belt that was too large for her. She eventually just left it "hooked up onto one of the lines, but it was laying over the edge of the floor." When the superintendent found her still working later that afternoon, he told her he'd assumed she'd fallen and died. While the super was admonishing her for not wearing the belt,

I look down and the laborer that I was paired up to was taking a sledgehammer and just demolishing my little red Volkswagen. It was like, "What did I do?" Well, he explained to me that we don't drive Communist cars onto union parking lots.

I couldn't leave my tools at work, because the gang boxes were full. I'm over in the middle of nowhere, with no way to get home, and I can't leave my tools. So I just put my toolbox on my shoulder and we hitched a ride. This farmer picked me up alongside of the road about a half mile from the job site. I got home, though, several hours later than I should have. And the husband was real upset. He was like, "Where's your car?" That was the nicest car that we owned. "Well, we don't have it anymore." "What do you mean, we don't have it anymore?" And then I explained. And it was like, "Well, you have to press charges against this guy. You can't let him do this shit to you." "No, I can't do that. You don't understand. I will get pushed off the building. You can't do those things."

I eventually got it towed home. We used parts off of it. It had nice seats and a nice shifter. But as far as the car—he had taken a cutting torch and cut the frame. I would assume it would have to be on work time, because I had the car at lunchtime. When I went back to work from lunch, it was fine.

After getting chewed out by this superintendent because I had left my safety belt and it was hanging over the edge of the floor and he thought that I had died, it was like, "Did you even go down to see if I was there?" "No, I just figured I'd worry about it when I got down there." Well, that told me where I stood. So that's why I was not going to press charges on my little Volkswagen. We just gritted our teeth and went on and bought a really old Volkswagen, and took and drove it to work. But from then on I parked it two or three blocks away from the job site.

These were real strong-valued people. It was not a union-made car and it represented to them, definitely I had to be a communist. I was driving a Volkswagen. I was a woman wanting to be a carpenter. So I had to be. That was my first day of work. Welcome to the real world.

Asking for help was not necessarily a more useful response, as Yvonne Valles learned. Attracted by the opportunity to work with her hands and the hope that she'd be able to buy a home once she made a journey-level painter's salary, she was an eager first-year apprentice. She joined painters hanging vinyl wallpaper at a hotel in Los Angeles, and within the first two weeks faced harassment from her foreman.

I'm still kind of traumatized by the second job I got. The foreman on the job was a real jerk. Him and a couple of the other painters would always be talking real dirty about women all the time. They used to leave magazines of naked women in the bathroom that I'd use. They'd leave the book wide open and it would show. They'd think it was funny. They were harassing from day one.

There was a young kid apprentice that was about eighteen years old. My foreman used to talk verbally abusive to him, call him a dickhead and all kinds of names. With me, I heard him making a crack one time, called me a dyke. Anyway, he was always bragging on breaks. He'd be talking to the guys, but I could overhear him because we'd eat in the same room. I mean, where was I going to go eat lunch? He used to pick up prostitutes. He'd be saying, I'm going to see so-and-so tonight.

One day, I was hanging up some wallpaper and he came to me, I was kneeling down. He goes, "Hey, you want to see some pictures of my girlfriend?" And I said, "No." He said, "Oh, come on, I'm training her to be an apprentice, too. Don't you want to see some pictures of how I train my apprentices?" I said, "No, why don't you just leave me alone?"

So anyway, I was kneeling down, spreading the wallpaper on the walls. All of a sudden he stuck a Polaroid picture in front of my face and he goes, "Look." And I looked. And he starts laughing.

It was a picture of a young woman laying down with her legs open and she had what they call in wallpapering a seam roller. It's got a little handle with the roller on it, you lay the seams down flat with that to get the air bubbles out. She had the handle inside her vagina. And he starts, "Yeah, that's how I train my apprentices."

Oh, man. I just said, "Get out of here, I don't want to see that!" I was really upset. I went home that day and I called the apprenticeship school and I told the head of the apprentice school, "I got a problem on the job. I'm being harassed and I just want you to know what's going on."

I told him about it, and I started crying 'cause I was really humiliated. He says, "Oh, gee, I'm sorry," and "That asshole," and he goes, "Yvonne, it's not always going to be like that." He says, "I'll talk to him."

But nothing ever happened. He had told me too, "You know, Yvonne, I can report this but it might not be good for you."

I said, "Well, there's only one thing I'm afraid of. I've heard that women that file lawsuits against their companies, they end up getting blackballed. I wouldn't want to have that mark against me." He said, "That's true, that could happen."

They don't care. They want to discourage you. It's like contractors have this attitude, from what I've heard, if a woman sues them—fine, they won't hire any more women at all.

I hated that guy. He was disgusting. He used to ask me if I'd want to snort some cocaine with him after work. I just kept my mouth shut because I needed the job. I needed to pay my rent, so I just tolerated it.

Any new worker wants to make the workplace more comfortable by developing congenial relationships with co-workers. Yet as Melinda Hernandez, a new electrical apprentice learned, friendliness could set off an invisible minefield.

On that job there was an apprentice—he wasn't a piece of shit, he was *the* piece of shit of life, the lowest of the low. But I didn't know this, see. He came off very nice. He happened to be Puerto Rican, too.

And he says, "Oh, it's nice to have a girl working side by side, why don't we hang out one day? We'll go out to dinner after work." So I didn't know. "It's just dinner. What's the big thing? What, are you afraid of me or something?" But he came off very nicely, so I said, All right. Maybe I can make a friend, you know, in the industry starting out.

So we went to dinner, and after dinner he wanted to go out dancing or whatever. And I said, "No, you know, I told you that I have someone, that I'm involved."

To make a long story short, that Monday we went to work, I think he told everybody what every man wants to hear—that we got intimate (and that's a very refined word coming from this character, okay). He did me, you know.

He became very nasty, openly, verbally cursing a lot, talking about who he screwed the night before to the men. And I'm sitting in the men's locker because the women weren't given their own locker. One day he actually brought in pornographic material, pictures that he had taken of a woman close up, with a flashlight. The reason I know this was because he was describing to them the pictures when I was in the room. And they were laughing. But none of them ever took a stand. I thought in their minds they figured, Well, it's not my daughter, or it's her own kind, it's a Puerto Rican just like her doing it to her. It's not us. Whatever it was, they

justified it. Nobody ever said anything. And I remember there was a guy in the room that was sitting in the corner, he was a born-again Christian, reading a Bible.

I got up and I walked out, I just stepped out of the room. I realized that I was in for a long haul, because that was my first job. Wow, you know, what a drag. But I hoped. I had high hopes that things would get better.

Family support was key for Cheryl Camp when she faced hostility on her second job. The knowledge that her union rotated apprentices to a different shop every six months meant that even if treatment didn't improve, it would at least end. And the fact that men on her first job had been particularly supportive helped her ride through the hard times.

There was an electrician on the job, a younger guy, too. And a minority, he was black. He went out of his way to harass me. It really irritated him to know that there was a female electrician on the job. And plus, I was an apprentice. He had gone through the trainee program and, you know, there was a stigma always attached to the people that came through the trainee program. I can't repeat the things that he said. He had the filthiest mouth, I mean really filthy, the things that he would say. And then he would describe his outings the night before with ladies of the night and go off into really intricate details of his endeavors and make sure that I could hear every single word. If I was walking someplace, he would start walking behind me and making rude comments about how women are.

What I really hated was, all the guys on the job knew that he was doing this to me, that he was harassing me. And no one intervened and talked to him to tell him, Why don't you back off and leave her alone. They knew that I was new, that I was an apprentice, and as an apprentice you're supposed to be seen and not heard, you're lower than whale crap. You really aren't supposed to have anything to say to a journeyman as an apprentice, other than asking questions, *if* they allow you to ask questions. I really don't think that they even considered my feelings in the matter. When I told them that I was taking him up on charges for harassment, they told me, Well, this is just the way he is, and Don't let it bother you. But that's impossible for it not to bother you.

There was another female on this job. She was a plumber, but we didn't work in the same area. He was harassing her too, but her husband is also a plumber, so he straightened him out so he didn't say anything else to her. But I had no one to intervene for me. And he was the type of individual that you could not just approach personally, and say, Why don't you just back off and leave me alone. It was the foreman that came through and ended up having him apologize to me. He ignored me after that.

I was under so much stress with him, from what he was saying and the way that he made me feel every day, I was ready to quit the trade at that time. My mother talked to me and was saying, "Well, Cheryl, you don't remember what your ultimate goals are. You wanted to finish this and see it through. You know the first shop that you worked for was so great and the guys were different there, so it's not going to always be this way. Just bear with it and try to see it through and it could get better." My mom was a real source of comfort.

The effect of a harasser's action was compounded when others on the job knew about it but did not intervene—as though he were acting on their behalf. Contractors and unions tended to underestimate the gravity of harassment and in some instances even condoned the behavior, tacitly or explicitly. Institutional procedures for prevention or punishment were rare.

Acts of passive aggression could cause serious injury without anyone's seeming to be responsible. Although with an inexperienced worker it might be difficult to distinguish between a true accident and an intended one, it was the responsibility of the supervising journeyman to look out for an apprentice's safety, and the responsibility of the training program to properly prepare apprentices. Karen Pollak saw the failure to train apprentices in the proper use of power tools not as some malevolent attack on women, but merely as the result of assuming that apprentices knew how to use them, which had traditionally been true. Karen had been trained to use a skill saw safely when she was five or six years old (by her grandfather, who showed the grandchildren his missing finger). But other female apprentices received

Lots and lots of injuries. Eye injury. Feet. Hands. We had a woman that lost three fingers. Because no one told her how to use the table saw. Another one was cutting stakes out on the job site, cut off her whole hand. All because no one took the time to really, really explain that these things can hurt you. I knew how to use the tools. I had an unfair advantage to a lot of the women. Basically what they taught you was how to put the saw

blade into the saw and make sure that the guard worked, if there was a guard. That was about it.

They would say to the woman that it happened to, See? I told you, you should have stayed home. A broom wouldn't do that to you. And then they would make it a point that *you knew* that someone had gotten hurt.

They told me when the lady cut her hand off. She was using a big radial arm saw, a 16-incher, out on the job site. She had put her hand down to hold the material. The material started to move. The saw got bound. And somehow or another her hand got back behind the saw, so it pulled itself right back across her. They were able to save it, but she didn't have full function of her hand. It's not the same. And never will be. That's something that could have been easily prevented.

Even if it began as an unintentional oversight, once women started to experience so many injuries, an adjustment should have been quickly made to incorporate power-tool safety into the training. Instead, the pattern of accidents became not only proof that women didn't belong, but an amulet to frighten women into leaving.

Some job situations had the feel of trench warfare. Men who wanted to drive women out; women who were determined to stay. Knowledge of tools and experience at the trade did not prevent an "accident" that broke Karen Pollak's nose when a journeyman did not want her—not only a woman, but a Cherokee Indian—working with him.

I had a sledgehammer dropped on me. This was a job that they had to have a woman. And they needed a minority. It was like, Give me a black woman or somebody who I can mark as a double and then I only have to have one of them. It was just a little tiny library for the University of Kansas Medical Center.

We were down in the hole and I was stripping forms. The guy above me was on the next set of scaffolding working on the next layer. I kept noticing that hairpins, which are a form-type hardware, would fall down and hit the hard hat. Every once in a while it'd hit the bill and knock the hat off. You'd bend over and pick the hat up, look up and go, "Can't you be careful?" "Yep, I just dropped it, sorry."

The superintendent had yelled at him about something. I was standing below and he was going, "Well, make *her* do it. She doesn't do anything."

"She's stripping. That's all she's here to do."

I was going, "Well, I'm willing to learn. I can handle doing more things than just pulling nails."

"Nah. Not with me you're not." At lunchtime, the foreman said that I was going to go help him after lunch.

He got up on top of the wall before I did. He was standing up on the scaffolding he had just built. I was just starting to climb up the form. BAM! The sledgehammer hit me, it rang my bell.

It was like, Okay, that *could* have been an accident. He throws the rope down. I hook up the sledgehammer and he pulls it back up. I make sure I'm away from the rope. If he happens to slip again, no problem.

For some odd reason, he didn't nail down his scaffolding like you're supposed to do. He told me he did. I stepped on the far end of the board and the scaffolding went smack with the board right in the face. Straight down, back into the hole.

The hole had mud in it. And water. I had hip waders on earlier that day stripping it out. It was an ugly sight. I had broke my nose. The superintendent comes over and says, "Well, this isn't going to work. He doesn't really want you up there."

"Oh, I just thought it was an accident that the sledgehammer fell."

"Probably was on his part, Karen."

"And that's why he didn't nail down the boards, huh?"

"Well, maybe he was getting ready to move them over to the next set of scaffolding."

"Right. He knew I was climbing up there."

I stayed on the bottom and stripped. He would drop things if I was underneath him. I soon got the idea, Stay away from him.

The wisdom of Karen's response—to outwit her journeyman's efforts to injure her while keeping up production— is made clear by the actions of the superintendent, who both represents the contractor on the job and belongs to the union. The journeyman responsible for her safety not only drops a sledgehammer and other objects on her, but lies to her about the scaffolding being nailed down, resulting in her fall and broken nose. Rather than laying off the journeyman or bringing him up on charges in the union, the super accommodates his wishes. All three understand the same unspoken ground rules: not only is it acceptable to refuse to work with a woman, it is acceptable to communicate that refusal through actions which, out on the street, could result in prosecution for assault and battery with a dangerous weapon.

Harassment could result not only in a stressful work environment or physical injury but also in economic costs, both short- and long-term. It was not unusual for a tradeswomen to be transferred or laid off after attention was called to harassment. Barbara Trees found that her skill training was also affected.

I was a second-year apprentice working for this contractor doing ceilings—the concealed kind, the hard kind of ceiling—and I was really trying to learn them. The bar isn't revealed, you don't see it, so they're kind of complicated. I wasn't finding it easy to begin with. I was up on the Baker [staging] by myself and the electricians opened up the computer floor around me. They opened up enough tiles so I couldn't move my Baker. I said to them, "You know, I need to move this Baker. Will you put back those tiles?" They just wouldn't do it.

I'd be working on a Baker and they'd be having their coffee break and I would hear my name fairly continuously. "Barbara . . . Barbara . . . Barbara . . ." I got sick of it, so I called over to them and I said, "Is there something you want to say to me?" And, "Oh, no, no, there's nothing we want to say to you."

That was really all it took.

I went home that night and I came back into work the next morning and these guys obviously had written on my Baker in letters a foot high, "PROPERTY OF THE CUNT." I didn't know what to do about it. I didn't really think there was anything I *could* do about it. But what happened is that my subforeman came over and he saw it. I didn't really want him to see it or anything. I was embarrassed, actually. So he says, "What's this?" I said, "Well, I think those electrician guys wrote this on here, you know, because we had words yesterday." He says, "Well, we can't have this. I'll speak to the foreman." I was really surprised by his reaction. I felt he was trying to help me.

So the foreman came over to me and asked me what happened. And he said, "We can't have other trades harassing our carpenters. We're going to have a meeting of all the trades later in the day. I'll let them know that they can't do this." I thought, you know, this sounded good, this sounded like what he was supposed to say to me.

I guess they had the meeting and what happened is that I was transferred out of there. They just decided that I was too much trouble. I remember as I walked down the street I passed one of those electrician guys and he almost tried to hide in the building. He saw me and he kind of put his eyes down. I think he must have realized what he had done.

This was my introduction to how they help you out. This guy was so sincere—Oh, we can't have them harassing our carpenters, we're not going to put up with this. I remember thanking him, thinking, This is really great.

Whenever I see ceilings now, I sort of panic. I actually kind of get a cold sweat going. I started to realize what it's from is that the two opportunities I had to learn ceilings both ended where I was laid off or taken off the job. I still feel bad about this. That was my chance to learn.

So this is what happens. Your training suffers. You feel guilty. You don't know what you did wrong. You're feeling like kind of an awful person. And you don't learn your ceilings.

A tradeswoman who changed contractors or crews—particularly if she bounced between situations where co-workers were friendly and fair and situations where she faced hostility and humiliation—could find it hard to build self-confidence and gain her bearings as a developing mechanic. Like many tradeswomen, Helen Vozenilek, an apprentice electrician in Albuquerque, struggled to understand the cause of harassment, looking for how she might prevent or avoid it.

I made the shithouse walls. IT was something like, FUCKING LESBIAN ELECTRICIAN BITCH. I somehow knew that had to be me. You know, process of elimination.

On that job, the steward was terrible. I don't think he liked women. It was just a bad collection of people. You know how men can get—when they're alone, they're fine, they're actually brothers? And then they get in a group and they're just beasts? I think that was the situation there. They sort of got beastly.

I did feel really harassed there and I didn't quite get it. I remember going home a couple of nights and just crying myself to sleep. I think the steward had talked to me that day, said they were going to run me off or something—and it was like, I didn't get it. The hardest thing is the capriciousness, not knowing what you did or what you were being held responsible for, or irresponsible for.

Some of the men who saw tradeswomen as invaders of their domain marked territory with graffiti, pornography, or bodily fluids. Although Irene Soloway, a New York City carpenter, "really didn't experience a great deal of sexual harassment."

I had one incident that upset me for quite a while, which was a job that I was determined to do well on and keep. After six months of coming in every day, I took a day off. When I came back, the shanty had porno pictures all over it, real disgusting ones.

The foreman and I didn't get along. It turned out his brother had spent the entire day plastering the shanty on company time. I really was truly shocked, because I had been on the job for six months and pornography was not an issue. So I felt it was terribly personal. It's like, you don't even know where to look! The men were all sitting on their benches and I knew that they weren't comfortable with it, either. I mean, you have a shanty that's clean and decent, you have your little nail and your little hook and your little lunch, and then one day you come in and it's—you know, open cunts all over the wall. It made a lot of people uncomfortable, but I knew that nobody would say a word. I had a screaming fight with the foreman outside the shanty. I was a second-year apprentice.

The reason why I had a problem with the foreman in the first place was because I told him, in front of a group of men, "I'm an apprentice, I'm not an animal, and if you want to call me, I have a name." He used to call black people Nigger, you know. I guess he must have called me Girl. He was furious with me and he told me so in no uncertain terms. And then this happened. I ended up being sent off the job, and I never felt that I had any retribution for that.

They sent me to another job and then two days later I got laid off. So they sort of diffused it that way. I always felt I had to find some like really, really remarkable way to turn the situation around. You think you have to deal with this on your own and you have to be able to stay in the industry, you know. That was my philosophy. I always thought of how would I turn this around and have him be shocked and upset and angry. Which is stupid. I mean, he's the boss. I'm not. So you can't turn it around in that way, in a personal way. But that was the way I used to think.

As an apprentice plumber, Maura Russell never had the opportunity to work with another woman in her trade. On one job with several hundred workers, though, she was able to work with two other tradeswomen, an electrician and a taper, building apartments for the elderly.

We hung around together, which was really nice. But they have a hard time with women getting together on the jobs.

There was one time when the three of us were having lunch in K—'s car. This one guy who was there just for two days, an asphalt contractor putting in the parking lot, came over to where we were eating our lunch and pissed on the side of the car. Quite unbelievable. Looking at him coming over, at first I thought his truck must be parked next to us. And then K—is like, "Wait a minute! Is he doing what I think he's doing?" Really.

He'd left by this point. We convinced K—that what she should do is talk to the super. The guy's in his truck and he denies it. K—says, "Oh, bullshit, you did this." At which point, the super went insane that she swore. And just said, "If you talk like that, you don't deserve to be treated like a lady."

He was just going to walk away and not deal with it. And that was the point at which K—took out her little Swiss Army knife and told the guy that she would slash his tires if he didn't apologize. He'd been laughing at the incident, which is what really enraged her. He finally did say, "Oh, I'm sorry, I'm sorry, I'm sorry."

She said, "No. You got out of the car to piss on my car, and now you have to get out to apologize."

So he did. He was angry at that point that he was compelled to do that. And the super was jumping up and down livid, like she was a maniac. He didn't want her on his job anymore. He went running to the trailer to call her company to get her fired (which he was unsuccessful in doing).

But that incident later, we joked, would become that she had a ten-inch knife or something to this guy's throat—and it has pretty much gone around the circuit like that. But that was definitely, Talk like a lady if you expect to be treated like one.

Laborer boss said that to me later in the day, "My wife, she just would have turned her head."

Really.

Although, for women, responding in kind to harassment could bring on more trouble, Maura was sure that if there had been three men in that car,

They would absolutely have pummeled him. And what would the super have done about that? He would have turned his little head. He would have expected that. Oh, they would have gone insane if something like that had happened to a man.

That was really quite an interesting statement of, You're not welcome. Gross, really gross.

Hostility could be triggered by small acts of self-empowerment. Like three women sitting together in a car. Or a woman becoming more assertive. Doubly vulnerable, as an African-American woman, Gloria Flowers found that her worst harassment came when she decided to speak up for herself, after she reached "a point where I wanted to have some respect, I wanted to be talked to like I had some sense."

Towards the end of my apprenticeship I was really catching the blues. That last year, I said to myself, I'm not taking this crap anymore. I'm going to start telling some of these guys off. Well, that was the worst thing I could have done. It's almost like, when you get revenge, it's not as sweet as you think it's going to be.

That last year was my worst year by far. I remember this super telling me, maybe I shouldn't have gotten in the trade. "Why don't you just give up and give out?"

I fell out with a lot of the guys. Some of the guys I had liked previously, we ended up just rubbing each other the wrong way. They started rotating me, working me every other week. At the time I didn't know it was because they wanted to lay me off and couldn't figure out a way to really do it.

This one job I was on, the Ohio Bell Building, downtown Cleveland, there was this black guy on the job, he hated my guts for some reason. He had problems with women, he was like in his third or fourth marriage. That was the worst, the darkest period, I have to say, because he got physically abusive.

He pushed me, physically pushed me down stairs when nobody was watching, in a sub-basement. I remember being so mad and so hurt, I wanted to kill that guy. But he was a body builder, he was really built.

A lot of times they had raffles for different things on the jobs. It just so happened that on this job—I don't know why this happened to me, God was trying to show me something—they were raffling a .357 magnum. I don't know what made this guy ask me if I was interested that particular day. Generally I had my little blinders on. I was kind of kept in the dark on a lot of things.

But that particular time—and feeling the way I was feeling—I wanted in on that raffle. I remember coming home. I talked to a girlfriend about it, and she said, Pray about it, and don't do nothing stupid. You can't take on no man, blah, blah, blah.

She really brought me back down to the ground. I prayed about it and it ended up working out. He got laid off, and I got laid off shortly thereafter.

That guy wanted to hurt me. He did. I never told any of the guys about it because, you know, they didn't care. That job had gone sour for me. None of the guys wanted to have anything to do with me on that particular job because I just wasn't taking any stuff.

Accidents set up against women or people of color were particularly insidious. When "successful" they accomplished two things: eliminating or frightening the target, and framing them to look incompetent, not only as individuals but, by extension, as a representative of their gender or race. As an apprentice electrician, Nancy Mason learned to be extra cautious, in case work was sabotaged.

I was deliberately set up, actually, on two occasions. Once I had circuits turned on when I was trimming out receptacles in a high-rise office space. I don't know who turned the circuits on. And another time I'd been hooking up fire alarm exit signs and I went back to check some. I was up at a light exit sign, and someone had actually tied the ground wire into the hot wire on the other end of the Scotchlok and as I was taking it out, someone turned it on and it blew up in front of me.

I did not get hurt, but obviously someone was hoping I probably would have, or gotten scared or whatever. Those incidents both happened, I think, when I was a fourth-year apprentice. I was getting pretty tuned in to always checking stuff with my own meter. But the turning on the circuit while I was at that exit sign was probably the most dangerous thing, because of the higher voltage. It was a 277 situation.

Bernadette Gross, who went through her carpentry apprenticeship in Seattle, was on many jobs where "the object was to buck me off, and I rode them like that. It was like, I'm not going anywhere." But harassment, even when handled, carried an additional personal cost—to one's sense of trust in other people. On a job early in her apprenticeship, Bernadette fell from a ladder that was not properly secured.

I was up on a second story framing a window, and the ladder wasn't tied off and it slid from under me.

I had a sheet of plywood dropped on my hard hat. I mean, it hit my hard hat really hard. I was bent over and it could have broke my back, really—and there was just never anything done.

At that time I didn't have sense enough to think that someone had set out to hurt me. Just later on, it was like putting it all together. I was still pretty new, right? And then, I never had that many accidents after that. In my second year, I knew better. If somebody told me to go up a ladder. I'd check it, you know. But in life, it took me a long time to believe that people had malice in their heart. I always believed that they were sort of going their way and you got in the way and they knocked you over. It wasn't anything that they set out to say, I'm going to knock her over, you know.

But I found out that there were people who did, you know, sit down and plot that. It's kind of a hard blow for me.

Such experiences happened to women who graduated from apprenticeship programs. They cast an ironic light on the common explanation for those who did not, the new women apprentices who quit after only a day, a month, or a year, the ones who supposedly "found it wasn't for them."

Families

Families are a fundamental social unit. In families we develop a sense of ourselves as individuals and as members of a primary group. We internalize messages about our position in our communities, our nations, and the world. We are taught systems of belief, usually consistent with the society in which we live, about appropriate roles for particular kinds of people. For example, we learn to think differently about men and women, elders and children, and people of various races, classes, and social statuses. We also learn how we are expected to treat the people we encounter in the world around us.

It is within families that members of a society first develop ideas and feelings about themselves as gendered individuals. When we are children, the socialization we receive contains strong messages about the appropriate attitudes and behaviors for males and females. When we are adults, families are where we spend much of our time, divide up the work of meeting our physical and emotional needs, and care for others, such as children or aging family members. Families usually divide up these interpersonal roles according to what is considered appropriate for men or for women. Yet families come in many forms, even within one society. The normative family structure of a married mother and father with children no longer represents the majority of families. Instead, a family may be a single parent with children, a couple with no children, lesbian or gay parents and their children, or a group of people who decide to share a household. As a result, individuals' experiences in families vary widely.

Feminist scholars examine the family as a major source of the reproduction of sexism in society. Researchers ask questions about how the organization of family life supports women's oppression in society through its ideologies, economics, distribution of domestic tasks, and intimate relations. Reciprocally, researchers examine the impact of demographic, technological, economic, and political structures on women's and men's power and positions in their families.

At the same time, feminist researchers examine families as a source of women's strength and resistance. Alternative family forms are one way to restructure family lives; in addition, families may provide a source of resistance to other forms of oppression, such as racism or poverty. Feminist family studies emphasize the ways that race, ethnicity, sexuality, and class influence our family experiences.

In the first selection in Section Six, Pepper Schwartz examines some ways that heterosexual couples divide up household labor. "Peer Marriage" focuses on heterosexual marriages in which partners share responsibility, domestic work, earning power, roles, and decision making. Such marriages, she finds, while rare, are more stable and happier than marriages based on traditional gender roles. Joint child-rearing, Schwartz argues, helps men and women construct a strong intimate connection with each other and decreases divorce rates. This contradicts the conservative notion that divorce stems from the breakdown of the traditional family, where women stay home and raise the children and men

297

earn the income. Schwartz suggests that the steadily increasing importance of women's income, changing attitudes among young men, and the cultural emphasis on the emotional satisfaction of both partners all make egalitarian, companionate marriages more appealing. When women and men share parenting, whether because of an ideological commitment to equality or for pragmatic reasons such as work schedules or economic necessity, both parents and children benefit. Yet increasing women's earnings and power within marriages challenges deep-rooted gender dynamics and can be hard for couples to adjust to. In couples who believe in egalitarianism but do not actually achieve it, women are increasingly dissatisfied and resentful. Why does Schwartz think peer marriages are not more common, given these advantages? Would you find an egalitarian relationship appealing? Why or why not?

The ways that heterosexual women balance work and family vary according to class, ethnicity, culture, and nationality. Denise Segura analyzes how Chicana and Mexicana immigrant mothers view their lives as employed mothers in "Working at Motherhood: Chicana and Mexicana Immigrant Mothers and Employment." She finds that many Mexicana immigrants in the study viewed working for pay as an important part of motherhood because the income helped support their families. Many Chicana mothers, in contrast, who had grown up in the United States, had been socialized with the American notion of a separation between spheres of work and family and therefore expressed more ambivalence about combining employment and mothering. The article illustrates how the meaning and practice of motherhood are culturally constructed and thus vary among different groups of women. How is the relationship between working outside the home and raising children defined in the culture in which you grew up?

For single mothers, the meaning of motherhood depends largely on cultural attitudes of stigma or support. Rickie Solinger, in "Race and 'Value': Black and White Illegitimate Babies, 1945–1965," traces changing views of unwed mothers and their offspring following World War II. Unmarried white mothers were pressured to put their "desirable" babies up for adoption during this period. Black women, in contrast, were denigrated by dominant discourse as sexually irresponsible, yet they received more community support for keeping and raising their children than did white women. Solinger's article illustrates how ideologies about gender and race affect how categories of women and various family structures are viewed in public discourse. How are these ideologies toward unmarried white and black women who have babies apparent in current public policy debates over welfare and teen pregnancy?

Ellen Lewin also shows how different groups of women reinterpret the meaning of motherhood. She examines how lesbian mothers perceive and manage their dual identities in "Negotiating Lesbian Motherhood: The Dialectics of Resistance and Accommodation." Lesbian mothers, both those who have children from previous heterosexual relationships and those who choose to have children as lesbians, resist narrow formulations of women's mothering role and challenge stereotypes of lesbians. Yet because the identities "lesbian" and "mother" are culturally defined as mutually exclusive, lesbian mothers have difficulty juggling the two identities. How do the political debates over lesbian and gay parents that are described in the boxed insert "The New Activism" show the influence of the stereotypes and dilemmas Lewin discusses?

For most women, these articles suggest, family relationships are a complicated mixture of accommodation and resistance to gender oppression. How do women accept traditional definitions of their family roles? How do they make choices about the relationship of paid employment to mothering? How do they gain power and fulfillment through family relationships, and how do these relationships constrict them?

Peer Marriage

PEPPER SCHWARTZ

Our generation has been the first to witness the emergence of "partnership" or "peer" marriages on a large social scale. Such marriages differ from their traditional counterparts in at least four key respects: men and women in these relationships regard each other as full social equals; both pursue careers; partners share equal authority for financial and other decision making; and, not least important, husbands typically assume far greater responsibility for child-rearing than in the past. Many of us—including much of the feminist movement, of which I have been a part—tend to regard these marriages as a major social breakthrough, the culmination of an arduous, generation-long effort to redefine women's roles and to secure for women the same freedom and dignity that society has traditionally accorded to men.

Yet in recent years conservatives, particularly the adherents of the "pro-family" or "family values" movement, have increasingly called for a rejection of the peer marriage ideal and a return by society as a whole to the traditional role-differentiated model. Bolstering their case is a significant body of traditional social theory arguing for the superior stability of the role-differentiated marriage, in which the husband serves as sole provider and main figure of authority, and the wife bears the lion's share of responsibilities for child-rearing and day-to-day household maintenance.

Contemporary concerns with marital and family stability are certainly warranted. In a society with a 50 percent divorce rate—in which a host of social pathologies can be traced directly to havoc in fatherless or broken homes—policymakers and theorists are right to place a high priority on measures aimed at keeping families intact. Yet it is far from self-evident that the road to greater marital stability lies in a return to tradition. Over the past generation, I would

argue, broad changes in society—and in the expectations that men and women bring to the marital relationship—have undermined much of the original basis of the traditional model of marriage. In reality, as I will try to show here, peer marriage offers a new formula for family and marital stability that may be both more durable and better adapted to the demands of contemporary culture than the older form. New data from studies that I and others have conducted support the notion that peer marriages are at least as stable as traditional unions and may in the long run prove more resilient vis-à-vis the special social pressures that marriages confront today.

MARITAL STABILITY AND MARITAL SATISFACTION

There is a close connection between marital stability and happiness or satisfaction in marriage—in both practice and theory. Even the most hard-headed theorists of the traditional model—such as sociologist Talcott Parsons or economist Gary Becker—have invariably sought to reconcile their advocacy of gender-based role differentiation with the possibility of marital satisfaction. To justify the traditional division of labor in marriage purely on the basis of men's and women's different biological aptitudes, historical experience, or cultural training is, after all, not a difficult theoretical task. But to posit happiness and mutual satisfaction as the outcome of such a union is another matter.

This is not to say that happiness was or is impossible to achieve under the traditional marital regime. Many people, especially when the larger culture supports it, find happiness in holding up their part of the marital bargain: women who like to be in charge of the kitchen, and men who want to bring home the bacon but do not want to cook it. In the past, and even today, this contract has worked for many

299

people. Increasingly, however, it does not work as well as it used to. It did not work for me as well as it worked for my mother, and it didn't work for her all the time, either. The gender-based division of labor, so automatic for so much of history, increasingly fails to bring the promised emotional fulfillment that was supposed to be a major part of its contribution to family satisfaction and stability—emotional fulfillment which is increasingly vital to marital stability today.

We may contrast the experience of my mother's generation with that of my own. Like so many women of her era, my mother traded *service* for *support,* a transaction with which she usually seemed content. She bore almost complete responsibility for raising her children and at the same time had full charge of household upkeep: cooking, cleaning, keeping my father's closets and drawers impeccably neat, and so forth. My father, not atypical of his generation, was a man who never packed his own suitcase for a trip. In return, he provided handsomely—beyond my mother's wildest dreams, since she had grown up in poverty and was forced to drop out of high school to support her ailing mother and her youngest sisters. Having met my father as a secretary in his fledgling law office, my mother was very grateful to have been pulled from destitution into a different social class. Later she could afford to finish high school and college, raise three children, and become a docent in an art museum. Her lifestyle with my father was something secure and in a sense wonderful, exceeding all her childhood expectations.

The arrangement worked well for my father also. He was not born to privilege. The eldest of five growing up on a farm in Indiana, he put himself through law school, transferring from the University of Chicago to night school at Loyola when times got rough. He scrambled to better himself and his family. He and his wife had the same goal: to achieve the means for the good life. They entertained clients and traveled.

But my father also expected my mother to do everything he told her to do. After all, his own father had been dictatorial; it was something a woman owed a man—even though, in my grandfather's case, his wife had purchased the farm for the family. No matter. Leadership at home was owed a man as part of his birthright. When my mother—an intense, intelligent woman—would occasionally resist an order or talk back, my father's response to her was scathing and uninhibited.

What was the bargain my mother willingly made? She had a husband who loved her, who created an increasingly luxurious environment, and who ordered her around and reminded her—almost incessantly—about how lucky she was to have him. Love and what my generation of women would call patriarchal control went hand in hand. On my mother's side, gratitude, deep resentment, and anger all came in a neat package. The marriage lasted fifty-five years, until my mother's death. Children were launched. The marriage could be declared a success. Nevertheless, under today's circumstances, I would expect such a marriage to survive ten years at best.

Today my mother would have had a chance at her own career, at which she had the talent to excel. She would have had a new identity as a human being with core rights and her own sense of entitlement. (Surely, she promoted mine.) She would have had a different standard of equality and different ideas about equity. She would probably not have thought it enough to have been rescued from poverty. She would have felt entitled to a different style of family decision making, and she would have had the options—and the cultural support—to demand more. But if my father had remained the same man he was when I was growing up, he would not have acquiesced. Under contemporary circumstances, the marriage most probably would have broken up—much to my own, my siblings', and probably my parents' disadvantage.

And that is one reason why I believe peer marriage—a marriage founded on the principle of equality and supported by shared roles and a greater chance of shared sensibilities—is an adaptation in the direction of greater family stability rather than instability. Indeed, in contemporary culture, a peer or partner relationship between spouses has become increasingly vital to keeping families intact. It also offers new advantages to children, to which I will return in a moment.

We must be clear, however, that the mere existence of separate careers does not guarantee a peer marriage. Such a marriage also requires a comprehensive reconceptualization of the partners' roles. Dual incomes alone are insufficient to guarantee stability.

MONEY AND WORK

Indeed, much empirical research, some of it my own, indicates that labor force participation and achievement of high income by women destabilizes marriage. A number of studies, including the well-known Income Maintenance Study done out of the University of Michigan, found that when one raised the income of low-income women—hoping to stabilize families by reducing poverty—divorce increased substantially. Theorists have deduced that, under such circumstances; growth in income simply opens a new option for women to leave the relationship, an option that many of them exercise. Moreover, many studies show high-earning women with higher breakup rates. It is unclear whether high earnings make women less willing to tolerate unwanted behaviors or other disappointments on the part of their spouses, or whether men find women who are ambitious or aggressive (or who possess other traits consonant with career success) unsatisfying to be with in the long run. At any rate, the correlation is real enough.

Nor do couples necessarily adapt smoothly to equalization of income and status between partners. In *American Couples,* a study of 6,000 married, cohabiting, and lesbian and gay couples, Phil Blumstein and I found that a partner's power rose in relation to his or her relative income as compared with that of the spouse or live-in lover, but not necessarily in the ways we would have predicted. Women's power rose and became equal to their partners' when they had equal income—but only if they had a supportive ideology that allowed them to claim equal power. And power did not necessarily increase proportionally to the income differential. For example, more power did not release women from as much housework as one might expect. Higher-income career women did less, but not equivalently less, and their partners did not do proportionately more. (Male partners of high-earning women *did* feel their partners were entitled to do less housework, but did *not* feel required to do more themselves!) Feminists may be inclined to despair: Are men so resistant to participation in household labor that nothing will induce them to pitch in appropriately?

Yet—and this is the key point—it remains to be seen whether the tensions we found are the permanent consequence of change or merely transitional pains that arise as couples, and society as a whole, grope for a new definition of the marital relationship. Many men are clearly uncomfortable with the weakening of the traditional male role as sole provider. And, notably, there has been little effort—outside a small and probably unrepresentative "men's movement"—to reconceptualize the husband's role under these new economic circumstances. However, several changes are conspiring to move society as a whole beyond this sometimes painful transitional phase: transformations in the economy, in the attitudes of younger men, and in the cultural definition of marriage itself.

In the first place, in the contemporary economy female income has become an important ingredient of family prosperity (even, in many cases, a necessity). Economists have long recognized that household income has maintained sta-

bility in the United States over the past decades only through large-scale entry of women into the workforce. The two-income household, once an exception, is now increasingly the norm.

Furthermore, corporate restructuring and downsizing have tended to intensify the trend. Women's labor force participation has become increasingly vital to family stability in a society where job security is, for all but a few, a thing of the past. Men are now beginning to realize that their hold on continuous employment after age forty is, to say the least, shaky. By age fifty-five, less than half of all men are still fully employed. Women, having many of the skills necessary for a service-oriented society, stay employable longer and more steadily. Indeed, in our society, the nonworking wife is increasingly becoming a symbol of exceptional wealth or conspicuous consumption—or of a major ideological commitment either to the patriarchal family or to a vision of the female as the primary parent.

There are signs that these new economic realities are beginning to affect attitudes among men in their twenties. Young boys today are increasingly growing up in two-parent families where females are either the chief provider or an essential contributor to family income. Moreover, they understand their own economic futures as providers to be far from secure. Partly as a result, more and more young men are seeking in marriage someone to be part of an economic team rather than an exclusive parenting specialist. Just as women have in the past sought "a good provider," so, I predict, men will increasingly want to marry (and stay married to) a woman who can provide her share of economic stability.

But possibly the most important change has come in the subtle cultural redefinition of the marital relationship itself. In a society in which divorce is prevalent and the economic independence of both spouses is the rule, marital stability depends increasingly on factors of personal satisfaction and emotional fulfillment. The glue holding marriages together today is neither economic necessity nor cultural sanction, but emotion. Marital stability in contemporary society increasingly depends on sustaining the emotional satisfaction of *both* partners. It is here that peer marriage shows its special advantages.

Under these new economic and cultural circumstances, the ability of men and women to participate in each other's lives—to build companion status—becomes essential to marital survival. Equality is a crucial ingredient of this form of intimacy. When women have validation in the outside world through career, and when couples can operate as a team on both economic and home issues, partners become more similar to each other and achieve greater emotional compatibility—or so I would hypothesize on the basis of my research with peer couples. With more outside experiences to bring to the marital community, the woman becomes a more interesting companion for the long run. Moreover, whatever competition or tensions may result from this new arrangement, women today probably need some of these career-related personality traits simply to stay competitive with the women men increasingly meet in the workplace. This was less important in a society where home and family were sacrosanct and a mother and wife— no matter how far she was from being a "soul mate"—was automatically protected from outside contenders for her spouse. However, that is not the society we live in any more, nor is it likely to return. And even though income creates independence and therefore opportunities for separation, the recognition that spouses would lose their mutually constructed lifestyle if the marriage ended has its own stabilizing effect, as I have found in my interviews with dozens of peer couples.

LOVE VERSUS MONEY

Of course, even today, if one were to analyze marriage in purely economic terms, the traditional model can seem to offer certain advantages over the peer arrangement. Becker and others have contended that, at least during child-raising years, couples with the woman in a full-time mothering role tend to gain more income. And a few studies have shown that men with working wives have lower incomes than men with nonworking wives. Economically ambitious couples probably calculate correctly that one parent, usually the male, should be released from most parental duties to earn as much as he can; the payoff here will lie in enhanced family income and social status, in which both partners presumably will share.

But this approach fails to address the real problem at the base of today's shaky marital system—maintaining a high standard of emotional fulfillment. "Efficient" role allocation frequently leaves partners leading parallel and largely separate lives. Mom and Dad did that—each an expert in their separate spheres. It worked when there was less expectation that marriage should produce a soul mate, and when Mom's tolerance levels were higher for the habitual carping at dinner. While this system did and does work for some, it tends to diminish emotional partnership. People in such "parallel marriages," financially secure, look at each other ten years

later and say, "Why you?"—and they divorce, often with children in primary grades.

SECRETS OF PEER SUCCESS

One key to the success of peer unions lies in *joint child-rearing*—the creation of a male parenting niche in day-to-day family. Indeed, I would go so far as to say that joint child-rearing constitutes the secret of successful peer unions and a new pathway to marital and family stability in contemporary life. Joint child-rearing cements a new intimacy between husband and wife and, research shows, builds a critical and difficult-to-sever tie between the two parents and the children.

Some theorists in the past have actually argued *against* a model of significant daily paternal participation in parenting, on the grounds that male involvement will erode the natural dependence of men on women and that men, resenting the extra burden, will ultimately leave. Of course, a lot of men are leaving in any case. And certainly some studies, particularly among working-class men, show child care and household labor participation to be associated with lower marital satisfaction. Still other researchers have found large numbers of men whose perception of shared participation correlates with greater marital satisfaction.

On the woman's side, moreover, the picture is not at all ambiguous. Shared labor has a *major* impact on women's satisfaction in marriage—and since more women than men leave relationships, this is a significant finding. A 1996 study by Nancy K. Grote and others showed that the more traditional the division of labor, the lower marital satisfaction was for women (though *not* for men). However, *both* men and women reported higher erotic satisfaction and friendship with one another when household labor, including parenting, was shared more equitably.

My studies and others show several other important benefits to joint child-rearing: First, the more men participate, the more attached they are to their children. Second, the more they parent, the more grateful wives are. Third, under joint parenting, it becomes harder for either the husband or the wife to consider leaving. And finally, unless the men are manifestly awful parents, children benefit from their father's attention, skills, and additional perspective. This extra parenting and contact with the father can represent a real boon for children.

While my study draws from interviews with only about one hundred couples, some research based on large data sets reinforces my findings. In *Bitter Choices: Blue Collar*

Women In and Out of Work, E. I. Rosin showed that a substantial number of working-class women interpreted the husband's help with children and housework as an expression of love and caring. A very interesting study by Diane Lye at the University of Washington found, among other things, that men who had the lowest divorce rates had the highest interaction with their sons around traditionally male games—football, baseball etc. Interestingly, the same was true of men who participated in similar activities with their daughters. Other studies have found a lower divorce rate among men who attended prenatal classes.

Still, one may argue that we are talking here about atypical men. Only a certain kind of fellow will participate in a prenatal class: peer men are born, not made. Yet that is not what I found in my own research. Most men I interviewed in egalitarian marriages did not come to them by way of ideological motivation, nor were they married to women who described themselves as feminists. The usual road to peer marriage was happenstance. The four most common routes: (1) A serious desire on the part of the husband to father more, and more effectively, than he himself had been fathered (men in these situations were frequently wrestling with significant pain left over from paternal abuse, neglect, or abandonment). (2) A job that *required* shift work or role sharing and which, over time, greatly attached the father to the parenting role. (3) A strong-willed working partner who presumed egalitarian marriage; men in these cases were mostly prepared to structure the marriage any way their wives (often not declared feminists) preferred to have it. (4) The experience of an unsatisfactory, highly traditional first marriage in which the wife was perceived as too emotionally dependent during the marriage and too economically helpless after it was over; men in these cases consciously selected a different kind of spouse and marital bargain in the second marriage.

Were they happy with their new bargain? Most of these men expressed pride in themselves, their wives, and their home life. Were these typical egalitarian marriages? It is impossible to say. But these marriages, while not invulnerable, looked more stable for their integration—in much the way traditional marriages often appear: integrated, independent, and satisfied.

"NEAR PEERS"

Some of the most troubled contemporary marriages, I have found, are those, in essence, caught between the old and the new paradigm—marriages that are neither fully traditional nor fully peer. I called such couples "near peers," since they professed belief in equal participation but failed to achieve it in practice. I believe the experience of such "near peers" may lie behind some of the frustrations that lead conservatives and others today to declare, in effect, that "We have tried equality and it has failed." In reality, what many couples have tried is inequality under the label of equality—an experience which has given equality, in some quarters, a bad name.

In "near peer" marriages, the wife typically devoted vastly more energy to the children while holding down a job. Although the husband made certain contributions to child-rearing and household upkeep, and professed an eagerness to do more, actual male performance fell short of the intended ideal, stirring the wife's resentment. In most cases, "near peer" men still controlled the finances and exercised veto power over the wife. The wife, performing a full-time job outside the home with little or no relief inside of it, was typically caught in a "slow burn" of inward anger. Paradoxically, such women did not long for more equality, since they assumed it would bring more of the same—increased responsibilities with no substantial male contribution. These women felt trapped and overwhelmed and many of them, I found, would have been happy to leave the workforce if it were financially possible. Furthermore, all their power—and much of their pleasure—continued to reside in the mothering role. They loved their children, felt compromised at the inadequacy of parenting time, and, perhaps surprisingly, rarely considered that one answer might be greater paternal participation. In truth, many such women were unwilling to surrender hegemony at home.

In such marriages, each spouse typically clings to his or her traditional powers while simultaneously craving a more partnership-oriented relationship. The result is emotional disappointment and conflict. Women in such relationships lend to view egalitarian gender roles as oppressive—seeing more respect, security, and satisfaction in the role of full-time mother. Yet they simultaneously resent the husband's low participation and quasi-autocratic behavior, since they feel they have earned equality and crave it on an emotional level.

ROADBLOCKS AND SUGGESTED POLICY REFORMS

While I have found that there are many different routes to a stable peer marriage, achievement of such a relationship is not automatic, as the experiences of the "near peers" attest. Several barriers stand in the way.

In the first place, it is often hard to avoid role differentiation, especially when partners have been strongly socialized to one or the other role. For example, it is simply not in the couple's best interests for the "bad cook" to prepare dinner while the good one does dishes. Even though cooking can be learned—quite easily, in fact—the startup costs (bad meals for a while) stop most couples in their tracks. The better the homemaker-parent and the more outstanding the provider, the less likely there is to be taste for change.

Other inhibitors to peer marriages include the gender-based organization of jobs in the outside world (which affect evaluations of each partner's career prospects), and the overall pull of the status quo. Yet in a sense, the biggest roadblock we face is our sense of the possible. Many women and men simply do not believe an egalitarian marriage is feasible—unless they happen to be in one. Even many who desire the peer model do not believe it can be achieved within ordinary working schedules. And most women expect significant male resistance and see a risk in asserting themselves, fearing that conflict with their husbands will lead to defeat and deeper resentment on their own part, or even divorce.

These are all reasonable cautions. The pleasure of sharing the day-to-day administration of home and family is not apparent to many men, especially those socialized to the older model. Nonetheless, today we find an increasing number of young men and remarried men actually yearning to be an involved parent. This represents a shift in ideology, a new view of "what is important in life."

However, women, too, need to change. Many women are used to being taken care of and are trained for submissive interaction with men. In effect, they set up during courtship many of the inequities they will complain about in marriage—and ultimately flee from. They want intimacy, yet they often establish conditions—such as maximization of mate income—that subvert family time and marital closeness.

In addition, there are several public policy reforms that might assist in the formation of peer marriages and thereby help anchor families of the future. Such reforms might include classes on marriage and the family in high school, where young men and women can learn a model of partnership, equity, and friendship; more pressure on employers to offer flextime and on-site child care, so that individuals are not penalized for their parenting choices; and after-school care in the public schools (until 6 PM).

There also needs to be more cultural support from the larger society. Most parents do not want to see their sons in the role of primary parent, do not want their sons' careers compromised, and still view a woman's work—including care for children—as unmanly. Moreover, most women are not encouraged to think of themselves as potential providers; only recently have they come to imagine themselves as fully committed to careers. I know there is a great split of opinion over whether young mothers should work at all, much less be encouraged to be responsible for their own economic welfare. But I would suggest that too much specialization in parenting and insufficient equality of experience may be more injurious in the long run than the difficulties involved when both partners juggle work and home.

CONCLUSIONS

We must recognize that there is no one form of marital organization appropriate for all couples. But I believe the "pro-family" or "family values" movement has been needlessly antagonistic to feminist models of marriage. After all, the two sides in this dialogue share some important goals: we do not want marriages to break up unless they absolutely have to; we want children to be loved and cherished and brought to adulthood in an intact family if there is any way it can be accomplished without punishment to either the children or the parents; we want people to want to form lasting bonds that strengthen the extended family.

The big question is how best to accomplish this. I suggest that shared parenting and increased spousal satisfaction are the most effective routes to family stability. I think that newfound feelings about equity and emotional closeness are essential to modern marital durability. Peer relationships will be good for women, children, and families—and a great benefit for men as well. Peer marriage is not a feminist or elitist vision. It is a practical plan to lower the divorce rate. But in order to see how well it works, society needs to offer the cultural and structural support to permit both men and women to parent, to participate in each other's lives, and to have the time together that a strong relationship requires. Whether peer marriage will actually work better than traditional marriage is, at this point, a matter of conjecture. We do know, however, that traditional roles have failed to ensure stability. The new model is an experiment we can ill afford to ignore.

Working at Motherhood: Chicana and Mexicana Immigrant Mothers and Employment[1]

DENISE A. SEGURA

In North American society, women are expected to bear and assume primary responsibility for raising their children. This socially constructed form of motherhood encourages women to stay at home during their children's early or formative years, and asserts activities that take married mothers out of the home (for instance, paid employment) are less important or "secondary" to their domestic duties.[2] Motherhood as a social construction rests on the ideological position that women's biological abilities to bear and suckle children are "natural," and therefore fundamental to women's "fulfillment." This position, however, fails to appreciate that motherhood is a culturally formed structure whose meanings can vary and are subject to change.

Despite the ideological impetus to mother at home, over half of all women with children work for wages.[3] The growing incongruence between social ideology and individual behaviors has prompted some researchers to suggest that traditional gender role expectations are changing (for example, greater acceptance of women working outside the home).[4] The profuse literature on the "ambivalence" and "guilt" employed mothers often feel when they work outside the home, however, reminds us that changes in expectations are neither absolute nor uncontested.

Some analysts argue that the ambivalence felt by many employed mothers stems from their discomfort in deviating from a socially constructed "idealized mother," who stays home to care for her family.[5] This image of motherhood, popularized in the media, schoolbooks, and public policy,

implies that the family and the economy constitute two separate spheres, private and public. Dubois and Ruiz argue, however, that the notion of a private–public dichotomy largely rests on the experiences of white, leisured women and lacks immediate relevance to less privileged women (for instance, immigrant women, women of color), who have historically been important economic actors both inside and outside the home.[6] The view that the relationship between motherhood and employment varies by class, race, and/or culture raises several important questions. Do the ideology of motherhood and the "ambivalence" of employed mothers depicted within American sociology and feminist scholarship pertain to women of Mexican descent in the United States? Among these women, what is the relation between the ideological constructions of motherhood and employment? Is motherhood mutually exclusive from employment among Mexican-heritage women from different social locations?

In this chapter I explore these questions using qualitative data gathered from thirty women of Mexican descent in the United States—both native-born Chicanas (including two Mexico-born women raised since preschool years in the US) and resident immigrant Mexicanas.[7] I illustrate that notions of motherhood for Chicanas and Mexicanas are embedded in different ideological constructs operating within two systems of patriarchy. Contrary to the expectations of acculturation models, I find that Mexicanas frame motherhood in ways that foster a more consistent labor market presence than do Chicanas. I argue that this distinction—typically bypassed in the sociological literature on motherhood, women and work, or Chicano Studies—is rooted in their dissimilar social locations—that is, the "social spaces" they engage within the social structure created by the intersection of class, race, gender, and culture.[8]

I propose that Mexicanas, raised in a world where economic and household work often merged, do not dichotomize social life into public and private spheres, but appear to view employment as one workable domain of motherhood. Hence, the more recent the time of emigration, the less ambivalence Mexicanas express regarding employment. Chicanas, on the other hand, raised in a society that celebrates the expressive functions of the family and obscures its productive economic functions, express higher adherence to the ideology of stay-at-home motherhood and correspondingly more ambivalence toward full-time employment—even when they work.

These differences between Mexicanas and Chicanas challenge current research on Mexican-origin women that treats them as a single analytic category (for instance, "Hispanic") as well as research on contemporary views of motherhood that fails to appreciate diversity among women. My examination of the intersection of motherhood and employment among Mexican immigrant women also reinforces emerging research focusing on women's own economic and social motivations to emigrate to the United States (rather than the behest of husbands and/or fathers).[9]

My analysis begins with a brief review of relevant research on the relationship between motherhood and employment. Then I explore this relationship in greater detail, using in-depth interview data. I conclude by discussing the need to recast current conceptualizations of the dilemma between motherhood and employment to reflect women's different social locations.

THEORETICAL CONCERNS

The theoretical concerns that inform this research on Chicana/Mexicana employment integrate feminist analyses of the hegemonic power of patriarchy over work and motherhood with a critique of rational choice models and other models that overemphasize modernity and acculturation. In much of the literature on women and work, familial roles tend to be portrayed as important constraints on both women's labor market entry and mobility. Differences among women related to immigrant status, however, challenge this view.

Within rational choice models, motherhood represents a prominent social force behind women's job decisions. Becker and Polachek, for example, argue that women's "preference" to mother is maximized in jobs that exact fewer penalties for interrupted employment, such as part-time, seasonal, or clerical work.[10] According to this view,

women's pursuit of their rational self-interest reinforces their occupational segregation within low-paying jobs (for example, clerical work) and underrepresentation in higher-paying, male-dominated jobs that typically require significant employer investments (for example, specialized training). Employers may be reluctant to "invest" in or train women workers who, they perceive, may leave a job at any time for familial reasons.[11] This perspective views motherhood as a major impediment to employment and mobility. But it fails to consider that the organization of production has developed in ways that make motherhood an impediment. Many feminist scholars view this particular development as consistent with the hegemonic power of patriarchy.

Distinct from rational choice models, feminist scholarship directs attention away from individual preferences to consider how patriarchy (male domination/female subordination) shapes the organization of production, resulting in the economic, political, and social subordination of women to men.[12] While many economists fail to consider the power of ideological constructs such as "family" and "motherhood" in shaping behavior among women, employers, and the organization of production itself, many feminist scholars focus on these power dynamics.

Within feminist analyses, motherhood as an ideology obscures and legitimizes women's social subordination because it conceals particular interests within the rubric of a universal prerogative (reproduction). The social construction of motherhood serves the interest of capital by providing essential childbearing, child care, and housework at a minimal cost to the state, and sustains women as a potential reservoir of labor power, or a "reserve army of labor."[13] The strength of the ideology of motherhood is such that women continue to try to reconcile the "competing urgencies"[14] of motherhood and employment despite the lack of supportive structures at work or within the family.

Because employers view women as mothers (or future mothers), they encounter discrimination in job entry and advancement.[15] Because women are viewed as mothers, they also work a "second shift" at home.[16] The conflict between market work and family work has caused considerable ambivalence within women. Berg, for example, notes that one of the dominant themes in analyzing women and work is the "guilt" of employed mothers based on "espousing something different" from their own mothers.[17]

The notion Berg describes of "conflict" or "guilt" rests on several suppositions. The first assumption is that motherhood is a unilaterally oppressive state; the second, that employed mothers feel guilt; and the third, that today's employed mothers do not have working mothers (which partially explains their "guilt feelings"). Inasmuch as large numbers of working-class, immigrant, and racial ethnic women have long traditions of working in the formal and informal economic sectors, such assumptions are suspect.

Research on women of Mexican descent and employment indicates their labor force participation is lower than that of other women when they have young children.[18] Moreover, Chicanas and Mexicanas are occupationally segregated in the lowest-paying of female-dominated jobs.[19] Explanations for their unique employment situation range from analyses of labor market structures and employer discrimination[20] to deficient individual characteristics (for instance, education, job skills)[21] and cultural differences.[22]

Analyses of Chicana/Mexicana employment that utilize a cultural framework typically explain the women's lower labor force participation, higher fertility, lower levels of education, and higher levels of unemployment as part of an ethnic or cultural tradition.[23] That is, as this line of argument goes, Chicano/Mexican culture emphasizes a strong allegiance to an idealized form of motherhood and a patriarchal ideology that frowns upon working wives and mothers and does not encourage girls to pursue higher education or employment options. These attitudes are supposed to vary by generation, with immigrant women (from Mexico) holding the most conservative attitudes.[24]

There are two major flaws in the research on Chicana/Mexicana employment, however. First, inconsistency in distinguishing between native-born and resident immigrant women characterizes much of this literature. Second, overreliance on linear acculturation persists. Both procedures imply either that Chicanas and Mexicanas are very similar, or that they lie on a sort of "cultural continuum," with Mexican immigrants at one end holding more conservative behaviors and attitudes grounded in traditional (often rural) Mexican culture, and U.S.-born Chicanos holding an amalgamation of cultural traditions from Mexico and the United States.[25] In terms of motherhood and employment, therefore, Mexicanas should have more "traditional" ideas about motherhood than U.S.-born Chicanas. Since the traditional ideology of motherhood typically refers to women staying home to "mother" children rather than going outside the home to work, Mexicanas theoretically should not be as willing to work as Chicanas or North American women in general—unless there is severe economic need. This formulation, while logical, reflects an underlying emphasis on modernity—or the view that "traditional" Mexican culture lags behind North American culture in developing behaviors and attitudes conducive to participating fully in modern society.[26] Inasmuch as conventional North American views

of motherhood typically idealize labor market exit to care for children, embracing this prototype may be more conducive to maintaining patriarchal privilege (female economic subordination to men) than facilitating economic progress generally. In this sense, conceptualizations of motherhood that affirm its economic character may be better accommodating to women's market participation in the United States.

The following section discusses the distinct views of motherhood articulated by Chicanas and Mexicanas and their impact on employment attitudes and behaviors. In contrast to the notion that exposure to North American values enhances women's incentives to work, proportionately more Chicanas than Mexicanas express ambivalence toward paid employment when they have children at home. I analyze these differences among a selected sample of clerical, service, and operative workers.

METHOD AND SAMPLE

This paper is based on in-depth interviews with thirty Mexican-origin women—thirteen Chicanas and seventeen Mexicanas—who had participated in the 1978 to 79 or 1980 to 81 cohorts of an adult education and employment training program in the greater San Francisco Bay Area.[27] All thirty respondents had been involved in a conjugal relationship (either legal marriage or informal cohabitation with a male partner) at some point in their lives before I interviewed them in 1985, and had at least one child under eighteen years of age. At the time of their interviews, six Chicanas and fourteen Mexicanas were married; seven Chicanas and three Mexicanas were single parents.

On the average, the married Chicanas have 1.2 children at home; the Mexicanas report 3.5 children. Both Chicana and Mexicana single mothers average 1.6 children. The children of the Chicanas tend to be preschool age or in elementary school. The children of the Mexicanas exhibit a greater age range (from infant to late adolescence), reflecting their earlier marriages and slightly older average age.

With respect to other relevant characteristics, all but two Mexicanas and five Chicanas had either a high school diploma or its equivalent (GED). The average age was 27.4 years for the Chicanas and thirty-three years for the Mexicanas.[28] Upon leaving the employment training program, all the women secured employment. At the time of their interviews, about half of the Chicanas ($n = 7$); and three-fourths of the Mexicanas ($n = 12$) were employed. Only two out of the seven (28 percent) employed Chicanas worked full-time (thirty-five or more hours per week) whereas nine out of the twelve (75 percent) employed Mexicanas worked full-time. Most of the Chicanas found clerical or service jobs (for example, teacher assistants); most of the Mexicanas labored in operative jobs or in the service sector (for example, hotel maids), with a small minority employed as clerical workers.

I gathered in-depth life and work histories from the women to ascertain:

1. What factors motivated them to enter, exit, and stay employed in their specific occupations;
2. whether familial roles or ideology influenced their employment consistency; and
3. whether other barriers limited their job attachment and mobility.

My examination of the relationship between motherhood and employment forms part of a larger study of labor market stratification and occupational mobility among Chicana and Mexican immigrant women.[29]

MOTHERHOOD AND EMPLOYMENT

Nearly all of the respondents, both Chicana and Mexicana, employed and nonemployed, speak of motherhood as their most important social role. They differ sharply in their employment behaviors and views regarding the relationship between motherhood and market work. Women fall into four major groups. The first group consists of five *Involuntary Nonemployed Mothers,* who are not employed but care full-time for their children. All of these women want to be employed at least part time. They either cannot secure the job they want and/or feel pressured to be at home mothering full-time.

The second group consists of six *Voluntary Non-employed Mothers* who are not employed but remain out of the labor force by *choice.* They feel committed to staying at home to care for preschool and/or elementary school age children.

The third category, *Ambivalent Employed Mothers,* includes eleven employed women. They have either preschool or elementary school age children. Women in this group believe that employment interferes with motherhood and feel "guilty" when they work outside the home. Despite these feelings, they are employed at least part-time.

The fourth group, *Nonambivalent Employed Mothers,* includes eight employed women. What distinguishes these women from the previous group is their view that employment and motherhood seem compatible social dynamics irrespective of the age of their children. All eight women are Mexicanas. Some of these women believe employment could be problematic, however, *if* a family member could not care for their children or be at home for the children when they arrived from school.

Chicanas tend to fall in the second and third categories, whereas Mexicanas predominate in the first and fourth groups. Three reasons emerged as critical in explaining this difference:

1. the economic situations of their families;
2. labor market structure (four-fifths of the nonemployed Mexicanas were involuntarily unemployed); and
3. women's conceptualizations of motherhood, in particular, their expressed *need* to mother.

Age of the women and number of children did not fall into any discernible pattern, therefore I did not engage them in depth within my analysis.

First, I consider the situation of the Voluntary Nonemployed Mothers, including three married Chicanas, one single-parent Mexicana, and one single-parent Chicana. All but one woman exited the labor market involuntarily (for reasons such as layoffs or disability). All five women remain out of the labor force by choice. Among them, the expressed need to mother appears strong—overriding all other concerns. They view motherhood as mutually exclusive from employment. Lydia, a married Chicana with a small toddler, articulates this perspective:

> Right now, since we've had the baby, I feel, well he [her husband] feels the same way, that I want to spend this time with her and watch her grow up. See, because when I was small my grandmother raised me so I felt this *loss* [her emphasis] when my grandmother died. And I've never gotten that *real love,* that mother love from my mother. We have a friendship, but we don't have that "motherly love." I want my daughter to know that I'm here, especially at her age, it's very important for them to know that when they cry that mama's there. Even if it's not a painful cry, it's still important for them to know that mommy's there. She's my number one— she's all my attention . . . so working-wise, it's up to [her husband] right now.

Susana, a Chicana single parent with a five-year-old child, said:

I'm the type of person that has always wanted to have a family. I think it was more like I didn't have a family-type home when I was growing up. I didn't have a mother and a father and the kids all together in the same household all happy. I didn't have that. And that's what I want more than anything! I want to be different from my mother, who has worked hard and is successful in her job. I don't want to be successful in the same way.

Lydia, Susana, and the other voluntarily unemployed Chicanas adamantly assert that motherhood requires staying home with their children. Susana said: "A good mother is there for her children all the time when they are little and when they come home from school." All the Chicanas in this category believe that motherhood means staying home with children—even if it means going on welfare (AFDC). This finding is similar to other accounts of working-class women.[30]

The sense shared among this group of women that motherhood and employment are irreconcilable, especially when children are of preschool age, is related to their social locations. A small minority of the Chicanas had been raised by nonemployed mothers ($n = 3$). They feel they should stay at home with their children as long as it's economically feasible. Most of the Chicanas, however, resemble Lydia and Susana, who had been raised by employed mothers. Although these women recognize that their mothers had worked out of economic need, they believe they did not receive sufficient love and care from their mothers. Throughout their interviews, this group of Chicanas expressed hostility and resentment against their employed mothers for leaving them with other caretakers. These feelings contribute to their decisions to stay at home with their children, and/or their sense of "guilt" when they are employed. Their hostility and guilt defy psychoanalytic theories that speculate that the cycle of gender construction locking women into "exclusive mothering" roles can be broken if the primary caretaker (the mother) undertakes more diverse roles.[31] Rather, Chicanas appear to value current conceptionalizations of motherhood that prioritize the expressive work of the mother, as distinct from her economic activities.

This group of Chicanas seems to be pursuing the social construction of motherhood that is idealized within their ethnic community, their churches, and society at large.[32] Among Chicanos and Mexicanos the image of *la madre* as self-sacrificing and holy is a powerful standard against which women often compare themselves.[33] The Chicana informants also seem to accept the notion that women's primary duty is to provide for the emotional welfare of the children, and that economic activities which take them outside the home are secondary. Women's desire to enact the socially constructed motherhood ideal was further strengthened by their conviction that many of their current problems (for instance, low levels of education, feelings of inadequacy, single parenthood) are related to growing up in families that did not conform to the stay-at-home mother/father-as-provider configuration. Their evaluation of the close relationship between motherhood and economic or emotional well-being of offspring parallels popular emphasis on the primacy of individual efforts and the family environment to emotional vigor and achievement (Parsons and Bales 1955; Bradley and Caldwell 1984; Caspi and Elder 1988; Parcel and Menaghan 1990).[34]

Informants in this group speak to a complex dimension of mothering and gender construction in the Chicano/Mexicano communities. These women reject their employed mothers' organization of family life. As children, most had been cared for by other family members, and now feel closer to their grandmothers or other female relatives than to their own biological mothers. This causes them considerable pain—pain they want to spare their own children. Many, like Susana, do not want to be "successful" in the tradition of their own employed mothers. Insofar as "success" means leaving their children with other caretakers, it contradicts their conceptualization of motherhood. Rather, they frame "success" in more affective terms: having children who are happy and doing well in school. This does not suggest that Chicanas disagree with the notion that having a good job or a lucrative career denotes "success." They simply feel that successful careers could and should be deferred until their children are older (for instance, in the upper grades of elementary school) and doing well academically and emotionally.

Only one married Mexicana, Belen, articulated views similar to those of the Chicanas. Belen left the labor market in 1979 to give birth and care for her newborn child. It is important to note that she has a gainfully employed husband who does not believe mothers should work outside the home. Belen, who has two children and was expecting a third when I interviewed her, said:

I wanted to work or go back to school after having my first son, but my husband didn't want me to. He said, "no one can take care of your child the way you can." He did not want me to work. And I did not feel right having someone else care for my son. So I decided to wait until my children were older.

Belens' words underscore an important dynamic that impacted on both Mexicana and Chicana conceptualizations of motherhood: spousal employment and private patriarchy. Specifically, husbands working in full-time, year-round jobs with earnings greater than those of their wives tended to pressure women to mother full-time. Women who succumb to this pressure become economically dependent on their husbands and reaffirm male authority in the organization of the family. These particular women tend to consider motherhood and employment in similar ways. This suggests that the form the social construction of motherhood takes involves women's economic relationship to men as well as length of time in the United States.

Four Mexicanas and one Chicana were involuntarily nonemployed. They had been laid off from their jobs or were on temporary disability leave. Three women (two Mexicanas/one Chicana) were seeking employment; the other two were in the last stages of pregnancy but intended to look for a job as soon as possible after their child's birth. All five women reported feeling "good" about being home with their children but wanted to rejoin the labor force as soon as possible. Ideologically these women view motherhood and employment as reconcilable social dynamics. As Isabel, an unemployed production worker, married with eight children, said:

> I believe that women always work more. We who are mothers work to maintain the family by working outside, but also inside the house caring for the children.

Isabel voiced a sentiment held by all of the informants—that women work hard at motherhood. Since emigrating to the U.S. about a decade ago, Isabel had been employed nearly continuously, with only short leaves for childbearing. Isabel and nearly all of the Mexicanas described growing up in environments where women, men, and children were important economic actors. In this regard they are similar to the Nonambivalent Employed Mothers—all of whom are also Mexicanas. They tended not to dichotomize social life in the same way as the Voluntary Nonemployed Chicanas and Ambivalent Employed informants.

Although all of the Chicanas believe that staying home best fulfills their mother roles, slightly fewer than half actually stay out of the labor market to care for their young children. The rest of the Chicanas are employed and struggling to reconcile motherhood with employment. I refer to these women as Ambivalent Employed Mothers. They express guilt about working and assert they *would not work*

if they did not have to for economic reasons. Seven of these women are Chicanas; four are Mexicanas.

To try and alleviate their guilt and help meet their families' economic goals, most of the Chicanas work in part-time jobs. This option permits them to be home when their children arrive from school. Despite this, they feel guilty and unhappy about working. As Jenny, a married Chicana with two children, ages two and four, who is employed part-time, said:

> Sure, I feel guilty. I *should* [her emphasis] be with them [her children] while they're little. He [her husband] really feels that I should be with my kids all the time. And it's true.

Despite their guilt, most of the women in this group remain employed because their jobs offer them the means to provide for family economic betterment—a goal that transcends staying home with their children. However, women's utilization of economic rationales for working sometimes served as a smokescreen for individualistic desires to "do something outside the home" and to establish a degree of autonomy. Several women, for example, stated that they enjoyed having their "own money." When I asked these women to elaborate, they typically retreated to a familistic stance. That is, much of *her* money is used *for the family* (for example, child care, family presents, clothing). When money is used *for the woman* (makeup, going out with the girls) it is often justified as necessary for her emotional well-being, which in turn helps her to be a good wife and mother.

The Mexicana mothers who are employed express their ambivalence somewhat differently from the Chicanas. One Mexicana works full-time; the other three are employed part-time. Angela, a Mexicana married with one child and employed full-time as a seamstress, told me with glistening eyes:

> Always I have had to work. I had to leave my son with the baby-sitter since he was six months old. It was difficult. Each baby-sitter has their own way of caring for children, which isn't like yours. I know the baby-sitter wouldn't give him the food I left. He always had on dirty diapers and was starving when I would pick him up. But there wasn't any other recourse. I had to work. I would just clean him and feed him when I got home.

Angela's "guilt" stemmed from her inability to find good, affordable child care. Unlike most of the Mexicanas, who had extensive family networks, Angela and her husband had few relatives to rely on in the US. Unlike the Chicana informants, Angela did not want to exit the labor market to care for her child. Her desire is reinforced by economic need; her husband is irregularly employed.[35] For the other three Mexicanas in this group, guilt as an employed mother appears to have developed with stable spousal employment. That is, the idea of feeling guilty about full-time employment emerged *after* husbands became employed in secure, well-paying jobs and "reminded" them of the importance of stay-at-home, full-time motherhood. Lourdes, who was married with eight children and working as a part-time hotel maid said:

I was offered a job at a—factory, working from eleven at night to seven in the morning. But I had a baby and so I wasn't able to work. I would have liked to take the job because it paid $8.25 an hour. I couldn't though, because of my baby. And my husband didn't want me to work at night. He said, "If we both work at night, who will take care of the children?" So I didn't take the job.

To thwart potential guilt over full-time employment and to ease marital tension (if she had taken this job she would have earned more money than her husband), Lourdes declined this high-paying job. When her child turned two, she opted to work part-time as a hotel maid. Lourdes, and the other Mexicanas employed part-time, told me that they *would* work full-time *if* their husbands supported their preferences. Mexicanas' ambivalence, then, is related to unease about their children's child care situations, as well as to anger at being held accountable to a narrow construction of motherhood enforced by their husbands.

All Ambivalent Employed Mothers report worrying about their children while at work. While this does not necessarily impair their job performance, it adds another psychological or emotional burden on their shoulders. This burden affects their ability to work full-time (overtime is especially problematic) or seek the means (especially schooling) to advance in their jobs.

Women seem particularly troubled when they have to work on weekends. This robs them of precious family time. As Elena, a Chicana single parent with two children, ages nine and three, who works part-time as a hotel maid, said:

Yes, I work on weekends. And my kids, you know how kids are—they don't like it. And it's hard. But I hope to find a job soon where the schedule is fixed and I won't have to work on weekends—because that time should be for my kids.

There is a clear sense among the women I interviewed that a boundary between *time for the family* and *market time* should exist. During times when this boundary folds, women experience both internal conflict (within the woman herself) and external conflict (among family members). They regard jobs that overlap on family time with disfavor and unhappiness. When economic reasons compel women to work during what they view as family time, they usually try to find as quickly as possible a different job that allows them to better meet their mother roles.

Interestingly, the Chicanas appear less flexible in reconciling the boundaries of family time and market time than the Mexicanas. That is, Chicanas overwhelmingly "choose" part-time employment to limit the amount of spillover time from employment on motherhood and family activities. Mexicanas, on the other hand, overwhelmingly work full-time ($n = 9$) and attempt to do both familial caretaking and market work as completely as possible.

This leads us to consider the fourth category I call Nonambivalent Employed Mothers. This category consists of Mexicana immigrants, both married and single-parent (six and two women, respectively). Mexicanas in this group do not describe motherhood as a *need* requiring a separate sphere for optimal realization. Rather, they refer to motherhood as one function of womanhood compatible with employment insofar as employment allows them to provide for their family's economic subsistence or betterment. As Pilar, a married Mexicana with four children, employed full-time as a line supervisor in a factory, said: "I work to help my children. That's what a mother should do." This group of Mexicanas does not express *guilt* over leaving their children in the care of others so much as *regret* over the limited amount of time they could spend with them. As Norma, a Mexicana full-time clerical worker who is married with two children ages three and five, said:

I don't feel guilty for leaving my children because if I didn't work they might not have the things they have now. . . . Perhaps if I had to stay at home I would feel guilty and frustrated. I'm not the type that can stay home twenty-four hours a day. I don't think that would help my children any because I would feel pressured at being cooped up [*encerrada*] at home. And that way I wouldn't have the same desire to play with my daughters. But now, with the time we have together, we do things that we want to, like run in the park, because there's so little time.

All of the Mexicanas in this group articulate views similar to Norma's. Their greater comfort with the demands of market and family work emanates from their social locations. All of the Mexicanas come from poor or working-class families, where motherhood embraced both economic and affective features. Their activities were not viewed as equal to those of men, however, and ideologically women saw themselves as *helping* the family rather than *providing* for it.

Few Mexicanas reported that their mothers were wage-laborers ($n = 3$), rather, described a range of economic activities they remembered women doing "for the family."[36] Mexicanas from rural villages ($n = 7$) recounted how their mothers had worked on the land and made assorted products or food to sell in local marketplaces. Mexicanas from urban areas ($n = 5$) also discussed how their mothers had been economically active. Whether rural or urban, Mexicanas averred that their mothers had taught them to "help" the family as soon as possible. As Norma said:

> My mother said: "it's one thing for a woman to lie around the house but it's a different thing for the work that needs to be done. As the saying goes, work is never done; the work does you in *[el trabajo acaba con uno; uno nunca acaba con el trabajo]*.

Lourdes and two other Mexicanas cleaned houses with their mothers after school. Other mothers sold clothes to neighbors, cooked and sold food, or did assorted services for pay (for example, giving penicillin shots to neighbors). The Mexicanas do not view these activities as "separate" or less important than the emotional nurturing of children and family. Rather, they appreciate both the economic and the expressive as important facets of motherhood.

Although the Mexicanas had been raised in worlds where women were important economic actors, this did not signify gender equality. On the contrary, male privilege, or patriarchy, characterizes the organization of the family, the economy, and the polity in both rural and urban Mexican society.[37] In the present study, Mexicanas indicated that men wielded greater authority in the family, the community, and the state than women. Mexicanas also tended to uphold male privilege in the family by viewing both domestic work and women's employment as "less important" than the work done by men. As Adela, a married Mexicana with four children, said: "Men are much stronger and do much more difficult work than women." Mexicanas also tended to defer to husbands as the "head" of the family—a position they told me was both "natural" and "holy."[38]

WORKING AT MOTHERHOOD

The differences presented here between the Chicanas and Mexicanas regarding motherhood and employment stem from their distinct social locations. Raised in rural or working-class families in Mexico, the Mexicanas described childhoods where they and their mothers actively contributed to the economic subsistence of their families by planting crops, harvesting, selling homemade goods, and cleaning houses. Their situations resonate with what some researchers term a family economy, where all family members work at productive tasks differentiated mainly by age and sex.[39] In this type of structure, there is less distinction between economic life and domestic life. Motherhood in this context is both economic and expressive, embracing employment as well as child-rearing.

The family economy the Mexicanas experienced differs from the family organization that characterizes most of the Chicanas' childhoods. The Chicanas come from a world that idealizes a male wage earner as the main economic "provider," with women primarily as consumers and only secondarily as economic actors.[40] Women in this context are mothers first, wage earners second. Families that challenge this structure are often discredited, or perceived as dysfunctional and the source of many social problems.[41] The ambivalence Chicanas recurrently voice stems from their belief in what Kanter calls "the myth of separate worlds."[42] They seek to realize the popular notion or stereotype that family is a separate structure—a haven in a heartless world. Their attachment to this ideal is underscored by a harsh critique of their own employed mothers and themselves *when* they work full-time. Motherhood framed within this context appears irreconcilable with employment.

There are other facets to the differences between Chicanas and Mexicanas. The Mexicanas, as immigrant women, came to the United States with a vision of improving the life chances of their families and themselves. This finding intersects with research on "selective immigration." That is, that Mexican immigrants tend to possess higher levels of education than the national average in Mexico, and a wide range of behavioral characteristics (for instance, high achievement orientation) conducive to success in the United States.[43]

The Mexicanas emigrated hoping to work—hence their high attachment to employment, even in physically demanding, often demeaning jobs. Mexican and Chicano husbands support their wives' desires to work *so long as* this employment does not challenge the patriarchal structure of the family. In other words, so long as the

Mexicanas: (1) articulate high attachment to motherhood *and* family caretaker roles, (2) frame their employment in terms of family economic goals, and (3) do not ask men to do equal amounts of housework or child care, they encounter little resistance from husbands or other male family members.

When Mexican and Chicano husbands secure good jobs, however, they begin pressuring wives to quit working or to work only part-time. In this way, Mexican and Chicano men actively pursue continuity of their superordinate position within the family. This suggests that the way motherhood is conceptualized in both the Mexican and Chicano communities, particularly with respect to employment, is wedded to male privilege, or patriarchy. Ironically, then, Mexicanas' sense of employment's continuity with motherhood enhances their job attachment but does not challenge a patriarchal family structure or ethos.

Similarly, Chicanas' preference for an idealized form of motherhood does not challenge male privilege in their community. Their desire to stay at home to mother exercised a particularly strong influence on the employment behavior of single-parent Chicanas and women with husbands employed in relatively good jobs. This preference reflects an adherence to an idealized, middle-class lifestyle that glorifies women's domestic roles, as well as to maintenance of a patriarchal family order. Chicanas feel they should stay at home to try and provide their children with the mothering they believe children should have—mothering that many of them had not experienced. Chicanas also feel compelled by husbands and the larger community to maintain the status of men as "good providers." Men earning wages adequate to provide for their families' needs usually urged their wives to leave the labor market. While the concept of the good provider continues to be highly valued in our society, it also serves as a rationale that upholds male privilege ideologically and materially, and reinforces the myth of separate spheres that emanates from the organization of the family and the economy.

CONCLUSION

By illustrating how Chicanas and Mexicanas differ in their conceptualizations and organization of the motherhood and employment nexus, this study demonstrates how motherhood is a culturally formed structure with various meanings and subtexts. The vitality of these differences among a group who share a common historical origin and many cultural attributes underscores the need for frameworks that analyze diversity among all groups of women. Most essential to such an undertaking is a critique of the privileging of the "separate spheres" concept in analyses of women and work.

The present study provides additional coherence to recent contentions that the private–public dichotomy lacks immediate relevance to less privileged women (for instance, Chicana and Mexican immigrant women). In the process of illustrating how Chicanas and Mexicanas organized the interplay between motherhood and employment, it became clear that a more useful way of understanding this intersection might be to problematize motherhood itself. Considering motherhood from the vantage point of women's diverse social locations revealed considerable heterogeneity in how one might speak of it. For example, motherhood has an economic component for both groups of women, but it is most strongly expressed by Mexicana immigrants. The flavor of the expressive, however, flows easily across both groups of women, and for the Mexicanas embraces the economic. What this suggests is that the dichotomy of the separate spheres lacks relevance to Chicanas and Mexicanas and other women whose social origins make economic work necessary for survival.

This leads us to consider the relative place and function of the ideology of motherhood prevalent in our society. Motherhood constructed to privilege the woman who stays at home serves a myriad of functions. It pushes women to dichotomize their lives rather than develop a sense of fluidity across roles, responsibilities, and preferences. Idealized, stay-at-home motherhood eludes most American women with children. As an ideology, however, it tells them what "should be," rendering them failures *as women* when they enter the labor market. Hence the feelings of ambivalence that characterized employed mothers' lives for the most part—except those who had not yet internalized these standards. The present research provided examples of such women, along with the understanding that other women from different social locations may demonstrate distinct ways of organizing the motherhood–employment nexus as well.

Feminist analyses of women and work emphasize the role of patriarchy to maintain male privilege and domination economically and ideologically. It is important to recognize that male privilege is not experienced equally by all men, and that patriarchy itself can be expressed in different ways. The present study found that notions of motherhood among Mexicanas and Chicanas are embedded in different ideological constructs operating within two systems of patriarchy. For Mexicanas, patriarchy takes the form of a corporate family model, with all members contributing to the common good. For Chicanas, the patriarchal structure centers more closely around a public–private dichotomy that idealizes men as economic providers and women primarily as caretakers-consumers.

The finding that women from more "traditional" backgrounds (such as rural Mexico) are likely to approach full-time employment with less ambivalence than more "American" women (such as the Chicanas) rebuts linear acculturation models that assume a negative relationship between ideologies (such as motherhood) constructed with-

in "traditional" Mexican society and employment. It also complements findings on the negative relationship between greater length of time in the United States and high aspirations among Mexicans.[44] This suggests that employment problems (for example, underemployment, unemployment) are related less to "traditional" cultural configurations than to labor market structure and employment policies. Understanding the intersections between employment policy, social ideology, and private need is a necessary step toward expanding possibilities for women in our society.

NOTES

1. This article is a revised version of "Ambivalence or Continuity?: Motherhood and Employment among Chicanas and Mexican Immigrant Women," *AZTLAN, International Journal of Chicano Studies Research* (1992). I would like to thank Maxine Baca Zinn, Evelyn Nakano Glenn, Arlie Hochschild, Beatriz Pesquera, and Vicki Ruiz for their constructive feedback and criticism of earlier drafts of this paper. A special thanks goes to Jon Cruz for his assistance in titling this paper. Any remaining errors or inconsistencies are my own responsibility. This research was supported in part by a 1986–87 University of California President's Postdoctoral Fellowship.

2. Betsy Wearing, *The Ideology of Motherhood, A Study of Sydney Suburban Mothers* (Sydney: George Allen and Unwin, 1984); Barbara J. Berg, *The Crisis of the Working Mother, Resolving the Conflict between Family and Work* (New York: Summit Books, 1986); Nancy Folbre "The Pauperization of Motherhood: Patriarchy and Public Policy in the United States," *Review of Radical Political Economics* 16 (1984). The view that mothers should not work outside the home typically pertains to married women. Current state welfare policies (e.g., Aid to Families with Dependent Children [AFDC], workfare) indicate that single, unmarried mothers belong in the labor force, not at home caring for their children full-time. See Naomi Gerstel and Harriet Engel Gross, "Introduction," in N. Gerstel and H. E. Gross, eds., *Families and Work* (Philadelphia: Temple University Press, 1987), pp. 1–12; Deborah K. Zinn and Rosemary C. Sarri, "Turning Back the Clock on Public Welfare," in *Signs: Journal of Women in Culture and Society* 10 (1984), pp. 355–370; Nancy Folbre "The Pauperization of Motherhood"; Nancy A. Naples, "A Socialist Feminist Analysis of the Family Support Act of 1988," AFFILIA 6 (1991), pp. 23–38.

3. Allyson Sherman Grossman, "More than Half of All Children Have Working Mothers," Special Labor Force Reports— Summaries, *Monthly Labor Review* (February 1982), pp. 41–43; Howard Hayghe, "Working Mothers Reach Record Number in 1984," *Monthly Labor Review* 107 (December 1984), pp. 31–34;

U.S. Bureau of The Census "Fertility of American Women: June 1990," *Current Population Report,* Series P-20, No. 454, (Washington D.C.: United States Government Printing Office, 1991). In June 1990, over half (53.1 percent) of women between the ages of 18–44 who had had a child in the last year were in the labor force. This proportion varied by race: 54.9 percent of white women, 46.9 percent of Black women, and 44.4 percent of Latinas were in the labor force. See U.S. Bureau of the Census (1991), p. 5.

4. Simon and Landis report that a 1986 Gallup Poll indicates that support for married women to work outside the home is considerably greater than 1938 levels: 76 percent of women and 78 percent of men approve (1989: 270). Comparable 1938 levels are 25 percent and 19 percent, respectively, of women and men. The 1985 Roper Poll finds the American public adhering to the view that a husband's career supersedes that of his wife: 72 percent of women and 62 percent of men agree that a wife should quit her job and relocate if her husband is offered a good job in another city (189: 272). In the reverse situation, 20 percent of women and 22 percent of men believe a husband should quit his job and relocate with his wife (1989: 272). Simon and Landis conclude: "The Women's Movement has not radicalized the American woman: she is still prepared to put marriage and children ahead of her career and to allow her husband's status to determine the family's position in society" (1989: 269). Rita J. Simon and Jean M. Landis, "Women's and Men's Attitudes about a Woman's Place and Role," *Public Opinion Quarterly* (1989), 53: 265–276.

5. Arlie Hochschild with Anne Machung, *The Second Shift, Working Parents and the Revolution at Home* (New York: Viking Penguin Books, 1989); Kathleen Gerson, *Hard Choices* (Berkeley, California: University of California Press, 1985); Barbara J. Berg, *The Crisis of the Working Mother, Resolving the Conflict between Family and Work* (New York: Summit Books, 1986). The concept of "separate spheres" is approached in a variety of ways and often critiqued. See Michele Barrett, *Women's Oppression Today, Problems in Marxist Feminist Analysis* (London, Verso Press,

1980); Nona Glazer "Servants to capital: Unpaid domestic labor and paid work," *Review of Radical Economics* 16 (1984), pp. 61–87. Zaretsky contends that distinct family and market spheres arose with the development of industrial capitalism: "men and women came to see the family as separate from the economy, and personal life as a separate sphere of life divorced from the larger economy." See Eli Zaretsky, *Capitalism, The Family and Personal Life* (New York: Harper Colophon Books, 1976), p. 78. This stance is substantially different from that of early radical feminist approaches, including Firestone, who argued that the separation antedates history. See Shulamith Firestone, *The Dialectic of Sex* (New York: Bantam Books, 1970). Other scholars assert that the relations of production and reproduction are intertwined and virtually inseparable. See Heidi Hartmann, "Capitalism, Patriarchy and Job Segregation by Sex," in Martha Blaxall and Barbara Reagan, eds., *Women and the Work Place* (Chicago, Illinois: University of Chicago Press, 1976), pp. 137–169.

6. Hood argues that the "ideal" of stay-at-home motherhood and male provider has historically been an unrealistic standard for families outside the middle and upper classes. She points out that early surveys of urban workers indicate between 40 and 50 percent of all families supplemented their income with the earnings of wives and children. See Jane C. Hood, "The Provider Role: Its Meaning and Measurement," *Journal of Marriage and the Family* 48 (May 1986), pp. 349–359.

7. It should be noted that native-born status is not an essential requirement for the ethnic label "Chicana/o." There are numerous identifiers used by people of Mexican descent, including: Chicana/o, Mexican, Mexican-American, Mexicana/o, Latina/o, and Hispanic. Often people of Mexican descent use two or three of the above labels, depending on the social situation (e.g., "Mexican-American" in the family or "Chicana/o" at school). See John A. Garcia, "Yo Soy Mexicano . . . : Self-identity and Socio-demographic Correlates," *Social Science Quarterly* 62 (March, 1981), pp. 88–98; Susan E. Keefe and Amado M. Padilla, *Chicano Ethnicity* (Albuquerque, NM: University of New Mexico Press, 1987). My designation of study informants as either "Chicana" or "Mexicana" represents an analytic separation that facilitates demonstrating the heterogeneity among this group.

8. Patricia Zavella, "Reflections on Diversity among Chicanos," *Frontiers* 2 (1991), p. 75.

9. See Rosalia Solorzano-Torres, "Female Mexican Immigrants in San Diego County," in V. L. Ruiz and S. Tiano, eds., *Women on the U.S.-Mexico Border: Responses to Change* (Boston: Allen and Unwin, 1987), pp. 41–59; Reynaldo Baca and Bryan Dexter, "Mexican Women, Migration and Sex Roles," *Migration Today* 13 (1985), pp. 14–18; Sylvia Guendelman and Auristela Perez-Itriago, "Double Lives: The Changing Role of Women in Seasonal Migration," *Women's Studies* 13 (1987), pp. 249–271.

10. Gary S. Becker, "Human Capital, Effort, and the Sexual Division of Labor," *Journal of Labor Economics* 3 (1985 Supplement), pp. S33–S58; Gary S. Becker, *A Treatise on the Family* (Cambridge, MA: Harvard University Press, 1981); Solomon W. Polachek, "Occupational Self-Selection: A Human Capital Approach to Sex Differences in Occupational Structure," *Review of Economics and Statistics* 63 (1981), pp. 60–69; S. Polachek, "Occupational Segregation among Women: Theory, Evidence, and a Prognosis" in C. B. Lloyd, E. S. Andrews and C. L. Gilroy, eds., *Women in the Labor Market* (New York: Columbia University Press, 1981), pp. 137–157; S. Polachek, "Discontinuous Labor Force Participation and Its Effect on Women's Market Earnings," in C. Lloyd, ed., *Sex Discrimination and the Division of Labor* (New York: Columbia University Press, 1975), pp. 90–122. Becker's classic treatise, *Human Capital,* uses the following example borrowed from G. Stigler, "The Economics of Information," *Journal of Political Economy* (June 1961): "Women spend less time in the labor force than men and, therefore, have less incentive than residents of the area to invest in knowledge of specific consumption activities." See Gary S. Becker, *Human Capital* (Chicago: University of Chicago Press, 1975), p. 74.

11. Some institutional economists argue that "statistical discrimination" is one critical labor market dynamic that often impedes women and minorities. See Kenneth Arrow, "Economic Dimensions of Occupational Segregation: Comment I," *Signs; Journal of Women in Culture and Society* 1 (1987), pp. 233–237; Edmund Phelps, "The Statistical Theory of Racism and Sexism," in A. H. Amsden, ed., *The Economics of Women and Work* (New York: St. Martin's Press, 1980), pp. 206–210. This perspective suggests that prospective employers often lack detailed information about individual applicants and therefore utilize statistical averages and normative views of the relevant group(s) to which the applicant belongs in their hiring decisions (e.g., college-educated men tend to be successful and committed employees; all women are potential mothers; or women tend to exit the labor force for childbearing).

Bielby and Baron pose an important critique to the underlying rationale of statistical discrimination. They argue that utilizing perceptions of group differences between the sexes is "neither as rational nor as efficient as the economists believe." That is, utilizing stereotypical notions of "men's work" and "women's work" is often costly to employers and therefore irrational. This suggests that sex segregation is embedded in organizational policies which reflect and reinforce "belief systems that are also rather inert." See William T. Bielby and James N. Baron, "Undoing Discrimination: Job Integration and Comparable Worth," in C. Bose and G. Spitze, eds., *Ingredients for Women's Employment Policy* (New York: State University of New York Press, 1987), p. 216, pp. 221–222.

12. Annette Kuhn, "Structure of Patriarchy and Capital in the Family," in A. Kuhn and Annemarie Wolfe, eds., *Feminism and Materialism: Women and Modes of Production* (London: Routledge and Kegan Paul, 1978); Heidi Hartmann, "Capitalism, Patriarchy, and Job Segregation by Sex," in Martha Blaxall and Barbara Reagan, eds., *Women and the Work Place* (Chicago: University of Chicago Press, 1976), pp. 137–169; H. Hartmann, "The Family as the Locus of Gender, Class, and Political Struggle: The Example of Housework," *Signs: Journal of Women in Culture and Society* 6 (1981), pp. 366–394; Michele Barrett, *Women's Oppression Today, Problems in Marxist Feminist Analysis* (London: Verso Press, 1980).

13. Lourdes Beneria and Martha Roldan, *The Crossroads of Class and Gender, Industrial Homework, Subcontracting, and Household Dynamics in Mexico City* (Chicago: The University of Chicago Press, 1987); L. Beneria and Gita Sen, "Accumulation, Reproduction, and Women's Role in Economic Development: Boserup Revisited," in E. Leacock and H. I. Safa, eds., *Women's Work: Development and Division of Labor by Gender* (Massachusetts: Bergin and Garvey Publishers, 1986), pp. 141–157; Dorothy Smith, "Women's Inequality and the Family," in N. Gerstel and H. E. Gross, eds., *Families and Work* (Philadelphia: Temple University Press, 1987), pp. 23–54.

14. This phrase was coined by Arlie R. Hochschild and quoted in Lillian B. Rubin, *Intimate Strangers, Men and Women Together* (New York: Harper and Row, 1983).

15. Rosabeth Moss Kanter, *Men and Women in the Corporation* (New York: Basic Books, 1977). Bielby and Baron note: "employers expect certain behaviors from women (e.g., high turnover) and therefore assign them to routine tasks and dead-end jobs. Women respond by exhibiting the very behavior employers expect, thereby reinforcing the stereotype." Bielby and Baron, "Undoing Discrimination: Job Integration and Comparable Worth," p. 221.

16. Arlie Hochschild with Anne Machung, *The Second Shift, Working Parents and the Revolution of Home* (New York: Viking Penguin Books, 1989).

17. Barbara J. Berg, *The Crisis of the Working Mother, Resolving the Conflict between Family and Work* (New York: Summit Books, 1986), p. 42.

18. Howard Hayghe, "Working Mothers Reach Record Number in 1984," *Monthly Labor Review* 107 (December, 1984), pp. 31–34; U.S. Bureau of the Census, "Fertility of American Women: June 1990" in Current Population Report, Series P-20, No. 454 (Washington D.C.: United States Government Printing Office, 1991); U.S. Bureau of Census Report, "Fertility of American Women: June 1986" in Current Population Report, Series P-20. No. 421 (Washington, D.C.: United States Printing Press). In June 1986 (the year closest to the year I interviewed the respondents where I found relevant data), 49.8 percent of all women with newborn children were in the labor force. Women demonstrated differences in this behavior: 49.7 percent of white women, 51.1 percent of Black women, and 40.6 percent of Latinas with newborn children were in the labor force. See U.S. Bureau of the Census "Fertility of American Women: June 1986" (1987), p. 5.

19. Bonnie Thornton Dill, Lynn Weber Cannon, and Reeve Vanneman, "Pay Equity: An Issue of Race, Ethnicity, and Sex" (Washington D.C.: National Commission on Pay Equity, February, 1987); Julianne Malveaux and Phyllis Wallace, "Minority Women in the Workplace," in K. S. Koziara, M. Moskow, and L. Dewey Tanner, eds., *Women and Work: Industrial Relations Research Association Research Volume* (Washington D.C.: Bureau of National Affairs, 1987), pp. 265–298; Vicki L. Ruiz, " 'And Miles to go. . . .': Mexican Women and Work, 1930–1985" in L. Schlissel, V. L. Ruiz, and J. Monk, eds., *Western Women, Their Land, Their Lives* (Albuquerque: University of New Mexico Press, 1988), pp. 117–136.

20. Mario Barrera, *Race and Class in the Southwest: A Theory of Racial Inequality* (Notre Dame, IN: University of Notre Dame Press, 1979); Tomas Almaguer, "Class, Race, and Chicano Oppression," in *Socialist Revolution* 5 (1975), pp. 71–99; Denise Segura, "Labor Market Stratification: The Chicana Experience," *Berkeley Journal of Sociology* 29 (1984), pp. 57–91.

21. Marta Tienda and P. Guhleman, "The Occupational Position of Employed Hispanic Women," in G. J. Borjas and M. Tienda, eds., *Hispanics in the U.S. Economy* (New York: Academic Press, 1985), pp. 243–273.

22. Edgar J. Kranau, Vicki Green, and Gloria Valencia-Weber, "Acculturation and the Hispanic Woman: Attitudes towards Women, Sex-Role Attribution, Sex-Role Behavior, and Demographics," *Hispanic Journal of Behavioral Sciences* 4 (1982), pp. 21–40; Alfredo Mirande and Evangelina Enriquez, *La Chicana, The Mexican American Woman* (Chicago: The University of Chicago Press, 1979).

23. Kranau, Green, and Valencia-Weber, "Acculturation and the Hispanic Woman," pp. 21–40; Alfredo Mirande, *The Chicano Experience: An Alternative Perspective* (Notre Dame: University of Notre Dame Press, 1985).

24. Vilma Ortiz and Rosemary Santana Cooney, "Sex-Role Attitudes and Labor Force Participation among Young Hispanic Females and Non-Hispanic White Females," *Social Science Quarterly* 65 (June, 1984), pp. 392–400.

25. Susan E. Keefe and Amado M. Padilla, *Chicano Ethnicity* (Albuquerque, NM: University of New Mexico Press, 1987); Richard H. Mendoza, "Acculturation and Sociocultural Variability," in J. L. Martinez Jr. and R. H. Mendoza, eds., *Chicano Psychology,* 2nd ed. (New York: Academic Press, 1984), pp. 61–75.

26. Maxine Baca Zinn, "Mexican-American Women in the Social Sciences," *Signs: Journal of Women in Culture and Society* 8 (1982), pp. 259–272. M. Baca Zinn, "Employment and Education of Mexican-American Women: The Interplay of Modernity and Ethnicity in Eight Families," *Harvard Educational Review* 50 (February 1980), pp. 47–62. M. Baca Zinn, "Chicano Family Research: Conceptual Distortions and Alternative Directions," *Journal of Ethnic Studies* 7 (1979) pp. 59–71.

27. For additional information on the methods and sample selection, I refer the reader to Denise A. Segura, "Chicanas and Mexican Immigrant Women in the Labor Market: A Study of Occupational Mobility and Stratification," unpublished Ph.D. dissertation, Department of Sociology, University of California, Berkeley (1986).

28. The ages of the Chicanas range from 23 to 42 years. The Mexicanas reported ages from 24 to 45. The age profile indicates that most of the women were in peak childbearing years.

29. Denise A. Segura, "Chicanas and Mexican Immigrant Women in the Labor Market."

30. For an example, see Betsy Wearing, *The Ideology of Motherhood, A Study of Sydney Suburban Mothers* (Sydney: George Allen and Unwin, 1984).

31. For an example, see Nancy Chodorow, *The Reproduction of Mothering* (Berkeley: University of California Press, 1979).

32. Manuel Ramirez III and Alfredo Castaneda, *Cultural Democracy, Bicognitive Development, and Education* (New York: Academic Press, 1974); Robert F. Peck and Rogelio Diaz-Guerrero, "Two Core-Culture Patterns and the Diffusion of Values Across Their Borders," *International Journal of Psychology* 2 (1967), pp. 272–282; Javier I. Escobat and E. T. Randolph, "The Hispanic and Social Networks," in R. M. Becerra, M. Karno, and J. I. Escobar, eds., *Mental Health and Hispanic Americans: Clinical Perspectives* (New York: Grune and Stratton, 1982).

33. Alfredo Mirande and Evangelina Enriquez, *La Chicana, The Mexican American Woman* (Chicago: The University of Chicago Press, 1979); Margarita Melville, "Introduction" and "Matrascence" in M. B. Melville, ed., *Twice a Minority: Mexican American Women* (St. Louis: The C.V. Mosby Co., 1980), pp. 1–16; Gloria Anzaldúa, *Borderlands, La Frontera: The New Mestiza* (San Francisco: Spinsters/Aunt Lute Book Co., 1987); Linda C. Fox, "Obedience and Rebellion: Re-Vision of Chicana Myths of Motherhood," *Women's Studies Quarterly* (Winter, 1983), pp. 20–22.

34. Talcott Parsons and Robert Bales, *Family, Socialization, and Interaction Processes* (New York: Free Press, 1955); Robert H. Bradley and Bettye M. Caldwell, "The Relation of Infants' Home Environments to Achievement Test Performance in First Grade: A Follow-up Study," *Child Development* 55 (1984), pp. 803–809; Toby L. Parcel and Elizabeth G. Menaghan, "Maternal Working Conditions and Child Verbal Facility: Studying the Intergenerational Transmission of Inequality from Mothers to Young Children," *Social Psychology Quarterly* 53 (1990), pp. 132–147; Avshalom Caspi and Glen H. Elder, "Emergent Family Patterns: The Intergenerational Construction of Problem Behavior and Relationships," in R. Hinde and J. Stevenson Hinde, eds., *Understanding Family Dynamics* (New York: Oxford University Press, 1988).

35. For a full discussion of the interplay between economic goals and economic status of the respondents and their employment decisions, I refer the reader to Denise Segura, "The Interplay of Familism and Patriarchy on Employment among Chicana and Mexican Immigrant Women," in the *Renato Rosaldo Lecture Series Monograph* 5 (Tucson, AZ: The University of Arizona, Center for Mexican American Studies, 1989), pp. 35–53.

36. Two of the Mexicanas reported that their mothers had died while they were toddlers and therefore they were unable to discuss their economic roles.

37. Patricia M. Fernandez-Kelly, "Mexican Border Industrialization, Female Labor-Force Participation and Migration," in J. Nash and M. P. Fernandez-Kelly, eds., *Women, Men, and the International Division of Labor* (Albany: State University of New York Press, 1983), pp. 205–223; Sylvia Guendelman and Auristela Perez-Itriago, "Double Lives: The Changing Role of Women in Seasonal Migration," *Women's Studies* 13 (1987), pp. 249–271; Reynaldo Baca and Dexter Bryan, "Mexican Women, Migration and Sex Roles," *Migration Today* 13 (1985), pp. 14–18.

38. Research indicates religious involvement plays an important role in gender beliefs. See Ross K. Baker, Laurily K. Epstein, and Rodney O. Forth, "Matters of Life and Death: Social, Political, Religious Correlates of Attitudes on Abortion," *American Politics Quarterly* 9 (1981), pp. 89–102; Charles E. Peek and Sharon Brown, "Sex Prejudice among White Protestants: Like or Unlike Ethnic Prejudice?" *Social Forces* 59 (1980), pp. 169–185. Of particular interest for the present study is that involvement in fundamentalist Christian churches is positively related to adherence to traditional gender role ideology. See Clyde Wilcox and Elizabeth Adell Cook, "Evangelical Women and Feminism: Some Additional Evidence," *Women and Politics* 9 (1989), pp. 27–49; Clyde Wilcox, "Religious Attitudes and Anti-Feminism: An Analysis of the Ohio Moral Majority," *Women and Politics* 48 (1987), pp. 1041–1051. Half of the Mexicanas (and all but two Chicanas) adhered to the Roman Catholic religion; half belonged to various fundamentalist Christian churches (e.g., Assembly of God). Two Chicanas belonged to other Protestant denominations. I noticed that the women who belonged to the Assembly of God tended to both work full-time in the labor market and voice the strongest convictions of male authority in the family. During their interviews many of the women brought out the Bible and showed me the biblical passages that authorized husbands to "rule" the family. Catholic women also voiced traditional beliefs regarding family structure but did not invoke God.

39. Frances Rothstein, "Women and Men in the Family Economy: An Analysis of the Relations Between the Sexes in Three Peasant Communities," *Anthropological Quarterly* 56 (1983), pp. 10–23. Ruth Schwartz Cowan, "Women's Work, Housework, and History: The Historical Roots of Inequality in Work-Force Participation," in N. Gerstel and H. E. Gross, eds., *Families and Work* (Philadelphia: Temple University, 1987), pp. 164–177. Louise A. Tilly and Joan W. Scott, *Women, Work, and Family* (New York: Holt, Rinehart, and Winston, 1978).

40. Jessie Bernard, "The Rise and Fall of the Good Provider Role," *American Psychologist* 36 (1981), pp. 1–12; J. Bernard, *The Future of Motherhood* (New York: Penguin Books, 1974); Jane C. Hood, "The Provider Role: Its Meaning and Measurement," *Journal of Marriage and the Family* 48 (May, 1986), pp. 349–359.

41. Lorraine O. Walker and Mary Ann Best, "Well-Being of Mothers with Infant Children: A Preliminary Comparison of Employed Women and Homemakers," *Women and Health* 17 (1991), pp. 71–88; William J. Doherty and Richard H. Needle, "Psychological Adjustment and Substance Use among Adolescents Before and After a Parental Divorce," *Child Development* 62 (1991), pp. 328–337; Eugene E. Clark and William Ramsey, "The Importance of Family and Network of Other Relationships in Children's Success in School," *International Journal of Sociology of the Family* 20 (1990), pp. 237–254.

42. Rosabeth Moss Kanter, *Men and Women of the Corporation* (New York: Basic Books, 1977).

43. John M. Chavez and Raymond Buriel, "Reinforcing Children's Effort: A Comparison of Immigrant, Native-Born Mexican American and Euro-American Mothers," *Hispanic Journal of Behavioral Sciences* 8 (1986), pp. 127–142. Raymond Buriel, "Integration with Traditional Mexican-American Culture

and Sociocultural Adjustment" in J. L. Martinez, Jr. and R. H. Mendoza, eds., *Chicano Psychology,* 2nd ed. (New York: Academic Press, 1984), pp. 95–130; Leo R. Chavez, "Households, Migration and Labor Market Participation: The Adaptation of Mexicans to Life in the United States," *Urban Anthropology* 14 (1985), pp. 301–346.

44. Raymond Buriel, "Integration with Traditional Mexican-American Culture and Sociocultural Adjustment," in J. L. Martinez, Jr. and R. H. Mendoza, eds., *Chicano Psychology,* 2nd ed. (New York: Academic Press, 1984), pp. 95–130. In their analysis of differences in educational goals among Mexican-Americans, Buriel and his associates found that: "third-generation Mexican Americans felt less capable of fulfilling their educational objectives." See Raymond Buriel, Silverio Caldaza, and Richard Vasquez, "The Relationship of Traditional Mexican American Culture to Adjustment and Delinquency among Three Generations of Mexican American Adolescents," *Hispanic Journal of Behavioral Sciences* 4 (1982), p. 50. Similar findings were reported by Nielsen and Fernandez: "we find that students whose families have been in the U.S. longer have *lower* [their emphasis] aspirations than recent immigrants." See Francois Nielsen and Roberto M. Fernandez, *Hispanic Students in American High Schools: Background Characteristics and Achievement* (Washington D.C.: United States Government Printing Office, 1981), p. 76.

In their analysis of Hispanic employment, Bean and his associates reported an unexpected finding—that English-proficient Mexican women exhibit a greater "constraining influence of fertility" on their employment vis-à-vis Spanish-speaking women. They speculate that more acculturated Mexican women may have "a greater desire for children of higher quality," and therefore "be more likely to devote time to the informal socialization and education of young children." They wonder "why this should hold true for English-speaking but not Spanish-speaking women." See Frank D. Bean, C. Gray Swicegood, and Allan G. King, "Role Incompatibility and the Relationship between Fertility and Labor Supply among Hispanic Women" in G. J. Borjas and M. Tienda, eds., *Hispanics in the U.S. Economy* (New York: Academic Press, 1985), p. 241.

R E A D I N G   3 0

Race and "Value": Black and White Illegitimate Babies, 1945–1965

RICKIE SOLINGER

There are two histories of single pregnancy in the post-World War II era, one for Black women and one for white. But for girls and women of both races, being single and pregnant has revealed that, either publicly or privately, their fertility can become a weapon used by others to keep such females vulnerable, defenseless, dependent and, without male protection, in danger. One aspect of single pregnancy that sharply and powerfully illustrates both the common vulnerability of unwed mothers and the racially distinct treatment they have received is the question of what an

Rickie Solinger, "Race and 'Value': Black and White Illegitimate Babies. 1945–1965" from *Mothering: Ideology, Experience, and Agency,* edited by Evelyn Nakano Glenn, Grace Chang, and Linda Rennie Forcey. Copyright © 1994 by Routledge. Reprinted with the permission of Routledge, Inc.

unmarried girl or woman can or will do with her illegitimate child.

Throughout my study of unwed pregnancy in the pre-*Roe v. Wade* era,[1] racially distinct ideas about the "value" of the illegitimate baby surface again and again as central to an unmarried mother's fate. In short, after World War II, the white bastard child was no longer the child nobody wanted. The Black illegitimate baby became the child white politicians and taxpayers loved to hate. The central argument of this essay is that the "value" of illegitimate babies has been quite different in different historical eras, and that in the United States during the mid-twentieth century, the emergence of racially specific attitudes toward illegitimate babies, including ideas about what to do with them, fundamentally shaped the experiences of single mothers.

Social, cultural, and economic imperatives converged in the postwar era in such a way as to sanction very narrow and rigid, but different, options for Black and white unwed mothers, no matter what their personal preferences. Black single mothers were expected to keep their babies, as most unwed mothers, Black and white, had done throughout the history of the United States. Unmarried white mothers, for the first time in this country's history, were urged to put their babies up for adoption. These racially specific prescriptions exacerbated racism and racial antagonism in postwar America, and have influenced the politics of female fertility into our own time.

During the Progressive era of the late nineteenth and early twentieth centuries up through the 1930s, social commentators and social service professionals typically considered an illegitimate baby a "child of sin," the product of a mentally deficient mother.[2] As such, this child was tainted and undesirable. The girl or woman, Black or white, who gave birth to it was expected by family, by the community, and by the state to bring it up. Commentators assumed that others rarely wanted a child who stood to inherit the sinful character—the mental and moral weaknesses—of its parent. Before World War II, state laws and institutional regulations supported this mandate, not so much because there were others vying for the babies, but so as to ensure that the mothers would not abandon the infants. State legislators in Minnesota and elsewhere required mothers seeking care in maternity homes to breast-feed their babies for three months and more, long enough to establish unseverable bonds between infant and mother.[3]

Prewar experts stressed that the biology of illegitimacy stamped the baby permanently with marks of mental and moral deficiency, and affirmed that moral conditions were embedded in and revealed by these biological events.[4] Likewise, the unwed mother's pregnancy both revealed her innate biological and moral shortcomings and condemned her, through the illicit conception and birth, to carry the permanent stain of biological and moral ruin. The biological experience she underwent was tied to her moral status in a fixed, direct, and inexorable relationship. Equally important, her motherhood was immutable. While the deficiencies, the stain, and her ruination violated her biological integrity, as well as her social and moral standing in the community, the unwed mother's maternal relation to the child was not compromised. That was also fixed directly and inexorably by the biological facts of conception and birth.

These attitudes reflected, in part, the importance of bridal virginity and marital conception in mainstream American culture. They also reflected early twentieth-century ideas among moral and medical authorities regarding the strong link between physical, mental, and moral degeneracy and the degeneracy of sex. Until the 1940s, illegitimacy usually carried one meaning; cultural, racial, or psychological determinants which admitted group or individual variability were not sought to explain its occurrence. In this prewar period, social, religious, and educational leaders rarely called for the rehabilitation of unwed mothers or suggested that there were steps they could take to restore their marriageability and their place in the community. What was lost could not be regained; what was acquired could not be cast off. Consequently, most unwed mothers did not have choices to make in that era about the disposition of the bastard child.

WHITE UNWED MOTHERS AND THEIR BABIES: THE POSTWAR ADOPTION MANDATE

After the war, state-imposed breast-feeding regulations and institutional policies asserting the immutability of the white unwed mother's relationship to her illegitimate baby became harder to sustain in the face of a complex and changing set of social conditions. First, the demographic facts of single pregnancy were changing. White birth control and abortion remained illegal and hard to obtain. More girls and women were participating in nonmarital, heterosexual intercourse; thus more of them became pregnant and carried babies to term.[5] As nonmarital sex and pregnancy became more common (and then very common during the later postwar period), it became increasingly difficult to sequester, punish, and insist on the permanent ruination of ever larger numbers of girls and women. This was particularly the case since many of these single pregnant females were members of the growing proportion of the population that considered itself middle class. As a result, it became increasingly difficult for parents and the new service professionals, themselves members of the middle class, to sanction treating "our daughters" as permanently ruined.

In addition, a strain of postwar optimism emerged that rejected the view that the individual, white, unwed mother was at the mercy of harmful environmental or other forces having the power to determine her fate. The modern expert offered the alternative claim that illegitimacy reflected an emotional and psychological, not environmental or biological, disorder. It was, in general, a symptom of individual, treatable neuroses. Reliance on the psychological explanation redeemed both American society and the individual female. Moreover, by moving the governing imperative from the body (biology) to the mind (psychology), all of the fixed relationships previously defining white illegitimacy became mutable, indeterminate, even deniable.

Psychological explanations transformed the white unwed mother from a genetically tainted unfortunate into a maladjusted woman who could be cured. While there was no solvent that could remove the biological stain of illegitimacy, the neuroses that fostered illegitimacy could respond to treatment. The white out-of-wedlock child, therefore, was no longer a flawed by-product of innate immorality and low intelligence.[6] The child's innocence was restored and its adoptability established. At the same time, psychologists argued that white unwed mothers, despite their deviant behavior, could be rehabilitated, and that a successful cure rested in large measure on the relinquishment of the child.[7] The white unwed mother no longer had an immutable relationship to her baby.

In postwar America, the social conditions of motherhood, along with notions about the psychological status of the unwed mother, became more important than biology in defining white motherhood. Specifically, for the first time, it took more than a baby to make a white girl or woman into a mother. Without a preceding marriage, a white female could not achieve true motherhood. Leontine Young, the prominent authority on social casework theory in the area of unwed mothers, cautioned in 1954, "The caseworker has to clarify for herself the differences between the feelings of the normal [married] woman for her baby and the fantasy use of the child by the neurotic unmarried mother."[8] Accepting these new imperatives, social authorities insisted on the centrality of the male to female adult roles, thereby offsetting postwar concerns that women were aggressively undermining male prerogatives in the United States. Experts explained that the unwed mother who came to terms with the baby's existence, symbolically or concretely, and relinquished the child, enhanced her ability to "function [in the future] as a healthy wife and mother."[9]

Release from the biological imperative represented a major reform in the treatment of the many white unwed mothers who desperately desired a way out of trouble, a way to undo their life-changing mistake. The rising rate and numbers of white single pregnancy, particularly among unmarried, middle-class women, would have created an ever larger number of ruined girls and women if unwed mothers continued to have no option but to keep their illegitimate children. In a postwar society that increasingly privileged couples, marriage, children, families, and confor-

mity, this prospect would not have been a happy one. The option of placing an illegitimate child for adoption became, in a sense, an unplanned but fortuitous safety valve for white girls and women who became unwed mothers but—thanks to the sanctioning of adoption—could go on to become properly married wives and mothers soon thereafter.

This arrangement could work only if there was a sizable population of white couples who wanted to adopt infants, and who didn't mind if the babies had been born to unwed mothers. In the postwar period, this condition was met in part because the postwar family imperative put new pressures on infertile couples who in the past would have remained childless. A social scientist in the mid-1950s referred to illegitimate babies as "the silver lining in a dark cloud":

> Over one in ten of all marriages are involuntarily childless. Since most of these couples desire to adopt a baby, illegitimacy is a blessing to [them]. Curiously, from their standpoint there are not enough illegitimate births because most of these couples must wait one or two or three years in order to adopt a baby, and some are never able to have one because there is not enough for all who want them.[10]

In the early 1950s a leading social work theorist, using what was becoming a popular metaphor, worried about "the tendency growing out of the demand for babies to regard unmarried mothers as breeding machines . . . [by people intent] upon securing babies for quick adoptions."[11]

Through adoption, then, the unwed mother could put the mistake—both the baby *qua* baby, and the proof of nonmarital sexual experience—behind her. Her parents were not stuck with a ruined daughter and a bastard grandchild for life. And the baby could be brought up in a normative family, by a couple prejudged to possess all the attributes and resources necessary for successful parenthood.

Some unmarried pregnant girls considered abortion the best way to efface their mistake, but the possibility in the mid-1950s of getting a safe, legal, hospital abortion was slim, in fact, slimmer than it had been in the prewar decades. If a girl or woman knew about hospital abortions, she might appeal to a hospital abortion committee, a (male) panel of the director of obstetrics/gynecology, and the chiefs of medicine, surgery, neuropsychiatry and pediatrics. In hospitals, including Mt. Sinai in New York, which set up an abortion committee in 1952, the panel of doctors met once a week and considered cases of women who could bring letters from two specialists diagnosing them as psychologically impaired and unfit to be mothers.[12]

By the early 1950s, doctors claimed that new procedures and medications had eliminated the need for almost all medically indicated abortions.[13] That left only psychiatric grounds, which might have seemed promising for girls and women desperate not to have a child.[14] After all, psychiatric explanations were in vogue, and white unwed mothers were categorically diagnosed as deeply neurotic, or worse. There was, however, a catch. These abortion committees had been set up to begin with because their very existence was meant to reduce requests for "therapeutic" abortions, which they did.[15] It was, in fact, a matter of pride and competition among hospitals to have the highest ratio of births to abortions on record.[16] But even though psychiatric illness was the only remaining acceptable basis for request, many doctors did not believe in these grounds. A professor of obstetrics in a large university hospital said, "We haven't done a therapeutic abortion for psychiatric reasons in ten years. . . . We don't recognize psychiatric indications."[17] So an unwed pregnant girl or woman could be diagnosed and certified as disturbed, probably at considerable cost, but she couldn't convince the panel that she was sick enough. The committee may have, in fact, agreed with the outside specialists that the abortion petitioner was psychotic, but the panel often claimed the problem was temporary, with sanity recoverable upon delivery.[18]

The doctors were apparently not concerned with questions about when life begins. They were very concerned with what they took to be their responsibility to protect and preserve the links between femininity, maternity, and marriage. One doctor spoke for many of his colleagues when he complained of the "clever, scheming women, simply trying to hoodwink the psychiatrist and obstetrician" in their appeals for permission for abortions.[19] The mere request, in fact, was taken, according to another doctor, "as proof [of the petitioner's] inability and failure to live through the destiny of being a woman."[20] If such permission were granted, one claimed, the woman "will become an unpleasant person to live with and possibly lose her glamour as a wife. She will gradually lose conviction in playing a female role."[21] An angry committee member, refusing to grant permission to one woman, asserted, "Now that she has had her fun, she wants us to launder her dirty underwear. From my standpoint, she can sweat this one out."[22]

For many doctors, however, condemning the petitioner to sweat it out was not sufficient punishment. In the mid-1950s, in Maryland, a doctor would almost never agree to perform a therapeutic abortion unless he sterilized the woman at the same time.[23] The records of a large, midwestern, general hospital showed that between 1941 and 1950, seventy-five percent of the abortions performed there were accompanied by sterilization.[24] The bottom line was that, if you were single and pregnant (and without rich or influential parents who might, for example, make a significant philanthropic gesture to the hospital), your chances with the abortion committee were pretty bleak. Thousands of unhappily pregnant women each year got illegal abortions, but for thousands of others, financially, morally, or otherwise unable to arrange for the operation, adoption seemed their only choice.

Service agencies, however, found the task of implementing the adoption mandate complicated. Many who worked with white unwed mothers in maternity homes, adoption agencies, or public welfare offices in this period had to braid unmatched strands into a coherent plan. Agency workers were deeply uneasy about separating babies from the one individual who until recently had been historically and culturally designated as best suited, no matter what her marital status, to care for her own baby. In addition, the community response to out-of-wedlock pregnancy and maternity in the United States had historically been punitive.[25] Keeping mother and child together was simultaneously in the child's best interest and the earned wages of sin for the unwed mother. Until the postwar era, most social workers had trained and practiced in this tradition.[26]

After World War II, social workers struggled to discard the two most basic assumptions that had previously guided their work with white unwed mothers. These girls and women were no longer considered the best mothers for their babies. And they would no longer be expected to pay for their illicit sexual experience and illegitimate pregnancy by living as ruined women and outcast mothers of bastard children. Social workers were now to offer them a plan which would protect them from lasting stigma and rehabilitate them for normative female roles. The psychological literature supporting definitions of unwed mothers as not-mothers, the interest of many white couples in obtaining newborn babies, and postwar concepts of family helped social workers accept new ideas about the disposition of illegitimate white babies.

After the war, in all parts of the country, public agencies, national service organizations, and maternity homes allocated the resources and developed techniques for separating mother and child. Services became increasingly so streamlined that in many maternity homes, such as the Florence Crittenton Home in Houston, "Babies [went] directly from the hospital to children's [adoption] agencies."[27] Indeed, public and private agencies were functioning in an environment in which the separation of single mother and child was becoming the norm. In Minnesota, for example, in 1925 there were two hundred such separations; in 1949, one thousand; between 1949 and 1955, approximately seventeen hundred each year. Nationally, by 1955, ninety thousand babies born out of wedlock were being placed for adoption, an 80 percent increase since 1944.[28]

To meet the demand and to justify their own existence, agencies and individual operators not infrequently resorted to questionable tactics, including selling babies for profit. When the federal government undertook to investigate widespread coercive and profit-oriented adoption practices in the United States in the 1950s, the task was assigned to Senator Estes Kefauver's Subcommittee to Investigate Juvenile Delinquency. This committee was charged with redressing the problem of adoption for profit and assuring the "suitability of the home" for adoptable children, a criterion which could not, by definition, be met in homes headed by unmarried mothers.[29] While illegitimate pregnancy and babies had, in the past, been a private matter handled by family members, perhaps assisted by charity workers, by mid-century these issues had become public concerns and public business.

The Kefauver committee and the organizations and individuals it investigated defined white unmarried mothers out of their motherhood. If not by law, then de facto, they were not parents. This judgment was in line with and supported various forms of state control over single, pregnant girls and women and those who might become pregnant, including, of course, the state's formal and informal proscriptions against birth control for unmarried girls and women, its denial of access to safe, legal abortion, and its tolerance in many places of unsafe, illegal abortions. The state determined what types of agencies and individuals an unmarried mother could deal with in planning for her child, and either strongly suggested or legislated which ones were "morally wrong." These state prerogatives allowed some agencies and individuals to abuse and exploit childbearing, single, white women.

A very articulate, eighteen-year-old, unmarried mother from Minnesota wrote to her governor in August 1950, illustrating how some public agencies took direct action to separate white babies from their mothers, even against the mother's will. She said that a welfare worker in her city told her she could not keep her baby, "that the baby should be brought up by both a mother and a father." Having gotten no satisfaction, she wrote in frustration and anger to President Truman:

With tears in my eyes and sorrow in my heart I'm trying to defend the rights and privileges which every citizen in the United States is supposed to enjoy under our Constitution [but are] denied me and my baby. . . . The Welfare Department refuses to give me my baby without sufficient cause or explanation. . . . I have never done any wrong and just because I had a baby under such circumstances the welfare agency has no right to condemn me and to demand my child be placed [for adoption].[30]

A year earlier, a young man living in Sterling, Colorado, wrote to the Children's Bureau about a similar case. In this situation, a young man and a young deaf woman had conceived a baby out of wedlock but planned to marry. When the man went to the Denver Welfare Department for assistance a few days before the baby was born, he found that the baby had already been targeted for adoption.

This case, in particular, demonstrates a couple of key assumptions underlying the behavior of some agency workers in matters of out-of-wedlock adoptions. The young mother was deaf. As a handicapped person and an unmarried girl, her maternity, as well as her child, was considered illegitimate, and could be rightfully terminated by the authorities. Physically defective women had curtailed rights as mothers, just as physically defective illegitimate babies had diminished opportunities to join the middle class. This case also suggests the very important notion that white babies were so valuable because in postwar America, they were born not only untainted but also *unclassed*. A poor, "white trash" teenager could have a white baby in Appalachia; it could be adopted by an upper-middle-class couple in Westport, Connecticut, and the baby would, in that transaction, become upper-middle-class also.

Finally, this case illustrates that agency workers believed that a successful separation often depended on an early and very quick transaction. This was noticed by contemporaries, including the authors of a state-certified report on adoption in Cook County, Illinois, that warned about the problems that arose when "mothers come into court service division to sign a consent either on the day they are released from the hospital, or shortly thereafter [and] are physically and emotionally upset to the extent that they are not capable of making rational decisions."[31]

Courts also facilitated adoption abuse. A chief probation officer in the Richmond County, Alabama, Juvenile Court spent a great deal of her time finding and "freeing" white babies for adoption, using her position to legitimize these activities. One unwed mother told of her encounter with the officer, a Miss Hamilton. She said:

Several hours after delivery [Miss Hamilton] informed me that my baby had been born dead. She told me that if I signed a paper she had, no one, my family or friends, would know about the situation, and that everything would be cleared up easily. She described the paper as being a consent authorizing the burial of the child. . . . I signed the paper without really looking at it, as I was in a very distressed and confused condition at the time.

This young woman went on to say that, "Two years later I was shocked to receive in the mail adoption papers from the Welfare Department in California since I was under the impression that the child was deceased."[32]

Illegalities and abuse existed in some mainstream institutions, but a great many of the worst abuses were committed by individual baby brokers—lawyers, doctors, and non-professionals cashing in on the misfortune of unwed mothers. In postwar, consumerist America, institutions promoted services and attitudes to protect the out-of-wedlock child from market-driven deals and to see that it was well placed. On the other hand, these same institutions were themselves behaving in market-oriented ways as they promoted a specific, socially beneficial product: the two-parent/two-plus-child family. This double message justified the baby brokers' commoditylike treatment of unwed mothers and their babies. Charlton G. Blair, a lawyer who handled between thirty and sixty adoptions a year in the late 1950s, justified his operation by denying he ever "paid one red cent" to a prospective mother of an illegitimate child to persuade her to part with the baby. But in suggesting why the adopting parents were willing to pay up to $1,500 for a child, which included the lawyer's fee, Blair defined his sense of the transaction very clearly: "If they're willing to pay $3,000 for an automobile these days, I don't see why they can't pay this much for a child."[33] A baby broker in Texarkana, Texas, boasted to an employee that she had sold 993 illegitimate babies throughout the United States and that she wanted to make it one thousand before she died.[34]

A case which dramatically captures the plight of poor, white, unwed mothers was presented at the Kefauver hearings by Mary Grice, an investigative reporter for the *Wichita Beacon*. Grice testified about a woman, "Mrs. T.," who had been in the adoption business since 1951 or 1952. "Mrs. T." warehoused unwed, pregnant girls in the basement of her home. "She would have them on cots for prospective adoptive parents [who] would come in and she would take them downstairs, and she would point to the girls and say, 'Point out the girl that you want to be the

mother of your child.' " Grice's investigation revealed that "Mrs. T." kept on average seven unmarried mothers in her basement at a time, and that she would oversee a number of the deliveries herself in the basement. According to Grice, between 150 and 164 adoptions each year of this sort were taking place in Sedgwick County, Kansas. "Mrs. T." often collaborated with Grace Schauner, a Wichita abortionist. Unmarried pregnant girls and women would first see Schauner, and if they decided not to have an abortion, they would be referred to "Mrs. T.," who would "care for them and sell their infants after birth."[35]

"Mrs. T's" girls were the ones whose class, gender, and race combined to render them most vulnerable. Because they were poor, they did not have the information or other resources to resist baby-market operators. Because they were female (specifically, white females), their socially mandated shame precluded self-protection and motherhood. Because they were white, their babies had value. This combination of poverty, race and gender—in a context which defined white unwed mothers as not-mothers, and defined their babies as valuable—put some white unwed mothers in a position of extreme vulnerability.

Again, there is no question that for many white unwed mothers, the opportunity to place their babies independently meant that they could get exactly what they needed when they needed it: money to live on, shelter, medical care, and assurances about the placement of the baby, all with no questions asked. These girls and women were often spared the delays, the layers of authority, the invasions of privacy, the permanent black mark engraved in the files of the welfare department, and they were spared the pressure to reveal the father's name, all of which characterized the bureaucratic agency approach.[36] Their experience demonstrated how difficult it was for institutions to perform simultaneously as agents of social control and as sources of humanitarian assistance for the needy and vulnerable.

The stories of unwed mothers abused by the baby market reveal how class, gender, and (white) race together created the possibilities to use these girls and women for profit. Cultural constructions of female sexuality and maternity in the postwar decades, and the sanctions against sexual and maternal nonconformity, sent unwed mothers with few resources into the anonymous marketplace, which offered, simultaneously, protection and danger.

An intruder in the courtroom in Miami, Florida, where a section of the Kefauver hearings was held in November 1955, expressed the frustration of some girls and women who felt they had lost control over the disposition of their illegitimate children. This woman stood up, unbidden, and lectured the men before her in a loud voice. She said,

> Excuse me. I am not leaving no court. . . . You have to carry these children nine months and then you have them taken away by the Catholic Charities, and then they throw you out and drag you all over the street. . . . I'm no drunk, I'm no whore. . . . I gave birth to two children and had them taken away from me. I don't sleep nights thinking about my children. What do you people care? Don't take my picture. You people have no feelings at all. That man [a judge testifying that there are plenty of services available for unwed mothers] is sitting there and lying—lying. These people just take other people's children away from them. All that he has said is a lie. My baby was born . . . and I haven't seen it since. . . . How would you like it? Year after year you have to go to the people . . . and ask them why you can't have your children.[37]

Clark Vincent, a sociologist who closely followed the treatment of white unwed mothers in this era, offered the following vision of a world in the near future where the state would have unrestrained authority to determine who is a mother.

> If the demand for adoptable infants continues to exceed the supply; if more definitive research . . . substantiates that the majority of unwed mothers who keep their children lack the potential for "good motherhood"; and if there continues to be an emphasis through laws and courts on the "rights of the child" superseding the "rights of the parents"; then it is quite probable that in the near future unwed mothers will be "punished" by having their children taken away from them at birth. Such a policy would not be enacted nor labeled overtly as "punishment." Rather it would be implemented under such pressures and labels as "scientific finding," "the best interests of the child," "rehabilitation goals for the unwed mother," and the "stability of the family and society."[38]

THE BLACK UNWED MOTHER AND HER CHILD: A TAXPAYERS' ISSUE

In postwar America, there was only one public intention for white, unwed mothers and their babies: separate them.

Toward Black, single mothers and their babies, however, there were three broadly different public attitudes.[39] One attitude, often held by middle-of-the-road politicians, social service administrators, and practitioners, maintained that Blacks had babies out of wedlock because they were Negro, because they were ex-Africans and ex-slaves, irresponsible and immoral, but baby-loving. According to this attitude, the state and its institutions and agencies could essentially ignore breeding patterns, since Blacks would take care of their children themselves. And if Blacks did not, they were responsible for their own mess. Adopting Daniel Moynihan's famous phrase from this period, I call this public attitude toward Black illegitimacy *benign neglect*.

A second response to Black mothers and babies was *punitive*. The conservative, racist politicians who championed this position argued simply that the mothers were bad and should be punished. The babies were expendable because they were expensive and undesirable as citizens. Public policies could and should be used to punish Black unmarried mothers and their children in the form of legislation enabling states to cut them off from welfare benefits, and to sterilize or incarcerate "illegitimate mothers."[40]

I label the third way of seeing this group *benevolent reformist*. Employees at the United States Children's Bureau and many in the social work community who took this position maintained that Black girls and women who had children out of wedlock were just like whites who did the same. Both groups of females were equally disturbed and equally in need of help, particularly in need of social casework. Regarding the baby, benevolent reformers held that Black, unwed mothers should be accorded every opportunity to place the infant for adoption, just like whites.

Despite these different attitudes toward Black women and their babies, proponents of all three shared a great deal. First, they shared the belief that the Black, illegitimate baby was the product of pathology. This was the case whether it was a pathology grounded in race, as it was for the benign neglecters and the punishers, or in gender, as it was for the benevolent reformers. Second, all commentators agreed that the baby's existence justified a negative moral judgment about the mother and the mother-and-baby dyad. The Black illegitimate infant was proof of its mother's moral incapacities; its illegitimacy suggested its own probable tendencies toward depravity. Because of the eager market for white babies, this group was cleared of the charge of inherited moral taint, while Black babies were not. Indeed, proponents of each of the three perspectives agreed that the unwed, Black mother must, in almost every case, keep her baby. Where they differed was in explaining why this was so. The different answers reflected different strains of racism and carried quite different implications for public policies and practices regarding the Black, unmarried mother and her child.

The benign neglecters began to articulate their position at about the same time that the psychologists provided new explanations for white, single pregnancy. In tandem, these developments set Black and white, unwed mothers in different universes of cause and effect. According to these "experts," Black and white single mothers were different from each other in several ways. When Black, single girls and women had intercourse, it was a sexual, not a psychological, act, and Black mothers had "natural affection" for their children, whatever their birth status. The white, unwed mother had only neurotic feelings for her out-of-wedlock child. The "unrestrained sexuality" of Black women, and their capacity to love the resulting illegitimate children, were perceived as inbred traits, and unchangeable parts of Black culture.

Thus, by becoming mothers, even unwed mothers, Black women were simply doing what came naturally. There was no reason for social service workers or policymakers to interfere. It was also important in this regard that the operative concept of "culture" excised considerations of environment. Environment was not a primary factor in shaping female sexual behavior or the mother's relationship to her illegitimate baby. These were determined by "culture," an essentially biological construct. Therefore, since professionals could only have an impact on the immediate situation—and could not penetrate or rearrange Black "culture," it was doubly futile to consider interfering. The absence of services for these women and their children was justified in this way. Issues regarding Blacks and adoption were quickly dismissed by those who counseled neglect. Agencies claimed that Blacks didn't want to part with their babies, and, just as important, Black couples didn't want to adopt children.[41]

White policymakers and service providers often pointed to the Black grandmothers—willing, able, loving, and present—to justify their contentions that the Black family would take care of its own, and that no additional services were necessary. Yet when grandmothers rendered such service, policymakers labeled them "matriarchs" and blamed them for "faulty personality growth and for maladaptive functioning in children."[42] The mother was similarly placed in a double bind. She was denied services because she was black, an alleged cultural rather than a racial distinction,

and then she was held responsible for the personal and social consequences.[43] The social service system was, in this way, excused from responsibility or obligation to Black, unwed mothers.

The punishers, both Southern Dixiecrats and Northern racists, drew in part on the "cultural" argument to target both the unwed mother and her baby. They held that Black culture was inherited, and that the baby would likely be as great a social liability as its mother. Moreover, they claimed that for a poor, Black woman to have a baby was an act of selfishness, as well as of pathology, and deserved punishment.[44] Once the public came to believe that Black illegitimacy was not an innocuous social fact, but carried a direct and heavy cost to white taxpayers, many whites sanctioned their political representatives to target Black, unwed mothers and their babies for attack.[45]

The willingness to attack was expressed, in part, by a special set of tropes which drew on the language and concepts of the marketplace. The "value" assigned to the illegitimate child-as-commodity became useful in classifying the violation of the Black, unwed mother in a consumer society. Repeatedly, Black, unmarried mothers were construed as "women whose business is having illegitimate children."[46] This illicit "occupation" was portrayed as violating basic consumerist principles, including good value in exchange for a good price, for a product which, in general, benefits society. Black, unmarried mothers, in contrast, were said to offer bad value (Black babies) at a high price (taxpayer-supported welfare grants) to the detriment of society, demographically and economically. The behavior of these women—most of whom did not receive Aid to Dependent Children grants for their illegitimate children[47]— was construed as meeting only the consumerist principle that everything can, potentially, be a commodity. These women were accused of treating their reproductive capacities and their children as commodities, with assigned monetary values. From this perspective, Black, unmarried mothers were portrayed as "economic women," making calculated decisions for personal, financial gain.[48]

The precise economic principle most grossly violated by these women was, according to many, that they got something (ADC) for nothing (another Black baby); they were cheating the public with a bad sell. The fact that it was, overwhelmingly, a buyers' market for Black babies "proved" the valuelessness of these children, despite their expense to the taxpaying public.[49] White babies entered a healthy sellers' market, with up to ten couples competing for every one adoptable infant.[50]

Spokespeople for this point of view believed that Black, unmarried mothers should pay dearly for the bad bargain they foisted on society, especially on white taxpayers. But many felt that rather than paying for their sins, Black women were being paid, by ADC grants, an exchange which encouraged additional sexual and fiscal irresponsibility.[51] Thus, society was justified in punishing Black, unwed mothers. In addition, the Black unmarried woman, allegedly willing to trade on her reproductive function, willing to use her body and her child so cheaply, earned the state's equal willingness to regard her childbearing capacity cheaply, and take it away, for example, by sterilization legislation.

The ironic truth was that ADC benefits were such inadequate support (and employment and child care opportunities so meager or nonexistent) that government policies had the effect of causing, not responding to, the economic calculations a woman made that might lead to pregnancy. The average welfare payment per child, per month, was $27.29, with monthly averages less than half that amount in most Southern states.[52] The following encounter illustrates the relationship between illegitimacy and economics, from one woman's point of view.

> When the case analyst visited the family, the little girl came in with a new dress and shoes. The mother explained that it was the last day of school and the child had begged for new clothes like the other children had. She got them, but the mother's comment was, "I hope that dress does not cause me another baby."[53]

This mother's economic and sexual calculations were rooted in poverty and maternal concern, not in some desire to multiply inadequate stipends through additional pregnancies.

In Florida, the assumptions of welfare officials and legislators concerning the "business" intentions of Black, unwed mothers received a jolt in the early 1960s, when mothers withdrew from the ADC program rather than risk having their children taken away from them and sent, for example, to the homes of married relatives, under the state's "suitable home" law. This law aimed to punish illegitimate mothers who "persisted" in having babies, while saving taxpayers' money by reducing welfare rolls. "At least some [social workers] anticipated that among Negro families, the 'extended family pattern' would ease the pain of separation and rarely generate resistance to placement. But as one mother said, 'People give away puppies and kittens, but they don't give away their children.' "[54] In the face of the persistence of a slave owners' mentality among Florida's welfare professionals and politicians, and the commodization of children this view supported, Black women demonstrated their adherence to a value system which placed their children and their bodies outside of the economic nexus, as far as the government and the welfare system were concerned.[55]

The public's interest in casting Black, unwed mothers and their babies as consumer violators was reflected in opinion polls that suggested the American public wanted to withhold federal support, or food money, from illegitimate, Black babies.[56] Among dissenters were people who believed it was wrong "to deny food to children because of the sins of the parents."[57] Both groups, however, fell into a trap set by conservative politicians who found it politically profitable to associate Black illegitimacy in their constituent's minds with the rising costs of public welfare grants. The Aid to Dependent Children caseload increased in the postwar period for many reasons, including the basic increase in numbers of children and families, and the increase in households headed by women because of divorce, separation, desertion, *and* illegitimacy. Between 1953 and 1959, the number of families headed by women rose 12.8 percent, while the number of families rose only 8.3 percent.[58] While white sentiment was being whipped up to support punitive measures against Black "subsidized immorality,"[59] only about 16 percent of nonwhite, unwed mothers were receiving ADC grants.[60] Adoption, which was not an option for most Blacks, was the most important factor in removing white children from would-be ADC families. Of unwed, white mothers who kept their children, 30 percent, or nearly twice as large a percentage as Blacks, were receiving Aid to Dependent Children grants in 1959.[61] Yet in the minds of large segments of the white public, Black, unwed mothers were being paid, in welfare coin, to have children. The "suitable home" laws, which were originally designed, it was claimed, to protect the interests of children, were not instrumental in stopping those payments. The children in question represented low value to politicians leading the attacks on welfare costs. These were politicians who had no qualms about using Black, illegitimate children as pawns in their attempt to squash Black "disobedience" via morals charges.[62]

Led by Annie Lee Davis, a Black social worker at the United States Children's Bureau, many members of the social work community worked unceasingly to convert benign neglecters and punishers into benevolent reformers. Davis was a committed integrationist. She was dedicated to convincing the white social service establishment that Black, unmarried mothers needed and deserved the same services as their white counterparts. In 1948, Davis addressed this message to her colleagues: "Within minority groups, unmarried mothers suffer guilt and shame as in the majority group." She added, "I know there are those who will challenge this statement," but, she insisted, "In the process of adopting the cultural traits of the dominant group in America all groups are striving to be American."[63]

Davis insisted white public officials and social workers be brought to believe that Black, unwed mothers were psychologically and morally the equals of whites. Only then would Blacks be eligible for the best available services. Ironically, Davis believed that a key element of proof was to establish that Blacks were as interested in adoptive placements for their illegitimate babies as whites were urged to be. Her task was to convince her colleagues that lack of alternative options alone created the custom and the necessity that Blacks kept their illegitimate children.

Benevolent reformers typically took the position that it was unacceptable and potentially racist to assume that Blacks did not want every opportunity that whites had, including adoption. But it was extremely difficult for the reformers to suggest that some Black, single mothers wanted their children, and others did not. It was not simply unwed mothers and their babies at issue, it was the race. For the reformers, constructing an equivalency between Black and white unmarried mothers was the most promising and practical route to social services and social justice.

But even if a Black, single mother did consider placing her child for adoption, she knew that the likelihood that the agency would expeditiously approve a couple as adoptive parents was slim.[64] While a white, unwed mother could expect a rapid placement, the Black one knew that her child would be forced, in part because of agency practices, to spend months in foster homes or institutions before placement, if that was ever achieved. For example, adoption agencies frequently rejected Blacks who applied for babies, claiming they did not meet the agency's standards for adoptive parents. They also neglected to work with schools and hospitals in contact with Black, unwed mothers to improve referral services between these institutions and the agencies, because they feared recruiting Black babies when there might not be homes for them. In these ways the organizations that reformers depended on to provide services for Black, unwed mothers equal to those for whites, and to make it more possible for society to perceive these Blacks in the same way as they saw whites, did not hold up their end. The reformers had their integrationist vision, but the institutions of society would not cooperate, even when some Black, unwed mothers did.

In fact, the evidence from postwar Black communities suggests that the Black, unwed mother accepted responsibility for her baby as a matter of course,[65] even when she was sorry to have gotten pregnant.[66] A study in the mid-1960s cautioned the social work profession: "Social work wisdom is that Negroes keep because there is no place to give the baby up, but the study showed . . . that Negroes did not favor adoption, opportunities or their absence notwithstanding." Findings showed that the issue of disposition of the child was the only one that consistently yielded a difference between Black and white respondents, no matter whether they were the unwed mother, her parents, or professional staff. In fact, the Blacks revealed their determination to keep mother and child together and the whites their determination to effect separation, "no matter how [the investigator] varied the content of the questions."[67]

In the same period in Cincinnati, several researchers captured the comments of the mothers themselves. Some girls and women focused on the needs of the baby. One typical respondent claimed, "An innocent child should not be denied his mother's love." Joyce Ladner's subjects in another Midwestern city considered the illegitimate baby as "a child who had the right to be cared for and reared in the community of his parents without stigmatization."[68] Others in the Cincinnati study focused on the strength of their own needs, "I'd grieve myself to death if I let my baby go." A few predicted they would have had nervous breakdowns if they hadn't been allowed to keep their babies. A representative outlook drew on the sanctified status of motherhood: "The Lord suffered for you to have a baby. He will suffer for you to get food for the baby." Still others expressed themselves in forward-looking, practical terms, "You were less apt to have regrets if you kept the baby than if you let him go."[69]

For many Black, unwed mothers, the reasons to keep a baby were simply grounded in an immutable moral code of maternal responsibility. A young, Black woman said, "Giving a child away is not the sort of thing a good person would do"; and a teenager asserted, "My parents wouldn't let me give up the baby for adoption."[70] Two Black women in Philadelphia subscribed to this morality. One said:

> I sure don't think much of giving babies up for adoption. The mother mightn't be able to give it the finest and best in the world, but she could find a way like I did. My mother had thirteen heads and it was during the Depression. . . . *She* didn't give us away.

The other commented, "If you have a child, bring it up. Take the responsibility. Hard or easy, it's yours."[71]

The central question for all of these Black, single mothers was how good a mother you were, not whether you were legally married.[72] The overriding stimulus in structuring the personal decisions of these girls and women was a "powerful drive toward family unity, even if the family is not the socially approved one of father, mother and children."[73] In a study of thirty poor, single, Black mothers, only two told the investigators that they would advise another woman in their situation to give the baby up, and both cited difficulties with the welfare office as their reason.[74] The author of the study referred to the "vehemence" of most Black, single mothers about their decision to keep the child.[75]

Helen Harris Perlman, recognizing the negative attitudes of social workers toward girls and women who failed to relinquish illegitimate babies, counseled her colleagues in the 1960s, "Even if more opportunities for adoption of Negro babies become possible, there is a strong probability that most Negro mothers—indeed, most unwed mothers—will want to keep their babies."[76]

CONCLUSION

A research team in North Carolina investigating illegitimacy concluded in the early 1960s that one major difference between white and Black unwed mothers was that the white girl generally felt that a "new maturity" had come with the experience of conceiving out of wedlock. The team claimed that this was not true for the Black subjects, and explained: "The white subculture demands learning from experience," so the white unwed mother must learn her lesson. The white girl "has probably been encouraged to look within herself for the reasons for her mistake because the white subculture stresses individual responsibility for error."[77]

These observations capture a great deal of the intentionality underlying the white culture's treatment of unwed mothers under the adoption mandate. For these girls and women, the "lesson" was twofold: no baby without a husband; and no one is to blame but yourself. Learning the lesson meant stepping on the road to maturity and womanhood. The illegitimate child was an encumbrance or an obstacle to following this route. The ability to relinquish was constructed as the first, most crucial step in the right direction.

Joyce Ladner, in her study of Black women in the 1960s, dealt with the same issue—the relationship between illegitimacy and maturity. She suggested a strikingly different finding:

The adolescent Black girl who became pregnant out of wedlock changed her self-conception from one who was

approaching maturity to one who had attained the status of womanhood. . . . Mothers were quick to say that their daughters had become grown, that they have "done as much as I have done."[78]

The road to maturity for Black unwed mothers was unmediated. Maturity accompanied maternity, the baby's legal status notwithstanding.

Both Black and white women in the postwar era were subject to a definition of maturity that depended on motherhood. The most pervasive, public assumption about Black and white unwed mothers, however, was that their nonmarital childbearing did not constitute maternity in the culturally sanctioned sense. The treatment of these girls and women reinforced the notion that legitimation of sexuality and maternity was the province of the state and the community and was not the rights of individual girls and women. In the case of white, unwed mothers, the community (including the mother herself, and her family), with government support, was encouraged to efface episodes of illicit sex and maternity. Outside of marriage neither the sex nor the resulting child had "reality" in the community or in the mother's life. They became simply momentary mental aberrations. In the case of Black, unwed mothers, sexuality was brute biology and childbearing its hideous result. The state, with the support of public institutions, could deface the Black, single mother's dignity, diminish her resources, threaten her right to keep her child, and even threaten her reproductive capacity.

In both cases, the policies and practices which structured the meanings of race and gender, sexuality, and motherhood for unwed mothers were tied to social issues—such as the postwar adoption market for white babies, and the white, taxpaying public's hostile identification of ADC as a program to support Black, unwed mothers and their unwanted babies—which used single, pregnant women as resources and scapegoats.

In the immediate pre-*Roe v. Wade* era, the uses of race combined with the uses of gender, sexuality, and maternity in ways that dealt Black and white unwed mothers quite different hands. According to social and cultural intentions for the white, unwed mother and her baby, relinquishment of the baby was meant to place all scent of taint behind them and thus restore good value to both. The Black, unwed mother and her child, triply devalued, had all their troubles before them.

NOTES

1. This essay is taken from a larger study, *"Wake Up Little Susie": Single Pregnancy and Race in the pre-*Roe v. Wade *Era* (New York: Routledge, 1992).

2. See, for example, Charlotte Lowe, "Intelligence and Social Background of the Unmarried Mother," *Mental Hygiene* 4 (October 1927), pp. 783–794; and Henry C. Schumacher, M.D., "The Unmarried Mother: A Socio-Psychiatric Viewpoint," *Mental Hygiene* 4 (October 1927), pp. 775–782.

3. Maryland passed such a law in 1919 and Wisconsin in 1922. It was claimed that these laws would reduce high infant mortality rates, although they were never shown to do so. Maternity home residents were targeted since this group was considered most likely, in its search for secrecy, to abandon its babies. See Elza Virginia Dahlgren, "Attitudes of a Group of Unmarried Mothers toward the Minnesota Three Months Nursing Regulation and Its Application," M.A. thesis, University of Minnesota, 1940.

4. See, for example, Percy Kammerer, *The Unmarried Mother* (Boston: Little, Brown & Co., 1918) and Schumacher, "The Unmarried Mother."

5. Even though many studies published in this era claimed that rates of illicit coition were not rising in the postwar era, the fact that the illegitimacy rates and illegal abortion rates were higher than ever suggests otherwise. See, for example, Alfred C. Kinsey, Wardell B. Pomeroy, Clyde E. Martin, and Paul H. Gebhard, *Sexual Behavior in the Human Female* (Philadelphia: W. B. Saunders Company, 1953), chap. 8. Also see Phillips Cutright, "Illegitimacy in the United States: 1920–1968," in Charles F. Westoff and Robert Parke, Jr., eds., *Demographic and Social Aspects of Population Growth* (Washington, D.C.: Commission on Population Growth and the American Future), p. 384.

6. See Viviana A. Zelizer, *Pricing the Priceless Child: The Changing Social Value of Children* (New York: Basic Books, 1985) for an interesting discussion of related issues.

7. See, for example, Mary Lynch Crockett, "An Examination of Services to the Unmarried Mother in Relation to Age at Adoption Placement of the Baby," *Casework Papers, 1960* (New York: Columbia University Press, 1960), pp. 75–85.

8. Leontine Young, *Out of Wedlock* (New York: McGraw Hill, 1954), p. 216.

9. Janice P. Montague, "Acceptance or Denial—The Therapeutic Uses of the Mother/Baby Relationship," paper presented at the Florence Crittenton Association of America Northeast Conference, 1964.

10. Winston Ehrmann, "Illegitimacy in Florida II: Social and Psychological Aspects of Illegitimacy," *Eugenics Quarterly* 3 (December 1956), p. 227.

11. Leontine Young, "Is Money Our Trouble?" paper presented at the National Conference on Social Work, 1953.

12. Mary Calderone, ed., *Abortion in the United States* (New York: Harper and Brothers, 1958), pp. 92–93, 139; Alan Guttmacher, "Therapeutic Abortion: The Doctor's Dilemma," *Journal of Mt. Sinai Hospital* 21 (1954), p. 111; Lewis Savel,

"Adjudication of Therapeutic Abortion and Sterilization," in Edmund W. Overstreet, ed., *Therapeutic Abortion and Sterilization* (New York: Harper and Row, 1964), pp. 14–21.

13. Calderone, ed., *Abortion in the United States*, pp. 86–88.

14. See, for example, J. G. Moore and J. H. Randall, "Trends in Therapeutic Abortion: A Review of 137 Cases," *American Journal of Obstetrics and Gynecology* 63 (1952), p. 34.

15. Harry A. Pearce and Harold A. Ott, "Hospital Control of Sterilization and Therapeutic Abortion," *American Journal of Obstetrics and Gynecology* 60 (1950), p. 297; James M. Ingram, H.S.B. Treloar, G. Phillips Thomas, and Edward B. Rood, "Interruption of Pregnancy for Psychiatric Indications—A Suggested Method of Control," *Obstetrics and Gynecology* 29 (1967), pp. 251–55.

16. See, for example, Charles C. Dahlberg, "Abortion," in Ralph Slovenko, ed., *Sexual Behavior and the Law* (Springfield, IL.: Charles Thomas, 1965), p. 384.

17. Arthur Mandy, "Reflections of a Gynecologist," in Harold Rosen, ed., *Therapeutic Abortion* (New York: The Julian Press, 1954), p. 291.

18. Gregory Zillboorg, "The Clinical Issues of Postpartum Psychopathology Reactions," *American Journal of Obstetrics and Gynecology* 73 (1957), p. 305; Roy J. Heffernon and William Lynch, "What Is The Status of Therapeutic Abortion in Modern Obstetrics?" *American Journal of Obstetrics and Gynecology* 66 (1953), p. 337.

19. Nicholson J. Eastman, "Obstetric Forward," in Rosen, *Therapeutic Abortion*, p. xx.

20. Theodore Lidz, "Reflections of a Psychiatrist," in Rosen, *Therapeutic Abortion*, p. 279.

21. Flanders Dunbar, "Abortion and the Abortion Habit," in Rosen, *Therapeutic Abortion*, p. 27.

22. Mandy, "Reflections," p. 289.

23. Manfred Guttmacher, "The Legal Status of Therapeutic Abortion," in Rosen, *Therapeutic Abortion*, p. 183. Also see Nanette Davis, *From Crime to Choice: The Transformation of Abortion in America* (Westport CT.: Greenwood Press, 1985), p. 73; Johan W. Eliot, Robert E. Hall, J. Robert Willson, and Carolyn Hauser, "The Obstetrician's View," in Robert E. Hall, ed., *Abortion in a Changing World,* vol. 1 (New York: Columbia University Press, 1970), p. 93: Kenneth R. Niswander, "Medical Abortion Practice in the United States," in David T. Smith, ed., *Abortion and the Law* (Cleveland: The Press of Case Western Reserve University, 1967), p. 57.

24. David C. Wilson, "The Abortion Problem in the General Hospital," in Rosen, *Therapeutic Abortion*, pp. 190–1. Also see Myra Loth and H. Hesseltine, "Therapeutic Abortion at the Chicago Lying-In Hospital," *American Journal of Obstetrics and Gynecology* 72 (1956), pp. 304–311, which reported that 69.4% of their sample were sterilized along with abortion. Also relevant are Keith P. Russell, "Changing Indications for Therapeutic Abortion: Twenty Years' Experience at Los Angeles County Hospital,"

Journal of the American Medical Association (January 10, 1953), pp. 108–111, which reported an abortion-sterilization rate of 75.6%; and Lewis E. Savel, "Adjudication of Therapeutic Abortion and Sterilization," *Clinical Obstetrics and Gynecology* 7 (1964), pp. 14–21.

25. See, for example, Michael W. Sedlak, "Young Women and the City: Adolescent Deviance and the Transformation of Educational Policy, 1870–1960," *History of Education Quarterly* 23 (1983), pp. 1–28.

26. See Lillian Ripple, "Social Work Standards of Unmarried Parenthood as Affected by Contemporary Treatment Formulations," Ph.D. Dissertation, University of Chicago, 1953.

27. *Directory of Maternity Homes* (Cleveland: National Association of Services for Unmarried Parents, 1960).

28. U.S. Congress, Senate Judiciary Committee, Subcommittee to Investigate Juvenile Delinquency, Interstate Adoption Practices, July 15–16, 1955, 84th Congress, 1st sess. (Washington, D.C.: Government Printing Office, 1955), p. 200.

29. U.S. Congress, Senate Judiciary Committee, Subcommittee to Investigate Juvenile Delinquency, Commercial Child Adoption Practices, May 16, 1956, 84th Congress, 2nd sess. (Washington, D.C.: Government Printing Office, 1956), p. 6.

30. Duluth, Minnesota to Governor Luther Youngdahl, August 2, 1950, and to President Truman, August 14, 1950, Box 457, File 7-4-3-3-4. Record Group 102, National Archives.

31. U.S. Congress, Commercial Child Adoption Practices, May 16, 1956, p. 86.

32. Ibid., p. 120.

33. *New York Times* (July 10, 1958).

34. U.S. Congress, Senate Committee on the Judiciary, Subcommittee to Investigate Juvenile Delinquency in the United States, 84th Congress, 2nd sess., Unpublished Hearing, May 11, 1956.

35. U.S. Congress, Senate Judiciary Committee, *Hearings Before the Subcommittee to Investigate Juvenile Delinquency, Interstate Adoption Practices,* Miami, Florida, November 14–15, 1955, 84th Congress, 1st sess. (Washington, D.C.: Government Printing Office, 1956), pp. 54–56.

36. U.S. Congress, Interstate Adoption Practices, July 15–16, 1955, p. 206.

37. U.S. Congress, Interstate Adoption Practices, Miami, Florida, November 14–15, 1955, p. 245.

38. Clark Vincent, "Unwed Mothers and the Adoption Market: Psychological and Familial Factors," *Journal of Marriage and Family Living* 22 (May 1960), p. 118.

39. See Solinger, *"Wake Up Little Susie"* chap. 7 for a fuller discussion of these three public perspectives.

40. See Winifred Bell, *Aid to Dependent Children* (New York: Columbia University Press, 1965); and Julius Paul, "The Return of Punitive Sterilization Proposals," *Law and Society Review* 3 (August 1968), pp. 77–106.

41. See, for example, Andrew Billingsley and Jeanne Giovannoni, *Children of the Storm* (New York: Harcourt, Brace and Jovanovich, Inc., 1972), p. 142.

42. Patricia Garland, "Illegitimacy—A Special Minority-Group Problem in Urban Areas," *Child Welfare* 45 (February 1966), p. 84.

43. Ibid.

44. See, for example, the editorial, "It Merits Discussion," Richmond News Leader, March 22, 1957.

45. During the period considered here, Black women in the South were among the first in the United States to receive publicly subsidized birth control, sterilization, and abortion services. See Thomas Shapiro, *Population Control Politics: Women, Sterilization and Reproductive Choice* (Philadelphia: Temple University Press, 1985); Gerald C. Wright, "Racism and the Availability of Family Planning Services in the United States," *Social Forces* 56 (June 1978), pp. 1087–1098; and Martha C. Ward, *Poor Women, Powerful Men: America's Great Experiment in Family Planning* (Boulder: Westview Press, 1986).

46. See, for example, the *New York Times,* August 28, 1960, which quotes Louisiana Governor Jimmie H. Davis justifying the recent state legislation targeting "those who make it their business to produce illegitimate children."

47. See *Illegitimacy and Its Impact on the Aid to Dependent Children Program,* Bureau of Public Assistance, Social Security Administration, U.S. Department of Health, Education and Welfare (Washington, D.C.: Government Printing Office, 1960).

48. The *Atlanta Constitution,* January 25, 1951. The *Constitution* reported that the Georgia State Welfare Director, making an argument for denying Aid to Dependent Children grants to mothers with more than one illegitimate child, noted that "Seventy percent of all mothers with more than one illegitimate children are Negro. . . . Some of them, finding themselves tied down to one child, are not adverse to adding others as a business proposition." A Philadelphia judge recommended in 1958 that mothers of three or more illegitimate children be jailed [because it is] apparent that childbearing has become a business venture to collect relief benefits." *New York Times,* March 4, 1958.

49. "A Study of Negro Adoptions," *Child Welfare* 38 (February 1959), p. 33, quoting David Fanshel, *A Study in Negro Adoptions* (New York: Child Welfare League of America, 1957): "In moving from white to Negro adoptions we are moving from what economists would call a 'seller's market' . . . to a 'buyer's market.' "

50. See, for example, Lydia Hylton, "Trends in Adoption," *Child Welfare* 44 (February, 1966), pp. 377–386. Hylton cites the figures of 182 white applicants for every 100 white infants in the mid-1960s, although higher ratios were obtained earlier in the period of this study. In 1960, a government report claimed that in some communities, there were ten suitable applicants for every white infant, *Illegitimacy and Its Impact,* p. 28.

51. One of a number of readers responding irately to a *New York Times'* editorial in support of giving welfare grants to unmarried mothers, wrote to the *Times,* "As for your great concern for those careless women who make a career of illicit pregnancy, they should either bear the expense or be put where they can no longer indulge in their weaknesses." *New York Times,* July 7, 1961.

52. *New York Times,* August 9, 1959. In late 1958, average monthly family grants in the ADC program were $99.83 nationally,

but in the South, they ranged between \$27.09 in Alabama and \$67.73 in Texas. Bell, *Aid to Dependent Children,* p. 224.

53. Hazel McCalley, "The Community Looks at Illegitimacy," Florence Crittenton Association of America Papers, Box 3, folder: FCAA Annual 11th, 1960–61, Social Welfare History Archives, University of Minnesota (hereafter cited as SWHA). See *Facts, Fallacies and the Future—A Study of the ADC Program of Cook County, Illinois* (New York: Greenleigh Associates, 1960), p. 29, for a prominent, contemporary discussion concerning how small welfare grants to single mothers were directly responsible for increasing these women's financial and social dependence on men.

54. "Suitable Home Law," (Jacksonville: Florida Department of Public Welfare, 1962), pp. 25–26; quoted in Bell, *Aid to Dependent Children,* p. 132.

55. An excellent study of Black single mothers' strategies in this era is Renee M. Berg, "A Study of a Group of Unmarried Mothers Receiving ADC," Doctor of Social Work dissertation, University of Pennsylvania School of Social Work, 1962.

56. A Gallup Poll conducted in 1960 found that only "one in ten [respondents] favored giving aid to further children born to unwed parents who have already produced an out of wedlock child." *St. Louis Post Dispatch,* August 8, 1961.

57. *Milwaukee Journal,* August 9, 1961.

58. *Illegitimacy and Its Impact,* p. 30.

59. *Buffalo Currier Express,* December 5, 1957.

60. *Illegitimacy and Its Impact,* p. 36.

61. Ibid.

62. See "The Current Attack on ADC in Louisiana," September 16, 1960, Florence Crittenton Association of America Papers, Box 3, folder: National Urban League, New York City, SWHA.

63. Annie Lee Davis, "Attitudes toward Minority Groups: Their Effect on Services for Unmarried Mothers," paper presented at the National Conference on Social Work, 1948.

64. See Seaton W. Manning, "The Changing Negro Family: Implications for the Adoption of Children," *Child Welfare* 43 (November 1964), pp. 480–485; Elizabeth Herzog and Rose Bernstein, "Why So Few Negro Adoptions?" *Children* 12 (January–February 1965), pp. 14–15; Billingsley and Giovannoni, *Children of the Storm;* Fanshel, *A Study in Negro Adoption;* Trudy Bradley, "An Exploration of Caseworkers' Perceptions of Adoptive Applicants," *Child Welfare* 45 (October 1962), pp. 433–443.

65. Elizabeth Tuttle, "Serving the Unmarried Mother Who Keeps Her Child," *Social Welfare* 43 (October 1962), p. 418.

66. See *Facts, Fallacies and Future,* pp. 19–20; 552 out of 619 mothers of illegitimate children in this study did not want another child but reported that they had no information about how to prevent conception.

67. Deborah Shapiro, "Attitudes, Values and Unmarried Motherhood," in *Unmarried Parenthood: Clues to Agency and Community Action* (New York: National Council on Illegitimacy, 1967), p. 60.

68. Joyce Ladner, *Tomorrow's Tomorrow: The Black Woman* (New York: Doubleday and Co., 1971), pp. 2, 8.

69. Ellery Reed and Ruth Latimer, *A Study of Unmarried Mothers Who Kept Their Babies* (Cincinnati: Social Welfare Research, Inc., 1963), p. 72.

70. Shapiro, "Attitudes, Values," p. 61.

71. Renee Berg, "Utilizing the Strengths of Unwed Mothers in the AFDC Program," *Child Welfare* 43 (July 1964), p. 337.

72. Ibid.

73. Berg, "A Study of a Group of Unwed Mothers Receiving ADC," p. 96.

74. Ibid., p. 93.

75. Ibid., p. 95.

76. Helen Harris Perlman, "Observations on Services and Research," in *Unmarried Parenthood: Clues to Agency and Community Action* (New York: National Council on Illegitimacy, 1967), p. 41.

77. Charles Bowerman, Donald Irish, and Hallowell Pope, *Unwed Motherhood: Personal and Social Consequences* (Chapel Hill: University of North Carolina, 1966), p. 261.

78. Ladner, *Tomorrow's Tomorrow,* pp. 214–215.

READING 31

Negotiating Lesbian Motherhood: The Dialectics of Resistance and Accommodation[1]

ELLEN LEWIN

When I first began to assemble resources for a study of lesbian mothers in 1976, very few people were aware of the existence of such a category, and if they were, they usually saw it as an oxymoron. Lesbian mothers occasionally gained the attention of the general public when they were involved in custody cases that received publicity, but such notoriety was infrequent and typically fleeting. In fact, aside from those who had lesbian mothers in their social circles, even the wider lesbian population was aware of lesbian mothers mainly in connection with custody cases. In the early collections of articles on lesbian issues that emerged from the lesbian feminist movement, lesbian mothers were almost never mentioned except in connection with their vulnerability to custody litigation.[2] Mothers in these cases either lost custody of their children, or won custody only under highly compromised conditions, sometimes with the stipulation that the child have no contact with the mother's partner.[3]

Well-known custody cases in the 1970s demonstrated the likelihood that lesbian mothers would face considerable discrimination in court. The Mary Jo Risher case, in which a mother lost custody of her younger son after her teenage son testified against her, was perhaps the best documented of these, particularly after the story was dramatized as a made-for-TV movie.[4] And the case of Sandy and Madeleine, two mothers who became lovers and subsequently had custody challenged by both ex-husbands, was extensively publicized in the lesbian community with the circulation of a film called *Sandy and Madeleine's Family.*

Ellen Lewin, "Negotiating Lesbian Motherhood: The Dialectics of Resistance and Accommodation" from *Mothering: Ideology, Experience, and Agency,* edited by Evelyn Nakano Glenn, Grace Chang, and Linda Rennie Forcey. Copyright © 1994 by Routledge. Reprinted with the permission of Routledge, Inc.

The case demonstrated that lesbian mothers' custody could be challenged repeatedly, even after a favorable ruling in court, at least until the children achieved majority. The film, originally produced for use in court, emphasized the strong religious values of the mothers, their involvement in wholesome activities with both sets of children, and the warmth and nurturance of the family environment they provided.[5]

All these images of lesbian mothers were defensive. When lesbian mothers found themselves in court, they necessarily had to convince the judge (and in the Risher case, the jury) that they were as good at being mothers as any other women, that they were, in fact, *good* in the sense of possessing the moral attributes of altruism and nurturance that are culturally demanded of mothers in North American cultures. In these formulations, mothers are assumed to be *naturally* equipped to place their children's interests ahead of their own, to be selfless in a way that precludes or overshadows their own sexuality;[6] such assumptions are at the heart of twentieth-century presumptions of maternal suitability for custody.[7] When mothers are lesbians, however, the courts, reflecting popular views of homosexuality as "unnatural," tend to view them as morally flawed, and thus as unfit parents. Their task in dealing with the legal system, therefore, is to demonstrate that they possess the "natural" attributes expected of mothers and are thus worthy of receiving custody of their children. Maternal virtue, therefore, shifts from being a quality inherent to women to being a behavior one must actively demonstrate in order to pursue a claim to custody.[8]

While many lesbian mothers understood that the way to keep custody of their children was to show that they were "as good as" heterosexual mothers, they firmly believed that they would eventually be shown to be superior parents who were bringing new, nonsexist families into being. They viewed the two-parent, heterosexual, nuclear family as the arena in which the patriarchy inscribed gender expectations onto both women and men. If the power dynamics of that family form were largely responsible for the continuing devalued status of women, and for a variety of abusive practices, then a domestic arrangement based on presumably nongendered relations between two "equal" women partners would constitute a first step toward the better sort of world feminists dreamed of. Jeanne Vaughn, the coeditor of *Politics of the Heart: A Lesbian Parenting Anthology,* put it this way:

> We have an opportunity for radical social change beginning in our homes, change that requires rethinking our views of family, of kinship, of work, of social organization. We need to develop some specifically lesbian-feminist theories of family. How would/did/could we mother our children without the institution of compulsory heterosexuality?[9]

The image many lesbian mothers conjured up was utopian, resembling the broad outlines of Charlotte Perkins Gilman's *Herland,* a fictional society of women in which motherhood and caring were elevated to the center of the inhabitants' lives. Without the need to serve and please powerful males, without the degradations of daily experience in a patriarchal society, Gilman's image suggests, women might be free to express their true, nurturant natures. They would reveal abilities unlikely to emerge in male-dominated society, and would focus on creative, constructive projects rather than on frivolities such as fancy dress and (hetero)sexuality.[10]

The popular images of mothers and families that dominated the lesbian community in the 1970s, then, focused on the ways in which being a mother and having a family could constitute a form of resistance to traditional, and thereby patriarchal, family forms. In particular, success at motherhood (as measured by how well one's child turned out) would demonstrate that children did not need the structure of a heterosexual family, and, most significantly, the regular contribution of a father, to develop normally. The achievement of lesbian mothers would both counteract the notion that lesbianism and motherhood are inherently contradictory and, in fact, redefine and desexualize what it means to be a lesbian.

At the same time, however, the complexities of living as a mother required lesbian mothers to reinstate the dichotomy of natural/unnatural and mother/nonmother that their redefinition of lesbianism sought to subvert. Negotiating the daily issues of being a mother and meeting obligations to one's children brought them into conflict both with the dominant heterosexist society and with lesbians who had not chosen motherhood.

FEMINIST VIEWS OF RESISTANCE

When many of us took up a feminist agenda in our scholarship, directing our attention to documenting the experience of women from their point of view, it seemed that we had no choice but to concentrate on describing a depressing history of victimization and oppression. As we examined the social and cultural lives of women, not only in familiar terrain, but also outside western traditions, we found over and over again that women were confined to secondary social status, relegated to devalued cultural roles, and often brutalized and demeaned in their daily lives. The evidence of despair poured in, bolstered at every turn by the grim discoveries we continued to make about our own society and our own lives.[11]

In many instances, the best it seemed that we could offer to help remedy this situation was to produce astute, woman-centered descriptions of the conditions under which women's lives were lived, paired with analyses geared toward change. In many instances, feminist scholars directed their energies toward the documentation of women's point of view, focusing on ways to dissolve the hegemony of male-centered assumptions about the organization of social life and women's place in it. In anthropology, such work often proposed alternative views of traditionally patriarchal institutions.[12] But in other instances, feminist interpretations came to center on resistance, looking at how even clearly oppressed women might take action on their own behalf, either by directly sabotaging the instruments of male dominance, or by constituting their consciousness in a way that undermined their subordination.[13]

Feminist scholars have most commonly applied the concept of resistance to studies of women in the workforce. Bonnie Thornton Dill's research on Black women household workers, for example, focuses on the way they manage their relationships with employers to enhance their own self-respect. She documents how these workers organized "strategies for gaining mastery over work that was socially defined as demeaning and . . . actively resisted the depersonalization of household work."[14]

Along similar lines, Aihwa Ong, writing about women factory workers in Malaysia, shows how labor practices introduced by capitalism lead to the reconstruction of meanings of gender and sexuality. In response to proletari-anization, Malay women organize cultural responses to their changing status, most markedly in the form of episodes of spirit possession. "Spirit attacks," Ong tells us, "were indirect retaliations against coercion and demands for justice in personal terms within the industrial milieu."[15]

Notions of resistance have also informed studies of women outside the workplace. Emily Martin, for example, has contrasted women's ideas about their bodies and the ideology of mainstream medicine, describing instances in which women resist medical assumptions at variance with their own experience. She sees working-class women as most able to reject scientific metaphors of women's bodies, particularly those that focus on production and failed pro-duction, perhaps because "they have less to gain from pro-ductive labor in the society." [16] Self-consciousness and ver-bal protest are taken as evidence of resistance in Martin's analysis, as are instances of sabotage or outright refusal to cooperate with medical instructions.

Louise Lamphere's study of immigrant factory workers in New England also looks carefully at resistance, but frames it as one of several strategies women can mount to cope with employers' efforts to control their lives. She views women "as active strategists, weighing possibilities and devising means to realize goals, and not as passive acceptors of their situations."[17] Lamphere cautions, how-ever, against viewing all of women's actions on their own behalf as resistance. Rather, she emphasizes the importance of distinguishing between "strategies of resistance" and "strategies of accommodation," pointing out that some strategies may best be seen as adjustments that allow women to cope with their place in the labor market by dif-fusing employers' control of the workplace. Such strategies ought not to be viewed, Lamphere says, as resistance only, since they may not be based in purposeful opposition to the employer, and since they may only result in continuing exploitation of the workers, and, as such, constitute a kind of consent to existing relations of domination.[18]

Taking a different approach, Judith Butler has proposed that scholars reconsider their dependence on the concept of gender, arguing that gender, as a dualistic formulation, rests on the same asymmetry that feminists seek to overturn. She urges the adoption of strategies that would "disrupt the oppositional binary itself,"[19] and suggests that calling into question the "continuity and coherence" of gender identi-ties, sabotaging the "intelligibility" of gender, would under-mine the "regulatory aims" of gender as a cultural system.[20] Butler's claim seems to be that lesbianism, or other sexual stances at odds with normative heterosexuality, could con-stitute a kind of resistance to the very existence of gender. She locates gender continuities within the domain of sexu-ality, viewing "intelligible" genders . . . as those which in some sense institute and maintain relations of coherence and continuity among sex, gender, sexual practice, and desire."[21] The decisions one takes with regard to one's iden-tity, then, and in particular, the extent to which they may be said to destabilize conventional expectations and represen-tations, may constitute resistance not only to specific forms of oppression but to the oppressive effects of gender as an ideological straitjacket.

All of these approaches to resistance reveal a commit-ment to render women as active subjects. While these scholars are reluctant to blame women for their subordina-tion, neither are they willing to cast them as hapless victims of actions wholly beyond their control. Women are thus seen as capable of framing strategies for enhancing their situations, whether the battleground be material—as when women's resistance improves their working conditions—or symbolic—as when refusal to conform to common conven-tions of gender may be interpreted as constituting sabotage of the larger system.

This concern with subjectivity and agency raises signifi-cant questions for the study of women who seem to defy gender limitations in any aspect of their lives. Just as Butler has suggested that incongruent sexuality might be viewed as resistance, one might ask whether other "disorders" of sexuality and gender could also be viewed in this light. The question becomes particularly pressing when women them-selves explain their behavior as subversive. We must then ask whether apparently conscious refusals by lesbian moth-ers, or any other group of women, to accept the strictures of gender are best understood as instances of resistance.

LESBIAN MOTHERS AND RESISTANCE TO HETEROSEXISM

By the time I was well into my research, at the end of the 1970s, the custody problems that had concerned me at the outset were no longer the only issues facing lesbian moth-ers. Pregnant women were starting to appear at lesbian social gatherings, at political meetings and concerts, some-times alone and sometimes in the company of their lovers. These women were not, for the most part, new to lesbian life; most had never been married, and child custody fears did not figure prominently for them. They certainly had not become pregnant by accident. While some of the mothers and mothers-to-be had had romantic interludes with men, more explained how they had "made themselves pregnant" by arranging a sexual situation with a man, or by using some form of "insemination."[22]

The emphasis in these women's accounts of their experiences was on how they had to overcome their earlier fears that being lesbian would preclude motherhood. Lesbians reported that they had often thought of themselves as not being suitable mothers, having internalized images of homosexuals as self-serving, immature, or otherwise not capable of the kind of altruism basic to maternal performance.

Sarah Klein,[23] a lesbian who lives with her one-year-old daughter and her lover, explained the conflict as she perceived it:

I've always wanted to have a child. In terms of being real tied up with being gay, it was one of the reasons that for a long time I was hesitant to call myself a lesbian. I thought that automatically assumed you had nothing to do with children. . . . I felt, well, if you don't *say* you're a lesbian, you can still work with children, you can still have a kid, you can have relationships with men. But once I put this label on myself, [it would] all [be] over.

By having a child, Sarah repudiated the boundaries she had once associated with being a lesbian; she has claimed what she sees as her right to be a mother.

But other lesbians' accounts indicate that not all perceive themselves as having had a lifelong desire for motherhood. Among those who claim not to remember wanting children when they were younger was Kathy Lindstrom. She had a child by insemination when she was in her early thirties, but says that she never considered the possibility until a few years earlier. She could only explain her behavior as arising from some sort of "hormonal change."

It just kind of came over me. It wasn't really conscious at first. It was just a need.

Kathy's understanding of her desire to be a mother as something "hormonal," that is, natural, suggests an implicit assertion that this is something so deep and so essentially part of her that nothing, including her lesbianism, can undermine it. Her account indicates that she refuses to allow the associations others have with her status as a lesbian to interfere with her own perception of herself and her needs.

Other lesbian mothers view their urge to have a child as stemming from a desire to settle down, to achieve adulthood, and to counteract forces toward instability in their lives. Ruth Zimmerman, who had a five-year-old son from a relationship with a man she selected as a "good" father, had ended the relationship soon after she became pregnant.

I definitely felt like I was marking time, waiting for something. I wasn't raised to be a career woman. I was raised to feel like I was grown up and finished growing up and living a regular normal life when I was married and had kids. And I knew that the married part wasn't going to happen. I feel like I've known that for a long time.

Like Kathy, Ruth defined her progress as a human being, and as a woman, in terms that are strikingly conventional and recall traditional feminine socialization. While clearly accepting motherhood as a marker of adulthood and "living a normal life," Ruth tried to overcome the equally conventional limits placed on lesbians in order to have her child.

The notion that having a child signifies adulthood, the acceptance of social responsibility, and demonstrates that one has "settled down" appears in the accounts of many lesbian mothers. Most often, lesbian mothers speak of their lives before motherhood as empty and aimless, and see the birth of their children as having centered them emotionally. They frequently cite new interests in education, nutrition, and health, and reconciliations with family members with whom they had not been on good terms, as evidence of their new maturity. As Louise Green, a young lesbian mother who describes herself as a former hippie, explains: "I think [having my daughter] has turned my life into this really good thing."

Louise describes herself as living a marginal, disorganized existence until she finally decided that she would have a child. She did not consider using mainstream medicine to get pregnant, assuming that such resources would never be available to her, both for financial reasons and because she would be viewed with hostility by medical professionals. Instead, she went about asking men she met whether they would like to be sperm donors; she finally located a willing prospect and obtained a sperm sample from him. Louise never told this man her real name, and once she had conceived she left the area, concerned that he could somehow pose a threat to her relationship with her child.

Louise's account focuses on conception and birth as spiritual transitions to a higher and better existence. She became pregnant on her first attempt, which she explained as evidence that mystical forces "meant" for this to happen. She wanted very much to have a home delivery, but after a protracted and complicated labor, she was transferred to a hospital, where she finally gave birth with the aid of multiple technological interventions. Despite this interference with the kind of spiritual environment she had hoped to give birth in, Louise describes the entire experience in mystical terms.

> It was about the best thing I ever experienced. I was totally amazed. The labor was like I had died. . . . I had just died. The minute she came out, I was born again. It was like we'd just been born together.

Louise did not allow either her counterculture lifestyle or her status as a lesbian to interfere with the spiritual agenda she felt destined to complete. She says the mystical process she underwent in becoming a mother has permitted her to become more fully herself, to explore aspects of her being that would have remained hidden if she allowed lesbianism alone to define who she is.

> [After] I had [my daughter] I felt it was okay to do these things I've been wanting to do real bad. One of them is to paint my toenails red. I haven't done it yet, but I'm going to do it. I felt really okay about wearing perfume and I just got a permanent in my hair. . . . I feel like I'm robbing myself of some of the things I want to do by trying to fit this lesbian code. I feel like by my having this child, it has already thrown me out in the sidelines.

Louise has used the process of becoming a mother to construct her identity in a way that includes being a lesbian but also draws from other sources. She sees her need to do this as essential and intended, and has moved along her path with the assurance that she is realizing her destiny.

Not all lesbians become mothers as easily as Louise. On a purely practical level, of course, the obstacles to a lesbian becoming pregnant can be formidable. Even if she knows a man who is interested in such a venture, she might not contemplate a heterosexual liaison with enthusiasm and might be equally reluctant to ask him to donate sperm. Mainstream medicine may not seem like an option either, because of financial considerations, or because of fears that doctors will be unwilling to inseminate a lesbian or even a single woman—a realistic concern, of course.

Once one has defined oneself as a lesbian, the barriers to becoming a mother are so significant, in fact, that many of

the formerly married lesbian mothers I interviewed explained that they had gone through with marriages (sometimes of long duration) because this seemed the only way to realize their dream of being mothers and being normal in the eyes of their families and communities.

Harriet Newman, an artist who lives with her two daughters in a rural area north of San Francisco, fell in love with another woman during her first year in college. Her parents discovered the affair and forced her to leave school and to see a psychiatrist. The experience convinced her that it would be safer "to be a regular person in the world." When she met a gay man who also wanted to live more conventionally, they married, and almost immediately had their two children.

> The main thing that made us decide to get married was that we very much wanted to part of the mainstream of life, instead of on the edges. We wanted to be substantial . . . part of the common experience.

For lesbians who become mothers through insemination or some other method,[24] then, conscious resistance to rigid formulations of "the lesbian" seems to be central to their intentions. Unwilling to deny their identity as lesbians, they also demand the right to define what that identity constitutes. The intrinsic benefits of motherhood—the opportunity to experience birth and child development—are experiences they do not want to forego. In particular, once the relatively simple technology of donor insemination became widely known, and given the haphazard controls exerted over access to sperm donations, lesbians have come to understand that they can, indeed, be mothers. Access to motherhood thus comes to be viewed as a "civil right" not dissimilar to equal opportunity in the job market or other rights lesbians and gay men now demand with increasing insistence.

In some instances, women explained that their age made having a child imperative. Laura Bergeron, who had two sons from a relationship prior to coming out, decided to find a donor for a third child when she entered her late thirties.

> I really did want to have a girl, and I was getting older. . . . I was feeling that I didn't really want to have children past the appropriate childbearing age. I had been doing too much reading about retardation and mongoloids and everything else . . . so I put some ads [for donors] in the paper.

Annabel Jessop voices similar concerns, explaining that she decided to use artificial insemination to become pregnant even though she would have preferred being settled in a long-term relationship before embarking on motherhood.

> I decided that I wanted to have a kid, and that because I'm in my thirties my time was limited. I look at it as a life choice. There's only so many things you can do in your life, and this is one of the things I wanted to do, and it was time to do it. Waiting wasn't going to do any good. Professionally, I was together, I was as stable as I was ever going to be financially, I had a little put away, and there was just no reason not to do it now.

Becoming a mother is central to being able to claim an identity as a "good" woman, drawn from one's association with children. Mothers describe childhood as a time of innocence and discovery, and a mother can gain spiritual benefits through her contribution to a child's development. One lesbian mother explained:

> You get to have a lot of input in another human being's very formative years. That's real special to have that privilege of doing that, and you get to see them growing and developing and it's sort of like you put in the fertile soil and . . . hopefully what will happen is that they grow and blossom and become wonderful. . . . I think it's definitely the most important thing that people do . . . to build the next generation.

As Louise Green's narrative indicated, lesbians often characterize their transformation into mothers as a spiritual journey, an experience that gives them access to special knowledge and that makes them worthier than they otherwise could have been. Regina Carter, whose daughter is six, put it this way:

> My kid has given me more knowledge than any other experience in my life. She's taught me more than all the teachings I've ever learned as far as education, and I mean that as far as academic education, spiritual education. Taught me things that no other person, place, or thing could possibly teach me. And those are, you know, those things are without words.

Similarly, Bonnie Peters echoed these views when she told me that being a mother connected her with sources of honesty and worthiness.

> I've become more at peace with me [since having my daughter]. She's given me added strength; she's made

me—it's like looking in the mirror in many ways; she's made me see myself for who I am. She's definitely given me self-worth. I've become, I think, a more honest person.

Motherhood, then, can draw a woman closer to basic truths, sensitizing her to the feelings of others and discovering a degree of altruism they had not perceived in themselves prior to having a child. It may provide the opportunity for a woman to make clear her involvement with a kind of authenticity, a naturalness, that brings her closer to profound, but ineffable, truths.

MANAGING LESBIAN MOTHERHOOD

While the accounts given by some lesbian mothers suggest that they have resisted the cultural opposition between "mother" and "lesbian" and demanded the right to be both, the ongoing management of being a lesbian mother may depend on separating these two statuses, thus intensifying their dichotomization. Lesbian mothers frequently speak of these two dimensions of their identities as competing or interfering with each other; conflicts with lesbians who are not mothers sometimes further solidify these divisions.

Tanya Petroff, who lives with her seven-year-old daughter in an East Bay city, speaks evocatively of how being a mother overshadows her identity as a lesbian.

> The mothering thing, the thing about being a mother seems to be more important to me than my sexual orientation. . . . I've had [lesbians] tell me that I had chosen a privileged position in having a child and if it was going to be difficult for me then it was too goddam bad.

For Tanya, the conflict is most acute when she is developing a new relationship with another woman. She must then make clear that she views herself and her daughter as an indivisible social unit that takes precedence over other attachments.

> I'm definitely part of a package deal. I come with my daughter and people who can't relate to both of us are not people I want to relate to for very long.

What this means in terms of other relationships is that Tanya sees other mothers, regardless of whether they are gay or straight, as the people with whom she has the most in common. Since relocating to the Bay Area from a town in the Midwest, Tanya has tended to minimize her contact with what she calls the "lesbian community" in favor of socializing with other mothers. She feels that she is better able to resist pressures to raise her daughter to be a "little amazon," an expectation she believes common to lesbians who are not mothers. Beyond this, Tanya feels that there are simply too many practical obstacles to meaningful friendships with women who are not mothers. Living alone and having a demanding job mean that Tanya has to plan ahead to arrange child care. People who don't have children are no help with this; she accounts for this by explaining that they are "single," meaning that they have no children. There is such a deep gulf between mothers and nonmothers, in her view, that there is simply no meaningful basis for understanding or trust.

> There is a difference between people who have children and people who don't have children. People who don't have children, to my way of thinking, are very selfish. . . . They needn't consider anyone other than themselves. They can do exactly what they want to do at any given time. And though I admire that, it's not possible for me to do that and I guess for that reason most of my friends are single mothers, because it's hard for me to coordinate my needs and my time with someone who's in a completely different head set. "Why can't you get a sitter for the kid?"—that kind of thing. . . . I just prefer being with people who have some sense of what it's like to be me, and I understand where they are too.

Tanya's belief that she can only find truly supportive friends among those whose situations closely mirror her own with respect to single motherhood grows not only out of her very real need for material assistance, but also from the importance she places on having friends who affirm or validate her identity. The most essential aspect of her identity, by this account, is that of being a mother. It supersedes her sexual orientation, her ethnicity, her job.

For some lesbian mothers, difficult experiences with lovers parallel disappointments with the wider lesbian community. Leslie Addison, who lives alone with her twelve-year-old daughter, describes a long series of conflicts with lesbian community groups over support for mothers. While she can easily explain the failure of these women to be conscious about mothers as stemming from their being "single," she has had a harder time dealing with lovers and prospective lovers who do not understand or are unwilling to accommodate her needs as a mother. Shortly after her divorce, she began her first relationship with a woman with the expectation that a woman lover would naturally help her with her child and be eager to participate in their family activities. Leslie found instead that her lover was reluctant to spend more than minimal amounts of time with her daughter, never offering to help with child care or domestic responsibilities. Ironically, when she was straight, she says that she could always get a boyfriend to baby-sit for her; as a lesbian, she finds that women usually refuse to do child care.

> That wasn't quite what I expected. I expected there would be more sharing between women of the child. But I found it's really not, because another woman has a role identity crisis. She can't be the mother, because you're already the mother. She can't be the father, because she's not the father, whereas the men sort of played that role. It was easier for them to fall into it. They could just play daddy, I could play momma, and everybody'd be happy.

The stark separation between "mother" and "lesbian" as elements of identity may be even more sharply drawn for women concerned with maintaining secrecy about their sexual orientation. In these instances, daily life is segregated into time when they are "mothers" and time when they are "lesbians," creating constant concern about information management and boundary maintenance. While some mothers who voice these concerns are motivated by fears about custody, others seem to be more worried by what they understand to be broad community standards. Segregation may seem the best way to protect children from being stigmatized, but in addition, lesbian mothers know that motherhood itself tends to preclude their being suspected of homosexuality. As one mother explained, "Of course, I have the mask. I have a child. I'm accepted [as heterosexual] because I have a child and that kind of protection."

Laura Bergeron, who had three children outside of marriage, is not only secretive about her lesbianism in her relations with the wider community, but she has not allowed her children to find out that she is a lesbian. Her lover, a married woman, is unwilling to do anything that might disrupt current arrangements, and Laura explains that her lover's situation is the major reason for her secrecy. But she is also concerned that the father of her two sons might try to get custody if he knew about her sexual orientation, despite the fact that he only agreed to help her get pregnant with the stipulation that he would never have any formal obligations to their children. And she fears that her civil service job would somehow be compromised as well were her sexual orientation known.

> There's just no way that we could ever be anything but heavily closeted. We have a lot of women's activities that go on here, but we don't mix the worlds. . . . That's why my children can't know. . . . I've set up my life so that it doesn't include my children.

Laura has made complicated arrangements for supervising her children before and after school and, in order to spend more time with her lover, has installed an intercom between the two houses that enables her to monitor her kids' activities. Meeting both her children's and her lover's needs means that she has little time for herself, and she sees most of her time with her children as mechanical. While she describes motherhood as separate from her "life," it is clear that managing the division between the two worlds creates a problem in organizing her identity.

For some women who maintain strict separation between their identities as mothers and as lesbians, the threat of custody litigation is more than an abstract fear. Theresa Baldocchi, whose son is nine years old, survived a protracted custody trial at the time she divorced her former husband, John. Her legal expenses and liability for debts incurred by John during their marriage left her virtually bankrupt, and it has taken years for her to solidify her financial situation. Theresa was not a lesbian at the time of the divorce, but John made allegations that she was. Now that she has come out, she is convinced that she must carefully separate her life as a mother and as a lesbian, lest her former husband decide to institute another custody case against her. Despite the fact that John has an extensive history of psychiatric hospitalization and that she is a successful professional, she is sure that her chances of winning in such a trial would be slim.

> Now that I'm gay, I'd lose. There's just no way in the world I would win, after having had my fitness questioned when I was Lady Madonna, let alone now.

Theresa has decided that living in a middle-class suburban area and arranging her home in an impeccably conventional fashion help shield her from suspicion of being anything other than a typical "mom." The Bay Bridge, which she must cross each day between her home and San Francisco, where she works and socializes with her lesbian friends, symbolizes her strategy. She feels that each trip involves a palpable transition, as she prepares herself to meet the requirements of her destination—home or San Francisco. Most crucial for her strategy is not telling her son that she is a lesbian, since she feels it would be inappropriate to expect him to maintain her secret.

If Theresa was concerned only with managing information about her homosexuality, she would probably avoid seeing her former husband, and thus be able to relax, at least, at home. But Theresa firmly believes that being a good mother demands that she take every opportunity to maximize her son's contact with John, a model father in her eyes. Because John is not regularly employed, he has offered to take care of their son each day while Theresa is at work. This arrangement has meant both that Theresa does not have to obtain paid child care during these hours, and that her son has daily contact with his father. It also means that she has virtually no privacy. She must control the kinds of friends who visit her, and must make sure that nothing that might reveal her sexual orientation can be found in her home. Most poignantly, she must limit her lover's access to her home for fear that her presence would somehow make the situation transparent. She consigns her most reliable potential source of support to the background, leaving herself isolated and anxious much of the time.

In other instances, lesbian mothers may separate the two aspects of their lives in order to maintain fragile relationships with their families. Rita García, who lives in San Francisco with her eight-year-old son and her lover, Jill Hacker, has made arrangements with her family that she believes can be sustained only if she avoids mention of her partner and their relationship. She comes from a large and close Mexican-American family. When they first learned that she was a lesbian, shortly after her divorce, they were so angry, and so convinced that she was no longer a fit parent, that they briefly considered supporting her husband's claim for custody. Once the case finally came to trial, however, Rita's husband abandoned his interest in custody. The family learned, during these proceedings, that he had abused her on numerous occasions, once beating her so severely that she had to go to the hospital. They withdrew their support from her husband, but also refused to communicate with Rita.

Rita did not see her parents at all for over a year. When Rita's grandmother had surgery and demanded to see her favorite granddaughter, the family relented, and Rita became a central figure in the grandmother's nursing care. The crisis allowed her to be reintegrated into the family, and she began once again to be her mother's closest confidante. This rapprochement, however, was founded on an unspoken agreement that Rita not mention her lover or anything about her home life.

The situation had stabilized, with Rita spending a great deal of time with her parents. Her son attends a Catholic school in her parents' neighborhood, so she drops him off there each day on her way to work. Rita's mother makes him breakfast every morning, and after school he returns to his grandparents' house to play and do his homework. Before Rita picks him up in the evening, he usually eats dinner as well, which allows Rita to work overtime at her job. Whenever Rita and Jill have plans in the evening, he spends the night with his grandparents. Besides this kind of practical support, Rita depends on her father for help with her car and for advice about financial matters. She is close to her sister, and often exchanges overnight baby-sitting with her.

But Rita never mentions her lover to her family, and her parents have established a strict policy of never visiting her home. Jill is never invited to family events, spending Christmas and Thanksgiving with her own family. While her parents know that she is a lesbian, Rita has decided not to tell her son, reasoning that it might be difficult for him to manage his relations with his grandparents if he had to be secretive about this topic. Separating her identity as a lesbian from her identity as a mother is consistent with her notion of being a good mother. Her son's welfare is enhanced by his ties to his grandparents, and Rita is able to provide better for him with the assistance they provide. Anything that might undermine that relationship would have the effect of harming her child, and that would make her a bad mother, undeserving, should the issue come up again, of being the custodial parent.

Other mothers explain the separation of motherhood from other dimensions of their lives, and the centrality of being a mother, to framing their identities more practically, citing the weighty and unrelenting obligations faced by parents. Peggy Lawrence, who lives with her lover, Sue Alexander, her ten-year-old daughter, and Sue's two sons, spoke at length about the effects of being a mother on her personal freedom. Being a mother means that she must be concerned about continuity and stability in ways that constrain her spontaneity, and earning money must be a priority no matter how oppressive her work. Peggy and Sue live in a neighborhood close to their children's school, and have chosen to live in San Francisco because they think their children will encounter less discrimination here as the children of lesbians than in the Midwest, where they would prefer to live. Peggy explains what being a mother means to her:

Being a mother, to me—being a mother is more consuming than any other way that I could possibly imagine identifying myself . . . any other way that I identify myself is an identification of some part of my being a mother. I am a lesbian mother, I am a working mother—"mother" hardly ever modifies any other thing. Mother is always the primary—it's always some kind of mother, but it's never a mother-anything. Mother is—mother, for mothers, is always the thing that is more consuming.

But others understand motherhood to mean the uniquely intense feelings that exist between mother and child. Lisa Stark, who describes the weightiness of single parenthood as almost unbearable, has come to see her children as the reason she can continue to struggle with her obligations, paradoxically the explanation for both her suffering and her very survival.

I've . . . never had to live for myself. The only reason I get up in the morning is to get them off to school. For me to trot off to work in order to earn the money to support them. I don't know what I'd do if I didn't have them. They're everything I've got. . . . I love them so much that it really is painful.

Having a child or being a mother may be said to create and reinforce meaningful ties with the world, and to make struggle worthwhile. While being a lesbian mother can be difficult, and may make a woman's life complicated and stressful, children offer significant intrinsic rewards—most importantly, a way to experience feelings of special intimacy, and to be connected to higher-order, spiritual values. Motherhood allows lesbians to be more like other women, at least with respect to the most defining feminine role expectation, but segregating these two dimensions of the self becomes the most efficient way to manage practical obligations and intensifies the dichotomization of "lesbian" and "mother."

LESBIAN MOTHERHOOD: RESISTANCE OR ACCOMMODATION?

The goals motherhood allows lesbians to enhance are, of course, no different from those heterosexual women describe for themselves. Being a mother, in particular, becoming a mother, is perceived as a transformative experience, an accomplishment that puts other achievements in their proper perspective. It is also construed as an individual achievement, something a woman can "do" to make herself a mother, that is, to transform herself into an altruistic, spiritually aware human being. In a culture that elevates what has been characterized as "mythic individualism" as a central value, individuals idealize autonomy, self-reliance, and the notion that one must "find oneself" and "make something" of oneself.[25]

> Clearly, the meaning of one's life for most Americans is to become one's own person, almost to give birth to oneself.[26]

Women in America have particular difficulty living up to this cultural ideal. Individualistic and assertive behaviors valued in men are discouraged in women. Dependency, particularly through marriage, is represented as a specifically feminine sort of success. I have discussed elsewhere the remarkable congruences I observed in accounts both lesbian and heterosexual women offered of their divorces, and the similarities between these stories and lesbians' coming-out narratives.[27] These narratives are constructed around themes of agency, independence, and individuality, and celebrate women's ability to define their own lives, to decide how to represent their identities, and to achieve adulthood and autonomy. Despite the fact that both divorce and coming out as a lesbian are popularly understood to be problematic, and, indeed, have historically been defined as stigmatized statuses, women represent them as odysseys of self-discovery leading to more authentic formulations of the self.

Accounts of becoming a mother, in similar fashion, focus on the power of the individual to construct herself as a mother, to negotiate the formation of her self and to bring something good into her life. For lesbians, particularly for lesbians who decided to become mothers once their identification as lesbians was firm, the process of becoming a mother demands agency. At the same time, to the extent that wanting to be a mother is perceived as a *natural* desire, one unmediated by culture or politics, then becoming a mother permits a lesbian to move into a more natural or normal status than she would otherwise achieve. In this sense, becoming a mother represents a sort of conformity with conventional gender expectations. At the same time, to the extent that becoming a mother means overcoming the equation of homosexuality with *unnaturalness,* then this transformation allows the lesbian mother to resist gendered constructions of sexuality. This act of resistance is paradoxically achieved through compliance with conventional expectations for women, so it may also be construed as a gesture of accommodation.

Placing motherhood at the center of one's identity often involves, as we have seen, simultaneously placing other aspects of the self, most notably lesbianism, at the margins. Demanding the right to be a mother suggests a repudiation of gender conventions that define "mother" and "lesbian" as inherently incompatible identities, the former natural and intrinsic to women, organized around altruism, the latter unnatural, and organized around self-indulgence. But living as a mother means making other choices, and these choices reinscribe the opposition between "mother" and "lesbian." Subversion of orderly gender expectations is hypothetical, at best, in the lives of many lesbian mothers, at the same time that knowledge of their existence can only be imagined by the wider public as a rebellion of the most fundamental sort.

The model I would suggest based on the accounts presented here is that lesbian mothers are neither resisters nor accommodators—or perhaps that they are both. A more accurate way of framing their narratives is that they are strategists, using the cultural resources offered by motherhood to achieve a particular set of goals. That these are the goals framed by past experience in a heterosexist and perhaps patriarchal society, and that these resources are culturally constrained and shaped by the exigencies of gender, does not simplify the analysis. While such women are often conscious resisters, others gladly organize their experience as a reconciliation with what they view as traditional values. At the same time that some outsiders may see their behavior as transgressive (and thereby label them resisters or subversives), others perceive lesbian motherhood (along with other indications of compliance with conventional behaviors, such as gay/lesbian marriage) as evidence that lesbians (and other "deviants") can be domesticated and tamed.[28]

The search for cultures of resistance continues to be a vital dimension of the feminist academic enterprise. At the same time that we cannot limit our analyses of women's lives to accounts of victimization, we cannot be complacent when we discover evidence of resistance and subversion. Either interpretation may fail to reveal the complex ways in which resistance and accommodation, subversion and compliance, are interwoven and interdependent, not distinct orientations, but mutually reinforcing aspects of a single strategy. Lesbian mothers are, in some sense, both lesbians and mothers, but they shape identity and renegotiate its meanings at every turn, reinventing themselves as they make their way in a difficult world.

NOTES

1. This paper draws on research conducted with the support of National Institute of Mental Health Grant MH-30890 and a grant from the Rockefeller Foundation Gender Roles Program. A more extensive treatment of this material appears in Ellen Lewin, *Lesbian Mothers: Accounts of Gender in American Culture* (Ithaca, N.Y.: Cornell University Press, 1993).

2. See, for example, Ginny Vida, ed., *Our Right to Love: A Lesbian Resource Book* (Englewood Cliffs, N.J.: Prentice-Hall, 1978).

3. Donna Hitchens, "Social Attitudes, Legal Standards, and Personal Trauma in Child Custody Cases," *Journal of Homosexuality,* vol. 5, (1979), pp. 89–95; Ellen Lewin, "Lesbianism and Motherhood: Implications for Child Custody," *Human Organization,* vol. 40, no. 1, (1981), pp. 6–14; Rhonda R. Rivera, "Our Strait-Laced Judges: The Legal Position of Homosexual Persons in the United States," *Hastings Law Journal* 30, (1979), p. 799.

4. Clifford Guy Gibson, *By Her Own Admission: A Lesbian Mother's Fight to Keep Her Son* (Garden City, N.Y.: Doubleday, 1977).

5. Sherrie Farrell, John Gordon Hill, and Peter M. Bruce, *Sandy and Madeleine's Family* (film) (San Francisco: Multi Media Resource Center, 1973).

6. Not only lesbians, but heterosexual mothers whose sexual activity comes to the attention of the authorities, may be vulnerable in cases where their custody is challenged. See Nancy D. Polikoff, "Gender and Child Custody Determinations: Exploding the Myths," in Irene Diamond, ed., *Families, Politics, and Public Policy: A Feminist Dialogue on Women and the State* (New York: Longman, 1983), pp. 183–202.

7. Nan Hunter and Nancy D. Polikoff, "Custody Rights of Lesbian Mothers: Legal Theory and Litigation Strategy," *Buffalo Law Review* 25, (1976), p. 691; Lewin, "Lesbianism and Motherhood."

8. Ellen Lewin, "Claims to Motherhood: Custody Disputes and Maternal Strategies," in Faye Ginsburg and Anna Lowenhaupt Tsing, eds., *Uncertain Terms: Negotiating Gender in American Culture* (Boston: Beacon Press, 1990), pp. 199–214.

9. Jeanne Vaughn, "A Question of Survival," in Sandra J. Pollack and Jeanne Vaughn, eds., *Politics of the Heart: A Lesbian Parenting Anthology* (Ithaca, N.Y.: Firebrand Books, 1987), p. 26.

10. Charlotte Perkins Gilman, *Herland* (1915, New York: Pantheon Books, 1979).

11. A number of works that have chronicled the second wave of feminism in the United States have noted that the treatment of agency and victimization has been a central issue in the framing of feminist theory. See, for example, Alice Echols, *Daring to Be Bad: Radical Feminism in America, 1967–1975* (Minneapolis: University of Minnesota Press, 1989); Hester Eisenstein, *Contemporary Feminist Thought* (Boston: G. K. Hall, 1983); Alison M. Jaggar, *Feminist Politics and Human Nature* (Totowa, N.J.: Rowman & Allanheld, 1983). Central issues giving rise to these theories, particularly the essentialist stances taken by adherents of cultural feminism, were those of violence and abuse—rape, incest, battering, and the like.

12. See, for example, Jane Goodale, *Tiwi Wives: A Study of the Women of Melville Island, North Australia* (Seattle: University of Washington Press, 1971); Annette B. Weiner, *Women of Value, Men of Renown: New Perspectives in Trobriand Exchange* (Austin: University of Texas Press, 1976); Margery Wolf, *Women and the Family in Rural Taiwan* (Stanford: Stanford University Press, 1972).

13. Lila Abu-Lughod has reviewed the diverse forms an emphasis on resistance has taken in anthropology and in other disciplines in "The Romance of Resistance: Tracing Transformations of Power through Bedouin Women," *American Ethnologist,* vol. 17, no. 1 (February 1990), pp. 41–55. Abu-Lughod urges us not to romanticize resistance, but to use its appearance "to teach us about the complex interworkings of historically changing structures of power."

Some scholars, notably James Scott, have suggested that interest in resistance has blossomed as scholars on the left have been forced to confront the failure of socialist revolutions. See *Weapons of the Weak: Everyday Forms of Peasant Resistance* (New Haven: Yale University Press, 1985).

14. Bonnie Thornton Dill, "Domestic Service and the Construction of Personal Dignity," in Ann Bookman and Sandra Morgen, eds., *Women and the Politics of Empowerment* (Philadelphia: Temple University Press, 1988), p. 33.

15. Aihwa Ong, *Spirits of Resistance and Capitalist Discipline: Factory Women in Malaysia* (Albany: State University of New York Press, 1987), p. 220.

16. Emily Martin, *The Woman in the Body: A Cultural Analysis of Reproduction* (Boston: Beacon Press, 1987), p. 110.

17. Louise Lamphere, *From Working Daughters to Working Mothers: Immigrant Women in a New England Industrial Community* (Ithaca, N.Y.: Cornell University Press, 1987), pp. 29–30.

18. Lamphere, *From Working Daughters to Working Mothers,* p. 30.

19. Judith Butler, *Gender Trouble: Feminism and the Subversion of Identity* (New York: Routledge, 1990), p. 27.

20. Butler, *Gender Trouble,* p. 17.

21. Ibid.

22. Although artificial insemination is often included among the "new" reproductive technologies such as in vitro fertilization, embryo transfer, and sex predetermination, there is actually nothing particularly new about the procedure. Originally developed for use in animal husbandry, artificial insemination by donor (AID) conceptions are estimated as accounting for thousands of births in the United States each year. See Martin Curie-Cohen, Lesleigh Luttrell, and Sander Shapiro, "Current Practice of Artificial Insemination by Donor in the United States," *New England Journal of Medicine* 300 (11) (1979), pp. 585–590.

The procedure itself introduces sperm into the vagina with a needle-less syringe at a time calculated to coincide with the woman's ovulation. Once methods for freezing sperm were perfected in 1949, the possibility of expanded use presented itself (both for animals and for humans), as sperm banks and various sorts of matching services came into existence; Gena Corea, *The Mother Machine: Reproductive Technologies from Artificial Insemination to Artificial Wombs* (New York: Harper and Row, 1985), p. 36. At present, there is only minimal government regulation of artificial insemination or of sperm banks. Sperm banks and access to medically supervised insemination are controlled almost exclusively by physicians, who act as gatekeepers in terms of who may have access to frozen sperm. This means both that medical screening of donors is far from consistent or reliable and that physicians tend to use their personal values to determine who should have access to these services; Judith N. Lasker and Susan Borg, *In Search of Parenthood: Coping with Infertility and High-Tech Conception* (Boston: Beacon Press, 1987). Since frozen sperm can be expensive, unmarried women, as well as low-income patients may not have the same access to insemination as affluent couples: Curie-Cohen, Luttrell, and Shapiro, "Current Practice of Artificial Insemination"; Maureen McGuire and Nancy Alexander, "Artificial Insemination of Single Women," *Fertility and Sterility* 43 (1985), pp. 182–184; Carson Strong and Jay Schinfeld, "The Single Woman and Artificial Insemination by Donor," *Journal of Reproductive Medicine* 29 (1984), pp 293–299.

Despite these obstacles, the low-tech nature of artificial insemination and the possibility of mobilizing alternatives to physician-controlled sperm banks have meant that women, in fact, can easily retain control of the procedure. Women whose physicians may be unwilling to inseminate—whether they be single, low-income, or lesbian—can use their informal networks to carry out insemination outside conventional medical settings; Rona Achilles, "Donor insemination: The Future of a Public Secret," in Christine Overall, ed., *The Future of Human Reproduction* (Toronto: The Women's Press, 1989), pp. 105–119; Francie Hornstein, "Children by Donor Insemination: A New Choice for Lesbians," in Rita Arditti, Renate Duelli Klein, and Shelley Minden, eds., *Test-Tube Women: What Future for Motherhood?* (London: Pandora Press, 1984),

pp. 373–381; Ellen Lewin, "By Design: Reproductive Strategies and the Meaning of Motherhood," in Hilary Homans, ed., *The Sexual Politics of Reproduction* (London: Gower, 1985), pp. 123–138.

In the late 1970s, this process was generally called "artificial insemination." Within a few years, however, mothers began to use alternate language, labeling the procedure either "donor insemination" or simply "insemination" in an effort to downplay the implication that there was anything intrinsically "unnatural" about getting pregnant in this way.

23. Names and some other details have been changed to preserve the anonymity of women whom I interviewed. For a detailed account of the methods used in this research, see Lewin, *Lesbian Mothers.*

24. Adoption, though difficult, was another approach used by lesbians who wished to become mothers. Because of the large number of two-parent families who wish to adopt, and the small number of healthy newborn babies available for adoption, single women (and men) are rarely considered prime candidates as adoptive parents. Their chances are, of course, even slighter if they are known to be lesbian or gay. Adoption is more in reach of these prospective parents if they can arrange a private adoption or if they are willing to adopt an older, disabled, abused, or minority/mixed-race child—those considered less desirable. See Editors of the Harvard Law Review, *Sexual Orientation and the Law* (Cambridge, MA: Harvard University Press, 1989).

25. Robert Bellah, et al., *Habits of the Heart: Individualism and Commitment in American Life* (Berkeley: University of California Press, 1985), p. 65.

26. Bellah, *Habits of the Heart,* p. 82.

27. Lewin, *Lesbian Mothers.*

28. See Ellen Lewin, *Lesbian Mothers,* and "On the Outside Looking In: The Politics of Lesbian Motherhood," in Faye Ginsburg and Rayna Rapp, eds., *Conceiving the New World Order: Local/Global Intersections in the Politics of Reproduction* (Berkeley: University of California Press, 1995, for a discussion of how the popular media has accommodated images of lesbian families and poses them in opposition to still-abnormal childless lesbians.

THE NEW ACTIVISM: LESBIAN AND GAY PARENTING

CHRIS BULL

It was enough to strike terror in the heart of any parent. To support legislation to ban adoption and foster care by lesbian and gay parents, a right-wing organization took the unprecedented step of singling out one couple and their children as targets for political purposes. The group's method: sending a letter to every member of the Texas legislature challenging the lesbian couple's adoption of twins on the grounds that the children would be better off in a "traditional family."

The women in question were Elizabeth Birch, executive director of the Human Rights Campaign, the nation's largest gay advocacy organization, and Hilary Rosen, president of the Recording Industry Association of America, a trade group. In the fall of 1998 the couple had arranged to adopt twins, who were born the following January 7 to a woman in Texas and whom they named Jacob and Anna Rosen-Birch.

"Hillary and I have always had gay rights issues in the forefront of our lives, but we have never had anything cut as close to our souls as becoming parents," Birch says. "The bonding process with your children is so deep that we would do anything to protect it from those who threaten it. What we did in adopting is a very private thing, and when the Right got ahold of it, it felt very mean and personal."

The Birch–Rosen adoption was indeed finalized, despite popular support for the antigay-parenting bill. But the fear it caused the couple was familiar to millions of gay parents across America who seek legal and social recognition for their children. If Birch and Rosen—well connected Washington power brokers—could be threatened with losing a child, it could happen to almost anyone.

Of course, there have always been parents who happened to be gay. But now their open embrace of home and hearth has taken on increasingly political overtones, extending their demands for equal rights to school-

houses and day care centers, where gay activists have traditionally been outsiders. "It wasn't that long ago that gay parenting was thought to be a contradiction in terms," says C. Ray Drew, executive director of the Family Pride Coalition, a national parenting support and advocacy group based in San Diego. "Nor gay people realize that they do not have to negate that part of their lives, and they are putting tremendous pressure on the system to accommodate their needs in raising children."

The politics of gay parenting has breathed new energy into more traditional gay rights measures as well. Many parents have taken on sodomy laws, which have repeatedly been cited to deny gay parents custody on the grounds that they are habitual lawbreakers. Antidiscrimination ordinances are increasingly seen as protecting not only the jobs of gay parents but also the health insurance that covers their children. National and state bans on marriage are sending many same-sex parents scurrying to find other means of legal recognition to formalize some aspects of their families.

While it is difficult to measure precisely the number of children raised by gay parents, most experts put the number well into the millions. Gay men and lesbians travel many roads to parenthood. Some are rearing kids from previous heterosexual marriages. Others, however, approached parenthood as openly gay or lesbian individuals or couples. They have planned families through means that range from biological coparenting with an opposite-sex friend to artificial insemination to adoption and foster care.

Anecdotal evidence suggests that gay parenting is booming. Gay churches and synagogues, for instance, minister to so many gay parents that they have opened child care centers for their members. Parks in predominantly gay neighborhoods like the Castro and Noe Valley in San Francisco and New York City's Greenwich Village overflow with gay parents and their children.

"In talking with doctors and attorneys, it's clear there are more gay parents than ever," says Kelly Taylor, founder and editor of *Alternative Family* magazine, a bimonthly publication for gay parents. "Lesbians have always been parents, but now men are increasingly interested as well. Many we've spoken to really did not believe they could become parents until recently." Taylor started the magazine shortly after the birth of her daughter in 1998.

Moreover, parenting has transformed ordinary gay men and lesbians into cultural warriors, changing the face of gay life and politics forever. "It's hard to believe that just a few years ago Michael and I were just a couple of queens living in a fabulous apartment in New York," says Jon Galluccio, who changed his surname to that of his partner, Michael, on the couple's sixteenth anniversary last year. "It has politicized us beyond our wildest dreams." In 1997 they won the right to coadopt their son, Adam, making them the first same-sex couple in New Jersey to be granted this right. On May 17 they finalized the adoption of another foster child, Madison. They are also planning to adopt Madison's six-year-old stepsister, Rosa.

The political ramifications are far from clear, however. The new emphasis on family matters puts gays and lesbians on a collision course with the religious right, which seeks to define family in strict. "Leave It to Beaver" terms: mom, pop, and a couple of kids. For instance, in a January 12 press release decrying Birch and Rosen's adoption, the Family Research Council, a Washington, D.C.-based conservative religious group, declared that "homosexual activists put their personal desires above the rights of these children to have a chance at normal family life with a father and a mother." Gary Bauer, FRC's former president who resigned to seek the Republican presidential nomination, has vowed to raise the issue on the campaign trail.

But gay parenting coincides with a broader reconfiguration of households and kinship. "The definition of family has been changing at an exponential pace, and you better believe the change is not just about gay people," says Pepper Schwartz, a professor of sociology at the University of Washington in Seattle. "More heterosexuals are having children through surrogates, there are more children of divorced parents, and there are more single moms and dads than ever before. The public is in the process of realizing the family is not its structure—it's what you make of it as long as there is a lifetime commitment to children."

In the meantime, however, lesbians and gay men are facing a backlash as the most visible—and most politi-

cally vulnerable—part of the changing family dynamic. "Frankly, gay parents are the weakest link among nontraditional families," Schwartz says. "The public is wary of the changes in the family, which is still seen as mom and apple pie. It's a lot easier to go after homosexuals than single moms."

It took the case of Sharon Bottoms to draw many Americans' attention to the plight of gay families. In her case the Virginia supreme court in 1995 upheld the 1993 ruling of a county juvenile court judge, which stripped Bottoms, the biological mother of a two-year-old boy, of custody solely because she is a lesbian. In granting custody of the boy to Bottoms's mother, the judge ruled that Bottoms was an unfit parent because she had both acted immorally and violated the state's sodomoy law by engaging in lesbian sex.

Other gay parents are determined to avoid Bottom's fate. Like Birch and Rosen, the Galluccios were targeted by the religious right. On its Internet portal, FRC labeled the Galluccios "twisted" and listed them among the "bad of 1998." Jon Galluccio credits a January 13 Frank Rich column in the *New York Times,* titled "Family Values Stalkers," with stemming the personal attacks. "The public exposure showed how ugly they really are—attacking not just people but their kids as well—and they just couldn't deny it," he says. "We've accepted a public role, so we are ready for criticism. But don't dehumanize our children."

Even for people accustomed to political battles, parenthood dramatically raises the stakes. Many agonize over the potential that public scrutiny—to say nothing of the often viciously personal attacks—has to violate the privacy of their intimate relationships with their children. Daniel Zingale is a case in point. The executive director of AIDS Action, a Washington, D.C., AIDS lobby group, Zingale and his partner, Chuck Supple, adopted a baby boy in 1997. But Zingale declines to state his son's country of birth, saying it could open the door to challenges by antigay activists or the country's government, even though the adoption has legal standing in the United States. "By its very nature there is nothing more personal than a bond with a child," he says. "And we want to keep it that way."

Zingale says parenthood has changed his worldview. "When I heard about the murder of Matthew Shepard, I experienced it first as a parent and second as a gay man, whereas in the past I would have seen it primarily as a gay man who could be vulnerable to violence myself," he says. "I felt a kinship with parents who are concerned about the safety of their kids. I believe there is a commonality that transcends sexual orientation, and that will help us politically in the long run."

Although Galluccio sympathizes with those who seek to protect their children by staying away from the public spotlight, he says, "We knew from the beginning that we would have to be out in ways we could never imagine. I can't tell you how many times I've been at ShopRite with Adam in the shopping cart and someone will say, "Is it Mommy's day off? and I will respond, 'There is no mom. Adam has another dad.' Everyone wants to create a better life for theirs kids than they had. In our lifetime we want to see a world where kids of gay parents are accepted just like everyone else."

As one of the most visible activists in the county, Birch is also worried about the effect the publicity generated by her activism will have on her children. On many workdays she brings them into the HRC office in Washington, D.C., where the staff takes great pleasure in playing with them. But she will not allow the news media to photograph them. "I've admired the way the president and Mrs. Clinton have kept Chelsea out of the spotlight, and the press has generally been respectful of that," she says. "We want our children to make up their own minds when they are old enough about how public they will be."

For some gays and lesbians, parenting is the very thing that made them public figures. Stacy Jolles and Nina Beck say parenting has helped them overcome vestiges of their own homophobia. In 1995 Beck gave birth to a boy, Noah, who had a congenital heart defect. Jolles adopted Noah, who died in 1997. "I did most of my growing up as a parent," Jolles says. "We knew he was going to have a short life, and having to make life-and-death decisions for a child was a very sobering experience. We wanted to make sure that we're secure enough in our own identity as lesbian parents that we did not pass along any doubt to our child."

That experience in turn prompted the couple to sign on as plaintiffs in *Baker v. Vermont,* a lawsuit seeking same-sex marriage in the state. The Vermont supreme court heard oral arguments in November and may issue a ruling by the end of the year. "Our marriage activism grew naturally out of the parenting experience," Beck

says. "While we have legal parenting right as the biological and adoptive parents, marriage would offer us further protection by allowing us to have our house in both our names, for instance. It would bring more stability to our family."

Despite the qualms of parents involved in politics, this is one battle gay rights activists are confident they will win in the end. Many gay leaders have a personal stake in the outcome as well. In addition to Birch and Zingale, Joan Garry, executive director of the Gay and Lesbian Alliance Against Defamation, and Rebecca Isaacs, political director of the National Gay and Lesbian Task Force, among others, are raising children. "Americans are very reluctant to interfere in personal decisions about parenting," Birch says. "They don't want the religious right making the decision for them."

Still, antigay groups are not the only critics of gay parenting. As lesbians and gays turn their attention to family rights, advocates of sexual liberation fear that the gay movement is losing its political and sexual edge. Michael Bronski, author of *The Pleasure Principle: Sex, Backlash, and the Struggle for Gay Freedom,* says that like heterosexual families, many gay parents give up active roles in the larger urban community for a cloistered existence in the suburbs. "I'm worried that gay parenting could drain energy from grassroots politics," he says. "There are so few people who are really active in the gay movement anyway, and I don't think that many parents really do get involved in suburban school boards or PTAs. Urban gay areas have been the heart and soul of gay life, and they are threatened by this trend."

The battle may ultimately hinge on which family structure is deemed best for children. On that score lesbians and gay men are bolstered by a growing body of scientific literature indicating the children of gay parents are just as healthy and well-adjusted as those raised by opposite-sex couples. A 1992 survey of the findings of thirty studies of the children of gay parents published in the psychological journal *Child Development* concluded that the studies were nearly unanimous in their findings that the children had developed normally. FRC and other conservative groups cite a 1983 study by the right-wing Family Research Institute that indicated children of gay parents were more likely to be gay themselves. But that out-of-date study is hampered by a small sample size and the reputation of its author, Paul Cameron, a widely discredited antigay researcher.

"The mainstream research shows that gay parents are as talented as any other parent," Schwartz says. "Voluntary adoptive parents, whether gay or straight, tend to be among the best parents because they really want to be parents. Children need to know that they are wanted. Once courts and legislators look at the studies rather than the stereotypes, it will make a big difference."

But surveys never tell the whole story. Beck is pregnant again. Like all parents who have lost a child, Beck and Jolles are experiencing a combination of trepidation and hope. But unlike nongay parents, they have special lessons they want to impart to their child. "I want our child to know that no matter what the rest of the world thinks," Beck says, "being brought up in a lesbian household is just fine and dandy."

SECTION SEVEN

Sexuality

The processes of socialization encourage women and men to develop different views of and approaches to sexuality and intimate relationships. Women learn strong interpersonal and emotional skills in preparation for roles as wives and mothers and for employment in professions associated with nurturing, such as teaching and nursing. At the same time, women's and men's different positions in social institutions mean that we enter our intimate and sexual relationships with different amounts and kinds of resources, power, networks, and expectations. In addition, we are surrounded by a culture that portrays women and men as having intrinsically different sexual needs, desires, and obligations. The readings in this section discuss how sexuality is gendered, showing how even such a seemingly personal matter as sexuality is *socially constructed* in various ways in different contexts.

The first two readings show how two very different groups of women interpreted their same-sex relationships during the 1940s and 1950s. They raise fascinating questions about how people make sense of their sexual experiences in various ways. In "Oral History and the Study of Sexuality in the Lesbian Community: Buffalo, New York, 1940–1960," Madeline Davis and Elizabeth Lapovsky Kennedy document the sexual, social, and political evolution of a lesbian community. In constructing that community, lesbians created sexual roles that validated women's sexuality and laid the groundwork for the feminist and gay liberation movements. By paying careful attention to the practices of participants in

the Buffalo community during this time, the reading underscores how groups construct and understand sexuality and intimacy in various ways according to the social context.

Leila Rupp provides another illustration of the various interpretations women develop of their intimate lives in " 'Imagine My Surprise': Women's Relationships in Mid-Twentieth-Century America." Women's relegation to the "private sphere," combined with changing expectations for how women should conduct themselves in relationships, makes it difficult to interpret women's sexual and intimate lives. Rupp explores the difficulty of labeling women's intimate relationships with other women as lesbian relationships, given changing definitions of lesbianism in different social and historical contexts. By allowing the letters and other documents of women to speak for themselves, Rupp offers us insight into our foremothers' lives and provides an example of feminist historical analysis. The article contrasts with Davis and Kennedy's account of the Buffalo lesbian community: Although both groups of women formed intimate relationships with other women, the working-class lesbians of Davis and Kennedy's study interpreted their relationships very differently from Rupp's middle-class subjects. What do you think explains the differences in the identities and communities these two groups constructed?

The next article, "Doing Desire: Adolescent Girls' Struggles for/with Sexuality," by Deborah Tolman, examines how another group of females—adolescent girls—understand their sexuality. Adolescents have

349

been the subject of considerable recent public debate over sexuality, with many politicians suggesting that teenage sexual activity should be discouraged. Yet, Tolman notes, adolescence is the life stage during which we begin to develop our sexual selves and form a sense of our intimate connections to others. Tolman examines how adolescent girls construct desire, tracing the complex mix of pleasure and desire with danger and fear, and highlighting differences of sexual orientation. As a result of the cultural repression of women's sexuality, Tolman argues, adolescent girls are "denied full access to the power of their own desire." How do the girls Tolman discusses come to understand their sexual selves in this context? Can you think of examples of how teenage sexuality is understood in discussions of public policy or sex education?

The final article examines the social construction of men's sexuality. Bachelor parties are a pervasive cultural ritual that Jason Schultz argues often reinforce a model of male sexuality that depends on objectifying women. In "Getting Off on Feminism," Schultz describes his attempt to organize a nonsex-

ist, yet still "sexy," bachelor party, and in the process begins to show what a nonsexist model of male heterosexuality could look like. He argues that honesty and communication about sexual desires and experiences can move us toward a sexuality that is not defined by reproduction and doesn't rely on conventional models of men's aggression and women's passivity. What is the traditional model of straight male sexuality? What does Schultz think an egalitarian model of male heterosexuality would be? What would a nonsexist model of heterosexual sex look like for women? Do you agree with Schultz that constructing a "new feminist sexuality for men" is important?

Like family life, sexuality and intimate relationships are both a source of support and strength for women and a location of oppression. What do these readings suggest about how women find sexuality to be a means of fulfillment and an expression of self-definition? In contrast, how do the readings show sexuality to be a means of social control? In short, how are women oppressed and how do they resist in their intimate and sexual lives?

Oral History and the Study of Sexuality in the Lesbian Community: Buffalo, New York, 1940–1960

MADELINE DAVIS and ELIZABETH LAPOVSKY KENNEDY

We began a study of the history of the Buffalo lesbian community, 1940–1960, to determine that community's contribution to the emergence of the gay liberation movement of the 1960s.[1] Because this community centered around bars and was highly role defined, its members often have been stereotyped as low-life societal discards and pathetic imitators of heterosexuality. We suspected instead that these women were heroines who had shaped the development of gay pride in the twentieth century by forging a culture for survival and resistance under prejudicial conditions and by passing this sense of community on to newcomers; in our minds, these are indications of a movement in its prepolitical stages.[2] Our original research plan assumed the conceptual division between the public (social life and politics) and the private (intimate life and sex), which is deeply rooted in modern consciousness and which feminism has only begun to question. Thus we began our study by looking at gay and lesbian bars—the public manifestations of gay life at the time—and relegated sex to a position of less importance, viewing it as only incidentally relevant. As our research progressed we came to question the accuracy of this division. This article records the transformation in our thinking and explores the role of sexuality in the cultural and political development of the Buffalo lesbian community.

At first, our use of the traditional framework that separates the public and private spheres was fruitful.[3] Because the women who patronized the lesbian and gay bars of the past were predominantly working class and left no written records, we chose oral history as our method of study.

Madeline Davis and Elizabeth Lopovsky Kennedy. "Oral History and the Study of Sexuality in the Lesbian Community: Buffalo, New York, 1940–1960." *Feminist Studies* 12, no. 1 (Spring 1986). Copyright © 1986 by Feminist Studies, Inc. Reprinted with the permission of Feminist Studies, Inc.

Through the life stories of over forty narrators, we found that there were more bars in Buffalo during the forties and fifties than there are in that city today. Lesbians living all over the city came to socialize in these bars, which were located primarily in the downtown area. Some of these women were born and raised in Buffalo; others had migrated there in search of their kind. In addition, women from nearby cities, Rochester and Toronto, came to Buffalo bars on weekends. Most of the women who frequented these bars had full-time jobs. Many were factory workers, taxi drivers, bartenders, clerical workers, hospital technicians; a few were teachers or women who owned their own businesses.[4]

Our narrators documented, beyond our greatest expectations, the truth of our original hypothesis that this public bar community was a formative predecessor to the modern gay liberation movement. These bars not only were essential meeting places with distinctive cultures and mores, but they were also the central arena for the lesbian confrontation with a hostile world. Participants in bar life were engaged in constant, often violent, struggle for public space. Their dress code announced them as lesbians to their neighbors, to strangers on the streets, and of course to all who entered the bars. Although confrontation with the straight world was a constant during this period, its nature changed over time. In the forties, women braved ridicule and verbal abuse but rarely physical conflict. One narrator of the forties conveys the tone: "There was a great difference in looks between a lesbian and her girl. You had to take a streetcar—very few people had cars. And people would stare and such."[5] In the fifties, with the increased visibility of the established gay community, the concomitant postwar rigidification of sex roles, and the political repression of the McCarthy era, the street dyke emerged. She was a full-time "queer," who frequented the bars even on week-nights and was ready at any time to fight for her space and dignity. Many of our fifties narrators were both aware and proud that their fighting contributed to a safer, more comfortable environment for lesbians today.

> Things back then were horrible, and I think that because I fought like a man to survive I made it somehow easier for the kids coming out today. I did all their fighting for them. I'm not a rich person; I don't even have a lot of money; I don't even have a little money. I would have nothing to leave anybody in this world, but I have that that I can leave to the kids who are coming out now, who will come out into the future, that I left them a better place to come out into. And that's all I have to offer, to leave them. But I wouldn't deny it; even though I was getting my brains beaten up I would never stand up and say, "No, don't hit me, I'm not gay, I'm not gay." I wouldn't do that.

When we initially gathered this material on the growth and development of community life, we placed little emphasis on sexuality. In part we were swept away by the excitement of the material on bars, dress, and the creation of public space for lesbians. In addition, we were part of a lesbian feminist movement that opposed a definition of lesbianism based primarily on sex. Moreover, we were influenced by the popular assumption that sexuality is natural and unchanging and the related sexist assumption of women's sexual passivity—both of which imply that sexuality is not a valid subject for historical study. Only recently have historians turned their attention to sexuality, a topic that used to be of interest mainly to psychologists and the medical profession. Feminists have added impetus to this study by suggesting that women can desire and shape sexual experience. Finally, we were inhibited by the widespread social reluctance to converse frankly about sexual matters. Thus for various reasons, all stemming, at least indirectly, from modern society's powerful ideological division between the public and the private, we were indisposed to consider how important sexuality might have been to the women we were studying.

The strength of the oral history method is that it enables narrators to shape their history, even when their views contradict the assumptions of historians. As our work progressed, narrators volunteered information about their sexual and emotional lives, and often a shyly asked question would inspire lengthy, absorbing discourse. By proceeding in the direction in which these women steered us, we came to realize that sexuality and sexual identity were not incidental but were central to their lives and their community. Our narrators taught us that although securing public space was indeed important, it was strongly motivated by the need to provide a setting for the formation of intimate relationships. It is the nature of this community that it created public space for lesbians and gay men, while at the same time it organized sexuality and emotional relationships. Appreciation of this dynamic interconnection requires new ways of thinking about lesbian history.

What is an appropriate framework for studying the sexual component of a lesbian community's history and for revealing the role of sexuality in the evolution of twentieth-century lesbian and gay politics? So little research has been done in this area that our work is still exploratory and tentative. At present, we seek primarily to understand forms of lesbian sexual expression and to identify changes in sexual norms, experiences, and ideas during the 1940s and 1950s. We also look for the forces behind these changes in the evolving culture and politics of the lesbian community. Our goal has been to ascertain what part, if any, sexuality played in the developing politics of gay liberation. As an introduction to this discussion, we shall present our method of research because it has been crucial in our move to study sexuality, and so little has been written on the use of oral history for research on this topic.

USING ORAL HISTORY TO CONSTRUCT THE HISTORY OF THE BUFFALO LESBIAN COMMUNITY

The memories of our narrators are colorful, illuminating, and very moving. Our purpose, however, was not only to collect individual life stories, but also to use these as a basis for constructing the history of the community. To create from individual memories a historically valid analysis of this community presented a difficult challenge. The method we developed was slow and painstaking.[6] We treated each oral history as a historical document, taking into account the particular social position of each narrator and how that might affect her memories. We also considered how our own point of view influenced the kind of information we received and the way in which we interpreted a narrator's story. We juxtaposed all interviews with one another to identify patterns and contradictions and checked our developing understanding with other sources, such as newspaper accounts, legal cases, and labor statistics.

As mentioned earlier, we first focused on understanding and documenting lesbian bar life. From the many vibrant and humorous stories about adventures in bars and from the mountains of seemingly unrelated detail about how people spent their time, we began to identify a chronology of bars and to recognize distinctive social mores and forms of lesbian consciousness that were associated with different time periods and even with different bars. We checked and supplemented our analysis by research into newspaper accounts of bar raids and closings and actions of the State Liquor Authority. Contradictions frequently emerged in our material on bars, but, as we pursued them, we found they were rarely due to idiosyncratic or faulty memory on the part of our narrators but to the complexity of bar life. Often the differences could be resolved by taking into account the different social positions of our narrators or the kinds of questions we had asked to elicit the information we received. If conflicting views persisted, we tried to return to our narrators for clarification. Usually we found that we had misunderstood our narrators or that contradictions indeed existed in the community at the time. For instance, narrators consistently told us about the wonderful times in bars as well as how terrible they were. We came to understand that both of these conditions were part of the real experience of bar life.

When we turned our attention to sexuality and romance in this community, we were at first concerned that our method would not be adequate. Using memories to trace the evolution of sexual norms and expression is, at least superficially, more problematic than using them to document social life in bars. There are no concrete public events or institutions to which the memories can be linked. Thus, when a narrator talks about butch–fem sexuality in the forties, we must bear in mind the likelihood that she has modified her view and her practice of butch–fem sexuality in the fifties, sixties, seventies, and eighties. In contrast, when a narrator tells about bars in the forties, even though social life in bars might have changed over the last forty years, she can tie her memories to a concrete place like Ralph Martin's bar, which existed during a specific time period. Although not enough is known about historical memory to fully evaluate data derived from either type of narrative, our guess is that, at least for lesbian communities, they are equally valid.[7] The vividness of our narrators' stories suggests that the potential of oral history to generate full and rich documents about women's sexuality might be especially rich in the lesbian community. Perhaps lesbian memories about sexual ideals and experiences are

not separated from the rest of life because the building of public communities is closely connected with the pursuit of intimate relationships. In addition, during this period, when gay oppression marked most lesbians' lives with fear of punishment and lack of acceptance, sexuality was one of the few areas in which many lesbians found satisfaction and pleasure. This was reinforced by the fact that, for lesbians, sexuality was not directly linked with the pain and/or danger of women's responsibility for childbearing and women's economic dependence on men. Therefore, memories of sexual experience might be more positive and more easily shared. But these ideas are tentative. An understanding of the nature of memory about sexuality must await further research.

The difficulty of tying memories about sexual or emotional life to public events does present special problems. We cannot identify specific dates for changes in sexual and emotional life, such as when sex became a public topic of conversation or when role-appropriate sex became a community concern. We can talk only of trends within the framework of decades. In addition, we are unable to find supplementary material to verify and spark our narrators' memories. There are no government documents or newspaper reports on lesbian sexuality. The best one can find are memoirs or fiction written about or by residents in other cities, and even these don't exist for participants in working-class communities of the forties.[8] In general, we have not found these problems to require significant revision of our method.

Our experience indicates that the number of people interviewed is critical to the success of our method, whether we are concerned with analyzing the history of bar life or of emotional and sexual life. We feel that between five and ten narrators' stories need to be juxtaposed in order to develop an analysis that is not changed dramatically by each new story. At the present time, our analysis of the white lesbian community of the fifties is based on oral histories from over fifteen narrators. In contrast, we have only five narrators who participated in the white community of the forties, four for the black community of the fifties, and one from the black community of the forties. Therefore, we emphasize the fifties in this article and have the greatest confidence in our analysis of that decade. Our discussion of the forties must be viewed as only tentative. Our material on the black community is not yet sufficient for separate treatment; so black and white narrators' memories are interspersed throughout the article. Ultimately, we hope to be able to write a history of each community.

SEXUALITY AS PART OF THE CULTURAL POLITICAL DEVELOPMENT OF THE BUFFALO LESBIAN COMMUNITY

Three features of lesbian sexuality during the forties and fifties suggest its integral connection with the lesbian community's cultural-political development. First, butch–fem roles created an authentic lesbian sexuality appropriate to the flourishing of an independent lesbian culture. Second, lesbians actively pursued rich and fulfilling sexual lives at a time when sexual subjectivity was not the norm for women. This behavior was not only consistent with the creation of a separate lesbian culture, but it also represented the roots of a personal and political feminism that characterized the gay liberation movement of the sixties. Third, although butch–fem roles and the pursuit of sexual autonomy remained constant throughout this period, sexual mores changed in relation to the evolving forms of resistance to oppression.

Most commentators on lesbian bar life in the forties and fifties have noted the prominence of butch–fem roles.[9] Our research corroborates this; we found that roles constituted a powerful code of behavior that shaped the way individuals handled themselves in daily life, including sexual expression. In addition, roles were the primary organizer for the lesbian stance toward the straight world as well as for building love relationships and for making friends.[10] To understand butch–fem roles in their full complexity is a fundamental issue for students of lesbian history; the particular concern of this article is the intricate connection between roles and sexuality. Members of the community, when explaining how one recognized a person's role, regularly referred to two underlying determinants: image, including dress and mannerism, and sexuality.[11] Some people went so far as to say that one never really knew a woman's role identity until one went to bed with her. "You can't tell butch–fem by people's dress. You couldn't even really tell in the fifties. I knew women with long hair, fem clothes, and found out they were butches. Actually I even knew one who wore men's clothes, haircuts, and ties, who was a fem."

Today, butch–fem roles elicit deep emotional reactions from many heterosexuals and lesbians. The former are affronted by women assuming male prerogatives; the latter by lesbians adopting male-defined role models. The hostility is exemplified by the prevalent ugly stereotype of the butch–fem sexual dyad: the butch with her dildo or penis substitute, trying to imitate a man, and the simpering passive fem who is kept in her place by ignorance. This representation evokes pity for lesbians because women who so

interact must certainly be sexually unfulfilled; one partner cannot achieve satisfaction because she lacks the "true" organ of pleasure, and the other is cheated because she is denied the complete experience of the "real thing." Our research counters the view that butch–fem roles are solely an imitation of sexist heterosexual society.

Inherent in butch–fem relationships was the presumption that the butch is the physically active partner and the leader in lovemaking. As one butch narrator explains, "I treat a woman as a woman, down to the basic fact it'd have to be my side doin' most of the doin'." Insofar as the butch was the doer and the fem was the desired one, butch–fem roles did indeed parallel the male/female roles in heterosexuality. Yet unlike the dynamics of many heterosexual relationships, the butch's foremost objective was to give sexual pleasure to a fem; it was in satisfying her fem that the butch received fulfillment. "If I could give her satisfaction to the highest, that's what gave me satisfaction." As for the fem, she not only knew what would give her physical pleasure, but she also knew that she was neither object nor receptacle for someone else's gratification. The essence of this emotional/sexual dynamic is captured by the ideal of the "stone butch," or untouchable butch, that prevailed during this period. A "stone butch" does all the "doin' " and does not ever allow her lover to reciprocate in kind. To be untouchable meant to gain pleasure from giving pleasure. Thus, although these women did draw on models in heterosexual society, they transformed those models into an authentically lesbian interaction. Through role playing they developed distinctive and fulfilling expressions of women's sexual love for women.

The archetypal lesbian couple of the 1940s and 1950s, the "stone butch" and the fem, poses one of the most tantalizing puzzles of lesbian history and possibly of the history of sexuality in general.[12] In a culture that viewed women as sexually passive, butches developed a position as sexual aggressor, a major component of which was untouchability. However, the active or "masculine" partner was associated with the giving of sexual pleasure, a service usually assumed to be "feminine." Conversely, the fem, although the more passive partner, demanded and received sexual pleasure and in this sense might be considered the more self-concerned or even more "selfish" partner. These attributes of butch–fem sexual identity remove sexuality from the realm of the "natural," challenging the notion that sexual performance is a function of biology and affirming the view that sexual gratification is socially constructed.

Within this framework of butch–fem roles, individual lesbians actively pursued sexual pleasure. On the one hand, butch–fem roles limited sexual expression by imposing a definite structure. On the other hand, this structure ordered and gave a determinant shape to lesbian desire, which allowed individuals to know and find what they wanted. The restrictions of butch–fem sexuality, as well as the pathways it provided for satisfaction, are best captured and explored by examining what it meant for both butch and fem that the butch was the doer; how much leeway was there before the butch became fem, or the fem became butch?

Although there was complete agreement in the community that the butch was the leader in lovemaking, there was a great deal of controversy over the feasibility or necessity of being a "stone butch." In the forties, most butches lived up to the *ideal* of "the untouchable." One fem, who was in a relationship with an untouchable butch at that time, had tried to challenge her partner's behavior but met only with resistance. Her butch's whole group—those who hung out at Ralph Martin's—were the same. "Because I asked her one time, I said, 'Do you think that you might be just the only one?' 'Oh no,' she said. 'I know I'm not, you know, that I've discussed with . . . different people.' [There were] no exceptions, which I thought was ODD, but, I thought, well, you know. This is how it is."

In the fifties, the "stone butch" became a publicly discussed model for appropriate sexual behavior, and it was a standard that young butches felt they had to achieve to be a "real" or "true" butch. In contrast to the forties, a fifties' fem who was out in the community would not have had to ask her butch friend why she was untouchable and if there were others like her. She would have known it was the expected behavior for butches. Today our narrators disagree over whether it was, in fact, possible to maintain the ideal and they are unclear about the degree of latitude allowed in the forties or fifties before a butch harmed her reputation. Some butches claim that they were absolutely untouchable; that was how they were, and that's how they enjoyed sex. When we confronted one of our narrators, who referred to herself as an "untouchable," with the opinion of another narrator, who maintained that "stone butches" had never really existed, she replied, "No, that's not true. I'm an 'untouchable.' I've tried to have my lover make love to me, but I just couldn't stand it. . . . I really think there's something physical about that." Like many of our butch narrators, this woman has always been spontaneously orgasmic; that is, her excitement level peaks to orgasm while making love to another woman. Another "stone butch" explains: "I wanted to satisfy them [women], and I wanted to make love—I love to make love. I still think

that's the greatest thing in life. But I don't want them to touch me. I feel like that spoils the whole thing—I am the way I am. And I figure if a girl is attracted to me, she's attracted to me because of what I am."

Other butches who consider themselves, and have the reputation of being, untouchable claim that it is, as a general matter, impossible to be completely untouchable. One, when asked if she were really untouchable, replied, "Of course not. How would any woman stay with me if I was? It doesn't make any sense. . . . I don't believe there was ever such a class—other than what they told each other." This woman preferred not to be touched, but she did allow mutual lovemaking from time to time during her long-term relationships. A first time in bed, however:

> There's no way in hell that you would touch me . . . if you mean untouchable like that. But if I'm living with a woman, I'd have to be a liar if I said that she hadn't touched me. But I can say that I don't care for it to happen. And the only reason it does happen is because she wants it. It's not like something I desire or want. But there's no such thing as an untouchable butch—and I'm the finest in Buffalo and I'm telling you straight—and don't let them jive you around it—no way.

This narrator's distinction between her behavior on a first night and her behavior in long-term relationships appeared to be accepted practice. The fact that some—albeit little—mutuality was allowed over the period of a long relationship did not affect one's reputation as an untouchable butch, nor did it counter the presumption of the butch as the doer.

This standard of untouchability was so powerful in shaping the behavior of fifties' butches that many never experienced their fems making love to them. By the seventies, however, when we began our interviewing, norms had changed enough so that our butch narrators had had opportunities to experience various forms of sexual expression. Still, many of them—in fact all of those quoted above on "stone butches"—remained untouchable. It was their personal style long after community standards changed. Today these women offer explanations for their preference that provide valuable clues about both the personal importance and the social "rightness" of untouchability as a community norm in the forties and fifties. Some women, as indicated in one of the above quotes, continue to view their discomfort with being touched as physical or biological. Others feel that if a fem were allowed the physical liberties usually associated with the butch role, distinctions would blur and the relationship would become confusing. "I feel that if we're in bed and she does the same thing to me that I do her, we're the same thing." Another narrator, reflecting on the fact that she always went to bed with her clothes on, suggests that "what it came to was being uncomfortable with the female body. You didn't want people you were with to realize the likeness between the two." Still other butches are hesitant about the vulnerability implicit in mutual lovemaking. "When the first girl wanted to make a mutual exchange sexually, . . . I didn't want to be in the position of being at somebody's disposal, or at their command that much—maybe that's still inside me. Maybe I never let loose enough."

But many untouchables of the fifties did try mutual lovemaking later on, and it came as a pleasant surprise when they found they enjoyed being touched. "For some reason . . . I used to get enough mental satisfaction by satisfying a woman . . . then it got to the point where this one woman said, 'Well, I'm just not gonna accept that,' and she started venturing, and at first I said, 'No, no,' and then I said, 'Well, why not?' and I got to enjoy it." This change was not easy for a woman who had spent many years as an "untouchable." At first she was very nervous and uncomfortable about mutual sex, but "after I started reaching physical climaxes instead of just mental, it went, that little restlessness about it. It just mellowed me right out, y'know." The social pressure of the times prevented some women from experiencing expanded forms of sexual expression they might have enjoyed, and it also put constraints upon some women who had learned mutual sex outside of a structured community. One of our narrators had begun her sex life with mutual relations and enjoyed it immensely, but in order to conform to the community standard for butches, adopted untouchability as her sexual posture. She accepted this behavioral change willingly and saw it as a logical component of her role during this period.

How was a community able to monitor the sexual activities of its members, and how might people come to know if a butch "rolled over"—the community lingo for a butch who allowed fems to make love to her? The answer is simple: fems talked! A butch's reputation was based on her performance with fems.

Despite the fact that sexual performance could build or destroy a butch's reputation, some butches of the fifties completely ignored the standard of untouchability. Our narrators give two reasons for this. One reason is the opinion that a long-term relationship requires some degree of mutuality to survive. One butch, a respected leader of the community because of her principles, her affability, and her organizational skills, was not only "touchable" but also suspects that most of the butches she knew in the fifties were not "stone butches." "Once you get in bed or in your bedroom and the lights go out, when you get in between those sheets, I don't think there's any male or there's any female or butch or fem, and it's a fifty–fifty thing. And I think that any relationship . . . any true relationship that's gonna survive has got to be that way. You can't be a giver and can't be a taker. You've gotta both be givers and both gotta be takers." The second reason is the pleasure of being touched. Some women experienced this in the fifties and continued to follow the practice.

> When it came to sex [in the fifties] butches were untouchable, so to speak. They did all the lovemaking, but love was not made back to them. And after I found out how different it was, and how great it was, I said, "What was I missing?" I remember a friend of mine, that I had, who dressed like a man all her life . . . and I remember talking to [her] and saying to her, you know you've got to stop being an untouchable butch, and she just couldn't agree. And I remember one time reaching over and pinching her and I said, "Did you feel that?" and she said, "Yes," and I said, "It hurt, didn't it? Well, why aren't you willing to feel something that's good?"

We do not know if in the forties, as in the fifties, butches who preferred a degree of mutuality in lovemaking existed side by side with the ideal of untouchability because we have considerably less information on that decade. Therefore, we cannot judge whether there was in fact a development toward mutual sexuality, the dominant form of lesbian lovemaking of the sixties and seventies, or whether the "stone butch" prescribed ideal and mutual lovemaking couples existed side by side consistently throughout the forties and fifties.

Our information on fem sexuality is not as extensive as that on butch sexuality because we have been able to contact fewer fem narrators. Nevertheless, from the fems we have interviewed and from comments by butches who sought them out and loved them, we do have an indication that fems were not passive receivers of pleasure, but for the most part knew what they wanted and pursued it.[13] Many butches attributed their knowledge of sex to fems, who educated them by their sexual responsiveness as well as by their explicit directions in lovemaking.

As implied by our discussion of butch sexuality, many fems had difficulty accepting "untouchability." One fem narrator of the forties had a ten-year relationship with an untouchable butch, and the sexual restrictions were a source of discomfort for her. "It was very one-sided, you know, and . . . you never really got a chance to express your love. And I think this kind of suppressed . . . your feelings, your emotions. And I don't know whether that's healthy. I don't think so." But at the same time the majority of these fems appreciated being the center of attention; they derived a strong sense of self-fulfillment from seeking their own satisfaction and giving pleasure—by responding to their butches. "I've had some that I couldn't touch no parts of their bodies. It was all about me. Course I didn't mind! But every once in a while I felt like, well, hey, let me do something to you. I could NEVER understand that. 'Cause I lived with a girl. I couldn't touch any part of her, no part. But boy, did she make me feel good, so I said . . . All right with me . . . I don't mind laying down."

What emerges from our narrators' words is in fact a range of sexual desires that were built into the framework of role-defined sexuality. For butches of the period, we found those who preferred untouchability; those who learned it and liked it; those who learned it and adjusted to it for a time; those who preferred it, but sensed the need for some mutuality; and those who practiced mutuality regularly. For fems, we found those who accepted pleasure, thereby giving pleasure to their lovers; usually such women would aggressively seek what they wanted and instruct their lovers with both verbal and nonverbal cues. Some fems actively sought to make love to their butches and were successful. And finally, we found some women who were not consistent in their roles, changing according to their partners. In the varied sex lives of these role-identified women of the past, we can find the roots of "personal–political" feminism. Women's concern with the ultimate satisfaction of other women is part of a strong sense of female and potentially feminist agency and may be the wellspring for the confidence, the goals, and the needs that shaped the later gay and lesbian feminist movement. Thus, when we develop our understanding of this community as a predecessor to the gay liberation movement, our analysis must include sexuality. For these lesbians actively sought, expanded, and shaped their sexual experience, a radical undertaking for women in the 1940s and 1950s.

Although butch–fem roles were the consistent framework for sexual expression, sexual mores changed and developed throughout this period; two contradictory trends emerged. First, the community became more open to the acceptance of new sexual practices, the discussion of sexual matters, and the learning about sex from friends as well as lovers. Second, the rules of butch–fem sexuality became more rigid, in that community concern for the role-appropriate behavior increased.

In the forties there were at least two social groups, focused in two prominent bars, Ralph Martin's and Winters. According to our narrators, the sexual mores of these two groups differed: the former group was somewhat conservative; the latter group was more experimental, presaging what were to become the accepted norms of the fifties. The lesbian patrons of Ralph Martin's did not discuss sex openly, and oral sex was disdained. "People didn't talk about sex. There was no intimate conversation. It was kind of hush, hush . . . I didn't know there were different ways." By way of contrast, this narrator recalls a visit to Winters, where other women were laughing about "sixty-nine" "I didn't get it. I went to [my partner] and said, 'Somebody says "sixty-nine" and everybody gets hysterical.' " Finally her partner learned what the laughter was all about. At that time our narrator would have mentioned such intimacies only with a lover. It wasn't until later that she got into bull sessions about such topics. Not surprisingly, this narrator does not recall having been taught about sex. She remembers being scared during her first lesbian experience, then found that she knew what to do "naturally." She had no early affairs with partners older than herself.

The Winters' patrons had a more open, experimental attitude toward sex; they discussed it unreservedly and accepted the practice of oral sex. These women threw parties in which women tried threesomes and daisy chains. "People would try it and see how it worked out. But nothing really happened. One person would always get angry and leave, and they would end up with two." Even if their sexual adventures did not always turn out as planned, these women were unquestionably innovative for their time. Our narrator from the Winters' crowd reminisced that it was always a contrast to go home to the serene life of her religious family. She also raved about two fems who were her instructors in sexual matters, adding, "I was an apt pupil."

During the fifties the picture changed, and the mores of the Ralph Martin's group virtually disappeared. Sex came to be a conversation topic among all social groups. Oral sex became an accepted form of lovemaking, so that an individual who did not practice it was acting on personal preference rather than on ignorance or social proscription. In addition, most of our fifties' butch narrators recall having been teachers or students of sex. As in the Winters' group in the forties, an important teacher for the butch was the fem. "I had one girl who had been around who told me. I guess I really frustrated the hell out of her. And she took a piece of paper and drew me a picture and she said, 'Now you get this spot right here.' I felt like a jerk. I was embarrassed that she had to tell me this." According to our narrator, the lesson helped, and she explains that "I went on to greater and better things."

The fifties also saw the advent of a completely new practice—experienced butches teaching novice butches about sex. One narrator remembers that younger women frequently approached her with questions about sex: "There must be an X on my back. They just pick me out. . . ." She recalls one young butch who "had to know every single detail. She drove me crazy. Jesus Christ, y'know, just get down there and do it—y'get so aggravated." The woman who aggravated her gives the following account of learning about sex:

> And I finally talked to a butch buddy of mine. . . . She was a real tough one. I asked her "What do you do when you make love to a woman?" And we sat up for hours and hours at a time. . . . "I feel sexually aroused by this woman, but if I take her to bed, what am I gonna do?" And she says, "Well, what do you feel like doing?" and I says "Well, the only thing I can think of doing is . . . all I want to do is touch her, but what is the full thing of it . . . you know." So when [she] told me I says, "Really," well there was this one thing in there, uh . . . I don't know if you want me to state it. Maybe I can . . . well, I won't . . . I'll put in terms that you can understand. Amongst other things, the oral gratification. Well, that kind of floored me because I never expected something like that and I thought, well, who knows, I might like it.

She later describes her first sexual experience in which she was so scared that her friend had to shove her into the bedroom where the girl was waiting.

At the same time that attitudes toward discussions of and teachings about sexuality relaxed, the fifties' lesbian community became stricter in enforcing role-appropriate sexuality. Those who deviated from the pattern in the forties might have identified themselves as "lavender butch" and might have been labeled by others as "comme çi, comme ça." Although their divergence from the social norm would have been noticed and discussed, such women were not stigmatized. But the community of the fifties left little room to deviate. Those who did not consistently follow one role in bed were considered "ki-ki" (neither–nor), or more infrequently, "AC/DC," both pejorative terms imposed by the community. Such women were viewed as disruptive of the social order and not to be trusted. They not only elicited negative comments, but they also were often ostracized from social groups. From the perspective of the 1980s, in which mutuality in lovemaking is emphasized as a positive quality, it is important to clarify that "ki-ki" did not refer to an abandonment of role-defined sex but rather to a shifting of sexual posture depending upon one's bed partner. Therefore, it was grounded absolutely in role playing. One of our narrators in fact defined "ki-ki" as "double role playing."[14]

These contradictory trends in attitudes and norms of lesbian sexuality parallel changes in the heterosexual world. Movement toward open discussion of sex, the acceptance of oral sex, and the teaching about sex took place in the society at large, as exemplified by the publication of and the material contained in the Kinsey reports.[15] Similarly, the lesbian community's stringent enforcement of role-defined behavior in the fifties occurred in the context of straight society's postwar move toward a stricter sexual division of labor and the ideology that accompanied it.[16] These parallels indicate a close connection between the evolution of heterosexual and homosexual cultures, a topic that requires further research.[17] At this point, we wish to stress that drawing parallels with heterosexuality can only partially illuminate changes in lesbian sexual mores. As an integral part of lesbian life, lesbian sexuality undergoes transformations that correspond with changing forms of the community's resistance to oppression.

Two developments occurred in this prepolitical period that are fundamental for the later emergence of the lesbian and gay liberation movement of the sixties. The first development was the flourishing of a lesbian culture; the second was the evolving stance of public defiance. The community of the forties was just beginning to support places for public gatherings and socializing, and during this period lesbians were to be found in bars only on weekends. Narrators of the forties do not remember having role models or anyone willing to instruct them in the ways of gay life. The prevalent feeling was that gay life was hard, and if people wanted it, they had to find it for themselves. In the fifties, the number of lesbian bars increased, and lesbians could be found socializing there every night of the week. As bar culture became more elaborate and open, lesbians more freely exchanged information about all aspects of their social lives, including sexuality. Discussion of sex was one of the many dimensions of an increasingly complex culture. The strengthening of lesbian culture and the concomitant repression of gays in the fifties led the community to take a more public stance. This shift toward public confrontation subsequently generated enough sense of pride to counter the acknowledged detriments of gay life so that members of the community were willing to instruct newcomers both socially and sexually. Almost all our narrators who came out in the fifties remember a butch who served as a role model or remember acting as a role model themselves. Instruction about sexuality was part of a general education to community life that developed in the context of expanding community pride.

However, the community's growing public defiance was also related to its increased concern for enforcing role-appropriate behavior in the fifties. Butches were key in this process of fighting back. The butches alone, or the butch–fem couple, were always publicly visible as they walked down the street, announcing themselves to the world. To deal effectively with the hostility of the straight world, and to support one another in physical confrontations, the community developed, for butches in particular, rules of appropriate behavior and forms of organization and exerted pressure on butches to live up to these standards. Because roles organized intimate life, as well as the com-

munity's resistance to oppression, sexual performance was a vital part of these fifties' standards.

From the vantage point of the 1980s and twenty more years of lesbian and gay history, we know that just as evolving community politics created this tension between open discussion and teaching about sex and strict enforcement of role-appropriate sexual behavior, it also effected the resolution. Our research suggests that in the late sixties in Buffalo, with the development of the political activities of gay liberation, explicitly political organizations and tactics replaced butch–fem roles in leading the resistance to gay oppression. Because butch–fem roles were no longer the primary means for organizing the community's stance toward the straight world, the community no longer needed to enforce role-appropriate behavior.[18] This did not mean that butch–fem roles disappeared. As part of a long tradition of creating an authentic lesbian culture in an oppressive society, butch–fem roles remain, for many lesbians, an important code of personal behavior in matters of either appearance, sexuality, or both.

ACKNOWLEDGMENTS

This article is a revision of a paper originally presented at the International Conference on Women's History and Oral History, Columbia University, New York, November 18, 1983. We want to thank Michael Frisch, Ellen DuBois, and Bobbi Prebis for reading the original version and offering us helpful comments. We also want to thank Rayna Rapp and Ronald Grele for their patience throughout the revision process.

NOTES

1. This research is part of the work of the Buffalo Women's Oral History Project, which was founded in 1978 with three goals: (1) to produce a comprehensive, written history of the lesbian community in Buffalo, New York, using as the major source oral histories of lesbians who came out prior to 1970; (2) to create and index an archive of oral history tapes, written interviews, and relevant supplementary materials; and (3) to give this history back to the community from which it derives. Madeline Davis and Elizabeth (Liz) Kennedy are the directors of the project. Avra Michelson was an active member from 1978 to 1981 and had a very important influence on the development of the project. Wanda Edwards has been an active member of the project since 1981, particularly in regard to research on the black lesbian community and on racism in the white lesbian community.

2. This hypothesis was shaped by our personal contact with Buffalo lesbians who came out in the 1940s and 1950s, and by dis-

cussion with grassroots gay and lesbian history projects around the country, in particular the San Francisco Lesbian and Gay History Project, the Boston Area Gay and Lesbian History Project, and the Lesbian Herstory Archives. Our approach is close to and has been influenced by the social constructionist tendency of lesbian and gay history. See in particular Jonathan Katz, *Gay American History: Lesbians and Gay Men in the U.S.A.* (New York: Crowell, 1976); Gayle Rubin, Introduction to *A Woman Appeared to Me,* by Renée Vivien (Nevada: Naiad Press, 1976), iii–xxxvii; Jeffrey Weeks, *Coming Out: Homosexual Politics in Britain from the Nineteenth Century to the Present* (London: Quartet Books, 1977). We want to thank all these sources, which have been inspirational to our work.

3. The Buffalo Women's Oral History Project has written two papers on bar life, both by Madeline Davis, Elizabeth (Liz) Kennedy, and Avra Michelson: "Buffalo Lesbian Bars in the Fifties," presented at the National Women's Studies Association,

Bloomington, Indiana, May 1980, and "Buffalo Lesbian Bars: 1930–1960," presented at the Fifth Berkshire Conference on the History of Women, Vassar College, Poughkeepsie, N.Y., June 1981. Both papers are on file at the Lesbian Herstory Archives, P.O. Box 1258, New York, New York 10116.

4. We think that this community could accurately be designated as a working-class lesbian community, but this is not a concept many members of this community would use; therefore, we have decided to call it a public bar community.

5. All quotes are taken from the interviews conducted for this project between 1978 and 1984. The use of the phrase "lesbian and her girl" in this quote reflects some of our butch narrators' belief that the butch member of a couple was the lesbian and the fem member's identity was less clear.

6. A variety of sources were helpful for learning about issues and problems of oral history research. They include the Special Issue on Women's Oral History, *Frontiers* 2 (Summer 1977); Willa K. Baum, *Oral History for the Local Historical Society* (Nashville, Tenn.: American Association for State and Local History, 1975); Michael Frisch, "Oral History and *Hard Times:* A Review Essay," *Oral History Review* (1979): 70–80; Ronald Grele, ed., *Envelopes of Sound: Six Practitioners Discuss the Method, Theory, and Practice of Oral History and Oral Tradition* (Chicago: Precedent Publishing, 1975); Ronald Grele, "Can Anyone over Thirty Be Trusted?: A Friendly Critique of Oral History," *Oral History Review* (1978): 36–44; "Generations: Women in the South," *Southern Exposure* 4 (Winter 1977); "No More Moanin'," *Southern Exposure* 1 (Winter 1974); Peter Friedlander, *The Emergence of a UAW Local, 1936–1939* (Pittsburgh: University of Pittsburgh Press, 1975); William Lynwood Montell, *The Saga of Coe Ridge: A Study in Oral History* (Knoxville: University of Tennessee Press, 1970); Studs Terkel, *Hard Times: An Oral History of the Great Depression* (New York: Pantheon Books, 1970); Martin B. Duberman, *Black Mountain: An Exploration in Community* (Garden City, N.Y.: Doubleday, 1972); Sherna Gluck, ed., *From Parlor to Prison: Five American Suffragists Talk about Their Lives* (New York: Vintage, 1976); and Kathy Kahn, *Hillbilly Women* (New York: Doubleday, 1972).

7. For a helpful discussion of memory, see John A. Neuenschwander, "Remembrance of Things Past: Oral Historians and Long-Term Memory," *Oral History Review* (1978): 46–53. Many sources cited in the previous note also have relevant discussions of memory; in particular, see Frisch; Grele, *Envelopes of Sound;* Friedlander; and Montell.

8. See for instance Joan Nestle, "Esther's Story: 1960," *Common Lives/Lesbian Lives* 1 (Fall 1981):5–9; Joan Nestle, "Butch–Fem Relationships: Sexual Courage in the 1950s," *Heresies* 12 (1981): 21–24; Audre Lorde, "Tar Beach," *Conditions* no. 5 (1979): 34–47 and Audre Lorde, "The Beginning," in *Lesbian Fiction,* ed. Elly Bulkin (Watertown, Mass.: Persephone Press, 1981), 225–74. Lesbian pulp fiction can also provide insight into the emotional and sexual life of this period; see, for instance, Ann Bannon's *I Am a Woman* (Greenwich, Conn.: Fawcett, 1959) and *Beebo Brinker* (Greenwich, Conn.: Fawcett, 1962).

9. See, for instance, Nestle, "Butch–Fem Relationships"; Lorde, "Tar Beach"; Del Martin and Phyllis Lyon, *Lesbian/Woman* (New York: Bantam, 1972); John D'Emilio, *Sexual Politics, Sexual Communities: The Making of a Homosexual Minority in the United States 1940–1970* (Chicago: University of Chicago Press, 1983).

10. For a full discussion of our research on butch–fem roles, see Madeline Davis and Elizabeth (Liz) Kennedy, "Butch–Fem Roles in the Buffalo Lesbian Community, 1940–1960" (paper presented at the Gay Academic Union Conference, Chicago, October 1982). This paper is on file at the Lesbian Herstory Archives.

11. These two main determinants of roles are quite different from what would usually be considered as indicators of sex roles in straight society; they do not include the sexual division of labor.

12. The origins of the "stone butch" and fem couple are beyond the scope of this paper. For an article that begins to approach these issues, see Esther Newton, "The Mythic Mannish Lesbian: Radclyffe Hall and the New Woman," *Signs* 9 (Summer 1984): 557–75.

13. Our understanding of the fem role has been enhanced by the following: Nestle's "Butch–Fem Relationships" and "Esther's Story"; Amber Hollibaugh and Cherrie Moraga, "What We're Rolling Around in Bed With: Sexual Silences in Feminism: A Conversation toward Ending Them," *Heresies* 12 (1981):58–62.

14. For indications that "ki-ki" was used nationally in the lesbian subculture, see Jonathan Katz, *Gay/Lesbian Almanac: A New Documentary* (New York: Harper & Row, 1983), 15, 626.

15. Alfred C. Kinsey, Wardell B. Pomeroy, and Clyde E. Martin, *Sexual Behavior in the Human Male* (Philadelphia: W. B. Saunders, 1948); and Alfred Kinsey et al., *Sexual Behavior in the Human Female* (Philadelphia: W. B. Saunders, 1953). Numerous sources document this trend; see, for instance, Ann Snitow, Christine Stansell, and Sharon Thompson, eds., *Powers of Desire: The Politics of Sexuality* (New York: Monthly Review Press, 1983), in particular, Introduction, sec. 2, "Sexual Revolutions," and sec. 3, "The Institution of Heterosexuality," 9–47, 115–71, 173–275; and Katz, *Gay/Lesbian Almanac.*

16. See Mary P. Ryan, *Womanhood in America: From Colonial Times to the Present* (New York: Franklin Watts, 1975).

17. A logical result of the social constructionist school of gay history is to consider that heterosexuality is also a social construction. Katz, in *Gay/Lesbian Almanac,* begins to explore this idea.

18. Although national homophile organizations began in the fifties, no such organizations developed in Buffalo until the formation of the Mattachine Society of the Niagara Frontier in 1969. But we do not think that the lack of early homophile organizations in this city made the bar community's use of roles as an organizer of its stance toward the straight world different from that of cities where homophile organizations existed. In general, these organizations, whether mixed or all women, did not draw from or affect bar communities. Martin and Lyon in chap. 8, "Lesbians United," *Lesbian/Woman* (238–79), present Daughters of Bilitis (DOB) as an alternative for those dissatisfied with bar life, not as an organization to coalesce the forces and strengths of the bar community. Gay liberation combined the political organization of DOB and the defiance and pride of bar life and therefore affected and involved both communities.

"Imagine My Surprise": Women's Relationships in Mid-Twentieth-Century America

LEILA J. RUPP

When Carroll Smith-Rosenberg's article "The Female World of Love and Ritual" appeared in the pages of *Signs* in 1975, it revolutionized the way in which women's historians look at nineteenth-century American society and even served notice on the historical profession at large that women's relationships would have to be taken into account in any consideration of Victorian society.[1] Since then we have learned more about relationships between women in the past, but we have not reached consensus on the issue of characterizing these relationships.

Debate within the women's movement has centered around the work of two writers. In 1980, Adrienne Rich published "Compulsory Heterosexuality and Lesbian Existence," in which she argued for the concept of a lesbian continuum based on solidarity among women and resistance to patriarchy rather than on identity or sexual behavior.[2] The next year, Lillian Faderman's *Surpassing the Love of Men,* which traced the history of women's relationships, suggested that the nineteenth-century phenomenon of romantic friendship involved a deep commitment and sensuality but not, ordinarily, genital sexuality.[3] As a result of the controversy that has swirled around these works, we have no simple answer to the question, asked of a variety of historical figures: Was she a lesbian?

Meanwhile, outside the feminist world, Smith-Rosenberg's work has increasingly been misused to deny the sexual aspect of relationships between prominent women in the past. In response, feminist scholars have reacted to such distortions by bestowing the label "lesbian"

on women who would themselves not have used the term. The issue goes beyond labels, however, because the very nature of women's relationships is so complex. The problem of classification becomes particularly thorny in twentieth-century history with the establishment of a lesbian identity. I would like to consider here the issue of women's relationships in the twentieth century by reviewing the conflicting approaches to lesbian labeling, by tracing the continuity of romantic friendship into the mid-century, and, finally, by suggesting a conceptual approach that recognizes the complexity of women's relationships without denying the common bond shared by all women who have committed their lives to other women in the past.

Looking first at what Blanche Cook proclaimed "the historical denial of lesbianism," we find the most publicized and most egregious example in Doris Faber's *The Life of Lorena Hickok: E. R.'s Friend,* the story of the relationship of Eleanor Roosevelt and reporter Lorena Hickok.[4] Author Doris Faber presented page after page of evidence that delineated the growth and development of a love affair between the two women, yet she steadfastly maintained that a woman of Eleanor Roosevelt's "stature" could not have *acted* on the love that she expressed for Hickok. This attitude forced Faber to go to great lengths with the evidence before her. For example, she quoted a letter Roosevelt wrote to Hickok and asserted that it is "particularly susceptible to misinterpretation." Roosevelt's wish to "lie down beside you tonight and take you in my arms," Faber claimed, represented maternal—"albeit rather extravagantly" maternal—solicitude. For Faber, "there can be little doubt that the final sentence of the above letter does not mean what it appears to mean" (p. 176).

Faber's book received far more public attention than serious works of lesbian history because the idea of a famous and well-respected—even revered—woman engaging in lesbian acts was titillating. An article about the Hickok book was even carried in the *National Enquirer,* which, for a change, probably presented the material more accurately, if more leeringly, than the respectable press.[5]

Faber's interpretation, unfortunately, is not an isolated one. She acknowledged an earlier book, *Miss Marks and Miss Woolley,* for reinforcing her own views "regarding the unfairness of using contemporary standards to characterize the behavior of women brought up under almost inconceivably different standards."[6] Anna Mary Wells, the author of the Marks and Woolley book, set out originally to write a biography of Mary Woolley, a president of Mount Holyoke, but almost abandoned the plan when she discovered the love letters of the two women. Ultimately Wells went ahead with a book about the relationship, but only after she decided, as she explained in the preface, that there was no physical relationship between them.

Another famous women's college president, M. Carey Thomas of Bryn Mawr, received the same sort of treatment in a book that appeared at the same time as the Hickok book, but to less fanfare.[7] The discovery of the Woolley–Marks letters sparked a mild panic among Mount Holyoke alumnae and no doubt created apprehension about what might lurk in Thomas's papers, which were about to be microfilmed and opened to the public.[8] But Marjorie Dobkin, editor of *The Making of a Feminist: Early Journals and Letters of M. Carey Thomas,* insisted that there was nothing to worry about. Thomas admittedly fell for women throughout her life. At fifteen, she wrote: "I think I must feel towards Anna for instance like a boy would, for I admire her so . . . and then I like to touch her and the other morning I woke up and she was asleep and I admired her hair so much that I kissed it. I never felt so much with anybody else." And at twenty: "One night we had stopped reading later than usual and obeying a sudden impulse I turned to her and asked, 'Do you love me?' She threw her arms around me and whispered, 'I love you passionately.' She did not go home that night and we talked and talked." At twenty-three, Thomas wrote to her mother: "If it were only possible for women to elect women as well as men for a 'life's love!' . . . It is possible but if families would only regard it in that light!" (pp. 72, 118, 229).

Thomas did in fact choose women for her "life's loves," but Dobkin, who found it "hard to understand why anyone should very much care" about personal and private behavior and considered the question of lesbianism "a relatively inconsequential matter," assured us that "physical contact" unquestionably played a part in Thomas's relationships with women, but, making a labored distinction, insisted that "sexuality" just as unquestionably did not (pp. 79, 86).

The authors of these three books were determined to give us an "acceptable" version of these prominent women's relationships in the past, and they seized gratefully on Smith-Rosenberg's work to do it. Likewise, Arthur Schlesinger, Jr., in the *New York Times Book Review,* found the question of whether Hickok and Roosevelt were "lovers in the physical sense" an "issue of stunning inconsequence," but cited Smith-Rosenberg's work to conclude that the two women were "children of the Victorian age," which accepted celibate love between women.[9]

As Blanche Cook pointed out in her review of Faber's book, however, it is absurd to pretend that the years 1932 to 1962 now belong to the nineteenth century.[10] Although it is vitally important not to impose modern concepts and standards on the past, we have gone entirely too far with the notion of an idyllic Victorian age in which chaste love between people of the same sex was possible and acceptable.

It is not surprising, in light of such denials of sexuality, that many feminist scholars have chosen to claim as lesbians all women who have loved women in the past. Blanche Cook has concluded firmly that "women who love women, who choose women to nurture and support and to create a living environment in which to work creatively and independently, are lesbians."[11] Cook named as lesbians Jane Addams, the founder of Hull House, who lived for forty years with Mary Rozet Smith; Lillian Wald, also a settlement house pioneer, who left evidence of a series of intense relationships with women; and Jeannette Marks and Mary Woolley. All, Cook insisted, in the homophobic society in which we live, must be claimed as lesbians.

In the simplest terms, we are faced with a choice between labeling women lesbians who might have violently rejected the notion or glossing over the significance of women's relationships by considering them asexual and Victorian.[12] But what is problematic enough when we are dealing with a period in which the concept of lesbianism did not exist becomes even more troubling when we turn to the twentieth century.

What the research increasingly suggests is that two separate largely class-bound forms of relationships between women existed. We seem to have little trouble identifying the working-class phenomena—"crossing" women who dressed and worked as men and who married women, and lesbian communities that grew up around the bars and, eventually, in the military—as sexual and, therefore, lesbian. But what about the middle- and upper-class romantic friends? It is not a question of nineteenth-century romantic friends becoming lesbians in the twentieth century. Despite the sexualization of American society at the turn of the century and the concomitant "discovery of lesbianism," romantic friendship and "Boston marriage" continued to exist.[13] I would like to illustrate this continuity, and therefore the complexity of women's relationships in historical perspective, with examples from the American women's rights movement in the late 1940s and 1950s.

I have found evidence of a variety of relationships in collections of women's papers and in the records of women's organizations from this period. I do not have enough information about many of these relationships to characterize them in any definitive way, nor can I even offer much information about some of the women. But we cannot afford to overlook whatever evidence women have left us, however fragmentary. Since my research focuses on feminist activities, the women I discuss here are by no means a representative group of women. The women's rights movement in the period after the Second World War was composed primarily of white, privileged women who maintained a preexisting commitment to feminism by creating an isolated and homogeneous feminist community.[14]

Within the women's rights movement were two distinct phenomena—couple relationships and intense devotion to a charismatic leader—that help clarify the problems that face us if we attempt to define these relationships in any cut-and-dried fashion. None of the women who lived in couple relationships and belonged to the women's rights movement in the post-1945 period would, as far as can be determined, have identified themselves as lesbians. They did, however, often live together in long-term committed relationships, which were accepted in the movement, and they did sometimes build a community with other women like themselves. Descriptions of a few relationships that come down to us in the sources provide some insight into their nature.

Jeannette Marks and Mary Woolley, subjects of the biography mentioned earlier, met at Wellesley College in 1895 when Marks began her college education and Woolley arrived at the college as a history instructor. Less than five years later they made "a mutual declaration of ardent and exclusive love" and "exchanged tokens, a ring and a jeweled pin, with pledges of lifelong fidelity."[15] They spent the rest of their lives together, including the many years at Mount Holyoke, where Woolley served as president and Marks taught English. Mary Woolley worked in the American Association of University Women and the Women's International League for Peace and Freedom. Jeannette Marks committed herself to suffrage and, later,

through the National Woman's Party, to the Equal Rights Amendment. It is clear from Marks's correspondence with women in the movement that their relationship was accepted as a primary commitment. Few letters to Marks in the 1940s fail to inquire about Woolley, whose serious illness clouded Marks's life and work. One married woman, who found herself forced to withdraw from Woman's Party work because of her husband's health, acknowledged in a letter to Marks the centrality of Marks's and Woolley's commitment when she compared her own reason for "pulling out" to "those that have bound you to Westport," the town in which the two women lived.[16] Mary Woolley died in 1947, and Jeannette Marks lived on until 1964, devoting herself to a biography of Woolley.

Lena Madesin Phillips, the founder of the International Federation of Business and Professional Women's Clubs, lived for some thirty years with Marjory Lacey-Baker, an actress whom she first met in 1919. In an unpublished autobiography included in Phillips's papers, she straightforwardly wrote about her lack of interest in men and marriage. As a young girl, she wrote that she "cared little for boys," and at the age of seven she wrote a composition for school that explained: "There are so many little girls in the school and the thing i [sic] like about it there are no boys in school. i [sic] like that about it."[17] She noted that she had never taken seriously the idea of getting married. "Only the first of the half dozen proposals of marriage which came my way had any sense of reality to me. They made no impression because I was wholly without desire or even interest in the matter." Phillips seemed unperturbed by possible Freudian and/or homophobic explanations of her attitudes and behavior. She explained unabashedly that she wanted to be a boy and suffered severe disappointment when she learned that, contrary to her father's stories, there was no factory in Indiana that made girls into boys. She mentioned in her autobiography the "crushes" she had on girls at the Jessamine Female Institute—nothing out of the ordinary for a young woman of her generation, but perhaps a surprising piece of information chosen for inclusion in the autobiography of a woman who continued to devote her emotional energies to women.

In 1919, Phillips attended a pageant in which Lacey-Baker performed and she inquired about the identity of the woman who had "[t]he most beautiful voice I ever heard."[18] Phillips "lost her heart to the sound of that voice," and the two women moved in together in the 1920s. In 1924, according to Lacey-Baker's notes for a biography of Phillips, the two women went different places for Easter; recording this caused Lacey-Baker to quote from *The*

Prophet: "Love knows not its own depth until the hour of separation."[19] Phillips described Lacey-Baker in her voluminous correspondence as "my best friend," or noted that she "shares a home with me."[20] Phillips's friends and acquaintances regularly mentioned Lacey-Baker. One male correspondent, for example, commented that Phillips's "lady-friend" was "so lovely, and so devoted to you and cares for you."[21] Phillips happily described the tranquillity of their life together to her many friends: "Marjory and I have had a lovely time, enjoying once more our home in summertime. . . . Marjory would join in the invitation of this letter and this loving greeting if she were around. Today she is busy with the cleaning woman, while I sit with the door closed working in my study."[22] "We have had a happy winter, with good health for both of us. We have a variety of interests and small obligations, but really enjoy most the quiet and comfort of Apple Acres."[23] "We read and talk and work."[24]

Madesin Phillips's papers suggest that she and Marjory Lacey-Baker lived in a world of politically active women friends. Phillips had devoted much of her energy to international work with women, and she kept in touch with European friends through her correspondence and through her regular trips to Europe accompanied by Lacey-Baker. Gordon Holmes, of the British Federation of Business and Professional Women, wrote regularly to "Madesin and Maggie." In a 1948 letter she teased Phillips by reporting that "two other of our oldest & closest Fed officers whom you know could get married but are refusing—as they are both more than middle-aged (never mind their looks) it suggests 50–60 is about the new dangerous age for women (look out for Maggie!)."[25] Phillips reported to Holmes on their social life: "With a new circle of friends around us here and a good many of our overseas members coming here for luncheon or tea with us the weeks slip by."[26] The integral relationship between Phillips's social life and her work in the movement is suggested by Lacey-Baker's analysis of Phillips's personal papers from the year 1924: "There is the usual crop of letters to LMP following the Convention [of the BPW] from newly-met members in hero-worshipping mood—most of whom went on to be her good friends over the years."[27] Lacey-Baker was a part of Phillips's movement world, and their relationship received acceptance and validation throughout the movement, both national and international.

The lifelong relationship between feminist biographer Alma Lutz and Marguerite Smith began when they roomed together at Vassar in the early years of the twentieth century. From 1918 until Smith's death in 1959, they shared a Boston apartment and a summer home, Highmeadow, in the Berkshires. Lutz and Smith, a librarian at the Protestant Zion Research Library in Brookline, Massachusetts, worked together in the National Woman's Party. Like Madesin Phillips, Lutz wrote to friends in the movement of their lives together: "We are very happy here in the country—each busy with her work and digging in the garden."[28] They traveled together, visiting Europe several times in the 1950s. Letters to one of them about feminist work invariably sent greetings or love to the other. When Smith died in 1959, Lutz struggled with her grief. She wrote to her acquaintance Florence Kitchelt, in response to condolences: "I am at Highmeadow trying to get my bearings. . . . You will understand how hard it is. . . . It has been a very difficult anxious time for me."[29] She thanked another friend for her note and added, "It's a hard adjustment to make, but one we all have to face in one way or another and I am remembering that I have much to be grateful for."[30] In December she wrote to one of her regular correspondents that she was carrying on but it was very lonely for her.[31]

The fact that Lutz and Smith seemed to have many friends who lived in couple relationships with other women suggests that they had built a community of women within the women's rights movement. Every year Mabel Vernon, a suffragist and worker for peace, and her friend and companion Consuelo Reyes, whom Vernon had met through her work with the Inter-American Commission of Women, spent the summer at Highmeadow. Vernon, one of Alice Paul's closest associates during the suffrage struggle, had met Reyes two weeks after her arrival in the United States from Costa Rica in 1942. They began to work together in Vernon's organization, People's Mandate, in 1943, and they shared a Washington apartment from 1951 until Vernon's death in 1975.[32] Reyes received recognition in Vernon's obituaries as her "devoted companion" or "nurse-companion."[33] Two other women who also maintained a lifelong relationship, Alice Morgan Wright and Edith Goode, also kept in contact with Lutz, Smith, Vernon, and Reyes. Sometimes they visited Highmeadow in the summer.[34] Wright and Goode had met at Smith and were described as "always together" although they did not live together.[35] Like Lutz and Smith, they worked together in the National Woman's Party, where they had also presumably met Vernon. Both Wright and Goode devoted themselves to two causes, women's rights and humane treatment for animals. Wright described herself as having "fallen between two stools—animals and wimmin."[36] The two women traveled together and looked after each other as age began to take its toll.

These examples illustrate what the sources provide: the bare outlines of friendship networks made up of woman-committed women. Much of the evidence must be pieced together, and it is even scantier when the women did not live together. Alma Lutz's papers, for example, do not include any personal correspondence from the post-1945 period, so what we know about her relationship with Marguerite Smith comes from the papers of her correspondents. Sometimes a relationship surfaces only upon the death of one of the women. For example, Agnes Wells, chairman of the National Woman's Party in the late 1940s, explained to an acquaintance in the party that her "friend of forty-one years and house-companion for twenty-eight years" had just died.[37] When Mabel Griswold, executive secretary of the Woman's Party, died in 1955, a family member suggested that the party send the telegram of sympathy to Elsie Wood, the woman with whom Griswold had lived.[38] This kind of reference tells us little about the nature of the relationship involved, but we do get a sense of acceptance of couple relationships within the women's rights movement.

A second important phenomenon found in the women's rights movement—the charismatic leader who attracted intense devotion—also adds to our understanding of the complexity of women's relationships. Alice Paul, the founder and leading light of the National Woman's Party, inspired devotion that bordered on worship. One woman even addressed her as "My Beloved Deity."[39] But, contrary to both the ideal type of the charismatic leader and the portrait of Paul as it exists now in historical scholarship, Paul maintained close relationships with a number of women she had first met in the suffrage struggle.[40] Paul's correspondence in the National Woman's Party papers does not reveal much about the nature of her relationships, but it does make it clear that her friendships provided love and support for her work.

It is true that many of the expressions of love, admiration, and devotion addressed to Paul seem to have been one-sided, from awestruck followers, but this is not the only side of the story. Paul maintained close friendships with a number of women discussed earlier who lived in couple relationships with other women. She had met Mabel Vernon when they attended Swarthmore College together, and they maintained contact throughout the years, despite Vernon's departure from the Woman's Party in the 1930s.[41] Of Alice Morgan Wright, she said that, when they first met, they ". . . just became sisters right away."[42] Jeannette Marks regularly sent her love to "dear Alice" until a conflict in the Woman's Party ruptured their relationship.[43]

Other women, too, enjoyed a closer relationship than the formal work-related one for which Paul is so well known.

Paul obviously cared deeply, for example, for her old friend Nina Allender, the cartoonist of the suffrage movement. Allender, who lived alone in Chicago, wrote to Paul in 1947 of her memories of their long association: "No words can tell you what that [first] visit grew to mean to me & to my life. . . . I feel now as I did then—only more intensely—I have never changed or doubted—but have grown more inspired as the years have gone by. . . . There is no use going into words. I believe them to be unnecessary between us."[44] Paul wrote that she thought of Allender often and sent her "devoted love."[45] She worried about Allender's loneliness and gently encouraged her to come to Washington to live at Belmont House, the Woman's Party headquarters, where she would be surrounded by loving friends who appreciated the work she had done for the women's movement.[46] Paul failed to persuade her to move, however. Two years later Paul responded to a request from Allender's niece for help with the cost of a nursing home with a hundred-dollar check and a promise to contact others who might be able to help.[47] But Allender died within a month at the age of eighty-five.

Paul does not seem to have formed an intimate relationship with any one woman, but she did live and work within a close-knit female world. When in Washington, she lived, at least some of the time, at Belmont House; when away she lived either alone or with her sister, Helen Paul, and later with her lifelong friend Elsie Hill. It is clear that Alice Paul's ties—whether to her sister or to close friends or to admirers—served as a bond that knit the Woman's Party together. That Paul and her network could also tear the movement asunder is obvious from the stormy history of the Woman's Party.[48]

Alice Paul is not the only example of a leader who inspired love and devotion among women in the movement. One senses from Marjory Lacey-Baker's comment, quoted above—that "newly met members in hero-worshipping mood" wrote to Lena Madesin Phillips after every BPW convention—that Phillips too had a charismatic aura. But the best and most thoroughly documented example of a charismatic leader is Anna Lord Strauss of the League of Women Voters, an organization that in the post-1945 years distanced itself from women's rights.

Strauss, the great-granddaughter of Lucretia Mott, came from an old and wealthy family; she was prominent and respected, a staunch liberal who rejected the label of "feminist." She never married and her papers leave no evidence of intimate relationships outside her family. Yet Strauss was the object of some very strong feelings on the part of the women with whom she worked. She, like Alice Paul and Madesin Phillips, received numerous hero-worshipping letters from awestruck followers. But in her case we also have evidence that some of her co-workers fell deeply in love with her. It is hard to know how the women discussed here would have interpreted their relationship with Strauss. The two women who expressed their feelings explicitly were both married women, and in one case Strauss obviously had a cordial relationship with the woman's husband and children. Yet there can be no question that this League officer fell in love with Strauss. She found Strauss "the finest human being I had ever known" and knowing her "the most beautiful and profound experience I have ever had."[49] Loving Strauss—she asked permission to say it—made the earth move and "the whole landscape of human affairs and nature" take on a new appearance.[50] Being with Strauss made "the tone and fiber" of her day different; although she could live without her, she could see no reason for having to prove it all the time.[51] She tried to "ration and control" her thoughts of Strauss, but it was small satisfaction.[52] When Strauss was recovering from an operation, this woman wrote: "I love you! I can't imagine the world without you. . . . I love you. I need you."[53]

Although our picture of this relationship is completely one-sided—for Strauss did not keep copies of most of her letters—it is clear that Strauss did not respond to such declarations of love. This woman urged Strauss to accept her and what she had to say without "the slightest sense of needing to be considerate of me because I feel as I do." She understood the "unilateral character" of her feelings, and insisted that she had more than she deserved by simply knowing Strauss at all.[54] But her hurt, and her growing suspicion that Strauss shunned intimacy, escaped on occasion. She asked: "And how would it hurt you to let someone tell you sometime how beautiful—how wonderful you are? Did you ever let anyone have a decent chance to try?"[55] She realized that loving someone did not always make things easier—that sometimes, in fact, it made life more of a struggle—but she believed that to withdraw from love was to withdraw from life. In what appears to have been a hastily written note, she expressed her understanding—an understanding that obviously gave her both pain and comfort—that Strauss was not perfect after all: "Way back there in the crow's nest (or at some such time) you decided not to become embroiled in any intimate human relationship, except those you were, by birth, committed to. I wonder. . . . There is something you haven't mastered. Something you've been afraid of after all."[56]

This woman's perception that Strauss avoided intimacy is confirmed elsewhere in Strauss's papers. One old friend was struck, in 1968, by Strauss's ability to "get your feelings out and down on paper!" She continued: "I know you so well that I consider this great progress in your own inner state of mental health. It is far from easy for you to express your feelings. . . ."[57] This aspect of Strauss's personality fits with the ideal type of the charismatic leader. The other case of a woman falling in love with Strauss that emerges clearly from her papers reinforces this picture. This woman, also a League officer, wrote in circuitous fashion of her intense pleasure at receiving Strauss's picture. In what was certainly a reference to lesbianism, she wrote that she hoped Strauss would not think that she was "one of those who had never outgrown the emotional extravaganzas of the adolescent." Before she got down to League business, she added:

> But, Darling, as I softly close the door on all this—as I should and as I want to—and as I must since all our meetings are likely to be formal ones in a group—as I go back in the office correspondence to "Dear Miss Strauss" and "Sincerely Yours," . . . as I put myself as much as possible in the background at our March meeting in order to share you with the others who have not been with you as I have—as all these things happen, I want you to be very certain that what is merely under cover is still there—as it most surely will be—and that if all the hearts in the room could be exposed there'd be few, I'm certain, that would love you more than . . . [I].[58]

Apparently Strauss never responded to this letter, for a month later, this woman apologized for writing it: "I have had qualms, dear Anna, about that letter I wrote you. (You knew I would eventually of course!)." Continuing in a vein that reinforces the previously quoted perception of Strauss's inability to be intimate, she wrote of imagining the "recoil . . . embarrassment, self-consciousness and general discomfort" her letter must have provoked in such a "reserved person." She admitted that the kind of admiration she had expressed, "at least in certain classes of relationships (of which mine to you is one)—becomes a bit of moral wrongdoing."[59] She felt ashamed and asked forgiveness.

What is clear is that this was a momentous and significant relationship to at least one of the parties. Almost twenty years later, this woman wrote of her deep disappointment in missing Strauss's visit to her city. She had allowed herself to dream that she could persuade Strauss to stay with her a while, even though she knew that others would have prior claims on Strauss's time. She wrote:

> I have not seen you since that day in Atlantic City when you laid the gavel of the League of Women Voters down. . . . I do not look back on that moment of ending with any satisfaction for my own behavior, for I passed right by the platform on which you were still standing talking with one of the last persons left in the room and shyness at the thought of expressing my deep feeling about your going—and the fact that you were talking with someone else led me to pass on without even a glance in your direction as I remember though you made some move to speak to me! . . . But if I gave you a hurt it is now a very old one and forgotten, I'm sure—as well as understood.[60]

Whatever the interpretation these two women would have devised to explain their feelings for Strauss, it is clear that the widely shared devotion to this woman leader could sometimes grow into something more intense. Strauss's reserve and her inability to express her feelings may or may not have had anything to do with her own attitude toward intimate relationships between women. One tantalizing letter from a friend about to be married suggests that Strauss's decision not to marry had been made early: "I remember so well your answer when I pressed you, once, on why you had never married. . . . Well, it is very true, one does not marry unless one can see no other life."[61] A further fragment, consisting of entries in the diary of Doris Stevens—a leading suffragist who took a sharp swing to the right in the interwar period—suggests that at least some individuals suspected Strauss of lesbianism. Stevens, by this time a serious red-baiter and, from the evidence quoted here, a "queerbaiter" as well, apparently called a government official in 1953 to report that Strauss was "not a bit interested in men."[62] She seemed to be trying to discredit Strauss, far too liberal for her tastes, with a charge of "unorthodox morals."[63]

Stevens had her suspicions about other women as well. She recorded in her diary a conversation with a National Woman's Party member about Jeannette Marks and Mary Woolley, noting that the member, who had attended Wellesley with Marks, "Discreetly indicated there was 'talk.' "[64] At another point she reported a conversation with a different Woman's Party member who had grown disillusioned about Alice Paul. Stevens noted that her informant related "weird goings on at Wash. hedqts wherein it was clear she thought Paul a devotee of Lesbos & afflicted with Jeanne d'Arc identification."[65] Along the same lines, the daughter of a woman who had left the National Woman's Party complained that Alice Paul and another leader had sent her mother a telegram that "anybody with sense" would think "was from two people who were adolescent [*sic*] or from two who had imbied [*sic*] too much or else Lesbians to a Lesbian."[66]

Such comments suggest that the intensity of women's relationships and the existence and acceptance of couple relationships in women's organizations had the potential, particularly during the McCarthy years, to attract denunciation. Doris Stevens herself wrote to the viciously right-wing and antiSemitic columnist Westbrook Pegler to "thank you for knowing I'm not a queerie" despite the fact that she considered herself a feminist.[67] Although the association between feminism and lesbianism was not new in the 1950s, the McCarthyite connection between political deviance and homosexuality seemed to fuel suspicion.[68] How real the threat was for women is suggested by two further incidents involving opposition to the appointment of women, both described in the memoirs of India Edwards, a top woman in the Truman administration.[69]

In 1948, opposition to tax court judge Marion Harron's reappointment to the bench arose from Harron's fellow judges, who cited her lack of judicial temperament and "unprovable charges of an ethical nature." Although Edwards did not specify the nature of the charges, we know from *The Life of Lorena Hickok* that Harron had written letters to "E. R.'s friend" that even Doris Faber had to admit were love letters. The other case that Edwards described left no doubt about what ethical and moral charges were involved. When Truman appointed Kathryn McHale, longtime executive director of the American Association of University Women, to the Subversive Activities Control Board, Senator Pat McCarran advised Truman to withdraw her name and threatened to hold public hearings during which "information would be brought out that she was a lesbian."

On the whole, though, the feminists who lived in couple relationships managed to do so respectably, despite the emergence of a lesbian culture and the occasional charges of lesbianism. This was because they worked independently or in professional jobs, had the money to buy homes together, and enjoyed enough status to be beyond reproach in the world in which they moved. Women who later identified as lesbians but did not attach an identity to their emotions and behaviors in the 1950s describe that period as one in which women might live together without raising any eyebrows, but it is important to remember that even the class privilege that protected couple relationships would not necessarily suffice if women sought to enter powerful male-dominated institutions.[70]

What exactly should we make of all this? In one way it is terribly frustrating to have such tantalizingly ambiguous glimpses into women's lives. In another way, it is exciting to find out so much about women's lives in the past. I think it is enormously important not to read into these relationships what we want to find, or what we think we should find. At the same time, we cannot dismiss what little evidence we have as insufficient when it is all we have; nor can we continue to contribute to the conspiracy of silence that urges us to ignore what is not perfectly straightforward. Thus, although it is tempting to try to speculate about the relationships I have described here in order to impose some analysis on them, I would rather simply lay them out, fragmentary as they are, in order to suggest a conceptual approach that recognizes the complexities of the issue.

It is clear, I think, that none of these relationships can be easily categorized. There were women who lived their entire adult lives in couple relationships with other women, and married women who fell in love with other women. Were they lesbians? Probably they would be shocked to be identified in that way. Alice Paul, for example, spoke scornfully of *Ms.* magazine as "all about homosexuality and so on."[71] Another woman who lived in a couple relationship distinguished between the (respectable) women involved in the ERA struggle in the old days and the "lesbians and bra-burners" of the contemporary movement.[72] Sasha Lewis, in *Sunday's Women,* reported an incident we would do well to remember here. One of her informants, a lesbian, went to Florida to work against Anita Bryant and stayed with an older cousin who had lived for years in a marriagelike relationship with another woman. When Lewis's informant saw the way the two women lived—sharing everything, including a bedroom—she remarked about the danger of Bryant's campaign for their lives. They were aghast that she would think them lesbians, since, they said, they did not do anything sexual together.[73] If even women who chose to share beds with other women would reject the label "lesbian," what about the married women, or the women who avoided intimate relationships?

What is critical here, I would argue, is that these women lived at a time during which some women *did* identify as lesbians. The formation of a lesbian identity, from both an individual and historical perspective, is enormously significant. So far, most of the historical debate over the use of the term "lesbian" has focused on earlier periods.[74] Passionate love between women has existed, but it has not always been named. Since it *has* been named in the twentieth century,

and since there *was* such a thing as a lesbian culture, we need to distinguish between women who identify as lesbians and/or who are part of a lesbian culture, where one exists, and a broader category of women-committed women who would not identify as lesbians but whose primary commitment, in emotional and practical terms, was to other women. There is an important difference between, on the one hand, butch–fem couples in the 1950s who committed what Joan Nestle has aptly called an act of "sexual courage" by openly proclaiming the erotic aspect of their relationships, and, on the other, couples like Eleanor Roosevelt and Lorena Hickok or Alma Lutz and Marguerite Smith.[75]

We know that identity and sexual behavior are not the same thing.[76] There are lesbians who have never had a sexual relationship with another woman and there are women who have had sexual experiences with women but do not identify as lesbians. This is not to suggest that there is no difference between women who loved each other and lived together but did not make love (although even that can be difficult to define, since sensuality and sexuality, "physical contact" and "sexual contact" have no distinct boundaries) and those who did. But sexual behavior—something about which we rarely have historical evidence anyway—is only one of a number of relevant factors in a relationship. Blanche Cook has said everything that needs to be said about the inevitable question of evidence: "Genital 'proofs' to confirm lesbianism are never required to confirm the heterosexuality of men and women who live together for twenty, or fifty, years." Cook reminds us of the publicized relationship of General Eisenhower and Kay Summersby during the Second World War: They "were passionately involved with each other. . . . They were inseparable. But they never 'consummated' their love in the acceptable, traditional, sexual manner. Now does that fact render Kay Summersby and Dwight David Eisenhower somehow less in love? Were they not heterosexual?"[77]

At this point, I think, the best we can do as historians is to describe carefully and sensitively what we do know about a woman's relationships, keeping in mind both the historical development of a lesbian identity (Did such a thing as a lesbian identity exist? Was there a lesbian culture?) and the individual process that we now identify as "coming out" (Did a woman feel attachment to another woman or women? Did she act on this feeling in some positive way? Did she recognize the existence of other women with the same commitment? Did she express solidarity with those women?). Using this approach allows us to make distinctions among women's relationships in the past—intimate friendships, supportive relationships growing out of common political work, couple relationships—without denying their significance or drawing fixed boundaries. We can recognize the importance of friendships among a group of women who, like Alma Lutz, Marguerite Smith, Mabel Vernon, Consuelo Reyes, Alice Morgan Wright, and Edith Goode, built a community of women but did not identify it as a lesbian community. We can do justice to both the woman-committed woman who would angrily reject any suggestion of lesbianism and the self-identified lesbian without distorting their common experiences.

This approach does not solve all the problems of dealing with women's relationships in the past, but it is a beginning. The greatest problem remains the weakness of sources. Not only have women who loved women in the past been wisely reluctant to leave evidence of their relationships for the prying eyes of a homophobic society, but what evidence they did leave was often suppressed or destroyed.[78] Furthermore, as the three books discussed at the beginning show, even the evidence saved and brought to light can be savagely misinterpreted.

How do we know if a woman felt attachment, acted on it, recognized the existence of other women like her, or expressed solidarity? There is no easy answer to this, but it is revealing, I think, that both Doris Faber and Anna Mary Wells are fairly certain that Lorena Hickok and Jeannette Marks, respectively, did have "homosexual tendencies" (although Faber insists that even Hickok cannot fairly be placed in the "contemporary gay category"), even if the admirable figures in each book, Eleanor Roosevelt and Mary Woolley, certainly did not. That is, both of these authors, as hard as they try to deny lesbianism, find evidence that forces them to discuss it, and both cope by pinning the "blame" on the women they paint as unpleasant—fat, ugly, pathetic Lorena Hickok and nasty, tortured, arrogant Jeannette Marks.

So we present what evidence we have, being careful to follow Linda Gordon's advice and "listen quietly and intently" to the women who speak to us from the sources.[79] In the case of twentieth-century history, we may also have the opportunity to listen to women speak in the flesh. We may privately believe that all the evidence suggests that a woman was a lesbian, but what do we do if she insisted, either explicitly or implicitly, that she was not? That is why the process of coming out is so important to us as historians. In a world in which some women claimed a lesbian identity and built lesbian communities, the choice to reject that identification has a meaning of its own. It is imperative that we not deny the reality of any woman's historical experience by blurring the distinctions among different kinds of choices. At the same time, recognition of the common bond of commitment to women shared by diverse women throughout history strengthens our struggle against those who attempt to divide and defeat us.

ACKNOWLEDGMENTS

Holly Near's song "Imagine My Surprise," celebrates the discovery of women's relationships in the past. The song is recorded on the album *Imagine My Surprise,* Redwood Records. I am grateful to Holly Near and Redwood Records for their permission to use the title here.

This is a revised version of an article originally published in *Frontiers: A Journal of Women Studies* 5 (Fall 1980). The original research was made possible by a fellowship from the Radcliffe Research Scholars Program. Additional research, funded by the National Endowment for the Humanities, was undertaken jointly with Verta Taylor for our book *Survival in the Doldrums: The American Women's Rights Movement* (1987).

NOTES

1. Carroll Smith-Rosenberg, "The Female World of Love and Ritual: Relations between Women in Nineteenth Century America," *Signs* 1 (1975): 1–29.

2. Adrienne Rich, "Compulsory Heterosexuality and Lesbian Existence," *Signs* 5 (1980): 631–60. See also Ann Ferguson,

Jacquelyn N. Zita, and Kathryn Pyne Addelson, "On Compulsory Heterosexuality and Lesbian Existence: Defining the Issues," *Signs* 7 (1981): 158–99.

3. Lillian Faderman, *Surpassing the Love of Men: Romantic Friendship and Love between Women from the Renaissance to the*

Present (New York: William Morrow, 1981). See also Faderman's *Scotch Verdict* (New York: Quill, 1983), a compelling re-creation of the trial of two Edinburgh schoolteachers accused of having sex together (the model for Lillian Hellman's *The Children's Hour*). Faderman argues against a sexual component in the two women's relationship, suggesting that "for many women, what *ought* to be, in fact *was*" (p. 126).

For examples of reviews that discussed the controversial nature of Faderman's argument, see the Muriel Haynes's review of *Surpassing the Love of Men* in *Ms.* 9 (June 1981): 36; and reviews of *Scotch Verdict* by Karla Jay in *Women's Review of Books* 1 (December 1983):9–10 and by Terry Castle in *Signs* 9 (1984): 717–20.

4. Blanche Wiesen Cook, "The Historical Denial of Lesbianism," *Radical History Review* 20 (1979): 60–65; Doris Faber, *The Life of Lorena Hickok: E.R.'s Friend* (New York: William Morrow, 1980).

5. Edward Sigall, "Eleanor Roosevelt's Secret Romance—the Untold Story," *National Enquirer,* November 13, 1979, pp. 20–21.

6. Anna Mary Wells, *Miss Marks and Miss Woolley* (Boston: Houghton Mifflin, 1978); Faber, *Lorena Hickok,* p. 354. Cook, "Historical Denial," is a review of the Wells book.

7. Marjorie Housepian Dobkin, *The Making of a Feminist: Early Journals and Letters of M. Carey Thomas* (Kent, Ohio: Kent State University Press, 1980).

8. *New York Times,* August 21, 1976, p. 22.

9. Arthur Schlesinger, Jr., "Interesting Women," *New York Times Book Review,* February 17, 1980, p. 31.

10. Cook, review of *The Life of Lorena Hickok, Feminist Studies* 6 (1980): 511–16.

11. Cook, "Female Support Networks and Political Activism: Lillian Wald, Crystal Eastman and Emma Goldman," *Chrysalis* 3 (1977): 48.

12. In a review of books on Frances Willard, Alice Paul, and Carrie Chapman Catt, Gerda Lerner criticized the denial of sexuality in relationships in which women shared their lives "in the manner of married couples." In an attempt to bridge the two approaches, Lerner suggested that perhaps Paul, Willard, Catt, along with Susan B. Anthony, Anna Dickinson, and Jane Addams, were "simply what Victorian 'lesbians' looked like. Gerda Lerner, "Where Biographers Fear to Tread," *Women's Review of Books* 11 (September 1987): 11–12.

13. On the significance of class, see Myriam Everard, "Lesbian History: A History of Change and Disparity," *Journal of Homosexuality* 12 (1986): 123–37 and "Lesbianism and Medical Practice in the Netherlands, 1897–1930," paper presented at the Berkshire Conference of Women Historians, Wellesley, Massachusetts, 1987. Not all the lesbian communities we know of prior to the 1950s were working class, however. There were middle- and upper-class communities in Europe and, to a lesser extent, among American bohemians at the turn of the century. On "crossing" women, see Jonathan Katz, *Gay American History* (New York: Thomas Y. Crowell, 1976), and *Gay/Lesbian Almanac* (New York: Harper & Row, 1983). On the emergence of a lesbian community,

see Madeline Davis and Elizabeth Lapovsky Kennedy, "Oral History and the Study of Sexuality in the Lesbian Community: Buffalo, New York, 1940–1960," in this volume; Joan Nestle, "Butch–Fem Relationships: Sexual Courage in the 1950s," *Heresies: The Sex Issue* 12 (1981): 21–24; Allan Bérubé, "Coming Out under Fire," *Mother Jones* (February/March 1983): 23–45; and John D'Emilio, *Sexual Politics, Sexual Communities: The Making of a Homosexual Minority in the U.S. 1940–1970* (Chicago: University of Chicago Press, 1983).

On the "discovery of lesbianism," see Nancy Sahli, "Smashing: Women's Relationships before the Fall," *Chrysalis* 8 (1979): 17–27; George Chauncey, Jr., "From Sexual Inversion to Homosexuality: Medicine and the Changing Conceptualization of Female Deviance," *Salmagundi* 58/59 (Fall 1982/Winter 1983): 114–46; Christina Simmons, "Women's Sexual Consciousness and Lesbian Identity, 1900–1940" (paper presented at the Berkshire Conference of Women Historians, Northhampton, Massachusetts, 1984); Esther Newton, "The Mythic Mannish Lesbian: Radclyffe Hall and the New Woman."

14. See Leila J. Rupp and Verta Taylor, *Survival in the Doldrums: The American Women's Rights Movement, 1945 to the 1960s* (New York: Oxford University Press, 1987).

15. Wells, *Miss Marks and Miss Woolley,* p. 56.

16. Caroline Babcock to Jeannette Marks, February 12, 1947, Babcock papers, box 8 (105), Schlesinger Library, Radcliffe College, Cambridge, Massachusetts. I am grateful to the Schlesinger Library for permission to use the material quoted here.

17. "The Unfinished Autobiography of Lena Madesin Phillips," Phillips papers, Schlesinger Library.

18. "Chronological Records of Events and Activities for the Biography of Lena Madesin Phillips, 1881–1955," Phillips papers, Schlesinger Library.

19. "Chronological Records of Events and Activities for the Biography of Lena Madesin Phillips, 1881–1955," Phillips papers, Schlesinger Library.

20. Lena Madesin Phillips to Audrey Turner, January 21, 1948, Phillips papers, Schlesinger Library; Phillips to Olivia Rossetti Agresti, April 26, 1948, Phillips papers, Schlesinger Library.

21. Robert Heller to Phillips, September 26, 1948, Phillips papers, Schlesinger Library.

22. Phillips to Mary C. Kennedy, August 20, 1948, Phillips papers, Schlesinger Library.

23. Phillips to Gordon Holmes, March 28, 1949, Phillips papers, Schlesinger Library.

24. Phillips to [Ida Spitz], November 13, 1950, Phillips papers, Schlesinger Library.

25. Holmes to Madesin & Maggie, December 15, 1948, Phillips papers, Schlesinger Library.

26. Phillips to Holmes, March 28, 1949, Phillips papers, Schlesinger Library.

27. "Chronological Record of Events and Activities for the Biography of Lena Madesin Phillips, 1881–1955," Phillips papers, Schlesinger Library.

28. Alma Lutz to Florence Kitchelt, July 1, 1948, Kitchelt papers, box 6 (177), Schlesinger Library.

29. Lutz to Kitchelt, July 29, 1959, Kitchelt papers, box 7 (178), Schlesinger Library.

30. Lutz to Florence Armstrong, August 26, 1959, Armstrong papers, box 1 (17), Schlesinger Library.

31. Lutz to Rose Arnold Powell, December 14, 1959, Powell papers, box 3 (43), Schlesinger Library.

32. Mabel Vernon, "Speaker for Suffrage and Petitioner for Peace," an oral history conducted in 1972 and 1973 by Amelia R. Fry, Regional Oral History Office, University of California, 1976. Courtesy, the Bancroft Library.

33. Press release from Mabel Vernon Memorial Committee, Vernon, "Speaker for Suffrage"; obituary in the *Wilmington Morning News,* September 3, 1975, Vernon, "Speaker for Suffrage."

34. Alice Morgan Wright to Anita Pollitzer, July 9, 1946, National Woman's Party papers, reel 89. The National Woman's Party papers have been microfilmed and are distributed by the Microfilming Corporation of America. I am grateful to the National Woman's Party for permission to quote the material used here.

35. Alice Paul, "Conversations with Alice Paul: Woman Suffrage and the Equal Rights Amendment," an oral history conducted in 1972 and 1973 by Amelia R. Fry, Regional Oral History Office, University of California, 1976, p. 614. Courtesy, the Bancroft Library. Nora Stanton Barney to Alice Paul, n.d. [received May 10, 1945], National Woman's Party papers, reel 86.

36. Wright to Pollitzer, n.d. [July 1946], National Woman's Party papers, reel 89.

37. Agnes Wells to Pollitzer, August 24, 1946, National Woman's Party papers, reel 89.

38. Paul to Dorothy Griswold, February 2, 1955, National Woman's Party papers, reel 101.

39. Lavinia Dock to Paul, May 9, 1945, National Woman's Party papers, reel 86.

40. See, for example, Susan D. Becker, *The Origins of the Equal Rights Amendment: American Feminism between the Wars* (Westport, Conn.: Greenwood Press, 1981), and Christine A. Lunardini, *From Equal Suffrage to Equal Rights: Alice Paul and the National Woman's Party, 1910–1928* (New York: New York University Press, 1986).

41. Vernon, "Speaker for Suffrage."

42. Paul, "Conversations," p. 197.

43. Jeannette Marks to Paul, March 25, 1945, National Woman's Party papers, reel 85; Marks to Paul, March 30, 1945, National Woman's Party papers, reel 85; Marks to Paul, April 27, 1945, National Woman's Party papers, reel 85.

44. Nina Allender to Paul, January 5, 1947, National Woman's Party papers, reel 90.

45. Paul to Allender, March 9, 1950, National Woman's Party papers, reel 96.

46. Paul to Allender, November 20, 1954, National Woman's Party papers, reel 100; Kay Boyle to Paul, December 5, 1954, National Woman's Party papers, reel 100; Paul to Allender, December 6, 1954, National Woman's Party papers, reel 100.

47. Boyle to Paul, February 13, 1957, National Woman's Party papers, reel 103; Paul to Boyle, March 5, 1957, National Woman's Party papers, reel 103.

48. See Leila J. Rupp, "The Women's Community in the National Woman's Party, 1945 to the 1960s," *Signs* 10 (1985): 715–40.

49. Letter to Anna Lord Strauss, December 22, 1945, Strauss papers, box 6 (118), Schlesinger Library. Because of the possibly sensitive nature of the material reported here, I am not using the names of the women involved.

50. Letter to Strauss, September 19, 1946, Strauss papers, box 6 (119), Schlesinger Library.

51. Letter to Strauss, May 9, 1947, Strauss papers, box 6 (121), Schlesinger Library.

52. Letter to Strauss, June 28, 1948, Strauss papers, box 6 (124), Schlesinger Library.

53. Letter to Strauss, February 26, 1951, Strauss papers, box 1 (15), Schlesinger Library.

54. Letter to Strauss, December 22, 1945, Strauss papers, box 6 (118), Schlesinger Library.

55. Letter to Strauss, May 9, 1947, Strauss papers, box 6 (121), Schlesinger Library.

56. "Stream of consciousness," March 10, 1948, Strauss papers, box 6 (124), Schlesinger Library.

57. Augusta Street to Strauss, n.d. [1968], Strauss papers, box 7 (135), Schlesinger Library.

58. Letter to Strauss, February 11, 1949, Strauss papers, box 6 (125), Schlesinger Library.

59. Letter to Strauss, March 3, 1949, Strauss papers, box 6 (125), Schlesinger Library.

60. Letter to Strauss, March 8, 1968, Strauss papers, box 7 (135), Schlesinger Library.

61. Lilian Lyndon to Strauss, April 23, 1950, Strauss papers, box 1 (14), Schlesinger Library.

62. Diary entries, August 30, 1953 and September 1, 1953, Doris Stevens papers, Schlesinger Library.

63. Diary entry, August 24, 1953, Doris Stevens papers, Schlesinger Library.

64. Diary entry, February 4, 1946, Doris Stevens papers, Schlesinger Library.

65. Diary entry, December 1, 1945, Doris Stevens papers, Schlesinger Library.

66. Katharine Callery to Stevens, Aug. 17, 1944, Stevens papers, Schlesinger Library.

67. Stevens to Westbrook Pegler, May 3, 1946, Stevens papers, Schlesinger Library.

68. See Margaret Jackson, "Sexual Liberation or Social Control? Some Aspects of the Relationship between Feminism and the Social Construction of Sexual Knowledge in the Early Twentieth Century," *Women's Studies International Forum* 6 (1983): 1–17; Carroll Smith-Rosenberg, "Discourses of Sexuality and Subjectivity: The New Woman, 1870–1936," in this volume; and John D'Emilio, "The Homosexual Menace: The Politics of Sexuality in Cold War America," unpublished paper presented at

the Organization of American Historians Conference, Philadelphia, 1982.

69. India Edwards, *Pulling No Punches* (New York: Putnam's 1977), pp. 189–90.

70. Interviews by Leila J. Rupp and Verta Taylor; see Rupp and Taylor, *Survival in the Doldrums.*

71. Paul, "Conversations," pp. 195–96.

72. Interview conducted by Taylor and Rupp, December 10, 1979.

73. Sasha Gregory Lewis, *Sunday's Women: A Report on Lesbian Life Today* (Boston: Beacon Press, 1979), p. 94.

74. See, for an example, the discussion in Judith C. Brown, *Immodest Acts: The Life of a Lesbian Nun in Renaissance Italy* (New York: Oxford University Press, 1986), pp. 171–73.

75. Nestle, "Butch–Fem Relationships."

76. Much of the literature on lesbianism emphasizes this crucial distinction between identity and experience. See, for example,

Barbara Ponse, *Identities in the Lesbian World: The Social Construction of Self* (Westport, Conn.: Greenwood Press, 1978); and E. M. Ettore, *Lesbians, Women and Society* (London: Routledge & Kegan Paul, 1980).

77. Cook, "Historical Denial," p. 64.

78. The Mount Holyoke administration closed the Marks-Woolley papers when Wells discovered the love letters, and the papers are open to researchers now only because an American Historical Association committee, which included Blanche Cook as one of its members, applied pressure to keep the papers open after Wells, to her credit, contacted them. Faber describes her unsuccessful attempts to persuade the archivists at the FDR Library to close the Lorena Hickok papers.

79. Linda Gordon, "What Should Women's Historians Do: Politics, Social Theory, and Women's History," *Marxist Perspectives* 3 (1978), 128–36.

IN PRAISE OF "BEST FRIENDS": THE REVIVAL OF A FINE OLD INSTITUTION

BARBARA EHRENREICH

All the politicians, these days, are "profamily," but I've never heard of one who was "profriendship." This is too bad and possibly shortsighted. After all, most of us would never survive our families if we didn't have our friends.

I'm especially concerned about the fine old institution of "best friends." I realized that it was on shaky ground a few months ago, when the occasion arose to introduce my own best friend (we'll call her Joan) at a somewhat intimidating gathering. I got as far as saying, "I am very proud to introduce my best friend, Joan . . ." when suddenly I wasn't proud at all: I was blushing. "Best friend," I realized as soon as I heard the words out loud, sounds like something left over from sixth-grade cliques: the kind of thing where if Sandy saw you talking to Stephanie at recess, she might tell you after school that she wasn't going to be your best friend anymore, and so forth. Why couldn't I have just said "my good friend Joan" or something *grown-up* like that?

But Joan is not just any friend, or even a "good friend"; she is my best friend. We have celebrated each other's triumphs together, nursed each other through savage breakups with the various men in our lives, discussed the Great Issues of Our Time, and cackled insanely over things that were, objectively speaking, not even funny. We have quarreled and made up; we've lived in the same house and we've lived thousands of miles apart. We've learned to say hard things, like "You really upset me when . . ." and even "I love you." Yet, for all this, our relationship has no earthly weight or status. I can't even say the name for it without sounding profoundly silly.

Why is best friendship, particularly between women, so undervalued and unrecognized? Partly, no doubt, because women themselves have always been so undervalued and unrecognized. In the western tradition, male best friendships are the stuff of history and high drama. Reread Homer, for example, and you'll realize that Troy did not fall because Paris, that spoiled Trojan prince, loved Helen, but because Achilles so loved Patroclus. It was Patroclus' death, at the hands of the Trojans, that made Achilles snap out of his sulk long enough to slay the Trojans' greatest warrior and guarantee victory to the Greeks. Did Helen have a best friend, or any friend at all? We'll never know, because the only best friendships that have survived in history and legend are man-on-man: Alexander and Hephaestion, Orestes and Pylades, Heracles and Iolas.

Christianity did not improve the status of female friendship. "Every woman ought to be filled with shame at the thought that she is a woman," declaimed one of the early church fathers, Clement of Alexandria, and when two women got together, the shame presumably doubled. Male friendship was still supposed to be a breeding ground for all kinds of upstanding traits—honor, altruism, courage, faith, loyalty. Consider Arthur's friendship with Lancelot, which easily survived the latter's dalliance with Queen Guinevere. But when two women got together, the best you could hope for, apparently, was bitchiness, and the worst was witchcraft.

Yet, without the slightest encouragement from history, women have persisted in finding best friends. According to recent feminist scholarship, the nineteenth century seems to have been a heyday of female best friendship. In fact, feminism might never have gotten off the ground at all if it hadn't been for the enduring bond between Elizabeth Cady Stanton, the theoretician of the movement, and Susan B. Anthony, the movement's first great pragmatist.

And they are only the most famous best friends. According to Lilian Faderman's book *Surpassing the Love of Men*, there were thousands of anonymous female couples who wrote passionate letters to each other, exchanged promises and tokens of love, and suffered through the separations occasioned by marriage and migration. Feminist scholars have debated whether these great best friendships were actually lesbian, sexual relationships—a question that I find both deeply fascinating (if these were lesbian relationships, were the women involved conscious of what a bold and subversive step they had taken?) and somewhat beside the point. What matters is that these women honored their friendships, and sought ways to give them the kind of coherence and meaning that the larger society reserved only for marriage.

In the twentieth century, female best friendship was largely eclipsed by the new ideal of the "companionate marriage." At least in the middle-class culture that celebrated "togetherness," your *husband* was now supposed to be your best friend, as well, of course, as being your

lover, provider, coparent, housemate, and principal heir. My own theory (profamily politicians please take note) is that these expectations have done more damage to the institution of marriage than no-fault divorce and the sexual revolution combined. No man can be all things to even one woman. And the foolish idea that one could has left untold thousands of women not only divorced, but what is in the long run far worse—friendless.

Yet even feminism, when it came back to life in the early seventies, did not rehabilitate the institution of female best friendship. Lesbian relationships took priority, for the good and obvious reason that they had been not only neglected but driven underground. But in our zeal to bring lesbian relationships safely out of the closet, we sometimes ended up shoving best friendships further out of sight. "Best friends?" a politically ever-so-correct friend once snapped at me, in reference to Joan, "why aren't you lovers?" In the same vein, the radical feminist theoretician Shulamith Firestone wrote that after the gender revolution, there would be no asexual friendships. The coming feminist Utopia, I realized sadly, was going to be a pretty lonely place for some of us.

Then, almost before we could get out of our jeans and into our corporate clone clothes, female friendship came back into fashion—but in the vastly attenuated form of "networking." Suddenly we are supposed to have dozens of women friends, hundreds if time and the phone bill allow, but each with a defined function: mentors, contacts, connections, allies, even pretty ones who might be able to introduce us, now and then, to their leftover boyfriends. The voluminous literature on corporate success for women is full of advice on friends: whom to avoid ("turkeys" and whiners), whom to cultivate (winners and potential clients), and how to tell when a friend is moving from the latter category into the former. This is an advance, because it means we are finally realizing that women are important enough to be valued friends and that friendship among women is valuable enough to write and talk about. But in the pushy new dress-for-success world, there's less room than ever for best friendships that last through thick and thin, through skidding as well as climbing.

Hence my campaign to save the institution of female best friendship. I am not asking you to vote for anyone, to pray to anyone, or even to send me money. I'm just suggesting that we all begin to give a little more space, and a little more respect, to the best friendships in our lives. To this end, I propose three rules:

1. Best friendships should be given social visibility. If you are inviting Pat over for dinner, you would naturally think of inviting her husband, Ed. Why not Pat's best friend, Jill? Well, you may be thinking, how childish! They don't have to go everywhere together. Of course they don't, but neither do Pat and Ed. In many settings, including your next dinner party or potluck, Pat and Jill may be the combination that makes the most sense and has the most fun.

2. Best friendships take time and nurturance, even when that means taking time and nurturance away from other major relationships. Everyone knows that marriages require "work." (A ghastly concept, that. "Working on a marriage" has always sounded to me like something on the order of lawn maintenance.) Friendships require effort, too, and best friendships require our very best efforts. It should be possible to say to husband Ed or whomever, "I'm sorry I can't spend the evening with you because I need to put in some quality time with Jill." He will be offended only if he is a slave to heterosexual couple-ism—in which case you shouldn't have married him in the first place.

3. Best friendship is more important than any work-related benefit that may accrue from it, and should be treated accordingly. Maybe your best friend will help you get that promotion, transfer, or new contract. That's all well and good, but the real question is: Will that promotion, transfer, or whatever help your best friendship? If it's a transfer to San Diego and your best friend's in Cincinnati, it may not be worth it. For example, as a writer who has collaborated with many friends, including "Joan," I am often accosted by strangers exclaiming, "It's just amazing that you got through that book [article, or other project] together and you're still friends!" The truth is, in nine cases out of ten, that the friendship was always far more important than the book. If a project isn't going to strengthen my friendship—and might even threaten it—I'd rather not start.

When I was thinking through this column—out loud of course, with a very good friend on the the the phone—she sniffed, "So what exactly do you want—formal legalized friendships, with best-friend licenses and showers and property settlements in case you get in a fight over the sweaters you've been borrowing from each other for the past ten years?" No, of course not, because the beauty of best friendship, as opposed to, say, marriage, is that it's a totally grassroots creative effort that requires no help at all from the powers that be. Besides, it would be too complicated. In contrast to marriage—and even to sixth-grade cliques—there's no rule that says you can have only one "best" friend.

Doing Desire: Adolescent Girls' Struggles for/with Sexuality

DEBORAH L. TOLMAN

In order to perpetuate itself, every oppression must corrupt or distort those various sources of power within the culture of the oppressed that can provide energy for change. For women, this has meant suppression of the erotic as a considered source of power and information within our lives.

(Lorde 1984, 53)

Recent research suggests that adolescence is the crucial moment in the development of psychological disempowerment for many women (e.g., Brown and Gilligan 1992; Gilligan 1990). As they enter adolescence, many girls may lose an ability to speak about what they know, see, feel, and experience evident in childhood as they come under cultural pressure to be "nice girls" and ultimately "good women" in adolescence. When their bodies take on women's contours, girls begin to be seen as sexual, and sexuality becomes an aspect of adolescent girls' lives; yet "nice" girls and "good" women are not supposed to be sexual outside of heterosexual, monogamous marriage (Tolman 1991). Many girls experience a "crisis of connection," a relational dilemma of how to be oneself and stay in relationships with others who may not want to know the truth of girls' experiences (Gilligan 1989). In studies of adolescent girls' development, many girls have demonstrated the ironic tendency to silence their own thoughts and feelings for the sake of relationships, when what they

think and feel threatens to be disruptive (Brown and Gilligan 1992). At adolescence, the energy needed for resistance to crushing conventions of femininity often begins to get siphoned off for the purpose of maintaining cultural standards that stand between women and their empowerment. Focusing explicitly on embodied desire, Tolman and Debold (1993) observed similar patterns in the process of girls learning to look at, rather than experience, themselves, to know themselves from the perspective of men, thereby losing touch with their own bodily feelings and desires. It is at this moment in their development that many women will start to experience and develop ways of responding to their own sexual feelings. Given these realities, what are adolescent girls' experiences of sexual desire? How do girls enter their sexual lives and learn to negotiate or respond to their sexuality?

Despite the real gains that feminism and the sexual revolution achieved in securing women's reproductive rights and increasing women's sexual liberation (Rubin 1990), the tactics of silencing and denigrating women's sexual desire are deeply entrenched in this patriarchal society (Brown 1991). The Madonna/whore dichotomy is alternately virulent and subtle in the cultures of adolescents (Lees 1986; Tolman 1992). Sex education curricula name male adolescent sexual desire; girls are taught to recognize and to keep a lid on the sexual desire of boys but not taught to acknowledge or even to recognize their own sexual feelings (Fine 1988; Tolman 1991). The few feminist empirical studies of girls' sexuality suggest that sexual desire is a complicated, important experience for adolescent girls about which little is known. In an ethnographic study, Fine noticed that adolescent girls' sexuality was acknowledged by adults in school, but in terms that denied the sexual subjectivity of girls; this "missing discourse of desire" was, however, not

Deborah L. Tolman, "Doing Desire: Adolescent Girls" Struggles for/with Sexuality," from *Gender & Society* 8, no. 3 (September 1994). Copyright © 1994 by Sociologists for Women in Society. Reprinted with the permission of Sage Publications, Inc.

always absent from the ways girls themselves spoke about their sexual experiences (Fine 1988). Rather than being "educated," girls' bodies are suppressed under surveillance and silenced in the schools (see also Lesko 1988). Although Fine ably conveys the existence of girls' discourse of desire, she does not articulate that discourse. Thompson collected 400 girls' narratives about sexuality, romance, contraception, and pregnancy (Thompson 1984, 1990) in which girls' desire seems frequently absent or not relevant to the terms of their sexual relationships. The minority of girls who spoke of sexual pleasure voiced more sexual agency than girls whose experiences were devoid of pleasure. Within the context of girls' psychological development, Fine's and Thompson's work underscores the need to understand what girls' experiences of their sexual desire are like.

A psychological analysis of this experience for girls can contribute an understanding of both the possibilities and limits for sexual freedom for women in the current social climate. By identifying how the culture has become anchored in the interior of women's lives—an interior that is birthed through living in the exterior of material conditions and relationships—this approach can keep distinct women's psychological responses to sexual oppression and also the sources of that oppression. This distinction is necessary for avoiding the trap of blaming women for the ways our minds and bodies have become constrained.

METHODOLOGICAL DISCUSSION

Sample and Data Collection

To examine this subject, I interviewed thirty girls who were juniors in an urban and a suburban public high school ($n = 28$) or members of a gay and lesbian youth group ($n = 2$). They were 16.5 years old on average and randomly selected. The girls in the larger study are a heterogeneous group, representing different races and ethnic backgrounds (Black, including Haitian and African American; Latina, including Puerto Rican and Colombian; Euro-American, including Eastern and Western European), religions (Catholic, Jewish, and Protestant), and sexual experiences. With the exception of one Puerto Rican girl, all of the girls from the suburban school were Euro-American; the racial/ethnic diversity in the sample is represented by the urban school. Interviews with school personnel confirmed that the student population of the urban school was almost exclusively poor or working class and the students in the suburban school were middle and upper-middle class. This information is important in

that my focus is on how girls' social environments shape their understanding of their sexuality. The fact that girls who live in the urban area experience the visibility of and discourse about violence, danger and the consequences of unprotected sex, and that the suburban girls live in a community that offers a veneer of safety and stability, informs their experiences of sexuality. Awareness of these features of the social contexts in which these girls are developing is essential for listening to and understanding their narratives about sexual experiences.

The data were collected in one-on-one, semistructured clinical interviews (Brown and Gilligan 1992). This method of interviewing consists of following a structured interview protocol that does not direct specific probes but elicits narratives. The interviewer listens carefully to a girl, taking in her voice, and responding with questions that will enable the girl to clarify her story and know she is being heard. In these interviews, I asked girls direct questions about desire to elicit descriptions and narratives. Most of the young women wove their concerns about danger into the narratives they told.

Analytic Strategy

To analyze these narratives, I used the Listening Guide—an interpretive methodology that joins hermeneutics and feminist standpoint epistemology (Brown et al. 1991). It is a voice-centered, relational method by which a researcher becomes a listener, taking in the voice of a girl, developing an interpretation of her experience. Through multiple readings of the same text, this method makes audible the "polyphonic and complex" nature of voice and experience (Brown and Gilligan 1992, 15). Both speaker and listener are recognized as individuals who bring thoughts and feelings to the text, acknowledging the necessary subjectivity of both participants. Self-consciously embedded in a standpoint acknowledging that patriarchal culture silences and obscures women's experiences, the method is explicitly psychological and feminist in providing the listener with an organized way to respond to the coded or indirect language of girls and women, especially regarding topics such as sexuality that girls and women are not supposed to speak of. This method leaves a trail of evidence for the listener's interpretation, and thus leaves room for other interpretations by other listeners consistent with the epistemological stance that there is multiple meaning in such stories. I present *a* way to understand the stories these young women chose to tell me, our story as I have heard and understood it. Therefore, in the interpretations that follow I include my responses, those of an adult woman, to these girls' words, providing information about girls' experiences of sexual desire much like countertransference informs psychotherapy.

Adolescent Girls' Experiences of Sexual Desire

The first layer of the complexity of girls' experiences of their sexual desire was revealed initially in determining whether or not they felt sexual feelings. A majority of these girls (two-thirds) said unequivocally that they experienced sexual desire; in them I heard a clear and powerful way of speaking about the experience of feeling desire that was explicitly relational and also embodied. Only three of the girls said they did not experience sexual feelings, describing silent bodies and an absence of or intense confusion about romantic or sexual relationships. The remaining girls evidenced confusion or spoke in confusing ways about their own sexual feelings. Such confusion can be understood as a psychic solution to sexual feelings that arise in a culture that denigrates, suppresses, and heightens the dangers of girls' sexuality and in which contradictory messages about women's sexuality abound.

For the girls who said they experienced sexual desire, I turned my attention to how they said they responded to their sexual feelings. What characterized their responses was a sense of struggle; the question of "doing desire"—that is, what to do when they felt sexual desire—was not straightforward for any of them. While speaking of the power of their embodied feelings, the girls in this sample described the difficulties that their sexual feelings posed, being aware of both the potential for pleasure and the threat of danger that their desire holds for them. The struggle took different shapes for different girls, with some notable patterns emerging. Among the urban girls, the focus was on how to stay safe from bodily harm, in and out of the context of relational or social consequences, whereas among the suburban girls the most pronounced issue was how to maintain a sense of themselves as "good" and "normal" girls (Tolman 1992). In this article, I will offer portraits of three girls. By focusing on three girls in depth, I can balance an approach to "variance" with the kind of case study presentation that enables me to illustrate both similarities and differences in how girls in the larger sample spoke about their sexual feelings. These three girls represent different sexual preferences—one heterosexual, one bisexual, and one lesbian.[1] I have chosen to forefront the difference of sexual preference because it has been for some women a source of empowerment and a route to community; it has also been a source of divisiveness among feminists. Through this approach, I can illustrate *both* the similarities and differences in their experiences of sexual desire, which are nested in their individual experiences as well as their social contexts. Although there are many other demarcations that differentiate these girls—social class, race, religion, sexual experience—and this is not the most pervasive difference in this sample,[2] sexual preference calls attention to the kinds of relationships in which girls are experiencing or exploring their sexual desire and which take meaning from gender arrangements and from both the presence and absence of institutionalization (Fine 1988; Friend 1993). Because any woman whose sexuality is not directly circumscribed by heterosexual, monogamous marriage is rendered deviant in our society, all adolescent girls bear suspicion regarding their sexuality, which sexual preference highlights. In addition, questions of identity are heightened at adolescence.

Rochelle Doing Desire   Rochelle is a tall, larger, African-American girl who is heterosexual. Her small, sweet voice and shy smile are a startling contrast to her large body, clothed in white spandex the day of our interview. She lives in an urban area where violence is embedded in the fabric of everyday life. She speaks about her sexual experience with a detailed knowledge of how her sexuality is shaped, silenced, denigrated, and possible in relationships with young men. As a sophomore, she thought she "had to get a boyfriend" and became "eager" for a sexual relationship. As she describes her first experience of sexual intercourse, she describes a traditional framing of male–female relationships:

> I felt as though I had to conform to everything he said that, you know, things that a girl and a guy were supposed to do, so like, when the sex came, like, I did it without thinking, like, I wish I would have waited . . . we started kissing and all that stuff and it just happened. And when I got, went home, I was like, I was shocked, I was like, why did I do that? I wish I wouldn't a did it.
>
> *Did you want to do it?*
>
> Not really. Not really. I just did it because, maybe because he wanted it, and I was always like tryin' to please him and like, he was real mean, mean to me, now that I think about it. I was like kind of stupid, cause like I did everything for him and he just treated me like I was nothing and I just thought I had just to stay with him because I needed a boyfriend so bad to make my life complete but like now it's different.

Rochelle's own sexual desire is absent in her story of defloration—in fact, she seems to be missing altogether. In a virtual caricature of dominant cultural conventions of femininity, Rochelle connects her disappearance at the moment of sex—"it just happened"—to her attempts to fulfill the cultural guidelines for how to "make [her] life complete." She has sex because "he wanted it," a response that holds no place for whether or not she feels desire. In reflecting on this arrangement, Rochelle now feels she was "stupid . . . to do everything for him" and in her current relationship, things are "different." As she explains: "I don't take as much as I did with the first guy, cause like, if he's doin' stuff that I don't like, I tell him, I'll go, I don't like this and I think you shouldn't do it and we compromise, you know. I don't think I can just let him treat me bad and stuff."

During the interview, I begin to notice that desire is not a main plot line in Rochelle's stories about her sexual experiences, especially in her intimate relationships. When I ask her about her experiences of sexual pleasure and sexual desire, she voices contradictions. On one hand, as the interview unfolds, she is more and more clear that she does not enjoy sex: "I don't like sex" quickly becomes "I hate sex . . . I don't really have pleasure." On the other hand, she explains that

> there are certain times when I really really really enjoy it, but then, that's like, not a majority of the times, it's only sometimes, once in a while . . . if I was to have sex once a month, then I would enjoy it . . . if I like go a long period of time without havin' it then, it's really good to me, cause it's like, I haven't had something for a long time and I miss it. It's like, say I don't eat cake a lot, but say, like every two months, I had some cake, then it would be real good to me, so that's like the same thing.

Rochelle conveys a careful knowledge of her body's hunger, her need for tension as an aspect of her sexual pleasure, but her voiced dislike of sex suggests that she does not feel she has much say over when and how she engages in sexual activity.

In describing her experiences with sexuality, I am overwhelmed at how frequently Rochelle says that she "was scared." She is keenly aware of the many consequences that feeling and responding to her sexual desire could have. She is scared of being talked about and getting an undeserved reputation: "I was always scared that if I did that (had sexual intercourse) I would be portrayed as, you know, some-

thing bad." Even having sex within the confines of a relationship, which has been described by some girls as a safe haven for their sexuality (Rubin 1990; Tolman 1992), makes her vulnerable; she "could've had a bad reputation, but luckily he wasn't like that"; he did not choose to tell other boys (who then tell girls) about their sexual activity. Thinking she had a sexually transmitted disease was scary. Because she had been faithful to her boyfriend, having such a disease would mean having to know that her boyfriend cheated on her and would also make her vulnerable to false accusations of promiscuity from him. Her concern about the kind of woman she may be taken for is embedded in her fear of using contraception: "When you get birth control pills, people automatically think you're having sex every night and that's not true." Being thought of as sexually insatiable or out of control is a fear that many girls voice (Tolman 1992); this may be intensified for African-American girls, who are creating a sexual identity in a dominant cultural context that stereotypes Black women as alternately asexual and hypersexual (Spillers 1984).

Rochelle's history provides other sources of fear. After her boyfriend "flattened [her] face," when she realized she no longer wanted to be with him and broke off the relationship, she learned that her own desire may lead to male violence. Rochelle confided to me that she has had an abortion, suffering such intense sadness, guilt, and anxiety in the wake of it that, were she to become pregnant again, she would have the baby. For Rochelle, the risk of getting pregnant puts her education at risk, because she will have to sacrifice going to college. This goal is tied to security for her; she wants to "have something of my own before I get a husband, you know, so if he ever tries leavin' me, I have my own money." Given this wall of fears, I am not surprised when Rochelle describes a time when simply feeling desire made her "so scared that I started to cry." Feeling her constant and pervasive fear, I began to find it hard to imagine how she can feel any other feelings, including sexual ones.

I was thus caught off guard when I asked Rochelle directly if she has felt desire and she told me that she does experience sexual desire; however, she explained "most of the time, I'm by myself when I do." She launched, in breathless tones, into a story about an experience of her own sexual desire just the previous night:

> Last night, I had this crank call. . . . At first I thought it was my boyfriend, cause he likes to play around, you know. But I was sitting there talking, you know, and thinking of him and then I found out it's not him, it was so crazy weird, so I hang the phone up and he called

back, he called back and called back. And then I couldn't sleep, I just had this feeling that, I wanted to have sex so so bad. It was like three o'clock in the morning. And I didn't sleep the rest of the night. And like, I called my boyfriend and I was tellin' him, and he was like, what do you want me to do, Rochelle, I'm sleeping! [Laughs.] I was like, okay, okay, well I'll talk to you later, bye. And then, like, I don't know, I just wanted to, and like, I kept tossin' and turnin'. And I'm trying to think who it was, who was callin' me, cause like, it's always the same guy who always crank calls me, he says he knows me. It's kinda scary. . . . I can't sleep, I'm like, I just think about it, like, oh I wanna have sex so bad, you know, it's like a fever, drugs, something like that. Like last night, I don't know, I think if I woulda had the car and stuff, I probably woulda left the house. And went over to his house, you know. But I couldn't, cause I was baby-sitting.

When I told her that it sounds a little frightening but it sounds like there's something exciting about it, she smiled and leaned forward, exclaiming, "Yeah! It's like sorta arousing." I was struck by the intensity of her sexual feelings and also by the fact that she is alone and essentially assured of remaining alone due to the late hour and her responsibilities. By being alone, not subject to observation or physical, social, emotional, or material vulnerability, Rochelle experienced the turbulent feelings that are awakened by this call in her body. Rochelle's desire has not been obliterated by her fear; desire and fear both reverberate through her psyche. But she is not completely alone in this experience of desire, for her feelings occur in response to another person, whom she at first suspects is her boyfriend speaking from a safe distance, conveying the relational contours of her sexual desire. Her wish to bring her desire into her relationship, voiced in her response of calling her boyfriend, is in conflict with her fear of what might happen if she did pursue her wish—getting pregnant and having a baby, a consequence that Rochelle is desperate to avoid.

I am struck by her awareness of both the pleasure and danger in this experience and how she works the contradiction without dissociating from her own strong feelings. There is a brilliance and also a sadness in the logic her body and psyche have played out in the face of her experiences with sexuality and relationships. The psychological solution to the dilemma that desire means for her, of feeling sexual desire only when she cannot respond as she says she would like to, arises from her focus on these conflicts as personal experiences, which she suffers and solves private-

ly. By identifying and solving the dilemma in this way, Rochelle is diminished, as is the possibility of her developing a critique of these conflicts as not just personal problems but as social inequities that emerge in her personal relationships and on her body. Without this perspective, Rochelle is less likely to become empowered through her own desire to identify that the ways in which she must curtail herself and be curtailed by others are socially constructed, suspect, and in need of change.

Megan Doing Desire   Megan, a small, freckled, perky Euro-American, is dressed in baggy sweats, comfortable, unassuming, and counterpointed by her lively engagement in our interview.[3] She identifies herself as "being bisexual" and belongs to a gay youth group; she lives in a city in which wealth and housing projects coexist. Megan speaks of knowing she is feeling sexual desire for boys because she has "kind of just this feeling, you know? Just this feeling inside my body." She explains: "My vagina starts to kinda like act up and it kinda like quivers and stuff, and like I'll get like tingles and and, you can just feel your hormones (laughing) doing something weird, and you just, you get happy and you just get, you know, restimulated kind of and it's just, and Oh! Oh!" and "Your nerves feel good." Megan speaks about her sexual desire in two distinct ways, one for boys and one for girls. In our interview, she speaks most frequently about her sexual feelings in relation to boys. The power of her own desire and her doubt about her ability to control herself frighten her: "It scares me when I'm involved in a sexual situation and I just wanna go further and further and cause it just, and it scares me that, well, I have control, but if I even just let myself not have control, you know? . . . I'd have sex and I can't do that." Megan knows that girls who lose control over their desire like that can be called "sluts" and ostracized.

When asked to speak about an experience of sexual desire, Megan chooses to describe the safety of a heterosexual, monogamous relationship. She tells me how she feels when a boyfriend was "feeling me up"; not only is she aware of and articulate about his bodily reactions and her own, she narrates the relational synergy between her own desire and his:

I just wanted to go on, you know? Like I could feel his penis, you know, 'cause we'd kinda lied down you know, and, you just really get so into it and intense and, you just wanna, well you just kinda keep wanting to go on or something, but it just feels good. . . . His penis being on my leg made, you know, it hit a nerve or something, it did something because it just made me start to get more horny or whatever, you know, it just made me want to do more things and stuff. I don't know how, I can't, it's hard for me to describe exactly how I felt, you know like, (intake of breath) . . . when he gets more excited then he starts to do more things and you can kind of feel his pleasure and then you start to get more excited.

With this young man, Megan knows her feelings of sexual desire to be "intense," to have a momentum of their own, and to be pleasurable. Using the concrete information of his erection, she describes the relational contours of her own embodied sexual desire, a desire that she is clear is her own and located in her body but that also arises in response to his excitement.

Although able to speak clearly in describing a specific experience she has had with her desire, I hear confusion seep into her voice when she notices that her feelings contradict or challenge societal messages about girls and sexuality:

It's so confusing, 'cause you have to like say no, you have to be the one to say no, but why should you be the one to, cause I mean maybe you're enjoying it and you shouldn't have to say no or anything. But if you don't, maybe the guy'll just keep going and going, and you can't do that, because then you would be a slut. There's so [much] like, you know, stuff that you have to deal with and I don't know, just I keep losing my thought.

Although she knows the logic offered by society—that she must "say no" to keep him from "going and going," which will make her "a slut"—Megan identifies what is missing from that logic, that "maybe you're"—she, the girl—"the one who is enjoying it." The fact that she may be experiencing sexual desire makes the scripted response—to silence his body—dizzying. Because she does feel her own desire and can identify the potential of her own pleasure, Megan asks the next logical question, the question that can lead to outrage, critique, and empowerment: "Why should you have to be the one to [say no]?" But Megan also gives voice to why sustaining the question is difficult; she knows that if she does not conform, if she does not "say no"—both to him and to herself—then she may be called a slut, which could lead to denigration and isolation. Megan is caught in the contradiction between the reality of her sexual feelings in her body and the absence of her sexual feelings in the cultural script for adolescent girls' sexuality. Her confusion is an understandable response to this untenable and unfair

choice: a connection with herself, her body, and sexual pleasure or a connection with the social world.

Megan is an avid reader of the dominant culture. Not only has she observed the ways that messages about girls' sexuality leave out or condemn her embodied feelings for boys, she is also keenly aware of the pervasiveness of cultural norms and images that demand heterosexuality:

Every teen magazine you look at is like, guy this, how to get a date, guys, guys, guys, guys, guys. So you're constantly faced with I have to have a boyfriend, I have to have a boyfriend, you know, even if you don't have a boyfriend, just [have] a fling, you know, you just want to kiss a guy or something. I've had that mentality for so long.

In this description of compulsory heterosexuality (Rich 1983), Megan captures the pressure she feels to have a boyfriend and how she experiences the insistence of this demand, which is ironically in conflict with the mandate to say no when with a boy. She is aware of how her psyche has been shaped into a "mentality" requiring any sexual or relational interests to be heterosexual, which does not corroborate how she feels. Compulsory heterosexuality comes between Megan and her feelings, making her vulnerable to a dissociation of her "feelings" under this pressure.

Although she calls herself bisexual, Megan does not describe her sexual feelings for girls very much in this interview. In fact, she becomes so confused that at one point she says she is not sure if her feelings for girls are sexual:

I mean, I'll see a girl I really really like, you know, because I think she's so beautiful, and I might, I don't know. I'm so confused. . . . But there's, you know, that same mentality as me liking a guy if he's really cute, I'm like, oh my God, you know, he's so cute. If I see a woman that I like, a girl, it's just like wow, she's so pretty, you know. See I can picture like hugging a girl; I just can't picture the sex, or anything, so, there's something being blocked.

Megan links her confusion with her awareness of the absence of images of lesbian sexuality in the spoken or imagistic lexicon of the culture, counterpointing the pervasiveness of heterosexual imagery all around her. Megan suggests that another reason that she might feel "confused" about her feelings for girls is a lack of sexual experience. Megan knows she is feeling sexual desire when she can identify feelings in her own body—when her "vagina acts up"—and these feelings occur for her in the context of a sexual relationship, when she can feel the other person's desire. Because she has never been in a situation with a girl that would allow this embodied sexual response, she posits a connection between her lack of sexual experience with girls and her confusion.

Yet she has been in a situation where she was "close to" a girl and narrates how she does not let her body speak:

> There was this one girl that I had kinda liked from school, and it was like really weird 'cause she's really popular and everything. And we were sitting next to each other during the movie and, kind of her leg was on my leg and I was like, wow, you know, and that was, I think that's like the first time that I've ever felt like sexual pleasure for a girl. But it's so impossible, I think I just like block it out, I mean, it could never happen. . . . I just can't know what I'm feeling. . . . I probably first mentally just say no, don't feel it, you know, maybe. But I never start to feel, I don't know. It's so confusing. 'Cause finally it's all right for me to like a girl, you know? Before it was like, you know, the two times that I really, that it was just really obvious that I liked them a lot, I had to keep saying no no no no, you know, I just would not let myself. I just hated myself for it, and this year now that I'm talking about it, now I can start to think about it.

Megan both narrates and interprets her dissociation from her embodied sexual feelings and describes the disciplinary stance of her mind over her body in how she "mentally" silences her body by saying "no," preempting her embodied response. Without her body's feelings, her embodied knowledge, Megan feels confused. If she runs interference with her own sexual feelings by silencing her body, making it impossible for her to feel her desire for girls, then she can avoid the problems she knows will inevitably arise if she feels sexual feelings she "can't know"—compulsory heterosexuality and homophobia combine to render this knowledge problematic for her. Fearing rejection, Megan keeps herself from feelings that could lead to disappointment, embarrassment, or frustration, leaving her safe in some ways, yet also psychologically vulnerable.

Echoing dominant cultural constructions of sexual desire, Megan links her desire for girls with feelings of fear: "I've had crushes on some girls . . . you can picture yourself kissing a guy but then if you like a girl a lot and then you picture yourself kissing her, it's just like, I can't,

you know, oh my God, no (laughs), you know it's like scary . . . it's society . . . you never would think of, you know, it's natural to kiss a girl." Megan's fear about her desire for girls is different from the fears associated with her desire for boys; whereas being too sexual with boys brings the stigma of being called a "slut," Megan fears "society" and being thought of as "unnatural" when it comes to her feelings for girls. Given what she knows about the heterosexual culture in which she is immersed—the pressure she feels to be interested in "guys" and also given what she knows about homophobia—there is an inherent logic in Megan's confused response to her feelings for girls.

Melissa Doing Desire Melissa, dressed in a flowing gypsy skirt, white skin pale against the lively colors she wears, is clear about her sexual desire for girls, referring to herself as "lesbian"; she is also a member of a gay/lesbian youth group. In speaking of her desire, Melissa names not only powerful feelings of "being excited" and "wanting," but also more contained feelings; she has "like little crushes on like millions of people and I mean, it's enough for me." Living in a world defined as heterosexual, Melissa finds that "little crushes" have to suffice, given a lack of opportunity for sexual exploration or relationship: "I don't know very many people my age that are even bisexual or lesbians . . . so I pretty much stick to that, like, being hugely infatuated with straight people. Which can get a little touchy at times . . . realistically, I can't like get too ambitious, because that would just not be realistic."

At the forefront of how Melissa describes her desire is her awareness that her sexual feelings make her vulnerable to harm. Whereas the heterosexual girls in this study link their vulnerability to the outcomes of responding to their desire—pregnancy, disease, or getting a bad reputation—Melissa is aware that even the existence of her sexual desire for girls can lead to anger or violence if others know of it: "Well I'm really lucky that like nothing bad has happened or no one's gotten mad at me so far, that, by telling people about them, hasn't gotten me into more trouble than it has, I mean, little things but not like, anything really awful. I think about that and I think it, sometimes, I mean, it could be more dangerous." In response to this threat of violence, Melissa attempts to restrain her own desire: "Whenever I start, I feel like I can't help looking at someone for more than a few seconds, and I keep, and I feel like I have to make myself not stare at them or something." Another strategy is to express her desire covertly by being physically affectionate with other girls, a behavior that is common and acceptable; by keeping her sexuality secret, she can "hang all over [girls] and stuff and they wouldn't even think that I meant anything by it." I am not surprised that Melissa associates feeling sexual desire with frustration; she explains that she "find(s) it safer to just think about the person than what I wanna do, because if I think about that too much and I can't do it, then that'll just frustrate me," leading her to try to intervene in her feelings by "just think[ing] about the person" rather than about the more sexual things she "want(s) to do." In this way, Melissa may jeopardize her ability to know her sexual desire and, in focusing on containing what society has named improper feelings, minimize or exorcise her empowerment to expose that construction as problematic and unjust.

My questions about girls' sexual desire connect deeply with Melissa's own questions about herself; she is in her first intimate relationship, and this interview proves an opportunity to explore and clarify painful twinges of doubt that she had begun to have about it. This relationship began on the initiative of the other girl, with whom she had been very close, rather than out of any sexual feelings on Melissa's part. In fact, Melissa was surprised when her friend had expressed a sexual interest, because she had not "been thinking that" about this close friend. After a history of having to hold back her sexual desire, of feeling "frustrated" and being "hugely infatuated with straight people," rather than having the chance to explore her sexuality, Melissa's response to this potential relationship was that she "should take advantage of this situation." As the interview progresses, Melissa begins to question whether she is sexually attracted to this girl or "it's just sort of like I just wanted something like this for so long that I'm just taking advantage of the situation."

When I ask Melissa questions about the role of her body in her experience of sexual desire, her confusion at first intensifies:

Is that [your body] part of what feels like it might be missing?

(eight-second pause) It's not, well, sometimes, I mean I don't know how, what I feel all the time. It's hard like, because I mean I'm so confused about this. And it's hard like when it's actually happening to be like, OK, now how do I feel right now? How do I feel right now? How am I gonna feel about this? . . . I don't know, 'cause I don't know what to expect, and I haven't been with anyone else so I don't know what's supposed to happen. So, I mean I'm pretty confused.

The way she speaks about monitoring her body suggests that she is searching for bodily feelings, making me wonder

what, if anything, she felt. I discern what she does not say directly; that her body was silent in these sexual experiences. Her hunger for a relationship is palpable: "I really wanted someone really badly, I think, I was getting really sick of being by myself. . . . I would be like God, I really need someone." The desperation in her voice, and the sexual frustration she describes, suggest that her "want" and "need" are distinctly sexual as well as relational.

One reason that Melissa seems to be confused is that she felt a strong desire to be "mothered," her own mother having died last year. In trying to distinguish her different desires in this interview, Melissa began to distinguish erotic feelings from another kind of wanting she also experienced: she said that "it's more of like but I kind of feel like it's really more of like a maternal thing, that I really want her to take care of me and I just wanna touch someone and I just really like the feeling of just how I mean I like, when I'm with her and touching her and stuff. A lot, but it's not necessarily a sexual thing at this point." In contrast to her feelings for her girlfriend, Melissa describes feeling sexually attracted to another girl. In so doing, Melissa clarifies what is missing in these first sexual adventures, enabling her to know what had bothered her about her relationship with her girlfriend:

I don't really think I'm getting that much pleasure, from her, it's just, I mean it's almost like I'm getting experience, and I'm sort of having fun, it's not even that exciting, and that's why I think I don't really like her . . . because my friend asked me this the other day, well, I mean does it get, I mean when you're with her does it get really, I don't remember the word she used, but just really, like what was the word she used? But I guess she meant just like, exciting [laughing]. But it doesn't, to me. It's weird, because I can't really say that, I mean I can't think of like a time when I was really excited and it was like really, sexual pleasure, for me, because I don't think it's really like that. I mean not that I think that this isn't good because, I don't know, I mean, I like it, but I mean I think I have to, sort of realize that I'm not that much attracted to her, personally.

Wanting both a relationship and sexual pleasure, a chance to explore closeness and her sexual curiosity, and discovering that this relationship leaves out her sexual desire, Melissa laments her silent body: "I sort of expect or hope or whatever that there would be some kind of more excited feeling just from feeling sexually stimulated or whatever. I would hope that there would be more of a feeling than I've gotten so far." Knowing consciously what she "knows" about the absence of her sexual feelings in this relationship has left her with a relational conflict of large proportions for her: "I'm not that attracted to her and I don't know if I should tell her that. Or if I should just kind of pretend I am and try to . . . anyway." I ask her how she would go about doing that—pretending that she is. She replies, "I don't think I could pretend it for too long." Not being able to "pretend" to have feelings that she knows she wants as part of an intimate relationship, Melissa faces a dilemma of desire that may leave her feeling isolated and lonely or even fraudulent.

ADOLESCENT GIRLS' SEXUAL DESIRE AND THE POSSIBILITIES OF EMPOWERMENT

All of the girls in this study who said they felt sexual desire expressed conflict when describing their responses to their sexual feelings—conflict between their embodied sexual feelings and their perceptions of how those feelings are, in one way or another, anathema or problematic within the social and relational contexts of their lives. Their experiences of sexual desire are strong and pleasurable, yet they speak very often not of the power of desire but of how their desire may get them into trouble. These girls are beginning to voice the internalized oppression of their women's bodies; they knew and spoke about, in explicit or more indirect ways, the pressure they felt to silence their desire, to dissociate from those bodies in which they inescapably live. Larger societal forces of social control in the form of compulsory heterosexuality (Rich 1983), the policing of girls' bodies through school codes (Lesko 1988), and media images play a clear part in forcing this silence and dissociation. Specific relational dynamics, such as concern about a reputation that can easily be besmirched by other girls and by boys, fear of male violence in intimate relationships, and fear of violent repercussion of violating norms of heterosexuality are also audible in these girls' voices.

To be able to know their sexual feelings, to listen when their bodies speak about themselves and about their relationships, might enable these and other girls to identify and know more clearly the sources of oppression that press on their full personhood and their capacity for knowledge, joy, and connection. Living in the margins of a heterosexual society, the bisexual and lesbian girls voice an awareness of these forces as formative of the experiences of their bodies and relationships; the heterosexual girls are less clear and less critical about the ways that dominant constructions of their sexuality impinge on their embodied and relational

worlds. Even when they are aware that societal ambivalence and fears are being played out on their minds and bodies, they do not speak of a need for collective action, or even the possibility of engaging in such activities. More often, they speak of the danger of speaking about desire at all. By dousing desire with fear and confusion, or simple, "uncomplicated" denial, silence, and dissociation, the girls in this study make individual psychological moves whereby they distance or disconnect themselves from discomfort and danger. Although disciplining their bodies and curbing their desire is a very logical and understandable way to stay physically, socially, and emotionally safe, it also heightens the chance that girls and women may lose track of the fact that an inequitable social system, and not a necessary situation, renders women's sexual desire a source of danger rather than one of pleasure and power in their lives. In "not knowing" desire, girls and women are at risk for not knowing that there is nothing wrong with having sexual feelings and responding to them in ways that bring joy and agency.

Virtually every girl in the larger study told me that no woman had ever talked to her about sexual desire and pleasure "like this"—in depth, listening to her speak about her own experiences, responding when she asked questions about how to masturbate, how to have cunnilingus, what sex is like after marriage. In the words of Rubin: "The ethos of privacy and silence about our personal sexual experience makes it easy to rationalize the refusal to speak [to adolescents]" (1990, 83; Segal 1993). Thompson (1990) found that daughters of women who had talked with them about pleasure and desire told narratives about first intercourse that were informed by pleasure and agency. The recurrent strategy the girls in my study describe of keeping their desire under wraps as a way to protect themselves also keeps girls out of authentic relationships with other girls and women. It is within these relationships that the empowerment of women can develop and be nurtured through shared experiences of both oppression and power, in which collectively articulated critiques are carved out and voiced. Such knowledge of how a patriarchal society systematically keeps girls and women from their own desire can instigate demand and agency for social change. By not talking about sexual desire with each other or with women, a source for empowerment is lost. There is a symbiotic interplay between desire and empowerment: to be empowered to desire one needs a critical perspective, and that critical perspective will be extended and sustained through knowing and experiencing the possibilities of desire and healthy embodied living. Each of these girls illustrates the phenomenon observed in the larger study—the difficulty for girls in having or sustaining a critical perspective on the culture's silencing of their sexual desire. They are denied full access to the power of their own desire and to structural supports for that access.

Common threads of fear and joy, pleasure and danger, weave through the narratives about sexual desire in this study, exemplified by the three portraits. Girls have the right to be informed that gaining pleasure and a strong sense of self and power through their bodies does not make them bad or unworthy. The experiences of these and other adolescent girls illustrate why girls deserve to be educated about their sexual desire. Thompson concludes that "to take possession of sexuality in the wake of the anti-erotic sexist socialization that remains the majority experience, most teenage girls need an erotic education" (1990, 406). Girls need to be educated about the duality of their sexuality, to have safe contexts in which they can explore both danger and desire (Fine 1988), and to consider why their desire is so dangerous and how they can become active participants in their own redemption. Girls can be empowered to know and act on their own desire, a different educational direction than the simplistic strategies for avoiding boys' desire that they are offered. The "just say no" curriculum obscures the larger social inequities being played out on girls' bodies in heterosexual relationships and is not relevant for girls who feel sexual feelings for girls. Even adults who are willing or able to acknowledge that girls experience sexual feelings worry that knowing about their own sexual desire will place girls in danger (Segal 1993). But keeping girls in the dark about their power to choose based on their own feelings fails to keep them any safer from these dangers. Girls who trust their minds and bodies may experience a stronger sense of self, entitlement, and empowerment that could enhance their ability to make safe decisions. One approach to educating girls is for women to speak to them about the vicissitudes of sexual desire—which means that women must let themselves speak and know their own sexual feelings, as well as the pleasures and dangers associated with women's sexuality and the solutions that we have wrought to the dilemma of desire: how to balance the realities of pleasure and danger in women's sexuality.

Asking these girls to speak about sexual desire, and listening and responding to their answers and also to their questions, proved to be an effective way to interrupt the standard "dire consequences" discourse adults usually employ when speaking at all to girls about their sexuality. Knowing and speaking about the ways in which their sexuality continues to be unfairly constrained may interrupt the appearance of social equity that many adolescent girls (especially white, middle-class young women) naively and trustingly believe, thus leading them to reject feminism as unnecessary and mean-spirited and not relevant to their lives. As we know from the consciousness-raising activities that characterized the initial years of second-wave feminism, listening to the words of other girls and women can make it possible for girls to know and voice their experiences, their justified confusion and fears, their curiosities. Through such relationships, we help ourselves and each other to live in our different female bodies with an awareness of danger, but also with a desire to feel the power of the erotic, to fine-tune our bodies and our psyches to what Audre Lorde has called the "yes within ourselves" (Lorde 1984, 54).

NOTES

1. The bisexual girl and the lesbian girl were members of a gay/lesbian youth group and identify themselves using these categories. As is typical for members of privileged groups for whom membership is a given, the girls who feel sexual desire for boys and not for girls (about which they were asked explicitly) do not use the term "heterosexual" to describe themselves. Although I am aware of the debate surrounding the use of these categories and labels to delimit women's (and men's) experience, because my interpretive practice is informed by the ways society makes meaning of girls' sexuality, the categories that float in the culture as ways of describing the girls are relevant to my analysis. In addition, the bisexual and lesbian girls in this study are deeply aware of compulsory heterosexuality and its impact on their lives.

2. Of the thirty girls in this sample, twenty-seven speak of a desire for boys and not for girls. This pattern was ascertained by who appeared in their desire narratives and also by their response to direct questions about sexual feelings for girls, designed explicitly to interrupt the hegemony of heterosexuality. Two of the thirty girls described sexual desire for both boys and girls and one girl described sexual desire for girls and not for boys.

3. Parts of this analysis appear in Tolman (1994).

REFERENCES

Brown, L. 1991. Telling a girl's life: Self authorization as a form of resistance. In *Women, Girls and Psychotherapy: Reframing Resistance,* ed. C. Gilligan, A. Rogers, and D. Tolman. New York: Haworth.

Brown, L., E. Debold, M. Tappan, and C. Gilligan. 1991. Reading narratives of conflict for self and moral voice: A relational method. In *Handbook of Moral Behavior and Development: Theory, Research, and Application,* ed. W. Kurtines and J. Gewirtz. Hillsdale, NJ: Lawrence Erlbaum.

Brown, L., and C. Gilligan. 1992. *Meeting at the Crossroads: Women's Psychology and Girls' Development.* Cambridge, MA: Harvard University Press.

Fine, Michelle. 1988. Sexuality, schooling and adolescent females: The missing discourse of desire. *Harvard Educational Review* 58:29–53.

Friend, Richard. 1993. Choices, not closets. In *Beyond Silenced Voices,* ed. M. Fine and L. Weis. New York: State University of New York Press.

Gilligan, Carol. 1989. Teaching Shakespeare's sister. In *Making Connections: The Relational World of Adolescent Girls at Emma Willard School,* ed. C. Gilligan, N. Lyons, and T. Hamner. Cambridge, MA: Harvard University Press.

———. 1990. Joining the resistance: Psychology, politics, girls and women. *Michigan Quarterly Review* 29:501–36.

Lees, Susan. 1986. *Losing Out: Sexuality and Adolescent Girls.* London: Hutchinson.

Lesko, Nancy. 1988. The curriculum of the body: Lessons from a Catholic high school. In *Becoming Feminine: The Politics of Popular Culture,* ed. L. Roman. Philadelphia: Falmer.

Lorde, Audre. 1984. The uses of the erotic as power. In *Sister Outsider: Essays and Speeches.* Freedom, CA: Crossing Press.

Miller, Jean Baker. 1976. *Towards a New Psychology of Woman.* Boston: Beacon Press.

Rich, Adrienne. 1983. Compulsory heterosexuality and lesbian existence. In *Powers of Desire: The politics of sexuality,* ed. A.

Snitow, C. Stansell, and S. Thompson. New York: Monthly Review Press.

Rubin, Lillian. 1990. *Erotic Wars: What Happened to the Sexual Revolution?* New York: HarperCollins.

Segal, Lynne. 1993. Introduction. In *Sex Exposed: Sexuality and the Pornography Debate,* ed. L. Segal and M. McIntosh. New Brunswick, NJ: Rutgers University Press.

Spillers, Hortense. 1984. Interstices: A small drama of words. In *Pleasure and Danger: Exploring Female Sexuality,* ed. C. Vance. Boston: Routledge and Kegan Paul.

Thompson, Sharon. 1984. Search for tomorrow: On feminism and the reconstruction of teen romance. In *Pleasure and Danger: Exploring Female Sexuality,* ed. C. Vance. Boston: Routledge and Kegan Paul.

———. 1990. Putting a big thing in a little hole: Teenage girls' accounts of sexual initiation. *Journal of Sex Research* 27:341–61.

Tolman, Deborah L. 1991. Adolescent girls, women and sexuality: Discerning dilemmas of desire. *Women, Girls, and Psychotherapy: Reframing Resistance,* ed. C. Gilligan, A. Rogers, and D. Tolman. New York: Haworth.

———. 1992. Voicing the body: A psychological study of adolescent girls' sexual desire. Unpublished dissertation, Harvard University.

———. 1994. Daring to desire: Culture and the bodies of adolescent girls. In *Sexual Cultures: Adolescents, Communities and the Construction of Identity,* ed. J. Irvine. Philadelphia: Temple University Press.

Tolman, Deborah, and Elizabeth Debold. 1993. Conflicts of body and image: Female adolescents, desire, and the no-body. In *Feminist Treatment and Therapy of Eating Disorders,* ed. M. Katzman, P. Failon, and S. Wooley. New York: Guilford.

SEX ED: HOW DO WE SCORE?

CAROLYN MACKLER

The 12:55 bell rings at Ridgewood High School and a flock of freshmen filter into Evelyn Rosskamm Shalom's Health 9 class. Greeting the sea of navy blue baseball caps and capri pants, Shalom announces that today's lesson will commence with the "question box" and instructs students to proceed as quietly as possible to the Magic Carpet. In a stampede evocative of July in Pamplona, twenty-five pairs of Nikes and clunky sandals clamor onto a dingy gray rug at the back of the room and, with one brave male exception, self-segregate by gender: girls on one side, boys on the other, a puerile triad huddled in the back. Shalom, joking about her recent fiftieth birthday, treats herself to a metal chair at the mouth of the circle and produces slips of folded white paper.

"Any more to add before I begin?" she asks, casually tucking a wayward strand of auburn hair behind one ear.

Braces-revealing smirks ripple through the crowd, especially among the Peanut Gallery trio, who menacingly ooze "spitball" from every pore of their bodies.

Shalom quickly scans a crumpled selection. "Have I already answered: 'Why do people have oral sex?'"

The Peanut Gallery erupts and a handful of mid-pubescents dutifully nod their heads. Shalom, a sixteen-year veteran of Ridgewood High School who has been described as someone who rules a class with velvet-gloved discipline, allows the rascals a heartbeat to blow off steam before skillfully channeling their discomfort into a lively debate in response to the next questions: "What is the right age to have sex?" Once Shalom takes the floor to address the query, a hush falls over the Magic Carpet. The only discernable sound is the buzzing of florescent lights above. Fifty eyes are intent on Shalom. Even the Peanut Gallery is hooked.

So goes a typical health class at Ridgewood High School in suburban New Jersey. The Ridgewood school district is renowned for its comprehensive and thorough family-life education curriculum. Following a 1980

statewide mandate that all New Jersey schoolchildren were to have sex education, Ridgewood Public Schools formed an advisory committee to consult with the school regarding its ever-evolving curriculum. Ridgewood students receive health education every year of their public school careers, beginning with instruction from a certified nurse specialist in elementary school and progressing to classes taught by high school teachers, such as Shalom, who has a master's degree in health education.

Fade from the Magic Carpet to a school district in Franklin County, North Carolina, where, in the fall of 1997, a scissors-toting parent-volunteer was summoned to the high school to slice chapters 17, 20, and 21 out of ninth-graders' health textbooks. The culpable text—covering contraception, sexually transmitted diseases (STDs), and relationship—didn't comply with the statewide abstinence-only curriculum, ruled the school board. Apparently, in a state where in 1996 there were 25,240 recorded pregnancies among fifteen- to nineteen-year-olds, the board hoped that if they obliterated a discourse on condoms, getting down wouldn't dawn on youngsters.

Unfortunately, this sort of scene is business as usual with the politically explosive issue of school-based sex education. While a uniform national curriculum does not exist, barrels of federal money are being siphoned into abstinence-only-until-marriage programs, frequently laden with wrath-of-God scare tactics. Comprehensive sexuality education the likes of Ridgewood's, designed to reinforce sexuality as a positive and healthy part of being human, is available to only about 5 percent of school children in the United States. Sexuality education is an across-the-school-boards contentious subject, bound to generate controversy, even among well-meaning feminists; sexuality is not a one-size-fits-all equation, and the messages appropriate for one kid may not work for the girl or boy at the adjacent desk.

And then there's the Great Antipleasure Conspiracy. Translation: adults swindling kids (especially girls) by trying to convince them that sex is no fun, in the hope that they won't partake, a practice exemplified by the shocking omission of the clitoris—whose sole function is to deliver female pleasure—from most high school biology textbooks. The notion of women experiencing erotic pleasure—or possessing full sexual agency—clearly scares the boxer shorts off conservative educators. Analogous to attempting to eradicate pizza by withholding Italy from a map of Europe, not including the clitoris in a textbook depiction of female genitalia is a frightening misleading excuse for education.

Tiptoeing around any of these issues—from pleasure to power to pregnancy prevention—is denying youngsters their basic right to health information. It is catapulting them into life-threatening sexual scenarios without sufficient tools to protect themselves. It is jeopardizing their chance to lay sturdy foundations for a sexually healthy adulthood. It's time to wake up and smell the hormones.

Ridgewood boasts one of the most progressive school districts in a "mixed landscape," explains Susan N. Wilson, the executive coordinator of the Network for Family Life Education, a nonprofit organization based at the Rutgers School for Social Work in Piscataway, New Jersey, that promotes comprehensive sexuality education in schools and communities. Wilson . . . explains that over the past several years there has been progress in the quantity of sex education in the schools. "In most places, it exists; something is being taught," she says, "but there are many school districts where students receive the bare minimum—HIV education—and very, very late in their school lives." Wilson points out that many politicians have embraced AIDS education with open arms. "In a true intertwining of church and state, they've jumped at the chance to reveal that sex does, in fact, equal death."

Debra Haffner, president of the Sexuality Information and Education Council of the United States (SIECUS), a nonprofit group that advocates for sexuality education and sexual rights, describes how most young people in this country get hurried through sex-abuse prevention in early grade school, the Puberty Talk in fifth grade, a lesson on HIV and STDs in middle school, and possibly a health elective in high school. "There's currently a great emphasis on abstinence in this country," she adds, "partially driven by federal pro-

grams, but partially driven by the conservative influence in communities."

Abstinence-only lessons, though varying from classroom to classroom, often revolve around a "pet your dog, not your date" theme. One resoundingly sexist message is that the onus of restricting foreplay should fall on the girl, encouraging her to use "self-control" rather than "birth control." A pseudoscientific chart from Sex Respect, a fear-based abstinence curriculum, depicts how male genitalia become aroused during "necking," while female genitalia lag behind until "petting." The girl-cum-gatekeeper's pleasure gets swept to the side, leaving her to ward filthy, boys-will-be-boys paws off her silky drawers.

The overwhelming bulk of scientific research underscores the failure of abstinence-only education in doing anything but eclipsing the erotic with the neurotic. A recent report by the National Campaign to Prevent Teen Pregnancy revealed that "the weight of the current evidence indicates that these abstinence programs do not delay the onset of intercourse." In a country where a mere 6.9 percent of men and 21 percent of women ages eighteen to fifty-nine hold out for their honeymoon, force-feeding "Just Say No" to teenagers sends them scurrying to the playground or onto the Web in search of information—usually to find misinformation—and frolicking under the covers all the same. But the risks of leaving kids without sufficient skills and facts range from the obvious—pregnancy and STDs—to sexual abuse, date rape, and sexual powerlessness.

Reducing adolescent pregnancy and the risk of sexually transmitted diseases is clearly paramount. But Susan Wilson, who's convinced that the right wants to "stamp out" teen sexuality altogether, wonders whether the effort is "on a collision course with healthy sexuality."

Debra Haffner echoes similar sentiments. "My mentor from twenty years ago used to call that 'Sex is dirty. Save it for someone you love,' " she scoffs. "We cannot ingrain in young people the message that sexual intercourse violates another person, kills people, and leaves you without a reputation, and then expect that the day they put a wedding band on their finger they're going to forget all that."

She pauses and adds wryly, "It just creates adults who are in sex therapy because they can't have fulfilling relationships with their spouses and partners."

In 1996, SIECUS published the second edition of its *Guidelines for Comprehensive Sexuality Education: K–12,* which it had originally developed earlier in the decade with a task force that included the Centers for Disease Control and Prevention, Planned Parenthood Federation of America, and the National School Boards Association. The guidelines serve as a framework to facilitate the development of a comprehensive sex education program arising from the belief that "young people explore their sexuality as a natural process of achieving sexual maturity." Accordingly, emphasis should be placed on informed decision making about intercourse by acknowledging—not condemning—the broad range of adolescent sexual behaviors.

The SIECUS sexuality education model is designed to spiral through the school years, with age-appropriate lessons at all grade levels. . . . Proponents of comprehensive sexuality education believe that by high school, teenagers should have processed enough information to make responsible choices surrounding sex. And the research is on their side: studies reveal that teenagers who partake in discussions that include all options, from chastity belts to condoms, often delay sexual intercourse or reduce its frequency. By cultivating in adolescents a sense of sexual self-determination—with empowerment and gratification and honest communication being central—things tend to fall into place; unwanted pregnancy and sexually transmitted diseases remain on the periphery, not at the hub of their ideas about human sexuality.

Back to the Great Antipleasure Conspiracy. There's reluctance even among liberal adults—most likely due to their own discomfort surrounding sexuality—to acknowledge that the majority of sex is for recreation, not procreation. Scarier still is the notion of pleasuring oneself. Wilson points out that masturbation is a subject "avoided assiduously by teachers." It is essential for schools to employ educators who will not blanch at the mention of, say, a clitoris (and who, like Shalom, boycott clitoris-free textbooks). "Nobody invests money in training," says Wilson, who points out that often sex ed teachers hit the chalkboard with only a weekend workshop under their belt. "A basic course in human sexuality for everyone in the helping professions should be commonplace."

It doesn't take a logician to deduce that the future of sex education is in serious jeopardy, but perhaps it's going to take feminists to do something about it. With a paucity of children receiving comprehensive sexuality education and gobs of federal money flying into reactionary, fear-based instruction, there's plenty of action to be taken, in the form of rallying school districts, educators, politicians, and parents to support education designed to empower, enlighten, and, yes, even excite youth about sexuality. And while we'll be sorry to see sex therapists hard-pressed for clients, we can envision a world where girls and boys grow into adults who regard their sexuality as anything but a one-way ticket to disease and unplanned pregnancy.

As I lean across Shalom's metal desk to hit the off button on my tape recorder, she interjects one final comment. "I see how kids respond to this stuff every single day," she reports. "They are just waiting for adults to share the tools with them. And it's not 'share the tools so I can go out and do it,' it's 'please help me learn how to grow up.'"

Getting Off on Feminism

JASON SCHULTZ

When it comes to smashing a paradigm, pleasure is not the most important thing. It is the only thing.

—Gary Wolf, Wired magazine

Minutes after my best friend told me he was getting married, I casually offered to throw a bachelor party in his honor. Even though such parties are notorious for their degradation of women, I didn't think this party would be much of a problem. Both the bride and groom considered themselves feminists, and I figured that most of the men attending would agree that sexism had no place in the celebration of this union. In fact, I thought the bachelor party would be a great opportunity to get a group of men together for a social event that didn't degenerate into the typical antiwomen, homophobic male-bonding thing. Still, ending one of the most sexist traditions in history—even for one night—was a lot tougher than I envisioned.

I have to admit that I'm not a *complete* iconoclast: I wanted to make the party a success by including at least some of the usual elements, such as good food and drink, great music, and cool things to do. At the same time, I was determined not to fall prey to traditional sexist party gimmicks such as prostitutes, strippers jumping out of cakes, or straight porn. But after nixing all the traditional lore, even *I* thought it sounded boring. What were we going to do except sit around and think about women?

"What about a belly dancer?" one of the ushers suggested when I confided my concerns to him. "That's not as bad as a stripper." I sighed. This was supposed to be an occasion

for the groom and his male friends to get together, celebrate the upcoming marriage, and affirm their friendship and connection with each other as men. "What the fuck does hiring a female sex worker have to do with any of that?" I shouted into the phone. I quickly regained my calm, but his suggestion still stung. We had to find some other way.

I wanted my party to be as "sexy" as the rest of them, but I had no idea how to do that in the absence of female sex workers. There was no powerful alternative image in our culture from which I could draw. I thought about renting some gay porn, or making it a cross-dressing party, but many of the guests were conservative and I didn't want to scare anyone off. Besides, what would it say about a bunch of straight men if all we could do to be sexy was act queer for a night?

Over coffee on a Sunday morning, I asked some of the other guys what they thought was so "sexy" about having a stripper at a bachelor party.

"Well," David said, "it's just a gag. It's something kinda funny and sexy at the same time."

"Yeah," A. J. agreed. "It's not all that serious, but it's something special to do that makes the party cool."

"But *why* is it sexy and funny?" I asked. "Why can't we, as a bunch of guys, be sexy and funny ourselves?"

" 'Cause it's easier to be a guy with other guys when there's a chick around. It gives you all something in common to relate to."

"Hmm. I think I know what you mean," I said. "When I see a stripper, I get turned on, but not in the same way I would if I was with a lover. It's more like going to a show or watching a flick together. It's enjoyable, stimulating, but it's not overwhelming or intimate in the same way that sex is. Having the stripper provides a common emotional context for us to feel turned on. But we don't have to do anything about it like we would if we were with a girlfriend, right?"

"Well, my girlfriend would kill me if she saw me checking out this stripper," Greg replied. "But because it's kind of a male-bonding thing, it's not as threatening to our relationship. It's not because it's the stripper over her, it's because it's just us guys hanging out. It doesn't go past that."

Others agreed. "Yeah. You get turned on, but not in a serious way. It makes you feel sexy and sexual, and you can enjoy feeling that way with your friends. Otherwise, a lot of times, just hanging out with the guys is pretty boring. Especially at a bachelor party. I mean, that's the whole point, isn't it—to celebrate the fact that we're bachelors, and he"—referring to Robert, the groom—"isn't!"

Through these conversations, I realized that having a female sex worker at the party would give the men permission to connect with one another without becoming vulnerable. When men discuss sex in terms of actions—who they "did," and how and where they did it—they can gain recognition and validation of their sexuality from other men without having to expose their *feelings* about sex.

"What other kinds of things make you feel sexy like the stripper does?" I asked several of the guys.

"Watching porn sometimes, or a sexy movie."

A. J. said, "Just getting a look from a girl at a club. I mean, she doesn't even have to talk to you, but you still feel sexy and you can still hang out with your friends."

Greg added, "Sometimes just knowing that my girlfriend thinks I'm sexy, and then talking about her with friends, makes me feel like I'm the man. Or I'll hear some other guy talk about his girlfriend in a way that reminds me of mine, and I'll still get that same feeling. But that doesn't happen very often, and usually only when talking with one other guy."

This gave me an idea. "I've noticed that same thing, both here and at school with my other close guy friends. Why doesn't it happen with a bunch of guys, say at a party?"

"I don't know. It's hard to share a lot of personal stuff with guys," said Adam, "especially about someone you're seeing, if you don't feel comfortable. Well, not comfortable, because I know most of the guys who'll be at the party, but it's more like I don't want them to hassle me, or I might say something that freaks them out."

"Or you're just used to guys talking shit about girls," someone else added. "Like at a party or hanging out together. They rag on them, or pick out who's the cutest or who wants to do who. That's not the same thing as really talking about what makes you feel sexy."

"Hmm," I said. "So it's kind of like if I were to say that I liked to be tied down to the bed, no one would take me

seriously. You guys would probably crack up laughing, make a joke or two, but I'd never expect you to actually join in and talk about being tied up in a serious way. It certainly wouldn't feel 'sexy,' would it? At least not as much as the stripper."

"Exactly. You talking about being tied down here is fine, 'cause we're into the subject of sex on a serious kick and all. But at a party, people are bullshitting each other and gabbing, and horsing around. The last thing most of us want is to trip over someone's personal taste or start thinking someone's a little queer."

"You mean queer as in homosexual?" I asked.

"Well, not really, 'cause I think everyone here is straight. But more of queer in the sense of perverted or different. I mean, you grow up in high school thinking that all guys are basically the same. You all want the same thing from girls in the same way. And when someone like you says you like to be tied down, it's kinda weird—almost like a challenge. It makes me have to respond in a way that either shows me agreeing that I also like to be tied down or not. And if someone's a typical guy and he says that, it makes you think he's different—not the same guy you knew in high school. And if he's not the same guy, then it challenges you to relate to him on a different level."

"Yeah, I guess in some ways it's like relating to someone who's gay," Greg said. "He can be cool and all, and you can get along totally great. But there's this barrier that's hard to cross over. It kinda keeps you apart. And that's not what you want to feel toward your friends, especially at a party like this one, where you're all coming together to chill."

As the bachelor party approached, I found myself wondering whether my friends and I could "come together to chill"—and affirm our status as sexual straight men—without buying into homophobic or sexist expressions. At the same time, I was doing a lot of soul-searching on how we could challenge the dominant culture's vision of male heterosexuality, not only by deciding against having a stripper at our party but also by examining and redefining our own relationships with women.

SEX AND THE SENSITIVE MAN

According to the prevailing cultural view, "desirable" hetero men are inherently dominant, aggressive, and, in many subtle and overt ways, abusive to women. To be sexy and powerful, straight men are expected to control and contrive a sexuality that reinforces their authority. Opposing these notions of power subjects a straight guy to being branded "sensitive," submissive, or passive—banished to the nether regions of excitement and pleasure, the unmasculine, asexual, "vanilla" purgatory of antieroticism. Just as hetero women are often forced to choose between the images of the virgin and the whore, modern straight men are caught in a cultural tug-of-war between the Marlboro Man and the Wimp.

So where does that leave straight men who want to re-examine what a man is and change it? Can a good man be sexy? Can a sexy man be good? What is good sex, egalitarian sex? More fundamentally, can feminist women and men coexist comfortably, even happily, within the same theoretical framework—or the same bedroom?

Relationships with men remain one of the most controversial topics among feminists today. Having sex, negotiating emotional dependency, and/or raising children force many hetero couples to balance their desire to be together with the oppressive dymanics of sexism. In few other movements are the oppressor group and the oppressed group so intimately linked.

But what about men who support feminism? Shouldn't it be okay for straight feminist women to have sex with them? Straight men aren't always oppressive in their sexuality, are they?

You may laugh at these questions, but they hold serious implications for straight feminist sex. I've seen many relationships between opposite-sex activists self-destruct because critical assumptions about power dynamics and desires were made in the mind, but not in the bed. I've even been told that straight male feminists can't get laid without A) feeling guilty; B) reinforcing patriarchy; or C) maintaining complete passivity during sexual activity. Each of these three options represents common assumptions about the sexuality of straight men who support feminism. Choice A, "feeling guilty," reflects the belief that straight male desire inherently contradicts the goals of feminism and fails to contribute to the empowerment of women. It holds that any man who enjoys sex with a woman must be benefiting from sexist male privilege, not fighting against it. In other words, het sex becomes a zero-sum game where if men gain, feminism loses.

Choice B represents the assumption that hetero male sex is inherently patriarchal. Beyond merely being of no help, as in Choice A, straight male sexuality is seen as part of the problem. Within this theory, one often hears statements such as "all heterosexual sex is rape." Even though these statements are usually taken out of context, the ideas behind them are problematic. In essence, they say that you can never have a male/female interaction that isn't caught up in oppressive dynamics. Men and women can never be together, especially in such a vulnerable exchange as sexuality, without being subject to the misdistribution of power in society.

The third choice, "maintaining complete passivity," attempts a logical answer to the above predicament. In order to come even close to achieving equality in heterosexuality (and still get laid), men must "give up" all their power through inactivity. A truly feminist man should take no aggressive or dominant position. He should, in fact, not act at all; he should merely lie back and allow the woman to subvert male supremacy through her complete control of the situation. In other words, for a man and a woman to share sexuality on a "level playing field," the man must remove all symptoms of his power through passivity, even though the causes of that inequality (including his penis!) still exist.

I know of one feminist man whose girlfriend *insisted* that she always be on top when they had intercourse. Her reasoning was simple: a man in a dominant sexual position represents sexist oppression incarnate. Therefore, the only possible way to achieve female empowerment was to subvert this power through her dominance. She even went so far as to stop intercourse before he reached orgasm, as a protest against male sexual entitlement.

The above story represents the *assumption* that sexism functions within male sexuality in a uniform, unvarying way, and that straight women must adapt and strategize within their personal relationships accordingly.

Does it have to be this way? Must male heterosexuality always pose a threat to feminism? What about the sensitive guy? Wasn't that the male cry (whimper) of the nineties? Sorry, but all the media hype about sensitivity never added up to significant changes in behavior. Straight male sexuality still remains one of the most underchallenged areas of masculinity in America. Some men *did* propose a different kind of sexuality for straight men in the 1970s, one that emphasizes feelings and sensitivity and emotional connection. But these efforts failed to affect our ideas in any kind of revolutionary way. Now, instead of a "sexy" sensitive guy, men's magazines are calling for the emergence of the "Post-Sensitive Man," while scientific studies tell us that women prefer Clint Eastwood over Michael Bolton.

Why did sensitivity fail? Were straight women, even feminists, lying to men about what they wanted? The answer is "yes" and "no." I don't think sensitivity was the culprit. I think the problem was men's passivity, or more specifically, men's lack of assertiveness and power.

In much of our understanding, power is equated with oppression: images of white supremacists dominating people of color, men dominating women, and the rich dominating the poor underline the histories of many cultures and societies. But power need not always oppress others. One can, I believe, be powerful in a nonoppressive way.

In order to find this sort of alternative, we need to examine men's experience with power and sexuality further. Fortunately, queer men and women have given us a leg up on the process by re-energizing the debate about what is good sex and what is fair sex. Gay male culture has a long history of exploring nontraditional aspects of male sexuality, such as cross-dressing, bondage and dominance, and role playing. These dynamics force gay men to break out of a singular experience of male sexual desire and to examine the diversity within male sexuality in the absence of gender oppression. Though gay men's culture still struggles with issues such as the fetishizing of men of color and body fascism, it does invite greater exploration of diversity than straight male culture. Gay culture has broader and more inclusive attitudes about what is sexy and a conception of desire that accommodates many types of sex for many types of gay men. For straight men in our culture, there is such a rigid definition of "sexy" that it leaves us few options besides being oppressive, overbearing, or violent.

Part of the success that gay male culture enjoys in breaking out of monolithic notions of male sexuality lies in the acceptance it receives from its partners and peers. Camp, butch, leather, drag-queer culture is constantly affirming the powerful presence of alternative sexualities. Straight male culture, on the other hand, experiences a lack—a void of acceptance—whenever it tries to assert some image other than the sexist hetero male. Both publicly and in many cases privately, alternative straight nude sexualities fail to compete for attention and acceptance among hetero men and women.

HOT, HEAVY, AND HETEROSEXUAL

Without role models and cultural messages to affirm them, new forms of desire fail to stick around in our heads and our hearts. Therefore, straight men and women need to get hot and heavy for an alternative male heterosexuality. Often, women who desire nontraditional types of straight men fail to assert their desires publicly. If and when they find these men, they do so through friendships, in long-term relationships, or by accident. They rarely seek them out in bars, one-night stands, or house parties. Sexual desire that results from a friendship or long-term relationship can be wonderful, but it fails to hold the popular "sexy" status that active dating, flirtation, or seduction does. If we truly hope to change straight male sexuality, we must move beyond private one-on-one affirmations and change public and cultural ones.

Unfortunately, it's easier said than done. Whenever I've tried to assert a nonoppressive sexuality with women, I've sunk into a cultural quagmire. I get caught riding that fine line between being a Sensitive New Age Guy and an asshole. Many straight women (both feminist and not) still find an aggressive, dominant man sexy. Many straight women still desire a man to take charge when it comes to romance or intimacy, especially when initiating intercourse. Yet many of the same straight feminist women constantly highlight the abuse and discrimination that many of these men inflict. They often complain about a man who is misogynist while affirming his desirability. This dichotomy of desire is confusing and frustrating.

Admittedly, much of my frustration relates to my own experience. I've always found fierce, independent women attractive—women who say they want a man to support them emotionally, listen to them, and not fight them every step of the way. Yet in reality, these women often lost respect for me and for other men who tried to change our sexuality to meet these needs.

I'd try to play the game, moving in as the aggressive man and then showing a more sensitive side after I'd caught the person's attention. But more often than not, the result was frustrating. I didn't catch a clue until one night when I had an enlightening conversation with one of these women who called herself a feminist. I asked her why guys who tried to accommodate the political desires of straight feminists always seemed to lose out in the end. She said she thought it was because a lot of young straight women who confront gender issues through feminism are constantly trying to redefine themselves in relation to culture and other people in their lives. Therefore, if they pursue relationships with men, many consciously seek out a *traditional* man— not only because it is the kind of man they have been taught to desire, but because he is familiar to them. He is strong, stable, predictable, and powerful. As the woman's identity shifts and changes, she can use the man she is dating as a reference point and source of strength and stability.

If she chooses to become involved with a feminist man who feels the same need to examine assumptions about gender (including his own masculinity) on a political and personal level, both partners are in a state of flux and instability. Both are searching for an understanding of their relationship, but each questions how that relationship is defined, even down to assumptions about men, women, sex, and commitment. Within this shifting matrix, straight feminist men who explore alternative ways of being sexual are often perceived as passive, weak, and in many cases, undesirable. In the end, it seems much easier to choose the traditional male.

OUT OF THE BREEDING BOX

We need to assert a new feminist sexuality for men, one that competes with the traditional paradigm but offers a more inviting notion of how hetero men can be sexual while tearing apart the oppressive and problematic ways in which so many of us have experienced sexuality in the past. We need to find new, strong values and ideas of male heterosexuality instead of passive identities that try to distance us from sexist men. We need to stop trying to avoid powerful straight sexuality and work to redefine what our power means and does. We need to find strength and desire outside of macho, antiwomen ways of being masculine.

Take the notion of "breeding." Many cultures still assume that the male desire to breed and procreate is the primary purpose of sexuality. This idea, based on outdated notions of Darwinism and evolutionary prophecy, forces us to think of heterosexual men as having a single sexual purpose—ejaculating inside a fertile woman. Be hard, be strong, and cum into any woman's vagina you can find. It's all about sowing seed and proving heterosexuality through the conquest of women. Through this mechanism, reproductive sex is seen as "natural" and most desirable; all other forms of sexual interaction are seen as warm-ups or "foreplay." Breeding prioritizes heterosexuality, and within straight sex, limits its goal to the act of vaginal intercourse.

Yet in a pro-birth-control, increasingly queer-friendly world, breeding has become a minuscule aspect of sexuality. Few heterosexual men and women have sex strictly to breed, and gay men and women almost never do. Within this new context, notions of what is "sexy" and what straight men desire have much more to do with how we fuck or how we feel than with what we produce.

Even among young people who have no intention of creating children, breeder assumptions continue to define male heterosexuality. For instance, many of my friends, especially queer ones, will harass me after I've been dating a woman for a while and give me flack for being a "breeder." They assume that the reason I'm with her—the goal of my relationship—is to make sure I cum inside her. Even if I

don't want a child, even if I hate intercourse, the assumption about my male heterosexuality is that I will at least act like I'm trying to procreate when I'm having sex. Any possibility of a hetero nonbreeder sexuality doesn't exist. I'm forced into the breeding box, no questions permitted.

I've tried to confront these assumptions actively, but it's difficult. Usually I respond with something crass, such as, "Funny, I don't feel like breeding, just fucking." Or by talking about how *I* prefer to be penetrated sometimes. This may seem extreme, but that's how challenging it feels to try to present a different idea of straight male sexuality—one that isn't predicated on notions of being vanilla or being a breeder.

My critique of breeding is not an attempt to discredit fatherhood. Parenting is as much a part of the revolution as any other personal act. My point is that if we want hetero men to change, we have to give them viable choices. There has to be a difference between acting straight and acting like a breeder. And breeding is just *one* of the many assumptions that our culture applies to male heterosexuality.

It's up to straight men to change these assumptions. Gay men and lesbians have engaged in a cultural dialogue around sexuality over the last twenty-five years; straight women are becoming more and more vocal. But straight men have been almost completely silent. This silence, I think, stems in large part from fear: our cultures tell us that being a "real" man means not being feminine, not being gay, and not being weak. They warn us that anyone who dares to stand up to these ideas becomes a sitting target to have his manhood shot down in flames.

BREAKING THE SILENCE

Not becoming a sitting target to have *my* manhood shot down was high on my mind when the evening of my best friend's bachelor party finally arrived. But *I* was determined not to be silent about how I felt about the party and about new visions for straight men within our society.

We decided to throw the party two nights before the wedding. We all gathered at my house, each of us bringing a present to add to the night's activities. After all the men had arrived, we began cooking dinner, breaking open beer and champagne, and catching up on where we had left off since we last saw each other.

During the evening, we continued to talk off and on about why we didn't have a stripper or prostitute for the party. After several rounds of margaritas and a few hands of poker, tension started to build around the direction I was pushing the conversation.

"So what don't you like about strippers?" David asked me.

This was an interesting question. I was surprised not only by the guts of David to ask it, but also by my own mixed feelings in coming up with an answer. "It's not that I don't like being excited, or turned on, per se," I responded. "In fact, to be honest, watching a female stripper is an exciting and erotic experience for me. But at the same time, it's a very uncomfortable one. I get a sense when I watch her that I'm participating in a misuse of pleasure, if that makes sense."

I looked around at my friends. I couldn't tell whether the confused looks on their faces were due to the alcohol, the poker game, or my answer, so I continued. "Ideally, I would love to sit back and enjoy watching someone express herself sexually through dance, seduction, flirtation—all the positive elements I associate with stripping," I said. "But at the same time, because so many strippers are poor and forced to perform in order to survive economically, I feel like the turn-on I get is false. I feel like I get off easy, sitting back as the man, paying for the show. No one ever expects me to get up on stage.

"And in that way, it's selling myself short sexually. It's not only saying very little about the sexual worth of the woman on stage, but the sexual worth of me as the viewer as well. By *only* being a viewer—just getting off as a member of the audience—the striptease becomes a very limiting thing, an imbalanced dynamic. If the purpose is for me to feel sexy and excited, but not to act on those feelings, I'd rather find a more honest and direct way to do it. So personally, while I would enjoy watching a stripper on one level, the real issues of economies, the treatment of women, and the limitation of my own sexual personae push me to reject the whole stripper thing in favor of something else."

"But what else do you do to feel sexy?" A. J. asked.

"That's a tough question," I said. "Feeling sexy often depends on the way other people act toward you. For me, right now, you guys are a huge way for me to feel sexy. [Some of the men cringe.] I'm not saying that we have to challenge our sexual identities, although that's one way. But we can cut through a lot of this locker-room macho crap and start talking with each other about how we feel sexually, what we think, what we like, etc. Watching the stripper makes us feel sexy because we get turned on through the dynamic between her performance and our voyeurism. We can find that same erotic connection with each other by re-creating that context between us. In such a case, we're still heterosexual—we're no more having sex with each other than we are with the stripper. But we're not relying on the imbalanced dynamic of sex work to feel pleasure as straight men."

I took a deep breath. All right, I thought. Here we go. "What makes me feel sexy? I'll tell you. I feel sexy when I say how much I love licking chocolate off a partner's back. Not just that I like to do it, or talking about how often I do it, but that it feels amazing to taste her sweat and her skin mixed in with the sweetness of the chocolate. I feel sexy when I think about running my fingers through her hair in the shower, or watching her put a condom on me with her tongue. I feel sexy remembering how my muscles stretch and strain after being tied down to the bed, or the difference between leather, lace, and silk rubbing up and down my body. That's some of what makes me feel sexy."

The guys were silent for a few seconds, but soon afterwards, the ice seemed to break. While most of the guys weren't completely satisfied with or prepared for my answer, they seemed to feel that it was a step in the right direction. They agreed that, as heterosexual men, we should be able to share with each other what we find exciting and shouldn't *need* a female stripper to feel sexy. In some ways it may have been the desire to define their own sexuality that changed their minds; in others it may have been a traditionally masculine desire to reject any dependency on women. In any case, other men began to speak of their own experiences with pleasure and desire, and we continued to talk throughout the night, exploring the joys of hot sex, one-night stands, and even our preferences for certain brands of condoms. We discussed the ups and down of monogamy versus "open" dating and the pains of long-distance relationships.

Some men continued to talk openly about their desire for straight pornography or women who fit the traditional stereotype of femininity. But others contradicted this, expressing their wish to move beyond that image of women in their lives. The wedding, which started out as the circumstance for our gathering, soon fell into the background of our thoughts as we focused away from institutional ideas of breeder sexuality and began to find common ground through our real-life experiences and feelings as straight men. In the end, we all toasted the groom, sharing stories, jokes, and parts of our lives that many of us had never told. Most importantly, we were able to express ourselves sexually without hiding who we were from each other.

Thinking back on the party, I realized that the hard part was figuring out what we all wanted and how to construct a different way of finding that experience. The other men there wanted it just as much as I did. The problem was that we had no ideas of what a different kind of bachelor party might look like. Merely eliminating the old ways of relating (i.e., the female sex workers) left a gap, an empty space which in many ways *felt* worse than the sexist connection that existed there before; we felt passive and powerless. Yet we found a new way of interacting—one that embraced new ideas and shared the risk of experiencing them.

Was the party sexy? Did we challenge the dominance of oppressive male sexuality? Not completely, but it was a start. I doubt anyone found my party as "sexy" as traditional ones might be, but the dialogue has to start somewhere. It's going to take a while to generate the language and collective tension to balance the cultural image of heterosexual male sexuality with true sexual divinity. Still, one of my friends from high school—who's generally on the conservative end of most issues—told me as he was leaving that of all the bachelor parties he had been to, this was by far the best one. "I had a great time," he said. "Even without the stripper."

PUBLIC PLEASURE AND THE PURSUIT OF POLITICAL CHANGE

> We need to affirm one another, support one another, help, enable, equip, and empower one another to deal with the present crisis, but it can't be uncritical, because if it's uncritical, then we are again refusing to acknowledge other people's humanity. If we are serious about acknowledging other people's humanity, then we are committed to trusting and believing that they are forever in process. Growth, development, maturation happens in stages. People grow, develop, and mature along the lines in which they are taught. Disenabling critique and contemptuous feedback hinders.
>
> —Cornel West

The bachelor party was but a small example of the dialogue straight men need to—and can—create. Some of the most amazing conversations I have had have been with other straight and bisexual men about the *pleasure* of sex with women. These conversations have been far from passive, boring, or placid. They have ranged from the many uses of cock rings to issues of consent within S/M and B&D acts to methods of achieving multiple male orgasms. The difference between these conversations and typical sexist male dialogue is that our discourse strives to bypass the mythological nature of straight male bravado and pornographic fantasy and to emphasize straight men asserting themselves as strong voices for equality *and* pleasure in cultural discourses on sexuality.

These public dialogues have been immensely helpful in dispelling overemphasized issues like impotence and premature ejaculation; such conversations have also allowed us to move past the degrading and pornographic lingo used in high-school locker rooms to describe sex with women and have pushed us to focus our energy on honest questions, feelings, and *desires*. These are the kinds of voices straight men must claim publicly.

When it comes to sex, feminist straight men must become participants in the discourse about our own sexuality. We have to fight the oppressive images of men as biological breeders and leering animals. We must find ways in which to understand our diverse backgrounds, articulate desires that are not oppressive, and acknowledge the power we hold. We must take center stage when it comes to articulating our views in a powerful voice. I'm not trying to prescribe any particular form of sexuality or specify what straight men should want. But until we begin to generate our own demands and desires in an honest and equitable way for feminist straight women to hear, I don't think we can expect to be both good *and* sexy any time soon.

Bodies

It might seem that women's physical bodies and health are biological matters rather than social. In fact, however, factors like access to health care, working conditions, and nutrition are all socially determined. In addition, cultural ideologies about women's bodies affect how we perceive our own bodies, as well as how social institutions regulate women's bodies and health. Women's bodies are contested terrain, the subject of struggle over political rights, reproductive health care, and medical research. Much feminist scholarship and activism focuses on health issues. The ability to control reproduction, to live and work in conditions not injurious to their health, and to receive safe, effective, and affordable medical care are central to women's welfare. Feminists have devoted considerable energy to changing public health policy on women's behalf and to increasing research funding to women's health issues during the last two decades.

In the 1970s, a women's health movement developed in the United States as an outgrowth of the feminist and consumer health movements. Women's health advocates criticized and challenged the medical establishment's tendency to view women as abnormal and inherently diseased simply because the female reproductive cycle deviates from the male. Women today across the world are asserting the right to control their own bodies by exposing and resisting the medical abuse of women in forms ranging from forced sterilization and sex selection against females to pharmaceutical experimentation.

Women are also increasing their control over their own health care by enhancing access to information and specialized training that allow them to more accurately assess their health care needs and make informed decisions about medical treatment. These movements focused on improving women's health care have recently worked alongside other movements, such as those organizing against AIDS or working for improved nutrition and preventive health care for the poor in the United States and Third World countries.

This section explores the social construction of women's bodies, the role of medicine in the maintenance of gender inequality, and issues related to women's health, including what illness tells us about women's position in society.

Suzanne Kessler's article in Section Two ("The Medical Construction of Gender") showed that the medical system actively constructs sex categories. In "Hormonal Hurricanes: Menstruation, Menopause, and Female Behavior," Anne Fausto-Sterling discusses additional ways that medicine shapes our understandings of gender. She examines traditional research on menstruation and menopause and finds that it reflects a deep bias against women by advancing the view that women are "slaves of their reproductive physiologies." Reviewing feminist studies of premenstrual syndrome and menopause, Fausto-Sterling suggests other approaches to women's health issues. Her work forces us to realize that social contexts deeply affect medical interpretations of the female reproductive cycle. Can you think of additional examples of how beliefs about gender are reflected in medical approaches to women's or men's reproductive health?

Social contexts also shape and create health problems. Becky Wangsgaard Thompson examines the social roots of women's eating problems in " 'A Way Outa No Way': Eating Problems among African-American, Latina, and White Women." Thompson argues that compulsive eating, compulsive dieting, anorexia, and bulimia are coping strategies that women employ in response to sexual abuse, poverty, heterosexism, racism, and "class injuries." Eating problems thus are not just about conforming to a norm of physical appearance but are also a "serious response to injustices." Thompson's article illustrates how examining women's multiple oppressions—race, class, and sexuality, as well as gender—can alter feminist analyses. What kinds of social change would be necessary to eliminate eating problems?

Angela Davis examines the ways that racism and class inequality have shaped the ideology and practice of motherhood and reproduction in the United States in "Outcast Mothers and Surrogates: Racism and Reproductive Politics." Davis shows how motherhood and reproduction have been constructed differently for women of color and poor women than for white middle-class women. She traces the historical view of enslaved African women as breeders and "surrogate mothers" to the children of white slave owners. Contemporary women of color and poor women are denigrated when they are single teen mothers. They lack access to abortion and remain subject to involuntary sterilization. Motherhood has been glorified, on the other hand, for white middle- or upper-class women, and current infertility technologies encourage women with the financial means to become biological mothers at any cost. In short, Davis illustrates how racism and class inequality affect the politics of reproduction. Can you find examples of the dynamics Davis describes in media coverage of infertility or of low-income mothers?

The final article in this section, "The Politics of Breast Cancer," by Susan M. Love, MD, documents women's attempts to increase funding for breast cancer research. Breast cancer remains largely a medical mystery, with little known about its causes, prevention, or effective treatment. Nevertheless, Love shows, it received little attention and few resources from the federal government until breast cancer survivors began intensive protest and lobbying efforts. These activists' success in raising money and affecting the direction of scientific research provides an illustration of women's resistance to their treatment by male-dominated medical institutions. Along these lines, how do the other readings in this section illustrate women's resistance?

Hormonal Hurricanes:
Menstruation, Menopause, and Female Behavior

ANNE FAUSTO-STERLING

Woman is a pair of ovaries with a human being attached, whereas man is a human being furnished with a pair of testes.

—*Rudolf Virchow, MD (1821–1902)*

Estrogen is responsible for that strange mystical phenomenon, the feminine state of mind.

—*David Reuben, MD, 1969*

In 1900, the president of the American Gynecological Association eloquently accounted for the female life cycle:

Many a young life is battered and forever crippled in the breakers of puberty; if it crosses these unharmed and is not dashed to pieces on the rock of childbirth, it may still ground on the ever-recurring shadows of menstruation and lastly upon the final bar of the menopause ere protection is found in the unruffled waters of the harbor beyond the reach of the sexual storms.[1]

Since then we have amassed an encyclopedia's worth of information about the existence of hormones, the function of menstruation, the regulation of ovulation, and the physiology of menopause. Yet many people, scientists and nonscientists alike, still believe that women function at the beck and call of their hormonal physiology. In 1970, for example, Dr. Edgar Berman, the personal physician of former Vice President Hubert Humphrey, responded to a female member of Congress:

Even a Congresswoman must defer to scientific truths . . . there just are physical and psychological inhibitants that limit a female's potential. . . . I would still rather have a male John F. Kennedy make the Cuban missile crisis decisions than a female of the same age who could possibly be subject to the curious mental aberrations of that age group.[2]

In a more grandiose mode, Professor Steven Goldberg, a university sociologist, writes that "men and women differ in their hormonal systems . . . every society demonstrates patriarchy, male dominance, and male attainment. The thesis put forth here is that the hormonal renders the social inevitable."[3]

At the broadest political level, writers such as Berman and Goldberg raise questions about the competency of *any and all* females to work successfully in positions of leadership, while for women working in other types of jobs, the question is, Should they receive less pay or more restricted job opportunities simply because they menstruate or experience menopause? And further, do women in the throes of premenstrual frenzy frequently try to commit suicide? Do they really suffer from a "diminished responsibility" that should exempt them from legal sanctions when they beat their children or murder their boyfriends?[4] Is the health of large numbers of women threatened by inappropriate and even ignorant medical attention—medical diagnoses that miss real health problems, while resulting instead in the prescription of dangerous medication destined to create future disease?

The idea that women's reproductive systems direct their lives is ancient. But whether it was Plato, writing about the disruption caused by barren uteri wandering about the body,[5] Pliny, writing that a look from a menstruating woman will "dim the brightness of mirrors, blunt the edge of steel, and take away the polish from ivory,"[6] or modern scientists writing about the changing levels of estrogen and progesterone, certain messages emerge quite clearly. Women, by nature emotionally erratic, cannot be trusted in positions of responsibility. Their dangerous, unpredictable furies warrant control by the medical profession,[a] while ironically, the same "dangerous" females also need protection because their reproductive systems, so necessary for the procreation of the race, are vulnerable to stress and hard work.

"The breakers of puberty," in fact, played a key role in a debate about higher education for women, a controversy that began in the last quarter of the nineteenth century and still echoes today in the halls of academe. Scientists of the late 1800s argued on physiological grounds that women and men should receive different types of education. Women, they believed, could not survive intact the rigors of higher education. Their reasons were threefold: first, the education of young women might cause serious damage to their reproductive systems. Energy devoted to scholastic work would deprive the reproductive organs of the necessary "flow of power," presenting particular problems for pubescent women, for whom the establishment of regular menstruation was of paramount importance. Physicians cited cases of women unable to bear children because they pursued a course of education designed for the more resilient young man.[7] In an interesting parallel to modern nature—nurture debates, proponents of higher education for women countered biological arguments with environmental ones. One anonymous author argued that, denied the privilege afforded their brothers of romping actively through the woods, women became fragile and nervous.[8]

Opponents of higher education for women also claimed that females were less intelligent than males, an assertion based partly on brain size itself but also on the overall size differences between men and women. They held that women cannot "consume so much food as men . . . [because] their average size remains so much smaller; so that the sum total of food converted into thought by women can never equal the sum total of food converted to thought by men. It follows, therefore, that *men will always think more than women.*"[9] One respondent to this bit of scientific reasoning asked the thinking reader to examine the data: Aristotle and Napoleon were short, Newton, Spinoza,

Shakespeare, and Comte delicate and of medium height, Descartes and Bacon sickly, "while unfortunately for a theory based upon superior digestion, Goethe and Carlyle were confirmed dyspeptics."[10] Finally, as if pubertal vulnerability and lower intelligence were not enough, it seemed to nineteenth-century scientists that menstruation rendered women "more or less sick and unfit for hard work" "for one quarter of each month during the best years of life."[11]

Although dated in some of the particulars, the turn-of-the-century scientific belief that women's reproductive functions make them unsuitable for higher education remains with us today. Some industries bar fertile women from certain positions because of workplace hazards that might cause birth defects, while simultaneously deeming equally vulnerable men fit for the job.[b] Some modern psychologists and biologists suggest that women perform more poorly than do men on mathematics tests because hormonal sex differences alter male and female brain structures; many people believe women to be unfit for certain professions because they menstruate. Others argue that premenstrual changes cause schoolgirls to do poorly in their studies, to become slovenly and disobedient, and even to develop a "nymphomaniac urge [that] may be responsible for young girls running away from home . . . only to be found wandering in the park or following boys."[12]

If menstruation really casts such a dark shadow on women's lives, we ought certainly to know more about it—how it works, whether it can be controlled, and whether it indeed warrants the high level of concern expressed by some. Do women undergo emotional changes as they progress through the monthly ovulatory cycle? And if so, do hormonal fluctuations bring on these ups and downs? If not—if a model of biological causation is appropriate—how else might we conceptualize what happens?

THE SHADOWS OF MENSTRUATION: A READER'S LITERATURE GUIDE

The Premenstrual Syndrome

> SCIENCE UPDATE: PREMENSTRUAL STRAIN LINKED TO CRIME
>
> —*Providence Journal*

> ERRATIC FEMALE BEHAVIOR TIED TO PREMENSTRUAL SYNDROME
>
> —*Providence Journal*

VIOLENCE BY WOMEN IS LINKED TO MENSTRUATION

—*National Enquirer*

Menstruation makes news, and the headlines summarize the message. According to Dr. Katharina Dalton, premenstrual syndrome (PMS) is a medical problem of enormous dimensions. Under the influence of the tidal hormonal flow, women batter their children and husbands, miss work, commit crimes, attempt suicide, and suffer from up to 150 different symptoms, including headaches, epilepsy, dizziness, asthma, hoarseness, nausea, constipation, bloating, increased appetite, low blood sugar, joint and muscle pains, heart palpitations, skin disorders, breast tenderness, glaucoma, and conjunctivitis.[13] Although the great concern expressed in the newspaper headlines just quoted may come from a single public relations source,[14] members of the medical profession seem eager to accept at face value the idea that "70 to 90 percent of the female population will admit to recurrent premenstrual symptoms and that 20 to 40 percent report some degree of mental or physical incapacitation."[15]

If all this is true, then we have on our hands nothing less than an overwhelming public health problem, one that deserves a considerable investment of national resources in order to develop understanding and treatment. If, on the other hand, the claims about premenstrual tension are cut from whole cloth, then the consequences are equally serious. Are there women in need of proper medical treatment who do not receive it? Do some receive dangerous medication to treat nonexistent physiological problems? How often are women refused work, given lower salaries, taken less seriously because of beliefs about hormonally induced erratic behavior? In the game of PMS the stakes are high.

The key issues surrounding PMS are so complex and interrelated that it is hard to know where to begin. There is, as always, the question of evidence. To begin with we can look, in vain, for credible research that defines and analyzes PMS. Despite the publication of thousands of pages of allegedly scientific analyses, the most recent literature reviews simultaneously lament the lack of properly done studies and call for a consistent and acceptable research definition and methodology.[16] Intimately related to the question of evidence is that of conceptualization. Currently held theoretical views about the reproductive cycle are inadequate to the task of understanding the emotional ups and downs of people functioning in a complex world. Finally, lurking beneath all of the difficulties of research design, poor methods, and muddy thinking is the medical

world's view of the naturally abnormal woman. Let's look at this last point first.

If you're a woman you can't win. Historically, females who complained to physicians about menstrual difficulties, pain during the menstrual flow, or physical or emotional changes associated with the premenstruum heard that they were neurotic. They imagined the pain and made up the tension because they recognized menstruation as a failure to become pregnant, to fulfill their true role as a woman.[17] With the advent of the women's health movement, however, women began to speak for themselves.[18] The pain is real, they said; our bodies change each month. The medical profession responded by finding biological/hormonal causes, proposing the need for doctor-supervised cures. A third voice, however, entered in: that of feminists worried about repercussions from the idea that women's natural functions represent a medical problem capable of preventing women from competing in the world outside the home. Although this multisided discussion continues, I currently operate on the premise that some women probably do require medical attention for incapacitating physical changes that occur in synchrony with their menstrual cycle. Yet in the absence of any reliable medical research into the problem it is impossible to diagnose true disease or to develop rational treatment. To start with, we must decide what is normal.

The tip-off to the medical viewpoint lies in its choice of language. What does it mean to say "70 to 90 percent of the female population will admit to recurrent premenstrual symptoms"?[19] The word *symptom* carries two rather different meanings. The first suggests a disease or an abnormality, a condition to be cured or rendered normal. Applying this connotation to a statistic suggesting 70 to 90 percent symptom formation leads one to conclude that the large majority of women are by their very nature diseased. The second meaning of *symptom* is that of a sign or signal. If the figure of 70 to 90 percent means nothing more than that most women recognize signs in their own bodies of an oncoming menstrual flow, the statistics are unremarkable. Consider then the following, written in 1974 by three scientists:

> It is estimated that from 25 percent to 100 percent of women experience some form of premenstrual or menstrual emotional disturbance. Eichner makes the discerning point that the few women who do not admit to premenstrual tension are basically unaware of it but one only has to talk to their husbands or co-workers to confirm its existence.[20]

Is it possible that up to 100 percent of all menstruating women regularly experience emotional disturbance? Compared to whom? Are males the unstated standard of emotional stability? If there is but a single definition of what is normal and men fit that definition, then women with "female complaints" must by definition be either crazy or in need of medical attention. A double bind indeed.

Some scientists explicitly articulate the idea of the naturally abnormal female. Professor Frank Beach, a pioneer in the field of animal psychology and its relationship to sexuality, suggests the following evolutionary account of menstruation. In primitive hunter–gatherer societies adult women were either pregnant or lactating, and since life spans were so short they died well before menopause; low-fat diets made it likely that they did not ovulate every month; they thus experienced no more than ten menstrual cycles. Given current life expectancies as well as the widespread use of birth control, modern women may experience a total of 400 menstrual cycles. He concludes from this reasoning that "civilization has given women *a physiologically abnormal status* which may have important implications for the interpretation of psychological responses to periodic fluctuations in the secretion of ovarian hormones"—that is, to menstruation (emphasis added).[21] Thus the first problem we face in evaluating the literature on the premenstrual syndrome is figuring out how to deal with the underlying assumption that women have "a physiologically abnormal status."

Researchers who believe in PMS hold a wide variety of viewpoints (none of them supported by scientific data) about the basis of the problem. For example, Dr. Katharina Dalton, the most militant promoter of PMS, says that it results from a relative end-of-the-cycle deficiency in the hormone progesterone. Others cite deficiencies in vitamin B$_6$, fluid retention, and low blood sugar as possible causes. Suggested treatments range from hormone injection to the use of lithium, diuretics, megadoses of vitamins, and control of sugar in the diet[22] (see Table 1 for a complete list). Although some of these treatments are harmless, others are not. Progesterone injection causes cancer in animals. What will it do to humans? And a recent issue of the *New England Journal of Medicine* contains a report that large doses of vitamin B$_6$ damage the nerves, causing a loss of feeling in one's fingers and toes.[23] The wide variety of PMS "causes" and "cures" offered by the experts is confusing, to put it mildly. Just what *is* this syndrome that causes such controversy? How can a woman know if she has it?

With a case of the measles it's really quite simple. A fever and then spots serve as diagnostic signs. A woman said

TABLE I ALLEGED CAUSES AND PROPOSED TREATMENTS OF PMS

Hypothesized Causes of Premenstrual Syndrome	Various PMS Treatments (used but not validated)
Estrogen excess	Oral contraceptives
Progesterone deficiency	(combination estrogen
Vitamin B deficiency	and progesterone pills)
Vitamin A deficiency	Estrogen alone
Hypoglycemia	Natural progesterone
Endogenous hormone allergy	Synthetic progestins
Psychosomatic	Valium or other tranquilizers
Fluid retention	Nutritional supplements
Dysfunction of the neurointermediate lobe of the pituitary	Minerals
Prolactin metabolism	Lithium
	Diuretics
	A prolactin inhibitor/ dopamine agonist
	Exercise
	Psychotherapy, relaxation, education, reassurance

SOURCES: Robert L. Reid and S. S. Yen, "Premenstrual Syndrome," *American Journal of Obstetrics and Gynecology* 139 (1981): 85–104; and Judith Abplanalp, "Premenstrual Syndrome: A Selective Review," *Women and Health* 8 (1983): 107–24.

to have PMS, however, may or may not have any of a very large number of symptoms. Furthermore, PMS indicators such as headaches, depression, dizziness, and loss or gain of appetite show up in everyone from time to time. Their mere presence cannot (as would measle spots) help one to diagnose the syndrome. In addition, whether any of these signals connote disease depends upon their severity. A slight headache may reflect nothing more than a lack of sleep, but repeated, severe headaches could indicate high blood pressure. As one researcher, Dr. Judith Abplanalp, succinctly put it: "There is no one set of symptoms which is considered to be the hallmark of or standard criterion for defining the premenstrual syndrome."[24] Dr. Katharina Dalton agrees but feels one can diagnose PMS quite simply by applying the term to "any symptoms or complaints which regularly come just before or during early menstruation but are absent at other times of the cycle."[25] Dalton contrasts this with men suffering from potential PMS "symptoms," because, she says, they experience them randomly during the month while women with the same physical indications acknowledge them only during the premenstruum.

PMS research usually bases itself on an ideal, regular, twenty-eight-day menstrual cycle. Researchers eliminate as subjects for study women with infrequent, shorter, or longer cycles. As a result, published investigations look at a skewed segment of the overall population. Even for those women with a regular cycle, however, a methodological problem remains because few researchers define the premenstrual period in the same way. Some studies look only at the day or two preceding the menstrual flow, others look at the week preceding, while workers such as Dalton cite cases that begin two weeks before menstruation and continue for one week after. Since so few investigations use exactly the same definition, research publications on PMS are difficult to compare with one another.[26] On this score if no other, the literature offers little useful insight, extensive as it is.

Although rarely stated, the assumption is that there is but *one* PMS. Dalton defines the problem so broadly that she and others may well lump together several phenomena of very different origins, a possibility heightened by the fact that investigators rarely assess the severity of the symptoms. Two women, one suffering from a few low days and the other from suicidal depression, may both be diagnosed as having PMS. Yet their difficulties could easily have different origins and ought certainly to receive different treatments. When investigators try carefully to define PMS, the number of people qualifying for study decreases dramatically. In one case a group used ten criteria (listed in Table 2) to define PMS only to find that no more than 20 percent of those who had volunteered for their research project met them.[27] In the absence of any clearly agreed-upon definition(s) of PMS, examinations of the topic should at least state clearly the methodology used; this would enable comparison between publications and allow us to begin to accumulate some knowledge about the issues at hand (Table 2 lists suggested baseline information). At the moment the literature is filled with individual studies that permit neither replication nor comparison with one another— an appropriate state, perhaps, for an art gallery but not for a field with pretensions to the scientific.

Despite the problems of method and definition, the conviction remains that PMS constitutes a widespread disorder, a conviction that fortifies and is fortified by the idea that women's reproductive function, so different from that of "normal" men, places them in a naturally diseased state. For those who believe that 90 percent of all women suffer from a disease called PMS, it becomes a reasonable research strategy to look at the normally functioning menstrual cycle for clues about the cause and possible treat-

TABLE 2   TOWARD A DEFINITION PREMENSTRUAL SYNDROME

Experimental criteria (rarely met in PMS studies):
Premenstrual symptoms for at least six preceding cycles
Moderate to severe physical and psychological symptoms
Symptoms *only* during the premenstrual period, with marked relief at onset of menses
Age between 18 and 45 years
Not pregnant
Regular menses for six previous cycles
No psychiatric disorder; normal physical examination and laboratory test profile
No drugs for preceding four weeks
Will not receive anxiolytics, diuretics, hormones, or neuroleptic drugs during the study

Miminal descriptive information to be offered in published studies of PMS (rarely offered in the current literature):
Specification of the ways in which subjects were recruited
Age limitations
Contraception and medication information
Marital status
Parity
Race
Menstrual history data
Assessment instruments
Operational definition of PMS
Pschiatric history data
Assessment of current psychological state
Criteria for assessment of severity of symptoms
Criteria for defining ovulatory status of cycle
Cutoff criteria for "unacceptable" subjects

SOURCE: Judith Abplanalp, "Premenstrual Syndrome: A Selective Review," *Women and Health* 8 (1983): 107–24.

ment. There are, in fact, many theories but no credible evidence about the origins of PMS. In Table 1 I've listed the most frequently cited hypotheses, most of which involve in some manner the hormonal system that regulates menstruation. Some of the theories are ingenious and require a sophisticated knowledge of human physiology to comprehend. Nevertheless, the authors of one recent review quietly offer the following summary: "To date no one hypothesis has adequately explained the constellation of symptoms composing PMS."[28] In short, PMS is a disease in search of a definition and cause.

PMS also remains on the lookout for a treatment. That many have been tried is attested to in Table 1. The problem is that only rarely has the efficacy of these treatments been tested with the commonly accepted standard of a large-scale, double-blind study that includes placebos. In the few properly done studies "there is usually (1) a high placebo response and (2) the active agent is usually no better than a placebo."[29] In other words, women under treatment for PMS respond just as well to sugar pills as to medication containing hormones or other drugs. Since it is probable that some women experience severe distress caused by malfunctions of their menstrual system, the genuinely concerned physician faces a dilemma. Should he or she offer treatment until the patient says she feels better even though the drug used may have dangerous side effects; or should a doctor refuse help for as long as we know of no scientifically validated treatment for the patient's symptoms? I have no satisfactory answer. But the crying need for some scientifically acceptable research on the subject stands out above all. If we continue to assume that menstruation is itself pathological, we cannot establish a baseline of health against which to define disease. If, instead, we accept in theory that a range of menstrual normality exists, we can then set about designing studies that define the healthy female reproductive cycle. Only when we have some feeling for *that* can we begin to help women who suffer from diseases of menstruation.

Many of those who reject the alarmist nature of the publicity surrounding PMS believe nevertheless that women undergo mood changes during their menstrual cycle. Indeed, most western women would agree. But do studies of large segments of our population support this generality? And if so, what causes these ups and downs? In trying to answer these questions we confront another piece of the medical model of human behavior, the belief that biology is primary, that hormonal changes cause behavioral ones, but not vice versa. Most researchers use such a linear, unicausal model without thinking about it. Their framework is so much a part of their belief system that they forget to question it. Nevertheless it is the model from which they work, and failure to recognize and work skeptically with it often results in poorly conceived research combined with implausible interpretations of data. Although the paradigm of biological causation has until very recently dominated menstrual-cycle research, it now faces serious and intellectually stimulating challenge from feminist experts in the field. . . .

MENOPAUSE: THE STORM BEFORE THE CALM

An unlikely specter haunts the world. It is the ghost of former womanhood . . . "unfortunate women abounding in the streets walking stiffly in twos and threes, seeing little and observing less. . . . The world appears [to them] as through a grey veil, and they live as docile, harmless creatures missing most of life's values." According to Dr. Robert Wilson and Thelma Wilson, though, one should not be fooled by their "vapid cow-like negative state" because "there is ample evidence that the course of history has been changed not only by the presence of estrogen, but by its absence. The untold misery of alcoholism, drug addiction, divorce, and broken homes caused by these unstable estrogen-starved women cannot be presented in statistical form."[30]

Rather than releasing women from their monthly emotional slavery to the sex hormones, menopause involves them in new horrors. At the individual level one encounters the specter of sexual degeneration, described so vividly by Dr. David Reuben: "The vagina begins to shrivel, the breasts atrophy, sexual desire disappears. . . . Increased facial hair, deepening voice, obesity . . . coarsened features, enlargement of the clitoris, and gradual baldness complete the tragic picture. Not really a man but no longer a functional woman, these individuals live in the world of intersex."[31] At the demographic level, writers express foreboding about women of the baby-boom generation, whose life span has increased from an average forty-eight years at the turn of the century to a projected eighty years in the year 2000.[32] Modern medicine, it seems, has played a cruel trick on women. One hundred years ago they didn't live long enough to face the hardships of menopause but today their increased longevity means they will live for twenty-five to thirty years beyond the time when they lose all possibility of reproducing. To quote Dr. Wilson again: "The unpalatable truth must be faced that all postmenopausal women are castrates."[33]

But what medicine has wrought, it can also rend asunder. Few publications have had so great an effect on the lives of so many women as have those of Dr. Robert A. Wilson, who pronounced menopause to be a disease of estrogen deficiency. At the same time in an influential popular form, in his book *Feminine Forever,* he offered a treatment: estrogen replacement therapy (ERT).[34] During the first seven months following publication in 1966, Wilson's book sold one hundred thousand copies and was excerpted in *Vogue* and *Look* magazines. It influenced thousands of physicians to prescribe estrogen to millions of women, many of whom had no clinical "symptoms" other than cessation of the menses. As one of his credentials Wilson lists himself as head of the Wilson Research Foundation, an outfit funded by Ayerst Labs, Searle, and Upjohn, all pharmaceutical giants interested in the large potential market for estrogen. (After all, no woman who lives long enough can avoid menopause.) As late as 1976 Ayerst also supported the Information Center on the Mature Woman, a public relations firm that promoted estrogen replacement therapy. By 1975 some six million women had started long-term treatment with Premarin (Ayerst Labs' brand name for estrogen), making it the fourth or fifth most popular drug in the United States. Even today, two million of the forty million postmenopausal women in the United States contribute to the $70 million grossed each year from the sale of Premarin-brand estrogen.[35] The "disease of menopause" is not only a social problem: it's big business.[36]

The high sales of Premarin continue despite the publication in 1975 of an article linking estrogen treatment to uterine cancer.[37] Although in the wake of that publication many women stopped taking estrogen and many physicians became more cautious about prescribing it, the idea of hormone replacement therapy remains with us. At least three recent publications in medical journals seriously consider whether the benefits of estrogen might not outweigh the dangers.[38] The continuing flap over treatment for this so-called deficiency disease of the aging female forces one to ask just what *is* this terrible state called menopause? Are its effects so unbearable that one might prefer to increase, even ever so slightly, the risk of cancer rather than suffer the daily discomforts encountered during "the change of life"?

Ours is a culture that fears the elderly. Rather than venerate their years and listen to their wisdom, we segregate them in housing built for "their special needs," separated from the younger generations from which we draw hope for the future. At the same time we allow millions of old people to live on inadequate incomes, in fear that serious illness will leave them destitute. The happy, productive elderly remain invisible in our midst. (One must look to feminist publications such as *Our Bodies, Ourselves* to find women who express pleasure in their postmenopausal state.) Television ads portray only the arthritic, the toothless, the wrinkled, and the constipated. If estrogen really is the hormone of youth and its decline suggests the coming of old age, then its loss is a part of biology that our culture ill equips us to handle.

There is, of course, a history to our cultural attitudes toward the elderly woman and our views about menopause. In the nineteenth century physicians believed that at menopause a woman entered a period of depression and increased susceptibility to disease. The postmenopausal body might be racked with "dyspepsia, diarrhea . . . rheumatic pains, paralysis, apoplexy . . . hemorrhaging . . .

tuberculosis . . . and diabetes," while emotionally the aging female risked becoming irritable, depressed, hysterical, melancholic, or even insane. The more a woman violated social laws (such as using birth control or promoting female suffrage), the more likely she would be to suffer a disease-ridden menopause.[39] In the twentieth century, psychologist Helene Deutsch wrote that at menopause "woman has ended her existence as a bearer of future life and has reached her natural end—her partial death—as a servant of the species."[40] Deutsch believed that during the postmenopausal years a woman's main psychological task was to accept the progressive biological withering she experienced. Other well-known psychologists have also accepted the idea that a woman's life purpose is mainly reproductive and that her postreproductive years are ones of inevitable decline. Even in recent times postmenopausal women have been "treated" with tranquilizers, hormones, electroshock, and lithium.[41]

But should women accept what many see as an inevitable emotional and biological decline? Should they believe, as Wilson does, that "from a practical point of view a man remains a man until the end," but that after menopause "we no longer have the 'whole woman'—only the 'part woman' "?[42] What is the real story of menopause?

The Change: Its Definition and Physiology

In 1976, under the auspices of the American Geriatric Society and the medical faculty of the University of Montpellier, the First International Congress on the Menopause convened in the south of France. In the volume that emerged from that conference, scientists and clinicians from around the world agreed on a standard definition of the words *menopause* and *climacteric*. "Menopause," they wrote, "indicates the final menstrual period and occurs during the climacteric. The climacteric is that phase in the aging process of women marking the transition from the reproductive stage of life to the nonreproductive stage."[43] By consensus, then, the word *menopause* has come to mean a specific event, the last menstruation, while *climacteric* implies a process occurring over a period of years.[c]

During the menstrual cycle, the blood levels of a number of hormones rise and fall on a regular basis. At the end of one monthly cycle, the low levels of estrogen and progesterone trigger the pituitary gland to make follicle-stimulating hormone (FSH) and luteinizing hormone (LH). The FSH influences the cells of the ovary to make large amounts of estrogen, and induces the growth and maturation of an oocyte. The LH, at just the right moment, induces ovulation and stimulates certain ovarian cells to form a progesterone-secreting structure called a corpus luteum. When no pregnancy occurs the life of the corpus luteum is limited and, as it degenerates, the lowered level of steroid hormones calls forth a new round of follicle-stimulating and luteinizing hormone synthesis, beginning the cycle once again. Although the ovary produces the lion's share of these steroid hormones, the cells of the adrenal gland also contribute, and this contribution increases in significance after menopause.

What happens to the intricately balanced hormone cycle during the several years preceding menopause is little understood, although it seems likely that gradual changes occur in the balance between pituitary activity (FSH and LH production) and estrogen synthesis.[44] One thing, however, is clear: menopause does not mean the *absence* of estrogen, but rather a gradual lowering in the availability of *ovarian* estrogen. Table 3 summarizes some salient information about changes in steroid hormone levels during the menstrual cycle and after menopause. In looking at the high point of cycle synthesis and then comparing it to women who no longer menstruate, the most dramatic change is seen in the estrogenic hormone estradiol.[d] The other estrogenic hormones, as well as progesterone and testosterone, drop off to some extent but continue to be synthesized at a level comparable to that observed during the early phases of the menstrual cycle. Instead of concentrating on the notion of estrogen deficiency, however, it is more important to point out that (1) postmenopausally the body makes different kinds of estrogen; (2) the ovaries synthesize less and the adrenals more of these hormones; and (3) the monthly ups and downs of these hormones even out following menopause.

While estrogen levels begin to decline, the levels of FSH and LH start to increase. Changes in these hormones

appear as early as eight years before menopause.[45] At the time of menopause and for several years afterward, these two hormones are found in very high concentrations compared to menstrual levels (FSH as many as fourteen times more concentrated than premenopausally, and LH more than three times more). Over a period of years such high levels are reduced to about half their peak value, leaving the postmenopausal woman with one-and-one-half times more LH and seven times more FSH circulating in her blood than when she menstruated regularly.

It is to all of these changes in hormone levels that the words *climacteric* and *menopause* refer. From these alterations Wilson and others have chosen to blame estrogen for the emotional deterioration they believe appears in postmenopausal women. Why they have focused on only one hormone from a complex system of hormonal changes is anybody's guess. I suspect, however, that the reasons are (at least) twofold. First, the normative biomedical disease model of female physiology looks for simple cause and effect. Most researchers, then, have simply assumed estrogen to be a "cause" and set out to measure its "effect." The model or framework out of which such investigators work precludes an interrelated analysis of all the different (and closely connected) hormonal changes going on during the climacteric. But why single out estrogen? Possibly because this hormone plays an important role in the menstrual cycle as well as in the development of "feminine" characteristics such as breasts and overall body contours. It is seen as the quintessential female hormone. So where could one better direct one's attention if, to begin with, one views menopause as the loss of true womanhood?

Physical changes do occur following menopause. Which, if any, of these are caused by changing hormone levels is another question. Menopause research comes equipped with its own unique experimental traps.[46] The

TABLE 3 HORMONE LEVELS AS A PERCENTAGE OF MID-MENSTRUAL-CYCLE HIGH POINT

Stage of Menstrual Cycle	TYPE OF ESTROGEN			Progesterone	Testosterone	Androstenedione
	Estrone	Estradiol	Estriol			
Premenopausal stage						
Early (menses)	20%	13%	67%	100%	55%	87%
Mid (ovulation)	100	100	—	—	100	100
Late (premenstrual)	49	50	100	—	82	—
Postmenopausal stage	17	3	50	50	23	39

SOURCE: Wulf H. Utian, *Menopause in Modern Perspectives* (New York: Appleton-Century-Crofts, 1980), 32.

most obvious is that a postmenopausal population is also an aging population. Do physical and emotional differences found in groups of postmenopausal women have to do with hormonal changes or with other aspects of aging? It is a difficult matter to sort out. Furthermore, many of the studies on menopause have been done on preselected populations, using women who volunteer because they experience classic menopausal "symptoms" such as the hot flash. Such investigations tell us nothing about average changes within the population as a whole. In the language of the social scientist, we have no baseline data, nothing to which we can compare menopausal women, no way to tell whether the complaint of a particular woman is typical, a cause for medical concern, or simply idiosyncratic.

Since the late 1970s feminist researchers have begun to provide us with much-needed information. Although their results confirm some beliefs long held by physicians, these newer investigators present them in a more sophisticated context. Dr. Madeleine Goodman and her colleagues designed a study in which they drew information from a large population of women ranging in age from thirty-five to sixty. All had undergone routine multiphasic screening at a health maintenance clinic, but none had come for problems concerning menopause. From the complete clinic records they selected a population of women who had not menstruated for at least one year and compared their health records with those of women who still menstruated, looking at thirty-five different variables, such as cramps, blood glucose levels, blood calcium, and hot flashes, to see if any of these symptoms correlated with those seen in postmenopausal women. The results are startling. They found that only 28 percent of Caucasian women and 24 percent of Japanese women identified as postmenopausal "reported traditional menopausal symptoms such as hot flashes, sweats, etc., while in nonmenopausal controls, 16 percent in Caucasians and 10 percent in Japanese also reported these same symptoms."[47] In other words, 75 percent of menopausal women in their sample reported no remarkable menopausal symptoms, a result in sharp contrast to earlier studies using women who identified themselves as menopausal.

In a similar exploration, researcher Karen Frey found evidence to support Goodman's results. She wrote that menopausal women "did not report significantly greater frequency of physical symptoms or concern about these symptoms than did pre-or post-menopausal women."[48] The studies of Goodman, Frey, and others[49] draw into serious question the notion that menopause is generally or necessarily associated with a set of disease symptoms. Yet at least three physical changes—hot flashes, vaginal dryness

and irritation, and osteoporosis—and one emotional one—depression—remain associated in the minds of many with the decreased estrogen levels of the climacteric. Goodman's work indicates that such changes may be far less widespread than previously believed, but if they are troublesome to 26 percent of all menopausal women they remain an appropriate subject for analysis.

We know only the immediate cause of hot flashes: a sudden expansion of the blood flow to the skin. The technical term to describe them, *vasomotor instability,* means only that nerve cells signal the widening of blood vessels, allowing more blood into the body's periphery. A consensus has emerged on two things: (1) the high concentration of FSH and LH in blood probably causes hot flashes, although exactly how this happens remains unknown; and (2) estrogen treatment is the only currently available way to suppress the hot flashes. One hypothesis is that by means of a feedback mechanism, artificially raised blood levels of estrogen signal the brain to tell the pituitary to call off the FSH and LH. Although estrogen does stop the hot flashes, its effects are only temporary; remove the estrogen and the flashes return. Left alone, the body eventually adjusts to the changing levels of FSH and LH. Thus a premenopausal woman has two choices in dealing with hot flashes: she can either take estrogen as a permanent medication, a course Wilson refers to as embarking "on the great adventure of preserving or regaining your full femininity,"[50] or suffer some discomfort while nature takes its course. Since the longer one takes estrogen, the greater the danger of estrogen-linked cancer, many health care workers recommend the latter.[51]

Some women experience postmenopausal vaginal dryness and irritation that can make sexual intercourse painful. Since the cells of the vaginal wall contain estrogen receptors, it is not surprising that estrogen applied locally or taken in pill form helps with this difficulty. Even locally applied, however, the estrogen enters into the bloodstream, presenting the same dangers as when taken in pill form. There are alternative treatments, though, for vaginal dryness. The Boston Women's Health Collective, for example, recommends the use of nonestrogen vaginal creams or jellies, which seem to be effective and are certainly safer. Continued sexual activity also helps—yet another example of the interaction between behavior and physiology.

Hot flashes and vaginal dryness are the *only* climacteric-associated changes for which estrogen unambiguously offers relief. Since significant numbers of women do not experience these changes and since for many of those that do the effects are relatively mild, the wisdom of ERT must be examined carefully and on an individual basis. Both men and women undergo certain changes as they age, but Wilson's catastrophic vision of postmenopausal women—those ghosts gliding by "unnoticed and, in turn, notic[ing] little"[52]—is such a far cry from reality that it is a source of amazement that serious medical writers continue to quote his work.

In contrast to hot flashes and vaginal dryness, osteoporosis, a brittleness of the bone which can in severe cases cripple, has a complex origin. Since this potentially life-threatening condition appears more frequently in older women than in older men, the hypothesis of a relationship with estrogen levels seemed plausible to many. But as one medical worker has said, a unified theory of the disease "is still nonexistent, although sedentary lifestyles, genetic predisposition, hormonal imbalance, vitamin deficiencies, high-protein diets, and cigarette smoking all have been implicated."[53] Estrogen treatment seems to arrest the disease for a while, but may lose effectiveness after a few years.[54]

Even more than in connection with any physical changes, women have hit up against a medical double bind whenever they have complained of emotional problems during the years of climacteric. On the one hand physicians dismissed these complaints as the imagined ills of a hormone-deficient brain, while on the other they generalized the problem, arguing that middle-aged women are emotionally unreliable, unfit for positions of leadership and responsibility. Women had two choices: to complain and experience ridicule and/or improper medical treatment, or to suffer in silence. Hormonal changes during menopause were presumed to be the cause of psychiatric symptoms ranging from fatigue, dizziness, irritability, apprehension, and insomnia to severe headaches and psychotic depression. In recent years, however, these earlier accounts have been supplanted by a rather different consensus now emerging among responsible medical researchers.

To begin with, there are no data to support the idea that menopause has any relationship to serious depression in women. Postmenopausal women who experience psychosis have almost always had similar episodes premenopausally.[55] The notion of the hormonally depressed woman is a shibboleth that must be laid permanently to rest. Some studies have related irritability and insomnia to loss of sleep from nighttime hot flashes. Thus, for women who experience hot flashes, these emotional difficulties might, indirectly, relate to menopause. But the social, life history, and family contexts in which middle-aged women find themselves are more important links to emotional changes occurring during the years of the climacteric. And these, of course, have nothing whatsoever to do with hormones. Quite a number of studies suggest that the majority of women do not consider menopause a time of crisis. Nor do most women suffer from the so-called "empty nest syndrome" supposedly experienced when children leave home. On the contrary, investigation suggests that women without small children are less depressed and have higher incomes and an increased sense of well-being.[56] Such positive reactions depend upon work histories, individual upbringing, cultural background, and general state of health, among other things.

In a survey conducted for *Our Bodies, Ourselves,* one which in no sense represents a balanced cross section of U.S. women, the Boston Women's Health Collective recorded the reactions of more than two hundred menopausal or postmenopausal women, most of whom were suburban, married, and employed, to a series of questions about menopause. About two-thirds of them felt either positively or neutrally about a variety of changes they had undergone, while a whopping 90 percent felt okay or happy about the loss of childbearing ability![57] This result probably comes as no surprise to most women, but it flies in the face of the long-standing belief that women's lives and emotions are driven in greater part by their reproductive systems.

No good account of adult female development in the middle years exists. Levinson,[58] who studied adult men, presents a linear model of male development designed primarily around work experiences. In his analysis, the male climacteric plays only a secondary role. Feminist scholars Rosalind Barnett and Grace Baruch have described the difficulty of fitting women into Levinson's scheme: "It is hard to know how to think of women within this theory—a woman may not enter the world of work until her late thirties, she seldom has a mentor, and even women with life-long career commitments rarely are in a position to reassess their commitment pattern by age forty," as do the men in Levinson's study.[59]

Baruch and Barnett call for the development of a theory of women in their middle years, pointing out that an adequate one can emerge only when researchers set aside preconceived ideas about the central role of biology in adult female development and listen to what women themselves say. Paradoxically, in some sense we will remain unable to understand more about the role of biology in women's middle years until we have a more realistic *social* analysis of women's postadolescent psychological development. Such an analysis must, of course, take into account ethnic, racial, regional, and class differences among women, since once biology is jettisoned as a universal cause of female behavior, it no longer makes sense to lump all women into a single category.

Much remains to be understood about menopause. Which biological changes, for instance, result from ovarian degeneration and which from other aspects of aging? How does the aging process compare in men and women? What causes hot flashes and can we find safe ways to alleviate the discomfort they cause? Do other aspects of a woman's life affect the number and severity of menopausally related physical symptoms? What can we learn from studying the experience of menopause in other, especially nonwestern, cultures? A number of researchers have proposed effective ways of finding answers to these questions.[60] We need only time, research dollars, and an open mind to move forward.

CONCLUSION

The premise that women are by nature abnormal and inherently diseased dominates past research on menstruation and menopause. While appointing the male reproductive system as normal, this viewpoint calls abnormal any aspect of the female reproductive life cycle that deviates from the male's. At the same time, such an analytical framework places the essence of a woman's existence in her reproductive system. Caught in her hormonal windstorm, she strives to attain normality but can do so only by rejecting her biological uniqueness, for that too is essentially deformed: a double bind indeed. Within such an intellectual structure no medical research of any worth to women's health can be done, for it is the blueprint itself that leads investigators to ask the wrong questions, look in the wrong places for answers, and then distort the interpretation of their results.

Reading through the morass of poorly done studies on menstruation and menopause, many of which express deep hatred and fear of women, can be a discouraging experience. One begins to wonder how it can be that within so vast a quantity of material so little quality exists. But at this very moment the field of menstrual-cycle research (including menopause) offers a powerful antidote to that disheartenment in the form of feminist researchers (both male and female) with excellent training and skills, working within a new analytical framework. Rejecting a strict medical model of female development, they understand that men and women have different reproductive cycles, *both* of which are normal. Not binary opposites, male and female physiologies have differences *and* similarities. These research pioneers know too that the human body functions in a social milieu and that it changes in response to that context. Biology is not a one-way determinant but a dynamic component of our existence. And, equally important, these new investigators have learned not only to *listen* to what women say about themselves but to *hear* as well. By and large, these researchers are not in the mainstream of medical and psychological research, but we can look forward to a time when the impact of their work will affect the field of menstrual-cycle research for the better and for many years to come.

NOTES

a. In the nineteenth century, control took the form of sexual surgery such as ovarietomies and hysterectomies, while twentieth-century medicine prefers the use of hormone pills. The science of the 1980s has a more sophisticated approach to human physiology, but its political motives of control and management have changed little. For an account of medicine's attitudes toward women, see Barbara Ehrenreich and Deidre English, *For Her Own Good: 150 Years of Experts' Advice to Women* (New York: Doubleday, 1979); and G. J. Barker-Benfield, *The Horrors of the Half-Known Life* (New York: Harper & Row, 1977).

b. The prohibited work usually carries a higher wage.

c. There is also a male climacteric, which entails a gradual reduction in production of the hormone testosterone over the years as part of the male aging process. What part it plays in that process is poorly understood and seems frequently to be ignored by researchers, who prefer to contrast continuing male reproductive potency with the loss of childbearing ability in women.[61]

d. Estrogens are really a family of structurally similar molecules. Their possibly different biological roles are not clearly delineated.

REFERENCES

1. Carroll Smith-Rosenberg and Charles Rosenberg, "The Female Animal: Medical and Biological Views of Woman and Her Role in 19th Century America," *Journal of American History* 60(1973):336.

2. Edgar Berman, Letter to the Editor, *New York Times,* 26 July 1970.

3. Steven Goldberg, *The Inevitability of Patriarchy* (New York: William Morrow, 1973), 93.

4. Herbert Wray, "Premenstrual Changes," *Science News* 122(1982):380–81.

5. Ilza Veith, *Hysteria: The History of a Disease* (Chicago: University of Chicago Press, 1965).

6. Pliny the Elder, quoted in M. E. Ashley and Montagu, "Physiology and Origins of the Menstrual Prohibitions," *Quarterly Review of Biology* 15(1940):211.

7. Smith-Rosenberg and Rosenberg, "The Female Animal"; Henry Maudsley, "Sex in Mind and in Education," *Popular Science Monthly* 5(1874):200; and Joan Burstyn, "Education and Sex: The Medical Case against Higher Education for Women in England 1870–1900," *Proceeds of the American Philosophical Society* 177(1973):7989.

8. Carroll Smith-Rosenberg, "The Hysterical Woman: Sex Roles and Role Conflict in 19th Century America," *Social Research* 39(1972):652–78.

9. M. A. Hardaker, "Science and the Woman Question," *Popular Science Monthly* 20(1881):583.

10. Nina Morais, "A Reply to Ms. Hardaker on: The Woman Question," *Popular Science Monthly* 21(1882):74–75.

11. Maudsley, "Sex in Mind and in Education," 211.

12. Katharina Dalton, *Once a Month* (Claremont, Calif.: Hunter House, 1983), 78.

13. Ibid.; Katharina Dalton, *The Premenstrual Syndrome* (London: William Heinemann Medical Books, 1972).

14. Andrea Eagan, "The Selling of Premenstrual Syndrome," *Ms.* Oct. 1983, 26–31.

15. Robert L. Reid and S. S. Yen, "Premenstrual Syndrome," *American Journal of Obstetrics and Gynecology* 139(1981):86.

16. J. Abplanalp, R. F. Haskett, and R. M. Rose, "The Premenstrual Syndrome," *Advances in Psychoneuroendocrinology* 3(1980):327–47.

17. Dalton, *Once a Month.*

18. Boston Women's Health Collective, *Our Bodies, Ourselves* (New York: Simon and Schuster, 1979).

19. Reid and Yen, "Premenstrual Syndrome," 86.

20. John O'Connor, M. Shelley Edward, and Lenore O. Stern, "Behavioral Rhythms Related to the Menstrual Cycle," in *Biorhythms and Human Reproduction,* ed. M. Fern et al. (New York: Wiley, 1974), 312.

21. Frank A. Beach, Preface to chapter 10, in *Human Sexuality in Four Perspectives* (Baltimore: Johns Hopkins University Press, 1977), 271.

22. M. B. Rosenthal, "Insights into the Premenstrual Syndrome," *Physician and Patient* (April 1983):46–53

23. Herbert Schaumberg et al., "Sensory Neuropathy from Pyridoxine Abuse," *New England Journal of Medicine* 309(1983):446–48.

24. Judith Abplanalp, "Premenstrual Syndrome: A Selective Review," *Women and Health* 8(1983):110.

25. Dalton, *Once a Month,* 12.

26. Abplanalp, Haskett, and Rose, "The Premenstrual Syndrome"; and Abplanalp, "Premenstrual Syndrome: A Selective Review."

27. Abplanalp, "Premenstrual Syndrome: A Selective Review."

28. Reid and Yen, "Premenstrual Syndrome," 97.

29. G. A. Sampson, "An Appraisal of the Role of Progesterone in the Therapy of Premenstrual Syndrome," in *The Premenstrual Syndrome,* ed. P. A. vanKeep and W. H. Utian (Lancaster, England: MTP Press Ltd. International Medical Publishers, 1981), 51–69; and Sampson, "Premenstrual Syndrome: A Double-Bind Controlled Trial of Progesterone and Placebo," *British Journal of Psychiatry* 135 (1979):209–15.

30. Robert A. Wilson and Thelma A. Wilson, "The Fate of the Nontreated Postmenopausal Woman: A Plea for the Maintenance of Adequate Estrogen from Puberty to the Grave," *Journal of the American Geriatric Society* 11(1963):352–56.

31. David Reuben, *Everything You Always Wanted to Know about Sex but Were Afraid to Ask* (New York: McKay, 1969), 292.

32. Wulf H. Utian, *Menopause in Modern Perspectives* (New York: Appleton-Century-Crofts, 1980).

33. Wilson and Wilson, "The Fate of the Nontreated Postmenopausal Woman," 347.

34. Robert A. Wilson, *Feminine Forever* (New York: M. Evans, 1966).

35. Marilyn Grossman and Pauline Bart, "The Politics of Menopause," in *The Menstrual Cycle,* vol. 1, ed. Dan, Graham, and Beecher.

36. Kathleen MacPherson, "Menopause as Disease: The Social Construction of a Metaphor," *Advances in Nursing Science* 3(1981):95–113; A. Johnson, "The Risks of Sex Hormones as Drugs," *Women and Health* 2(1977):8–11.

37. D. Smith et al., "Association of Exogenous Estrogen Endometrial Cancer," *New England Journal of Medicine* 293(1975):1164–67.

38. H. Judd et al., "Estrogen Replacement Therapy," *Obstetrics and Gynecology* 58(1981):267–75; M. Quigley, "Postmenopausal Hormone Replacement Therapy: Back to Estrogen Forever?" *Geriatric Medicine Today* 1(1982):78–85; and Thomas Skillman, "Estrogen Replacement: Its Risks and Benefits," *Consultant* (1982):115–27.

39. C. Smith-Rosenberg, "Puberty to Menopause: The Cycle of Femininity in 19th Century America," *Feminist Studies* 1(1973):65.

40. Helene Deutsch, *The Psychology of Women* (New York: Grune and Stratton, 1945), 458.

41. J. H. Osofsky and R. Seidenberg, "Is Female Menopausal Depression Inevitable?" *Obstetrics and Gynecology* 36(1970): 611.

42. Wilson and Wilson, "The Fate of the Nontreated Postmenopausal Woman," 348.

43. P. A. vanKeep, R. B. Greenblatt, and M. Albeaux-Fernet, eds., *Consensus on Menopause Research* (Baltimore: University Park Press, 1976), 134.

44. Utian, *Menopause in Modern Perspectives.*

45. Ibid.

46. Madeleine Goodman, "Toward a Biology of Menopause," *Signs* 5(1980):739–53.

47. Madeleine Goodman, C. J. Stewart, and F. Gilbert, "Patterns of Menopause: A Study of Certain Medical and Physiological Variables among Caucasian and Japanese Women Living in Hawaii," *Journal of Gerontology* 32(1977):297.

48. Karen Frey, "Middle-Aged Women's Experience and Perceptions of Menopause," *Women and Health* 6(1981):31.

49. Eve Kahana, A. Kiyak, and J. Liang, "Menopause in the Context of Other Life Events," in *The Menstrual Cycle,* vol. 1, ed. Dan, Graham, and Beecher, 167–78.

50. Wilson, *Feminine Forever,* 134.

51. A. Voda and M. Eliasson, "Menopause: The Closure of Menstrual Life," *Women and Health* 8(1983):137–56.

52. Wilson and Wilson, "The Fate of the Nontreated Postmenopausal Woman," 356.

53. Louis Avioli, "Postmenopausal Osteoporosis: Prevention vs. Cure," *Federation Proceedings* 40(1981):2418.

54. Voda and Eliasson, "Menopause: The Closure of Menstrual Life."

55. G. Winokur and R. Cadoret, "The Irrelevance of the Menopause to Depressive Disease," in *Topics in Psychoendocrinology,* ed. E. J. Sachar (New York: Grune and Stratton, 1975).

56. Rosalind Barnett and Grace Baruch, "Women in the Middle Years: A Critique of Research and Theory," *Psychology of Women Quarterly* 3(1978):187–97.

57. Boston Women's Health Collective, *Our Bodies, Ourselves.*

58. D. Levinson et al., "Periods in the Adult Development of Men: Ages 18–45," *The Counseling Psychologist* 6(1976): 21–25.

59. Barnett and Baruch, "Women in the Middle Years," 189.

60. Ibid.; Goodman, "Toward a Biology of Menopause"; and Voda, Dinnerstein, and O'Donnell, eds., *Changing Perspectives on Menopause.*

61. Marcha Flint, "Male and Female Menopause: A Cultural Put-on," in *Changing Perspectives on Menopause,* ed. A. M. Voda, M. Dinnerstein, and S. O'Donnell (Austin: University of Texas Press, 1982).

IF MEN COULD MENSTRUATE—

GLORIA STEINEM

A white minority of the world has spent centuries conning us into thinking that a white skin makes people superior—even though the only thing it really does is make them more subject to ultraviolet rays and to wrinkles. Male human beings have built whole cultures around the idea that penis envy is "natural" to women—though having such an unprotected organ might be said to make men vulnerable, and the power to give birth makes womb envy at least as logical.

In short, the characteristic of the powerful, whatever they may be, are thought to be better than the characteristics of the powerless—and logic has nothing to do with it.

What would happen, for instance, if suddenly, magically, men could menstruate and women could not?

The answer is clear—menstruation would become an enviable, boast-worthy, masculine event:

Men would brag about how long and how much.

Boys would mark the onset of menses, that longed-for proof of manhood, with religious ritual and stag parties.

Congress would fund a National Institute of Dysmenorrhea to help stamp out monthly discomforts.

Sanitary supplies would be federally funded and free. (Of course, some men would still pay for the prestige of commercial brands such as John Wayne Tampons, Muhammad Ali's Rope-a-dope Pads, Joe Namath Jock Shields—"For Those Light Bachelor Days," and Robert "Barretta" Blake Maxi-Pads.)

Military men, right-wing politicians, and religious fundamentalists would cite menstruation ("*menstrua-*

tion") as proof that only men could serve in the Army ("you have to give blood to take blood"), occupy political office ("can women be aggressive without that steadfast cycle governed by the planet Mars?"), be priests and ministers ("how could a woman give her blood for our sins?"), or rabbis ("without the monthly loss of impurities, women remain unclean").

Male radicals, left-wing politicians, and mystics, however, would insist that women are equal, just different; and that any woman could enter the ranks if only she were willing to self-inflict a major wound every month ("you *must* give blood for the revolution"), recognize the preeminence of menstrual issues, or subordinate her selfness to all men in their Cycle of Enlightenment.

Street guys would brag ("I'm a three-pad man") or answer praise from a buddy ("Man, you lookin' *good!*") by giving fives and saying, "Yeah, man, I'm on the rag!"

TV shows would treat the subject at length. ("Happy Days": Richie and Potsie try to convince Fonzie that he is still "The Fonz," though he has missed two periods in a row.) So would newspapers. (SHARK SCARE THREATENS MENSTRUATING MEN. JUDGE CITES MONTHLY STRESS IN PARDONING RAPIST.) And movies. (Newman and Redford in *Blood Brothers!*)

Men would convince women that intercourse was *more* pleasurable at "that time of the month." Lesbians would be said to fear blood and therefore life itself—though probably only because they needed a good menstruating man.

Of course, male intellectuals would offer the most moral and logical arguments. How could a woman master any discipline that demanded a sense of time, space, mathematics, or measurement, for instance, without that in-built gift for measuring the cycles of the moon and planets—and thus for measuring anything at all? In the rarefied fields of philosophy and religion, could women compensate for missing the rhythm of the universe? Or for their lack of symbolic death-and-resurrection every month?

Liberal males in every field would try to be kind: the fact that "these people" have no gift for measuring life or connecting to the universe, the liberals would explain, should be punishment enough.

And how would women be trained to react? One can imagine traditional women agreeing to all these arguments with a staunch and smiling masochism. ("The ERA would force housewives to wound themselves every month": Phyllis Schlafly. "Your husband's blood is as sacred as that of Jesus—and so sexy, too!": Marabel Morgan.) Reformers and Queen Bees would try to imitate men, and *pretend* to have a monthly cycle. All feminists would explain endlessly that men, too, needed to be liberated from the false idea of Martian aggressiveness, just as women needed to escape the bonds of menses envy. Radical feminists would add that the oppression of the nonmenstrual was the pattern for all other oppressions. ("Vampires were our first freedom fighters!") Cultural feminists would develop a bloodless imagery in art and literature. Socialist feminists would insist that only under capitalism would men be able to monopolize menstrual blood. . . . In fact, if men could menstruate, the power justifications could probably go on forever.

If we let them.

"A Way Outa No Way": Eating Problems among African-American, Latina, and White Women

BECKY WANGSGAARD THOMPSON

Bulimia, anorexia, binging, and extensive dieting are among the many health issues women have been confronting in the last twenty years. Until recently, however, there has been almost no research about eating problems among African-American, Latina, Asian-American, or Native American women, working-class women, or lesbians.[1] In fact, according to the normative epidemiological portrait, eating problems are largely a white, middle, and upper-class heterosexual phenomenon. Further, while feminist research has documented how eating problems are fueled by sexism, there has been almost no attention to how other systems of oppression may also be implicated in the development of eating problems.

In this article, I reevaluate the portrayal of eating problems as issues of appearance based in the "culture of thinness." I propose that eating problems begin as ways women cope with various traumas including sexual abuse, racism, classism, sexism, heterosexism, and poverty. Showing the interface between these traumas and the onset of eating problems explains why women may use eating to numb pain and cope with violations to their bodies. This theoretical shift also permits an understanding of the economic, political, social, educational, and cultural resources that women need to change their relationship to food and their bodies.

Becky Wangsgaard Thompson. "'A Way Outa No Way': Eating Problems among African American, Latina, and White Women," *Gender & Society* 6, no. 4 (December 1992). Copyright © 1994 by Sociologists for Women in Society. Reprinted with the permission of the author.

EXISTING RESEARCH ON EATING PROBLEMS

There are three theoretical models used to explain the epidemiology, etiology, and treatment of eating problems. The biomedical model offers important scientific research about possible physiological causes of eating problems and the physiological dangers of purging and starvation (Copeland 1985; Spack 1985). However, this model adopts medical treatment strategies that may disempower and traumatize women (Garner 1985; Orbach 1985). In addition, this model ignores many social, historical, and cultural factors that influence women's eating patterns. The psychological model identifies eating problems as "multidimensional disorders" that are influenced by biological, psychological, and cultural factors (Garfinkel and Garner 1982). While useful in its exploration of effective therapeutic treatments, this model, like the biomedical one, tends to neglect women of color, lesbians, and working-class women.

The third model, offered by feminists, asserts that eating problems are gendered. This model explains why the vast majority of people with eating problems are women, how gender socialization and sexism may relate to eating problems, and how masculine models of psychological development have shaped theoretical interpretations. Feminists offer the culture-of-thinness model as a key reason why eating problems predominate among women. According to this model, thinness is a culturally, socially, and economically enforced requirement for female beauty. This imperative makes women vulnerable to cycles of dieting, weight loss, and subsequent weight gain, which may lead to anorexia and bulimia (Chernin 1981; Orbach 1978, 1985; Smead 1984).

Feminists have rescued eating problems from the realm of individual psychopathology by showing how the difficulties are rooted in systematic and pervasive attempts to control women's body sizes and appetites. However, researchers have yet to give significant attention to how race, class, and sexuality influence women's understanding of their bodies and appetites. The handful of epidemiological studies that include African-American women and Latinas casts doubt on the accuracy of the normative epidemiological portrait. The studies suggest that this portrait reflects which particular populations of women have been studied rather than actual prevalence (Andersen and Hay 1985; Gray, Ford, and Kelly 1987; Hsu 1987; Nevo 1985; Silber 1986).

More important, this research shows that bias in research has consequences for women of color. Tomas Silber (1986) asserts that many well-trained professionals have either misdiagnosed or delayed their diagnoses of eating problems among African-American and Latina women due to stereotypical thinking that these problems are restricted to white women. As a consequence, when African-American women or Latinas are diagnosed, their eating problems tend to be more severe due to extended processes of starvation prior to intervention. In her autobiographical account of her eating problems, Retha Powers (1989), an African-American woman, describes being told not to worry about her eating problems since "fat is more acceptable in the Black community" (p. 78). Stereotypical perceptions held by her peers and teachers of the "maternal Black woman" and the "persistent mammy-brickhouse Black woman image" (p. 134) made it difficult for Powers to find people who took her problems with food seriously.

Recent work by African-American women reveals that eating problems often relate to women's struggles against a "simultaneity of oppression" (Clarke 1982; Naylor 1985; White 1991). Byllye Avery (1990), the founder of the National Black Women's Health Project, links the origins of eating problems among African-American women to the daily stress of being undervalued and overburdened at home and at work. In Evelyn C. White's (1990) anthology, *The Black Woman's Health Book: Speaking for Ourselves,* Georgiana Arnold (1990) links her eating problems partly to racism and racial isolation during childhood.

Recent feminist research also identifies factors that are related to eating problems among lesbians (Brown 1987; Dworkin 1989; Iazzetto 1989; Schoenfielder and Wieser 1983). In her clinical work, Brown (1987) found that lesbians who have internalized a high degree of homophobia are more likely to accept negative attitudes about fat than are lesbians who have examined their internalized homophobia. Autobiographical accounts by lesbians have also indicated that secrecy about eating problems among lesbians partly reflects their fear of being associated with a stigmatized illness ("What's Important" 1988).

Attention to African-American women, Latinas, and lesbians paves the way for further research that explores the possible interface between facing multiple oppressions and the development of eating problems. In this way, this study is part of a larger feminist and sociological research agenda that seeks to understand how race, class, gender, nationality, and sexuality inform women's experiences and influence theory production.

METHODOLOGY

I conducted eighteen life history interviews and administered lengthy questionnaires to explore eating problems among African-American, Latina, and white women. I employed a snowball sample, a method in which potential respondents often first learn about the study from people who have already participated. This method was well suited for the study since it enabled women to get information about me and the interview process from people they already knew. Typically, I had much contact with the respondents prior to the interview. This was particularly important given the secrecy associated with this topic (Russell 1986; Silberstein, Striegel-Moore, and Rodin 1987), the necessity of women of color and lesbians to be discriminating about how their lives are studied, and the fact that I was conducting across-race research.

To create analytical notes and conceptual categories from the data, I adopted Glaser and Strauss's (1967) technique of theoretical sampling, which directs the researcher to collect, analyze, and test hypotheses during the sampling process (rather than imposing theoretical categories onto the data). After completing each interview transcription, I gave a copy to each woman who wanted one. After reading their interviews, some of the women clarified or made additions to the interview text.

Demographics of the Women in the Study

The eighteen women I interviewed included five African-American women, five Latinas, and eight white women. Of these women, twelve are lesbian and six are heterosexual. Five women are Jewish, eight are Catholic, and five are Protestant. Three women grew up outside of the United

States. The women represented a range of class backgrounds (both in terms of origin and current class status) and ranged in age from nineteen to forty-six years old (with a median age of 33.5 years).

The majority of the women reported having had a combination of eating problems (at least two of the following: bulimia, compulsive eating, anorexia, and/or extensive dieting). In addition, the particular types of eating problems often changed during a woman's life span. (For example, a woman might have been bulimic during adolescence and anorexic as an adult.) Among the women, 28 percent had been bulimic, 17 percent had been bulimic and anorexic, and 5 percent had been anorexic. All of the women who had been anorexic or bulimic also had a history of compulsive eating and extensive dieting. Of the women, 50 percent were compulsive eaters and dieters (39 percent) or compulsive eaters (11 percent) but had not been bulimic or anorexic.

Two-thirds of the women have had eating problems for more than half of their lives, a finding that contradicts the stereotype of eating problems as transitory. The weight fluctuation among the women varied from 16 to 160 pounds, with an average fluctuation of 74 pounds. This drastic weight change illustrates the degree to which the women adjusted to major changes in body size at least once during their lives as they lost, gained, and lost weight again. The average age of onset was eleven years old, meaning that most of the women developed eating problems prior to puberty. Almost all of the women (88 percent) consider themselves as still having a problem with eating, although the majority believe they are well on the way to recovery.

THE INTERFACE OF TRAUMA AND EATING PROBLEMS

One of the most striking findings in this study was the range of traumas the women associated with the origins of their eating problems, including racism, sexual abuse, poverty, sexism, emotional or physical abuse, heterosexism, class injuries, and acculturation.[2] The particular constellation of eating problems among the women did not vary with race, class, sexuality, or nationality. Women from various race and class backgrounds attributed the origins of their eating problems to sexual abuse, sexism, and emotional and/or physical abuse. Among some of the African-American and Latina women, eating problems were also associated with poverty, racism, and class injuries. Heterosexism was a key factor in the onset of bulimia, compulsive eating, and extensive dieting among some of the

lesbians. These oppressions are not the same nor are the injuries caused by them. And certainly, there are a variety of potentially harmful ways that women respond to oppression (such as using drugs, becoming a workaholic, or committing suicide). However, for all these women, eating was a way of coping with trauma.

Sexual Abuse

Sexual abuse was the most common trauma that the women related to the origins of their eating problems. Until recently, there has been virtually no research exploring the possible relationship between these two phenomena. Since the mid-1980s, however, researchers have begun identifying connections between the two, a task that is part of a larger feminist critique of traditional psychoanalytic symptomatology (DeSalvo 1989; Herman 1981; Masson 1984). Results of a number of incidence studies indicate that between one-third and two-thirds of women who have eating problems have been abused (Oppenheimer et al. 1985; Root and Fallon 1988). In addition, a growing number of therapists and researchers have offered interpretations of the meaning and impact of eating problems for survivors of sexual abuse (Bass and Davis 1988; Goldfarb 1987; Iazzetto 1989; Swink and Leveille 1986). Kearney-Cooke (1988) identifies dieting and binging as common ways in which women cope with frequent psychological consequences of sexual abuse (such as body image disturbances, distrust of people and one's own experiences, and confusion about one's feelings). Root and Fallon (1989) specify ways that victimized women cope with assaults by binging and purging: bulimia serves many functions, including anesthetizing the negative feelings associated with victimization. Iazzetto's innovative study (1989), based on in-depth interviews and art therapy sessions, examines how a woman's relationship to her body changes as a consequence of sexual abuse. Iazzetto discovered that the process of leaving the body (through progressive phases of numbing, dissociating and denying) that often occurs during sexual abuse parallels the process of leaving the body made possible through binging.

Among the women I interviewed, 61 percent were survivors of sexual abuse (eleven of the eighteen women), most of whom made connections between sexual abuse and the beginning of their eating problems. Binging was the most common method of coping identified by the survivors. Binging helped women "numb out" or anesthetize their feelings. Eating sedated, alleviated anxiety, and combated loneliness. Food was something that they could trust and was accessible whenever they needed it. Antonia (a pseudonym) is an Italian-American woman who was first sexually abused by a male relative when she was four years old. Retrospectively, she knows that binging was a way she coped with the abuse. When the abuse began, and for many years subsequently, Antonia often woke up during the middle of the night with anxiety attacks or nightmares and would go straight to the kitchen cupboards to get food. Binging helped her block painful feelings because it put her back to sleep.

Like other women in the study who began binging when they were very young, Antonia was not always fully conscious as she binged. She described eating during the night as "sleep walking. It was mostly desperate—like I had to have it." Describing why she ate after waking up with nightmares, Antonia said, "What else do you do? If you don't have any coping mechanisms, you eat." She said that binging made her "disappear," which made her feel protected. Like Antonia, most of the women were sexually abused before puberty; four of them before they were five years old. Given their youth, food was the most accessible and socially acceptable drug available to them. Because all of the women endured the psychological consequences alone, it is logical that they coped with tactics they could do alone as well.

One reason Antonia binged (rather than dieted) to cope with sexual abuse is that she saw little reason to try to be the small size girls were supposed to be. Growing up as one of the Italian Americans in what she described as a "very WASP town," Antonia felt that everything from her weight and size to having dark hair on her upper lip were physical characteristics she was supposed to hide. From a young age she knew she "never embodied the essence of the good girl. I don't like her. I have never acted like her. I can't be her. I sort of gave up." For Antonia, her body was the physical entity that signified her outsider status. When the sexual abuse occurred, Antonia felt she had lost her body. In her mind, the body she lived in after the abuse was not really hers. By the time Antonia was eleven, her mother put her on diet pills. Antonia began to eat behind closed doors as she continued to cope with the psychological consequences of sexual abuse and feeling like a cultural outsider.

Extensive dieting and bulimia were also ways in which women responded to sexual abuse. Some women thought that the men had abused them because of their weight. They believed that if they were smaller, they might not have been abused. For example when Elsa, an Argentine woman, was sexually abused at the age of eleven, she thought her chubby size was the reason the man was abusing her. Elsa said, "I had this notion that these old perverts

liked these plump girls. You heard adults say this too. Sex and flesh being associated." Looking back on her childhood, Elsa believes she made fat the enemy partly due to the shame and guilt she felt about the incest. Her belief that fat was the source of her problems was also supported by her socialization. Raised by strict German governesses in an upper-class family, Elsa was taught that a woman's weight was a primary criterion for judging her worth. Her mother "was socially conscious of walking into places with a fat daughter and maybe people staring at her." Her father often referred to Elsa's body as "shot to hell." When asked to describe how she felt about her body when growing up, Elsa described being completely alienated from her body. She explained,

> Remember in school when they talk about the difference between body and soul? I always felt like my soul was skinny. My soul was free. My soul sort of flew. I was tied down by this big bag of rocks that was my body. I had to drag it around. It did pretty much what it wanted and I had a lot of trouble controlling it. It kept me from doing all the things that I dreamed of.

As is true for many women who have been abused, the split that Elsa described between her body and soul was an attempt to protect herself from the pain she believed her body caused her. In her mind, her fat body was what had "bashed in her dreams." Dieting became her solution, but, as is true for many women in the study, this strategy soon led to cycles of binging and weight fluctuation.

Ruthie, a Puerto Rican woman who was sexually abused from twelve until sixteen years of age, described bulimia as a way she responded to sexual abuse. As a child, Ruthie liked her body. Like many Puerto Rican women of her mother's generation, Ruthie's mother did not want skinny children, interpreting that as a sign that they were sick or being fed improperly. Despite her mother's attempts to make her gain weight, Ruthie remained thin through puberty. When a male relative began sexually abusing her, Ruthie's sense of her body changed dramatically. Although she weighed only 100 pounds, she began to feel fat and thought her size was causing the abuse. She had seen a movie on television about Romans who made themselves throw up and so she began doing it, in hopes that she could look like the "little kid" she was before the abuse began. Her symbolic attempt to protect herself by purging stands in stark contrast to the psychoanalytic explanation of eating problems as an "abnormal" repudiation of sexuality. In fact, her actions and those of many other survivors indicate a girl's logical attempt to protect herself (including her sexuality) by being a size and shape that does not seem as vulnerable to sexual assault.

These women's experiences suggest many reasons why women develop eating problems as a consequence of sexual abuse. Most of the survivors "forgot" the sexual abuse after its onset and were unable to retrieve the abuse memories until many years later. With these gaps in memory, frequently they did not know why they felt ashamed, fearful, or depressed. When sexual abuse memories resurfaced in dreams, they often woke feeling upset but could not remember what they had dreamed. These free-floating, unexplained feelings left the women feeling out of control and confused. Binging or focusing on maintaining a new diet were ways women distracted or appeased themselves, in turn, helping them regain a sense of control. As they grew older, they became more conscious of the consequences of these actions. Becoming angry at themselves for binging or promising themselves they would not purge again was a way to direct feelings of shame and self-hate that often accompanied the trauma.

Integral to this occurrence was a transference process in which the women displaced onto their bodies painful feelings and memories that actually derived from or were directed toward the persons who caused the abuse. Dieting became a method of trying to change the parts of their bodies they hated, a strategy that at least initially brought success as they lost weight. Purging was a way women tried to reject the body size they thought was responsible for the abuse. Throwing up in order to lose the weight they thought was making them vulnerable to the abuse was a way to try to find the body they had lost when the abuse began.

Poverty

Like sexual abuse, poverty is another injury that may make women vulnerable to eating problems. One woman I interviewed attributed her eating problems directly to the stress caused by poverty. Yolanda is a Black Cape Verdean mother who began eating compulsively when she was twenty-seven years old. After leaving an abusive husband in her early twenties, Yolanda was forced to go on welfare. As a single mother with small children and few financial resources, she tried to support herself and her children on $539 a month. Yolanda began binging in the evenings after putting her children to bed. Eating was something she could do alone. It would calm her, help her deal with loneliness, and make her feel safe. Food was an accessible commodity that was cheap. She ate three boxes of macaroni and cheese when nothing else was available. As a single mother with little

money, Yolanda felt as if her body was the only thing she had left. As she described it,

> I am here, [in my body] 'cause there is no where else for me to go. Where am I going to go? This is all I got . . . that probably contributes to putting on so much weight cause staying in your body, in your home, in yourself, you don't go out. You aren't around other people . . . You hide and as long as you hide you don't have to face . . . nobody can see you eat. You are safe.

When she was eating, Yolanda felt a momentary reprieve from her worries. Binging not only became a logical solution because it was cheap and easy but also because she had grown up amid positive messages about eating. In her family, eating was a celebrated and joyful act. However, in adulthood, eating became a double-edged sword. While comforting her, binging also led to weight gain. During the three years Yolanda was on welfare, she gained seventy pounds.

Yolanda's story captures how poverty can be a precipitating factor in eating problems and highlights the value of understanding how class inequalities may shape women's eating problems. As a single mother, her financial constraints mirrored those of most female heads of households. The dual hazards of a race- and sex-stratified labor market further limited her options (Higginbotham 1986). In an article about Black women's health, Byllye Avery (1990) quotes a Black woman's explanation about why she eats compulsively. The woman told Avery,

> I work for General Electric making batteries, and, I know it's killing me. My old man is an alcoholic. My kid's got babies. Things are not well with me. And one thing I know I can do when I come home is cook me a pot of food and sit down in front of the TV and eat it. And you can't take that away from me until you're ready to give me something in its place. (p. 7)

Like Yolanda, this woman identifies eating compulsively as a quick, accessible, and immediately satisfying way of coping with the daily stress caused by conditions she could not control. Connections between poverty and eating problems also show the limits of portraying eating problems as maladies of upper-class adolescent women.

The fact that many women use food to anesthetize themselves, rather than other drugs (even when they gained access to alcohol, marijuana, and other illegal drugs), is partly a function of gender socialization and the competing demands that women face. One of the physiological consequences of binge eating is a numbed state similar to that experienced by drinking. Troubles and tensions are covered over as a consequence of the body's defensive response to massive food intake. When food is eaten in that way, it effectively works like a drug with immediate and predictable effects. Yolanda said she binged late at night rather than getting drunk because she could still get up in the morning, get her children ready for school, and be clearheaded for the college classes she attended. By binging, she avoided the hangover or sickness that results from alcohol or illegal drugs. In this way, food was her drug of choice since it was possible for her to eat while she continued to care for her children, drive, cook, and study. Binging is also less expensive than drinking, a factor that is especially significant for poor women. Another woman I interviewed said that when her compulsive eating was at its height, she ate breakfast after rising in the morning, stopped for a snack on her way to work, ate lunch at three different cafeterias, and snacked at her desk throughout the afternoon. Yet even when her eating had become constant, she was still able to remain employed. While her patterns of eating no doubt slowed her productivity, being drunk may have slowed her to a dead stop.

Heterosexism

The life history interviews also uncovered new connections between heterosexism and eating problems. One of the most important recent feminist contributions has been identifying compulsory heterosexuality as an institution which truncates opportunities for heterosexual and lesbian women (Rich 1986). All of the women interviewed for this study, both lesbian and heterosexual, were taught that heterosexuality was compulsory, although the versions of this enforcement were shaped by race and class. Expectations about heterosexuality were partly taught through messages that girls learned about eating and their bodies. In some homes, boys were given more food than girls, especially as teenagers, based on the rationale that girls need to be thin to attract boys. As the girls approached puberty, many were told to stop being athletic, begin wearing dresses, and watch their weight. For the women who weighed more than was considered acceptable, threats about their need to diet were laced with admonitions that being fat would ensure becoming an "old maid."

While compulsory heterosexuality influenced all of the women's emerging sense of their bodies and eating patterns, the women who linked heterosexism directly to the beginning of their eating problems were those who knew they were lesbians when very young and actively resisted heterosexual norms. One working-class Jewish woman, Martha, began compulsively eating when she was eleven years old, the same year she started getting clues of her lesbian identity. In junior high school, as many of her female peers began dating boys, Martha began fantasizing about girls, which made her feel utterly alone. Confused and ashamed about her fantasies, Martha came home every day from school and binged. Binging was a way she drugged herself so that being alone was tolerable. Describing binging, she said, "It was the only thing I knew. I was looking for a comfort." Like many women, Martha binged because it softened painful feelings. Binging sedated her, lessened her anxiety, and induced sleep.

Martha's story also reveals ways that trauma can influence women's experience of their bodies. Like many other women, Martha had no sense of herself as connected to her body. When I asked Martha whether she saw herself as fat when she was growing up she said, "I didn't see myself as fat. I didn't see myself. I wasn't there. I get so sad about that because I missed so much." In the literature on eating problems, *body image* is the term that is typically used to describe a woman's experience of her body. This term connotes the act of imagining one's physical appearance. Typically, women with eating problems are assumed to have difficulties with their body image. However, the term *body image* does not adequately capture the complexity and range of bodily responses to trauma experienced by the women. Exposure to trauma did much more than distort the women's visual image of themselves. These traumas often jeopardized their capacity to consider themselves as having bodies at all.

Given the limited connotations of the term body image, I use the term *body consciousness* as a more useful way to understand the range of bodily responses to trauma.[3] By body consciousness I mean the ability to reside comfortably in one's body (to see oneself as embodied) and to consider one's body as connected to oneself. The disruptions to their body consciousness that the women described included leaving their bodies, making a split between their body and mind, experiencing being "in" their bodies as painful, feeling unable to control what went in and out of their bodies, hiding in one part of their bodies, or simply not seeing themselves as having bodies. Binging, dieting, or purging were common ways women responded to disruptions to their body consciousness.

Racism and Class Injuries

For some of the Latinas and African-American women, racism coupled with the stress resulting from class mobility related to the onset of their eating problems. Joselyn, an African-American woman, remembered her white grandmother telling her she would never be as pretty as her cousins because they were lighter skinned. Her grandmother often humiliated Joselyn in front of others, as she made fun of Joselyn's body while she was naked and told her she was fat. As a young child, Joselyn began to think that although she could not change her skin color, she could at least try to be thin. When Joselyn was young, her grandmother was the only family member who objected to Joselyn's weight. However, her father also began encouraging his wife and daughter to be thin as the family's class standing began to change. When the family was working class, serving big meals, having chubby children, and keeping plenty of food in the house was a sign the family was doing well. But, as the family became mobile, Joselyn's father began insisting that Joselyn be thin. She remembered, "When my father's business began to bloom and my father was interacting more with white businessmen and seeing how they did business, suddenly thin became important. If you were a truly well-to-do family, then your family was slim and elegant."

As Joselyn's grandmother used Joselyn's body as territory for enforcing her own racism and prejudice about size, Joselyn's father used her body as the territory through which he channeled the demands he faced in the white-dominated business world. However, as Joselyn was pressured to diet, her father still served her large portions and bought treats for her and the neighborhood children. These contradictory messages made her feel confused about her body. As was true for many women in this study, Joselyn was told she was fat beginning when she was very young even though she was not overweight. And, like most of the women, Joselyn was put on diet pills and diets before even reaching puberty, beginning the cycles of dieting, compulsive eating, and bulimia.

The confusion about body size expectations that Joselyn associated with changes in class paralleled one Puerto Rican woman's association between her eating problems and the stress of assimilation as her family's class standing moved from poverty to working class. When Vera was very young, she was so thin that her mother took her to a doctor who prescribed appetite stimulants. However, by the time Vera was eight years old, her mother began trying to shame Vera into dieting. Looking back on it, Vera attributed her mother's change of heart to competition among extended family members that centered on "being white, being successful, being middle class, . . . and it was always, 'Ay Bendito. She is so fat. What happened?' "

The fact that some of the African-American and Latina women associated the ambivalent messages about food and eating to their family's class mobility and/or the demands of assimilation while none of the eight white women expressed this (including those whose class was stable and changing) suggests that the added dimension of racism was connected to the imperative to be thin. In fact, the class expectations that their parents experienced exacerbated standards about weight that they inflicted on their daughters.

EATING PROBLEMS AS SURVIVAL STRATEGIES

Feminist Theoretical Shifts

My research permits a reevaluation of many assumptions about eating problems. First, this work challenges the theoretical reliance on the culture-of-thinness model. Although all of the women I interviewed were manipulated and hurt by this imperative at some point in their lives, it is not the primary source of their problems. Even in the instances in which a culture of thinness was a precipitating factor in anorexia, bulimia, or binging, this influence occurred in concert with other oppressions.

Attributing the etiology of eating problems primarily to a woman's striving to attain a certain beauty ideal is also problematic because it labels a common way that women cope with pain as essentially appearance-based disorders. One blatant example of sexism is the notion that women's foremost worry is about their appearance. By focusing on the emphasis on slenderness, the eating-problems literature falls into the same trap of assuming that the problems reflect women's "obsession" with appearance. Some women were raised in families and communities in which thinness was not considered a criterion for beauty. Yet, they still developed eating problems. Other women were taught that women should be thin, but their eating problems were not primarily in reaction to this imperative. Their eating strategies began as logical solutions to problems rather than problems themselves as they tried to cope with a variety of traumas.

Establishing links between eating problems and a range of oppressions invites a rethinking of both the groups of women who have been excluded from research and those whose lives have been the basis of theory formation. The construction of bulimia and anorexia as appearance-based disorders is rooted in a notion of femininity in which white middle- and upper-class women are portrayed as frivolous, obsessed with their bodies, and overly accepting of narrow gender roles. This portrayal fuels women's tremendous shame and guilt about eating problems—as signs of self-centered vanity. This construction of white middle- and upper-class women is intimately linked to the portrayal of working-class white women and women of color as their opposite: as somehow exempt from accepting the dominant standards of beauty or as one step away from being hungry and therefore not susceptible to eating problems. Identifying that women may binge to cope with poverty contrasts the notion that eating problems are class bound. Attending to the intricacies of race, class, sexuality, and gender pushes us to rethink the demeaning construction of middle-class femininity and establishes bulimia and anorexia as serious responses to injustices.

Understanding the link between eating problems and trauma also suggests much about treatment and prevention.

Ultimately, their prevention depends not simply on individual healing but also on changing the social conditions that underlie their etiology. As Bernice Johnson Reagon sings in Sweet Honey in the Rock's song "Oughta Be a Woman," "A way outa no way is too much to ask/too much of a task for any one woman" (Reagon 1980).[4] Making it possible for women to have healthy relationships with their bodies and eating is a comprehensive task. Beginning steps in this direction include insuring that (1) girls can grow up without being sexually abused, (2) parents have adequate resources to raise their children, (3) children of color grow up free of racism, and (4) young lesbians have the chance to see their reflection in their teachers and community leaders. Ultimately, the prevention of eating problems depends on women's access to economic, cultural, racial, political, social, and sexual justice.

NOTES

1. I use the term *eating problems* as an umbrella term for one or more of the following: anorexia, bulimia, extensive dieting, or binging. I avoid using the term *eating disorder* because it categorizes the problems as individual pathologies, which deflects attention away from the social inequalities underlying them (Brown 1985). However, by using the term *problem* I do not wish to imply blame. In fact, throughout, I argue that the eating strategies that women develop begin as logical solutions to problems, not problems themselves.

2. By trauma I mean a violating experience that has long-term emotional, physical, and/or spiritual consequences that may have immediate or delayed effects. One reason the term *trauma* is useful conceptually is its association with the diagnostic label *post-traumatic stress disorder (PTSD)* (American Psychological Association 1987). PTSD is one of the few clinical diagnostic categories that recognize social problems (such as war or the Holocaust) as responsible for the symptoms identified (Trimble 1985). This concept adapts well to the feminist assertion that a woman's symptoms cannot be understood as solely individual, considered outside of her social context, or prevented without significant changes in social conditions.

3. One reason the term *consciousness* is applicable is its intellectual history as an entity that is shaped by social context and social structures (Delphy 1984; Marx 1964). This link aptly applies to how the women described their bodies because their perceptions of themselves as embodied (or not embodied) directly relate to their material conditions (living situations, financial resources, and access to social and political power).

4. Copyright © 1980. Used by permission of Songtalk Publishing.

REFERENCES

American Psychological Association. 1987. *Diagnostic and Statistical Manual of Mental Disorders.* 3rd ed. rev. Washington, DC: American Psychological Association.

Andersen, Arnold, and Andy Hay. 1985. Racial and socioeconomic influences in anorexia nervosa and bulimia. *International Journal of Eating Disorders* 4:479–87.

Arnold, Georgiana. 1990. Coming home: One Black woman's journey to health and fitness. In *The Black Women's Health Book: Speaking for Ourselves,* Evelyn C. White. Seattle, WA: Seal Press.

Avery, Byllye Y. 1990. Breathing life into ourselves: The evolution of the National Black Women's Health Project. In *The Black Women's Health Book: Speaking for Ourselves,* Evelyn C. White. Seattle, WA: Seal Press.

Bass, Ellen, and Laura Davis. 1988. *The Courage to Heal: A guide for Women Survivors of Child Sexual Abuse.* New York: Harper & Row.

Brown, Laura S. 1985. Women, weight and power: Feminist theoretical and therapeutic issues. *Women and Therapy* 4:61–71.

———. 1987. Lesbians, weight and eating: New analyses and perspectives. In *Lesbian psychologies,* the Boston Lesbian Psychologies Collective. Champaign: University of Illinois Press.

Chernin, Kim. 1981. *The Obsession: Reflections of the Tyranny of Slenderness.* New York: Harper & Row.

Clarke, Cheryl. 1982. *Narratives.* New Brunswick, NJ: Sister Books.

Copeland, Paul M. 1985. Neuroendocrine aspects of eating disorders. In *Theory and Treatment of Anorexia Nervosa and Bulimia: Biomedical, Sociocultural, and Psychological Perspectives,* Steven Wiley Emmett. New York: Brunner/Mazel.

Delphy, Christine. 1984. *Close to Home: A Materialist Analysis of Women's Oppression.* Amherst: University of Massachusetts Press.

DeSalvo, Louise. 1989. *Virginia Woolf: The Impact of Childhood Sexual Abuse on Her Life and Work.* Boston, MA: Beacon.

Dworkin, Sari H. 1989. Not in man's image: Lesbians and the cultural oppression of body image. In *Loving Boldly: Issues Facing Lesbians,* Ester D. Rothblum and Ellen Cole. New York: Harrington Park Press.

Garfinkel, Paul E., and David M. Garner. 1982. *Anorexia Nervosa: A Multidimensional Perspective.* New York: Brunner/Mazel.

Garner, David. 1985. Iatrogenesis in anorexia nervosa and bulimia nervosa. *International Journal of Eating Disorders* 4:701–26.

Glaser, Barney G., and Anselm L. Strauss. 1967. *The Discovery of Grounded Theory: Strategies for Qualitative Research.* New York: Aldine DeGruyter.

Goldfarb, Lori. 1987. Sexual abuse antecedent to anorexia nervosa, bulimia and compulsive overeating: Three case reports. *International Journal of Eating Disorders* 6:675–80.

Gray, James, Kathryn Ford, and Lily M. Kelly. 1987. The prevalence of bulimia in a Black college population. *International Journal of Eating Disorders* 6:733–40.

Herman, Judith. 1981. *Father-Daughter Incest.* Cambridge, MA: Harvard University Press.

Higginbotham, Elizabeth. 1986. We were never on a pedestal: Women of color continue to struggle with poverty, racism and sexism. In *For Crying Out Loud,* Rochelle Lefkowitz and Ann Withorn. Boston, MA: Pilgrim Press.

Hsu, George. 1987. Are eating disorders becoming more common in Blacks? *International Journal of Eating Disorders* 6:113–24.

Iazzetto, Demetria. 1989. When the body is not an easy place to be: Women's sexual abuse and eating problems. Ph.D. diss., Union for Experimenting Colleges and Universities, Cincinnati, Ohio.

Kearney-Cooke, Ann. 1988. Group treatment of sexual abuse among women with eating disorders. *Women and Therapy* 7:5–21.

Marx, Karl. 1964. *The Economic and Philosophic Manuscripts of 1844.* New York: International.

Masson, Jeffrey. 1984. *The Assault on the Truth: Freud's Suppression of the Seduction Theory.* New York: Farrar, Strauss & Giroux.

Naylor, Gloria. 1985. *Linden Hills.* New York: Ticknor & Fields.

Nevo, Shoshana. 1985. Bulimic symptoms: Prevalence and the ethnic differences among college women. *International Journal of Eating Disorders* 4:151–68.

Oppenheimer, R., K. Howells, R. L. Palmer, and D. A. Chaloner. 1985. Adverse sexual experience in childhood and clinical eating disorders: A preliminary description. *Journal of Psychiatric Research* 19:357–61.

Orbach, Susie. 1978. *Fat Is a Feminist Issue.* New York: Paddington.

———. 1985. Accepting the symptom: A feminist psychoanalytic treatment of anorexia nervosa. In *Handbook of Psychotherapy for Anorexia Nervosa and Bulimia,* David M. Garner and Paul E. Garfinkel. New York: Guilford.

Powers, Retha. 1989. Fat is a Black women's issue. *Essence,* Oct., 75, 78, 134, 136.

Reagon, Bernice Johnson. 1980. "Oughta be a woman." On Sweet Honey in the Rock's album *Good News.* Music by Bernice Johnson Reagon; lyrics by June Jordan. Washington, DC: Songtalk.

Rich, Adrienne. 1986. Compulsory heterosexuality and lesbian existence. In *Blood, Bread and Poetry.* New York: Norton.

Root, Maria P. P., and Patricia Fallon. 1988. The incidence of victimization experiences in a bulimic sample. *Journal of Interpersonal Violence* 3:161–73.

———. 1989. Treating the victimized bulimic: The functions of binge—purge behavior. *Journal of Interpersonal Violence* 4:90–100.

Russell, Diana E. 1986. *The Secret Trauma: Incest in the Lives of Girls and Women.* New York: Basic Books.

Schoenfielder, Lisa, and Barbara Wieser, eds. 1983. *Shadow on a Tightrope: Writings by Women about Fat Liberation.* Iowa City, IA: Aunt Lute Book Co.

Silber, Tomas. 1986. Anorexia nervosa in Blacks and Hispanics. *International Journal of Eating Disorders* 5:121–28.

Silberstein, Lisa, Ruth Striegel-Moore, and Judith Rodin. 1987. Feeling fat: A woman's shame. In *The Role of Shame in Symptom Formation,* Helen Block Lewis. Hillsdale, NJ: Lawrence Erlbaum.

Smead, Valerie. 1984. Eating behaviors which may lead to and perpetuate anorexia nervosa, bulimarexia, and bulimia. *Women and Therapy* 3:37–49.

Spack, Norman. 1985. Medical complications of anorexia nervosa and bulimia. In *Theory and Treatment of Anorexia Nervosa and Bulimia: Biomedical, Sociocultural, and Psychological Perspectives,* Steven Wiley Emmett. New York: Brunner/Mazel.

Swink, Kathy, and Antoinette E. Leveille. 1986. From victim to survivor: A new look at the issues and recovery process for adult incest survivors. *Women and Therapy* 5:119–43.

Trimble, Michael. 1985. Post-traumatic stress disorder: History of a concept. In *Trauma and Its Wake: The Study and Treatment of Post-traumatic Stress Disorder,* C. R. Figley. New York: Brunner/Mazel.

What's important is what you look like. 1988. *Gay Community News,* July, 24–30.

White, Evelyn C., ed. 1990. *The Black Women's Health Book: Speaking for Ourselves.* Seattle, WA: Seal Press.

———. 1991. Unhealthy appetites. *Essence,* Sept., 28, 30.

Outcast Mothers and Surrogates: Racism and Reproductive Politics

ANGELA Y. DAVIS

The historical construction of women's reproductive role, which is largely synonymous with the historical failure to acknowledge the possibility of reproductive self-determination, has been informed by a peculiar constellation of racist and misogynist assumptions. These assumptions have undergone mutations even as they remain tethered to their historical origins. To explore the politics of reproduction in a contemporary context is to recognize the growing intervention of technology into the most intimate spaces of human life: from computerized bombings in the Persian Gulf, that have taken life from thousands of children and adults as if they were nothing more than the abstract statistics of a video game, to the complex technologies awaiting women who wish to transcend biological, or socially induced infertility. I do not mean to suggest that technology is inherently oppressive. Rather, the socioeconomic conditions within which reproductive technologies are being developed, applied, and rendered accessible or inaccessible maneuver them in directions that most often maintain or deepen misogynist, antiworking-class, and racist marginalization.

To the extent that fatherhood is denied as a socially significant moment in the process of biological reproduction, the politics of reproduction hinge on the social construction of motherhood. The new developments in reproductive technology have encouraged the contemporary emergence of popular attitudes—at least among the middle classes—that bear a remarkable resemblance to the nineteenth-

century cult of motherhood, including the moral, legal, and political taboos it developed against abortion. While the rise of industrial capitalism led to the historical obsolescence of the domestic economy and the ideological imprisonment of (white and middle-class) women within a privatized home sphere, the late twentieth-century breakthroughs in reproductive technology are resuscitating that ideology in bizarre and contradictory ways. Women who can afford to take advantage of the new technology—who are often career women for whom motherhood is no longer a primary or exclusive vocation—now encounter a mystification of maternity emanating from the possibility of transcending biological (and socially defined) reproductive incapacity. It is as if the recognition of infertility is now a catalyst—among some groups of women—for a motherhood quest that has become more compulsive and more openly ideological than during the nineteenth century. Considering the antiabortion campaign, it is not difficult to envision this contemporary ideological mystification of motherhood as central to the efforts to deny all women the legal rights that would help shift the politics of reproduction toward a recognition of our autonomy with respect to the biological functions of our bodies.

In the United States, the nineteenth-century cult of motherhood was complicated by a number of class- and race-based contradictions. Women who had recently immigrated from Europe were cast, like their male counterparts, into the industrial proletariat, and were therefore compelled to play economic roles that contradicted the increasing representation of women as wives/mothers. Moreover, in conflating slave motherhood and the reproduction of its labor force, the moribund slave economy effectively denied motherhood to vast numbers of African women. My female ancestors were not led to believe that, as women, their primary vocation was motherhood. Yet slave women were imprisoned within their reproductive role as well. The same sociohistorical reasons for the ideological location of European women in an increasingly obsolete domestic economy as the producers, nurturers, and rearers of children caused slave women to be valued in accordance with their role as breeders. Of course, both motherhood, as it was ideologically constructed, and breederhood, as it historically unfolded, were contingent upon the biological birth process. However, the one presumed to capture the moral essence of womaness, while the other denied, on the basis of racist presumptions and economic necessity, the very possibility of morality and thus also participation in this motherhood cult.

During the first half of the nineteenth century, when the industrial demand for cotton led to the obsessive expansion of slavery at a time when the importation of Africans was no longer legal, the "slaveocracy" demanded of African women that they bear as many children as they were biologically capable of bearing. Thus, many women had fourteen, fifteen, sixteen, seventeen, eighteen, nineteen, twenty children. My own grandmother, whose parents were slaves, was one of thirteen children.

At the same time, therefore, that nineteenth-century white women were being ideologically incarcerated within their biological reproductive role, essentialized as mothers, African women were forced to bear children, not as evidence of their role as mothers, but for the purpose of expanding the human property held by slave owners. The reproductive role imposed upon African slave women bore no relationship to a subjective project of motherhood. In fact, as Toni Morrison's novel *Beloved,* indicates—inspired as it is by an actual historical case of a woman killing her daughter—some slave women committed infanticide as a means of resisting the enslavement of their progeny.

Slave women were *birth mothers* or *genetic mothers*— to employ terms rendered possible by the new reproductive technologies—but they possessed no legal rights as mothers of any kind. Considering the commodification of their children—and indeed, of their own persons—their status was similar to that of the contemporary *surrogate mother.* I am suggesting that the term *surrogate mother* might be invoked as a retroactive description of their status because the economic appropriation of their reproductive capacity reflected the inability of the slave economy to produce and reproduce its own laborers—a limitation with respect to the forces of economic production that is being transformed in this era of advanced capitalism by the increasing computerization and robotization of the economy.

The children of slave mothers could be sold away by their owners for business reasons or as a result of a strategy of repression. They could also be forced to give birth to children fathered by their masters, knowing full well that the white fathers would never recognize their Black children as offspring. As a consequence of the socially constructed invisibility of the white father—a pretended invisibility strangely respected by the white and Black community alike—Black children would grow up in an intimate relation to their white half-brothers and sisters, except that their biological kinship, often revealed by a visible physical resemblance, would remain shrouded in silence. That feature of slave motherhood was something about which no one could speak. Slave women who had been compelled—or had, for their own reasons, agreed—to engage in sexual intercourse with their masters would be committing the equivalent of a crime if they publicly revealed the fathers of their children.[1] These women knew that it was quite likely that their children might also be sold or brutalized or beaten by their own fathers, brothers, uncles, or nephews.

If I have lingered over what I see as some of the salient reproductive issues in African-American women's history, it is because they seem to shed light on the ideological context of contemporary technological intervention in the realm of reproduction. Within the contemporary feminist discourse about the new reproductive technologies—in vitro fertilization, surrogacy, embryo transfer, etc.—concern has been expressed about what is sometimes described as the "deconstruction of motherhood"[2] as a unified biological process. While the new technological developments have rendered the fragmentation of maternity more obvious, the economic system of slavery fundamentally relied upon alienated and fragmented maternities, as women were forced to bear children, whom masters claimed as potentially profitable labor machines. Birth mothers could not therefore expect to be mothers in the legal sense. Legally these children were chattel and therefore motherless. Slave states passed laws to the effect that children of slave women no more belonged to their biological mothers than the young of animals belonged to the females that birthed them.[3]

At the same time, slave women and particularly those who were house slaves were expected to nurture and rear and mother the children of their owners. It was not uncommon for white children of the slave-owning class to have relationships of a far greater emotional intensity with the slave women who were their "mammies" than with their own white biological mothers. We might even question the meaning of this conception of "biological motherhood" in light of the fact that the Black nurturers of these white children were frequently "wet nurses" as well. They nourished the babies in their care with the milk produced by their own hormones. It seems, therefore, that Black women were not only treated as surrogates with respect to the reproduction of slave labor, they also served as surrogate mothers for the white children of the slave owners.

A well-known lullaby that probably originated during slavery has been recorded in some versions that powerfully reflect the consciousness of slave women who were compelled to neglect their own children, while lavishing their affection on the children of their masters. "Hushaby, / Don't you cry / Go to sleep, little baby. / And when you wake, / You shall have a cake / And all the pretty little ponies."[4]

In all likelihood, this version—or verse—was directed to the white babies, while the following one evoked the forced isolation of their own children: "Go to sleep, little baby, / When you wake / You shall have / All the mulies in the stable. / Buzzards and flies / Picking out its eyes, / Pore little baby crying, / Mamma, mamma!"[5]

A similar verse was sung to a lullaby entitled "Ole Cow": "Ole cow, ole cow, / Where is your calf? / Way down yonder in the meadow / The buzzards and the flies / A-pickin' out its eyes, / The po' little thing cried, Mammy."[6]

The economic history of African-American women—from slavery to the present—like the economic history of immigrant women, from both Europe and colonized or formerly colonized nations, reveals the persisting theme of work as household servants. Mexican women and Irish women, West Indian women and Chinese women have been compelled, by virtue of their economic standing, to function as servants for the wealthy. They have cleaned their houses and—our present concern—they have nurtured and reared their employers' babies. They have functioned as surrogate mothers. Considering this previous history, is it not possible to imagine the possibility that poor women—especially poor women of color—might be transformed into a special caste of hired pregnancy carriers? Certainly such fears are not simply the product of an itinerant imagination. In any event, whether or not such a caste of women baby-bearers eventually makes its way into history, these historical experiences constitute a sociohistorical backdrop for the present debate around the new reproductive technologies. The very fact that the discussion over surrogacy tends to coincide, by virtue of corporate involvement and intervention in the new technologies, with the debate over surrogacy for profit, makes it necessary to acknowledge historical economic precedents for surrogate motherhood.

Those patterns are more or less likely to persist under the impact of the technology in its market context. The commodification of reproductive technologies, and, in particular, the labor services of pregnant surrogate mothers, means that money is being made and that, therefore, someone is being exploited.

Once upon a time—and this is still the case outside the technologically advanced capitalist societies—a woman who discovered that she was infertile would have to reconcile herself to the impossibility of giving birth to her own biological offspring. She would therefore either try to create a life for herself that did not absolutely require the presence of children, or she chose to enter into a mothering relationship in other ways. There was the possibility of foster motherhood, adoptive motherhood, or play motherhood.[7] This last possibility is deeply rooted in the Black community tradition of extended families and relationships based both on biological kinship—though not necessarily biological motherhood—and on personal history, which is often as binding as biological kinship. But even within the biological network itself, relationships between, for example, an aunt and niece or nephew, in the African-American and other family traditions, might be as strong or stronger than those between a mother and daughter or son.

My own mother grew up in a family of foster parents with no siblings. Her best friend had no sisters and brothers either, so they invented a sister relation between them. Though many years passed before I became aware that they were not "really" sisters, this knowledge had no significant impact on me: I considered my Aunt Elizabeth no less my aunt later than during the earlier years of my childhood. Because she herself had no children, her relation to me, my sister, and two brothers was one of a second mother.

If she were alive and in her childbearing years today, I wonder whether she would bemoan the fact that she lacked the financial resources to employ all the various technological means available to women who wish to reverse their infertility. I wonder if she would feel a greater compulsion to fulfill a female vocation of motherhood. While working-class women are not often in the position to explore the new technology, infertile women—or the wives/partners of infertile men—who are financially able to do so are increasingly expected to try everything. They are expected to try in vitro fertilization, embryo transplants, surrogacy. The availability of the technology further mythologizes motherhood as the true vocation of women. In fact, the new reproductive medicine sends out a message to those who are capable of receiving it: motherhood lies just beyond the next technology. The consequence is an ideological compulsion toward a palpable goal: a child one creates either via one's own reproductive activity or via someone else's.

Those who opt to employ a surrogate mother will participate in the economic as well as ideological exploitation of her services. And the woman who becomes a surrogate mother earns relatively low wages. A few years ago, the going rate was $20,000. Considering the fact that pregnancy is a 24-hour-a-day job, what might seem like a substantial sum of money is actually not even a minimum wage. This commodification of motherhood is quite frightening in the sense that it comes forth as permission to allow women and their partners to participate in a program that is generative of life. However, it seems that what is really generated is sexism and profits.

The economic model evoked by the relationship between the surrogate mother and the woman [or man] who makes use of her services is the feudalistic bond between servant and her employer. Because domestic work has been primarily performed in the United States by women of color, native-born as well as recent immigrants (and immigrant women of European descent), elements of racism and class bias adhere to the concept of surrogate motherhood as potential historical features, even in the contemporary absence of large numbers of surrogate mothers of color.

If the emerging debate around the new reproductive technologies is presently anchored to the socioeconomic conditions of relatively affluent families, the reproductive issues most frequently associated with poor and working-class women of color revolve around the apparent proliferation of young single parents, especially in the African-American community. For the last decade or so, teenage pregnancy has been ideologically represented as one of the greatest obstacles to social progress in the most impoverished sectors of the Black community. In actuality, the *rate* of teenage pregnancy in the Black community—like that among white teenagers—has been waning for quite a number of years. According to a National Research Council study, fertility rates in 1960 were 156 births per 1,000 Black women aged fifteen to nineteen and 97 in 1985.[8] What distinguishes teenage pregnancy in the Black community today from its historical counterpart is the decreasing likelihood of teenage marriage. There is a constellation of reasons for the failure of young teenagers to consolidate traditional two-parent families. The most obvious one is that it rarely makes economic sense for an unemployed young woman to marry an unemployed young man. As a consequence of shop closures in industries previously accessible to young Black male workers—and the overarching deindustrialization of the economy—young men

capable of contributing to the support of their children are becoming increasingly scarce. For a young woman whose pregnancy results from a relationship with an unemployed youth, it makes little sense to enter into a marriage that will probably bring in an extra adult as well as a child to be supported by her own mother/father/grandmother, etc.

The rise of single motherhood cannot be construed, however, as synonymous with the "fall" of the nuclear family within the Black community—if only because it is an extremely questionable proposition that there was such an uncontested structure as the nuclear family to begin with. Historically, family relationships within the Black community have rarely coincided with the traditional nuclear model. The nuclear family, in fact, is a relatively recent configuration, integrally connected with the development of industrial capitalism. It is a family configuration that is rapidly losing its previous, if limited, historical viability: presently, the majority of US families, regardless of membership in a particular cultural or ethnic group, cannot be characterized as "nuclear" in the traditional sense. Considering the gender-based division of labor at the core of the nuclear model, even those families that consist of the mother-father-children nucleus—often popularly referred to as "nuclear families"—do not, rigorously speaking, conform to the nuclear model. The increasingly widespread phenomenon of the "working mother," as opposed to the wife/mother whose economic responsibilities are confined to the household and the children, thoroughly contradicts and renders anachronistic the nuclear family model. Not too many mothers stay at home by choice anymore; not too many mothers can afford to stay at home, unless, of course, they benefit from the class privileges that accrue to the wealthy. In other words, even for those whose historical realities were the basis of the emergence of this nuclear family model, the model is rapidly losing its ability to contain and be responsive to contemporary social/economic/psychic realities.

It angers me that such a simplistic interpretation of the material and spiritual impoverishment of the African-American community as being largely rooted in teenage pregnancy is so widely accepted. This is not to imply that teenage pregnancy is unproblematic. It is extremely problematic, but I cannot assent to the representation of teenage pregnancy as "the problem." There are reasons why young Black women become pregnant and/or desire pregnancy. I do not think I am far off target when I point out that few young women who choose pregnancy are offered an alternative range of opportunities for self-expression and development. Are those Black teenage girls with the potential for higher education offered scholarships permitting them to study at colleges and universities like Le Moyne? Are teenagers who choose pregnancy offered even a vision of well-paying and creative jobs?

Is it really so hard to grasp why so many young women would choose motherhood? Isn't this path toward adulthood still thrust upon them by the old but persisting ideological constructions of femaleness? Doesn't motherhood still equal adult womanhood in the popular imagination? Don't the new reproductive technologies further develop this equation of womanhood and motherhood? I would venture to say that many young women make conscious decisions to bear children in order to convince themselves that they are alive and creative human beings. As a consequence of this choice, they are also characterized as immoral for not marrying the fathers of their children.

I have chosen to evoke the reproductive issue of single motherhood among teenagers in order to highlight the absurdity of locating motherhood in a transcendent space— as the antiabortion theorists and activists do—in which involuntary motherhood is as sacred as voluntary motherhood. In this context, there is a glaring exception: motherhood among Black and Latina teens is constructed as a moral and social evil—but even so, they are denied accessible and affordable abortions. Moreover, teen mothers are ideologically assaulted because of their premature and impoverished entrance into the realm of motherhood while older, whiter, and wealthier women are coaxed to buy the technology to assist them in achieving an utterly commodified motherhood.

Further contradictions in the contemporary social compulsion toward motherhood—contradictions rooted in race and class—can be found in the persisting problem of sterilization abuse. While poor women in many states have effectively lost access to abortion, they may be sterilized with the full financial support of the government. While the "right" to opt for surgical sterilization is an important feature of women's control over the reproductive functions of their bodies, the imbalance between the difficulty of access to abortions and the ease of access to sterilization reveals the continued and tenacious insinuation of racism into the politics of reproduction. The astoundingly high—and continually mounting—statistics regarding the sterilization of Puerto Rican women expose one of the most dramatic ways in which women's bodies bear the evidence of colonization. Likewise, the bodies of vast numbers of sterilized indigenous women within the presumed borders of the United States bear the traces of a 500-year-old tradition of genocide. While there is as yet no evidence of large-scale steril-

ization of African-American and Latina teenage girls, there is documented evidence of the federal government's promotion and funding of sterilization operations for young Black girls during the 1960s and 70s. This historical precedent convinces me that it is not inappropriate to speculate about such a future possibility of preventing teenage pregnancy. Or—to engage in further speculation—of recruiting healthy young poor women, a disproportionate number of whom would probably be Black, Latina, Native American, Asian, or from the Pacific Islands, to serve as pregnancy carriers for women who can afford to purchase their services.

A majority of all women in jails and prisons are mothers and 7 to 10 percent are pregnant.[9] On the other hand, women's correctional institutions still incorporate and dramatically reveal their ideological links to the cult of motherhood. Even today, imprisoned women are labeled "deviant," not so much because of the crimes they may have committed, but rather because their attitudes and their behavior are seen as blatant contradictions of prevailing expectations—especially in the judicial and law enforcement systems—of women's place. They are mothers who have failed to find themselves in motherhood.

Since the onset of industrial capitalism, women's "deviance" has been constructed in psychological terms; the site of female incarceration has been less the prison and more the mental institution. For this reason, the population of jails and prisons is majority male and a minority female, while the reverse is the case in the mental institutions. The strategic role of domesticity in the structure and correctional goals of women's prisons revolves around the notion that to rehabilitate women, you must teach them how to be good wives and good mothers. Federal prisons such as Alderson Federal Reformatory for women in West Virginia and state institutions like the California Institute for Women and Bedford Hills in the state of New York attempt to architecturally—albeit mechanistically—evoke family life. Instead of cells there are cottages; here women have historically "learned" how to keep house, wash and iron clothes, do the dishes, etc. What bearing does this have on the politics of reproduction? I would suggest that there is something to be learned from the egregious contradiction of this emphasis on training for motherhood within a prison system that intransigently refuses to allow incarcerated women to pursue any meaningful relationship with their own children.

In the San Francisco Bay area, there are only three alternative institutions where women serving jail sentences may live with their children—the Elizabeth Fry Center, Mandela House, and Keller House. In all three places combined, there is space for about twenty to twenty-five women. In the meantime, thousands of women in the area suffer the threat—or reality—of having their children taken away from them and made wards of the court. Imprisoned women who admit that they have drug problems and seek to rehabilitate themselves often discover that their admissions are used as evidence of their incapacity to be good mothers. In the jails and prisons where they are incarcerated, they are presumably being taught to be good mothers, even as they are powerless to prevent the state from seizing their own children. Excepting a small minority of alternative "correctional" institutions, where social stereotypes are being questioned (although in most instances, the structure of incarceration itself is left unchallenged), the underlying agenda of this motherhood training is to turn aggressive women into submissive and dependent "mothers," whose children are destined to remain motherless.

The process through which a significant portion of the population of young Black, Latina, Native American, Asian, and Pacific women are criminalized, along with the poor European women, who, by their association with women of color are deemed criminal, hinges on a manipulation of a certain ideological representation of motherhood. A poor teenage Black or Latina girl who is a single mother is suspected of criminality simply by virtue of the fact that she is poor and has had a child "out of wedlock." This process of criminalization affects the young men in a different way—not as fathers, but rather by virtue of a more all-embracing racialization. Any young Black man can be potentially labeled as criminal: a shabby appearance is equated with drug addiction, yet an elegant and expensive self-presentation is interpreted as drug dealing. While it may appear that this process of criminalization is unrelated to the construction of the politics of reproduction, there are significant implications here for the expansion of single motherhood in Black and Latino communities. The 25 percent of African-American men in jails and prisons,[10] for example, naturally find it difficult, even in a vicarious sense, to engage in any significant parenting projects.

In pursuing a few of the ways in which racism—and class bias—inform the contemporary politics of reproduction, I am suggesting that there are numerous unexplored vantage points from which we can reconceptualize reproductive issues. It is no longer acceptable to ground an analysis of the politics of reproduction in a conceptual construction of "woman" as a sex. It is not enough to assume that female beings, whose bodies are distinguished by vaginas, ovarian tubes, uteri, and other biological features related to reproduction should be able to claim such "rights" to

exercise control over the processes of these organs, as the right to abortion. The social/economic/political circumstances that oppress and marginalize women of various racial, ethnic, and class backgrounds, and thus alter the impact of ideological conceptions of motherhood, cannot be ignored without affirming the same structures of domination that have led to such different—but related—politics of reproduction in the first place.

In conclusion, I will point to some of the strategic constellations that should be taken into consideration in reconceiving an agenda of reproductive rights. I do not present the following points as an exhaustive list of such goals, but rather I am trying to allude to a few of the contemporary issues requiring further theoretical examination and practical/political action. While the multiple arenas in which women's legal abortion rights are presently being assaulted and eroded can account for the foregrounding of this struggle, the failure to regard economic accessibility of birth control and abortion has equally important results in the inevitable marginalization of poor women's reproductive rights. With respect to a related issue, the "right" and access to sterilization is important, but again, it is equally important to look at those economic and ideological conditions that track some women toward sterilization, thus denying them the possibility of bearing and rearing children in numbers they themselves choose.

Although the new reproductive technologies cannot be construed as inherently affirmative or violative of women's reproductive rights, the anchoring of the technologies to the profit schemes of their producers and distributors results in a commodification of motherhood that complicates and deepens power relationships based on class and race. Yet, beneath this marriage of technology, profit, and the assertion of a historically obsolete bourgeois individualism lies the critical issue of the right to determine the character of one's family. The assault on this "right"—a term I have used throughout, which is not, however, unproblematic—is implicated in the ideological offensive against single motherhood as well as in the homophobic refusal to recognize lesbian and gay family configurations—and especially in the persisting denial of custody (even though some changes have occurred) to lesbians with children from previous heterosexual marriages. This is one of the many ways in which the present-day ideological compulsion toward motherhood that I have attempted to weave into all of my arguments further resonates. Moreover, this ideology of motherhood is wedded to an obdurate denial of the very social services women require in order to make meaningful choices to bear or not to bear children. Such services include health care—

from the prenatal period to old age—child care, housing, education, jobs, and all the basic services human beings require to lead decent lives. The privatization of family responsibilities—particularly during an era when so many new family configurations are being invented that the defi- nition of family stretches beyond its own borders—takes on increasingly reactionary implications. This is why I want to close with a point of departure: the reconceptualization of family and of reproductive rights in terms that move from the private to the public, from the individual to the social.

NOTES

1. See Harriet A. Jacobs. *Incidents in the Life of a Slave Girl.* Edited and Introduction by Jean Fagan Yellin. Cambridge, Mass.: Harvard University Press, p. 1087.

2. See Michelle Stanworth, ed. *Reproductive Technologies: Gender, Motherhood and Medicine.* Minneapolis: University of Minnesota Press, 1987.

3. See Paula Giddings. *When and Where I Enter: The Impact of Black Women on Race and Sex in America.* New York: William Morrow, 1984.

4. Dorothy Scarborough. *On the Trail of Negro Folksongs,* Hatboro, Pennsylvania: Folklore Associates, Inc, 1963. (original edition published by Harvard University Press, 1925), p. 145.

5. *Ibid.,* p. 148.

6. *Ibid.*

7. The tradition of Black women acting as "play mothers" is still a vital means of inventing kinship relations unrelated to bio- logical origin.

8. Gerald David Jaynes and Robin M. Williams, Jr., ed. *A Common Destiny: Blacks and American Society,* Washington, D.C.: National Academy Press, 1989, p. 515.

9. See Ellen M. Barry, "Pregnant Prisoners," *Harvard Women's Law Journal,* vol. 12, 1989.

10. See Marc Mauer. "Young Black Men and the Criminal Justice System: A Growing National Problem." A Report by the Sentencing Project, 918 F Street, N. W. Suite 501, Washington, D.C. 20004, February 1990.

WHEN THE POLITICAL BECOMES THE PERSONAL OR AN ABORTION THAT WASN'T AN ABORTION; A RIGHT THAT HARDLY SEEMS SUCH

ELEANOR MILLER

I never thought I'd need an abortion. In 1980 we were referred to New York Hospital's Infertility Clinic. I remember Dale and I sitting in the waiting room; each man held a small container through which one could see the semen he had just collected in the bathroom. The next year we moved to Milwaukee. A lay midwife

Eleanor Miller, "When the Political Becomes the Personal or an Abortion That Wasn't an Abortion; A Right that Hardly Seems Such," from *Midwest Feminist Papers* 1, New Series (1991), edited by Michael R, Hill and Mary Jo Deegan. Copyright © 1991 by Midwest Sociologists for Women in Sociology. Reprinted with the permission of *Midwest Feminist Papers.*

referred us to *the* infertility expert in town, one of the few physicians who would provide backup for the lay midwives who practice illegally here. Sounded like someone I would like, and I did.

He immediately noticed my congenital heart defect. No reason not to try to have a baby; we just needed to be careful. This next part of the story is a well-known one; invasive tests, temperature charts, dashes home fol- lowed by postcoital exams, clomid. Finally, in August of 1983, Samantha was born (with the crash cart outside my door in case of heart failure and intravenous antibi- otics to reduce the risk of endocarditis). I was thirty-six.

When Sam was eight months old we discovered that Dale had thyroid cancer. Given my age and history of infertility and the fact that Dale's prognosis was good, we decided that it was now or never if we wanted a second child. Radiation has a distinctive impact on male fertility, however. I remember staring at bent and pinheaded sperm through our ob/gyn's microscope. We had the same experiences we had the first time—miscarriage in my office, followed within the hour by a D&C without anesthesia in my ob/gyn's office. In 1987 Jill was born. I was very tired, but very happy.

Given my age and health and Dale's, we were sure we didn't want any more children. Then in September of 1989, noticing that I was feeling exhausted and nauseous, I realized I was pregnant. I called Dale. He said he would be right home. After I hung up, I called my ob/gyn's office. A nurse who knew me answered. "I'm pregnant," I said. "I need. . . ." "Congratulations," says she. "No," I reply. "I want to arrange to have an abortion." She says she will have the doctor call me, nothing more.

He tells me that I am not too old to have another child. He volunteers that he could do a tubal ligation at the same time. But I'm too exhausted, I argue, and I still have a baby in diapers (not to mention that I have a good chance of soon being elected president of SWS and chair of my department). He jokes that his wife and he will raise the child until it's three and then, becoming more serious, asks me whether I've really thought long and hard about this decision and whether I've discussed it with Dale. I can't believe this conversation. He says finally, "You know, I don't do abortions; but I will refer you to a friend I trust who does." He gives me the person's name; he's on the staff of an abortion clinic. We hang up. I feel betrayed, angry, silly. Why did I think it would be easy? Why did I trust this man?

I call the abortion clinic to set up an appointment. I notice that it is in the heart of Milwaukee's poorest, most segregated area; in fact it is the area in which I do my research. When I arrive there three days later, I'm grateful that there aren't any protesters. We park in the unpaved, litter-strewn lot beside the two-story cinderblock building that houses the abortion clinic. The first story has large aqua and orange plastic squares decorating it. There is no sign. When we enter, we approach a glass-enclosed office and I fill out a sheet that asks for basic demographic information as well as insurance information. I am then asked for $200. I begin to write a check. The receptionist looks askance. Don't I know

they only accept cash? I tell her that I wasn't told. "Oh, you're Dr. So-and-so's patient; I guess it's alright." I write my check and am asked to wait in the basement of the building. I descend the stairs, holding Dale's hand.

There are four or five couples seated in orange plastic chairs, all silently staring into space or looking at a TV chained to the wall. An African-American woman is standing. She and a very young-looking African-American couple are the only nonwhites in the room. With one exception, the white couples are older and appear to be married. Dale and I wait there a long time, two hours to be exact. During that time I am called to have a brief medical history taken and to have some bloodwork done. The nurse who pricks my finger to take the blood says: "I see you're a doctor; well, let's make this clear. I'll be your nurse today; you do what I say; you're my patient." I am puzzled by this obvious exercise of social control and status jockeying. I had given no indication that I thought any other situation existed. The interesting thing is that I never see her again.

I am later called into a tiny office off the small main waiting room. Here a rosy-cheeked social worker inquiries as to whether I really know what I am doing and asks me whether or not my decision has been coerced. She asks me what form of birth control I had been using and looks critical when I say that I had been using none. I don't try to explain. She also asks me what sort I intend to use when I leave that day. I tell her that my husband will probably have a vasectomy, but I feel intruded upon by her questions. In fact, I hadn't thought about birth control at all, either in the past or for the future.

At about 11:00, I am ushered upstairs into a small, green room where I am asked to undress. I put on a hospital gown and a nurse helps me onto the table and into the stirrups. She turns on the vacuum aspirator; she says it would be good for me to hear what it sounds like, so as not to be alarmed later. She records my blood pressure in my chart and notes that I have been referred by Dr. So-and-so. She ventures that she is in the market for a fertility expert since she is having difficulty conceiving. I describe my ob/gyn in vaguely positive terms and then I pour out my story to her. I tell her what a cruel trick I think it is that someone with my history should find herself pregnant. I feel human for a moment.

The doctor, pale, bespectacled, enters the room. He seems embarrassed. He says his name. He looks at my chart, puts it down and inserts the speculum. He says, "You're starting to have a spontaneous abortion; it often happens in women your age." "Look," he says to the nurse, stepping back, "see the tissue." "I am going to give you an injection of lidocaine; it will make your mouth *[sic]* numb." At this point the nurse took my right arm. I thought she was trying to hold my hand, but, as I groped for hers, it became clear that she was actually pinning my right arm to table. I hear the vacuum switch on and the procedure is over in about two or three minutes. The nurse rolls me over to my left side, away from the vacuum aspirator, and tells me to bring my knees up. A brief time later, I feel something moving swiftly up my legs as she puts on my underpants, to which she has attached a sanitary napkin. She tells me to dress and then leads me to the recovery room.

Three or four women are on the other cots, but most of the women who had been in the basement are in an adjoining room having soda and cookies. The nurse takes my blood pressure and massages my uterus several times. After a while she says she needs to see how much I am bleeding. I tell her I didn't think much, but she hauls me to my feet and asks me to take down my pants so she can see. While I am doing this, she holds a blanket between me and the other women. I am shocked as she goes from cot to cot doing this. She gives us instructions on aftercare and announces to the group that we should not call unless we are passing big clots or are filling, she emphasizes filling, four pads an hour. She says that we will have to listen to a talk about how to take birth-control pills and participate in a question and answer period before we can be discharged. She walks us into the room where the first women to have had abortions that morning are talking, eating, and reading magazines. They have apparently been detained there until all the abortions are completed. I listen to the lecture. Afterwards, there is only one question. A woman asks: "When will it be safe to lift a baby?" Dale is waiting for me. He has witnessed two C-sections, but has not been allowed into the room where I have just had my D&C. Yes, somehow my abortion had been magically transformed into a D&C, at least that's how my ob/gyn subsequently refers to what happened that morning when I next meet him.

As we ride home, I feel sad and angry. The whole process has been such a degradation ceremony. I chide myself for having panicked, for trusting my infertility specialist, for not having the presence of mind to think that I would have been better off at "Bread and Roses," a feminist clinic. I am angry about the stereotypes of the abortion seeker, particularly the one of the professional woman who is too self-absorbed to want to be bothered with children.

The next time I visit my internist, I ask him if he can recommend a gynecologist, someone who does abortions. He looks rather puzzled. I describe my experience. I make it clear that my request is a matter of politics, not immediate medical need. He replies, "Most gynecologists here don't do abortions; you know, they picket your house and things." I thought, " 'They' aren't the only ones who can picket."

R E A D I N G 3 9

The Politics of Breast Cancer

SUSAN M. LOVE, MD, with KAREN LINDSEY

If "everything is political," as they say, the politics of can- cer have their roots in the 1950s. In 1952 the American Cancer Society started the Reach to Recovery program. This was a group of women helping women: survivors of breast cancer helping newly diagnosed women. Members of Reach to Recovery, all of whom had had mastectomies, would visit the patient in the hospital and reassure her that there was life after mastectomy. They were, and continue to be, a wonderful resource for women with breast cancer.

From there, support groups for women with breast can- cer evolved. Women sat together and talked about their experiences and their feelings. It was tremendously helpful for these people to learn they were not alone in their feel- ings about a disease that was shrouded in so much mystery and fear.

All this underlined the fact that there was no psychoso- cial support from the medical profession—you had to get it from somewhere else. And since the disease remained one hidden from public view, there was still an aura of some- thing shameful and disreputable about it.

The politics of breast cancer accelerated in the 1970s, when Shirley Temple Black, Betty Ford, and Happy Rockefeller told the world they had breast cancer. Their openness began to create an environment in which breast cancer could be looked at as a dangerous disease that need- ed to be addressed by public institutions, rather than a pri- vate and shameful secret. There was a dramatic increase in the number of women in America who got mammograms, and in the number of breast cancer cases diagnosed.

Those were the days of the one-step procedure. You'd go in for the biopsy; it would be done under general anes-

thetic and, if the lump was positive, your breast would be immediately removed. You'd go under the anesthetic not knowing whether you'd have a breast when you woke up. There was no psychosocial support: your doctor wouldn't talk with you beyond telling you it was cancer (if they even told you that) and they removed your breast.

In 1977 Rose Kushner, a writer with breast cancer, wrote a terribly important book, *Why Me?* It ushered in the two-step procedure. Kushner saw no reason for a woman to have to decide whether to have a mastectomy before she even knew if she had breast cancer. She argued passionately that it was important for the woman to have her biopsy, learn if she had cancer, and then, if she did, decide what route to pursue. Doctors were still working on the erro- neous assumption that time was everything: if they didn't get the cancer out the instant they found it, it would spread and kill the patient. Kushner had done enough research to realize that wasn't the case—that a few weeks between diagnosis and treatment wouldn't do any medical harm, and would do a great deal of emotional good. She pushed for the two-step procedure, and her book influenced large num- bers of women to demand it for themselves. She became a national figure, representing women with breast cancer on the boards designing national studies, moving closer into the realm of politics. She died of breast cancer many years later, in January 1990.

Another force on the horizon at that time was Nancy Brinker. Brinker's sister, Susan G. Komen, was diagnosed with breast cancer in 1977 and died in 1980. In 1983 Brinker founded the Susan G. Komen Breast Cancer Foundation, which is based in Dallas, Texas. Ironically, she herself got breast cancer soon afterward. Since the mid- 1980s, they've been working to raise money for research. They also try to encourage funding for women to get mam- mography. They organize the yearly Race for the Cure, which takes place in a number of cities. Brinker's husband is a wealthy businessman, active in Republican politics, and through him she became acquainted with the Bushes, the Reagans, the Quayles, and other important Republicans whose support she was able to enlist in some of her breast-cancer work.

For a long time, that was pretty much all that was going on around breast cancer. Then in the late 1980s, almost spontaneously, in different parts of the country a number of political women's cancer groups sprang up. One was in the Boston area, started by a patient of mine, Susan Shapiro, who had breast cancer. When she was diagnosed, she began to search for anyone working on the political issues around women and cancer, and she couldn't find anything. Yet she was passionately convinced that were political implications to cancer, and particularly to women's cancers. She wrote an article in the feminist newspaper *Sojourner,* called "Cancer as a Feminist Issue," and at the end of it she announced a meeting at the Cambridge Women's Center. A lot of women showed up, women who had been as frustrated as she by the lack of political response to their disease. They formed the Women's Community Cancer Project. Their scope was fairly broad, including all cancers that women got and the role of women as caretakers for children, spouses, and parents with cancer. Inevitably, much of the focus was on breast cancer. Shapiro died in January 1990, but the project continues to flourish.

At about the same time the Women's Community Cancer Project was beginning, another group in Oakland, California, The Women's Cancer Resource Center, started, founded by a lesbian named Jackie Winnow. It too was a political group. There was a second group in the Bay Area, Breast Cancer Action, founded by Eleanor Pred, an older woman with breast cancer who modeled her work on some AIDS activism.

In Washington, DC, the Mary-Helen Mautner Project for Lesbians with Cancer was formed by Susan Hester after Mautner, her partner, died of breast cancer. Its purpose was to provide support for lesbians with cancer, based on the model of the AIDS buddy programs.

These four groups emerged at around the same time. There were obvious differences: in two cases, the focus was lesbians, and in two the focus was all cancers. But all were based on the premise that there were political, not just personal, aspects of cancer that affected women.

All of these groups were aware of the work the AIDS movement had been doing. For the first time we were seeing people with a killer disease aggressively demanding more money for research, changes in insurance bias, and job protection. Women with breast cancer took note of that—particularly those women who had been part of the feminist movement, and were geared, as the gay activists with AIDS were, to the idea of identifying oppression and confronting it politically.

At the time these groups were emerging, I was finishing work on the first edition of [my] book. As I went on my book tour, talking with women, I began to realize how deep women's anger was, and how ready they were to do something. The key moment for me was in Salt Lake City in June 1990, when I gave a talk for 600 women. It was the middle of the afternoon, during the week, and the audience was mostly older women. It was a pretty long talk, and at the end, I said, "We don't know the answers, and I don't know what we have to do to make President Bush wake up and do something about cancer. Maybe we should march topless on the white House." I was making a wisecrack, hoping to end a somber talk with a little lightness.

I got a great response, and afterward women came up to me asking when the march was, how they could sign up for it, and what they could do to help organize it. I realized that, throughout the country, this issue touched all kinds of women, and that they were all fed up with the fact that this virtual epidemic was being ignored. I saw that it wasn't just in the big centers like San Francisco and Boston and Washington, DC, where I'd expect to see political movements springing up. It was everywhere—everywhere women were ready to fight for attention to breast cancer.

I felt we needed to have some sort of national organization to give these women the hook they needed to begin organizing. I went to Washington to give a talk to the Mautner Project. Before the talk, I went out to dinner with Susan Hester, the founder of the project and two of her friends. I was talking about the thoughts I'd had after the Salt Lake City speech. My idea was that maybe we should have a big march, and end it with the formation of a new national organization. Hester thought we needed to go about it the other way around: if we formed the organization, we could get its members to come to a big march.

When I left, I called Amy Langer, the president of NABCO, the National Association of Breast Cancer Organizations, a group dedicated to giving individuals and groups breast cancer information. I asked what she thought of the idea, and she liked it. I also contacted Nancy Brinker of the Komen Foundation.

The four of us met for breakfast in Washington on December 11, 1990, during a breast cancer event—Susan, Amy, Nancy, and I—and we discussed it further. We all were enthusiastic and the result was a planning meeting. We invited Sharon Greene, the executive director of Y-Me, a very large support group organization in Chicago. Then we got Ann McGuire from the Women's Community Cancer Project, and we invited Eleanor Pred from Breast Cancer Action and Kim Calder from Cancer Care and Canact from New York.

We discussed whether or not any one of the existing groups wanted to take on the political piece, and although everyone was very enthusiastic no one felt they could handle this aspect, so we decided to go for a coalition of groups. The Komen Foundation dropped out and the other groups became the planning committee for the new coalition. We set up several task forces to figure out how we'd go about it and what our goals would be. Amy Langer used NABCO's list and others threw in their lists for an invitation to an organizing meeting in May 1991. Then we called an open meeting, to be held in Washington, and wrote to every women's group we knew of.

We had no idea who'd show up. On the day of the meeting the room was packed. There were representatives from all kinds of groups: the American Cancer Society and the American Jewish Congress were there. So was the Human Rights Campaign Fund, a big gay and lesbian group. There were members of breast cancer support groups from all around the country—such as Arm in Arm from Baltimore, the Linda Creed group from Philadelphia, and Share from New York. Overall there were about 100 or so individuals representing seventy-five organizations. We were overwhelmed, and we started the National Breast Cancer Coalition on the spot. Out of that meeting came the first Board of the Coalition.

NABCO agreed to be the administrator of the planning committee. Its expenses would be reimbursed from the other groups. As a result Amy chaired the meetings until bylaws and officers could be chosen. A year later Fran Visco, a lawyer from Philadelphia who had had breast cancer in her late thirties, became the first elected president. She has since taken a leave of absence from her law office and remains the president today.

From this first group of eager participants we formed a volunteer working board. Our first action, in the fall of 1991, was a project we called "Do the Write Thing." We wanted to collect and deliver to Washington 175,000 letters, representing the 175,000 women who would be diagnosed with breast cancer that year. The letters would go both to the president and to various members of Congress.

This was spring, and we were planning this for October, Breast Cancer Awareness Month. Not only did we want 175,000 letters altogether, we wanted the number from each state to match the number in that state who would get breast cancer. We managed to identify groups in each state who could work with us. In October, we ended up with 600,000 letters—it was an enormous response. We delivered them to the White House. The guards just stood there; nobody would help us lift the boxes. All these women who'd had mastectomies were lifting heavy boxes of letters onto the conveyer belt.

We were all certain that the letters would just be dumped into the shredder. To make things worse, we hardly got any media coverage, because the Clarence Thomas–Anita Hill hearings were going on. So we were afraid that our first action had been a flop. But in reality, we had succeeded in a number of ways.

For one thing, we had organized in such a way that we had a group in every state. That meant a large and potentially powerful organization. For another, even if the White House ignored us, the congresspeople didn't. When we started lobbying for increased research money the members of Congress granted us $43 million more, raising the 1993 appropriation to $132 million. That was a small triumph.

One of the things we realized, however, was that we had to do more research ourselves. When we lobbied, the congresspeople who were interested in what we had to say kept asking, "Well, how much money do you need?" And we didn't know.

We realized we had to find out, and quickly. Mary Jo Kahn from the Virginia Breast Cancer Group suggested that we ask the scientists themselves, and Amy Langer suggested we hold research hearings, which we did in February 1992. We invited scientists from around the country who studied breast cancer to come to the hearings. Since we had no money, they had to pay for their own trips. We got $10,000 from a donor in Philadelphia to fund the hearings, and there were other donations as well. We rented a hotel hall, and fifteen major research scientists came. They testified about what research wasn't getting done because of lack of funding, and how much money they thought they really needed.

Those hearings went on for a day, and it was one of the first times that scientists and activists interested in breast cancer had met together. The next morning we had a congressional breakfast; many of the scientists came with us and spoke to several of the congressional representatives.

We created an interesting coalition. If the scientists alone lobby for more research money, it looks like they're doing it out of self-interest. But our involvement made it clear that this wasn't about ivory-tower research, but about work that really could save human lives.

We met again after the hearings and came up with a figure: we needed $433 million for breast cancer research. The total 1992 budget was $93 million. So we started lobbying for $300 million more, armed with our report based on the scientists' testimony.

At first the reaction was overwhelmingly negative. Everybody in Congress kept saying there was no money and it would be impossible to come up with anything like another $300 million. People kept insisting that we should reduce it; we were defeating ourselves by demanding so much. But we insisted. What we were being "greedy" for was women's lives, and we weren't willing to compromise.

The National Cancer Institute didn't initially support our efforts. For one thing, it would have embarrassed them. The Institute is bound by law to give a budget to the president every year, called the bypass budget, which is *their* best estimate of how much money *they* need. (A leftover from the Nixon administration's War on Cancer, it's called the bypass budget because it bypasses Congress and goes straight to the president.) The bypass budget had *only* asked for something like $197 million, so they didn't feel like they could support a new demand for $433 million more.

But we kept at it, and when the politicians told us there wasn't any more money, we said, "Well, you found money for the savings and loan bailout. You found money for the Gulf War. We think you can find this money too, if you really decide it's important that women are dying." We testified at the Senate, and at the House. We lobbied, we sent faxes, and we called. Eventually we got somewhere—in the fall of 1992 Senator Tom Harkin, who was very sympathetic to us because his two sisters had died of breast cancer, was the chair of the Senate Appropriations Committee in charge of NIH funding. He made sure that the budgeted amount for breast cancer spending at the NIH was $220 million. But that wasn't enough. In order to get the rest of our $433 million total he tried to put forth a transfer amendment that would move money from the Defense Department to the domestic budget. It didn't work.

But we had another advantage at this point—this was the year of the woman. Because of Anita Hill, a lot of congressmen were looking bad when it came to women's issues. They needed to spiff up their images—especially since it was an election year. They realized that breast cancer was a safe thing. There was no racial issue, no question about whether someone was telling the truth or not, no important male judge's reputation at stake—just the stark fact that women were dying. Add to this the demographics of breast cancer—it's most prevalent among white and middle- to upper-class women. These men were being asked to support their own wives, mothers, and sisters, as well as the women who are most likely to vote. So we got a lot of support from men not usually known as feminists or progressives—Arlen Specter was running radio ads in Philadelphia about how important it was to fight breast cancer. Alphonse D'Amato in New York came up with an amendment saying Congress should take 3 percent of the Defense Department's budget to give us our $300 million.

We also, of course, had the more predictable allies—Ted Kennedy held hearings in my office at the Faulkner in Boston on breast-cancer research. And, of course, we had strong support from a number of congresswomen, who had their own understanding of the importance of fighting breast cancer.

Then Senator Harkin noticed that, amazingly, in the past there actually had been some money for breast cancer in the Defense Department—$25 million spent on mammogram machines for the army. At our urging he decided to try and increase that to $210 million.

The Defense Department people decided that with all these attacks on their budget, they didn't want to risk their budget being wiped out. If the money officially left their budget, they'd never get it back when they applied for the following year's budget. But if the money stayed in their budget, they could fund breast cancer research this year; and then next year, with the budget still the same or higher, they could spend that money on bombers or whatever else they decided was important. So they agreed to a bill using $210 million of defense money for breast-cancer research and it passed.

About twenty senators who had voted against it left while the roll call went on. When it became clear that it was going to pass, these senators literally ran back to the room and down to the podium to change their votes. Presumably they preferred to be on the winning side. Coalition vice president Jane Reese Colbourne and others watched on C-SPAN as the senators did their undignified but useful turn around. We ended up with a final vote of 89 to 4, with seven abstentions.

After all that, our victory was almost destroyed. President Bush challenged the decision because medical research funding was domestic spending and Department of Defense funding was military spending. As Jane Reese Colbourne describes it, "We ended up doing a vigil in front of the Senate while they had a meeting to determine whether we could really use that money. Senator Harkin fought for it. We were ready to call in people from Richmond and Baltimore to relieve us and keep the vigil going. Then Senator Inouye came out and told us we had the money."

So there was $210 million in the Department of Defense budget and the extra $220 million in the NCI budget. That's

$430 million total. Against all odds, we had succeeded. Part of it was being in the right place at the right time. But most of it was the enormous amount of work all the women in the coalition and around the country had put in. Overnight, we had an enormous amount of clout and were well recognized for a group that had just begun.

We were ready to move on to our next step. It was one thing to raise money, but we wanted to have a say in how it was spent. We wanted women from our groups, women with breast cancer, to be involved in the decision-making panels on review boards for grants, on the National Cancer Advisory Board, and in all the decision making. We started lobbying for that, and our next major project was to deliver 2.6 million signatures to the White House in October 1993 to represent the 2.6 million women living with breast cancer at the time—1.6 million who knew they had breast cancer, and 1 million who were yet to be diagnosed. We mobilized around the country collecting signatures, and we delivered our 2.6 million signatures to President Clinton on October 18. As a measure of how far we'd gone from October 1991 when the boxes went on the conveyor belt into the shredder, this time we were welcomed in the East Room, where Fran Visco and I shared the stage with both Hillary and Bill Clinton, along with Secretary of Health and Human Services Donna Shalala. The room was filled with 200 of our people. It was an awesome moment.

And President Clinton followed up. In December we had a meeting to set national strategy—a meeting of activists, politicians, scientists, doctors, laypeople, businesspeople. We came up with a National Action Plan. In each one of the subgroups working on this plan, there was one of our activist members. We were at the table and we were changing the policy of business as usual around breast cancer.

Being with the scientists, talking and working with them, the activists were able to learn that the answers aren't always easy, that scientists have to work months and years to come up with one useful discovery. The scientists saw that the activists weren't shrill, uninformed troublemakers, but intelligent, concerned people fighting to save their own and others' lives.

Meanwhile, as in any successful movement, there's been a backlash. It's come from two places. One is from the people who have been working with breast cancer for a long time. They see the National Breast Cancer Coalition as the brash new upstart trying to shake up the status quo. And indeed we are. Nothing had changed for years, and it is time that we had some action around this issue.

There's also been a backlash from some of the scientists. They're glad for the funding, but they don't like the idea of having medical research funds earmarked for specific diseases. They point out that some of the discoveries about breast cancer have come from studying other things—which is true. One gene found in studying a rare eye cancer turned out to be present also in breast cancer. But there are an awful lot of things they've studied that haven't told us anything about breast cancer. They have this romantic notion about how only the curiosity of a scientist can bring about a medical miracle—you throw seeds into the fields and among the weeds the wildflowers will come up. And we're saying, yes, but we'll get more of the particular flowers we need if we do a little cultivation.

What it's really about is power—who gets to decide how the money is spent. Should it be decided by the taxpayer, whose money, after all, it is? Or should it be decided by the scientists in terms of their curiosity? They say, "We can't just give the money to whoever yells the loudest, and we can't politicize research and science." But research and science have always been political—it just depends on whose research and whose politics it is. Is it Nixon's war on cancer, or Jerry Lewis's Muscular Dystrophy, or the Heart Association clamoring for more money and more research? What's different is that now there is a new group in the melee. And that's really what the backlash is about.

In fact, the National Breast Cancer Coalition has had a strict policy from the beginning to try not to rob one disease for another. We have always been clear that we want a bigger pie, not a bigger piece of a pie that's never been large enough in the first place. That's one of the reasons it's so important the increased funding we got *this year* came from the Department of Defense—not from AIDS research or asthma research or any other essential medical area.

The scientists then argue that eventually the money won't come from the military or some other budget, that it will come from some other disease research. But that "eventually" is a long way off—there's a lot of useless government spending that we can go after first.

The other argument is that the amount of money per case of cancer should be equal across all cancers. X amount of money per case of breast cancer, X amount for lung cancer. But that's too simplistic a way to measure it. The important measure is what we know about the disease. We know what causes lung cancer. But we don't know what to do about breast cancer yet. This doesn't mean the other diseases don't need money. We need to fight the tobacco industry and do better antismoking campaigns. But we need much more money for diseases like breast cancer, for which we don't yet have the information to get out to people.

The exciting thing is that one of the goals we had was to get researchers into the field. Generally speaking, there are only about eight centers that are specializing in breast cancer in the country.

One of the reasons we wanted the money from the Department of Defense was to attract new people, to get researchers working on new aspects of breast cancer. And it worked. With the $210 million made available by the Department of Defense, they got 2,400 grant applications. Many of these were people who had never done breast cancer research before.

And we now have representation at many of the levels at which decisions are made. Fran Visco sits as one of three members of the President's Cancer Panel. Kay Dickersin, from Arm in Arm in Maryland, was just appointed to the National Cancer Advisory Board. We were on the oversight committee for the Department of Defense money and involved in the study sections. We are forging the National Action Plan with the Department of Health and Human Services.

Our goals remain the same. We want access for all women to high-quality screening and treatment for breast cancer. The Mammography Quality Standards Act is a first step. Health care reform will be another. We want influence for women with breast cancer. We are currently training activists to be effective advocates and contribute when they get a seat at the table. And we want research into the cause of breast cancer, how to prevent it and how to cure it. The increase in environmental research as well as basic research is in part in response to our efforts. We want more basic research, rather than focusing our energies on how to treat existing disease. We need both, of course, but ultimately, the goal is to stop the cancer before a woman gets it in the first place.

I've learned through this that you really can affect how the government acts. A small group of committed people can do a lot. So few people let their feelings be known that the people who do it, and do it vociferously, get an undue amount of power. We didn't have any money—not like the gun lobby or the tobacco industry. But we organized. And now some of the groups with money started to help us—Revlon has been supporting women's lives as well as their looks. They paid for the petition campaign.

Many of the women in the coalition have never been involved in political action before, and they're finding themselves working side by side with baby boomers who marched in the 60s and learned the value of political protest—and now are confronting breast cancer, and realiz-ing that like civil rights and war resistance and the early women's movement issues, breast-cancer research needs to be fought for.

At the same time, breast cancer affects women of all ages, and all political stripes. Eighty-year-old women get breast cancer; thirty-year-old women get breast cancer. Democrats and Republicans and radicals and conservatives get breast cancer. Heterosexual and bisexual and lesbian women get breast cancer. Caucasian, African-American, Hispanic, and Asian women get breast cancer.

This is an issue we can all agree on and one we have to all fight for. We can't afford to be good girls any longer. We can't let this disease pass on to another generation. Our lives and the lives of our daughters depend on it.

Last year at the Los Angeles Breast Cancer Coalition "War Mammorial" the Coalition put white plastic casts of women's torsos, 1,300 of them, on a hill. From a distance they looked like graves but up close they showed the variety of women's bodies: large breasts, small breasts, some with mastectomies and some with implants. Katie, my five-year-old daughter, was walking around trying to figure out which breasts she wanted when she grew up. Then she turned serious.

"Are these the graves of women with breast cancer?" she asked.

"No, these women are all alive," I told her. "But some women do die from breast cancer."

"Well, you're trying to stop that, aren't you, Mommy?"

"Yes, Katie, I would like to stop breast cancer before you grow up."

She thought about that a minute. "What if you die first?" she asked.

"I'd like to stop breast cancer before I die," I replied. She thought again, then turned to me and said, "If there is breast cancer left after you die it is a big problem. Because I'm not going to be a breast surgeon. I'm going to be a bal-lerina."

Well, Katie doesn't have to worry—she can go ahead and be a ballerina. And she won't be haunted, as so many women are now, by the fear of getting breast cancer. As long as we keep fighting, the discoveries we're making, buttressed by the political activism that lets the scientists and the government know that we won't let up until we've ended breast cancer, will bring about her wish. That's what keeps me going. Twenty years from now, a comfortable retiree with no more breast cancer to worry about, I can sit in the audience waiting for the curtain to rise and my beautiful, healthy daughter to pirouette across the stage.

ASSESSING OLDER LESBIANS' HEALTH NEEDS

SHARON DEEVEY

During the course of [my] research. I worked as a contingent staff nurse on a geropsychiatric unit in a local private hospital. One shift I was assigned to care for a sixty-year-old retired nurse named Ann who had been diagnosed with depression. The psychiatrist's admitting note reported that Ann had "no family," but had lived for thirty-five years with a female roommate.

After I had met Ann, I returned to the nursing station and speculated quietly that this particular patient might be an older lesbian woman. The other nurses knew about my research and one of them asked, "What makes you think that?"

"Well," I said, not exactly sure myself, "because she has lived for thirty-five years with her roommate, and . . . she has a Gertrude Stein haircut!" How could I explain the "sense" of recognizing someone like myself?

From my research about older gay and lesbian people, I knew to avoid direct discussion of sexual orientation with older clients. Gay men and lesbian women who grew up before the Gay Liberation Movement are frequently unwilling or unable to discuss their personal lives with strangers. In the 1940s and 1950s, exposure of "homosexuality" almost guaranteed loss of family, job, and basic safety.

Ann was on suicide precautions and needed to be escorted when leaving the unit. I went with her to the laundry room, and while she washed her clothes, I chatted with her and learned something of her situation.

She had met her roommate thirty-five years ago when Dorie moved in next door. They'd been friends right away, had moved from the small town where they'd lived to the city of Columbus, and had helped each other through school. Ann had worked in several nursing jobs, and Dorie was a retired dietitian.

Things were hard now, Ann reported, because they could not get around much. Their younger woman friend who had been living with them had become seriously ill with cancer and had returned to her family in California. Dorie needed cataract surgery and could not see to drive. Ann had been having crying spells and angry outbursts. She had read about our special geropsychiatric unit and decided to come for help. She spoke very quietly, rarely made eye contact, and answered little more than specifically asked. Both her answers and her guarded manner seemed to confirm my speculation about her lifestyle.

The following weekend, I was assigned to the adjoining locked adult unit. I asked the nurse in charge on the geropsychiatric unit to tell me if Ann's roommate came to visit.

A couple of hours later, the nurse came looking for me. "I think you're right about them," she said. "There's something about seeing them together. . . . Why don't you come over and talk to them during your break?"

They were sitting in the corner of the dayroom, talking quietly. Ann looked up in recognition. Her partner Dorie stood as I introduced myself. She had very short, pure white hair and startlingly blue eyes that I knew could see very little.

After a few introductory pleasantries (while I wracked my brain trying to figure out how to support these women), I said, "You seem to be very important to each other."

"Oh, yes," Dorie said. "Neither of us has any other family . . . just a nephew of mine in Cleveland."

"You need to be clear with your doctor and the nurses about that," I said. "You have the right to be treated as each other's family."

"I'm afraid someone will sneer," Dorie said, looking away. I was right. If they were just roommates they would have no reason to be afraid.

"I can't promise that everyone will understand," I answered, being intentionally vague. "This hospital generally respects what patients want, but you'll have to ask to be treated as family to each other." When I reported the conversation to Ann's primary nurse, she agreed about the importance of supporting the relationship and managing the issue sensitively.

Ann was gone the following weekend. In a team meeting, the primary nurse had mentioned the probability of Ann's lesbian sexual orientation to the other team members.

The psychiatrist was adamant. The primary nurse told me that he said no one was to discuss sex with his patient.

"I tried to convince him," she went on, "it's not about sexuality. It's about social isolation, and why Ann's so distrustful of staff and so guarded with other patients in the dayroom. He wouldn't listen. He just kept repeating, 'no one is to discuss sex with her.' " As it turned out, Ann signed herself out of the hospital against medical advice.

It was the first time I was tempted to follow a patient home from the hospital, but I knew I could not rescue Ann and Dorie by myself. I returned with renewed determination to my research. When I am aging, or ill, and need health care, I can only hope that nurses and physicians will know more about lesbian women and treat me with the same sensitivity and respect they offer anyone else.

Violence against Women

Violence against women manifests itself in many forms. Verbal harassment, sexual imposition, sexual assault, rape, domestic battering, lesbian bashing, and child abuse all contribute to a social climate that encourages women to comply with men's desires or to restrict their activities in order to avoid assault. The threat of violence against women is pervasive across cultures. Feminist analyses of violence against women focus on the extent to which violence serves as a means for the institutionalized control of women and children by men. The articles in this section analyze various forms of violence against women and contrast beliefs and actualities about various kinds of male violence. Often, sexist ideologies encourage us to accept violence against women as either harmless or deserved. Feminist analyses take the position that this violence constitutes a system through which men frighten and therefore control and dominate women.

Patricia Yancey Martin and Robert A. Hummer also explore the implications of heterosexual male bonding in "Fraternities and Rape on Campus." Fraternity members' negative attitudes toward women, rigid ideas about masculinity, and pressures to demonstrate simultaneously their heterosexuality and their utter loyalty to the "brotherhood" create fraternity cultures in which men use women to demonstrate their masculinity and worth. What are some other social contexts in which similar pressures for men to be hypermasculine exist?

In contrast, John Stoltenberg discusses how some men's experiences with sexual violence have led

them to work against rape. In "I Am Not a Rapist!" Stoltenberg records a conversation among young men involved in an antiviolence organization. The men describe hearing from women friends who have been raped and discuss their awareness of how these experiences affect their friends' relationships with them and with other men. They lament the fact that women fear them as potential rapists when they pass on the street at night. Overall, they argue that the effects of sexual violence are pervasive for men as well as for women. Stoltenberg suggests that such men represent a new movement of young men who oppose violence against women because of their personal experiences with that violence. He argues that this movement of men has the potential to transform gender politics. How do you think sexual violence affects men? What is men's role in working to end sexual violence?

Hate crimes are crimes motivated by prejudice against particular groups. Because violence against women is so widespread, we sometimes fail to recognize it as a crime of hate. Gloria Steinem argues that mass killings in schools such as Columbine, Colorado, and Jonesboro, Arkansas, serial killings by criminals such as Edmund Kemper and Son of Sam, and other multiple sadistic killings of strangers are linked to male domination. In "Supremacy Crimes," Steinem argues that we should regard most such crimes not as individual and apolitical assaults by deranged men. Rather, they are crimes against women as a group, committed for the most part by white heterosexual males and motivated by men's

439

desire for power and superiority. Think about the coverage of the mass killings in schools that occurred at the end of the 1990s. Did the media acknowledge the sex of the killers and most of the victims and the role gender might have played in what happened?

Violence against women, as all these articles point out, is not simply the act of individual men against individual women. Instead, it is created and perpetuated by social institutions. The final article in this section, "Accountability or Justice? Rape as a War Crime," by Mary Ann Tétreault, documents the use of rape as "an instrument of policy" in wartime. Focusing on the Iraqi invasion of Kuwait and the war in Bosnia-Herzogovina, Tétreault examines the use of rape and charges of rape as political fodder against the enemy, the treatment of rape victims by their own communities and governments, and the responses of war-crimes tribunals to rape charges. She argues that, as in other forms of rape, shame prevents many women from reporting their assaults or seeking damages from war-crimes tribunals. How is rape in wartime similar to and different from rape in the contexts described in the other articles in this section?

"The Man in the Street": Why He Harasses

CHERYL BENARD and EDIT SCHLAFFER

It is a violation of my natural external freedom not to be able to go where I please, and to experience other restrictions of this kind. . . . Even though the body and life are something external, just like property, nevertheless my personality is wounded by such experiences, because my most immediate identity rests in my body.

Hegel, *Texte zur philosophischen Propaedeutik*

I am standing at Wittenbergplatz waiting for the light to turn green, in my left hand I am carrying a bag filled with groceries . . . behind me I sense the approach of two men and turn my head, at that moment the man on my left reaches for my hair which falls to my shoulders colored with henna, he runs his fingers through my hair experimentally and says to his friend: great hair. . . . An ordinary everyday experience for the colonized in a city of the First World.

Verena Stefan, *Haeutungen*

By the time we are in our twenties we have become accustomed to the laws of the street. The abrupt but regular interruptions of our daily movements have become familiar, we have acquired the habit of overhearing comments, we are graceful at dodging straying hands, we have the skill of a general in making rapid strategic evaluations, we can usually tell at a glance whether that group of young men leaning against a car door might use physical intimidation or just jokes, whispered comments, laughter, whether it's worth crossing over to the other side of the street or enough to act

nonchalant and cultivate deafness. It's no longer frightening, just annoying, sometimes jolting when one is called abruptly out of a train of thought or a moment of absent-mindedness. One gets used to it.

Is all of this normal, inevitable? It was a question I had stopped asking myself by the time I spent a year abroad at the university in Beirut. In the dorm I shared a room with Widad from Bahrein, an eighteen-year-old who wanted to be a teacher. At home, Widad always wrapped an abaya around her jeans and T-shirt when she went out of the house, and to Widad, the behavior of men on the street was news. Not yet hardened by long experience, Widad spent her first week in Beirut in tears. Sobbing with anger and confusion, she would report on the insulting and unbelievable things that had been said to her, the grabbing, the pushing, the comments, the aggressive looks, the smacking lips, the hissing in her ear. The abaya, she would conclude, has nothing to do with women. In Bahrein we wear it because of the men, someday maybe we won't have to but right now, this is how they are, and who can stand it? The final outcome, I am sorry to report, was not that Widad became hardened and militant, schooled in the martial arts and an example to us all, but that she was instrumental in organizing a group of Bahreini men, so that for the rest of the academic year the women from Bahrein moved through the city like a convoy flanked by a string of guards ready to fight at the sign of a covetous glance.

For the American women, this was an occasion to think again about the kind of world we have learned to accept as normal. On public streets, we plan our routes and our timing as if we were passing through a minefield. We are touched, harassed, commented upon in a stream of constant small-scale assaults, and in a culture which values privacy and anonymity in crowds these intimacies are considered inevitable. Secretly, women like it, popular opinion believes, and posters of men whistling after a woman are thought by advertising agencies to sell their product. Besides, popular opinion goes on to explain, women provoke it, with their fashions, their manner of walking, their behavior. These are familiar arguments; we hear them whenever the subject of violence against women comes up. There are few facts to hold up against them. Stamped as trivial, the harassment of women has received no attention from sociology, and cities that regulate almost everything from bicycles and dogs to the use of roller skates in order to keep the traffic moving have no ordinances or rules to guarantee women the right to free passage.

What kinds of men harass women, what do they think they are doing, how do women feel about it? Diaries and essays by women, and reports from other times and cultures, give some very sketchy information. For a more systematic picture, we observed the behavior of men in four cities (Berlin, Los Angeles, Rome, and Vienna) over the period of a year, allowing for differences in season, time of day, and part of town. Interviews with women provided information on how the victims feel. Some of the results were surprising and some were depressingly predictable.

That the behavior of the "man on the street" has received so little attention is odd, because it captures in quintessential, almost primordial form the combination of the ordinary and the bizarre which we have learned to regard as normal. The "man on the street" is a synonym for everyone, which in our society means every man. The behavior he casually accords to randomly passing women he has never seen before serves to identify him as a member of the ruling group, to whom the streets and the society belong. And at the same time this behavior, looked at with an analytic eye, is very peculiar. The anthropologist from outer space, that popular device for viewing the world with a bit more perspective, would be very astonished to find adult males moaning, jumping, whistling, singing, honking, winking, contorting face and body, hissing obscenities, laughing hysterically, and mumbling hoarse endearments to perfect strangers without apparent provocation. However odd, though, these single and seemingly irrational instances add up to a pattern, and the pattern spells intimidation.

Women are assigned, in this interaction, an inevitably passive part. They have a number of available responses, but their response makes little difference. A woman can ignore what she sees or hears, she can reply, she can curse, keep walking, stop, try for a disarming smile, get angry, start a discussion. What she does has little influence. A friendly answer may stop the man, or it may encourage him to further intimacies; threats and curses may silence him, or they may prompt genuine aggression. The language itself

puts us at a permanent disadvantage; it is hard to exchange serious insults without using sexual put-downs that invariably go against women. And passersby, far from supporting a woman who defends herself, will shed their former indifference to disapprove of feminine vulgarity.

It is commonly supposed that certain countries and cultures display this behavior more than others; the Mediterranean cultures, particularly, are assumed to be swarming with papagallos dedicated to the female foreign tourist. In fact, this form of male behavior is distributed quite evenly across the continents, races, and generations. The nationalist author Qasim Amin deplored the harassment of the heavily veiled Egyptian women at the turn of the century and in fact attributed masculine aggression to the veil. As a sign of women's inferior status, he argued, it encouraged men to treat them with disrespect and take liberties. This interpretation comes very close to the truth. Like other forms of sexual violence, harassment has little to do with the individual woman and nothing to do with sex; the issue is power.

Whether you wear a slit skirt or are covered from head to foot in a black chador, the message is not that you are attractive enough to make a man lose his self-control but that the public realm belongs to him and you are there by his permission as long as you follow his rules and as long as you remember your place. Badr-al-Moluk Bamdad recalls in her book on growing up in Iran that there was no way for a woman to win this game; if, in the opinion of any passing male, one's veil was not wrapped with sufficient modesty, one could be insulted, reprimanded, and threatened, while if obediently covered one would be followed and taunted by boys and young men shouting that one looked like a "black crow or an inkwell."[1]

Harassment of women is timeless, but the notion that women really like it and feel flattered is a refinement that has been added more recently. Women's own accounts have always shown a clear awareness of the essential hostility implied by these male attentions, even when they didn't put that awareness into the context of any more general picture of sexist structures. Descriptions have been handed down to us from many different sources. Evelyn Scott, an American woman who later was to become a successful author, spent the year of 1916 in Brazil with her lover. They were poor, she was pregnant. In her diary, she wrote that, in Rio, "something objectionable always occurred" when she went outdoors unaccompanied. "Perhaps it is because I am only twenty years old," she wrote. "Perhaps it is because I am shabbily dressed. I know perfectly well that I am not particularly pretty. Inwardly shrinking and cold with an obscure fear, I make it a point to look very directly at all the men who speak to me. I want to shame them by the straightforwardness of my gaze. Perhaps I am ridiculous. If I could consider sex more factually and with less mystical solemnity I might find amusement in the stupidity of these individuals who can't be so sinister after all."[2]

Anger and an "obscure fear" are the most common responses of women, and those feelings are all the greater when the situation seems too intimidating to allow a reply. Pretending to have heard nothing, looking away, hoping the men will get bored and stop or will be too busy with the woman walking in front of you to attend to you are calculations that increase the impact of the experience. A twenty-two-year-old law student remembered one pivotal incident in her life: "I was seventeen, and just walking around downtown with my friend Marie. Two men started talking to us, making jokes and telling us to come with them. They grabbed our arms and tried to pull us along. Marie got angry and told them to let us go. The men pushed her against a building and started shaking her and saying she was unfriendly and stuck up and should watch out. Finally they left. It was afternoon and there were a lot of people around, but nobody said anything. At the time I learned from that that it was better to ignore men who talked to you like that. If you act like you don't care, they usually let you go without any trouble. I don't think that's a very good conclusion to draw, but I still don't know how to act in situations like that without getting into trouble."

What is going on in the minds of the men who do this? Not much, judging from their difficulties in articulating their intentions. We interviewed sixty men, choosing a range of age groups out of those who addressed us on the street. (Incidentally, this was the only female response we found that genuinely and predictably disarms the harassing male, so if you want to transform a lewdly smirking man into a politely confused one within a matter of seconds you need only pull a mimeographed questionnaire out of your bag and inform him that he is part of a research project. This method, however, is rather time-consuming.) Pressed for an explanation of their behavior, most of the men initially played it down. Boredom and a feeling of youthful camaraderie that came over them when discussing women with other men emerged as the most frequent feelings prompting harassment. The notion that women disliked this and felt infringed upon in their freedom of movement was a novel one for most men, not because they had another image of the woman's response but because they had never given it any thought at all. Only a minority, around 15 percent, explicitly set out to anger or humiliate their victims. This is

the same group that employs graphic sexual commentary and threats. Other forms of antagonism often become mixed up with the sexual. Some migrant laborers or construction workers insult not so much the woman as the snobbish privileged class she symbolizes to them. Another minority of men believes with firm conviction that women enjoy receiving their attention. One forty-five-year-old construction worker portrayed himself as a kind of benefactor to womanhood and claimed to specialize in older and less attractive women to whom, he was sure, his display of sexual interest was certain to be the highlight in an otherwise drab and joyless existence. A significant group of men, around 20 percent, said that they would not engage in this behavior when alone, but only in the company of male friends. This supports the explanation that the harassment of women is a form of male bonding, of demonstrating solidarity and joint power.

The symbolic nature of the behavior is its most important attribute. A surprising finding was that harassment declines in the late evening and during the night, and that men are then more likely to display the kind of behavior typical of the avoidance usually shown to strangers in public or crowded situations: averting one's eyes, accelerating the pace of walking to keep a distance, etc. At first glance, this finding is surprising. It would seem that harassment would be even more effective at night, even more intimidating to the woman. Probably, this is precisely the reason it declines during the night; on a deserted street, it would be *too* effective. The woman, not merely annoyed or unnerved but genuinely alarmed, might well be driven to an "extreme" response (such as calling for help) that the good citizen would not like to have to explain. In the daytime, he takes no such risk. The age, education, and income of the man make little difference; in their street behavior, they revert to a primordially uniform condition across the lines of class and generation. Younger men tend to be more aggressive, and older men to lower their voices and whisper hastily as they pass you. Some areas are exempt altogether: small villages, where all the inhabitants know each other, and residential suburban areas.

The genuinely *public* world is the main arena for harassment. The street, as a place where strangers encounter each other, is also the place where societies have always taken care to clearly mark the lines of order and status. It is on the streets that members of subordinate groups have to wear special clothing or identifying marks, that they must salute, take off their hat, or jump down from the sidewalk to make way for the members of the superior group. Harassment is a way of ensuring that women will not feel at ease, that they will remember their role as sexual beings available to men and not consider themselves equal citizens participating in public life. But the ritual of harassment does more than that. By its seeming harmlessness and triviality, it blurs the borders of women's right to personal integrity, and encourages men who would never commit a violent crime against a strange woman to participate in minor transgressions against her right to move freely, to choose which interactions to participate in and which people to communicate with. By making of the "man on the street," the average man, a minor sex offender, it also makes him an accomplice in the more massive forms of violence against women.

NOTES

1. Badr-al-Molak Bamdad, *Women's Emancipation in Iran* (New York, 1977)

2. Mary Jane Moffat and Charlotte Painter, eds., *Revelations: Diaries of Women* (New York: Vintage, 1974), p. 100.

R E A D I N G   4 1

Fraternities and Rape on Campus

PATRICIA YANCEY MARTIN and ROBERT A. HUMMER

Rapes are perpetrated on dates, at parties, in chance encounters, and in specially planned circumstances. That group structure and processes, rather than individual values or characteristics, are the impetus for many rape episodes was documented by Blanchard (1959) thirty years ago (also see Geis 1971), yet sociologists have failed to pursue this theme (for an exception, see Chancer 1987). A recent review of research (Muehlenhard and Linton 1987) on sexual violence, or rape, devotes only a few pages to the situational contexts of rape events, and these are conceptualized as potential risk factors for individuals rather than qualities of rape-prone social contexts.

Many rapes, far more than come to the public's attention, occur in fraternity houses on college and university campuses, yet little research has analyzed fraternities at American colleges and universities as rape-prone contexts

Patricia Yancey Martin and Robert A. Hummer, "Fraternities and Rape on Campus," *Gender & Society* 3, no. 4 (December 1989). Copyright © 1989 by Sociologists for Women in Society. Reprinted with the permission of Sage Publications, Inc.

(cf. Ehrhart and Sandler 1985). Most of the research on fraternities reports on samples of individual fraternity men. One group of studies compares the values, attitudes, perceptions, family socioeconomic status, psychological traits (aggressiveness, dependence), and so on, of fraternity and nonfraternity men (Bohrnstedt 1969; Fox, Hodge, and Ward 1987; Kanin 1967; Lemire 1979; Miller 1973). A second group attempts to identify the effects of fraternity membership over time on the values, attitudes, beliefs, or moral precepts of members (Hughes and Winston 1987; Marlowe and Auvenshine 1982; Miller 1973; Wilder, Hoyt, Doren, Hauck, and Zettle 1978; Wilder, Hoyt, Surbeck, Wilder, and Carney 1986). With minor exceptions, little research addresses the group and organizational context of fraternities or the social construction of fraternity life (for exceptions, see Letchworth 1969; Longino and Kart 1973; Smith 1964).

Gary Tash, writing as an alumnus and trial attorney in his fraternity's magazine, claims that over 90 percent of all gang rapes on college campuses involve fraternity men (1988, p. 2). Tash provides no evidence to substantiate this claim, but students of violence against women have been concerned with fraternity men's frequently reported involvement in rape episodes (Adams and Abarbanel 1988). Ehrhart and Sandler (1985) identify over fifty cases of gang rapes on campus perpetrated by fraternity men, and their analysis points to many of the conditions that we discuss here. Their analysis is unique in focusing on conditions in fraternities that make gang rapes of women by fraternity men both feasible and probable. They identify excessive alcohol use, isolation from external monitoring, treatment of women as prey, use of pornography, approval of violence, and excessive concern with competition as precipitating conditions to gang rape (also see Merton 1985; Roark 1987).

The study reported here confirmed and complemented these findings by focusing on both conditions and processes. We examined dynamics associated with the social construction of fraternity life, with a focus on processes that foster the use of coercion, including rape, in fraternity men's relations with women. Our examination of men's social fraternities on college and university campuses as groups and organizations led us to conclude that fraternities are a physical and sociocultural context that encourages the sexual coercion of women. We make no claims that all fraternities are "bad" or that all fraternity men are rapists. Our observations indicated, however, that rape is especially probable in fraternities because of the kinds of organizations they are, the kinds of members they have, the practices their members engage in, and a virtual absence of university or community oversight. Analyses that lay blame for rapes by fraternity men on "peer pressure" are, we feel, overly simplistic (cf. Burkhart 1989; Walsh 1989). We suggest, rather, that fraternities create a sociocultural context in which the use of coercion in sexual relations with women is normative and in which the mechanisms to keep this pattern of behavior in check are minimal at best and absent at worst. We conclude that unless fraternities change in fundamental ways, little improvement can be expected.

METHODOLOGY

Our goal was to analyze the group and organizational practices and conditions that create in fraternities an abusive social context for women. We developed a conceptual framework from an initial case study of an alleged gang rape at Florida State University that involved four fraternity men and an eighteen-year-old coed. The group rape took place on the third floor of a fraternity house and ended with the "dumping" of the woman in the hallway of a neighboring fraternity house. According to newspaper accounts, the victim's blood-alcohol concentration, when she was discovered, was .349 percent, more than three times the legal limit for automobile driving and an almost lethal amount. One law enforcement officer reported that sexual intercourse occurred during the time the victim was unconscious: "She was in a life-threatening situation" (*Tallahassee Democrat,* 1988b). When the victim was found, she was comatose and had suffered multiple scratches and abrasions. Crude words and a fraternity symbol had been written on her thighs (*Tampa Tribune,* 1988). When law enforcement officials tried to investigate the case, fraternity members refused to cooperate. This led, eventually, to a five-year ban of the fraternity from campus by the university and by the fraternity's national organization.

In trying to understand how such an event could have occurred, and how a group of over 150 members (exact figures are unknown because the fraternity refused to provide a membership roster) could hold rank, deny knowledge of the event, and allegedly lie to a grand jury, we analyzed newspaper articles about the case and conducted openended interviews with a variety of respondents about the case and about fraternities, rapes, alcohol use, gender relations, and sexual activities on campus. Our data included over 100 newspaper articles on the initial gang rape case; open-ended interviews with Greek (social fraternity and sorority) and non-Greek (independent) students (n = 20); university administrators (n = 8, five men, three women); and alumni advisers to Greek organizations (n = 6). Openended interviews were held also with judges, public and private defense attorneys, victim advocates, and state prosecutors regarding the processing of sexual assault cases. Data were analyzed using the grounded theory method (Glaser 1978; Martin and Turner 1986) . In the following analysis, concepts generated from the data analysis are integrated with the literature on men's social fraternities, sexual coercion, and related issues.

FRATERNITIES AND THE SOCIAL CONSTRUCTION OF MEN AND MASCULINITY

Our research indicated that fraternities are vitally concerned—more than with anything else—with masculinity (cf. Kanin 1967). They work hard to create a macho image and context and try to avoid any suggestion of "wimpishness," effeminacy, and homosexuality. Valued members display, or are willing to go along with, a narrow conception of masculinity that stresses competition, athleticism, dominance, winning, conflict, wealth, material possessions, willingness to drink alcohol, and sexual prowess vis-à-vis women.

Valued Qualities of Members

When fraternity members talked about the kind of pledges they prefer, a litany of stereotypical and narrowly masculine attributes and behaviors was recited and feminine or woman-associated qualities and behaviors were expressly denounced (cf. Merton 1985). Fraternities seek men who are "athletic," "big guys," good in intramural competition, "who can talk college sports." Males "who are willing to drink alcohol," "who drink socially," or "who can hold their liquor" are sought. Alcohol and activities associated with the recreational use of alcohol are cornerstones of fraternity social life. Nondrinkers are viewed with skepticism and rarely selected for membership.[1]

Fraternities try to avoid "geeks," nerds, and men said to give the fraternity a "wimpy" or "gay" reputation. Art, music, and humanities majors, majors in traditional women's fields (nursing, home economics, social work, education), men with long hair, and those whose appearance or dress violate current norms are rejected. Clean-cut, handsome men who dress well (are clean, neat, conforming, fashionable) are preferred. One sorority woman commented that "the top-ranking fraternities have the best looking guys."

One fraternity man, a senior, said his fraternity recruited "some big guys, very athletic" over a two-year period to help overcome its image of wimpiness. His fraternity had won the interfraternity competition for highest grade-point average several years running but was looked down on as "wimpy, dancy, even gay." With their bigger, more athletic recruits, "our reputation improved; we're a much more recognized fraternity now." Thus a fraternity's reputation and status depend on members' possession of stereotypically masculine qualities. Good grades, campus leadership, and community service are "nice" but masculinity dominance—for example, in athletic events, physical size of members, athleticism of members—counts most.

Certain social skills are valued. Men are sought who "have good personalities," are friendly, and "have the ability to relate to girls" (cf. Longino and Kart 1973). One fraternity man, a junior, said: "We watch a guy [a potential pledge] talk to women . . . we want guys who can relate to girls." Assessing a pledge's ability to talk to women is, in part, a preoccupation with homosexuality and a conscious avoidance of men who seem to have effeminate manners or qualities. If a member is suspected of being gay, he is ostracized and informally drummed out of the fraternity. A fraternity with a reputation as wimpy or tolerant of gays is ridiculed and shunned by other fraternities. Militant heterosexuality is frequently used by men as a strategy to keep each other in line (Kimmel 1987).

Financial affluence or wealth, a male-associated value in American culture, is highly valued by fraternities. In accounting for why the fraternity involved in the gang rape that precipitated our research project had been recognized recently as "the best fraternity chapter in the United States," a university official said: "They were good-looking, a big fraternity, had lots of BMWs [expensive, German-made automobiles]." After the rape, newspaper stories described the fraternity members' affluence, noting the high number of members who owned expensive cars (*St. Petersburg Times,* 1988).

The Status and Norms of Pledgeship

A pledge (sometimes called an associate member) is a new recruit who occupies a trial membership status for a specific period of time. The pledge period (typically ranging from ten to fifteen weeks) gives fraternity brothers an opportunity to assess and socialize new recruits. Pledges evaluate the fraternity also and decide if they want to become brothers. The socialization experience is structured partly through assignment of a Big Brother to each pledge. Big Brothers are expected to teach pledges how to become a brother and to support them as they progress through the trial membership period. Some pledges are repelled by the pledging experience, which can entail physical abuse; harsh discipline; and demands to be subordinate, follow orders, and engage in demeaning routines and activities, similar to those used by the military to "make men out of boys" during boot camp.

Characteristics of the pledge experience are rationalized by fraternity members as necessary to help pledges unite into a group, rely on each other, and join together against outsiders. The process is highly masculinist in execution as well as conception. A willingness to submit to authority, follow orders, and do as one is told is viewed as a sign of loyalty, togetherness, and unity. Fraternity pledges who find the pledge process offensive often drop out. Some do this by openly quitting, which can subject them to ridicule by brothers and other pledges, or they may deliberately fail to make the grades necessary for initiation or transfer schools and decline to reaffiliate with the fraternity on the new campus. One fraternity pledge who quit the fraternity he had pledged described an experience during pledgeship as follows:

> This one guy was always picking on me. No matter what I did, I was wrong. One night after dinner, he and two other guys called me and two other pledges into the chapter room. He said, "Here, X, hold this 25-pound bag of ice at arms' length 'til I tell you to stop." I did it even though my arms and hands were killing me. When I asked if I could stop, he grabbed me around the throat and lifted me off the floor. I thought he would choke me to death. He cussed me and called me all kinds of names. He took one of my fingers and twisted it until it nearly broke. . . . I stayed in the fraternity for a few more days, but then I decided to quit. I hated it. Those guys are sick. They like seeing you suffer.

Fraternities' emphasis on toughness, withstanding pain and humiliation, obedience to superiors, and using physical force to obtain compliance contributes to an interpersonal style that de-emphasizes caring and sensitivity but fosters intragroup trust and loyalty. If the least macho or most critical pledges drop out, those who remain may be more receptive to, and influenced by, masculinist values and practices that encourage the use of force in sexual relations with women and the covering up of such behavior (cf. Kanin 1967).

Norms and Dynamics of Brotherhood

Brother is the status occupied by fraternity men to indicate their relations to each other and their membership in a particular fraternity organization or group. Brother is a male-specific status; only males can become brothers, although women can become "Little Sisters," a form of pseudomembership. "Becoming a brother" is a rite of passage that follows the consistent and often lengthy display by pledges of appropriately masculine qualities and behaviors. Brothers have a quasifamilial relationship with each other, are normatively said to share bonds of closeness and support, and are sharply set off from nonmembers. Brotherhood is a loosely defined term used to represent the bonds that develop among fraternity members and the obligations and expectations incumbent upon them (cf. Marlowe and Auvenshine [1982] on fraternities' failure to encourage "moral development" in freshman pledges).

Some of our respondents talked about brotherhood in almost reverential terms, viewing it as the most valuable benefit of fraternity membership. One senior, a business-school major who had been affiliated with a fairly high-status fraternity throughout four years on campus, said:

> Brotherhood spurs friendship for life, which I consider its best aspect, although I didn't see it that way when I joined. Brotherhood bonds and unites. It instills values of caring about one another, caring about community, caring about ourselves. The values and bonds [of brotherhood] continually develop over the four years [in college] while normal friendships come and go.

Despite this idealization, most aspects of fraternity practice and conception are more mundane. Brotherhood often plays itself out as an overriding concern with masculinity and, by extension, femininity. As a consequence, fraternities comprise collectivities of highly masculinized men with attitudinal qualities and behavioral norms that predispose them to sexual coercion of women (cf. Kanin 1967; Merton 1985; Rapaport and Burkhart 1984). The norms of masculinity are complemented by conceptions of women and femininity that are equally distorted and stereotyped and that may enhance the probability of women's exploitation (cf. Ehrhart and Sandler 1985; Sanday 1981, 1986).

Practices of Brotherhood

Practices associated with fraternity brotherhood that contribute to the sexual coercion of women include a preoccupation with loyalty, group protection and secrecy, use of alcohol as a weapon, involvement in violence and physical force, and an emphasis on competition and superiority.

Loyalty, Group Protection, and Secrecy Loyalty is a fraternity preoccupation. Members are reminded constantly to be loyal to the fraternity and to their brothers. Among other ways, loyalty is played out in the practices of group protection and secrecy. The fraternity must be shielded from criticism. Members are admonished to avoid getting the fraternity in trouble and to bring all problems "to the chapter" (local branch of a national social fraternity) rather than to outsiders. Fraternities try to protect themselves from close scrutiny and criticism by the Interfraternity Council (a quasigoverning body composed of representatives from all social fraternities on campus), their fraternity's national office, university officials, law enforcement, the media, and the public. Protection of the fraternity often takes precedence over what is procedurally, ethically, or legally correct. Numerous examples were related to us of fraternity brothers' lying to outsiders to "protect the fraternity."

Group protection was observed in the alleged gang rape case with which we began our study. Except for one brother, a rapist who turned state's evidence, the entire remaining fraternity membership was accused by university and criminal justice officials of lying to protect the fraternity. Members consistently failed to cooperate even though the alleged crimes were felonies, involved only four men (two of whom were not even members of the local chapter), and the victim of the crime nearly died. According to a grand jury's findings, fraternity officers repeatedly broke appointments with law enforcement officials, refused to provide police with a list of members, and refused to cooperate with police and prosecutors investigating the case (*Florida Flambeau,* 1988).

Secrecy is a priority value and practice in fraternities, partly because full-fledged membership is premised on it (for confirmation, see Ehrhart and Sandler 1985; Longino and Kart 1973; Roark 1987). Secrecy is also a boundary-maintaining mechanism, demarcating in-group from out-group, us from them. Secret rituals, handshakes, and mottoes are revealed to pledge brothers as they are initiated into full brotherhood. Since only brothers are supposed to know a fraternity's secrets, such knowledge affirms membership in the fraternity and separates a brother from others. Extending secrecy tactics from protection of private knowledge to protection of the fraternity from criticism is a predictable development. Our interviews indicated that individual members knew the difference between right and wrong, but fraternity norms that emphasize loyalty, group protection, and secrecy often overrode standards of ethical correctness.

Alcohol as Weapon   Alcohol use by fraternity men is normative. They use it on weekdays to relax after class and on weekends to "get drunk," "get crazy," and "get laid." The use of alcohol to obtain sex from women is pervasive—in other words, it is used as a weapon against sexual reluctance. According to several fraternity men whom we interviewed, alcohol is the major tool used to gain sexual mastery over women (cf. Adams and Abarbanel 1988; Ehrhart and Sandler 1985). One fraternity man, a twenty-one-year-old senior, described alcohol use to gain sex as follows: "There are girls that you know will fuck, then some you have to put some effort into it. . . . You have to buy them drinks or find out if she's drunk enough. . . ."

A similar strategy is used collectively. A fraternity man said that at parties with Little Sisters: "We provide them with 'hunch punch' and things get wild. We get them drunk and most of the guys end up with one." " 'Hunch punch,' " he said, "is a girls' drink made up of overproof alcohol and powdered Kool-Aid, no water or anything, just ice. It's very strong. Two cups will do a number on a female." He had plans in the next academic term to surreptitiously give hunch punch to women in a "prim and proper" sorority because "having sex with prim and proper sorority girls is definitely a goal." These women are a challenge because they "won't openly consume alcohol and won't get openly drunk as hell." Their sororities have "standards committees" that forbid heavy drinking and easy sex.

In the gang rape case, our sources said that many fraternity men on campus believed the victim had a drinking problem and was thus an "easy make." According to newspaper accounts, she had been drinking alcohol on the evening she was raped; the lead assailant is alleged to have given her a bottle of wine after she arrived at his fraternity house. Portions of the rape occurred in a shower, and the victim was reportedly so drunk that her assailants had difficulty holding her in a standing position (*Tallahassee Democrat,* 1988a). While raping her, her assailants repeatedly told her they were members of another fraternity under the apparent belief that she was too drunk to know the difference. Of course, if she was too drunk to know who they were, she was too drunk to consent to sex (cf. Allgeier 1986; Tash 1988).

One respondent told us that gang rapes are wrong and can get one expelled, but he seemed to see nothing wrong in sexual coercion one-on-one. He seemed unaware that the use of alcohol to obtain sex from a woman is grounds for a claim that a rape occurred (cf. Tash 1988). Few women on campus (who also may not know these grounds) report date rapes, however; so the odds of detection and punishment are slim for fraternity men who use alcohol for "seduction" purposes (cf. Byington and Keeter 1988; Merton 1985).

Violence and Physical Force   Fraternity men have a history of violence (Ehrhart and Sandler 1985; Roark 1987). Their record of hazing, fighting, property destruction, and rape has caused them problems with insurance companies (Bradford 1986; Pressley 1987). Two university officials told us that fraternities "are the third riskiest property to insure behind toxic waste dumps and amusement parks." Fraternities are increasingly defendants in legal actions brought by pledges subjected to hazing (Meyer 1986; Pressley 1987) and by women who were raped by one or more members. In a recent alleged gang rape incident at another Florida university, prosecutors failed to file charges but the victim filed a civil suit against the fraternity nevertheless (*Tallahassee Democrat*, 1989).

Competition and Superiority   Interfraternity rivalry fosters in-group identification and out-group hostility. Fraternities stress pride of membership and superiority over other fraternities as major goals. Interfraternity rivalries take many forms, including competition for desirable pledges, size of pledge class, size of membership, size and appearance of fraternity house, superiority in intramural sports, highest grade-point averages, giving the best parties, gaining the best or most campus leadership roles, and, of great importance, attracting and displaying "good-looking women." Rivalry is particularly intense over members, intramural sports, and women (cf. Messner 1989).

FRATERNITIES' COMMODIFICATION OF WOMEN

In claiming that women are treated by fraternities as commodities, we mean that fraternities knowingly, and intentionally, *use* women for their benefit. Fraternities use women as bait for new members, as servers of brothers' needs, and as sexual prey.

Women as Bait

Fashionably attractive women help a fraternity attract new members. As one fraternity man, a junior, said, "They are good bait." Beautiful, sociable women are believed to impress the right kind of pledges and give the impression that the fraternity can deliver this type of woman to its members. Photographs of shapely, attractive coeds are printed in fraternity brochures and videotapes that are distributed and shown to potential pledges. The women pictured are often dressed in bikinis, at the beach, and are pictured hugging the brothers of the fraternity. One university official says such recruitment materials give the message: "Hey, they're here for you, you can have whatever you want," and, "we have the best-looking women. Join us and you can have them too." Another commented: "Something's wrong when males join an all-male organization as the best place to meet women. It's so illogical."

Fraternities compete in promising access to beautiful women. One fraternity man, a senior, commented that "the attraction of girls [i.e., a fraternity's success in attracting women] is a big status symbol for fraternities." One university official commented that the use of women as a recruiting tool is so well entrenched that fraternities that might be willing to forgo it say they cannot afford to unless other fraternities do so as well. One fraternity man said, "Look, if we don't have Little Sisters, the fraternities that do will get all the good pledges." Another said, "We won't have as good a rush [the period during which new members are assessed and selected] if we don't have these women around."

In displaying good-looking, attractive, skimpily dressed, nubile women to potential members, fraternities implicitly, and sometimes explicitly, promise sexual access to women. One fraternity man commented that "part of what being in a fraternity is all about is the sex" and explained how his fraternity uses Little Sisters to recruit new members:

> We'll tell the sweetheart [the fraternity's term for Little Sister], "You're gorgeous; you can get him." We'll tell her to fake a scam and she'll go hang all over him during a rush party, kiss him, and he thinks he's done wonderful and wants to join. The girls think it's great too. It's flattering for them.

Women as Servers

The use of women as servers is exemplified in the Little Sister program. Little Sisters are undergraduate women who are rushed and selected in a manner parallel to the recruitment of fraternity men. They are affiliated with the fraternity in a formal but unofficial way and are able, indeed required, to wear the fraternity's Greek letters. Little Sisters are not full-fledged fraternity members, however; and fraternity national offices and most universities do not register or regulate them. Each fraternity has an officer called Little Sister Chairman who oversees their organization and activities. The Little Sisters elect officers among themselves, pay monthly dues to the fraternity, and have well-defined roles. Their dues are used to pay for the fraternity's social events, and Little Sisters are expected to attend and hostess fraternity parties and hang around the house to make it a "nice place to be." One fraternity man, a senior, described Little Sisters this way: "They are very social girls, willing to join in, be affiliated with the group, devoted to the fraternity." Another member, a sophomore, said: "Their sole purpose is social—attend parties, attract new members, and 'take care' of the guys."

Our observations and interviews suggested that women selected by fraternities as Little Sisters are physically attractive, possess good social skills, and are willing to devote time and energy to the fraternity and its members. One undergraduate woman gave the following job description for Little Sisters to a campus newspaper:

It's not just making appearances at all the parties but entails many more responsibilities. You're going to be expected to go to all the intramural games to cheer the brothers on, support and encourage the pledges, and just be around to bring some extra life to the house. [As a Little Sister] you have to agree to take on a new responsibility other than studying to maintain your grades and managing to keep your checkbook from bouncing. You have to make time to be a part of the fraternity and support the brothers in all they do. (*The Tomahawk,* 1988)

The title of Little Sister reflects women's subordinate status; fraternity men in a parallel role are called Big Brothers. Big Brothers assist a sorority primarily with the physical work of sorority rushes, which, compared to fraternity rushes, are more formal, structured, and intensive. Sorority rushes take place in the daytime and fraternity rushes at night so fraternity men are free to help. According to one fraternity member, Little Sister status is a benefit to women because it gives them a social outlet and "the protection of the brothers." The gender-stereotypic conceptions and obligations of these Little Sister and Big Brother statuses indicate that fraternities and sororities promote a gender hierarchy on campus that fosters subordination and dependence in women, thus encouraging sexual exploitation and the belief that it is acceptable.

Women as Sexual Prey

Little Sisters are a sexual utility. Many Little Sisters do not belong to sororities and lack peer support for refraining from unwanted sexual relations. One fraternity man (whose fraternity has sixty-five members and eighty-five Little Sisters) told us they had recruited "wholesale" in the prior year to "get lots of new women." The structural access to women that the Little Sister program provides and the absence of normative supports for refusing fraternity members' sexual advances may make women in this program particularly susceptible to coerced sexual encounters with fraternity men.

Access to women for sexual gratification is a presumed benefit of fraternity membership, promised in recruitment materials and strategies and through brothers' conversations with new recruits. One fraternity man said: "We always tell the guys that you get sex all the time, there's always new girls. . . . After I became a Greek, I found out I could be with females at will." A university official told us that, based on his observations, "no one [i.e., fraternity men] on this campus wants to have 'relationships.' They just want to have fun [i.e., sex]." Fraternity men plan and execute strategies aimed at obtaining sexual gratification, and this occurs at both individual and collective levels.

Individual strategies include getting a woman drunk and spending a great deal of money on her. As for collective strategies, most of our undergraduate interviewees agreed that fraternity parties often culminate in sex and that this outcome is planned. One fraternity man said fraternity parties often involve sex and nudity and can "turn into orgies." Orgies may be planned in advance, such as the Bowery Ball party held by one fraternity. A former fraternity member said of this party:

The entire idea behind this is sex. Both men and women come to the party wearing little or nothing. There are pornographic pinups on the walls and usually porno movies playing on the TV. The music carries sexual overtones. . . . They just get schnockered [drunk] and, in most cases, they also get laid.

When asked about the women who come to such a party, he said: "Some Little Sisters just won't go. . . . The girls who do are looking for a good time, girls who don't know what it is, things like that."

Other respondents denied that fraternity parties are orgies but said that sex is always talked about among the brothers and they all know "who each other is doing it with." One member said that most of the time, guys have sex with their girlfriends "but with socials, girlfriends aren't allowed to come and it's their [members'] big chance [to have sex with other women]." The use of alcohol to help them get women into bed is a routine strategy at fraternity parties.

CONCLUSIONS

In general, our research indicated that the organization and membership of fraternities contribute heavily to coercive and often violent sex. Fraternity houses are occupied by same-sex (all men) and same-age (late teens, early twenties) peers whose maturity and judgment is often less than ideal. Yet fraternity houses are private dwellings that are mostly off-limits to, and away from scrutiny of, university and community representatives, with the result that fraternity house events seldom come to the attention of outsiders. Practices associated with the social construction of fraternity brotherhood emphasize a macho conception of men and masculinity, a narrow, stereotyped conception of women and femininity, and the treatment of women as commodities. Other practices contributing to coercive sexual relations and the cover-up of rapes include excessive alcohol use, competitiveness, and normative support for deviance and secrecy (cf. Bogal-Allbritten and Allbritten 1985; Kanin 1967).

Some fraternity practices exacerbate others. Brotherhood norms require "sticking together" regardless of right or wrong; thus rape episodes are unlikely to be stopped or reported to outsiders, even when witnesses disapprove. The ability to use alcohol without scrutiny by authorities and alcohol's frequent association with violence, including sexual coercion, facilitates rape in fraternity houses. Fraternity norms that emphasize the value of maleness and masculinity over femaleness and femininity and that elevate the status of men and lower the status of women in members' eyes undermine perceptions and treatment of women as persons who deserve consideration and care (cf. Ehrhart and Sandler 1985; Merton 1985).

Androgynous men and men with a broad range of interests and attributes are lost to fraternities through their recruitment practices. Masculinity of a narrow and stereotypical type helps create attitudes, norms, and practices that predispose fraternity men to coerce women sexually, both individually and collectively (Allgeier 1986; Hood 1989; Sanday 1981, 1986). Male athletes on campus may be similarly disposed for the same reasons (Kirshenbaum 1989; Telander and Sullivan 1989).

Research into the social contexts in which rape crimes occur and the social constructions associated with these contexts illumine rape dynamics on campus. Blanchard (1959) found that group rapes almost always have a leader who pushes others into the crime. He also found that the leader's latent homosexuality, desire to show off to his peers, or fear of failing to prove himself a man are frequently an impetus. Fraternity norms and practices contribute to the approval and use of sexual coercion as an accepted tactic in relations with women. Alcohol-induced compliance is normative, whereas, presumably, use of a knife, gun, or threat of bodily harm would not be because

the woman who "drinks too much" is viewed as "causing her own rape" (cf. Ehrhart and Sandler 1985).

Our research led us to conclude that fraternity norms and practices influence members to view the sexual coercion of women, which is a felony crime, as sport, a contest, or a game (cf. Sato 1988). This sport is played not between men and women but between men and men. Women are the pawns or prey in the interfraternity rivalry game; they prove that a fraternity is successful or prestigious. The use of women in this way encourages fraternity men to see women as objects and sexual coercion as sport. Today's societal norms support young women's right to engage in sex at their discretion, and coercion is unnecessary in a mutually desired encounter. However, nubile young women say they prefer to be "in a relationship" to have sex while young men say they prefer to "get laid" without a commitment (Muehlenhard and Linton 1987). These differences may reflect, in part, American puritanism and men's fears of sexual intimacy or perhaps intimacy of any kind. In a fraternity context, getting sex without giving emotionally demonstrates "cool" masculinity. More important, it poses no threat to the bonding and loyalty of the fraternity brotherhood (cf. Farr 1988). Drinking large quantities of alcohol before having sex suggests that "scoring" rather than intrinsic sexual pleasure is a primary concern of fraternity men.

Unless fraternities' composition, goals, structures, and practices change in fundamental ways, women on campus will continue to be sexual prey for fraternity men. As all-male enclaves dedicated to opposing faculty and administration and to cementing in-group ties, fraternity members eschew any hint of homosexuality. Their version of masculinity transforms women, and men with womanly characteristics, into the out-group. "Womanly men" are ostracized; feminine women are used to demonstrate members' masculinity. Encouraging renewed emphasis on their founding values (Longino and Kart 1973), service orientation and activities (Lemire 1979), or members' moral development (Marlowe and Auvenshine 1982) will have little effect on fraternities' treatment of women. A case for or against fraternities cannot be made by studying individual members. The fraternity qua group and organization is at issue. Located on campus along with many vulnerable women, embedded in a sexist society, and caught up in masculinist goals, practices, and values, fraternities' violation of women—including forcible rape—should come as no surprise.

ACKNOWLEDGMENTS

We gratefully thank Meena Harris and Diane Mennella for assisting with data collection. The senior author thanks the graduate students in her fall 1988 graduate research methods seminar for help with developing the initial conceptual framework. Judith Lorber and two anonymous *Gender & Society* referees made numerous suggestions for improving our article and we thank them also.

NOTES

1. Recent bans by some universities on open-keg parties at fraternity houses have resulted in heavy drinking before coming to a party and an increase in drunkenness among those who attend. This may aggravate, rather than improve, the treatment of women by fraternity men at parties.

REFERENCES

Allgeier, Elizabeth. 1986. "Coercive Versus Consensual Sexual Interactions." G. Stanley Hall Lecture to American Psychological Association Annual Meeting, Washington, DC, August.

Adams, Aileen, and Gail Abarbanel. 1988. *Sexual Assault on Campus: What Colleges Can Do.* Santa Monica, CA: Rape Treatment Center.

Blanchard, W. H. 1959. "The Group Process in Gang Rape." *Journal of Social Psychology* 49:259–66.

Bogal-Allbritten, Rosemarie B., and William L. Allbritten. 1985. "The Hidden Victims: Courtship Violence among College Students." *Journal of College Student Personnel* 43:201–4.

Bohrnstedt, George W. 1969. "Conservatism, Authoritarianism and Religiosity of Fraternity Pledges." *Journal of College Student Personnel* 27:36–43.

Bradford, Michael. 1986. "Tight Market Dries Up Nightlife at University." *Business Insurance* (March 2):2, 6.

Burkhart, Barry. 1989. Comments in Seminar on Acquaintance/Date Rape Prevention: A National Video Teleconference, February 2.

Burkhart, Barry R., and Annette L. Stanton. 1985. "Sexual Aggression in Acquaintance Relationships." Pp. 43–65 in *Violence in Intimate Relationships,* ed. G. Russell. Englewood Cliffs, NJ: Spectrum.

Byington, Diane B., and Karen W. Keeter. 1988. "Assessing Needs of Sexual Assault Victims on a University Campus." Pp. 23–31 in *Student Services: Responding to Issues and Challenges.* Chapel Hill: University of North Carolina Press.

Chancer, Lynn S. 1987. "New Bedford, Massachusetts, March 6, 1983–March 22, 1984: The 'Before and After' of a Group Rape." *Gender & Society* 1:239–60.

Ehrhart, Julie K., and Bernice R. Sandler. 1985. *Campus Gang Rape: Party Games?* Washington, DC: Association of American Colleges.

Farr, K. A. 1988. "Dominance Bonding through the Good Old Boys Sociability Network." *Sex Roles* 18:259–77.

Florida Flambeau. 1988. "Pike Members Indicted in Rape." (May 19):1, 5.

Fox, Elaine, Charles Hodge, and Walter Ward. 1987. "A Comparison of Attitudes Held by Black and White Fraternity Members." *Journal of Negro Education* 56:521–34.

Geis, Gilbert. 1971. "Group Sexual Assaults." *Medical Aspects of Human Sexuality* 5:101–13.

Glaser, Barney G. 1978. *Theoretical Sensitivity: Advances in the Methodology of Grounded Theory.* Mill Valley, CA: Sociology Press.

Hood, Jane. 1989. "Why Our Society Is Rape-Prone." *New York Times,* May 16.

Hughes, Michael J., and Roger B. Winston, Jr. 1987. "Effects of Fraternity Membership on Interpersonal Values." *Journal of College Student Personnel* 45:405–11.

Kanin, Eugene J. 1967. "Reference Groups and Sex Conduct Norm Violations." *The Sociological Quarterly* 8:495–504.

Kimmel, Michael, ed. 1987. *Changing Men: New Directions in Research on Men and Masculinity.* Newbury Park, CA: Sage.

Kirshenbaum, Jerry. 1989. "Special Report, An American Disgrace: A Violent and Unprecedented Lawlessness Has Arisen among College Athletes in all Parts of the Country." *Sports Illustrated* (February 27):16–19.

Lemire, David. 1979. "One Investigation of the Stereotypes Associated with Fraternities and Sororities." *Journal of College Student Personnel* 37:54–57.

Letchworth, G. E. 1969. "Fraternities Now and in the Future." *Journal of College Student Personnel* 10:118–22.

Longino, Charles F., Jr., and Cary S. Kart. 1973. "The College Fraternity: An Assessment of Theory and Research." *Journal of College Student Personnel* 31:118–25.

Marlowe, Anne F., and Dwight C. Auvenshine. 1982. "Greek Membership: Its Impact on the Moral Development of College Freshmen." *Journal of College Student Personnel* 40:53–57.

Martin, Patricia Yancey, and Barry A. Turner. 1986. "Grounded Theory and Organizational Research." *Journal of Applied Behavioral Science* 22:141–57.

Merton, Andrew. 1985. "On Competition and Class: Return to Brotherhood." *Ms.* (September):60–65, 121–22.

Messner, Michael. 1989. "Masculinities and Athletic Careers." *Gender & Society* 3:71–88.

Meyer, T. J. 1986. "Fight Against Hazing Rituals Rages on Campuses." *Chronicle of Higher Education* (March 12):34–36.

Miller, Leonard D. 1973. "Distinctive Characteristics of Fraternity Members." *Journal of College Student Personnel* 31:126–28.

Muehlenhard, Charlene L., and Melaney A. Linton. 1987. "Date Rape and Sexual Aggression in Dating Situations: Incidence and Risk Factors." *Journal of Counseling Psychology* 34:186–96.

Pressley, Sue Anne. 1987. "Fraternity Hell Night Still Endures." *Washington Post* (August 11):B1.

Rapaport, Karen, and Barry R. Burkhart. 1984. "Personality and Attitudinal Characteristics of Sexually Coercive College Males." *Journal of Abnormal Psychology* 93:216–21.

Roark, Mary L. 1987. "Preventing Violence on College Campuses." *Journal of Counseling and Development* 65:367–70.

Sanday, Peggy Reeves. 1981. "The Socio-Cultural Context of Rape: A Cross-Cultural Study." *Journal of Social Issues* 37:5–27.

———. 1986. "Rape and the Silencing of the Feminine." Pp. 84–101 in *Rape,* ed. S. Tomaselli and R. Porter. Oxford: Basil Blackwell.

St. Petersburg Times. 1988. "A Greek Tragedy." (May 29):1F, 6F.

Sato, Ikuya. 1988. "Play Theory of Delinquency: Toward a General Theory of 'Action.' " *Symbolic Interaction* 11:191–212.

Smith, T. 1964. "Emergence and Maintenance of Fraternal Solidarity." *Pacific Sociological Review* 7:29–37.

Tallahassee Democrat. 1988a. "FSU Fraternity Brothers Charged" (April 27):1A, 12A.

———. 1988b. "FSU Interviewing Students about Alleged Rape" (April 24):1D.

———. 1989. "Woman Sues Stetson in Alleged Rape" (March 19):3B.

Tampa Tribune. 1988. "Fraternity Brothers Charged in Sexual Assault of FSU Coed." (April 27):6B.

Tash, Gary B. 1988. "Date Rape." *The Emerald of Sigma Pi Fraternity* 75(4):1–2.

Telander, Rick, and Robert Sullivan. 1989. "Special Report, You Reap What You Sow." *Sports Illustrated* (February 27):20–34.

The Tomahawk. 1988. "A Look Back at Rush, A Mixture of Hard Work and Fun" (April/May):3D.

Walsh, Claire. 1989. Comments in Seminar on Acquaintance/Date Rape Prevention: A National Video Teleconference, February 2.

Wilder, David H., Arlyne E. Hoyt, Dennis M. Doren, William E. Hauck, and Robert D. Zettle. 1978. "The Impact of Fraternity and Sorority Membership on Values and Attitudes." *Journal of College Student Personnel* 36:445–49.

Wilder, David H., Arlyne E. Hoyt, Beth Shuster Surbeck, Janet C. Wilder, and Patricia Imperatrice Carney. 1986. "Greek Affiliation and Attitude Change in College Students." *Journal of College Student Personnel* 44:510–19.

"I Am Not a Rapist!" Why College Guys Are Confronting Sexual Violence

JOHN STOLTENBERG

What follows is an emotionally charged conversation among members of a Duke University student organization called Men Acting for Change (MAC), one of many new men's groups at colleges and universities across the United States and Canada. Besides meeting regularly to talk personally, MAC members present programs about gender and sexuality, focusing on sexual violence and homophobia, to fraternities and other campus groups.

MAC came to national prominence in the United States when members appeared in a segment about pornography on the ABC newsmagazine program "20/20." On January 28, 1993, millions of viewers heard these college-age males speak graphically about the negative effects of pornography, including *Playboy,* on their sex lives and their relationships with women.

A year earlier, Kate Wenner, an ABC producer, asked to pick my brains about how to do a pornography story that hadn't been done before. Over an amiable lunch at a café near Lincoln Center, I suggested she report how pornography has become a primary form of sex education for young men. She liked the idea and tracked down MAC. The resulting broadcast included footage of frank conversations among both female and male Duke students and was perhaps the most astute coverage of pornography's interpersonal effects yet to appear on network television.

After the "20/20" segment aired, MAC members were invited to appear on "Oprah," "Donahue," "Jerry Springer," "Maury Povich," and "Montel Williams," but they declined

John Stoltenberg, " 'I Am Not A Rapist!' Why College Guys are Confronting Sexual Violence" from *Feminism and Men: Reconstructing Gender Relations,* edited by Steven P. Schact and Doris W. Ewing (New York: New York University Press, 1998). Reprinted with the permission of the Elaine Markson Literary Agency.

to have their stories sensationalized. Meanwhile *Playboy* went ballistic and, in an apparent attempt at damage control, ridiculed them in print as "the pointy-headed, wet-behind-the-scrotum boys at Duke."

In January 1994, curious to know what makes MAC tick, I traveled to Durham, North Carolina, to attend the third annual Student Conference on Campus Sexual Violence, to be held at Duke. The brochure promised "focus on student activism and involvement in the anti-rape movement" and quoted Jason Schultz, a conference organizer and "20/20" participant: "Through our work against rape, we take control of our future and generate the skills and perspectives that we need to help make it a better, safer place for both women and men." The afternoon before the conference opened, Jason arranged a private conversation in his home among five MAC members. They understood that I would sit in, ask questions, and try to get an edited transcript of their conversation published where it could contribute to more accurate understanding of the student movement against sexual violence.

As I listened, I realized that these young men had taken the meaning of sexual violence to heart in some intensely personal and generationally specific new ways. Everyone in the group knew friends who had been sexually assaulted. At one point I asked them to estimate how many. One said that one in five of his friends had told him this. Another said fifty. Another said that among his twenty to twenty-five friends who had been sexually assaulted, he also knew the perpetrator in half the cases.

At another point one told something he had never before shared with his fellow MAC members: he himself had been sexually molested in his youth. That dramatic moment was generationally specific too, I realized. Such a disclosure would never have occurred among college-age males even a decade before. The vocabulary and sense of social safety would simply not have existed.

I came to understand that what these college-age males had to say is historically unprecedented: they had each become aware, through personal experience, of their own stake in confronting sexual violence.

There is a newsworthy story here, I thought to myself, a trend to be watched. An extraordinary new student-based social-change movement has begun; yet no major news-gathering medium has thought to listen in to the generationally specific experience represented by these five members of MAC.[1] Although they spoke as individuals and from particular viewpoints—the group was a mix of straight, bi, and gay; white and black—they also seemed at times to speak on behalf of many more male agemates than themselves. Quite matter-of-factly, without any prompting, they each described an experience now so common that it may define their generation more profoundly than any war ever has: how it feels to be perceived by female peers as a potential rapist.

Ever since the women's movement began to bring sexual violence to light in the early 1970s, the extent of rape and the extent of women's fears of it have been trivialized, refuted, and ridiculed by mainstream media. Today the aspirations of campus activists to radical gender egalitarianism and eroticized equality are similarly distorted in the popular press. For example, in the early 1990s students at Antioch College developed a comprehensive, nine-page policy spelling out the meaning of consent in sexual contact and conduct; defining and prohibiting a list of offenses that included rape, sexual assault, "sexual imposition," and nondisclosure of a known HIV-positive status; and detailing fair hearing procedures and remedies in case of violation. This pathbreaking, gender-neutral, ethically acute initiative was widely sneered at by media commentators who had never read it, never talked to the students who drafted and implemented it. During the 1960s and early 1970s, many "with it" magazine and book editors reveled in the ribald romance of covering the radical student antiwar movement in depth and at length. By contrast, today's middle-age male media decision makers act as if their journalistic radar screens got stuck in time along with the anachronistic sexual politics of their youth. Nostalgic for the 1960s "sexual revolution" days before feminism made "no" even an option for women—when, in the hustle of the time, "Girls say yes to [sex with] boys who say no [to the military]"— today's middle-age male media decision makers package smug blather about "date-rape hysteria" (a *New York* magazine cover story) or "sexual correctness" (a *Newsweek* cover story) or "do-me feminism" (an *Esquire* cover story)

and sign up execrably researched diatribes about "morning-after misgivings" (Katie Roiphe) or "the new Victorianism" (Rene Denfield). Today's middle-age male media decision makers just don't get it.

What this conversation reveals, however, is that a significant subset of young males have started to get it. Typical of a brand-new kind of self-selected peer group, they voice values that do not much resemble the sexual politics of most men their fathers' age. Within their transient, education-centered communities, the social and relational meaning of sexual violence to young women has become apparent to them as an everyday, lived reality. Never before have so many young males struggled to take this reality on board in their moral map of the world, and never before have so many known that others are doing so also.

In the student antiwar movement of the 1960s, many young women of conscience organized politically on behalf of young men whose bodies were then regarded as most at risk—deployable as cannon fodder in an immoral military operation. Today, more and more young men of conscience have begun to understand their vital role in the student movement against sexual violence, and this time it is they who have put their lives on the line in behalf of the women whose bodies are most at risk.

For older menfolk—especially those who hold jobs in academia and are therefore in a position to offer material support and substantive resources—this movement presents a classic challenge for teachers: to listen to and learn from students.

When student antiwar activists of the 1960s brought new ideals and values into their subsequent work, family, and civic lives, the cultural and political impact of that movement was felt throughout the larger society for decades. As I write, the president of the United States is a man who in his student days protested the Vietnam war. Who would have guessed back then that the fledgling youth counterculture, vibrantly antimilitarist, would not only help halt a war but one day inform this nation's governance at the highest level?

Today, too, it is easy not to reckon the profound cultural and political shift portended by the values and ideals of young people in the burgeoning campus antirape movement. But who knows? One day this country could elect a president who in her or his student days protested, and helped end, men's war against women.

Q: Why did you get involved in Men Acting for Change?
WARREN HEDGES (30, PHD CANDIDATE IN ENGLISH)[2]: I got
    involved because of women I was close to and things

they had survived. When I walk on campus at night and a woman in front of me sees I'm a man walking behind her, her shoulders tense up and she starts walking more quickly. Her keys come out of her pocket in case she needs them to defend herself from me. It wouldn't do any good to try and convince her I'm a nice guy or "enlightened." I'm perceived as something that doesn't fit with what I want to be, and the only way to change that is by changing the broader social structure—laws and economic relations and things like that.

In our culture having a penis is supposed to be a package deal: You're supposed to have specific desires (for women) and pursue them in specific ways (aggressively, competitively), identify with men instead of women, have specific—and usually boring—sexual practices. There's this broad cultural discourse saying, "This is who you should be if you happen to have this particular organ." I can't create a space where I can express myself and be more upfront about my desires and my identifications and my practices and so forth without trying to change the larger social structures.

ANDY MOOSE (21, PRELAW ENGLISH MAJOR):   My reason for doing this came through a slow process, especially with MAC meetings, of having the space to really reflect about how I felt about a lot of emotional and personal issues that I hadn't spent much time as a man thinking about before. I'm in a fraternity and have seen a lot of abuses that go on within that system. I want to stay in there and work to improve the situation so that my fraternity brothers get to that process as well. I've felt it could help them, and also stop a lot of the abuses that were going on to other friends. It's personal for me, rather than seeing a great deal of violence and wanting to work towards stopping that. That's a major concern, but the bigger driving force for me is the personal gains that I see possible for people in working with these issues.

CARLTON LEFTWICH (25, PREMED):   I'm *twenty-five* years old and I have come to the realization that I've never had a healthy relationship with a woman. There's a lot of issues here that make me reflect on my opinion of women and how I treat them, how I deal with them, and how I could develop a healthy relationship with one. Healthy to me is looking at them and not saying. "Oh, that's a *woman's* point of view"— making everything that she says or feels inferior. I'd like to get on an even keel when discussing some-

thing with a woman and not just look at her and say, "She's a totally different kind of thing."

ERICK FINK (22, PSYCH MAJOR AND WOMEN'S STUDIES MINOR):   I took this intro to women's studies class and it hit me that this feminist stuff made a lot of sense. Like, even though you've never raped anyone or even thought about it, other men are doing that in your name and they're hurting people that you love in your name. All the pressure that men feel to act a certain way and do a certain thing and fit a certain mold—maybe it *used* to work, but it's not working now. And now I'm here, and I'm going to try to do something about it. I feel like I and people with penises have something to gain from the women's movement, a lot to gain: being able to be exactly who you are without having to be "a man" in the traditional sense.

I've felt very limited by patriarchy. My sense of masculinity mostly came from where everybody else's does, TV—"If you do this, chicks will dig you." That was what was masculine for me—how to attract the opposite sex. But I didn't want to be this macho guy. It's not that I didn't want to be; I just wasn't.

CARLTON: I never could identify with what straight was— this rugby-playing kind of rough-and-tumble guy, always having to prove that I was macho—so I just automatically thought that I had to be gay, because I was very sensitive and I loved classical music. I was not a quote unquote normal young man, because I never liked football. And I always heard, "Well, all guys like football—if you don't play football you're a sissy."

JASON SCHULTZ (22, PUBLIC POLICY MAJOR AND WOMEN'S STUDIES MINOR):   In high school I was one of the top ten in my class academically. The other nine were all girls. They were brilliant and they taught me—about math, physics, English. Learning from female peers really had a big influence. The culture tells you women are bimbos, don't know anything, and are ditzes, sex objects; but my reality was different. I had good relationships with women who were intellectual and spoke their mind and wouldn't let me get away with shit—in a very loving way. Not "Get the fuck out" but "You better change or *I'm* going to get the fuck out." When I got to college, the intelligent, assertive, self-confident women started calling themselves feminists, and these were the people I loved to hang out with—"Oh, sure I'll go to your meeting. Oh, that sounds like an interesting class"—and I started to get involved. But for me there was a piece missing. I went through fraternity rush, didn't find any men that I really liked to hang out with, and felt really stupid. Women in women's studies classes were focusing on women's experience, women's perspective—which made a lot of sense, because it's left out of traditional academia—but nothing was speaking to me on a first-person level. At that time there were a couple other men on campus who wanted the same thing, and it was framed as men interested in confronting sexual violence. It was this group that I felt could look at the other component, the part that I needed to match—not to feel isolated as much as I was sometimes, not to feel like I had to speak for men.

Q: How have you personally been affected by sexual violence?

JASON: My first year in college, a good friend of mine, a female friend, was avoiding me. We weren't communicating; we didn't have the intimacy I enjoyed so much. And I'm like, "What's up with you? What's bugging you? Did you flunk some test or something?" I knew that she had gone out with this guy, and I knew who he was, and she told me the story in brief detail: She was raped. And she was like, "That's why I don't feel comfortable around you— it's because I don't know who to trust anymore." I didn't blame her at all. I was pissed at him. I was *really* pissed at him. It made me angry that this guy had ruined a friendship of mine with somebody I cared about. Then when I saw this men-concerned-with-sexual-violence thing, it came together.

As a man doing this kind of work you get stories and stories—it's just exponential. I probably know fifty survivors personally—most of them through campus.

WARREN: The first person who told me she had survived a rape—here on campus by another Duke student on Valentine's Day—was during my first year in graduate school. For me it was a real hard lesson learning that just me being sensitive is not enough. This sort of thing was happening to women and it was going to change the way they reacted to all or most men, especially initially. And that prompted me to get involved with this program in Durham with men who batter their wives.

Once it became known on campus that I was concerned about these issues, and once I had a chance to speak at a Take Back the Night march, the number of stories I heard from women just seemed to multiply. One reason MAC has been so important to me is that I feel I've got an emotional support network now— not just feeling utterly overwhelmed by the number of stories that seemed to come flooding in. Probably one in five friends told me—attempted rapes and assaults, but usually rape.

CARLTON: When I was growing up I was abused sexually. I just internalized everything and left it there. It was through MAC I could come in contact with people who had a rape encounter and see how they handled it, how they were surviving it, without actually having to admit that I was someone who had been raped also. That was really difficult for me. But to see women have the courage to pick up their lives and keep on going—it's really empowering. I can feel for women a lot more now that I know that it was something that I had no control over and that it wasn't my fault. I can understand that helplessness and that dirty feeling, the pain and sorrow.

Most guys are like, "Well, how do you rape a male?" There are a lot of ways to rape a male. And I would say to any other male survivor, "Don't be ashamed." Even if it happened ten, fifteen, twenty years ago, it still happened, and you're going to have to deal with it. You're going to have to address those feelings. It's not going to be easy, but try and hook up with a group of guys that can really feel for you and care about you. And by caring for women—I guess I took that assumption, that these guys care about women—then they're obviously going to care about my plight and respect me.

ERICK: For the women I know that have been sexually assaulted or raped— I'd say 20 to 25 percent—it sticks with them; it changes their lives.

CARLTON: Your sense of security is gone, and once you lose your sense of security you're never going to get it back.

ERICK: There's an awful lot of fear out there—like if there's a woman sitting in a room with me alone, and we're sitting there talking, there's the chance that she is fearful of me.

CARLTON: Sometimes I just want to shout, "I'm not going to hurt you!"

JASON: Holding up a sign: "not a rapist"?

CARLTON: Yeah.

ANDY: My first experience of sexual violence was from the other side, knowing the male who was being accused. During freshman year at Duke, I was faced with a rape case that was going to the Judi [Judicial] Board. This was a huge shock for me—becoming aware of the size of the problem and the frequency with which these acts were going on. It was something I was completely unaware of in high school. Having a very dear personal friend share with me that they were assaulted, coupled with knowing someone accused of the rape—those two things at the same time forced me to try to understand how this could happen. I couldn't just say, "Well, it's obvious these people are incredibly violent," because I wasn't seeing that. How could this happen around me every day and these people don't show me any signs of violent tendencies? How could this be happening with such frequency?

As you begin to get involved, a lot more people, a shocking number, tell you things. It takes you aback, the numbers—between twenty and twenty-five good friends, very close. Mostly women, 90-some percent. I had one male friend share like that. And there were a number of stories where the male was someone I knew, probably a fourth of them. Actually more than that—probably half.

Talking with other people in MAC and doing programs on sexual violence helped me, because I felt I could do something. In a very basic way that feels good, to fight a situation that before you felt really helpless in. I have a little bit more understanding of how the event could happen—so it's not so much burning hatred towards that individual. I'm not so quick just to discard that person and say, "OK, he raped this woman so now I'm just going to not communicate with him any longer." I don't want to do that. There's definitely resentment and anger, a great deal of anger, and I try to suppress that as much as I can, because when you have these sorts of numbers around you, it's vital that you don't hate and cut that person off just because—. I mean, you become very lonely, obviously.

Q: How do you reach other men?

JASON: Standing up to them never seems to work. It seems to push them farther away, make them reactive. It's a balance of making them feel like I care what they say and being willing to sit down and listen to them for a long time, but then be willing to challenge them. Not saying, "Oh, you're a sexist pig—get the fuck outta here," but when the opportunity is there to say, "What you're saying really bothers me" or "I'd really like to talk to you about this because I'm learning where this is coming from."

CARLTON: Don't make men feel like a minority. There are a lot of men out there who really want to understand themselves and their feelings a lot more, and you can really turn somebody off with that raw anger that seems to be associated with feminists. That's intimidating to men. I know it is to me.

ANDY: A lot of the successes that I've been a part of talking with fraternity men came from catching them off guard. The minute some discussion on sexual violence comes up they become defensive. When they've gotten in these discussions with women or with non-Greek men, oftentimes it's led to an argument, they didn't feel very good about it, they don't want to talk about it, and so they don't deal with it. If there's something being discussed about a Greek function, they immediately assume that the fraternity men are going to be blamed, and they're going to defend themselves as not being a rapist or whatever. So a lot of the successes have come from surprise, when they realize there's a real conversation that's going to happen and it's not going to become some heated argument—because a lot of men haven't really thought about it much at all, and people really enjoy having an opportunity to reflect about their opinions, to recognize, "Wow, you know, I've thought about this and it really helped."

ERICK: I was talking to a good friend and he said, "You know what I think date rape is? I think this woman has sex with this guy and the next morning she decides she shouldn't have done it, so she just screams rape." And I'm like, "Well, you know, I remember not long ago I felt the same way. But if you really think about it, things like that can happen. On a date maybe with somebody that you might know very well or have been seeing for a long time, you could get violent with that person, couldn't you?" And he said, "Uh, I don't know." And I'm like, "Well, have you ever gotten so angry or so frustrated with your girlfriend that you could just—" And he's like, "Sure, I guess so." And there was a relation there, where I could see how he was feeling, and he could see how I was feeling too. I think if he had said that to a woman, she would be very offended—and rightfully so.

ANDY: You have to have discussions for the potential rapist, but also focus on how people contribute to an environment or make it easier for a rape to happen. A lot of times they don't recognize how they in a much more subtle way contribute or make these sorts of things easier to happen, by a comment or a particular action in a situation.

WARREN: Or by no action.

ANDY: Right, exactly, because so quickly they say, "Well, *I'm* not a rapist." They don't think about what environment you're establishing when you're having a party or you're making some joke or you don't say anything in a particular situation. It's better to have dialogue about those issues.

JASON: A lot of men don't hear what feminists are actually saying when it's coming from women. Their words are so devalued, and we value men's words more. My experience has been that it takes some patience, because if somebody said something sexist like "Oh, she deserved to be raped, look at how she's dressed," there's an instinct to want to confront that. But what seems to be more beneficial is to ask questions, maybe let the story weave itself a little more, find a deeper belief system, and figure out what about that issue to confront. I think with some men you can definitely do that.

WARREN: My formative experience thinking about male violence was working with men who beat their wives. They were ordered by the courts to attend. The men couldn't leave the program angry because they might go home and beat their partner. That was a real constraint on my need to be vindictive and self-righteous. There was a counselor who put it very well when he said, "Dealing with abusive men is like judo; you gotta grab ahold of their energy and move them someplace they don't expect to end up."

NOTES

1. I tried for two years to get this conversation into print. Among the publications that passed on it are *Cosmopolitan, Details, Elle, Glamour, Mademoiselle, Ms., On the Issues, Rolling Stone,* and the *Village Voice.*

2. Ages and academic concentrations are given as of the date of this conversation.

BEHIND CLOSED DOORS

KRISTEN GOLDEN

MAGGIE: When I was growing up, we moved every few years because my dad was an executive who was transferred often. I got to like moving. I'd think: "A whole new life—I'll start fresh and have all these new possibilities." I was married to Jennifer's father from when I was twenty-one until I was thirty-five. He got cancer in his early thirties. He was treated and was fine for a few years and we forgot all about it, thinking, "This will never come back." Suddenly he had a recurrence. He was in the hospital a while, and then he came home. There was nothing left for the doctors to do. He had a hospital bed in the middle of our living room, so I could take care of him and be with Jennifer, who was about eleven then. His illness took over my life, but I was so busy I hardly noticed. . . .

After he died, I started going out with somebody we'd been friends with. For years my husband had taken all my attention. I didn't feel restless when he was sick, but when he was gone, I thought, "Wow, here I am, thirty-five, and I'm ready for life." Maybe the timing was wrong, but I think your children are never actually going to like your going out with someone else. Jennifer didn't dislike Peter, but we all had a hard time.

Peter was recently divorced when we started seeing each other. Quite soon we said we'd like to get married, but somehow that didn't happen for a long time. Our situation turned out to be so difficult that our marriage didn't last too long, although I was actually very fond of him. He is the father of my younger daughter, Theresa.

Frank was the next one. I met him through some friends. We decided we wanted to get married. . . .

In the beginning, Frank and Jennifer didn't have a lot to do with each other. Before he came along, it was just the three of us, and my daughters and I had become closer than ever. Jennifer was trying to be supportive and helpful and, make me feel OK. She wanted me to be happy, so she tried to like Frank as best she could, but she didn't very much. I guess later she felt like she was the one who was right.

Frank was different from most people I'd known. Frank was a very quiet person—articulate but with a quiet voice. He was a real storyteller and pretty interesting for me to talk to. He was fond of my younger daughter. When we were dating, we'd often go out in the evenings, but when we saw each other in the day, my little one was always with us. He seemed to want more children. He had one that he had lost touch with through divorce. I wanted a father for my daughter and I liked the way he was with her. . . .

I don't know exactly when the violence started. I know we hadn't been together that long, maybe a few months. He was really sweet to me before we married, but one eye-opening thing happened on our honeymoon. There wasn't any physical violence, but he had been drinking and he was goading me. He told me what he really thought of my kids. That sure made my alarm bells go off. I don't really have a temper, but everybody has a point. We didn't exactly fight, but I was quite surprised at what he said. Then he was all sweet in the morning. It wasn't really verbal abuse—but in a way, it was.

Gradually Frank started to drink more and push me more. I never figured out what he wanted me to do or say. I felt like he thought he had to make me angry— and inevitably he would. He was intelligent, more so than Jennifer thought. He'd select the things about me that I prided myself on and say that they weren't true. Sometimes I would raise my voice when we fought, which my children were quite shocked at because I had never raised my voice to them.

After about a month and a half of that kind of treatment, I got really angry one night. I'm pretty sure this was the first time he was violent. The kids had gone to sleep. You know how traditionally a woman might slap a man's face once in a while, if he's extremely goading? I felt like he wanted to bring me to that point. I was never one to even spank children, but Frank made me so angry that I slapped him. That seemed to be the signal for him to go wild. I was shocked to suddenly be thrown around the room. Afterward he was all contrite—he had given me a black eye—but he said, "Well, you started it." I guess that's true. I thought, "Well, look what I did."

The next day you could see my black eye. I think anybody whose husband beats them up feels ashamed. I don't know why they should. Husbands should be ashamed, but they don't feel that way somehow. I guess you just feel like such an idiot to be staying with this person that you don't want to talk about it. And you don't suddenly stop loving someone just one night; it takes longer than that.

I still cared about Frank and didn't want to run him down with my children, so I didn't talk about it with the kids. Jennifer was busy with her own life, and her friends were really her life. Frank was very nice after that. I found out later that a lot of these things are just the usual pattern, but I hadn't had any experience with this sort of thing before.

There were a lot of good things in our relationship. The violence didn't really have anything to do with it. Of course, we would argue, but he would be really nice for a while and then gradually he would get back to criticizing me. The violence would always escalate when he'd been drinking, so I'd think, "If only he could give up drinking."

One time when he was drunk, he hit me so hard, I flew across the room and broke my arm. That was scary. I didn't feel like he was going to stop beating me, no matter what happened. I was in so much pain, I could barely talk, so it was hard for me to say anything, but that didn't calm him down. He kept going, even when he started to sober up. I was terrified. Finally, he felt bad and took me to the hospital.

When we got there, I didn't want to tell people what had happened. I guess I felt protective toward him. But also, this man is right there glaring at me. Having him go to jail seemed silly, because if I sent him there I would be pretty frightened when he came out. It was a mixture of protecting him and being afraid.

And Frank was genuinely frightened by the possibility that the police might be notified. One time—before the broken-arm episode—he was being violent, and Jennifer called the police. When they arrived, I didn't want to say, "Take this person away." So I said, "I'm all right. I don't want to charge him." The police said, "Are you sure?" I said yes and they went away.

And I *was* sure because I could feel that Frank was so shocked by the police coming that that would be it for that occasion, at least. Jennifer was quite stunned that I did not turn him in. I think your kids often don't understand why you do certain things. If he had ever touched either of my kids, I would have done something. Strange that you can't think more of yourself. And the kids weren't really afraid of him. I would say Jennifer is a fairly strong woman and, if anything, he was probably a little afraid of her. I don't think he would have done anything to the girls. There's something about wives, though.

After the broken-arm thing, of course, I realized this was getting serious. At the hospital he said he was going to give up drinking. He was very contrite, and he asked for one more try. We talked for a few hours and I thought, "Well, one more try," but I suggested that we sell the house we bought together and separate our finances in case it didn't work out. I wasn't feeling too hopeful. Quite often I'm sure women want to leave but don't know what they would do for money. You can't just leave the house and wonder, "How will I get him out of there? How will I support my family?"

A few months later, he beat me again. I decided to leave then and there. After having gone through the episode with my arm, this time I thought it could be life or death, and I wasn't going to let myself be killed. Jennifer had already said to me that while she couldn't make me leave, she wouldn't let me die. I was really scared, but I started to fight back physically. I was quite angry—all those promises and here we were again. But fighting back didn't make me feel powerful.

He just kept hitting me. Finally, I said I had to go to the bathroom and fled the room. I grabbed Theresa and ran out the door. Fortunately, someone was driving by. Although I didn't even know him and my clothes were torn, I flagged him down. I said, "Please help me, this man is trying to hurt me." He told me he'd drive me wherever I wanted to go. I figured he was a better bet than what I was running from. Frank came out of the house, but he just stood there. The abuse plays a little differently when it's outside. I got in the car and asked the man to take us to where Jennifer was working. My little daughter and I sat there and waited until the end of Jennifer's shift, and then we all went to the women's shelter.

I had a very unsympathetic boss at the time. So here I was: I had to go to work, look normal, and then go to the shelter at night. But the shelter was very helpful for me. I got to tell my story confidentially. Everyone was supportive. I got a lot of counseling and coaching on the law, although it seemed really quite boring that the whole thing was so predictable. You know: the men are always so sweet afterward and say they would never do it again; they're usually controlling, manipulative people who run down your self-esteem so you think you deserve being hit. . . .

It's been a few years now—four years ago that we got married—so I've pretty much been able to shake what Frank did to me. Maybe I'm not as sure of myself as I would want to be, but he didn't convince me I was a bad person. I think, "Perhaps I'm not really so great, but I still didn't deserve this." These men make you feel so bad about yourself. They have no right to say that you're not a worthy person. No right at all. Every person in the world is much too important to lose.

I'm sorry for my children—it was so hard on them. But I've found it interesting to be able to understand why I did the things I did. I was like everyone else. I used to think, "Why, why do women stay after the first minute of violence?" So if my telling my story gets even just one of those women out, even though it's not much, I'd feel like something in my life has made a difference.

R E A D I N G   4 3

Supremacy Crimes

GLORIA STEINEM

From domestic violence to sexual harassment, naming a crime has been the first step toward solving it. But another crime is hiding in plain sight. You've seen the ocean of television coverage, you've read the headlines: "How to Spot a Troubled Kid," "Twisted Teens," "When Teens Fall Apart."

After the slaughter in Colorado that inspired those phrases, dozens of copycat threats were reported in the same generalized way: "Junior high students charged with conspiracy to kill students and teachers" (in Texas); "Five honor students overheard planning a June graduation bombing" (in New York); "More than 100 minor threats reported statewide" (in Pennsylvania). In response, the White House held an emergency strategy session titled "Children, Violence, and Responsibility." Nonetheless, another attack was soon reported: "Youth With 2 Guns Shoots 6 at Georgia School."

I don't know about you, but I've been talking back to the television set, waiting for someone to tell us the obvious: it's not "youth," "our children," or "our teens." It's our sons—and "our" can usually be read as "white," "middle class," and "heterosexual." We know that hate crimes, violent and otherwise, are overwhelmingly committed by white men who are apparently straight. The same is true for an even higher percentage of impersonal, resentment-driven, mass killings like those in Colorado; the sort committed for no economic or rational gain except the need to say, "I'm superior because I can kill." Think of Charles Starkweather, who reported feeling powerful and serene after murdering ten women and men in the 1950s; or the shooter who climbed the University of Texas Tower in 1966, raining down death to gain celebrity. Think of the engineering student at the University of Montreal who

resented females' ability to study that subject, and so shot to death fourteen women students in 1989, while saying, "I'm against feminism." Think of nearly all those who have killed impersonally in the workplace, the post office, McDonald's.

White males—usually intelligent, middle class, and heterosexual, or trying desperately to appear so—also account for virtually all the serial, sexually motivated, sadistic killings, those characterized by stalking, imprisoning, torturing, and "owning" victims in death. Think of Edmund Kemper, who began by killing animals, then murdered his grandparents, yet was released to sexually torture and dismember college students and other young women until he himself decided he "didn't want to kill *all* the coeds in the world." Or David Berkowitz, the Son of Sam, who murdered some women in order to feel in control of all women. Or consider Ted Bundy, the charming, snobbish young would-be lawyer who tortured and murdered as many as forty women, usually beautiful students who were symbols of the economic class he longed to join. As for John Wayne Gacy, he was obsessed with maintaining the public mask of masculinity, and so hid his homosexuality by killing and burying men and boys with whom he had had sex.

These "senseless" killings begin to seem less mysterious when you consider that they were committed disproportionately by white, nonpoor males, the group most likely to become hooked on the drug of superiority. It's a drug pushed by a male-dominant culture that presents dominance as a natural right; a racist hierarchy that falsely elevates whiteness; a materialist society that equates superiority with possessions, and a homophobic one that empowers only one form of sexuality.

As Elliott Leyton reports in *Hunting Humans: The Rise of the Modern Multiple Murderer*, these killers see their behavior as "an appropriate—even 'manly'—response to the frustrations and disappointments that are a normal part of life." In other words, it's not their life experiences that are the problem, it's the impossible expectation of dominance to which they've become addicted.

This is not about blame. This is about causation. If anything, ending the massive cultural cover-up of supremacy crimes should make heroes out of boys and men who reject violence, especially those who reject the notion of superiority altogether. Even if one believes in a biogenetic component of male aggression, the very existence of gentle men proves that socialization can override it.

Nor is this about attributing such crimes to a single cause. Addiction to the drug of supremacy is not their only root, just the deepest and most ignored one. Additional reasons why this country has such a high rate of violence include the plentiful guns that make killing seem as unreal as a video game; male violence in the media that desensitizes viewers in much the same way that combat killers are desensitized in training; affluence that allows maximum access to violence-as-entertainment; a national history of genocide and slavery; the romanticizing of frontier violence and organized crime; not to mention extremes of wealth and poverty and the illusion that both are deserved.

But it is truly remarkable, given the relative reasons for anger at injustice in this country, that white, nonpoor men have a near-monopoly on multiple killings of strangers, whether serial and sadistic or mass and random. How can we ignore this obvious fact? Others may kill to improve their own condition—in self-defense, or for money or drugs; to eliminate enemies; to declare turf in drive-by shootings; even for a jacket or a pair of sneakers—but white males addicted to supremacy kill even when it worsens their condition or ends in suicide.

Men of color and females are capable of serial and mass killing, and commit just enough to prove it. Think of Colin Ferguson, the crazed black man on the Long Island Railroad, or Wayne Williams, the young black man in Atlanta who kidnapped and killed black boys, apparently to conceal his homosexuality. Think of Aileen Carol Wuornos, the white prostitute in Florida who killed abusive johns "in self-defense," or Waneta Hoyt, the upstate New York woman who strangled her five infant children between 1965 and 1971, disguising their cause of death as sudden infant death syndrome. Such crimes are rare enough to leave a haunting refrain of disbelief, as evoked in Pat Parker's poem "jonestown": "Black folks do not/ Black folks do not/Black folks do not commit suicide." And yet they did.

Nonetheless, the proportion of serial killings that are not committed by white males is about the same as the propor-

tion of anorexics who are not female. Yet we discuss the gender, race, and class components of anorexia, but not the role of the same factors in producing epidemics among the powerful.

The reasons are buried deep in the culture, so invisible that only by reversing our assumptions can we reveal them.

Suppose, for instance, that young black males—or any other men of color—had carried out the slaughter in Colorado. Would the media reports be so willing to describe the murderers as "our children"? Would there be so little discussion about the boys' race? Would experts be calling the motive a mystery, or condemning the high school cliques for making those young men feel like "outsiders"? Would there be the same empathy for parents who gave the murderers luxurious homes, expensive cars, even rescued them from brushes with the law? Would there be as much attention to generalized causes, such as the dangers of violent video games and recipes for bombs on the Internet?

As for the victims, if racial identities had been reversed, would racism remain so little discussed? In fact, the killers themselves said they were targeting blacks and athletes. They used a racial epithet, shot a black male student in the head, and then laughed over the fact that they could see his brain. What if *that* had been reversed?

What if these two young murderers, who were called "fags" by some of the jocks at Columbine High School, actually had been gay? Would they have got the same sympathy for being gay-baited? What if they had been lovers? Would we hear as little about their sexuality as we now do, even though only their own homophobia could have given the word "fag" such power to humiliate them?

Take one more leap of the imagination: suppose these killings had been planned and executed by young women— of any race, sexuality, or class. Would the media still be so uninterested in the role played by gender-conditioning? Would journalists assume that female murderers had suffered from being shut out of access to power in high school, so much so that they were pushed beyond their limits? What if dozens, even hundreds of young women around the country had made imitative threats—as young men have done—expressing admiration for a well-planned massacre and promising to do the same? Would we be discussing their youth more than their gender, as is the case so far with these male killers?

I think we begin to see that our national self-examination is ignoring something fundamental, precisely because it's like the air we breathe: the white male factor, the middle-class and heterosexual one, and the promise of superiority it carries. Yet this denial is self-defeating—to say the least. We will never reduce the number of violent Americans, from bullies to killers, without challenging the assumptions on which masculinity is based: that males are superior to females, that they must find a place in a male hierarchy, and that the ability to dominate *someone* is so important that even a mere insult can justify lethal revenge. There are plenty of studies to support this view. As Dr. James Gilligan concluded in *Violence: Reflections on a National Epidemic,* "If humanity is to evolve beyond the propensity toward violence . . . then it can only do so by

recognizing the extent to which the patriarchal code of honor and shame generates and obligates male violence."

I think the way out can only be found through a deeper reversal: just as we as a society have begun to raise our daughters more like our sons—more like whole people—we must begin to raise our sons more like our daughters—that is, to value empathy as well as hierarchy; to measure success by other people's welfare as well as their own.

But first, we have to admit and name the truth about supremacy crimes.

A LETTER FROM CLAUDIA BRENNER

January 1991

Dear Friend,

On May 13, 1988, my lover, Rebecca, was murdered. I survived, with five bullet wounds.

At the trial of the attacker, it was proven that we were attacked because of who we were—two lesbians, two women living our lives and our love for each other.

There is no way to lessen the horror of that moment. . . .

On May 13, Rebecca and I were hiking on the Appalachian trail in Adams County, Pennsylvania. At our campsite that morning, Rebecca was stopped by a man who asked her for a cigarette. He hadn't been there when we arrived at the site the previous evening, and must have arrived very late at night.

Later that day, we broke camp and continued our hike. As we checked a map at a fork in the trail, we were surprised to see the same man walking behind us. He had a rifle.

He asked us if we were lost. We said no, and turned left, onto a side trail. He continued along the main trail. The encounter made both Rebecca and me uneasy. We kept looking behind to see if the man was following us, but we never saw him again.

Claudia Brenner, "A Letter from Claudia Brenner." Reprinted with the permission of Claudia Brenner.

Late that afternoon, Rebecca and I stopped and made camp near a stream. It was a secluded spot, some distance from the trail. We ate, made love, and rested.

Suddenly, there were gunshots. The shots were *so* sudden, *so* loud, *so* violent, *so* world-changing that at first I didn't even realize that they were gunshots and that we were the targets—except there was so much blood.

Because I was between the attacker and Rebecca, I was hit first. I was shot in the upper arm, twice in the neck, in the head and face. Rebecca told me to run behind a nearby tree. As she followed me, Rebecca was shot in the head and back.

The shooting finally stopped. We were both behind a large tree. In my frantic shock and fear, I didn't understand how badly hurt we were. But Rebecca had the presence of mind to tell me what to do. She told me to stop the bleeding. I believe she saved my life.

My only thought was to get us out of there and get help. I brought Rebecca her sneakers, but she couldn't see them. She was losing her vision. I tried to lift her, but she kept slumping to the ground.

Someplace deep within me, I began to understand how badly hurt Rebecca was. If the situation could get worse, it came with the realization that I had to go for help alone. I covered Rebecca, gave her all the first aid I could think of, and started out for help.

Before I left, Rebecca was unconscious. We never had a chance to say goodbye.

Soaked in blood, I walked on the rugged trail about two miles to a forest road. I was completely terrified that whoever had attacked us might be following and attack again. I walked on the road another two miles before I finally saw a car. I stopped the car, and the driver rushed me to the police in nearby Shippensburg.

All I could think about was Rebecca. The State Police immediately began a search for her.

That evening, I was airlifted to the Hershey Medical Center trauma unit. I had emergency surgery that night. The next day I learned that the police had found Rebecca's body. She died from the bullet wound that hit her back and exploded in her liver.

But my ordeal did not end with the horror of Rebecca's death.

The State Police caught the man who murdered Rebecca—the same man who had followed us on the trail—Stephen Roy Carr. We now know that Stephen Roy Carr stalked us, hid eighty-five feet away in the woods while we made camp, shot to kill, and left us for dead.

During the legal proceedings that followed, it became clear that Carr had attacked us because we were lesbians. Carr's lawyer even implied—during the trial and the appeal—that Rebecca and I had provoked the attack.

The implication that Rebecca and I had "teased" Carr with our sexuality, and that we were responsible for this man stalking us, spying on us, and shooting to kill us was not only outrageous, it was disgusting.

Fortunately, the trial judge refused to allow this line of argument. On October 27, 1988, Stephen Roy Carr was convicted of first-degree murder and later sentenced to life in prison without parole.

I survived the attack, but in the months that followed I was consumed with grief and fear. My world centered on the knowledge that Rebecca was dead and that somehow I was alive.

I had always known that the world was not a safe place for lesbians. But somehow, I believed that nothing this terrible would ever happen to me.

I believed that all I needed to do was not to look like a stereotypical lesbian and be discreet about my expressions of affection to other women. That security was shattered by the bullets. . . .

Sincerely,

Claudia Brenner

Accountability or Justice? Rape as a War Crime

MARY ANN TÉTREAULT

WARTIME RAPE AS A NORMATIVE ISSUE

Whether and how to treat rape as a war crime are complex questions. Rape is a contested issue in domestic criminal law, an assault for which the victim is blamed as much or more than the criminal—she asked for it, people say (Brownmiller 1975:373). This perversity is rationalized as the outcome of cultural traditions that associate female chastity with family honor (e.g., Peristiany 1965; Tillion 1983), and underlies some of the shame associated with being a rape victim. Shame contributes to the low likelihood that the rapist will be charged with his crime if the victim can conceal what has happened to her. Victim reluctance to suffer the social and legal repercussions of rape also shields rapists who commit their crimes during a war (e.g., Asia Watch & Physicians for Human Rights 1993:1). Even though concealment also limits the support the victim can claim from her family and friends, shame and the fear of social ostracism work for the rapist whether he is an acquaintance, a stranger, or a soldier.

But the victim is not the only person influencing the kind and amount of publicity given to rape. When rape is an instrument of policy, rapists themselves and their bureaucratic superiors publicize the act as part of the crime. Here, the purpose of rape is precisely to shame the victim, her family, and her nation, and to terrorize her entire community. "Rape [is] an act of conquest and subjugation of whole societies, involving deliberate national humiliation as a means of suppression and social control. . . ." (Makiya 1993:294). This technique is used domestically, against ethnic minorities and opposition groups, as well as against for-

eign populations. Kanan Makiya notes that the government of Iraq employs "official rapists," civil servants whose job it is to rape selected Iraqi women and thus "dishonor an entire family name" (289). Other regimes, for example Jordan (Makiya 1993), Pakistan (Makiya 1993; Asia Watch 1992), Haiti (Human Rights Watch National Coalition for Haitian Refugees 1994), and India (Asia Watch & Physicians for Human Rights 1993) also rape female citizens to control dissident populations.

Rape in war is often read as the criminal—or, even worse, the inevitable—behavior of individuals (Brownmiller 1975:73). It is far more accurate to view wartime rape as an instrument of policy. Military organizations, with their hierarchical chains of command, are designed so that leaders can direct the behavior of subordinates. To argue that rapes committed by soldiers are individual acts, particularly if military rapists go uncharged and unpunished, is simply untenable (Amnesty International 1993:4). Rather, as is rape domestically when routinely performed by state employees, wartime rape is undertaken to implement strategies of genocide and terror.

Genocide, the obliteration of an enemy's social formation,[1] has been practiced since ancient times and nearly always involves the sexual violation of women (Smith 1994a). Where slavery was institutionalized—for example, in ancient Greece, Old Testament Israel, or premodern Arabia—the defeat of an enemy on his own territory resulted in killing as many men as possible, destroying the city, and capturing women and children to become concubines and slaves (Garlan 1988; Mernissi 1991; Smith 1994a).[2] This practice destroyed the enemy as an organic community.

Rape has replaced capture as the primary sexual instrument of genocide. Following the battle of Culloden in 1746, English troops used rape to destroy the organization of Scottish tribes (clans) supporting a Stuart claimant to the throne (Brownmiller 1975:38–40). The army of Pakistan

Mary Ann Tétreault, "Accountability or Justice? Rape as a War Crime" (previously unpublished paper). Reprinted with the permission of the author.

systematically raped more than 200,000 Bengali women before being routed by the Indian army in 1971 (Roy 1975); today, the Indian army uses rape against Muslim women in Kashmir (Asia Watch & Physicians for Human Rights 1993). Rape was an integral element of the genocide committed by the Nazis against the Jews and by the Khmer Rouge against other Khmer (Smith 1994b). It is used today in "ethnic cleansing" campaigns in Bosnia-Herzegovina (Amnesty International 1993; *New York Times* October 22, 1993:A4).

Wartime rape plus coerced pregnancy combine the ancient mechanism of capture with the perennial mechanism of rape to carry out another version of ethnic warfare. Women are raped repeatedly until pregnancies are confirmed and then detained until their pregnancies are too advanced for safe abortions to be performed. Reports from Bosnia indicate that this pattern was followed in camps maintained by the Bosnian Serbs (e.g., Personal Narratives 1992; Burns 1992; Lewin 1993). However, most reports from Bosnia indicate that rape victims are more likely to be killed than held to bear the children of the rapists (Amnesty International 1993:2; Burns 1993).

A similar pattern of coerced pregnancy has been reported in Rwanda, but with a twist.

[D]uring the atrocities, women of the opposite ethnic group were raped to humiliate and harm them (and they were often killed afterward). In this later phase . . . the preference was for women of the same ethnic group as the perpetrators, this time to reproduce the group. There are many stories . . . of young Tutsi women being held in Kigali by the RPF forces (mostly Tutsi) as walking wombs, where the yearnings of youth mixed with the strategies of statesmen to capture women of reproductive age—especially women of one's [own] ethnicity. . . . [I]n this case the fighting has ended up by conquering women of the same group as the soldiers (Newbury 1995).

This strategy of replenishing the group depends both on ancient beliefs that women are merely the vessels in which men breed their own descendants, and principles followed by many nation-states whereby nationality passes from father to son independently of the mother (Yuval-Davis and Anthias 1989; Tétreault and al-Mughni 1995).

Rape and the threat of rape are also terror tactics that drive people out of their homes and villages, making it easier for enemy forces to extend their control over territory (Thomas and Ralph 1993). Rape is a crime against women that effectively removes male combatants from enemy ranks. The fear of rape explains why men who might otherwise remain to defend their homes will flee with their families to protect their women—and themselves: Though wartime rape of men is uncommon, it is not unknown (Tétreault 1992; Thomas and Ralph 1993; Riding 1993). Families that stay behind risk more than physical security. The rape of a family member devastates family life; those who watch feel impotent and vulnerable because they cannot protect the victims (Morton and Sangrey 1979). In cultures where shame is connected to the loss of female chastity, a raped woman is both humiliated by her attacker and rejected by family members. Indeed, rape in war, like other forms of torture, is frequently performed in front of family members to maximize its effectiveness in achieving social, emotional, and cognitive disorientation, terrorizing the community, and making it easier to control (e.g., Simons 1994; al-Mughni and al-Turkait 1994).

The unparalleled power of rape to effect or mark subjection has been exploited since ancient times. K. J. Dover (1978) notes that herms, stone markers carved to represent the face and erect penis of the god Hermes, also represented the threat of sexual retaliation against anybody encroaching on the territory of Greek property owners. The equation of penetration with subordination was so strong in ancient Athens that a man who permitted his body to be penetrated during homosexual acts risked his citizenship, while the forcible penetration of an Athenian citizen constituted the crime of hubris and required the execution of the offender to restore the victim to his former political status (103–4).

Despite the fact that both men and women can be raped, rape is overwhelmingly a crime committed by men against women. It is a crime intended to have collective and personal consequences. Rape is triggered by deep emotions and incites equally deep-seated reactions connected to the use of sexual symbolism to convey a whole range of concepts other than those dealing strictly with sexual acts. The symbolic connection between female chastity and group integrity, for example, is an important element motivating wartime rape. *Women* are living beings with personal lives and civil statuses; *woman* is the embodiment of complex constructions of community and nationality (Hunt 1984; Yuval-Davis & Anthias 1989; Mosse 1985; Theweleit 1987).

Wartime rape is a political crime against the symbol. It is a sacrilege. The group is shamed by the rape and injured as a result of the shame; however, the victim suffers both as the victim of a crime and as the scapegoat of their shame. This scapegoating has dire consequences for the sexually violated woman (Roy 1975; Brownmiller 1975; Tétreault 1992), but they are addressed—if they are addressed—as the problems of a person rather than a people. The appalling prevalence of rape in war and the even more appalling masses of evidence that it is neither inevitable nor unconnected to military strategy evoke questions about why wartime rape is personalized rather than treated as the severe human rights abuse that it is.

> Despite the pervasiveness of rape, it often has been a hidden element of war, a fact that is linked inextricably to its largely gender-specific character. The fact that the abuse is committed by men against women has contributed to its being narrowly portrayed as sexual or personal . . . a portrayal that depoliticizes sexual abuse in conflict and results in its being ignored as a war crime (Thomas & Ralph, 84).

Rape is often a prelude to murder. But whether victims live or die, rape is an engine of enormous devastation. It wreaks simultaneously physical, emotional, and psychological violence against a human being, a family, a community, and a people. It has grave physical consequences—injury, infection, pregnancy, and death (Quindlen 1993)—and lasting psychological consequences ranging from distaste for sexual intimacy and an impaired capacity for trust to insanity and even suicide (Hartman and Burgess 1988; Kilpatrick and Veronen 1983; Mann 1991; al-Mughni and al-Turkait 1994); and initiates a train of collective consequences that can end in the elimination of a community and its unique pattern of organized social and political life (Smith 1994a).

WARTIME RAPE AS A PRACTICAL ISSUE

In this section, I examine two contemporary cases of war in which rape was utilized strategically as part of a campaign of terror and/or genocide. These are the Iraqi invasion of Kuwait and the war in Bosnia-Herzegovina. I consider three aspects of rape as a human rights abuse: its politicization as a conflict strategy; the treatment of rape victims by families, communities, and governments; and two examples of international tribunals where victims can make claims or bring charges against rapists and those responsible for their actions.

Politicization

The politicization of rape is most likely to occur as part of an ongoing conflict, when it can motivate military and civil-

ian populations and possibly alter the strategic balance of forces. Politicization to motivate one's own armies is clearly an incitement to retaliatory behavior against women on the "other side" (Brownmiller 1975:64–72). Here I look at cases in which parties in a conflict use charges of enemy rape to mobilize external support for their side. Paradoxically, such a strategy tends to devalue the actual suffering of victims, and is rarely pursued either to seek justice for them once the fighting is over or to hold those responsible accountable for their crimes.

Susan Brownmiller (1975) discusses the politicization of wartime rape in the context of the two world wars. During World War I, the German army was charged with the "rape of Belgium" in atrocity stories aimed at aggravating anti-German feelings among civilian populations and Allied troops. After the war, those stories were reevaluated by scholars, who concluded that they were *merely* propaganda. A numbers game ensued—*only* so many rapes had occurred, fewer than originally reported (46–48). One writer implied that allegations of rape were made for their alliterative value in French rather than because they had actually occurred (47). The initial exaggeration was used to justify this later trivialization; the reality of the rapes disappeared.

The creation of tribunals to try war criminals on the losing side following World War II led to a somewhat different result in the cases of the "rape of Nanking" and the sexual torture of Jewish women under the Nazi regime. The conquest of Nanking was marked by horrible atrocities committed by Japanese troops against the Chinese civilian population. Reports featured the trope "rape of Nanking" because it was so literally as well as figuratively true. Yet a 1938 report by a missionary group detailing the consequences of the Japanese invasion and conquest of the city "excluded rape per se" as a category of damage, despite its inclusion of many less damaging injuries (57–58).

The Tokyo war crimes tribunal did not call rape victims to testify. However, witnesses testifying to other crimes also reported on the hundreds of rapes they had seen during the carnage. From this testimony, the tribunal estimated that 20,000 rapes had occurred in Nanking during the first month of occupation alone, and that widespread rape continued to be committed, along with other crimes, "at least six weeks after the city had been taken" (cited in Brownmiller 1975:61).[3]

Adopting a "rape of Belgium/Nanking" strategy, spokespersons for the Kuwaiti government in exile, desperately aware of its dependence on external forces to liberate Kuwait, made repeated claims about Iraqi atrocities that emphasized the rape of Kuwaiti women by Iraqi soldiers during the invasion and occupation.[4] Publication of these stories in the press and on television helped to build popular sympathy in the United States and Europe for the rollback of the invasion.

After liberation, some Kuwaitis who had remained in Kuwait during the occupation questioned the motivation for this strategy and criticized its terrorizing effects on Kuwaitis living under occupation. None disputed the charge that rapes had occurred and several reported that gang rape, other forms of sexual torture, and murder were routinely inflicted on women in the Resistance unfortunate enough to have been taken captive (e.g., Tétreault 1992; al-Mughni and al-Turkait 1994). An initially classified report by US army investigators released in 1993 supports the tenor of contemporary Kuwaiti allegations, though the estimates of numbers of all types of atrocities were lower than what had been alleged during the war. However, in the postliberation environment, the Kuwaiti regime was pressed by US officials to minimize public comments about human rights abuses committed during the occupation to calm Kuwaitis engaged in retributory rampages against scapegoats, primarily Palestinians, accused of being collaborators (Lancaster 1993).

Unlike the Iraqi rapes of Kuwaitis which appear to have been primarily acts of terror, humiliation, and pollution (al-Mughni and al-Turkait 1994),[5] a significant number of the rapes in Bosnia-Herzegovina were committed as part of a strategy of "ethnic cleansing" intended to remove members of "ethnic" groups other than the one represented by whichever army was victorious in a particular territory. As in the case of Jewish women victimized by the Nazis, some women were taken to concentration camps and repeatedly violated; others were raped in their homes, often in front of family members. Many rape victims were also murdered (Amnesty International 1993; In re Jane Doe et al. 1993; Simons 1994; MacKinnon 1993; Lewis 1994; Coll 1994).

The organized quality of so many rapes is revealed by the sequestration of the women in camps, barracks, and motels (*New York Times* 1992) and the recording of rapes on videotape. Catherine MacKinnon (1993) equates the filming of rapes by Serbs with the expression of a culture of pornography.[6] I see this differently, as part of a propaganda campaign to influence the environment of the conflict. The films are less indicative of pornographic qualities in a particular culture than the results of a sexualization of film and video entertainment visible worldwide. The films, by their nature, get viewers' attention, but they are primarily intended to persuade. Their content depends jointly on technical capability and the government's assessment of just how

much it can get away with in the process of creating and marketing its message.

The filming of the rapes is not incidental, however. It is part of the propaganda machine. According to MacKinnon, some rapes by Serb soldiers were staged to look as though they had been committed by Croatians (1993:27). Rape films are shown on Serbian television to whip up popular support for the war, and to Serb soldiers to encourage them to greater efforts (27–28). As a high school student, I watched similar (though, mercifully, far less graphic) films that had been produced during World War II by the US military for the same purposes.[7] MacKinnon notes that the Nazis also made films like this and used them to produce "sexually explicit antisemitic hate propaganda" (30).

In this context, arguments over the pornographic value of a particular country's propaganda have the same unfortunate consequences as the personalization of wartime rape: They shift attention from the issue of wartime rape as a human rights abuse to allegations about its possible psychological causes. The exploitation of photographs and video footage of someone's rape or mutilated or dying body should qualify as a war crime, a violation of the 1949 Geneva Convention prohibiting "outrages upon personal dignity." However, this is a separate issue.

All sides in the Bosnian war have used allegations of rape to mobilize supporters, neutralize opponents, and manipulate the balance of forces in the conflict. All of them have also engaged in rape (Amnesty International 1993:3; Riding 1993:1), though the United Nations has accused only Serb commanders of committing rape and other atrocities as part of a policy of genocide (Cohen 1995:1). Even though there are vast differences in the degree of criminal culpability among the three sides fighting in Bosnia-Herzegovina, to focus on rapes by one side only makes light of the abuses of women raped by non-Serbian forces. Their attackers are virtually acquitted in the court of public opinion: One side commits war crimes while the other is only responding in kind. This is the same attitude that excused an orgy of Russian rapes of German women at the end of World War II (Brownmiller 1975:66–72; Rubin 1992). In a similarly perverse way, a focus on "cultures of pornography" attenuates the individual and collective responsibility of rapists, their commanding officers, and the political leaders who oversee and condone their actions.

The Treatment of Victims

Immediately following the liberation, the Kuwaiti government sent female military personnel to interview war victims and record their testimony. Two recorders interviewed in 1992 said that they had talked with a number of rape victims, most of whom reported aggravated circumstances. Neither was willing to report the number of rape victims she had interviewed, nor to divulge any specific information regarding any of the rapes. A clinical psychologist also refused to report the number of wartime rape victims among his patients (Tétreault 1992). A recent estimate drawn from multiple sources, including medical records, concludes that approximately 2,000 Kuwaiti women were sexually assaulted by Iraqi military personnel during the conflict (al-Mughni and al-Turkait 1994).

A mechanism for processing claims for war damages was established under UN auspices (see below), but few Kuwaiti women presented claims for damages from wartime rape. Both the discretion of medical and military officials in possession of actual data and the refusal of the women themselves to press their claims have erased rape from discussions of reparation and restitution due Kuwait from Iraq. The primary public reason given for the quiet submersion of the issue of wartime rape in Kuwait is to respect the shame of rape victims and to avoid causing them any more pain than they have suffered already. The clinical psychologist mentioned above put it this way:

> [R]ape is a social and ethical stigma for the one [raped] and for their families. Many families keep their victims locked in the house. Married victims are being divorced. Most rape victims are being treated by traditional methods, reading the Quran, or taking them to special religious people. . . . Many cases with reactive anxiety are developing severe psychotic depression—even schizophrenia. . . . Virginity is a very precious concept to a Kuwaiti (Tétreault 1992).

Here we see again the most frequently cited reasons for the nonreporting of rape: social stigma, self-blame, prevention by family members or religious counselors, fear of rejection and repudiation, and severe mental illness. This psychologist also said that he knew of cases where male family members killed rape victims or encouraged them to commit suicide; others committed suicide despite the efforts of friends and family members to stop them (Tétreault 1992). Occasional press reports told similar stories (e.g., Mann 1991). Death is the most effective silencer.

The treatment of rape victims by investigators and medical personnel was generally humane in Kuwait, including the exemplary discretion practiced by individuals collecting their testimonies. Their treatment by families and neighbors was uneven, despite widespread verbal and occasional actual support for reintegrating victims into Kuwaiti society without stigma (Tétreault 1994b; p. 301). The treatment of rape victims by the state was ambiguous. On the one hand, medical and social services were made available to rape victims as to other victims of post-traumatic stress (al-Mughni and al-Turkait 1994), while rape victims' plight was not exploited publicly as a foreign policy tool. For example, rape victims have not been featured in Kuwaiti arguments to retain UN sanctions against Iraq.[8]

On the other hand, the political value of wartime rape was not totally forgone by domestic political actors. A whispering campaign alleged that rape had been far more widespread than was reflected in official reports, and that nearly every family that had remained behind was dishonored because it harbored at least one raped woman. Some who had remained in Kuwait during the occupation were convinced that the whispering campaign was a ploy to discredit the resistance and, by implication if not inclusion, others pressing for greater democratization (Tétreault 1992). At the same time, one well-known resistance rape and murder victim, Asrir al-Qabandy, was publicly honored as a martyr for Kuwait.

Given the climate faced by raped women in similar (though far from identical) cultural circumstances, the willingness of so many women in Bosnia-Herzegovina to testify publicly to their sexual abuse by armed forces is remarkable, and the reluctance of the others is understandable. At this juncture, there is not enough information to judge how well or how poorly rape survivors are being treated by families and communities. However, there is little reason to believe that the post-traumatic treatment of Bosnian women is any less hurtful than what happened to many Kuwaiti women. Well-intentioned individuals and groups gathering evidence for future legal actions carried out their inquiries in ways that brought individual raped women to public attention. Requests that survivors "tell their stories over and over again to reporters, even if the telling was traumatic," inflicted another kind of injury (Quindlen 1993b). Some Bosnian rape victims experienced the added trauma of being interviewed on television in the course of fact-gathering expeditions, many during the extensively covered 1992 trip by a delegation from the European Community to investigate charges about rape camps and pregnancies forced on Bosnian Muslim women (Riding 1993).

The outcomes of coerced pregnancies provide evidence that the treatment of Bosnian women by their government is tainted by instrumental concerns. An unknown number of these pregnancies were terminated by abortion and others ended in the delivery and subsequent abandonment of the infants (e.g., *New York Times* January 27, 1993:A3). The Bosnian government forbade the surrender of the infants for overseas adoption, wanting them to remain Bosnians to replace in however pitifully small numbers the tens of thousands of war dead. The babies were sequestered in orphanages financed by foreign donors, while government officials continued to apply pressure on those mothers whose identities were known to accept them into homes in which husbands were unaware of their existence, much less the circumstances of their conceptions (Williams 1993).

War-Crimes Tribunals

Because Iraq was not defeated by coalition forces but merely driven out of Kuwait, it was not considered possible to establish war-crimes tribunals like the ones set up after World War II. However, the invasion triggered a series of resolutions in the United Nations Security Council reflecting an intention to punish Iraq for violating Kuwait's sovereignty. Significantly with respect to an innovative approach to war crimes, the resolutions created a novel set of institutions to adjudicate damage claims. The Iraqi government has so far refused to contribute actively to reparations funds to pay these damages (Crook 1993:146).[9] Even so, the claims and payment process is well under way, thanks to the availability of funds to pay damages in the form of Iraqi assets sequestered under UN-directed economic sanctions imposed on August 6, 1990. As a result, some assessment of its utility as a vehicle for bringing justice to victims can be made.

The legal foundation for Iraq's liability is Security Council Resolution 687, a comprehensive cease-fire resolution passed in April 1991 following the end of hostilities. The resolution reaffirmed Iraq's responsibility for all damages caused by its illegal invasion and occupation of Kuwait. This attribution of responsibility to the state rests on principles established under the law of war, specifically the fourth Hague Convention (1907) and its provisions regarding the conduct of war on land, their interpretation by the International Military Tribunal at Nuremberg in 1946, and their reaffirmation in the 1949 Geneva Conventions (Crook 1993:147; also Reisman and Antoniou 1994). Of particular interest for those concerned with wartime rape, under these principles, "Iraq is responsible for all acts of its armed forces in Kuwait, including acts contrary to military orders or discipline for which a state might not normally be responsible in peacetime" (Crook 1993:148). The question of whether any crime committed was "private" rather than a

"war crime" thus never becomes an issue. The state is accountable in all cases.

The primary institution for collecting and assessing claims against Iraq for direct losses arising from the invasion and occupation of Kuwait is the United Nations Compensation Commission—the UNCC (Crook 1993). Created over the course of a year, the commission began sitting in July 1991, receiving its first set of claims from governments in June 1992. Governments transmitting these consolidated claims set up their own procedures to collect them. In Kuwait, the Public Authority for Assessment of Compensation for Damages Resulting from Iraqi Aggression—PAAC—was created by Amiri decree on May 27, 1991

> to serve as a national authority for Kuwaiti claims. PAAC has the responsibility to submit to the UNCC consolidated claims of Kuwaiti and certain [Gulf Cooperation Council][10] nationals, including claims of corporations and government institutions that suffered losses" (Asem and al-Mughni 1994:12).

PAAC opened five offices to process claims for compensation made under six damage categories established by the UNCC. These are claims for having had to leave Kuwait or remain out of Kuwait as a result of the invasion (category A); claims for serious personal injury or the death of a parent, spouse, or child (category B); individual claims for damages up to $100,000 (category C); individual claims for damages over $100,000 (category D); claims by corporations and other entities (category E); and claims by governments and international organizations (category F). Categories A and B carry fixed rates of compensation (Crook 1993; Asem and al-Mughni 1994).[11]

The UNCC/PAAC procedure is highly routinized, though great care is taken to protect claimants' legal rights. Claimants appear at one of the PAAC offices and fill out a form describing their injuries and losses. They must bring proof of damage such as death certificates, medical reports, receipts, statements by witnesses, and other independent corroboration. The claims are evaluated by PAAC staff members and then by a judicial committee to be sure that each meets the "threshold" standard set for each type of claim. During this process, every claim is reviewed by a lawyer. Consolidated claims are forwarded to the UNCC office in Geneva, where they are evaluated further to determine whether the claims appear to be "unauthorized, inflated or unsubstantiated." After a thorough review, a panel of commissioners recommends to the Governing Council of the UNCC the amount to be paid to each government. The Council decides how much will actually be paid (Crook 1993:153).

This streamlined procedure was directed by Decision 1 of the UNCC Governing Council and reflected the commission's desire to process small claims to compensate injured individuals, many of whom were likely to have very limited resources, as expeditiously as possible (Crook 1993:152, 154). The establishment of small fixed payments for A and B claims also makes the procedure easier on victims. The relatively small amount of the payments, given the limits of the fund available to pay them, ensures payment to a relatively large proportion of those injured; fixed payments concentrate attention on the fact of damage rather than on collateral—though important—issues such as the extent of financial losses from hasty departure and how much an individual suffered as the result of a personal injury. The inclusion of grounds such as "serious personal injury" and "mental pain and anguish" for category B claims led to a specification of the injuries that would qualify. Under Decision 3, the Governing Council listed among qualifying injuries "dismemberment, loss of use of an organ or function . . . [and] mental injury arising from sexual assault" (Crook 1993:153).

Category B payments can be supplemented by making claims under categories C and D, and here the difficulty in defining the scope of "mental pain and anguish" and therefore the extent of Iraq's liability presented problems bearing on the resolution of claims for compensation for sexual assault. Differences in "national approaches" made reaching conclusions based on anything other than what can be easily monetized—for example, losses of income or medical expenses as opposed to feelings of shame and pollution or the pain of family rejection—impossible to achieve. The potentially infinite mental anguish a victim might suffer moved the Council to establish ceilings for claims in seven categories of mental pain and anguish (Decision 8). These include a ceiling of "$5,000 for each incident of sexual assault, aggravated assault or torture. Various family and overall ceilings also apply" (Crook 1993:154).[12]

Although one might contest the justice of claims limitations or outright disqualification of some categories of damage, the UNCC/PAAC model offers substantial accountability and justice to wronged individuals through a procedure that grants the maximum dignity and privacy to victims of war crimes. At the most basic level, the fundamental principle of state responsibility obviates what is a near impossibility in most instances—that is, victims having to identify particular individuals who inflicted damage on them. It is independent of the whereabouts of war criminals, a critical advantage in cases in which victims have no reason to believe the national courts of their attackers will assist them. The principles and procedures of UNCC/PAAC provide a tribunal that is especially apt for the adjudication of claims of wartime rape: The crime is defined as having been committed to implement state policy; the victim is treated as injured by state policy and not a personal attack. The relative privacy of the proceedings is an additional protection for the sensibilities of victims and their families.

The small number of Kuwaiti claims for damages due to rape, universally attributed to the shame attached to being a rape victim, could be handled differently but in a way that comports with the principles and procedures of UNCC/PAAC. The rules might accommodate a separate, yet conforming, procedure for confirming sexual assault. PAAC officials had hoped to encourage rape victims to come forward by guaranteeing them anonymity. However, only three came forward (personal communications from two PAAC staff members). Rather than requiring rape victims to present their own claims, however, medical records and records obtained by the military recorders could be used as the basis of claims of publicly unnamed persons—Jane Does and John Does—and forwarded by the responsible agencies to PAAC for review. Any money collected could be held in an escrow account from which injured individuals could apply later for their compensation. The spectacle of aged Korean women mobilizing to demonstrate against the Japanese government, and demanding compensation for sexual assaults committed during World War II,[13] demonstrates both the persistence of suffering experienced by rape victims and their greater willingness to make claims when the prospect of public shame loses its power to make them fear for their life chances.

A second strategy for adjudicating war-crimes charges has been initiated in the Bosnian conflict. In Bosnia-Herzegovina, there is neither access by an international tribunal to territories and populations harboring persons accused of war crimes nor an international consensus regarding which, if any, of the belligerents is responsible for illegal acts. The ongoing nature of the conflict is a third and, perhaps in the end, the chief, obstacle to establishing anything like a satisfactory system of justice. Yet to wait for the conclusion of the conflict to move on the issue of war crimes was widely perceived as little more than an invitation for even more of them to be committed (e.g., Rubin 1992; Anthony Lewis 1994).

The ideology of ethnonationalism that shapes the discourse on the war in the former Yugoslavia is practiced as "ethnic cleansing," the elimination of persons on the basis of religion, ideology, dialect, or political allegiance from territory held by one or another victorious army. The discovery of Serb-run concentration camps in Bosnia in late summer 1992 (Engleberg 1992a–c; Crane-Engel 1994) provided evidence of genocide that was horrifyingly reminiscent of Nazi and Khmer death camps. Although the international situation remained as stalemated as ever with regard to a consensus on the war, making policy on war crimes proved to be possible though difficult.

The United Nations Security Council voted unanimously on October 6, 1992, to create a war-crimes commission, the first such body to be established since World War II. The commission was charged with collecting evidence about possible atrocities committed anywhere in the former Yugoslavia and making decisions about who should be prosecuted for them (Paul Lewis 1992). Diplomats were quoted as saying that the immediate aim of the new resolution was to deter atrocities by "send[ing] a clear message that those responsible for the atrocities and gross violations . . . must be brought to justice" (A1).

Problems with the commission concept were noted immediately by international jurists. Alfred Rubin (1992:A32) criticized the injustice in the mandate of the commission, confined as it was to investigations in the former Yugoslavia: "If the tribunal is a good idea, shouldn't it be open also to complaints against Iraq . . . the Irish Republican Army and the Royal Ulster Constabulary . . . [and] the Palestine Liberation Organization?" The commission's lack of jurisdiction to investigate charges of atrocities committed by armies of nation-states in addition to insurgent groups was also noted: If the PLO, why not the Israeli army? If the IRA or the RUC, why not the British army? And if Iraq, why not the US military? The Tokyo and Nuremburg tribunals were effective because they were the courts of victors; there were no victors in the former Yugoslavia—indeed, the likely winner was the primary target of the commission. Rubin concluded that the commission's flaws left deterrence through exposure as its only function.

Benjamin Ferencz (1992:A32) hoped that the commission would be just the first step toward the establishment of an international criminal court. Such an outcome would meet the objections to the commission made by Rubin and would be a permanent addition to the range of international organizations available to "enforce the rule of law." The logic of this position was compelling. In May 1993, the Security Council voted unanimously to establish a tribunal to hear charges of war crimes committed in the former Yugoslavia. US delegate Madeleine K. Albright stressed during the debate that rape charges would be among those the court would hear (Paul Lewis 1993a).

The commission had begun its work without investigators of its own or even subpoena powers, having to rely on information gathered by others, chiefly governments (Robbins 1993:A8). By July 1993, a war-crimes database compiled by law students at De Paul University in Chicago had counted "some 25,000 victims of rape, torture, murder, and ethnic cleansing" (A1). Despite this mounting evidence, disputes among members of the Security Council regarding the religion of a top candidate delayed the naming of the tribunal's chief prosecutor for a year. Like the eventually nominated chief prosecutor Richard Goldstone, a highly respected jurist from South Africa, none of the judges finally appointed was a Muslim.

The tribunal was not permitted to try anyone in absentia. In late 1992, a high US official had accused ten Yugoslavs of being war criminals, a list including Serbian president Slobodan Milosević and Bosnian Serb leader Radovan Karadzić, persons unlikely ever to be indicted, much less brought to trial (Robbins 1993:A8). The tribunal's lack of access to top war criminals has been criticized since its inception. However, on February 13, 1995, the tribunal handed down the first indictment for genocide ever made by an international court, against Zeljko Meakić, commander of the Omarska camp. The specific crimes committed under his direction include rape (Cohen 1995).

CONCLUSIONS

The repeated recurrence of wholesale rape as a strategy of conflict, together with the acute and long-lasting suffering rape inflicts on victims, support the logic and justice of treating rape as a war crime. Yet unlike other human rights abuses that inflict physical and mental harm, rape includes social opprobrium directed toward the victim as part of its repertoire of damage. This quality makes rape technically and morally difficult to prosecute successfully in domestic criminal courts. It is no less so in the context of civil or international conflict. However, the failure to prosecute offenders for wartime rape and other human rights abuses confers a kind of permission for it to continue. Ignoring rape as a war crime also has contributed to the persistent myth that rape is a crime for which the victim bears significant culpability.

It may be the similarity of rape in war to rape in domestic settings that explains the unwillingness of those responsible for charging and prosecuting offenders to treat rape the same way that other human rights abuses are treated. It is much easier to prove a case of domestic nonsexual assault in criminal court than a case of rape (Brownmiller 1975:373–74). This is not only because of men's fears that they will be falsely charged with rape but also because of the subordinate status of women and the widespread assumption that men as persons are entitled to a degree of physical dominance over women that women as persons are denied over men (Johnson 1988). Laws and customs permitting men to rape and beat their wives have no counterparts privileging violent criminal behavior by wives against husbands (Barry 1979).

The symbolic role of women and their sexual violation during war contributes to the complexity of formulating war-crimes charges. At the same time, the desire to avoid shame supports the privatization of rape rather than its treatment as an act of war. Still, evidence about rape contributes to charges of human rights abuses committed against civilians during a conflict. Thus, it strengthens claims for reparations and compensation or, failing that, retribution of some kind. A government's position on wartime rape depends on whether politicization is more likely than privatization to promote national interests.

The politicization of wartime rape guarantees neither consideration for the victims nor that the role of rape as a strategy of conflict will be pondered once the war is over. As the example of Nanking shows, even when evidence is overwhelming, an accounting of rapes may be omitted from assessments of damage. This lessens the likelihood that rape will appear on a list of war-crimes charges or as grounds for demands for compensation to victims. Such omissions contribute to collective amnesia about the myriad specific examples of wartime rape that contradict erroneous assumptions that rape is an opportunistic crime committed by depraved or deprived individuals. This assumption feeds deeply held prejudices about the nature of rape and the relative culpability of victims and rapists.

Myths of culpability also affect the treatment of victims. Shame makes victims reluctant to press charges or demand reparations. The ostensible protectors of victims are also culpable: the family that is helpless in the face of attackers, and the state and its army whose impotence failed to shield a civilian population from atrocities. States can defend their failure to press for justice for rape victims by insisting that they are protecting the victims from further pain and harm when, in reality, leaders of nations and their armies prefer that no one remember how they failed to perform their most fundamental obligation to protect.

Ignoring rape as a war crime reinforces assumptions connected to the symbolic role of women and denies what Hannah Arendt (1965) calls their "plurality," their individual identities. It also denies them standing as injured persons before the law. When women are denied justice, rapists, their commanding officers, and their governments escape accountability. Even if rape is included as a class of war crimes, however, accountability and justice will continue to be difficult to achieve. The ability of the United Nations to develop, under UNCC, an innovative procedure that confers so much autonomy on wronged individuals depended on the decision of the UN Security Council that Iraq's invasion and occupation of Kuwait were illegal. The Security Council was the effective court for war-crimes trials against Iraq. Resolutions passed by the Security Council in response to the Iraqi invasion reflected the United Nations' adjudication of the conflict. Having found Iraq guilty of the war and therefore of every crime committed in the war's prosecution, defining, collecting, and establishing the validity of individual claims for damages quickly became routine.

The drawbacks to such a procedure are also clear. Iraqi leaders from the president to field commanders escaped personal accountability for what were, after all, decisions made by people and not by an automaton—the Iraqi "state." For victims to whom "justice" includes the trial and punishment of the individuals personally responsible for breaking their bodies and ruining their lives, recognition that they were wronged and monetary compensation for the damages inflicted on them constitute incomplete rather than full justice. A second drawback is that the achievement of more than partial restitution is far from guaranteed. Iraq has so far rejected the opportunity to sell a limited amount of oil under UN supervision for humanitarian purposes, one of which is to provide money to pay damages to war crimes victims. Instead, it has flouted the Security Council's sanctions by smuggling oil out and selling it on black markets. This recalcitrance denies Iraq's responsibility for its war crimes as well as additional money to pay damage claims. A further impediment to restitution is the dependence of the replenishment of the fund on implementation by member states, some of whose interests conflict with those of war victims, once economic sanctions against Iraq are lifted. Despite these drawbacks, however, the principle of state responsibility and the procedures protecting victims that mark the operation of UNCC/PAAC are models for achieving limited but significant justice for victims of rape and other human rights abuses.

Neither accountability nor justice is an easy proposition for victims of wartime rape in Bosnia-Herzegovina. There is no international consensus on who is responsible for the conflict—whatever degree of accountability is achieved must be accumulated one defendant at a time. Unlike UNCC/PAAC, the tribunal established to try war crimes committed in the former Yugoslavia has yet to prove itself effective in achieving either accountability or justice. Under its rules, the tribunal is unlikely to indict or try those at the top of the pyramid of responsibility for policies that utilized rape as an instrument of terror and genocide, tainting the justice of trials of lower-level individuals directly involved in rape and other human rights abuses. In effect, the tribunal's necessarily retail approach to accountability reprivatizes rape and other human rights abuses as crimes committed by individuals against individuals or, at best, by a group of individuals against a helpless population.

To consider wartime rape as a human rights abuse encourages us to think about other brutal acts of war and question why so many survivors are so willing to forget them. Victims don't forget, of course, but as one moves away from the direct targets of abuse and the people who love them, shame, distaste, and denial characterize the responses of most of the rest. Much has been written about the German population and its callousness to the plight of Jews during the Nazi era. Yet people of every nationality, including Americans, dismiss human rights abuses as reasons for changing their opinions or their behavior when such actions cost money, strategic advantage, or status. Rape is more convoluted but not fundamentally different from other crimes against humanity. For every human rights abuse, accountability is too seldom demanded and justice far too rarely achieved.

ACKNOWLEDGMENTS

The author thanks Jennifer Louise Davis for her research assistance, and Martha Bailey, David Binder, Obrad Kesić, Haya al-Mughni, David Newbury, Roger Smith, Kristin Stilt, and Robin Teske for their advice and helpful comments on earlier drafts.

NOTES

1. A paradigm of genocide is developed by Helen Fein in "Defining Genocide as a Sociological Concept," *Current Sociology* 38:1 (Spring 1990), 25–30. It includes the notion of a collectivity as constituted by ideology or other forms of group identity *in addition to* ethnicity. Thus, the behavior of the Khmer Rouge in Cambodia is genocide even though the ethnic identities of killers and killed were both Khmer. Other chapters in the Fein volume discuss cases of genocide in addition to the ones noted in this text, and explore theories offering causal explanations.

2. That this practice in Greece was not confined to the Homeric period is evident in the Athenian treatment of Melos during the Peloponnesian War—see Thucycides, *The Peloponnesian War,* trans. Rex Warner (Baltimore: Penguin, 1959), 366.

3. The Nuremburg tribunal did not include rape on the list of war crimes. During the war there was no rerun in the European theater of allegations on the same level as stories of the World War I "rape of Belgium." Indeed, given both the volume of propaganda films produced by the Allies during World War II and the volume of evidence amassed afterward, contemporary charges of war crimes made against Germany during the war seem to have been vastly understated. Afterward, "sexual forms of torture, including rape, were documented at the [Nuremburg] trials" (MacKinnon 1993, 30; see also Brownmiller 1975).

4. Although most of the accusations were made on television, some also appeared in the press. See, for example, *New York Times,* December 2, 1990, 19; December 8, 1990, 8; December 16, 1990, 1. Kuwaitis whom I interviewed in 1992 said that during the war, they had heard reports that the number of Kuwaiti women raped amounted to 8,000.

5. The importance of ritual pollution to Iraqi behavior in Kuwait can be inferred from evidence other than the sexual assaults—for example, the many deposits of urine and feces on furniture, desks, documents, and other places in private homes and public buildings, and the type of vandalization of the works of Kuwaiti artists in the National Museum (Tétreault 1992).

6. "In the war-crimes trials for the genocidal war against Bosnia-Herzegovina and Croatia, will those who incited to genocide through rape, sexual torture, and murder—the Serbian pornographers as well as the high policymakers and the underlings—get what they deserve (1993:30)?"

7. I recall one in particular that showed Hitler beaming down on a tableful of naked infants that the voiceover said were babies whose young, unmarried, Aryan mothers had been impregnated in special camps by German soldiers specifically selected to breed new members of the German superrace. Of all the footage that I saw, that segment, along with another from a film shot in Russia during a rout of Russian forces by German troops which featured the death of the person holding the camera, are the only ones that I remember out of the scores of hours of propaganda films that I and my classmates were subjected to in the name of social studies education at the height of the Cold War. As an adult, I would classify both of these clips as pornographic, and as powerful incitements to fear and visceral hatred.

8. The victim group that is the primary subject of Kuwaiti arguments opposing the lifting of sanctions is the several hundred Kuwaitis taken prisoner by the Iraqis and never returned.

9. Money to pay claims was to be provided by assessing Iraq a percentage of its income from oil sales but no such sales have been made to date because of continuing UN economic sanctions against Iraq (Crook 1993:144). A special procedure was established under UN Security Council Resolution 706 (August 15, 1991) authorizing the sale of $1.6 billion worth of oil over six months, with 30 percent of that to go to the fund and the rest to administrative costs and the purchase, under strict supervision, of food, medicine, and other items to meet civilian needs (146). Iraq has refused to comply with the conditions specified in the resolution.

10. The Gulf Cooperation Council is an international organization modeled after the European Community that was established in 1981. Its members are Kuwait, Saudi Arabia, Bahrain, Qatar, Oman, and the United Arab Emirates.

11. In some cases, claims for damages in excess of the limits set in categories A and B were presented as A and B claims. The additional damages were assessed for things like uncompensated medical bills. This procedure enabled small claims to be processed in the A and B categories, whose settlement was the top priority of UNCC.

12. It should be clear that mental pain and anguish were recognized as resulting from injuries other than sexual assault. Ceilings were set in other areas as well. For example, the Council approved a ceiling of $15,000 for mental pain and anguish resulting from the death of a spouse, child, or parent (Crook 1993:154).

13. These are the so-called comfort women, who were kidnapped as girls and sequestered in military brothels for the entertainment of Japanese troops. The very existence of the comfort women was denied until very recently, and their claims for reparations have so far been dismissed by the Japanese government. [Editors' note: Some former "comfort women" have now received reparations.] One reason offered for the government's refusal to admit culpability and make even token payments to the survivors is that this would amount to a very large amount of money. This by itself points up the need to institutionalize procedures for assigning responsibility and assessing damages for wartime rape as a means to limit such behavior in the future.

REFERENCES

Amnesty International. 1993. *Bosnia-Herzegovina: Rape and Sexual Abuse by Armed Forces.* New York: Amnesty International.

Arendt, Hannah. 1965. *On Revolution.* New York: Compass.

Asia Watch and the Women's Rights Project. 1992. *Double Jeopardy: Police Abuse of Women in Pakistan.* New York: Human Rights Watch.

Asia Watch and Physicians for Human Rights. 1993. *Rape in Kashmir: A Crime of War.* New York: Asia Watch.

Asem, Adel, and Haya al-Mughni. 1994. "Claiming for Compensation through the United Nations Compensation Commission: The Case of Kuwait." Paper presented at the International Conference on the Effects of the Iraqi Aggression on Kuwait. Kuwait. April.

Bard, Morton, and Diane Sangrey. 1979. *The Crime Victim's Book.* New York: Basic Books.

Barry, Kathleen. 1979. *Female Sexual Slavery.* Englewood Cliffs, N.J.: Prentice-Hall.

Brownmiller, Susan. 1975. *Against Our Will: Men, Women and Rape.* New York: Simon and Schuster.

Burns, John F. 1992. "150 Muslims Say Serbs Raped Them in Bosnia." *New York Times* October 3:L5.

Cohen, Roger. 1993. "2 Serbs to Be Shot for Killings and Rapes." *New York Times* March 31:A6.

———. 1994. "Ex-Guard for Serbs Tells of Grisly 'Cleansing' Camp." *New York Times* August 1:A1, A8.

———. 1995. "Tribunal Charges Genocide by Serbs." *New York Times* February 14:A1–A2.

Coll, Steve. 1994. "War Crimes and Punishment: Bosnia in the Shadow of the Holocaust." *Washington Post Magazine* September 25.

Crane-Engel, Melinda. 1994. "Germany vs. Genocide." *New York Times Magazine* October 30.

Crook, John R. 1993. "The United Nations Compensation Commission—A New Structure to Enforce State Responsibility." *American Journal of International Law* 87.

In re Jane Doe et al. against Radovan Karadzić. United States District Court, Southern District of New York, Civ. 93-0878 PKL. 1993. "Complaint for Genocide: War Crimes and Crimes against Humanity; Summary Execution; Torture; Cruel,

Inhuman or Degrading Treatment; Wrongful Death; Assault and Battery; and Intentional Infliction of Emotional Harm. Class Action: Jury Trial Demand." February. "Memorandum in Support of Motion to Dismiss before Answer." May. "Reply Declaration of Lawrence W. Schilling in Support of Defendant's Motions to Dismiss." May. "Plaintiff's Memorandum of Points and Authorities in Opposition to Defendant's Motion to Dismiss before Answer." August. "Plaintiffs' Sur-Reply Brief in Opposition to Defendant's Motion to Dismiss Before Answer." October.

Dover, K. J. 1978. *Greek Homosexuality*. London: Duckworth.

Engelberg, Stephen. 1992a. "Bosnians Provide Accounts of Abuse in Serbian Camps. " *New York Times* August 4:A1.

———. 1992b. "Refugees from Camps Tell of Agony and Terror." *New York Times* August 7:A5.

———. 1992c. "Clearer Picture of Bosnia Camps: A Brutal Piece of a Larger Plan." *New York Times* August 16:1, 14.

Fein, Helen. 1990. "Genocide: A Sociological Perspective," *Current Sociology* 38:1 (Spring).

Ferencz, Benjamin B. 1992. Letter to the editor. *New York Times* October:A32.

Garlan, Yvon. 1988. *Slavery in Ancient Greece*. Rev. and expanded ed. Trans. Janet Lloyd. Ithaca: Cornell University Press.

Glenny, Misha. 1994. "Council of Despair." *New York Times* December 6:A15.

Hartman, Carol R., and Ann Wolbert Burgess. 1988. "Rape Trauma and Treatment of the Victim." In *Post-Traumatic Therapy and Victims of Violence*, ed. F. M. Ochberg. New York: Brunner Mazel.

Human Rights Watch National Coalition for Haitian Refugees. 1994. *Rape in Haiti: A Weapon of Terror*. Washington, D.C.: Human Rights Watch.

Hunt, Lynn. 1984. *Politics, Culture, and Class in the French Revolution*. Berkeley: University of California Press.

Johnson, Miriam. 1988. *Strong Mothers, Weak Wives*. Berkeley: University of California Press.

Kilpatrick, Dean G., and Lois J. Veronen. 1983. "Treatment for Rape-Related Problems: Crisis Intervention Is Not Enough." In *Crisis Intervention*, ed. L. H. Cohen, W. Claiborn, and G. Specter. New York: Human Sciences Press.

Lancaster, John. 1993. "Administration Releases Report on Iraqi War Crimes in Kuwait." *Washington Post* March 20:A18.

Lewin, Tamar. 1993. "The Balkans Rapes: A Legal Test for the Outraged." *New York Times* January 15:B15.

Lewis, Anthony. 1994. " 'The Civilized World.' " *New York Times* July 1:A17.

Lewis, Paul. 1992. "U.N. Sets Up War-Crimes Panel on Charges of Balkan Atrocities." *New York Times* October 7:A1, A6.

———. 1993a. "Security Council Establishes War-Crimes Tribunal for the Balkans." *New York Times* May 26:A13.

———. 1993b. "Disputes Hamper U.N. Drive for a War Crimes Tribunal." *New York Times* September 9:A10.

———. 1994. "If There Ever Were a Nuremburg for the Former Yugoslavia. . . ." *New York Times* June 12:E7.

MacKinnon, Catherine A. 1993. "Turning Rape into Pornography: Postmodern Genocide." *Ms.* July/August.

Makiya, Kanan. 1993. *Cruelty and Silence: War, Tyranny, Uprising, and the Arab World*. New York: Norton.

Mann, Judy. 1991. "Kuwaiti Rape a Doubly Savage Crime." *Washington Post* March 29:C3.

Mernissi, Fatima. 1991. *The Veil and the Male Elite: A Feminist Interpretation of Women's Rights in Islam*. Trans. Mary Jo Lakeland. Reading, Mass.: Addison Wesley.

Mosse, George L. 1985. *Nationalism and Sexuality: Respectability and Abnormal Sexuality in Modern Europe*. New York: Howard Fertig.

Al-Mughni, Haya, and Fawzia al-Turkait. 1994. "Dealing with Trauma: Cultural Barriers to Self-Recovery: The Case of Kuwaiti Women." Paper presented at the seminar on The Effective Methods for Encountering the Psychological and the Social Effects of the Iraqi Aggression, sponsored by the Social Development Office of the Amiri Diwan. Kuwait. March.

New York Times. 1992. "Rape—and Soldiers' Morale." Editorial December 7:A18.

Newbury, David. 1995. Personal communication.

Peristiany, J. G., ed. 1965. *Honor and Shame: The Values of Mediterranean Society*. London: Weidenfeld and Nicolson.

Personal Narratives. 1992. "Rape after Rape after Rape." *New York Times* December 13:E17.

Peterson, V. Spike. 1994. "Gendered Nationalisms." *Peace Review* 6:1.

Quindlen, Anna. 1993a. "Gynocide." *New York Times* March 10:A19.

———. 1993b. "The Rescuers." *New York Times* May 5:A23.

Reisman, W. Michael, and Chris T. Antoniou, eds. 1994. *The Laws of War: A Comprehensive Collection of Primary Documents on International Laws Governing Armed Conflict*. New York: Vintage.

Riding, Alan. 1993. "European Inquiry Says Serbs' Forces Have Raped 20,000." *New York Times* January 9:1, 4.

Robbins, Carla Anne. 1993. "Balkan Judgments: World again Confronts Moral Issues Involved in War-Crimes Trials." *Wall Street Journal* July 13:A1, A8.

Roy, K. K. 1975. "Feelings and Attitudes of Raped Women of Bangladesh towards Military Personnel of Pakistan." In *Victimology: A New Focus*, vol. 5, *Exploiters and Exploited: The Dynamics of Victimization*. Lexington, Mass.: D. C. Heath.

Rubin, Alfred P. 1992. Letter to the editor, *New York Times* October 23:A32.

Simons, Marlise. 1994. "Bosnian Rapes Go Untried by the U.N." *New York Times* December 7:A8.

Smith, Roger W. 1994a. "Genocide and the Politics of Rape: Historical and Psychological Perspectives." Presented at Remembering for the Future: Internation Conference on the Holocaust and Genocide. March 13–17. Berlin.

———. 1994b. "Women and Genocide: Notes on an Unwritten History." *Holocaust and Genocide Studies* 8:3 Winter.

Tétreault, Mary Ann. 1992. Interviews in Kuwait, March, September–October.

———. 1994a. Interviews in Kuwait, March.

———. 1994b. "Whose Honor? Whose Liberation? Women and the Reconstruction of Politics in Kuwait." In *Women and Revolution in Africa, Asia, and the New World,* ed. Mary Ann Tétreault. Columbia: University of South Carolina Press.

———, and Haya al-Mughni. 1995. "Women, Citizenship, and Nationalism in Kuwait." Paper presented at the annual meeting of the International Studies Association. February 21–25. Chicago.

Theweleit, Klaus. 1987. *Male Fantasies.* Vol. 1: *Women, Floods, Bodies, History,* trans. Stephen Conway. Minneapolis: University of Minnesota Press.

Thomas, Dorothy Q., and Regan E. Ralph. 1993. "Rape in War: The Tradition of Impunity." *SAIS Review* 14:1. Spring.

Tillion, Germaine. 1983. *The Republic of Cousins: Women's Oppression in Mediterranean Society,* trans. Quintin Hoare. London: Al Saqi Books.

Williams, Carol J. 1993. "Bosnia's Orphans of Rape: Innocent Legacy of Hatred." *Los Angeles Times* July 24:A1, A12.

Yuval-Davis, Nita, and Floya Anthias, eds. 1989. *Woman-Nation-State.* London: Macmillan.

P A R T   F O U R

Social Change

Thus far we have emphasized the *stability* of gender inequality. We have examined how socialization, social definitions of gender, and the structure and content of all the major institutional arenas of social life converge to produce a world in which males and females are understood as essentially different and are differentially valued and rewarded. The forces that perpetuate gender inequality are so intricately interwoven into the social fabric and so deeply embedded in the identities of individuals that changing them is beyond the power of anyone individual, no matter how well-intentioned that individual may be.

Yet societies can and do *change*. Anyone who has lived through the past three decades in the United States cannot help but notice that there has been substantial change in the position, behaviors, and consciousness of women and men. In earlier readings, we discussed some of the dynamic forces that have *unintentionally* recast gender consciousness and inequality, including new cultural meanings, technological innovations, demographic processes, and economic factors. To understand fully how systems of gender inequality change, we must also examine the ways that women have sought collectively and *intentionally* to reduce their disadvantage. Certainly every society or group contains individuals who are nonconformists, but significant and lasting social change is ultimately the result of collective action rather than individual action.

In Part Four, we turn our attention to struggles to transform culture and social institutions in two arenas. Section Ten focuses on the politicization of gender in the state and global politics. Section Eleven documents the rich history and diversity of the women's movement and examines continuity and change in the history of American feminism. To understand the part that women themselves have played in improving their status, we focus, on the one hand, on women's actions "within the system" by conventional and orderly means and, on the other, on women's collective actions "outside the system" by unconventional and disorderly means.

Politics is generally thought to refer to the institutionalized or authoritative system by which a society makes decisions, allocates power, and distributes resources. According to the traditional view, voting, campaigning, lobbying, conducting organizational activities, holding office, and working in political parties are classified as politics because they take place in the context of formal governmental structure.

Feminist scholars have pointed out that the standard definition of politics is too narrow, however, for understanding women's political participation. It not only assumes a particular type of state and political system but ignores the fact that in most industrialized societies women have been denied access to the formal political process until fairly recently.

In the United States, women were not allowed to vote, hold office, or sit on juries until the twentieth century. Even after women received the vote with the passage of the Nineteenth Amendment to the US Constitution in 1920, their participation in electoral politics, involvement in major political parties, and election to public offices lagged significantly behind men's. African-American women, moreover, remained effectively disenfranchised in southern states by racist voter-registration rules until the late 1960s.

It was not until a half century after women got the vote that the gap between men's and women's party involvement and office holding began to shrink, and even today women fare better in local and state politics than in the national arena. Voting turnout differences between women and men finally disappeared in 1976. But it took until 1980 for women to use the electoral process to express their collective dissatisfaction by voting in line with their interests in women's equality, creating for the first time what has come to be known as the "gender gap."

Elections, participation in party politics, running for office, and lobbying are not, however, the only ways to express grievances, influence public policy, and achieve social change. Politics also includes social movements, protests, and other group actions intended to change cultural beliefs and influence the distribution of power and resources in a state or community. This definition is broad enough to encompass women's long history of participation in collective action on their own behalf through the feminist movement as well as in pursuit of other human rights causes through female reform societies, women's church groups, alternative religious societies, women's clubs, and other social movements.

Social movements are collective attempts to bring about change. They originate outside the established political system, forge links between individuals and groups who share common concerns, and mobilize the people and resources needed to pursue the goal of social change. In democratic societies, social movements and the tactics they employ—marches, boycotts, strikes, demonstrations, protests—are a regular part of the democratic process. Movements act as pressure groups on behalf of people excluded from routine decision-making processes and the dominant power structure; they are a major source of new social patterns and cultural understandings.

Because participants in social movements typically challenge conventional ideas and behaviors, they are often stereotyped by the larger society as deviant and irrational and are accused of exaggerating their claims. If we take a historical perspective on social movements, however, we will often find that today's social institution is likely to have been yesterday's social movement. In other words, social movement participants are not qualitatively different from other kinds of social actors and their actions are governed by the same norms that underlie other groups.

Although popular opinion often presents the women's movement as a relatively recent phenomenon, its roots are well grounded historically. Indeed, the similarities between the views of contemporary feminists and earlier feminists are remarkable. More than 200 years ago, for example, Abigail Adams gave this warning to her husband, John, when he was fashioning the Constitution of the United States:

> In the new code of laws which I suppose will be necessary for you to make, I desire you would remember the ladies and be more generous and favorable to them than your ancestors. Do not put such unlimited power in the hands of husbands. Remember, all men would be tyrants if they could.
>
> If particular care and attention is not paid to the ladies, we are determined to foment a rebellion, and will not hold ourselves bound by any laws in which we have no voice or representation.

Unfortunately, John Adams failed to take his wife's warning seriously. He urged her to be patient and said there were more important issues than the rights of "ladies."

As this example illustrates, in the United States, as in much of the industrialized world, the history of feminist activism is long and rich. Until the past three decades, however, knowledge of the women's movement remained mostly buried. Initially most scholars studying the women's movement held that feminism in the United States has come in waves. The first wave began in the nineteenth century as a broad attack on male domination, continued for almost a century, and then died precipitously in 1920 with the passage of the suffrage amendment granting women the right to vote, which by then had become the movement's major goal. Supposedly, a forty-year lull followed before the second wave, or new feminist movement, erupted in the mid-1960s.

As a result of new research, a different interpretation of the history of the American women's movement has recently emerged that emphasizes the continuity and persistence of women's resistance. The newer work recognizes the great waves of mass feminist activism, but it also points to the survival of feminism in less highly mobilized periods. It focuses not only on the continuity of the movement but on changes in feminist ideology, goals, constituency, tactics, and organizational style. In addition to self-proclaimed feminists, working-class women and women of color also have a long history of struggle on their own behalf, in labor unions, socialist and communist groups, women's clubs, and within churches and communities. Any analysis of contemporary feminism and the backlash against it must consider the multiple forms of the enduring struggle against gender inequality.

The readings thus far suggest the depth, pervasiveness, and persistence of gender inequality and the intersection of gender inequality with inequalities of race, class, and sexuality. It is not surprising, then, that contemporary feminism encompasses a wide range of struggles, from local efforts to improve women's daily lives to broad visions of fundamentally restructuring all institutions that perpetuate and sustain male dominance. The media have repeatedly proclaimed the present period the "postfeminist era" and many women disavow the feminist label—yet, as we shall see, women's movements remain very much alive. Feminist groups can be found within every major institution: in the professions, academia, labor, religion, politics, the arts, music, and literature. Feminist groups have mobilized around practically every issue imaginable, including employment and equal pay issues, abortion rights, health, depression, substance abuse, pornography, prostitution, disability rights, spirituality, child care, nuclear weaponry, lesbianism, incest, battering, racism, and older women's rights. Feminists organize around sexual, racial and ethnic, and class identities.

The flourishing of women's organizing in these multiple forms can be considered a "third wave" of feminism that builds on the successes and lessons of earlier activism. Third-wave feminism is characterized by the view that gender is multiple and variable because it is also shaped by race, class, sexuality, nationality, and other factors. Because feminism addresses every facet of social life, it has had a major and lasting impact not only on economic, political, and cultural institutions but also on the consciousness and lives of individual women and men. Third-wave feminism grows as the women and men born after, and shaped by, the sweeping changes wrought by the 1970s women's movement reshape feminism and the larger world.

In Part Four, we examine the diversity of women's participation in politics and contemporary feminist movements, emphasizing the continuity and global nature of feminist challenges as well as changes and differences in feminist goals, constituencies, and tactics. The readings document the multiple forms that feminist resistance can take. They recognize that protest can be directed at the structural, cultural, or individual level and that resistance varies across cultural and national contexts. We conclude with an overview of the American women's movement and a look to the future. As you consider these readings, consider in what ways gender systems are shaped by national governments and transnational politics. In what ways have the efforts of women to transform gender succeeded?

Global Politics and the State

National governments, international relations, and transnational economies exert wide-ranging influence on gender systems. Government-controlled economies shape differences in women's and men's wages and the prices of goods that women and men produce and consume. National and international policies on education, welfare, health, and various forms of violence against women affect women's daily lives in profound ways.

Because governmental policies frequently reflect dominant sexist ideologies, they often serve to reinforce the disadvantaged position of women in most countries. The state, in fact, plays a central part in maintaining a social structure of inequality between women and men. The state plays a crucial role in perpetuating inequalities of class (through regulation of the labor market or of minimum wages, for example) and of race (through legislative policies regarding immigration or affirmative action, for example).

Feminist scholars focus on the ways that state actions and policies create and perpetuate gender categories, ideologies of women's inferiority, and differential access of women and men to valued resources and power. The state's role in upholding gender stratification, of course, is inextricably linked to its role in reinforcing race and class stratification, as the articles in this section point out.

The increasing interdependence of the world's countries means that women's lives are shaped not only by the governmental policies of their own country but also by transnational politics and economics as well. A complex web of interrelation-

ships among transnational corporations, states, groups within states, geography, technology, and ideologies of gender, race, ethnicity, and religion shapes relations among women, states, and global politics. In this section, contributors examine the relationships among constructions of gender, women's lives, and the state, both in the United States and internationally.

One of the major topics of analysis for feminist scholars of the state is the ways that governments regulate women's childbearing and family structures. The first reading looks at how the government regulates the lives of poor women with children. In "Surviving the Welfare System: How AFDC Recipients Make Ends Meet in Chicago," Kathryn Edin shows how AFDC payments provide too little money to support women and their children, forcing women to earn additional money by working under-the-table jobs. In contrast to the stereotypes of the lazy welfare mother, Edin shows that surviving on welfare requires hard work and ingenuity. Yet the low-wage jobs most welfare recipients are qualified for provide no better alternative. What kinds of social changes might alleviate the problems Edin describes?

Some early suffragists speculated that women's oppression by the state would end with women's access to the vote, a symbol of political participation. Yet women's suffrage did not, in fact, make the electoral process gender neutral. In "The Year of the Woman, the Angry White Male, and the Soccer Mom," Susan Carroll describes the changing frames the media use to portray gender in recent elections. Each of these catch phrases, Carroll argues, over-simplifies complicated gender trends in elections. The "soccer mom" was held up as a typical woman voter in the 1996 presidential elections—devoted to her family and concerned primarily about issues that affected her children. That media stereotype reflected only a fraction of the issues that concern women; it left out a range of issues, from welfare to reproductive rights to women's experiences in the workforce. Carroll points out that the media focus on "soccer moms" left other groups of women and other issues invisible. How have the media framed gender in the most recent elections? Do these frames reinforce or challenge traditional roles for women? Can you find examples of these frames in recent media coverage?

While Edin and Carroll examine how women's status is shaped by politics in the United States, the next two articles focus on the international politics of gender. The oppression of women in Third World countries is compounded by the fact that wealthy countries and poor countries occupy very different positions in the global economic system. In "Our Policies, Their Consequences: Zambian Women's Lives under 'Structural Adjustment,' " Amber Ault and Eve Sandberg show that the oppression of women in Third World countries is connected to the self-interested practices of wealthier countries like the United States and international agencies like the International Monetary Fund. Based on news coverage of international economic organizations such as the International Monetary Fund and the World Trade Organization, what are the effects of these policies on gender inequality?

Cynthia Enloe further discusses the international economics and politics of women's labor in "The Globetrotting Sneaker," suggesting that women workers' interests have been left behind as international trade has increased. Taking sneaker manufacturers as an example, Enloe shows how international corporations profit from the labor of underpaid and exploited women workers in Third World countries. She argues that women's acceptance of traditional submissive, family-oriented models for their lives makes them ideal workers for companies that want low-paid, compliant workers. Documenting the activism of women workers in South Korea, Enloe shows that Nike moved its manufacturing from South Korea to countries like China and Indonesia, where there was less organizing by workers. Yet, she suggests, increasing international organizing by women workers holds the potential for social change, particularly if women in the United States join them. Do you agree with Enloe that companies like Nike and Reebok should not employ women at such low wages? How does your standard of living depend on the work of the women workers that Enloe discusses? Where are your sneakers and clothing produced? Where is the clothing sold by your college or university manufactured? What might you and other Americans do to improve the living situation of women workers abroad?

Finally, Myra Marx Ferree describes how different state structures can shape different kinds of resistance by women. In "Patriarchies and Feminisms: The Two Women's Movements of Post-Unification Germany," Ferree argues that women in East and West Germany experienced patriarchy in vastly different ways before unification because of the difference between the capitalist and communist states. While women in West Germany were economically dependent on their husbands, women in East Germany were dependent on the state. As a result of these different experiences, even after the two Germanies unified, feminists from West Germany tended to focus on the oppressive nature of private family relationships, while those from East Germany emphasized the role of public policy and the state in women's oppression. Neither side is "right," Ferree suggests. Instead, we need to understand that gender inequality can play out in very different ways in different national contexts, and that as a result "feminism is intrinsically multiple in its analyses and emphases."

Once again, this section returns to the question of the commonalities and differences among women. Given the disparities of wealth and power among women around the world, do women have anything in common by virtue of their gender?

Surviving the Welfare System:
How AFDC Recipients Make Ends Meet in Chicago

KATHRYN EDIN

In the discourse surrounding public welfare, recipients of Aid to Families with Dependent Children (AFDC) have often been portrayed as passive dependents who rely on government handouts as their sole source of support. In this view, welfare creates dependency by discouraging people from seeking work, forcing them and their children into a permanent underclass (Mead 1989, Murray 1984, Novak 1987). During the 1980s, this image of the welfare recipient provided a rationale for state legislators to let benefit levels fall far behind inflation and prompted Congress to restrict benefits (with some exceptions) to those who can prove they are seeking work.

Those who argue that welfare engenders dependence ignore the fact that states set welfare benefits too low to live on. Because of this, recipients must work at regular or informal jobs. But they "work" the system as well: they make sure the money they earn does not come to the attention of the welfare department. They conceal outside income because if they told their caseworker they were working or receiving outside assistance, their welfare checks would soon be reduced by nearly the full amount of their earnings, leaving them as poor as before.

Using data from in-depth interviews with fifty Chicago-area welfare recipients. I show that single mothers did not receive enough money from AFDC to support their families. As a result, all the women I interviewed supplemented their checks and concealed this information from their caseworkers. Although many of these mothers had received

Kathryn Edin, "Surviving the Welfare System: How AFDC Recipients Make Ends Meet in Chicago," from *Social Problems* 38, no. 4 (November 1991). Copyright © 1991 by the Society for the Study of Social Problems. Reprinted with the permission of the author and University of California Press Journals.

welfare for most of their adult lives, none liked being on welfare or having to hide outside income, though they believed their actions were economically necessary. Despite their discomfort, most mothers stayed on welfare because they could not find jobs that made them better off.

In sum, many unskilled single mothers spend much of their adult lives on welfare not because welfare warps their personalities or makes them dependent but because while welfare pays badly, low-wage jobs do not pay any better. Most welfare mothers would leave welfare for work if they could end up with significantly more disposable income as a result.

In the pages below I first describe my methods of research. Then I construct budgets of expenses and income for the mothers in my sample. There is a wide shortfall between what they spent and what they received from welfare and food stamps. Finally, I explain how these women closed this gap by relying on friends, family, absent fathers, boyfriends, and most important, by working.

METHOD

My respondents came from Cook County (Chicago and its surrounding suburbs). Cook County provides AFDC benefits that approximate the national average and has a welfare population that is quite diverse. Between 1988 and 1990, a wide variety of individuals introduced me to fifty-nine mothers on AFDC. All but nine agreed to be interviewed for this study. These women represented thirty-three independent networks and resided in about one-third of Chicago's eighty-eight community areas and five suburbs. The sample included both never-married and divorced mothers, mothers at various educational levels, mothers of black, white, Hispanic, and Asian descent, mothers living in private and public housing, mothers of different age groups, and both long-term and short-term recipients.

My sample is 46 percent African-American (as compared to roughly 40 percent of welfare recipients nationally), 38 percent non-Hispanic white (as compared to 39 percent), 10 percent Hispanic, and 6 percent Asian.[1] Because I wanted to maximize my chances of finding recipients who lived on welfare alone, I oversampled those living in public housing (42 percent as compared to 18 percent nationally) (U.S. House of Representatives 1990: 580, 586).

I conducted most of these one- to three-hour interviews in respondents' homes. In initial interviews, I gathered topical life histories. In subsequent interviews, I collected detailed income and expenditure data. I asked respondents to estimate income and expenditures during the previous month. I then asked how much these monthly amounts had varied over the previous twelve months. Usually, respondents had copies of phone, electric, and gas bills on hand, which they showed me. Because their budgets were tight, respondents typically knew what they spent each month. Most knew the exact cost of each food and household item they purchased and spoke at length about which stores had the lowest prices. If they could not remember how much they spent, I asked them to keep track during the next month and report back. I had respondents estimate their monthly income and expenditures at least twice and asked them to account for any discrepancies. Finally, I asked if they had made large one-time purchases during the previous year (VCRs, furniture, appliances, bicycles, etc.). Respondents generally paid for these items in monthly installments. I spread lump-sum payments evenly over twelve months. I interviewed each respondent at least twice, most between three and five times. I tape-recorded, transcribed, coded, and analyzed each interview using a computer database program.

EXPENSES

The average woman in my sample spent $864 a month. Of this, food and housing accounted for $501. These figures appear in the first column of Table 1. The upper portion of the table is devoted to expenses and the lower portion to income. The amount of money paid for housing varied considerably depending on whether the mother lived in subsidized housing, shared housing with others, or paid the market rate for her own apartment. Because this so heavily influenced the budgets of these women, I have broken down the sample by housing category in columns two, three, and four. Those living in private market-rate housing paid $467 for housing compared to $208 for those who doubled up and $123 for those living in subsidized housing. Those living in private and subsidized housing spent about the same amount for food ($267 and $264 respectively), but those sharing housing spent far less because most of these mothers had only one child, whereas other mothers usually had two or three.

From Table 1 we see that those living in private housing spent far less for items other than housing and food. Car payments, disposable diapers, and burial or life insurance costs (included in miscellaneous expenses) account for most of this difference. Since no privately housed mothers lived in suburbs, they did not need cars. As only a few of these mothers had infants, most did not buy diapers. Finally, these primarily white mothers did not purchase burial insurance. Most black mothers—especially those living in Chicago's dangerous housing projects—said they could not do without burial insurance, for which local morticians charged about $20 per month. If we eliminate these three items, other expenses only varied by about $20 between groups.

At the bottom of Table 1, I have calculated several overall measures of expenses compared to income. The first measure, total expenses minus welfare income, shows the net overall shortfall was $343 for all the women. However, it was $432 for women living in private housing but only $320 for those who shared housing and $276 for women living in subsidized housing.[2]

A second measure, the cost of housing and food minus total income from welfare, shows how much money these women had left over each month for all other expenses once they had paid for food and housing. Overall, there was only $10 left over once rent and food were paid for. But for women living in subsidized housing there was $119. For those sharing housing there was $52 left over. In contrast, mothers living in private housing were already $147 in debt: their total welfare benefit failed by a wide margin even to pay for their rent and food.

From this we could say that women living in private housing were $266 worse off ($147 plus $119) each month than their counterparts living in subsidized housing, even though their welfare benefits were higher ($587 versus $506 because of larger average family sizes). Mothers who share housing are $62 ($119 minus $52) worse off than those with subsidies, but $199 ($147 plus $52) better off than those with their own market-rent apartments.

TABLE I   BUDGETS FOR 50 CHICAGO-AREA AFDC FAMILIES BY HOUSING CATEGORY

N	All, 50	Private Housing, 17	Shared Housing, 11	Subsidized Housing, 22
Expenses				
Housing[1]	$264	$467	$208	$123
Food	$247	$267	$181	$264
Other	$353	$285	$372	$396
Phone	$28	$23	$13	$40
Check cashing	$5	$5	$4	$6
Clothing/shoes	$47	$39	$60	$47
School supplies	$10	$8	$9	$12
Toiletries/cleaning	$30	$35	$31	$26
Laundry/dry cleaning	$32	$44	$16	$30
Transportation	$41	$39	$50	$38
Over-the-counter medical costs	$13	$13	$16	$11
Time payments[2]	$19	$22	$21	$15
Entertainment/travel	$22	$15	$22	$28
Cigarettes/alcohol	$27	$17	$30	$34
Lottery	$3	$5	$2	$1
Car payments	$22	$3	$49	$24
Misc.[3]	$54	$17	$48	$85
Total expenses	$864	$1,019	$761	$782
Income				
Welfare				
AFDC	$324	$349	$287	$320
Foods stamps	$197	$238	$154	$186
Income from other sources				
Unearned				
Friends/family	$59	$43	$111	$45
Boyfriends	$76	$123	$18	$69
Absent fathers	$30	$27	$37	$29
Other	$45	$70	$15	$40
Earned				
Work in the regular economy	$128	$88	$162	$141
Work in the underground economy	$38	$81	$19	$14
Total other sources	$376	$432	$362	$338
Total welfare income[4]	$521	$587	$441	$506
Total income all sources	$897	$1019	$803	$844
Shortfall				
Welfare income minus total expenses	−$343	−$432	−$320	−$276
Welfare income minus housing and food	+$10	−$147	+$52	+$119
Total income minus total expenses	−$33	+$0	−$42	−$62

1. Rent or mortgage, gas, and electricity. Gas is the main source of heat in Chicago.
2. Most of these expenses were for furniture or household appliances.
3. This category includes expenditures for baby care (diapers), hair care, cosmetics, jewelry, expenses for special occasions (gifts and party costs), moving expenses and insurance (life and burial). Burial insurance, for example, is common in black neighborhoods and costs about $20 per month.
4. Table has been somewhat changed from original publication, with permission of the author.

Although those paying market rents were clearly the worst off, all three categories faced the same fundamental reality—the system did not provide enough money to support a family, as several women indicated:

> I don't ever pay off all my bills, so there isn't ever anything left over. As soon as I get my check, it's gone, and I don't have anything left.

> What you have to live off isn't enough. Me myself, I just got back on, and I had been off for about six years because I was working. But having a baby I had to get back on the program. It's just not enough. You just can't live off it especially with three kids or two kids. . . . It is impossible the things you have to do, to last you 'til the next month. Me myself, I get $380 for three kids. The rent I pay is just impossible plus my other little bills.

> Oh yeah. It ain't enough! It ain't enough! Get a big sign saying "That is not enough!" We want more! More! It's just not enough what we're getting.

INCOME

My sample's total income averaged $897 a month, of which 58 percent, $521, came from AFDC and food stamps. Half of the remaining 42 percent came from work of various kinds and just under half from absent fathers, boyfriends, and relatives. Respondents obtained the remainder from student loans, insurance settlements, churches, and community organizations. Although no mother received income from all these sources, most combined several strategies to balance their budget. I divide these strategies in two categories: unearned and earned income.

Unearned Income

First, I discuss assistance received from others and not earned by working. This includes assistance from family, friends, boyfriends, absent fathers, churches, community organizations, student loans and grants, and legal settlements.

Assistance from Family and Friends   Nineteen recipients received contributions from family and friends. Thirteen respondents had parents, friends, and relatives who consistently helped. For the other six, friends and family helped in emergencies and on special occasions.

Recipients felt it was unreasonable that the welfare department required them to report such assistance. Since

families and friends gave support to "put food on the table" or to "pay the light bill before the electricity gets shut off," respondents maintained it was "crazy" to let welfare "take that away from us."

> A lot of people lie; I know that I have had to lie. Like that they get monies. Like my mom. If she gave me $100 to help me get through, to pay the bills that I've had overdue, or to help me get through, or whatever, I'm not going to claim that to the Public Aid!

Although respondents did not work for this assistance, they spent time and energy establishing and maintaining these relationships. Friends and relatives often pressured mothers to meet relational demands, pushed them to become self-supporting, and expected they take steps (i.e., attend educational or training programs) to achieve financial independence.

Boyfriends and Absent Fathers   Boyfriends were also a common source of unearned income. When boyfriends "lived in," mothers felt entitled to regular and substantial assistance. In my small sample, about half of the thirteen live-in boyfriends worked at regular jobs. Boyfriends who worked regular jobs were a more reliable source of financial support than those who only hustled on the street or worked in illegal activities.

> It's difficult around here to find a good man. Most of them don't work. They just work the streets, you know. They just steal and deal and stuff. That kind of thing is a drag. I mean, it's very risky, and though it brings in a lot of money, eventually they're going to lose it all and you're going down with them. My first husband worked the streets, and I know now enough to stay away from that kind.

Mothers claimed they had little difficulty convincing boyfriends to assist in supporting children who were, in most cases, not their own. They had more trouble convincing absent fathers to help (see Liebow 1967:74–102). Although almost every mother sampled cooperated with government officials to establish paternity for her children, many had no court-ordered support award. Further, support orders did not guarantee payment. Even when absent fathers met their obligation, Public Aid required that support payments be made through the department. Upon receiving payment, Public Aid kept all but $50, which it "passed through" to a recipient as exempt income.

Some mothers circumvented these rules and arranged for absent fathers to pay them directly without the knowledge of the welfare department. In this way they kept the full amount. Even then, support was seldom reliable or substantial, since many of the absent fathers in question worked irregularly or for low wages, had children by other women who also needed support, or were in prison. Mothers could not count on such income, and offered this as one reason why they did not report it.

> Well, the son's father had given me a little bit of money, here and there. But I'm not going to report that: that's not a steady income. I can't rely on him.

Almost all mothers were indignant that the welfare department expected them to report such income and felt welfare officials were "cheating" when they deducted support payments from welfare checks.

Churches and Community Agencies   A few tenacious respondents "got an income" by "hitting" or "begging from" churches and community agencies. Most Chicago churches and agencies give away small amounts of food and clothing. Some also give money for specific needs, like eyeglasses or dental work.

> Two weeks before the checks come out I hit the churches. The churches will let you come the week before you are getting your check, so I hit four different churches in a week. I get about $150 worth of groceries plus they give clothes.

In Chicago, enough churches and community groups offer assistance so a recipient can receive cash and in-kind aid from several sources in a single month.

> You know, getting around and getting the car payment or insurance payment made by churches is an income too. I had to go to one church after another. I would try to remember which one I hadn't gone to and ask them. Oh gosh, I think there were three churches that gave me money to get glasses. But [I only needed one pair], so I paid my car payment and insurance too.

Student Grants and Legal Settlements   Two respondents won large cash settlements for injuries. They did not report this income to Public Aid, as they would have been cut off from all assistance until they had depleted these resources.

Full-time student mothers partly relied on student loans and grants to make ends meet. By the time they paid tuition and books, they had only a few hundred dollars left per school term. Still, this extra cash was essential.

> After you pay for your books and everything you may get a refund whatever is left so I get about $200 or $300 a semester and I don't report that.

Earned Income

Just over half of those interviewed did not receive substantial outside assistance, and engaged in part-time or full-time unreported work to make ends meet. I divide earned income from unreported work into two categories: work in the regular economy and work in the underground economy.

Work in the Regular Economy   Seven mothers obtained false social security numbers and worked at regular jobs. They earned an average of $5 an hour. Mothers worked as teacher's aides, nurse's aides, fast-food workers, factory workers, and secretaries. Respondents reported that obtaining false social security cards was easy:

> [You'll find welfare mothers in] any factory. They have a whole network. [False] social security cards are easy to come by—they're a dime a dozen. I could take you to a place right now to get one where I used to work. I was told many times, "Just give me $25, and I'll get you a card." [At this factory] about 25 of them was doing it, and they offered to show me. They was making $5, $6 an hour plus the welfare they was getting.

In my sample, regular jobs taken under false identities proved more reliable and profitable than off-the-books work. Respondents expressed frustration that they "had" to conceal the fact they were working regular jobs because they didn't earn enough to forgo welfare.

> [I work] at [a fast-food place] for $4 an hour. It's still not enough. I wish I could go off aid and let them know that I work.

In addition to low pay, respondents cited frequent layoffs, uncertainty over the number of hours one could work, and lack of health benefits as reasons why they could not report their work. Their claim that "everybody knows" and "everybody does it" strengthened their belief that concealment was legitimate.

Twenty-two respondents worked part-time at regular jobs or odd jobs but were paid in cash off the books. Jobs included bartending, catering, house cleaning, child care, retail work, and sewing. Because these jobs paid cash, there was little chance AFDC could monitor earnings. Thus, although off-the-books jobs paid only about $3 an hour, most mothers preferred them to better-paid jobs requiring social security numbers.

> I really [have] trouble claiming my work. I know and everyone else knows [about off-the-books] work where you can make cash and not tell them about it. . . . It's the only way to survive.

Some employers reportedly colluded with recipients, offering the option of cash work at a slightly lower wage.

Off-the-books jobs ranged from jobs with regular hours at a single place of employment to highly irregular neighborhood odd jobs. Many said they worked odd jobs when other more reliable strategies failed. Odd jobs offered a type of unemployment insurance to those between what respondents sometimes dubbed "real" or more regular jobs. Nonworking mothers pursued odd jobs when they were between boyfriends or when a friend or relative failed to come through. Irregular jobs were also quite important to underground workers—those who made ends meet by selling sex, drugs, and stolen goods—a point addressed below.

Work in the Underground Economy Ten mothers worked in the underground economy: they engaged in activities that were against the law, in addition to violating the welfare rules. Those who sold drugs usually sold marijuana and made only a modest profit.[3] One respondent sold cocaine, but was murdered by her supplier during the course of the project because she owed him $600. Another mother said she stopped selling crack after a police officer told her the state would take custody of her children if she was caught. Some mothers fenced stolen goods, including meat, jewelry, and VCRs. The highest-paid work these women performed was selling sex, from which they earned about $40 per hour. Five mothers supplemented their welfare in this way.

To keep the frequency of their underground work to a minimum, respondents combined underground jobs with odd jobs they performed on a more routine basis.

> I might ask somebody if I could do their laundry so I could get some cigarettes, or [beg for money on the street]. I have done some of that in my day. And on a hot summer day, I might get an ounce of marijuana, roll some joints. It cost me $30, [and] I get $120 in profit. I don't do it often.
>
> I [buy joints wholesale] from a friend of mine and I sell them and make a profit. I do this about every other month, and I make about $150. I sell drugs, sell articles which aren't mine, pick up cans, do house chores, shovel snow, [and] cut grass.

These women did not call themselves "dealers," "fences," or "prostitutes." In fact, they distinguished themselves from "professionals," those who worked in the underground economy "for a living." Although those women who sold sex described their activities as "turning tricks," "selling ass," or "selling myself," they did not consider these activities prostitution, but rather, "a social thing," or "social prostitution." In keeping with this self-definition, they claimed they did not solicit openly or often. Most developed regular customers, often servicing only one or two for a period of time. This exclusivity lent some measure of legitimacy to the exchange of sex for money.

> I also think a lot of people have affairs with guys who will pay some of their bills. It's like a more legitimate prostitution. There is not really an exchange of money for services. It is more of a social thing. You are sleeping with this person, and in return he is taking care of a few things for you.

Informants claimed they wanted desperately to be good mothers and keep their families together. Most "professional" dealers, fences, and prostitutes they knew were not good parents to their children. Respondents believed the children of professionals were "trouble," and usually "[got] messed up at an early age." Some claimed they knew professionals who lost custody of their children through neglect or imprisonment.

Those working illegal jobs felt it was unacceptable to perform such activities unless they had exhausted all other resources and the well-being of their children was threatened.

> Like if I don't have food, I have to make some extra money by turning a few tricks. I also do hair, babysitting, clean the landlord's house, laundry; . . . [from the combination of these activities] I clear close to $200 a month.
>
> Once my bills were pretty high, and I had to pay them. So what I did was give my nephew my whole

check and went in with him to get a pound of reefer. And I got my interest out of that, so I was able to pay what I had to pay.

I've sold things that wasn't mine. . . . I've stolen out of the store to feed my kids. I was sent to the court and spent a day in jail for it. The judge understood and let me out.

PASSIVE DEPENDENCY OR MAINSTREAM VALUES?

Many women on welfare told me "I never thought I'd sink so low," or "I dream of the day that I can leave welfare behind." The overwhelming majority wanted to become self-sufficient through work, and a substantial minority had tried leaving welfare for reported work, only to return to welfare when they found they could not pay their bills. Respondents disliked concealing outside income from the welfare department. In nearly every interview, women used phrases like "I had no choice" or "I was forced to" to account for their actions.

Respondents felt particularly guilty about the lies welfare "forced" them to tell to conceal outside income.

Public Aid is an agency that I believe can teach a person how to lie. If you tell them the truth, you won't get any help. But if you go down there and tell them a lie, you get help. And I can't understand it, and every woman on Public Aid will tell you the same thing. It teaches you to lie. It won't accept the truth. So when you deal with Public Aid, you have to tell them a tale.

Respondents feared they would suffer real material hardship if they didn't "beat the system."

One thing about being on AFDC . . . you have to think. You have to set up a strategy on how to beat them and not let them beat you. You know it's bad that you have to think of [a strategy] though. And yet you have to go in there and beat the system. You cannot go in there and be totally honest, because you'll lose every time.

Some feared they would go hungry, end up on the streets, or lose custody of their children. Most could not imagine living solely on welfare; no one knew anyone who did.

These mothers insisted lying was out of character for them, something which they would not do normally. One mother remarked, "Public Aid forces you into deceit and dishonesty, things you normally would not think of doing." Respondents chose between being good mothers and good citizens. In every case, concern for their children's welfare outweighed moral qualms.

[So how did you feel about having to lie?] I felt guilty. I really did. I felt I was cheating my government, but on the other hand I had to think about my family. I was not about to let my children starve or have no clothes on their backs.

The dissonance between conscience and what mothers perceived as necessary dishonesty diminished self-respect. Most respondents spoke passionately about how receiving welfare made them "feel like dirt" or "feel so ashamed I could die." Their struggle to keep their families together increased their sense of being "on the bottom."

Sometimes you get so desperate you think the only way you can make ends meet is to be a prostitute. I think that is a gut-level feeling. You feel you are on the bottom anyhow.

Although recipients worried about day-to-day material survival, most viewed survival as not merely a matter of having adequate food, shelter, and clothing. They felt there were "psychological" and "social" aspects as well.

You know, we live in such a materialistic world. Our welfare babies have needs and wants too. They see other kids going to the circus, having toys and stuff like that. You gotta do what you gotta do to make your kid feel normal. There is no way you can deprive your child.

The above quote captures a common sentiment among the welfare recipients I interviewed: children need to have an occasional treat, and mothers who refuse may deprive their offspring of normalcy. On a more fundamental level, many mothers worried that if they did not provide a few extras— expensive tennis shoes, for example—their children would be tempted to sell drugs to get them.

My boy, he sees these kids that sell drugs. They can afford to buy these [tennis shoes] and he can't. So I have my little side job and [buy them for him]. You got to do it to keep them away from drugs and . . . from the streets.

The mothers themselves needed an occasional extra, too. Many women reported that by spending small amounts on cosmetics, cigarettes, alcohol, or the lottery, they could avoid feeling "like I'm not completely on the bottom," or "my life is not completely hopeless."

By setting benefits so low, welfare denies these needs and increases recipients' perceived isolation from society's mainstream. The following quote, offered by an unusually articulate respondent, reflects the commonly expressed belief that welfare fails to integrate the poor with the larger society.

I don't understand why [Public Aid is] punishing people who are poor if you want to mainstream them. If indeed, the idea is to segregate, to be biased, to create a widening gap between the haves and the have-nots, then the welfare system is working. If it is to provide basic needs, not just financial but psychological and social needs of every human being, then the system fails miserably.

WORK AND WELFARE: A DUAL DILEMMA

For the fifty Chicago-area recipients I interviewed, finding a job that paid more than welfare was nearly impossible. If welfare recipients could not live on their benefits, they could hardly live on wages resembling those benefits. Furthermore, leaving welfare has serious economic costs, since working mothers typically incur more health, transportation, and clothing expenses than their welfare counterparts.

Few of the jobs that unskilled or semiskilled single mothers can get offer health benefits. Although Medicaid currently covers those who leave welfare for work for one year, few employers provide family coverage after that year is up. Those who qualify for coverage usually must make a copayment they cannot afford.

They say that they want mothers to get back off the Aid and work, okay. There's a lot of mothers who want to work—okay—like me, I want to work. And then you work, [your employer] don't give you [medical insurance]. And sometimes, it depends on how much you make, they cut off your medical card, and when you go out and get those jobs you don't make enough to pay rent, then medical and bills. Then they'll probably get laid off, or they won't like it, and then they have to start all over again and it might be months before they get their benefits going again. . . . It's just another hassle.

The added costs of health care, child care, transportation, and clothing often mean wages do not cover expenses. As a result, mothers who want to work feel they cannot.

Just looking at it doesn't make sense to have to go to a job that pays the minimum wage when you consider that $2, [per hour] goes to pay the baby-sitter so you bring home $2 and you have to put your food, medical, your rent on $2 an hour—you can't make it. So you go down to welfare because it is cheaper to live for single parents.

I have applied all over, looking for [a job]. But a lot of places that are hiring are only paying me [minimum wage], and that's not enough for me to survive. I had a chance at [a fast food] place, but I figured out how much they were paying . . . and it just wasn't enough to cover my bills.

Since most low-wage entry-level workers experience periodic layoffs, mothers feared taking a reported job: if they lost it they would have had to reapply for welfare. In Chicago, eligibles wait four to six weeks for their benefits to start. In the interim, families are left without any means of support. About one-third of those I sampled had lost low-wage jobs in the past. Some had friends and family to tide them over, but others suffered severe material hardship—an experience they did not want to repeat.

I asked respondents how much they would have to make to leave welfare altogether. Mothers said they would not take a job paying less than $7 to $10 per hour. Jobs at this wage are hard to come by, especially for women with few skills.[4]

Recipients' estimates of an adequate hourly wage agree with data from the Consumer Expenditure Survey of 1984–85, which show that single mothers who work spend about $800 more for health care, $300 more for clothing, $500 more for transportation, and $1,200 more for child care than nonworking single mothers do. By adding these figures to the amounts privately-housed welfare mothers spent, I calculate that working mothers without housing subsidies, but with average child care, clothing, and transportation expenses, need to earn at least $14,800 per year to live as well as their welfare counterparts. Unless they too have substantial outside income, working mothers would need to earn $7.50 to $9.00 per hour to reach this amount, depending on how many hours they work (Jencks and Edin 1991). The average welfare mother cannot expect to earn much. Garfinkel and Michalopoulos (1989) estimate an average welfare mother can expect to earn $5.15 per hour (in 1989 dollars). Assuming they have average work-related expenses, this approximately equals the average welfare benefit package.

Beyond its economic costs, work has substantial noneconomic costs. Few day care centers accept newborns or children over twelve, so their mothers must find alternatives. Working mothers who stay home with sick children may lose their jobs, but they cannot send sick children to day care. Working mothers usually are not home when their school-aged children return from school. In the summer, mothers have difficulty finding responsible adults to watch their children. Unless mothers can afford after-school and summer day care, their children forfeit adult supervision for a substantial part of each day.

In Chicago ghetto neighborhoods, unsupervised children are vulnerable to gang activity, drug use, and teen pregnancy. In my sample, one women's twelve-year-old daughter was "sleeping around with a married man" while she was away at work. She found out from the man's wife, who threatened to kill her child. Another quit her job to make sure her fourteen-year-old son stayed in school. While she worked, her son skipped school repeatedly, ran with a dangerous gang, and was arrested for theft.

The following account reflects the frustration mothers experience when they try to function as full-time workers and mothers, especially when the resulting income is inadequate.

[It's] not worth it to go out working when you think about it, you know. It's not worth it 'cause you have kids and then they gonna be sick, and you gonna have to go to the doctor, and mainly that's why lots of mothers don't go out and get jobs because they don't think it's worth it. Going out there and working and then having a lot of problems and then can't even buy groceries and stuff like that.

DISCUSSION

The so-called "welfare trap" is not primarily one of behavioral dependency but one of economic survival. In a society where single mothers must provide financially for their children, where women are economically marginalized into unreliable jobs that pay little more than the minimum wage, where child support is inadequate or nonexistent, and where day care costs and health insurance (usually not provided by employers) are unaffordable for most, it should surprise no one that half the mothers supporting children on their own choose welfare over reported work.

While some argue welfare creates the very problems it tries to alleviate by setting up a system of perverse incentives that reward dependency rather than work (Mead 1989), I argue that the welfare system actually prohibits dependency by paying too little to make this possible.

The evidence presented here challenges the validity of three widely accepted stereotypes about welfare recipients: they do not work, they do not want to work, and their behaviors reflect values different from mainstream society. These findings have important implications for the debate about the underclass and current and future public policy but must be interpreted with care since the sample is not representative of mothers in other cities and states.

The obvious solution to the problem of inadequate benefits or low earnings is to increase one or the other. The expansion of AFDC benefits is politically unlikely. Since most Americans believe single mothers should work, non-workers will always be considered outside the mainstream (Garfinkel and McLanahan 1986).

Rather than focus on expanding benefits, I suggest we ensure that those who work full-time can earn a living wage. Several leading policy analysts have proposed that we increase single mothers' income through a child support assurance system and wage supplements of various kinds (Ellwood 1988, Garfinkel 1990, Garfinkel and McLanahan 1986, Jencks and Edin 1991, Orr 1991, Wilson 1987). Any set of solutions, however, must take into account that mothers need to roughly double their current potential earnings to make work a viable alternative to welfare.

Other barriers to employment include lack of affordable child care, insufficient health insurance coverage, and inadequate or nonexistent child support payments (Danzinger and Nichols-Casebolt 1990, Glass 1990; Marshall and Marx 1991). Providing these benefits to more families would significantly lower the cost of working and facilitate the transition from welfare to self-sufficiency through work.

ACKNOWLEDGMENTS

I wish to gratefully acknowledge the help of the fifty welfare households who participated in this study, who must remain anonymous. Christopher Jencks offered invaluable assistance in every phase of this research. Malcolm Spector gave important editing assistance. Arlene Kaplan Daniels, Susan Mayer, and Timothy J. Nelson also made helpful comments. Shirlee Garcia, Sonja Grant, and Deborah Hayes assisted with interviewing, and Julie Mittler contributed administrative support. Correspondence to Edin, 87B Wentworth Street, Charleston, SC 29401.

NOTES

1. As a white researcher, I was concerned that racial and class differences between me and respondents might limit my interviewing effectiveness. Because of this, I hired one Hispanic and two African-American interviewers. All three were former or current welfare recipients, and after careful training they helped me contact and interview 21 of the 27 black and Hispanic respondents in the sample.

2. Benefits in Chicago are slightly higher than average: no state provides benefits generous enough to cover what the 50 Chicago-area mothers reported spending. Cook County mothers needed at least $961 in cash and food stamps to meet their monthly expenses. It is unlikely that rents in any major city average more than $100 less than in Chicago, so welfare families probably did not get by on less than $750 anywhere. In 1988, a family of three received cash and food stamps worth $750 a month in Los Angeles and San Francisco and $701 in New York City, but these cities were all more expensive than Chicago. Benefits were $699 in Detroit, $589 in Philadelphia, $491 in Atlanta, and $412 in Houston and Dallas (U.S. House of Representatives 1990). Detroit is thus the only major city where a family might have gotten by on AFDC and food stamps. Families living in low-cost rural areas of high-benefit states might also get by. National figures and other small-scale studies are consistent with the story of these 50 Chicago-area recipients (Edin 1989, Gardiner and Lyman 1984, Halsey, Nold, and Block 1982, Jencks and Edin 1991, Sharff 1987).

3. I asked respondents to estimate the time they spent selling drugs and stolen goods and how much they made. A simple calculation of earnings over time spent shows these jobs paid approximately the minimum wage (from $3 to $5 an hour).

4. Approximately one-third said they would not take a job without benefits because they or their children had expensive health care needs.

REFERENCES

Danzinger, Sandra K., and Ann Nichols-Casebolt. 1990. "Child support in paternity cases." *Social Service Review* 64:458–74.

Ellwood, David T. 1988. *Poor Support: Poverty in the American Family.* New York: Basic Books.

Gardiner, John A., and Theodore R. Lyman. 1984. *The Fraud Control Game: State Responses to Fraud and Abuse in AFDC and Medicaid Programs.* Bloomington, Ind.: Indiana University Press.

Garfinkel, Irwin. 1990. "A new child support assurance system." Institute for Research on Poverty, Discussion Paper #916-90. Madison, University of Wisconsin.

Garfinkel, Irwin, and Sara McLanahan. 1986. *Single Mothers and Their Children.* Washington, D.C.: The Urban Institute.

Glass, Becky L. 1990. "Child support enforcement: An implementation analysis." *Social Service Review* 64:542–56.

Halsey, H., F. Nold, and M. Block. 1982. "AFDC: An analysis of grant overpay." Palo Alto, Calif.: Block and Nold Economic Consultants.

Jencks, Christopher, and Kathryn Edin. 1991. "Reforming welfare." In *Rethinking Social Policy,* ed. Christopher Jencks, 204–35. Cambridge, Mass.: Harvard University Press.

Liebow, Elliot. 1967. *Tally's Corner.* Boston: Little, Brown and Company.

Marshall, Nancy L., and Fern Marx. 1991. "The affordability of child care for the working poor." *Families in Society* 72:202–11.

Mead, Lawrence. 1989. "The logic of workfare: The underclass and work policy." In William Julius Wilson, ed., *The Ghetto Underclass: Social Science Perspectives,* 156–69. Newbury Park, Calif.: Sage.

Michalopoulos, Charles, and Irwin Garfinkel. 1989. "Reducing welfare dependence and poverty of single mothers by means of earnings and child support: Wishful thinking and realistic possibilities." Institute for Research on Poverty, Discussion paper #882-89. Madison: University of Wisconsin.

Murray, Charles. 1984. *Losing Ground.* New York: Basic Books.

Novak, Michael. 1987. *The New Consensus on Family and Welfare.* American Enterprise Institute for Public Policy Research. Milwaukee, Wi.: Marquette University.

Orr, Lloyd D. 1991. "Wage rate subsidies: Some new dimensions." Unpublished manuscript. Bloomington: Indiana University.

Sharff, Jagna Wojcicka. 1987. "The underground economy of neighborhood." In *Cities of the United States,* ed. Leith Mullings, 19–50. New York: Columbia University Press.

U.S. House of Representatives. 1990. "Background material and data on programs within the jurisdiction of the Committee on Ways and Means." Committee on Ways and Means. Washington, DC: Government Printing Office.

Wilson, William Julius. 1987. *The Truly Disadvantaged.* Chicago: University of Chicago Press.

R E A D I N G   4 6

The Year of the Woman, the Angry White Male, and the Soccer Mom: Media Framing of Gender in Recent Elections

SUSAN J. CARROLL

In every recent election the media have adopted a news frame for writing about gender. News frames serve a very useful function for journalists, who work under incredible time pressures. A news frame gives journalists a "hook" or a "peg" for their articles or stories; it helps them to decide what to focus on and what to ignore. Frames are also very important because they determine how citizens perceive the larger political world; they affect public perceptions. Media frames lead the electorate to focus on certain aspects of current events while ignoring others (Gitlin 1980, Entman 1991 and 1993, Norris 1997).

Susan Carroll, "Year of the Woman, the Angry White Male, and the Soccer Mom: Media Framing of Gender in Recent Elections" from *Fifth Women's Policy Research Conference Proceedings* (1998). Reprinted with the permission of the Institute for Women's Policy Research.

In this paper I examine media framing of gender-related phenomena in recent elections, with an emphasis on the Soccer Mom frame adopted by the media during the 1996 elections. In 1996 the media devoted considerable attention to women voters, a development which on the surface appeared far preferable to 1994, when journalists focused their attention on the Angry White Male and largely ignored women voters. However, from a feminist perspective, the Soccer Mom frame, which journalists employed in interpreting the significance of women voters in 1996, was nearly as problematic as the Angry White Male frame. Like the Angry White Male frame, the Soccer Mom frame rendered the vast majority of women voters invisible. When viewed through this frame, the diversity among women and the multifaceted nature of their lives disappeared from view. The Soccer Mom frame shifted the focus away from women to children and families, with women present only in their roles as self-sacrificing "moms."

THE YEAR OF THE WOMAN

In 1992 the frame that the media used for writing about women and the elections was, of course, the frame of "The Year of the Woman." Story after story was written about the record number of women running for Congress and the fact that 1992 was a breakthrough year for women candidates. Of course, "The Year of the Woman" was, as all media frames are, a distortion of the complete underlying picture of what happened in that election. While record numbers of women ran for and were elected to Congress, it was hardly a record year for women at all levels of office. For example, only three women ran as general election candidates for governor in 1992 compared to eight in 1990, and none of the women gubernatorial candidates was elected in 1992 while three were elected in 1990 (Center for the American Woman and Politics 1998a). Consequently, 1992 certainly was not "The Year of the Woman" for women running for governor.

Feminist activists and organizations were able to play some role in structuring the frame for the 1992 elections. Of course, feminists certainly did not come up with the name "The Year of the Woman." (Feminists never would have settled for just a year; rather, we would have demanded at least a decade and probably a century.) However, feminist activists did see that record numbers of women were running for Congress and chose to push that story with the media. And for the most part, those of us who were sources for stories about the 1992 elections did little to draw the attention of journalists to the fact that women were faring poorly at the gubernatorial level; we were content to let the media focus on the level of office where the gains for women were most dramatic.

In some respects, the "Year of the Woman" frame benefited feminists and women's organizations. For example, memberships and contributions to EMILY's List, a major Democratic prochoice donor network, soared. In the long run, however, "The Year of the Woman" frame proved to be a mixed blessing. One of the major down sides was that women candidates seemed to be old news after 1992, and the media paid very little attention to women candidates in 1994 or 1996. Women candidates were old news and the media went looking for new ways to frame subsequent elections. The fact that there were record high numbers of women running for statewide offices in 1994 and the U.S. House in 1996 (Center for the American Woman and Politics 1998b) went largely unnoticed despite attempts by some feminist organizations to draw the media's attention to these developments.

THE ANGRY WHITE MALE

In 1994 the media largely ignored gender in the weeks leading up to the elections, but then in the aftermath of the elections they "discovered" a phenomenon they called the "Angry White Male." A search of the major newspapers classification of the Lexis-Nexis database indicates that the first reference to the Angry White Male was in an article in the *Washington Post,* on November 10, 1994:

> Two years ago, it was the Year of the Woman. This time around, the election may come to be known as the Year of the Man, or the Year of the Angry Man (*Washington Post,* November 10, 1994).

Throughout the remainder of 1994 and into the spring and summer of 1995, news stories focusing on the Angry White Male spread like wildfire as the print media attempted to find an explanation for the results of the 1994 elections (Norris and Carroll 1997).

The media framing of 1994 as "The Year of the Angry White Male" seems to have been based on a single finding from a question asked in exit polls conducted on the day of the election. One of the questions that pollsters ask voters as they are leaving the polls is for whom they just voted in the congressional race in their district—the Republican candidate or the Democratic candidate. In response to this question, the pollsters found that women were about equally as likely to have voted for the Republican candidate for Congress in 1994 as they had been in 1992 and 1990; in other words, women voted about the same in 1994 as they had in the two previous elections. In contrast, men voted much more heavily Republican in 1994 than in the past two elections (Norris and Carroll 1997, Table 1). Since the electorate seemed disgruntled and elected a Republican Congress for the first time in several decades, journalists assumed that the results must be attributable to angry white men who flocked to the polls, abandoned the Democrats, and elected Republicans. This was despite the fact that when polls directly asked voters if they were angry, only a small proportion of voters—men or women—said they were.

Clearly, media emphasis on the Angry White Male in the aftermath of the 1994 elections was disadvantageous for women. Women were largely invisible in media coverage of the 1994 elections both as voters and as candidates.

THE SOCCER MOM

In 1996 the media rediscovered the gender gap. Women candidates and angry white men were by then old news. Searching for a new gender-related storyline, journalists turned their attention to women voters, stimulated in large part by poll results suggesting that the gender gap in preferences for the presidential candidates was larger than it had been in previous elections. Just as they had "discovered" the Angry White Male in 1994, in 1996 they "discovered" the Soccer Mom. Some journalists, including columnist Ellen Goodman (*Home News & Tribune,* November 10, 1996) and National Public Radio's Susan Stamberg (National Public Radio, 1996), even went so far as to label 1996 "The Year of the Soccer Mom." In fact, soccer moms received so much attention during the election that the American Dialect Society voted the term "soccer mom" Word of the Year for 1996 (*Washington Post,* January 12, 1998). Similarly, an Associated Press article written in early 1997 named Soccer Moms along with the macarena, Bob Dole, and rules girls as the four phenomena which will be forever associated with the year 1996 (*Associated Press,* December 30, 1996).

My research on the Soccer Mom frame, completed with the assistance of a Goldsmith Research Award from the Joan Shorenstein Center on the Press, Politics and Public Policy at Harvard University's Kennedy School of Government, is based on an examination of 211 articles published in fifty-five different major newspapers between July 1 and November 30, 1996. These articles were identified through a Lexis-Nexis search of the major newspapers classification, focusing on the key words "soccer moms" and "elections."

The first reference to soccer moms in the context of the 1996 elections appeared in an article in the *Washington Post* in July. The article, written by E. J. Dionne, Jr., quotes Alex Castellanos, a senior media advisor to Bob Dole, suggesting that Bill Clinton, following the advice of his pollster, Dick Morris, was targeting a voter whom Castellanos called the "soccer mom," defined in this article as "the overburdened middle income working mother who ferries her kids from soccer practice to scouts to school" (*Washington Post,* July 21, 1996).

Media interest in soccer moms picked up as the election approached. The number of articles on soccer moms in major newspapers increased from one in July to twelve in August and September to 198 in October and November. In large part, the intense media interest in soccer moms stemmed from the fact that they had become, at least in the eyes of the media, the most sought-after group of swing voters in the 1996 elections. Journalists noted repeatedly that soccer moms, who had tended to vote for Republicans in previous elections, leaned toward Clinton in 1996. According to media reports, if Dole were to have any chance of winning the election, he simply had to win back the soccer moms.

Defining the Soccer Mom and Erasing Other Subgroups of Women

The above quote by Alex Castellanos which appeared in the July *Washington Post* article makes clear that the Soccer Mom, at least in her political manifestation, was the creation of consultants involved in the presidential campaigns. Yet very few articles among those I examined pointed to the E. J. Dionne article or to the campaigns and political consultants in explaining the origins of the Soccer Mom.

By far the more popular explanation for the origins of the term "soccer mom" focused on Denver City Councilwoman Susan Casey, who ran for office in 1995 with the slogan "A Soccer Mom for City Council." She called herself a soccer mom, she said, because "That was my life" (*Rocky Mountain News,* October 30, 1996). Casey explained, "I've been a teacher, I have a PhD, I've managed national presidential campaigns, but when I wake up in the morning and when I go to bed at night, my heart and soul are in my family" (*Boston Herald,* October 24, 1996).

The repeated telling and retelling of the Casey story by journalists suggested that soccer moms were a "real" identity group in American society and not merely a name given by political consultants to a particular combination of demographic variables. In Susan Casey reporters had a woman who was willing to embrace the term Soccer Mom and to identify herself as such, and Susan Casey's labeling of herself as a Soccer Mom gave legitimacy to journalists' use of the label.

At first, the media focus on soccer moms seemed to offer the possibility that the media would move on to examine other specific subgroups of women voters and their interests in the election, thereby presenting a more complicated and realistic portrayal of women voters than had been offered in coverage of previous elections. However, this possibility was never realized. Instead, the media became fixated on soccer moms to the near-exclusion of serious discussion of other women voters and their concerns. For example, in 80.1 percent of the newspaper articles I examined, no other subgroup of women was mentioned even superficially. In the overwhelming majority of the articles on soccer moms, the, other subgroups of women were simply invisible.

The Soccer Mom herself was defined in many different ways, ranging from very simple descriptions such as "married women with children" (*Baltimore Sun,* November 29, 1996) or "Married, white, suburban women" (*Newsday,* October 31, 1996) to far more elaborate descriptions such as that provided by William Safire in the *New York Times Magazine:*

> She often drives a sports-utility vehicle or a minivan, carries snacks and orange juice for the kids, sometimes takes along extra lawn chairs. She can be a full-time homemaker or can also work outside the home. . . . soccer moms are not exclusively working class—many are upper-middle-class suburbanies. . . . [The soccer mom is] in her thirties, harried, family-oriented, carpool-pallored, ethnically diverse, with her vote up for grabs. And as the soccer mom goes, so goes the election, if she's not too tired to get to the polls (*New York Times,* October 27, 1996).

While there clearly was no agreed-upon definition of the Soccer Mom, some attributes were mentioned more frequently in press coverage than were others. Not surprisingly, motherhood was the most frequently mentioned attribute of the Soccer Mom. More than half (58.8 percent) of the newspaper articles I examined made explicit reference to what was implicit in the name Soccer Mom itself—that the Soccer Mom was a mother or a woman who had children. The next most frequently mentioned characteristics, in order, were: lives in the suburbs (41.2 percent of the articles); is a swing voter (30.8 percent); is busy, harried, stressed out, or overburdened (28.4 percent); works outside the home (24.6 percent); drives a minivan, station wagon (usually Volvo), or sports-utility vehicle (20.9 percent); is middle-class (17.1 percent); is married (13.7 percent); and is white (13.3 percent).

Despite the repeated reference to these characteristics, the boundaries around the definition of the Soccer Mom were fluid and constantly shifting. She was often described in contradictory ways. For example, while the Soccer Mom was often portrayed as thirty-something, some journalists included women in their twenties while others included women in their forties and even fifties. While most saw her as middle class, some described her as affluent; others included working-class women in the category soccer moms. According to some media accounts, only women who worked outside the home could be soccer moms. In other accounts homemakers were also included, and in a few descriptions soccer moms were limited to the ranks of career women and professionals. Taken as a whole, the media clearly provided a "big tent" conception of the Soccer Mom. Many women, perhaps even most, could fit into one description or another.

The plasticity of the category Soccer Mom and the inclusion of women with so many different characteristics only served to further the erasure of various subgroups of women in the 1996 elections. The category seemed to be large and ambiguous enough to include women of varying races and ethnicities, women from different social classes, and women who were not married (and perhaps not even heterosexual). Because enough women of varying characteristics were able to fit into one or another of the many different definitions that were employed, it was not clear which or how many women were excluded. If a more fixed and restrictive definition of the Soccer Mom had been used repeatedly and consistently, it would have been much more obvious how many and which types of women were being left out.

The Soccer Mom Comes to Represent All Women Voters and Women Are Erased

Various subgroups of women were not the only ones who were erased from view in the 1996 elections through the media's excessive focus on the Soccer Mom. In what may appear initially to be a paradoxical statement, the excessive focus on the Soccer Mom, a clearly gendered construct, ultimately led to the erasure of "women" as a collectivity which possessed agency or interests in the 1996 elections. The Soccer Mom became the symbolic representation of women voters; the interests of the Soccer Mom came to represent the interests of all women voters.

The erasure of women voters that occurred as a result of the Soccer Mom frame is perhaps best illustrated by examining the issue-based attempts by presidential candidates to appeal to voters, as reported in newspaper articles. There was a near-consensus about the concerns of the Soccer

Mom among reporters and the political practitioners whom they quoted. The Soccer Mom's interests focused on her children and her family. She was concerned about her children's futures, their education, and their safety. As Kellyanne Fitzpatrick, a Republican pollster noted, "If you are a soccer mom, the world according to you is seen through the needs of your children" (*New York Times*, October 20, 1996). The Soccer Mom, as portrayed in media reports, fit the stereotype of the self-sacrificing "mom," always placing the needs and interests of her children and family above any personal needs or interests she might have as an individual.

Newspaper articles frequently referred to the issues that candidates discussed in attempting to appeal to the Soccer Mom. Taxes and economic concerns were mentioned in one-eighth of the articles. Most of these references were due to the fact that Bob Dole talked repeatedly about his proposed 15 percent tax cut, which he argued would allow one parent in two-income families (presumably the soccer mom) to stay home with the children.

But *most* of the other issues mentioned in articles about soccer moms were more often associated with the Clinton campaign. Bill Clinton spoke out in favor of school uniforms and teen curfews, talked about the importance of installing V-chips in televisions, expressed opposition to cigarette advertising aimed at teenagers, took credit for and urged expansion of the Family and Medical Leave Act, and advocated longer hospital stays for childbirth. The articles examined for this analysis often reported on Clinton's attempts to appeal to soccer moms on the basis of these issues.

It is clear that most of the issues emphasized in candidate attempts to appeal to soccer moms had children as their target group—for example, education, V-chips, school uniforms, student financial aid, drug use among young people, smoking among children, and teen curfews. Even those issues that were not so obviously child and family centered often were talked about in a way that connect them to children and families. For example, crime was depicted as an issue that threatens family security, and gun control was viewed as a way to address the crime problem. Similarly, Clinton frequently talked about expanding parental leave so that parents (presumably most often mothers) could take time off from work to attend parent–teacher conferences. Perhaps most interesting are the issues that are absent from the Soccer Mom agenda as defined by the campaigns—for example, abortion, welfare reform, health care for women, sexual harassment, job training for women, pension reform,

and child care. Many of the issues that have been most closely associated with organized feminism do not appear among the issues that candidates emphasized in appealing to the Soccer Mom. Similarly, issues that deal with women's status or interests apart from their roles as mothers (for example, workplace issues) are missing.

In short, women seem to have been largely absent from the soccer-mom agenda as defined by the campaigns and reported by the media. For the most part, the focus was not or women, but rather on their children and their families. Women were represented only through their roles as moms.

CONCLUSION

In 1996 we witnessed the largest gender gap ever in a presidential contest. For the first time in history women could legitimately claim that their votes elected the president of the United States. Yet feminists and many other subgroups of women lost out because women, with their diverse interests and multifaceted lives, were effectively erased; only children, families, and self-sacrificing moms remained.

In the 1996 campaigns the presidential candidates talked about the concerns which seemed to be of interest to "soccer moms." They thereby appeared to be focusing on women voters while simultaneously ignoring voters who might have been politically unpalatable (e.g., women on welfare, women immigrants) or who might have pushed to have their concerns addressed in the campaign or placed on the president's agenda (e.g., feminists, women of color, prochoice activists, professional women). Middle-class, suburban mothers were not offensive to anyone, and there was no danger that a lobbyist was going to show up on the president's doorstep shortly after the election demanding attention to the issues of concern to soccer moms.

Clinton was re-elected following a campaign in which he espoused policies such as V-chips and school uniforms and bans on cigarette advertising. Feminism was not and is not part of this soccer-mom agenda. In fact, women and their interests (except in their roles as moms) seem to be largely absent from the soccer-mom agenda as the campaigns and the media defined it; for the most part, the target groups for this policy agenda are children and families.

Clearly, the frames that the media have utilized in talking about gender in the past three elections, especially the Angry White Male and the Soccer Mom frames, have not been advantageous to feminism or to advancing a feminist agenda. As feminist activists, we need to make sure that what happened in 1994 and 1996 does not happen again in the 1998 and 2000 elections. Since reporters have developed gender-related frames for interpreting each of the past three elections, the probability that the media will develop some frame for writing about gender in 1998 and 2000 is very great. As feminists we need to be *not merely* reactive, responding to the frame set by someone else, *but rather* proactive, helping to develop and establish the frame. Our goal should be to ensure that the frames which the media adopt in talking about gender in future elections reflect the multiplicity and diversity of women's lives while simultaneously advancing a feminist agenda. In trying to influence how gender is framed in upcoming elections, we need to think not only about what serves women's interests in the 1998 and 2000 election cycles, but also about how the frames which the media adopt will play out in the more distant future and affect our efforts to advance a feminist agenda in the years following 2000.

Of course, influencing how the media frame the elections is a very difficult and delicate task. The last thing the media want is to appear to be manipulated by feminists, so clearly our efforts have to be subtle. Nevertheless, now, in the months before the 1998 election season is in high gear, would seem the ideal time to give serious thought to how we might try to influence the way the media frames gender in the upcoming elections.

If, despite our best efforts, our attempts to be proactive in influencing the way women voters and candidates are portrayed in the media fall, and the media adopt news frames that work against a feminist agenda, we perhaps need to be more consciously resistant to the use of such frames. Instead of accepting media frames, like the Soccer Mom, which portray women according to traditional gender stereotypes, we need to find new, innovative ways to resist, disrupt, and challenge any news frames which work against or undermine our goals as feminists.

REFERENCES

Associated Press, December 30, 1996.

Baltimore Sun, November 29, 1996.

Boston Herald, October 24, 1996.

Center for the American Woman and Politics. 1998a. *Women Candidates for Governor 1970–1996.* Fact Sheet. New Brunswick, N.J.: Center for the American Woman and Politics.

———. 1998b. *Summary of Women Candidates for Selected Offices, 1968–1996.* Fact Sheet. New Brunswick, N.J.: Center for the American Woman and Politics.

Entman, Robert M. 1991. "Framing U.S. Coverage of International News: Contrasts in Narratives of the K.A.I. and Iran Air Incidents." *Journal of Communication* 41(4),6–27.

———. 1993. "Framing: Toward Clarification of a Fractured Paradigm." *Journal of Communication* 43(4):51–8.

Gitlin, Todd. 1990. *The Whole World Is Watching.* Berkeley; California.

Home News & Tribune, November 10, 1996.

National Public Radio. 1996. "Weekend Edition Saturday." October 19.

Newsday, October 31, 1996.

New York Times, October 20, 1996.

———. October 27, 1996.

Norris, Pippa. 1997. "Introduction: Women, Media, and Politics." In *Women, Media, and Politics.* ed. Pippa Norris, 1–18. New York: Oxford.

——— and Susan J. Carroll. 1997. "The Dynamics of the News Framing Process: From Reagan's Gender Gap to Clinton's Soccer Moms." Paper presented at the Annual Meeting of the Southern Political Science Association, Norfolk, Virginia, November 5–8.

Rocky Mountain News, October 30, 1996.

Washington Post, November 10, 1994.

———. July 21, 1996.

———. January 12, 1998.

REINVENTING THE WHEEL

MS. MAGAZINE, GULF DISPATCH

One fateful day last November, 47 Saudi women decided to drive a few yards in their own country (see Ms., January/February 1991). Now we have an eyewitness/participatory report on what actually took place in Riyadh, and on the aftermath. The author, a Saudi herself, must remain anonymous for her own safety.

3:00 P.M. Cars arrive in parking lot at Safeway supermarket on King Abdulaziz Road. Women sit beside male relatives or in the back of chauffeur-driven cars.

3:15 Fourteen women slide behind the wheels of as many cars. The men step away. Thirty-two other women join the fourteen, as passengers. None speak; they all move swiftly, as one black mass—wearing the traditional *gitwa* (head covering) and *abaya* (robe); all but five have their faces covered as well, with only their eyes showing.

3:22 The excitement in the air is overpowering. It is the first time the women have driven on their native soil. Furthermore, this is a country that does not favor public demonstrations of any kind, so this is a precedent. The convoy begins to move. Steady hands, heads held high.

3:25 Convoy moves out of the parking lot, turning north on King Abdulaziz Road. Some male relatives drive discreetly behind and alongside in support.

3:31 Turn west at the corner onto Mursalat Road. Two of the cars pull over by the Sheraton Hotel. People on the roads: a variety of expressions. Shock, horror, admiration. Some thumbs-up signals in encouragement, some smiles and fists held up in the air in solidarity, a few horns beeping in support.

3:35 Turn left, south on Olaya Road. Cars with curious (male) drivers begin to follow the convoy.

3:45 Another left. Four cars stopped at the traffic light are caught and pulled over by the police. The rest of the cars continue.

3:48 Back onto King Abdulaziz Road. En masse they decide to make the round one more time.

3:53 Stopped by police at the traffic light in front of the mosque. Afternoon prayers have just ended. The police don't know what to do. One officer leaves to call his superiors for instruction. They in turn call City Hall.

3:55 The imam of the mosque comes out to ask the police about the situation, then goes back in. Within minutes, about thirty *mutawa* (fundamentalists) emerge, screaming epithets: "Whores! Prostitutes! Sinners!" They surround the cars and pound on the windows and doors. The women sit silently inside.

4:00 The police move in. They ask the women what they think they are doing. "Driving," is the simple reply. "Why?" "In time of war mobilization and national emergency we need to, for the safety of our families." The police seem strangely awed, filled with respect. More *mutawa* appear, screaming and cursing, demanding that the women be taken to their own (religious) prisons. The police refuse, saying this is a secular matter.

4:30 The eight cars and the other two cars are allowed to drive to where the other four cars are parked. Now numbering well over fifty, the *mutawa* follow, becoming more abusive. The women no longer answer questions; they sit with the car windows rolled up while the fundamentalists surround and batter the cars.

5:15 Finally, a policeman takes the wheel of each car, with a *mutawa* sitting alongside him, haranguing the women. Only one carful of women refuses to permit the *mutawa* inside. The cars are driven to the Olaya police station, and the women are told to enter. They refuse to do so until a government representative is present.

5:50 The women are finally escorted into the police station. Seven *mutawa* insists on entering, and only after repeated requests by the police that they leave do they comply. The questioning begins.

Q: "Did your husbands or fathers or brothers know you were planning to do this?" A: "Does it matter?" Q: "Is this demonstration politically motivated?" A: "Why, no, it is a matter of safety during a time of national crisis." The women are polite and peaceable, courteous in giving the necessary information. One woman, assumed to be the ringleader, is taken to another room and questioned intensely. The other women chant. "We want her back with us. She is not our leader. This is a collective act." She is brought back, but later again sequestered for more interrogation. This continues for at least three hours.

9:30 Some of the husbands of the women appear. They are told to wait in an adjoining room.

12 MIDNIGHT Interrogation of the men begins—about a half hour each.

1:00 A.M. A government representative appears. The make relatives are urged to sign a document declaring that the women will never again participate in such an action, will never again drive or even speak of this matter, under threat of punishment or imprisonment. Only then will the women be released.

2:30 All the male relatives comply except one, who refuses as a matter of principle. Finally, so much pressure is put on him that he signs. Another male relative is so angered at his wife that he refuses to come to the police station at all; at last he too appears and complies. One of the women is single; her father is dead, and her brothers are in another city. Since she is not permitted to sign for herself, she names a male friend who appears to sign for her, so that she can be released. (Later, this man is harassed and called a criminal for having helped).

3:30 The entire group is finally permitted to leave the police station and go to their homes.

The Next Day

Handwritten copies of "police reports" (bearing no official stamps) appear as leaflets; these are distributed in government offices, pasted or nailed to the walls of public buildings, left on the front windows of cars, passed out in the streets. These so-called reports claim that the women in the driving demonstration were wearing shorts; that they hurled insults at religious men and condemned the government. Included in the allegations: the women were sluts; their husbands were secularist, westernized, communists pimps. . . .

Aftermath

The women and their families have been ceaselessly harassed, threatened, cursed—by telephone, mail, and in person. Some of the women are educators; their university offices were broken into and ransacked by fundamentalist students who believed the allegations. . . . The women have been fired from or suspended from their jobs, and they (and their husbands) are banned from traveling abroad. . . .

Postscript

January 15: Today I rang up my neighborhood civil defense office. I said that my brother is in the army, my father is dead, and my driver is too scared to drive me anywhere—he wants to stay in his room or go back to the Philippines right away. I told the civil defense office that I need tape and plastic to seal the windows against possible chemical warfare. I need bread and bottled water and basic supplies. May I have special dispensation to drive in this emergency?

"No," was the reply, "Call 999 emergency and they will bring you what you need." I called. They gave me another number. I have been trying to get through to this other number now for days. The line is continually busy.

Late January

We are at war.

In the midst of all this horror and uncertainty, last night a group of *mutawa* climbed over a fence to throw stones through the windows of the home of one of the women. They shouted threats for an hour before departing.

In a time of national crisis, they have nothing better to do than terrorize women?

Our Policies, Their Consequences: Zambian Women's Lives under "Structural Adjustment"

AMBER AULT and EVE SANDBERG

Women around the globe share many concerns, including meeting basic subsistence needs, improving the prevention and treatment of diseases like AIDS, providing for reproductive health and freedom, reducing infant mortality and childhood illness, preventing violence against women, ensuring gender equity in labor, law, and education, and increasing women's ability to exercise sexual self-determination. Because wealthy countries and poor countries occupy very different positions in the global economic system, however, the social, economic, and political oppression experienced by women of poor countries differs in form from that experienced by women in wealthy countries. Furthermore, the oppression of women in Third World countries does not exist in a vacuum that begins and ends at national borders. Indeed, much of the poverty, discrimination, disease, and violence experienced by Third World women results from the exploitation of their countries by wealthier countries and the international organizations that they control. As feminist scholars and activists in wealthy western countries, we must educate ourselves about our roles in supporting the systems of domination which perpetuate the exploitation of women elsewhere.

We do not argue that all women in industrialized nations enjoy vast, substantial advantages over all women in Third World countries. Indeed, many women in the United States live in extreme poverty, without decent housing, steady health care, stable employment, or any assurance of personal safety, while some women in poor nations enjoy relatively high standards of living. Nonetheless, because wealthy

western countries benefit from the labor of exploited Third World workers, western feminists need to understand the roles their governments play in women's oppression in other countries.

In this brief report, we use a case study to demonstrate how the self-interested practices of wealthier countries in one international organization exacerbate and sometimes create the oppression of Third World women as women, citizens, and workers. To explicate the connections between the United States government, one powerful international organization, and the lives of women in Third World countries, we recount the impact of an International Monetary Fund (IMF) Structural Adjustment Program in the African country of Zambia.

The International Monetary Fund constitutes an international agency designed to promote a stable world economy. As part of its mission, it provides loans to countries with failing economies. Capital for such loans comes from deposits made by the countries participating in the International Monetary Fund. The conditions each borrowing country must meet to secure a loan are contingent on the ultimate approval by the board of directors of the Fund, which includes representatives of the member states, whose votes are weighted relative to their countries' financial contributions; wealthy nations like the United States make large contributions and therefore enjoy great influence over the contingencies attached to loans the agency makes, as well as its policies and actions. Not surprisingly, the terms of loans to Third World countries reflect the economic and political interests and values of the world's wealthiest nations.

The "Structural Adjustment Program" constitutes one kind of loan package managed by this organization. The

Amber Ault and Eve Sandberg, "Our Policies, Their Consequences: Zambian Women's Lives under a Structural Adjustment." Reprinted with the permission of the authors.

International Monetary Fund makes financial assistance to Third World countries contingent upon borrower countries' willingness to make significant adjustments in their economic systems. The adjustments required by the International Monetary Fund reflect western capitalist economic ideologies. In addition, they often reflect a disregard for the structural, cultural, social, and technological features of the borrowing country. As a result, Structural Adjustment Programs administered by the International Monetary Fund frequently result in dramatic and devastating changes in the countries that adopt them. Nonetheless, because the International Monetary Fund constitutes one of the few sources of loan capital to which an indebted country can turn, countries suffering severe economic difficulty often accept the terms of Structural Adjustment Programs.

Such was the case of Zambia, a Black-governed country in South-Central Africa that implemented an IMF Structural Adjustment Program in October 1985 and wrestled with it in various forms until its termination in May, 1987. Before we describe the policies and outcomes of the Structural Adjustment Program in Zambia, we offer a brief description of some features of the country, so that readers may more fully grasp the ramifications of the program on the lives of citizens in general and women in particular.

At the time it instituted its IMF Structural Adjustment Program, Zambia reported that its population numbered about 6.7 million citizens. About 3.81 million Zambians over the age of 11 were working or actively seeking work, but only about 71 percent of these people could find jobs. While some urban Zambian women worked as teachers, nurses, secretaries, and waitresses, many more were self-employed as food sellers, street vendors, and charcoal producers, or in other jobs in the "informal sector"; in rural areas, women usually worked as farmers.

Then, as now, Zambia imported many goods. Government controls on foreign exchange rates held in check the cost to consumers of food and other goods imported by retailers before the implementation of the Structural Adjustment Program. Such controls helped to allow families in both urban and rural areas to meet their basic subsistence needs and were especially beneficial for women upon whom rests most of the responsibility of supporting the family.

Other government policies and programs helped to make life in Zambia manageable for its citizens before the Structural Adjustment Program. For example, the Zambian government made heavily subsidized health care available to all citizens, and ensured access to basic education.

Zambian governmental policies also kept domestic tensions in check by equitably distributing government-subsidized resources to the four separate geographic areas occupied by the country's four major ethnic groups.

Before it would disburse a loan to Zambia, the IMF required the Zambian government to promise to make major changes in the structure of its economy. According to the IMF, the required changes would allow the country to participate more successfully in the world market and, as a result, would allow it to repay its loan. Although many of the wealthy countries with controlling interests in the IMF do not have balanced national budgets, the IMF's Structural Adjustment Program packages are designed around the idea that Third World countries should achieve balanced budgets, and that they should do this in part by suspending support to domestic programs.

The International Monetary Fund required Zambia to devalue its currency, discontinue its subsidization of food, health, and education, suspend social welfare programs, lay off federal employees, and turn its attention to both diversifying and increasing its exports for international markets. The result: a socioeconomic nightmare for the country's people. The changes required by the IMF produced widespread unemployment; inflation of astronomical proportions; the suspension of the education of many people, especially girls; a dramatic decrease in access to health care; an increase in violence; conflict between the country's ethnic groups; and increased class stratification. While these problems affected most citizens, they made life especially arduous for women.

Overnight, the devaluation of Zambian currency and the suspension of government subsidies on imported goods produced massive inflation. The consumer prices of domestically produced products and services, including health care, school fees, and transportation, rose by 50 percent; the prices of many imported goods doubled. Women and girls were especially hard-hit by inflation. For example, because women are primarily responsible for feeding and clothing their children, the dramatic increases in the cost of food and household goods took a great toll on their limited incomes; with the increase in household expenses, and the end of nationally subsidized health care and education, medicine and schooling became increasingly beyond the means of most families. As a result, families made difficult decisions about who would receive the benefit of increasingly limited resources, and those decisions reflected entrenched patriarchal values. In the case of education, for example, families often reverted to traditions that promoted the education of male children over that of girls.

Sudden, massive unemployment exacerbated the problems resulting from inflation. The IMF required the Zambian government to lay off scores of government workers as a means of reducing expenditures. As a result of reduced consumer spending, private businesses and industry also let large numbers of workers go. In both spheres, women suffered great losses because their positions were frequently regarded as the most expendable. Joblessness, coupled with inflation, left Zambians destitute; sexist social structures disadvantaged women, even relative to men, who were suffering greatly.

For example, while the inflated price of gasoline made the cost of public transportation beyond most citizens' means and forced those who retained jobs to walk long distances to and from work, after-work hours were very different for men and women. Because they are responsible for feeding their families, many women had to extend their days with either extra income-producing activities or by obtaining land on which to create family gardens. Women's "double burden" of work and child care became even greater under the hardships of the Structural Adjustment Program.

Women also suffered directly at the hands of men as a result of the social stress the country experienced during the Structural Adjustment Program. Men, pressed to their limits, took advantage of women's resources and patriarchal social structures which allowed them to succeed in such efforts. For example, one woman farmer interviewed recounted how her brother had stolen from her: their father had willed them an ox to share, and every year she and her brother took turns using the animal to plow their fields; in the first year of the Structural Adjustment Program, the brother took the ox, refused to return it, and rented it to others for extra income, saying that his family could not survive if he did otherwise; the woman, in turn, could not plant enough to feed her family that year, and since customary law in the area did not recognize women's right to property, had no recourse. Such situations were not uncommon.

Nor was physical violence. In the years of the Structural Adjustment Program, the rate of violent crime in Zambia rose sharply. Women's increased activity away from home, as a result of their need to have extra income-generating activities, made them increasingly vulnerable to attack; women walking to and from work or their gardens, often distant from their homes, were fearful of being assaulted. At home, too, people were wary. One interviewee described how she and her husband took turns staying awake at night to protect themselves from prospective robbers.

These problems were further exacerbated by increasing conflict between groups in Zambia. As a result of IMF conditions, the government suspended its policy of distributing agricultural resources equitably throughout the country. Some areas of the country began to receive more and better supplies, setting the stage for conflicts between the ethnic groups living in different geographic regions. The Structural Adjustment Program also indirectly produced increased stratification among the country's women: those women farmers who happened to live along the country's supply roads received many more resources than those who lived in remote territories. While such women were among the few to benefit financially from the Structural Adjustment Program in Zambia, their prosperity rested on the deprivation of others.

Clearly, the imposition of the conditions of the IMF Structural Adjustment Program in Zambia wreaked havoc on the lives of the country's people. Similar IMF Structural Adjustment Programs throughout the Third World have produced equally devastating effects. We note that some IMF Structural Adjustment Programs in other impoverished countries have included a feature missing from the Zambian program: special encouragement for multinational corporations to promote exports. The mistreatment of women workers by such corporations has been well documented by other feminist scholars. (Nash and Fernandez-Kelly, 1983; Fuentes and Ehrenreich, 1983; Ward, 1990)

A small number of women entrepreneurs benefit from the free-market conditions created by IMf adjustment programs, and some women find empowerment and forge coalitions with other women in their efforts to resist the hardships the programs impose. Generally, however, throughout the Third World, people suffer greatly as a result of the conditions their governments must accept in order to procure loans designed to relieve the economic instability of their countries.

As voting members in the IMF, western governments, including that of the United States, condone and encourage the policies that so disrupt the lives of so many millions in Third World states. The United Nations Economic Social and Cultural Organization (UNESCO) and the United Nations Africa Economic Committee (UNAEC) have criticized the extraordinary toll that citizens in Third World states, especially women, are paying for their governments' Structural Adjustment Programs. In the 1990s, other organizations and individual citizens in western countries are also attempting to alter IMF policies. The Development Gap, for example, a Washington, DC-based nongovernmental organization concerned primarily with the environment, began a campaign in 1991 to urge the US Congress to use the US voting position in the International Monetary Fund to alter IMF Structural Adjustment Programs.

Western feminists can join or initiate efforts to alter the IMF's programs. Women from wealthy countries must recognize our collaboration in the global system that oppresses women. As citizens of the countries intimately involved with the implementation of international policies which foster the exploitation of women in the Third World, we can seek to change the system. Indeed, we must: to fail to act on behalf of the women suffering as a result of our government's involvement in the IMF is to perpetuate the oppression of others, even as we seek to relieve our own.

REFERENCES

Fuentes, Annette and Ehrenreich, Barbara, eds.: *Women in the Global Factory.* Boston: South End Press, 1983.

Nash, June and Fernandez-Kelly, Patricia, eds.: *Women, Men, and the International Division of Labor.* Albany: State University of New York Press, 1983.

Ward, Kathryn, ed.: *Women Workers and Global Restructuring.* Ithaca: Cornell University Press, 1990.

R E A D I N G   4 8

The Globetrotting Sneaker

CYNTHIA ENLOE

Four years after the fall of the Berlin Wall marked the end of the Cold War, Reebok, one of the fastest-growing companies in United States history, decided that the time had come to make its mark in Russia. Thus it was with considerable fanfare that Reebok's executives opened their first store in downtown Moscow in July 1993. A week after the grand opening, store managers described sales as well above expectations.

Reebok's opening in Moscow was the perfect post-Cold War scenario: commercial rivalry replacing military posturing; consumerist tastes homogenizing heretofore hostile peoples; capital and managerial expertise flowing freely across newly porous state borders. Russians suddenly had the "freedom" to spend money on US cultural icons like

athletic footwear, items priced above and beyond daily subsistence: at the end of 1993, the average Russian earned the equivalent of $40 a month. Shoes on display were in the $100 range. Almost 60 percent of single parents, most of whom were women, were living in poverty. Yet in Moscow and Kiev, shoe promoters had begun targeting children, persuading them to pressure their mothers to spend money on stylish, western sneakers. And as far as strategy goes, athletic shoe giants have, you might say, a good track record. In the United States many inner-city boys who see basketball as a "ticket out of the ghetto" have become convinced that certain brand-name shoes will give them an edge.

But no matter where sneakers are bought or sold, the potency of their advertising imagery has made it easy to ignore this mundane fact: Shaquille O'Neal's Reeboks are stitched by someone; Michael Jordan's Nikes are stitched by someone; so are your roommate's, so are your grandmother's. Those someones are women, mostly Asian women who are supposed to believe that their "opportunity" to make sneakers for US companies is a sign of their country's progress—just as a Russian woman's chance to spend two months' salary on a pair of shoes for her child allegedly symbolizes the new Russia.

As the global economy expands, sneaker executives are looking to pay women workers less and less, even though the shoes that they produce are capturing an ever-growing share of the footwear market. By the end of 1993, sales in the United States alone had reached $11.6 billion. Nike, the largest supplier of athletic footwear in the world, posted a record $298 million profit for 1993—earnings that had nearly tripled in five years. And sneaker companies continue to refine their strategies for "global competitiveness"—hiring supposedly docile women to make their shoes, changing designs as quickly as we fickle customers change our tastes, and shifting factories from country to country as trade barriers rise and fall.

The logic of it all is really quite simple; yet trade agreements such as the North American Free Trade Agreement (NAFTA) and the General Agreement of Tariffs and Trade (GATT) are, of course, talked about in a jargon that alienates us, as if they were technical matters fit only for economists and diplomats. The bottom line is that all companies operating overseas depend on trade agreements made between their own governments and the regimes ruling the countries in which they want to make or sell their products. Korean, Indonesian, and other women workers around the world know this better than anyone. They are tackling trade politics because they have learned from hard experience that the trade deals their governments sign do little to improve the lives of workers. Guarantees of fair, healthy labor practices, of the rights to speak freely and to organize independently, will usually be left out of trade pacts—and women will suffer. The recent passage of both NAFTA and GATT ensures that a growing number of private companies will now be competing across borders without restriction. The result? Big business will step up efforts to pit working women in industrialized countries against much lower-paid working women in "developing" countries, perpetuating the misleading notion that they are inevitable rivals in the global job market.

All the "New World Order" really means to corporate giants like athletic shoemakers is that they now have the green light to accelerate long-standing industry practices. In the early 1980s, the field marshals commanding Reebok and Nike, which are both US-based, decided to manufacture most of their sneakers in South Korea and Taiwan, hiring local women. L.A. Gear, Adidas, Fila, and Asics quick-

TABLE I HOURLY WAGES IN ATHLETIC FOOTWEAR FACTORIES

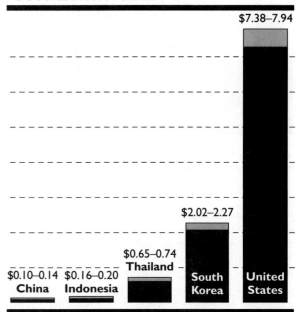

ly followed their lead. In short time, the coastal city of Pusan, South Korea, became the "sneaker capital of the world." Between 1982 and 1989 the United States lost 58,500 footwear jobs to cities like Pusan, which attracted sneaker executives because its location facilitated international transport. More to the point, South Korea's military government had an interest in suppressing labor organizing, and it had a comfortable military alliance with the United States. Korean women also seemed accepting of Confucian philosophy, which measured a woman's morality by her willingness to work hard for her family's well-being and to acquiesce to her father's and husband's dictates. With their sense of patriotic duty, Korean women seemed the ideal labor force for export-oriented factories.

US and European sneaker company executives were also attracted by the ready supply of eager Korean male entrepreneurs with whom they could make profitable arrangements. This fact was central to Nike's strategy in particular. When they moved their production sites to Asia to lower labor costs, the executives of the Oregon-based company decided to reduce their corporate responsibilities further. Instead of owning factories outright, a more efficient strategy would be to subcontract the manufacturing to

TABLE 2   A $70 PAIR OF NIKE PEGASUS: WHERE THE MONEY GOES

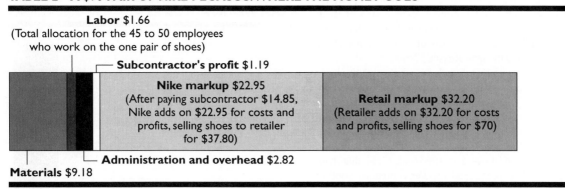

Labor $1.66
(Total allocation for the 45 to 50 employees
who work on the one pair of shoes)

— **Subcontractor's profit $1.19**

| **Nike markup $22.95**
(After paying subcontractor $14.85,
Nike adds on $22.95 for costs and
profits, selling shoes to retailer
for $37.80) | **Retail markup $32.20**
(Retailer adds on $32.20 for costs
and profits, selling shoes for $70) |

— **Administration and overhead $2.82**

Materials $9.18

wholly foreign-owned—in this case, South Korean—companies. Let them be responsible for workers' health and safety. Let them negotiate with newly emergent unions. Nike would retain control over those parts of sneaker production that gave its officials the greatest professional satisfaction and the ultimate word on the product: design and marketing. Although Nike was following in the footsteps of garment and textile manufacturers, it set the trend for the rest of the athletic footwear industry.

But at the same time, women workers were developing their own strategies. As the South Korean pro-democracy movement grew throughout the 1980s, increasing numbers of women rejected traditional notions of feminine duty. Women began organizing in response to the dangerous working conditions, daily humiliations, and low pay built into their work. Such resistance was profoundly threatening to the government, given the fact that South Korea's emergence as an industrialized "tiger" had depended on women accepting their "role" in growing industries like sneaker manufacture. If women reimagined their lives as daughters, as wives, as workers, as citizens, it wouldn't just rattle their employers; it would shake the very foundations of the whole political system.

At the first sign of trouble, factory managers called in government riot police to break up employees' meetings. Troops sexually assaulted women workers, stripping, fondling, and raping them "as a control mechanism for suppressing women's engagement in the labor movement," reported Jeong-Lim Nam of Hyosung Women's University in Taegu. It didn't work. It didn't work because the feminist activists in groups like the Korean Women Workers Association (KWWA) helped women understand and deal with the assaults. The KWWA held consciousness-raising

sessions in which notions of feminine duty and respectability were tackled along with wages and benefits. They organized independently of the male-led labor unions to ensure that their issues would be taken seriously, in labor negotiations and in the prodemocracy movement as a whole.

The result was that women were at meetings with management, making sure that in addition to issues like long hours and low pay, sexual assault at the hands of managers and health care were on the table. Their activism paid off: in addition to winning the right to organize women's unions, their earnings grew. In 1980, South Korean women in manufacturing jobs earned 45 percent of the wages of their male counterparts; by 1990, they were earning more than 50 percent. Modest though it was, the pay increase was concrete progress, given that the gap between women's and men's manufacturing wages in Japan, Singapore, and Sri Lanka actually *widened* during the 1980s. Last but certainly not least, women's organizing was credited with playing a major role in toppling the country's military regime and forcing open elections in 1987.

Without that special kind of workplace control that only an authoritarian government could offer, sneaker executives knew that it was time to move. In Nike's case, its famous advertising slogan—"Just Do It"—proved truer to its corporate philosophy than its women's "empowerment" ad campaign, designed to rally women's athletic (and consumer) spirit. In response to South Korean women workers' newfound activist self-confidence, the sneaker company and its subcontractors began shutting down a number of their South Korean factories in the late 1980s and early 1990s. After bargaining with government officials in nearby China and Indonesia, many Nike subcontractors set up shop in those countries, while some went to Thailand. China's government remains nominally Communist; Indonesia's ruling generals are staunchly anti-Communist. But both are governed by authoritarian regimes who share the belief that if women can be kept hard at work, low paid, and unorganized, they can serve as a magnet for foreign investors.

Where does all this leave South Korean women—or any woman who is threatened with a factory closure if she demands decent working conditions and a fair wage? They face the dilemma confronted by thousands of women from dozens of countries. The risk of job loss is especially acute in relatively mobile industries; it's easier for a sneaker, garment, or electronics manufacturer to pick up and move than it is for an automaker or a steel producer. In the case of South Korea, poor women had moved from rural villages into the cities searching for jobs to support not only themselves but parents and siblings. The exodus of manufacturing jobs has forced more women into the growing "entertainment" industry. The kinds of bars and massage parlors offering sexual services that had mushroomed around U.S. military bases during the Cold War have been opening up across the country.

But the reality is that women throughout Asia are organizing, knowing full well the risks involved. Theirs is a long-term view; they are taking direct aim at companies' nomadic advantage, by building links among workers in countries targeted for "development" by multinational corporations. Through sustained grassroots efforts, women are developing the skills and confidence that will make it increasingly difficult to keep their labor cheap. Many are looking to the United Nations conference on women in Beijing, China, this September [1996], as a rare opportunity to expand their cross-border strategizing.

The Beijing conference will also provide an important opportunity to call world attention to the hypocrisy of the governments and corporations doing business in China. Numerous athletic shoe companies followed Nike in setting up manufacturing sites throughout the country. This included Reebok—a company claiming its share of responsibility for ridding the world of "injustice, poverty, and other ills that gnaw away at the social fabric," according to a statement of corporate principles.

Since 1988, Reebok has been giving out annual human rights awards to dissidents from around the world. But it wasn't until 1992 that the company adopted its own "human rights production standards"—after labor advocates made it known that the quality of life in factories run by its subcontractors was just as dismal as that at most other athletic shoe suppliers in Asia. Reebok's code of conduct, for example, includes a pledge to "seek" those subcontractors who respect workers' rights to organize. The only problem is that independent trade unions are banned in China. Reebok has chosen to ignore that fact, even though Chinese dissidents have been the recipients of the company's own human rights award. As for working conditions, Reebok now says it sends its own inspectors to production sites a couple of times a year. But they have easily "missed" what subcontractors are trying to hide—like 400 young women workers locked at night into an overcrowded dormitory near a Reebok-contracted factory in the town of Zhuhai, as reported last August in the *Asian Wall Street Journal Weekly.*

Nike's cofounder and CEO, Philip Knight, has said that he would like the world to think of Nike as "a company with a soul that recognizes the value of human beings." Nike, like Reebok, says it sends in inspectors from time to time to check up on work conditions at its factories; in Indonesia, those factories are run largely by South Korean subcontractors. But according to Donald Katz in a recent book on the company, Nike spokesman Dave Taylor told an in-house newsletter that the factories are "[the subcontractors'] business to run." For the most part, the company relies on regular reports from subcontractors regarding its "Memorandum of Understanding," which managers must sign, promising to impose "local government standards" for wages, working conditions, treatment of workers, and benefits.

In April, the minimum wage in the Indonesian capital of Jakarta will be $1.89 *a day*—among the highest in a country where the minimum wage varies by region. And managers are required to pay only 75 percent of the wage directly; the remainder can be withheld for "benefits." By now, Nike has a well-honed response to growing criticisms of its low-cost labor strategy. Such wages should not be seen as exploitative, says Nike, but rather as the first rung on the ladder of economic opportunity that Nike has extended to workers with few options. Otherwise, they'd be out "harvesting coconut meat in the tropical sun," wrote Nike spokesman Dusty Kidd, in a letter to the *Utne Reader.* The all-is-relative response craftily shifts attention away from reality: Nike didn't move to Indonesia to help Indonesians; it moved to ensure that its profit margin continues to grow. And that is pretty much guaranteed in a country where "local standards" for wages rarely take a worker over the poverty line. A 1991 survey by the International Labor Organization (ILO) found that 88 percent of women working at the Jakarta minimum wage at the time—slightly less than a dollar a day—were malnourished.

A woman named Riyanti might have been among the workers surveyed by the ILO. Interviewed by the *Boston Globe* in 1991, she told the reporter who had asked about her long hours and low pay: "I'm happy working here. . . . I can make money and I can make friends." But in fact, the reporter discovered that Riyanti had already joined her co-workers in two strikes, the first to force one of Nike's Korean subcontractors to accept a new women's union and the second to compel managers to pay at least the minimum wage. That Riyanti appeared less than forthcoming about her activities isn't surprising. Many Indonesian factories have military men posted in their front offices who find no fault with managers who tape women's mouths shut to keep them from talking among themselves. They and their superiors have a political reach that extends far beyond the barracks. Indonesia has all the makings for a political explosion, especially since the gap between rich and poor is widening into a chasm. It is in this setting that the government has tried to crack down on any independent labor organizing—a policy that Nike has helped to implement. Referring to a recent strike in a Nike-contracted factory, Tony Nava, Nike representative in Indonesia, told the *Chicago Tribune* in November 1994 that the "troublemakers" had been fired. When asked about Nike policy on the issue, spokesman Keith Peters struck a conciliatory note: "If the government were to allow and encourage independent labor organizing, we would be happy to support it."

Indonesian workers' efforts to create unions independent of governmental control were a surprise to shoe companies. Although their moves from South Korea have been immensely profitable [see chart], they do not have the sort of immunity from activism that they had expected. In May 1993, the murder of a female labor activist outside Surabaya set off a storm of local and international protest. Even the US State Department was forced to take note in its 1993 worldwide human rights report, describing a system similar to that which generated South Korea's boom twenty years earlier: severely restricted union organizing, security forces used to break up strikes, low wages for men, lower wages for women—complete with government rhetoric celebrating women's contribution to national development.

Yet when President Clinton visited Indonesia last November, he made only a token effort to address the coun-try's human rights problem. Instead, he touted the benefits of free trade, sounding indeed more enlightened, more in tune with the spirit of the post-Cold War era than do those defenders of protectionist trading policies who coat their rhetoric with "America first" chauvinism. But "free trade" as actually being practiced today is hardly *free* for any workers—in the United States or abroad—who have to accept the Indonesian, Chinese, or Korean workplace model as the price of keeping their jobs.

The not-so-new plot of the international trade story has been "divide and rule." If women workers and their government in one country can see that a sneaker company will pick up and leave if their labor demands prove more costly than those in a neighbor country, then women workers will tend to see their neighbors not as regional sisters, but as competitors who can steal their precarious livelihoods. Playing women off against each other is, of course, old hat. Yet it is as essential to international trade politics as is the fine print in GATT.

But women workers allied through networks like the Hong Kong-based Committee for Asian Women are developing their own post-Cold War foreign policy, which means addressing women's needs: how to convince fathers and husbands that a woman going out to organizing meetings at night is not sexually promiscuous; how to develop workplace agendas that respond to family needs; how to work with male unionists who push women's demands to the bottom of their lists; how to build a global movement.

These women refuse to stand in awe of the corporate power of the Nike or Reebok or Adidas executive. Growing numbers of Asian women today have concluded that trade politics have to be understood by women on their own terms. They will be coming to Beijing this September [1995] ready to engage with women from other regions to link the politics of consumerism with the politics of manufacturing. If women in Russia and Eastern Europe can challenge Americanized consumerism, if Asian activists can solidify their alliances, and if US women can join with them by taking on trade politics—the post-Cold War sneaker may be a less comfortable fit in the 1990s.

ACKNOWLEDGMENTS

This article draws from the work of South Korean scholars Hyun Sook Kim, Seung-kyung Kim, Katherine Moon, Seungsook Moon, and Jeong-Lim Nam.

Patriarchies and Feminisms: The Two Women's Movements of Post-Unification Germany

MYRA MARX FERREE

In the nearly five years that have passed since the Berlin Wall was opened with such hope and joy, there have been many accounts of enormous problems in the now-unified Germany. Unemployment and anomie in the East (ex-GDR), higher taxes and greater competition in the West, and a resurgent racism in both parts have tempered the mood of celebration. Although many foretold the costs, particularly for women, the extent of these problems has been sobering for all. The phrase "women are the losers of the unification" has become virtually a cliché; moreover, it does reflect reality. Women's official unemployment rate (over 20 percent) is twice as high as men's, rises in the cost of living and the end to subsidies for basic goods have widened the gap in standards of living, leaving those with lower incomes (often women) relatively worse off, and benefits such as child care leaves and kindergarten subsidies have been slashed (Bialas and Ettl 1993). In addition, the change in abortion law has cost ex-GDR women their previous right to abortion on demand in the first trimester.

In this painful situation, feminists both East and West have actively drawn attention to women's problems, but have found it surprisingly difficult to establish a common ground from which to combat such issues. This article attempts to analyze certain aspects of the problems of mutual understanding that have arisen between East and West German feminists in particular and East and West German women more generally. I argue that some of these

tensions and incomprehensions have their roots in the different structures of state policy and in the resulting differences in women's experiences and collective identities in the two postwar Germanies. In this sense, the conflicts between East and West feminists can be understood as a specific case of a more general problem of feminist identity. Other conflicts over feminist identity—such as those between White and Black feminists[1] in the United States or between First and Third World feminists' globally—both illuminate and are illuminated by consideration of the dynamics of this specific case.

I suggest that these broad conflicts over interpretations of feminism are often rooted in different experiences of women with the state. States and state policies play a major role in systematically shaping women's experiences of paid work, marriage, and motherhood. Their effects may be seen in part in the interpretations of oppression and freedom that women construct based on personal and deeply felt experiences.

It is important to clarify at the outset that I am not arguing for a simplistic translation of women's experience into the politics of feminism in general or in either part of Germany specifically. In Germany, both before and after unification, there has been a complex process of debate both among feminists and between feminists and others that has contributed to shaping the understanding of the kinds of goals the women's movement stands for and of the appropriate means with which to accomplish those goals (Hampele 1991; Gerhard et al. 1990). In each locus of debate there arose what I call a "collective self-representation" of feminism, that is, a shared and yet personal sense of the meaning of a feminist collective identity. Such a collective identity links an interpretation of the past (women's experiences) to an interpretation of the future (women's aspirations). Collective identity is thus neither simply a reflection of past experience nor independent of it, but an actively constructed interpretation of shared history (Melucci 1988; Taylor and Whittier 1992).

Such feminist collective self-representation is different in important ways in each part of Germany; some of these differences arise from the nature of women's experiences with patriarchy when there were still two different countries. At the root, each system was organized around a fundamentally different sort of patriarchy. Following the lead offered by some feminist theorists of the welfare state (Siim 1987; Brown 1987; Jonasdottir and Jones 1988; Sassoon 1987), I distinguish between what has been called public and private patriarchy. At an abstract level, most analysts of gender oppression would agree that patriarchal power is both private and public and that both intrafamilial relations and state politics are arenas in which women's subordination is constructed and male domination is exercised on a daily basis. At a practical level, however, one or the other form of patriarchy may dominate certain women's concrete experiences and thus carry a disproportionate weight in the explanations of oppression and aspirations for freedom that these women develop for themselves. Such collective explanations and aspirations are invoked whenever women refer to themselves as "feminist." Jane Mansbridge (1995) calls this the "street theory" of feminism and I refer to it as their collective self-representation.

My core argument is that at least two such practical feminisms arose in postwar East and West Germany. Each reflected women's efforts to interpret experiences that were fundamentally different because each was predominantly structured by a different type of patriarchial state system: East Germany reflected principles of public patriarchy and West Germany those of private patriarchy. Because of this, mutual incomprehension, misunderstanding, and recriminations have become commonplace among feminists in unified Germany (Holland-Cunz 1990; Hampele, Helwerth, and Schwarz 1993; Rohnstock 1994). Even when there is a shared self-identification as "feminist," there are often different interpretations of what this term means. Some of the sources of these unanticipated communication difficulties are in the experiences of domination, competition, or recrimination in the period after unification; while these are also important, they are not my focus here (see Ferree 1992 for a fuller examination of these issues). In this article, I limit my discussion to factors that were already present before the Wall fell, problems that arise from the specific structures of state policy in each country, and the resulting differences in women's experiences and collective self-representations.

THE TWO GERMANIES AND THEIR POLICIES

The distinction between public and private patriarchy rests fundamentally on the role of the state as either supplanting or supporting the conventional authority and practical power of the individual male as household head. The state socialism of East Germany (German Democratic Republic, GDR) supplanted the individual male head and thus embodied principles of public patriarchy; the state policies undergirding the social market economy of West Germany (Federal Republic of Germany, FRG) are, in contrast, strongly oriented to sustaining private patriarchy. The issue defining this distinction is *not* whether the state is more or less influential in women's lives, but rather the nature of the effects that it strives for and accomplishes.

In the GDR, state policy tended to diminish the dependence of women on individual husbands and fathers, but it enhanced the dependence of women as mothers on the state (Ferree 1993; Bastian, Labsch, and Müller 1990). In the FRG, state policy instead followed the principle of subsidiarity and actively encouraged private dependencies. In particular, the state had a mandate to preserve "the" family, which it defined primarily as the husband–wife relationship as a context in which children can be raised (Moeller 1993; Ostner 1994). Thus, overall, the nature of the state's role in public patriarchy was to emphasize the *direct* relationship of mothers to the state; the nature of the state's role in private patriarchy was to encourage wives' dependence on husbands and children's on parents. In turn, this means that in public patriarchy women experienced their oppression as *mothers* and as more directly connected to the activities of the state as patriarch; in private patriarchy, women experienced their oppression as *wives* and as more directly connected to their individual dependence on their spouses.

To make these abstractions more concrete, compare the nature of women's ordinary life experiences in the two systems. In the former GDR, approximately one-third of all babies were born out of wedlock, and virtually all women were in the labor force and worked essentially full-time jobs, where they earned on average 40 percent of the family income. Out-of-home child care for children under three and kindergartens and after-school care for older children were universally available at low cost (which, incidentally, is an exception among socialist as well as nonsocialist countries). State subsidies for child care, rent, and other basic necessities reduced differences in the standards of living between single mothers and two-parent, two-income families. Divorce was easy to obtain; women were more often the ones who petitioned for divorce; and the divorce rate was the highest in the world.[2] Dependence on an individual husband appears to have been reduced to a minimum.

In the FRG, by contrast, 90 percent of babies were born within marriages. Living together was not uncommon, but when the baby arrived, so did marriage (87 percent of cohabiting relationships were childless compared to 18 percent of marriages). Having a child was structurally inconsistent with holding a full-time job, given the short and irregular school hours and scarcity of child care for preschool children. There were child care places for less than 5 percent of the children under three years of age. This incompatibility forced women to choose between having a baby or having a job. Of women aged thirty to fifty, only one-third had full-time jobs; on the other hand, fully 15 percent of women aged forty to fifty remained childless. A majority of employed mothers interrupted their careers for at least six years; even mothers of older children (fifteen years and older) were less likely than nonmothers to be in the labor force at all, not even considering the reductions they faced in the hours they worked or the status of their jobs. Given their restricted labor-force participation, it is not surprising that West German women provided on average only 18 percent of the family income and that the majority of employed women did not earn enough to support themselves independently, let alone raise a child. Tax subsidies such as income splitting further widened the gulf between the standard of living of two-parent families and single mothers; if a mother was confronted with the choice of keeping her job or keeping her marriage, the economic incentives strongly favored the latter.[3] Dependence on an individual husband was thus strongly institutionalized.

These differences are well known. The way they play themselves out in feminist identity and analysis is less obvious. There are several distinct areas where I think the differences between public and private patriarchy, and thus the structurally different experiences of dependency and oppression, were expressed in the specifics of feminist consciousness and politics before unification and which still carry a residue into current interactions.

FEMINIST IDENTITY AND THE STRUCTURES OF EXPERIENCE

The most central difference relevant for feminism may be how women's identities are shaped in relation to the dominant form of patriarchy in general and how patriarchy has been institutionalized in particular. In West Germany, there was a conceptual package invoked by the phrase "wife–

mother": these two roles were inseparably bundled together. This conceptualization has not carried over easily to the eastern part of unified Germany, where motherhood was not bound so structurally to wifehood. Thinking about mothers in the FRG shaded easily into imagining them only as wives; one needed to specify "single mother" and, in doing so, one invoked the image of mothers who were politically and culturally deviant as well as impoverished. In the East, the imagery of single mother was not so necessary: women were mothers and workers and they may or may not have chosen to be or stay married. Being unmarried and a mother was not an identity that carried a connotation of victimhood, deviance, or struggle.

The imagery of "woman" was more shaped by the wife role in the West; the "conventional" picture of womanhood was structured in terms of a woman's tenuous connection to the labor force, her need to attend to her appearance and to the care of the household, and to be sexually attractive to and able to depend on an individual man. Women's magazines instructed their readers in how they could achieve the current style of satisfying their husband's needs. Identity was expressed in "lifestyle," which for most women meant the nature of their consumer activities and personal appearances.

For East Germans, the conventional woman was not at the disposal of an individual man but instrumentalized by the state as patriarch. The image of woman was thus the "worker–mother" who contributed both reproductive and productive labor to a collectively male-defined state. The concept of worker–mother appears to have been as much a self-evident package as the West's concept of wife–mother; the ability to combine paid employment and motherhood was not questioned any more in the East than the ability to combine wife and mother roles was in the West. In both the conventional image and the self-understanding of GDR women, wifehood was much less salient than the role of worker. Not only did the GDR woman's constant work at home and in the labor force take precedence over her appearance or the appearance of her home in others' perceptions of her, but she identified her children and her job, not her spouse or her home, as her achievements. Consumption was a chore, not a means to identify and self-expression. That this was an issue of identity, not merely deprivation of consumer goods, is suggested by the collapse of western-style women's magazines in ex-GDR markets; indeed, the West German firm that bought the largest existing women's magazine in the GDR and tried to use it to market "glamour" to women in eastern Germany largely failed to attract an audience. Within a year the magazine ceased publication.

The exaggerations and stereotypes of each version of womanhood are distorted reflections of the differently organized patriarchal demands: on the one hand, the wife of leisure working on her appearance and waiting for her husband to come home; on the other, the single working mother who has the support of the state in attending to all of her responsibilities. Note that from each side, the dependency of the other woman is idealized; husbands support "their" wives, the state supports "its" mothers, and neither patriarch supposedly asks for anything in return. Envy of the "ease" and generous support offered to women in the other way of life is a theme that was used politically on both sides of the Wall. From inside either public or private patriarchy, it was never so simple, of course. The price for each of these "privileged" ways of life was more evident to the women paying it than to the women whose personal experiences were with patriarchy of a different sort.

In reality, neither public nor private patriarchy constitutes liberation for women, but each tends to shift the focus of women's attention to different aspects of their oppression. In the context of private patriarchy, the family, sexuality, and marital relations are initially at the forefront of theorizing (Janssen-Jurreit 1976; Millett 1970; Friedan 1963). The initial feminist idea is that if relationships between men and women as individuals could be put on a different footing, it would lead to structural change and vice versa— the structural changes that are sought are those that would change the balance of power within familial relationships. Power relationships within the family are often problematized and are seen as "spilling over" into the rest of social organization. In fact, rejecting marriage and seeking full-time employment, in the context of private patriarchy, are ways for women to challenge the status quo—to struggle against the individualized dependency prescribed by gender norms and almost invisibly upheld by state policy.

In the context of public patriarchy, the role of public policy and the state is more immediately central and obvious. The male domination of political decision making in all areas, the role of the state as the "guardian" who speaks for women rather than allowing them to speak for themselves, and the felt absence of collective political voice are all aspects of the sense of powerlessness that are directly evident in the experience of women's subordination by collective rather than by individual male power. Power relations within the family, if problematized at all, are seen as stemming from more fundamental policies and decisions taken at the public political level. Private relationships— whether lesbian or heterosexual—are experienced as irrelevant or secondary in comparison (e.g., Merkel et al. 1990;

Kahlau 1990; Hampele 1991). The common theme of feminist critiques is that women are "instrumentalized" by the state and that such state power must be challenged.

Neither of these experientially grounded perceptions is wholly wrong. Both the family and the state are arenas in which women's power and self-determination are restricted and where efforts to reconstitute social relations along less patriarchal lines are essential to the feminist project. Both forms of patriarchal organization, however, tend to encourage a distinctively one-sided form of analysis, because each type of model "fits" and explains certain gut-level experiences of oppression better. What is particularly instructive, albeit painful, is the collision between these two understandings.

THE DOUBLE VISION OF FEMINISM

Unlike the other Eastern European countries, the GDR in the 1980s had a slowly emerging feminist movement that became mobilized during the course of the transition and played an active political role in the process of Germany's restructuring. This movement was largely demobilized as the reform of the GDR was transformed into its absorption into the Federal Republic (Ferree 1994). In West Germany, there had been an active autonomous feminist movement and a variety of local feminist projects since the early 1970s (Ferree 1987). Each of these two differently grounded feminist identities that arose in these differently organized social contexts have been forced by unification now to share the same political space. Each has a tendency to disparage the degree of feminist understanding of the other with terms such as backward, hypocritical, arrogant, atheoretical, callous, naive, hypersensitive, know-it-all (Rohnstock 1994). The charges and countercharges go on and on and are unfortunately cast primarily in terms of the individual or collective personalities of the "other." Such attempts to define "better" and "worse" feminists, and in the process to defend one's own version of feminism as "more true," ultimately founder on the reality of difference.

This reality is that the contexts of public and private patriarchy and separate national experiences, which were independently theorized and from which two different women's movements emerged at two different times, are in practice differing organizations of oppression. What "feels true" as a collective self-representation has to resonate with each woman's experience of her own oppression to be accepted, and that feeling of authenticity varies based on the fundamental political structuring of personal experience. Given such different ways of structuring experience in public and private patriarchy, what "feels true" to a woman raised in one system will likely "feel alien" to a woman whose identity has been formed in the other. Because an authentic feminist politics has to "feel true," it cannot—and should not—aspire to universal priorities or any single dimension of "correctness." Although sustaining a view of feminism as intrinsically multiple in its analyses and emphases is difficult, such pluralism enriches and strengthens feminist practice.

This indicates the need to preserve as much as possible the perspective that arose out of the experience of public patriarchy in the GDR—not only for the insights it already generated into the contradictions and identity processes of such a system for women, but also because it continues to offer valuable insight into features of private patriarchy that women who live under it might otherwise tend to take for granted and allow to become theoretically invisible. Moreover, the comparison suggests the extent of analytical problems that women in eastern Germany will have to overcome as they attempt to grapple with understanding the costs and benefits of the new, imposed status of dependent wife.

Contrasts such as these help to expose the experiential preconditions of feminist theorizing and thus broaden and differentiate theories. Western European and North American feminists have already learned much from such critical contrasts drawn by women in Third World countries and from the differences in experience and interpretation between women of dominant and subordinate ethnic and racial groups in the industrialized countries. The common ethnicity and developed industrial economies that existed on both sides of the Wall may have made German feminists underestimate the difficulties of communication and the gulf in experience and identity that was still to be bridged when the Wall fell. The sheer unexpectedness of such fundamental differences blocked many attempts to listen to and learn from theory grounded in a significantly different structuring of women's lives. Nonetheless, the contrast between public and private patriarchy now being painfully articulated in both parts of Germany is worth attending to, rather than wishing away, because it may bind together a number of common experiences across specific situations.

One of the most interesting of these potential analogies is the way in which Black feminist thought has also attempted to come to terms with the greater significance of public patriarchy in African-American women's lives than in the lives of White American women. Using such an analogy should not be interpreted to suggest that African-American women's experience with a racist state is in any way identical to East German women's experience in the GDR, but rather to indicate that some of the elements that define public patriarchy, especially the direct relation of mothers to the state, may be responsible for observed similarities in identity and perspective that would otherwise be very surprising. Thus, despite dramatic differences in economic opportunity, family poverty, and social devaluation, among many other things, there are some points where African-American feminist thought touches closely on issues that women in eastern Germany have also been attempting to express (the best summary of the diverse insights from Black feminist thought is Collins [1990]). Such surprising commonalities need some explanation. One possibility is that they reflect some general characteristics of difference between public and private patriarchy.

First, there has been a tendency for feminists in eastern Germany to talk more positively about the family and to see a challenge for feminism in integrating men more fully into family life. In comparison to women under private patriarchy, they did not see men's exclusion from the family as offering a good in itself, nor did they define single parenting as freedom from male oppression—but they were also not so willing to marry, unless men met their expectations for family participation (e.g., Rohnstock 1994). Men's relationship to children was something that women valued and that the state ignored and actively marginalized. These are experiences on which African-American feminists have also had to insist and about which White feminists have been skeptical (Collins 1990).

The experience of family as a support system in opposition to the culture at large, of withdrawal into the family as a form of privacy from the state, is another theme that presents family in a positive light in African-American feminist writing; it is also echoed in some of the descriptions of the role of the family in state socialism in East Germany and elsewhere (e.g., Einhorn 1993; Funk and Mueller 1993). Because private patriarchy has not been so dominant in the experience of Black women or women in East Germany, it may be easier for them to imagine bringing men more centrally into families, without conceding patriarchal authority to them, than it is for many White American women or West German feminists. It seems at least possible that political practices that simply exclude men, as if changing them were either irrelevant or impossible, do not make nearly as much sense from a vantage point of public patriarchy as they do for women whose experiences have been more shaped by domination by individual men.

Second, women's labor-force participation is easy to connect to women's liberation in the context of private patriarchy since the extent of women's earnings are in practice directly related to their independence from individual husbands. This link is more problematic in public patriarchy, since women's labor is expected—even demanded—in the paid labor force as well as in unpaid domestic chores. For African-American feminists and feminists in East Germany, paid employment has provided a self-evident part of their identity as well as a burden—but it is hard to confuse it with "emancipation." The conditions of their integration into the paid labor force (e.g., ongoing discrimination), rather than the fact of employment itself, tend to draw theoretical attention and need more explanation.

For many feminists in West Germany, labor-market discrimination has clearly been a problem but one that apparently could be explained by women's frequent and extensive exclusion from the labor force in whole or in part when they have children. From this perspective, marginality rather than discrimination is the problem and creating compatibility between paid employment and motherhood is the solution; from a perspective of public patriarchy, the issue is the conditions under which such compatibility has already been produced and why and how women are made to pay for it. Such ongoing discrimination needs explanation in terms of something other than women's intermittent labor-force participation.

For women in eastern Germany, paid employment is certainly no longer self-evident. Thus, answering the question of what this growing exclusion from the labor force means is an entirely new issue, not a standard part of their feminist repertoire of self-understandings. As long as permanent or quasipermanent exclusion was simply inconceivable, it did not need to be theorized as a source of oppression. For women under public patriarchy, the idea of paid employment as somehow "an expression" of feminism did not make much sense, yet it was also not experienced as irrelevant to a feminist agenda. It was more the invisible precondition of experience and selfhood, parallel almost to the way literacy is taken for granted in industrialized countries.[4]

Third, within a framework of public patriarchy, it makes little sense to talk about doing politics that remains "autonomous" by virtue of keeping its hands out of the affairs of government for fear of being co-opted. Such a claim to autonomy has been a popular position among feminists in West Germany, albeit a stance that has been losing some support in recent years (Ferree 1987). Insofar as it is the state that is directly usurping the right of women to speak for themselves, as in public patriarchy, there is little alternative to pragmatically challenging this "guardianship" head-on. This means that women can and must find practical ways to restructure the state in less patriarchal ways. This concern with making policy and holding political office makes much less experiential sense to women in private patriarchy, who perceive their lives as being more directly shaped by nonstate actors and by cultural norms and expectations that are not formally enacted into law. Within the context of private patriarchy, the role of the state is more indirect and thus less visible, and the more obvious targets for action seem both more diffuse and more personalized. To those accustomed to public patriarchy, this focus can look like too much concern with symbolic issues, such as language, that are "trivial" compared to direct confrontations with policymakers.

For women who have lived under public patriarchy, the direct tie experienced between mothers and the state means that the state cannot so easily be felt as remote and irrelevant. The specific demands leveled at the state will vary by political context, of course. US women of color have pointed particularly to the significance of welfare levels, access to health insurance, and affordable housing as feminist issues of great and burning relevance to their daily lives, and they have directed attention to state policy in these areas, which White feminists have more easily overlooked. Women in eastern Germany have raised issues such as public child care, the antidiscrimination law, and representation in state and national politics higher on the feminist agenda in the postunification state by highlighting the immediacy of their impact. While feminist practice in West Germany even before unification had increasingly emphasized the importance of such state policies, this concern has been greatly accelerated by unification and its aftermath. It remains to be seen whether a national feminist organization aimed at influencing federal policy, such as originally favored by feminists in eastern Germany, will ultimately emerge as well.

CONCLUSION

The experience of family, paid employment, and state politics shows certain common threads between feminist concerns in East Germany and those raised by some women of color in the United States. These commonalities in theorizing and in critiques of pseudo-universalized theories that fail to reflect their experiences suggest that some common explanation might be sought. Such an explanation may rest in the different purposes that state intervention serves in public and private patriarchy. It is not a question of quantitative differences in the degree of state activism or state determination of people's life chances overall, but rather of the qualitative differences in the ends that such state intervention serves: either supporting the authority and power of an individual husband as patriarch or undermining it in favor of the collective authority of the male-dominated state for the benefit of men as a group.

As more Eastern European feminists find a voice with which to articulate their concerns, we may find that their collective self-representation of feminism, structured by their experiences of public patriarchy, may be even more different from the feminism arising from private patriarchy than is now apparently the case in unified Germany. What some have advanced as the reasons why there is "no women's movement" in Eastern Europe may yet become explanations for why the feminism that emerges there will take a distinctive form (Tatur 1992).

The experiences of the feminism articulated from "the other side" as not "really" being feminism, according to the standards of one's own collective self-representation, have contributed to the disillusionment and discouragement of both sides. The early efforts to deny differences, pointing instead to the always present indisputable commonalities, have over the course of the past five years largely been abandoned. The many practical experiences German feminists have had in conferences, workshops, meetings, and projects have provided ample evidence of difference. The model of public and private patriarchy outlined here suggests that the tensions and resentments that often accompany such expressions of difference are built up not just from political competition over scarce resources, new hierarchical relationships, and personal failures of empathy and understanding in the current crisis—important as such experiences have been—but also from threats to the collective self-representation of feminism itself. These varying self-representations may contain a large structural component reflecting the differently organized forms of patriarchy that women experienced. Thus, different aspects of feminist politics can "feel true" to women on each side of the now-crumbled Wall, and feminist authenticity for each set of women pushes them to reject and criticize claims that express understandings of what "women" are and need that are not validated by their own experiences.

Ultimately, however, the reality of such diversity in women's experiences—not just in their interpretations of them—demands a definition of feminism that encompasses difference. What is now so often expressed as "better" and "worse" versions of feminism in Germany should not be understood so much as matters of women being naive or antimale or careerist or statist–in other words, not as expressions of deficiencies of feminist analysis—but rather as reflections of the differences in the organization of patriarchy and of women's lives. Theorizing difference in this context takes on a new meaning and a new urgency.

ACKNOWLEDGMENTS

An earlier version of this article was presented at the conference "Crossing Borders," Stockholm, Sweden, May 1994. The research for this article was conducted with the support of research fellowship 3-53621 from the German Marshall fund of the United States and by a Provost's Award from the University of Connecticut Research Foundation. The article has benefited from the comments of many of the conference participants. Still earlier versions benefited from comments and suggestions from Christine Bose, Lisa D Brush, Irene Dölling, Christel Eckart, Jo Freeman, Ute Gerhard, Carol Hagemann-White, Eva Maleck-Lewy, Natalie Sokoloff, Verta Taylor, Wayne Villemez, Lise Vogel, Jane Wilkie, and Brigitte Young. My thanks to them, even though I (perversely) do not accept all the arguments they have offered.

NOTES

1. Black and White are used here as political terms and thus capitalized.

2. For details and statistics on the status of women in the DDR, see Einhorn (1993); Helwig and Nickel (1993); Maier (1992). For a history of policy that discusses its objectives and how it has secured these outcomes, see Penrose (1990).

3. For more extensive and detailed data on the status of women in the preunification Federal Republic of Germany, see Helwig and Nickel (1993); Maier (1992); Kolinsky (1989). For a history of policy that suggests how these outcomes were sought and institutionalized, see Moeller (1993) and Ostner (1994).

4. For differences in specific attitudes and experiences relating to paid work and family relations, see Institut für Demoskopie Allensbach (1993). As one illustration of the substantial gulf in expectations between East and West, consider the level of agreement with the statement "an employed mother can give a child just as much warmth and security as a mother who does not have a job." While 66 percent of East Germans agreed, only 39 percent of West Germans did. In this regard, it is the East Germans who are closer to the European average (61 percent agreement).

REFERENCES

Bastian, Katrin, Evi Labsch, and Sylvia Müller. 1990. "Zur situation von Frauen als Arbeitskraft in der Geschichte der DDR." Originally published in *Zaunreiterin* (Leipzig), reprinted in *Streit* 2:59–67.

Bialas, Christiana, and Wilfried Ettl. 1993. "Wirtschaftliche Lage, soziale Differenzierung und Probleme der Interessenorganisation in den neuen Bundesländern." *Soziale Welt* 44, no. 1:52–75.

Brown, Carol. 1987. "The New Patriarchy." Pp. 137–60 in *Hidden Aspects of Women's Work,* ed. Christine Bose, Roslyn Feldberg, and Natalie Sokoloff. New York: Praeger.

Collins, Patricia Hill. 1990. *Black Feminist Thought.* Boston: Unwin Hyman.

Einhorn, Barbara. 1993. *Cinderella Goes to Market: Citizenship, Gender, and Women's Movements in East Central Europe.* New York: Verso.

Ferree, Myra Marx. 1987. "Equality and Autonomy: Feminist Politics in the United States and West Germany." Pp. 172–95 in *The Women's Movements of the United States and Western Europe,* ed. Mary Katzenstein and Carol McClurg Mueller. Philadelphia, Pa.: Temple University Press.

———. 1992. "The Wall Remaining: Two Women's Movements in a Single German State." Paper presented at conference on German Unification, Western European Studies Program, Notre Dame University, South Bend, Ind.

———. 1993. "The Rise and Fall of 'Mommy Politics': Feminism and Unification in (East) Germany." *Feminist Studies* 19:89–115.

———. 1994. " 'The Time of Chaos Was the Best': The Mobilization and Demobilization of a Women's Movement in East Germany." *Gender and Society* 8, no. 4.

Friedan, Betty. 1963. *The Feminine Mystique.* New York: Dell.

Funk, Nanette, and Magda Mueller, eds. 1993. *Gender Politics and Post-communism.* New York: Routledge.

Gerhard, Ute, Metchthild Jansen, Andrea Maihofer, Pia Schmid, Irmgard Schultz, eds. 1990. *Differenz und Gleichheit.* Frankfurt a/M: Ulrike Helmer Verlag.

Hampele, Anne. 1991. "Der unabhängige Frauenverband." Pp. 221–82 in *Von der Illegalität ins Parlament* ed. Helmut Müller-Enbergs, Marrianne Schulz, and Jan Wielgohs. Berlin: LinksDruck Verlag.

———. 1993. " 'Arbeit mit, plane mit, regiere mit': Zur politischen Partizipation von Frauen in der *DDR*." Pp. 281–320 in *Frauen in Deutschland, 1945–1992,* ed. Gisela Helwig and Hildegard Maria Nickel. Bonn: Bundeszentral für politische Bildung.

Hampele, Anne, Helwerth Ulrike, and Gislinde Schwarz. 1993. "Drei Jahre nach der Wende: Zum Stand der Ost-West-Beziehungen in der Frauenbewegung," Paper presented at the Goethe Institute, New York.

Helwig, Gisela, and Hildegard Maria Nickel, eds. 1993. *Frauen in Deutschland, 1945–1992.* Band 318, Studien zur Geschichte und Politik. Bonn: Bundeszentrale für politische Bildung.

Holland-Cunz, Barbara. 1990. "Bemerkungen zur Lage der deutsch-deutschen Frauenbewegung." *Links* Sept.: 35–39.

Institut für Demoskopie Allensbach. 1993. *Frauen in Deutschland: Lebensverhältnisse, Lebensstile, und Zukunftserwartungen.* Köln: Bund Verlag.

Janssen-Jurreit, Marielouise. 1976. *Sexismus.* München: Carl Hanser Verlag.

Jonasdottir, Anna, and Kathleen B. Jones, eds. 1988. *The Political Interests of Gender: Developing Theory and Research with a Feminist Face.* London: Sage.

Kahlau, Cordula, ed. 1990. *Aufbruch! Frauenbewegung in der DDR.* Munich: Frauenoffensive.

Kolinsky, Eva. 1989. *Women in West Germany: Life, Work, and Politics.* Oxford: Berg.

Maier, Friederike. 1992. "Frauenerwerbstätigkeit in der DDR und BRD: Gemeinsamkeiten und Unterschiede." Pp. 23–35 in *Ein Deutschland—Zwei Patriarchate?,* ed. Gudrun-Axeli Knapp and Ursula Müller. Bielefeld: University of Bielefeld.

Mansbridge, Jane. 1995. "What Is Feminism?" In *Feminist Organizations: Harvest of the New Women's Movement,* ed.

Myra Marx Ferree and Patricia Yancey Martin. Philadelphia, Pa.: Temple University Press.

Melucci, Alberto. 1988. "Getting Involved: Identity and Mobilization in Social Movements." Pp. 329–48 in *From Structure to Action: Comparing Social Movement Research across Cultures.* ed. Bert Klandermans, Hanspeter Kriesi, and Sidney Tarrow. Greenwich, Conn.: JAI Press.

Merkel, Ina, Eva Schäfer, Sünne Andresen, Frigga Haug, Kornelia Hauser, Jutta Meyer-Siebart, Eva Stäbler, and Ellen Woll, eds. 1990. *Ohne Frauenistkein Staatzumachen.* Hamburg: Argument Verlag.

Millett, Kate. 1970. *Sexual Politics.* Garden City, N.Y.: Doubleday.

Moeller, Robert. 1993. *Protecting Motherhood: Women and the Family in the Politics of Postwar West Germany.* Berkeley: University of California Press.

Ostner, Ilona 1994. "Back to the Fifties: Gender and Welfare in Unified Germany." *Social Politics: International Studies in Gender, State, and Society* 1, no. 1:32–59.

Penrose, Virginia. 1990. "Vierzig Jahre SED-Frauenpolitik: Ziele, Strategien, Ergebnisse." *IFG: Frauenforschung* 4:60–77.

Rohnstock, Katrin. 1994. *Stiefschwestern: Was Ost-Frauen und West-Frauen voneinander denken.* Frankfurt a/M: Fischer.

Sassoon, Anne Showstack, ed. 1987. *Women and the State: The Shifting Boundaries between Public and Private.* London: Hutchinson.

Siim, Birte. 1987. "The Scandinavian Welfare States: Toward Sexual Equality or a New Kind of Male Domination?" *Acta Sociologica* 3/4:255–70.

Tatur, Melanie. 1992. "Why Is There No Women's Movement in Eastern Europe?" Pp. 61–75 in *Democracy and Civil Society in Eastern Europe,* ed. P. G. Lewis. London: Macmillan.

Taylor, Verta, and Nancy Whittier. 1992. "Collective Identity in Social Movement Communities: Lesbian Feminist Mobilization." Pp. 104–30 in *Frontiers of Social Movement Theory,* ed. Aldon Morris and Carol McClurg Mueller. New Haven, Conn.: Yale University Press.

Social Protest and the Feminist Movement

Throughout *Feminist Frontiers* we have begun to understand the breadth and magnitude of the social forces working to differentiate women and men and to disadvantage women. Socialization, the organization of social institutions, and social and economic policies all come together to hinder women's full political participation, self-determination, economic security, and even health and safety.

Despite the ubiquitous nature of sexism, racism, classism, nationalism, homophobia, and the other forms of inequality embedded in our social institutions, women resist. As we have seen, women often fight to undermine the forces of oppression in individual ways. Women also come together to take collective action to pursue social change. This section explores contemporary feminist movements, noting how feminist issues are different in particular cultures and historical contexts.

Women's resistance has a long history and has taken many different forms. In "Black Club Women and the Creation of the National Association of Colored Women" Stephanie Shaw documents African-American women's tradition of organizing against racism and sexism. The National Association of Colored Women, which served as the preeminent African-American organization during the late 1800s and early 1900s, built on existing community institutions and stressed "self-determination, self-improvement, and community development." The women Shaw writes about would not, by and large, have called themselves "feminist,"

because that term was appropriated by white activists of the time. Nevertheless, their resistance is central to a history of women's movements. In what ways were their goals and strategies similar to and different from what you know as "feminism" today?

Moving to the contemporary context, R. W. Connell discusses "Gender Politics for Men." Connell draws on observations of men's organizing to describe why and how men might challenge dominant models of masculinity. He suggests that the goal of such a movement would be "making the full range of gender symbolism and practice available to all people." Such a goal requires changing the political and economic relations of power between men and women and constructing egalitarian relationships between women and men and among men. These are long-term goals, but Connell points out the importance of building lives that are more egalitarian and less limited by gender now—from parenting to appearance and demeanor to educational curricula. What do you think men have to gain or lose from the political goals Connell advocates? What do women have to gain or lose from changes in masculinity? Do you think most men at your college or university would support changing masculinity? Why or why not?

Gender systems do not exist apart from other forms of inequality. Black lesbian, bisexual, and heterosexual feminist authors have repeatedly emphasized in their writings the intersectional nature of oppression, or the need to understand the multiple and interlocking nature of racial, sexual, heterosexual, and class domination. In "Punks, Bulldaggers, and Welfare Queens," Cathy J. Cohen discusses the origins of queer politics, a form of activism that emerged in the 1990s to promote an understanding of sexuality that rejects the idea of static, stable sexual identities and behaviors, such as gay and straight, that have been used to normalize and privilege some groups and to marginalize and subordinate others. Cohen embraces queer activists' in-your-face strategies intended to challenge the invisibility of gay, lesbian, bisexual, and transgendered people and to embrace sexual difference. But she criticizes the narrowness of queer politics for its overemphasis on deconstructing the historically and culturally recognized categories of homosexual and heterosexual. Such a strategy, she argues, exaggerates the similarities between individuals categorized under the label of "heterosexual" and ignores the way other systems of oppression regulate the lives of women and men of all races, classes, and sexualities.

In "The Next Feminist Generation: Imagine My Surprise," Ellen Neuborne describes her experiences as a young woman raised by feminist parents in a world that she believed had been changed by the women's movement. When she encounters sexism at work, she is taken aback to discover that she does not initially resist it. Her "programming" to accept gender inequality is both subtle and pervasive. Neuborne argues that sexism takes different forms now; rather than being expected to make coffee for their male co-workers, women are assigned to less challenging jobs (ostensibly as a favor), or seen as uncommitted employees if they have children. While the second-wave women's movement

transformed corporations' official policies to support gender equality, Neuborne suggests that the *practice* of gender equality in the workplace lags far behind. She concludes by telling young women: "[D]on't be fooled into thinking that feminism is old-fashioned. The movement is ours and we need it." Can you think of examples of "programming" in your own experience? How have your workplaces and schools been influenced by feminism? What forms of sexism or gender inequality have you observed? What do you think a feminist movement for the new century might look like?

In the anthology's final reading, Verta Taylor, Nancy Whittier, and Cynthia Fabrizio Pelak present an overview of the multiple ideologies and forms of the feminist movement in the United States from its emergence in the 1960s to the present. "The Women's Movement: Persistence through Transformation" considers the larger social and economic conditions responsible for the rise of women's movements in the western world and describes the international context of feminism. The analysis focuses on the way feminist movements have changed over time as a result of activists' own ideas and goals and the larger social and political context, including antifeminist countermovements that have arisen to oppose the aims of the women's movement.

Feminism, as this article demonstrates, has a long and vibrant history and strong prospects for the future. As women's movements enter the twenty-first century, they are becoming more diverse than ever and hold great promise for transforming the lives of both women and men for the better. As you finish reading *Feminist Frontiers,* what changes would you like to see in the gender system? How do you propose to accomplish these changes?

Black Club Women and the Creation
of the National Association of Colored Women

STEPHANIE J. SHAW

Much of what we know about black club women has been explained in the context of the creation of the National Association of Colored Women (NACW).[1] This scholarship often links black club women's activities to the most immediate and most obvious stimuli—the rising tide of Jim Crowism, the increase in lynching and other acts of mob violence, the vile verbal and literary attacks on the character of black women, and the general deterioration of race relations throughout the nation.[2] Historian Rayford Logan referred to these decades at the end of the nineteenth century as "the Nadir" in the history of American race relations.[3]

Club women themselves spoke out and wrote enough to suggest that those problems were important catalysts for their activism. Late-nineteenth-century journalist, community activist, and club leader Ida B. Wells Barnett launched her antilynching crusade not simply after the brutal killing of her good friend Thomas Moss, but also after her thorough investigation of lynching incidents concluded that the recent increase in lynching was carefully and deliberately orchestrated in response to black economic gains and political potential. Mary Church Terrell added the abuse of vagrancy laws, the convict lease system, and peonage to the increasing threats to black life and security. Prominent turn-of-the-century Virginia club woman Janie Porter Barrett summarized the feelings of sympathetic contemporary observers (and recent scholars) when she wrote: "No one can deny that the Negro race is going through the most trying period of its history. Truly these are days when we are 'being tried as by fire.' "[4]

Stephanie J. Shaw, "Black Club Women and the Creation of the National Association of Colored Women," from *Journal of Women's History* 3, no. 2 (Fall 1991) Copyright © 1991 by Indiana University Press. Reprinted with the permission of the publishers.

Considering the evidence that black club women left, it is not difficult to see why current-day scholars interpret the organization of the NACW as a response to these bad conditions. But such a conclusion ignores considerable evidence that reveals the obvious flaw in the interpretation. According to historian Willie Mae Coleman, the Colored Women's League, formed in Washington, DC, in 1892, was a coalition of 113 organizations. The more nationally oriented National Federation of Afro-American Women, formed in 1895, represented the combination of eighty-five organizations.[5] When these two federations combined in 1896 to form the NACW, the impetus and inclination for black women to form a collective was more than a few years old. In fact, it predated the so-called nadir of African-American history by generations.

The purpose of this article is to formulate a new interpretation of the creation of the national black women's club coalition of the 1890s—one that points to the internal traditions of the African-American community rather than activities in the white community. Numerous factors suggest the need for the alternative view. First, the history of "voluntary associations" among African Americans indicates a historical legacy of collective consciousness and mutual associations. Second, individual histories of diverse club women reveal early lessons in racial consciousness and community commitment. And third, the work of organized black women before the formation of the NACW was no different from the activities of club women after the creation of the NACW. Altogether, the founding of the NACW did not mark the beginning of the important organized work of black women against racism, sexism, and their effects, as earlier studies imply. Instead, the creation of the national organization represents another step in an internal historical process of encouraging and supporting self-determination, self-improvement, and community development.

At least as early as the advent of American slavery, African Americans consistently demonstrated inclinations toward community consciousness and collective activity. Historians of the antebellum South, slavery, and slave culture inform us that even under slavery, black men and women operated as a community within a community in which both personal and social identities developed and helped to ameliorate the harsh conditions of their enforced bondage.[6] Slaves often acted together in rebellion, or colluded afterwards to protect those implicated in acts of resistance.[7] Plantation child care situations, the forced secrecy surrounding organized religious ceremonies, and the potential for and actual loss of blood family members continually encouraged the development of group consciousness.[8] Folk tales provided lessons in group survival and examples of community ethics.[9] Historian Lawrence Levine writes that the most enduring characteristic of slave songs was their group nature. While they often functioned to set the pace of work for slaves, in improvised verses, one gang member might chastise another for not carrying his/her burden of the work. Structurally, through lining-out and call-and-response forms, the songs allowed a slave "at one and the same time to preserve his voice as a distinct entity and to blend it with those of his fellows."[10] Slaves in All Saints Parish, South Carolina, even imposed "a cooperative work ethos upon the highly individualist task system" of work which their owners used in an attempt to regulate their labor. Slaves adapted the labor system proposed by their masters and overseers "to their own sense of appropriateness" as they worked the crop in a row, hoeing and moving across the field synchronously to the rhythm of a work song.[11] Historian Deborah Gray White notes that slave women developed a network within the slave community that was supportive, empowering, and instrumental to their survival.[12]

Within the nonslave population of the antebellum period, the associations of individuals could take on more structure. They abounded in the North and South as benevolent and beneficial societies and intellectual and community uplift groups, among others. The Free African Society, formed in Philadelphia in 1787 by Richard Allen and Absolom Jones, is best known for the creation of the African Methodist Episcopal Church. From its inception, however, The Free African Society was also a mutual-aid society. The Female Benevolent Society of St. Thomas took over the organization in 1793, and two years later the all-male African Friendly Society of St. Thomas joined the women. The Daughters of Africa, which existed as early as 1821, was a mutual-aid organization of approximately 200 black working-class women. Members bought groceries and supplies for the needy, paid sick benefits, and lent money to society members in emergency situations. One scholar estimates that by 1850 there were at least 200 black mutual-aid societies in the country's major cities, with a total of 13,000 to 15,000 members.[13] This estimate is undoubtedly conservative, for in 1838 there were 119 such organizations with 7,372 members in Philadelphia alone.[14]

African-American women worked for self-improvement and racial advancement in a variety of settings during the antebellum period. Historian Linda Perkins writes that "the threads that held together the organizational as well as individual pursuits . . . were those of 'duty' and 'obligation' to the race. The concept of racial obligation was intimately linked with the concept of racial 'uplift' and 'elevation.'" Perkins notes the efforts of the Colored Female Produce Society, formed in 1831, to boycott slave-made products. Members of the Boston-based Afri-American Female Intelligence Society used their collected dues to buy newspapers and books and to rent a reading room. Also, members of at least one year were eligible for illness benefits. One reporter claimed that the Ohio Ladies Education Society had, by 1840, done "'more towards the establishment of schools for the education of colored people . . . in Ohio than any other organized group.'"[15]

When slavery ended, African Americans had considerable experience operating mutual associations, and carrying those practices through the Reconstruction period ensured future survival. Greater physical mobility, the tremendously unstable economy, and a determination to be free and independent of whites continued to encourage mutual associations. Historian Armstead Robinson writes that during the Reconstruction period, black men and women began to develop "their communal infrastructure."[16] To that end, among the many associations created during this period were agricultural societies concerned with planting, harvesting, contracting labor, and homesteading; savings and loan associations; insurance companies; trade unions; fire departments; burial, literary, social, educational, and business societies; and many others.[17] Even the educational institutions developed among former slaves during this period focused not simply on schooling the individual but on the educational needs and interests of the group in tandem.[18] Taken to the extreme, all-black towns formed in the south and west during and immediately after the Reconstruction period were radical and ultimate examples of mutual associations.[19]

Although federal Reconstruction organizations and institutions eventually collapsed, black self-help groups continued to thrive, and black women's activities were prominent. The Daughters of Zion, founded in 1867 in Memphis, Tennessee, was a church-affiliated group that served the same purpose that the earlier associations and later women's clubs served—individual and community self-help and uplift. With over 300 members at one time, the group organized relief efforts after the war, employed a physician to care for congregation members, and worked in various other public health and education activities.[20] Mary Prout founded The Independent Order of St. Luke (IOSL) in 1867. The Order began as a traditional beneficial society for women and later admitted men. Under the subsequent leadership of Maggie Lena Walker, the organization flourished financially and grew to 100,000 members in twenty-eight states. Walker also devised the plans for the St. Luke Penny Savings Bank, a major financial institution that came about as a result of community cooperation. And once in place, the bank fostered that tradition by becoming a symbol of accomplishment, a source of pride, and a facilitator of community development. Walker credited her success not simply to her own abilities but also to "the strength of the St. Luke collective as a whole and . . . the special strengths and talents of the inner core of the St. Luke women in particular." She linked black women as individuals to the advancement of the group by encouraging them to work to improve conditions of the home, community, and race.[21]

The details of Elsa Barkley Brown's study of Maggie Lena Walker indicate that the development of community consciousness and social responsibility was not accidental but a consequence of deliberate processes. Among black women in general, a variety of individuals participated in those processes. For example, if Clara Jones, a prominent Detroit librarian and club woman, had not heard it before, when she was preparing to leave home to attend college in the late 1920s, her grandfather, a former slave, reminded her: "You're going to get your education, and it's not yours. You're doing it for your people."[22] Jones later characterized her family as "a fiercely education-conscious family." And she added that "it was accepted that my four brothers and sisters and . . . [I] would all go to college to help our race. That was the way everyone thought in those days."[23]

Janie Porter Barrett's community activism is well known, but rarely do we get a glimpse of aspects of her early life that might help to explain her activism. Born in 1870, Barrett founded the Locust Street Settlement House in Hampton, Virginia, and the Peak Turnout, Virginia, Home for Delinquent Girls (later called the Girls' Industrial School). Her mother worked as a nurse for a wealthy white family, and she reared Janie in their home. Janie's mother apparently accepted her employer's educating Janie along with the white children of the family, but she left her position when the white woman of the house announced that she wanted to become Janie's legal guardian and send her to a northern white school for more education. Historian Tullia Brown Hamilton notes that the employer expected Janie to pass for white while attending the school. After quitting her job, Janie's mother sent her daughter to Hampton Institute instead. Obviously, Barrett's mother wanted to have control over her daughter's education, but we can also speculate about Barrett's mother's race consciousness. That is, it was not only unacceptable for her child to pass for white, but it was also important for Barrett to go to a black school. Not surprisingly, because of her upbringing in the comfortable white household, Barrett found the living conditions at Hampton in the 1880s to be very disappointing. After all, she had always enjoyed having a room that "was daintily furnished, and . . . surroundings [that] bespoke refinement and ease." Evidently, the white household did not foster the development of any realistic racial identity either. But Hampton could and did remedy that. Barrett wrote that when she first arrived at Hampton, she got tired of being drilled on her "duties to the race." She noted that she always woke up happy on Sundays, because on Sundays, she said, "I didn't have to do a single thing for my race." But students and faculty at Hampton succeeded at making Barrett more socially responsible and racially conscious. And when she created the Locust Street Settlement House in 1890—six years before the formation of the NACW and eighteen years before the creation of the Virginia Federation of Colored Women's Clubs (VFCWC)—she used money that she and her husband intended to use to install indoor plumbing in their home.[24]

Twenty-five years later, Barrett, a well-seasoned community activist, had held offices in the NACW and the VFCWC and was launching her project to create a home for delinquent black girls in Virginia. When Margaret Murray Washington, a principal at Tuskegee Institute and the wife of Booker T. Washington, offered her a principalship at Tuskegee Institute, Barrett wrote to Hollis Frissell (then president of Hampton Institute) that "Washington's letter makes me wish that I could be in two places at once. I should be glad to serve at Tuskegee, but I know I am going where I am needed [most?] and though this undertaking is most difficult, it isn't impossible, and if the friends will stand by me, this Home School will be, in time, a tremendous power for good." In fact, the home school became a model program, set up on the cottage plan and the honor system, with the VFCWC as one of its major financial supporters.[25]

Ida B. Wells (Barnett) was born a slave in Holly Springs, Mississippi, in 1862, of parents who insisted on educating their children, and some of Wells's first teachers were individuals who came to Holly Springs specifically to aid the recently freed men and women. Wells eventually left her hometown to continue her education, but after her parents died during the yellow fever epidemic of 1878, she and her surviving siblings immediately came under the guardianship of the Masons, a fraternal society of which her father was a member. Such fraternal societies traditionally assumed the responsibility for the surviving dependents of deceased members. While it is unlikely that this incident alone caused Wells to become an activist, surely the lesson in social responsibility was not lost. Within a short time, she became very active in civil rights causes. In 1884 she successfully sued the Chesapeake and Ohio Railroad for not allowing her to ride in a first-class car for which she had a ticket, but a higher court overturned the decision. Before the reversal occurred, railroad company lawyers offered Wells money to settle the case out of court, but she turned down their offers, dismissing the possibility of an individual payoff while pushing for a larger victory for the race. By the 1890s her articles on educational conditions for black residents in Memphis resulted in her being fired from her teaching position. More scathing pieces on lynching resulted in her fleeing for her life.[26] While she lived in exile, other black club women helped to support and protect her.[27] Wells wrote that most of the trouble she encountered with whites resulted from her actions on behalf of the race. But she said she owed it to herself and her race to tell the truth about white racism.[28]

Jane Edna Hunter, born in 1882 on a South Carolina plantation, grew up in a household with her parents that at one time also enjoyed the presence of her grandmother and great grandmother, both of whom were former slaves. Her parents appreciated the value of formal education but apparently could neither assume the right nor afford the privilege; Hunter worked her way through school. At the end of one summer of employment, because she needed all of her earnings to obtain school necessities, a friend agreed to purchase her return train ticket. When at the last minute it became apparent that the person who had offered to purchase the ticket would not follow through, the twenty or so proud friends and neighbors who gathered at the train station to see her off began to put together their change, ultimately collecting enough money for her ticket and fifty cents to spare.[29]

Hunter eventually finished secondary and nursing school, but when she relocated to Cleveland in 1905, she did not easily find housing or work. She had no family and few friends in that city, and the first place she lived turned out to be a residence for prostitutes. As soon as she established herself favorably in housing and in work, she and a few friends met to form the Working Girl's Home Association to build a home for "the poor motherless daughters of the race." The women who formed this voluntary association pledged to contribute five cents a week and committed themselves to recruiting new members. The first home opened in 1911. After the second facility opened in 1917, Hunter tried to explain her motivation:

> There was something . . . [that] kept urging and making me less content with what I was doing and calling me into a broader service. . . . Then the thought came to me that there were other girls who had come to Cleveland, perhaps under similar circumstances as myself and were strangers and alone and were meeting with the same difficulties and hardships in trying to establish themselves in a large city.

The Working Girl's Home Association proved to be a successful venture and its residence grew from a 23-room facility to a 72-room facility in 1917. By 1928 the institution had 135 bedrooms, four parlors, six clubrooms, a cafeteria, and a beauty salon.[30]

The creation of the Working Girl's Home Association represented a traditional response to a particular problem in that the black community historically turned to voluntary associations to resolve internal problems. But Jane Edna Hunter's organization also represented what was new about many of the black women's associations (more often called leagues or clubs after 1890) formed around this time. It was a voluntary association, but the women who came together to form the association did not share the common local history that the earlier church and/or community society members shared. Hunter and many of her colleagues were relative newcomers to Cleveland. In general, the origins of the membership of the late-nineteenth- to early-twentieth-century women's clubs were often different in this substantial way. These women were not necessarily total strangers to one another, but they were quite often newcomers to the geographic locales where they became prominently associated with club work.

Records of the Federation of Colored Women's Clubs of Colorado, for example, indicate that many of its members were not natives of Colorado. Gertrude Ross, who held numerous offices beginning in 1911, was from Illinois. Ruth Howard, one of Denver's most active residents, came to Colorado from Texas. Elizabeth Ensley, the founder of the Federation in 1903, came from Massachusetts by way of Washington, DC, and Mississippi. Among the many other examples, Bettey Wilkins, a member of several federated clubs in Colorado, came from Ohio.[31]

The few published accounts of black women's clubs suggest the same. Elizabeth Lindsay Davis provides brief biographical sketches of seventy-one Illinois club women in her book on the state federation. She notes the birthplace and location of the club work for thirty-nine of the women (54 percent). Only one of the women was active in club work in the place where she was born.[32] Delilah Beasley's 1919 work on black pioneers in California explicitly identifies nineteen women who were members of clubs, at least fourteen of whom were migrants to California.[33]

Tullia Brown Hamilton studied the leadership of the NACW and detailed similar statistics. Out of 108 women, Hamilton determined the birthplaces of seventy. Approximately half of that number were born in the antebellum slave states (while over 90 percent of the general population was born and still lived there in the 1890s), and of that number born in the south, 65 percent settled in the north or west after some migration within the south. Hamilton also concluded that even among northern club women, "in all likelihood [they] migrated to other areas of the North, West, or even the South before settling down."[34]

To be sure, because of turn-of-the-century migration patterns, many African Americans in the urban areas where clubs proliferated had migrated there.[35] More important, the clubs allowed women who had left their original communities to continue to associate with one another for individual and collective advancement as earlier mutual associations had. Significantly, the diverse geographic origins of the residents now meant that "the community" was no longer local; it had national roots. And so to effectively address the concerns of the members, the club network and many club activities became national.[36]

The twenty-five members of the Willing Worker's Club of Stamford, Connecticut, gave $2,000 to "needy causes throughout the city" between 1901 and 1907. The Art and Study Club of Moline, Illinois, enumerated among its functions visiting the sick and clothing the poor. Members of the Adelphi Club of St. Paul, Minnesota, read race literature, supported two elderly women, took fruit and magazines to city hospitals, gave food baskets to the needy on Easter and Thanksgiving, took clothes to a local orphanage, and supported a South Carolina kindergarten. Black club

women in Boston supported a kindergarten in Atlanta, Georgia. Although charters, bylaws, and objectives are not available for most turn-of-the-century clubs, the actions of members of many of them suggest that they also believed in a stated aim of the Neighborhood Union of Atlanta, Georgia: "to develop group consciousness and mass movements."[37]

Supporting the less able and improving standards of living meant providing services normally supported by local governments through public taxes. But providing these services pushed the activities of these women beyond traditional "charity work" and, in fact, represented community development. Charleston, South Carolina, club woman Susan Dart Butler operated a library for African Americans in a building owned by her father and stocked primarily with his books. Local black club women helped to maintain the facility until it became too expensive for them to operate. At that point, Butler leased it to the city for one dollar a year on the condition that public officials maintain it as a black library. Black club women in Atlanta, Georgia, helped the Neighborhood Union to establish and maintain a public-health clinic for black residents. They eventually leased it to the city, also, and thereby forced the public support that similar clinics in the white community always enjoyed. In both instances, the women ultimately donated the facilities to the city.[38]

In Delaware, Texas, Arkansas, West Virginia, Florida, Virginia, and Alabama the state federations of colored women's clubs created institutions for sheltering black juvenile delinquents who would otherwise have suffered incarceration with adult prison populations. In Missouri, Texas, North Carolina, Mississippi, Florida, Virginia, Alabama, Georgia, South Carolina, and Louisiana, black club women funded, built, and maintained public-health clinics and/or hospitals.[39] Club women also created homes for black working women in such urban areas as Cleveland, Chicago, New York, Newark, Boston, Little Rock, and Kansas City (Missouri). The Neighborhood Union House was a model settlement house that groups throughout the country sought to emulate. Other prominent settlements created by club women included the Locust Street Settlement in Hampton, Virginia, the Phillis Wheatley in Cleveland, and the Russel Plantation Settlement and the Calhoun Settlement in rural Alabama. In all of the former confederate states, in midwestern states including Kansas, Indiana, Ohio, Illinois, Minnesota, and in numerous northern and western states, black club women built, supported, and/or managed nursery schools and kindergartens, orphanages, and homes for the black elderly. The White Rose

Home in New York gained a national reputation for its work to protect black women migrants from the South. Altogether, the work of black club women on behalf of the race involved a broad range of activities. And even when their activities seemed explicitly directed to the benefit of women—as with the effort for women's suffrage and work with the YWCA movement—or some other less race-specific topic, they understood the consequences of all such work in terms of improving conditions for the race.[40]

The activities of NACW affiliates did not differ dramatically from earlier association activities. Club women provided aid to people in the community at large and therefore worked as the old benevolent societies worked. They provided emergency support for members and therefore functioned as the old mutual aid and beneficial associations functioned. And they worked for self-improvement and community uplift as both benevolent and beneficial societies of an earlier period had. But the NACW was different from those earlier associations not only in that it was a national black women's collective, but also, it was the country's leading national race organization—predating the creation of the National Association for the Advancement of Colored People (NAACP) by fifteen years. Even after the founding of the NAACP, the NACW remained, for some time, the leading black national organization working for the individual and collective advancement of African Americans, because the NAACP remained controlled by whites for many years.

Self-help and racial uplift were always important objectives of black women's public activism, but the focal points of the activism did change over time. In earlier decades, the shared conditions of slavery and the limited mobility that slaves enjoyed restricted their associations to groups that included but went beyond the "family" to embrace the whole slave community. Except for the antislavery societies, associations of free blacks in the antebellum period maintained a local orientation as well. In the postemancipation period, black women's organizations abounded, and many, like the ISOL, eventually had national connections. But the voluntary associations formed by club women around the turn of the century embraced local women with shared traditions and outlooks who were often no longer from the same families, churches, neighborhoods, or even regions. And not only did that aspect of diversity not preclude their organizing, but it encouraged the creation of a national structure to perpetuate the historical traditions of self-help, community development, and racial uplift despite the demographic shifts in progress.

If the formation of black women's clubs represents but one phase in a long history of group identification and mutual association, then the formation of the NACW represents not only the broadening base, vision, and abilities of black club women, but also another logical step in the effort to maintain and/or improve important historical mechanisms for racial self-help. Through this newly rationalized and nationalized structure, black women could speak more profoundly about problems specific to them as black women and problems that affected them as they affected the race. There is no need to defend black club women against charges of imitating white women (the General Federation of Women's Clubs) or compensating for exclusion by the white women. African-American women's tradition of mutual association predated the GFWC by many years. And black women were reformers long before the Progressive Era. It is equally inappropriate to interpret the creation of the national coalition of African-American women's clubs as a response to the contemporary attacks on black female morality. Such attacks undoubtedly gave the organizers an important "cause" that could evoke an immediate response from the black community. But those attacks rested on an historical tradition, too, and at best the attacks only became more public and more frequent at this time. White society had always maintained that black people were immoral and evil; black slavery itself had been rationalized through this explanation.[41] The formation of the NACW represented no psychosocial shift in the women's personal identities or in their social, political, and economic agendas. Rather, it was simply a new national voice through which black club women could continue the struggle to improve their personal lives and the general standard of life in the ever-broadening communities of which they were a part.

NOTES

1. See, for examples, Ruby M. Kendricks, " 'They Also Serve': The National Association of Colored Women, Inc.," *Negro History Bulletin* 42 (March 1954): 171–75; Tullia Kay Brown Hamilton, "The National Association of Colored Women, 1896–1920" (PhD diss., Emory University, 1978); Angela Y. Davis, *Women, Race and Class* (New York: Random House, 1983),

127–36. Activities of church and civic groups not associated with the NACW are included in Gerda Lerner's "Early Community Work of Black Club Women," *Journal of Negro History* 59 (April 1974): 158–62; and throughout Dorothy C. Salem's "To Better Our World: Black Women in Organized Reform, 1890–1920" (PhD diss., Kent State University, 1986). The most recent treatment of black women's organized self-help efforts is Anne Firor Scott, "Most Invisible of All: Black Women's Voluntary Associations," *Journal of Southern History* 56 (February 1990):3–22.

2. See Cynthia Neverdon-Morton, *Afro-American Women of the South and the Advancement of the Race, 1895–1925* (Knoxville: University of Tennessee Press, 1989), 191–201. And see local and state studies, including Darlene Clark Hine, *When the Truth Is Told: A History of Black Women's Culture and Community in Indiana, 1875–1950* (Indianapolis: National Council of Negro Women, 1981); Marilyn Dell Brady, "Kansas Federation of Colored Women's Clubs: 1900–1930," *Kansas History: A Journal of the Central Plains* 9 (Spring 1986): 19–30; Erlene Stetson, "Black Feminism in Indiana, 1893–1933," *Phylon* 64 (December 1983): 292–98; Earline Rae Ferguson, "The Woman's Improvement Club of Indianapolis: Black Women Pioneers in Tuberculosis Work, 1903–1933," *Indiana Magazine of History* 84 (September 1988): 237–61; Wilson Jeremiah Moses, "Domestic Feminism, Conservativism, Sex Roles, and Black Women's Clubs, 1893–1896," *Journal of Social and Behavioral Sciences* 24 (Fall 1987): 166–177. When historians discuss the attacks on black female morality as the most important reason for organizing the NACW, they usually point to the infamous James Jacks letter, in which he charged that all black women were prostitutes, liars, and thieves. Maude Thomas Jenkins, in "The History of the Black Woman's Club Movement in America" (EdD diss., Columbia University Teacher's College, 1984), does explore the complex range of issues that crystallized and encouraged the formation of the NACW. She also links black women's associations in general to an African tradition of mutual aid.

3. See Rayford Logan, *The Negro in American Life and Thought: The Nadir, 1877–1901* (New York: Dial Press, 1954). The revised version of this book was published with the title *The Betrayal of the Negro*.

4. Alfreda E. Duster, ed., *Crusade for Justice: The Autobiography of Ida B. Wells-Barnett* (Chicago: University of Chicago Press, 1968), 47–52; Ida B. Wells, *Southern Horrors: Lynch Law in All Its Phases* (New York: New York Age Print, 1892); and *A Red Record: Tabulated Statistics and Alleged Causes of Lynchings in the United States, 1892–1893–1894* (Chicago: Donohue and Henneberry Press, 1895); Mary Church Terrell, "Lynching from a Negro's Point of View," *North American Review* 178 (June 1904): 853–68; Janie Porter Barrett, *Locust Street Social Settlement: Founded and Managed by Colored* (Hampton, Va.: Hampton Normal and Agricultural Institute, 1912), 19 in the Harris and Janie Porter Barrett Collection, Huntington Library Archives, Hampton University, Hampton, Va.

5. Willie Mae Coleman, "Keeping the Faith and Disturbing the Peace. Black Women: From Anti-Slavery to Women's Suffrage" (PhD diss., University of California-Irvine, 1982), 75.

6. See, for examples, Sterling Stuckey, "Through the Prism of Folklore: The Black Ethos in Slavery," *The Massachusetts Review* 9 (Summer 1968): 417–37; John Blassingame, *The Slave Community* (New York: Oxford University Press, 1972); George Rawick, *From Sundown to Sun Up* (Westport, Conn.: Greenwood Publishing Co., 1972); Eugene Genovese, *Roll, Jordan, Roll: The World the Slaves Made* (New York: Pantheon Books, 1974); Herbert G. Gutman, *The Black Family in Slavery and Freedom, 1750–1925* (New York: Vintage Books, 1976).

7. See Angela Davis, "Reflections on the Black Woman's Role in the Community of Slaves," *The Black Scholar* 2 (December 1971): 2–15; Allan Kulikoff, *Tobacco and Slaves: The Development of Southern Cultures in the Chesapeake, 1680–1800* (Chapel Hill: University of North Carolina Press, 1986), 343–44; Herbert Aptheker, *American Negro Slave Revolts* (New York: Columbia University Press, 1943); and see note 6 above.

8. Orville Vernon Burton, *"In My Father's House Are Many Mansions": Family and Community in Edgeville, S.C.* (Chapel Hill: University of North Carolina Press, 1985), 164–65; Allan Kulikoff, *Tobacco and Slaves,* 345–51; Albert J. Raboteau, *Slave Religion: The "Invisible Institution" in the Antebellum South* (Oxford: Oxford University Press, 1978); Norrece T. Jones, Jr., *Born a Child of Freedom Yet a Slave: Mechanisms of Control and Strategies of Resistance in Antebellum South Carolina* (Hanover: University Press of New England, 1990).

9. Sterling Stuckey, "Through the Prism of Folklore"; Lawrence Levine, *Black Culture and Black Consciousness: Afro-American Folk Thought from Slavery to Freedom* (New York: Oxford University Press, 1977), 81–135; John Blassingame, *The Slave Community,* 127–30.

10. Lawrence Levine, *Black Culture and Black Consciousness,* 6, 7, 10, 33–34; Albert Raboteau, *Slave Religion,* 243–45.

11. Charles Joyner, *Down by the Riverside; A South Carolina Slave Community* (Urbana: University of Illinois Press, 1984), 58–59.

12. Deborah Gray White, *Ar'n't I a Woman: Female Slaves in the Plantation South* (New York: W. W. Norton & Co., 1985), 119–141.

13. Leonard P. Curry, *The Free Black in Urban America, 1800–1850* (Chicago: University of Chicago Press, 1981), 197–214; Dorothy Sterling, ed., *We Are Your Sisters: Black Women in the Nineteenth Century* (New York: W. W. Norton & Co., 1984), 104–07. See also Philip S. Foner, *History of Black Americans: From Africa to the Emergence of the Cotton Kingdom* (Westport, Conn.: Greenwood Press, 1975), 555–78; Herbert Aptheker, *A Documentary History of the Negro People in the US,* 3 vols. (New York: Citadel Press, 1951, 1973, 1974), passim; Dorothy Porter, "The Organized Educational Activities of Negro Literary Societies, 1828–1846," *Journal of Negro Education* 6 (October 1936): 555–576; Julie Winch, *Philadelphia's Black Elite: Activism, Accommodation, and the Struggle for Autonomy, 1787–1848* (Philadelphia: Temple University Press, 1988), 5–15.

14. Leonard P. Curry, *The Free Black in Urban America,* 202. An 1835 issue of *Niles Register* estimated that Baltimore had

35–40 black mutual-aid societies. Curry's estimate of 200 groups is baffling considering that he cites the individual statistics for Baltimore and Philadelphia.

15. Linda Perkins, "Black Women and Racial 'Uplift' Prior to Emancipation," in *The Black Woman Cross Culturally,* ed. Filomina Chioma Steady (Cambridge: Schenkman Publishing Co., 1981), 317–334.

16. Armstead Robinson, "Plans Dat Comed From God: Institution Building and the Emergence of Black Leadership in Reconstruction Memphis," in *Towards a New South? Studies in Post-Civil War Southern Communities,* ed. Orville Burton and Robert G. McMath (Westport, Conn.: Greenwood Press, 1982), 71–102.

17. See W. E. B. DuBois, ed., *Some Efforts of American Negroes for their Own Social Betterment* (Atlanta: Atlanta University Press, 1898); Guy B. Johnson, "Some Factors in the Development of Negro Social Institutions in the United States," *American Journal of Sociology* 30 (November 1934): 329–337; Inabel Burns Lindsay, "Some Contributions of Negroes to Welfare Services, 1865–1900," *Journal of Negro Education* 25 (Winter 1956): 18; Joel Williamson, *After Slavery: The Negro in South Carolina during Reconstruction, 1861–1877* (Chapel Hill: University of North Carolina Press, 1965), 321–23; Vernon Lane Wharton, *The Negro in Mississippi, 1865–1890* (Chapel Hill: University of North Carolina Press, 1947; reprint, New York: Harper & Row, 1965), 270–73; Peter Rachleff, *Black Labor in Richmond, 1865–1890* (Urbana: University of Illinois Press, 1989), passim; Elsa Barkley Brown, "Womanist Consciousness: Maggie Lena Walker and the Independent Order of St. Luke," *Signs: Journal of Women in Culture and Society* 14 (Spring 1989): 610–633. A scrap of paper dated 1898 in the Harris and Janie Porter Barrett collection at Hampton notes the creation of The People's Building and Loan Association of Hampton, Virginia, in 1889. The note claims that by 1898, the organization had loaned over $140,000 to members, earned over $30,000 in dividends, and helped stockholders purchase 250 houses.

18. See James D. Anderson, *The Education of Blacks in the South, 1860–1935* (Chapel Hill: University of North Carolina Press, 1988).

19. For examples of studies on black towns, see Nell Irvin Painter, *The Exodusters: Black Migration to Kansas after Reconstruction* (New York: Alfred A. Knopf, 1977); Kenneth M. Hamilton, *Black Towns and Profit: Promotion and Early Development in the Trans-Appalachian West* (Urbana: University of Illinois Press, 1990).

20. Kathleen C. Berkeley, " 'Colored Ladies also Contributed': Black Women's Activities from Benevolence to Social Welfare, 1866–1896," in *The Web of Southern Social Relations: Women, Family, and Education,* ed. Walter J. Fraser, Jr., R. Frank Saunders, Jr., and Jon L. Wakelyn (Athens: University of Georgia Press, 1985), 180–82.

21. Benjamin [Griffith] Brawley, *Negro Builders and Heroes* (Chapel Hill: University of North Carolina Press, 1937), 267–70; Elsa Barkley Brown, "Womanist Consciousness," 616–17.

22. See Mary Brinkerhoff, "Books, Blacks Beautiful to Her," *Dallas Morning News,* 23 July 1971, in vertical files, Biographical–women, "Clara Jones," Walter P. Reuther Archives of Labor History and Urban Affairs, Wayne State University, Detroit. (Hereafter cited as Labor Archives.)

23. Robert Kraus, "Black Library Chief Bears No Scars after Squabble," *Detroit Free Press,* February 18, 1971 in vertical files, Labor Archives; Maggie Kennedy, "A Librarian Who Speaks Her Mind," *Dallas Times Herald,* October 21, 1976, in 1970–76 Clippings box, Clara Jones Papers, Black Librarians' Archives, North Carolina Central University School of Library Science, Durham. Interestingly, when Jones read Joel Chandler Harris's Uncle Remus stories as an adult, she recognized them as stories she had heard all her life, but she was appalled by what she characterized as the "injected" racism. In their original form, the stories often included themes of collective consciousness.

24. Florence Lattimore, *A Palace of Delight (The Locust Street Settlement for Negroes at Hampton, Virginia)* (Hampton, Va: Hampton Normal and Agricultural Institute, 1915), 4–8; Sadie Iola Daniel, *Women Builders* (Washington, D.C.: Associated Publishers, 1970), 54–61; Tullia Brown Hamilton, "The National Association of Colored Women," 140.

25. "Virginia State Federation of Colored Women's Clubs: Its Origin and Objectives," and Edna M. Colson, "The Petersburg Women's Council," typescripts, Virginia Federation of Colored Women's Clubs Papers, Johnson Memorial Library Special Collections, Virginia State University, Petersburg, VA; William Anthony Aery, "Helping Wayward Girls: Virginia's Pioneer Work," *Southern Workman* 44 (November 1915): 598–604; Esther F. Brown, "Social Settlement Work in Hampton," *Southern Workman* 33 (July 1904): 393–96; Janie Porter Barrett to Dr. [Hollis P.] Frissell, December 25, 1915, Harris and Janie Porter Barrett Collection. Cited in full in note 4.

26. Alfreda M. Duster, *Crusade for Justice,* xiv–xix, 5, 15–20.

27. See Dorothy Salem, "To Better Our World: Black Women and Organized Reform," 24–25.

28. Alfreda M. Duster, *Crusade for Justice,* 69, 93. Wells-Barnett dedicated her autobiography to "our youth [who] are entitled to the facts of race history which only the participants can give." Ibid., 5.

29. Adrienne Lash Jones, "Jane Edna Hunter: A Case Study of Black Leadership, 1910–1950" (PhD diss., Case Western Reserve University, 1983), 49–64. Also note that black community residents of Norfolk, Virginia, were so proud of Lula McNeil and so optimistic about her potential for the community that, after she graduated at the top of the first graduating class of the first black high school in that city, they all contributed money for educating her further at the state normal school. After graduation, she taught school for a while and later returned to nursing school and became a public health nurse. See Lula Catherine McNeil interview transcript, Black Nurses Archives, Hampton University, Hampton, Va.

30. Adrienne Lash Jones, "Jane Edna Hunter," 93–100; Mayme V. Holmes, "The Story of the Phillis Wheatley Association of Cleveland," *Southern Workman* 57 (October 1928): 399–401; Jane

E. Hunter, "Phyllis [*sic*] Wheatley Association of Cleveland: An Institution Devoted to Better, Brighter Girls, Happier, Heartier Women," *The Competitor 1* (March 1920): 52–54.

31. Minutes of the Federation of Colored Women's Clubs of Colorado, June 28, 1911; June 13, 1917; June 9, 1920; June 14–17, 1932; June 11–13, 1946; "Autobiography of Mrs. Hattie Taylor"; "Biography of Mrs. Elizabeth Ensley, Founder of the State Federation of Colored Women's Clubs"; and "Biography of Betty Wilkins," in the Records of the Federation of Colored Women's Clubs of Colorado, Western History Division, Denver Public Library, Denver.

32. Elizabeth L. Davis, *The Story of the Illinois Federation of Colored Women's Clubs* (n.p.,n.d.), esp. chapter 6, "Who's Who," in the Henry P. Slaughter Collection, Woodruff Library, Atlanta University Center Archives, Atlanta.

33. Delilah L. Beasley, *The Negro Trail Blazers of California* (Los Angeles: Times Mirror Printing, 1919), esp. chapter 13, "Distinguished Women."

34. See Tullia Brown Hamilton, "The National Association of Colored Women," 39–53.

35. Hamilton notes that 42 of the 59 clubs represented at the first NACW Convention in Nashville in 1897 were from urban areas. Ibid., 55.

36. This is not to suggest that the "communications revolution" underway at the time had no impact on these women's efforts to create a national organization.

37. W. E. B. DuBois, *Efforts at Social Betterment among Negro Americans,* 45–50; Elizabeth Lindsay Davis, *The Story of the Illinois Federation of Colored Women's Clubs,* 6–10; Dorothy Salem, "To Better Our World," 155; "Neighborhood Union's Aim Granted by the Laws of Georgia under the Charter of the State of Georgia," box 3, 1. 1931, Neighborhood Union Collection, Atlanta University Center Archives, Atlanta.

38. Ethel Evangeline Martin Bolden, "Susan Dart Butler: Pioneer Librarian," (MA thesis, Atlanta University, 1959); Jacqueline Anne Rouse, *Lugenia Burns Hope: Black Southern Reformer* (Athens: University of Georgia Press, 1989), 71–73; Cynthia Neverdon-Morton, *Afro-American Women of the South and the Advancement of the Race,* 159–161. Janie Porter Barrett also eventually turned over the Industrial School to the state of Virginia.

39. Untitled typescript [a history of the Virginia State Federation of Colored Women's Clubs], 2–3 and Edna M. Colson, "The Petersburg Women's Council," typescript, The Virginia Federation of Colored Women's Club Papers; Frances Reynolds Keyser, "Florida Federation of Colored Women's Clubs Establish a Home for Delinquent Girls," *The Competitor* 3 (May 1921): 34; Dorothy Salem, "To Better Our World," 124–209; Tullia Brown Hamilton, "The National Association of Colored Women," 72, 76.

40. Dorothy Salem, Ibid; Paula Giddings, *When and Where I Enter: The Impact of Black Women on Race and Sex in America* (New York: William Morrow & Co., 1984), 135; isolated papers of the Kansas City, Mo., Federation of Colored Women's Clubs, b. 28–4, f. 96, Frederick Douglass Collection, Moorland-Spingarn Research Center, Howard University, Washington, D.C.; "The History of the Cincinnati Federation of Colored Women's Clubs (1904–1952)," typescript, Mirriam Hamilton Spotts Papers, Amistad Research Center, Tulane University, New Orleans; William Anthony Aery, "Helping Wayward Girls"; Pitt Dillingham, "Black Belt Settlement Work," *Southern Workman* 31 (July 1902): 383–388 and (August 1902): 437–444; Jane E. Hunter, "Phyllis [*sic*] Wheatley Association of Cleveland"; Mrs. Laurence C. Jones, "Mississippi's Bright Club Fields," *The Competitor* 3 (May 1921): 27–28; Mayme Holmes, "The Story of the Phillis Wheatley Association of Cleveland, Ohio." Almost every issue of *Woman's Era* and *National Notes* includes details of similar activities for NACW affiliates throughout the country. On suffrage and interracial cooperation, see Jane Olcott, *The Work of Colored Women* (New York: War Work Council, National Board of the YMCA, 1919), issued by the Colored Work Committee; Cynthia Neverdon-Morton, "The Black Women's Struggle for Equality in the South, 1895–1925," in *The Afro-American Woman: Struggles and Images,* ed. Sharon Harley and Rosalyn Terborg-Penn (Port Washington, N.Y.: Kennikat Press, 1978), 43–57; and Rosalyn Terborg-Penn, "Discontented Black Feminist: Prelude and Postscript to the Passage of the Nineteenth Amendment," in *Decades of Discontent: The Women's Movement,* 1920–1940, ed. Lois Scharf and Joan M. Jenson (Westport, Conn: Greenwood Press, 1983), 261–78.

41. See discussions on origins of American racism in Winthrop Jordan, *White over Black: American Attitudes toward the Negro, 1550–1812* (New York: Oxford University Press, 1974), or the abridged version, *The White Man's Burden.*

Gender Politics for Men

R. W. CONNELL

When I was about ten or eleven years old I played in a school rugby football team for a short time. Rugby is a game in which you clasp a pointed ball to your chest and try to run through a wall of opposing players to put the ball on the ground behind them. They attempt to throw you to the ground, seize the ball, and run through a wall of your players in order to put the ball on the ground behind you. When half the game is over, everyone turns around and runs the other way.

This is the most popular sport in Sydney, my hometown, and rightly so. It is closely related to great art. Each half of the game runs for about the same length of time as Beethoven's Ninth Symphony. The ball weighs about as much as a hardcover edition of Dante's *Inferno*. And at the end of the season, each player's face resembles a portrait by Picasso.

So, as a lover of the arts, I joined the school rugby team. Being a slow runner, I became a forward. This gave me the right and the duty to join in "scrums," where the forwards link up in a phalanx and try to push the other team off the ball by weight and strength. Those at the back of the scrum place their heads among the other player's buttocks to get leverage to push, and cannot see very well (though they can still smell). So I don't know who it was that—in a scrum during my second game—pulled out a tuft of my hair. I hope it was a member of the opposing team.

I changed to soccer the next week. This was a serious decision. In Australia in the 1950s soccer players were known to have limp wrists, and were thought to wear frilly nighties to bed. Even today soccer players in Australia are suspected of dilettantism. Now that my hair is coming out for quite different reasons, forty years later, I still remem-

ber the incident and in a sense I am still living with its consequences. It was one of the moments when I began my dissent from hegemonic masculinity.

There is, at present, an international questioning of the kind of masculinity I met on the rugby field and that others meet in the military, in corporate boardrooms, and in most governments in the world. "International" is no overstatement. Some of the best historical research on masculinity has been done in New Zealand, and some of the best sociology in Australia. Some of the best theory has been done in England, some of the best field observation in the United States. Some of the best youth work has been done in Germany, and some of the most important political work in Canada and South Africa.

This questioning has been provoked by an international feminist movement, which brought to light the oppression of women and the patriarchal character of major institutions and dominant forms of culture. It became clear that the questions politicians classify as "women's issues" are also issues about men. Men are gendered too. Once this is acknowledged, hard questions arise about how men become gendered, how masculinity is related to gender inequality, and how men can become part of the solution rather than part of the problem.

MEN'S INTERESTS

In the days of the attempt to set up a "men's liberation" movement, in the 1970s, it was assumed that feminism was good for men, because men too suffered from rigid sex roles. As women broke out of their sex role, men would be enabled to break out of theirs, and would have fuller, better, and healthier lives as a result.

The failure of any large number to sign on as the men's auxiliary to feminism, in the years since, suggests a flaw in this analysis. Men's dominant position in the gender order

R. W. Connell, "Gender Politics for Men" from *Feminism and Men: Reconstructing Gender Relations,* edited by Steven P. Schacht and Doris W. Ewing. Copyright © 1998. Reprinted with the permission of New York University Press.

has a material payoff, and the discussions of masculinity have constantly underestimated how big it is. In the rich capitalist countries such as the United States, men's average incomes are approximately double the average incomes of women. Men have ten times the political access of women worldwide (measured by representation in parliaments). Men have even greater control of corporate wealth (looking at top management in major corporations). Men control the means of violence, in the form of weapons and armed forces.

I call these advantages the "patriarchal dividend" for men, and this dividend is not withering away. The gender segregation of the workforce in the rich countries has declined little in recent years. Men's representation in parliaments worldwide has risen, not fallen, in recent years. As corporations have gone multinational—under the aegis of corporate hegemonic masculinity—they have increasingly escaped the national-level political structures through which women press for equal opportunity and an end to discrimination. The new international garment manufacturing and microprocessor assembly industries, for instance, are arenas of rampant sexism. Violence against women has not measurably declined.

Yet not all men are corporate executives or mass killers. Though men in general gain the patriarchal dividend, specific groups of men gain very little of it. For instance, working-class youth, economically dispossessed by structural unemployment, may gain no economic advantage at all over the women in their communities. Other groups of men pay part of the price, alongside women, for the maintenance of an unequal gender order. Gay men are systematically made targets of prejudice and violence. Effeminate and wimpish men are constantly put down. Black men, in the United States (as in South Africa) suffer massively higher levels of lethal violence than white men.

There are, then, divisions of interest among men on gender issues. I would also want to emphasize that not all interests are egotistic. Interests are also relational, that is, constituted in the social relations one shares with other people. Most men have relational interests that they share with particular women, for instance, as parents needing child care provision and good health services for children, or as workers, needing improved conditions and security. Gay men share with lesbians an interest in fighting discrimination.

When we look at men's lives concretely, we regularly find dense networks of relationships with women: with mothers, wives, partners, sisters, daughters, aunts, grandmothers, friends, workmates, neighbors. Very few men have a life-world that is blocked off from women, that is genuinely a "separate sphere."

Each of these relationships can be the basis for men's relational interest in reform. For instance, I have an interest in my wife's being free of the threat of intimidation or rape, in her having job security and equal pay, in her having the best possible health care. I have an interest in my daughter's being free of sexual harassment at school, in her having access to any kind of training and all occupations, in her growing up a confident and autonomous person.

Men's interest in gender hierarchy, defined by the patriarchal dividend, is real and large, but it is internally divided, and it is cross-cut by relational interests shared with women. Which of these interests is actually pursued by particular men is a matter of politics—politics in the quite familiar sense of organizing in the pursuit of programs.

Men who try to develop a politics in support of feminism, whether gay or straight, are not in for an easy ride. They are likely to be met with derision from many other men, and from some women. It is almost a journalistic cliché that women despise Sensitive New Age Guys. They will not necessarily get warm support from feminist women, some of whom are deeply distrustful of all men, most of whom are wary of men's power, and all of whom make a political commitment to solidarity with women. Since change in gender requires reconstructing personal relations as well as public life, there are many opportunities for personal hurt, mistaken judgments, and anger.

I do not think men seeking progressive reforms of masculinity can expect to be comfortable, while we live in a world marked by gendered violence and inequality. Masculinity therapy offers personal comfort as a substitute for social change. But this is not the only use for emotional support. As shown by John Rowan's book *The Horned God,* therapeutic methods and emotional exploration can be used to support men, as feminist therapy supports women, in the stresses of a project of social change.[1]

POLITICAL PURPOSES

Given the difficulties of the project, what might motivate men to press on into the flames? We need some conception of where the politics should be headed, a vision of the world we are trying to produce. Other forces certainly are making choices, which children and youth face here and now in a barrage of advertising masquerading as sport, militarism masquerading as entertainment, commercial sex masquerading as personal freedom.

The goal defined by sex-role reformers in the 1970s was the abolition of masculinity (and femininity) by a movement toward androgyny, the blending of the two existing sex roles. This grasped the fact that we have to change personal life, but underestimated the complexity of masculinities and femininities, put too much emphasis on attitudes and not enough on material inequalities and issues of power.

We might better think of the goal as "recomposing" the elements of gender: making the full range of gender symbolism and practice available to all people. Though this may sound exotic when formulated as a strategy, bits of it are quite familiar in practice. In schools, for instance, it is quite a common goal to "expand the options" for girls, by trying to make science and technology courses more available to them; and for boys, by encouraging them to learn to cook or to sew.

It has been argued that the most effective form of sex education with teenagers is "learning to be the opposite sex," that is, trying to get girls and boys to think through heterosexual relationships from the point of view of the other party. (Most school sex education is forbidden, however, to go beyond heterosexual thoughts.) Bronwyn Davies, an Australian feminist educator, wryly suggests that children are good poststructuralists, and readily learn to move among different gender positions in culture.[2]

The bodily dimension of gender is often thought to be the absolute limit of change. When I am interviewed about these issues on radio, interviewers often seem to think that bodily difference (either in sport or in reproduction) is a knockout question. But if we understand gender as being about the way bodies are drawn into a historical process, then we can recognize contradictions in existing embodiments and can see enormous possibilities of *re-embodiment* for men. There are different ways of using, feeling, and showing male bodies.

I am charmed to see, in shops selling artistic postcards and posters, a genre showing muscular male bodies cuddling babies. Why not make this a widespread pleasure? Provided, of course, the men are also sharing the other tactile experiences of baby care—getting the milk in, wringing out the nappies, and wiping up the shit.

But rearranging elements is not enough. As the American feminist Wendy Chapkis argues, playing with the elements of gender can be benign only if we unpack the "package deal" that, for women, links beauty and status, and for men links desirability and power.[3] We can rearrange difference only if we contest dominance. So a recomposing strategy requires a project of social justice.

Gender relations involve different spheres of practice, so there is an unavoidable complexity in gender politics. Theoretical work in social science distinguishes at least three spheres: the relations of power, the relations of pro-

duction, and the relations of cathexis.[4] In each case we can define directions for a politics of gender justice.

Pursuing justice in power relations means contesting men's predominance in the state, professions, and management, and ending violence against women.

Some groups of men have specifically focused on the issue of men's violence toward women. Generally maintaining a relationship (sometimes tense) with women's groups mobilizing around domestic violence or rape, such groups have worked with violent men to try to reduce the chance of further violence, and have launched wider educational campaigns. The most extensive has been the White Ribbon campaign in Canada, which arose from commemorations of the 1989 massacre of women at the University of Montreal. In this case, mass media and mainstream politicians as well as community groups have been brought into a campaign rejecting violence against women, with considerable impact at a national level.

Pursuing justice in economic relations means equalizing incomes, sharing the burden of household work, and equalizing access to education and training. A key vehicle for such politics is workers' organizations.

While male-controlled unions have often been antagonistic to women, even in totally masculinized industries some unions have taken progressive action. In 1979–80 the United Steel Workers successfully pressed for women to be hired at the Hamilton steelworks in Canada. A serious effort was made to encourage discussion of the issues by the male membership, and a fair level of support for the change was gained. A few years earlier, the Builders Labourers Federation in New South Wales sponsored the entry of women workers on exclusively male building sites. In this case, the women clerks in the union office had challenged the sexism of a left-wing male leadership and persuaded them to change their policy. In another Canadian example, in electrical manufacturing in Westinghouse plants, it was pressure from below that led to the integration of women into formerly all-male shops. Stan Gray, the activist who tells the story, notes that this was only the beginning of the process. A sprawling struggle, in the context of recession and layoffs, nevertheless moved on to campaigns against workplace sexism; some of the men came to see sexism as divisive and against their own interests as workers.[5]

Pursuing justice in the structure of cathexis means ending homophobia, reconstructing heterosexual relations on the basis of reciprocity not hierarchy, and disconnecting masculinity from pressures toward violence.

The peace movement is perhaps the longest-established forum where significant numbers of men have been engaged in a critique of an important part of hegemonic masculinity, violence. Quaker traditions, the Gandhian legacy, and the nonviolence civil rights movement in the United States are part of this heritage. Though the peace movement has not generally defined masculinity as its target (that connection being made by feminist groups in actions excluding men, such as the Greenham Common encampment in Britain), it has provided a forum for political action that in fact contests hegemonic masculinity.

Along these lines we can define an agenda for a progressive politics of masculinity, and can find many examples of worthwhile practice. That still leaves open the question of the overall form this politics should take.

A MEN'S MOVEMENT?

It is commonly assumed that a progressive politics of masculinity must take the form of a social movement. The usual model is feminism; many writers imply a close parallel between the women's movement and a men's movement. More remotely, the labor movement and civil rights movements serve as models.

I would argue that these parallels are not close, and may be seriously misleading. The movements just listed are mobilizations of oppressed or exploited groups to end their subordination. They seek the unity of the group and assert the dignity of a previously stigmatized identity.

"Men" as a group, and heterosexual men in particular, are not oppressed or disadvantaged (though that belief is now promoted by right-wing campaigns against affirmative action). As I have noted, men *in general* gain a patriarchal dividend. Hegemonic masculinity is not a stigmatized identity. Quite the opposite: the culture already honors it. Seeking the unity of "men" can only mean emphasizing the experiences and interests men have that separate them from women, rather than the interests they share with women that might lead toward social justice.

This is not an abstract theoretical point. It has happened in practice in the history of some antisexist men's groups, such as the American group MOVE studied by Paul Lichterman.[6] Initially involved both in antiviolence work with batterers and in raising public issues about masculinity, this group gradually moved toward a therapeutic ideology, developed a concern with being "positive" about men, and moved away from public stands and issues about the structure of power. What happened in this specific case also happened much more broadly in the transition from "men's liberation" in the early 1970s to masculinity therapy in the 1980s.

The evangelical Christian Promise Keepers and the African-American Million Man March of 1995 both follow the model of a social movement and both have been vehicles for promoting patriarchal understandings of masculinity in the context of the pursuit of evangelical religion or racial justice. The idea of a husband as the responsible "head of the family" has proved attractive in mobilizing middle-class men (and has proved attractive to many women, too, where the alternative is abandonment or violence). The definition and the movement are carefully policed against homosexuality (gay men, but not their gayness, are welcome in the Promise Keepers—they are seen as potential converts).

To fight for justice in gender relations often means, paradoxically, doing the opposite of the things that would create a "men's movement." That is, tackling issues that inevitably divide men rather than unite them: issues like homophobia, affirmative action for women, equal pay, sexual harassment, and violence.

This is not for a moment to doubt the importance of solidarity among the men, and the women, involved with these issues. Indeed, I would emphasize this point strongly. Experience has shown that work on these issues is stressful, often painful, and difficult to sustain without support. This points to the importance, for men engaged in such struggles, of networks such as the National Organization for Men against Sexism in the United States. Journals such as *Changing Men* in the United States, *XY* in Australia, and *Achilles Heel* in Britain are key elements in antisexist networks.

Rather than a grand "men's movement," we should be thinking of a variety of struggles in diverse sites, linked through networking rather than mass mobilization or formal organization. Men are likely to be detached from the defense of patriarchy in small numbers at a time, in a great variety of circumstances. So the likely political pattern is one of unevenness between situations, with differently configured issues and possibilities of action.

The examples discussed in the last section, the White Ribbon movement, the union movement, and the peace movement, illustrate these points. What is involved in all three cases is not a social movement of men focused on masculinity, but some kind of alliance politics. Here the project of social justice depends on the overlapping of interests or commitments between different groups. The overlapping may be temporary, but can be long term (a perfectly familiar situation in politics). Existing power resources can be used for new ends. We do not have to start from scratch all the time.

It is often assumed that alliance means compromise and therefore containment. The familiar militant gesture of insisting on revolutionary purity is not unknown in men's countersexist politics.[7] The chances of actually changing the world this way are slight.

Pluralism in alliance-making is necessary, but containment is not a necessary result. Given that patriarchy is a historical structure, not a timeless dichotomy of men abusing women, it will be ended by a historical process. The strategic problem is to generate pressures that will culminate in the long run in a transformation of the structure; and any initiative that sets up pressure in that direction is worth having. Lynne Segal, in the best feminist appraisal of issues about masculinity, is cool about the pace of change; her book is called *Slow Motion*. But she is in no doubt about the possibilities of change, through hard work in familiar institutions such as workplaces, unions, and political parties.[8]

In the long run, as Keynes remarked, we are all dead; and while we are still alive, we want to see something more than a rise in the probability of social justice in the distant future. So as well as long-term educational strategies, we also need what British feminists called "prefigurative politics"—at least samples of paradise, at least little bits of justice, here and now.

Again, this is familiar in principle. Progressive education hoped to prefigure the good society in democratic schools; industrial democracy hoped to prefigure a democratically controlled economy in each workplace. In my household (like many others) we hope to prefigure a society in which gender equality and sexual tolerance are routine, a bedrock of civilization.

However, the prefigurative politics of gender and sexuality are not necessarily rocklike. They may, on the contrary, be scandalous, hilarious, or disturbing. Halloween on Haight Street; Cal-PEP, an AIDS prevention program run by prostitutes and former prostitutes; the pleasures and dangers of queer culture; integrated sports. Prefiguration may also be peaceable: fathers taking toddlers and babies in push-chairs for an outing.

Much of the effective work done on masculinity is educational, above all. It involves attempts to reformulate knowledge, to expand understanding, to create new capacities for practice. I think we might value this fact and build on it. It is in education that we have some of the best chances to prefigure new ways of being men and boys. I will end, therefore, with some remarks on the problems of educational strategies.

EDUCATION

"Gender" in discussions of schools has mainly signaled issues about girls. The recent debate marks an important recognition that boys are gendered too. The commonest error is to assume that a strategy formulated for one situation must work for the other. Given the patriarchal dividend, which gives boys an interest in claiming the gender privilege open to them, a simple translation will not generally work.

Educational responses to issues about boys must have two sides. They must be concerned with the impact of the advantaged group's actions on the less advantaged group. (Thus, the issue of harassment of girls is rightly a major concern of programs concerned with boys.)

They must also be concerned with the *costs* paid for the situation of advantage. (Thus, the impact of harassment on boys, in the form of bullying among boys, and poisoned relationships with girls, is also a major concern.) The long-term costs to boys and men, though often hard to assess, may well be the most important.

Recent discussions of educational strategies for boys have rightly pointed to the negative impact on boys of narrow models of masculinity and obsolete ideas about men's and women's work. Such stereotypes, if adopted by the boys, severely limit their cultural experiences, their vocational choices, and their expectations about future personal relationships, both with men and with women.

These issues go beyond equity policy in the narrow sense to broad curriculum objectives. Educational policy about boys must concern the range of their experiences and their understanding of life options. Maximizing the range of pupils' knowledge, eliminating barriers to their awareness, interest, and tolerance, and widening the range of their own life choices are general educational goals that have specific applications in the education of boys.

These goals cannot be pursued if gender itself is not made an object of enquiry and learning. This has been an important trend in education for girls and women, both in "mainstream" curriculum areas and in the growth of new fields such as women's studies. Recent research on masculinity has produced a body of knowledge that makes it easier than before to develop a curriculum about gender that is gender inclusive and plainly relevant to boys.

This may require programs with a different structure from those most familiar in gender equity work. Gender equity work in English-speaking countries has emphasized *gender-specific* programs addressed to girls. The first generation of school-level programs concerned with boys has followed this logic, producing programs specifically *for* boys.

Youth work in Germany has made an important distinction between "gender-specific" and "gender-relevant" programs.[9] Both in welfare and in curriculum, schools may now have a need for more of the *gender-relevant* type of programs. These take gender relations as the object of inquiry, discussion, and learning; and they may be addressed to boys and girls together as well as separately.

Not all education occurs in schools, of course. Some of the most impressive recent antisexist work is educational work in difficult circumstances, such as prisons, and around difficult issues, such as violence. An example is the educational program for young men developed by the Australian group Men Against Sexual Assault.

As David Denborough explains the approach, it is possible to find respectful ways of working with young men without shying away from the hard issues of men's violence. Denborough draws on the new masculinity research to develop the strategy, encouraging young men not only to recognize the main narrative of masculinity in their community, but also to search for the counternarratives, the other possibilities that exist in the same situation. A search for countermeanings also appears in Don Sabo's work in an American prison. Sabo notes how sport and physical training at one level play into the cultivation of masculine hardness, but at another level represent a kind of self-care in a hostile and very unhealthy environment.[10]

Educational work on masculinity is not likely to be easy. People in this field are already aware of a number of problems: resistance by boys and men (including those who may be in most need of new programs), difficulties in defining purposes, skepticism from staff, ethical problems in relation to girls' programs, and shortages of materials and research.

Nevertheless, the expansion of young people's knowledge and capacity for choice and action about an important area of their current and future lives is a coherent and important educational goal. It is an issue where the agenda of justice in gender relations is linked to widely shared social purposes and has immediate practical possibilities.

ACKNOWLEDGMENTS

This essay began in presentations to a conference on Reproduction and Change in Masculinity, sponsored by the Hans Bockler Foundation of the German union movement, held at Munich in September 1994. It draws on the essay "The Politics of Changing Men," published in *Socialist Review,* 1995, and on research on "boys and schools" done for the New South Wales Department of School Education (which is of course not responsible for my views on the matter). I am grateful to Heinz Kindler, Gudrun Linne, Van Davy, and Lee Bell for making these projects possible.

NOTES

1. John Rowan, *The Horned God: Feminism and Men as Wounding and Healing* (London: Routledge and Kegan Paul, 1987).

2. Bronwyn Davies, *Shards of Glass* (Sydney: Allen and Unwin, 1993).

3. Wendy Chapkis, *Beauty Secrets: Women and the Politics of Appearance* (Boston: South End Press, 1986).

4. See R. W. Connell, *Gender and Power,* for a more detailed account of these structures (Cambridge: Polity Press, 1987).

5. June Corman et al., *Recasting Steel Labour,* Meredith Burgmann, "Revolution and Machismo," in Elizabeth Windschuttle, ed., *Women, Class and History* ([Sydney?], Australia: Fontana, 1980); Stan Gray, "Sharing the Shop Floor," in Michael Kaufman, ed., *Beyond Patriarchy: Essays by Men on Pleasure, Power, and Change* (Toronto: Oxford University Press, 1987).

6. Paul Lichterman, "Making the Politics of Masculinity," *Comparative Social Research* 11(1989):185–208.

7. See, for instance, John Stoltenberg, *Refusing to Be a Man* (London: Fontana, 1990).

8. Lynne Segal, *Slow Motion: Changing Masculinities, Changing Men* (London: Virago, 1990).

9. Heinz Kindler, *Maske(r)ade: Jungen- und Mannarerbeit für die Praxis* (Schwäbisch-Gmünd und Tabingen: Neuling Verlag, 1993).

10. David Denborough, *Step by Step: Developing Respectful Ways of Working with Young Men to Reduce Violence* (Sydney: Men Against Sexual Assault, 1994); Don Sabo, "Doing Time Doing Masculinity: Sports and Prison," in Michael A. Messner and Donald F. Sabo, eds., *Sex, Violence and Power in Sports: Rethinking Masculinity* (Freedom, CA: Crossing Press, 1994).

JUDAISM, MASCULINITY, AND FEMINISM

MICHAEL S. KIMMEL

In the late 1960s, I organized and participated in several large demonstrations against the war in Vietnam. Early on—it must have been 1967 or so—over 10,000 of us were marching down Fifth Avenue in New York urging the withdrawal of all US troops. As we approached one corner, I noticed a small but vocal group of counter-demonstrators, waving American flags and shouting patriotic slogans. "Go back to Russia!" one yelled. Never being particularly shy, I tried to engage him. "It's my duty as an American to oppose policies I disagree with. This is patriotism!" I answered. "Drop dead, you commie Jew fag!" was his reply.

Although I tried not to show it, I was shaken by his accusation, perplexed and disturbed by the glib association of communism, Judaism, and homosexuality. "Only one out of three," I can say to myself now, "is not especially perceptive." But yet something disturbing remains about that linking of political, religious, and sexual orientations. What links them, I think, is a popular perception that each is not quite a man, that each is less than a man. And while recent developments may belie this simplistic formulation, there is, I believe, a kernel of truth to the epithet, a small piece I want to claim, not as vicious smear, but proudly. I believe that my Judaism did directly contribute to my activism against that terrible war, just as it currently provides the foundation for my participation in the struggle against sexism.

What I want to explore here are some of the ways in which my Jewishness has contributed to becoming an antisexist man, working to make this world a safe environment for women (and men) to fully express their humanness. Let me be clear that I speak from a cultural heritage of Eastern European Jewry, transmuted by three generations of life in the United States. I speak of the culture of Judaism's effect on me as an American Jew, not from either doctrinal considerations—we all know the theological contradictions of a biblical reverence for

Michael S. Kimmel, "Judaism, Masculinity, and Feminism." *Changing Men* (Summer/Fall 1987). Copyright © 1987. Reprinted with the permission of the author.

women, and prayers that thank God for not being born one—nor from an analysis of the politics of nation states. My perspective says nothing of Middle Eastern machismo; I speak of Jewish culture in the diaspora, not of Israeli politics.

The historical experience of Jews has three elements that I believe have contributed to this participation in feminist politics. First, historically, the Jew is an *outsider*. Wherever the Jew has gone, he or she has been outside the seat of power, excluded from privilege. The Jew is the symbolic "other," not unlike the symbolic "otherness" of women, gays, racial and ethnic minorities, the elderly and the physically challenged. To be marginalized allows one to see the center more clearly than those who are in it, and presents grounds for alliances among marginal groups.

But the American Jew, the former immigrant, is "other" in another way, one common to many ethnic immigrants to the United States. Jewish culture is, after all, seen as an ethnic culture, which allows it to be more oppressive and emotionally rich than the bland norm. Like other ethnic subgroups, Jews have been characterized as emotional, nurturing, caring. Jewish men hug and kiss, cry and laugh. A little too much. A little too loudly. Like ethnics.

Historically, the Jewish man has been seen as less than masculine, often as a direct outgrowth of this emotional "respond-ability." The historical consequences of centuries of laws against Jews, of anti-Semitic oppression, are a cultural identity and even a self-perception as "less than men," who are too weak, too fragile, too frightened to care for our own. The cruel irony of ethnic oppression is that our rich heritage is stolen from us, and then we are blamed for having no rich heritage. In this, again, the Jew shares this self-perception with other oppressed groups who, rendered virtually helpless by an infantilizing oppression, are further victimized by the accusation that they are, in fact, infants and require the beneficence of the oppressor. One example of this cultural self-hatred can be found in the comments of Freud's colleague and friend Weininger (a Jew) who argued that "the Jew is saturated with femininity. The most feminine Aryan is more masculine than the most manly Jew. The Jew lacks the good breeding that is based upon respect for one's own individuality as well as the individuality of others."

But, again, Jews are also "less than men" for a specific reason as well. The traditional emphasis on literacy in Jewish culture contributes in a very special way. In my family, at least, to be learned, literate, a rabbi, was the highest aspiration one could possibly have. In a culture characterized by love of learning, literacy may be a mark of dignity. But currently in the United States literacy is a cultural liability. Americans contrast egghead intellectuals, divorced from the real world, with men of action—instinctual, passionate, fierce, and masculine. Senator Albert Beveridge of Indiana counseled in his 1906 volume *Young Man and the World* (a turn-of-the-century version of *Real Men Don't Eat Quiche*) to "avoid books, in fact, avoid all artificial learning, for the forefathers put America on the right path by learning from completely natural experience." Family, church and synagogue, and schoolroom were cast as the enervating domains of women, sapping masculine vigor.

Now don't get me wrong. The Jewish emphasis on literacy, on mind over body, does not exempt Jewish men from sexist behavior. Far from it. While many Jewish men avoid the Scylla of a boisterous and physically harassing misogyny, we can often dash ourselves against the Charybdis of a male intellectual intimidation of others. "Men with the properly sanctioned educational credentials in our society," writes Harry Brod, "are trained to impose our opinions on others, whether asked for or not, with an air of supreme self-confidence and aggressive self-assurance." It's as if the world were only waiting for our word. In fact, Brod notes, "many of us have developed mannerisms that function to intimidate those customarily denied access to higher educational institutions, especially women."[1] And yet, despite this, the Jewish emphasis on literacy has branded us, in the eyes of the world, less than "real" men.

Finally, the historical experience of Jews centers around, hinges upon our sense of morality, our ethical imperatives. The preservation of a moral code, the commandment to live ethically, is the primary responsibility of each Jew, male or female. Here, let me relate another personal story. Like many other Jews, I grew up with the words "Never Again" ringing in my ears, branded indelibly in my consciousness. For me they implied a certain moral responsibility to bear witness, to remember—to place my body, visibly, on the side of justice. This moral responsibility inspired my participation in the antiwar movement, and my active resistance of the draft *as a Jew.* I remember family dinners in front of the "CBS Evening News," watching Walter Cronkite recite the daily tragedy of the war in Vietnam. "Never again," I said to myself, crying myself to sleep after watching napalm fall on Vietnamese villagers. Isn't this the brutal terror we have sworn ourselves to preventing when we utter those two words? When I allowed myself to feel the pain of those people, there was no longer a choice; there was, instead, a moral imperative to speak out, to attempt to end that war as quickly as possible.

In the past few years, I've become aware of another war. I met and spoke with women who had been raped, raped by their lovers, husbands, and fathers, women who had been beaten by those husbands and lovers. Some were even Jewish women. And those same words—Never Again—flashed across my mind like a neon meteor lighting up the darkened consciousness.

Hearing that pain and that anger prompted the same moral imperative. We Jews say "Never Again" to the systematic horror of the Holocaust, to the cruel war against the Vietnamese, to Central American death squads. And we must say it against this war waged against women in our society, against rape and battery.

So in a sense, I see my Judaism as reminding me every day of that moral responsibility, the *special* ethical imperative that my life, as a Jew, gives to me. Our history indicates how we have been excluded from power, but also, as men, we have been privileged by another power. Our Judaism impels us to stand against any power that is illegitimately constituted because we know only too well the consequences of that power. Our ethical vision demands equality and justice, and its achievement is our historical mission.

NOTE

1. Harry Brod, "Justice and a Male Feminist" in *The Jewish Newspaper* (Los Angeles) June 6, 1985, p. 6.

Punks, Bulldaggers, and Welfare Queens: The Radical Potential of Queer Politics?

CATHY J. COHEN

On the eve of finishing this essay my attention is focused not on how to rework the conclusion (as it should be) but instead on news stories of alleged racism at Gay Men's Health Crisis (GMHC). It seems that three black board members of this largest and oldest AIDS organization in the world have resigned over their perceived subservient position on the GMHC board. Billy E. Jones, former head of the New York City Health and Hospitals Corporation and one of the board members to quit, was quoted in the *New York Times* as saying, "Much work needs to be done at GMHC to make it truly inclusive and welcoming of diversity. . . . It is also clear that such work will be a great struggle. I am resigning because I do not choose to engage in such struggle at GMHC, but rather prefer to fight for the needs of those ravaged by HIV." (Dunlap).

This incident raises mixed emotions for me, for it points to the continuing practice of racism many of us experience on a daily basis in lesbian and gay communities. But just as disturbingly it also highlights the limits of a lesbian and gay political agenda based on a civil rights strategy, where assimilation into, and replication of, dominant institutions are the goals. Many of us continue to search for a new political direction and agenda, one that does not focus on integration into dominant structures but instead seeks to transform the basic fabric and hierarchies that allow systems of oppression to persist and operate efficiently. For some of us, such a challenge to traditional gay and lesbian politics was offered by the idea of queer politics. Here we had a potential movement of young antiassimilationist activists committed to challenging the very way people understand and respond to sexuality. These activists promised to engage in struggles that would disrupt dominant norms of sexuality, radically transforming politics in lesbian, gay, bisexual, and transgendered communities.

Despite the possibility invested in the idea of queerness and the practice of queer politics, I argue that a truly radical or transformative politics has not resulted from queer activism. In many instances, instead of destabilizing the assumed categories and binaries of sexual identity, queer politics has served to reinforce simple dichotomies between heterosexual and everything "queer." An understanding of the ways in which power informs and constitutes privileged and marginalized subjects on both sides of this dichotomy has been left unexamined.

I query in this essay whether there are lessons to be learned from queer activism that can help us construct a new politics. I envision a politics where one's relation to power, and not some homogenized identity, is privileged in determining one's political comrades. I'm talking about a politics where the *nonnormative* and *marginal* position of punks, bulldaggers, and welfare queens, for example, is the basis for progressive transformative coalition work. Thus, if there is any truly radical potential to be found in the idea of queerness and the practice of queer politics, it would seem to be located in its ability to create a space in opposition to dominant norms, a space where transformational political work can begin.

EMERGENCE OF QUEER POLITICS AND A NEW POLITICS OF TRANSFORMATION

Theorists and activists alike generally agree that it was in the early 1990s that we began to see, with any regularity, the use of the term "queer."[1] This term would come to denote not only an emerging politics, but also a new cohort of academics working in programs primarily in the humanities centered around social and cultural criticism (Morton 121). Individuals such as Judith Butler. Eve Sedgwick, Teresa de Lauretis, Diana Fuss, and Michael Warner produced what are now thought of as the first canonical works of "queer theory." Working from a variety of postmodernist and poststructuralist theoretical perspectives, these scholars focused on identifying and contesting the discursive and cultural markers found within both dominant and marginal identities and institutions which prescribe and reify "heterogendered" understandings and behavior.[2] These theorists presented a different conceptualization of sexuality, one which sought to replace socially named and presumably stable categories of sexual expression with a new fluid movement among and between forms of sexual behavior (Stein and Plummer 182).

Through its conception of a wide continuum of sexual possibilities, queer theory stands in direct contrast to the normalizing tendencies of hegemonic sexuality rooted in ideas of static, stable sexual identities and behaviors. In queer theorizing the sexual subject is understood to be constructed and contained by multiple practices of categorization and regulation that systematically marginalize and oppress those subjects thereby defined as deviant and "other." And, at its best, queer theory focuses on and makes central not only the socially constructed nature of sexuality and sexual categories, but also the varying degrees and multiple sites of power distributed within all categories of sexuality, including the normative category of heterosexuality.

It was in the early 1990s, however, that the postmodern theory being produced in the academy (later to be recategorized as queer theory) found its most direct interaction with the real-life politics of lesbian, gay, bisexual, and transgendered activists. Frustrated with what was perceived to be the scientific "de-gaying" and assimilationist tendencies of AIDS activism, with their invisibility in the more traditional civil rights politics of lesbian and gay organizations, and with increasing legal and physical attacks against lesbian and gay community members, a new generation of activists began the process of building a more confrontational political formation—labeling it queer politics (Bérubé and Escoffier 12). Queer politics, represented most notoriously in the actions of Queer Nation, is understood as an "in your face" politics of a younger generation. Through action and analysis these individuals seek to make "queer" function as more than just an abbreviation for lesbian, gay, bisexual, and transgendered. Similar to queer theory, the queer politics articulated and pursued by these activists first and fore-

most recognizes and encourages the fluidity and movement of people's sexual lives. In queer politics sexual expression is something that always entails the possibility of change, movement, redefinition, and subversive performance—from year to year, from partner to partner, from day to day, even from act to act. In addition to highlighting the instability of sexual categories and sexual subjects, queer activists also directly challenge the multiple practices and vehicles of power which render them invisible and at risk. However, what seems to make queer activists unique, at this particular moment, is their willingness to confront normalizing power by emphasizing and exaggerating their own antinormative characteristics and nonstable behavior. Joshua Gamson, in "Must Identity Movements Self-Destruct? A Queer Dilemma," writes that

> queer activism and theory pose the challenge of a form of organizing in which, far from inhibiting accomplishments, the *destabilization* of collective identity is itself a goal and accomplishment of collective action.
>
> The assumption that stable collective identities are necessary for collective action is turned on its head by queerness, and the question becomes: *When and how are stable collective identities necessary for social action and social change?* Secure boundaries and stabilized identities are necessary not in general, but in the specific, a point social movement theory seems currently to miss. (403, original emphasis)

Thus queer politics, much like queer theory, is often perceived as standing in opposition, or in contrast, to the category-based identity politics of traditional lesbian and gay activism. And for those of us who find ourselves on the margins, operating through multiple identities and thus not fully served or recognized through traditional single-identity-based politics, *theoretical conceptualizations* of queerness hold great political promise. For many of us, the label "queer" symbolizes an acknowledgment that through our existence and everyday survival we embody sustained and multisited resistance to systems (based on dominant constructions of race and gender) that seek to normalize our sexuality, exploit our labor, and constrain our visibility. At the intersection of oppression and resistance lies the radical potential of queerness to challenge and bring together all those deemed marginal and all those committed to liberatory politics.

The problem, however, with such a conceptualization and expectation of queer identity and politics is that in its present form queer politics has not emerged as an encompassing challenge to systems of domination and oppression, especially those normalizing processes embedded in hetero-normativity. By "heteronormativity" I mean both those localized practices and those centralized institutions which legitimize and privilege heterosexuality and heterosexual relationships as fundamental and "natural" within society. I raise the subject of heteronormativity because it is this normalizing practice/power that has most often been the focus of queer politics (Blasius 19–20; Warner xxi–xxv).

The inability of queer politics to effectively challenge heteronormativity rests, in part, on the fact that despite a surrounding discourse which highlights the destabilization and even deconstruction of sexual categories, queer politics has often been built around a simple dichotomy between those deemed queer and those deemed heterosexual. Whether in the infamous "I Hate Straights" publication or queer kiss-ins at malls and straight dance clubs, very near the surface in queer political action is an uncomplicated understanding of power as it is encoded in sexual categories: all heterosexuals are represented as dominant and controlling and all queers are understood as marginalized and invisible. Thus, even in the name of destabilization, some queer activists have begun to prioritize sexuality as the primary frame through which they pursue their politics.[3] Undoubtedly, within different contexts various characteristics of our total being—for example, race, gender, class, sexuality—are highlighted or called upon to make sense of a particular situation. However, my concern is centered on those individuals who consistently activate only one characteristic of their identity, or a single perspective of consciousness, to organize their politics, rejecting any recognition of the multiple and intersecting systems of power that largely dictate our life chances.

It is the disjuncture, evident in queer politics, between an articulated commitment to promoting an understanding of sexuality that rejects the idea of static, monolithic, bounded categories, on the one hand, and political practices structured around binary conceptions of sexuality and power, on the other hand, that is the focus of this article. Specifically, I am concerned with those manifestations of queer politics in which the capital and advantage invested in a range of sexual categories are disregarded and, as a result, narrow and homogenized political identities are reproduced that inhibit the radical potential of queer politics. It is my contention that queer activists who evoke a single-oppression framework misrepresent the distribution of power within and outside of gay, lesbian, bisexual, and transgendered communities, and therefore limit the comprehensive and transformational character of queer politics.

Recognizing the limits of current conceptions of queer identities and queer politics, I am interested in examining the concept of "queer" in order to think about how we might construct a new political identity that is truly liberating, transformative, and inclusive of all those who stand on the outside of the dominant constructed norm of state-sanctioned white middle- and upper-class heterosexuality.[4] Such a broadened understanding of queerness must be based on an intersectional analysis that recognizes how numerous systems of oppression interact to regulate and police the lives of most people. Black lesbian, bisexual, and heterosexual feminist authors such as Kimberle Crenshaw, Barbara Ransby, Angela Davis, Cheryl Clarke, and Audre Lorde have repeatedly emphasized in their writing the intersectional workings of oppression. And it is just such an understanding of the interlocking systems of domination that is noted in the opening paragraph of the now famous black feminist statement by the Combahee River Collective:

> The most general statement of our politics at the present time would be that we are actively committed to struggling against racial, sexual, heterosexual, and class oppression and see as our particular task the development of *integrated* analysis and practice based upon the fact that the major systems of oppression are interlocking. The synthesis of these oppressions creates the conditions of our lives. As Black women we see Black feminism as the logical political movement to combat the manifold and simultaneous oppressions that all women of color face. (272)

This analysis of one's place in the world which focuses on the intersection of systems of oppression is informed by a consciousness that undoubtedly grows from the lived experience of existing within and resisting multiple and connected practices of domination and normalization. Just such a lived experience and analysis have determined much of the progressive and expansive nature of the politics emanating from people of color, people who are both inside and outside of lesbian and gay communities.

However, beyond a mere recognition of the intersection of oppressions, there must also be an understanding of the ways our multiple identities work to limit the entitlement and status some receive from obeying a heterosexual imperative. For instance, how would queer activists understand politically the lives of women—in particular women of color—on welfare, who may fit into the category of heterosexual, but whose sexual choices are not perceived as normal, moral, or worthy of state support? Further, how do queer activists understand and relate politically to those whose same-sex sexual identities position them within the category of queer, but who hold other identities based on class, race and/or gender categories which provide them with membership in and the resources of dominant institutions and groups?

Thus, inherent in our new politics must be a commitment to left analysis and left politics. Black feminists as well as other marginalized and progressive scholars and activists have long argued that any political response to the multilayered oppression that most of us experience must be rooted in a left understanding of our political, economic, social, and cultural institutions. Fundamentally, a left framework makes central the interdependency among multiple systems of domination. Such a perspective also ensures that while activists should rightly be concerned with forms of discursive and cultural coercion, we also recognize and confront the more direct and concrete forms of exploitation and violence rooted in state-regulated institutions and economic systems. The Statement of Purpose from the first Dialogue on the Lesbian and Gay Left comments specifically on the role of interlocking systems of oppression in the lives of gays and lesbians. "By leftist we mean people who understand the struggle for lesbian and gay liberation to be integrally tied to struggles against class oppression, racism, and sexism. While we might use different political labels, we share a commitment to a fundamental transformation of the economic, political and social structures of society."

A left framework of politics, unlike civil rights or liberal frameworks, brings into focus the systematic relationship among forms of domination, where the creation and maintenance of exploited, subservient, marginalized classes is a necessary part of, at the very least, the economic configuration. Urvashi Vaid, in *Virtual Equality,* for example, writes of the limits of civil rights strategies in confronting systemic homophobia:

> civil rights do not change the social order in dramatic ways; they change only the privileges of the group asserting those rights. Civil rights strategies do not challenge the moral and antisexual underpinnings of homophobia, because homophobia does not originate in our lack of full civil equality. Rather, homophobia arises from the nature and construction of the political, legal, economic, sexual, racial and family systems within which we live. (183)

Proceeding from the starting point of a system-based left analysis, strategies built upon the possibility of incorporation and assimilation are exposed as simply expanding and making accessible the status quo for more privileged members of marginal groups, while the most vulnerable in our communities continue to be stigmatized and oppressed.

It is important to note, however, that while left theorists tend to provide a more structural analysis of oppression and exploitation, many of these theorists and activists have also been homophobic and heterosexist in their approach to or avoidance of the topics of sexuality and heteronormativity. For example, Robin Podolsky, in "Sacrificing Queers and other 'Proletarian' Artifacts," writes that quite often on the left lesbian and gay sexuality and desire have been characterized as "more to do with personal happiness and sexual pleasure than with the 'material basis' of procreation—we were considered self-indulgent distractions from struggle . . . [an example of] 'bourgeois decadence' " (54).

This contradiction between a stated left analysis and an adherence to heteronormativity has probably been most dramatically identified in the writing of some feminist authors. I need only refer to Adrienne Rich's well-known article, "Compulsory Heterosexuality and Lesbian Existence," as a poignant critique of the white, middle-class heterosexual standard running through significant parts of feminist analysis and actions. The same adherence to a heterosexual norm can be found in the writing of self-identified black left intellectuals such as Cornel West and Michael Eric Dyson. Thus, while these writers have learned to make reference to lesbian, gay, bisexual, and transgendered segments of black communities—sparingly—they continue to foreground black heterosexuality and masculinity as the central unit of analysis in their writing—and most recently in their politics, witness their participation in the Million Man March.

This history of left organizing and the left's visible absence from any serious and sustained response to the AIDS epidemic have provoked many lesbian, gay, bisexual and transgendered people to question the relevance of this political configuration to the needs of our communities. Recognizing that reservations of this type are real and should be noted, I still hold that a left-rooted analysis which emphasizes economic exploitation and class structure, culture, and the systemic nature of power provides a framework of politics that is especially effective in representing and challenging the numerous sites and systems of oppression. Further, the left-centered approach that I embrace is one that designates sexuality and struggles against sexual normalization as central to the politics of all marginal communities.

THE ROOT OF QUEER POLITICS: CHALLENGING HETERONORMATIVITY?

In the introduction to the edited volume *Fear of a Queer Planet: Queer Politics and Social Theory*, Michael Warner asks the question: "What do queers want?" (vii). He suggests that the goals of queers and their politics extend beyond the sexual arena. Warner contends that what queers want is acknowledgment of their lives, struggles, and complete existence; queers want to be represented and included fully in left political analysis and American culture. Thus what queers want is to be a part of the social, economic, and political restructuring of this society; as Warner writes, queers want to have queer experience and politics "taken as starting points rather than as footnotes" in the social theories and political agendas of the left (vii). He contends that it has been the absence or invisibility of lived queer experience that has marked or constrained much of left social and political theories and "have posited and naturalized a heterosexual society" in such theories (vii).

The concerns and emerging politics of queer activists, as formulated by Warner and others interested in understanding the implications of the idea of queerness, are focused on highlighting queer presence and destroying heteronormativity not only in the larger dominant society but also in extant spaces, theories, and sites of resistance, presumably on the left. He suggests that those embracing the label of "queer" understand the need to challenge the assumption of heteronormativity in every aspect of their existence:

> Every person who comes to a queer self-understanding knows in one way or another that her stigmatization is connected with gender, the family, notions of individual freedom, the state, public speech, consumption and desire, nature and culture, maturation, reproductive politics, racial and national fantasy, class identity, truth and trust, censorship, intimate life and social display, terror and violence, health care, and deep cultural norms about the bearing of the body. Being queer means fighting about these issues all the time, locally and piecemeal but always with consequences. (xiii)

Now, independent of the fact that few of us could find ourselves in such a grandiose description of queer consciousness, I believe that Warner's description points to the fact that in the roots of a lived "queer" existence are experiences with domination and in particular heteronormativity that form the basis for genuine transformational politics. By transformational, again, I mean a politics that does not search for opportunities to integrate into dominant institutions and normative social relationships, but instead pursues a political agenda that seeks to change values, definitions, and laws which make these institutions and relationships oppressive.

Queer activists experiencing displacement both within and outside of lesbian and gay communities rebuff what they deem the assimilationist practices and policies of more established lesbian and gay organizations. These organizers and activists reject cultural norms of acceptable sexual behavior and identification and instead embrace political strategies which promote self-definition and full expression. Members of the Chicago-based group Queers United Against Straight-acting Homosexuals (QUASH) state just such a position in the article "Assimilation Is Killing Us: Fight for a Queer United Front" published in their newsletter, WHY I HATED THE MARCH ON WASHINGTON:

> Assimilation is killing us. We are falling into a trap. Some of us adopt an apologetic stance, stating "that's just the way I am" (read: "I'd be straight if I could."). Others pattern their behavior in such a way as to mimic heterosexual society so as to minimize the glaring differences between us and them. No matter how much [money] you make, fucking your lover is still illegal in nearly half of the states. Getting a corporate job, a fierce car and a condo does not protect you from dying of AIDS or getting your head bashed in by neo-Nazis. The myth of assimilation must be shattered.
>
>   . . . Fuck the heterosexual, nuclear family. Let's make families which promote sexual choices and liberation rather than sexual oppression. We must learn from the legacy of resistance that is ours: a legacy which shows that empowerment comes through grassroots activism, not mainstream politics, a legacy which shows that real change occurs when we are inclusive, not exclusive. (4)

At the very heart of queer politics, at least as it is formulated by QUASH, is a fundamental challenge to the heteronormativity—the privilege, power, and normative status invested in heterosexuality—of the dominant society.

It is in their fundamental challenge to a systemic process of domination and exclusion, with a specific focus on heteronormativity, that queer activists and queer theorists are tied to and rooted in a tradition of political struggle most often identified with people of color and other marginal groups. For example, activists of color have, through many historical periods, questioned their formal and informal inclusion and power in prevailing social categories. Through just such a process of challenging their centrality to lesbian and gay politics in particular, and lesbian and gay communities more generally, lesbian, gay, bisexual, and transgendered people of color advanced debates over who and what would be represented as "truly gay." As Steven Seidman reminds us in "Identity and Politics in a 'Postmodern' Gay Culture: Some Historical and Conceptual Notes," beyond the general framing provided by postmodern queer theory, gay and lesbian—and now queer— politics owes much of its impetus to the politics of people of color and other marginalized members of lesbian and gay communities.

> Specifically, I make the case that postmodern strains in gay thinking and politics have their immediate social origin in recent developments in the gay culture. In the reaction by people of color, third-world-identified gays, poor and working-class gays, and sex rebels to the ethnic/ essentialist model of identity and community that achieved dominance in the lesbian and gay cultures of the 1970s, I locate the social basis for a rethinking of identity and politics. (106)

Through the demands of lesbian, gay, bisexual, and transgendered people of color as well as others who did not see themselves or their numerous communities in the more narrowly constructed politics of white gays and lesbians, the contestation took shape over who and what type of issues would be represented in lesbian and gay politics and in larger community discourse.

While similarities and connections between the politics of lesbians, gay men, bisexuals, and transgendered people of color during the 1970s and 1980s and queer activists of today clearly exist, the present-day rendition of this politics has deviated significantly from its legacy. Specifically, while both political efforts include as a focus of their work the radicalization and/or expansion of traditional lesbian and gay politics, the politics of lesbian, gay, bisexual, and transgendered people of color have been and continue to be much broader in its understanding of transformational politics.

The politics of lesbian, gay, bisexual, and transgendered people of color has often been guided by the type of radical intersectional left analysis I detailed earlier. Thus, while the politics of lesbian, gay, bisexual, and transgendered activists of color might recognize heteronormativity as a primary system of power structuring our lives, it understands that heteronormativity interacts with institutional racism, patriarchy, and class exploitation to define us in numerous ways as marginal and oppressed subjects.[5] And it is this constructed subservient position that allows our sisters and brothers to be used either as surplus labor in an advanced capitalist structure and/or seen as expendable, denied resources, and thus locked into correctional institutions across the country. While heterosexual privilege negatively impacts and constrains the lived experience of "queers" of color, so too do racism, classism, and sexism.

In contrast to the left intersectional analysis that has structured much of the politics of "queers" of color, the basis of the politics of some white queer activists and organizations has come dangerously close to a single-oppression model. Experiencing "deviant" sexuality as the prominent characteristic of their marginalization, these activists begin to envision the world in terms of a "hetero/queer" divide. Using the framework of queer theory in which heteronormativity is identified as a system of regulation and normalization, some queer activists map the power and entitlement of normative heterosexuality onto the bodies of all heterosexuals. Further, these activists naively characterize all those who exist under the category of "queer" as powerless. Thus, in the process of conceptualizing a decentered identity of queerness, meant to embrace all those who stand on the outside of heteronormativity, a monolithic understanding of heterosexuality and queerness has come to dominate the political imagination and actions of many queer activists.

This reconstruction of a binary divide between heterosexuals and queers, while discernible in many of the actions of Queer Nation, is probably most evident in the manifesto "I Hate Straights." Distributed at gay pride parades in New York and Chicago in 1990, the declaration written by an anonymous group of queers begins,

> I have friends. Some of them are straight.
>
> Year after year, I see my straight friends. I want to see how they are doing, to add newness to our long and complicated histories, to experience some continuity.
>
> Year after year I continue to realize that the facts of my life are irrelevant to them and that I am only half listened to, that I am an appendage to the doings of a greater world, a world of power and privilege, of the laws of installation, a world of exclusion. 'That's not true,' argue my straight friends. There is the one certainty in the politics of power; those left out of it beg for inclusion, while the insiders claim that they already are. Men do it to women, whites do it to blacks, *and everyone does it to queers.*

. . . The main dividing line, both conscious and unconscious, is procreation . . . and that magic word—Family. (emphasis added)

Screaming out from this manifesto is an analysis which places not heteronormativity, but heterosexuality, as the central "dividing line" between those who would be dominant and those who are oppressed. Nowhere in this essay is there recognition that "nonnormative" procreation patterns and family structures of people who are labeled heterosexual have also been used to regulate and exclude *them.* Instead, the authors declare. "Go tell them [straights] to go away until they have spent a month walking hand in hand in public with someone of the same sex. After they survive that, then you'll hear what they have to say about queer anger. Otherwise, tell them to shut up and listen." For these activists, the power of heterosexuality is the focus, and queer anger the means of queer politics. Missing from this equation is any attention to, or acknowledgment of, the ways in which identities of race, class, and/or gender either enhance or mute the marginalization of queers, on the one hand, and the power of heterosexuals, on the other.

The fact that this essay is written about and out of queer anger is undoubtedly part of the rationale for its defense (Berlant and Freeman 200). But I question the degree to which we should read this piece as just an aberrational diatribe against straights motivated by intense queer anger. While anger is clearly a motivating factor for such writing, we should also understand this action to represent an analysis and politics structured around the simple dichotomy of straight and queer. We know, for instance, that similar positions have been put forth in other anonymously published, publicly distributed manifestos. For example, in the document *Queers Read This,* the authors write, "Don't be fooled, straight people own the world and the only reason you have been spared is you're smart, lucky or a fighter. Straight people have a privilege that allows them to do whatever they please and fuck without fear." They continue by stating that "Straight people are your enemy."

Even within this document, which seems to exemplify the narrowness of queer conceptions, there is a surprising glimpse at a more enlightened left intersectional understanding of what queerness might mean. For instance, the authors continue, "Being queer is not about a right to privacy; it is about the freedom to be public, to just be who we are. It means everyday fighting oppression; homophobia, racism, misogyny, the bigotry of religious hypocrites and our own self-hatred." Evident in this one document are the inherent tensions and dilemmas many queer activists currently encounter: how does one implement in real political struggle a decentered political identity that is not constituted by a process of seemingly reductive "othering"?

The process of ignoring or at least downplaying queers' varying relationships to power is evident not only in the writing of queer activists, but also in the political actions pursued by queer organizations. I question the ability of political actions such as mall invasions (pursued by groups such as the Queer Shopping Network in New York and the Suburban Homosexual Outreach Program [SHOP] in San Francisco), to address the fact that queers exist in different social locations. Lauren Berlant and Elizabeth Freeman describe mall invasion projects as

> [an attempt to take] the relatively bounded spectacle of the urban pride parade to the ambient pleasures of the shopping mall. "Mall visibility actions" thus conjoin the spectacular lure of the parade with Hare Krishna-style conversion and proselytizing techniques. Stepping into malls in hair-gelled splendor, holding hands and handing out fliers, the queer auxiliaries produce an "invasion" that conveys a different message. "We're here, we're queer, *you're* going shopping." (210)

The activity of entering or "invading" the shopping mall on the part of queer nationals is clearly one of attempted subversion. Intended by their visible presence in this clearly coded heterosexual family economic mecca is a disruption of the agreed-upon segregation between the allowable spaces for queer "deviant" culture and the rest of the "naturalized" world. Left unchallenged in such an action, however, are the myriad ways, besides the enforcement of normative sexuality, in which some queers feel alienated and excluded from the space of the mall. Where does the mall as an institution of consumer culture and relative economic privilege play into this analysis? How does this action account for the varying economic relationships queers have to consumer culture? If you are a poor or working-class queer the exclusion and alienation you experience when entering the mall may not be limited to the normative sexual codes associated with the mall, but may also be centered on the assumed economic status of those shopping in suburban malls. If you are a queer of color your exclusion from the mall may, in part, be rooted in racial norms and stereotypes which construct you as a threatening subject every time you enter this economic institution. Queer activists must confront a question that haunts most political organizing: How do we put into politics a broad and inclusive left analysis that can actually engage and mobilize individuals with intersecting identities?

Clearly, there will be those critics who will claim that I am asking too much from any political organization. Demands that every aspect of oppression and regulation be addressed in each political act seem, and are indeed, unreasonable. However, I make the critique of queer mall invasions neither to stop such events nor to suggest that every oppression be dealt with by this one political action. Instead, I raise these concerns to emphasize the ways in which varying relation to power exist not only among heterosexuals, but also among those who label themselves queer.

In its current rendition, queer politics is coded with class, gender, and race privilege, and may have lost its potential to be a politically expedient organizing tool for addressing the needs—and mobilizing the bodies—of people of color. As some queer theorists and activists call for the destruction of stable sexual categories, for example, moving instead toward a more fluid understanding of sexual behavior, left unspoken is the class privilege which allows for such fluidity. Class or material privilege is a cornerstone of much of queer politics and theory as they exist today. Queer theorizing which calls for the elimination of fixed categories of sexual identity seems to ignore the ways in which some traditional social identities and communal ties can, in fact, be important to one's survival. Further, a queer politics which demonizes all heterosexuals discounts the relationships—especially those based on shared experiences of marginalization—that exist between gays and straights, particularly in communities of color.

Queers who operate out of a political culture of individualism assume a material independence that allows them to disregard historically or culturally recognized categories and communities or at the very least to move fluidly among them without ever establishing permanent relationships or identities within them. However, I and many other lesbian and gay people of color, as well as poor and working-class lesbians and gay men, do not have such material independence. Because of my multiple identities, which locate me and other "queer" people of color at the margins in this country, my material advancement, my physical protection and my emotional well-being are constantly threatened. In those stable categories and named communities whose histories have been structured by shared resistance to oppression, I find relative degrees of safety and security.

Let me emphasize again that the safety I feel is relative to other threats and is clearly not static or constant. For in those named communities I also find versions of domina-

tion and normalization being replicated and employed as more privileged/assimilated marshal group members use their associations with dominant institutions and resources to regulate and police the activities of other marginal group members. Any lesbian, gay, bisexual, or transgendered person of color who has experienced exclusion from indigenous institutions, such as the exclusion many out black gay men have encountered from some black churches responding to AIDS, recognizes that even within marginal groups there are normative rules determining community membership and power (Cohen). However, in spite of the unequal power relationships located in marginal communities, I am still not interested in disassociating politically from those communities, for queerness, as it is currently constructed, offers no viable political alternative, since it invites us to put forth a political agenda that makes invisible the prominence of race, class, and to varying degrees gender in determining the life chances of those on both sides of the hetero/queer divide.

So despite the roots of queer politics in the struggles of "queer" people of color, despite the calls for highlighting categories which have sought to regulate and control black bodies like my own, and despite the attempts at decentralized grassroots activism in some queer political organizations, there still exist—for some, like myself—great misgivings about current constructions of the term "queer." Personally speaking, I do not consider myself a "queer" activist or, for that matter, a "queer" anything. This is not because I do not consider myself an activist; in fact I hold my political work to be one of my most important contributions to all of my communities. But like other lesbian, gay, bisexual, and transgendered activists of color, I find the label "queer" fraught with unspoken assumptions which inhibit the radical political potential of this category.

The alienation, or at least discomfort, many activists and theorists of color have with current conceptions of queerness is evidenced, in part, by the minimal numbers of theorists of color who engage in the process of theorizing about the concept. Further, the sparse numbers of people of color who participate in "queer" political organizations might also be read as a sign of discomfort with the term. Most important, my confidence in making such a claim of distance and uneasiness with the term "queer" on the part of many people of color comes from my interactions with other lesbian, gay, bisexual, and transgendered people of color who repeatedly express their interpretation of "queer" as a term rooted in class, race, and gender privilege. For us, "queer" is a politics based on narrow sexual dichotomies which make no room either for the analysis of oppression of those we might categorize as heterosexual, or for the privilege of those who operate as "queer." As black lesbian activist and writer Barbara Smith argues in "Queer Politics: Where's the Revolution?":

> Unlike the early lesbian and gay movement, which had both ideological and practical links to the left, black activism and feminism, today's "queer" politicos seem to operate in a historical and ideological vacuum. "Queer" activists focus on "queer" issues, and racism, sexual oppression and economic exploitation do not qualify, despite the fact that the majority of "queers" are people of color, female or working class. . . . Building unified, ongoing coalitions that challenge the system and ultimately prepare a way for revolutionary change simply isn't what "queer" activists have in mind. (13–14)

It is this narrow understanding of the idea of queer that negates its use in fundamentally reorienting the politics and privilege of lesbian and gay politics as well as more generally moving or transforming the politics of the left. Despite its liberatory claim to stand in opposition to static categories of oppression, queer politics and much of queer theory seem in fact to be static in the understanding of race, class, and gender and their roles in how heteronormativity regulates sexual behavior and identities. Distinctions between the status and the acceptance of different individuals categorized under the label of "heterosexual" go unexplored.

I emphasize the marginalized position of some who embrace heterosexual identities not because I want to lead any great crusade to understand more fully the plight of "the heterosexual." Rather, I recognize the potential for shared resistance with such individuals. This potential not only for coalitional work but for a shared analysis is especially relevant, from my vantage point, to "queer" people of color. Again, in my call for coalition work across sexual categories, I do not want to suggest that same-sex political struggles have not, independently, played an essential and distinct role in the liberatory politics and social movements of marginal people. My concern, instead, is with any political analysis or theory which collapses our understanding of power into a single continuum of evaluation.

Through a brief review of some of the ways in which nonnormative heterosexuality has been controlled and regulated through the state and systems of marginalization we may be reminded that differentials in power exist within all socially named categories. And through such recognition we may begin to envision a new political formation in which one's relation to dominant power serves as the basis of unity for radical coalition work in the twenty-first century.

HETEROSEXUALS ON THE (OUT)SIDE OF HETERONORMATIVITY

In this section I want to return to the question of a monolithic understanding of heterosexuality. I believe that through this issue we can begin to think critically about the components of a radical politics built not exclusively on identities, but on identities as they are invested with varying degrees of normative power. Thus, fundamental to my concern about the current structure and future agenda of queer politics is the unchallenged assumption of a uniform heteronormativity from which all heterosexuals benefit. I want again to be clear that there are, in fact, some who identify themselves as queer activists who do acknowledge relative degrees of power, and heterosexual access to that power, even evoking the term "straight queers." "Queer means to fuck with gender. There are straight queers, bi queers, tranny queers, lez queers, fag queers, SM queers, fisting queers in every single street in this apathetic country of ours" (anonymous, qtd. McIntosh 31).

Despite such sporadic insight, much of the politics of queer activists has been structured around the dichotomy of straight versus everything else, assuming a monolithic experience of heterosexual privilege for all those identified publicly with heterosexuality. A similar reductive dichotomy between men and women has consistently reemerged in the writing and actions of some feminists. And only through the demands, the actions, and the writing of many "feminists" and/or lesbians of color have those women who stand outside the norm of white, middle-class, legalized heterosexuality begun to see their lives, needs, and bodies represented in feminist theory (Carby; Collins; hooks). In a similar manner lesbian, gay, bisexual, and transgendered people of color have increasingly taken on the responsibility for at the very least complicating and most often challenging reductive notions of heteronormativity articulated by queer activists and scholars (Alexander; Farajaje-Jones; Lorde; Moraga and Anzaldúa; B. Smith).

If we follow such examples, complicating our understanding of both heteronormativity and queerness, we move one step closer to building the progressive coalition politics many of us desire. Specifically, if we pay attention to both historical and current examples of heterosexual relationships which have been prohibited, stigmatized, and generally repressed we may begin to identify those spaces of shared or similar oppression and resistance that provide a basis for radical coalition work. Further, we may begin to answer certain questions: In narrowly positing a dichotomy of heterosexual privilege and queer oppression under which we all exist, are we negating a basis of political unity that could serve to strengthen many communities and movements seeking justice and societal transformation? How do we use the relative degrees of ostracization all sexual/cultural "deviants" experience to build a basis of unity for broader coalition and movement work?

A little history (as a political scientist a little history is all I can offer) might be helpful in trying to sort out the various ways heterosexuality, especially as it has intersected with race, has been defined and experienced by different groups of people. It should also help to underscore the fact that many of the roots of heteronormativity are in white supremacist ideologies which sought (and continue) to use the state and its regulation of sexuality, in particular through the institution of heterosexual marriage, to designate which individuals were truly "fit" for full rights and privileges of citizenship. For example, the prohibition of marriages between black women and men imprisoned in the slave system was a component of many slave codes enacted during the seventeenth and eighteenth centuries. M. G. Smith, in his article on the structure of slave economic systems, succinctly states. "As property slaves were prohibited from forming legal relationships or marriages which would interfere with and restrict their owner's property rights" (71–72). Herbert G. Gutman, in *The Black Family in Slavery and Freedom, 1750–1925,* elaborates on the ideology of slave societies which denied the legal sanctioning of marriages between slaves and further reasoned that Blacks had no conception of family.

> The *Nation* identified sexual restraint, civil marriage, and family "stability" with "civilization" itself.
> Such mid-nineteenth-century class and sexual beliefs reinforced racial beliefs about Afro-Americans. As slaves, after all, their marriages had not been sanctioned by the civil laws and therefore "the sexual passion" went unrestrained. . . . Many white abolitionists denied the slaves a family life or even, often, a family consciousness because for them [whites] the family had its origins in and had to be upheld by the civil law. (295)

Thus it was not the promotion of marriage or heterosexuality per se that served as the standard or motivation of most slave societies. Instead, marriage and heterosexuality, as viewed through the lenses of profit and domination, and the ideology of white supremacy, were reconfigured to justify the exploitation and regulation of black bodies, even those presumably engaged in heterosexual behavior. It was this system of state-sanctioned, white male, upper-class, heterosexual domination that forced these presumably black *heterosexual* men and women to endure a history of rape, lynching, and other forms of physical and mental terrorism. In this way, marginal group members, lacking power and privilege although engaged in heterosexual behavior, have often found themselves defined as outside the norms and values of dominant society. This position has most often resulted in the suppression or negation of their legal, social, and physical relationships and rights.

In addition to the prohibition of marriage between slaves, A. Leon Higginbotham, Jr., in *The Matter of Color—Race and the American Legal Process: The Colonial Period,* writes of the legal restrictions barring interracial marriages. He reminds us that the essential core of the American legal tradition was the preservation of the white race. The "mixing" of the races was to be strictly prohibited in early colonial laws. The regulation of interracial heterosexual relationships, however, should not be understood as exclusively relegated to the seventeenth, eighteenth and nineteenth centuries. In fact, Higginbotham informs us that the final law prohibiting miscegenation (the "interbreeding" or marrying of individuals from different "races"—actually meant to inhibit the "tainting" of the white race) was not repealed until 1967:

> Colonial anxiety about interracial sexual activity cannot be attributed solely to seventeenth-century values, for it was not until 1967 that the United States Supreme Court finally declared unconstitutional those statutes prohibiting interracial marriages. The Supreme Court waited thirteen years after its *Brown* decision dealing with desegregation of schools before, in *Loving v. Virginia,* it agreed to consider the issue of interracial marriages. (41)

It is this pattern of regulating the behavior and denigrating the identities of those heterosexuals on the outside of heteronormative privilege, in particular those perceived as threatening systems of white supremacy, male domination, and capitalist advancement that I want to highlight. An understanding of the ways in which heteronormativity works to support and reinforce institutional racism, patriarchy, and class exploitation must therefore be a part of how we problematize current constructions of heterosexuality. As I stated previously. I am not suggesting that those involved in publicly identifiable heterosexual behavior do not receive political, economic, and social advantage, especially in comparison to the experiences of some lesbian, transgendered, gay, and bisexual individuals. But the equation linking identity and behavior to power is not as linear and clear as some queer theorists and activists would have us believe.

A more recent example of regulated nonnormative heterosexuality is located in current debates and rhetoric regarding the "underclass" and the destruction of the welfare system. The stigmatization and demonization of single mothers, teen mothers, and, primarily, poor women of color dependent on state assistance has had a long and suspicious presence in American "intellectual" and political history. It was in 1965 that Daniel Patrick Moynihan released his "study" entitled *The Negro Family: The Case for National Action.* In this report, which would eventually come to be known as the Moynihan Report, the author points to the "pathologies" increasingly evident in so-called Negro families. In this document were allegations of the destructive nature of Negro family formations. The document's introduction argues that

> the fundamental problem, in which this is most clearly the case, is that of family structure. The evidence—not final, but powerfully persuasive—is that the Negro family in urban ghettos is crumbling. A middle-class group has managed to save itself, but for vast numbers of the unskilled, poorly educated city working class the fabric of conventional social relationships has all but disintegrated.

Moynihan, later in the document, goes on to describe the crisis and pathologies facing Negro family structure as being generated by the increasing number of single-female-headed households, the increasing number of "illegitimate" births and, of course, increasing welfare dependency:

> In essence, the Negro community has been forced into a matriarchal structure which, because it is so out of line with the rest of the American society, seriously retards the progress of the group as a whole, and imposes a crushing burden on the Negro male and, in consequence, on a great many Negro women as well. . . . In a word, most Negro youth are in danger of being caught up in the tangle of pathology that affects their world, and probably a majority are so entrapped. . . . Obviously, not every instance of social pathology afflicting the Negro community can be traced to the weakness

of family structure. . . . Nonetheless, at the center of the tangle of pathology is the weakness of the family structure. (29–30)

It is not the nonheterosexist behavior of these black men and women that is under fire, but rather the perceived non-normative sexual behavior and family structures of these individuals, whom many queer activists—without regard to the impact of race, class, or gender—would designate as part of the heterosexist establishment or those mighty "straights they hate."

Over the last thirty years the demonization of poor women, engaged in nonnormative heterosexual relationships, has continued under the auspices of scholarship on the "underclass." Adolph L. Reed, in "The 'Underclass' as Myth and Symbol: The Poverty of Discourse about Poverty," discusses the gendered and racist nature of much of this literature, in which poor, often black and Latina women are portrayed as unable to control their sexual impulses and eventual reproductive decisions, unable to raise their children with the right moral fiber, unable to find "gainful" employment to support themselves and their "illegitimate children," and of course unable to manage "effectively" the minimal assistance provided by the state. Reed writes,

> The underclass notion may receive the greatest ideological boost from its gendered imagery and relation to gender politics. As I noted in a critique of Wilson's *The Truly Disadvantaged,* "family" is an intrinsically ideological category. The rhetoric of "disorganization," "disintegration," "deterioration" reifies one type of living arrangement—the ideal type of the bourgeois nuclear family—as outside history, nearly as though it were decreed by natural law. But—as I asked earlier—why exactly is out-of-wedlock birth pathological? Why is the female-headed household an indicator of disorganization and pathology? Does that stigma attach to *all* such households—even, say, a divorced executive who is a custodial mother? If not, what are the criteria for assigning it? The short answer is race and class bias inflected through a distinctively gendered view of the world. (33–34)

In this same discourse of the "underclass," young black men engaged in "reckless" heterosexual behavior are represented as irresponsible baby factories, unable to control or restrain their "sexual passion" (to borrow a term from the seventeenth century). And unfortunately, often it has been the work of professed liberals like William Julius Wilson, in his book *The Truly Disadvantaged,* that, while not using the word "pathologies," has substantiated in its own tentative way the conservative dichotomy between the deserving working poor and the lazy, Cadillac-driving, steak-eating welfare queens of Ronald Reagan's imagination. Again, I raise this point to remind us of the numerous ways that sexuality and sexual deviance from a prescribed norm have been used to demonize and to oppress various segments of the population, even some classified under the label "heterosexual."

The policies of politicians and the actions of law enforcement officials have reinforced, in much more devastating ways, the distinctions between acceptable forms of heterosexual expression and those to be regulated— increasingly through incarceration. This move toward the disallowance of some forms of heterosexual expression and reproductive choice can be seen in the practice of prosecuting pregnant women suspected of using drugs—nearly 80 percent of all women prosecuted are women of color; through the forced sterilization of Puerto Rican and Native American women: and through the state-dictated use of Norplant by women answering to the criminal justice system and by women receiving state assistance.[6] Further, it is the "nonnormative" children of many of these nonnormative women that Newt Gingrich would place in orphanages. This is the same Newt Gingrich who, despite his clear disdain for gay and lesbian "lifestyles," has invited lesbians and gay men into the Republican party. I need not remind you that he made no such offer to the women on welfare discussed above. Who, we might ask, is truly on the outside of heteronormative power—maybe *most* of us?

CONCLUSION: DESTABILIZATION AND RADICAL COALITION WORK

While all this may, in fact, seem interesting or troubling or both, you may be wondering: What does it have to do with the question of the future of queer politics? It is my argument, as I stated earlier, that one of the great failings of queer theory and especially queer politics has been their inability to incorporate into analysis of the world and strategies for political mobilization the roles that race, class, and gender play in defining people's differing relations to dominant and normalizing power. I present this essay as the beginning of a much longer and protracted struggle to acknowledge and delineate the distribution of power within and outside of queer communities. This is a discussion of how to build a politics organized not merely by reductive categories of straight and queer, but organized instead around a more intersectional analysis of who and what the enemy is and where our potential allies can be found. This analysis seeks to make clear the privilege and power embedded in the categorizations of, on the one hand, an upstanding, "morally correct," white, state-authorized, middle-class, male *heterosexual,* and on the other, a culturally deficient, materially bankrupt, state-dependent, *heterosexual* woman of color, the latter found most often in our urban centers (those that haven't been gentrified), on magazine covers, and on the evening news.

I contend, therefore, that the radical potential of queer politics, or any liberatory movement, rests on its ability to advance strategically oriented political identities arising from a more nuanced understanding of power. One of the most difficult tasks in such an endeavor (and there are many) is not to forsake the complexities of both how power is structured and how we might think about the coalitions we create. Far too often movements revert to a position in which membership and joint political work are based upon a necessarily similar history of oppression—but this is too much like identity politics (Phelan). Instead, I am suggesting that the process of movement building be rooted not in our shared history or identity, but in our shared marginal relationship to dominant power which normalizes, legitimizes, and privileges.

We must, therefore, start our political work from the recognition that multiple systems of oppression are in operation and that these systems use institutionalized categories and identities to regulate and socialize. We must also understand that power and access to dominant resources are distributed across the boundaries of "het" and "queer" that we construct. A model of queer politics that simply pits the grand "heterosexuals" against all those oppressed "queers" is ineffectual as the basis for action in a political environment dominated by Newt Gingrich, the Christian Right, and the recurring ideology of white supremacy. As we stand on the verge of watching those in power dismantle the welfare system through a process of demonizing poor and young, primarily poor and young women of color—many of whom have existed for their entire lives outside the white, middle-class, heterosexual norm—we have to ask if these women do not fit into society's categories of marginal, deviant, and "queer." As we watch the explosion of prison construction and the disproportionate incarceration rates of young men and women of color, often as part of the economic development of poor white rural communities, we have to ask if these individuals do not fit society's definition of "queer" and expendable.

I am not proposing a political strategy that homogenizes and glorifies the experience of poor heterosexual people of color. In fact, in calling for a more expansive left political identity and formation I do not seek to erase the specific historical relation between the stigma of "queer" and the sexual activity of gay men, lesbians, bisexual, and transgendered individuals. And in no way do I mean to, or want to, equate the experiences of marginal heterosexual women and men to the lived experiences of queers. There is no doubt that heterosexuality, even for those heterosexuals who stand outside the norms of heteronormativity, results in some form of privilege and feelings of supremacy. I need only recount the times when other women of color, more economically vulnerable than myself, expressed superiority and some feelings of disgust when they realized that the nice young professor (me) was "that way."

However, in recognizing the distinct history of oppression lesbian, gay, bisexual, and transgendered people have confronted and challenged, I am not willing to embrace every queer as my marginalized political ally. In the same way, I do not assume that shared racial, gender, and/or class position or identity guarantees or produces similar political commitments. Thus, identities and communities, while important to this strategy, must be complicated and destabilized through a recognition of the multiple social positions and relations to dominant power found *within* any one category or identity. Kimberle Crenshaw, in "Mapping the Margins: Intersectionality, Identity Politics, and Violence against Women of Color," suggests that such a project use the idea of intersectionality to reconceptualize or problematize the identities and communities that are "home" to us. She demands that we challenge those identities that seem like home by acknowledging the other parts of our identities that are excluded:

> With identity thus reconceptualized [through a recognition of intersectionality], it may be easier to understand the need to summon up the courage to challenge groups that are after all, in one sense, "home" to us, in the name of the parts of us that are not made at home. . . . The most one could expect is that we will dare to speak against internal exclusions and marginalizations, that we might call attention to how the identity of "the group" has been centered on the intersectional identities of a few. . . . Through an awareness of intersectionality, we can better acknowledge and ground the differences among us and negotiate the means by which these differences will find expression in constructing group politics. (1299)

In the same ways that we account for the varying privilege to be gained by a heterosexual identity, we must also pay attention to the privilege some queers receive from being white, male, and upper class. Only through recognizing the many manifestations of power, across and within categories, can we truly begin to build a movement based on one's politics and not exclusively on one's identity.

I want to be clear that what I and others are calling for is the destabilization, and not the destruction or abandonment, of identity categories.[7] We must reject a queer politics which seems to ignore, in its analysis of the usefulness of traditionally named categories, the roles of identity and community as paths to survival, using shared experiences of oppression and resistance to build indigenous resources, shape consciousness, and act collectively. Instead, I would suggest that it is the multiplicity and interconnectedness of our identities which provide the most promising avenue for the *destabilization and radical politicalization* of these same categories.

This is not an easy path to pursue because most often this will mean building a political analysis and political strategies around the most marginal in our society, some of whom look like us, many of whom do not. Most often, this will mean rooting our struggle in, and addressing the needs of, communities of color. Most often this will mean highlighting the intersectionality of one's race, class, gender, and sexuality and the relative power and privilege that one receives from being a man and/or being white and/or being middle class and/or being heterosexual. This, in particular, is a daunting challenge because so much of our political consciousness has been built around simple dichotomies such as powerful/powerless; oppressor/victim: enemy/comrade. It is difficult to feel safe and secure in those spaces where both your relative privilege and your experiences with marginalization are understood to shape your commitment to radical politics. However, as Bernice Johnson Reagon so aptly put it in her essay, "Coalition Politics: Turning the Century," "if you feel the strain, you may be doing some good work" (362).

And while this is a daunting challenge and uncomfortable position, those who have taken it up have not only survived, but succeeded in their efforts. For example, both the needle exchange and prison projects pursued through the auspices of ACT UP New York point to the possibilities and difficulties involved in principled transformative coalition work. In each project individuals from numerous identities—heterosexual, gay, poor, wealthy, white, black, Latino—came together to challenge dominant constructions of who should be allowed and who deserved care. No particular identity exclusively determined the shared political commitments of these activists; instead their similar positions, as marginalized subjects relative to the state—made clear through the government's lack of response to AIDS—formed the basis of this political unity.

In the prison project, it was the contention of activists that the government which denied even wealthy gay men access to drugs to combat this disease must be regarded as the same source of power that denied incarcerated men and women access to basic health care, including those drugs and conditions needed to combat HIV and AIDS. The coalition work this group engaged in involved a range of people, from formerly incarcerated individuals, to heterosexual men and women of color, to those we might deem privileged white lesbians and gay men. And this same group of people who came together to protest the conditions of incarcerated people with AIDS also showed up to public events challenging the homophobia that guided the government's and biomedical industries response to this epidemic. The political work of this group of individuals was undoubtedly informed by the public identities they embraced, but these were identities that they further acknowledged as complicated by intersectionality and placed within a political framework where their shared experience as marginal, nonnormative subjects could be foregrounded. Douglas Crimp, in his article "Right On, Girlfriend!," suggests that through political work our identities become remade and must therefore be understood as *relational*. Describing such a transformation in the identities of queer activists engaged in, and prosecuted for, needle exchange work, Crimp writes,

> But once engaged in the struggle to end the crisis, these queers' identities were no longer the same. It's not that "queer" doesn't any longer encompass their sexual practices; it does, but it also entails a *relation* between those practices and other circumstances that make very different people vulnerable both to HIV infection and to the stigma, discrimination, and neglect that have characterized the societal and governmental response to the constituencies most affected by the AIDS epidemic. (317–18)

The radical potential of those of us on the outside of heteronormativity rests in our understanding that we need not base our politics in the dissolution of all categories and communities, but we need instead to work toward the destabilization and remaking of our identities. Difference, in and of itself—even that difference designated through named categories—is not the problem. Instead it is the power invested in certain identity categories and the idea that bounded categories are not to be transgressed that serve as the basis of domination and control. The reconceptualization not only of the content of identity categories, but the intersectional nature of identities themselves, must become part of our political practice.

We must thus begin to link our intersectional analysis of power with concrete coalitional work. In real terms this means identifying political struggles such as the needle exchange and prison projects of ACT UP that transgress the boundaries of identity to highlight, in this case, both the repressive power of the state and the normalizing power evident within both dominant and marginal communities. This type of principled coalition work is also being pursued in a more modest fashion by the Policy Institute of the National Gay and Lesbian Task Force. Recently, the staff at the Task Force distributed position papers not only on the topics of gay marriages and gays in the military, but also on right-wing attacks against welfare and affirmative action. Here we have political work based in the knowledge that the rhetoric and accusations of nonnormativity that Newt Gingrich and other right-wingers launch against women on welfare closely resemble the attacks of nonnormativity mounted against gays, lesbians, bisexuals, and transgendered individuals. Again it is the marginalized relation to power, experienced by both of these groups—and I do not mean to suggest that the groups are mutually exclusive—that frames the possibility for transformative coalition work. This prospect diminishes when we do not recognize and deal with the reality that the intersecting identities that gay people embody—in terms of race, class, and gender privilege—put some of us on Gingrich's side of the welfare struggle (e.g., Log Cabin Republicans). And in a similar manner a woman's dependence on state financial assistance in no way secures her position as one supportive of gay rights and/or liberation. While a marginal identity undoubtedly increases the prospects of shared consciousness, only an articulation and commitment to mutual support can truly be the test of unity when pursuing transformational politics.

Finally, I realize that I have been short on specifics when trying to describe how we move concretely toward a transformational coalition politics among marginalized subjects. The best I can do is offer this discussion as a starting point for reassessing the shape of queer/lesbian/gay/bisexual/transgendered politics as we approach the twenty-first century. A reconceptualization of the politics of marginal groups allows us not only to privilege the specific lived experience of distinct communities, but also to search for those interconnected sites of resistance from which we can wage broader political struggles. Only by recognizing the link *between* the ideological, social, political, and economic marginalization of punks, bulldaggers, and welfare queens can we begin to develop political analyses and political strategies effective in confronting the linked yet varied sites of power in this country. Such a project is important because it provides a framework from which the difficult work of coalition politics can begin. And it is in these complicated and contradictory spaces that the liberatory and left politics that so many of us work for is located.

ACKNOWLEDGMENTS

The author would like to thank Mark Blasius, Nan Boyd, Ed Cohen, Carolyn Dinshaw, Jeff Edwards, Licia Fiol-Matta, Joshua Gamson, Lynne Huffer, Tamara Jones, Carla Kaplan, Ntanya Lee, Ira Livingston, and Barbara Ransby for their comments on various versions of this paper. All shortcomings are of course the fault of the author.

NOTES

1. The very general chronology of queer theory and queer politics referred to throughout this article is not meant to write the definitive historical development of each phenomenon. Instead, the dates are used to provide the reader with a general frame of reference. See Epstein for a similar genealogy of queer theory and queer politics.

2. See Ingraham for a discussion of the heterogendered imaginary.

3. I want to be clear that in this essay I am including the destruction of sexual categories as part of the agenda of queer politics. While a substantial segment of queer activists and theorists call for the *destabilization* of sexual categories, there are also those self-avowed queers who embrace a politics built around the *deconstruction* and/or elimination of sexual categories. For example, a number of my self-identified queer students engage in sexual behavior that most people would interpret as *transgressive* of sexual identities and categories. However, these students have repeatedly articulated a different interpretation of their sexual behavior. They put forth an understanding that does not highlight their transgression of categories, but one which instead represents them as individuals who operate outside of categories and sexual identities altogether. They are sexual beings, given purely to desire, truly living sexual fluidity, and not constrained by any form of sexual categorization or identification. This interpretation seems at least one step removed from that held by people who embrace the fluidity of sexuality while still recognizing the political usefulness of categories or labels for certain sexual behavior and communities. One example of such people might be those women who identify as lesbians and who also acknowledge that sometimes they choose to sleep with men. These individuals exemplify the process of destabilization that I try to articulate within this essay. Even further removed from the queers who would do away with all sexual categories are those who also transgress what many consider to be categories of sexual behaviors while they publicly embrace one stable sexual identity (for example, those self-identified heterosexual men who sleep with other men sporadically and secretly).

4. I want to thank Mark Blasius for raising the argument that standing on the outside of heteronormativity is a bit of a misnomer, since as a dominant normalizing process it is a practice of regulation in which we are all implicated. However, despite this insight I will on occasion continue to use this phrasing, understanding the limits of its meaning.

5. See Hennessy for a discussion of left analysis and the limits of queer theory.

6. For an insightful discussion of the numerous methods used to regulate and control the sexual and reproductive choices of women, see Shende.

7. See Jones for an articulation of differences between the destabilization and the destruction of identity categories.

REFERENCES

Alexander, Jacqui. "Redrafting Morality: The Postcolonial State and the Sexual Offences Bill of Trinidad and Tobago." *Third World Women and the Politics of Feminism,* ed. C. T. Mohanty, A. Russo, and L. Torres. Bloomington: Indiana UP, 1991. 133–52.

Berlant, Lauren, and Elizabeth Freeman. "Queer Nationality." Warner 193–229.

Bérubé, Allan, and Jeffrey Escoffier. "Queer/Nation." *Out/Look: National Lesbian and Gay Quarterly* II (Winter 1991): 12–14.

Blasius, Mark. *Gay and Lesbian Politics: Sexuality and the Emergence of a New Ethic.* Philadelphia: Temple UP, 1994.

Butler, Judith. *Gender Trouble.* New York: Routledge, 1990.

Carby, Hazel. *Reconstructing Womanhood: The Emergence of the Afro-American Woman Novelist.* New York: Oxford UP, 1987.

Clarke, Cheryl. "The Failure to Transform: Homophobia in the Black Community." Smith, *Home Girls* 197–208.

Cohen, Cathy J. "Contested Membership: Black Gay Identities and the Politics of AIDS." *Queer Theory/Sociology.* Ed. S. Seidman, Oxford: Blackwell, 1996. 362–94.

Collins, Patricia Hill, *Black Feminist Thought: Knowledge, Consciousness, and the Politics of Sociology Empowerment.* New York: Harper, 1990.

Combahee River Collective. "The Combahee River Collective Statement." Smith, *Home Girls* 272–82.

Crenshaw, Kimberle. "Mapping the Margins: Intersectionality, Identity Politics, and Violence against Women of Color." *Stanford Law Review* 43 (1991): 1241–99.

Crimp, Douglas. "Right On, Girlfriend!" Warner 300–20.

Davis, Angela Y. *Women, Race and Class.* New York: Vintage, 1983.

De Lauretis, Teresa. "Queer Theory: Lesbian and Gay Sexualities." *Differences* 3.2 (Summer 1991): iii–xviii.

Dunlap, David W. "Three Black Members Quit AIDS Organization Board." *New York Times* 11 Jan. 1996: B2.

Dyson, Michael Eric. *Between God and Gangsta Rap.* New York: Oxford UP, 1996.

Epstein, Steven. "A Queer Encounter: Sociology and the Study of Sexuality." *Sociological Theory* 12 (1994): 188–202.

Farajaje-Jones, Elias. "Ain't I a Queer." Creating Change Conference, National Gay and Lesbian Task Force, Detroit, Michigan, 8–12 Nov. 1995.

Fuss, Diana, ed. *Inside/Outside.* New York: Routledge, 1991.

Gamson, Joshua. "Must Identity Movements Self-destruct? A Queer Dilemma." *Social Problems* 42 (1995): 390–407.

Gutman, Herbert G. *The Black Family in Slavery and Freedom, 1750–1925.* New York: Vintage, 1976.

Hennessy, Rosemary. "Queer Theory, Left Politics," *Rethinking MARXISM* 7.3 (1994): 85–111.

Higginbotham, A. Leon, Jr. *In the Matter of Color—Race and the American Legal Process: The Colonial Period.* New York: Oxford UP, 1978.

hooks, bell. *Feminist Theory: From Margin to Center.* Boston: South End, 1984.

Ingraham, Chrys. "The Heterosexual Imaginary: Feminist Sociology and Theories of Gender." *Sociological Theory* 12 (1994): 203–19.

Jones, Tamara. "Inside the Kaleidoscope: How the Construction of Black Gay and Lesbian Identities Inform Political Strategies." Unpublished. Yale University, 1995.

Lorde, Audre, *Sister Outsider: Essays and Speeches by Audre Lorde.* New York: The Crossing P. 1984.

McIntosh, Mary. "Queer Theory and the War of the Sexes." *Activating Theory: Lesbian, Gay, Bisexual Politics,* ed. J. Bristow and A. R. Wilson. London: Lawrence and Wishart, 1993. 33–52.

Moraga, Cherríe, and Gloria Anzaldúa, eds. *This Bridge Called My Back: Writings by Radical Women of Color.* New York: Kitchen Table/Women of Color, 1981.

Morton, Donald. "The Politics of Queer Theory in the (Post) Modern Moment," *Genders* 17 (Fall 1993): 121–15.

Moynihan, Daniel Patrick. *The Negro Family: The Case for National Action.* Washington D.C.: Office of Policy Planning and Research. U.S. Department of Labor, 1965.

Phelan, Shane. *Identity Politics: Lesbian Feminism and the Limits of Community.* Philadelphia: Temple UP, 1989.

Podolsky, Robin. "Sacrificing Queer and other 'Proletarian' Artifacts." *Radical America* 25.1 (January 1991): 53–60.

Queer Nation. "I Hate Straights" manifesto. New York, 1990.

Queers United Against Straight-acting Homosexuals. "Assimilation Is Killing Us: Fight for a Queer United Front." WHY I HATED THE MARCH ON WASHINGTON (1993):4.

Ransby, Barbara, and Tracye Matthews. "Black Popular Culture and the Transcendence of Patriarchical Illusions." *Race & Class* 35.1 (July–September 1993): 57–70.

Reagon, Bernice Johnson. "Coalition Politics: Turning the Century." Smith, *Home Girls* 356–68.

Reed, Adolph L., Jr. "The 'Underclass' as Myth and Symbol: The Poverty of Discourse about Poverty." *Radical America* 24.1 (January 1990): 21–40.

Rich, Adrienne. "Compulsory Heterosexuality and Lesbian Existence." *Powers of Desire: The Politics of Sexuality,* ed. A. Snitow, C. Stansell and S. Thompson. New York: Monthly Review, 1983. 177–206.

Sedgwick, Eve. *The Epistemology of the Closet.* Berkeley: U of California P, 1990.

Seidman, Steven. "Identity and Politics in a 'Postmodern' Gay Culture." Warner 105–42.

Shende, Suzanne. "Fighting the Violence against Our Sisters: Prosecution of Pregnant Women and the Coercive Use of Norplant." *Women Transforming Politics: An Alternative Reader,* ed. C. Cohen, K. Jones, and J. Tronto, New York: New York UP, 1997.

Smith, Barbara. "Queer Politics: Where's the Revolution?" *The Nation* 257.1 (July 5, 1993): 12–16.

———, ed. *Home Girls: A Black Feminist Anthology.* New York: Kitchen Table/Women of Color, 1983.

Smith, M. G. "Social Structure in the British Caribbean about 1820." *Social and Economic Studies* 1.4 (August 1953): 55–79.

"Statement of Purpose." Dialogue on the Lesbian and Gay Left. Duncan Conference Center in Del Ray Beach, Florida. 1–4 April 1993.

Stein, Arlene, and Ken Plummer. " 'I Can't Even Think Straight': 'Queer' Theory and the Missing Sexual Revolution in Sociology." *Sociological Theory* 12 (1994): 178–87.

Vaid, Urvashi. *Virtual Equality: The Mainstreaming of Gay & Lesbian Liberation.* New York: Anchor, 1995.

Warner, Michael, ed. *Fear of a Queer Planet: Queer Politics and Social Theory.* Minneapolis: U of Minnesota P, 1993.

West, Cornel. *Race Matters.* Boston: Beacon, 1993.

Wilson, William Julius. *The Truly Disadvantaged: The Inner City, the Underclass, and Public Policy.* Chicago: U of Chicago P, 1987.

R E A D I N G   5 3

The Next Feminist Generation: Imagine My Surprise

ELLEN NEUBORNE

When my editor called me into his office and told me to shut the door, I was braced to argue. I made a mental note to stand my ground.

It was behind the closed door of his office that I realized I'd been programmed by the sexists.

We argued about the handling of one of my stories. He told me not to criticize him. I continued to disagree. That's when it happened.

He stood up, walked to where I was sitting. He completely filled my field of vision. He said, "Lower your voice when you speak to me."

And I did.

I still can't believe it.

This was not supposed to happen to me. I am the child of professional feminists. My father is a civil rights lawyer. My mother heads the NOW Legal Defense and Education Fund. She sues sexists for a living. I was raised on a pure, unadulterated feminist ethic.

That didn't help.

Looking back on the moment, I should have said, "Step back out of my face and we'll continue this discussion like humans."

I didn't.

I said, "Sorry."

Sorry!

I had no idea twenty-some years of feminist upbringing would fail me at that moment. Understand, it is not his actions I am criticizing; it is mine. He was a bully. But the response was my own. A man confronted me. My sexist programming kicked in. I backed off. I said, "Sorry."

I don't understand where the programming began. I had been taught that girls could do anything boys could do. Equality of the sexes was an unimpeachable truth. Before that day in the editor's office, if you'd asked me how I might handle such a confrontation, I never would have said, "I'd apologize."

I'm a good feminist. I would never apologize for having a different opinion.

But I did.

Programming. It is the subtle work of an unequal world that even the best of feminist parenting couldn't overcome.

It is the force that sneaks up on us even as we think that we are getting ahead with the best of the guys. I would never have believed in its existence. But having heard it, amazingly, escape from my own mouth, I am starting to recognize its pattern.

When you are told you are causing trouble, and you regret having raised conflict, that's your programming.

When you keep silent, though you know the answer—programming.

When you do not take credit for your success, or you suggest that your part in it was really minimal—programming.

When a man tells you to lower your voice, and you do, and you apologize—programming.

The message of this programming is unrelentingly clear: Keep quiet.

I am a daughter of the movement. How did I fall for this?

I thought the battle had been won. I thought that sexism was a remote experience, like the Depression. Gloria had taken care of all that in the seventies.

Imagine my surprise.

And while I was blissfully unaware, the perpetrators were getting smarter.

What my mother taught me to look for—pats on the butt, honey, sweetie, cupcake, make me some coffee—are not the methods of choice for today's sexists. Those were just the fringes of what they were really up to. Sadly, enough of them have figured out how to mouth the words of equality while still behaving like pigs. They're harder to spot.

At my first newspaper job in Vermont, I covered my city's effort to collect food and money to help a southern town ravaged by a hurricane. I covered the story from the early fund-raising efforts right up to the day before I was to ride with the aid caravan down South. At that point I was taken off the story and it was reassigned to a male reporter. (It wasn't even his beat; he covered education.) It would be too long a drive for me, I was told. I wouldn't get enough sleep to do the story.

He may as well have said "beauty rest." But I didn't get it. At least not right away. He seemed, in voice and manner, to be concerned about me. It worked. A man got the big story. And I got to stay home. It was a classic example of a woman being kept out of a plum project "for her own good," yet while in the newsroom, hearing this explanation about sleep and long drives, I sat there nodding.

Do you think you would do better? Do you think you would recognize sexism at work immediately?

Are you sure?

Programming is a powerful thing. It makes you lazy. It makes you vulnerable. And until you can recognize that it's there, it works for the opposition. It makes you lower your voice.

It is a dangerous thing to assume that just because we were raised in a feminist era, we are safe. We are not. They are still after us.

And it is equally dangerous for our mothers to assume that because we are children of the movement, we are equipped to stand our ground. In many cases, we are unarmed.

The old battle strategies aren't enough, largely because the opposition is using new weaponry. The man in my office who made a nuisance of himself by asking me out repeatedly did so through the computer messaging system. Discreet. Subtle. No one to see him being a pig. Following me around would have been obvious. This way, he looked perfectly normal, and I constantly had to delete his overtures from my e-mail files. Mom couldn't have warned me about e-mail.

Then there is the danger from other women. Those at the top who don't mentor other women because if they made it on their own, so should subsequent generations. Women who say there is just one "woman's slot" at the top power level, and to get there you must kill off your female competition. Women who maintain a conspiracy of silence, refusing to speak up when they witness or even experience sexism, for fear of reprisals. These are dangers from within our ranks. When I went to work, I assumed other women were my allies.

Again, imagine my surprise.

I once warned a newly hired secretary that her boss had a history of discrimination against young women. She seemed intensely interested in the conversation at the time. Apparently as soon as I walked away, she repeated the entire conversation to her boss. My heart was in the right place. But my brain was not. Because, as I learned that day, sisterhood does not pay the bills. For younger women who think they do not need the feminist movement to get ahead, sisterhood is the first sentiment to fall by the wayside. In a world that looks safe, where men say all the right things and office policies have all the right words, who needs sisterhood?

We do. More than we ever have. Because they are smooth, because they are our bosses and control our careers, because they are hoping we will kill each other off so they won't have to bother. Because of all the subtle sexism that you hardly notice until it has already hit you. That is why you need the movement.

On days when you think the battle is over, the cause has been won, look around you to see what women today still face. The examples are out there.

On college campuses, there is a new game called rodeo. A man takes a woman back to his room, initiates sexual intercourse, and then a group of his friends barges in. The object of this game is for the man to keep his date pinned as long as possible.

Men are still afraid of smart women. When Ruth Bader Ginsburg was nominated to the Supreme Court, the *New York Times* described her as "a woman who handled her intelligence gracefully." The message: If you're smarter than the men around you, be sure to keep your voice down. Wouldn't want to be considered ungraceful.

A friend from high school calls to tell me he's getting married. He's found the perfect girl. She's bright, she's funny and she's willing to take his last name. That makes them less likely to get divorced, he maintains. "She's showing me she's not holding out."

In offices, women with babies are easy targets. I've seen the pattern played out over and over. One woman I know put in ten years with the company, but once she returned from maternity leave, she was marked. Every attempt to leave on time to pick up her baby at day care was chalked up as a "productivity problem." Every request to work part-time was deemed troublemaking. I sat just a few desks away. I witnessed her arguments. I heard the editors gossip when she was absent. One Monday we came into work and her desk had been cleaned out.

Another woman closer to my age also wanted to work part-time after the birth of her son. She was told that was unacceptable. She quit. There was no announcement. No good-bye party. No card for everyone in the office to sign. The week she disappeared from the office, we had a party for a man who was leaving to take a new job. We also were asked to contribute to a gift fund for another man who had already quit for a job in the Clinton administration.

But for the women with babies who were disappeared, nothing happened. And when I talked about the fact that women with babies tended to vanish, I was hauled into my boss' office for a reeducation session. He spent twenty minutes telling me what a great feminist he was and that if I ever thought differently, I should leave the company. No question about the message there: Shut up.

I used to believe that my feminist politics would make me strong. I thought strong thoughts. I held strong beliefs. I thought that would protect me. But all it did was make me aware of how badly I slipped when I lowered my voice and apologized for having a divergent opinion. For all my right thinking, I did not fight back. But I have learned something. I've learned it takes practice to be a strong feminist. It's not an instinct you can draw on at will—no matter how equality-minded your upbringing. It needs exercise. You have to think to know your own mind. You have to battle to work in today's workplace. It was nice to grow up thinking this was an equal world. But it's not.

I have learned to listen for the sound of my programming. I listen carefully for the *Sorrys,* the *You're rights.* Are they deserved? Or did I offer them up without thinking, as though I had been programmed? Have you? Are you sure?

I have changed my ways. I am louder and quicker to point out sexism when I see it. And it's amazing what you can see when you are not hiding behind the warm, fuzzy glow of past feminist victories. It does not make me popular in the office. It does not even make me popular with women. Plenty of my female colleagues would prefer I quit rocking the boat. One read a draft of this essay and suggested I change the phrase "fight back" to "stand my ground" in order to "send a better message."

But after falling for the smooth talk and after hearing programmed acquiescence spew from my mouth, I know what message I am trying to send: Raise your voice. And I am sending it as much to myself as to anyone else.

I've changed what I want from the women's movement. I used to think it was for political theory, for bigger goals that didn't include my daily life. When I was growing up, the rhetoric we heard involved the theory of equality: Were men and women really equal? Were there biological differences that made men superior? Could women overcome their stigma as "the weaker sex"? Was a woman's place really in the home?

These were ideas. Important, ground-breaking, mind-changing debates. But the feminism I was raised on was very cerebral. It forced a world full of people to change the way they think about women. I want more than their minds. I want to see them do it.

The theory of equality has been well fought for by our mothers. Now let's talk about how to talk, how to work, how to fight sexism here on the ground, in our lives. All the offices I have worked in have lovely, right-thinking policy statements. But the theory doesn't necessarily translate into action. I'm ready to take up that part of the battle.

I know that sitting on the sidelines will not get me what I want from my movement. And it is mine. Younger feminists have long felt we needed to be invited to our mothers' party. But don't be fooled into thinking that feminism is old-fashioned. The movement is ours and we need it.

I am one of the oldest of my generation, so lovingly dubbed "X" by a disdainful media. To my peers, and to the women who follow after me, I warn you that your programming is intact. Your politics may be staunchly feminist, but they will not protect you if you are passive.

Listen for the attacks. They are quiet. They are subtle.

And listen for the jerk who will tell you to lower your voice. Tell him to get used to the noise. The next generation is coming.

R E A D I N G   5 4

The Women's Movement: Persistence through Transformation

VERTA TAYLOR, NANCY WHITTIER, and CYNTHIA FABRIZIO PELAK

INTRODUCTION

Popular authors and scholars alike described the 1980s and 1990s as a "postfeminist" era of political apathy during which former feminists traded their political ideals for career mobility and cell phones and younger women single-mindedly pursued career goals and viewed feminism as an anachronism. Yet this was not the first time that commentators proclaimed the death of feminism. In the 1920s, after women won the right to vote, images of young women abandoning the struggle for rights in favor of jobs and good times filled the media. Then as now, feminism changed form, but neither the movement nor the injustices that produced it have vanished. Of all the manifestations of social activism in the 1960s, feminism is one of the few that persist. We explore here continuity and change in the American women's movement from the 1960s to the present. First we consider the structural preconditions of women's movements in the western world and the international context for activism. Then we focus on the changing ideologies, structures, political contexts, and strategies of the women's movement in the United States. We conclude our discussion by considering historically specific antifeminist counter-

Verta Taylor, Nancy Whittier, and Cynthia Fabrizio Pelak. "The Women's Movement: Persistence Through Transformation." Reprinted with the permission of the authors.

movements that have emerged in response to challenges of the women's movement.

STRUCTURAL PRECONDITIONS OF WESTERN FEMINIST MOVEMENTS

From a social movement perspective, women have always had sufficient grievances to create the context for feminist activity. Indeed, instances of collective action on the part of women abound in history, especially if one includes female reform societies, women's church groups, alternative religious societies, and women's clubs. However, collective activity on the part of women directed specifically toward improving their own status has flourished primarily in periods of generalized social upheaval, when sensitivity to moral injustice, discrimination, and social inequality has been widespread in the society as a whole (Chafe 1977; Staggenborg 1998a). The first wave of feminism in the United States grew out of the abolitionist struggle of the 1830s and peaked during an era of social reform in the 1890s, and the contemporary movement emerged out of the general social discontent of the 1960s. Although the women's movement did not die between these periods of heightened activism, it declined sharply in the 1930s, 1940s, and 1950s after the passage of the Nineteenth Amendment to the Constitution guaranteeing women the right to vote as a response to the changing social, political, and economic context (Rupp and Taylor 1987). During this period, women who had played important roles in obtaining women's suffrage managed to keep the flames of feminism alive by launching a campaign to pass an Equal Rights Amendment (ERA) to the Constitution.

Despite national differences in feminist movements, scholars identify certain basic structural conditions that have contributed to the emergence of feminist protest in most parts of the western world (Oppenheimer 1973; Huber and Spitze 1983; Chafetz and Dworkin 1986). Broad societal changes in the patterns of women's participation in the paid labor force, increases in women's formal educational attainment, and shifts in women's fertility rates and reproductive roles disrupt traditional social arrangements and set the stage for women's movements. As industrialization and urbanization bring greater education for women, expanding public roles create role and status conflicts for middle-class women, who then develop the discontent and gender consciousness necessary for political action (Chafetz and Dworkin 1986). Specifically, when women, especially married middle-class women, enter the paid labor force, their gender consciousness increases because they are more likely to use men as a reference group when assessing their access to societal rewards. Similarly, women often experience strains and discrepancies in their lives as their gender consciousness is raised through formal education (Klein 1984).

Other important structural factors that serve as preconditions for feminist mobilization include changes in family relationships, marriage, fertility, and sexual mores (Ferree and Hess 1994). Declines in women's childbearing and increases in their age at first marriage can improve women's educational attainment and participation in the paid labor force—which, in turn, raise their gender consciousness (Klein 1984). Moreover, changes in the traditional relationships between women and men in marriage and in sexual mores, such as the shift from authoritarian marriages to romantic or companionate marriages at the turn of the last century in the United States and the "sexual revolution" of the 1960s, can politicize gender relations and create the motivations for feminist mobilization.

Certainly, the specific configuration of structural preconditions underlying the genesis of feminist collective mobilizations varies with historical and geographic context. Not only the political context but also the demographic, economic, and cultural processes that have given rise to feminist movements in the United States are different from those in Third World countries. Such political and cultural variations are reflected in national and regional variations in the way women define their collective interests, in the distinct ideologies, organizational forms, and strategies adopted by feminist movements in different times and places, and ultimately in the possibilities for feminist mobilization. Nonetheless, scholars recognize some important commonalties among women's movements around the world.

FEMINIST MOVEMENTS IN AN INTERNATIONAL CONTEXT

We focus here on the women's movement in the United States. It is nonetheless important to acknowledge the multiple forms of feminist resistance around the world and to underscore the importance of the historical and geographic specificity of feminist activism. Throughout modern history, women in all regions of the world have organized collectively against the injustice and oppression in their lives and communities (Basu 1995). Such mobilizations in diverse political, cultural, and historical contexts have varied widely in their organizations, strategies, ideologies, and structures. Gender oppression for some Third World feminists cannot be divorced from issues and histories of colonization, immigration, racism, or imperialism, and thus feminist activism in some Third World contexts may be organized around a constellation of oppressions rather than specifically around gender oppression (Jayawardena 1986; Mohanty, Russo, and Torres 1991).

In some instances, ideological, organizational, and strategic differences in women's movements lie in fundamental differences in the political culture of a region (Ray 1999). In Calcutta, India, for example, which is dominated by the Communist Party and a strong and traditional left culture, the women's movement functions more as a political party and uses the party structure to address issues such as employment, poverty, and literacy that do not directly threaten the gender status quo. The women's movement in Bombay, on the other hand, which exists in a more open, contested political field and culture, is more explicitly feminist and uses more autonomous forms of organizing to spotlight issues that are more threatening to men, such as violence against women, religious fundamentalism, and women's restricted roles in the family. Although national and regional differences exist, there are important commonalties that link women's movements over time and place (Chafetz and Dworkin 1986; Katzenstein and Mueller 1987; Giele 1995; Miles 1996).

Women's movements, particularly those in industrialized countries, generally have emerged in two waves of heightened activism. In their cross-cultural, historical analysis of forty-eight countries, Chafetz and Dworkin (1986) found that the mass-scale, independent women's movements of the first wave, such as those in European societies and the United States, occurred in the closing decades of the nineteenth century and the first decades of the twentieth century, while the second-wave women's movements have emerged since the 1960s. Major goals of the first wave of activism included women's suffrage, educational opportunities for women, basic legal reforms, inheritance and property rights, and employment opportunities for women. Women's demands during this first wave often were framed around middle-class women's roles as wives and mothers and reinforced gender difference by valorizing women's special virtues and moral superiority over men. Smaller-scale movements during the first wave were more likely to challenge basic role differentiation between women and men and to resist doctrines and images of femininity in the culture.

To the extent that the large-scale changes brought on by urbanization and industrialization in western countries created dramatic changes in the workplace, the family, and the lives of women and men, it is not surprising there was considerable ideological debate and diversity among first-wave feminists. In the United States, for example, some factions of the nineteenth-century women's movement were grounded in essentialist views of sex differences and were more interested in nonfeminist social reforms, for which the vote was only a prerequisite (Buechler 1990; Giele 1995). Other branches of the nineteenth-century women's movement rejected essentialist notions of gender and, by pursuing more radical changes such as sexual freedom and the expansion of women's roles in the workplace and politics, sought to transform the gender order in more fundamental ways (Cott 1987).

Women's movements of the second wave in western countries, blossoming since the 1960s, have mobilized around an even broader range of issues, such as reproductive rights, sexual and economic exploitation, and violence against women (Chafetz and Dworkin 1986; Ferree and Hess 1994). Modern feminist movements often have developed around women's commonalities, but differences of race, class, ethnicity, and nationality are also expressed in the collective identities deployed by feminists (Moraga and Anzaldúa 1981; Mohanty, Russo, and Torres 1991). African-American women have organized around interlocking structures of oppression that affect women differently depending on their ethnicity, class, or sexual identities (Collins 1990). For example, African-American and Latina

women from low-income urban neighborhoods have struggled for quality education, affordable and safe housing, and expanded child care services for their families and communities (Naples 1992).

Since the 1970s, there has been a phenomenal growth in regional, interregional, and international networking among feminist groups (Miles 1996), although the origins of international women's organizations date back to the closing decades of the nineteenth century (Rupp 1997). The United Nations' International Women's Year (1975) and Decade for Women (1975–1985) helped foster global feminist dialogues and stimulated independent, locally based feminist activities in all parts of the world. Since the beginning of the UN Decade for Women, there have been four official UN world conferences of government representatives devoted to women's issues, with four unofficial forums of women's groups running alongside each of these conferences. Since the first forum in Mexico City in 1975, participation by women in the unofficial forums has increased sharply, challenging the notion that feminism has died in recent years.

Although these conferences and forums have been sites of considerable debate and conflict over the meaning of "women's issues" and the definition of feminism, the events have sparked multiple forms and foci of feminist resistance and a global awareness of women's oppression that reaches beyond women's groups. Feminists are forging global relations around a diverse set of issues including "health, housing, education, law reform, population, human rights, reproductive and genetic engineering, female sexual slavery and trafficking in women, violence against women, spirituality, peace and militarism, external debt, fundamentalism, environment, development, media, alternative technology, film, art and literature, publishing, and women's studies" (Miles 1996:142). The trajectory of the US women's movement can be fully understood only in this global context.

THE CONTEMPORARY FEMINIST MOVEMENT: CONTINUITY AND CHANGE

Most scholarly analyses of the women's movement of the late 1960s—what scholars call the "second-wave feminist movement"—divide it into two wings, with origins in the grievances and preexisting organizations of two groups of women: older professional women, who formed bureaucratic organizations with a liberal ideology and adopted legal reform strategies, and younger women from the civil rights and New Left movements, who formed small collective organizations with radical ideology and employed "personal as political" strategies such as consciousness-raising groups (Freeman 1975; Cassell 1977; Ferree and Hess 1994; Buechler 1990). During a period of resurgence dating to the founding of the National Organization for Women (NOW) in 1966, the movement established itself, forming organizations and ideologies and moving into the public eye (Buechler 1990; Ryan 1992). By 1971, major segments of feminism had crystallized: liberal feminism, embodied in the formation of groups such as NOW, the Women's Equity Action League (WEAL) in 1967, and the National Women's Political Caucus (NWPC) in 1971; radical feminism and socialist feminism, emerging from consciousness-raising groups, theory groups, and small action groups such as Redstockings and the Feminists in 1969; and lesbian feminism, organized in such groups as Radicalesbians in 1970 and the Furies (initially called "Those Women") in 1971 (Echols 1989).

The year 1972 was pivotal both for the movement's success and for its opposition. The Equal Rights Amendment (ERA) passed the Congress, and Phyllis Schlafly launched her first antifeminist attacks. This can be considered the movement's heyday because the feminist revolution seemed to be on the move. The campaign to ratify the ERA in the states brought mass mobilization, fostering female solidarity and enlisting women into feminism; women's studies programs proliferated on college campuses; the number and variety of feminist organizations increased phenomenally; and the movement entered the political arena and encountered active opposition (Matthews and DeHart 1990; Ryan 1992). Not only did feminism flourish in the ERA ratification campaign but it spread into the political mainstream, while radical and lesbian feminist organizing heightened outside it.

Following the ERA's defeat in 1982, the women's movement entered a period of the doldrums, in which it developed new structural forms to survive a declining membership and an increasingly nonreceptive environment. The 1980s saw a turning away from the values of equality, human rights, and social justice and even a deliberate backlash against the feminist momentum of the 1970s. Rights won by feminists in the 1960s and 1970s—from affirmative action to legal abortion—were under siege throughout the 1980s and 1990s. Yet the so-called postfeminist era of the 1980s and 1990s no more marks the death of the women's movement than did the earlier premature announcements of feminism's demise. In fact, although the women's movement of the turn of the twenty-first century takes a different form than it did twenty years earlier, it remains vital and influential.

Feminist Ideology

While ideas do not necessarily cause social movements, ideology is a central component in the life of any social movement (Morris and Mueller 1992). The modern feminist movement, like most social movements, is not ideologically monolithic. Feminist ideology encompasses numerous ideological strands that differ in the scope of change sought, the extent to which gender inequality is linked to other systems of domination—especially class, race, ethnicity, and sexuality—and the significance attributed to gender differences. We focus here on the evolution of the dominant ideologies that have motivated participants in the two major branches of the feminist movement from its inception, liberal feminism and radical feminism.

The first wave of the women's movement in the nineteenth century was, by and large, a liberal feminist reform movement. It sought equality within the existing social structure and, indeed, in many ways functioned like other reform movements to reaffirm existing values within the society (Ferree and Hess 1994). Nineteenth-century feminists believed that if they obtained the right to an education, the right to own property, the right to vote, employment rights—in other words, equal civil rights under the law—they would attain equality with men. Scholars have labeled this thinking "individualist" or "equity" feminism, linking the goal of equal rights to gender assumptions about women's basic sameness with men (Offen 1988; Black 1989).

The basic ideas identified with contemporary liberal or "mainstream" feminism have changed little since their formulation in the nineteenth century, when they seemed progressive, even radical (Eisenstein 1981). Contemporary liberal feminist ideology holds that women lack power simply because we are not, as women, allowed equal opportunity to compete and succeed in the male-dominated economic and political arenas but, instead, are relegated to the subordinate world of home, domestic labor, motherhood, and family. The major strategy for change is to gain legal and economic equalities and to obtain access to elite positions in the workplace and in politics. Thus, liberal feminists tend to place as much emphasis on changing individual women as they do on changing society. For instance, teaching women managerial skills or instructing rape victims in "survival" strategies strikes a blow at social definitions that channel women into traditionally feminine occupations or passive behaviors that make them easy targets of aggression from men.

Liberal feminists ironically provided ideological support through the 1970s and 1980s for the massive transformation in work and family life that was occurring as the United States underwent the transition to a postindustrial order (Mitchell 1986; Stacey 1987). Some writers even contend that by urging women to enter the workplace and adopt a male orientation, the equal opportunity approach to feminism unwittingly contributed to a host of problems that further disadvantaged women (especially working-class women and women of color), including the rise in divorce rates, the "feminization" of working-class occupations, and the devaluation of motherhood and traditionally female characteristics (Gordon 1991).

Radical feminist ideology dates to Simone de Beauvoir's early 1950s theory of "sex class," which was developed further in the late 1960s among small groups of radical women who fought the subordination of women's liberation within the New Left (Beauvoir 1952; Firestone 1970; Millett 1971; Atkinson 1974; Rubin 1975; Rich 1976, 1980; Griffin 1978; Daly 1978; Eisenstein 1981; Hartmann 1981; Frye 1983; Hartsock 1983; MacKinnon 1983). The radical approach recognizes women's identity and subordination as a "sex class," emphasizes women's fundamental difference from men, views gender as the primary contradiction and foundation for the unequal distribution of a society's rewards and privileges, and recasts relations between women and men in political terms (Echols 1989). Defining women as a "sex class" means no longer treating patriarchy in individual terms but acknowledging the social and structural nature of women's subordination. Radical feminists hold that in all societies, institutions and social patterns are structured to maintain and perpetuate gender inequality and female disadvantage permeates virtually all aspects of sociocultural and personal life. Further, through the gender division of labor, social institutions are linked so that male superiority depends upon female subordination (Hartmann 1981). In the United States, as in most industrialized societies, power, prestige, and wealth accrue to those who control the distribution of resources outside the home, in the economic and political spheres. The sexual division of labor that assigns child care and domestic responsibilities to women not only ensures gender inequality in the family system but perpetuates male advantage in political and economic institutions as well.

To unravel the complex structure on which gender inequality rests requires, from a radical feminist perspective, a fundamental transformation of all institutions in society. To meet this challenge, radical feminists formulated influential critiques of the family, marriage, love, motherhood, heterosexuality, sexual violence, capitalism, reproductive policies, the media, science, language and culture, the beauty industry, sports, politics, the law, technology, and more. Radical feminism's ultimate vision is revolutionary in scope: a fundamentally new social order that eliminates the sex-class system and replaces it with new ways—based on women's difference—of defining and structuring experience. Central to the development of radical feminist ideology was the strategy of forming small groups for the purpose of "consciousness-raising." Pioneered initially among New Left women, consciousness-raising can be understood as a kind of conversion in which women come to view experiences previously thought of as personal and individual, such as sexual exploitation or employment discrimination, as social problems that are the result of gender inequality.

By the late 1970s, the distinction between liberal and radical feminism was becoming less clear (Carden 1978; Whittier 1995). Ideological shifts took place at both the individual and organizational levels. Participation in liberal feminist reform and service organizations working on such issues as rape, battering, abortion, legal and employment discrimination, and women's health problems raised women's consciousness, increased their feminist activism, and contributed to their radicalization as they came to see connections between these issues and the larger system of gender inequality (Schlesinger and Bart 1983; Whittier 1995). Women were also radicalized by working through their own personal experiences of sexual harassment, divorce, rape, abortion, and incest (Huber 1973; Klein 1984).

Radicalization has occurred at the group level as well. By the end of the 1970s, liberal feminist organizations such as NOW, the Women's Legal Defense Fund, and the National Abortion Rights Action League (NARAL) which had been pursuing equality within the law, began to adopt strategies and goals consistent with a more radical stance. NOW included in its 1979 objectives not only such legal strategies as the ERA and reproductive choice, but broader issues such as the threat of nuclear energy to the survival of the species, lesbian and gay rights, homemakers' rights, the exploitation of women in the home, and sex segregation in the workplace (Eisenstein 1981). Even the ERA, which sought equality for women within the existing legal and economic structure, was based on the fact that women are discriminated against as a "sex class" (Mansbridge 1986).

Beginning in the mid-1980s, with the defeat of the unifying issue of the ERA and the growing diversification of the movement, feminist ideology de-emphasized the question of women's similarity to or difference from men in favor of "deconstructing" the term *woman*. Women of color, Jewish women, lesbians, and working-class women challenged radical feminists' idea of a "sex class" that implied a distinctive and essential female condition. Since women are distributed throughout all social classes, racial and ethnic groupings, sexual communities, cultures, and religions, disadvantage for women varies and is multidimensional (Spelman 1988). The recognition that the circumstances of women's oppression differ has given way to a new feminist paradigm that views race, class, gender, ethnicity, and sexuality as interlocking systems of oppression, forming what Patricia Hill Collins (1990) refers to as a "matrix of domination."

Some scholars have charged that focusing on women's differences from one another has resulted in a retreat to "identity politics" and the demise of the women's movement. Alice Echols (1989) links disputes over difference and a focus on identity to a concentration on building an alternative women's culture rather than confronting and changing social institutions. In a similar vein, Barbara Ryan (1989) argues that internal debates over the correctness of competing feminist theories and the political implications of personal choices—what she terms "ideological purity"—tore the women's movement apart. But other scholars see the sometimes vehement arguments over women's differences from one another as a sign of life (Taylor and Rupp 1993). Feminists organizing around diverse identities sometimes seek out new arenas of challenge that differ from traditional definitions of political activism and thus extend the reach of feminism. Self-help movements focused on the self and the body, for example—drug and alcohol abuse, incest, postpartum depression, battering, breast cancer—offer a complex challenge to traditional notions of femininity, motherhood, and sexuality and carry the potential to mobilize new constituencies (Taylor and Van Willigen 1996; Gagné 1998).

In any case, ideas alone are an incomplete explanation of either the direction or the consequences of a social movement (Marx and Wood, 1975; McCarthy and Zald 1977). Much depends on a movement's structures and strategies, as well as on the larger political context.

Feminist Organizational Structures

Social movements do not generally have a single central organization or unified direction. Rather, the structure of any general, broad-based social movement is more diffuse—composed of a number of relatively independent organizations that differ in ideology, structure, goals, and tactics. A social movement is characterized by decentralized leadership; it is loosely connected by multiple and overlapping memberships and by friendship networks that work toward common goals (Gerlach and Hine 1970). The organizational structure of the modern feminist movement has conformed to this model from its beginnings (Freeman 1975; Cassell 1977; Ferree and Martin 1995). While the movement as a whole is characterized by a decentralized structure, the various organizations that comprise it vary widely in structure. The diversity of feminist organizational forms reflects both ideological differences and the movement's diverse membership base (Freeman 1979).

There have been two main types of organizational structure in the modern feminist movement since its resurgence, reflecting the two sources of feminist organizing in the late 1960s: bureaucratically structured movement organizations with hierarchical leadership and democratic decision-making procedures, such as the National Organization for Women; and smaller collectively structured groups that formed a more diffuse social movement community held together by a feminist political culture. Collectively organized groups, at least in theory, strove to exemplify a better way of structuring society by constructing a distinctive women's culture that valorized egalitarianism, the expression of emotion, and the sharing of personal experience. It is important to recognize, however, that while the two strands of the women's movement emerged separately, they have not remained distinct and opposed to each other. Most women's movement organizations are mixed in form from the outset. The two structures have increasingly converged as bureaucratic organizations adopted some of the innovations of collectivism and feminist collectives became more formally structured (Staggenborg 1988, 1989; Martin 1990; Ryan 1992; Ferree and Martin 1995; Whittier 1995). In addition, many individual activists are involved in a variety of organizations with differing structures.

The bureaucratically structured and professionalized movement organizations initially adopted by liberal groups such as NOW were well suited to work within the similarly structured political arena and to members' previous experience in professional organizations. The structures that radical feminist groups initially adopted, on the other hand, built on their prior involvement in the New Left (Evans 1979). Collectivist organizations grew from radical feminists' attempts to structure relations among members, processes of decision making, and group leadership in a way that reflected or prefigured the values and goals of the movement (Rothschild-Whitt 1979; Breines 1982).

Feminist collectivist organizations made decisions by consensus, rotated leadership and other tasks among members, and shared skills to avoid hierarchy and specialization. Such groups often failed to meet their ideals and did, in fact, spawn unacknowledged hierarchies (Freeman 1972/3). Nevertheless, the conscious effort to build a feminist collective structure has had a lasting impact on the women's movement and has led to the growth of a social movement community (Buechler 1990). That is, the movement consists of not only formal organizations but also more informally organized communities, made up of networks of people who share the movement's political goals and outlook and work toward common aims. The collectivist branch of the women's movement initially sparked the growth of a feminist social movement community in which alternative structures guided by a distinctively feminist women's culture flourished—including bookstores, theater groups, music collectives, poetry groups, art collectives, publishing and recording companies, spirituality groups, vacation resorts, self-help groups, and a variety of feminist-run businesses. This "women's culture," though it includes feminists of diverse political persuasions, has been largely maintained by lesbian feminists. It nurtures a feminist collective identity that is important to the survival of the women's movement as a whole (Taylor and Whittier 1992; Taylor and Rupp 1993).

Both bureaucratic organizations working within mainstream politics and the alternative feminist culture have expanded and converged since the movement's emergence in the 1960s. Organizations such as NOW and NARAL incorporated some of the innovations of collectivism, including consciousness-raising groups, modified consensus decision making, and the use of direct-action tactics and civil disobedience. A host of structural variations emerged, including formally structured groups that use consensus decision making, organizations with deliberately democratic structures, and groups that officially operate by majority-rule democracy but in practice make most decisions by consensus (Staggenborg 1988, 1989; Martin 1990; Ryan 1992; Taylor 1996). At the same time, feminist collectives shifted their focus from consciousness-raising and radical feminist critique to the development of feminist self-help and service organizations such as rape crisis centers, shelters for battered women, job training programs for displaced homemakers, and lesbian peer counseling groups. Moreover, many feminist collectives revised their structure to depend less on consensus decision making and to permit specialization of skills. The widespread acceptance of the feminist analysis of rape as an act of violence and power rather than

a strictly sexual act further attested to the impact of the feminist antirape movement. Feminist antirape groups received financial support from government agencies and private foundations to provide rape-prevention and treatment services in public schools and universities (Matthews 1994). The distinction between "working outside the system" and "working within the system," so important in the late 1960s, no longer had the same significance.

In conjunction with the ideological shift from a universal to a differentiated category of "woman," the structures of the women's movement diversified as well. Although individual women of color and working-class women had participated in the founding of NOW and in the early protests against sexism in the civil rights movement, the women's movement attracted primarily white middle-class women. Not that women of color and working-class or poor women experienced no oppression as women or opposed feminist goals. A 1989 *New York Times*/CBS News poll revealed that, while only 64 percent of white women saw a need for a women's movement, 85 percent of African-American women and 76 percent of Hispanic women thought the women's movement was needed (Sapiro 1991). Yet the feminist movement remained predominantly white both because it continued to define its goals based on the concerns of white middle-class women and because many Black women and other women of color placed a priority on working in their own racial communities to advance their collective interests, despite the recognition of sexism within such organizations (Barnett 1993; Robnett 1996).

Independent organizing by women of color did grow during the 1970s, and when African-American activists in the women's movement formed the National Black Feminist Organization in 1973 it grew to a membership of 1,000 within its first year (Deckard 1983). In the 1980s and 1990s, independent feminist organizations and networks of women of color such as the National Black Women's Health Project and the National Coalition of 100 Black Women emerged. Women of color also formed active caucuses within predominantly white feminist organizations, such as the National Women's Studies Association, to work against racism within the women's movement (Leidner 1993). Likewise, Jewish women, who had historically played important roles within the women's movement, organized their own groups in the 1980s and spoke out against antisemitism within the movement (Beck 1980; Bulkin, Pratt, and Smith 1984). Some scholars have argued that the Black feminist movement generally does not mobilize through institutionalized formal organizations but operates through informal networks in local communities. Such informal networks include self-help groups, book clubs, "girlfriend" (women-only) parties and gatherings, and explicitly political groups. For example, in the 1990s, after the much publicized appeal of convicted rapist and professional boxer Mike Tyson one such informal network served as a springboard to launch an antirape education program geared to the Black community (White 1999).

Union women played a significant role in the formation of NOW in 1966 by providing office space and clerical services until NOW's endorsement of the ERA in 1967 forced the women of the United Auto Workers, an organization that at the time opposed the ERA, to withdraw such support. Women committed to both feminism and the union movement, like women of color, formed their own organization, the Coalition of Labor Union Women (CLUW) in 1974 (Balser 1987). CLUW claimed 16,000 members by 1982 and had made progress in its fight to win AFL–CIO support for feminist issues. Union women also participated in deeply gendered ways in labor movement activity such as the 1985 Wheeling-Pittsburgh Steel strike, both affirming and challenging gender (Fonow 1998). The basic class and race composition of the movement may have changed little throughout the 1970s and 1980s, but by the beginning of the twenty-first century "a movement that began as unconsciously class-bound and race-bound has now become consciously class-bound and race-bound" (Buechler 1990:158).

Collective action by the women's movement has created new institutions and moved into almost every major institution of our society. However, in direct proportion to the successes of the women's movement, a countermovement successfully reversed some feminist gains, stalled progress on others, and changed the face of the women's movement.

The Antifeminist Political Context

The early 1980s saw a rapid decrease in the number of feminist organizations and a transformation in the form and activities of the women's movement. In part, this was a response to the successes of the New Right: so powerful were antifeminist sentiments and forces that members of the Republican party were elected in 1980 on a platform developed explicitly to "put women back in their place." After forty years of faithful support of the ERA, the Republican party dropped it from its platform, called for a constitutional amendment to ban abortion, and aligned itself with the economic and social policies of the New Right. After the election of the conservative Reagan administration in 1980, federal funds and grants were rarely available to feminist service organizations, and because other social service organizations were also hard hit by budget cuts, competition increased for relatively scarce money from private foundations. As a result, many feminist programs such as rape crisis centers, shelters for battered women, abortion clinics, and job training programs were forced to close or limit their services.

The failure of the ERA in 1982 seemed to reflect the changed political climate and set the stage for other setbacks throughout the 1980s. Abortion rights, won in 1973 with the Supreme Court's decision in *Roe v. Wade,* were curtailed in 1989 by the Supreme Court's decision in *Webster v. Reproductive Services* permitting states to enact restrictions on abortion (Staggenborg 1991:137–38). Following the Webster decision, state governments set increasingly tight restrictions on abortion, ranging from "informed consent" laws that required a waiting period before women could obtain abortion surgery, to parental consent laws for underage women, to outright bans on abortion unless the woman's life was in danger. In 1991, the Supreme Court further limited abortion rights by ruling that federally funded family planning clinics could be barred from providing information on abortion. The antiabortion movement also escalated and hardened its tactics in the late 1980s and 1990s: it bombed abortion clinics, picketed doctors who performed abortions, and attempted to dissuade women entering clinics from having abortions (Staggenborg 1991; Simonds 1996).

Further, women's studies programs in colleges and universities, which had been established in the 1970s in response to feminist agitation, came under attack by conservatives in the late 1980s and early 1990s. A backlash against "multiculturalism" and "political correctness" in academia sought to restore the traditional academic focus on the "great thinkers" of Western European history and thus to maintain the primacy of white male perspectives and experiences. Joining the attack, feminists such as Camille Paglia, Katie Roiphe, and Elizabeth Fox-Genovese drew media attention by holding radical and lesbian feminists responsible for alienating mainstream women and men from the women's movement.

The women's movement suffered not only from such attacks but also from its apparent success. Overt opposition to the feminist movement had been muted in the mid- to late 1970s. Elites in politics, education, and industry gave the appearance of supporting feminist aims through affirmative action programs and the appointment of a few token women to high positions in their respective areas. Meanwhile, the popular image of feminism advanced by the mass media suggested that the women's movement had won its goals. Despite the real-life difficulties women encountered trying to balance paid employment and a "second shift" of housework and child care (Hochschild 1989), the image of the working woman became the feminine ideal. The public discourse implied that since women had already achieved equality with men, they no longer needed a protest movement. Women who continued to press for gender equality were described increasingly in negative terms, as lesbians, man-haters, and, in the words of right-wing talk show host Rush Limbaugh, "feminazis."

But the women's movement did not die. Rather, it went into abeyance in order to survive in a hostile political climate. Movements in abeyance are in a holding pattern, during which activists from an earlier period maintain the ideology and structural base of the movement but few new recruits join (Taylor 1989). A movement in abeyance is primarily oriented toward maintaining itself rather than confronting the established order directly. Focusing on building an alternative culture, for example, is a means of surviving when external resources are not available and the political structure is not amenable to challenge. The structure and strategies of the women's movement have changed, then, as mass mobilization has declined and opposition to feminism has swelled. Nevertheless, feminist resistance continues—just in different forms.

Multiple Strategies and the Challenge to Gender

Gender resistance, challenge, and change can occur at three levels: the individual level of consciousness and interactions, the social structural level, and the cultural level (Collins 1990). This conceptualization of feminist activism allows us to recognize that movements adopt many strategies and to acknowledge the important role of women's movements in the reconstruction of gender.

Resisting Gender Practices　At the level of consciousness and social interactions, individual women can and do resist norms and expectations of the dominant gender system (Thorne 1994, 1995). It is, however, social movements or collectives, rather than isolated individuals, who perform the critical role of refashioning the gender code and calling institutions to account for gender inequality (Huber 1976; Chafetz 1990; Connell 1987). One of the primary goals of the modern feminist movement has been to change the unequal power relations between women and men. A general strategy used by feminists to achieve this goal has been

to resist and challenge sexist practices within a diverse set of social contexts, ranging from heterosexual marriage to the gender division of labor in rearing and nurturing children to the gendered workplace and male-dominated medical establishment.

The formation of consciousness-raising groups facilitated the process of resisting and challenging gender practices and politicizing everyday life. Because consciousness-raising enables women to view the "personal as political," for most women it is an identity-altering experience. Becoming a feminist can transform a woman's entire self-concept and way of life: her biography, appearance, beliefs, behavior, and relationships (Cassell 1977; Esterberg 1997). As women's consciousness changes through personalized political strategies, women individually and collectively defy traditionally feminine role expectations for women and, in so doing, reconstruct the meanings of women, femininity, and interpersonal relationships between women and men. For example, some breast cancer activists have chosen to resist societal conceptions of femininity that link women's sexuality to breast beauty by refusing to wear prostheses or displaying mastectomy scars following breast surgery.

Women active in the feminist movement of the 1960s and 1970s continued to shape their lives in the 1980s and 1990s around their feminist beliefs, even when they were not involved in organized feminist activity. They continued to choose leisure activities, significant relationships, dress, and presentation of self consistent with feminist ideology (Whittier 1995). Many held jobs in government, social service organizations, or women's studies departments and other academic programs that allowed them to incorporate their political goals into their work. Even the consciousness and lives of women who did not identify as feminist have been altered by the women's movement. In a study of gender and family life in the Silicon Valley of California, Judith Stacey (1987) found that in the 1980s some women incorporated portions of feminism into traditional family and work structures by combining a feminist emphasis on developing satisfying careers, sharing household work with husbands, and increasing men's emotional expressiveness with fundamentalist Christianity and its focus on the importance of the family. Such women critiqued men's absence from families and lack of emotional expression, reflecting both feminism and traditional religion. The effects of the women's movement stretch far beyond policies and practices that are explicitly labeled feminist.

Another example of women resisting gender practices at the interactional level is found among young African-American women involved in little sister fraternity programs on college campuses in the 1990s. Such women embrace a collective identity built on notions of sisterhood and womanly strength to challenge the sexist practices of fraternities (Stombler and Padavic 1997). Further, these women use the fraternity little sister program to satisfy their own agendas of community service and self-enhancement. Even within the most traditional male-dominated organizations, then, gender relations are not immutable and women are employing diverse strategies to resist gender inequality.

Challenging the Structure of Gender Inequality   The challenge to gender inequality and the dominant gender order is also waged at the social structural level. As we have seen, the liberal bureaucratic strand of the modern feminist movement has employed legal reform strategies and engaged in street protests to counter sex discrimination in the economic, education, political, and domestic spheres. The legislative campaigns for equal pay for work of comparable worth and for maternity leave policies in the workplace challenge institutions that essentialize differences between women and men and rank "masculine" values and attributes above those identified as "feminine" (Vogel 1993). The women's movement has created a feminist policy network of elected officials, lobbying organizations, social movement organizations, and individuals who have mobilized to address issues ranging from abortion rights, domestic violence, and pregnancy discrimination to day care, sexual harassment, and welfare rights (Ferree and Hess 1994; Staggenborg 1996; Gagné 1998).

As part of its legislative or legal strategies, the modern feminist movement has engaged in street protests such as picketing, mass demonstrations, and civil disobedience. Even within the conservative political climate of the 1980s, the feminist movement sparked some of the largest feminist demonstrations and actions in years. In April 1989, The National Organization for Women and abortion rights groups organized a national demonstration in Washington, DC, that drew between 300,000 and 600,000 women and men to protest restrictions on abortion. Additional national and local demonstrations followed. Prochoice activists organized electoral lobbying, defended abortion clinics, held conferences, and attempted to form coalitions across racial and ethnic lines and among women of different ages (Staggenborg 1991; Ryan 1992). The National Abortion Rights Action League experienced a growth in membership from 200,000 in 1989 to 400,000 in 1990 (Staggenborg 1991:138). NOW also continued to grow in the late 1980s

and 1990s. After a decline in the early 1980s, it reached a membership of 250,000 in 1989 and maintained that membership level throughout the 1990s.

A wide variety of feminist organizations continued to pursue social change at state and local levels in the late 1990s (Ferree and Martin 1995). The Lesbian Avengers, a direct-action group founded in the 1990s with affiliates in several large cities, uses dramatic street theater to focus on issues of sexism and homophobia. For example, outside a police station in Delaware, Lesbian Avengers protested the police department's lack of action to catch a serial rapist by drawing chalk outlines of bodies on the sidewalk to represent women who had been raped during the past year. Veteran feminist organizations, such as NOW, continued to hold public protests in the late 1990s. For instance, in 1999, NOW chapters across the country staged pickets outside Wal-Mart retail stores to protest the corporation's refusal to sell the emergency contraception kit PREVEN to those who wish to prevent unintended pregnancies.

Beyond street politics, feminist activism in the 1980s and 1990s moved into diverse institutional settings. As an indication of the success and influence of feminist mobilization in earlier years, women found niches from which to challenge and transform institutional policies and structures, from pay equity to sexual harassment to occupational sex segregation (Blum 1991). Women in the military, for example, have formed pressure groups such as Women Military Aviators, who fought for the opening up of combat aviation positions for women. In the Catholic Church, radical religious orders have become protected spaces for women who challenge hierarchy within the institutional church (Katzenstein 1998). In major corporations, feminists have joined with gay activists to campaign successfully for domestic partnership benefits for lesbian and gay employees. Such unobtrusive mobilization within institutional boundaries refutes the notion of the death of feminism (Katzenstein 1997). Although the form and location of feminist protest have changed, this does not mean the women's movement has been deradicalized. The transformative potential of feminist activism within institutional settings may in some contexts be greater than that of pressure from outside.

Reconstructing the Culture of Gender   At the cultural level, the feminist social movement community has challenged cultural values, beliefs, and norms around gender and the gender order through building alternative social and cultural institutions for women outside mainstream institutions. The strategy of creating autonomous institutions is rooted in radical feminist ideology, which emphasizes that women need to have places and events away from patriarchal society where they can develop strength and pride as women. Since the early years of the women's movement, an extensive network of institutions has emerged within which a feminist culture flourishes (Taylor and Whittier 1992). Feminist communities contribute to the reconstruction of the culture of gender by challenging the devaluation of the feminine and undermining androcentric values and beliefs at the same time that they rearticulate alternative femininities and woman-centered values and beliefs (Taylor and Rupp 1993).

Into the new century, the feminist cultural community has continued to thrive with events such as an "annual multicultural multiracial conference on aging" for lesbians (*Off Our Backs* 1991:12), feminist cruises, annual women's music festivals, and women's comedy festivals in different parts of the country (Staggenborg 1998b). Gatherings and conferences include groups such as Jewish lesbian daughters of holocaust survivors, women motorcyclists, fat dykes, pagans, Asian lesbians, practitioners of herbal medicine, and survivors of incest. Newsletters and publications exist for a multitude of groups, among them women recovering from addictions, women's music professionals and fans, lesbian separatists, disabled lesbians, lesbian mothers, feminists interested in sadomasochism, and feminists opposed to pornography.

The growth of the feminist community underscores the flowering of lesbian feminism in the late 1980s and 1990s (Esterberg 1997; Stein 1997). A wide variety of lesbian and lesbian feminist books and anthologies have been published on topics ranging from lesbian feminist ethics to separatism to sexuality to lesbian parenthood to commitment ceremonies for lesbian couples (see, for example, Hoagland 1988; Hoagland and Penelope 1988; Loulan 1990; Butler 1991), reflecting diverse perspectives that have been hotly debated in the pages of lesbian publications and at conferences and festivals. For example, a series of letters to the editor in a national lesbian newsletter during 1991 argued about the correct lesbian feminist response to lesbians serving in the armed forces in the Persian Gulf War: some readers held that the war was a manifestation of patriarchy and that lesbians in the military should be criticized; others argued that lesbian soldiers should be supported because they are lesbians in a homophobic institution, regardless of one's support of or opposition to the war; still others argued that the Gulf War was justified and that lesbian servicewomen should be celebrated for their patriotic service (*Lesbian Connection* 1991). Clearly, the task of building a community based on the identity "lesbian" has proven complex, if not impossible. Nevertheless, the institutional structure of the social movement community has continued to expand, and within the community feminists construct and reinforce a collective identity based on opposition to dominant conceptions of women and lesbians (Taylor and Whittier 1992).

Another example of resistance on the cultural level is the emergence of women's self-help groups, which sprang directly out of the early women's health movement and continue to model support groups on feminist consciousness-raising (Rapping 1996; Simonds 1996). Some feminist writers contend that women's self-help diverts the feminist agenda away from social and political change and directs women, instead, to change themselves (Kaminer 1992). Others argue that explicitly feminist self-help movements, such as strands of the postpartum depression and breast cancer movements, are contributing to the reconstruction of gender through the collective redefinition of womanhood and the cultural articulation of alternative femininities (Taylor 1996; Taylor and Van Willigen 1996; Klawiter 1999). These self-help movements are not depoliticized and purely individually focused; they perform a critical role of challenging institutional gender biases and refashioning the dominant gender code (Taylor 1996; Taylor 1999).

All of these diverse strategies, operating at different levels, challenge traditional societal definitions of femininity and masculinity and the dominant gender order. From the individual to the social structural to the cultural plane, we can see the continuous impact of the women's movement.

Movement Continuity and Change into the Twenty-first Century

Social movement scholars understand that social movements affect one another. The abolitionist movement in the mid-nineteenth century influenced the first wave of the women's movement in the United States, and the civil rights and New Left movements of the 1960s shaped the course of the second wave (Buechler 1990). In turn, the women's movement has had a substantial impact on other social movements. Meyer and Whittier (1994) argue that "the ideas, tactics, style, participants, and organizations of one movement often *spill over* its boundaries to affect other social movements" (277, emphasis in the original). The gay and lesbian movement, transgender, AIDS, recovery from addictions, New Age, and animal-rights movements have been profoundly influenced by feminist values and ideology, including the emphasis on collective structure and consensus, the notion of the personal as political, and the critique of patriarchy extended to the mistreatment of animals and ecological resources (Jasper and Poulsen 1995; Einwohner 1999).

The women's movement also trained a large number of feminist activists in the 1970s (particularly lesbians), who have participated in new social movements and integrated feminism into them (Cavin 1990; Whittier 1995). The gay and lesbian movement, for example, has expanded its health concerns to include breast cancer as well as AIDS and has used strategies of the feminist antirape movement to confront violence against gays and lesbians. In addition, feminists have renewed coalitions with the peace, environmental, socialist, anti-US intervention in Latin America, and antiapartheid movements, transforming these movements both by creating separate feminist organizations that address these issues and by moving into mixed-sex organizations (Whittier 1995). In a sense the women's movement has come full circle, rejoining the 1990s versions of the movements that composed the New Left in the 1960s, when many feminists split off to form a separate autonomous women's movement.

Although the women's movement has changed form and location, the level of mass mobilization and confrontation of the social structural system has clearly declined since the 1980s. Because feminism came to focus more on consciousness and culture and established roots in other social movements of the period, feminist protest is less visible than it was during the heyday of the women's movement. According to some studies (Schneider 1988; Dill unpublished), despite support for feminist goals, many young women do not identify themselves as feminists, apparently because the term is stigmatized. A feminist is seen as someone who deviates from gender norms by being unattractive, aggressive, hostile to men, unfeminine, opposed to marriage and motherhood, and lesbian. Despite the gain made by women in some areas, gender norms are still so rigid and deeply internalized that they successfully deter many women who support the feminist agenda from participating in the movement.

Yet some younger women have joined the women's movement despite the risks entailed in identifying with a stigmatized and unpopular cause. A new generation of women has been recruited to feminism primarily through women's studies courses and through the transmission of feminism from mothers to daughters. The institutionalized gains of the heyday of feminist activism in the 1970s are enabling the women's movement to survive and to disseminate its ideas to new recruits. What direction the self-proclaimed "third-wave" feminists (Kamen 1991; Walker 1992, 1995) will take is not at all clear, but the history of the women's movement suggests that a new constituency will revise feminist ideology, renovate existing structures, respond to a changing political climate, and further develop feminist strategies.

ANTIFEMINIST COUNTERMOVEMENTS

The emergence of organized opposition is one indication of the successes of feminist movements. In general, it is when social movements pose a serious threat to the status quo that countermovements appear (Chafetz and Dworkin 1987). Antifeminist resistance movements mobilized in response to first- and second-wave feminist movements in the United States when feminists began to gain political legitimacy and influence. For example, as the first wave of the women's movement was building support for suffrage in the late nineteenth century, an organized antisuffrage movement began to coalesce (Marshall 1997). Likewise, when the feminist movement of the 1970s was gaining political ground on the ratification of the Equal Rights Amendment, an anti-ERA movement blossomed (Marshall 1984).

Antifeminist countermovements, like feminist movements, are not monolithic. They vary over time and place by ideology, strategy, and organization (Marshall 1985; Buechler 1990; Blee 1991). Chafetz and Dworkin (1987) contend that antifeminist countermovements are composed of two constituencies: vested-interest groups, which are typically male-dominated and oppose feminist change movements on the basis of class interests; and voluntary grassroots associations made up of women who are reacting to the threat to their status as privileged traditional women.

Compared to the scholarship on movements, countermovements have been understudied and undertheorized (Meyer and Staggenborg 1996). Research on organized opposition to feminism by women is also limited (Klatch 1990; Marshall 1997). Women's participation in antifeminist countermovements challenges the radical feminist notion that women are a "sex class" with clearly defined gender interests (Luker 1984; Blee 1991). Scholars often characterize antifeminist women as victims of false consciousness or as women who are passively expressing their husbands' interests. Marshall (1997) argues that these are overly simplistic interpretations and that an appreciation for the ways in which antisuffragist leaders used their wealth, social networks, and political power to build an oppositional identity in the antisuffrage movement suggests "a conceptual shift of the locus of conflict over suffrage from culture to politics" (p. 13). In this light, antifeminist women should be viewed as political actors who take up gendered class interests independent of their husbands (Marshall 1997).

The interaction between opposing movements is a prominent feature of contemporary US society. Any social movement analysis is incomplete without a consideration of the interdependence of movements and countermovements. For example, we cannot fully understand the tactics, strategies, organizational forms, and feminist identities characteristic of the feminist movement during the 1980s and 1990s without considering the effects of the antiabortion mobilization and the rise of the New Right.

The modern women's movement in the United States has been opposed by a variety of conservative antifeminist groups. In the early 1970s, the Stop ERA campaign initiated by Phyllis Schlafly fought to block passage of the ERA by state legislatures. Through the 1970s, the New Right grew larger and more influential, linking conservative issues like opposition to busing, abortion, gay rights, the ERA, and governmental regulation of business through affirmative action and health and safety programs (Klatch 1990). With the election of Ronald Reagan to the presidency in 1980, the New Right gained state support for its agenda.

The antifeminist movement in the late 1980s and 1990s spent considerable energy opposing abortion, and its successes in that area have been impressive in terms of judicial and legislative gains and disruptive demonstrations at abortion clinics (Staggenborg 1991; Simonds 1996). Over the years a number of aggressive splinter groups, such as Operation Rescue, developed out of the mainstream National Right to Life Committee, which originated within the Catholic Church. The murders of Drs. David Gunn in Pensacola, Florida, and Barnett Slepian in Buffalo, New York, are potent examples of the radical tactics advocated by some antiabortion rights groups.

The prevalence of antifeminist resistance throughout history highlights the significance of the family, sexuality, and reproduction for the maintenance of the dominant social order. The growth of antifeminism, however, does not imply that the women's movement has failed or run its course. On the contrary, it attests to feminism's successful challenge to the status quo.

CONCLUSION

The history of the women's movement, and its present survival despite the challenges it has confronted from within its own ranks and from a conservative political climate, suggest that because feminism is a response to the fundamental social cleavage of gender it will continue to exist (Taylor and Rupp 1993). As one generation of feminists fades from the scene with its ultimate goals unrealized, another takes up the challenge (Rossi 1982).

But each new generation of feminists does not simply carry on where the previous generation left off. Rather, it speaks for itself and defines its own objectives and strategies, often to the dismay and disapproval of feminists from earlier generations. A new generation of feminists may organize a "warm line" for women suffering postpartum depression (Taylor 1996), or construct a public clothesline of T-shirts representing the victims of domestic violence to raise awareness of violence against women, or march together in a Take Back the Night event to empower survivors of sexual violence and reclaim the streets for women. They may put on "drag king" performances to challenge the restrictions placed on expressions of women's sexuality, or distribute condoms and dental dams to women for AIDS prevention, or organize "kiss-ins" with Queer Nation. While earlier generations of activists may not view such endeavors as feminist, as Myra Ferree and Beth Hess (1985:182) point out, "feminism is not simply a form of received wisdom" but something that evolves with each new cycle of feminist activism. Just as the women's movement of the twentieth century has endured and persisted through transformation, feminism of the twenty-first century will be characterized by continuity and change.

REFERENCES

Atkinson, T. G. (1974). *Amazon Odyssey.* New York: Links.

Balser, Diane. (1987). *Sisterhood and Solidarity: Feminism and Labor in Modern Times.* Boston: South End Press.

Barnett, Bernice McNair. (1993). Invisible southern black women leaders in the civil rights movement: The triple constraints of gender, race, and class. *Gender & Society,* 7, 162–182.

Basu, Amrita, ed. (1995). *The Challenge of Local Feminisms: Women's Movements in Global Perspective.* Boulder, CO: Westview Press.

Beauvoir, S. de. (1952). *The Second Sex.* New York: Bantam.

Beck, E. T. (1980). *Nice Jewish girls: A Lesbian Anthology.* Watertown, MA: Persephone.

Black, Naomi. (1989). *Social Feminism.* Ithaca, NY: Cornell University Press.

Blee, Kathleen M. (1991). *Women of the Klan: Racism and Gender in the 1920s.* Berkeley, CA: University of California Press.

Blum, Linda M. (1991). *Between Feminism and Labor: The Significance of the Comparable Worth Movement.* Berkeley, CA: University of California Press.

Breines, W. (1982). *Community and Organization in the New Left, 1962–68.* New York: Praeger.

Buechler, Steven M. (1990). *Women's Movements in the United States.* New Brunswick, NJ: Rutgers.

Bulkin, Elly, Minnie Bruce Pratt, & Barbara Smith. (1984). *Yours in Struggle: Three Feminist Perspectives on Anti-Semitism and Racism.* New York: Long Haul Press.

Butler, Becky. (1991). *Ceremonies of the Heart: Celebrating Lesbian Unions.* Seattle, WA: The Seal Press.

Carden, Maren. (1978). The proliferation of a social movement. In Louis Kriesberg, ed., *Research in Social Movements, Conflict, and Change,* vol. 1 (pp. 179–196). Greenwich, CT: JAI Press.

Cassell, J. (1977). *A Group Called Women: Sisterhood and Symbolism in the Feminist Movement.* New York: David McKay.

Cavin, Susan. (1990). The invisible army of women: Lesbian social protests, 1969–88. In Guida West & Rhoda Blumberg, eds. *Women and Social Protest* (pp. 321–332). New York: Oxford University Press.

Chafe, W. H. (1977). *Women and Equality: Changing Patterns in American Culture.* New York: Oxford University Press.

Chafetz, Janet. (1990). *Gender Equity: An Integrated Theory of Stability and Change.* Newbury Park, CA: Sage.

Chafetz, Janet, & Gary Dworkin. (1986). *Female Revolt.* Totowa, NJ: Rowman and Allenheld.

———. (1987). In the face of threat: Organized antifeminism in comparative perspective. *Gender & Society, 1,* 33–60.

Collins, Patricia Hill. (1990). *Black Feminist Thought.* New York: Routledge.

Connell, R. W. (1987). *Gender and Power.* Stanford, CA: Stanford University Press.

Cott, Nancy. (1987). *The Grounding of Modern Feminism.* New Haven, CT: Yale University Press.

Daly, Mary. (1978). *Gyn/ecology,* Boston: Beacon.

Deckard, Barbara Sinclair. (1983). *The Women's Movement.* New York: Harper and Row.

Dill, Kim. Unpublished. "Feminism in the nineties: The influence of collective identity and community on young feminist activists." Master's thesis, The Ohio State University, 1991.

Echols, Alice. (1989). *Daring to Be Bad: Radical Feminism in America 1967–1975.* Minneapolis: University of Minnesota Press.

Einwohner, Rachel L. (1999). Gender, class, and social movement outcomes: Identity and effectiveness in two animal rights campaigns. *Gender & Society, 13,* 56–76.

Eisenstein, Z. (1981). *The Radical Future of Liberal Feminism.* New York: Longman.

Esterberg, Kristin G. (1997). *Lesbian and Bisexual Identities: Constructing Communities, Constructing Selves.* Philadelphia: Temple University Press.

Evans, Sarah. (1979). *Personal Politics.* New York: Knopf.

Ferree, Myra Marx, & Beth B. Hess. [1985] (1994). *Controversy and Coalition: The New Feminist Movement.* Boston: Twayne.

Ferree, Myra Marx, & Patricia Yancey Martin. (1995). *Feminist Organizations: Harvest of the New Women's Movement.* Philadelphia: Temple University Press.

Firestone, S. (1970). *The Dialectic of Sex.* New York: William Morrow.

Fonow, Mary Margaret. (1998). Protest engendered: The participation of women steelworkers in the Wheeling-Pittsburgh steel strike of 1985. *Gender & Society,* 12, 710–728.

Freeman, Jo. (1972/3). The tyranny of structurelessness. *Berkeley Journal of Sociology,* 17, 151–164.

———. (1975). *The Politics of Women's Liberation.* New York: David McKay.

———. (1979). Resource mobilization and strategy: A model for analyzing social movement organization actions. In M. N. Zald & J. D. McCarthy, eds. *The Dynamics of Social Movements* (pp. 167–89). Cambridge, MA: Winthrop.

Frye, Marilyn. (1983). *The Politics of Reality: Essays in Feminist Theory.* Trumansburg, NY: Crossing Press.

Gagné, Patricia. (1998). *Battered Women's Justice: The Movement for Democracy and the Politics of Self-defense.* New York: Twayne Publishers.

Gerlach, L. P., & V. H. Hine. (1970). *People, Power, Change: Movements of Social Transformation.* Indianapolis: Bobbs-Merrill.

Giele, Janet Zollinger. (1995). *Two Paths to Women's Equality: Temperance, Suffrage, and the Origins of Modern Feminism.* New York: Twayne Publishers.

Gordon, Suzanne. (1991). *Prisoners of Men's Dreams.* New York: Little, Brown.

Griffin, S. (1978). *Women and Nature.* New York: Harper & Row.

Hartmann, Heidi. (1981). The family as the locus of gender, class, and political struggle: The example of housework. *Signs,* 6, 366–94.

Hartsock, Nancy. (1983). *Money, Sex, and Power: Toward a Feminist Historical Materialism.* New York: Longman.

Hoagland, Sarah Lucia. (1988). *Lesbian Ethics: Toward New Value.* Palo Alto, CA: Institute of Lesbian Studies.

Hoagland, Sarah Lucia, & Julia Penelope, eds. (1988). *For Lesbians Only.* London: Onlywomen Press.

Hochschild, Arlie. (1989). *The Second Shift.* New York: Avon.

Huber, Joan. (1973). From sugar and spice to professor. In A. S. Rossi & A. Calderwood, *Academic Women on the Move.* New York: Russell Sage Foundation.

———. (1976). Toward a sociotechnological theory of the women's movement. *Social Problems,* 23, 371–388.

Huber, Joan, & Glenna Spitze. (1983). *Sex Stratification: Children, Housework, and Jobs.* New York: Academic.

Jasper, James M., & Jane D. Poulsen. (1995). Recruiting strangers and friends: Moral shocks and social networks in animal rights and anti-nuclear protests. *Social Problems, 42,* 493–512.

Jayawardena, Kumari. (1986). *Feminism and Nationalism in the Third World.* London: Zed Books.

Kamen, Paula. (1991). *Feminist Fatale: Voices from the "Twenty-something" Generation Explore the Future of the Women's Movement.* New York: Donald I. Fine.

Kaminer, Wendy. (1992). *I'm Dysfunctional, You're Dysfunctional: The Recovery Movement and other Self-help Fashions.* Reading, MA: Addison-Wesley.

Katzenstein, Mary Fainsod. (1997). Stepsisters: Feminist movement activism in different institutional spaces. In David Meyer & Sidney Tarrow, eds. *A Movement Society? Contentious Politics for a New Century.* Boulder, CO: Rowland and Littlefield.

———. (1998). *Faithful and Fearless: Moving Feminist Protest inside the Church and Military.* Princeton, NJ: Princeton University Press.

Katzenstein, Mary Fainsod, & Carol McClurg Mueller. (1987). *The Women's Movements of the United States and Western Europe.* Philadelphia: Temple University Press.

Klatch, Rebecca. (1990). The two worlds of women of the new right. In Louise A. Tilly & Patricia Gurin, Eds. *Women, Politics and Change.* New York: Russell Sage Foundation.

Klawiter, Maren. (1999). Racing for the Cure, walking women, and toxic touring: Mapping cultures of action within the Bay Area terrain of breast cancer. *Social Problems, 46,* 104–126.

Klein, Ethel. (1984). *Gender Politics.* Cambridge, MA: Harvard University Press.

Leidner, Robin. (1993). Constituency, accountability, and deliberation: Reshaping democracy in the National Women's Studies Association. *NWSA Journal, 5,* 4–27.

Lesbian Connection (1991). Vols. 13 & 14. Lansing, MI: Ambitious Amazons.

Loulan, JoAnn. (1990). *The Lesbian Erotic Dance.* San Francisco: Spinsters Book Company.

Luker, Kristin. (1984). *Abortion and the Politics of Motherhood.* Berkeley: University of California Press.

MacKinnon, C. A. (1983). Feminism, Marxism, method, and the state: Toward feminist jurisprudence. *Signs, 8,* 635–68.

Mansbridge, Jane. (1986). *Why We Lost the ERA.* Chicago: University of Chicago Press.

Marshall, Susan E. (1984). Keep us on the pedestal: Women against feminism in twentieth-century America. In Jo Freeman, Ed., *Women: A Feminist Perspective* (pp. 568–581). Palo Alto: Mayfield.

———. (1985). Ladies against women: Mobilization dilemmas of antifeminist movements. *Social Problems, 32,* 348–362.

———. (1997). *Splintered Sisterhood: Gender and Class in the Campaign against Woman Suffrage.* Madison, WI: The University of Wisconsin Press.

Martin, Patricia Yancey. (1990). Rethinking feminist organizations. *Gender & Society, 4,* 182–206.

Marx, G. T., & J. L. Wood. (1975). Strands of theory and research in collective behavior. *Annual Review of Sociology, 1,* 363–428.

Matthews, Nancy. (1994). *Confronting Rape: The Feminist Anti-rape Movement and the State.* London: Routledge.

Matthews, Donald G., & Jane Sheffon DeHart. (1990). *Sex, Gender and the Politics of ERA: A State and the Nation.* New York: Oxford.

McCarthy, J. D., & M. N. Zald. (1977). Resource mobilization and social movements: A partial theory. *American Journal of Sociology, 82,* 1212–1239.

Meyer, David S., & Nancy Whittier. (1994). Social movement spillover. *Social Problems, 41,* 277–298.

Meyer, David S., & Suzanne Staggenborg. (1996). Movements, countermovements, and the structure of political opportunity. *American Journal of Sociology, 101,* 1628–1660.

Miles, Angela. (1996). *Integrative Feminisms: Building Global Visions, 1960s–1990s.* New York: Routledge.

Millett, K. (1971). *Sexual Politics.* New York: Avon.

Mitchell, Juliet. (1986). Reflections on twenty years of feminism. In Juliet Mitchell & Ann Oakley, eds. *What Is Feminism?* (pp. 34–48). Oxford: Basil Blackwell.

Mohanty, Chandra Talpade, Ann Russo, & Lordes Torres, eds. (1991). *Third World Women and the Politics of Feminism.* Bloomington, IN: Indiana University Press.

Moraga, Cherríe & Gloria Anzaldúa. (1981). *This Bridge Called My Back: Writings by Radical Women of Color.* Watertown, MA: Persephone.

Morris, Aldon D., & Carol McClurg Mueller, eds. (1992). *Frontiers in Social Movement Theory.* New Haven, CT: Yale University Press.

Naples, Nancy A. (1992). Activist mothering: Cross-generational continuity in the community work of women from low-income neighborhoods. *Gender & Society, 6,* 441–463.

Off Our Backs (1991). Passages 7—Beyond the barriers. Vol. 21 (6), 12.

Offen, Karen. (1988). Defining feminism: A comparative historical approach. *Signs, 14,* 119–157.

Oppenheimer, Valerie Kincade. (1973). Demographic influence on female employment and the status of women. In Joan Huber, Ed. *Changing Women in a Changing Society* (pp. 184–199). Chicago: University of Chicago Press.

Rapping, Elayne. (1996). *The Culture of Recovery: Making Sense of the Recovery Movement in Women's Lives.* Boston: Beacon Press.

Ray, Raka. (1999). *Fields of Protest: Women's Movements in India.* Minneapolis: University of Minnesota Press.

Rich, Adrienne. (1976). *Of Woman Born.* New York: Norton.

———. (1980). Compulsory heterosexuality and lesbian existence. *Signs, 5,* 631–660.

Robnett, Belinda. (1996). African-American women in the civil rights movement, 1954–1965: Gender, leadership, and micro-mobilization. *American Journal of Sociology, 101,* 1661–1693.

Rossi, Alice S. (1982). *Feminist in Politics: A Panel Analysis of the First National Women's Conference.* New York: Academic Press.

Rothschild-Whitt, Joyce. (1979). The collectivist organization: An alternative to rational-bureaucratic models. *American Sociological Review,* 44, 509–527.

Rubin, G. (1975). "Traffic in women: Notes on the 'political economy' of sex." In *Toward an Anthropology of Women,* Rayne Reiter, ed. New York: Monthly Review Press.

Rupp, Leila J. (1997). *Worlds of Women: The Making of an International Women's Movement.* Princeton, NJ: Princeton University Press.

Rupp, Leila J., & Verta Taylor. (1987). *Survival in the Doldrums: The American Women's Rights Movement, 1945 to 1960s.* New York: Oxford University Press.

Ryan, Barbara. (1989). Ideological purity and feminism: The U.S. women's movement from 1966 to 1975. *Gender & Society,* 3, 239–257.

———. (1992). *Feminism and the Women's Movement.* New York: Routledge.

Sapiro, V. (1991). In Janet Boles, ed. *The Annals of the American Academy of Political and Social Science,* May, 515.

Schlesinger, M. B., & P. Bart. (1983). Collective work and self-identity: The effect of working in a feminist illegal abortion collective. In L. Richardson & V. Taylor, eds. *Feminist Frontiers.* Reading, MA: Addison-Wesley.

Schneider, Beth. (1988). Political generations in the contemporary women's movement. *Sociological Inquiry,* 58, 4–21.

Simonds, Wendy. (1996). *Abortion at Work: Ideology and Practice in a Feminist Clinic.* New Brunswick, NJ: Rutgers University Press.

Spelman, Elizabeth. (1988). *Inessential Woman: Problems of Exclusion in Feminist Thought.* Boston: Beacon Press.

Stacey, Judith. (1987). Sexism by a subtler name? Postindustrial conditions and postfeminist consciousness. *Socialist Review,* 17, 7–28.

Staggenborg, Suzanne. (1988). The consequences of professionalization and formalization in the pro-choice movement. *American Sociological Review, 53,* 585–606.

———. (1989). Stability and innovation in the women's movement: A comparison of two movement organizations. *Social Problems, 36,* 75–92.

———. (1991). *The Pro-choice Movement.* New York: Oxford University Press.

———. (1996). The survival of the women's movement: Turnover and continuity in Bloomington, Indiana. *Mobilization, 1,* 143–158.

———. (1998a). *Gender, Family, and Social Movements.* Thousand Oaks, CA: Pine Forge Press.

———. (1998b). Social movement communities and cycles of protest: The emergence and maintenance of a local women's movement. *Social Problems, 45,* 180–204.

Stein, Arlene. (1997). *Sex and Sensibility: Stories of a Lesbian Generation.* Berkeley, CA: University of California Press.

Stombler, Mindy, & Irene Padavic. (1997). Sister acts: Resisting men's domination in black and white fraternity little sister programs. *Social Problems, 44,* 257–275.

Taylor, Verta. (1989). Social movement continuity: The women's movement in abeyance. *American Sociological Review, 54,* 761–775.

———. (1996). *Rock-a-by Baby: Feminism, Self-help, and Postpartum Depression.* New York: Routledge.

———. (1999). Gender and social movements: Gender processes and women's self-help movements. *Gender & Society, 13,* 8–33.

Taylor, Verta, & Leila Rupp. (1993). Women's culture and lesbian feminist activism: A reconsideration of cultural feminism. *Signs, 19,* 32–61.

Taylor, Verta, & Marieke Van Willigen. (1996). Women's self-help and the reconstruction of gender: The postpartum support and breast cancer movements. *Mobilization: An International Journal, 2,* 123–142.

Taylor, Verta, & Nancy Whittier. (1992). Collective identity in social movement communities: Lesbian feminist mobilization. In Aldon Morris & Carol Mueller, eds. *Frontiers of Social Movement Theory.* New Haven, CT: Yale University Press.

Thorne, Barrie. (1994). *Gender Play: Girls and Boys in School.* New Brunswick, NJ: Rutgers University Press.

———. (1995). Symposium on West and Fenstermaker's 'Doing Difference.' *Gender & Society, 9,* 498–499.

Vogel, Lise. (1993). *Mothers on the Job: Maternity Policy in the U.S. Workplace.* New Brunswick, NJ: Rutgers University Press.

Walker, Rebecca. (1992). Becoming the third wave. *Ms., 2* (January/February), 39–41.

———. (1995). *To Be Real: Telling the Truth and Changing the Face of Feminism.* New York: Anchor.

White, Aaronette M. (1999). Talking feminist, talking back: Micromobilization processes in a collective protest against rape. *Gender & Society, 13,* 77–100.

Whittier, Nancy E. (1995). *Feminist Generations: The Persistence of the Radical Women's Movement.* Philadelphia: Temple University Press.

LINKING ARMS AND MOVEMENTS

URVASHI VAID

More than 800 lesbians, bisexual women, transgendered women, queer women, and supportive straight women (and a handful of men) gathered at the Lesbian Rights Summit of the National Organization for Women April 23–25 [1999] in Washington, DC. The same weekend a contingent of more than 300 progressive queers of all colors marched on Philadelphia as part of the rally demanding freedom for Mumia Abu-Jamal, the black radical writer and activist many of us believe is falsely accused of murdering a police officer.

A tale of two lesbian movements could be written in the parallel trajectories of these two events. It would be easy, for example, to characterize the NOW meeting as the gathering of the white lesbian-feminist movement—but that would negate the participation and leadership of strong women of color. And it would be equally easy to dismiss the Mumia mobilization as the Left's issue du jour—but such a characterization would continue the false negation of the critical leadership role that lesbians of color and radical gay men have long played in the Left. It is the links between feminism and queerness that interest me in both of these gatherings.

Lesbian-feminist politics are across the board more multi-issue and progressive than mainstream gay, lesbian, bisexual, and transgender organizing. Dykes and queer girls see the connections and try to organize from the intersection of politics rather than from a single identity. Lesbian-feminist political theory owes much to lesbians of color and to radical women of all colors. The women at the NOW gathering are in many ways the offspring of this progressive tradition among lesbians. There were students, labor activists, mainstream political campaign workers, veteran dykes, and cultural lesbian feminists.

Many of the organizers and supporters of the queer contingent at the Mumia rally represent a who's who of a radical lesbian-feminist movement. Veteran activist and writer Barbara Smith gave a keynote speech noting that queer progressives had always been present inside people-of-color movements.

Lesbian feminism and queer progressive organizing share several points of connection. Both movements share the truth that economic and technological changes help shape our lives and influence public policy choices about the regulation of sexuality. Economic-based decisions shape policy about sex and birth control today. The welfare reform bill passed by Congress and endorsed by the administration contains population control measures such as efforts to reduce the "out of wedlock" birthrate and to promote heterosexual relationships and two-parent families. These measures are designed to control the sexual lives of poor or low-income women. For our queer movement's struggle to create families, those measures are especially dangerous.

There are at least four other links that bind a progressive movement for gay, lesbian, bisexual, and transgender liberation with women's liberation. First, there is an intimate connection between homophobia and sexism: Homophobia maintains gender inequality. Labels like "fag" or "dyke" are deployed to police the boundaries of sexual and gender expression.

Second, there is an intimate connection between sexism and gender rigidity and between the gay and lesbian liberation movement and gender nonconformity. Feminists have long argued that biology does not limit men or women to performing preassigned, gender-specific roles. Homophobia persecutes all those who are gender nonconformists—the sissy, the butch, the transgendered person.

Third, feminists and queers have long shared a critique of the limitations and pathologies of the traditional, patriarchal, nuclear family and a commitment to opening up other forms of family.

Fourth, both movements have worked hard to achieve and protect full sexual, reproductive, and personal autonomy and choice for women and men—a struggle that is far from over.

These are the links between the much more traditional politics of NOW's lesbian summit and a more radical lesbian-feminist movement. In the final analysis, both are lesbian movements built on a faith in an intersectional politics that focuses on the need for fundamental change in social institutions.